www.wadsworth.com

wadsworth.com is the World Wide Web site for Wadsworth Publishing Company and is your direct source to dozens of online resources.

At *wadsworth.com* you can find out about supplements, demonstration software, and student resources. You can also send e-mail to many of our authors and preview new publications and exciting new technologies.

wadsworth.com
Changing the way the world learns®

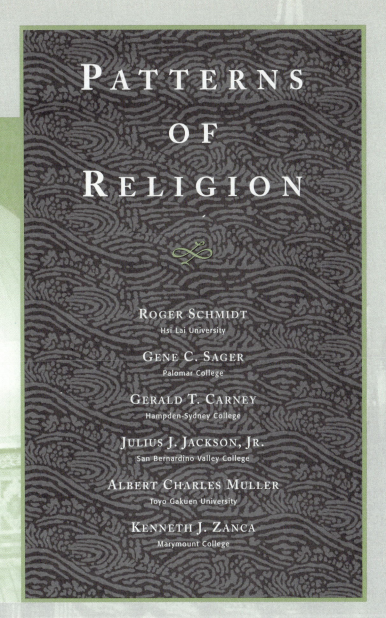

PATTERNS OF RELIGION

ROGER SCHMIDT
Hsi Lai University

GENE C. SAGER
Palomar College

GERALD T. CARNEY
Hampden-Sydney College

JULIUS J. JACKSON, JR.
San Bernardino Valley College

ALBERT CHARLES MULLER
Toyo Gakuen University

KENNETH J. ZANCA
Marymount College

Wadsworth Publishing Company

I T P® **An International Thomson Publishing Company**

Belmont, CA · Albany, NY · Boston · Cincinnati · Johannesburg · London · Madrid · Melbourne
Mexico City · New York · Pacific Grove, CA · Scottsdale, AZ · Singapore · Tokyo · Toronto

RELIGION EDITIOR: Peter Adams

ASSISTANT EDITOR: Kerri Abdinoor

EDITORIAL ASSISTANT: Mindy Newfarmer

DEVELOPMENTAL EDITOR: Vicki Nelson

MARKETING MANAGER: Dave Garrison

PRINT BUYER: Stacey Weinberger

PERMISSIONS EDITOR: Robert Kauser

PRODUCTION: The Book Company

COPY EDITOR: Mary Berry

PHOTO RESEARCH: Emspace Artwork

TEXT AND COVER DESIGNER: William Seabright and Associates

COVER IMAGE: Corbis Images

COMPOSITION: Irene Imfeld Graphic Design

PRINTER: R.R. Donnelley

Printed in the United States of America
1 2 3 4 5 6 7 8 9 10

For more information, contact Wadsworth Publishing Company, 10 Davis Drive, Belmont, CA 94002,
or electronically at http://www.wadsworth.com

International Thomson Publishing Europe
Berkshire House
168-173 High Holborn
London, WC1V 7AA, United Kingdom

International Thomson Editores
Seneca, 53
Colonia Polanco
11560 México D.F. México

Nelson ITP, Australia
102 Dodds Street
South Melbourne
Victoria 3205, Australia

International Thomson Publishing Asia
60 Albert Street
#51-01 Albert Complex
Singapore 189969

Nelson Canada
1120 Birchmount Road
Scarborough, Ontario
Canada M1K 5G4

International Thomson Publishing Japan
Hirakawa-cho Kyowa Building, 3F
2-2-1 Hirakawacho, Chiyoda-ku
Tokyo 102 Japan

International Thomson Publishing Southern Africa
Building 18, Constantia Square
138 Sixteenth Road, P.O. Box 2459
Halfway House, 1685 South Africa

ISBN 0534 506 496

See Credits on page 707 which is a continuation of this copyright page.

♻ This book is printed on acid-free recycled paper.

In appreciation of the first World's Parliament of Religions.

Chicago, 1893.

ROGER SCHMIDT

Roger Schmidt is chair of the Department of Religious Studies at Hsi Lai University (Rosemead, California), a university grounded in Buddhist traditions and values. He is a graduate of the University of Redlands and the Claremont Graduate School. He taught philosophy and religion for thirty years at San Bernardino Valley College and its sister institution Crafton Hills College, retiring as a professor emeritus in 1993. Schmidt is the author of *Exploring Religion* (Wadsworth, 2d edition, 1988); co-author of *San Bernardino Valley College Sports, 1926–1996*; and contributor to *The Study of Religion in Two-Year Colleges* (1975) and *So There's a Community College in Your Town* (1975). He was a member of the American Academy of Religion project on the Study of Religion in Two-Year Colleges (1974) funded by the Charles E. Merrill Trust, a recipient of a National Endowment for the Humanities Fellowship (1975), Teacher of the Year at San Bernardino Valley College (1985), and the recipient of an honorary Litt. D. (1998). He is deeply indebted to his mentors Gordon Atkins, Douglas Eadie, Floyd Ross, and Edwin S. Gaustad, and to his wife, Ann Mattison Schmidt.

GENE C. SAGER

Gene Sager is professor of religious studies and philosophy at Palomar College, San Marcos, California. He was awarded a National Endowment for the Humanities Fellowship for the school year 1976–1977. Much of his research has been stimulated by the experience of living abroad, especially a four-year stay in Japan, where he studied with and translated for one of Japan's leading scholars, Professor Keiji Nishitani

of Kyoto University. In addition to a translation of Nishitani's article "Tradition and Modernization in Japan" (*Japan Studies*, 1969), Sager has authored articles, including "Teaching Asian Philosophy" (*Aitia*, 1974), "An Experiment in Interdisciplinary Studies" (*Interdisciplinary Perspectives*, 1977), and "Japanese Religion Today" (*Darshana International*, 1989). His articles on contemporary moral and spiritual issues include "Diet and the Environment" (*Sustainable Development*, 1995) and "Ecotourism" (*Natural Life*, 1996). He is founder and director of the Palomar College Religious Studies Program and recipient of teaching excellence awards in 1993, 1996, and 1998. He stands most indebted to his wife, Margarita, for her love and support.

GERALD T. CARNEY

Gerald T. Carney is professor of religion at Hampden-Sydney College in Virginia. He received his Ph.D. in the history of religions from Fordham University where he studied with Thomas Berry, Jose Pereira, and Ewert Cousins. He has published articles on Vaishnava devotional traditions and religious aesthetics in the *Journal of Dharma* and the *Journal of Vaishnava Studies*. He has contributed chapters to *Shaping Bengali Worlds, Public and Private* and to *The International Challenge of Raimon Panikkar*, the latter a study of the contributions of Panikkar's Christology to interreligious dialogue. Carney's early research focused on the development of Bengal Vaishnava dramatic traditions, especially the drama of Kavikarnapura, the *Caitanyacandrodaya*. He is presently working on the biography of Baba Premananda Bharati, an early Bengal Vaishnava missionary to the West. From 1992 to 1994, Carney served as president of the Virginia Consortium for Asian

Studies. At Hampden-Sydney College, he was associate dean for academic support from 1996 to 1999. Hampden-Sydney College provided support for the period during which the first draft of the chapter of Hinduism was completed.

Repeated extraordinary opportunities to experience the Hindu religious traditions were made possible by the personal and intellectual support of Srivatsa Goswami, the director of the Sri Chaitanya Prema Sansthana in Vrindaban. Carney is deeply grateful to Srivatsaji and to this father Sri Purushottama Goswami; to the other Goswamis of Radha Raman Temple; to his colleagues at Jai Singh Ghera; and in a particular way, to the late Asim Krishna Das for their help in deepening his experience of Hindu life and practice. In the deepest way, he cherishes the companionship of his wife, Ellen DeLuca, on their shared personal and spiritual journey.

JULIUS J. JACKSON, JR.

Julius J. Jackson, Jr., is an associate professor and department chair in the Department of Philosophy and Religious Studies at San Bernardino Valley College. His degrees include a B.A. in religious studies from Alma College; an M.Div. from Duke University; and a Ph.D. in religious studies from Syracuse University, where his areas of specialization were hermeneutic theory and religion and culture. Prior to taking the position at San Bernardino Valley College, Jackson taught at Syracuse University; California State University, Long Beach; the University of Redlands; Crafton Hills College; and California State University, San Bernardino, where he continues to teach upper-division classes in the School of Humanities. He is the author of *A Guided Tour of John Stuart Mill's Utilitarianism* (Mayfield, 1993). In addition, he has authored two case studies—on Gandhi and Muhammad—in the Hartwick Humanities in Management Institute's series on leadership, written short articles and book reviews, and presented papers at twenty different national and international conferences. Most recently, he has authored interactive, multimedia computer tutorials for both Allyn & Bacon and Mayfield to accompany college textbooks in the areas of classical mythology, the

Western humanities, introduction to philosophy, and world religions. His mentors and friends influential in his career include Ron Massanari; David Miller; Patricia Cox Miller; and most important, his wife, Janice Ropp Jackson.

ALBERT CHARLES MULLER

A. Charles Muller is a professor of East-West comparative thought at Toyo Gakuen University in Chiba, Japan. His primary field of study is Korean Buddhism, having received his Ph.D. from the Program in Korean Studies at SUNY Stony Brook, where his area of research was the history of Sŏn soteriological theory. Muller is the author of *The Sutra of Perfect Enlightenment: Korean Buddhism's Guide to Meditation*, and he is currently working on a translation of Wŏnhyo's *Meaning of the Two Hindrances*. In conjunction with his researches in Buddhism and, on a broader scale, East Asian thought, he has compiled two extensive Chinese-English lexicons (a dictionary of Buddhist terms and a dictionary of literary Chinese), which are available on CD-ROM, as well as on his Web site (http://www.acmuller.gol.com). He is also the moderator of the Internet discussion forum *ZenBuddhism*. He is currently involved in a number of international projects concerning the digitization of East Asian canonical texts and reference materials.

KENNETH J. ZANCA

Kenneth J. Zanca is professor of Religious Studies at Marymount College, Palos Verdes, California. He received his Ph.D. from Fordham University, where he studied systematic theology with a specialty in Christian ethics. He is the author of several books, most recently *American Catholics and Slavery, 1789–1866* (1994) and an ethics textbook, *How to Arrive at a Considered Opinion* (1996). He has also contributed articles to encyclopedias and presented papers at such learned societies as the Society for Christian Ethics, Society for the Sociology of Religion, College Theology Society, and Catholic Theological Society of America. Zanca's teaching has been recognized with Marymount College's Outstanding Faculty Member Award in 1993, 1994, 1995, and 1997.

BRIEF CONTENTS

PREFACE   XVII

CHAPTER   1   STUDYING RELIGION 2

CHAPTER   2   ANCIENT SPIRITUALITY 50

CHAPTER   3   TRIBAL RELIGIONS IN HISTORICAL TIMES 126

CHAPTER   4   HINDUISM 206

CHAPTER   5   BUDDHISM 278

CHAPTER   6   TAOISM 336

CHAPTER   7   CONFUCIANISM 396

CHAPTER   8   JUDAISM 444

CHAPTER   9   CHRISTIANITY 514

CHAPTER   10   ISLAM 582

EPILOGUE   MILLENNIAL RELIGIONS 638

APPENDIX   A   JAINISM AND SIKHISM 651

APPENDIX   B   SHINTO 658

APPENDIX   C   WEB SITE OF WORLD RELIGIONS 669

NOTES   672

INDEX   691

CONTENTS

PREFACE   XVIII

CHAPTER   1   **STUDYING RELIGION** 2
Roger Schmidt

Religion and the Term *"Religion"*   4

Defining Religion   5

Perceptions of the Sacred   10

Forms of Religious Expression   15

Classifying Religions   17

Magic and Religion   25

Religion in Traditional and Secular Societies   26

Approaches to the Study of Religion   27

Religion and Truth   29

Some Observations   32

Glossary of Religious Terms   33

For Further Study   36

Readings   37

    1.1   What Is Religion?, Gudo Wafu Nishijima   37

    1.2   Atheists for Jesus?, Daniel C. Maguire   38

    1.3   What Faith Is, Paul Tillich   41

    1.4   Truth and the Religions of the World, Sarvepalli Radhakrishnan   43

    1.5   What Will Happen to God?, Naomi R. Goldenberg   45

    1.6   The Virtue of Sympathy, Simone Weil   48

CHAPTER 2 ANCIENT SPIRITUALITY 50
Roger Schmidt

Dead and Living Religions 52

The Problem of Naming 52

Prehistory 54

Prehistoric Religion: Beliefs and Practice 61

Ancient Urban Societies 67

Ancient Urban Religions: Beliefs and Practices 75

Ancient Spirituality in Modern Thought 93

Glossary of Ancient Spirituality 100

For Further Study 102

Readings 104

2.1 Stone Age Burials and the Afterlife, Mircea Eliade 104

2.2 Was There a Neanderthal Religion?, Peter Rowley-Conwy 104

2.3 The Goddess and the Dawn of Religion, Merlin Stone 106

2.4 Blood Sacrifice, Walter Burkert 110

2.5 The Making of Humans: A Maya Myth 112

2.6 The Quest for Immortality: *Gilgamesh* 116

2.7 Judgement at the Court of Osiris:
Egyptian Book of the Dead 117

2.8 Transformed by Isis: *The Golden Ass of Apuleius,*
Lucius Apuleius 120

CHAPTER 3 TRIBAL RELIGIONS IN HISTORICAL TIMES 126
Roger Schmidt

Problems of Naming 128

Tribal Religions and Societies 129

Religious Beliefs of Tribal Peoples 132

Religious Practice of Tribal Peoples 144

Indigenous Peoples in Historical Times 153

Contemporary Indigenous Peoples and Spirituality 167

Glossary of Tribal Religions 169

For Further Study 171

Readings   173

   3.1   Symbolism, John Lame Deer   173

   3.2   In the Beginning: A Barotse Creation Myth   176

   3.3   Beyond the Dome We Call the Sky:
A Seneca Myth of Origins   177

   3.4   A Conversation with Ogotemmêli: A Dogon
Creation Story, Marcel Griaule   184

   3.5   Seeking a Vision: The Sioux Vision Quest,
George Sword (Long Knife)   189

   3.6   !Kung Healing, Marjorie Shostak   191

   3.7   Chief Seattle's Speech of 1854, Chief Seattle   197

   3.8   Santería: A Revitalization Movement, Joseph M. Murphy   200

CHAPTER   4   HINDUISM   206

Gerald T. Carney

Hindu Beliefs   210

Hindu Practice   213

History of Hinduism   221

Contemporary Hinduism   241

Glossary of Hinduism   248

For Further Study   252

Readings   254

   4.1   The Primal Sacrifice: The *Rig Veda*   254

   4.2   The *Katha Upanishad*   255

   4.3   Selections from the *Brihadaranyaka*
and *Chandogya Upanishads*   258

   4.4   *Bhagavad Gita* (Books 3 and 9)   260

   4.5   Vaishnava Devotional Poetry   268

   4.6   Poems to Shiva, Basavanna   271

   4.7   The Need for a More Humane Morality and a
Purer Mode of Worship, Ram Mohan Roy   272

   4.8   Religion and the Practice of Politics, Mohandas K. Gandhi   273

   4.9   The Hindu Way of Life, Radhakrishnan   275

CHAPTER 5   **BUDDHISM 278**
Albert Charles Muller

Buddhist Beliefs 281

Buddhist Practice 290

History of Buddhism 299

Contemporary Buddhism 311

Glossary of Buddhism 319

For Further Study 322

Readings 323

     5.1   Questions Which Lead Not to Edification, *The Majjhima-Nikaya* 323

     5.2   Contemplation of the Impurity of the Body: *Visuddhi-Magga* 325

     5.3   Realizing the Four Noble Truths: The *Mahavastu* 326

     5.4   Expedient Means: Three Parables from the *Lotus Sutra* 327

     5.5   *The Heart Sutra* 329

     5.6   Stabilizing Meditation and Observational Meditation: *The Awakening of Mahayana Faith* 330

     5.7   The *Sutra of Perfect Enlightenment:* Contemplation of Impurity and How to Find a Qualified Teacher 331

     5.8   How to Contemplate: The *Mu Koan* 333

CHAPTER 6   **TAOISM 336**
Gene C. Sager

Taoist Beliefs 338

Taoist Practice 346

History of Taoism 353

Contemporary Taoism 375

Glossary of Taoism 377

For Further Study 379

Readings 380

     6.1   Chinese Divination: *I Ching*, John Blofeld 380

     6.2   The Founder's Words: *Tao Te Ching* 382

     6.3   The Mystic Philosopher: *Chuang-tzu* 386

6.4   The Power of the Precious Names: "The Heaven-Honored One of the Primal Beginnings Speaks the Scripture of the Precious Names of the Three Controllers"   388

6.5   The Jade Emperor's Birthday, Peter Goullart   390

6.6   Women's Spirituality: *Immortal Sisters*   391

6.7   Taoist Meditation in Motion: T'ai-Chi Ch'uan, Gene C. Sager   394

CHAPTER   7   CONFUCIANISM   396
Gene C. Sager

Confucian Beliefs   398

Confucian Practice   405

History of Confucianism   413

Contemporary Confucianism   427

Glossary of Confucianism   429

For Further Study   430

Readings   432

7.1   The Founder's Words: *Analects of Confucius*   432

7.2   The Second Great Confucian: Mencius   434

7.3   The Great Ultimate of Chu Hsi: The *Chu Tzu Ch'uan-shu*   436

7.4   The Relevance of Confucianism Today, Herbert Fingarette   438

7.5   Confucianism and the Future of China, Tu Wei Ming   440

CHAPTER   8   JUDAISM   444
Roger Schmidt

Judaic Beliefs   446

Judaic Practice   456

History of Judaism   464

Contemporary Judaism   489

Glossary of Judaism   492

For Further Study   496

Readings   497

8.1 "When God Began to Create . . ." *Genesis* 1:1–2:4a 497

8.2 A Second Account of Creation: *Genesis* 2:4b–3:24 498

8.3 The Coming of Lilith, Judith Plaskow 501

8.4 The Abrahamic Covenant: *Genesis* 17:1–14 503

8.5 The Mosaic Covenant: *Exodus* 19:1–20:14 504

8.6 The Law of Holiness: *Levicitus* 19 506

8.7 A Summation of the Commandments: The *Talmud* 507

8.8 Trying a Capital Case: The *Talmud* 508

8.9 Selections from the *Mishnah Tractate Avot* 510

CHAPTER 9   CHRISTIANITY 514
Kenneth J. Zanca

Christian Beliefs 516

Christian Practice 526

History of Christianity 530

Contemporary Christianity 554

Glossary of Christianity 559

For Further Study 563

Readings 564

9.1 The Oldest Non-Christian Account of Jesus:
Testimonium Flavinium, Flavius Josephus 564

9.2 The Account of the Empty Tomb:
Matthew, Mark, and *Luke* 564

9.3 An Early Prayer: From the *Didache* 566

9.4 The Nicene Creed 566

9.5 Living in Two Cities: *The City of God*, Augustine of Hippo 567

9.6 Living the Monastic Life:
Excerpts from *Rule*, Benedict of Nursia 569

9.7 What Is a Sacrament? *Summa Theologica*, Thomas Aquinas 571

9.8 Against Indulgences: *Ninety-five Theses, or Disputation
on the Power and Efficacy of Indulgences*, Martin Luther 574

9.9 Reply to Luther: *Exsurge Domine*, Pope Leo X 577

9.10 The Protestant Declaration: From
the *Augusburg Confession*, Martin Luther and Philip Melanchton 577

CHAPTER 10　　**ISLAM** 582

Julius J. Jackson, Jr.

Islamic Beliefs　584

Islamic Practice　591

History of Islam　602

Contemporary Islam　616

Glossary of Islam　621

For Further Study　623

Readings　624

10.1　The "Lord's Prayer" of Islam: *Quran, Sura* 1　624

10.2　On God: The *Quran*　624

10.3　On Piety and Social Justice: The *Quran*　628

10.4　On Christians and Jews: The *Quran*　631

10.5　Sufi Poetry, Jalal al-Din　633

10.6　Making the *Hajj:* Malcolm X after Mecca, Malcolm X　634

EPILOGUE　　**MILLENNIAL RELIGIONS** 638

Julius J. Jackson, Jr.

The Phenomenon of Millennialism　639

Twentieth-Century Millennial Groups　640

Millennialism as a Focus for Religious Studies　644

Ends and Beginnings　648

Glossary of Millennialism　649

For Further Study　650

APPENDIX A　　**JAINISM AND SIKHISM** 651

Gerald T. Carney

APPENDIX B　　**SHINTO** 658

Gene C. Sager

APPENDIX C　　**WORLD WIDE WEB RESOURCES** 669

Julius J. Jackson, Jr.

NOTES　　672

INDEX　　691

PREFACE

Patterns of Religion is an introduction to the religions of the world with an emphasis on seven of the most influential traditions: Buddhism, Christianity, Confucianism, Hinduism, Islam, Judaism, and Taoism. The book also includes chapters on ancient patterns of spirituality and tribal religions in historical times; an epilogue on millennial religions; and appendixes on Jainism, Sikhism, Shinto, and the Web sites of the religions that are the subjects of the text. Other traditions such as Zoroastrianism and Chinese folk religions are discussed at the points at which they intersect with the traditions that are the focus of the text. The book is comprehensive (it covers all of the major living traditions and touches on many lesser-known traditions) and includes readings from the scripture of each of the major traditions. With the exception of Chapters 1 and 2, each chapter has the same four-part internal organization (beliefs, practice, history, and contemporary context).

Patterns of Religion has ten chapters. Chapter 1, "Studying Religion," introduces concepts important to the interpretation of religion. It begins with issues related to the terms *religion* and *religious*, as well as the definition of religion. Subsequent sections introduce the basic forms of religious expression and selected classifications of religions. Concluding sections distinguish between traditional and secular societies, discuss different approaches to the study of religion, and touch on the question of truth and religious belief.

Chapter 2, "Ancient Spirituality," focuses on prehistoric and ancient urban religions. The origins of religion are rooted in prehistory, thousands of years before the appearance of written texts. The story of ancient urban religions begins with the emergence of cities in Mesopotamia (modern Iraq) approximately 5,500 years ago. Subsequently, at different times, urban civilizations and religious systems developed in Egypt, the Indian subcontinent, China, Europe, the Americas, and sub-Saharan Africa. Chapter 2 begins with the problem of labeling ancient spirituality and then, in turn, covers prehistoric religion and ancient urban religions.

Chapter 3, "Tribal Religions in Historical Times," returns to the subject of oral religious traditions introduced in Chapter 2 but shifts the narrative from prehistoric to historical times. After the invention of writing and the rise of urban societies, oral peoples maintained their traditional ways in areas of the world where the influence of state systems either did not reach them or did not overwhelm them. Hundreds of tribal societies survived into modern times, particularly in sub-Saharan Africa, the Americas, the Arctic, and Oceania, where only in the past four hundred years, and especially the past two hundred years, have traditional societies been deeply affected by the religions, technologies, economies, and political dominance of modern states.

The focus of Chapter 4 is Hinduism, India's principal religion and the third largest in the world, numbering nearly 747 million devotees.[1] The Indian subcontinent (the area of modern Bangladesh, Bhutan, India, Nepal, and Pakistan) is the birthplace not only of Hinduism but also of Buddhism, Jainism, and Sikhism; it is also home to Christians, Muslims, and Zoroastrians. Jainism (with 4 million adherents) and Sikhism (with 22.5 million) are mentioned in Chapter 4 and covered in more detail in Appendix A.

Buddhism, the subject of Chapter 5, has around 353 million devotees and is the principal religion of Bhutan, Cambodia, Laos, Mongolia, Myanmar (formerly Burma), South Korea, Sri Lanka (Ceylon), Thailand, Tibet, and Vietnam. Buddhism and Shinto are the dominant religious traditions in Japan; Buddhism and Chinese folk religion (a mixture of ancestor veneration, popular deities, Confucian values, Buddhism, and religious Taoism) predominate in Taiwan. Significant Buddhist populations also exist in China, Malaysia, Mongolia, Nepal, Singapore, Europe, and the Americas.

Chapters 6 and 7 focus on traditions indigenous to China. Chapter 6 covers religion in prehistoric China, Chinese folk religion, and classical Chinese philosophy as contexts for understanding religious Taoism. Confucianism is the subject of Chapter 7. In spite of an inhospitable environment in the People's Republic of China, China's indigenous traditions continue to be part of Chinese life and culture on the mainland and among Chinese outside the mainland (for example, Taiwan, Singapore, Malaysia, and the United States).

Judaism, the focus of Chapter 8, shares with Hinduism the distinction of being the oldest of the major religious traditions. In numbers of adherents it is relatively small (16 million); however, the influence of its religious and ethical beliefs has been enormous. Judaic monotheism and prophecy (belief that God speaks through prophets) are historical antecedents directly linked to Christianity and Islam and indirectly linked to Sikhism and other monotheistic traditions, such as Baha'i.

Christianity, covered in Chapter 9, is the world's largest religion, numbering nearly 2 billion believers, or one-third of the total human population. It has expanded from its geographical and cultural base in ancient Palestine to nearly every nation on earth. A truly global movement, Christianity is established in Europe (552 million adherents), the Americas (675 million), Africa (351 million), Asia (289 million), and Oceania (24 million).

Islam, the most recent of the seven religions that are the focus of this text and second only to Christianity in number of adherents, is the subject of Chapter 10. Muslims, the followers of Islam, total about 1 billion people. Islam has spread from its birthplace in Arabia eastward throughout Asia and westward to Africa, Europe, and the Americas. It is the primary faith of over forty modern states, including Afghanistan, Albania, Algeria, Azerbaijan, Bangladesh, Chad, Egypt, Guinea, Indonesia, Iran, Iraq, Kuwait, Libya, Malaysia, Mali, Nigeria, Pakistan, Saudi Arabia, Senegal, Sierra Leone, Sudan, Syria, Tajikistan, Tanzania, Tunisia, Turkey, and Yemen. Large minority Muslim populations exist in many countries including Ethiopia, France, India, and the United States.

THE ORGANIZATION OF THIS BOOK

Chapters 3 through 10 are divided into four main sections: (1) beliefs, (2) practice, (3) history, and (4) the contemporary context. A similar format is followed in the treatment of Jainism, Sikhism, and Shinto in the appendixes and a modified form of it is used in Chapter 2. This innovative ordering permits readers to acquire an overview of a religious tradition's beliefs and practices before being plunged into the details of its historical development. Putting the initial focus on beliefs and practice has advantages for students and instructors. For students, this approach makes the reading of the history section a richer and more meaningful experience. Because the beliefs and practice sections are designed to stand alone, the four-part internal division of the chapters lends itself to teaching approaches and assignments that stress one or more of the divisions and that omit or give less attention to others. For instructors who stress beliefs and practice, the chapter organization provides greater flexibility in coverage and choice of reading assignments. This module approach is especially useful in one-semester courses that cover a range of religions; two-semester courses can draw on the full resources of the text.

BELIEFS

Each religious tradition includes a belief system or worldview through which adherents understand the world and their place in it. A religious worldview provides a view of the whole of things (beliefs about life and the cosmos) and of what is ultimately real. Sections on beliefs provide an overview of a tradition's doctrines about the ultimate (for example, God), the cosmos, the nature and destiny of human beings, and evil. In those traditions with a historical founder and master figure, the section on beliefs begins with the life and teaching of the foundational figure (for example, Buddha, Christ, Confucius, and Muhammad). This approach allows readers to learn something about the charismatic figure who inspired and continues to inspire believers and outsiders as well. The sections on beliefs concentrate on beliefs that are traditional and mainstream and give less attention to nontraditional and sectarian beliefs. This approach may convey a false sense of doctrinal agreement, because considerable variation in belief exists within the major religious traditions, and no single set of beliefs adequately expresses the diversity of beliefs of the major subgroups or of the individuals within a tradition. To offset the impression of doctrinal unity conveyed in the beliefs sections, a wider spectrum of beliefs is covered in the history sections.

PRACTICE

Lived religion is not simply a matter of believing; it is something that is done, an acting out in words and gestures of what ultimately matters. Thus, each religious tradition constitutes a way of life or ethos, as well as a worldview. Sections in the text on practice focus on the religions' moral, ritual, social, and institutional dimensions. Each religion involves moral commands or guidelines respecting how life ought to be lived and a sense of what constitutes the good life. Each religion, to one degree or another, perform rituals or ceremonies. Ritual is the element of practice that gives each religion a distinctive social and cultural personality and that shapes a tradition's

calendar. Each religion is a social and institutional entity with a set of values, codes of conduct, and relationships respecting gender, marriage, leadership, organization, governance, and decision making. The social character of a religion is reflected in the name by which it is identified as a communal entity: the Buddhist *sangha*, the Christian *church*, the Jewish *synagogue*, the Muslim *umma*, and so on.

HISTORY

The history sections of the chapters cover the development and the major turning points of each of the seven major traditions plus Jainism, Sikhism, and Shinto in Appendixes A and B. They also provide a historical context for prehistoric, ancient urban, and recent tribal traditions. For traditions associated with a foundational figure, the history section begins with the period following the death of the founder. The histories introduce important figures, events, movements, and disputes that may have been neglected or passed over in the sections on beliefs, and they also illustrate the point that all religions change over time. In dating events within a common chronology, we have substituted the religiously neutral acronyms B.C.E. (before the common era) and C.E. (of the common era) for the Christian conventions B.C. (before Christ) and A.D. (*Anno Domini*, "in the year of the Lord").

THE CONTEMPORARY CONTEXT

The concluding sections of Chapters 3 through 10 and Appendixes A and B place each religion in its contemporary context. Violence, racism, sexism, and poverty are some of the features of modern life that have profound implications for religious life. The concluding sections touch on some of these issues and on the challenges that secularism, science, and religious pluralism pose for religion. However, they primarily focus on areas of concern that are internally vexing, such as conversion, religious intermarriage, the role of women, ordination, homosexuality, reproductive issues, and the clash of fundamentalists and modernists. Because the religions introduced in

Chapter 2 are dead rather than living entities, this chapter's concluding section introduces modern assessments of ancient spirituality that involve issues and judgments respecting social and religious primitivism, the origin of religion, and gender roles and goddesses in prehistoric and ancient urban religions.

READINGS

A special feature of *Patterns of Religion* is the inclusion of readings at the end of each chapter, including selections from scriptures and other important texts that are usually unavailable in surveys of the religions of the world. An introduction to each reading provides a context for the reading's interpretation and includes questions about content. Each chapter also includes a glossary and bibliographical suggestions for further study.

TABLES AND TIME LINES

Chapters 2 through 10 include time lines that provide a chronological overview of important events or persons, as well as tables that delineate the principal scriptures and internal divisions or movements within each of the major religious traditions.

GEOPOLITICAL FRAMEWORK

Geopolitical references are made throughout the text, and maps are provided to help readers locate themselves spatially and temporally. The world map on the next page identifies the six humanly inhabited continents (Africa, the Americas, the Arctic, Asia, Australia, and Europe) and the area known as Oceania. The map also identifies the major geographical and cultural regions that are referred to frequently in the text, along with the birthplaces of twelve of the major living religions.

The areas north and south of the Sahara Desert constitute the two main geographical and cultural regions of the African continent: *North Africa* and *sub-Saharan Africa*. *The Americas* is a collective term for North and South America and the Caribbean islands. The *Arctic* comprises the region surrounding the North Pole and a cultural area that includes Greenland and northern

portions of Russia, Scandinavia, Canada, and Alaska. *Europe* is separated from Asia in the east by the Ural Mountains and is bounded to the west by the Atlantic Ocean and to the South by the Mediterranean Sea. *Europe* includes the insular cultures of Ireland, Britain, and Iceland. *Eurasia* is a term for the conjoined continents Europe and Asia. *Oceania* refers to the islands and cultures of Melanesia, Micronesia, and Polynesia and, in this text, includes *Australia*.

Asia is a geographical term for the continent bounded to the west by Europe and the Red Sea, to the east by the Pacific Ocean, to the north by the Arctic Ocean, and to the south by the Indian Ocean. Scholars have subdivided Asia by culture and geography into five main regions: East, South, Southwest, Southeast, and Central Asia. *Southwest Asia* and Africa's Nile River valley gave rise to the civilizations of ancient Egypt, Mesopotamia, and Persia and to Judaism, Zoroastrianism, Christianity, Islam, and Baha'i. Southwest Asia and North Africa constitute the *Middle East*. China and Japan were the principal centers of the civilizations and indigenous religions of *East Asia* (Confucianism, Taoism, and Shinto). The Indian subcontinent gave birth to the civilizations of *South Asia* and to Hinduism, Buddhism, Jainism, and Sikhism. Indian and Chinese influences on the cultures of *Southeast Asia* (for example, Burma, Cambodia, Thailand, and Vietnam) are reflected in the older designation of the region as Indochina. *Central Asia* is a designation for western China, Tibet, and Mongolia.

ASIAN AND WESTERN RELIGIOUS TRADITIONS

Although Asia is the birthplace of the seven religions that are the chief subjects of *Patterns of Religion*, these religions are frequently divided into Asian and Western traditions. Judaism, Christianity, and Islam originated in Southwest Asia, but because formative periods in the histories of Judaism and Christianity have been grounded in Europe, and because Judaism and Christianity have profoundly influenced Western cultures, they are often referred to as *Western*

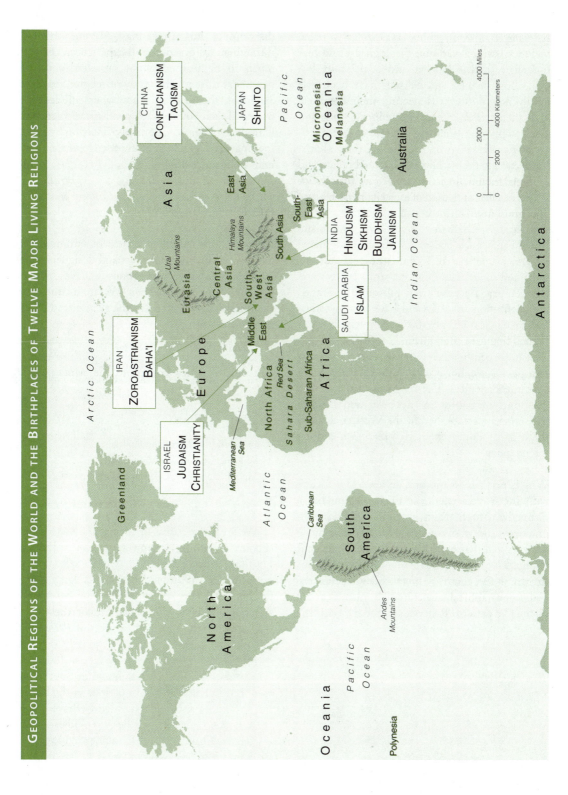

GEOPOLITICAL REGIONS OF THE WORLD AND THE BIRTHPLACES OF TWELVE MAJOR LIVING RELIGIONS

religious traditions. This classification also includes Islam, a tradition theologically and historically related to Judaism and Christianity, but one whose peoples and cultures have been primarily non-Western. Reflecting their historical and theological interconnectedness, Judaism, Christianity, and Islam are sometimes referred to as *Abrahamic religions* (because of their shared connection to the Israelite patriarch Abraham and to the religion of ancient Israel) or as *monotheistic religions* (a category that includes Zoroastrianism, Sikhism, Baha'i, and other religions).

Like the Abrahamic traditions, Hinduism, Buddhism, Confucianism, and Taoism originated in Asia, but unlike them, these traditions remained in an Asian context until the twentieth century. Because they profoundly shaped the civilizations of Asia and have less historical and theological affinity to the Abrahamic traditions, Hinduism, Buddhism, Confucianism, and Taoism are commonly referred to as *Asian religious traditions*. Note, however, that these divisions are chiefly pedagogical. The reality is that Western traditions are rooted in the East, and Eastern traditions are established in the West, and today there is an unprecedented interaction among the religions.

Why is *patterns* an appropriate term to associate with the world's religions? Each religion has a distinctive pattern, that is, a set of beliefs, symbols, practices, and traditions that forms a meaningful story and that provides guides and models for living. The various elements of the religions (myths, rituals, doctrines, moral codes, institutions, and so on) also have an internal coherence and distinctive pattern. Patterns are not always easily discernible, but they may become evident through study, practice, and experience. There is much to be learned about ourselves and our neighbors through the study of religion. In such a pursuit, the dictum "Know yourself" encompasses "Teach yourself." A good place to start is with the wisdom of Confucius: "He who by reanimating the Old can gain knowledge of the New is fit to be a teacher."

ACKNOWLEDGMENTS

Many persons including reviewers, editors, copy editors, production managers and designers, colleagues, students, and spouses have helped produce *Patterns of Religion*. We are indebted to the following reviewers for their close reading of the manuscript:

Maura O'Neill, Chaffey College
Gregory Elder, Riverside City College
James P. McDermott, Canisius College
Lawrence Dunlop, Marymount College
Bruce Hanson, Fullerton College
Deborah Wallin, Skagit Valley College
Leslie Aldritt, Northland College
William Ashcraft, Carlton College
Mary Ellen Young, Lakewood Community College
and
Arnold Johanson, Moorhead State University.

We are appreciative of their work and for the support of editors Tammy Goldfeld, Katherine Hartlove, Sheryl Fullerton, Vicki Nelson, and Peter Adams. Additionally, we thank Mary Berry for her final edit; Betsy Martin for her photo selection and Dusty Friedman for coordination.

PATTERNS
OF
RELIGION

CHAPTER 1

STUDYING RELIGION

Tents set up below Mount Kailas, a sacred mountain in southwestern Tibet, a region of the People's Republic of China. Mount Kailas is holy to Hindus, who associate it with the god Siva and to Tibetan Buddhists, who identify it as the center of the cosmos.

A good way to start a study of the world's religions is to reflect on the proposition that "a person who knows only one religion knows none." It seems obvious that knowledge of more than a single religious tradition is needed to make informed judgments about other religions, but is it also plausible that "to know one religion is to know all?" Some interpreters insist that the various religions, in spite of their differences, share a common core; thus, to know the truth of one religion is to know the truth of all. Does this perspective require familiarity with other religions, or is knowledge of one sufficent? Is it possible to know a religion without believing in and practicing it? If it is not, can we ever, at any point in time, "know" more than one religion? What is implied by the distinction between possessing "knowledge about" and "knowledge of and for" a religious tradition?

Religion is an important feature of human existence. The earth is home to about 5.8 billion humans. Slightly over half of them identify themselves as Christians (1.9 billion) or Muslims (1.1 billion). Another 1.1 billion are Hindus (747 million) or Buddhists (353 million). Millions more identify themselves as Baha'is, Confucians, Jains, Jews, Parsis, Shintoists, Sikhs, and so on. Approximately 16 percent of the world's people see themselves as nonreligious.[1] The accuracy of statistics on adherents is problematic, but the figures do indicate that the overwhelming majority of humans are concerned with matters of the spirit and that most people mediate those concerns within concrete communities of faith. Thus, however we resolve issues related to the assertion that "to know one religion is to know none," in an age of global communication it is difficult to remain isolated from religions different from our own.

Chapter 1 introduces subjects and categories that scholars have devised to study religious phenomena. These categories are not ones through which foundational religious figures (for example, Buddha, Christ, and Muhammad) understood their experiences. In fact, there is nothing "religious" about these categories, but they are useful to the study of religion. We begin with some remarks about the terms *religion* and *religious*.

RELIGION AND THE TERM "RELIGION"

Although what we now label as religious behavior is extremely ancient, humans existed for thousands of years before they came to think of themselves as having a "religion" or as being "religious." As historian of religion Wilfred Cantwell Smith has argued, it is likely that the languages of prehistoric peoples, like those of the first literate societies, did not include a word that might be translated as religion or its cognate "religious."[2] The terms *religion* and *religious* are derived from the Latin *religio* and *religiosus*. In early Roman times, *religio* signified the oaths and obligations that families observed in relationship to powers external to human beings. Individuals who were diligent in performing their obligations were *religiosi* (devout or pious), and the places in which such duties were performed were considered "religious," or sacred. The Roman philosopher Cicero (ca. 45 B.C.E.) noted that *religio* was derived from the root *religere*, a term meaning "to gather together" and "to go over again" in the sense of one who is care-

ful and constant in performing ceremonies in the service of the gods. Early Christians understood *religio* to signify the careful performance of rites and duties in respect to God. Awareness that a group's religion differed from that of others eventually led to the distinction between true and false religion.[3]

The emergence of self-conscious forms of religiosity such as Christianity provided the precedent for movements such as Manichaeism and Islam to identify themselves as religions. The Manichaean founder Mani (216–277 C.E.) was aware that he was creating a religious "system" that he hoped would encompass all of humankind.[4] The *Quran*—God's revelation to Muhammad (570–632 C.E.)—uses *din* (Arabic for "religion") and *islam* (meaning "submission to God") to signify both the name of the Muslim religion *("I have approved Islam for your religion")* and surrender to God's law as the essence of true religion *("The true religion with God is Islam")*.[5]

What are some of the implications of the absence of the categories *religion* and *the religions* in ancient times and their emergence in the first millennium C.E. as generic terms for "religious phenomena" and "religious communities"? First, the question that moderns take for granted—What is your religion?—could not have been asked prior to the creation and assimilation of such categories.

Second, peoples without linguistic equivalents for the term *religion* have no names for their "religion." Thus, we speak of the spirituality of Native American peoples such as the Hopi as the "religion" of the Hopis and of the spirituality of archaic urban societies such as the Egyptians as the "religion" of the ancient Egyptians. Further, the naming of most of the traditions studied in this text occurred after their foundational periods. Judaism was not a name for the traditions of ancient Israel until late in the biblical period. Jesus referred neither to his disciples as Christians nor to his movement as Christianity. *Hindu* was initially a label that Muslims applied to non-Muslims in the Indian subcontinent; eventually it became a Hindu self-designation. For centuries, the Chinese thought of Confucianism and Taoism as schools of thought rather than as religions.[6]

Third, the distinction between the *religious* and the *nonreligious* and the perception of "the religions" as "religions" made it possible for "religion" to become an object of study. Initially such studies were conducted by religious insiders, but the advent of modern science and secular societies provided the conditions for the emergence of the scientific study of religious phenomena by "dispassionate" outsiders. The latter development constituted a dramatic shift in orientation. As Smith has noted, outsiders regard the elements of an insider's faith simply as aspects of that person's religion rather than as constituting reality: "Heaven and Hell, to a believer, are stupendous places into one or other of which irretrievably he is about to step. To an observer, they are items in the believer's mind. To the believer, they are parts of the universe; to the observer, they are parts of a religion."[7]

Fourth, the absence of comparable equivalents for *religion* in non-Western cultures raises the possibility that the term does not point to a common feature present in all religions. There is no consensus on this subject. On one side are those who believe that all religions share a common core, an underlying unity. On the other side are those who argue that there is no single feature or set of features common to all religions.

DEFINING RELIGION

Without saying so, we have introduced several definitions of the term *religion*. We noted that *religio* signified being bound to powers external to humans with conscientious attention to accompanying obligations and ceremonies. The adjective *religiosus* was applied to the rites and obligations performed and to those objects, persons, or groups that were regarded as religious. Modern lexical definitions have preserved those meanings. In *Webster's New World Dictionary of the American Language* (1956), *religion* signifies "belief in a divine or superhuman power or powers" and "expression of this belief in conduct and ritual." Those who are religious are characterized as "devout, pious; godly" and as "careful and conscientious."

We have also implicitly used *religion* and *religious* as general terms for all of those things to which they apply. The extension of the word *religion* denotes all of those things that belong to the class *religion* (Buddhism, Islam, and so on), and the word *religious* denotes all those things characterized as "religious" (deities, temples, and so on). But these extensions or *denotations* get fuzzy at the edges. What should be included or excluded? Are philosophies and movements such as communism, fascism, and humanism religions? Prayer is considered a form of religious expression, but what about other human behaviors? If "God is love," are loving acts, irrespective of belief, religious? If, as Mohandas K. Gandhi (1869–1948) declared, "Truth is God," are scientific truths, even when at odds with traditional belief, religious?

The problem of where to draw the line between religion and nonreligion brings us to *intension* or connotation, that aspect of meaning that involves identifying features shared by the things within a term's extension. Intensional definitions require decisions respecting similarities and differences. Definitions of this type were first systematized by the Greek philosopher Aristotle (384–322 B.C.E.) and are typically referred to as definition by genus and difference. When this approach is applied to religion, we find ourselves engaged in thinking about features religions have in common. This leads us to the issue of whether there is a feature or a set of features that makes religion what it is and not something else. Jonathan Z. Smith's analysis of monothetic and polythetic definitions of religion is helpful here.[8]

MONOTHETIC DEFINITIONS

Monothetic definitions identify a single, decisive trait that all members of a class invariably have in common and often entail the conviction that definitions ought to identify either a thing's essence or a term's essential meaning.[9] In classical Western philosophy, the "true" or "real" meanings of general terms were believed to correspond to the essential features of the things symbolized. This is evident in Plato's (ca. 429–347 B.C.E.) dialogues, in which the philosopher Socrates (ca. 470–399 B.C.E.) challenges his fellow Athenians to think through such concepts as justice, love, and piety in order to arrive at their "real" meanings, and in Aristotle's observation that names ought to have one meaning. Like the efforts of these philosophers, attempts to identify the single distinctive feature of religion have been inconclusive. As we shall see, however, the discourse has been instructive.

SUPERNATURAL BEINGS The view that belief in one or more deities is the decisive feature of all religions is widespread, especially in the West. It is articulated in anthropologist Edward Burnett Tylor's (1832–1917) characterization of religion as "belief in Spiritual Beings."[10] Tylor's definition places religion in the class *belief system*, a category that includes atheistic ideologies such as communism but distinguishes religion from these ideologies by identifying belief in spiritual beings as that which invariably makes religion, religion.

Tylor's conception of religion is supported by a substantial body of empirical evidence, because belief in divinities is a common feature of most religions. His definition also reflects how most westerners conceive of religion, a generalization corroborated in part by standard dictionary definitions that mention devotion to God or gods. Contemporary advocates of this perspective include scholars of religion, as in Melford E. Spiro's defense of Tylor's definition: "I would argue that the belief in superhuman beings and in their power to assist or to harm man approaches universal distribution, and this belief—I would insist—is the core variable which ought to be designated by any definition of religion."[11]

One objection to defining religion in terms of belief in spiritual beings is that such a definition excludes some traditions that are conventionally included in the class *religion*. There are, for example, traditions within Buddhism and Confucianism in which divinities are either unimportant or have their existence explicitly denied. Deities are not the decisive feature of these traditions. To Confucian philosopher Chu Hsi (1130–1200 C.E.), the "Great Ultimate" is the transcendent foundation of heaven and earth and is immanent in everything. The Great Ultimate is a principle, not a divine person. For Buddhists, the historical Buddha (Siddhartha Gautama, 563–483 B.C.E.) is not a creator deity but the embodiment of enlightened human existence. Buddha is the teacher of the gods and humankind; he transcended the gods, and the eternal truth *(Dharma)* he discovered is the vehicle through which others can become Buddhas, or "enlightened ones." In defense of Tylor's and Spiro's definitions, traditional Buddhist claims of Gautama Buddha's omniscience and of the capacity of other transcendent beings to assist human beings clearly fit within the category *superhuman being*. However, Buddhists who see the Buddha in humanistic terms reject claims of his omniscience and of the transcendence of other enlightened beings.[12]

Another objection is that belief in deity is not even universal among contemporary Jews and Christians. A poll conducted for *Reader's Digest's Young Britain* indicated that among young Britons who identified themselves as Anglican or Roman Catholic Christians, 19 and 11 percent, respectively, did not believe in God.[13] Disbelief in God is not simply a reflection of the trials of adolescence, however. Some Jews and Jewish groups have rejected belief in God but insist that they have not abandoned Judaism, arguing that the Jewish people and culture are the core of Judaism. Indicative of this phenomenon in Christianity is a remark attributed to English novelist and barrister John Mortimer: "I have come to the conclusion that I am Christian. Except of course that I don't believe in God." Mortimer meant that his culture and values are Christian.

THE SACRED   Although Tylor's and Spiro's definitions exclude those movements in which spirit beings are either unimportant or explicitly rejected from the category *religion,* there are monothetic definitions broad enough to include such movements. One is the view that the human perception of **the sacred** or **the holy** (understood here as synonymous terms) is the unique feature of religion. An advantage of this perspective is that the "sacred" (transcendent reality) is sufficiently open ended to function as a symbol for spirit beings and impersonal ultimates such as Nirvana and the Tao (Dao).

Belief that the sacred is the decisive feature of religion is shared by several scholars, two of whom were Rudolf Otto (1869–1937) and Mircea Eliade (1907–1986). Otto, a Christian theologian, believed that religion is grounded in experiences of the holy, which he described as a feeling of being in the presence of the **numinous,** a mysterious and awesome power.[14] He was influenced by the theology of Friedrich Schleiermacher (1768–1834), who, in response to the argument that claims about the nature and existence of God are logically and scientifically unprovable, shifted the focus of religion from what is believed to what is experienced. Schleiermacher identified the universal religion-making characteristic as "a feeling of absolute dependence," a view reflected in Otto's conviction that religions are rooted in experiences of the numinous. A historian of religion, Eliade regarded the sacred as "the one unique and irreducible element" of religion but held that no definitive definition is possible, because each tradition has a unique perception of the sacred.[15]

THE ULTIMATE   Another monothetic definition identifies belief in the ultimate as the feature all religions have in common. **The ultimate** may be conceived of as a spiritual being, an impersonal absolute, or a way of being, among other ways. Christian theologian Paul Tillich (1886–1965) shared Otto's view that "the universal religious basis is the experience of the Holy within the finite,"[16] but he also spoke of the holy as the ultimate—as "that which matters to us unconditionally." An analogous sense of the ultimate is evident in the observation by Japanese Buddhist Master Zenkei Shibayama that Zen—understood as the "Truth, or the Absolute" rather than as a school of Buddhism—"is the basis of all religions and all philosophies."[17]

Just as there are problems with identifying belief in supernatural beings as the decisive or essential feature of religion, there are objections to using the sacred and the ultimate as well. Otto's idea of the holy has been criticized because in reflecting Christian and Judaic perceptions of God, it fails the test of universality on which it is predicated. The notion of the sacred or holy is not as applicable to Asian patterns of faith. In the Zen Buddhist tradition, for example, humans work out their own salvation through meditation and a scrupulous attention to those moral and ceremonial duties that shape one into the fullness of being rather than through surrender to the holy conceived of as a mysterious and powerful being.

Critics also contend that although terms such as *the sacred* and *the ultimate* avoid being too restrictive, they are equally too general to be of value as a category for defining religion.[18] Jonathan Z. Smith argues that monothetic definitions are unjustifiably reductive, stressing similarity at the expense of those differences that make "all the difference."[19] The view that the holy or the ultimate is the essential feature of religion replaces each tradition's unique conception of the holy or the ultimate with a general term that obscures the differences among traditions. God, Buddhahood (Enlightenment), and Tao are symbols of what ultimately matters, but remarkably dissimilar and perhaps incommensurable ones.

Efforts to isolate the essential feature of a specific religious tradition are subject to similar objections. Dutch scholar Gerardus van der Leeuw's (1890–1950) identification of the ideal form of the following traditions is indicative of the distortions to which this approach is susceptible. For this renowned scholar, Judaism was the religion of will and of obedience. Hinduism was the religion of the infinite and ascetic renunciation, and Buddhism the religion of nothingness and compassion. Islam was the religion of God's majestic power and judgment, and Christianity the religion whose essence was love.[20]

Definitions like these ignore important differences within the traditions. God and God's commands are important features of traditional forms of Judaism, but they are not important to all Judaic groups. Are Jews who do not believe in God but who place Israel (understood as a people and as a land) at the center of Judaism Judaists? A conviction that God was in Christ is at the heart of traditional Christian theology, but there is no understanding of Christ that all Christians everywhere and always have shared. Are those who identify themselves as Christians but believe in neither God nor the divinity of Christ Christians? Perhaps it is advisable, as theologian John Cobb observed of Christianity, to look for continuity in a group's self-identification as a community of memory rather than in an unchanging essence: "The unity of Christianity is the unity of an historical movement. That unity does not depend on any self-identity of doctrine, vision of reality, structure of existence, or style of life. It does depend on demonstrable continuities, the appropriateness of creative change, and the self-identification of people in relation to a particular history."[21]

Religious traditions are usually so internally diverse that it is impossible, except arbitrarily, to isolate a single, decisive characteristic of any of them. Divisions are so common to the major religious traditions that the names of these traditions might be best thought of as umbrella terms for a range of groups, each of which has distinctive beliefs, practices, and histories. Thus, it is perhaps more appropriate to speak of several Buddhisms, Christianities, Hinduisms, Islams, and Judaisms than to assume that there is an essential Buddhism, Christianity, Hinduism, Islam and Judaism. Christianity, for example, is a label for over twenty-two thousand autonomous denominations (for example, Roman Catholic, Greek Orthodox, Southern Baptist, American Baptist, Assemblies of God, African Methodist Episcopal, and Seventh-day Adventist).

POLYTHETIC DEFINITIONS

A **polythetic definition,** as articulated by Jonathan Z. Smith, replaces the idea of a single, decisive feature that all members of a class invariably have in common with the following proposition: A class consists of a set of *features* or *properties*. Each member of the class possesses several but not all features of the class and no single feature is "possessed by every member of the class."[22] Monothetic definitions often assume that true definitions identify the essence of the thing defined and thus correspond to reality. Polythetic definitions, in contrast, assume that things, including definitions, change and that there is no empirical evidence for the notion that biological or cultural traits are immutable.[23]

Ludwig Wittgenstein's (1889–1951) analogy of "family resemblance" is helpful here. Religions are best thought of as a family. Like members of human families, some religions resemble each other very much, and others do not. This view accommodates the evidence that *most*, but *not all*, members of the family *religions* include a belief in spirit beings. The view also has the flexibility to include in the class *religion* Jewish groups that reject belief in God and that ground Judaism in the Jewish people and the land of Israel.

Sociologist Talcott Parsons's (1902–1979) definition of religion as "a set of beliefs, practices, and institutions which men have evolved in various societies" is a polythetic one. Unfortunately, this definition is so general that it fails as a tool for discriminating between groups that are religious and those, such as political parties, that presumably are not. Another polythetic approach sharpens the focus by identifying a more expansive and more limiting set of features typical of religions: doctrines, rituals, social structures, moral guides, and narratives (myth, scripture, and so on).

FUNCTIONAL DEFINITIONS

Because of problems associated with monothetic definitions of religion and the desirability of developing alternative models through which religious phenomena could be studied, some scholars shifted their attention from the content of religious belief systems to an analysis of how these belief systems serve the intellectual, emotional, and social needs of humans. Functionally speaking, the importance of religion is derived from its capacity to serve human needs. For example, religion has been defined functionally as a form of social control, as morality tinged with emotion, and as a way of investing life with meaning.

Some functionalists see religious belief systems as grounded in the need of humans to interpret and understand the world in which they find themselves. Others stress the emotional function, characterizing religion as a response to human fear and feelings of powerlessness. Still others emphasize the social aspect of religion. The latter is evident in sociologist Emile Durkheim's (1858–1917) understanding of religion as a "science of social control" grounded in a society's sense of the sacred. In Durkheim's words, "A religion is a unified system of beliefs and practices relative to sacred things, that is to say things set apart and forbidden, beliefs and practices which unite into one single moral community . . . all those who adhere to them."[24] For Durkheim, the sacred is not a supernatural being but an aggregate of human values perceived as transcendent and authoritative for group life.

Religious beliefs and practices conceal the collective ideal, but humans are not mistaken in insisting on the importance of these beliefs and practices as they consecrate those values and conventions that sustain communal life.

A more encompassing approach defines religion as a *meaning-giving* activity that serves emotional and social, as well as cognitive, functions. Meaning giving involves more than stories of how things came to be, such as the Greek myth that fire was a gift of Prometheus, and the biblical myth that different languages came from God's confusion of tongues at the Tower of Babel. Sociologist Max Weber (1864–1920) saw religion as a way of investing life with meaning in response to those features of human existence (suffering, evil, and death) that are not resolvable in scientific terms. As anthropologist Clifford Geertz observed, religious symbol systems provide a context for making suffering "bearable, supportable, something, as we say sufferable."[25]

Contemporary scholars often combine Weberian and Durkheimian insights. Christian theologian George Lindbeck sees religions as "comprehensive interpretive schemes" that mold and organize all of life; they provide a view of the "general order of existence" (the relationships of humans, society, and the world) and serve to create those relationships.[26] Religious worldviews help humans reconcile and transcend the unsatisfactory character of human existence. The religious message is that meaningful life is possible through a conformation of human life to, in Lindbeck's phrase, the "ultimate reality and goodness that lies at the heart of things."[27]

Sociologist Hans J. Mol argues that "systems of meaning" are "necessary for the wholeness (and wholesomeness) of individuals and society."[28] Identity—a sense of where one belongs and how one fits in—is very important, and in Mol's view religion is the "sacralization of identity." **Sacralization** (the process of becoming or making sacred) protects identity through a commitment to a worldview sustained by the reiteration of rites and stories. Religions are not the only systems of meaning, but they are important ones. Art, philosophy, and science are other ways that humans create order out of chaos.

What might we conclude from our discussion of definitions? First, there is no such thing as religion in general. The religions are concrete communities of faith with distinctive beliefs and practices. Second, *religion* is a term for such a wide range of religions that it is misleading to identify a single, decisive characteristic that they all have in common. Third, no definition of religion or of a specific religion is the right or final one. In this vein, philosopher W. Richard Comstock suggests that we should think of definitions as *open,* that is, as contextual and provisional. Such an approach involves the judgment that definitions express the meanings of words rather than the essence of things and that meanings are a function of their linguistic and cultural contexts. In this light, open definitions of religion (whether monothetic or polythetic) are, in Comstock's words, "a context-determined proposal" of an aspect of "religion worthy of further investigation."[29]

Before concluding this section, we would be remiss if we didn't formulate a definition of our own. Religions, then, are systems of meaning embodied in a pattern of life, a community of faith, and a worldview that articulate a view of the sacred and of what ultimately matters. Our definition identifies three principal ways that religions resemble each other: (1) a pattern of life or ethos (a way of living, including moods, shared attitudes, and rituals), (2) a community of faith (social structures and institutions), and (3) a worldview (a view of what is ultimately real and what ultimately matters). The definition assumes that the sacred is an adequate symbol for a range of things, including, for example, spirit beings and Israel understood as a land and a people. We agree with Mircea Eliade that there can be no definitive or final definition of the sacred, because religious movements perceive it differently; thus, descriptions of the sacred ought to be faithful to the ways in which it is understood and manifested in concrete communities of faith.

A test of any definition is what it includes and excludes. Our definition does not invalidate the spirituality of individuals who do not participate in a community of faith but who see themselves as religious or spiritual, but it does exclude their private faith from qualifying as a discrete religion. In linking a religious worldview to the sacred, we concur with the view that belief in spirit beings or an impersonal ultimate is an important feature of religious belief systems.

PERCEPTIONS OF THE SACRED

As noted, *the sacred* is a general term devised to speak about a feature most religions share: the perception of a transcendent and enduring order of things. In this sense, the sacred is a symbol of what is ultimately real. As the ultimate (the highest that can be conceived), the sacred is absolute, eternal, incomparable, and unsurpassable. The eternal is, as a Buddhist scripture declares, that which delivers us from *"the born, the made, the compounded."*[30] In a second sense of ultimacy, the sacred is a symbol of what ultimately matters, of what makes human life worth living.

The sacred has been perceived as both personal and impersonal. As a divine person, the sacred is known as a Goddess (for example, Demeter, Isis, Kali) or a God (for example, Allah, Krishna, Yahweh). Sometimes deity is conceived of as both male and female, as in Christian theologian Rosemary Ruether's use of the term *God/ess* as a metaphor of the Primal Matrix who creates and liberates.[31] Deities are addressed in familial terms as Grandfather, Grandmother, Mother, Father, Sister, and Brother. They have been exalted as Lord and King and called by their attributes—for example, as the Almighty and the Merciful. The sacred has been thought of as a nonpersonal power or force, a liberating truth, a state of being, and a process. Spoken of impersonally, it has been referred to, for example, as Nirvana; the Tao; and the True, the Good, and the Beautiful.

EXPERIENCES OF THE SACRED

What distinguishes religious experiences from other experiences? In one perspective, **religious experiences** are socially approved and mediated interpretations of physiologically generated sensations. Interpretation is what makes an experience a religious one: "A person identifies an experience as religious when he comes to believe that the best explanation of what has happened to him is a religious one."[32]

Others argue that it is the sacred or the holy that distinguishes religious experience from other experiences. Rudolf Otto's term *the numinous* points to a nonrational quality in the human experience of the holy, a feeling Otto characterized as being in the presence of an overwhelming power.[33] Otto noted that the holy is both fascinating and repelling, a feature of religious experience articulated by the Christian monk Joachim of Fiore (1135–1202): "almost every page of scripture proclaims both how lovable and how terrifying God is," so that paradoxically "a person can rejoice for love's sake in his fear and tremble with dread in the midst of love." [34]

Otto's understanding of religious experience as being in the presence of an awesome power resonates with Christianity and Islam and other deity-centered traditions, but less so with those traditions in which deities are not central. Buddhists and an important strand of Hindu tradition often describe intense religious experiences as incomparable bliss or peace. For Zen Buddhist philosopher Kitarō Nishida (1875–1945), the essential religious ideal (the "blowing out of the self") consists of becoming a being that denies itself: "There is a seeing without a seeing one, and a hearing without a hearing one. This is salvation. . . . In the religious consciousness, body and soul disappear and we unite ourselves with absolute Nothingness."[35]

Sociologist of religion Joachim Wach believed that experiences of the sacred entail a total response

of one's whole being "to what is apprehended as ultimate reality."[36] In his view, such experiences are the most intense ones of which humans are capable. Such an intensity is evident in Sioux holy man John Fire/Lame Deer's description of how he was affected by holding the sacred pipes of his people: "I held the pipes. . . . I felt a power surging from them into my body, filling all of me. Tears were streaming down my face. And in my mind I got a glimpse of what the pipe meant. . . . I knew that when I smoked the pipe I was at the center of all things, giving myself to the Great Spirit."[37] Religious experiences are usually less intense and total than this one, however. They range in intensity from mildly uplifting to ecstatic experiences in which people feel themselves metaphorically "standing outside of themselves."[38] Praying, reading scripture, attending religious services, and sitting in meditation may confirm the value of such activities, but they are usually only mildly transformational.

Religious experiences are not always positive. Sometimes religiously "sanctioned" behavior seems more pathological and dis-eased than ecstatic and liberating. Visions and voices sometimes prompt individuals to kill and maim or to be mentally and emotionally abusive. Religious communities have sanctioned holy wars, crusades, inquisitions, the torture and execution of heretics and witches, sacrifice, and other forms of violence, including self-destruction. Blood sacrifice has been an important religious behavior, but human sacrifice is now universally condemned. Animal sacrifice continues, but humans are at odds as to its moral or religious sanction. Faith healing and rejection of blood transfusions and other medical treatments on religious grounds, ingestion of hallucinogens to facilitate visions, and female circumcision are other examples of the complex and ambiguous character of religious behavior.

Religion typically involves both an awareness of the unsatisfactory aspects of human existence and a conviction that it can be overcome fully or in part by experiences that subordinate or harmonize one's being with the sacred. In this sense, religions are **soteriological**—that is, they are modes

A Dharma-Chakra, an eight-spoked wheel symbolizing the teachings of the Buddha. Jobehand Temple, Lhasa, Tibet, People's Republic of China, 1986.

of deliverance or transformation. Van der Leeuw's study of religious phenomena led him to conclude that "religion is always directed towards salvation, never to life as it is given, and in this respect all religion with no exception, is the religion of deliverance."[39] Holy communities and symbol systems provide contexts through which afflicted and fragmented persons can be delivered from misfortune, disease, and even the finality of death.

Religious groups differ on the question of how salvation is accomplished. Traditions such as Christianity and Pure Land Buddhism proclaim that we cannot save ourselves, that we are saved by a higher power. Others, such as Zen Buddhism and Jainism, emphasize that each one of us must work out

our own salvation. Groups acknowledging that salvation comes from a higher power disagree about what humans must do to be saved. Some insist that we are saved by faith alone, whereas others complement faith with good works or other efficacious acts. Confucianism, a tradition that stresses human rather than divine deliverance, teaches that we are shaped into fully responsible human beings through personal effort and such social structures as education, ritual, and filial respect. Sacred rites can be instruments of deliverance, as is evident in rites performed to deliver the afflicted from disease and in the Mormon practice of baptizing the living on behalf of those who are deceased.

SPEAKING OF THE SACRED

Religious traditions typically affirm that the holy is known in human experience and yet is always more than humans can comprehend. Buddhists say that Nirvana is a form of consciousness that no words can adequately define or describe. A Hindu text declares that Brahman, the reality that underlies and permeates all things, "cannot be known through language, nor by the mind, nor by sight." Christian theologians, such as Saint Thomas Aquinas (1225–1274), and Jewish theologians, such as Moses Maimonides (1135–1204), have insisted that humans cannot speak unequivocably of God. In Thomas's words, "To know God by any created likeness is not to know the essence of God."[40]

If the holy is paradoxically revealed in human experience yet ineffable, then one problem of religious language is whether literal, or factually descriptive speech about the ultimate is possible. If it is impossible to speak unambiguously of the eternal, then nonliteral modes of speech are required. To better understand religious uses of language, we examine in turn symbols, metaphors, sacraments, and sacred stories.

SYMBOLS   **Symbols** are things (words, gestures or objects) that mean or signify something. For example, the word *cup* reminds us of the object cup, and in some contexts, forming a V with the index and middle fingers signifies peace. Most symbols—

and most philosophers and linguists would claim all symbols—are representational; that is, by convention or stipulation they stand for the things they symbolize. Representational symbols do not make present, except to the mind, what they symbolize; thus, the use of the word *cow* does not make a hoofed, cud-chewing animal appear.

Of course, scholars recognize that symbols do much more than point to or stand for what they represent. For example, symbols play a fundamental role in what is humanly thinkable. As parameters or boundaries of the thinkable, symbols shape for humans their perceptions of themselves, others, society, and the world. Religionists often make bolder claims, insisting that some symbols have a likeness to, or even make present, what they symbolize. Symbols that are said to involve a likeness to what they symbolize are referred to here as **metaphors,** and those that make present what they symbolize are called **sacraments.**

METAPHORS An array of symbols have served as metaphors of the sacred. Christians often speak of God as "Father," a metaphor that rests on an analogy between fathers and God. The analogy does not assume that God is one's natural father but rather is like a caring, authoritative parent. Mother is another metaphor for divinity. People speak of the "Holy One" as "our Mother" who cares for them as a mother cares for her children. The sun has been a metaphor for deity. Aztec sages saw a likeness between the life-giving function of the sun and that of the divine Giver of Life. Fire, light, and sky, like the sun, have been regarded as natural metaphors for the sacred. The expansive sky is a symbol for the infinite and incomparable. Light is a metaphor for truth and eternal wisdom. Fire symbolizes both the transforming and the destructive power of the holy.

SACRAMENTS Symbols that function *sacramentally* are believed to make present the thing symbolized. Words, gestures, and objects are employed in prayers and rites to invoke—not merely to call to mind—an invisible, sacred presence. Christians assume that when they gather together in the Lord's name, the Lord is also present, and many of them believe that Christ is present through the consecrated bread and wine of Holy Communion. Nichiren Buddhists believe blessings flow from worship before a *mandala* (a visual art form) of the *Lotus Sutra* and recitation of the *mantra Namu Myoho Renge Kyo.* Aztec sages regarded the sun not simply as a likeness to the Giver of Life but as a sacrament through which the Giver of Life was physically present.

Although some religionists believe that symbols may have a likeness to the sacred or even make it present, they usually insist that symbols and the symbolized are not identical. In his study of the Nuer, an East African people, anthropologist E. E. Evans-Pritchard (1902–1973) noted that although a material symbol of divinity cannot, by its very nature, be identical with what it symbolizes, in Nuer spirituality a symbol always has a close association with what it represents. The Nuer believe that God (Kwoth) is unseen and, in part, unknowable, but they also believe that metaphors such as wind, air, and light are similar to Kwoth's invisible and omnipresent character and that although oxen and crocodiles are not identical with Kwoth, they are sacraments through which he is made present. Thus, in Nuer theology, it is appropriate to say of rain that "it is God" or of a crocodile that "it is Spirit," but it is inappropriate to say the obverse, "God is rain" or "Spirit is a crocodile." Rain and crocodiles have a likeness to divinity and are even sacraments through which divinity is made present, but they are not identical with it.[41]

SACRED STORIES From a religious standpoint, the holy is infinitely more than humans can conceive. It is an inexpressible and indescribable mystery, a mystery that cannot be cleared up by gathering more data, performing additional experiments, or thinking more clearly. In the words of the poet Emily Dickinson (1830–1886), the unknown "is the largest need of the intellect, though for it, no one thinks to thank God."[42] If the sacred is an essential mystery, it follows that talk about the sacred is a form of story rather than factually descriptive speech. Seen from the perspective that all speech of the sacred is metaphor and story, we can appreciate the importance of story forms to religious language.

The notion that human perceptions of what is ultimately real are stories, or what scholars refer to as *myths,* rather than descriptions of reality is, of course, debatable. Muslim traditionalists believe that Allah has revealed his nature and what he would have humans do in the *Quran,* which they proclaim is God's inerrant word rather than fallible human speech. For many Christians, knowledge of God's nature is not nearly as inaccessible as theologians such as Saint Thomas believed. Christian **fundamentalists** contend that the *Bible* reveals a nonmetaphorical knowledge of God, especially of God's will, and an inerrant and nonmythical record of the course and ultimate end of history. Nevertheless, those who believe that religious language can be descriptive as well as figurative also insist that God is always something more than humans are capable of understanding.

MYTHS   Broadly conceived, **myth** refers to speech about the sacred whether it is articulated in nonstory form (creed, sermon, or treatise) or in story form (myth, legend, or parable). In this perspective, all religions include mythic conceptions. Christianity reduced to its mythical elements might be characterized in this fashion:

> In the beginning God created the Heavens and the Earth; human beings, the culmination of God's creative activity, were created in the image of God. Though created in God's image, humans are imperfect beings who, as a consequence of their disobedience, have become alienated from God and stand in need of redemption. God's redemptive work—prompted by divine love rather than human merit—was accomplished through the person of Jesus the Christ, the Son of God, and our Lord and Saviour. God's redemption of humankind through Christ is available to all who have faith and will culminate in an eternal, joyous life with God.

It is arbitrary and artificial to reduce Christianity or any other religious traditions to their mythical

elements. However, it is important to understand that all religious traditions have mythological conceptions and that to speak of Christian or Buddhist myths is not a scholarly conceit suggesting that such myths are untrue. Myths concern what lies beyond the reaches of historical and scientific inquiry; they are not so much true or false as they are stories to live by.

Broadly defined, all talk about the sacred is mythological, but in a narrow sense, myth is a form of story that has as its subject a time outside of time, especially at the beginning or end of time. *Origin myths* speak of the beginnings of the world and of all living things. They include stories about the alienation of the divine and human and motifs such as the loss of paradise and humans who survived a primeval flood. *End-time myths,* or **eschatologies,** are about "last things" and the ultimate destiny of human beings.

Like dreams, myths speak of situations that suspend the limitations of space and time and otherwise shatter the normal and ordinary. The subject matter is often a mixture of the momentous and bizarre, and myths are often populated with exotic creatures with human attributes. For example, a Native American myth relates that death became a feature of human existence as a result of Coyote's speech-act that if a rock he hurled into a river sank, people would die, and if it floated, people would live forever.

Myths are often dismissed as stories that reflect the misconceptions and naïveté of premodern peoples. At best, myths are regarded as amusing fictions. In the study of religion, however, myths are understood as stories that embody a people's understanding of the world and their place in it. It is difficult to exaggerate the significance of myths, as is evident in this synthesis of the creation narratives in *Genesis:*

> In the beginning God created the heavens and earth and all living things and saw that creation is very good. Humankind, the culmination of God's creation, was made in the image of God. The primeval male, Adam, was placed in a paradisal garden, the Garden of Eden. God saw

that it was not good for Adam to be alone, that humankind was not yet complete, and created Eve. The couple ate of the forbidden fruit of the Tree of Knowledge. Suffering, death, and expulsion from the Garden were consequences of their disobedience.

The myth sustains several meanings: The cosmos is purposive; creation is good; male and female complete each other. Such stories shape our sense of who we are and to whom we belong. Stories—historical and mythological—constitute our collective memory. As a sage in one of Isaac Bashevis Singer's stories observed, "Today we live, but by tomorrow today will be a story. The whole world, all human life, is one long story."[43]

FORMS OF RELIGIOUS EXPRESSION

There are many forms of religious expression, but most can be subsumed under the following categories: belief, morality, ritual, scripture, and community. They are introduced here so that you will have a set of meanings to associate with them.

BELIEF

Each religious tradition entails a belief system—a set of beliefs embodied in symbols, sacred stories, doctrines, and codes of conduct—that constitutes, in Lindbeck's terminology, a "comprehensive interpretive scheme" that provides believers with an orientation to life. Religious belief systems address perennial human concerns: Who am I? Why must I suffer and die? What is my destiny? What ought I to do? Is there something that can deliver us from misfortune, heal our afflictions, or otherwise deliver us from the unsatisfactory aspects of human existence? Our study of the beliefs of each religion focuses on conceptions of the sacred and of what ultimately matters, the nature and destiny of human beings, evil, and the cosmos.

MORALITY

Morality includes codes of conduct and principles concerning right and wrong, good and bad, and virtue and vice. All religious communities have, to one degree or another, a body of moral and practical wisdom. Such wisdom includes codes of conduct that regulate and guide human interaction, as well as beliefs about what constitutes the good life. In tandem, moral wisdom and sacred rites constitute and give form to a way of life. Moral guides are particularly important in those areas of human existence with the most potential to disrupt communal life. Sanctions against incest, in-group violence, and theft are nearly universal. Believers evaluate the legitimacy of moral directives in different ways. Some see them as divine commands that must be obeyed. Others believe that the moral order is woven into the fabric of the cosmos and failure to live in the way that the universe is ordered results in disharmony. Still others regard moral directives as guides subject to the claims of conscience and ethical reflection.

RITUAL

Ritual is perhaps the quintessential religious act. It is a means of sanctification—of putting things in their proper places.[44] Purity and pollution observances are examples of such ritualized behaviors. Hindus avoid contact with what are considered sources of defilement, including such bodily excretions as sweat, menstrual discharge, and feces. Mosaic law permits Jews to eat seafood with fins and scales and cud-chewing animals with cloven hooves but enjoins them to abstain from eating unclean ones. *Sanctification* usually involves acts of purification, supplication, and thanksgiving—actions in humankind's religious history that have often been facilitated by sacrifices of cereal or blood.

Rituals are acted out in response to a wide range of human concerns. Scholars refer to rituals that provide individuals and groups with a way to mediate transition points in the human life cycle (for example, birth, the transition from child to adult, marriage, and death) and other changes of status (ordination, initiation, and so on) as **rites of passage.** Rituals associated with the human life cycle are also known as **life cycle rites. Calendrical rites** are ceremonies performed to recreate or commemorate important events in the life of the group, to celebrate and sustain the rhythms of nature (for example, planting and harvesting), and to observe regularly scheduled daily and weekly worship. **Periodic rites** are rituals conducted as the need arises—for example, in relationship to personal healing or traveling.

Rituals are complex events. Three aspects of rituals—the performative, repetitive, and communal—are commented on here. Rituals are *performative;* they are acted out in word and deed. Ceremonies make a difference; that is, they bring things about. A marriage rite, for example, changes the status of a couple and unites two families. Rituals are *repetitive;* they are structured rather than unstructured, familiar rather than unfamiliar. Of course, new ceremonies can be created, and old ones are subject to change. Rituals are *communal;* they provide patterns that bind a group together and set the group's members apart from others. In this sense, rituals express the distinctive personality of each religious community. For example, circumcision, dietary rules, and Sabbath day worship have helped forge and sustain Jewish identity. In the words of philosopher Benedict Spinoza (1632–1677), "So great is the importance that I attach to the sign of circumcision . . . that I am persuaded that it is sufficient by itself to maintain the separate existence of the [Jewish] nation forever."[45]

Myths are often ritually acted out. Oral peoples link themselves to what matters most by recreating in words and gestures what the gods and ancestral spirits did in the beginning. In addition to recreating primordial time, rituals may commemorate momentous historical events. Jews commemorate their liberation from bondage in Egypt through their Passover festival. Muslims journey to Mecca to worship God and relive the formative events in the life of their community of faith. The Christian calendar from Advent through Easter celebrates events in the life of Christ.

Blood sacrifice has been an important and, for moderns, puzzling feature of sacred rites. The practice has had a long history. Some scholars believe there is evidence of animal and human sacrifice dating from around forty thousand to fifty thousand years ago, and it was a common feature of late prehistoric and ancient urban religions. Ancient Israelite religion involved animal sacrifices, and in the late biblical period, blood sacrifices were offered daily in the Temple in Jerusalem. Although Muslims do not regard it as sacrifice, they slaughter animals in commemoration of Abraham's willingness, in accord with God's command, to sacrifice his son Ishmael, and as a form of almsgiving to the poor. Like Buddhism and postbiblical Judaism, Christianity eschews sacrifice. However, the connection of sacrifice to Christ's Crucifixion and the Christian doctrine of Atonement is evident in the *New Testament* passage that avers that *"without the shedding of blood there is no forgiveness of sins."*[46] Sacrifice is not simply an archaic, premodern behavior; animal sacrifice continues to have a prominent place in tribal traditions, strands of Hinduism, and religions such as Santería.

Sacrifice is a vivid example of the intersection of religion and violence. In *Violence and the Sacred,* French scholar René Girard has argued that human violence and the need to contain it are "the heart and secret soul of the Sacred." In his view, religion originated as a response to violence (murder) and was embodied in rituals intended to restore the social order: "Religion in its broadest sense, then, must be another term for that obscurity that surrounds man's efforts to defend himself by curative or preventative means against his own violence."[47] Sacrifice, Girard believes, provided an outlet for violent human impulses and helped maintain communal order by sanctioning violence against outsiders, scapegoats, and surrogate (substitute) victims.

SCRIPTURE

Scripture consists of a body of oral or written tradition that a group turns to again and again both as a guide to live by and as an understanding of what is ultimately real. Scriptures in oral traditions are embodied in myths. Those in literate traditions are embodied in holy writs such as the *Vedas* (Hindu), the *Torah* (Jewish), the *Bible* (Christian), and the *Quran* (Muslim). Scripture is a body of literature that a community of faith believes embodies eternal truth and that functions as the authoritative measure by which the group organizes reality and evaluates what matters most. The authoritative character of scripture is derived from the conviction that it is divinely revealed (for example, God's revelation to Muhammad) or is a human discovery of timeless truth (for example, Buddha's apprehension of the *dharma*).

Scripture requires interpretation, because sacred texts rarely have only one meaning. Scholars within each community of faith have devised approaches and guidelines that have been fruitful in drawing out the meanings of texts. Because interpretive strategies are introduced in subsequent chapters, only one form of **hermeneutics,** or mode of interpretation—namely, **scripture criticism**—is introduced here. Scripture criticism interprets scripture through modern historical and literary methods. Its conclusions can be unsettling. For example, scholars employing its methods have rejected the traditional Judaic and Christian teaching that Moses authored the *Pentateuch,* the first five books of the *Bible.* Buddhologists note that the earliest Buddhist scriptures *(Sutras)* were written approximately four hundred years after the Buddha's death, and some of these scholars have concluded that what the texts report the Buddha said and did are largely the creation of the Buddhist community.

Until recently, believers in each religion have thought of their scripture as *the* scripture, the only embodied truth. This is an understanding that many believers continue to hold, but it has been challenged by a growing awareness of the scriptures of other traditions and of the scholarship of scripture criticism. For some contemporary religionists, *the* scripture has become *a* scripture—one of many—a truth in a forest of truths.

COMMUNITY

Religions contain social structures and institutions that provide procedures and processes for relating to others, resolving problems and providing for the general welfare. Studies of the social dimensions of holy communities include, for example, attention to organization, leadership, class (influence and affluence), caste (hereditary status and vocation), and gender. Religious forms of governance (polities) range from those in which the governing process may be nothing more than a consensus of its members to those in which power is highly centralized. In hierarchical structures, leadership is provided by professional clergy **(priests)** who conduct the sacred rites and reiterate the sacred stories. Other forms of leadership include **prophets, sages, shamans,** and **avatars** (deities incarnate in human form or some other life form).

Gender is important to the study of religion because it is a factor in determining the roles and status of men and women, in interpreting and shaping religious experiences, and in constructing belief systems. Within most of the religions studied in this text, women have traditionally been subordinate to men and excluded from positions of leadership. They were counseled to find fulfillment in childbirth; domestic activities; and familial, political, and religious subordination to men. In some contexts, gender was destiny: it was believed that women as women could not be delivered from the cycle of rebirth or achieve enlightenment, or that their salvation was linked to having children. Today, religious institutions are being challenged by men and women of faith who reject the moral and religious legitimacy of patriarchy and its subordination of women and who are reformulating their faith in more compatible idioms.

CLASSIFYING RELIGIONS

Religions can be separated into subclasses or types based on a similarity that members of a subclass have in common but that is not shared by all religions. Three classifications are introduced here: theistic and nontheistic, ethnic and universal, and established and new. Jonathan Z. Smith has pointed out that such binary classifications usually entail the judgment that one of the binaries is superior to the other.[48] The categories introduced here are intended to be descriptive. Theistic traditions are not viewed as superior to nontheistic ones, or universal religions superior to ethnic religions, or established religions superior to new religions.

THEISTIC AND NONTHEISTIC RELIGIONS

The distinction between personal and impersonal conceptions of the sacred is the basis for classifying religions as theistic or nontheistic. In **theistic religions,** the sacred is primarily conceived of as a divine person (God) or divine persons (gods and other spirit beings) with whom humans interact. This classification includes, for example, Christianity, Hinduism, Islam, Judaism, Shinto, Sikhism, Zoroastrianism, tribal religions, and the religions of the first urban societies.

In **nontheistic religions,** the sacred is primarily conceived of in an impersonal form—as, for example, a power, a process, a liberating truth, or a way of being. This category includes, for example, Buddhism, Confucianism, Jainism, and secular or humanistic Judaism. It can also be extended to include quasi-religious movements such as communism and humanism, which affirm nontheistic and explicitly atheistic worldviews, and therapeutic movements such as Scientology.

The qualification *primarily* is used advisedly. Religious traditions usually include both theistic and nontheistic ways of speaking and thinking about the sacred. It is a matter of emphasis. Christians primarily think of God as a personal being (for example, as a loving parent and as incarnate in Jesus), but some speak of God impersonally, as Being Itself or as Truth. Hinduism is primarily a theistic tradition, but an important strand of it distinguishes between *nirguna* Brahman, the godhead that has neither form nor attribute, and *saguna* Brahman, the absolute manifested and worshiped

as a God. Tribal religions are overwhelmingly theistic, but they are not bereft of nontheistic conceptions of sacred power. Buddhist traditions focus on impersonal perceptions of the ultimate (for example, Sunyatta, or Nothingness), but they are not atheistic; they reject belief in a creator deity but acknowledge the existence of gods and include a galaxy of enlightened, transcendent beings such as the historical Buddha, Maitreya Buddha, and Amitabha Buddha. China's traditions include theistic and nontheistic elements. Religious Taoism, Chinese folk religion, and most Buddhist sects include a host of spirit beings from whom help can be obtained, whereas Confucians and "rationalistic" Buddhists conceive of an impersonal Ultimate. Table 1.1 gives examples of theistic and nontheistic religions.

ETHNIC AND UNIVERSAL RELIGIONS

The distinction between ethnic and universal religions is based on whether participation in them is primarily a function of birth and culture or of doctrine. **Ethnic religions** bind people together by ancestry and culture. In contrast, **universal religions** seek converts across the lines of kinship and culture and weld them into a holy community on the basis of doctrine.

Ethnic religions can be further divided into simple and complex. *Simple ethnic* and *tribal* are collective terms that describe the preurban societies and traditions of oral peoples. The characterization does not mean that oral peoples are simpleminded or that their worldviews are less developed but rather that their modes of subsistence, social organization, and material development are less developed and differentiated than those of centralized, urban states. Because the chief principle for inclusion in simple ethnic societies is common ancestry, each society constitutes a natural and relatively closed religious group. Incorporation of outsiders is by intermarriage, capture, and other forms of contact rather than by conversion. Simple ethnic (tribal) religions include those of peoples who lived before the invention of writing (see Chapter 2) and those of oral peo-

	THEISTIC AND NONTHEISTIC RELIGIONS	
Table 1.1	**PRIMARILY THEISTIC**	**PRIMARILY NONTHEISTIC**
	Baha'i (c-e)	Buddhism (c-e)
	Chinese folk religion (eth-e)	Confucianism (eth-e)
	Christianity (c-e)	Jainism (eth-e)
	Hinduism (eth-e)	Scientology (c-n)
	Islam (c-e)	Society for Humanistic Judaism (eth-e)
	Judaism (eth-e)	Theosophical Society (c-e)
	Mandaean (eth-e)	Transcendental Meditation (c-n)
	Shinto (eth-e)	
	Sikhism (eth-e)	
	Zoroastrianism (eth-e)	

eth = primarily ethnic; c = primarily conversionist (universal); e = established; n = new.

ples who lived or are living in historic times (see Chapter 3). Many who follow tribal religions today are literate and knowledgeable about modern as well as traditional life.

Complex ethnic religions or *national religions* are identified with the cultures of particular peoples, but unlike tribal religions, they are grounded in societies with urban centers and centralized forms of governance. They are usually, but not always, literate traditions. Complex ethnic religions are not missionary religions, but when they function as the dominant religion of a centralized, urban state they may integrate and subsume other peoples and cultures through conquest and other forms of contact (trade, treaties, and so on). National religions often exist in contexts in which there are multiple religious groups and subgroups.

The emergence of the first complex ethnic religions coincided with advancements in agriculture. Intensive agricultural production supported larger populations and urban centers and required more complex social and religious institutions. Power was usually concentrated in monarchs whose authority was validated by religious beliefs. Royal palaces and elaborate temples with a priestly class to attend them were typically erected. The first urban society, the city-states of Sumer, emerged in Mesopotamia

(modern Iraq) approximately 5,500 years ago and soon thereafter in Egypt. Premodern urban societies subsequently developed in South Asia (the Indus Valley), East Asia (China), Europe, Central and South America, and sub-Saharan Africa.

Some complex ethnic religions are living, and others are dead. Extinct national traditions include, for example, the state cults of the ancient urban civilizations of Egypt, Mesopotamia, Greece, Rome, and Central and South America (the subjects of Chapter 2). Living ethnic-national religions include the subjects of subsequent chapters and appendixes (Confucianism, Hinduism, Jainism, Judaism, Shinto, and Taoism) and traditions that are not covered (for example, Druze and Mandaean).

Confucianism and Taoism have profoundly influenced non-Chinese cultures in East and Southeast Asia, but they are primarily Chinese traditions, and participation in them as schools of thought or religious movements is primarily a function of individual choice within a Chinese cultural context. Shinto (see Appendix B) is a Japanese tradition in a landscape shared with other religions. Judaism is the religious tradition of the Jews. Conversion to Judaism regularly occurs but is rarely associated with proselytizing.

A stone carving of the Star of David from ancient Palestine (Israel) ca. first century C.E. Photo 1980.

The Hindu population is widely distributed—in 109 countries—but the overwhelming majority (around 720 million) live in Mother India, and a high percentage of Hindus who live abroad are of Indian ancestry. Hinduism's influence and presence spread to Southeast Asia (persevering in Bali, a part of Indonesia) and in modern times to Africa, Europe, and the Americas by nonmissionary forms of contact (for example, intermarriage and trade) and by Indian immigrants who have maintained their Hindu faith. However, cross-cultural conversions do occur through Hindu movements such as the Ramakrishna Mission (Vedanta Societies) and the International Society for Krishna Consciousness (Hare Krishna).

Although the primary factors in religious associations are still birth and culture, universal religions diminish their import by stressing doctrinal commitment. Universal religions are associated with exemplary founders such as Buddha, Christ, and Muhammad. They are conversionist, seeking converts wherever their resources and conditions permit. Christianity, Islam, and Buddhism have, in that order, the largest number of adherents

among the conversionist religions, and as each is widely distributed around the world, they are clearly cross-cultural.

There are many other conversionist or universal religions, including well-established ones such as Baha'i, the Church of Jesus Christ of Latter-day Saints (Mormons), and Sikhism and recently emergent ones such as Scientology, Transcendental Meditation, and the Unification Church. Baha'i and Latter-day Saints were established in the nineteenth century. The Mormons are a rapidly growing Christian movement with over 10 million members worldwide. Baha'i has extended far beyond its Iranian origins and has over 7 million adherents.

Like ethnic religions, universal religions are not always sustainable. Mithraism, a group involving worship of the deity Mithras, and Manichaeism, founded by the prophet Mani (216–277 C.E.), were once popular throughout the Middle East; both movements have disappeared altogether. Zoroastrianism, a theistic tradition founded by the Persian prophet Zoroaster (ca. 628–551 B.C.E.), made converts throughout most of the Persian Empire and influenced contiguous worldviews as well (for example Judaism, Christianity, and Islam). When Persia became Islamic, a group of Zoroastrians fled to India, where their descendants, known as Parsis, keep the faith alive. Parsis are now ethnically exclusive and nonconversionist. They number around 272,000.

Conversionist faiths sometimes find it difficult to export their symbol systems from one culture to another and therefore remain chiefly within an ethnic orbit. Jainism, a religious movement established in India by the sage Mahavira (sixth century B.C.E.), was initially a voluntary and conversionist group, but it has remained within an ethnic orbit and no longer seeks converts. Jains now number slightly over 4 million devotees: over 85 percent live in India, and Jains who live abroad are of Indian ancestry (see Appendix A). Sikhism was founded in the Punjab region of India by Guru Nanak (1469–1530 C.E.) and now numbers around 22 million adherents (see Appendix A). Sikhs seek converts, but they have had limited success in con-

The distinction between ethnic and universal religions is useful if we remember the following caveats. First, simple and complex ethnic religions do not seek converts from other cultures, but their worldviews are universal—that is, they are "comprehensive interpretive systems" of the whole of reality. Second, each religion, whether ethnic or conversionist, may include subgroups in which membership may be either a condition of birth or voluntary. Third, participation in universal religions is voluntary, but the religion of each generation is usually that of their parents.

ESTABLISHED AND NEW RELIGIONS

The classification of a religion as established or new is based on the longevity of the tradition. *Established religions* have lasted over time; they have survived the death of their foundational figures and everyone who had personal contact with them. Established religions can be further divided into dominant and minority. *Dominant* religious groups are relatively large and have a stake in the well-being of the society in which they are situated. State religions are a type of dominant religion. **Denominations,** another dominant type, share their legitimacy with other denominations in a context of religious toleration and liberty.

Established *minority* religious groups are on the margins of society in terms of power and influence. Like dominant groups, they have persisted over time, but they have remained small and set apart from the dominant culture. Like most marginal groups, they have suffered from persecution, especially in their foundational periods, but perhaps in part because of their longevity they have obtained a degree of respectability and public tolerance. Examples of long-established groups that have remained on the margins of society include, for example, the Old Order Amish, the Druze, and the Mandaeans (a group in modern Iraq and Iran that dates from the beginnings of the common era).

New religions span the lives of their foundational figures and all of those who had contact with them; for our purposes, a religion is no longer "new" when it persists beyond the life spans of adherents

A torii gate, a gateway associated with Shinto shrines. Hiroshima, Japan, 1980–1990s.

verting non-Indians. Most Sikhs reside in the Punjab, and those living outside of India are primarily of Indian ancestry. Tenrikyo, a monotheistic faith founded by Nakayama Miki (1798–1887), has over 3 million adherents, but efforts to establish Tenrikyo outside of Japan and Japanese living abroad have not been very successful.

We pointed out earlier that the names of religions are typically general terms for numerous subgroups, each with their distinctive beliefs, practices, and histories. Because of internal divisions, religions classified as ethnic or universal may include traditions that do not fit the classification as a whole. As an example, Christianity and Islam are for the most part conversionist, but there are Christian groups such as the Old Order Amish (founded around 1693) and Islamic groups such as the Druze (a nonorthodox movement founded in 1017 and active today in Lebanon and Syria) that were once conversionist but have ceased missionary activities.

THE NEW RELIGIONS: A SAMPLING WITH FOUNDERS IN PARENTHESES

Table 1.2

ESTABLISHED 1800–1899

Baha'i (Baha Allah)

Christian Science (Mary Baker Eddy)

Church of Jesus Christ of Latter-day Saints (Joseph Smith, Jr.)

Jehovah's Witnesses, official name since 1931 (Charles Taze Russell)

Konkokyo (Kawate Bunjiro)

Santería (grew out of the experiences of Africans in Cuba)

Seventh-day Adventist (Ellen G. White)

Societies for Ethical Culture (Felix Adler)

Tenrikyo (Nakayma Miki)

Theosophical Society (Helena Blavatsky, Henry Steel Olcutt, etc.)

Unity School of Christianity (Charles and Myrtle Fillmore)

Vedanta Society (Swami Vivekananda)

ESTABLISHED 1900–1949

amaNazaretha Baptist Church of South Africa (Isaiah Shembe)

Ancient and Mystical Order of the Rosae Crucis (H. Spencer Lewis)

Assemblies of God (Pentecostal denomination organized in 1914)

Branch Davidians (Victor T. Houteff)

Cao Dai (organized in 1926 in Vietnam)

International Church of the Foursquare Gospel (Aimee Semple McPherson)

Nation of Islam (Wallace Fard)

Native American Church (incorporated in 1918)

Rastafarianism (several foundational figures)

Rissho Koseikai Buddhism (Niwano Nikkyo and Naganuma Myoko)

Soka Gakkai, a.k.a. Nichiren Shoshu of America (Makiguichi Tsunesaburo)

United House of Prayer for All People (Bishop Charles E. "Daddy" Grace)

Universal Peace Mission (M. J. "Father" Divine)

Won Buddhism (Sot'aesan Pak Chungbin)

Worldwide Church of God (Herbert W. Armstrong)

who lived in the foundational period. Most new religions offer personal salvation as an antidote to the spiritual emptiness or malaise that they believe afflicts their contemporaries. Usually (but not always) these religions are founded by a charismatic leader who reveals or embodies the saving, liberating truth. New religions are small. To grow, they must seek converts either from the ranks of the religiously nonaffiliated or from other religious groups or communities. New religions are manifestations of social change; they are responses to and adaptations of other traditions (fusions of old

CONTINUED

Table 1.2

ESTABLISHED 1950–1999

Aum Shinrikyo (Shoko Asahara)

Branch Davidians (David Koresh, split from earlier Branch Davidians)

Church of All Worlds (Tim Zell, neopagan)

Church of God (David Berg)

Church of Israel (Dan Gayman, Christian Identity)

Church of Satan (Anton LaVey)

Church of Scientology (L. Ron Hubbard)

Church Universal and Triumphant (Mark and Elizabeth Clare Prophet)

Earth People (Mother Earth)

ECKANKAR (Paul Twitchell)

EST, a.k.a. the Forum (Werner Erhard, a.k.a. Jack Rosenberg)

Fo Guang Shan Buddhism (Venerable Master Hsing Yun)

Heaven's Gate (Marshall Applegate and Bonnie Lu Nettles)

International Society for Krishna Consciousness (A. C. Bhaktivedanta Swami Prabhupada)

Kimbanguist Church (established in the 1950s, but derived from the ministry of Simon Kimbangu of Zaire; largest independent Christian church in Africa)

People's Temple (Rev. James Jones)

Society for Humanistic Judaism (Rabbi Sherwin Wine)

Transcendental Meditation (Maharishi Mahesh Yogi)

Unification Church (Rev. Sun Myung Moon)

Women's Aglow Fellowship International (founded by a group of women)

and new) and are stimulated by conquest, colonization, and other cultural anxieties and dislocations (for example, the end of a millennium; see the Epilogue).

New religions can be divided into those that accommodate and those that reject the world. Movements such as Scientology and Transcendental Meditation seek integration into, and legitimation by, mainstream society. World-rejecting movements such as the Children of God and the International Society for Krishna Consciousness see themselves as exclusively in possession of Truth and regard society as hopelessly corrupt. As minority groups, new religions have less at stake in the well-being of the larger society and, in the case of world-rejecting movements, feel alienated from

it. They do not have the respectability that comes with familiarity and longevity.

Whatever their view of the larger society, new religions are to one degree or another set apart from established ones. Their set apartness stems from both an inner and an outer perception of otherness. Insiders believe that they have discovered a truth and way of life superior to those taught by the established traditions. Outsiders often view new groups as alien because "their ways are not our ways" and because family members have been converted by emissaries of the new religions. Perceptions of new religions as alien or threatening are evident in the labels for them. They are called **cults** (a term suggesting that they are dangerously deviant) or referred to by the older, somewhat less pejorative term **sects.**

New groups often suffer from real and imagined persecution. Conflict between dominant and marginal nonaccommodating groups can be tragic, as in the suicide-murders of 913 adherents of Rev. James Jones's People's Temple in Jonestown, Guyana (November 1978); the fiery deaths of eighty-six of David Koresh's Branch Davidians in Waco, Texas (April 1993); and twelve deaths from the release of the nerve gas sarin at a subway station in Yokohama, Japan (March 1995), by members of Shoko Asahara's Aum Shinrikyo movement.

All established, universal religions were initially new religions; thus, we can speak of the Jesus sect or the Mormon sect. The founders of many were persecuted by their contemporaries: Jesus was crucified. Muhammad fled Mecca in fear of his life. Baha Allah (the foundational figure of Baha'i) was imprisoned and exiled, and Joseph Smith, Jr. (the founder of the Mormon tradition) was murdered. Of course, founders can go gently into the "night." Gautama Buddha lived a long, relatively serene life, and Muhammad died of natural causes.

Patterns of Religion is about older religious traditions and has little to say about sectarian religious movements that were formed in the nineteenth and twentieth centuries. Nonetheless, the latter are an important part of the religious history of humankind and a word about them is appropriate. Many religions were established in the nineteenth century, including, for example, Baha'i (founded in 1863), the Latter-day Saints (founded in the late 1820s), and Jehovah's Witnesses (founded by Charles Taze Russell in 1872). These three movements are theistic, universal, and by our definition, established rather than new religions. After decades as a persecuted minority, Mormons have a place among the dominant religious groups in the United States. Baha'i is a persecuted minority religion in the land of its birth (Iran), but it is a respected minority in many nations. Jehovah's Witnesses has 2 million to 3 million adherents worldwide but remains aloof from other groups and on the margins of the states in which it operates.

The twentieth century has witnessed an explosion of new religions. In the United States, new Christian movements such as Campus Crusade for Christ (founded by William Bright in 1951), Children of God (by David Berg in 1969), Women's Aglow Fellowship International (by a group of women in 1967), and Promise Keepers (by Bill McCartney in 1990) have shared the stage with New Age and neopagan movements and humanist philosophies. The United States is not alone. Japan has given birth to an estimated one thousand religious groups since 1946, and sub-Saharan Africa is home to hundreds of new and predominantly indigenous Christian churches.

Communism, a movement with nineteenth-century philosophical antecedents and with religious overtones and ideological fervor, has been the most expansive and powerful of the new religions (by virtue of being the state ideology of the Soviet Union, the People's Republic of China, Cuba, and other nations). In the twentieth century, it has been a major force in the lives of millions but appears to be disintegrating as a viable ideology and as an alternative to traditional religions.

It is too early to assess the survivability and exportability of the new religions. The Vietnamese religion Cao Dai (established in 1926) is an example of a popular theistic movement that has not been exportable. Movements that have had cross-cultural success include Pentecostal Christian groups such as the Assemblies of God (organized in 1914), whose missions have inspired similar entities outside the United States. Other groups that have had some success in spreading their message across ethnic lines include Rissho Koseikai (a Buddhist group founded by Niwano Nikkyo and Naganuma Myoko in Japan in 1938), Scientology (by L. Ron Hubbard in the United States in 1953), the Unification Church (by Rev. Sun Myung Moon in Korea in 1954), and the International Society for Krishna Consciousness (by A. C. Bhaktivedanta Swami Prabhupada in the United States in 1965). Pan-Indian movements, such as the Native American Church, have successfully cut across tribal boundaries in the United States. Groups such as Rastafarianism (originated in Jamaica in the twentieth century), which synthesize African tribal traditions with Christianity, along with older, established religious movements such as Santería (Cuba) and Vodou (Haiti), have had success in the Caribbean and among African Americans who migrated from the region to Europe and the United States. Table 1.2 lists a sampling of new religions.

MAGIC AND RELIGION

Magic is the acquisition and exercise of supernatural power to bring about desired results. In traditional societies, magic has been inseparable from religion. Scientific and religious modernists see it as based on a mistaken understanding of how the world works. They are troubled by its persistence in popular culture and are sharply divided on its relationship to religion. One side sharply separates the two, regarding magic as a misguided and selfish attempt of humans to extend their control over events by a manipulation of sacred power through the magical arts (curses, spells, and other ritualized behaviors), and religion as the supplication of, and communion with, divinity. The other side rejects the notion of a decisive difference between magic and religion, regarding them as inseparable and complementary. Efforts to manipulate and control divinities or divine cosmic forces are so entwined with supplication and communion, says this side, that it is impossible to know where one ends and the other begins.

A magico-religious worldview sees the universe as a complex web of relationships and assumes that power is derived from such knowledge. This worldview affirms that nothing happens by chance and that magic, properly performed, will bring about the desired results. **Imitative magic** involves the belief that like produces like—for example, in simulating thunder and lightning to produce rain. **Contagious magic** assumes that something that was once part of something else continues to share in its vitality and power—for example, belief that a person's shorn hair continues to be part of that person and that, in the hands of a malevolent magician, it can be used to harm the person.

Divination is a term for the methods that magicians use to determine the applicability of magico-religious knowledge to the problems of clients and to recommend appropriate courses of action. **Wisdom divination** assumes that knowledge of the magico-religious structure of the cosmos is essential to human well-being. Knowledge of the heavens (astrology) and of the elements (alchemy) are examples of the complexity that wisdom divination can entail. Other methods divine solutions to problems and manipulate sacred power through incantations, casting lots, reading omens, functioning as a medium for spirit beings, and other behaviors. Supernatural power is acquired in various ways, including dreams, visions, trance states, and apprenticeship to a teacher who has mastered the magical arts.

Religious traditions usually assume that sacred power can be used benevolently or malevolently. Benevolent magicians (commonly referred to as diviners and shamans) are agents of well-being; they use their magico-religious power to heal, exorcise evil spirits, resolve problems, and see into the future. Malevolent magicians (commonly referred to as **witches** and **sorcerers**) use magic to harm others. In folk societies and popular culture, they are believed to use their supernatural power for evil purposes such as bewitching others and causing disease, barrenness, and death. It is not surprising that violence is often directed at those suspected of **witchcraft** or **sorcery**. For example, the *Los Angeles Times* reported that between July 1992 and July 1993, forty-four men and women of western Kenya were burned to death by their neighbors as witches and, as is usually the case, without evidence of their guilt.

In medieval and early modern Europe, Christians associated witchcraft with intentional evildoing, and witches were believed to be subjects of Satan. Some Christians continue to link witches and witchcraft with evil. Communities within England and the United States have struggled with accusations of satanic cults and ritual abuse and with individuals whose evil deeds involve satanic symbols. Some evil is done in the name of Satan (some is also done in the name of God), but cases involving charges of satanic ritual abuse often falter in the legal system for lack of evidence. Along the way the reputations of the accused are compromised.

Devotees of neopagan religious movements vigorously protest the identification of witchcraft with intentional evil. In *neopaganism,* witchcraft is an ancient life-affirming faith centered in the worship of the Mother Goddess and in folk traditions in which women had integral roles as healers and priests. These devotees believe that this tradition and craft were cruelly suppressed by patriarchal and misogynist Christian traditions, a suppression evident in the disproportionate number of women who were accused and executed as witches. The scapegoating of women as witches occurred on a large scale. Historian Anne Llewellyn Barstow estimates that 200,000 Europeans were accused of witchcraft in the period 1550 to 1750 and that around 100,000 were killed. Eighty percent or more of the accused were women. Typically, the victims were older, illiterate, widowed, and poor, and some of them functioned as midwives and healers.[49]

RELIGION IN TRADITIONAL AND SECULAR SOCIETIES

In traditional societies, religion has functioned as a unifying element of all the other aspects of individual and collective life. Wilfred Cantwell Smith notes the following about the pervasive and integrative character of Islam:

> Islam is not a "factor" in the life of Muslims, except insofar as they may have succumbed to the corrosive pressures of a modern-Western way (largely secular) of analyzing life. Rather, Islamic religiousness is the quality nurtured by the Islamic tradition by which the various factors of life cohere into a significant pattern. His faith is

not one item along with others in a Muslim's life, it is the meaning that all the items have for him, insofar as life has meaning. We understand Muslims and their faith only when someone can explain to us how politics, and economics, and all the other matters that the West calls secular, appear to a Muslim *qua* Muslim.[50]

In most modern states, religion no longer integrates the other elements of public life (for example, art, economics, education, medicine, and politics). In philosopher of religion Louis Dupre's words, "religion in the 20th century has ceased to integrate public life altogether."[51] This is particularly the case in most of Europe and North America, where the dominant traditional religion (Christianity) is situated in contexts in which there are numerous other religions and no authoritative form of Christianity. Dupre's assertion is also applicable to East Asia (China, Japan, Korea, Mongolia, and Taiwan) but much less so to North Africa, the Middle East, and South Asia. Religious establishments that integrate public life continue in Thailand (Buddhism), Nepal (Hinduism), and several Islamic states (for example, Algeria, Bangladesh, Iran, Libya, Pakistan, and Saudi Arabia). There are exceptions in Europe as well. Armenia (Apostolic), Greece (Eastern Orthodox), and Ireland (Roman Catholic) are nations in which a dominant form of Christianity profoundly influences public life. Even in countries in which Christians are in the majority (for example, Australia, Canada, New Zealand, Mexico, and the United States) but do not function as a dominant religious body, the beliefs and values of Christians are not entirely shut out of public life. With these exceptions in mind, it is valid to observe that in many modern states, there are many religions and no dominant religion. In such contexts, religions integrate the lives of their adherents but do not unify a society as a whole.

Secularism, human migrations, cultural pluralism, and challenges to traditional beliefs by modern science and philosophy are factors that make it both difficult and undesirable for many modern societies to achieve cultural integration through a single set of religious symbols. **Secularism**—separation of religion from other aspects of public life—is a feature of modern Western societies and non-Western ones that have been influenced by the conception of religion as a private affair separated from the conduct of public life. Many secular societies legitimate both belief and disbelief by the principle of intellectual and religious liberty, a legitimation that nurtures **religious pluralism** (the presence of different religious groups within a nation-state) and protects new and established minority religions.

Anthropologist Louis Dumont noted that the "holistic" character of traditional societies has been replaced in modern Western societies by an emphasis on the individual as an independent and "essentially non-social being" who can be religious outside a community of faith.[52] An autonomous and private conception of religion is evident in Thomas Jefferson's remark, "I am a sect by myself as far as I know." Another variation is found in Emily Dickinson's poem contrasting churchgoing with the spiritual resources available at home and through nature:

> Some keep the Sabbath going to Church—
> I keep it, staying at Home—
> With a Bobolink for a Chorister—
> And an Orchard, for A Dome—
>
> . . . .
>
> So instead of getting to Heaven, at last—
> I'm going, all along.[53]

The phenomenon of individual-centered rather than community-centered religion is evident in the remarks of one Sheila Larson, who, in a recent study of American values, is reported to have described her religion as "Sheilaism." Hers is an atomistic faith consisting of Sheila and her affirmation of discovering God within her own being, self-love, and concern for others independent of a religious community.[54] Larson's "orientation to life" is a relatively common modern phenomenon; many people see themselves as "religious" or "spiritual" outside of organized religions. Such orientations are often cafeteria-style faiths in which believers cobble together their religious worlds of meaning by integrating bits and pieces from different sources.

Where religion does not function as an integrative and pervasive cultural force, perhaps believers must, as Louis Dupre has urged Christians to do, "personally integrate what tradition did in the past."[55] The obligation of individuals to cultivate their interior lives within or outside a faith community and to integrate their interior lives with other elements of life may ring true for many readers. Nonetheless, we need to be aware of the social and cultural pervasiveness of traditional religions and to recognize that in nonsecular societies, individuals rarely choose their religion or are religious outside a community of faith.

APPROACHES TO THE STUDY OF RELIGION

We have introduced several subjects and categories for the study of religious phenomena. Here we describe the perspectives of the investigators.

SCIENTIFIC AND THEOLOGICAL PERSPECTIVES

Science and **theology** have much in common. Both are rational activities concerned with evidence and logical inference, with knowing and understanding. However, their assumptions and contexts are different. **Scientific studies of religion** are conducted by scholars who stand, at least for the purposes of their study, outside a circle of faith and who are committed to interpreting religious phenomena irrespective of the consequences for faith. For our purposes, this category includes historical, social, and behavioral studies, but it is not devoid of philosophical suppositions. Such studies account for religious phenomena on nonreligious grounds (for example historical, economic, sociological, and psychological grounds) and either discount or set aside religious explanations.

Theological studies of religion, in contrast, are conducted within a believing community. They entail a self-conscious effort of believers to critically examine and defend their beliefs. Like scientific studies, theological studies are concerned with clarity, evidence, and logical consistency, but they also aim at nurturing and deepening faith. Theology is transformational as well as informational. It is salvation reflected on. It is faith seeking understanding. Because the term *theology* is derived from the Greek term for God, it is not a satisfactory description of reasoned discourse on matters of belief in nontheistic traditions. In the absence of such a term, however, we are using theology as a symbol for the critical examination and defense of belief in both theistic and nontheistic traditions.

PROJECTIVIST AND RESPONSIVIST PERSPECTIVES

Projectivists believe that religious belief systems are illusory (misconceptions of reality) and explain the origin of religion and its ongoing importance in human life on functional grounds. **Responsivists** believe that the sacred or ultimate order of things is real and that some or all religions originated as responses to it.[56] An introduction to representative projectivists and responsivists provides a fuller and more nuanced understanding of the two perspectives.

E. B. Tylor, Emile Durkheim, Karl Marx (1818–1883), and Sigmund Freud (1836–1959) shared the projectivist view that as interpretations of reality, religious worldviews are illusory. Each of them evaluated religious phenomena in functional terms and speculated about the origin and evolution of religion. Tylor believed that religion had its origin in the need of humans to explain and otherwise make sense of their experiences. He surmised that the ideas of "soul" and "spirit beings" grew out of the need of prehistoric peoples to explain such threatening aspects of human existence as death and such puzzling phenomena as dreams and visions. Tylor theorized that the idea of a shadow self or soul capable of functioning independently of corporeal existence originated as a reasonable interpretation of such experiences. Tylor

singled out belief in spiritual beings as the essential characteristic of religion, but he did not believe that such beings exist. In his judgment, religion serves an indispensable human function (understanding), but it is not indispensable; scientific explanations will eventually replace religious ones and make the latter superfluous.

Durkheim viewed religion as a means whereby a people is organized into a moral community. In his view, a sense of the sacred is fundamental to community building, but the sacred is not God or the gods; it is a system of social relations and values, moral codes, and **taboos** that functions as a means of social control and as a force for the preservation of group life. Religious experiences are not entirely illusory, but as Durkheim noted, "it does not follow that the reality which is its foundation conforms objectively to the ideal which believers have of it." The "objective cause" of those sensations "out of which religious experience is made, is society." Thus, "society is the soul of religion."[57] In Durkheim's judgment, religious beliefs do not, as science does, add to our knowledge, but they do something every bit as valuable: they help us to live. And this is accomplished through the human creation of a sacralized world "which does not exist except in thought" but serves as a collective ideal for the daily round of human existence.[58] For Durkheim, religious belief systems are mistaken in their understanding of reality, but they are indispensable to "collective existence."

Marx believed that religion serves the interests of both the oppressor and the oppressed by commanding the submissiveness of the latter and by offering hope to them in the form of rewards in the hereafter. Religion helps preserve the position of the ruling class and serves as a druglike antidote for the despairing masses. In Marx's words, "Religion is the sigh of the oppressed creature, the heart of a heartless world, and the soul of soulless conditions. It is the opium of the people."[59] Religion provides a respite from human suffering, but like all opiates, it fails to change the conditions and underlying causes of human distress. Marx believed that once the working class was liberated, religion would no longer be needed.

In *Totem and Taboo,* Freud argued that the first stages of religion, politics, and morality had their origin in a primal crime, the murder of a primeval father by his sons. Freud imagined that in the beginning, families were ruled by fathers who fiercely defended their sexual monopolies of the females in their respective families. When sons matured and sought sexual congress with their mothers and sisters, they were killed or driven away by their fathers. In Freud's words, "One day the expelled brothers joined forces, slew and ate the father. . . . This violent primal father had surely been the envied and feared model for each of the brothers. Now they accomplished their identification with him by devouring him and each acquired a part of his strength."[60]

Freud believed that the brothers were acting out a fundamental feature of the unconscious life of all male children—sexual desire for their mothers and competition with their fathers for their mother's love—which he labeled the *Oedipus complex.* A figure in Greek mythology, Oedipus was disturbed by a prophecy that he would kill his father and marry his mother, so he fled his presumed parents' home, only to later kill in anger a stranger, his natural father, and to marry the victim's wife, his natural mother.

In Freud's analysis, the primal crime was truly momentous: it triggered the emergence of a new social organization and the beginnings of morality, religion, and sacrifice.[61] The brothers replaced the old social order (father rule) with a new one (heads of clans) in which authority was shared by the brothers. To circumvent ongoing sexual violence, they renounced sexual union with their mothers and sisters and thereby initiated the incest taboo, which, in Freud's view, was the first moral rule. The brothers absolved themselves of guilt by sacrificing an animal that functioned as a symbolic substitute for their father. The substitution was at once the first form of religion **(totemism)** and a primal rite of blood sacrifice with a surrogate victim. The brothers "undid their deed" by declaring that the surrogate for their father was not to be killed or eaten except in a ritual context. Thus, the murdered father rose triumphant as totemic symbol and sacramental feast. Freud speculated that as time passed, the ancestral father/totemic guardian spirit was transformed into a father God: "Psychoanalytic investigation of the individual teaches that god is in every case modelled after the father and that our personal relation to god is dependent upon our relation to our physical father, fluctuating and changing with him, and that god at bottom is nothing but an exalted father."[62] For Freud, religion is deeply rooted in human experience, but it can be surpassed through human rationality.

In contrast, responsivists believe that the religious dimension of human existence is a response to an enduring and transcendent aspect of reality. Rudolf Otto spoke of it as the Holy, Paul Tillich as the Ultimate, Mircea Eliade as the Sacred, Zenkai Shibayama as the Truth or Absolute, and Wilfred Cantwell Smith as the "transcendent reality" to which the religious traditions point. Of this sense of reality, Eliade observed, "Sacredness is above all *real.* The more religious a man *is* the more real he is, and the more he gets away from the unreality of a meaningless life."[63]

Responsivists may concur with projectivists that religions are human creations, but they insist that that is not the whole story. Responsivists believe that there is an enduring and transcendent reality and that religions are responses of humans to their experiences of this reality. For example, as a Christian, Gerardus van der Leeuw believed that "the origin of religion lies in God,"[64] and as a historian of religion, he believed that religions are shaped by historical and cultural forces. Belief in the responsive aspect of religion is compatible with the conviction that what is ultimately real is divinely revealed or intuitively grasped, as well as with the proposition that religions are human creations.

RELIGION AND TRUTH

The range of perspectives on religion we have surveyed here raises questions about the relationship of religious beliefs to truth. If no belief or set of beliefs is common to all religions, and the belief systems of the religions of the world articulate dissimilar and often incompatible beliefs, can all religions be, as they claim to be, true? Is there truth in all religions, in none of them, in some of them, or in only one of them? There are advocates of each of these options.

An insider clearly regards his or her religious belief system as true. Foundational figures such as Buddha, Christ, Muhammad, and Joseph Smith, Jr., regarded their doctrines, whether divinely revealed or intuited, as universal truths, not as conditional and relative. Likewise, theologians speak from inside communities of memory and articulate truths that cohere with received tradition.

Some believers proclaim that only their religion is true. For example, some (not all) Christians believe that the gospel is exclusively true and that salvation is through Christ alone. Other faith communities acknowledge the legitimacy of religions with whom they have theological and historical affinities. Muslims believe that true religion was revealed and established by God, and that it is embodied in Islam and the monotheistic traditions (Judaism, Christianity, Zoroastrianism) that preceded God's revelation to Muhammad.

Outsiders take different stances. Scientists may set aside or suspend the question of the truth of religious beliefs or, like those in the projectivist camp, believe that as interpretations of reality, all religions are false. It is clear that projectivists and scientific studies view religious subjects from the outside, but so do those responsivists who affirm that religion is true in respect to belief in an ultimate order of things but who cannot give assent to all of the doctrinal truths held by concrete religious communities.

Some responsivists believe that there is truth and saving power in all religions. This view was articulated by the Hindu sages Gandhi and Ramakrishna (1834–1886). "After long study and experience," Gandhi concluded "that (1) all religions are true, (2) all religions have some error in them." Ramakrishna wrote that "different creeds are but different paths to reach the Almighty. . . . Every religion is nothing but one of such paths that lead to God."[65] F. Max Müller (1823–1900), the scholar behind the proposition that "to know one religion is to know none," believed that the basic feature of all religion is "the perception of the infinite" and that no religion is devoid of truth. Christian theologian John Hick has suggested that all religions at their experiential roots are in contact with the same ultimate reality: "the different encounters with the transcendent within the different religious traditions may all be encounters with one infinite reality, though with partially different and overlapping aspects of that reality."[66]

The dichotomy of true and false religion accompanied by a perception that adherents of "false" religions are to be converted, expelled, or eradicated has been, in some historical contexts, a feature of Christianity and Islam. Other faiths have been more accommodating of doctrinal differences. Adherents of the major Chinese traditions (Buddhism, Confucianism, and Taoism) typically see these traditions as complementing rather than negating each other and as not requiring an exclusive commitment. Hindus teach that each of the orthodox schools of Hindu philosophy is true up to a point and that no single school is the exclusive custodian of truth. Jainism is remarkable for its doctrinal tolerance. The Jain doctrine of the many-sidedness of reality entails two teachings: (1) because they are historically conditioned, all viewpoints are only partial expressions of truth, and (2) no statement ever encompasses the whole truth, and therefore, all statements should be preceded by the term *maybe*. Baha'is teach that religious truths are provisional and change over time in response to new insights and revelations, and adherents affirm the truth of all religious traditions. It is worth noting that a religion may be doctrinally tolerant but intolerant on other grounds. India's first prime minister, Jawaharlal Nehru (1889–1964), once described his homeland, the birthplace of Hinduism, Buddhism, and Jainism, as "the least tolerant nation in social forms while the most tolerant in the realm of ideas."

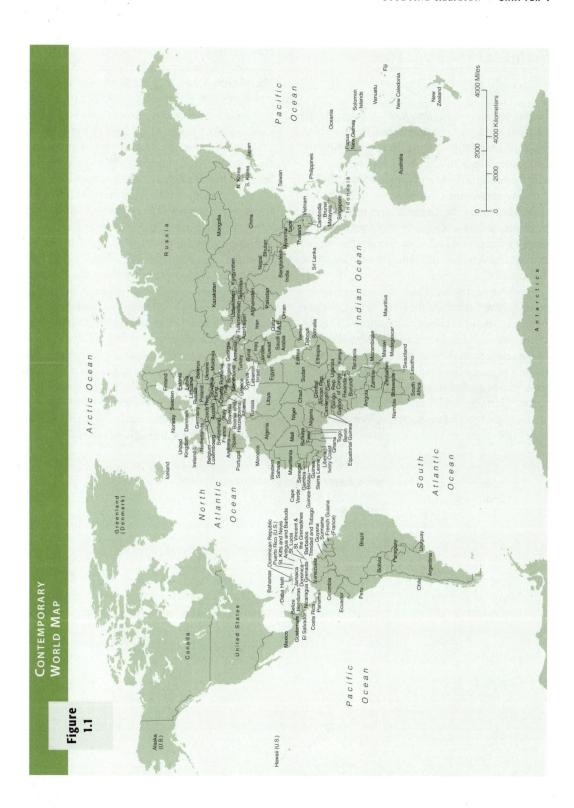

CONTEMPORARY
WORLD MAP

Figure
1.1

SOME OBSERVATIONS

For the purposes of our study, we have defined religion as a system of meaning embodied in a pattern of life, a community of faith, and a worldview that articulates a view of the sacred and of what ultimately matters. As you plunge into the study of concrete communities of faith, try to understand their patterns of life, the character of their communities, and the complexity of their worldviews. Seek to understand what each tradition regards as sacred and to become familiar with its stories and rituals.

We have introduced numerous categories that scholars have devised for the study of religious phenomena. Apply the classifications *theistic* and *nontheistic, ethnic* and *universal,* and *established* and *new* to the religions in the text, but remember the limitations of these classifications. To avoid the "tyranny of present-mindedness," keep in mind the distinction between traditional and secular societies. To avoid the "tyranny of categories," remember that today there are so many forms of interaction between religious worlds of meaning and so many ways of being religious that the boundaries that the classifications demark have been blurred.

Patterns of Religion is a scientific rather than a theological study, but we do not assume that religion can be exclusively explained in terms of nonreligious processes. We come at our subjects from the outside, but we have attempted to reconstruct religious beliefs and practices in a way that believers will find compatible with their faith. We seek to inform rather than to transform, to understand rather than to convert. Nevertheless, a person's beliefs may be profoundly influenced by such an approach. From the inside, a religious worldview is an apprehension of reality; from the outside, it is a perspective among other perspectives. A study of other traditions challenges our own belief system and threatens to turn its truth into a perspective, but it is a risk worth taking. When we do so, we experience some of the wonder of being human and plunge more deeply into the quest for truth. As you pursue your studies, reflect on the advice of one of the world's great teachers, Confucius: "I wasn't born knowing what I teach you. Being fond of the past, I sought it through diligence."[67]

GLOSSARY OF RELIGIOUS TERMS

avatar	a deity incarnate in human form or some other life form (for example, God incarnate in Jesus of Nazareth and Lord Krishna embodied as a charioteer in the *Bhagavad Gita*).
calendrical rite	a ritual associated with the celebration of the seasons or the commemoration of momentous events.
contagious magic	the idea that a material entity that was once part of another entity continues to participate in that entity; for example, that shorn human hair participates in the spirit of the person from whom it came and can be used in a ritual context to affect that person.
cult	(1) a collective body united by a common devotional practice, that is, a religion or religious subgroup; (2) a religious movement regarded as deviant, dangerous, and even pathological; a pejorative term for new religious groups.
denomination	a term for a mainstream religious group that recognizes the legitimacy of other religious groups.
divination	divining or solving problems, including the diagnosis of the causes of sickness or misfortune through contact with spirit beings or knowledge of esoteric wisdom.
eschatology	having to do with "last things" or end-time, such as belief in the return of Christ or the coming of Maitreya Buddha.
ethnic religion	a religion associated with a particular people and culture that does not seek converts across the boundaries of lineage, family, race, and culture.
fundamentalism	movements that preserve, renew, and defend traditional religious belief and practice and, in particular, the absolute veracity of scripture. For example, fundamentalist Christians believe that the *Bible* cannot be in error, because God is the ultimate author.
hermeneutics	the science or art of interpretation; the methodologies involved in interpreting a text.
the holy	as a noun, a term for an ineffable and unsurpassable power. As an adjective, an attribute of things (holy place, holy book, and so on) or persons. In this text, *the holy* is a synonym for *the sacred*.
imitative magic	the belief that like produces like; for example, that sounds or gestures that imitate thunder and rain will magically produce rain.
life cycle rite	a ritual performed at a specific transition point in the human life cycle (for example, at birth, puberty, marriage, or death).
magic	the mastery and exercise of sacred power for the purpose of bringing about desired events or conditions. See **contagious magic** and **imitative magic.**

metaphor	a figure of speech that makes an analogy between two or more things, such as speaking of God as King or as Mother or speaking of Nirvana as Emptiness.
monothetic definition	a definition of a term according to a single, decisive feature of the thing symbolized.
morality	a set of guides, codes, or commandments. Used as a synonym for *ethics*, it refers to discourse about what makes a right action right and the ends to which behavior ought to be directed.
myth	in a broad sense, all speech about the holy. In a narrow sense, a story about the cosmic origins of the world, humans, evil, and the like.
nontheistic religion	a religion in which the ultimate is conceived of as an impersonal process, power, liberating truth, or way of being.
numinous	Rudolf Otto's word for both the holy and the nonrational aspect of human experiences of the holy.
periodic rite	a ceremony performed as the need arises—for example, for healing, exorcisms, rainmaking, installations, war making, and so on.
polythetic definition	a definition of a term according to features that most, but not all, members of the symbolized have in common.
priest	a member of a professional class of leaders who serve as intermediaries between the community and the sacred, especially through the performance of rituals.
projectivist	in this text, one who believes that religious worldviews are illusory and who explains the role of religion in terms of its functions.
prophet	a messenger of divinity; one who speaks for God or a god.
religious experience	an experience that differs from other human experience by virtue of being associated with the sacred or ultimate.
religious pluralism	the existence of multiple religious groups within a society along with a recognition of the legitimacy of other religions.
responsivist	in this text, one who believes that religions are responses to what is ultimately real.
rite of passage	a ceremony performed at transition points in life; includes life cycle and status elevation rites.
ritual	a formalized social act commemorating sacred occasions and invoking a sacred presence.
sacralization	making something sacred or the process of becoming sacred.
sacrament	a symbolic act involving words, gestures, and things through which the sacred is manifested.

the sacred	in this text, a synonym for *the holy*. The sacred is set apart from *the profane* (the unhallowed or ordinary). As an adjective, an attribute of something or someone that is venerated.
sage	a figure whose religious status is associated with wisdom.
scientific study of religion	the study of religious phenomena through the methods of social scientists and historians.
scripture	a body of oral or written literature that a religious body regards as authoritative.
scripture criticism	the examination of scripture through historical-literary methods.
sect	See **cult.** A sect is a new religious group or established group that is set apart from established mainstream religious groups.
secularism	the view that public life should be conducted independant of religious institutions and symbols.
shaman	(1) a specialist in sacred matters, including the magical arts in tribal societies; functions as healer, diviner, and medium; (2) an ecstatic religious figure in tribal traditions who serves as a medium through which spirit beings are made present and controlled.
sorcery, sorcerer	the exercise of magical power for benevolent or malevolent purposes; synonyms for *witchcraft, witch*. Generally, sorcerers and witches use their magical powers with malevolent intent.
soteriology	the study of experiences in which humans are converted, saved, transformed, or enlightened.
symbol	broadly conceived, a word, gesture, or object that stands for, participates in, or makes present the thing symbolized.
taboo	that which is set apart as sacred or as dangerous and forbidden.
theistic religion	a religion in which belief in divine beings is central.
theology	a critical examination and defense of religious belief.
theological study of religion	a critical examination of religious beliefs and practices from within a circle of faith.
totemism	regarding a deified animal or plant as a benefactor and ancestor of a family, clan, or tribe.
the ultimate	the ultimate reality, the incomparable, that which matters most.
universal religion	(also conversionist religion) a religion in which membership is linked to a doctrinal affirmation of faith and that seeks converts across the boundaries of lineage, family, race, and ethnicity.
witchcraft/witch	knowledge and mastery of sacred power and use of the magical arts for good or ill. In both ordinary and academic discourse, a witch is a person who uses magical power to do evil. Synonym for *sorcery, sorcerer.*

FOR FURTHER STUDY

Resources are also included in the chapter notes, located at the end of this volume.

Abingdon Dictionary of Living Religions. Edited by Keith Crim. Nashville, Tenn.:
Abingdon, 1981.
   A valuable resource for contemporary religion.

Carmody, Denise L. *Women and World Religions.* 2d ed. Englewood Cliffs, N. J.:
Prentice-Hall, 1988.
   A solid introduction to the roles and status of women in the major religious traditions.

Carmody, Denise L., and John T. Carmody. *How To Live Well: Ethics in the World
Religions.* Belmont, Calif.: Wadsworth, 1988.
   An introduction to the morality and ethics of the world religions.

The Encyclopedia of Religion. 16 vols. Edited by Mircea Eliade. Chicago: University of
Chicago Press, 1986.
   The most comprehensive reference work for the study of religious phenomena.

The HarperCollins Dictionary of Religion. Edited by Jonathan Z. Smith and William
Scott Green. New York: HarperCollins, 1995.
   An excellent, up-to-date resource on a wide range of religious subjects.

The Holy Book in Comparative Perspective. Edited by Frederick M. Denny and Rodney
L. Taylor. Columbia, S.C.: University of South Carolina Press, 1993.
   Contains chapters on the scripture of each of the major religious traditions.

O'Neill, Maura. *Women Speaking, Women Listening.* Maryknoll, N.Y.: Orbis Books,
1990.
   *An interreligious dialogue of women on issues of gender in theological anthropology,
   epistemology, values, theology, feminism, and language.*

Paden, William E. *Religious Worlds: The Comparative Study of Religion.* Boston: Beacon
Press, 1988.
   A comparative study of God, myth, ritual and other subjects.

Schmidt, Roger. *Exploring Religion.* 2d ed. Belmont, Calif.: Wadsworth, 1988.
   *An introduction to varieties of religious expression and experience and to subjects
   addressed in the philosophical study of religion (for example, God, evil, and human
   destiny).*

Van Voorst, Robert E. *Anthology of World Scriptures.* Belmont, Calif.: Wadsworth,
1994.
   An introduction to the world religions through their scripture.

More comprehensive texts on the religions of the world are available through
Wadsworth Publishing Company (Belmont, Calif.): Kenneth Cragg, *The House of
Islam;* Byron Earhart, *Japanese Religion;* Sam Gill, *Native American Religions;* Thomas
Hopkins, *The Hindu Religious Tradition;* Noel King, *African Cosmos;* Jacob Neusner,
The Way of Torah; Richard Robinson, *The Buddhist Religion;* Lawrence Thompson,
Chinese Religion; and Mary Jo Weaver, *Introduction to Christianity.*

READINGS

Reading 1.1   WHAT IS RELIGION?   Gudo Wafu Nishijima

At the outset of *To Meet the Real Dragon*, the Buddhist priest Gudo Wafu Nishijima addresses the issue of what religions have in common. What, in his judgment, are features that all religions share? Why do some students of religion exclude Buddhism from the family of religions? Do you agree with Nishijima that all humans have a religion?

> People generally have rather strong feelings about religion. Either they accept religion as a natural and necessary part of their lives, or they carefully avoid any thing which resembles religion or religious thought. Very few people really consider the meaning of religion itself. But I think it is important to look closely at that which we call religion. I think we should ask ourselves a very fundamental question: What is religion anyway?
>
> This question became important to me many years ago. I was one of those people who are naturally attracted to religious ideas. I became interested in Buddhism when I was rather young, and I read many books about it. In some of those books, I found a very interesting debate. It seemed that some scholars doubted whether or not Buddhism was a religion. They insisted that a "true religion" must recognize the existence of a god, a supernatural realm, or a power in the universe which is beyond and apart from the material world. But Buddhism does not have such a belief. Buddhism looks no further than this place and time for its inspiration. Buddhism affirms this world. It was this affirmation of the real world that the religious scholars found troubling, and because of it, many of them could not bring themselves to include Buddhism in the family of true religions. This was very surprising to me. There was something strange about a definition of religion which could not accept the possibility of a "realistic" religion. In my life, Buddhism was religion itself. How could it not be a religion? But here in these books, scholars were seriously debating whether Buddhism was a religion or not. So I began to wonder what "religion" was. I asked myself what all religions had in common.
>
> Finding a common ground for all religions was not so easy. When I studied the religions of the world, I found great diversity in their beliefs and practices. In some cases, those beliefs and practices appeared to be similar, but there were also many fundamental differences. There were exceptions to every rule. It seemed that every definition of religion was either too narrow and limited or too complicated to be really useful. Then one day I noticed a very simple fact. I saw that while religious beliefs and practices were very diverse, the simple existence of such beliefs and practices was something all religions had in common. At first this observation seemed too simple and obvious to be of much importance, but later I realized that it was, in fact, very useful in clarifying the fundamental nature of religion. Every religion has its philosophy, its particular understanding of life. The followers of the religion believe in that philosophy and they act according to their belief. This is, I

think, the essence of religion. I think all religions have these two factors in common; that is, belief in a certain theory or philosophy and actual conduct in accord with that belief.

This simple definition of religion has rather far reaching implications. When we think of religion in this way, many of our common-sense notions about religion become untenable. Usually we think that there are religious people and irreligious people, that life divides itself neatly between the religious and the secular, the sacred and the profane. But if we use my simple definition of religion, such a division becomes irrelevant. All men have a philosophy, some understanding of the world which guides them in their day-to-day lives. They may not adhere to any formal religion or philosophy, but still they have their own very personal understanding of life and the world they live in. Some philosophers call this personal understanding of life our "world-view." It is this world-view which serves all people as the standpoint from which to decide their actions, their conduct in society. So I think religion is something much more basic and universal than most people realize. At the most fundamental level, I think that all men have a religion; that they cannot, in fact, live without a religion. What do you think?

Source: Gudo Wafu Nishijima and Jeffrey Alan Bailey, *To Meet the Real Dragon: Seeking the Truth in a World of Chaos* (Japan: Wind-bell, 1984), pp. 24–26. Reprinted by permission of Wind-bell Publications.

Reading 1.2 ATHEISTS FOR JESUS? Daniel C. Maguire

In the following reading, Daniel C. Maguire, a professor of theology, reflects on his experience at a Freedom from Religion Conference. Why did he feel both at odds and at home with the participants? On what grounds does Maguire include atheistic and agnostic humanism within the category *religion?* Do you agree or disagree? What is Maguire's definition of religion? Are all humans, in his view, religious?

My brother, Pat, once a priest, now an atheist, came to Madison, Wisconsin, recently to speak at a Freedom from Religion Conference. I attended and found myself in the unusual role of a stodgy conservative who still took God-talk seriously. At first, I felt removed from the other attenders, who were devoutly antireligious, right down to their jokes. These are the people who picket and sue when a crèche or a Star of David makes its way onto public property.

During the course of a long evening, however, I began to feel more at home with them than with many of my religious peers. On issues of racism, sexism, heterosexism, violence and the political abuse of power, their passions and commitments were biblical. Their concern for the poor, for the environment, for justice and for peace was fervid and intelligent. Two of them, brothers who were collaborating on a book tracing the historic evils of religion, were caring for their aged mother at home. They could well afford to put her in a care facility, but she abhorred the idea and they honored her preference. Indeed, they were structuring their lives around her needs.

So there I was, morally and cordially at home with people who hated my religious language. But language was the main thing that separated us. They rejected the symbols, the dogmas and the theology of religion, but not religion itself. My faith and their faith were sibling-close. I was at that time writing my now-published book *The Moral Core of Judaism and Christianity* (Fortress, 1993), and I was planning to include a diagram which at that point had seven spokes representing the seven major world religions. I realized this evening that I was one spoke short. I went back and added "Atheistic or Agnostic Humanism" as the eighth world religion. My dinner companions would not have appreciated being included in such a diagram. Why would I put them there?

Because religion is a response to the sacred, it is ubiquitous; there is no one who finds nothing sacred. (Not all call the right things holy; theology helps by locating the misplaced sacred.) We are *homo sacralis,* inveterate seekers of the transcendent. There is hope in this for our future and for the political and economic pacification of humankind. Civilization rests upon shared perceptions of the sacred. Without religion thus understood, we will all perish, atheists and theists alike.

We do not all express the experience of the sacred in the same way. It need not be translated into "religious language" or even into a belief in God. In Theravada Buddhism, for example, one of the major world religions, we look in vain for our concept of a personal deity. Nevertheless, the perception of the sacred is the pulsing heart of all moral sensibility. As Reinhold Niebuhr said, "Every genuine passion for social justice will always contain a religious element within it." The group known as "atheists for Niebuhr" proved him right. In my terms, they rejected his theology, his symbol system, his dogmatic language, but not his religion.

As the eight world religions take their historical and symbol-making journeys through time, they become further and further apart. This trajectory seems to provide little hope for human unity. But hope lies at the point of their beginning, at their common moral starting point.

Religion is born when human consciousness sees the wonder of our being, the smiles of infants, the beauty of the mallard, the gentle budding of the rose, the generous fecundity of the earth, the fire of heroism, the ecstatic promise of intelligence—when it sees all this and says, "Wow!" Do not let the informality of the expression undermine the point. This is the birth zone of awe-full respect and reverent gratitude for the mystery that marks our terrestrial genesis. From this primal awe, moral claims are born; from this primal reverence, religion emanates. The moral response names the gift good; the religious response goes on to proclaim it holy. This is the foundational moral and religious experience and the basis of all civilization.

This moment of moral and religious awakening is marked by a sense of giftedness, whether or not we go on to infer a divine Giver. Human moral intelligence is born in appreciative respect and religious esteem for the marvel into which we have been gratuitously and mysteriously cast. Some religions have one or many incarnations of the sacred; some have none and do not dare to call the sacred by name. All of this is rich religio-poetic experience, and we can enter into one another's journeys and visit one another's symbols with profit, not with fear. Beneath the sprawling diversity of all the radii is the root experience of the good which is also holy. (The term "sanctity of life" is meaningful even to nontheists.)

Idealistic atheists and agnostic humanists also experience the sacred and respond to it—sometimes even heroically. They lay down their lives for their friends. They merit a place among the religions.

The freedom-from-religion people with whom I met are not typical. They are confident atheists and, as such, seem to belong to the cocksure 19th century when popes, scientists, religionists and nontheists alike could all fancy themselves infallible. As the 20th century moves into the 21st, modest agnosticism is the more common currency. The foundations of easy dogmatism have been shaken on all fronts. Ambiguity characterizes our time. Agnosticism, even about the existence of a personal God, has found a place at our table, in the pew, in religious education and in our seminaries. How do we deal with it when we find it in neighbors, parishioners or in our own children?

To go back to the "Wow!" point: Behind churches, synagogues, mosques, and professions of agnostic or atheistic humanism lie the roots of a common spirituality that consists of our active, lived response to the sacred. Those who eschew God-talk and find the church a bore, but who hunger and thirst for justice and believe in hope, are spiritually bonded with us. All ecumenism starts at the moral core. The purpose of mission is not to transplant my model or to coopt another's, but to meet others at the moral, mystical core. There in shared awe, we can tell our symbolic stories and walk a bit on one another's paths. Since God was ecumenical before we were, we should be as good at listening as at witnessing. Perhaps after hearing our story, people will want to travel with us and share the biblical excitement about God. Perhaps not. But the encounter will benefit all participants.

As for nontheists and modern agnostics, they cannot ignore talk about God. Some of the deepest insights into human existence are enfolded in talk of divinity. Many of our most cherished values were born in the very religions now disregarded by many. If you had told Aristotle that all persons are created equal, he would have thought you uneducated, since women and slaves were obviously (for Aristotle) not the equals of men—at least not of Greek men.

Early Israel pioneered a better idea and we are its beneficiaries. The ancient world used the symbol "image of God" only to designate the sublimity of monarchs and pharaohs. Israel would have none of this. Instead, early Israel said, "If you would see the image of God, look at the baby in my arms. Look at my failing grandmother by the fire, and look in the reflecting pond. That is the image of God, and let no one call it unholy!"

Imago dei is a symbol wrapped in language about God, and our modern bills of rights and due-process theories of justice are genetically in debt to it. And this is but one of the treasures that came to us in religious dress. Agnostics and atheists who ignore religion ostracize themselves from a principal font of human wisdom and from a major struggle of the human mind. The sins of religionists should not keep them away.

My atheist brother was asked a few years ago to give the invocation at the graduation ceremony of the college where he taught philosophy. The students knew his views on God, yet they came to him for spiritual inspiration. He began on an atheistic note: "I ask you to bow your heads to no one because I believe there is no one to whom you should bow your heads." Then he urged them to have compassion for all that lives. He invited them to use their educations not just for personal aggrandizement but to build an earth of justice and peace marked by passionate commitment to the poor and the powerless. His words were heart-to-heart with those of Isaiah, Jesus, the Mary of the Magnificat, and his students. His invocation was greeted—as many invocations are not—with an ovation. To rephrase an observation of Simone Weil's: sometimes those denying God are closer to the reality called God than those who use the name without care.

Source: Daniel C. Maguire, "Atheists for Jesus? The Moral Core of Religious Experience," *The Christian Century* (Chicago: Christian Century Foundation, December 8, 1993), pp. 1228–1230. Copyright 1993 Christian Century Foundation. Reprinted by permission from the December 8, 1993 issue of the Christian Century.

Reading 1.3   WHAT FAITH IS   Paul Tillich

Protestant theologian Paul Tillich (1886–1965) defines faith here as the state of being ultimately concerned. What is involved in such a state? Is *faith* a synonym for *religious experience?* What does it mean to refer to faith as a "centered act"? In Tillich's view, what is the source of faith? How is faith related to the holy?

1. FAITH AS ULTIMATE CONCERN

Faith is the state of being ultimately concerned: faith are the dynamics of man's ultimate concern. Man, like every living being, is concerned about many things, above all about those which condition his very existence, such as food and shelter. But man, in contrast to other living beings, has spiritual concerns—cognitive, aesthetic, social, political. Some of them are urgent, often extremely urgent, and each of them as well as the vital concerns can claim ultimacy for a human life or the life of a social group. If it claims ultimacy it demands the total surrender of him who accepts this claim, and it promises total fulfillment even if all other claims have to be subjected to it or rejected in its name. If a national group makes the life and growth of the nation its ultimate concern, it demands that all other concerns, economic well-being, health and life, family, aesthetic and cognitive truth, justice and humanity, be sacrificed. The extreme nationalisms of our century are laboratories for the study of what ultimate concern means in all aspects of human existence, including the smallest concern of one's daily life. Everything is centered in the only god, the nation—a god who certainly proves to be a demon, but who shows clearly the unconditional character of an ultimate concern.

But it is not only the unconditional demand made by that which is one's ultimate concern, it is also the promise of ultimate fulfillment which is accepted in the act of faith. The content of this promise is not necessarily defined. It can be expressed in indefinite symbols or in concrete symbols which cannot be taken literally, like the "greatness" of one's nation in which one participates even if one has died for it, or the conquest of mankind by the "saving race," etc. In each of these cases, it is "ultimate fulfillment" that is promised, and it is exclusion from such fulfillment which is threatened if the unconditional demand is not obeyed. . . .

2. FAITH AS A CENTERED ACT

Faith as ultimate concern is an act of the total personality. It happens in the center of the personal life and includes all its elements. Faith is the most centered act of the human mind. It is not a movement of a special section or a special function of man's total being. They all are united in the act of faith. But faith is not the sum total of their impacts. It transcends every special impact as well as the totality of them and it has itself a decisive impact on each of them. . . .

Faith as the embracing and centered act of the personality is "ecstatic." It transcends both the drives of the nonrational unconscious and the structures of the rational conscious. It transcends them, but it does not destroy them. The ecstatic character of faith does not exclude its rational character although it is not identical with it, and it includes nonrational strivings without being identical with them. In the ecstasy of faith there is an awareness of truth and of ethical value; there are also past loves and hates, conflicts and reunions, individual and collective influences. "Ecstasy" means "standing outside of oneself"—without ceasing to be oneself— with all the elements which are united in the personal center. . . .

3. THE SOURCE OF FAITH

We have described the act of faith and its relation to the dynamics of personality. Faith is a total and centered act of the personal self, the act of unconditional, infinite and ultimate concern. The question now arises: what is the source of this all-embracing and all-transcending concern? The word "concern" points to two sides of a relationship, the relation between the one who is concerned and his concern. In both respects, we have to imagine man's situation in itself and in his world. The reality of man's ultimate concern reveals something about his being, namely, that he is able to transcend the flux of relative and transitory experiences of his ordinary life. Man's experiences, feelings, thoughts are conditioned and finite. They not only come and go, but their content is of finite and conditional concern— unless they are elevated to unconditional validity. But this presupposes the general possibility of doing so; it presupposes the element of infinity in man. Man is able to understand in an immediate personal and central act the meaning of the ultimate, the unconditional, the absolute, the infinite. This alone makes faith a human potentiality.

Human potentialities are powers that drive toward actualization. Man is driven toward faith by his awareness of the infinite to which he belongs, but which he does not own like a possession. . . .

4. FAITH AND THE DYNAMICS OF THE HOLY

He who enters the sphere of faith enters the sanctuary of life. Where there is faith, there is an awareness of holiness. . . . What concerns one ultimately becomes holy. The awareness of the holy is awareness of the presence of the divine, namely of the content of our ultimate concern. This awareness is expressed in a grand way in the Old Testament from the visions of the patriarchs and Moses to the shaking experiences of the great prophets and psalmists. It is a presence which remains mysterious in spite of its appearance, and it exercises both an attractive and a repulsive function on those who encounter it. In his classical book, *The Idea of the Holy,* Rudolph Otto has described these two functions as the fascinating and the shaking character of the holy. . . . They can be found in all religions because they are the way in which man always encounters the representations of his ultimate concern. The reason for these two effects of the holy is obvious if we see the relation of the experience of the holy to the experience of ultimate concern. The human heart seeks the infinite because that is where the finite wants to rest. In the infinite, it sees its own fulfillment. This is the reason for the ecstatic attraction and fascination of everything in which ultimacy is manifest. On the other hand, if ultimacy is manifest and exercises its fascinating attraction, one realizes at the same time the infinite distance of the finite from the infinite and, consequently, the negative judgment over any finite attempts to reach the infinite. The feeling of being consumed in the presence of the divine is a profound expression of man's relation to the holy. It is implied in every genuine act of faith, in every state of ultimate concern.

Source: Paul Tillich, *Dynamics of Faith* (New York: Harper & Row, 1957), pp. 1–13. Copyright © 1957 by Paul Tillich, renewed © 1985 by Hanna Tillich. Reprinted by permission of HarperCollins Publishers, Inc.

Reading 1.4   TRUTH AND THE RELIGIONS OF THE WORLD

Sarvepalli Radhakrishnan

Are religious conceptions about the ultimate nature of reality true, or are they illusory? Is it appropriate to speak of religious truth claims as true or false? Is one religion or one revelation of ultimacy true and all others false? What does Sarvepalli Radhakrishnan (1888–1975), a philosopher, Hindu theologian, and former president of India, believe about the truth of the world's religions? What is your viewpoint?

Protests are heard now and again against a comparative study of religion.

One reason for this is that the scientific study of religion is imagined to be a danger to religion itself. For a scientific student of religion is required to treat all religions in a spirit of absolute detachment and impartiality. To him one religion is as good as another; but such an attitude of cold neutrality in matters of religion does not appeal to the majority of mankind. Religion, it is argued, is nothing if not partisan and particularist. To compare the sacred books of the East with the holy scriptures of the West is to ignore that feeling of warmth and reverence which each individual has for his own religion. To such an objection it must be replied that truth is higher than any religion and a truly scientific attitude in these matters will ultimately result in gain immeasurably greater than any loss we may incur in the process. At the same time, while we may surrender our exclusive claims, the religion in which we were brought up will still exert a peculiar charm and fascination over us.

Another objection is that comparison means resemblance; and if one religion is like another, what happens to the claims of superiority and uniqueness? Certainly Comparative Religion notes the facts of resemblance as well as of difference. But a recognition of the points of similarity does not mean that the points of difference are negligible. Even if we wish to set forth the superior claims of one religion, it is necessary for us to know and appreciate the claims and contents of others.

Again, it is urged, if Comparative Religion tells us that higher religions possess features in common with the low and the primitive, then the inference is legitimate that our religious beliefs are of a degrading and childish character. . . . Here again, all that need be said is that it is illogical to confuse questions of origin and of value.

The tracing of the historical derivation of religious ideas is quite different from a critical determination of their value. . . .

Comparative Religion tells us that all religions have had a history and that none is final or perfect. Religion is a movement, a growth; and in all true growth the new rests on the old. Every religion has in it survivals from the old. Further, even if we are not satisfied with the present forms of religion, we may anticipate a better one. If religious forms were final and infallible expressions of divine will, we should have to accept slavery, subservience of women to men and many other evils as God's work.

If we are frank, we will admit that the characters of the gods we worshipped have not been, by any means, ideal. Every conceivable crime and cruelty have been attributed to the gods, though this did not interfere with the fervent worship of them by their devout followers. . . . It is consoling therefore to realize that no expression of religion is exhaustive and absolute. Such a belief may not help us to win the world for Buddha or for Christ, but it performs the more important task of interpreting and reconciling religious differences, and preserving religion itself from the decay which is overtaking existing systems. . . . [I]t is not the aim of Comparative Religion to demonstrate that this or that religion is the highest manifestation of the religious spirit. For the absoluteness of any religion is difficult to maintain when analogous phenomena are daily discovered among peoples of other faiths. The strength of the absolutist claim rests on the widespread belief that its own specific dogmas and legends are wholly unique; but Comparative Religion shows this to be erroneous. The original leaders of the study of Comparative Religion had the breadth of mind to realize this truth. God does not spurn the prayers which ascend to Him from the lips of those who do not profess our faith. Max Müller is emphatic on this point. He says: "I hold that there is a divine element in every one of the great religions of the world. I consider it blasphemous to call them the work of the devil, when they are the work of God; and I hold that there is nowhere any belief in God except as the result of a divine revelation, the effect of a divine spirit working in man. I could not call myself a Christian if I were to believe otherwise, if I were to force myself against all my deepest instincts to believe that the prayers of Christians were the only prayers that God could understand. All religions are mere stammerings, our own as much as that of the Brahmins. They all have to be translated; and I have no doubt they all will be translated whatever their shortcomings may be." The same attitude was adopted by Dr. Estlin Carpenter: "He would confess that he could not himself share the belief that there was any absolute form of religion. He would explain that his own studies convinced him that it was profitable to remember that Christianity is not the only form of theism or the only vehicle of moral energy that history presents and that it did not appear to him that the surviving records were adequate to justify the isolation of the Christian religion from the fraternity of human nature and normal human experience." It is only when we adopt such open-mindedness that we can understand another's faith. It will remain merely a cold intellectual proposition until we make it a part of our inner being. We must experience the impression that has thrilled the follower of another faith if we wish to understand him. . . .

We can no longer say that truth has found its home in one part of the world alone. We are able to realize more vividly than did our forefathers that God has made Himself known to men in diverse manners. We no more assume that all that is good and true and valuable is found in any one religion, while those who do not chance to adopt it are doomed to everlasting pain. Such religious chauvinism would sound very strange on our lips. We have now a nobler and truer view of God.

With regard to religions, therefore, the question is not of truth or falsehood but life or death. Is it a dead curiosity or a going concern? Every living religion has its part in the spiritual education of the race. Many of our religious paradoxes and perplexities are due to the narrowness of our horizon. By enlarging our sympathies, we raise our thought above the narrow controversies of the day. We are all familiar with Goethe's paradox: "He who knows one language knows none." The poet asked "What does he know of England who only England knows?" What is true of language and history is true of religion also. We cannot understand our own religion unless it be in relation to one or more of the other faiths. By an intelligent and respectful study of other religions we gain a new understanding and appreciation of their traditions and our own.

Source: Sarvepalli Radhakrishnan, *East and West in Religion* (London: George Allen & Unwin, 1954), pp. 15ff.

Reading 1.5   WHAT WILL HAPPEN TO GOD?   Naomi R. Goldenberg

One of the momentous challenges to traditional religious beliefs and practices has been the emergence of feminism, a movement demanding justice for women, the empowering of women, and the dismantling of male hierarchies. Women are interpreting their religious traditions in the light of their experiences as women. Some women prefer to reform existing structures. Others have turned to Goddess traditions and have invented new religions centered in the feminine sacred. Do you agree with Naomi R. Goldenberg that Judaism and Christianity will be transformed by women? What new gods or reinterpretations of God do you anticipate?

What will happen to God? I first asked myself this question in 1971. I was sitting in a circle of women in Westchester, New York. We were all "housewives" with families and homes to care for. Some of us worked outside the home as well. It was the first consciousness-raising group I had ever attended.

Each woman had agreed to address the question "What prevented me from doing something I wanted to do?" I spoke about my recent decision to leave graduate school before completing my degree. . . .

Most of the other women also discussed their failure to achieve particular career goals. Some had begun training to become lawyers, journalists or doctors and felt that either family conflicts or the discouragement of male teachers and colleagues had caused them to drop out. A few felt that they didn't have enough energy to pick up the same career aspirations again.

Several women, however, had more hope. They were beginning their training all over again—this time armed with political insight, which they felt would enable them to understand the sexism they were bound to encounter and to suffer through it to attain their objectives. . . .

I enjoyed listening to the determination in their voices. "Such women will change the world," I thought. I felt that when enough women like them entered traditional professions, the structure of those professions could not remain the same. Female values and female ways of life would eventually have to be accommodated by the male hierarchies and would transform the hierarchies themselves. I felt I was living at the beginning of a major social revolution and wanted to participate with any talent I might possess.

The most important story I heard that night was one of a woman who had wanted to be a minister. She had begun study at Drew University, but had dropped out after a year and a half of course work. "They didn't know how to act around me in seminary classes," she said. "The men all kept asking me why I wanted to be a minister and expected me to give up. I had to argue with them and justify myself every day. I finally left seminary." . . . "The clergy can't accept women in their ranks," she said.

"The clergy will have to accept women," I thought. The feminist revolution will not leave religion untouched. Eventually, all religious hierarchies would be peopled with women. I imagined women functioning as rabbis, priests and ministers. I pictured women wearing clerical garb and performing clerical duties and suddenly *I saw a problem.* How could women represent a male god?

Everything I knew about Judaism and Christianity involved accepting God as the ultimate in male authority figures. If enough women claimed to represent "His" authority—to embody "His" presence in synagogues and on pulpits—congregations would have to stop seeing God as male. God would begin to look like "His" female officials. "And what would these women priests, ministers and rabbis read to their communities?" I wondered. They could certainly not use the Bible. A society that accepted large numbers of women as religious leaders would be too different from the biblical world to find the book relevant, let alone look to it for inspiration.

"God is going to change," I thought. "We women are going to bring an end to God. As we take positions in government, in medicine, in law, in business, in the arts and, finally, in religion, we will be the end of Him. We will change the world so much that He won't fit in anymore."

I found this line of thought most satisfying. I had no great tie to God anyway. He never seemed to be relevant to me at all. Reflection on His cultural demise left me with no sense of loss. Yet there was a magnificence attached to the idea of watching Him go. I felt part of a movement that would challenge religions that had been in force for millennia. "What will happen to God in His last years?" I wondered. "And who or what will replace Him?"

I knew these were important questions. Here was no issue of only scholarly interest. The end of God and the transformation of religion was of major significance to human life. . . . The reforms that Christian and Jewish women are proposing are major departures from tradition. When feminists succeed in changing the position of women in Christianity and Judaism, they will shake these religions at their roots. . . .

New Gods Are Coming

Many scholars of religion disagree with the radical direction I have predicted. They say that Christianity and Judaism can survive the very basic changes that will have to be made when these religions adapt to nonsexist culture. These scholars insist that a religion is whatever its followers define it to be. Christianity and Judaism, therefore, are said to consist of whatever those who call themselves Christians and Jews practice as religion. Theoretically then, Christianity could exist without Christ and Judaism could exist without Yahweh's laws as long as Christians and Jews *thought* of these departures from tradition as being in basic harmony with their faiths. Texts could be altered, female imagery could be added to the concept of God, new rituals and doctrines could be invented without bringing about the end of the faiths. Scholars who believe this is possible point out that Western religions have survived many changes over the past centuries and can be expected to survive many more in years to come.

I wonder. Judaism and Christianity have never been challenged to the extent that they will be in the next decades. The images of Christ and Yahweh will be questioned because of the very basic quality of maleness. All of the roles that men and women have been taught to consider as God-given will be re-evaluated. Although it is certainly true that small groups of Christians and Jews have departed from tradition by conceiving of God in female terms and by experimenting with new roles for men and women, such sects have been rather small-scale religious anomalies. The women's movement will being about religious changes on a massive scale. These changes will not be restricted to small numbers of individuals practicing nonsexist religions within a sexist society. Society itself will be transformed to the point that it will no longer be a patriarchy. For if men are no longer supreme rulers on earth, how could one expect them to retain sovereignty in heaven?

There will of course be nothing to prevent people who practice new religions from calling themselves Christians or Jews. Undoubtedly, many followers of new faiths will still cling to old labels. But a merely semantic veneer of tradition ought not to hide the fact that very nontraditional faiths will be practiced. Those of us who fancy ourselves scholars of religion will perceive what is happening more clearly if we do not pretend that we are watching minor metamorphoses occurring within the Jewish and Christian traditions.

What will we be watching? What sort of religious forces are beginning in this era of death for the great male gods? Surely new gods will be born. Since "gods" always reflect the styles of behavior we see as possible, as our range of the possible expands so must our pantheon.

Up until very recently, the only kind of legitimate public authority most of us could imagine was that of an adult male. As long as this image held us, we could picture God only as an old man. Now a growing number of us are able to imagine authority in new guises. Feminism is pushing us into an age of experimentation with new personifications of authority. We can picture public power held by a woman or group of women, shared by both sexes or rotated between the sexes. These more fluid concepts of hierarchy are certain to affect our view of God. In order for systems of religions to prove inspiring in this new age such ideals of pluralism and experimentation will have to be reflected in religious doctrine and practice.

Source: Naomi R. Goldenberg, *Changing of the Gods: Feminism and the End of Traditional Religions* (Boston: Beacon Press, 1979), pp. 1–9. *Changing of the Gods* by Naomi R. Goldenberg © 1979 by Naomi R. Goldenberg. Reprinted by permission of Beacon Press, Boston.

Reading 1.6 THE VIRTUE OF SYMPATHY   Simone Weil

Sympathy, the capacity to see phenomena through the eyes of insiders, to walk empathically in someone else's shoes is a virtue. Here Simone Weil (1909–1943) speaks of the importance of sympathy to a study of religion. Weil, a French Jew, identified so completely with the plight of the Jews during the Holocaust that she literally starved herself to death, and also experienced God unexpectedly in the person of Christ. How does she regard conversions from one religion to another?

All religions pronounce the name of God in their particular language. As a rule it is better for a man to name God in his native tongue rather than in one that is foreign to him. Except in special cases the soul is not able to abandon itself utterly when it has to make the slight effort of seeking for the words in a foreign language, even when this language is well known.

A writer whose native language is poor, difficult to manipulate and not widely known thoughout the world, is very strongly tempted to adopt another. There are a few like Conrad who have done so with startling success. But they are very rare. Except in special cases such a change does harm, both thought and style suffer, the writer is always ill at ease in the adopted language and cannot rise above mediocrity.

A change of religion is for the soul like a change of language for a writer. All religions, it is true, are not equally suitable for the recitation of the name of the Lord. Some, without any doubt, are very imperfect mediums. . . .

But in general the relative value of the various religions is a very difficult thing to discern, it is almost impossible, perhaps quite impossible. For a religion is only known from inside. Catholics say this of Catholicism, but it is true of all religions. Religion is a form of nourishment. It is difficult to appreciate the flavour and food-value of something one has never eaten.

The comparison of religions is only possible, in some measure, through the miraculous virtue of sympathy. We can know men to a certain extent if at the same time as we observe them from outside we manage by sympathy to transport our own soul into theirs for a time. In the same way the study of different religions does not lead to a real knowledge of them unless we transport ourselves for a time by faith to the very centre of whichever one we are studying.

This scarcely ever happens, for some have no faith, and the others have faith exclusively in one religion and only bestow upon the others the sort of attention we give to strangely shaped shells. There are others again who think they are capable of impartiality because they only have a vague religiosity which they can turn indifferently in any direction, whereas, on the contrary, we must have given all our attention, all our faith, all our love to a particular religion in order to think of any other religion with the high degree of attention, faith and love which is proper to it. In the same way, only those who are capable of friendship can take a real heart-felt interest in the fate of an utter stranger. . . .

In Europe today, and perhaps even in the whole world, the knowledge of comparative religion amounts to just about nothing. People have not even a notion of the possibility of such a knowledge. Even without the prejudices which get in our way, it is still very difficult for us even to form an idea of it. Among the different forms of religion there are, as it were, partial compensations for the visible differences, certain hidden equivalents which can only be caught sight of by the most penetrating discernment. Each religion is an original combination of explicit and implicit truths; what is explicit in one is implicit in another. The implicit adherence to a truth can in some cases be worth as much as the explicit adherence, sometimes even a great deal more. He who knows the secrets of all hearts, alone knows the secret of the different forms of faith. He has never revealed this secret, whatever anyone may say.

If one is born into a religion which is not too unsuitable for pronouncing the name of the Lord, if one loves this native religion with a well directed and pure love, it is difficult to imagine a legitimate motive for giving it up, before direct contact with God has placed the soul under the guidance of the divine will itself. After that the change is only legitimate if it is made in obedience. History shows that in fact this happens but rarely. Most often, perhaps always, the soul which has reached the highest realms of spirituality is confirmed in its love of the tradition which served it as a ladder.

Source: Simone Weil, *Waiting for God* (New York: Harper & Row, 1973), pp. 117–119. Reprinted by permission of the Putnam Publishing Group from WAITING FOR GOD by Simone Weil. Copyright © 1951 by G. P. Putnam's Sons; Renewed © 1979 by G. P. Putnam's Sons.

CHAPTER 2

ANCIENT

SPIRITUALITY

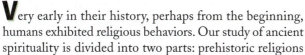

Very early in their history, perhaps from the beginning, humans exhibited religious behaviors. Our study of ancient spirituality is divided into two parts: prehistoric religions and religions of ancient urban societies. The category *prehistoric religions* refers to human spirituality before the invention of writing; these religions are examples of what we identified in Chapter 1 as simple ethnic or tribal religions. Ancient urban religions were rooted in societies with urban centers and centralized political institutions; this category includes complex ethnic (national) and universal (conversionist) religions. As in tribal religions, participation in complex ethnic religions is principally a function of ancestry and culture, whereas universal religions seek converts across the boundaries of ethnicity and nationality. Ancient urban states had several layers of religion, including national and folk religions. By the first millennium B.C.E., initiation cults (for example, cults of Dionysus and Isis), schools of thought (for example, those of Plato and Confucius), and conversionist religions (for example, Buddhism and Zoroastrianism) were part of the mix. In fact, each of the seven religions that are the subjects of Chapters 4 through 10 originated in premodern societies.

Stonehenge, a stone circle of standing stones with lintels, located near Salisbury in Wiltshire, England. This phase of the megalith construction began around 2000 B.C.E. Standing stones were erected on the site as early as 3100 B.C.E.

DEAD AND LIVING RELIGIONS

Our subjects here are, for the most part, dead rather than living traditions—religious systems that are no longer believed in or acted out. It is likely that living tribal traditions have some affinities to the beliefs and practices of prehistoric peoples, but it is impossible through scientific methods to identify religious systems that have persisted from prehistoric times to now. Likewise, the ancient urban religions that concern us here are, with few exceptions, dead rather than living entities. This is true of the state cults of ancient Egypt, Mesopotamia, pre-Hispanic America, the Canaanite and Greek city-states, and republican and imperial Rome. It is also true of the initiation cults. However, it is not true of the traditional religions of sub-Saharan African kingdoms that persist today in modern African states (for example, the religion of the Yoruba of Nigeria). Religions of African kingdoms are touched on here and in Chapter 3.

Claims have been made for the persistence of prehistoric and ancient urban religions among contemporary tribal peoples. It is contended, for example, that Australian Aboriginal spirituality has a pedigree of thirty thousand to forty thousand years and that the religions of the Maya and Inca survive as folk traditions among Indians of Central America and the Andean region. Whether these contemporary manifestations of faith are continuous with their alleged forebears is disputed, but most observers agree that elements of ancient religions survive today. Thus, features of the religion of the pre-Hispanic Maya survive in the folk traditions of Guatemala and southern Mexico in a blending of Maya traditions and Christianity. The religion of the ancient Indus Valley civilization ceased to be a living faith nearly four millennia ago, but elements of it have survived in Hinduism (see Chapter 4). Likewise, aspects of the folk spirituality of ancient China persist in modern Chinese religiosity (see Chapter 6).

THE PROBLEMS OF NAMING

A problem in speaking about the religions of tribal and ancient urban societies is how to label or describe them. It is complicated by the fact, as noted in Chapter 1, that such societies did not have words comparable to *religion* in their languages and did not name their "religions." Naming is no trifling matter. Labels and categories function as parameters of what is thinkable, and they have a powerful influence on our perceptions of things. If labels influence what is thinkable, what are the implications of the practice of characterizing tribal societies and religions as **primitive** and ancient polytheistic urban religions as **pagan?** In a nonpejorative sense, *primitive* is a category for societies whose technology and social organization were less developed and whose language was preliterate. Historically, however, the meaning of *primitive* has usually been extended to describe the culture and intelligence of oral peoples: their art was judged more magic than art, their religion mere superstition, their behavior savagery, and their thinking childish. The habit of categorizing ancient national religions as pagan is entwined with the antipathies that separated monotheists and polytheists in imperial Rome. In the process, *pagan* became a pejorative label for followers of polytheistic faiths, especially those of ancient Greece and Rome. Monotheists viewed pagans as idolaters (peoples who worshiped false gods) and as heathens (uncivilized and defiled peoples). Eventually, *pagan* became a label for all polytheistic religions, whether ancient or modern, oral or literate.

Recent scholarship has tried to avoid negative associations by substituting neutral terms. Religions and peoples classified as *primitive* have been collectively identified as *indigenous, nonliterate, primal, simple ethnic, traditional,* and *tribal. Complex ethnic* and *national* are neutralized alternatives to *pagan.* The revival of *pagan* in academic circles as a nonpejorative naming for such traditions coincides with an advance of knowledge about them and the emergence of contemporary groups who identify themselves as *neopagan.* No single label is completely satisfactory. We usually use *tribal* and *national* but in some contexts have turned to other labels, including *primitive* and *pagan,* but without the connotations of "backward," "savage," "idolatrous," or "heathen." Judgments that separate humans into insiders and outsiders have been a persistent feature of human existence. Tribal peoples saw themselves as "the people" and other peoples as "not my people." Similarly, ancient urban peoples viewed themselves as civilized and regarded tribalists as barbarians.

It may be difficult to get excited about dead religions or to overcome perceptions of tribal and archaic national religions as primitive and pagan. The talmudic proverb *"We do not see things as they are; we see things as we are"* reminds us that our perceptions of reality are influenced by our life situations and suggests that as we change, our understanding changes. It took years and several trips to the British Museum before I took an interest in ancient societies other than Greece and Rome and realized that I need not and ought not to "know" the Egyptians, Canaanites, Assyrians, and Babylonians only through the *Bible,* or to "see" the Persians only through the eyes of classical Greece, or to "see" the Aztecs and Incas only through their conquerors. An analogous transition had to be made before I could see the complexity and beauty of tribal systems. Humans living today and those who lived in prehistoric times and ancient urban societies are worlds apart, but in the quest for meaning they are one.

We have opted to speak in general terms of the religions of prehistoric and ancient urban peoples. This approach is unavoidable for prehistoric religions, because the evidence does not permit us to isolate specific traditions. In contrast, several ancient uban religions (for example, Egyptian,

Greek, and Aztec religions) are well documented. Nonetheless, in a brief treatment of ancient urban religions, a collective overview is as reasonable an approach as any.

Unlike Chapters 3 through 10, Chapter 2 has two subjects (prehistoric religions and ancient urban religions). To accommodate this fact, we have replaced the organization followed in other chapters (beliefs, practice, history, and contemporary context) with the following sequence: The discussion of prehistoric religions begins with a sketch of prehistory, followed by an overview of prehistoric religious beliefs and practices. The discussion of ancient urban religions begins with an introduction to ancient urban societies, followed by an overview of ancient urban religious beliefs and practices. The concluding section examines some of the ways that ancient spirituality has been perceived in modern thought.

PREHISTORY

Human **prehistory** is a vast period of time beginning with the appearance of the first human species around 2.5 million years ago and ending with the emergence of literate, urban civilizations around 3500 to 3000 B.C.E. If, as scientists believe, humans ancestral to modern humans emerged 2.5 million years ago, then 99.8 percent of the human story took place before the creation of writing. Prehistory is roughly coterminous with the **Stone Age,** a period beginning with the human production of stone tools approximately 2 million years ago and ending with the transition from stone to bronze tools around 3500 B.C.E. in Southwest Asia and at later dates elsewhere.

Scholars have divided the Stone Age into the Old Stone (Paleolithic) Age and the New Stone (Neolithic) Age chiefly on the basis of the principal means of subsistence. **Paleolithic** peoples subsisted by gathering edible plants, hunting animals, and scavenging the kills of predators. **Neolithic** peoples were farmers and, secondarily, hunters and gatherers. The Paleolithic dates from the production of stone tools around 2 million years ago to the agri-

cultural revolution, the transition from food gathering to food production around 8000 B.C.E. Because the Paleolithic is such a vast period of time, we have followed the convention of dividing it into the Early, Middle, and Late Paleolithic. The Neolithic began with the agricultural revolution and ended between 3500 and 3000 B.C.E. with the emergence of cities and the invention of writing. Stone Age cultures persisted in historical times in isolated environments and along the edges of urban societies. In fact, small populations of hunter-gatherers and simple agriculturalists survive today within modern states, but their societies are not pristine remnants of the chronological Stone Age because they have been influenced by contact with modern societies. Figure 2.1 shows the world dispersion of hunter-gatherers throughout prehistory and history.

The scientific study of human prehistory is relatively new. In the nineteenth century, the first fossil remains of prehistoric peoples were discovered, anthropology was established as a scientific discipline, and the division of prehistory into the Paleolithic and Neolithic was created. The primary sci-

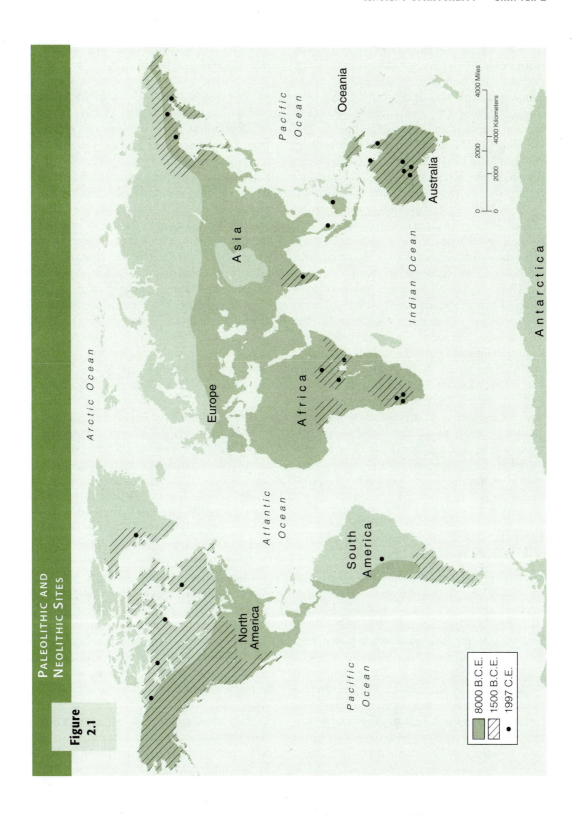

Figure 2.1

PALEOLITHIC AND NEOLITHIC SITES

ences for studies of prehistory—archaeology and paleontology—are fields within anthropology. Archaeologists study the material culture of ancient humans to describe and explain their behavior. Paleontologists interpret the fossil evidence. Other fields contribute to our understanding of prehistory, including ethnology (the branch of anthropology that conducts field studies of human groups). Extrapolations from ethnology to prehistory are problematic. As archaeologist Margaret Ehrenberg noted, it is a "very real possibility that no societies either today or in the recent past share social, political or religious patterns with some of those in the distant past, even if they do share superficial technological and economic features."[1]

Difficulties in reconstructing the worlds of meaning of prehistoric peoples are monumental. Conservative paleoanthropologists argue that because ideas and social patterns cannot be fossilized, interpretation should be limited to dating fossils and artifacts and identifying changes in material culture. Moderates believe that the evidence warrants modest judgments about the invisible culture (for example, ideas, rituals, and social structures) of prehistoric peoples. Less constrained scholars are willing to take more risks. In the absence of written evidence, reconstructions of the belief systems of prehistoric peoples must always be problematic.

THE PALEOLITHIC (2,000,000–10,000 YEARS B.P.)

The story of hominids (human-like beings) begins with Australopithecus, the genus evolutionists believe is ancestral to the genus *Homo* (humankind). Australopithecines emerged in Africa around 5 million years B.P. (before the present) and did not disappear until about 1.3 million years ago. The genus *Homo* began over 2 million years ago with the appearance of the species *habilis* (handyman) in sub-Saharan Africa. Australopithecines used rocks and sticks for utilitarian purposes, but it is likely that homo habilines were the first toolmakers. A new species, *Homo erectus*, appeared in Africa around 1.8 million years ago. *Homo erectus* gave rise

to *Homo sapiens* or reached a dead end around 200,000 years ago; before they disappeared, however, they had spread to Europe and Asia, produced the first standardized tools, made use of fire, and perhaps communicated through speech.[2]

Premodern forms of *Homo sapiens* emerged from *Homo erectus* over 200,000 years ago. They had larger brains and smaller jaws and teeth than their predecessors. Anatomically modern human beings emerged around 100,000 years ago and, in the intervening years, have undergone little in the way of biological change. All humans living today—irrespective of their differences—belong to a single biological genus and species *(Homo sapiens sapiens)*. Geographical separation of human populations over time produced distinctive biological and ethnic groupings. As *Homo erectus* was ancestral to archaic *Homo sapiens*, early modern *Homo sapiens* were ancestral to the primary geographical groupings observable today: Australian Aboriginals, Africans, Native Americans, Asians, Europeans, Polynesians, Micronesians, and Melanesians.

CHANGE IN THE EARLY PALEOLITHIC (2,000,000 –100,000 B.P.)

Change among ancient hominids was slow—nearly imperceptible. It proceeded on two intersecting levels: the biological and the cultural. Bipedalism evolved 4 million to 6 million years ago. Brain and body sizes gradually increased. Evidence of tool use dates from over 3 million B.P., and toolmaking dates about 2 million B.P. Evidence of fire use dates around 1.6 million B.P., but its mastery may have come a million years later. Change was slow but momentous. Bipedalism made hominids more adaptive to new environments, freed their hands for more effective tool use, and changed how parents carried their infants (in their arms and on their hips). Mastery of fire allowed hominids to extend their range into colder environments. Toolmaking was an extraordinary advancement that ultimately led to modern material culture.

The most momentous biological change was the evolution in the size and complexity of the human brain. Evolution of the human brain undergirded cultural change. Developments in the brain associated with speech and the structure of the human pharynx made speech possible. Spoken language permitted humans to construct a complex symbolic universe and transmit it to subsequent generations. In the words of paleontologist Stephen Jay Gould, "Our large brain is the biological foundation of intelligence; intelligence is the ground of culture; and cultural transmission builds a new mode of evolution more effective than Darwinian processes in its limited realm—the 'inheritance' and modification of learned behavior."[3]

SOCIAL AND RELIGIOUS BEHAVIOR IN THE EARLY PALEOLITHIC Early Paleolithic peoples lived in small groups consisting of adult males and females and their children. They sustained themselves by collecting and hunting food. It is likely that their groups had the characteristics of bands, a type of social organization common to hunter-gatherers in historical times. Bands typically number less than seventy members and consist of a few extended family groups. Social relations are nonhierachical and egalitarian: there are no divisions of class or rank. Decision making is usually consensual, relying on persuasion rather than force.

Although it is not an exceptionless rule, among recent hunter-gatherers women are primarily gatherers and men primarily hunters. Paleolithic hominids may have had a similar division of labor. Presumably, this division of responsibilities was linked to the primacy of mothers in child rearing and, secondarily, to the size and aggressiveness of males. Human progeny are incapable of surviving without constant and prolonged care, and nursing dictated that children remained near their mothers. Consequently, mothers, children, and others who provided child care harvested edible foods near their camps. The physiology and genetic makeup of males may have also contributed to the division of labor. As improved technologies made hunting larger animals feasible, sexual dimorphism (on average, males are bigger and stronger than females) and male aggressiveness better suited men to be the primary hunters.[4]

The evidence does not permit us to speak of habilines, erectines, or early sapiens as religious,

but they did exhibit behaviors that have profound moral and religious implications. Pair bonding and child rearing have been cited as evidence of altruism (acting for the welfare of others at some cost to one's self-interest) among ancient hominids. Father-parenting is atypical of nonhuman primates: male chimpanzees and gorillas provide their mates with little assistance in the care of infants. Unlike women, other female primates have estrus cycles, a period during which they are sexually attractive and active. In contrast, humans can copulate at any time, and it is possible that the loss or absence of estrus in women and their ongoing sexual attractiveness contributed to adult male-female pair bonding.[5]

Some scholars contend that tendencies for parental love, pair bonding, and other altruistic behaviors have been passed along genetically, as well as culturally.[6] They theorize that the genetic makeup that survived from generation to generation was that of couples who formed pairs and assisted each other in rearing children. On a darker note, fossil evidence of human injuries inflicted by humans supports the inference that ancient hominids were sometimes violent. Whether altruism and aggression were behaviors that hominids passed along genetically, as well as culturally, is disputed, but such behaviors clearly have moral and religious implications.

THE MIDDLE PALEOLITHIC (100,000–35,000 B.P.) During the Middle Paleolithic, humans were established in Africa; Asia; Europe; Australia; and by the end of the period, the Americas. Two species of the human family *(Homo sapiens sapiens* and *Homo neandertalensis)* were active during the Middle Paleolithic. Scholars are divided as to whether Neandertals were a separate species of the genus *Homo* or a subspecies of *Homo sapiens.* Our focus is on the Neandertals, but their behaviors were similar to those of *Homo sapiens.*

The first Neandertal fossils were discovered in 1856 in the Neander Valley near Dusseldorf, Germany. The discovery was disconcerting: Were the skull and bones those of an abnormal human or an archaic one? At that time—before Darwinian

evolution provided a convincing scientific explanation—few westerners believed humans had existed in any but their modern form, as such a belief
was contrary to the Christian view that humankind
began with Adam and Eve.[7] However, the Neander Valley fossils were no aberration. Other Neandertal skeletal remains were discovered in Belgium
and France, and it was thought that Neandertals
were a European population of humankind adapted to the glacial cold and cut off by the Ice Age
from cultural and genetic interaction with other
Homo sapiens. The extent of their geographical and
genetic isolation, however, has been challenged by
recent fossil finds that have placed similar peoples
in western and central Asia, as well as Europe.

The oldest extant human burials (ca. 60,000
years ago) are Neandertal. Corpses were buried
in shallow pits with their legs slightly flexed or in
crouched positions and with their heads pointed
to the east. Sometimes the graves contained animal bones, tools, or stones. At a cave site (Shanidar)
in the hills of northern Iraq, a remarkable fossil was
discovered. There, around 45,000 years ago, an adult
male Neandertal appears to have been buried. His
bones were found amid fossilized flower pollens,
suggesting that his body was garlanded in an assortment of wildflowers. A man in his forties, he
appears to have been blind from childhood and
to have had his right forearm amputated. The burial at Shanidar suggests that Neandertals formed
caring communities capable of supporting someone who was not able to hunt but who was valued for other reasons. It also suggests that they
mourned his death.

If caring and grief were aspects of Neandertal existence, so were deprivation and violence.
Life was short: remains of Neandertals who lived
past fifty are rare. Skeletal remains suggest that
broken bones, wounding, and malnutrition were
common. There are indications that humans killed
other humans; for example, a Neandertal skull
found at one site appears to be that of a man killed
by a blow to the head. Cannibalism may have
occurred; the evidence is disputed, but it appears
that some Neandertals were cooked and eaten and
their bones split for their marrow. In some cases,

skulls may have been widened at the base to extract
the brains.

Tangible evidence of humans as ***homo religiosus*** (religious beings) is evident with *Homo neandertalensis* and their contemporaries, *Homo sapiens
sapiens.* In the absence of writing, the meanings of
the symbolic universe of Neandertals have vanished, but the material residue of their behavior
is suggestive. Skeptics argue that their shallow
graves resulted from other factors (natural deaths
and detritus accumulated over time) and therefore
were not true burials, but the majority opinion is
that Neandertals buried their dead and that this
indicates that they believed something survived
death. Related behaviors, such as positioning
corpses so their heads pointed to the rising sun and
sprinkling human and animal bodies with red ocher
(the color of the life force, blood), also suggest that
they believed the deceased were reborn.

Other archaeological finds point to other
aspects of Neandertal spirituality. The bones and
skulls of cave bears (large European bears extinct
by 12,000 B.P.) may have had special value. A stone
chest covered by a stone slab and containing seven
bear skulls arranged with their snouts facing the
entrance of a cave was found in the Swiss Alps.
Other caves have yielded bear skulls arranged in
niches in the walls. The meaning of these discoveries is disputed. Some scholars believe that Neandertals regarded the cave bear as an ancestral,
guardian spirit. Others argue that the stone chests
were merely fallen slabs, and they attribute the position of the bones to chance.

THE LATE PALEOLITHIC (35,000–10,000 B.P.)

The Late Paleolithic is bounded by the disappearance of *Homo neandertalensis* (ca. 35,000 B.P.) and
the transition to agriculture (ca. 10,000 B.P.). The
first fossil remains of anatomically modern humans
were found in 1868 at Cro-Magnon, the name of
a rock shelter in southwestern France. Subsequent
finds were discovered at sites from Britain across
Europe and North Africa to Southwest Asia, but
Cro-Magnon stuck as a label for early sapient Europeans. Modern human groups moved into Neandertal territories equipped with more advanced

technologies and survival strategies, and gradually, through assimilation or conquest, the Neandertals disappeared.

Late Paleolithic *Homo sapiens* augmented their stone tool kits with blades, chisels, and awls, and by the end of the Paleolithic, they had made bows and arrows and spear throwers; sewed fur clothes with bone needles and fiber threads; and fished with nets, fishing lines, lances, and fishhooks. Late Paleolithic peoples were also accomplished artists. They drew and painted on the walls of caves and cliffs; sculpted figures from soft stone, bone, ivory, or baked clay; and made music with hollowed bone flutes and drumlike instruments made of mammoth bones.

Late Paleolithic paintings and drawings are awesome by virtue of their quality and puzzling by virtue of their location. They were often painted or drawn on cave walls in relatively inaccessible places. The subjects were usually animals. When humans were depicted, they usually had animal attributes or were hybrid animal-human figures. Why did Late Paleolithic peoples paint and draw, and what prompted them to do so in locations removed from everyday life? One theory sees cave art as magico-religious behavior: depictions of animals (some pierced by spears) were part of ritual re-creations of the hunt intended to insure successful hunting. Another view contends that cave art was part of an initiation rite in which the caves functioned as surrogate wombs from whence youths ascended to adulthood.

Observers have noted that cave art often depicts animal sexuality. Some scholars see such images as fertility symbols intended to magically replenish the animals upon which humans depended for food. Others have pointed out that the animals depicted are predominantly bison and horses—animals that constituted only a fraction of the diet of early Europeans—and argue that the art had other significations. French anthropologist Andre Leroi-Gourhan suggested that images of animal sexuality symbolized the belief that the sexual union of dual forces (male and female) was central to all life forms. In his reading of Paleolithic cave art, maleness is symbolized by horses, bears,

spears, and clubs and femaleness by bison, mammoths, and enclosed figures. It is worth noting that another interpreter, Annette Laming, shared the view that the images symbolized sexuality but concluded that the horses were female and the bison male.[8]

Late Paleolithic sculpture is less majestic than the paintings, but every bit as suggestive. Here the primary subject shifts from animals to humans and, particularly, to women with undefined facial features and large, exaggerated breasts, hips, and stomachs. Figurines of animals, men, and sexually indeterminate human beings were sculpted, but female subjects are more prominent in terms of distribution and number. Female figures dating from 29,000 to 15,000 B.P. have been found at sites ranging from western France to Siberia, and they outnumber male figures by roughly 10 to 1. Presumably, figurines with large breasts and distended stomachs symbolized fertility and a Mother Goddess. We return to this subject under "Prehistoric Beliefs."

THE NEOLITHIC (8000–3500 B.C.E.)

The New Stone Age dates from the beginnings of agriculture, around 8000 B.C.E., to the shift from stone to bronze tools around 3500 B.C.E. It is chiefly distinguished by a shift from hunting and gathering food to its production, and from nomadic to village life. Two momentous additions to material culture occurred during the Neolithic period: pottery and metallurgy. Another fascinating development was the creation of stone monuments. The production of bronze tools marks the chronological end of the Neolithic, and the invention of writing around 3000 B.C.E. marks the end of prehistory. However, Neolithic, cultures persisted in historic times, continuing in Britain and northern Europe for another thousand years and, in other contexts, into the twentieth century.

The first phase of the agricultural revolution (planting and harvesting crops and domesticating and breeding animals) was incipient farming (a combination of food gathering and food production). Incipient farming villages emerged between 8000 and 7000 B.C.E. in Southwest Asia and New Guinea (Oceania). In Southwest Asia—an area that contained grains and animals that could be domesticated—farming communities were established in what is now modern Turkey, Syria, and Israel. In the same millennium, villagers in the New Guinea highlands made the transition to food production, growing root crops and raising pigs. In China, rice was cultivated in the Yangtze River valley and millet in the Yellow River valley by 6000 B.C.E. Incipient farming cultures existed in southeastern Europe by 6000 B.C.E. and elsewhere in Europe between 6000 and 4000 B.C.E. Farming was established in Egypt by 5000 B.C.E., and Mesoamerican farmers cultivated pumpkins and beans by 6000 B.C.E.[9]

Advancements in agriculture facilitated a transition to effective farming villages (permanent settlements supported by agriculture). Hunter-gatherers persisted on every inhabited continent, but by the end of the Neolithic, effective farming villages were established in Asia, Africa, Europe, Oceania, and the Americas. Wheat, corn, rice, potatoes, and other grains and vegetables were being grown. Dogs, cattle, goats, pigs, sheep, fowl, horses, and llamas were domesticated. Food storage was improved, and irrigation systems increased crop yields. By the fourth millennium B.C.E. in Southwest Asia, cattle were being used as draft animals and two important technological developments—the plow and wheel—occurred.

Incipient farming villages were small. Jarmo, a village in Iraqi Kurdistan dating around 7000 B.C.E., appears to have contained twenty or more multiroomed huts and a population of roughly 150 people. Effective farming villages were significantly larger. At Catal Huyuk on the Anatolian Plateau (in modern Turkey), a town of around a thousand houses with a population of three thousand or more was occupied from 6200 to 5400 B.C.E. Villages of the Linear Pottery culture (a European culture that flourished between 5500 and 4800 B.C.E.) consisted of about a dozen large, rectangular longhouses and collectively housed several hundred villagers.[10]

Farming and village life changed the lives of Stone Age people. Population growth provided labor that excelled in nonfarming crafts such as art, building, pottery, toolmaking, weaponry, weaving, and metallurgy. Pottery was created as containers for foodstuffs and water by 7000 B.C.E. and developed into a decorative art before the Neolithic came to a close. Copper was used for small, precious items by 6500 B.C.E. in Anatolia, and bronze was widely used in the Middle East for casting tools, weapons, and ornaments by 3000 B.C.E. Surplus food and expanded material production created opportunities for trade and the exchange of ideas and technologies.

SOCIAL STRATIFICATION AND GENDER IN THE NEOLITHIC

Society was deeply affected by the shift to food production and sedentary life. As concentrations of population increased, social patterns changed and contributed to the formation of still larger population centers. Settled life provided the context for a division of labor into farmers, craftspeople, and political-religious elites. Making decisions through consensus worked for hunter-gatherers, but it was not as workable for villagers and townspeople. In farming villages and towns, decisions were made by councils of elders or chiefs or, in some preurban contexts, monarchs. Evidence of social ranking is scarce, but Neolithic sites in which there are disparities in grave goods (items buried with the deceased) and the size of homes support such a conclusion.

Many scholars believe that women had a dominant role in food production. If Paleolithic men were primarily hunters and women primarily gatherers, then women were probably more familiar with the growth patterns and uses of plants. Thus, it is likely that women were the first to harvest wild grains and vegetables and to domesticate them. That women were the first farmers is supported by the evidence. Among the grave goods of the Linear Pottery culture, hand-operated mills containing used mill flour were found exclusively in female burial sites. In a study of 104 recent horticultural societies (hoe rather than plow farmers), women were solely responsible for farming in 50 percent of them, whereas men were solely responsible for agriculture in only 17 percent; in the other 33 percent, men and women cooperatively farmed.[11]

The social implications of women's role in farming is an area of contention. Some scholars argue that the prominence of women in agriculture was paralleled by a social status equal to or greater than that of men. They cite the predominance of female images in Neolithic art as indicative of the high status of women. Other scholars disagree. The theological meanings of the images are also disputed. Were the female figurines dolls, votive offerings, ancestral spirits, fertility **fetishes** (objects imbued with magical power), images of goddesses, or perhaps all of these things? Because these issues loom large in contemporary scholarship, gender and the female sacred are addressed more fully at the end of the chapter.

MEGALITHS AND TUMULI: THE FIRST RELIGIOUS MONUMENTS   The Neolithic gave birth to the first religious architectural monuments in the form of stone monuments **(megaliths)** and earthen mounds **(tumuli).** Before Egypt's first stone pyramid was constructed (ca. 2600 B.C.E.), Neolithic peoples in Europe began setting in place gigantic stones that functioned as burial sites and open-air temples for worship and communal activities. Later, similar efforts were undertaken in Neolithic cultures in Asia, Oceania, and North America. Megaliths and tumuli are awesome witnesses to Neolithic spirituality and craftsmanship.

Between 4000 and 1500 B.C.E., thousands of megaliths were erected in western Europe. Dolmens—two or more upright stones covered by a flat capping stone and creating a chamber between them—functioned as tombs for generations of villagers. Chamber tombs were protected by mounds of earth, some of which covered several square yards of acreage. At some sites, subterranean passages led to and from the tombs. Menhirs (single upright stones) are another megalithic wonder. Sacred places were often marked off by one or two menhirs, but several sites involved numerous stones.

For example, at Carnac, France, 2,935 menhirs were aligned in parallel rows. Menhirs were often arranged in semicircles or circles (henges), as is evident at Stonehenge in Wiltshire, England. Silbury Hill in Wiltshire is one of the largest and oldest human-made earthen mounds (130 feet high and 525 feet in diameter).

Megaliths and earthen monuments were erected outside Europe as well. Stone figurines were set in place in prehistoric Japan, and mounds enclosed within a rectangular embankment covered the dead at Hopewell, a Neolithic site in the United States (Ohio and Illinois). Neolithic stone monuments have been discovered at many sites in Southeast Asia and Oceania, but the most widely known are the gigantic stone figures on Easter Island (ca. 1050 –1650 C.E.).

PREHISTORIC RELIGION: BELIEFS AND PRACTICE

Prehistoric religion is a convenient but misleading label. First, it wrongly suggests that prehistoric peoples had a single religion. The symbol systems of Stone Age peoples resembled one another, but it is very unlikely that a single universe of meaning was common to all. Prehistoric peoples were separated by geography, lineage, and culture. They were also separated by time; for example, the Middle and Late Paleolithic span a period of over ninety thousand years. Second, the label implies that prehistoric religion was an organized social entity. Like tribal peoples in historical time, it is unlikely that Stone Age peoples separated religion from other aspects of their lives; thus, the labels *prehistoric religion* and *Stone Age religion* do not refer to the types of organizations we are familiar with today. If we think of religion as a social institution, prehistoric peoples did not have a religion, but they were religious. Our treatment of Stone Age religious beliefs and practices is divided into sections

CHRONOLOGY OF PREHISTORY AND PREHISTORIC RELIGIONS

CA. **4.6 billion** B.P.	Formation of the earth
CA. **3.6 billion** B.P.	Beginning of life: single-celled life
CA. **5 million** B.P.	Emergence of hominid genus ancestral to humankind: *Australopithecus*
CA. **2 million** B.P.	Stone toolmaking begins with *Homo habilis*
CA. **500,000** B.P.	Use of fire by *Homo erectus*
CA. **200,000** B.P.	Emergence of early *Homo sapiens*
CA. **100,000** B.P.	Emergence of anatomically modern *Homo sapiens sapiens* and *Homo neandertalensis*
CA. **60,000** B.P.	Oldest known human burials (Neandertal)
CA. **30,000** B.P.	Paleolithic cave painting, sculpture, and music; disappearance of Neandertals
CA. **12,000** B.P.	First villagers: hunting, gathering, and fishing in Japan; hunting, gathering, and harvesting wild grains in Southwest Asia

on the cosmos, life after death, spirit beings, sacred persons, and sacrifice.

THE COSMOS

The archaeological record does not permit us to confidently reconstruct a Stone Age view of the cosmos, but it is probable that, like recent tribal peoples, prehistoric peoples perceived the world as being permeated with spirit. Mircea Eliade labeled this unity of the divine, natural, and human spheres as **cosmic religion.** Prehistoric peoples were deeply influenced by their efforts to survive in a harsh and dangerous environment. Life and death, food and fertility dominated their lives and shaped their worlds of meaning. The dependence of Paleolithic hunter-gatherers on edible plants and animals fostered what Eliade characterized as a "mystical solidarity" that bound hunter and hunted together.[12] Animal and plant species were more than sim-

ply something to eat; they embodied spirit beings endowed with supernatural power.

The agricultural revolution stimulated a new orientation, one that centered on the new food sources that sustained human life: Domesticated plants and animals. In the process, the mystical identification of cultivators with the cultivated gradually overshadowed that of the hunter and the hunted. Neolithic farmers were profoundly influenced by the fact that their lives were centered in a cycle of planting, ripening, and harvesting. Presumably, they saw in the fertility of living things and the cycles of domestic crops a microcosm of the cosmos. The world moved in a pattern of birth, death, and rebirth that seemed to be operative everywhere.

LIFE AFTER DEATH

The primary evidence of archaic religiosity is derived from human burials of the dead. What

CA. 8000 B.C.E.	First farmers: cultivation of barley and wheat and domestication of sheep, goats, and cattle in Southwest Asia; the Neolithic begins
CA. 7000 B.C.E.	Farming in Indus Valley, New Guinea (Oceania), and South America; pottery products begin in West Asia
CA. 6500 B.C.E.	Copper metallurgy begins
CA. 6200 B.C.E.	Protourban center: Catal Huyuk (Anatolia); farming in Greece and Aegean islands
CA. 6000 B.C.E.	Cultivation of rice and millet in China; growing of beans and pumpkins in Mesoamerica
CA. 4000 B.C.E.	Erection of megaliths in Europe (France); domestication of horses in southern Ukraine; maize (corn) farming in South America
CA. 3500 B.C.E.	Bronze metallurgy begins in Southwest Asia; plow agriculture begins and invention of the wheel in Southwest Asia
CA. 3000 B.C.E.	Farming and pastoralism in South Asia (India), Southeast Asia, Korea, and Japan; Stonehenge is begun

motivated humans to bury their dead? The life situation of Paleolithic nomads did not necessitate such behavior, so perhaps the burials are indicative of an affection that the living felt for the deceased. Possibly their sensibilities could not bear leaving the bodies of loved ones exposed to the elements and foraging carnivores. It is also possible that burials were prompted by fear of the dead.

But is that all that ancient burials meant? Is it not likely that they reflect the belief that humans, in some way, survived death? Several Paleolithic funerary behaviors support such a conclusion. Belief in life after death is supported by burials that include grave goods (for example, stone tools), a practice suggesting that such objects were regarded by Paleolithic hunter-gatherers as useful to the dead. At some Paleolithic sites, animals appear to have been sacrificed to accompany the dead. Animal bones have been found near corpses, and at some Neandertal sites, the dead appear to have been

covered with large animal bones Sometimes the deceased were sprinkled with a red ocher and buried with red grave goods. Scholars speculate that the bones and the red ocher (perhaps a substitute for the life force, blood) were part of a ritual process intended to restore the grave's occupants to life in the hereafter. At some Paleolithic sites, the dead were interred in fetal-like positions, a posture that suggests an association of the grave with the womb, of death with a second birth; heads of the deceased were usually pointed to the east, the direction of the rising sun, another symbol of renewal. The preservation of human skulls in the Late Paleolithic is also suggestive of the belief that some aspect of human existence survives death.

The funerary behaviors of Neolithic peoples provide evidence that they, like their predecessors, believed that some aspect of human existence survived death. Neolithic burials usually included grave goods, and the practical character of the goods (for example, tools, weapons, and pottery) implies that Neolithic villagers believed that the life of the dead was similar to this life. Sprinkling bodies with red ocher is also evident at several Neolithic sites. The most dramatic development was in the size and scope of Neolithic funerary monuments. Megaliths were erected and tumuli formed in conjunction with interments in western Europe and elsewhere. These monuments functioned both as memorials for ancestors and as a symbolic affirmation that humans survived death and that, in a seascape of change, something endures.

In addition to being burial sites, megaliths and tumuli had other religious functions and meanings. They were open-air temples where rituals were performed and worship occurred, and monuments such as Stonehenge may have had astronomical and calendrical applications and uses. Archaeologist Marija Gimbutas (1921–1994) argued that the earthen mounds symbolized the pregnant womb of the Great Goddess, who was both the Mother of the Earth and the mother of the dead laid to rest within it. Gimbutas regarded underground passages leading to and from the burial mounds as symbols of the Great Goddess's womb; their openings were vulvas and their passages vaginas leading to the uterus. Gimbutas also contended that Paleolithic caves functioned as symbols of the divine Mother's womb.[13] As in the case of tumuli and caves, Gimbutas saw a connection between megaliths and the Goddess. She suggested that megalithic sites were points where worshipers symbolically entered Mother Earth's womb and gave themselves to her.[14]

SPIRIT BEINGS

We cannot be sure what prehistoric peoples believed about spirit beings, but it is likely that spirit beings symbolized and embodied things in nature (for example, heavenly bodies, the earth, animals, and plants). It is also likely that prehistoric peoples believed in different types of spirits, including gods, goddesses, ancestral spirits, and totemic spirits. Speech about spirit beings usually involves **anthropomorphism**: the attribution of human qualities and features to divinities. This was very likely true

of prehistoric peoples. Thus, it is likely that at least some Stone Age humanlike figurines symbolized divinities. The archaeological evidence is suggestive of belief in **totemic spirits** (animal or nature spirits associated with the origins of families and clans) and **theriomorphic divinities** (those with animal or mixed animal and human bodies). **Ancestral spirits** (deified ancestors) may have also been part of the mix of deities.

ANCESTRAL SPIRITS   We noted that two beliefs can be inferred from Stone Age burials and grave goods: some aspect of human existence survived death, and the dead continued to have need for everyday things. Veneration of ancestral spirits involves a third belief: the conviction that the dead have an ongoing relationship with the living. Presumably, belief that humans transcended death was accompanied by the conviction that the dead interacted for good or ill with the living and that their veneration (including fear of them) was warranted. The veneration of ancestral spirits can be inferred from the preservation of human skulls in the Late Paleolithic. Evidence from the Neolithic includes burials of skulls or complete skeletons under the floors of houses and altars and, at one archaeological site in Southwest Asia, a room of skulls covered with plaster and given individualized figures. The preservation of human skulls and bones and the creation of burial monuments suggest that Stone Age peoples believed in an ongoing connection between the living and the dead through the skulls, bones, and burial sites.

NATURE DIVINITIES   The evidence suggests that Paleolithic peoples deified the animals that gave them life or otherwise captivated their consciousness, and that in the Neolithic, domestic crops and animals replaced or assumed a place alongside wild animals as symbols of divinity. For example, although some scholars believe that the skulls and long bones of bears found in caves occupied by Neandertals were the result of chance (bears inhabited the caves before humans did), it is possible that the bones were arranged by design and that cave bears had a divine status.

Analogous beliefs and practices have been reported in recent times. Arctic peoples have had complex relations with bears. One group places the skull and long bones of bears on a platform as an offering to a supreme being. Another group preserves bear skulls and long bones for a guardian divinity of wild animals to restore to life. Traditional Ainu, a people of Hokkaido (the large northern island of Japan), think of bears as intermediaries to the spirit world. Bears were not the only animals associated with prehistoric peoples. Burial sites contain the bones of other animals, and animals (for example, owls and horses) are depicted in prehistoric art. In some contexts, these depictions are suggestive of deified animals.

TOTEMIC SPIRITS A deity associated with protecting animals—watching over animals and restoring slain animals to life—is sometimes identified by scholars as a **Master of Animals.** The care of animal bones in prehistory was probably part of rituals of restoration and thanksgiving to guardians of animals, but it is also possible that bears, bison, horses, and other animals were totemic deities who were regarded as ancestors and guardians of the people who worshiped them.

GODDESSES AND GODS The human form also served as symbols of the sacred, embodiments of divinity. Carved statuettes of beings with human features have been found in Late Paleolithic sites from western France to Siberia and were even more widely distributed in Neolithic times. Most of the figurines with a determinable sex are women with broad hips, large stomachs, and pendulous breasts. Scholars are at odds as to their meaning. Some interpreters believe the figurines were symbols for a Mother Goddess and the reproductive power of women. Reflecting this perspective, the figures were labeled **Venus figurines,** after the Roman goddess of love. Another viewpoint regards the statuettes as dolls with little or no religious significance. A third perspective links their meaning to their location; because many of the statuettes were discovered in hearth and home sites, this is taken to mean that the figurines were regarded as guardian spirits. A fourth interpretation associates the fecund figures with imitative magic; Stone Age women who desired to get pregnant assisted the process by acquiring or fashioning pregnant models of themselves. Similar practices have been reported in indigenous cultures in historic times.

The female figurines probably had several meanings, but their association with goddesses seems warranted. Venus figurines are so common to the residue of Late Paleolithic hunter-gatherers and Neolithic cultivators that it appears that worship of goddesses was widespread in prehistory. Goddesses were depicted as women and as theriomorphic beings—for example, as women with the features of snakes or birds. Secondary depictions may also have occurred: owls, serpents, frogs, and other iconographic subjects may have been associated with goddesses, and bulls and axes with gods.[15] Goddess figures predominate in prehistoric sculpture, but we should not conclude that gods were unknown or inconsequential. The archaeological record includes statuettes of males and sexually

Venus figurine found at the Late Paleolithic burial site of Grimaldi on the French-Italian border.

indeterminate humans, and it is likely that some of these figures, as well as some depictions of animals (for example, bulls), symbolized gods.

Fertility and regeneration were dominant motifs in prehistoric spirituality. Female images were often corpulent and pregnant. Male figurines with phalli and depictions of humanlike figures coupled in sexual union are also part of what survives of Stone Age art. Some scholars regard depictions of human coupling as symbolic of a mythological holy marriage *(hieros gamos)* uniting male and female, God and Goddess. It is likely that prehistoric peoples made a connection between earth's fertility and that of women; the earth brought forth vegetation, and women bore children. In the larger equation of fertility and regeneration, the earth may have been seen as a goddess bearing life-sustaining food and to whom people returned when they died.

Ethnology supports this interpretation. The association of foods that sustain human life with a goddess is a mythological theme among recent cultivators from Melanesia to North America and, in some contexts, involves the death of a goddess. In the mythology of the Seneca, one of the tribes of the Iroquois Confederacy, the Mother Goddess gave birth to a daughter and forbade her to play in water; the daughter transgressed and was impregnated with twins by the water. The twins fought within her womb; one (Good Spirit) was born without complication, but the other (Bad Spirit) burst from his mother's side and killed her. The goddess buried her daughter, and from her body came corn and other edible plants.

SACRED PERSONS: THE *SHAMAN*

Shamanism, a type of religious leadership associated with hunter-gatherers and nomadic pastoralists in historic times, was probably part of Paleolithic religion. *Shamans* are human intermediaries between humans and spirit beings. They acquire their magico-religious power and authority through direct and ecstatic contact with guardian spirits: during trance states, *shamans* contact guardian spirits either through soul travel (their souls leave their

bodies and travel to the spirit realm) or **spirit possession** (a spirit enters their body). Mastery of sacred power enables these ecstatic magicians to solve problems, to heal, and to deliver or protect others from misfortunes. With the rise of villages and towns and of chiefdoms and kingdoms in the Neolithic, new forms of religious leadership emerged (for example, chiefs, kings, and priests); *shamanism,* however, has persisted from Paleolithic times to the present.

The case for the antiquity of *shamanism* relies on Paleolithic art. Drawings that reveal the skeletons and internal organs of animals are reminiscent of recent *shamanic* practice. As Eliade observed, "It is an art specifically characteristic of hunting cultures, but the religious ideology with which it is saturated is shamanic. For it is only the shaman who, by virtue of his supernatural vision, is able to 'see his own skeleton.'"[16] *Shamans* are also believed to be able to transform themselves into animal forms; thus, in Eliade's judgment, Paleolithic figures with mixed animal and human characteristics are further evidence of *shamanism.*

Shamanic power to heal, divine what is hidden, and otherwise harness supernatural power for human purposes involves the magical arts. Paleolithic paintings of animals and weapons of the hunt suggest hunting magic and *shamanic* practice. Ancient peoples may have assumed that depictions of speared bison accompanied by the requisite words and gestures would produce the desired result (imitative magic): the spearing of bison in the hunt. Belief that an item that was once part of something else continues to share in its power (contagious magic) may have occurred through integration of animal relics (antlers, hides, and the like) into the ritual drama.

SACRIFICE

Animal sacrifice appears to have been part of Paleolithic religion. Burials that include animal remains suggest that the attendant funerary rites involved animal sacrifice. At a cave site in Lebanon, deer fossils dating to approximately

50,000 years ago were discovered that indicate that the deer had been dismembered and sprinkled with red ocher. The discovery suggests a ritual of thanksgiving for that which gives life (the body of the deer) and a supplication to the spirit world for its renewal. Rituals associated with animals slain by hunters may have involved offering a portion of the animals to the spirit world, but it is likely that such offerings were a means of giving thanks to the spirit world rather than examples of animal sacrifice.

Human sacrifice and cannibalism may have been part of Paleolithic religion. There is evidence suggestive of human sacrifice in the Paleolithic, but apparently it was rare and continued to be a rare behavior in hunting and gathering societies in historical times. There is little evidence that humans were sacrificed to accompany the dead, a fairly common practice in the first urban civilizations. Cannibalism is alleged to have occurred among Neandertals. Presumably, Neandertal skulls that were widened at the base were widened to remove the brains for human consumption. Similar behaviors have been reported in historical times among peoples who viewed the eating of parts of a sacrificial victim (for example, the brain or heart) as a means of acquiring the victim's desirable attributes.[17]

Blood sacrifice increased in the Neolithic. Animals were sacrificed in conjunction with human burials and presumably at important junctures in vegetation cycles (for example, planting and harvesting) and on special occasions (sickness, famine, war, and so on). The victims were chiefly domestic animals (for example, goats, oxen, and sheep). Human sacrifice also occurred and, in some contexts, involved cannibalism. The victims were usually females and children. For example, the remains of two young girls found in a bog in Denmark (dating from approximately 3500 B.C.E.) suggest that the girls, who had been strangled, clubbed, and drowned, were sacrificed and cannibalized. Substitutionary sacrifices—those in which symbolic representations of living beings were placed in graves and no life was taken—were also part of Neolithic practice.

ANCIENT URBAN SOCIETIES

The agricultural revolution led to the emergence of the first cities, a phenomenon sometimes referred to as the urban revolution. Like the agricultural revolution, the development of urban centers involved fundamental changes in the way people lived and profoundly influenced religious expression. Scholars believe that the first cities emerged in southern Mesopotamia in the area known as Sumer between 3500 and 3000 B.C.E. Subsequently, societies with urban centers developed in Egypt (ca. 3100 B.C.E.), Palestine and Syria (ca. 2600 B.C.E.), the Indus Valley (ca. 2500 B.C.E.), China (ca. 2000 B.C.E.), Anatolia (ca. 2000 B.C.E.), Crete (ca. 2000 B.C.E.), Elam (ca. 2000 B.C.E.), Sudanic East Africa (ca. 2000 B.C.E.), Greece (ca. 1500 B.C.E.), America (ca. 1000 B.C.E.), Italy (ca. 700 B.C.E.), and sub-Saharan West Africa (700 C.E.).

Mesopotamia (the area of modern Iraq) was home to several states (the city-states of Sumer and the kingdoms of the Akkadians, Babylonians, Kassites, Assyrians, and Chaldeans). The Mesopotamian states were separate entities, but they shared elements of culture that persisted until the conquest of the Chaldeans (Neo-Babylonians) by the Persians in 539 B.C.E. Ancient Palestine (also known as Canaan) is the home of modern Israel and Lebanon; it was home to many peoples, including the Israelites, Phoenicians, Canaanites, and Philistines. Anatolia is part of modern Turkey; in ancient times it was home to the Hurrians, Hittites, and Lydians. The Indus Valley civilization was centered in what is now Pakistan. Ancient Elam was located in what is now southwestern Iran. The Aegean Sea was home to the urbanized island culture of Minoan Crete. Greece was home to the Mycenaeans, a Greek-speaking people who may have been the victors in the war (ca. 1190 B.C.E.) against Troy, a prosperous city in Asia Minor (modern Turkey).

By 525 B.C.E. the state systems of West Asia (ancient Egypt, Mesopotamia, Elam, Palestine, and Anatolia) and the Aegean had waxed and waned. During the next millennium, the Persians (550–330 B.C.E. and 226–651 C.E.), the Greeks (490–323 B.C.E.), the empire of Alexander the Great (356–323 B.C.E.), and the Romans (509 B.C.E.–476 C.E.) took center stage in southern Europe and the Middle East. In a different span of time, an analogous phenomenon involving the rise and fall of urban states took place in Central and South America as the first urban centers and centralized states (for example, the Olmec and Chavin cultures) gave way to subsequent states (for example, the Mochica, Maya, Zapotec, Toltec, Inca, and Aztec states).

Ancient Persia (the area of modern Iran) was home to the Persian empires, as well as the Achaemenid (ca. 550–331 B.C.E.) and Sassanid (226–651 C.E.) dynasties. Zoroastrianism became the state religion during the Achaemenid dynasty and had a similar status during the Sassanid dynasty. Centralized urban states emerged in Sudanic East Africa (the kingdom of Kush) in the second millennium B.C.E., and Kushite kings ruled the kingdoms of Kush and Egypt from around 747 to 656 B.C.E. Urban states established in West Africa between 500 and 1500 C.E. (for example, the kingdoms of Ghana, Mali, Benin, and Oyo).

CHARACTERISTICS OF ANCIENT URBAN CIVILIZATIONS

The term *civilization* has numerous connotations, including those that resonate in historian Gordon Childe's (1892–1957) characterization of the antecedents of civilization as "Paleolithic Savagery" and "Neolithic Barbarism."[18] If we set aside the assumptions about primitives implicit in Childe's categories, the term *civilization* is a useful symbol for a set of characteristics that were typical of ancient urban societies: cities, centralized governance, intensive agriculture, writing, monumental buildings, social ranking, craft specialization, metallurgy, trade, taxes, and mathematics. Some of these features (for example, metallurgy and trade) were already present in Neolithic societies, and some (for example, writing) were not common to all ancient urban civilizations. Figure 2.2 shows centers of ancient urban civilization.

INTENSIVE AGRICULTURE AND CENTRALIZED POLITICAL SYSTEMS   The emergence of urban civilizations coincided with advancements in agriculture. The transition from incipient to effective agricultural production supported larger populations and permanent settlements. The next phase—intensive food production—involved irrigation, greater diversification of domesticated crops and animals, and technological advances such as the plow. Because the oldest civilizations developed along great rivers—the Tigris and Euphrates (Mesopotamia), the Nile (Egypt), the Yellow (China), and the Indus (India)—and included hydraulic projects, some scholars maintain that irrigated farming was a necessary antecedent of the urban revolution. Other scholars argue that the development of new patterns of social organization, especially central regulative systems capable of incorporating several ethnic groups and directing labor-intensive projects (for example, irrigation works and public monuments), was as fundamental as intensive farming to the transition from villages to cities.

The transition from the noncentralized forms of governance of nomadic bands and farming villages to the centralized polities of ancient urban states consisted of several stages. Neolithic farming villages were probably organized in various ways. Some villages were probably led by councils, and others may have had a headman or headwoman. A new social organization involving the authority of chiefs and the ranking of descent groups by their relationship to the chief emerged in the Neolithic. Chiefdom societies united multiple villages around the leadership of the chief. A central village housed the chief and his or her retinue and functioned as a capital with shrines, priests, and protocols respecting the office and sacerdotal role of the chief.

Gradually, centralized state systems emerged with the power and authority to regulate their members and their relations with other states. States typically included a coercive policing authority, a system of taxation or tributes, a formal system of law, and a bureaucracy to administer public affairs. The first centralized states were city-states, those

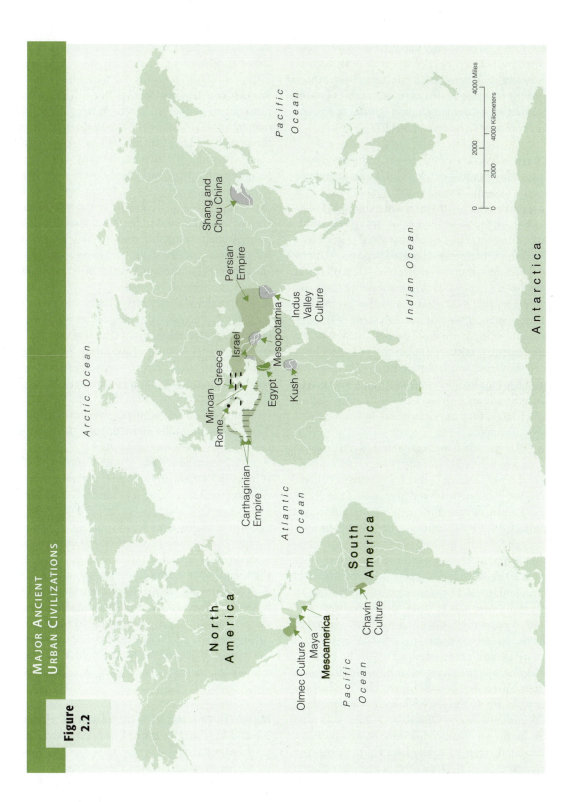

**Figure
2.2**

in which adjacent villages and rural areas were governed by a capital city. With exceptions, such as democratic Athens and republican Rome, most ancient urban societies were monarchies (states ruled by a monarch) or empires (groups of nations or peoples ruled by an emperor).

CITIES   Scholars identify several elements as constitutive of the first cities: a city is a settlement of several thousand (five thousand or more) that serves as a center for smaller settlements; conducts large-scale trade; and possesses monumental public buildings, extensive granaries, and advanced crafts. Some Neolithic settlements supported large populations and had some traits of urban centers. Catal Huyuk supported a population of as many as five thousand people in 6000 B.C.E., but it and other protourban centers in Southwest Asia lacked some of the elements associated with the first cities. By 3500 B.C.E., settlements with populations of at least two thousand people existed in Sumer. Over the next five hundred years, the first cities were established, including Uruk, a city with a population much larger than its predecessors and that housed several temples.

Ancient cities were regarded as holy places. Typically, they were associated with a patron divinity who was believed to dwell, figuratively or literally, in a house (temple) and in images of the divinity. Patron deities and their divine associates protected the inhabitants of cities from their enemies and the afflictions to which humans are subject. In return, the gods and goddesses of the city were attended to by the people and their priestly representatives. The cult center of the Sumerian sky deity Anu was at Uruk. Enki, the Sumerian god of primordial water and wisdom, reigned at Eridu. In some contexts, the city was regarded as an *axis mundi,* the sacred center of the cosmos. Marduk was the city-god of Babylon, the place from whence the cosmos began. The Yoruba holy city, Ila-Ife, is the place where the creator deity Olorun and his sons Obatala and Odudua created the earth and breathed life into the first humans. Cuzco, the capital of the Inca Empire, was the sacred center of the Inca cosmos and was near the mountain caves from whence the ancestors of the Inca emerged.

SOCIAL AND GENDER RELATIONS   More complex patterns of association accompanied the development of urban societies. The egalitarianism of Stone Age bands and farming villages gave way to class structures and ranking systems with commoners (peasants, servants, and slaves) at the bottom; merchants, artisans, and warriors in the middle; and priests and aristocrats at the top. At the apex of monarchical systems was the ruler, whose prestige was measured in part by the grandeur of his activities and the sumptuousness of his consumption (palaces, monuments, feasts, retainers, spouses, and so on).

Ethnicity was another complicating factor. Unlike tribal peoples, urban societies were composed of multiple ethnic groups, each of whom had its own lineages, traditions, and ethos. Social hierarchies and ethnic differences separated rulers from the ruled, aristocrats from commoners, masters from slaves, and priests from the uninitiated. Distinctions of class and ethnicity were reflected in a "high" faith of the elite and a "popular" faith of the lower classes and ethnic minorities.

Male dominance was typical of ancient urban cultures. Most monarchs, as well as the leaders of democratic Athens and republican Rome, were men. Queen Hatshepsut (ca. 1503–1482 B.C.E.) and Queen Cleopatra (ca. 51–30 B.C.E.) ruled Egypt; Bilqis, the Queen of Sheba, reigned in southern Arabia; and at least five women ruled in the kingdom of Kush (ca. 600 B.C.E.–300 C.E.). This does not exhaust the list of women monarchs, but male rule was the norm. The social and gender relationships that predominated in ancient urban societies paralleled those operative among the divinities; like monarchs, the heads of ancient national pantheons (collections of divinities) were usually male.

MATERIAL CULTURE AND MONUMENTS   Urban life and food surpluses freed people to develop a varied material culture. New industries and commercial ventures led to crafts that specialized in the

The great temple pyramid (ca. 1000–1200 C.E.) of the ancient Maya city Chichén Itzá, located in what is now the state of Yucatán, Mexico.

production and mechandising of nonagricultural products. Metallurgy and pottery were highly developed crafts. Gold and silver were primarily used in the decorative arts, and copper, bronze, and iron were the principal metals for the production of tools and weapons. Bronze—an alloy of copper and tin—was in production for tools, weapons, and ornaments by 3000 B.C.E. in the Middle East, China, India, and Greece. The Bronze Age (3000–1000 B.C.E.) was followed by the transition from bronze to iron tools and weaponry (the Iron Age) beginning around 1200 B.C.E. in West Asia.

Elaborate public buildings and monuments were the most spectacular embodiments of the material culture of ancient civilizations. Private homes were small, but urban centers housed large public buildings, including the ruler's palace, assembly halls, granaries, temples, shrines, and mortuary monuments. Temples were the dwelling places of gods and goddesses, housing their images and serving as a point of intersection between humankind and the divinities. Palaces—the residences of monarchs—were also sacred. They often included smaller temples, shrines, sacred groves, and emblems of the king's office and ancestry.

Pyramids and temples were the quintessential sacred monuments of ancient urban civilizations. Temples were often built on mounds or high places—surrogate mountains—that symbolized the center of the world. The ziggurats of Mesopotamia

and the temple-pyramids of Mesoamerica are spectacular examples. Ziggurats were quadrangular, terraced structures that rose from a base platform with a temple situated on the top and accessible by stairs or ramps. Temple-pyramids were built on an elevated, and usually artificially constructed, foundation with a temple adorned with panels, moldings, and sculptures situated on the upper platform. Ziggurats and pyramids resembled the mound of creation, and their height and massive solidity soared toward the abode of the gods and were awesome witnesses to the sacred.

Tombs, especially those of monarchs, were sometimes monumental. The pyramids of Egypt (massive stone burial structures with a rectangular base and four sharply sloping sides meeting at the apex) were both the "eternal homes" of Egyptian royalty and sacred necropolises (cities of the dead) surrounded by temples, guardian statues (for example, sphinxes), settlements, and the tombs of officials and lesser nobles. The massiveness and enduring qualities of the pyramids were vivid testimonies to the Egyptian belief in immortality, and their triangularity was an eloquent symbol of the Egyptian hierarchy, with the king at the apex, his officials aligned below him, and the masses constituting the supporting base of the pyramids. Funerary monuments were also characteristic of imperial China. For example, the tomb and large earthen burial mound of China's first emperor, Qin Shi Huang

(259–210 B.C.E.), was accompanied by temples and protected by an army of more than six thousand armed terra-cotta figures.

WRITING The emergence of urban centers and elite classes was accompanied by the invention of writing. The earliest known system of writing dates from around 3200 B.C.E. It was found in Sumer at the site of the ancient city of Uruk. Egyptian writing may be as old, but the oldest extant evidence dates from early in the first dynasty (ca. 2950–2770 B.C.E.). Chinese writing may be as venerable, but the oldest examples of it date from the second millennium B.C.E. Writing was not a feature of the civilizations of the Andean region and sub-Saharan Africa. The civilizations of the Minoans and the Indus Valley did have writing, but their scripts have not been deciphered.

Writing gradually restructured human consciousness: reading and seeing took precedence over speaking and hearing, and an unprecedented level of abstraction evolved.[19] Writing was a precondition of advances in mathematics and the sciences, the construction of calendars, the formalization of law, the issuing of edicts, and the emergence of sacred writ. With exceptions such as the high cultures of South America and sub-Saharan Africa, ancient urban religions were literate traditions. Table 2.1 lists some of the most important sacred texts of ancient urban religions.

THE EMERGENCE OF THE WORLD RELIGIONS

The period from 550 B.C.E. to 650 C.E. was a remarkable time in the history of religion. It was a period illuminated by Buddha, Confucius, Christ, and Muhammad—the foundational figures of Buddhism, Confucianism, Christianity, and Islam—and by lesser-known founders such as Mani (Manichaeism) and Mahavira (Jainism). It was also a period of philosophers whose thought profoundly influenced the history of ideas: Mencius and Chuang-tzu in China, Plato and Aristotle in Greece, and Nagarjuna and Patanjali in India.

As contacts between urban states increased through trade, alliance, and conquest and as states expanded and became more ethnically mixed, a cosmopolitan perspective emerged in southern Europe and the Middle East that entailed a sense of belonging to all of the (known) world rather than to an ethnically restrictive piece of it. This perspective ripened during the reign of Alexander the Great (336–323 B.C.E.), the Hellenistic Age (323–27 B.C.E.), and the Roman Empire (27 B.C.E.–476 C.E.). As articulated by Stoic philosophers, all humans should be regarded as belonging to one state and as sharing one standard of life and justice. This outlook was accompanied by the rise of religious groups and associations that offered personal salvation and that appealed to devotees across the boundaries of ethnicity, class, and caste.

Before 600 B.C.E., conversionist religions were rare. Zoroastrianism may have been the first. The dating is disputed; some scholars believe Zoroastrianism was founded around 1000 B.C.E. or even earlier by the Persian prophet and reformer Zoroaster; others believe he lived in the late seventh and early sixth centuries B.C.E. Zoroastrianism, Buddhism, Jainism, Christianity, Manichaeism, Islam, and other conversionist movements changed the religious landscape dramatically, providing people with alternatives to the traditions that had previously framed their religious life. In the same period, **initiation cults,** also known as **mystery religions,** were established in Greece, Egypt, and other areas of the Middle East and subsequently spread beyond their original ethnic-national orbits. Initiation cults (for example, cults associated with the worship of Demeter, Dionysus, Isis, Cybele, and Mithras) offered personal and saving experiences of the sacred through rituals that were voluntary and secret. Philosophical and religious movements that provided alternatives to tradition emerged in Europe (for example, Platonism, Epicureanism, and Stoicism), India (for example, Ajivika, Carvaka, Buddhism, and Jainism), and China (for example, Confucianism, Mohism, and Taoism).

The period was a momentous one for ethnic religions as well. Oblivion was the fate of most; for example, the national religious traditions of ancient

SACRED TEXTS OF ANCIENT URBAN RELIGIONS

Table 2.1

Avesta	The primary collection of Zoroastrian sacred texts (first millennium B.C.E.), including the *Gathas*, seventeen hymns ascribed to Zoroaster.
Code of Hammurabi	A legal code said to have been commissioned by the god of justice, the sun god Shamash, and decreed by the Babylonian (Amorite) King Hammurabi (ca. 1725 B.C.E.) It was originally carved on a rock and set in the temple of Marduk in Babylon.
Corpus Hermeticum	A collection of books of religious and philosophical traditions and practices dating from the second to fourth century C.E., attributed to, and associated with, the Greco-Egyptian deity Hermes Trismegistos.
Egyptian *Book of the Dead*	A text to guide the deceased in his or her passage through the underworld and to life with the gods. It regularly appeared on tombs and coffins.
Elder Edda	Myths and stories about pre-Christian Icelandic (Nordic) religion.
Enuma Elish	A creation myth sacred to the Babylonians. The final section directs devotees to memorize and repeat the poem.
Gilgamesh Epic	A Mesopotamian epic poem committed to writing in late Sumerian times (ca. 2100 B.C.E.) and incorporated into a larger Babylonian version of the epic ca. 1800 B.C.E.
Iliad	A Greek epic poem attributed to Homer (ca. 800 B.C.E.). The poem is about the Trojan War, the battles and heroes, Greek values, the role of the gods, sacrifice, and other religious beliefs and practices.
Popol Vuh	A book of the Quiche Maya compiled in the sixteenth century, after Spanish conquest, but containing pre-Hispanic Maya traditions.
Theogony	A poem written by the Greek poet Hesiod (ca. 700 B.C.E..) that delineates the genealogy of the Olympian gods and their predecessors.
The Treasure of Life	Among the sacred texts written by Mani (216–ca. 277 C.E..), the founder of Manichaeism.

Egypt, Mesopotamia, Greece, and Rome ceased to be living faiths. Nonetheless, these traditions had remarkable staying powers. The religion of ancient Egypt was formed in predynastic times and endured for roughly 2,500 years as a state religion and for another 800 years as an ethnic religion under Persian, Greek, and Roman domination, a longevity that Christianity and Islam—traditions that subsequently dominated the Egyptian landscape and that brought an end to nearly all of the national and initiation cults of the ancient Middle East and Mediterranean—have not yet equaled. The Egyptian temples still functioning in the Christianized Roman Empire were closed by the emperor Justinian (527–565 C.E.) in 529 C.E. Elements of the religious traditions of ancient Mesopotamia were shared by the kingdoms and empires of Mesopotamia for over three thousand years. Greek and Roman paganism were not as long-lived as Egyptian and Mesopotamian religions, but they were living traditions for around a thousand years.

A death knell did not sound for all ethnic-national religions. It was a creative period for Judaism, Hinduism, and Shinto. Between 550 and 350 B.C.E., the earlier traditions of ancient Israel

CHRONOLOGY OF ANCIENT URBAN SOCIETIES AND RELIGIONS

CA. 3500–3000	First cities emerge in Sumer; writing is invented
CA. 3100	Unification of Upper and Lower Egypt
CA. 2686–2181	Period of the Old Kingdom in Egypt
CA. 2500	Indus Valley civilization
CA. 2350	Akkadians under Sargon I subdue Sumerian city-states
CA. 2100	Code of Law of Sumerian king Ur-Nammu; elements of the *Gilgamesh Epic* traceable to 2100
CA. 1900	Abraham, the patriarch of Judaism
CA. 1725	Babylonians (Amorites) rule Mesopotamia; Code of Hammurabi
CA. 1500–1069	Period of the New Kingdom in Egypt; *Book of the Dead* emerges as a sacred text
CA. 1400–1200	Period of the Hittite Empire; Hittites develop iron metallurgy; Iron Age begins
CA. 1400	Collapse of Minoan civilization (Crete)

(those of Abraham, Moses, and David) were knit to later traditions to form Judaism, and between 200 and 650 C.E., Israel's rabbis had laid the foundations of Rabbinic Judaism. A similar ferment—the dissolution or re-formation of traditional spirituality and the birth of new forms of spirituality—occurred in South and East Asia. India's priests and sages produced the Hindu classics—the *Upanishads* and the *Bhagavad Gita*—and gave shape to classical Hinduism. Chinese sages gave birth to the Confucian and Taoist schools of thought. By the second century C.E., Lao-tzu had been deified and had revealed a new faith to Chang Tao-ling, the first Master of the Way of the Celestial Masters, a Taoist group that survives in China today. By the sixth century C.E., Shinto had emerged from Japanese prehistoric folk traditions and was established as an indigenous alternative to movements imported from China.

Ethnic religionists were potential participants in the initiation cults and potential converts to universal religions. Because the initiation cults were not exclusive, devotees could participate in them and in ethnic traditions as well; the boundaries of the mystery cults and of most ethnic-national traditions were not sharply drawn and did not require ideological exclusiveness. As a consequence, considerable adaptation and assimilation occurred in paganism, including the integration of foreign deities into the pantheons of accommodating national traditions and the establishment of religious associations such as the cults of Isis-Osiris and Orpheus across ethnic-national lines. The absence of ideological exclusiveness was part of the Chinese experience as well, permitting the Chinese to draw on elements of Confucianism, Taoism, Buddhism, and folk religion. This flexibility was less true of Judaism, Christianity, and Islam. The monotheistic faiths were exclusive, demanding loyalty to the one true God and rejection of the polytheistic theologies and ritual behaviors of paganism.

CA. 1353–1339	Rule of King Akhenaten in Egypt
CA. 1250	Possibly the time of Moses and the Exodus
CA. 1200–612	Assyrian dominance in Mesopotamia
CA. 1200–400	Olmecs: Mesoamerian mother civilization
CA. 776	First Olympic Games (Greece)
CA. 570	Birth of the Greek philosopher Pythagoras (d. 500)
CA. 563	Birth of Siddhartha Gautama, Shakyamuni Buddha
CA. 550	First historical reference to Orpheus
CA. 539	Persians under Cyrus the Great conquer the Chaldeans (Neo-Babylonians)
CA. 469	Birth of Socrates (d. 399)
CA. 323	Death of Alexander the Great
CA. 4	Birth of Jesus of Nazareth

ANCIENT URBAN RELIGIONS: BELIEFS AND PRACTICES

As a category, ancient urban religion casts a very wide net. It includes the national religions of ancient Egypt, Mesopotamia (for example, the religions of the Sumerians, Akkadians, Babylonians, Assyrians, and Chaldeans), Palestine (for example, the religions of the Canaanites, Israelites, Philistines, and Phoenicians), Anatolia (the religions of the Hurrians, Hittites, and Lydians), Crete (the Minoan religion), the Greek city-states, Rome, China, India, Mesoamerica (for example, the religions of the Maya, Olmecs, Toltecs, and Aztecs), the Andean region (for example, the religions of the Mochica and Inca), and Africa (for example, the religions of the kingdoms of Kush, Ghana,

Benin, and Oyo). The category also includes conversionist religions (Zoroastrianism, Buddhism, Christianity, Mandaean, Manichaeism, Orphism, and Islam, among others), mystery religions, and schools of thought that had religious overtones (for example, Pythagoreanism and Platonism). And this list does not nearly exhaust the groups that fit within this classification.

Given the number and variety of ancient urban religions, it is not surprising that there are few beliefs and practices common to all. Our focus is on ancient national religions, with less attention to the mystery and conversionist religions. The primary difference in reconstructing prehistoric and ancient urban spirituality is the availability of written texts. There are vast gaps in the written record and scripts that are still undeciphered, but unlike prehistoric spirituality, the thoughts of ancient urban peoples are available in their own voices through written texts. Our treatment of the beliefs and practices of ancient national religions is divided into sections on the cosmos, divinities, sacred persons (the king), the nature and destiny of humans, morality, and sacrifice.

THE COSMOS

Like modern humans, archaic peoples longed for order and harmony in the cosmos and human society. Most ancient national religions envisioned such an order within the framework of what we previously identified as cosmic religion, grounding the order and unity of the cosmos and the well-being of human society in a spiritual order that was manifested in the rhythms and cycles of the world and the agency of the gods. In contrast, the theologies of the Abrahamic religions (Judaism, Christianity, and Islam) saw nature as a mirror of God's creation and therefore as pregnant with meaning, but they rejected theologies that saw aspects of the cosmos (for example, the sun, earth, or animals) as embodiments and metaphors of divinity.

Humans have a passion for organizing their worlds into meaningful patterns, for creating order out of disorder. This human concern and passion for order is evident in the myths and calendars of ancient urban spirituality. The myths of ancient national religions often depicted an intelligible, orderly, and differentiated cosmos as emerging out of a preexistent and formless watery abyss or, more rarely, as being created by a self-existent deity.

The oldest extant Egyptian origin myth (from the third millennium B.C.E.) begins with a dark and inert primal water personified as the god Nun, from whence emerged Atum, the god of the sun and the *"Lord of the limits of the sky."* Atum emerged out of the watery chaos of Nun, stood on a primeval mound, and masturbated the twin deities—the god Shu and the goddess Tefnut—into being. The following text depicts Atum's act of creation: *"All manifestations came into being after I developed . . . no sky existed no earth existed . . . I created on my own being . . . I copulated with my hand . . . I sneezed out Shu . . . I spat out Tefnut."*[20] Subsequently, Shu (air) and Tefnut (moisture) produced the god Geb (earth) and the goddess Nut (sky). The sexual union of earth and sky produced Osiris (the god of the

underworld), Isis (the wife of Osiris and goddess of the Egyptian throne), Seth (the god of chaotic forces and slayer of his brother Osiris), and Neththys (the consort of Seth and the funerary goddess). Atum and his descendants formed the Ennead, the company of the nine deities of Heliopolis (the city and cult center of the Ennead and the holy place where the world, mythologically speaking, began).

A deity who creates the world out of nothing other than his own thought or being is another motif in Egyptian mythology. In Memphis, the Egyptian capital during the Old Kingdom (ca. 2686–2181 B.C.E.), Ptah , the creator and supreme god of Memphite theology, was depicted as conceiving and speaking the cosmos into being. In the city of Thebes, a theology emerged in the New Kingdom (ca. 1550–1069 B.C.E.) that regarded the sun god Amun as the king of the gods and the creator of the world. In Theban mythology, Amun fashioned himself into being and was the primal mound or cosmic egg from whence came the gods and all subsequent divinities. In another creation myth, the sun god Re (Ra), perhaps preeminent of all of the Egyptian high gods, emerged out of the primal water and created the world.

According to the *Enuma Elish*, a Babylonian creation myth (ca. 1200 B.C.E.), in the beginning *"when skies above were not yet named/nor earth below pronounced by name,"*[21] nothing existed except the primordial waters personified as Apsu, the god of freshwater, and Tiamat, the goddess of saltwater. From their intermingling, various gods and goddesses emerged, including Anu (sky) and his sons. The noisy and rude behavior of Anu and his offspring annoyed the primal couple, and Apsu resolved to destroy them. In the ensuing conflict, Anu's son Enki killed Apsu and replaced him as lord of the freshwater, whence he and his spouse brought forth Marduk. In response to the murder of Apsu, Tiamat, in concert with monsters she had created, prepared to make war on the gods. Marduk agreed to battle Tiamat on the condition that he would rule over the gods and that his utterances would determine destinies. After killing the goddess Tiamat, Marduk created the universe from her body and proposed that Babylon be built as a place of assembly for the gods. After the deities agreed to build the city, Marduk delegated to each god and goddess their duties and created humans to serve them.

In some contexts, origin myths were ritually acted out, an indication that the celebrants believed that a repetition of the myth helped renew the cosmos. For example, the Babylonian New Year's festival (ca. 1000 B.C.E.) involved the recitation of the *Enuma Elish* before the statue of Marduk, the patron god of the city of Babylon and the supreme god of the Babylonians. The twelve-day festival recreated the victory of divine order over chaos as it happened in the beginning. In reenacting Marduk's triumph over Tiamat and his subsequent rule of the cosmos, the king was divested of his royal insignia and slapped across the face by the high priest—actions that symbolized the setbacks that Marduk endured in his cosmic struggle. Humbled, the king knelt before the statue of Marduk and assured the deity that he had discharged his duties to the gods, Babylon, its citizens, and the temple. He was then reinvested with his royal insignia and authority.

In the eighth century B.C.E., the Greek poet Hesiod composed, with help from the Muses (goddesses who inspired artists), a detailed account of the origin of the cosmos. In the beginning was Chaos, an abyss, whence Mother Earth (Gaia) and Love (Eros) emerged. Gaia gave birth to Sky (Ouranos). From Mother Earth and Father Sky came plants; animals; rivers; lakes; and numerous offspring, including three Cyclops, twelve Titans, and three hundred other deities. Provoked by her husband, Gaia called upon the Titans to attack their father, Ouranos. Led by the Titan Kronus, the Titans surprised the sleeping Ouranos and castrated him. Knowing that he, like his father, was fated to be overthrown by one of his sons, Kronus swallowed the first five children of his union with his sister Rhea. Enraged, Rhea secretively gave birth to her third son, Zeus, in a mountain cave on the island of Crete. When she returned to her husband, Rhea cleverly wrapped a stone in the fashion of infants and presented it to him. Mistaking

it for the child, Kronus swallowed it. Later Zeus, using a strategem devised by the goddess Metis, forced his father to regurgitate the gods and goddesses he had swallowed and confined Kronus forever in Tartarus, a world below the earth's surface.

Following their victory over the Titans, the sons of Kronus and Rhea drew lots to determine their spheres of power: Zeus, the king of the Olympians (the gods who dwell on Mount Olympus), ruled the earth and sky; Poseidon, the seas; and Hades, the underworld and the dead. Their sisters ruled over domestic and vegetative spheres: Hestia was the virgin goddess of the hearth; Demeter the goddess of crops; and Hera, the wife of Zeus, the goddess of marriage and female sexuality. After becoming king of the Olympians, Zeus married his first wife, Metis, whose intelligence had helped him gain the throne. To protect himself from a repetition of the cycle of violence (the slaying of the father by a son), Zeus swallowed Metis before she could give birth to a child that could displace him. She, as an inner voice, then warns him, by virtue of her unsurpassable knowledge, of what the future holds so that he can deflect potentially undesirable outcomes.[22]

In pre-Hispanic Mexico, the Aztecs, or Mexica, likewise envisioned the world as being preceded by a dark, chaotic, and watery primordium out of which an orderly but unstable cosmos came into being. From this primordium arose a male and female deity, Ometeotl, the dual god who created himself/herself and is mother and father to all other divinities and the ultimate source of all that is. The first to emerge from the dual god were his/her four sons: the Red, Black, White, and Blue Tezcatlipocas, who subsequently did most of the work of creation (bringing forth the heavens, earth, and underworld; initiating life; making fire; and creating the calendar).[23]

Like origin myths, myths of regeneration are indicative of the understanding of the cosmos in ancient national spirituality. Cosmic order and embodied deities were evident in the alternation of the seasons; the daily dying and rising of the sun; and the process of planting, germinating, and harvesting. The sun (a god) figuratively dies and is reborn each day. The seasons move in a cycle that parallels the separation and return of spirit beings. This perception of the ongoing need of regeneration can be illustrated by Aztec mythology. The Aztecs believed that the world must be renewed each day. Each morning, the sun and war god, Huitzilopochtli (the Blue Tezcatlipoca), was born anew from the goddess of the earth, Coatlicue, whom he fought daily to save the world from the nocturnal powers associated with the gods of darkness.

Calendars were an important part of the human construction of an intelligible cosmos. They permitted ancient elites to predict solar and lunar eclipses; calculate solstices, equinoxes, and other celestial events; and pinpoint New Year's Day and other ceremonial occasions. Calendars were instrumental in arranging years into cycles of years, making historical time lines such as king's lists, and organizing time into ages. Calendars were a tangible element in the effort of ancient urban elites (priests and scribes) to make the past more concrete—to make what had gone before into historical events, as well as mythological ones.

The Aztecs constructed a calendar of 260 days composed of thirteen weeks of twenty days each as well as an annual solar calendar of 365 days composed of eighteen twenty-day months and a final period of five days that made up for the difference. Each day of the twenty-day week had an astrological sign and number that assisted astrologers in helping people born on an ominous day to avoid or counteract an evil fortune. Each day was associated with a deity. Most of the festivals were regulated by the solar calendar, and several of them combined celebration of crucial junctures in agriculture with portrayals of the lives of the relevant deities.

The Aztecs were keenly aware of their own history and placed themselves within the history of the cosmos, which they organized into Five Suns or Five Ages. At the time of the Spanish conquest of Mexico, they believed they were living in the Fifth Sun. Each of the Five Suns was dated; the first began nearly three thousand years ago. Each age ended catastrophically and involved divine intentionality. The First Sun lasted 676 years, and

the human beings, a race of giants created by the Black Tezcatlipoca, were eaten by jaguars associated with Quetzalcoatl, the White Tezcatlipoca. The Second Sun was destroyed by the Red Tezcatlipoca and a fierce wind. The Third Sun was consumed by a fire caused by Quetzalcoatl. The Fourth Sun was terminated by water, and the fifth was fated to end with earthquakes and hunger. At the end of each age, the work of divine creation began again.[24]

The origin myths and calendars of ancient urban religions have much to teach us: The world is cosmos and not chaos. Each element has its appointed place. Conflict and cooperation were part of creation, and both persist in the cosmos. Humans are grounded in both primordial and historical time. Even the diversity and contradictions of ancient mythologies are instructive; they indicate the willingness of ancient peoples to modify existing narratives and integrate new elements into them.

DIVINITIES

Nearly all ancient national religions were polytheistic. As philosopher Walter Burkert observed, "polytheism means that many gods are worshipped not only at the same place and at the same time, but by the same community and by the same individual; only the totality of the gods constitutes the divine world. However much a god is intent on his honour, he never disputes the existence of any other god; they are all everlasting ones. . . . What is fatal is if a god is overlooked."[25] The divinities did not demand exclusive attention or loyalty, and they often shared cities, temples, shrines, and priestly attendants. They exercised hegemony and leadership over their jurisdiction or sphere of influence and expected to receive their proper due. To ignore them was to invite disaster.

The gods and goddesses of polytheistic systems were symbolized by and embodied in all manner of things, but their behaviors and purposes were similar to human behaviors and purposes. They married, had affairs, produced children, argued, fought, took part in contests, did not respond kindly to insults or assaults on their honor, demanded the praise and service of human beings, were angry if they did not receive their due, and sometimes overstepped the bounds of the divine order of things (with adverse consequences). They differed from humans in the degree of their power, status, and permanence. The gods and goddesses were usually immortal, but not eternal, beings; like other elements of the cosmos, they came into being. Their power and knowledge far surpassed that of humans, but they were neither all powerful (omnipotent) nor all knowing (omniscient). The divinities were also limited in jurisdiction: they were associated with cities, peoples, localities, and functions (for example, arts, rain, fertility, healing, and war). Deities were often paired, bound together by marriage, affairs, or bipolarities (for example, good/evil, day/night, or heaven/earth).

The pantheon of a polytheistic religion is usually extensive. Shinto tradition speaks of 800,000 spirits *(kami)*, and Hindu traditions place the number of deities at 3,300 or, more remarkably, at 33 million. Perhaps the incomprehensibility of such estimates is a way of saying that divinities are everywhere. An extensive survey of divinities is beyond the scope of this text, but a familiarity with some divinities is instructive as to their nature, jurisdiction, and form.

The pantheons of the Sumerians and Akkadians, the principal peoples of southern Mesopotamia in the third millennium B.C.E., numbered around two thousand divinities. In addition, individuals had personal gods or guardian spirits who were responsive to their needs and petitioned the gods on their behalf. Each Sumerian city had a patron deity and a host of supporting divinities. Enlil replaced Anu as king of the Sumerian gods and keeper of the tablets of destiny by which the fates of humans and the gods were decreed until Marduk assumed preeminence in Babylonian mythology. Inanna (Ishtar), *"she who even 120 lovers could not exhaust,"* was the principal goddess. A goddess of war as well as love, Inanna-Ishtar survived the eclipse of Sumer and Akkad to become one of the most popular deities in western Asia.

The Greeks had an extensive pantheon, but a small coterie of gods dominated their theological landscape. The twelve primary Olympians included the foundational divinities (Zeus, Hera, Poseidon, Demeter, and in some lists, Hestia) plus Athena, Apollo, Artemis, Aphrodite, Hermes, Dionysus, Hephaistos, and Ares. The daughter of Metis and Zeus, Athena (Minerva in the Roman pantheon) was the virgin goddess of wisdom, war, and the arts, as well as the guardian deity of Athens. Apollo, the son of Zeus and the Titan Leto, was the god of healing, music, and prophecy. Artemis (Diana), the daughter of Zeus and Leto, was the goddess of childbirth and wild animals. Aphrodite (Venus), the goddess of love, was the daughter of Zeus and the Titan Dione or, in an alternative myth, emerged from the foam of the severed genitals of Ouranos. Hermes (Mercury), son of Zeus and the goddess Maia, was the messenger of the gods and guide of travelers. Dionysus (Bacchus), son of Zeus and a human mother Semele, was the god of wine and vegetation. Hephaistos (Vulcan), son of Zeus and Hera or, alternatively, born of Hera alone, was the god of fire and patron of metalworking. Ares (Mars), son of Zeus and Hera, was the god of war.

In ancient urban religions, everything in the cosmos was under the jurisdiction of a divinity or group of divinities, demons (beings intermediary between gods and humans), or amorphous spirits. Previous examples and the Aztec pantheon illustrate this point. Quetzalcoatl was associated with the planet Venus, wind, the west, and a feathered serpent (snake); depicted as a bearded old god, he was the wise patron of priests and learning. Black Tezcatlipoca was the god of night and the north, and he was the patron of sorcerers. The sun god Huitzilopochtli was associated with hummingbirds, the south, sacrifice, war, warriors, and the neverending battle against darkness. Xipe Totec represented vegetation and was depicted as wearing human skin; he was associated with the east, sacrifice, and goldsmiths. The earth goddess Coatlicue consumed filth (corpses, dirt, and human sin) and was associated with confessions of sin. The snake goddess Cihuacoatl was the patron of women in childbirth.

The divinities of ancient urban religions were associated with natural life forms and other nonhuman entities, but their behaviors and images were primarily anthropomorphic. Ea's symbol was a ram's head with the body of a fish, and Inanna-Ishtar was embodied in the morning and evening star (the planet Venus). Like most Mesopotamian deities, however, they were thought of as anthropomorphic divinities. In the form of a swan, Zeus (Jupiter in the Roman pantheon) seduced Leda, but Zeus and the other divinities that dominated the Greek and Roman pantheons were primarily depicted as humanlike beings. The symbolism was more ambiguous in Egypt. Isis, Osiris, and Ptah were symbolized in human form, but theriomorphic images were common. The sun god Re was depicted with a human body and a falcon head. Thoth, the god of learning and the scribe at the judgment of the dead, was portrayed as having a human body and an ibis or baboon head.

Pagan systems were not doctrinally or theologically exclusive. Gods and goddesses were often conflated or assimilated into the pantheons of other state cults. Roman religion was profoundly influenced by Etruscan (a people assimilated by Rome) and Greek antecedents and, to a lesser extent, by the spirituality of Germanic and Celtic tribes. This is evident in the Roman conflation of Greek, Celtic, Germanic, and Roman deities. For example, the Celtic god Lugh is identified with Mercury, the Germanic god Thor with Jupiter, and Greek deities with Roman deities.

THE ONE AND THE MANY Although polytheism was the predominant theology of ancient urban states, theologies that unified or conflated many gods into one were common to many cultures. The movement to bring order out of the profusion of divine beings is reflected in various ways. It is evident in polytheistic theologies that include supreme gods who brought the cosmos into being and ruled over a pantheon of divine beings. It is evident in contexts in which one god was exclusively worshiped without denying the existence of other deities (**henotheism**) and those in which the high gods of national religions were equated with a single, universal God. The attractiveness of ideas that

tie everything together is especially evident in monistic and monotheistic conceptions.

By the first millennium B.C.E., and perhaps earlier in the time of Moses (the thirteenth century), Israel's prophets and priests had forged a monotheistic theology out of a cultural landscape liberally populated by gods and goddesses. In the same period, the Persian prophet Zoroaster articulated a theology grounded in the ultimate triumph of the one God (Ahura Mazda) over evil, personified as Angra Mainyu. Monotheistic conceptions were articulated in ancient Egypt but were never developed into an exclusively monotheistic religion. In texts dating from the tenth dynasty (ca. 2130 B.C.E.)—the *Book of Two Ways* (a text inscribed on a coffin found at the necropolis of Hermopolis) and a king's instruction to his son Merikare—Re, the "All Lord," has the attributes of an omniscient, provident, and just creator deity. Later, but in the century before Moses, the Egyptian king Akhenaten (1353–1339 B.C.E.) had gravitated to the worship of one God, the solar deity Aten.[26] In acknowledging the absence of a sustained monotheism in ancient Egypt, it is fair to add that in Israelite religion, worship of the one true God (Yahweh) was usually accompanied by worship of other gods. As late as the seventh century B.C.E., the Canaanite goddess Asherah was worshiped alongside Yahweh in Jerusalem, and other Canaanite deities, such as the god Baal and the goddess Astarte, were worshiped by Israelites (*2 Kings* 23:7).

A theology that regarded all divinities as subordinate to one God or as manifestations of one God is evident in the conflations of the Egyptian sun deities Re and Amun into Amun-Re, as well as in theologies in which Re or Amun-Re were said to have given birth to the first divinities and to be present in all of them. By the end of the first millennium B.C.E., Hindu sages resolved the problem of the one and the many with the belief that all divinities were manifestations of one divine reality, Brahman.

Theologies that subordinated the many to the one also emerged in ancient Greece. The Greek philosopher Xenophanes (ca. 570–480 B.C.E.)

enjoined his contemporaries to displace the Olympians with belief in a God who "is one, supreme among gods and men, not at all like mortals in body or in mind."[27] Xenophanes was not alone. In later theologies, Zeus had acquired a set of attributes not unlike those attributed to God in Judaic and Christian theology.

Monistic conceptions of the divine were also articulated in pre-Columbian America. Aztec sages united the one and the many in one dual Supreme Being, the "god of dualities" Ometeotl, who was regarded as the "cosmic energy upon which everything depended."[28] The dual nature of Ometeotl was manifested in paired divinities who symbolized the elements of cooperation and conflict that pervade the cosmos. The cosmos and the Aztec pantheon that the dual God engendered reflect the dual and yet unified character of the whole of reality; this paired cooperation and conflict is manifested in male and female, good and evil, light and dark.

GODS, GOD, AND PHILOSOPHERS   The attraction of monistic explanations to urban elites was not simply a matter of logical and aesthetic beauty. The form and moral character of the divinities, as well as their number, were troubling. Divinities with human bodies and reprehensible moral behavior lost their appeal. Nature divinities gave way to humanlike gods and goddesses, and they, in turn, were eclipsed by monotheistic conceptions of an incorporeal being or by philosophies that displaced divine persons by disembodied absolutes (for example, the Good). In the science and much of the philosophy of classical Greece and Alexander's empire, the world was thought to work by natural rather than supernatural forces. Consequently, there was nothing left of a Zeus who hurled thunderbolts or of an Egyptian sun god Re who battled the forces of darkness each night and emerged triumphant at sunrise.[29]

The philosopher Xenophanes struck a telling blow against anthropomorphism. He believed that humans have made the gods in their own image, supposing that "the gods have been born, that they have voices and bodies and wear clothing like men."[30] Reason, he argued, leads us to conclude that one Supreme Being is superior to multiple supreme beings, because in the latter case, no divinity can really be supreme. A God who is eternal is superior to gods who, like Zeus, come into being. Xenophanes reduced anthropomorphism to an absurdity: "If oxen or lions had hands which enabled them to draw and to paint pictures as men do, they would portray their gods as having bodies like their own: horses would portray them as horses, and oxen as oxen."[31] Xenophanes was also critical of the behavior of the gods, which, by the standards of human morality, was immoral: "Homer and Hesiod attributed to the gods all sorts of actions which when done by men are disreputable and deserving of blame—such lawless deeds as theft, adultery, and mutual deception."[32] The Greek playwright Euripides (ca. 480–406 B.C.E.) asked rhetorically, "Who would pray to such a deity?"

Greek philosophers displaced divine persons with disembodied absolutes. In Plato's (ca. 429–347 B.C.E.) philosophy, the ultimate reality is the Good, an immaterial form (idea) that is the apex of the eternal, unchangeable, and invisible world of forms that lies behind, and is the foundation of, the visible world. The Good is analogous to the sun in the visible world; the sun is the source of the visibility of things and the cause of their generation and growth. In the invisible world, the Good is the cause of intelligibility and the grounds of intelligible being. The forms are known through human understanding rather than divine revelation.

Skeptics launched an even more devastating attack on the gods and traditional religion. The Greek Sophist, Protagoras of Abdera (480–411 B.C.E.), articulated what might be regarded as a foundational statement of **agnosticism**: "As for the gods, I have no way of knowing either that they exist or that they do not exist; nor, if they exist, what form they are. For the obstacles to that sort of knowledge are many, including the obscurity of the matter and the brevity of human life."[33] Harsher voices declared that God, whether one or many, did not exist at all **(atheism)**. The Sophist and playwright Critias (fifth century B.C.E.) suggested through the artifice of one of his characters that "fear of the gods" was invented by a clever person to help insure public order by making people believe that the gods police their deeds and thoughts. Euhemerus (ca. 300 B.C.E.) opined that the gods of Greece were apotheosized rulers and heroes who had become the objects of worship. In such a vortex of opinions, it seemed to the comic playwright Aristophanes (ca. 448–385 B.C.E.) that a chaotic wind ruled the world and had unseated Zeus.

Analogous ideas were articulated in India. Buddhists did not excise the gods altogether but radically reduced their importance. The historical Buddha (ca. 563–483 B.C.E.), the founder of Buddhism, taught that humans must work out their salvation independent of the gods. The Carvakas, an atheistic movement, rejected belief in God and rebirth and declared that the only worthy object in life is sensual pleasure. Philosophies that focused on the good life (Confucianism) or the way of the universe (Taoism) with little more than a nod to the gods were articulated in China as well.

The national religions and initiation cults of ancient Greece, Rome, Mesopotamia, and Egypt endured the criticism, but they were ultimately obliterated by Christianity. Centuries later the national religions of Central and South America suffered the same fate. The Christian emperor Theodosius I (347–395 C.E.) issued edicts in 391 and 392 that prohibited the worship of pagan gods. In 391, the Temple of Serapis in Alexandria and the library it housed was destroyed by monks. Serapis was a sun and fertility deity of Egyptian origin that had achieved popularity throughout the Roman Empire. A battle fought in 394, pitting those who sided with Jupiter and Hercules and those who fought for Christ, ended in a decisive Christian victory and the effective end of pagan religion. Pagan philosophers and intellectuals suffered similar blows. The Egyptian mathematician and Neoplatonist philosopher Hypatia (ca. 370–415 C.E.) was murdered and her body and library burned by a Christian mob in Alexandria. In 529, Justinian (483–565 C.E.), the emperor of the eastern portion of the Roman Empire, forbade

pagans and Christian heretics to teach any subject and closed the schools of pagan philosophy in Athens, including the academy established by Plato around 387 B.C.E. Pagan intellectuals reestablished themselves beyond the reach of the Christianized empire, and over the centuries, pre-Christian philosophies and science were assimilated into Christian thought. Pagan religion suffered a more grievous fate. The gods and goddesses were silenced, the temples were closed, and blood sacrifice was terminated. Only the myths and the remains of the sacred monuments survived.

SACRED PERSONS: THE KING

Ancient urban societies had a variety of sacred persons, including *shamans*, diviners, sages, priests, prophets, founders of movements, and even ascetics who renounced the world, but the most important figures for a society as a whole were usually kings. Ancient urban monarchies typically had a theology of sacred kingship, the belief that the ruler either embodied or represented the divine on earth. Rule by god-kings was the pattern in ancient Egypt, pre-Hispanic America, and Japan. Monarchs who represented the divine was the dominant pattern in Mesopotamia, Palestine, Persia, and China. **Sacred kings** were the symbolic center of most ancient urban societies, the chief intermediaries between the gods and humankind and the nexus that united all elements of society.

Egypt's kings were regarded as god-kings. Egyptian mythology affirmed that the monarch's office was established at the time of creation and that Egypt's kings ruled under the protective wings of the falcon-headed deities Horus and Re. By virtue of assuming the throne, the pharaoh became the visible image and beloved son of Re, who created the cosmos and gave it order. As the physical embodiment of the sun god, the responsibility for sustaining the cosmic order rested on the god-king. The Egyptian throne was also identified with the sky god Horus, his father, Osiris, and his mother, Isis. The connection was grounded in the myth of Osiris's murder, his restoration to life, and the enthronement of Horus. As the first son of the earth god Geb and the sky goddess Nut, Osiris inherited the right to rule Egypt and was its legendary first king. He was murdered by his brother Seth, the god of chaotic forces, who usurped the throne. The goddess Isis, the devoted sister-wife of Osiris, gathered his dismembered body and magically restored him to life. They copulated and conceived Horus to avenge Osiris's death and to reclaim the throne. Before a tribunal of the gods, Horus pressed his claim (as Osiris's son) to the throne; eventually, through the guile, intelligence, and magical power of Isis, Seth renounced his claim, and Horus was enthroned. Subsequently, Osiris became the Lord of the Underworld.

Aztec kings were likewise regarded as divine beings. They were descendants of the war god Huitzilopochtli, the god Quetzalcoatl, and the priest-king Topiltzin Quetzalcoatl, who ruled at Tollan, the capital of the Toltec civilization. At their birth, Aztec kings received the "heart" of Huitzilopochtli and other supernatural powers.

In ancient Israel, Mesopotamia, and China, kings were normally representatives of God; they were human rather than divine beings whose authority was legitimated by divinity. In predynastic China, kings were the chief intermediaries between the mundane and spiritual worlds and representatives of the heavenly will, but they were not (with some exceptions) regarded as gods. Similarly, in dynastic China, emperors were human rather than divine beings. They ruled by the "Mandate of Heaven," an authority derived from God and the transcendent order of things, and were therefore, figuratively speaking, "Sons of Heaven."

Roman emperors had considerable spiritual power. They were the chief priests of the Roman state religion and were associated in popular piety with the well-being of the empire, including the fertility of its animals, freedom from misfortune, victory in battle, and bountiful crops. Some emperors were deified in office, but they were usually elevated to divine status after their deaths by a pronouncement of the Roman Senate or, as in the case of unpopular rulers such as Nero, were denied apotheosis. Rome's first emperor, Caesar Octavian Augustus (r. 31 B.C.E.–14 C.E.), was voted the title of

Augustus (the fortunate and blessed) by the Senate and was deified after his death. Caesar Augustus added a new dimension to the Roman religion, the cult of the emperor, by constructing temples in honor of his deified adoptive father, Julius Caesar (d. 43 B.C.E.), and in homage to Augustus (the imperial office) and Roma (the personified Roman state).

Sacred kings were regulated by taboos and purity rules that set them apart from other mortals. In Africa, Shilluk and Shona kings wore veils so their faces could not be seen by the public, and Baganda rulers walked on a special mat or were carried so that their feet would not be polluted by touching the ground. Inca kings never wore the same ceremonial clothes twice and were transported in golden vehicles. Because of their status, kings could violate taboos that would spell disaster for others, such as breaking incest rules by marrying their sisters or mothers. The marriage of Isis and Osiris was the prototype for the marriage of brothers and sisters in the royal families of Egypt. The brother-sister union of the foundational ancestors of the Inca royal family justified the marriage of the Inca king and a sister-wife.

Living and dead kings were sacred. Prayers and rites were conducted before the statues of Egypt's god-kings. Reigning Egyptian kings built temples to house cults dedicated in their names that would continue after their deaths; usually the royal temple was in a complex that contained the royal tomb (pyramid), and the royal funeral was a defining moment for the temple. The spiritual potency of kings persisted after their death in temples, burial monuments, necropolises, and mummies. Inca kings addressed the mummified bodies of their predecessors, and mediums channeled the messages of the spirits of the ancestral potentates.

The deaths of monarchs were periods fraught with uncertainty and the potential for chaos. The transfer of power from the dead king to a new one was a delicate procedure involving lines of succession and conflicts between contending parties. In some contexts, the death of the ruler was marked by the extinguishing of a sacred fire, which was not relit until a successor was installed in office. African peoples such as the Shilluk and Shona reportedly killed their kings when they were old or weak or if their reign was unsatisfactory in order to transfer their spirits unharmed to their successors and to insure the ongoing vitality of the throne and the nation's well-being.[34] How widespread sanctioned regicide was in Africa and elsewhere is disputed.

THE NATURE AND DESTINY OF HUMANS

In ancient wisdom, humans are at once mystifying and transparent, transcendent and mundane, good and evil, sinful and redeemable. A passage in *Antigone,* a tragedy written by the Greek playwright Sophocles (ca. 495–406 B.C.E.), speaks to the capacity of humans to attract and repel: "Much there is that is strange, but none stranger than man." The historical Buddha (sixth century B.C.E.) was so troubled and fascinated by the human condition that he concentrated his mental efforts on the liberation of himself, his fellow humans, and all other sentient beings. In the same century, an inscription on the temple at Delphi advised those seeking Apollo's advice to "Know yourself." We have grouped ancient urban beliefs about humans around human nature, human interaction with divinities, and death and human destiny.

HUMAN NATURE   Origin myths reveal a great deal about how human nature was perceived in ancient national religions. They usually taught that the gods had something to do with the creation of humankind. In the Babylonian creation epic, the *Enuma Elish,* humans were created by the gods out of clay, as well as the blood and bones of the leader of the monsters that Tiamat had created to aid her in battle against Marduk. In Egyptian mythology, the artisan god Khnum molded humankind from clay on his potter's wheel and breathed life into his creation. In other Egyptian myths, humans are spoken into being by Ptah or come forth from Re's tears.[35]

A motif typical of myths of human origins is that humans have both earthly and spiritual dimensions of their being. This motif is evident in Marduk's forming of humans from clay (earth) and the bones and blood of a spirit being, as well as in Khnum's breathing the life force into a clay model of humankind. It is also evident in this Aztec story: After the creation of the Fifth Sun, Quetzalcoatl journeyed to the Land of the Dead to gather the bones of the people of the previous Sun and re-create human life. After a harrowing adventure, Quetzalcoatl escaped with the bones and ground them into powder. Then the gods wounded themselves and bled on the bones, and from the bones of humans and the blood of the gods, the people of the Fifth Sun were produced. A compelling variation of the motif of the spiritual aspect of human existence are myths in which humans are made in a likeness of god. This perspective is articulated in the *Bible* (*Gen.* 1:26–27) and the *Instructions to Merikare* (ca. 2130 B.C.E.), an Egyptian text that predates the verses in *Genesis* by over a thousand years. In the *Instructions to Merikare,* humans are said to come forth from the sun god Re in the likeness of Re.[36]

For what purpose were humans created? A prominent theme in ancient mythology is that humans were made to serve and honor the gods. The *Enuma Elish* states that humans were created to serve the *"gods that they might be at ease"*[37] The *Popol Vuh,* a Maya text, tells us that the gods made four models before they were able to form satisfactory human beings—that is, intelligent beings who would praise and respect the gods and who would provide for and nurture creation. The first human design produced deer and birds, but their behavior and language was inappropriate for what the gods had in mind. The second human model was formed from mud, but it was dissolved by water. The third design was constructed of wood, and that, too, proved inadequate. The fourth and final human prototype was modeled from yellow and white corn and proved suitable as a material to fashion humans. The first people (four men) were handsome and possessed perfect vision and understanding. But they were also flawed: their perfect vision and understanding violated the boundaries of what beings who were products of the gods should be. Surely, if left to their own devices, the first humans would *"become as great as gods."* Thus, the gods blurred their vision and limited their understanding. Later, the Maya gods formed the first four women.[38]

Myths about the failure of humans to achieve the purposes of their creation are common. A corollary of such myths is that because humans had offended the gods, the gods resolved to destroy them. The motif usually includes either human survivors of the destruction or, following the destruction, the divine creation of a new race of humans. In Aztec mythology, the people who lived in the first four Suns (worlds) were destroyed by animals, wind, fire, and flood. Egyptian mythology contains an episode in which humans plot against their creator, Re. Re and the divine council agree to send the cow goddess Hathor to slay humankind, but they relent and, through the artifice of beer, deflect the drunken goddess from completing the bloodletting.

Mythologically speaking, the gods have destroyed humans and the worlds they inhabit by wind, fire, and ice, but floods seem to be the catastrophe of choice. In Greek mythology, Zeus sets out to destroy humans through a great flood because of their impiety (in this case, a plot to feed Zeus human flesh). Zeus's purpose was thwarted by the Titan Prometheus, who told his son Deucalion to build a boat. Deucalion and his wife, Pyrrha, survived the calamity.[39] In the *Gilgamesh Epic*, Utnapishtim, who with his wife survived the flood, recounts the story of the flood to the Sumerian king, Gilgamesh. According to Utnapishtim, the gods (among them Anu, Enlil, and Inanna) gathered in council and decided to create a great flood to destroy humankind. The god of wisdom, Enki, was present at the council and subsequently advised Utnapishtim to build a boat. The cube-shaped boat had seven decks and nine chambers on each deck to house food, wine, precious metals, seeds, animals, Utnapishtim's family, and anyone in the city who wished to join them. The rains came and flooded everything. After the crisis passed, the war god, Enlil, blessed Utnapishtim and his wife, saying, *"Before this you were just a man, but now you and your wife shall be like gods."*[40]

INTERACTING WITH DIVINITIES   Ancient urban peoples, aside from the skeptics, believed that the gods were involved in what happened to them and the world they lived in. Human life was precarious. Wars, insurrections, and lawlessness toppled kingdoms and empires, and the defenses against such afflictions (for example, armies, diplomacy, laws, and courts) were often ineffective. Humans looked to the gods for protection and deliverance from disease and misfortune (war, injuries, marital discord, indebtedness, enslavement, assaults, theft, floods, and the like). They also believed that disease and misfortune resulted from the failure of humans to fulfill their obligations to the gods or were caused by malevolent spirits or malevolent humans (sorcerers). Thus, the Greeks spoke of human afflictions as the "arrows of Zeus," and a Mesopotamian text speaks of human suffering as being doled out by god as punishment for sin.[41]

Fear of the gods was the proper human response. People who feared the gods were likely to do what is proper in respect to both the gods and humankind. People who did not fear the gods were likely to conduct themselves improperly with respect to humans and to suffer at the "hands" of the divinities they offended. Humans interacted with the spirit beings that populated their world through prayer, ritual, divination, oblations (offerings), and sacrifice. Rituals, including those involving sacrifice, provided divinities their due and helped preserve the cosmic and social order. Votive offerings—gifts for prayers granted or petitions requested—were often left at temples and shrines.

Signs and omens (portents) of the spirit world were present everywhere and required masters of the magical arts (**diviners**) to interpret them. The range of omens and occult interpretation in ancient spirituality included, for example, interpreting dreams, palms, heavenly bodies, flights of birds, and animal livers. The interpretation of dreams was especially important, as divinities often revealed their purposes to humans through dreams. Deities also communicated through modes of **divination** that involved spirit possession, such as glossolalia, prophecy, and oracular utterances. Messages from the gods delivered by ecstatic and entranced mediums (oracles) were particularly sought. Thus, seekers came to the temple at Delphi to consult Apollo on a range of subjects (for example, marriage, sickness, travel, and affairs of state). Apollo's messages were channeled through a priestess, who in a trance state responded to inquiries put to her by the high priest of the temple. This type of oracular consultation occurred infrequently at Delphi. Oracular instruction was usually given through the interpretation of lots; this method involved drawing a lot (usually a bean) and determining its application to the supplicant's question.

Ancient urban medicine involved a knowledge of herbs, drugs, massage, and other empirical practices including surgery, but like traditional tribal medicine, it was permeated by magico-religious conceptions and practices (for example, prayer, divination, sacrifice, exorcism, curses, and spells). Egypt's lion-headed goddess Sakhmet was associated with healing, and her priests had a curing function. The Greeks had several gods of healing, including Apollo and his son Asclepius. Restoration to well-being is a form of salvation, and Asclepius was honored by devotees as a savior.

DEATH AND HUMAN DESTINY   Ancient urban religions were of different minds as to whether death was the end of human existence or a passage to other worlds. Some religious traditions taught that humans survived death and that the hereafter was a highly desirable place. Other traditions subscribed to the view that humans survived death as joyless ghosts. The national religions of Mesopotamia, Greek Olympian religion, and Israelite religion (the religion of Israel's tribes and Moses) assumed that death was humankind's destiny. The gods are immortal; humans are mortal. In contrast, belief in an afterlife was part of Egyptian religion and the national religions of pre-Hispanic America.

The *Gilgamesh Epic* articulates the view of human destiny that predominated in Mesopotamia. The epic's principal subjects are Gilgamesh, the legendary priest-king of the city-state of Uruk (ca. 2650 B.C.E.) and his friend Enkidu. The story

is about friendship, the death of Enkidu, Gilgamesh's quest for **immortality** to restore Enkidu to life, and his harrowing journey to Utnapishtim (the man who survived the flood and gained immortality) to find the secret of immortality. At the end of his journey, Gilgamesh resigned himself to the truth that mortality is the fate of humankind. In the words of one of the poem's characters:

> When the gods created mankind,
> Death for mankind they set aside,
> Life in their own hands retaining.[42]

In Olympian religion (the national religion of the Greek city-states), the land of the dead (Hades) is a shadowy land beneath the earth, a land of ghostlike beings (shades) from whence no one returns. The Greeks believed that it was better to be engaged in earthly activities than to wander without human faculties in the house of the god Hades. The Greek underworld was not exclusively a land of disembodied and emotionless shades, however. It included the Islands of the Blessed (the Elysian Fields), where mortals favored by the gods (for example, Achilles and Menelaus) lived happy and active lives, and Tartarus, the subterranean chamber far beneath Hades that was the prison of Cronus and other Titans who had warred against the gods. Some very special persons escaped the underworld altogether. For example, after his death, Heracles was awarded a place among the gods on Mount Olympus because of his heroic deeds.

The Aztecs, Inca, and Egyptians saw in death a passage to eternal life. The Inca believed that humans had two souls. At death, one of the souls journeyed to the land of the souls. The second soul continued to reside in the body and had needs similar to the living. The Aztecs believed that after humans died, they were destined to live in one of the many realms of the dead. The destination of the dead was primarily determined by social status and the manner in which death occurred. The Aztecs had thirteen heavens and several worlds below the earth. Most people were destined for Mictlan. The journey to Mictlan led through nine netherworlds, entailed many obstacles, and took four years to complete. Warriors who died in battle or as human sacrifices dwelled in the House of the Sun in the east; after four years in this joyous place they were reborn as hummingbirds (birds of the war god Huitzilopochti). People killed by lightning lived in a world of abundance, and women who died in childbirth resided in the House of the Sun in the west.

The Egyptians believed that although death disrupted the continuity of human life, it was not the end of human existence. Death was a passage to eternity. Initially, eternal life was the destiny only of Egypt's divine kings, but by around 2000 B.C.E., nobles and commoners could hope to join the gods in the sky. The Egyptian self was composed of the body, the heart (the seat of life), and three spirits (the *ba, ka,* and *akh*). The body was preserved in a tomb, usually as a mummified presence. The *ba* could leave or return to the body and, together with the body, formed the self's personality in the beyond. At death, the *ka* resided in the statues of the deceased that were placed in the tomb and protected it. The *akh* existed apart from the embalmed body and was associated with the eternal light of the heavens. Because the body was the physical basis of ongoing human existence, attention was given to its care. Mummification perpetuated the body, and ornate coffins and tombs stocked with grave goods provided for the ongoing care of Egyptian selves.

The Egyptian journey to the celestial realm of the immortals was facilitated by the *Book of the Dead,* a collection of spells, rites, and formulas inscribed on coffins and tombs and intended to be recited by the soul on its journey in the hereafter. The Egyptians did not connect life in the hereafter to a judgment of the earthly life of the deceased until around 1700 B.C.E. In this judgment, each person was taken after death before Osiris, the god of the dead, and "his or her heart weighed on scales against the figure of the goddess Right [Maat]; the good passed through to the new life as transfigured spirits, but the hearts of the wicked were tossed to Amemet," the underworld god who swallowed wicked hearts. Forty-two gods listened to

Anubis, the Egyptian canine-headed god of embalming, mummification, and cemeteries, conducted the dead to judgment in the underworld. Located in the Tomb of Sennedjem, Valley of the Kings, Luxor, Egypt.

the testimony (denials of wrongdoing by the deceased) and decided if it was true.[43]

Like ancient national religions, the great philosophers of antiquity were divided on the issue of whether humans survive death. As he awaited death, Socrates (ca. 469–399 B.C.E.) constructed an argument for the immortality of the soul. Plato, Socrates' most gifted student, believed that it is the human body that dies and that the human soul survives death and can be reborn again. In contrast, Aristotle (384–322 B.C.E.), Plato's most renowned student, believed that the soul was inseparable from the body and that death marked the end of individual human existence.

Belief in multiple selves was not uncommon in ancient spirituality as is evident in the theological anthropology of the Egyptians and Inca, but the most enduring conception of the self is that of a perishable body and immortal soul. Hindus believed that an indestructible aspect of their being, the *atman,* survived the death of the body and was reborn according to their *karma* (deeds). The dualistic character of Zoroastrian theology (dualisms of good and evil and body and soul) is evident in its understanding of the hereafter. In Zoroastrian teaching, following the death of the body, souls must be judged respecting their good and evil thoughts, words, and deeds to see if they are fit to undertake the journey to heaven or if they should be punished in hell or reside in the "dwelling place of shadows where there is neither joy nor torment."[44]

Ancient urban peoples heard voices and had visions. Spirits appeared to them in dreams and trance states, but saving experiences were generally confined to ritually mediated deliverances from disease and misfortune. However, by the first millennium B.C.E., personal transforming experiences of the sacred and promises of life after death or of liberation from the world of becoming were features of the initiation cults of Demeter, Cybele, Isis-Osiris, Dionysus, and Mithras, as well as of religious movements such as Buddhism, Jainism, Pythagoreanism, and Orphism.

Spiritual rebirth through ritual purification and identification with the sacred was a feature of the initiation cults. This is evident in the myth and cult of Demeter, the Greek goddess of growing things, and her daughter, Persephone. Because Demeter's principal sanctuary was at Eleusis, her cult is known as the Eleusinian mysteries. In the myth, the beautiful Persephone, the daughter of Zeus and Demeter, was abducted with the consent of Zeus by Hades, the lord of the dead. After discovering that Persephone had been abducted and raped, Demeter traveled the earth in sorrow and anger, rendering the fertile land barren for an entire year and endangering the survival of humans and other life forms. Zeus dispatched a messenger to his brother, Hades, demanding the return of Persephone. Hades consented but gave Persephone a pomegranate seed to eat, a gift that carried with it the fate that anyone who ate the food of Hades had to spend a third of the year in the underworld. Persephone was reunited with her mother, but because she had eaten the seed, she was obligated to spend a third of each year in the company of Hades as goddess of the underworld. Demeter's grief in her annual separation from her beloved daughter manifested itself as

winter, and her joy in Persephone's return was manifested in months of renewal, fertility, and plenty.[45] In the Eleusinian mysteries, devotees experienced, in a ritual context, a dying and rising to new life. This pattern of spiritual rebirth was characteristic of the mystery religions.

The cult of Demeter and Persephone promised initiates a privileged status in the Greek beyond (a place in the Elysian Fields), but Pythagoreanism, Orphism, and other movements offered devotees even more: deification. The Greek mathematician and philosopher Pythagoras (ca. 570–500 B.C.E.) was the founder of a religious movement that persisted for several centuries. Pythagoras and his followers believed that a person's true self is the soul and that it is possible to be liberated from the physical aspect of human existence (the body) and to become immortal through a process that extended over several lifetimes (reincarnations). The process of deification required the purification of the self through periods of silence, study, physical exercise, and diet.[46]

Orphism was reportedly founded by Orpheus, a legendary minstrel of the sixth century B.C.E. According to Greek myth, Orpheus descended into the underworld, determined to gain the release of his wife, Eurydice. He played the flute so beautifully that Hades and Persephone were willing to part with Eurydice on the condition that Orpheus would not look at her until they were safely home. He was unable to fulfill the condition, and Eurydice remained in the land of the shades. Upon returning home, Orpheus was torn to pieces by a group of women maddened by the god Dionysus. At this point in the myth, Orphism gave a new twist to Greek theological anthropology by tracing human origins to the death and dismemberment of the god Dionysus and his subsequent restoration to life. In this version of the myth, after Zeus had raped Persephone and sired Dionysus, Hera responded by sending the Titans to destroy the child. The Titans tore the child to pieces and cooked and ate him. Zeus responded by destroying the Titans with a thunderbolt. From the ashes of the Titans, Dionysus was restored to life by Zeus, and humans came forth with a divine, as well as human, nature. Orphism involved a life of purifi-cation to make amends for the murder of Diony-sus and a ceremonial dying and rising with Dionysus to new life.

MORALITY

The moralities of ancient national religions were grounded in human obedience to divinities and the divine order of things. They were not critically reflective (for example, concerned with what makes a right action right), but they included moral direc-tives (rules of conduct and judgments of ought, for example) and teachings about the good life. Fear of the gods was in the foreground of their moral understanding; this fear involved human obliga-tions to the gods (worship; prayer; sacrifice; and rules respecting diet, corpses, and so on) and moral directives respecting human relations. The latter included negative moral directives (for example, do not steal, murder, covet, or engage in sexual mis-conduct) and positive ones (for example, honor par-ents, treat strangers hospitably, and be solicitous of the poor and weak). The moral perspective of ancient urban spirituality was often accompanied by a sense that righteousness is rewarded and immorality punished.

The Aztecs and Inca linked a person's place in the hereafter to social status and the manner of dying (childbirth, drowning, battle, and so on) rather than to morality or right belief, but their confessions of sin and penitential behaviors involved acknowledging moral transgressions (murder, theft, false testimony, and so forth). Moral instruction, propriety, love of family, and an under-standing of the good life permeated the practical wisdom that Aztec fathers and mothers passed on to their sons and daughters. Such concerns are evi-dent in the Aztec ideal of the good father: "He raises children, he educates, he instructs, he admonishes, he teaches them to live. He places before them a large mirror" of culturally and personally reflective self-knowledge.[47] Christian missionary Father Bartolome de las Casas (1476–1566) opined that neither the great pagan philosophers (Socrates, Plato, and Aristotle) nor

Christian morality could offer any further wisdom to better "transform human life into virtuous action."[48]

Like the morality of Central and Andean America, the morality of Egypt and Mesopotamia is reflected in confessions of sin. A Mesopotami-an list of sins (compiled in the second millennium B.C.E.) identified two hundred sins of commission and omission, including, for example, promoting discord in the family, killing animals unnecessar-ily, and speaking differently from what one thinks. Mesopotamians were aware of a multitude of sin-ful behaviors, and their wisdom literature taught that even the most righteous human beings were guilty of sin: "Never has a sinless child been born to its mother."[49] Mesopotamians did not hope for a better life in the hereafter, but they praised the gods and petitioned them for deliverance from earthly afflictions. Also, as an antidote for these afflic-tions, they prescribed both attending to the gods and practicing moral behavior.

Unlike Mesopotamian peoples, Egyptians anticipated spending eternity with the gods, and by the late third millennium B.C.E. they associat-ed this end with proper behavior in respect to both humans and the gods. In the funerary text *The Book of the Two Ways*, the All Lord Re declares that *"in order to silence evil,"* he established four things at creation that were intended to give humans equal opportunity:

> I made the four winds that every man might breathe
> thereof like his fellow in his time.
>
> I made the great flood waters that the poor man
> might have rights in them like the great man.
>
> I made every man like his fellow. I did not command
> that they might do evil, it was their hearts that
> violated what I had said.
>
> I made that their hearts should cease from forgetting
> the west [the region of eternal life], in order that
> the divine offerings might be made to the gods of
> the provinces.[50]

In another coffin text from the same period (ca. 2130 B.C.E.), the *Instructions to Merikare*, the king admonished his son to prepare his place in eternity by being just and straightforward: *"more acceptable is the character of the straightforward man than the ox of the wrongdoer."* Therefore, serve God by providing for humankind.[51]

By 1700 B.C.E. the place of Egyptians in the hereafter involved formulaic disclaimers of wrongdoing against the divine and humankind before the court of Osiris. In the *Book of the Dead*, the deceased is depicted as confessing to the court a list of wrongs that he had not done against humans:

> *I have not oppressed my family, I have not ill-treated servants, I have not defrauded the oppressed, I have not caused pain, I have made no person to be hungry or to weep. I have done no murder and have had no murder done for me. I have not fornicated. I have not cheated.*

Denials of wrongdoing against humanity were interspersed with wrongs that the deceased had not done (negative confessions) against the gods:

> *I have not scorned God. I have not done what is abominable to the gods. I have not defrauded the temples of their oblations or purloined the cakes of the gods. I have not polluted holy places. I have not repulsed God in his manifestations. I am pure.*[52]

The morality and ideas of social justice of ancient urban peoples are also reflected in legal codes. The authority of ancient legal codes was regarded as being derived from the gods and conferred upon their representatives or embodiments on earth, the monarchs. The Sumerian king Ur-Nammu (ca. 2112–2095 B.C.E.) was history's first known lawgiver; on the authority of the city-god of Ur, the king established courts and set forth a law code that protected the rights of orphans, widows, and the poor. The legal code of the Babylonian king Hammurabi (ca. 1728–1686 B.C.E.) was said to be commissioned by the sun god Shamash, and Israelite laws were believed to have been given by God to Moses on Mount Sinai.

Pagan morality has often been summarily dismissed, but such a judgment seems unwarranted. The ancient virtues—industry, frugality, humility, loyalty, courage, wisdom, moderation, and justice—have not been displaced by superior ones. Embedded in ancient wisdom traditions were exhortations to honor one's parents and a hierarchical network of obedience and mutual obligation between spouses, parents and children, siblings, and rulers and subjects, a pattern of values and relationships that do not seem unwarranted today. Of course, there was much in the ancient world that is morally objectionable today, including blood sacrifice, slavery, social and gender inequalities, infanticide, and social injustice. Monarchs were constrained by ideas of social justice and the interplay of contending factions, but the costs of kingship were enormous and abuses of power commonplace. Slavery was probably rare in prehistory, but it was a prominent feature of ancient urban civilizations. Some voices were raised against slavery in ancient times, and legal limits were placed upon it, but slavery was not universally condemned until the outset of the twentieth century.

SACRIFICE

Blood sacrifice—presenting an offering to a divinity in a ritual context that involves the destruction of the offering—was a common feature of ancient national religions. Animal sacrifice appears to have been a universal feature of prehistoric and ancient urban spirituality. Whether human sacrifice was part of Paleolithic religion is disputed, but there is a consensus that it occurred during the Neolithica. Human sacrifice was common to most ancient urban societies. It was practiced sparingly in ancient Egypt, Mesopotamia, Palestine, Greece, India, China, and Japan and on an unprecedented scale in Mesoamerica. It is estimated that the Aztecs sacrificed between twenty thousand to fifty thousand humans annually (in the fourteenth and fifteenth centuries C.E.) by a variety of methods, including drowning, strangulation, and dismemberment (cutting the hearts out of victims, dismembering their bodies, removing their skins, and eating them).[53]

Sacrificial offerings were of two sorts: blood offerings of animals and humans and bloodless offerings of food, drink, flowers, and material culture. Blood sacrifices involved gifts of life through killing the sacrificial victim or gifts of the life force (blood) through nonfatal self-wounding (sacrifices of blood or body parts). The divinity to whom the oblation was given received the offering through those elements that were believed to be readily transferred to the spirit world (for example, by the spilling of blood on a sacrificial altar or on the ground or by burning portions of the offering and converting it into smoke). Normally, the sacrificers ate the portions of animals that were not given to the divinity, and in some contexts, humans were cannibalized. However, in some ritual contexts, every part of the sacrifice was consumed by fire.

Sacrifices were performed in conjunction with death, the renewal of the cosmos, and times of risk and danger. Blood sacrifices occurred in association with death. Animals were sacrificed and buried with the deceased in order to provide food and service in the hereafter, and humans (servants, soldiers, wives, lovers) were sacrificed and buried with their masters to serve, protect, and provide companionship for them. Burial sacrifices were also indicators of social rank: the number and kind of grave wealth and sacrifices reflected the status of the deceased. The most elaborate funerary sacrifices were associated with kings and nobles. A tomb (ca. 1500–1400 B.C.E.) unearthed in China that dates from the Shang dynasty contains the sacrificial remains of a company of soldiers, four charioteers, and their chariots and horses. Ritual killings of attendants occurred intermittently in ancient Egypt and Mesopotamia.[54]

Sacrifices of cosmic regeneration involved the preservation and renewal of the cosmic order. Daily offerings and those performed at junctures in the seasons (planting and harvesting) served to renew the cosmos. Blood was conceived as a life force and was believed to strengthen the productivity of fields and herds. The Maya sacrificed a youth to the corn god Ah Mun to strengthen the new crop of corn. Chinese emperors offered food, wines, valuable objects, and animal sacrifices to Heaven and Earth

as a symbol of their mandate to rule and as a means of renewing the cosmos.

As in prehistoric religions, some myths associated the death and dismemberment of deity with the origin of the foods that sustain human life. Early Vedic literature speaks of the different elements of the cosmos and human society as emerging from the dismembered body of the primal man, *Purusha*. Some scholars believe that the myth was ritually reenacted in pre-Vedic times as a means of cosmic regeneration and involved killing a man, horse, ox, sheep, and goat.

Aztec myths linked the urgent need for human sacrifice to the creation of humans through the self-wounding of divinities and the daily struggle of the gods to sustain the cosmos against the powers of darkness and death. In one Aztec myth, the humans of the Fifth Sun were given life by the blood of the gods who had wounded themselves to give humans the gift of life. Sacrifice was seen as the proper human response to the self-sacrifice of the gods. In a myth even more fundamental to the Aztec justification of sacrifice, the sun god Huitzilopochtli is born each day of the earth goddess Coatlicue and struggles daily to defeat the nocturnal powers that try to destroy her. By rising victorious each day, Huitzilopochtli prevents the destruction of life. Humans participated in this daily battle by providing the sun god with blood, the nectar of the gods, through human sacrifice and auto-sacrifice (self-woundings).

Sacrifice was made in dangerous situations (war, hunger, drought, sickness, and so on) and in potentially perilous transitions (childbirth, marriage, installations, and the like). To prevent droughts, the Aztecs offered children or prisoners to Tlaloc, the god of life-giving rain. New beginnings such as erecting a home called for sacrifice. Such occasions were usually accompanied by animal or bloodless oblations, but sacrifices of children in conjunction with the laying of foundation stones occurred in Anatolia, Mesopotamia, and Palestine. The *Bible* reports that during the reign of King Ahab of Israel (ca. 869–850 B.C.E.), the builder of Jericho sacrificed his firstborn under the foundations of the city and his youngest son under the gates (*1 Kings* 16:34). Presumably, this was done to insure good fortune and protection. Infant sacrifice may have been connected to offerings of firstborn children, firstborn animals, and first yields of harvests. Biblical ordinances that direct the Israelites to sacrifice the firstborn of their livestock and redeem their firstborn children by purchasing their freedom (*Exod.* 13:11–15 and *Num.* 18:15–18) reflect the ancient practice of offerings of firstlings of harvests, hunts, and herds.

Crises elicited sacrifices. Animals were sacrificed in conjunction with disease, misfortune, disputes, and momentous occasions. Humans were also sacrificed. Jephthah, an Israelite who delivered the Israelites from dominance by their enemies (*Judg.* 11:30–40), vowed to give sacrifice in exchange for victory in battle. When he returned home victorious, by the conditions of his vow, Jephthah was obligated to sacrifice his daughter. Agamemnon, the legendary king of Mycenae, sacrificed his daughter Iphigenia to placate the goddess Artemis and thereby gain favorable winds for Greek ships to cross the sea and attack Troy.

What purposes did blood sacrifice serve? Interpretations—both scholarly and religious—have viewed blood sacrifice as a gift to divinity. The logic of gifts entails an assumption that they will be repaid—that those who give will receive a gift in return. The reciprocity of gift giving is expressed by the Latin phrase **do–ut des** (I give that you will give). In this perspective, sacrifices functioned as a means of giving thanks for gifts received and as oblations to the spirit world for petitions not yet granted. The dialectic of gift exchange includes sacrifices offered as expiation or atonement for some fault or offense. In some contexts, sacrifice appears to involve more than an exchange of gifts. For example, a transposition of identities is evident in sacrifices in which the sacrificer ritually assumed the identity of the sacrificed and symbolically gave his or her life to divinity through the surrogate victim.

Over the centuries, human sacrifice has lost its moral and religious sanctity; it is no longer a holy act. The movement away from human sacrifice was well advanced even in ancient times. The first step back took the form of the substitution of bloodless sacrifices. This alternative was perhaps as old as blood sacrifice, because grave goods at some Neolithic sites include animal and human figurines that may have been regarded as substitutes for animals and humans. Humans were sacrificed in association with the deaths of monarchs and nobles in the initial phases of nearly all ancient urban civilizations, but substitutions of small effigies or life-size statues gradually became the norm. For example, humans were sacrificed on the death of Chinese kings and nobility in the Shang dynasty (ca. 1527–1027 B.C.E.), but the use of bloodless oblations and substitutionary figures, such as the terra-cotta soldiers of Emperor Qin Shi Huang, was the dominant pattern thereafter. However, concubines were buried alive to provide companionship for emperors as late as the Ming dynasty (1368–1644 C.E.).

Human sacrifice ended in Central and Andean America with the Spanish conquest, and though it and cannibalism continued in some regions of the world into the twentieth century, human sacrifice was on the wane in most ancient urban civilizations, for both practical and moral-religious reasons, in the first millennium B.C.E. Animal sacrifice continued on a regular basis as a means of exchange, purification, thanksgiving, and atonement. Sheep and cakes were daily oblations to Yahweh in his temple in Jerusalem, and additional sacrifices were made on the Sabbath and special occasions until the temple was destroyed by the Romans in 70 C.E. Vedic (early Hindu) rites called for the daily sacrifice of animals. Animal sacrifice persists today, but in many of the world's religions it has lost both its moral and religious legitimacy.

During the first millennium B.C.E., voices were raised and positions taken that removed the religious sanction from human sacrifice and, in some instances, animal sacrifice. The first precept of Buddhist moral teaching is to avoid injury to all sentient beings, including animals. Guided by the directive that "one should not harm or kill others," Buddhists rejected blood sacrifice (bloodless offerings were acceptable). The same precept led many Buddhists to become vegetarians. Jainism, a movement contemporary to Buddhism, also made non-injury to living things central to its teaching and, in so doing, struck a blow against animal and human sacrifice. In Greece, Zeus was depicted as condemning human sacrifice, and noninjury to animals and vegetarianism as a means of purifying the immortal soul were advocated by Orphism. Christianity was the dominant force in turning westerners away from blood (animal or human) sacrifice. In Christian doctrine, Christ's death and resurrection was the end of sacrifice; his death atoned once and for all for the sins of all humans. Christ was at once the perfect sacrifice (without blemish or sin) and the sacrificer (the self-giving Son of God and High Priest).

Stories that either condemned human sacrifice or provided an alternative to it were common in ancient literature. The shedding of blood often involves terrible consequences, even if it is clothed in sacrifice to a divinity. Thus, when the Greek hero Agamemnon sacrificed his daughter to appease the goddess Artemis, he unleashed a cycle of violence and unfaithfulness that eventually destroyed himself and his family. In one version of this story, Artemis replaced Iphigenia with an animal and made the young virgin a priestess. A similar substitution appears in the book of *Genesis:* Yahweh is pictured as commanding Abraham to sacrifice his son Isaac to the Lord, who at the last moment provided a ram as a substitute. The message that God does not require human sacrifice is also a feature of the story of an Indian king who vowed to immolate his first son if the god Varuna would bless him with many children. Following the birth of his first child, the king did not keep his vow, and the god gave him dropsy. The king resolved to purchase the son of a high-born man as a substitute for his own son, but as the king prepared to sacrifice the substitute, an advisor suggested that the king recite hymns pleasing to the god and substitute a goat for the boy. And the king did so.

ANCIENT SPIRITUALITY IN MODERN THOUGHT

Prehistoric and most ancient national religions may be dead rather than living entities, but they continue to fascinate moderns. Scholarly reflection has centered around three issues: (1) the minds of "primitives," (2) the origin of religion, (3) women and the female sacred. Each topic has been the subject of debate. Were the minds of oral peoples prelogical? How did religion begin? Was Goddess worship central to ancient spirituality? Were the sexes equal, or did one sex dominate the other?

ISSUE 1: THE MINDS OF "PRIMITIVES"

From the vantage point of modern Western thought and culture, the material and intellectual achievements of nonliterate societies have seemed alien and primitive. English anthropologist E. B. Tylor (1832–1917) accounted for the otherness and material simplicity of their cultures by locating them within an evolutionary scheme. In Tylor's view, Stone Age hunter-gatherers were at a savage stage of human development; savagery was followed by barbarism, a simple farming stage betweeen savagery and civilization. Tribal peoples who persisted after the rise of civilization were survivors of humankind's childhood.

Tylor believed that the minds of "savages" and 'barbarians" were comparable to those of moderns, but some interpreters were less charitable. Oral peoples were judged to be morally and intellectually deficient and incapable of self-government. Samuel George Morton, an American physician, characterized the Hottentots, a people of southern Africa, as "the nearest approximation to the lowest animals." Morton had a low opinion of Native Americans as well, averring that they were "incapable of a continued process of reasoning on abstract subjects."[55] Such assessments were sometimes extended to all non-Western peoples, as is evident in the remarks of Scottish philosopher

David Hume (1711–1776): "There never was a civilized nation of any other complexion than white. . . . No ingenious manufacturers amongst them, no arts, no sciences. . . . Such a uniform and constant difference could not happen in so many countries and ages, if nature had not made an original distinction between these breeds of men."[56]

Various explanations about human intelligence have been advanced by westerners to account for disparities in human achievement and cultures. Distinguished scientists (usually white males) ranked human groups according to such reputed criteria of intelligence as level of civilization, brain size, and inherited intelligence. Almost invariably they ranked white males at the top, followed by Asians, Native Americans, and black Africans. Women of every color have been seen as inferior to men. In 1879, psychologist Gustave Le Bon opined that women's intelligence is "closer to children and savages than to an adult, civilized man. They excel in fickleness, inconstancy, absence of thought and logic, and incapacity to reason."[57]

Such views are harder to defend today. The brains of *Homo sapiens* do not appear to have changed since the appearance of early modern humans in the Middle Paleolithic, and genetic research and brain measurements do not support claims that women are inferior to men or that some geographical races are inferior to others. Today, few scholars believe there is a single reliable measure of intelligence and most insist that intelligence is both heritable and malleable. Further, studies of non-Western cultures have undermined the view that Western culture is superior to all others.

Prehistoric and recent oral peoples are not intellectually inferior, but there is a difference between how they and **modernists** (those whose understanding has been shaped by modern science) understand their respective worlds. Oral peoples believe the world is infused with spirits and that nonhuman entities (earth and sky, animals and plants) speak, feel, and act. Modernists see the world as composed of animate and inanimate things and believe that what happens is caused by natural forces. Traditional peoples dance for rain. Modernists seed clouds. Modernists ask "what" caused *x*, whereas traditional peoples ask "who" caused it.

French philosopher Lucien Levy-Buhl (1857–1939) accounted for this difference by distinguishing between "primitive" and "civilized" minds. Primitive minds were prelogical (not fully rational). They failed to separate symbols from the symbolized and lacked knowledge of causal relationships. Their magico-religious reasoning attributed the causes of events to spirits whose powers were divined through dreams, visions, and omens. In contrast, civilized minds seek natural explanations and do not attribute personhood or spirit to animals, plants, and nonliving things.

Levy-Buhl later retracted this distinction, and the preponderance of recent scholarly opinion maintains that the idea of magico-religious (prerational) and civilized (rational) mentalities as evolutionary stages is unwarranted. In *The Savage Mind*, anthropologist Claude Levi-Strauss (b. 1908) argued that primitive thought included scientific and magico-religious modes of reasoning. Citing as evidence the detailed animal and plant taxonomies of oral peoples, he concluded that "primitive" thought is founded on a demand for order and that this demand is a feature of both magico-religious and scientific thought. For Levi-Strauss, magico-religious reasoning is neither irrational nor prelogical but rather has a logic of its own, including modes of acquiring knowledge and articulating models for explaining human experience.

In Levi-Strauss's view, there are two distinct modes of scientific thought; one is concrete and the other theoretical. Whereas the science of oral peoples is primarily concrete (the science of an experimental, do-it-yourself person), modern science is both concrete and theoretical. The science of traditional peoples is embedded in a magico-religious system; modern science is embedded in a secular belief system that sets aside supernatural explanations. Relevant to the interpretation of prehistoric religion is Levi-Strauss's contention that the human mastery of the great arts of civilization (farming, domestication of animals, pottery, and weaving) was preceded by methodical observation and experimentation: "There is no doubt that all these achievements required a genuinely scientific attitude, sustained and watchful interest and a desire for knowledge for its own sake.... Neolithic, or early historical man, was therefore the heir of a long scientific tradition."[58]

ISSUE 2: THE ORIGIN OF RELIGION

In the nineteenth and early twentieth centuries, scholars were not only interested in the origin of religion but also believed they could scientifically account for it. The quest did not involve an attempt to pinpoint religion's beginning in time but rather to provide a "plausible" explanation for the origin of religion and its evolution over time. As sociologist Emile Durkheim (1832–1917) observed, "if by origin we are to understand the very first beginning, the question has nothing scientific about it, and should be resolutely discarded. There was no given moment when religion began to exist."[59] Today scholars are even less confident of the legitimacy of the pursuit of origins and have either abandoned it or reformulated the issues involved.[60]

The search for origins entailed speculation about religion's primal form. Tylor coined the term **animism**—a belief system in which potentially everything is believed to have spirit and intentionality—as a label for the primal form of religion. Some scholars concurred with anthropologist Robert R. Marett's (1866–1943) contention that belief in an impersonal supernatural power was antecedent to the belief that nature abounded with spirits. Marett was indebted to the work of anthropologist and Anglican priest Robert H. Codrington (1830–1932) on Melanesian religion. *Mana,* a Melanesian term for an awesome power common to objects, persons, or spirits, was regarded as the prototypical conception of an impersonal supernatural power that preceded the personification of the holy as spirit. Durkheim and Sigmund Freud (1836–1939) opined that **totemism** was the initial form of religion. Ethnologist and Roman Catholic priest Wilhelm Schmidt (1868–1954) found belief in **high gods** (supreme beings) to be common among recent tribal peoples and speculated that a primordial monotheism was humankind's first conception of deity.

Recent scholarship has questioned the adequacy of animism, *mana,* or totemism as the first stage of religion and has rejected them as accurate labels for the belief systems of tribal religions. As Lawrence E. Sullivan observed: "Theories of superstition and animism have maligned the myths and obscured the rites of most of humankind. Suppositions about prelogical mentality, infantilism, and primitivism are revealing poses of modern thought and . . . mirror back to us the illusory self-definitions that flaunt a fragile, even wistful, hope for a privileged place in human history."[61]

ISSUE 3: WOMEN AND THE FEMALE SACRED IN PREHISTORY

Archaeological evidence of the female sacred in the Stone Age and studies of gender in recent small-scale societies have provided new resources for rethinking issues of gender and divinity. A controversial aspect of this reorientation is the contention that "Old Europe" (Late Paleolithic and Neolithic Europe) and Minoan Crete were idyllic times in which Goddess worship was preeminent and women were equal or superior in status and power to men.

GODDESSES   It is clear from the number and distribution of Late Paleolithic and Neolithic female figurines that images of women had considerable significance in prehistory. The controversy swirling around the figurines and other symbols of women involves the following contentions: (1) that the preeminent deities of the Stone Age were female; (2) that worship of a Mother Goddess preceded that of a Father God; (3) that a Mother Goddess was worshiped by early modern peoples across all of Europe; (4) that such worship constituted a single Stone Age cult; and (5) that Goddess worship was embedded in societies that were relatively peaceful, matrifocal (women centered), and either governed by women (matriarchal) or egalitarian.

Several scholars have made a case for the preeminence of goddesses in the Late Paleolithic and Neolithic. At Catal Huyuk (a Neolithic site), archaeologist James Mellaart found a depiction of what he interpreted as a Goddess giving birth to a bull (a symbol for male deity). Thus, for him, the Goddess gave birth to God (her son), a view congenial to the priority of Goddess worship. Marija Gimbutas granted that the religion of Old Europe included gods and goddesses but argued that it was dominated by worship of a "Great Goddess" who, as Creatrix, gave birth to life and, as Regeneratrix, renewed it.[62] Mellaart's and Gimbutas's research undergirds art historian Merlin Stone's vivid proclamation that "in the beginning people prayed to the Creatress of Life, the Mistress of Heaven. At the very dawn of religion, God was a woman."[63]

It is very likely that prehistoric peoples linked the earth's fertility to a Goddess whose body bore life-sustaining food, but does the evidence point to the worship of a single Mother Goddess across all of Old Europe that constituted a single religion? Gimbutas granted that religion in Old Europe involved more than one cult but argued that worship of a Mother Goddess was preeminent from the Late Paleolithic to the Neolithic and persisted in the Bronze Age island cultures of Crete, Malta, and Sardinia until around 1500 B.C.E. In Gimbutas's view, Stone Age art provides abundant evidence of Goddess worship. Female figures with snakelike hands and feet symbolized a fertility goddess. Owl images depicted a goddess of death and regeneration. Venus figurines signified the Earth Mother. Gimbutas synthesized the many images of goddesses into one "Great Goddess" who was the giver of life, death-wielder, and source of well-being: "The Goddess in all her manifestations was a symbol of the unity of all life in Nature. Her power was in water and stone, in tomb and cave, in animals and birds, snakes and fish, hills, trees, and flowers."[64]

Critics have raised several objections to scholars who, like Gimbutas, argue for the priority of Goddess worship and the existence of an ancient, unified Goddess religion. Anthropologist Joan B. Townsend's critique is representative. First, Townsend notes that the archaeological record is too discontinuous to support the claim of a continuous, unified Goddess tradition dating from the Late Paleolithic to the Neolithic. Second, ethnological studies indicate that belief in a single preeminent deity does not cut across the boundaries of small-scale societies in historic times and thus was unlikely to have done so in prehistoric times. Third, the thesis of the preeminence of Goddess worship does not adequately account for male and nonsexed human figurines and symbols in Stone Age art. Fourth, there is no necessary connection between snakes, owls and other symbols that Gimbutas linked to goddesses. Fifth, it is unwarranted to assume that symbols such as snakes have the same meaning across the boundaries of cultures, regions, and periods.[65] The Goddess movement has contributed to the rediscovery and reaffirmation of the feminine sacred and the bonding of women, but the claim that a Mother Goddess religion has persisted from the Late Paleolithic to the present is, in Townsend's judgment, "ludicrous."[66]

GENDER, RELIGION, AND SOCIETY   Have men been the dominant sex since time immemorial, or have there been societies in which women dominated or were equal in status and power? Classicist Johann J. Bachofen (1815–1887) argued that goddesses were not only the primary metaphor for deity in prehistory but also a reflection of the sex in power; thus, in humankind's social evolution, matriarchies preceded patriarchies. What Bachofen labeled "Mother right" was preceded by a primal stage of humankind marked by unregulated sexuality and male brutality. It was displaced by a matriarchal stage in which women were "the repository of all culture" and was eclipsed by a still higher patriarchal culture. For Bachofen, mother love preceded paternal love, as "the woman learns earlier than the man to extend her loving care beyond the limits of the ego to another creature, and to direct whatever gift of invention she possesses to the preservation and improvement of this other's existence."[67] The triumph of patriarchy brought "with it the liberation of the spirit from the manifestations of nature, a sublimation of human existence over the laws of material life. . . . Maternity pertains to the physical side of man, the only thing he shares with the animals: the paternal-spiritual principle belongs to him alone."[68] Most scholars reject Bachofen's stages of social evolution and insist that true matriarchies have never existed.[69]

Archaeological evidence for female dominance in prehistory is tenuous. It may be inferred from burials in which women were interred with elaborate grave goods and men were not, but gender inequality is not a common or widespread feature of Neolithic burials. Grave goods at Neolithic sites in Anatolia and Old Europe contain little that suggests gender inequality. In fact, the absence of evidence of gender inequality led Mellaart and Gimbutas to conclude that egalitarianism, rather than social stratifications based on sex or class, was the norm. In Gimbutas's words, "A division of labor between the sexes is indicated, but not a superiority of either."[70]

The evidence for Stone Age gender egalitarianism is also inconclusive. Neolithic burials of men often include weapons, an indication that men dominated the sphere of violence and which some interpreters see as confirmation of male domination. Ethnology provides some evidence that women and men are relatively equal in status in societies that are matrilineal (descent is through the female line) and matrilocal (married couples reside with the wife's mother's family). Women have been influential among the matrilineal and matrilocal Iroquois. In traditional Iroquois society, clan mothers nominated and, with the advice of their clans, elected the fifty male chiefs of the Iroquois Confederacy; they also had the power to remove a chief from the council and to exclude men from the longhouses. Decisions opposed by the clan mothers could not be implemented. Based on a study of thirty-seven recent simple ethnic societies, anthropologist Melvin Ember found that larger houses are typical of matrilocal societies and smaller ones, of patrilocal societies.[71] Extrapolating from Ember's research, the large houses at some Neolithic sites may be indicative of matrilocal, matrilineal, and egalitarian societies. However, ethnological studies indicate that there is no invariable relationship between matriliny, matrilocality,

and gender egalitarianism. In societies with matrilineal descent and matrilocal residence, women often have influential positions; power, however, is either shared with or dominated by men, and in some cases, men have more authority and higher status than women.

Many scholars argue that matriarchy and patriarchy are inappropriate categories for small-scale societies. Recent hunter-gatherers live in small groups governed by consensus and characterized by gender equality. A similar pattern may have been true of Paleolithic peoples. Sedentarism complicated group life, but it is unlikely that social stratifications based on class or gender were part of Neolithic farming villages because these divisions are not typical of recent horticultural villages.[72]

Assuming that Paleolithic and Neolithic cultures were relatively egalitarian, why did patriarchy become the dominant pattern by the end of the Neolithic? Anthropologists have identified three developments that contributed to the rise of patriarchy: the plow, nomadic pastoralism, and increased warfare.[73] All three are activities that men, by virtue of their larger size and perhaps their biopsychological makeup, are better suited to perform than women.

With the introduction of plows and draft animals, men gradually took over food production, and the status of women declined. Pastoralism—the raising and care of domestic herds as the primary means of subsistence—also emerged in the Neolithic and produced a more male oriented life than that of farming villages. In modern preindustrial societies where plow agriculture or pastoralism predominates, women tend to be subordinate to men. Thus, there is a high correlation between plow agriculture, draft animals, patriliny, land ownership, and a lower status of women, along with a high correlation between nonplow agriculture and a higher status of women.[74]

Anthropologists argue that war changed how Neolithic societies were organized by contributing to the emergence of chiefdoms under the leadership of warrior chiefs who were usually male.[75] Women have been and are warriors, but war has been primarily the province of men. In the past, war and weaponry favored those who were stronger; because men are, on average, taller, heavier, more muscular, and faster than women, men have dominated the technologies and strategies of war. Studies also indicate that women are less likely to be violent against those within or outside their group. To account for this dichotomy, scholars speculate that men are either biogenetically more aggressive than women or that, in warrior cultures, their aggression is useful and less socially constrained than that of women.[76] In small-scale societies, women have been more valuable than men biologically (they give birth to and nurture the young) and economically (they provide a high percentage of the food consumed), but men have had more value as warriors. As anthropologist Marvin Harris observed, "Warfare inverts the relative value of the contribution made by males and females to a group's prospects for survival."[77]

War, intensive agriculture, and pastoralism placed men in positions of power and situated them to acquire wealth and influence. Patriarchal societies and religions grew out of the shift from stone to iron tools and weapons and coincided with the emergence of warrior cultures and urban centers. The transition was marked by the subordination and devaluation of women and the dominance of men.

IDYLLIC OLD EUROPE   Gimbutas, Riane Eisler, and others also contend that the cultures of Late Paleolithic and Neolithic Old Europe and of Bronze Age Crete were earth centered, peaceful, and matrifocal. In their view, these idyllic cultures were destroyed by invasions (beginning in the fourth millennium B.C.E.) of nomadic and patrifocal pastoralists from the steppes of Eurasia. As a result of these clashes of cultures, women were subordinated to men and Goddess worship was suppressed. In Gimbutas's words, Old European civilization "was a long-lasting period of remarkable creativity and stability, an age free of strife." As evidence, she cited the relative absence in the archaeological record of (1) artistic depictions of violence, (2) lavish "chieftain" burials, (3) military fortifications, and (4) human sacrifice. The idyllic character of Old Europe could be inferred, Gimbu-

tas believed, from evidence of matriliny, egalitarianism, Goddess worship, and an artistic ethos of joy and harmony.[78]

In *The Chalice and the Blade,* Eisler juxtaposes alternative models of society. The "dominator model" is marked by aggression and war, social hierarchies, and male dominance. The "partnership model" is sexually egalitarian, cooperative, relatively peaceful, and less hierarchical. Eisler points to Old Europe and Minoan Crete as partnership societies that demonstrate that war and gender inequality "are neither divinely nor biologically ordained." Of Minoan culture, she writes that "there are no signs of war." It was the last time "a spirit of harmony between women and men as joyful and equal participants in life appears to pervade."[79]

Critics rebut the claims that a peaceful Old European culture was destroyed by invasions of Indo-European warriors. First, they contend that the case for "an age free of strife" is overstated. The archaeological record indicates that Old European towns had walls and other defensive measures, and the presence of weapons in male burials and skeletal head wounds at Catal Huyuk is indicative of violence.[80] The relative absence of war in the Paleolithic and Early Neolithic was chiefly a function of the absence of competition for resources. Second, in the judgment of anthropologist Colin Renfrew, the archaeological record does not support the view that successive waves of Indo-European nomadic pastoralists—originating from the steppes of southern Russia—invaded Europe in the late Neolithic.[81]

The issue of a peaceful Old Europe raises wider issues concerning human aggression, the origins of war, and the interplay of religion and violence. Violence appears to have been part of human existence from the beginning, as is borne out by evidence of human deaths at the hands of other humans in the Old Stone Age. Some scholars argue that humans have a biogenetic tendency to violence and lack the "inhibiting instincts" that prevent other animals from attacking their own. Others stress the relationship of violence to culture and insist that we should not confuse our heritable capacity for violence with its necessity.

THE LESSONS OF THE STUDY OF ANCIENT SPIRITUALITY

What lessons can be drawn from a study of ancient spirituality? Our understanding of the past is constantly in need of reassessment, because new research and interpretations invalidate old interpretations. The legitimacy of this observation is especially clear from our review of the pioneering studies of primitives and the origin of religion. Several lessons can be drawn from this. One lesson is that much of what is written here about ancient spirituality will appear out of date to future readers. Another lesson is that ideas and studies, including scientific ones, are colored by individual circumstance, time, place, and culture. Earlier scholarship about primitives and the origin of religion reveals a great deal about how Western ideas about ancient peoples have been shaped by factors such as colonialism, imperialism, sexism, slavery, and the presumed superiority of Western culture.

Recent scholarship has looked beyond the criticisms of paganism that were voiced in ancient times and repeated through the centuries (the anthropomorphism and immorality of the gods). The ancient world gave birth to the great wisdom traditions (for example, Buddhism, Confucianism, Hinduism, Judaism, Christianity, and Islam) that have provided moral guidelines and conceptions of how life ought to be lived through the intervening centuries. In recent scholarship, these traditions were not radically discontinuous from the moral directives and concepts of the good life of pagan spiritualities. The religious systems that inspire and nurture people today were connected to what preceded them. A message here is that even though pagan myths and theologies are no longer acted out or believed, they encoded a system of values and ideas that are worthy of respect and study.

Humans have been religious for a very long time. Both the antiquity and persistence of religious behaviors and beliefs over time suggest that spirituality is an important, perhaps even a fundamental, feature of human existence. This tells us something about what kind of creatures we are. Another important lesson of the study of ancient spirituality is that we should not assume that because a people's material culture is less developed, their worldview is simple or inferior.

Beyond the lessons that can be drawn from a study of ancient spirituality, does ancient spirituality itself have lessons to teach? Reflect on this chapter and the readings that follow, and see what conclusions you draw about the value of the integration of heaven and earth, the importance of the female sacred, and other elements of ancient spirituality.

GLOSSARY OF ANCIENT SPIRITUALITY

agnosticism	the view that there is insufficient evidence to believe or disbelieve in God.
ancestral spirit	a spirit of deceased kin believed to live on and have an ongoing relationship with the living.
animism	the belief that the world is pervaded by spirits or souls. E. B. Tylor coined the term as a designation for the first form of religious belief, and it is often used as a label for the belief systems of tribal religions.
anthropomorphism	attributing human attributes to nonhuman beings and things.
atheism	the belief that God and the gods do not exist.
axis mundi	a place or point that is the center of the universe; typically, the place or navel of creation.
cosmic religion	a belief system in which the unity of the divine, human, and natural spheres is unbroken.
divination, diviner	the magico-religious art of uncovering the causes of things and predicting the future through reading signs or omens, interpreting dreams, and serving as a medium for spirits.
do-ut des	Latin phrase from classical times translated here as "I give that you will give." Modern scholars interpret the phrase as a rule of gift exchange and as applicable to human petitions and gifts to divinities.
fetish	an object used in magico-religious practice that is believed to have supernatural power or an object symbolizing religious authority.
henotheism	loyalty and worship of one high god without disbelieving in others.
hieros gamos	Greek for "sacred marriage"; a union between a god or goddess and a human being, especially a monarch (for example, the mythological and ritual marriage of Heaven and Earth).
high god	a term coined by Andrew Lang for a supreme being ("deathless creator deities") in "primitive" religions.
homo religiosus	humans as religious beings.
immortality	eternal life; the condition of not being subject to death.
initiation cult	a label for religious groups during the Greco-Roman period that initiated devotees into its mysteries and secrets. Also known as *mystery religions,* initiation cults offered a ritual process in which devotees experienced a mystical identification with God or the gods of the cult and spiritual rebirth. Initiation cults included those centered around Demeter, Dionysus, Cybele, Isis, and Mithras.

mana	a Melanesian term associated with a supernatural, impersonal power immanent in things.
Master of Animals	a guardian spirit or deity associated with the well-being of a species or group of animal species.
megalith	a large stone aligned alone or in various patterns and used as tombs and temples during the Neolithic period.
modernist	a person whose worldview has been shaped by the Enlightenment (a label for a perspective that emerged in Europe in the seventeenth and eighteenth centuries) and modern science.
mystery religion	see **initiation cult.**
Neolithic	New Stone Age; the period in which humans discovered how to raise crops and domesticate animals. The Neolithic commenced around 8000 B.C.E. and ended around 3500 to 3000 B.C.E. with the transition from stone to bronze tools and weapons and the discovery of writing.
oracle	(1) a mode of divination involving a message from God or the gods delivered through a medium; (2) the shrine or temple where messages are received.
pagan	a derogatory term for persons who followed the traditional polytheistic religions of ancient Greece and Rome. By extension, it is a label for all polytheistic and tribal religionists.
Paleolithic	Old Stone Age; the period (ca. 2,000,000–8000 B.C.E.) in human history in which all humans subsisted by hunting and gathering.
prehistory	the period before the invention of writing.
primitive	a term for societies that exist by hunting and gathering or simple agriculture and that are nonliterate.
sacred king	a monarch who, by virtue of his or her office is sacred. A sacred king was regarded as God or a representative of God who ruled by divine authority.
shaman, shamanism	a specialist in sacred things in tribal societies; a person whose power to heal and divine is derived from direct contact with the spirit world; an ecstatic magician; practices and beliefs associated with a *shaman.*
spirit possession	the belief that spirits may enter other beings (for example, humans and animals) and speak or otherwise act through them.
Stone Age	the period in human history in which the principal tools were made of stone. Chronologically it spans the beginning of stone tool production (ca. 2,000,000 B.C.E.) to the transition to the Bronze Age (ca. 3500–3000 B.C.E.).
theriomorphic divinity	
	a deity depicted as an animal or as having an animal and human body.

totemic spirit	an animal or nature spirit associated with the origins of a family or clan.
totemism	the identification of an animal or some other entity with the origins of a family or clan. Emile Durkheim and Sigmund Freud believed that totemism was the primal form of religion.
tumuli	human-made earthen mounds, often constructed in conjunction with burials.
Venus figurine	a Late Paleolithic figurine of a naked and apparently pregnant female with large breasts and buttocks. Venus figurines were made of materials such as ivory, stone, and clay and have been found throughout Europe; most date between 29,000 and 22,000 B.C.E. They are named after Venus, the Roman goddess of sex and generation.

FOR FURTHER STUDY

Bottero, Jean. *Mesopotamia: Writing, Reasoning, and the Gods.* Chicago: University of Chicago Press, 1992.
  A thorough study of Mesopotamian religion and culture.

Burenhult, Goran, ed. *The Illustrated History of Humankind.* Vols. 1–4. San Francisco: HarperSan Francisco, 1993.
  An up-to-date telling of the human story from hominid antecedents of Homo sapiens to the end of the Stone Age (ca. 3500 B.C.E.) and the rise of urban states.

Burkert, Walter. *Greek Religion.* Translated by John Raffan. Cambridge, Mass.: Harvard University Press, 1985.
  One of the very best studies of Greek religion, including Homeric religion, the initiation cults, and Greek philosophy.

Eisler, Riane. *The Chalice and the Blade: Our History, Our Future.* San Francisco: HarperSan Francisco, 1987.
  An argument for a culture of gender cooperation rather than male or female dominance that finds precedents for it in Stone Age Europe and Minoan Crete.

Eliade, Mircea. *A History of Religious Ideas: From the Stone Age to the Eleusinian Mysteries.* Vol. 1. Translated by Willard R. Trask. Chicago: University of Chicago Press, 1978.
  An introduction to prehistoric religion and the religions of ancient Sumer, Egypt, and India.

Gimbutas, Marija. *The Language of the Goddess.* San Francisco: HarperCollins, 1991.
  A good introduction to Gimbutas's view of the matrifocal and peaceful character of Old Europe and the preeminence of Goddess worship.

Hultkrantz, Ake. *The Religions of the American Indians.* Translated by Monica Setterwall. Berkeley and Los Angeles: University of California Press, 1980.
Covers the beliefs and practices of the tribal and the ancient urban religions of the Americas.

Marinatos, Nanno. *Minoan Religion: Ritual, Image, and Symbol.* Columbia: University of South Carolina Press, 1993.
A scholarly study of Minoan religion.

Quirke, Stephen. *Ancient Egyptian Religion.* London: British Museum Publications, 1992.
An analysis of the principal features of Egyptian religion.

Pritchard, James B., ed. *The Ancient Near East: An Anthology of Texts and Pictures.* 2 vols. Princeton, N. J.: Princeton University Press, 1958.
A collection of texts from the civilizations of ancient West Asia, including myths, legal texts, and the Gilgamesh Epic.

READINGS

Reading 2.1   STONE AGE BURIALS AND THE AFTERLIFE   Mircea Eliade

Many scholars infer belief in survival after death from the ancient human practice of burying the dead. What reasons does Mircea Eliade (1907–1986) cite for this conclusion? Is fear of the dead compatible with the belief that something survives death? What is the significance of the grave goods?

> Belief in a survival after death seems to be demonstrated, from the earliest times, by the use of red ocher as a ritual substitute for blood, hence as a symbol for life. The custom of dusting corpses with ocher is universally disseminated in both time and space, from Choukoutien [China] to the western shores of Europe, in Africa as far as the Cape of Good Hope, in Australia, in Tasmania, in America as far as Tierra del Fuego. As to the religious meaning of burials, it has been the subject of vigorous controversy. There can be no doubt that the burial of the dead should have a justification—but which one? . . . belief in survival is confirmed by burials; otherwise there would be no understanding the effort extended in interring the body. This survival could be purely spiritual, that is, conceived as a postexistence of the soul, a belief corroborated by the appearance of the dead in dreams. But certain burials can equally well be interpreted as a precaution against the possible return of the deceased; in these cases the corpses were bent and perhaps tied. On the other hand, nothing makes it impossible that the bent position of the dead body, far from expressing fear of "living corpses" (a fear documented among certain peoples), on the contrary signifies the hope of a rebirth; for we know of a number of cases of intentional burial in the fetal position. . . .
>
> During the Upper Paleolithic, the practice of inhumation appears to have become general. Corpses sprinkled with red ocher are buried in graves in which a certain number of objects intended for personal adornment (shells, pendants, necklaces) have been found. It is probable that the animal skulls and bones discovered near graves are the remains of ritual feasts, if not of offerings. . . . the presence of such objects implies not only belief in a personal survival but also the certainty that the deceased will continue his particular activity in the other world. Similar ideas are abundantly documented, and on various levels of culture. . . .
>
> To sum up, we may conclude that the burials confirm the belief in survival.

Source: Mircea Eliade, *A History of Religious Ideas: From the Stone Age to the Eleusinian Mysteries,* vol. 1, trans. Willard R. Trask (Chicago: University of Chicago Press, 1978), pp. 9–11. Reprinted by permission.

Reading 2.2   WAS THERE A NEANDERTHAL RELIGION?   Peter Rowley-Conwy

In this essay, archaeologist Peter Rowley-Conwy proffers alternative interpretations of the evidence on which claims of Neanderthal religious behaviors are based. What explanation does he suggest for the proximity of Neanderthal artifacts and cave bear bones? Is hunger or greed a more plausible explanation for what appears to be evidence of cannibalism than the claim that ritual cannibalism occurred? Although

Rowley-Conwy does grant that Neanderthals occasionally buried their dead, why, in his opinion, is this not indicative of belief in an afterlife?

It is a common archaeological joke that any finding that cannot be explained in practical terms is labelled "ritual"—and the joke contains more than a grain of truth. The main text of this chapter refers to a number of finds that have often been thought to reflect ritual behavior of some kind among Neanderthals. Recently, these finds have come under renewed scrutiny. Here is a brief summary of three of the best-known claims, with the case against accepting them as fact. . . .

Popularized by Jean Auel's novel *The Clan of the Cave Bear* some years ago, this theory now has few, if any, supporters. It was based on the fact that quite a large number of caves have been found containing Neanderthal artifacts and thousands of bear bones. All this shows is that these early people occasionally visited a cave in which the huge bears hibernated and sometimes died. It does not show that Neanderthal people killed any of these bears, and still less that any ritual was involved.

There was also a reported finding from Drachenloch cave, in Switzerland, of several bear skulls set inside an arrangement of stone slabs—clear proof, it was claimed, of ritual behavior. But two mutually contradictory drawings of this were published at different times, no photographs exist, and it was recently established that the excavator was not even present on the day that the find was made. The whole thing, in fact, was reconstructed from the descriptions of the unskilled workmen who had carried out the excavation. Slabs of stone often fall from cave roofs and lie at unusual angles on the floor below, where the bones of dead cave bears would also lie. Verdict: a chance arrangement magnified by wishful thinking. . . .

Even if Neanderthals did eat each other, this of itself need indicate nothing more than hunger or greed. In a cave at Monte Circeo, in Italy, a Neanderthal skull was found in what was said to be a circle of stones, but, again, no photographs were taken before the skull was removed. Drawings made later by the person who found (and removed) the skull show a rough heap of stones rather than a regular circle, and nothing to suggest that the stones were deliberately arranged. The skull has no marks made by cutting tools, but appears to have been gnawed by a carnivore. Hyenas commonly carry animal skulls into their dens, and this is a more likely, if more prosaic, explanation of the presence of the skull. Verdict: a hyena settled on top of a rock fall to eat a grisly meal. . . .

These are less easily dismissed. Certainly, some are doubtful, including the often quoted burial of a boy inside a circle of ibex horns at Teshik-Tash, in Uzbekistan. This in fact comprises a few bones (not the whole skeleton) of a 12-year-old Neanderthal boy found in close proximity to a few ibex horns. There is no evidence that the horns were ever in a circle, there is no sign of a grave pit, and we have already seen that hyenas commonly take skulls into their dens. Verdict: another hyena meal.

There are also strong doubts about the famous "flower burial" from Shanidar, in Iraq. Not only is no grave pit visible, but the cause of death was a large roof slab that fell and crushed the Neanderthal man beneath it. Only a concentration of flower pollen suggests ritual activity; the heaping of flowers on the corpse, a scene reconstructed in many textbooks and films. Given the complexities of cave deposits, however, the pollen could have got there in various ways—indeed, even during the archaeological excavation. Verdict: an unfortunate Neanderthal who stood in the wrong place at the wrong time.

But at least two burials do seem to stand up to scrutiny. A skeleton from La Chapelle-aux-Saints, in France, was found in a steep-sided pit, and the findings were published in 1908. The pit seems too regular to be a natural depression into which the Neanderthal man simply crawled and died. It has been suggested that the hole may have been formed by floodwater, but it looks so square-cut that it appears to be a regular grave pit. The clearest grave pit found from this period is that in which a Neanderthal skeleton from Kebara, in Israel, was buried. This must have been deliberately dug. Verdict: these two Neanderthal men were buried, certainly, but does this prove that the Neanderthals had a religion or believed in an afterlife? It is not impossible that what we see is the simple disposal of dead bodies, and that nothing more complex than this was ever involved.

Source: Peter Rowley-Conwy, "Was There a Neanderthal Religion?" in *The First Humans: Human Origins and History to 10,000 B.C.,* ed. Goran Burenhult (San Francisco: HarperSan Francisco, 1993), p. 70. Copyright © 1993 by Weldon Owen Pty. Ltd./Bra Bocker AB. Reprinted by permission of HarperCollins Publishers Inc.

Reading 2.3   THE GODDESS AND THE DAWN OF RELIGION   Merlin Stone

Art historian Merlin Stone makes a spirited argument that deity was, in the beginning, a Goddess. Is there something missing in Father-God religions? Do Father-God religions provide theological justification for the dominance of men and the suppression of women? Would it be more theologically defensible to speak of God as male and female (masculine and feminine), or as beyond gender? Why is gender an important issue in theological reflection and in speech about God?

Though we live amid high-rise steel buildings, formica countertops and electronic television screens, there is something in all of us, women and men alike, that makes us feel deeply connected with the past. Perhaps the sudden dampness of a beach cave or the lines of sunlight piercing through the intricate lace patterns of the leaves in a darkened grove of tall trees will awaken from the hidden recesses of our minds the distant echoes of a remote and ancient time, taking us back to the early stirrings of human life on the planet. For people raised and programmed on the patriarchal religions of today, religions that affect us in even the most secular aspects of our society, perhaps there remains a lingering, almost innate memory of sacred shrines and temples tended by priestesses who served in the religion of the original supreme deity. In the beginning, people prayed to the Creatress of Life, the Mistress of Heaven. At the very dawn of religion, God was a woman. Do you remember?

For years something has magnetically lured me into exploring the legends, the temple sites, the statues and the ancient rituals of the female deities, drawing me back in time to an age when the Goddess was omnipotent, and women acted as Her clergy, controlling the form and rites of religion.

Perhaps it was my training and work as a sculptor that first exposed me to the sculptures of the Goddess found in the ruins of prehistoric sanctuaries and the earliest dwellings of human beings. Perhaps it was a certain romantic mysticism, which once embarrassed me, but to which I now happily confess, that led me over the years into the habit of collecting information about the early female religions and the veneration of female deities. Occasionally I tried to dismiss my fascination with this subject as overly fanciful and certainly disconnected from my work (I was building electronic sculptural environments at the time). Nevertheless, I would find myself continually perusing archaeology journals and poring over texts in museum or university library stacks.

As I read, I recalled that somewhere along the pathway of my life I had been told—and accepted the idea—that the sun, great and powerful, was naturally worshiped as male, while the moon, hazy, delicate symbol of sentiment and love, had always been revered as female. Much to my surprise I discovered accounts of Sun Goddesses in the lands of Canaan, Anatolia, Arabia and Australia, while Sun Goddesses among the Eskimos, the Japanese and the Khasis of India were accompanied by subordinate brothers who were symbolized as the moon.

I had somewhere assimilated the idea that the earth was invariably identified as female, Mother Earth, the one who passively accepts the seed, while heaven was naturally and inherently male, its intangibility symbolic of the supposedly exclusive male ability to think in abstract concepts. This too I had accepted without question—until I learned that nearly all the female deities of the Near and Middle East were titled Queen of Heaven, and in Egypt not only was the ancient Goddess Nut known as the heavens, but her brother-husband Geb was symbolized as the earth.

Most astonishing of all was the discovery of numerous accounts of the female Creators of all existence, divinities who were credited with bringing forth not only the first people but the entire earth and the heavens above. There were records of such Goddesses in Sumer, Babylon, Egypt, Africa, Australia and China.

In India the Goddess Sarasvati was honored as the inventor of the original alphabet, while in Celtic Ireland the Goddess Brigit was esteemed as the patron deity of language. Texts revealed that it was the Goddess Nidaba in Sumer who was paid honor as the one who initially invented clay tablets and the art of writing. She appeared in that position earlier than any of the male deities who later replaced Her. The official scribe of the Sumerian heaven was a woman. But most significant was the archaeological evidence of the earliest examples of written language so far discovered; these were also located in Sumer, at the temple of the Queen of Heaven in Erech, written there over five thousand years ago. Though writing is most often said to have been invented by *man*, however that may be defined, the combination of the above factors presents a most convincing argument that it may have actually been woman who pressed those first meaningful marks into wet clay.

In agreement with the generally accepted theory that women were responsible for the development of agriculture, as an extension of their food-gathering activities, there were female deities everywhere who were credited with this gift to civilization. In Mesopotamia, where some of the earliest evidences of agricultural development have been found, the Goddess Ninlil was revered for having provided

Her people with an understanding of planting and harvesting methods. In nearly all areas of the world, female deities were extolled as healers, dispensers of curative herbs, roots, plants and other medical aids, casting the priestesses who attended the shrines into the role of physicians of those who worshiped there.

Some legends described the Goddess as a powerful, courageous warrior, a leader in battle. The worship of the Goddess as valiant warrior seems to have been responsible for the numerous reports of female soldiers, later referred to by the classical Greeks as the Amazons. More thoroughly examining the accounts of the esteem the Amazons paid to the female deity, it became evident that women who worshiped a warrior Goddess hunted and fought in the lands of Libya, Anatolia, Bulgaria, Greece, Armenia and Russia and were far from the mythical fantasy so many writers of today would have us believe.

I could not help noticing how far removed from contemporary images were the prehistoric and most ancient historic attitudes toward the thinking capacities and intellect of woman, for nearly everywhere the Goddess was revered as wise counselor and prophetess. The Celtic Cerridwen was the Goddess of Intelligence and Knowledge in the pre-Christian legends of Ireland, the priestesses of the Goddess Gaia provided the wisdom of divine revelation at pre-Greek sanctuaries, while the Greek Demeter and the Egyptian Isis were both invoked as law-givers and sage dispensers of righteous wisdom, counsel and justice. The Egyptian Goddess Maat represented the very order, rhythm and truth of the Universe. Ishtar of Mesopotamia was referred to as the Directress of People, the Prophetess, the Lady of Vision, while the archaeological records of the city of Nimrud, where Ishtar was worshiped, revealed that women served as judges and magistrates in the courts of law.

The more I read, the more I discovered. The worship of female deities appeared in every area of the world, presenting an image of woman that I had never before encountered. As a result, I began to ponder upon the power of myth and eventually to perceive these legends as more than the innocent childlike fables they first appeared to be. They were tales with a most specific point of view.

Myths present ideas that guide perception, conditioning us to think and even perceive in a particular way, especially when we are young and impressionable. Often they portray the actions of people who are rewarded or punished for their behavior, and we are encouraged to view these as examples to emulate or avoid. So many of the stories told to us from the time we are just old enough to understand deeply affect our attitudes and comprehension of the world about us and ourselves. Our ethics, morals, conduct, values, sense of duty and even sense of humor are often developed from simple childhood parables and fables. From them we learn what is socially acceptable in the society from which they come. They define good and bad, right and wrong, what is natural and what is unnatural among the people who hold the myths as meaningful. It was quite apparent that the myths and legends that grew from, and were propagated by, a religion in which the deity was female, and revered as wise, valiant, powerful and just provided very different images of womanhood from those which we are offered by the male-oriented religions of today. . . .

As I considered the power of myth, it became increasingly difficult to avoid questioning the influential effects that the myths accompanying the religions that worship male deities had upon my own image of what it meant to be born a female, another Eve, progenitress of my childhood faith. As a child, I was told that Eve had been made from Adam's rib, brought into being to be his companion and helpmate, to keep him from being lonely. As if this assignment of permanent second mate, never to be captain, was not oppressive enough to my future plans as a developing member of society, I next learned that Eve was considered to be foolishly gullible. My elders explained that she had been easily tricked by the promises of the perfidious serpent. She defied God and provoked Adam to do the same, thus ruining a good thing—the previously blissful life in the Garden of Eden. Why Adam himself was never thought to be equally as foolish was apparently never worth discussing. But identifying with Eve, who was presented as the symbol of all women, the blame was in some mysterious way mine—and God, viewing the whole affair as my fault, chose to punish *me* by decreeing: "I will greatly multiply your pain in childbearing; in pain you shall bring forth children, yet your desire shall be for your husband and he shall rule over you" (Gen. 3:16).

So even as a young girl I was taught that, because of Eve, when I grew up I was to bear my children in pain and suffering. As if this was not a sufficient penalty, instead of receiving compassion, sympathy or admiring respect for my courage, I was to experience this pain with guilt, the sin of my wrongdoing laid heavily upon me as punishment for simply being a woman, a daughter of Eve. To make matters worse, I was also supposed to accept the idea that men, as symbolized by Adam, in order to prevent any further foolishness on my part, were presented with the right to control me—to rule over me. According to the omnipotent male deity, whose righteousness and wisdom I was expected to admire and respect with a reverent awe, men were far wiser than women. Thus my penitent, submissive position as a female was firmly established by page three of the nearly one thousand pages of the Judeo-Christian Bible. . . .

It is time to bring the facts about the early female religions to light. They have been hidden away too long. With these facts we will be able to understand the earliest development of Judaism, Christianity and Islam and their reactions to the female religions and customs that preceded them. With these facts we will be able to understand how these reactions led to the political attitudes and historical events that occurred as these male-oriented religions were forming—attitudes and events that played such a major part in formulating the image of women during and since those times. With these facts we will be able to clear away the centuries of confusion, misunderstanding and suppression of information, so that we may gain the vantage point necessary for examining the image, status and roles still assigned to women today. With these facts we will gain the historical and political perspective that will enable us to refute the ideas of "natural or divinely ordained roles," finally opening the way for a more realistic recognition of the capabilities and potential of children and adults, whether female or male, as individual human beings. When the ancient sources of the gender stereotyping of today are better understood, the myth of the Garden of Eden will no longer be able to haunt us.

Source: Merlin Stone, *When God Was a Woman* (New York: Dial Press, 1976), pp. 1–7, 240–241. From WHEN GOD WAS A WOMAN by Merlin Stone. Copyright © 1976 by Merlin Stone. Used by permission of Doubleday, a division of Bantam Doubleday Dell Publishing Group, Inc.

Reading 2.4   BLOOD SACRIFICE   Walter Burkert

Walter Burkert's description of animal sacrifice in ancient Greece provides an example of blood sacrifice, an important feature of ancient urban spirituality. Burkert focuses on Greek practice in historical times, but he links the origin of sacrifice to the symbiotic relationship between prehistoric hunters and the hunted and comments on the sacrifices of Neolithic farmers. What animals were sacrificed? Why were domestic animals the victims? Outline the steps involved in the rituals. What aspect of the rituals suggests rebirth or restoration? What portion of the sacrifice is allotted to the gods? How does myth explain the division of the portions? What is meant by the fiction or "comedy of innocence?" What, in Burkert's view, is the meaning of sacrifice for humankind?

> The essence of the sacred act, which is hence often simply termed doing or making sacred or working sacred things, is in Greek practice a straightforward and far from miraculous process: the slaughter and consumption of a domestic animal for a god. The most noble sacrificial animal is the ox, especially the bull; the most common is the sheep, then the goat and the pig; the cheapest is the piglet. The sacrifice of poultry is also common, but other birds—geese, pigeons—to say nothing of fish, are rare.
>
> The sacrifice is a festive occasion for the community. The contrast with everyday life is marked with washing, dressing in clean garments, and adornment, in particular, wearing a garland woven from twigs on the head—a feature which does not yet appear in Homer. The animal chosen is to be perfect, and it too is adorned, entwined with ribbons, with its horns gilded. A procession escorts the animal to the altar. Everyone hopes as a rule that the animal will go to the sacrifice complaisantly, or rather voluntarily; edifying legends tell how animals pressed forward to the sacrifice on their own initiative when the time had come. A blameless maiden at the front of the procession carries on her head the sacrificial basket in which the knife for sacrifice lies concealed beneath grains of barley or cakes. A vessel containing water is also borne along, and often an incense burner; accompanying the procession is one or several musicians, normally a male or female flute-player. The goal is the stone altar or pile of ashes laid down or erected of old. Only there may and must blood be shed.
>
> Once the procession has arrived at the sacred spot, a circle is marked out which includes the site of sacrifice, the animal, and the participants: as the sacrificial basket and water vessel are borne around in a circle, the sacred is delimited from the profane. All stand around the altar. As a first communal action water is poured from the jug over the hands of each participant in turn: this is to begin, *archesthai*. The animal too is sprinkled with water, causing it to jerk its head, which is interpreted as the animal nodding its assent. The god at Delphi pronounced through the oracle: 'That which willingly nods at the washing of hands I say you may justly sacrifice.' A bull is given water to drink: so he too bows his head.
>
> The participants each take a handful of barley groats *(oulai, oulochytai)* from the sacrificial basket. Silence descends. Ceremonially and resoundingly, and with arms raised to the sky, the sacrificer recites a prayer, invocation, wish, and vow. Then, as if in confirmation, all hurl their barley groats forward onto the altar and the

sacrificial animal; in some rituals stones are thrown. This, together with the washing of hands, is also called a beginning, *katarchesthai.*

The sacrificial knife in the basket is now uncovered. The sacrificer grasps the knife and, concealing the weapon, strides up to the victim: he cuts some hairs from its forehead and throws them on the fire. This hair sacrifice is once more and for the last time a beginning, *aparchesthai.* No blood has flowed, but the victim is no longer inviolate.

The slaughter now follows. Smaller animals are raised above the altar and the throat is cut. An ox is felled by a blow with an axe and then the artery in the neck is opened. The blood is collected in a basin and sprayed over the altar and against the sides: to stain the altar with blood *(haimassein)* is a pious duty. As the fatal blow falls, the women must cry out in high, shrill tones: the Greek custom of the sacrificial cry marks the emotional climax. Life screams over death.

The animal is skinned and butchered; the inner organs, especially the heart and the liver *(splanchna),* are roasted on the fire on the altar first of all. Occasionally the heart is torn still beating from the body before all else. To taste the entrails immediately is the privilege and duty of the innermost circle of participants. The inedible remains are then consecrated: the bones are laid on the pyre prepared on the altar in just order. In Homer, beginnings from all limbs of the animal, small pieces of meat, are also placed on the pyre: the dismembered creature is to be reconstituted symbolically. Later texts and paintings emphasize the pelvic bones and the tail; in the Homeric formula it is the thigh bones which are burned. Food offerings, cakes and broth, are also burned in small quantities; above all, the sacrificer pours wine over the fire so that the alcohol flames up. Once the *splanchna* have been eaten and the fire has died down, the preparation of the actual meat meal begins, the roasting or boiling; this is generally of a profane character. Nevertheless, it is not infrequently prescribed that no meat must be taken away: all must be consumed without remainder in the sanctuary. The skin falls to the sanctuary or to the priest.

The ritual of animal sacrifice varies in detail according to the local ancestral custom, but the fundamental structure is identical and clear; animal sacrifice is ritualized slaughter followed by a meat meal. In this the rite as a sign of the sacred is in particular the preparation, the beginning, on the one hand, and the subsequent restitution on the other: sacralization and desacralization about a central act of killing attended with weapons, blood, fire, and a shrill cry. . . .

Historically, this ritual of the sacrificial meal may be traced to the situation of man before the discovery of agriculture: hunting, especially big-game hunting for cattle and horses, was the prime task of the male, and the principal source of food for the family. Killing to eat was an unalterable commandment, and yet the bloody act must always have been attended with a double danger and a double fear: that the weapon might be turned against a fellow hunter, and that the death of the prey might signal an end with no future, while man must always eat and so must always hunt. Important elements of the rites that came before and after the sacrifice may accordingly be traced to hunting customs, in particular the laying down of the bones, especially the thigh bones, the raising up of the skull, and the stretching out of the skin: attempts to restore the slain animal at least in outline. What Karl

Meuli called the 'comedy of innocence', the fiction of the willingness of the victim for sacrifice, is also to be seen in this context. In the sacrificial ritual, of course, these customs are closely interwoven with the specific forms of Neolithic peasant animal husbandry. The fact that the domestic animal, a possession and a companion, must nevertheless be slaughtered and eaten creates new conflicts and anxieties which are resolved in the ritual: the animal is consecrated, withdrawn from everyday life and subjugated to an alien will; not infrequently it is set free, turned back into a wild animal. The fruits of agriculture, corn and wine, are also incorporated into the execution of the deed, as beginning and end, marking as it were the boundaries of domesticated life from between which death erupts as from an atavistic chasm when the fruits of the earliest agriculture, the groats of barley, are transformed into symbolic missiles.

However difficult it may be for mythological and for conceptual reflection to understand how such a sacrifice affects the god, what it means for men is always quite clear: community, *koinonia*. Membership of the community is marked by the washing of hands, the encirclement and the communal throwing; an even closer bond is forged through the tasting of the *splanchna*. From a psychological and ethological point of view, it is the communally enacted aggression and shared guilt which created solidarity. The circle of the participants has closed itself off from outsiders; in doing so, the participants assume quite distinct roles in the communal action. First there is the carrying of the basket, the water vessel, the incense burner, and the torches, and the leading of the animals; then come the stages of the beginning, the praying, the slaughter, the skinning, and the dismemberment; this is followed by the roasting, first of the *splanchna,* then of the rest of the meat, then the libations of wine, and finally the distribution of the meat. Boys and girls, women and men all have their place and their task. Directing the action is the sacrificer, the priest, who prays, tastes, and makes libation; in his awe of the divine he also demonstrates his own power, a power which, although it brings in reality only death, appears *e contrario* to embrace life as well. The order of life, a social order, is constituted in the sacrifice through irrevocable acts; religion and everyday existence interpenetrate so completely that every community, every order must be founded through a sacrifice.

Source: Reprinted by permission of the publisher from *Greek Religion* by Walter Burkert, Cambridge, Mass: Harvard University Press, Copyright © 1985 by Basil Blackwell Publisher and Harvard University Press. Originally published–German as GRIECHISCHE RELIGION DER ARCHAISHEN UND KLASSISCHEN EPOCHE copyright © 1977 by Verlag Kohlhammer, Stuttgart.

Reading 2.5   THE MAKING OF HUMAN BEINGS: A MAYA MYTH

According to the Maya text the *Popul Vuh,* in the beginning there was only sky and sea and the gods. After the world received its order, the gods began the process of making humans, but they were dissatisfied with their first three attempts, as the humans they molded into being were flawed. The first model could not work or speak. The second model could not reproduce. The third model forgot to pray and failed to live according to the sacred calendar. The fourth attempt to make humans was successful, and it is this part of the Maya creation epic that is reproduced here. The *Popul Vuh* was written in the sixteenth century, after the conquest of Mesoamerica by the Spanish, but it contains an account of pre-Hispanic Maya myths, theology, and culture as seen through the eyes of the Quiche Maya, a people who occupied the Maya kingdom in the area of what is now Guatemala.

In this segment of the Maya myth, how many people were initially created? What were they made of? What are some of the implications of creating men first and later creating women? What did the gods regard as the flaw in this human model? What did they do to correct the flaw? Is there a similarity between the flawed character of the first people in this Maya creation account and the book of *Genesis*? After Adam and Eve had eaten of the tree of knowledge in disobedience to God's command, God is depicted as saying, *"See, the man has become like one of us, knowing good and evil; and now, he might reach out his hand and take also from the tree of life, and eat, and live forever"* (*Gen.* 3:22).

And here is the beginning of the conceptions of humans, and of the search for the ingredients of the human body. So they spoke, the Bearer, Begetter, the Makers, Modelers named Sovereign Plumed Serpent:

"The dawn has approached, preparations have been made, and morning has come for the provider, nurturer, born in the light, begotten in the light. Morning has come for humankind, for the people of the face of the earth," they said. It all came together as they went on thinking in the darkness, in the night, as they searched and they sifted, they thought and they wondered.

And here their thoughts came out in clear light. They sought and discovered what was needed for human flesh. It was only a short while before the sun, moon, and stars were to appear above the Makers and Modelers. Split Place, Bitter Water Place is the name: the yellow corn, white corn came from there.

And these are the names of the animals who brought the food: fox, coyote, parrot, crow. There were four animals who brought the news of the ears of yellow corn and white corn. They were coming from over there at Split Place, they showed the way to the split.

And this was when they found the staple foods.

And these were the ingredients for the flesh of the human work, the human design, and the water was for the blood. It became human blood, and corn was also used by the Bearer, Begetter.

And so they were happy over the provisions of the good mountain, filled with sweet things, thick with yellow corn, white corn, and thick with pataxte and cacao, countless zapotes, anonas, jocotes, nances, matasanos, sweets—the rich foods filling up the citadel named Split Place, Bitter Water Place. All the edible fruits were there: small staples, great staples, small plants, great plants. The way was shown by the animals.

And then the yellow corn and white corn were ground, and Xmucane did the grinding nine times. Food was used, along with the water she rinsed her hands with, for the creation of grease; it became human fat when it was worked by the Bearer, Begetter, Sovereign Plumed Serpent, as they are called.

After that, they put it into words:

the making, the modeling of our first mother-father,
with yellow corn, white corn alone for the flesh,
food alone for the human legs and arms,
for our first fathers, the four human works.

It was staples alone that made up their flesh.

These are the names of the first people who were made and modeled.

This is the first person: Jaguar Quitze.

And now the second: Jaguar Night.

And now the third: Not Right Now.

And the fourth: Dark Jaguar.

And these are the names of our first mother-fathers. They were simply made and modeled, it is said; they had no mother and no father. We have named the men by themselves. No woman gave birth to them, nor were they begotten by the builder, sculptor, Bearer, Begetter. By sacrifice alone, by genius alone they were made, they were modeled by the Maker, Modeler, Bearer, Begetter, Sovereign Plumed Serpent. And when they came to fruition, they came out human:

They talked and they made words.

They looked and they listened.

They walked, they worked.

They were good people, handsome, with looks of the male kind. Thoughts came into existence and they gazed; their vision came all at once. Perfectly they saw, perfectly they knew everything under the sky, whenever they looked. The moment they turned around and looked around in the sky, on the earth, everything was seen without any obstruction. They didn't have to walk around before they could see what was under the sky; they just stayed where they were.

As they looked, their knowledge became intense. Their sight passed through trees, through rocks, through lakes, through seas, through mountains, through plains. Jaguar Quitze, Jaguar Night, Not Right Now, and Dark Jaguar were truly gifted people.

And then they were asked by the builder and mason:

"What do you know about your being? Don't you look, don't you listen? Isn't your speech good, and your walk? So you must look, to see out under the sky. Don't you see the mountain-plain clearly? So try it," they were told.

And then they saw everything under the sky perfectly. After that, they thanked the Maker, Modeler:

"Truly now,
double thanks, triple thanks
that we've been formed, we've been given
our mouths, our faces,
we speak, we listen,
we wonder, we move,
our knowledge is good, we've understood
what is far and near,
and we've seen what is great and small
under the sky, on the earth.

Thanks to you we've been formed,
we've come to be made and modeled,
our grandmother, our grandfather,"

they said when they gave thanks for having been made and modeled. They understood everything perfectly, they sighted the four sides, the four corners in the sky, on the earth, and this didn't sound good to the builder and sculptor:

"What our works and designs have said is no good:

'We have understood everything, great and small,' they say." And so the Bearer, Begetter took back their knowledge:

"What should we do with them now? Their vision should at least reach nearby, they should see at least a small part of the face of the earth, but what they're saying isn't good. Aren't they merely 'works' and 'designs' in their very names? Yet they'll become as great as gods, unless they procreate, proliferate at the sowing, the dawning, unless they increase."

"Let it be this way: now we'll take them apart just a little, that's what we need. What we've found out isn't good. Their deeds would become equal to ours, just because their knowledge reaches so far. They see everything," so said

the Heart of Sky, Hurricane,
Newborn Thunderbolt, Sudden Thunderbolt,
Sovereign Plumed Serpent,
Bearer, Begetter,
Xpiyacoc, Xmucane,
Maker, Modeler,

as they are called. And when they changed the nature of their works, their designs, it was enough that the eyes be marred by the Heart of Sky. They were blinded as the face of a mirror is breathed upon. Their vision flickered. Now it was only from close up that they could see what was there with any clarity.

And such was the loss of the means of understanding, along with the means of knowing everything, by the four humans. The root was implanted.

And such was the making, modeling of our first grandfather, our father, by the Heart of Sky, Heart of Earth.

And then their wives and women came into being. Again, the same gods thought of it. It was as if they were asleep when they received them, truly beautiful women were there with Jaguar Quitze, Jaguar Night, Not Right Now, and Dark Jaguar. With their women there they really came alive. Right away they were happy at heart again, because of their wives.

Red Sea Turtle is the name of the wife of Jaguar Quitze.

Prawn House is the name of the wife of Jaguar Night.

Water Hummingbird is the name of the wife of Not Right Now.

Macaw House is the name of the wife of Dark Jaguar.

So these are the names of their wives, who became ladies of rank, giving birth to the people of the tribes, small and great.

Source: *Popol Vuh: The Mayan Book of the Dawn of Life,* trans. Dennis Tedlock (New York: Touchstone, 1996), pp. 145–149. Copyright © 1985 by Dennis Tedlock. Reprinted by permission.

Reading 2.6   THE QUEST FOR IMMORTALITY: THE STORY OF GILGAMESH

Gilgamesh was the legendary king of the Sumerian city-state Uruk (ca. 2650 B.C.E.) who was deified after his death. Tales of the exploits of Gilgamesh were committed to writing in Sumer around 2100 B.C.E. and were unified into a single text in Babylonia around 1800 B.C.E. A longer version of the adventures of Gilgamesh was compiled by the end of the second millennium. The *Gilgamesh Epic* includes heroic combat; the intervention of the gods; the domestication of the wild man Enkidu; the friendship formed by Gilgamesh and Enkidu; the death of the latter; the quest for immortality; and a harrowing journey to talk to Utnapishtim, the man who survived the flood and was deified by the gods. The epic ends with Gilgamesh's acceptance of human mortality. The section reprinted here is about Gilgamesh's grieving the death of his friend Enkidu. What does it mean that Gilgamesh felt singled out for loss? What kind of conversion accompanies the loss of someone who is loved dearly? Describe Gilgamesh's sense of aloneness. Why does he resolve to talk to Utnapishtim?

Gilgamesh wept bitterly for his friend.
He felt himself now singled out for loss
Apart from everyone else. The word Enkidu
Roamed through every thought
Like a hungry animal through empty lairs
In search of food. The only nourishment
He knew was grief, endless in its hidden source
Yet never ending hunger.

All that is left to one who grieves
Is convalescence. No change of heart or spiritual
Conversion, for the heart has changed
And the soul has been converted
To a thing that sees
How much it costs to lose a friend it loved.

It has grown past conversion to a world
Few enter without tasting loss
In which one spends a long time waiting
For something to move one to proceed.
It is that inner atmosphere that has
An unfamiliar gravity or none at all
Where words are flung out in the air but stay
Motionless without an answer,
Hovering about one's lips
Or arguing back to haunt
The memory with what one failed to say,
Until one learns acceptance of the silence
Amidst the new debris
Or turns again to grief
As the only source of privacy,
Alone with someone loved.

It could go on for years and years,
And has, for centuries,
For being human holds a special grief
Of privacy within the universe
That yearns and waits to be retouched
By someone who can take away
The memory of death.

Gilgamesh wandered through the desert
Alone as he had never been alone
When he had craved but not known what he craved;
The dryness now was worse than the decay.
The bored know nothing of this agony
Waiting for diversion they have never lost.
Death has taken the direction he had gained.
He was no more a king
But just a man who now had lost his way
Yet had a greater passion to withdraw
Into a deeper isolation. Mad,

Perhaps insane, he tried
To bring Enkidu back to life
To end his bitterness,
His fear of death.
His life became a quest
To find the secret of eternal life
Which he might carry back to give his friend.

He had put on the skins of animals
And thrown himself in the dust, and now
He longed to hear the voice of one
Who still used words as revelations;
He yearned to talk to Utnapishtim,
The one who had survived the flood
And death itself, the one who knew the secret.

Source: *Gilgamesh: A Verse Narrative,* trans. Herbert Mason (New York: New American Library, 1972), pp. 53–55. Excerpt from Gilgamesh. Copyright © 1970 by Herbert Mason. Reprinted by permission of Houghton Mifflin Co. All rights reserved.

Reading 2.7   THE EGYPTIAN *BOOK OF THE DEAD:*
JUDGMENT AT THE COURT OF OSIRIS

The Book of the Dead, as it is commonly called, consists of numerous texts created in different times and places and edited into a somewhat standard text by around 1400 B.C.E. It is principally a book of magical charms to enable the deceased to pass safely through the perilous journey in the underworld to life eternal. The following excerpt is known as the *Negative Confession.* It is an assertion of innocence by the deceased before forty-two divinities who sit in judgment at the court of Osiris. Each of the forty-two assertions of innocence in the *Negative Confession* begins with a warm greeting ("Hail, thou") to a divinity or supernatural power. How many of the assertions of innocence involve disclaiming wrongful behaviors in respect to humans? How many involve disclaiming wrongful behaviors in respect to the gods? What do the wrongdoings against humans and the gods teach us about Egyptian belief about gaining immortality? Do you believe that the dead were as innocent as they proclaimed, or were the assertions exaggerated? If they were exaggerated, what was their purpose?

The scribe Nebseni, triumphant, saith:

1. *"Hail, thou whose strides are long, who comest forth from Annu (Heliopolis), I have not done iniquity.*

2. *"Hail, thou who art embraced by flame, who comest forth from Kher-aba, I have not robbed with violence.*

3. *"Hail, thou divine Nose (Fenti), who comest forth from Khemennu (Hermopolis), I have not done violence to any man.*

4. *"Hail, thou who eatest shades, who comest forth from the place where the Nile riseth, I have not committed theft.*

5. *"Hail, Neha-hau, who comest forth from Re-stau, I have not slain man or woman.*

6. *"Hail, thou double Lion-god, who comest forth from heaven, I have not made light the bushel.*

7. *"Hail, thou whose two eyes are like flint, who comest forth from Sekhem (Letopolis), I have not acted deceitfully.*

8. *"Hail, thou Flame, who comest forth as thou goest back, I have not purloined the things which belong unto God.*

9. *"Hail, thou Crusher of bones, who comest forth from Suten-henen (Heracleopolis), I have not uttered falsehood.*

10. *"Hail, thou who makest the flame to wax strong, who cometh forth from Het-ka-Ptah (Memphis), I have not carried away food.*

11. *"Hail, Qerti, (i.e., the two sources of the Nile), who come forth from Amentet, I have not uttered evil words.*

12. *"Hail, thou whose teeth shine, who comest forth from Ta-she (i.e., the Fayyum), I have attacked no man.*

13. *"Hail, thou who dost consume blood, who comest forth from the house of slaughter, I have not killed the beasts, which are the property of God.*

14. *"Hail, thou who dost consume the entrails, who comest forth from the* mabet *chamber, I have not acted deceitfully.*

15. "Hail, thou god of Right and Truth, who comest forth from the city of double Maati, I have not laid waste the lands which have been plowed.

16. "Hail, thou who goest backward, who comest forth from the city of Bast (Bubastis), I have never pried into matters to make mischief.

17. "Hail, Aati, who comest forth from Annu (Heliopolis), I have not set my mouth in motion against any man.

18. "Hail, thou who art double evil, who comest forth from the nome of Ati, I have not given way to wrath concerning myself without a cause.

19. "Hail, thou serpent Uamemti, who comest forth from the house of slaughter, I have not defiled the wife of a man.

20. "Hail, thou who lookest upon what is brought to him, who comest forth from the Temple of Amsu, I have not committed any sin against purity.

21. "Hail, Chief of the divine Princes, who comest forth from the city of Nehatu, I have not struck fear into any man.

22. "Hail, Khemiu (i.e., Destroyer), who comest forth from the Lake of Kaui, I have not encroached upon sacred times and seasons.

23. "Hail, thou who orderest speech, who comest forth from Urit, I have not been a man of anger.

24. "Hail, thou Child, who comest forth from the Lake of Heq-at, I have not made myself deaf to the words of right and truth.

25. "Hail, thou disposer of speech, who comest forth from the city of Unes, I have not stirred up strife.

26. "Hail, Basti, who comest forth from the Secret city, I have made no man to weep.

27. "Hail, thou whose face is turned backward, who comest forth from the Dwelling, I have not committed acts of impurity, neither have I lain with men.

28. "Hail, Leg of fire, who comest forth from Akhekhu, I have not eaten my heart.

29. "Hail, Kenemti, who comest forth from the city of Kenemet, I have abused no man.

30. "Hail, thou who bringest thine offering, who comest forth from the city of Sau (Sais) I have not acted with violence.

31. "Hail, thou god of faces, who comest forth from the city of Tchefet, I have not judged hastily.

32. "Hail, thou who givest knowledge, who comest forth from Unth, I have not . . . and I have not taken vengeance upon the god.

33. "Hail, thou lord of two horns, who comest forth from Satiu, I have not multiplied my speech overmuch.

34. "Hail, Nefer-Tem, who comest forth from Het-ka-Ptah (Memphis), I have not acted with deceit, and I have not worked wickedness.

35. "Hail, Tem-Sep, who comest forth from Tattu, I have not uttered curses on the King.

36. "Hail, thou whose heart doth labor, who comest forth from the city of Tebti, I have not fouled water.

37. "Hail, Ahi of the water, who comest forth from Nu, I have not made haughty my voice.

38. "Hail, thou who givest commands to mankind, who comest forth from Sau, I have not cursed the god.

39. "Hail, Neheb-nefert, who comest forth from the Lake of Nefer, I have not behaved with insolence.

40. "Hail, Neheb-kau, who comest forth from thy city, I have not sought for distinctions.

41. "Hail, thou whose head is holy, who comest forth from thy habitations, I have not increased my wealth, except with such things as are justly mine own possessions.

42. "Hail, thou who bringest thine own arm, who comest forth from Aukert (underworld), I have not thought scorn of the god who is in my city."

Source: "The Book of the Dead," trans. E. A.W. Budge, in *Sacred Books and Early Literature of the East*, vol. 2 (New York: Parke, Austin, and Lipscomb, 1917), pp. 258–261.

Reading 2.8   TRANSFORMED BY ISIS: *THE GOLDEN ASS OF APULEIUS*

Lucius Apuleius

The Golden Ass of Apuleius or *The Metamorphoses of Lucius Apuleius* was written by the Roman writer and Platonic philosopher Lucius Apuleius (ca. 124–170 C.E.). *The Golden Ass* is a novel about the adventures of a young man who was transformed by magic into an ass and, after numerous adventures and misadventures, was restored to human form by the goddess Isis. Book 11, which is excerpted here, begins with Lucius, embodied in an ass, purifying himself in the sea and praying to the Queen of Heaven variously identified as Ceres, Venus, Diana (the goddess of childbirth), and Proserpine, or by whatever name she was known. The goddess Isis manifested herself to Lucius in a dream. How does Isis identify herself? How does the idea of Isis as a single godhead venerated over all the earth under manifold forms provide a resolution to the problem of the relationship of one God to the many divinities? Isis was responsive to Lucius's petition and transformed him from the body of an ass to that of a man, but what spiritual transformation did the goddess demand of Lucius in return? Although this reading is abstracted from a novel, it provides a glimpse of the conversion or salvation experiences associated with the initiation cults or mystery religions.

About the first watch of the night I was aroused by sudden panic. Looking up I saw the full orb of the Moon shining with peculiar luster and that very moment emerging from the waves of the sea. Then the thought came to me that this was the hour of silence and loneliness when my prayers might avail. For I knew that the moon was the primal Goddess of supreme sway; that all human beings are the creatures of her providence; that not only cattle and wild beasts but even inorganic objects are vitalized by the divine influence of her light; that all the bodies which are on earth, or in the heavens, or in the sea, increase when she waxes, and decline when she wanes. Considering this, therefore, and feeling that Fate was now satiated with my endless miseries and at last licensed a hope of salvation, I determined to implore the august image of the risen Goddess.

So, shaking off my tiredness, I scrambled to my feet and walked straight into the sea in order to purify myself. I immersed my head seven times because, according to the divine Pythagoras, that number is specially suited for all ritual acts; and then, speaking with lively joy, I lifted my tear-wet face in supplication to the irresistible Goddess:

"Queen of Heaven *(regina caeli),* whether you are fostering Ceres the motherly nurse of all growth, who, gladdened at the discovery of your lost daughter, abolished the brutish nutriment of the primitive acorn and pointed the way to gentler food, as is yet shown in the tilling of the fields of Eleusis; or whether you are celestial Venus who in the first moment of Creation mingled the opposing sexes in the generation of mutual desires, and who, after sowing in humanity the seeds of indestructible continuing life, are now worshiped in the wave-washed shrine of Paphos; or whether you are the sister of Phoebus, who by relieving the pangs of childbirth travail with soothing remedies have brought safe into the world lives innumerable, and who are now venerated in the thronged sanctuary of Ephesus; or whether you are Proserpine, terrible with the howls of midnight, whose triple face has power to ward off all the assaults of ghosts and to close the cracks in the earth, and who wander through many a grove, propitiated in divers manners, illuminating the walls of all cities with beams of female light, nurturing the glad seeds in the earth with your damp heat, and dispensing abroad your dim radiance when the sun has abandoned us—O by whatever name, and by whatever rites, and in whatever form, it is permitted to invoke you, come now and succour me in the hour of my calamity. Support my broken life, and give me rest and peace after the tribulations of my lot. Let there be an end to the toils that weary me, and an end to the snares that beset me. Remove from me the hateful shape of a beast, and restore me to the sight of those that love me. Restore me to Lucius, my lost self. But if an offended god pursues me implacably, then grant me death at least since life is denied me."

Having thus poured forth my prayer and given an account of my bitter sufferings, I drowsed and fell asleep on the same sand-couch as before. But scarcely had I closed my eyes before a god-like face emerged from the midst of the sea with lineaments that gods themselves would revere. Then gradually I saw the whole body, resplendent image that it was, rise out of the scattered deep and stand beside me. . . .

"Behold, Lucius," she said, "moved by your prayer I come to you—I, the natural mother of all life, the mistress of the elements, the first child of time, the supreme divinity, the queen of those in hell, the first among those in heaven, the uniform manifestation of all gods and goddesses—I, who govern by my nod the crests of light in the sky, the purifying wafts of the ocean, and the lamentable silences of hell—I, whose single godhead is venerated all over the earth under manifold forms, varying rites, and changing names. Thus, the Phrygians that are the oldest human stock call me Pessinuntia, Mother of the Gods. The aboriginal races of Attica call me Cecropian Minerva. The Cyprians in their island-home call me Paphian Venus. The archer Cretans call me Diana Dictynna. The three-tongued Sicilians call me Stygian Proserpine. The Eleusinians call me the ancient goddess Ceres. Some call me Juno. Some call me Bellona. Some call me Hecate. Some call me Rhamnusia. But those who are enlightened by the earliest rays of that divinity the sun, the Ethiopians, the Arii, and the Egyptians who excel in antique lore, all worship me with their ancestral ceremonies and call me by my true name, Queen Isis.

"Behold, I am come to you in your calamity. I am come with solace and aid. Away then with tears. Cease to moan. Send sorrow packing. Soon through my providence shall the sun of your salvation arise. Hearken therefore with care unto what I bid. Eternal religion has dedicated to me the day which will be born from the womb of this present darkness. Tomorrow my priests will offer to me the first fruits of the year's navigation. They will consecrate in my name a new-built ship. For now the tempests of the winter are lulled; the roaring waves of the sea are quieted; and the waters are again navigable. You must await this ceremony, without anxiety and without wandering thoughts. For the priest at my suggestion will carry in the procession a crown of roses attached to the sistrum in his right hand; and you must unhesitatingly push your way through the crowd, join the procession, and trust in my good will. Approach close to the priest as if you meant to kiss his hand, and gently crop the roses. Instantly you will slough the hide of this beast on which I have long looked with abhorrence.

"Fear for no detail of the work to which I once put my hand. Even at this moment of time in which I appear before you, I am also in another place instructing my priest in a vision what is to be brought to pass. By my command the crush of people will open to give you way; and despite all the gay rites and ferial revelries not one of my worshipers will feel disgust because of the unseemly shape in which you are incarcerated. Neither will any one of them misinterpret your sudden metamorphosis or rancorously use it against you.

"Only remember, and keep the remembrance fast in your heart's deep core, that all the remaining days of your life must be dedicated to me, and that nothing can release you from this service but death. Neither is it aught but just that you should devote your life to her who redeems you back into humanity. You shall live blessed. You shall live glorious under my guidance; and when you have traveled your full length of time and you go down into death, there also, on that hidden side of earth, you shall dwell in the Elysian Fields and frequently adore me for my favors. . . .

"More, if you are found to merit my love by your dedicated obedience, religious devotion, and constant chastity, you will discover that it is within my power to prolong your life beyond the limit set to it by Fate."

At last the end of this venerable oracle was reached, and the invincible Goddess ebbed back into her own essence. No time was lost. Immediately snapping the threads of sleep, and wrung with a sweat of joy and terror, I wakened. Wondering deeply at so direct a manifestation of the Goddess's power, I sprinkled myself with salt water; and eager to obey her in every particular, I repeated over to myself the exact words in which she had framed her instructions. Soon the sun of gold arose and sent the clouds of thick night flying; and lo, a crowd of people replenished the streets, filing in triumphal religious procession. It seemed to me that the whole world, independent of my own high spirits, was happy. Cattle of every kind, the houses, the very day, all seemed to lift serene faces brimful with jollity. For sunny and placid weather had suddenly come upon us after a frosty yesterday; and the tuneful birdlets, coaxed out by the warmths of the Spring, were softly singing sweet hymns of blandishment to the Mother of the Stars, the Producer of the Seasons, the Mistress of the Universe. The trees also, both those that blossomed into fruit and those that were content to yield only sterile shade, were loosed by the southerly breezes; and glistening gaily with their budded leaves, they swished their branches gently in sibilant sighs. The crash of storm was over; and the waves, no longer mountainous with swirling foam, lapped quietly upon the shore. The dusky clouds were routed; and the heavens shone with clear sheer splendor of their native light.

By this time the forerunners of the main procession were gradually appearing, every man richly decked as his votive fancy suggested. One fellow was girded about the middle like a soldier; another was scarfed like a huntsman with hunting-knife and shoes; another, wearing gilt sandals, silken gown, and costly ornaments, walked with a woman's mincing gait; another with his leg-harness, targe, helm, and sword, looked as if he had come straight from gladiatorial games. Then, sure enough, there passed by a man assuming the magistrate with fasces and purple robe, and a man playing the philosopher with cloak, staff, wooden clogs, and goat's beard; a fowler with bird-lime elbowing a fisherman with hooks. I saw also a tame she-bear dressed as a matron and carried in a sedan-chair; an ape with bonnet of plaited straw and saffron-hued garment, holding in his hand a golden cup and representing Phrygian Ganymede the shepherd; and lastly, an ass with wings glued on his back ambling after an old man—so that you could at once have exclaimed that one was Pegasus and the other Bellerophon, and would have laughed at the pair in the same breath.

Into this playful masquerade of the overflowing populace the procession proper now marched its way. Women glowing in their white vestments moved with symbolic gestures of delight. Blossomy with the chaplets of the Spring, they scattered flowerets out of the aprons of their dresses all along the course of the holy pageant. Others, who bore polished mirrors on their backs, walked before the Goddess and reflected all the people coming after as if they were advancing towards the Image. Others, again, carrying combs of ivory, went through the various caressive motions of combing and dressing the queenly tresses of their Lady; or they sprinkled the street with drops of unguent and genial balm.

There was a further host of men and women who followed with lanterns, torches, waxtapers, and every other kind of illumination in honor of Her who was begotten of the Stars of Heaven. Next came the musicians, interweaving in sweetest measures the notes of pipe and flute; and then a supple choir of chosen youths, clad in snow-white holiday tunics, came singing a delightful song which an expert poet, by grace of the Muses, had composed for music, and which explained the antique origins of this day of worship. Pipers also, consecrated to mighty Sarapis, played the tunes annexed to the god's cult on pipes with transverse-mouthpieces and reeds held sidelong towards the right ear; and a number of officials kept calling out, "Make way for the Goddess!"

Then there came walking a great band of men and women of all classes and ages, who had been initiated into the Mysteries of the Goddess and who were all clad in linen garments of the purest white. The women had their hair anointed and hooded in limpid silk; but the men had shaven shining polls. Terrene stars of mighty deity were these men and women; and they kept up a shrill continuous tingle upon sistra of brass and silver and even gold. The chief ministers of the ceremony, dressed in surplices of white linen tightly drawn across the breast and hanging loose to the feet, bore the relics of the mighty gods exposed to view. The first priest held on high a blazing lamp—not at all like the lamps that illumine our evening suppers; for its long bowl was gold, and it thrust up from an aperture in the middle a fat flame. The second priest was similarly vestured, but he carried in both hands model altars to which the auxiliary love of the supreme Goddess has given the fitting title of Auxilia. The third priest grasped a palm-tree with all its leaves subtly wrought in gold, and the wand of Mercury. The fourth priest displayed the Symbol of Equity; a left hand molded with open palm, since the left hand seemed to be more adapted to administer equity than the busier, craftier right hand. The same man also bore a vessel of gold rounded into the shape of a woman's breast, from which he let milk trickle to the ground. The fifth priest had a winnowing-fan constructed with thickset sprigs of gold; and the sixth priest had an amphora.

After these came the Gods themselves, deigning to walk before our eyes on the feet of men. First we saw the dreadful messenger of the gods of heaven and hell, Anubis, with his face blackened on one side and painted gold on the other, lifting on high his dog's head and bearing his rod in his left hand. Close upon his heels followed a Cow, emblem of the Goddess that is fruitful mother of all, sitting upright upon the proud shoulders of her blessed worshiper. Another man carried the chest that contained the Secret Things of her unutterable mystery. Another bore in his beatified bosom a venerable effigy of Supreme Deity, which showed no likeness to any bird or beast, wild or tame, or even to man, but which was worthy of reverence because of its exquisite invention and originality: a symbol inexpressible of the true religion that should be veiled in Deep Silence. This effigy was of burnished gold, made as follows: a small urn was delicately hollowed out with a round bottom; the strange hieroglyphs of the Egyptians covered its outside; the spout was shaped rather low but jutting out like a funnel; the handle on the other side projected with a wide sweep; and on this stood an asp, stretching up his scaly, wrinkled, swollen throat and twining round the whole length.

At last the glorious moment which the presiding Goddess had promised me was at hand. For the priest, adorned exactly as she had described, neared with the instrument of my salvation. In his right hand he carried the Goddess's sistrum and a crown of roses. Ah, by Hercules, a crown indeed it was for me, since by the providence of the overmastering gods, after so many toils of experience, I was now to find my efforts crowned with victory over Fortune, my cruel foe.

However, though shaken with up-bubbling joy, I did not dash immediately forwards; for I did not want the peaceful order of the holy procession to be disturbed by an unruly beast. Instead, I nosed through the crowd with a polite all-but-human tread and a sidelong twist of my body; and, as the people, clearly by the Goddess's dispensation, disparted to let me through, I slowly approached the flowers. But the priest, as was obvious to me, recollected his admonitory vision of the night. He at once stopped stock-still; and spontaneously raising his right hand, he held the bunch up to my mouth. Trembling, with a thudding heart; I seized the crown in which some fine rose blooms were brightly woven; and greedily I masticated the whole lot.

Nor did the heavenly promise fail. At once my ugly and beastly form left me. My rugged hair thinned and fell; my huge belly sank in; my hooves separated out into fingers and toes; my hands ceased to be feet and adapted themselves to the offices of my erected state; my long neck telescoped itself; my face and head became round; my flapping ears shrank to their old size; my stony molars waned into human teeth; and my tail, the worst cross of my ass-days, simply disappeared.

The populace stood in blinking wonder; and the devotees adored the Goddess for the miraculous revelation of her power in a metamorphosis which partook of the shifting pageantry of a dream. Lifting their hands to heaven, with one voice the beholders rendered testimony to the lovingkindness of the Goddess thus signally declared. As for me, I remained nailed to the spot in mute stupefaction; for my wits were scattered by the shock of joy, and I was quite at a loss. What was the right utterance with which to begin my new life? Where was my voice to come from? How was I most auspiciously to employ my newborn tongue? What phrases could I choose to express my gratitude to so great a Goddess?

Source: *Apuleius: The Golden Ass,* trans. Jack Lindsay (Bloomington: Indiana University Press, 1962), pp. 235–243. Reprinted by permission of Indiana University Press.

CHAPTER 3

TRIBAL RELIGIONS
IN HISTORICAL TIMES

Navajo shaman *Gray Squirrel blends the sands of a sand painting as part of a four-day ritual to bring rain (Farmington, New Mexico, ca. 1978).*

The range and number of tribal peoples have been steadily reduced by the extension, in both ancient and modern times, of politically centralized states. Today, the entire inhabitable earth is under the jurisdiction of state systems. Consequently, tribal peoples are no longer autonomous; they are ethnic groups with varying degrees of self-determination within modern states. They have been changed by their interaction with dominant cultures, but they are very much alive. Data reported by the International Labour Organisation in 1993 estimated the population of indigenous people (those who subsist by hunting and gathering, horticulture, or pastoralism) at slightly over 300 million (about 5 percent of the earth's population) and the number of distinct tribes at 5,000.

The number of people who follow tribal religions is difficult to determine. There is no one-to-one relationship between traditional religionists and the 300 million indigenous peoples, because many of the latter have been incorporated into other religions. Furthermore, this figure does not include those tribal peoples engaged in nontraditional occupations who are cultural traditionalists. Demographics compiled by David B. Barrett and Todd M. Johnson in the *1998 Britannica Book of the Year* placed the number of tribal and *shamanistic* religionists at 231.7 million, or 4 percent of the total world population. But this does not take into account tribal ethnics who participate in pantribal religions or who see themselves as both traditionalists and nontraditionalists (for example, Christians).

There are reasons to be optimistic about the future of tribal religions, but their displacement has been extensive. At the outset of the twentieth century, there were over one thousand African traditional religions, and a majority of Africans south of the Sahara were traditionalists. At the century's end, around 10 percent of Africa's 700 million people maintain traditional faiths, and almost 90 percent are Christians or Muslims.[1] Sharp declines have occurred elsewhere, but as in Africa, traditional religions survive in the Americas, the Arctic, Asia, Eurasia, and Oceania.

PROBLEMS OF NAMING

As we saw in Chapter 2, the naming of oral peoples is a contentious subject. Modern Westerners have been both attracted to and repelled by peoples they regarded as "primitive." Some pronounced them animalistic, mendacious, and lascivious and wondered if they had souls. Native Americans and black Africans were regarded as naturally inferior to civilized peoples and thus suited to be servants or slaves. Such a judgment was articulated in 1550 during deliberations about the status of Indians at Valladolid, Spain, by the Spanish scholar Juan Gines de Sepulveda: the Indians, he said, "are inferior to the Spanish as are children to adults, women to men, and indeed, one might even say, as apes are to men."[2] Other westerners took a different but equally distorted position, depicting traditional peoples as "noble savages," that is, as generous, innocent, and unrepressed primal beings.

Older scholarship and popular usage characterize the religions of oral peoples as *animistic, totemistic, primitive,* and *pagan.* Recent scholarship has countered the negative connotations of such labels by referring to tribal peoples and their religions collectively as *indigenous, nonliterate, primal, simple ethnic, traditional,* and *tribal.* A similar sensitivity is evident in their geographical and cultural grouping by designations such as *African traditional* and *Native American. First Peoples* has also surfaced in Canada and the United States as a collective term for Indians and Eskimos.

There are problems with these "neutral" labels as well. **Tribal religions** and traditions are no longer exclusively oral or nonliterate; they are articulated through the written, as well as the spoken, word. *Primal* connotes "original," but **primal religions** in historic times are far removed from the prehistoric beginnings of religion. *Simple ethnic* has limited value, because such societies no longer exist as autonomous entities. *Traditional* and *indigenous* are general terms that are applicable, for example, to traditional Jews and indigenous Italians, as well as to tribalists. Furthermore, when indigenous peoples are defined as peoples whose social structures and modes of subsistence are preurban and preindustrial, this definition excludes peoples ordinarily included in the category. For example, black Africans are indigenous in the sense of being native to Africa but the majority are not indigenous in the narrow meaning of the term.

Tribal is also a flawed label. In some contexts, a *tribe* is defined as a type of preurban farming society composed of social segments based on lineage. So defined, tribes are sometimes seen as a rudimentary stage in the evolution of human culture from bands to tribes to chiefdoms to kingdoms. Indigenous peoples have a different perspective; they argue that recognition of their existence as tribes by modern states implicitly acknowledges their existence as nations. In these peoples' struggle for autonomy and self-determination, the term, *nation* (defined as a people united by culture, kinship, language, and territory) is a preferred alternative to *tribe* (for example, the Navajo Nation).

No labeling of oral societies and religions is entirely satisfactory. We use the terms preferred by contemporary scholarship (**indigenous** and **traditional**) but also employ the more problematic term *tribal. Indigenous* and *tribal* are used here in two senses. First, they refer to the societies and religions of oral peoples whose social structures ranged from bands to chiefdoms and who subsisted by hunting and gathering, farming, pastoralism, or some combination thereof. The terms **simple ethnic society** and **simple ethnic religion** have similar meanings. Second, because autonomous simple ethnic societies no longer exist, *tribal* and *indigenous* refer to people who maintain some aspects of their traditional culture within modern state systems, a meaning that permits us to include religions formerly grounded in premodern African kingdoms. As noted in Chapter 1, tribal peoples did not name their "religions"; thus, discourse about their religions has been coupled with discussion of their identity as a people (for example, the religion of the Navajo).

TRIBAL RELIGIONS AND SOCIETIES

Over the course of prehistoric and historic time there have been thousands of tribal societies. Each one has been unique, but the features described here are generally applicable to all of them before they became ethnic groups within state systems. Simple ethnic societies were composed of people who shared a common language, tradition, worldview, ethos, and morality. Each was a kinship circle united by real or assumed biological relationships. Kinship and peoplehood were so engrained that tribes often identified themselves with what is prototypically human; for example, the self-naming of the Navajo is *Dineh*, meaning "the people." Ethnocentrism is not exclusive to tribal ethnics, and its persistence suggests that the insider-outsider dyad is deeply engrained in human consciousness.

Tribal societies were characterized by preliterate languages, relatively unstratified social structures, decentralized polities, simple technologies, and modes of subsistence ranging from hunting and gathering to nonintensive forms of agriculture.

Dancers at the Old Basilica of Guadalupe during the annual pilgrimage to the shrine of Mexico's patron saint, the Virgin of Guadalupe integrate Christian and Native American elements.

Political processes ranged from consensus among adult members of bands to village councils made up of heads of families to a collection of villages led by a chief. Group decisions were usually by consensus and noncoercive; clans or subgroups that disagreed were not obligated to follow the will of the majority. In contrast, state systems (monarchies, oligarchies, and democracies) had the power to maintain order coercively. Tribal ethnics are no longer autonomous or necessarily nonliterate, but they continue to value kinship, oral traditions, and consensus. Many live in urban centers and engage in nontraditional vocations, but some sustain themselves through ancient patterns of existence in nonurban and nonindustrial contexts.

ORALITY AND RELIGIOUS EXPRESSION

It is axiomatic of scientific studies of religion to emphasize that society and culture influence religious expression. No feature of tribal culture affected primal religions more than their orality. In tribal societies, all knowledge was passed orally from generation to generation. Imagine yourself in a society in which nothing was written down. Knowledge of one's ancestors; artistic and technological expertise; knowledge of plants, animals, and seasons; and a complex body of stories, rites, and medicines were memorized and preserved orally. The consequences for religion were enormous. There were no sacred books. Everything sacred—knowledge of spirit beings and of the power that healed, transformed, and empowered—was handed down orally. Procedures for preserving and transmitting the principal "texts" of oral societies were complex and involved the mastery of extensive bodies of tradition. A vivid image of the awesome power of human memory and the vulnerability of an entirely oral tradition is contained in an African philosopher's observation: "When an old man dies, a library is destroyed."

Oral traditions, like written ones, are embodied in a complex symbolic universe. A Sioux ceremonial pipe is not simply a pipe. As contemporary Sioux holy man John Lame Deer observed, every part of the sacred pipe is symbolic. The bison calf carved on it represents the earth; the twelve eagle feathers hanging from its stem stand for the sky and twelve moons. The four ribbons attached to the stem represent the four cardinal directions: a red ribbon symbolizes the east, white the north, yellow the south, and black the west. The pipe's bowl signifies the blood of the Sioux, the stem their backbone, the bowl their head, the opening in the bowl their mouth, and "the smoke rising from it is our breath, the visible breath of our people." Sioux pipes unite "as one, earth, sky, and all living things."[3]

Traditional peoples regard words as having power, as magically accomplishing their ends. Prayer and song, blessing and cursing, incantation and spell are potent speech acts. In some traditions, creation is depicted as an act of speech. For example, in a Dogon creation myth, the Supreme Being (Amma) spoke seven creative "words" that were essential to bringing forth the world. Belief in the power of the spoken word is evident in the traditional African approach to everyday life: "Sowing alone is not sufficient to make the maize germinate and grow; speech and song must be added, for it is the word that makes the grasses germinate, the fruits grow, the cow go in calf and give milk. Even handicrafts need the word if they are to succeed."[4] This sense of the power of language is shared by contemporaries who, like Chickasaw novelist and poet Linda Hogan, have embraced the written as well as the spoken word: "I hold to the traditional Indian views on language, that words have power, that words become entities. When I write I keep in mind that it is a form of power and salvation that is for the planet. If it is good and enters the world, perhaps it will counteract the destruction that seems to be getting so close to us. I think of language and poems, even fiction, as prayers and small ceremonies."[5]

Myths are the sacred "texts" of oral traditions. They are stories of when the gods and the first human beings established the order of life and the way life should be lived. Myths were sometimes acted out, a union of saying and doing evident in John Lame Deer's remark: "Dancing and praying—it's the same thing."[6] An adage of the Acoma people of New Mexico reminds us that "telling stories is reliving the experience." This wisdom applies not only to individual and collective stories but also to the manner in which tribal peoples entered the time of origins by retelling and ritually recreating the myths. Myth and ritual are "arrows" of transcendence—that is, rhythmic and sometimes ecstatic modes of expression with a narrative thread and dramatic resonance that are at once gifts from the sacred and gateways to the sacred. Words of the Inuit (Eskimo) *shaman* Orpingalik bear witness to their power: "All my being is song, and I sing as I draw breath. . . . It is just as necessary for me to sing as it is to breathe."[7] Those who lacked stories and songs felt spiritually impoverished, as evidenced by the lament of a Navajo who had mastered none of his people's ceremonial songs: "I have always been a poor man, I do not know a single song."[8]

The individual and corporate identities of humans are shaped by stories and rituals. Destruction of a people's identity entails a loss of stories and ceremonies. This is evident in the Cheyenne saying, "We will always remember who we are as long as we keep dancing."[9] It is apparent in the following excerpt from Leslie Marmon Silko's novel *Ceremony*, in which the conflict between Native American and Euro-American traditions underlies the words. Silko is a member of the Laguna Pueblo in New Mexico.

> I will tell you something about stories,
>   [he said]
>   They aren't just entertainment.
>   Don't be fooled.
> They are all we have, you see,
>   all we have to fight off
>   illness and death.
> You don't have anything
>   if you don't have the stories.
>   Their evil is mighty
> but it can't stand up to our stories.
> So they try to destroy the stories
> let the stories be confused or forgotten.
>   They would like that
>   They would be happy
> Because we would be defenseless then.[10]

SOCIAL STRUCTURES AND TRIBAL SPIRITUALITY

Tribal spirituality is rooted in the life of a particular people and cannot easily be extended beyond the tribal circle. A simple ethnic society constituted a natural religious group in which inclusion followed from birth rather than from conversion and creedal affirmation. Such societies often included voluntary associations based on age, gender, or special interest, but the principle of inclusion in the society as a whole was kinship. Incorporation of outsiders occurred by intermarriage, capture, and other nonconversionist forms of contact.

Generally, the more differentiated the society, the more formalized religious leadership and institutions become. *Shamanic* leadership was typical of food gatherers and pastoralists. Such figures were authenticated by direct contact with the spirit world rather than the authority of a formalized office. In more stratified societies, priests were the chief intermediaries. Aware of his people's lack of elaborate religious institutions, the Apache warrior and Christian convert Geronimo noted in his autobiography that they had nonetheless a religious life: "We had no churches, no religious organization, no sabbath day, no holidays, and yet we worshipped. Sometimes the whole tribe would assemble to sing and pray, sometimes a smaller number perhaps only two or three."[11]

Religion was involved in every aspect of tribal life. Its pervasiveness is evident in African Christian John Mbiti's observation that "wherever the African is, there is his religion: he carries it to the fields where he is sowing seeds or harvesting a new crop, he takes it with him to the beer party or to attend a funeral. . . . Although many African languages do not have a word for religion as such, it nevertheless accompanies the individual from long before his birth to long after his physical death."[12]

The interplay of religion and society can be illustrated by the Dinka, an African people of the southern Sudan. Cattle are central to the Dinka, and references to cattle permeate their lives. Male names often begin with the prefix for "bull" or "ox" and those of women with the prefix for "cow." A man courts a woman by parading his ox and praising it in song and poetry. Cattle are the Dinka's chief form of compensation: they are gifts of exchange to a bride's family and compensatory satisfaction for offenses such as homicide or adultery. Cattle are also the Dinka's chief ceremonial link between the divine and the human. As gifts from the gods, ultimately cattle belong to the supreme God and are returned to him on special occasions through sacrifice.[13]

TRADITION AND CHANGE IN TRIBAL SOCIETIES

Simple ethnic societies were relatively "closed": each was autonomous and ethnically homogeneous. Roles were limited. Each generation followed in the footsteps of their parents. Authentic life repeated the patterns established by the gods and ancestors in the beginning, and human behavior was modeled on their example. What was handed down was familiar and reassuring. "Go the way many people go," advises an African proverb, "If you're alone, you will have reason to lament."

Nonetheless, tribal societies did change. Internally induced social change was triggered by developments in material culture, migrations, and revelations from the spirit world. Externally induced change resulted from interaction with other peoples and changes in the natural environment. Internecine violence usually did not involve major revisions in customs and worldview. Changes resulting from contact with outsiders were both noncoercive (ideas and material culture) and coercive (conquest and forced migrations). The imposition of state systems has been the most coercive source of change.[14] Innovations spread from one group to another through **cultural diffusion** or developed independently, a phenomenon referred to as **parallel development.** Cultural diffusion is evident in the gradual spread of agriculture from Southwest Asia to Greece and subsequently throughout Europe. Parallel development is evident in the independent origins of agriculture in Asia, Oceania, and America.

RELIGIOUS BELIEFS OF TRIBAL PEOPLES

The beliefs of tribal peoples are embodied in stories and rituals rather than in formalized doctrines and creeds. As noted, myths (sacred stories) constitute the normative texts or scriptures of tribal religions. Their principal themes—creation, past worlds, the origins of alienation and death, and the destruction and restoration of the world—are set in a time out of time. From within a tribal worldview, myths are perceived as descriptive or figurative truth in a way analogous to Christian and Judaic beliefs about Adam and Eve and God's revelation to Moses. Tribal mythologies are open rather than closed; that is, they can be modified to accommodate change.

As we saw in Chapter 2, we treat the religions of tribal peoples in historical times in general terms even though several are well documented. There is no specific tribal religion to which our treatment applies, but beliefs like those we will now discuss are typical of many of them. Tribal beliefs include concepts of spirit beings, the cosmos, humankind, death and human destiny, and evil.

SPIRIT BEINGS

The religions of tribal peoples, and perhaps most religions, involve a human quest for supernatural power. As the Katzie (a people of western Canada) healer Old Pierre observed, "Life is full of unseen hazards and dangers. Without power of some kind, men would float helplessly on its surface like corks."[15] For tribalists, the world is filled with holy power. What happens or can be made to happen is often a function of this transcendent power. Tribal religion, and perhaps all religion, teaches the art of acquiring this power or, in less manipulative terms, of being open to and empowered by it.

In some contexts, tribal peoples have thought of the supernatural in nontheistic terms. The Melanesian term *mana* is often used as a symbol for primal conceptions of an impersonal, supernatural power. Believed to insure successful human undertakings, *mana* is a power that can be acquired from anything in which it is present. In the words of anthropologist and Anglican priest Robert H. Codrington (1830–1922), "All Melanesian religion consists, in fact, in getting this Mana for one's self or getting it used for one's benefit."[16] *Mana* is present in some things and not in others. Spirits have *mana*, but *mana* is also present in things and conditions that have neither spirit nor personality. **Fetishes**—objects infused with *mana*—may be associated with spirits but are not themselves spirits. They can be acquired and controlled by humans—for example, for use in curing and witchcraft. Another form of tribal nontheism conceives of a single, impersonal power that is inherent in all things. According to some scholars, **pantheism**—belief that the world is permeated with an unlimited and monistic (one) cosmic force—is present in the theologies of the Sioux and the Bantu, as well as in other primal traditions.[17]

Tribal religions include nontheistic conceptions, but they preeminently conceive of supernatural power as *theistic*—that is, as being an attribute of spirit beings. Tribal theologies include an abundance of spirits. For example, the pantheon of the Ifugao of the Philippines includes 40 categories of divinities and an estimated 1,500 different supernatural beings; that of the Yoruba of West Africa numbers over 400 gods and goddesses. We have ordered this profusion of deities into the following categories: supreme beings, divinities embodied in nature, and other types of spirit beings.

A Supreme Being   Belief in a **Supreme Being** or High God is common to many tribal peoples. Scholars disagree about whether such beliefs were indigenous or borrowed from monotheistic traditions, but they appear to be very old. Tribal theologies are not strictly monotheistic: a High God is supreme within a pantheon of divinities but has many attributes in common with the God of monotheistic religions.

The Supreme Being is sovereign among the gods and spirits. As the Ruanda of Central Africa

teach, God (Imana) has no equal. The Supreme Being is believed to be the ultimate source of power, but his or her power is usually shared with, and diffused through, other beings and objects. In some myths, God is an eternal being or one who "came of Himself into being" and existed prior to everything else, but typically he or she comes from some preexistent phenomenon—as, for example, the emergence of Dasan, the high god of the Pomo of California, from the ocean. Typically, God is believed to see all and to be present everywhere. A saying of the Ila of central Zambia declares that "God has nowhere and nowhen that He comes to an end."[18] Sioux holy man George Sword (Long Knife) reported that his people "believed that *Wakan Tanka* was everywhere all the time and observed everything" that was done or thought.[19] Sky and air were metaphors of God's omniscience and omnipresence: the all-seeing God dwells in the sky yet, like air or wind, is present everywhere.

The Supreme Being is usually associated with creation. The Mende of Sierra Leone believe that God alone created the world and everything in it, including the divinities, but belief that the Supreme Being delegated some aspects of creation to others is typical. In Yoruba mythology, Olorun, the Lord of Heaven, was assisted in creation by his sons, Obatala and Obuduwa. A myth of the Yaruro of South America depicts the goddess Kuma as creating the world with the help of two brothers, the Water Serpent and the Jaguar. The Supreme Being is often depicted as making the world from formless primordial material, but in Dogon mythology God (Amma) created within his own being the pattern of all subsequent existence. Through the power of language, the Pomo High God talked the world into being.

One of the most striking features of the High God is that he or she is paradoxically both far away and near at hand. On the one hand, the Supreme Being is a mysterious, incomparable being who has withdrawn from human affairs (a phenomenon referred to as *deus otiosis*) and, as a consequence, is not the focus of worship. On the other hand, God is present in the world, "the one on whom men lean and do not fall."[20] For example, Olorun is seen as being far away in the sky, and unlike other deities in the Yoruba pantheon, he has no temples or cults to serve as a focus of sacrifice and worship. But Olorun knows, and is somehow present in, all that humans do. Olorun controls the course of events and sanctions the moral order, but the Lord of Heaven's will is primarily carried out through divinities with whom people deal directly.

The theology of the Lugbara, a people of Uganda and Zaire, provides another example of the paradox of the near and far. The Lugbara point out that the Supreme Being cannot be compared to anything else. Strictly speaking, God is not a person, for the creator of the first person can hardly be a person. The Lugbara say, "We do not know what God is like; he is everywhere, in the wind and in the sky. He is far away and we do not sacrifice to him."[21] God's immutable will cannot be modified by prayer or sacrifice, but he touches the lives of everyone through other deities.

DIVINITIES EMBODIED IN NATURE Tribal divinities, including High Gods, have usually been associated with some aspect of nature, a feature that prompted the judgment that primal religions were simply nature religions. Oral peoples personified the world around them, as the Canadian Indian Walking Buffalo remarked: "Did you know that trees talk? Well they do. They talk to each other, and they'll talk to you if you listen."[22] Perhaps everything in the natural world has been, in some context, deified.

The sky (heaven) and the sun have been universal symbols of deity. Heaven is often the dwelling place of the Supreme Being. As an Ewe tribesman put it, "Where heaven is, there is God."[23] The sun is frequently associated with the Supreme Being, the giver of life and light. Among the Natchez, a people who lived along the lower Mississippi River, the Supreme Being was embodied in the sun and symbolized by an eternal fire. The sun was the symbol of Kane, the Hawaiian god of sunlight and fresh water and the creator of humans and nature. The sun is usually male, but in some pantheons it is female. In the mythology of the Karraru of Australia, the Sun Mother emerged from her cave and

stirred the universe into life. Moon deities are also common. Hina, a Hawaiian goddess, was associated with the moon, as was the Shawnee creator goddess. Sun and moon were conjoined by the Fon of Benin in the Supreme Being Mawu-Lisa, who as Mawu was female and moon and as Lisa was male and sun. Rain, wind, thunder, stars, and other sky elements were deified.

The earth is often a goddess of fertility and vegetation. Asase Ya, an earth goddess of the Ashanti and other Akan peoples, is associated with conception and vegetation. Sacrifices to her are made at plowing and harvesting times, and on Thursdays, her sacred day, farming is forbidden. Cultivators were not alone in deifying the earth. Remarks voiced by Smohalla, a leader of the Sahapatin tribe in the 1880s in the state of Washington, to an Indian agent trying to persuade his people to farm reflect both a mystical identification with the earth and a hunter's aversion to farming: "You ask me to plow the ground. Shall I take a knife and tear my mother's bosom? Then when I die she will not take me to her bosom to rest."[24]

Myths sometimes depict creation as the sexual union of a Sky Father and an Earth Mother. The Ila of Zambia believe that all things originated from a union of the Sky Father, Leza, and the Earth Mother, Bulongo. A similar view is implicit in the words of the Sioux holy man Black Elk: "Is not the sky a father and the earth a mother, and are not all living things with feet or wings or roots their children?"[25]

Animals and plants have been regarded as gifts from spirit beings and as entities through which such beings were present in the world. The primary crops of the Iroquois were sacralized as sister goddesses: Corn Sister, Bean Sister, and Squash Sister. The Ainu of Japan had a mystical bond with bears, Northwest Coast Indians with salmon, and Plains Indians with buffalo. Sometimes Masters of Animals were believed to rule over the animals of one or more species and to see that they were not killed capriciously. Thus, the Inuit goddess Sedna lived in a cave under the sea and withheld or released animals according to the behavior of those who hunted them. In some contexts, animal spir-

Deceased village elders remummified and on display in the Asaro Caves in Papua, New Guinea (ca. 1992). Ancestor veneration is a feature of several tribal religions.

its are **tricksters,** spirits who are both clever and stupid, lawmakers and pranksters. Tricksters bestow gifts but also, through capriciousness or clumsiness, inflict misfortune.

OTHER TYPES OF SPIRIT BEINGS   Other important categories include ancestral, totemic, and culture divinities. Totemic spirits (see Chapter 1) are guardian and tutelary beings associated with descent groups (clans, lineages) and symbolized by totemic emblems. Each is linked with an animal or plant species or some other phenomenon and is often mythologically joined to the origin of a descent group. For example, Hopi clans trace their origins to their respective ancestral spirit beings (for example, bear, spider, sun, eagle, corn, or rain). The animal and plant ancestors are said to be "relatives." Members of the Hopi eagle clan are both descendants of the eagle spirit and related to eagles.

Respect for ancestors is typical of nonliterate societies, but the veneration of the spirits of deceased ancestors is less common. The pantheon of the Torajas of Indonesia includes a High God and the life-sustaining goddess of rice, but the Torajas also revere and pray to the spirits of their ancestral dead. Among the Lugbara, families are obligated to remember the spirits of deceased fathers: "They are our fathers and we are their children

whom they have begotten. Those that have died stay near us in our homes and we feed and respect them."[26] Veneration of ancestral spirits assumes that the relationship between the living and what Mbiti referred to as the "living dead" is an ongoing one. The living speak to the spirits of their dead through their own devices or through mediums who serve as bridges between the worlds. If the "living dead" are remembered and a proper relationship with them maintained, health and prosperity follow. If they are neglected or otherwise offended, disease and misfortune result.

Cultural elements and activities are also deified. The Yoruba deity Ogun is a god of iron and the patron of those who work with it. The Celtic sanctification of metals was embodied in Goibhniu, the deity of smiths and weaponry. The provinces of Ogun and Goibhniu were not narrowly prescribed. Ogun was associated with circumcision, scarification, and oaths. The Feast of Goibhniu was associated with healing and with a sacred potion that immunized partakers against aging. As war loomed larger in human affairs, war was deified, and warrior cults and societies emerged. Ogun and Goibhniu were associated with war, and the Celtic deity Lugh was a god of war as well as of arts and crafts. Domestic deities have been part of sedentary life. Among the Ainu, the hearth, the sacred center of the home, is associated with Kamui Fuchi, the "Supreme Ancestress," who protects the home from evil spirits and punishes wrongdoers.

THE ONE AND THE MANY: GOD AND THE GODS

How are we to interpret the deification of nature in tribal theologies? Were oral peoples unable to distinguish between the animate and the inanimate, the sentient and the nonsentient, the symbol and the thing symbolized? When they associated air with God, did they mean that air was God or a metaphor for God, who, like air, is present everywhere? There are no simple answers to these questions. Like all societies, simple ethnic groups included reflective and nonreflective personalities and popular and esoteric levels of understanding. A. I. Hallowell's work with the Ojibwa convinced him that they distinguished between the animate and the inanimate and the sentient and the nonsentient, but that they applied these categories differently than westerners do. When Hallowell asked, "Are *all* the stones we see about us alive?" he received the reply, "No! But some are!" Hallowell interpreted this response to mean that experience was key to the Ojibwa's understanding. In some contexts, a stone was simply a stone, but other times a stone was experienced as animate and sentient.[27]

Tribal theologies are complex. Depending on the context, they may be described as animistic, pantheistic, polytheistic, totemistic, or monotheistic. Some tribal religions have integrated the profusion of spirit beings into a theology that African scholar E. Bolaji Idowu has described as **diffused monism** (God is many, yet one).[28] The synthesis of the one and the many is evident in the theologies of the Dinka, Hopi, Nuer, and Sioux. The Dinka pantheon includes the Supreme Being, Nhialic, and a host of clan and nonclan divinities, but the Dinka also believe that Nhialic and the powers are one.[29] Thus, Nhialic is thought of as a single transcendent power manifested in numerous spirit beings. The Hopi term for ultimate reality is *a'ni himu,* the mysterious, ineffable power, which can be rendered as "very something" or "mighty something." In John D. Loftin's

view, "All Hopi deities should be understood as so many refractions of *a'ni himu*. The Hopi are not polytheistic; rather, they worship one spiritual substance that manifests itself in many modes of being."[30] A theology in which God is both immanent and transcendent was also articulated by Black Elk: "All things are the works of the Great Spirit. We should know that He is within all things: the trees, the grasses, the rivers, the mountains, and all the fourlegged animals, and the winged peoples; and even more important, we should understand that He is also above all these things and peoples."[31]

The Nuer believe that the Supreme Being, Kwoth, the Spirit of the sky, is the creator of the universe. Kwoth is not literally the sky but is present through it and is, like the air, present everywhere, including fetishes and divinities. As E. E. Evans-Pritchard put it, the spirits "are all God in different figures"; that is, they are refractions of God.[32] The Nuer speak to God directly or through one of the spirits. As transcendent, Kwoth "is everywhere and in nothing in particular, Spirit as it is in itself, God." As immanent, God is manifested in the spirits. Evans-Pritchard noted that the Nuer perceived they were dealing "with Spirit at different levels of thought and experience, Spirit in itself, Spirit in persons, Spirit in beasts, and Spirit in things."[33]

The Dinka, the Nuer, the Hopi, and the Sioux have had extended contact with monotheistic traditions, and it is likely that their diffused monistic theologies reflect this interaction. Acculturation is evident in the Dinka and Nuer belief that the Supreme Being is known as Kwoth to the Nuer, Nhialic to the Dinka, Allah to the Muslim, and God to the Christian.[34] Black Elk was both a Christian and a traditionalist, and he believed "that Christianity and traditional Lakota religion are essentially identical."[35] Acculturation and adaptation are to be expected. Christianity is not less authentic by having integrated elements from Greek, Roman, Celtic, Germanic, Oceanic, African, Asian, and Native American traditions into the life of the church. The same observation applies to the integration of external elements into tribal theologies.

THE COSMOS

Human conceptions of the world involve an orientation in time and space. Typical of tribal constructions of a sacred cosmos are (1) an ordering of everyday life in relationship to a sacred time of origins, when the gods and ancestors "did everything for the first time, creating the primal images that control the flow of the real,"[36] and (2) a mystical attachment to a sacred place.

SACRED TIME   Tribal peoples mark time by seasonal rhythms and ceremonies. Human activities are seen in relation to the position of the sun, the cycle of the moon, the passage of the seasons, and the human life cycle. Seasonal time is cyclical and repetitive. Living things follow a cycle of birth or germination, growth, death, and rebirth. Human occupations and rites are in concert with established patterns: hunters with the hunted, farmers with planting and harvesting, and pastoralists with herds and pastures.

Tribal peoples also associated time with events, positioning events in terms of before and after and dividing time into past, present, and future. They looked to the past—to the time of origins and to foundational events—for the patterns of authentic existence. The primordial, normative, and timeless past was recoverable by retelling and ritually acting out creation myths and by modeling everyday human behavior after the exemplary patterns laid out by the gods and ancestral spirits in the beginning. In Evan Zuesse's words, for peoples "to forget those first dramas of being is to destroy the forms that hold the universe together. Meaningless chaos is the only possible result. Life lived at its deepest, therefore, is truly a remembering and a *re*living."[37]

Primordial or sacred time can be illustrated by the concept of "the Dreaming," found among the Aboriginal peoples of Australia. According to the Mardu, a people of Australia's Western Desert, before the Dreaming the land was featureless and lifeless. During the Dreaming, Spirit creatures emerged from their slumbers beneath the earth's surface and gave the landscape the shape that it has

now. From them, all earthly life came. The behaviors of living things were laid out, including those that governed human existence. "Men hunted with spears and spear-throwers, and Mardu women gathered with digging sticks and wooden bowls, because those were the tools given them by the Dreaming ancestors."[38] Taboos and other behavioral guides established exogamous marriages and avoidance rules respecting sons-in-law and mothers-in-law. After creation was completed, the ancestral spirit beings remained in the hills, deserts, and water holes they created, but the Dreaming did not end; it is perpetuated each day by the actions of humans.[39] The Dreaming is an eternal time that both was and is, a cosmic past-present recoverable through rites, stories, and everyday human behaviors that repeat what the ancient ones did in the beginning.

Historical events were also integrated into tribal interpretations of the cosmos. **Foundational events**—events that signaled a turning point in the life of a people—were, like the time of origins, enshrined and preserved in myths and legends. The establishment of the Iroquois Confederacy is one such example. Prior to contact with Europeans, this confederacy, also called the League of the Five Nations (Cayugas, Oneidas, Onondagas, Mohawks, and Senecas), was established. Its organization united the five tribes into a confederacy based on kinship loyalties and transtribal alliances, liberating them from the endemic intertribal warfare and domestic violence that had afflicted them. There are different versions of the establishment of this confederacy (ca. 1450–1550 C.E.), all of which were recorded after contact. Our retelling integrates elements from two sources.[40]

In the beginning, Good Mind—the son and grandson of fertility goddesses and the twin of Evil Mind—imprisoned Evil Mind in a cave and created humans. He taught humans many things, including how to hunt and eat the fruits of the land and how to give the incense of tobacco to the Spirit Beings. He directed humans to live together as friends. After Good Mind vanished into the sky, a disagreement led the five nations to separate, speak different languages, and war with one another.

Later, a young woman became pregnant and, when her mother pressed her for an explanation, insisted that she had not had sexual intercourse. The mother was vexed by her daughter's condition, but Good Mind came to her in a dream and indicated that her daughter was a virgin and that the daughter's child "would do the work of the divinities on earth."[41] The grandmother feared what the child (named Deganawida) might do and tried, without success, to drown him three times. Deganawida's mission was to bring peace and government to the five nations, which suffered from warfare, feuds, cannibalism, and starvation: "The Great Creator from whom we all are descended sent me to establish the Great Peace among you. No longer shall you kill one another and nations shall cease warring upon each other."[42]

At the outset of his mission, Deganawida visited a woman (the Mother of Nations) and urged her to desist from feeding war parties. After he explained the principles of his message, she accepted it and in doing so gave the clan mothers priority in the polity of the Iroquois. Next, Deganawida converted the cannibal Hiawatha to his cause, and Hiawatha came to see himself in his victims and understood that he should not engage in "killing people and eating their flesh."[43] Deganawida's and Hiawatha's mission of peace was thwarted by the monster Tadadaho who in one version of the myth is associated with Evil Mind. Hiawatha's daughters were killed by Tadadaho, and as the people had become indifferent to one another's sorrows, no one comforted Hiawatha. Gradually, the grieving father overcame his bereavement and worked out a plan to present the mission of peace to the five nations. The proposal by Deganawida and Hiawatha was accepted by the Oneidas, Cayugas, Senecas, and Mohawks, and together they journeyed to Tadadaho, the chief of the Onondagas. On condition that he be made the main chief, Tadadaho accepted the league and was ritually transformed from a monster into a calm and peaceable man. The confederacy united the five nations as "one great family" based on mutual self-defense, local autonomy, a common set of symbols, and a social structure for maintaining public order.

Tribal conceptions of the cosmos and the human condition were chiefly articulated in stories about primordial origins and foundational events rather than in stories about the future. As Zuesse observed, the future is potential time and is therefore "not important because no relationships yet exist in it and between it and the present."[44] Eschatological (end-time) myths are atypical, but the future was not devoid of significance, as we shall see in the Hopi and Germanic myths that follow.

Hopi prophecy provides an example of end-time thinking and illustrates how discordant events have been integrated into Hopi mythology. The Hopi live in villages on a reservation in northeastern Arizona. Traditional Hopi believe that this world was preceded by three others and that the fourth, like the previous worlds, will come to an end. Destruction of the previous worlds was related to human behaviors that deviated from the plan of creation. Each of the worlds had lost its balance, and the peoples who survived and migrated to the next world were those who had not abandoned the way that the spirit beings had laid out for them. Prophecies of the end of the fourth world are related to the coming of Euro-Americans and to the extreme danger that the way of the whites poses for the Hopi way. The direst prophecy envisions an end to Hopi ceremonies and to the Hopi plan of life, but others speak of a return of the "true white brother" (a spirit being) and the establishment of a world in which the Hopi and the whites will become as one people. How the future will play out is implicit in the failure of past worlds. Like its predecessors, the fourth world is out of balance, but those Hopi who hold to the ways set for them at their emergence into this world will survive.[45]

Germanic myths link creation to the cosmic battle at the end of time. In the beginning there was nothing. The primeval frost giant Ymir was killed by Odin and his brothers, who took Ymir's body to the center of the great void. From the giant's blood the sea and lakes were formed; from his flesh came the earth, and from his skull the sky. At the center of the earth, the gods established a home for humankind, and Odin and two other deities created the first human couple from tree trunks. Brave warriors who died in battle were taken to Odin's castle, Valhalla (hall of the slain), where they prepared for a final cosmic battle (a vision of end-time that may reflect Christian influence). Death and destruction are the fate of both the gods and humankind. The final battle, known as Ragnarok, will pit the gods and the warriors of Valhalla against the forces of destruction: the World Serpent, the giants, the demons of the underworld, and Fenriswolf. It will commence when the World Serpent emerges from the sea and Fenriswolf breaks his chains. Thor leads the gods in the cosmic battle, killing the World Serpent but dying from its poison. Odin is consumed by Fenriswolf, who is in turn killed by one of Odin's sons. In one version of the myth, the World Tree (Yggdrasill) is destroyed, but in another it survives the cataclysm and from it a new age emerges. In another variation, two humans survive the destruction and from them comes a new family of humankind.[46]

SACRED SPACE   For instructional purposes, we have separated our discussions of time and space, but experientially they are inseparable. Humans locate objects and events in space and time. Objects occupy space and change over time, and events happen in a spatial and temporal context. Spatial-temporal categories interlock regardless of whether what has taken place occurred in historic or cosmic time, or in this world or some other plane.[47]

The intersection of time and space is evident in Hopi mythology. The multilayered Hopi cosmos consists of the earth, the worlds beneath the earth's surface, and the heavens above. Each of these worlds is occupied by beings peculiar to it. In the First World, "there was only the Creator, Taiowa. All else was endless space. There was no beginning and no end, no time, no shape, no life. . . . Then he, the infinite, conceived the finite."[48] Taiowa created Sotuknang and instructed him to lay out the worlds "in proper order so they may work harmoniously with one another according to my plan." After the creation of the worlds, the Creator directed Sotuknang to create life. He created Spider Woman, who clothed the First World with trees, plants, seeds, birds, and animals, giving them life and naming them. Taiowa, the Creator, saw that the world was very good and ready for humankind. Spider Woman took the four colors of the earth (yellow, red, white, and black) and mixed them with the liquid of her mouth to create the first male and female beings. She presented them to Sotuknang, who gave the ancestors of us all the gifts of speech, wisdom, and sexual reproductivity, along with this stipulation: "There is only one thing I ask of you. To respect the Creator at all times. Wisdom, harmony and respect for the love of the Creator who made you. May it grow and never be forgotten among you as long as you live."

The First People lived harmoniously. They knew that the earth was a living being and the mother of living things, and they honored her as Mother Earth and Corn Mother. They knew the sun as their father and as the face of the Creator, Taiowa. "The first People knew no sickness" and were in harmony with the animals, but gradually, as humans multiplied, they lost their way, became sick, and practiced sorcery. Animals drew away from them, and the people were divided by race and language and by "those who remembered the plan of Creation and those who did not." Sotuknang gathered those who followed the plan of creation in the great mound of the Ant People, where they were safe from the fire that destroyed the First World. When the people emerged from the ant mound into the Second World, they built homes and villages, made things with their hands, and began to trade with one another. The more goods they acquired, the more they wanted, and soon they began to quarrel and fight. The Second World was turned into ice, but as before, those "who sang the song of their Creation" were saved in the underground world of the Ant People.[49]

Eventually, the survivors emerged to the Third World, where they multiplied and created cities and countries. In the process, it became harder and harder to remain harmonious and to follow the plan of creation. Sotuknang instructed Spider Woman to have the righteous ones make a boat as a place of refuge from the flood that destroyed the Third World. The people sailed upon the waters toward the rising sun until they came to land and, after a long journey, arrived at the point of their emergence into the Fourth World. Many peoples emerged from the navel of the Fourth World—the Whites, the Paiutes, the Pueblos, the Navajo—and migrated to the places where they are now.

A sense of being rooted in a particular land is typical of the tribal sacralization of the cosmos. This sense of place is evident in remarks of Seattle, chief of the Suquamish and the Duwamish: "Every part of this soil is sacred in the estimation of my people. Every hillside, every valley, every plain and grove, has been hallowed by some sad or happy event in days long vanished."[50] Sometimes the sense of place is conceived as the sacred center of the cosmos, an *axis mundi*. The function of the sacred center as a point in the cosmos where the different realms (the earth, the above, and the below) and the "multiple planes of being intersect" is expressed in a complex range of symbols. The sacred center has been symbolized by trees, mountains, and other things that point to a pattern of ascent and descent between the various worlds.

The Sioux think of the cosmos as a spiritual power moving, like the sun, in a circle. As Black Elk observed, "Nothing can live well except in a manner that is suited to the way the sacred Power of the World lives and moves."[51] This perception is symbolically embodied in laying out camps in a circle, in metaphors of the Sioux Nation as a hoop with a sacred stick at its center, and in circular ceremonial dances. Tipis form circles, and the fires at the center of sweat lodges are seen as centers of the universe. Ceremonial pipes—a gift of White Buffalo Calf Woman—are sacramental centers of the spiritualized universe and a means for the Sioux to become one with it.

The villages and homes of the Dogon of Mali are arranged according to a pattern that reflects their conception of the cosmos. In the beginning, the creator God, Amma, existed alone, shaped as an egg. Amma transformed the egg into a double placenta and placed in each a set of twins, male and female. Dogon villages embody this cosmic twinness. Structures within each village are regarded as male or female. The north end of the village represents the head—the men's meetinghouse, where collective decisions are made. The village altar represents the penis, and the stone on which women crush fruit symbolizes female sexuality.

The Hopi point of emergence into the Fourth World (the earth's navel) is symbolically present as a hole in the floor of the Hopi *kivas* (religious lodges). Prior to their emergence, the various peoples were given their choice of life-sustaining activities. The Hopi chose an ear of blue corn (a variety of corn) and became farmers. The hard work and techniques of farming were taught to them by the caretaker of this world, the god Masau'u, and in replicating this work the Hopi return to "the timeless past when everything was one with the sacred." Weaving is another activity sacralized by its association with the time and place of origins. When the Hopi emerged from the earth's navel, Spider Woman taught them the techniques and patterns of weaving: "To recall that era through the timelessness of weaving is to regenerate the world. For the beginning all was fresh and pure, unspoiled by the passage of time."[52]

In the tribal ordering of the cosmos, no sharp divisions separate divinity, nature, and humankind. Earth and sky, animals and plants, humans and spirit beings are all related. A sense of kinship with the cosmos is part of the Hopi way. Masau'u, the god of death and of the renewal of life, taught the Hopi to revere the earth as a relative. As Loftin observed, "The perception of the earth as a relative is essential for the Hopi to produce a life-yielding harvest. To treat the earth without respect is to neglect the feelings of humility and harmony the ancestors chose in the beginning when they selected the short blue corn. Proper thoughts and feeling are, according to Hopi experience, necessary for fruitful communication with the sacred."[53]

The relationship of the timeless to everyday life is neither static nor inevitable in tribal religion. The cosmos is conceived of as a conflict of forces and wills in which the outcome cannot be taken for granted. Humans do their part by joining spirit beings in the work of sustaining and renewing the cosmos. Creation is renewed by the repetition of primal archetypes. The rising sun—signaling victory over the dark forces of the underworld—is greeted by prayer. Alternation in the seasons, planting, and harvesting are occasions for ceremonies. Hunters pray to the guardian spirits of animals and take care not to offend them lest the animals go away. Discordant human behavior (anger, envy, murder, and violations of taboos) affects the spirits and the operation of the world. The rain may not come, hunters may return empty-handed, and disease may strike unless harmony is restored.

HUMANKIND

Belief that individuals are composed of multiple selves or souls is typical of tribal constructions of the self. The idea of multiple selves is similar to, but more complicated than, the notion that individuals show different personality traits and mental faculties (for example, memory, aptitudes, or intelligence); rather, each person is regarded as a complex association of selves.

Ake Hultkrantz's distinction between body souls and free souls helps clarify the notion of multiple selves.[54] **Body souls** give life and movement to the body. Sometimes they are referred to as breath and are associated with the lungs or nasal passages. A body soul is localized in a specific human body and is inseparable from it. When individuals die, their body souls die. **Free souls,** in contrast, can leave the body during dreams, trances, or times of stress such as a high fever or the death of a relative. If free souls fail to return from their journeys, the individual dies. Individuals may have more than one body soul and more than one free soul. There are different types of free souls, but the most common ones are associated with individuality or personality. Free souls usually do not die.

Beliefs of the Mnong Gar of Vietnam and the Katzie of Canada provide examples of primal conceptions of multiple selves. The Mnong Gar conceive of a tripartite self: each person has a body soul located in the head that orients the body, a free soul that can separate from the body, and a disembodied guardian soul that lives in the sky and dies when the individual dies. The Katzie self includes the corporeal body and special talents that perish with the death of the individual, as well as three free souls. One free soul, a transcendent soul identified with "He Who Dwells Above," returns to the Supreme Being at death. A second free soul, vitality-thought, is associated with personality and the life force and is responsible for memory. It is free, during dreams or trances, to leave the body and journey to the spirit world. At death, vitality-thought merges with a third free soul, reflection, and becomes a shade or ghost.

In tribal thought, the self or some aspect of it is believed to permeate one's entire being. For example, the Katzie believe that the free soul vitality-thought pervades their entire bodies and that the loss of parts of the body diminishes one's soul and can change one's character. Phenomena that appear to be exterior to the self are regarded as part of it: Shadows are extensions of the self, not mere reflection. Others can be blessed or harmed by them, particularly by the shadows of kings and chiefs. Names are also regarded as part of the self. One's name, like other aspects of the individual, is concealed from one's enemies lest they use such knowledge to harm one. The complexity of primal conceptions of the self is captured by an African proverb that declares, "The spirit of man is without boundaries."[55]

DEATH AND HUMAN DESTINY

Tribal wisdom teaches that life is inseparable from the process of dying. Some humans die with equanimity, quietly accepting life's end. Some oral traditions depict holy men and women as having foreknowledge of their approaching death and as being prepared for it. Others taunt and flaunt death. Sioux warriors hurtled into battle with the cry, "It is a good day to die." Captured Iroquois joked about the torture and death that was their fate.

Tribal peoples sometimes recklessly court or stolidly accept death, but it is also perceived as dangerous and defiling, fearsome and disquieting. "Death," Evans-Pritchard noted, "is a subject Nuer do not care to speak about."[56] In some societies, the dead are feared. One reason for this reaction is the conviction that the spirits of the dead are capable of harming the living. Ghosts of those who die violently or prematurely are particularly dangerous. Thus, it is advisable to take measures to protect oneself. In West Africa, people fear that the dead may return and steal children; widows protect themselves and their children by an extended period of mourning. Corpses are often regarded as polluting. The Katzie take ceremonial baths and cleanse their homes to remove the pollution associated with corpses.

Death is disquieting. Sioux and Iroquois warriors were not all impervious to death. Sioux Crazy Dogs took vows to join the action where the danger was greatest or even to die in battle, but some men, through the custom of *berdache,* assumed the role and dress of women, thereby avoiding the warrior life and its ethos of dying young. Iroquois warriors had no way of stepping aside from their roles, but surviving traditions indicate that some feared they would be incapable of a courageous death.

Death is a time of mourning, of separation and sorrow. Rituals enable mourners to express their grief and behave properly and respectfully in regard to the dead and the living. In some contexts, the grieving and funerary process extends over long periods. For example, the Torajans of Indonesia do not bury their dead for months, or even years, in preparation for their highly formalized familial and communal expression of grief. Generally, as in the case of the Torajans, the more important the deceased, the more elaborate the funeral. Like many traditionalists, Torajans believe that the violation of their burial grounds may result in sickness. Mourning may be complicated by feelings other than grief; the dead may have been both loved and resented, especially where their roles and property were coveted.

Most tribal peoples share Chief Seattle's conviction that the dead are neither powerless nor really dead: "There is no death, only a change of worlds."[57] The souls of humans are believed to survive the death of the body. Rituals assist in the soul's transposition from death to life in the spirit world, and their performance is a serious responsibility.

Releasable souls are often believed to have a momentary existence near the corpse and a permanent one in the realm of the spirits. Traditional Sioux believe the human spirit is like a shadow. At death, it lingers for a time near the living and tries to communicate with them. Eventually it undertakes the journey to the land of the shadows, usually accompanied by the spirits of a ritually sacrificed animal and by other provisions laid near the body. Akan-speaking peoples of West Africa believe that one of their souls returns to the Supreme Being and that a second free soul goes to the land of the ancestors, where the dead live in much the same fashion as those in the visible world. The Torajans sacrifice animals to accompany souls to the land of the spirits. Although the spirits of the dead may be feared and, if not mollified, may be dangerous, they usually have an ongoing and positive relationship with the living through dreams and other modes of contact. Thus, tribal peoples' sense of place involves an attachment to the dwelling place of the spirits of their dead.

Belief in **reincarnation** (rebirth of souls in new bodies) is not uncommon. It is usually selective rather than automatic and universal; thus, in some societies, the souls of children who died are believed to receive another body, whereas those of adults are not reborn. Among the Yoruba, when an individual's free soul arrives before Olorun and his son Obatala, it may, if it has been good, choose either an afterlife with no sorrow or reincarnation as a child. The Ma'anyan Dayaks of Borneo preserve their dead for months for a mass cremation ceremony that enables the souls of the deceased to journey to the Land of the Dead, where they will someday be reborn.

The spirit world is sometimes a shadowy place where the souls of the dead lack individuality and cannot be contacted, but it is usually a mirror image of the visible world, a place where the living dead exist in a manner similar to the living. Spatially, the spirit world is typically at a distance from the living, in the sky or under the earth's surface. Multiple spirit worlds are not unusual. The Apu Tanis of northeastern India believe those who die a natural death go to a place below the earth, and those who die a violent death go to a spirit world in the sky. Good and evil are sometimes a factor in the destiny of souls, but the distinction between non-violent and violent deaths is often, as in the case of the Apu Tanis, the primary determinant.

EVIL

Although tribal peoples are primarily life affirming and "this worldly" rather than "other worldly," they are keenly aware of evil—that is, of sickness, injury, death and other misfortunes. Tribal resolutions to the problem of evil address three issues: (1) Why is evil a feature of human existence? (2) Why is this evil happening to me or our group? (3) What is the relationship of spirit beings to evil?

Death and suffering are seen as stemming from the time of origins and, consequently, as being a fundamental feature of human existence, but belief that they were not original features of creation is a common theme. In myths with the latter motif, primordial existence is initially paradisiacal—a time when death and suffering were unknown. In Nuer mythology, God, animals, and humans initially lived together harmoniously; humans did not die, and there was no killing and eating of animals. Sky and earth were connected by a rope that humans descended to gather food from the earth. When humans aged, they ascended the rope and were rejuvenated in the sky.

The loss of paradise is usually depicted as the consequence of some offense committed by humans or the result of the behavior of spirit beings, such as the thwarting of the Creator's will by a trickster spirit. In some myths, evil is depicted as originating in opposition to good, a motif sometimes embodied in stories about twins, such as the Seneca myth of the twin divinities, Good and Evil Mind. Alienation of the gods by humans was traceable to a wide range of offenses, including disobedience, the breaking of a taboo, or other objectionable behaviors. A myth shared by several African peoples relates that God moved far away because he was bumped by an old woman pounding foodstuffs.

In the mythology of the Mbuti of central Africa, the moral order was broken by a Mbuti who stole fire from the elderly mother of the god Tore. Because his mother died from the cold, Tore cursed humans with the fate of his mother; thus, through a human offense, death entered the world. A rarer mythological perspective points to an altruistic origin of death: humans chose death because without it, there would be too many people.

Tricksters are often the ultimate agents of evil. The Nuer say that as a prank, Hyena cut the rope uniting heaven and earth, making it impossible for aging humans to be rejuvenated. The thwarting of God's intention for creation is frequently associated with the motif of the perverted message. In one variation of this theme, God sent a messenger with the message that humans would not die. A trickster spirit heard God's instruction and, as a cruel joke, hurried ahead of God's emissary and delivered the message that humans must die. In another, God threw a piece of a gourd into the water to indicate that just as it would float, so humans would live forever. He sent a barren woman who, perhaps from spite, falsified God's message by throwing a piece of pottery into the water and pronouncing that just as it sank, so would humans die. In another myth, God sent two messengers, because he had not fully resolved the issue and was willing to leave the outcome to the race; the messenger of death won.

Myths provide a way of understanding why evil is a permanent feature of existence. They do not, however, account for the immediate cause of affliction: Why is this misfortune happening to me? As in the case of the origins of evil, the immediate causes of affliction have been seen as intentional rather than "natural." Oral peoples know that suffering and death are inescapable features of human life and distinguish between natural and violent deaths, but in practice the question that dominates their thinking about death and other afflictions is, Who caused it? Who caused the crops to fail, hunters to return without game, and people to die? The connection between intentionality and evil is articulated in several ways. In some societies, people believe newborns die because their spirits decide to return to the spirit world, a rationalization that helps parents deal with their loss. A typical understanding is the belief that afflictions result from human offenses such as neglecting spirit beings or violating a taboo. In such situations, misfortune is, in a sense, deserved. Suffering is also attributed to the malevolence of evil spirits or of humans (sorcerers or witches) who use their magical powers to harm others. Deliverance from evil is effected through ceremonies that appease the offended spirits, remove the fault of the afflicted, or counteract the power of malevolent beings.

Tribal peoples grapple with the problem of reconciling the existence of evil with the goodness of God. As Black Elk put it, "How could men get fat by being bad, and starve by being good?"[58] Efforts to resolve or mediate the problem tend to disassociate or exonerate the Supreme Being from evil, a tendency evident in the mythological motif that Divinity did not originally intend that humans suffer and die. God was distanced from evil by the alienation of the divine and the human through some human fault or by the frustration of God's intention by a trickster spirit. The latter is the case in the following Native American myth: In the beginning, all living things spoke the same language and lived together harmoniously. One day Coyote, a trickster, stayed away from the others; he was weary of company and of eating plants and fruits. In a dream, an evil one put meat before Coyote's nose and urged him to eat. Coyote was so enamored by the flesh that he killed a cottontail, thereby giving birth to the fear of other living things. Subsequently, the common language that bound all living beings together harmoniously was forgotten.

In tribal theologies in which all power is ultimately that of Divinity, God at least permits evil and is therefore either directly or indirectly involved in it. A Nuer invocation captures the dilemma: "God, now thou hast given us badness, or is it simply the lot of creation?"[59] Either evil directly comes from God, or it is an inescapable feature of creation. In diffused monistic theologies like that of the Lugbara, God is the agent of death but is only indirectly responsible for other human afflictions and misfortunes through the diffusion of his power in the gods. In some theologies, death and other aspects of existence are predestined. The Yoruba believe that a person's destiny is chosen by his or her guardian ancestral spirit and confirmed by Olorun in heaven before birth. Ancestral guardian spirits, if properly venerated, help persons realize the best part of their destinies. Although human destinies cannot be completely abrogated, an undesirable destiny can be ritually modified and a desirable one subverted.

RELIGIOUS PRACTICE OF TRIBAL PEOPLES

We will discuss the religious practice of tribal peoples in sections on sacred rites, sacred persons, traditional medicine, and tribal values.

SACRED RITES

Ritual is an indispensable dimension of tribal religious practice. Sacred rites are contexts through which humans experience the presence of the sacred, a deep sense of community with their companions, and deliverance from disease and misfortune. Re-creations of the time of origins and of foundational events enable participants to link the present to the eternal and become one with the transcendent. Life cycle and healing rites help shape identity and contribute to well-being. As Benjamin Ray observed, in tribal societies, individual and social well-being are mediated through ceremonies: "Through ritual man transcends himself and communicates directly with the divine. The coming of divinity to man and of man to divinity happens repeatedly with equal validity on almost every ritual occasion. The experience of salvation is thus a present reality, not a future event."[60]

Rites are performed to heal the sick, renew the ecosystem, restore social and familial harmony, secure good fortune, and acquire a vision. Rainmakers perform rituals to bring forth rain, diviners to know the future and modify a client's fate, and healers to cure. Cultivators conduct ceremonies to celebrate and sustain seasonal rhythms and harvests. Hunters sanctify their hunts and give thanks for their kills. Visions, trance states, and other ecstatic experiences are also mediated through ritual.

The most complicated and momentous rituals require the services of specialists, men and women of goodwill with the requisite knowledge and supernatural power to be agents of salvation or deliverance. Tribal specialists often have considerable expertise. Navajo ceremonials take years to memorize and are so complex that even the most learned and accomplished chanters or singers never master all of them. Chants may last as many as nine days and include such elements as baths, induced vomiting, medicines, fetishes, and over five hundred songs, each of which must be properly uttered and intoned if the rite is to be effective.

Indigenous peoples believe that rituals work (accomplish their purposes). Humans are not helpless. As Jonathan Z. Smith observed, rituals provide "a means of performing the way things ought to be in conscious tension to the ways things are," of creating a "controlled environment" where, for example, the sick are cured and the barren made fertile.[61] Rituals aim at keeping humans in harmony or balance with the multiple layers and beings of the universe. The efficacy of rituals to bring about such ideal outcomes is linked to their proper performance. In the words of Sioux holy man George Sword (Long Knife), "Every word and every motion said or done in the ceremony must be right. If a ceremony is not done right it does no good, and may do much harm."[62] Sword (Long Knife) may have overstated the case, but rituals require an attention to detail. Rituals are not seen as mere human contrivances. The Sioux believe that their rites and sacred pipe are gifts of the goddess White Buffalo Calf Woman. Katzie healer Old Pierre believed that He Who Dwells Above gave rites to the Katzie to increase their joy and to comfort them

in their grief. As gifts both from and to the spirit world, spirit beings found the performance of rites pleasing and were less likely to reject them.

Belief that the proper performance of a ceremony produces the desired result has merit, particularly when the purposes are social and moral. When feuds disrupted the community, Dinka Masters of the Fishing Spear (a priestly order) restored social harmony and the moral order through a complicated ritual process. Warring factions were brought together in a ritual context; if the feud involved a loss of life, an animal sacrifice was made and a compensation agreed upon that satisfied God and the family of the deceased. Life cycle rites also produced the desired results. For example, the privileges and responsibilities of adulthood were conferred in rites that socially effected the transition from child to adult. It is less clear how a celebration performed at the winter solstice contributed to the return of the sun or those performed in conjunction with planting insured a good crop. Likewise, sacred rites did not always accomplish their purposes. The sick did not always get well, feuds were not always resolved, and amulets did not always protect one from injury or insure a safe journey.

Tribal rites involve expressions and acts of praise, thanksgiving, supplication, and purification or expiation. Participants often prepare by cleansing themselves of impurities through such activities as washing, sweating (for example, Native American sweat lodges), and fasting. Prayers are an integral component of the ritual process and of the daily life of traditional peoples. Ceremonies typically begin by invoking the attentive presence of a spirit being, as in this Dinka prayer: "Divinity, I call you in my invocation because you help everyone and you are great towards all people, and all people are your children."[63] Because it is pleasing to the Supreme Being and to all the spirits, Sioux invocations involve smoking the sacred pipe, as well as uttering prayers. At some point in the ritual process, the master of ceremonies or one of the other participants petitions a specific deity for assistance: heal this child, enable this woman to conceive, grant a bountiful hunt or harvest.

SACRIFICE   Sacrifices—the presentation and transfer of gifts by means of their destruction to spirit beings—have often been part of tribal ceremonies. Sacrifice can be blood (killing animals and humans) or nonblood (presenting beer, cereal, fruit, milk, tobacco, or tubers) offerings. The more momentous the situation or the greater the danger, the more likely that blood sacrifice has been part of the ritual process. Among the Nuer, sacrifices of cereal and beer were associated with less stressful situations, whereas offerings of domestic animals were associated with crises such as sickness, pollution, barrenness, war, and the translation of souls from this world to the next. Among farmers, domestic animals have been the principal victims; among hunters and fishers, game animals.

Some of the purposes of sacrifice can be illustrated by examples from the practice of the Ainu (an indigenous people of Japan) and Santería (a movement originating in Cuba in the nineteenth century that blends Christianity and Yoruba religion). The Ainu "feast of sending away" culminates in the immolation of the most revered animal, the bear, and a communal eating of its flesh and blood. The death of the bear serves as both a gift of thanksgiving and as a messenger to the spirit world bearing the petitions of the Ainu for progeny, plenty, and protection from disease and misfortune. The Ainu believe the ceremony releases the spirit of the bear to the spirit world and that it will be returned by the gods as a reincarnated bear. By eating the bear, celebrants participate in the mysterious, sacred potency of the victim. Identification of the sacrificers with the sacrificed is so complete that the bear becomes a substitute for the celebrants; in the process, the faults, disease, and misfortune of the celebrants are transferred to the victim and die with it. Santeros (devotees of Santería) present spirit beings with gifts of life as a form of praise and sustenance (spirits must eat to live) and as a means of exchange (giving gifts in expectation that the divinities will give back). Typical of traditional practice, Santería sacrifices (for example, chickens, goats, and sheep) are consumed by the participants.

Firstling rites—those associated with hunting, fishing, and harvests—often involve gifts of animal and plant life. Hunters and fishers typically give a portion of their kills, and farmers and pastoralists offer the first fruits of harvests and flocks to spirit beings. Native Americans of the Northwest Coast region hold a First Salmon ceremony in conjunction with the first catch of the season, eating the fish and returning its bones to its watery home to restore it to life and to appease the Salmon spirits for killing salmon. Because firstling offerings are linked to what humans eat to survive, scholars disagree as to whether they should be regarded as sacrifices.

Animal sacrifice was a widely distributed behavior among tribal peoples in historical times, and it continues to be part of contemporary traditional religions and syncretistic movements such as Santería. Human sacrifice was less common, but it did occur and was sometimes accompanied by ritual cannibalism and head-hunting. For example, the Yanomamo, a people who live in the rain forest along the Brazil-Venezuela border, used to practice human sacrifice, collect human heads as trophies, and consume human flesh. In some contexts, tribal peoples sacrificed and consumed members of their own tribes, but usually the victims were members of other groups. Sacrifice and ritual cannibalism were sometimes a component of feuds and war, behaviors that provided revenge and a way for the sacrificers to acquire the power of the victims. Unsanctioned cannibalism was usually associated with witches, and allegations of witchcraft sometimes include charges of cannibalism. Such ritualized behaviors are not practiced or sanctified by tribal ethnics today.

In some tribal cultures, human sacrifice was associated with life-sustaining foods; for example, the Pawnee sacrificed a captive, usually a female, in an annual rite associated with the regeneration of game and cultivated foods. The association of the origin of domestic foods with the death and dismemberment of a goddess or, less frequently, of a god was widespread among cultivators, and such myths may have legitimated human sacrifice. In the Melanesian myth of Hainuwele, from the Island of Ceram, Ameta—a member of the nine original families that emerged in the beginning from

Mount Nunusaku—found a drowned wild boar with a coconut stuck to its tusk. Ameta took the coconut home and covered it with a cloth bearing the figure of a snake. A figure appeared to Ameta in a dream and instructed him to plant the coconut. In a short time, the coconut became a tree rich with blossoms. When the man climbed the tree to harvest the blossoms, he cut his finger, and his blood dropped upon a blossom. A young woman was formed from the blossom and the blood, and Ameta named her Hainuwele. During a great celebration, she stood at the center of the festival and passed betel nuts to the dancers. On the second evening of the festival Hainuwele gave the dancers gifts of precious coral, and on subsequent nights her presents included Chinese porcelain, copper boxes, and golden earrings. The people grew resentful and fearful of Hainuwele and resolved to kill her. On the ninth and concluding day of the celebration, Hainuwele was pressed into a large hole in the center of the dance ground and covered with dirt. Ameta recovered her body, cut it in pieces and buried the parts in locations around the village, from whence grew the first tubers, the primary food of the Melanesians.

Whatever the connection of myths involving the death and dismemberment of primordial beings to sacrifice, as Jonathan Z. Smith pointed out, the Hainuwele myth also demonstrates the adaptability of myth to changing conditions. Clearly, the material gifts produced by Hainuwele were not part of traditional culture, and her death and dismemberment can be interpreted as a rejection of nontraditional culture and a reaffirmation of the traditional life of the Ceramese.[64]

LIFE CYCLE RITES   Like other traditions, the ceremonies of tribal peoples include those associated with momentous transition points in the human life cycle (birth, puberty, marriage, and death). As rites associated with death were touched on earlier and marriage is discussed later in the "Tribal Values" section, examples of birth and initiation rites are provided here. The reproductive process from conception to birth was usually marked by ceremonies and attendant taboos. Particular foods and objects were regarded as dangerous to the process and were to be avoided by expectant parents. In some cultures, men were not allowed to be present at birth, and sexual intercourse between husband and wife was interdicted from some prenatal point until two or more years following childbirth.

Birth and childhood rites can be illustrated by practices of the Gikuyu of Kenya. In the period immediately following childbirth, Gikuyu families are not permitted to wash themselves in the river, sweep their houses, or take fire from one house to another in the village. After a period of seclusion, the mother's head is shaved, and her husband sacrifices a sheep in thanksgiving to God and the ancestral spirits. The shaving of the head symbolizes the transition from one state to another: the hair represents the mother's pregnancy that is completed with the birth of the child, and the new hair is a symbol of new life as well as a symbol that the child now belongs to the Gikuyu. Between the ages of six and ten, Gikuyu children participate in a ceremony that signals the end of childhood. In a reenactment of their birth, youngsters are placed between the legs of their mothers and bound to them by the intestines of goats. When the intestines are cut, the children imitate a baby's cry. The mothers' heads are shaved again, and the house is swept to mark the birth of the new being. When the children reach puberty, another rite completes the transition from youth to adult.[65]

Initiation rites—the socioreligious transposition from child to adult—are elaborate affairs of the entire community. They usually require the initiates to endure deprivations and ordeals. In the first stage of the initiation rites of the Akamba of Kenya, a boy is circumcised, and the clitoris of a girl is excised. The sexual woundings parallel the cutting of the umbilical cord at birth and, in concert with other aspects of the initiation, prepare the initiates, both male and female, for adult life by searing the experience in their memories. Members of another African tribe, the Maasai, perform initiations every four or five years for youths between twelve and sixteen. Initiates are assembled and covered with white clay, a symbol of new birth. After spending two months wandering about, the youths are washed in cold water as preparation for their circumcision the following day. After the circumcision, the initiates are secluded for four days. Subsequently, in a reversal of roles, they reappear dressed and adorned like women. When their circumcisions heal, the initiates' heads are shaved and the change of status from youth to adult effected. Through the ritual process, youths are reborn as adults and bonded into an age group that extends over their entire lives.

SACRED PERSONS

Personal experiences of the spirit world that are manifested in visions validate and empower tribal specialists in sacred matters and are highly valued by nonspecialists as well. The importance of visions is evident in the observation of George Sword that "no Lakota should undertake anything of great importance without first seeking a vision relative to it. *Hanble* [a vision] is a communication from Wakan Tanka or a spirit to one of mankind. It may come at any time or in any manner to anyone. . . . It may come unsought for or it may come by seeking it."[66]

Revelations from spirit beings come during dreams; trance states; and less ecstatic modes of awareness, such as intuition and insight. Because such disclosures are believed to have momentous implications for an individual's destiny, youths, and especially young men, are expected to seek them. Typically, these young people are isolated from others, endure austerities such as fasting, and spend their time in prayer and reflection. Visions are usually shared with, and interpreted by, the larger community.

A better understanding of tribal experiences of the sacred can be gained by taking a closer look at the experiences of those who function as specialists in sacred things. The range of such figures includes diviners, *shamans*, rainmakers, herbalists, elders, and in socially stratified and centralized societies, priests, chiefs, and monarchs. By virtue of their office, the chiefs and monarchs functioned as the principal priests and intermediaries between the visible and invisible worlds. They were assisted in their sacerdotal roles by a priestly class that conducted the nation's public rituals and cared for its shrines and temples.

In less socially complex societies, diviners and *shamans* have functioned as the chief intermediaries between humans and spirit beings. Through magico-religious powers, they assist their clients in the resolution of problems and the restoration of their well-being. As healers, they diagnose the causes of disease and misfortune and perform the proper actions to restore health to their clients. In addition, they divine what is unseen in the present and past, foresee the future, and in some contexts, modify their clients' fate. Diviners generally accomplish their purposes through ecstatic and nonecstatic methods, whereas *shamans* do so principally through ecstatic ones. This distinction can be illustrated by distinguishing between wisdom divination and possession divination. In **wisdom divination,** the religious specialist divines and heals by acquiring, through rigorous training, an extensive body of knowledge that can help resolve the problems of his or her clients. In **possession divination,** the specialist divines and heals through a trance state in which either a guardian spirit enters his or her body **(spirit possession)** and speaks through it, or alternatively, the specialist's free soul travels to the spirit world and returns with a diagnosis and cure. Spirit possession is often accompanied by spirit-filled speech **(glossolalia)** and convulsive body movement.

Our word *shaman* is derived from the Siberian *saman* (he who knows), describing figures who possess the power to heal the sick and to communicate with spirit beings in an ecstatic state. In historical times, *shamanism* has been common among hunter-gatherers and pastoralists in the Arctic, the Americas, Asia, and Oceania. *Shamans* acquire their magico-religious power through spirit-filled experiences, apprenticeship, and even inheritance or purchase, but the power is usually grounded in a sense of being chosen by Divinity. Often this experience of being chosen occurs during a serious illness, a trance state, or a dream. In such a condition, the subject is either possessed by a benefactor spirit or his or her free soul travels to the spirit world and acquires a guardian spirit. The control and assistance of such spirits enable *shamans* to heal, cast spells, change themselves into animals, divine secrets, control fetishes, and guard their turf against competitors. *Shamanic* powers are mediated through self-induced trance states (often assisted by music, dance, and stimulants such as tobacco) during which the *shaman's* soul journeys to the spirit world and brings back the information necessary to perform the task at hand.

Experiences of the Katzie healer Old Pierre illustrate both the ecstatic and ritualized character of the formation and legitimation of a *shaman*. By the time of his "power-vision" in his teens, Pierre had spent several winters memorizing Katzie traditions and going through ordeals that tested his seriousness and suitability. He spent extended periods of time in isolation, fasting, praying, and purifying himself. When his vision occurred, Pierre had been praying so fervently and fasting so strenuously that he had lapsed into a trance state. He reported that in that state his free soul left his body and followed the voice of a medicine spirit to a faraway place. From the medicine spirit he learned how to draw sickness out either by laying his hands on the afflicted person or by sucking the alien element out: "Now I had power—power in my hands and wrists to draw out sickness, power in my mouth to swallow it, and power to see all over the world and to recover minds that had strayed from their bodily homes. I was a medicine man: I could heal the sick, I could banish their diseases. . . . But not always. Whenever He Who Dwells Above had decided to take someone's soul, I could do nothing."[67] Old Pierre's vision produced in him a remarkable clarity: "Then at last my mind and body became really clean. My eyes were opened and I beheld the whole universe."[68]

Wisdom diviners may have originally been chosen through a direct experience of Divinity, but trance states, including spirit possession and soul travel, are not involved in their divining. As Ray observed, a wisdom diviner combines "all the known factors into a coherent picture" and from this makes a judgment, recommends a course of action, or

makes a statement from which clients may draw their own conclusions.[69] The Babalawo, diviner-priests of the Yoruba Ifa cult, make contact with the gods through a complex body of poetry and 256 divination figures. The Babalawo forecast the future, discern destinies, and provide their clients with models for making decisions in the following way: The diviner selects one of the 256 figures by shaking sixteen palm nuts and lifting as many nuts as he can out of his left hand with his right hand. The nuts remaining in his left hand determine the mark the diviner records on his divination tray. One of the 256 divination figures is formed by repeating the action eight times. The poems and figures provide models for resolving typical human problems and concerns. During sessions, clients do not directly pose the question or problem that is troubling them to the Babalawo. God knows the question, and through the divining process the Babalawo recites the poems appropriate to the figure on his diviner's tray. Clients choose the poem that provides a resolution to their problem. Wisdom divination requires a rigorous apprenticeship. Babalawo novices are trained for ten to twelve years by senior priests before they are able to master the traditions and technical knowledge required of them. Novices must memorize at least four poems for each of the 256 divination figures, a body of 1,024 poems.

TRADITIONAL MEDICINE

In tribal communities, religion and medicine have been inseparable. Like most people, tribalists value good health, progeny, longevity, and plenty. Afflictions and misfortunes are the converse of such goods, and deliverance from them is so urgently desired that all tribal religions—or perhaps as I. M. Lewis observed, "all religions—are cults of affliction."[70] Both aspects of the human condition (good and ill health, fortune and misfortune) are linked to matters of spirit, and the practice of medicine requires a knowledge of spiritual, as well as physical, maladies. Deliverance is chiefly from destructive forces rather than from earthly existence. Ascetic austerities such as fasting and sexual abstinence are periodic and limited in duration, and long-term austerities, such as a life-long commitment to celibacy with its renunciation of sexuality and marriage, are rare.

The range of tribal and folk practitioners includes herbalists, midwives, bone setters, and spiritual healers (men and women who specialize in the nexus between spirit beings and human well-being). Plant medicines are used by herbalists and spiritual healers (*shamans* and diviners) to cure, for example, diarrhea, skin infections, and aches and pains. Such remedies often involve a prodigious knowledge of medicinal plants. On the basis of fieldwork in the Amazon, Mark J. Plotkin reported: "A single shaman of the Wayana tribe in the northeast Amazon, for example, may use over 100 different species for medicinal purposes alone."[71]

When herbal medicines fail or are inapplicable, traditional peoples turn to spiritual healers for deliverance. Although spirit beings are directly or indirectly involved in every aspect of existence, including the practices of herbalists and midwives, their relation to traditional medicine is most evident in magico-religious curing, which is based on the premise that the affliction is the result either of some human violation of the moral or spiritual order or of the malevolence of humans (sorcery). Magico-religious healers (referred to here as *shamans* and diviners and in earlier terminology as witch doctors and medicine men) diagnose the cause of their patients' illnesses or misfortunes to determine whether their afflictions are the result of an offense of their own doing or of sorcery. The diagnosis typically involves extensive discussion among the healer, the patient, and the patient's family about the illness and its treatment, as well as wisdom (reading signs or interpreting dreams) or trance divination. In the latter, the soul or guardian spirit of the healer travels to the spirit world to learn the cause of the illness or misfortune, or the healer hosts a guardian divinity in his or her body that determines which spirit being has been offended, what standard of the social order has been violated, or whether sorcery is involved.

If witchcraft or sorcery is suspected, steps are taken to counter the malevolent power. **Exorcism**

(extracting a life-threatening spirit or object from the patient's body) is a typical procedure, because those who are believed to be enchanted or bewitched are often seen as being possessed by an evil spirit or as having an alien object lodged in them. If the offending witches are near at hand, they are exiled or killed. However, if the affliction or misfortune is diagnosed as stemming from a spirit being—usually an ancestral spirit that has been neglected or that is offended by a breach of the social order—appeasement and reconciliation are sought through offerings appropriate to the offense. Animal sacrifice is a typical means of assuaging offended spirits and restoring individual and community well-being.

Magico-religious curing is a ritualized process involving such components as prayers, songs, dances, purification, acts of atonement, and exorcism. Healers possess a collection of objects important to their craft, such as herbs, tobacco, pollens, fetishes, and amulets. In Navajo curing, the singer (Navajo healer) begins by inducing a trancelike state through which he divines the cause of the affliction at hand and the ceremony appropriate to it. A singer who has mastered that ceremony is contacted, and the ceremony is arranged. The family of the patient prepares for the ceremony by cleaning its hogan and gathering the necessary materials. The process of removing the affliction, depending on its cause, takes place over two to nine days and involves the participation of the patient's family. The singer or his assistants construct designs of colored sand on the floor of a ceremonial lodge through which the holy beings associated with the cause and cure of the disease are made present. The patient is placed in the center of the drypainting (sandpainting), and the singer petitions, through a series of chants and gestures, the holy ones to remove the patient's affliction and restore his or her well-being. Herbal medicines are also used.

As we have seen, spiritual healers see themselves as chosen by spirit beings, and they see their power as derived from these spirits. Usually their visions stem from a personal quest or occur during a serious illness or upon the heels of some adversity, but their techniques and remedies are honed by apprenticeship and experience. The importance of healers can hardly be overestimated. As Godfrey Lienhardt observed, healing rites "represent the conversion of a situation of death into a situation of life."[72]

TRIBAL VALUES

Tribal values are embedded in particular societies and vary accordingly. Courage and physical prowess are important virtues in warrior societies and less so in peaceful ones. In farming societies, where power and prestige are measured by the accumulation and redistribution of goods, loyalty and generosity are important. Our treatment of tribal values focuses on community well-being and morality.

COMMUNITY WELL-BEING   In tribal societies and values, the well-being of the community is more important than that of individuals. Humans cannot survive alone; we are dependent upon others. A West African proverb speaks to this fact: "Man is no palm nut, self-contained."[73] In marked contrast to French philosopher René Descartes's "I think, therefore I am" (which is regarded by some scholars as the starting point of modern Western philosophy), Mbiti formulated the traditional African sense of self as being grounded in a particular ethnic community in this fashion: "I am, because we are; and since we are, therefore I am."[74]

Tribal communities are bound together by ancestry and culture. In such societies, who we are is separable from the communities to which we belong. The circle of ancestry includes ancestral spirits, lineages, clans, and families. Everyone is related by real and/or mythological ancestors from whence lines of descent are reckoned. Mbiti's comments about kinship in African tribal communities apply to non-African tribal communities as well:

> It is kinship which controls social relationships between people in a given community: it governs marital customs and regulations, it determines the behaviour of one individual towards another. Indeed, this sense of kinship binds together the entire life of the "tribe," and is even extended to cover animals, plants and non-living objects through the "totemic" system. . . . This it is which largely governs the . . . life of the individual in the society of which he is a member.[75]

At the center of the tribal community is the extended family, a group of relatives reckoned by blood and marriage that includes parents and their children, grandparents, uncles, aunts, in-laws, and cousins. A contemporary Sioux woman, Mary Crow Dog, describes the extended family as being "like a warm womb cradling all within it. Kids were never alone, always fussed over by not one but several mothers, watched and taught by several fathers."[76] Even death does not separate the living and the "living dead," because the spirits of ancestors are seen as links between families, the larger community, and the spirit world; conversations, prayers, and ritualized forms of exchange continue among them.

Marriage and procreation are the lifeblood of community. Some societies provide alternatives (contexts in which men could assume the roles of women or women the roles of men), but for the most part those who do not marry are at odds with traditional beliefs about what is involved in being human. Barrenness is regarded as a curse and grounds for separation. Persons who do not marry and procreate are in danger of having no one to perform their funerary rites, perpetuate their name, or placate their spirits, because each generation constitutes "the link between the ancestors and the living family."[77] Generally speaking, large families and many children are signs of well-being that further guarantee the "immortality" of the family.

In communities in which shared existence is the highest value, the loss of community is the paramount evil. Antisocial individuals act as if they have no family, and such persons are often suspected of sorcery. In many tribal worldviews, the order of how things ought to be was established in the beginning and is maintained through taboos, rituals, and other behavior guides. Men and women who follow the cosmic order obey such guides. Those who transgress threaten themselves, the community, and the divine order on which the community is predicated. Persons who violate the moral and religious order have stepped outside the model of what it means to be human.

MORALITY Tribal morality was formerly judged to be prereflective, primitive, and circumscribed by taboos and customs rather than grounded in reflection and embedded in individual conscience. Like many assessments grounded in early theories of social evolution, this judgment is not as convincing as it once was. If regard for others is the mark of morality, tribal morality usually meets such a standard, because it is typically grounded in the primacy of the well-being of the community and is undergirded by guidelines of mutual obligation.

Regard for others and mutal obligation are essential to shared life. It took months of living with Canadian Eskimos (Inuit) for French ethnologist Gontran de Poncins to understand this truth. He lived with them before World War II, when their way of life was only slightly changed by contact with the West. Initially, he was exasperated by the Eskimos' helping themselves to his property but was eventually mollified by recognizing that in their way of life, things were not exclusively owned: "It was not that everything here was owned in common, for it was not; it was better than that. . . . Each member of the community was concerned to see that all the others were provided for."[78] It became clear to de Poncins that individual existence depended upon corporate existence: "It is the community that remains alive here, not the men; it is the community that has had a poor hunting season or a good one, that is hungry or well-fed, that has reason to rejoice or to despair."[79] A morality centered on regard for others and the common good is also evident in the subordination of personal advantage to the good of the society as a whole among Bantu peoples, as well as in the linkage of the welfare of each individual to the welfare of others among the Navajo.[80]

In addition to being other-regarding, tribal morality involves beliefs about what constitutes a good life. As noted, each individual is situated in time and space and is part of a web of social relationships that include those of family, tribe, and spirit beings. In many traditional societies, human well-being—the good life—requires a proper balance of these relationships, that is, of being in harmony with one's world and being content with one's circumstance. Thus, in the Navajo tradition, the happy person is one who lives a long life "walking" in harmony and beauty with patience and equanimity and who dies of old age.

The harmonious life involves a deep identification with the earth. As Chief Seattle reportedly said: "This we know, All Things are connected, Like the blood which unites one family, All things are connected. Whatever befalls the earth, befalls the sons of the earth. Man did not weave the web of life; he is merely a strand in it. Whatever he does to the web, he does to himself."[81] In tribal theologies, the earth and the things of the earth are perceived as relatives. In such a sacralized world, human existence is grounded in a religious and moral orientation rather than a scientific one. As Richard Hart said of the nurturing character of Zuni farming, it is "conservation from the point of view of caring for a relative and not from a scientific point of view of conserving a natural resource."[82]

Human well-being is inseparable from the land and the beings that inhabit it. That this calls for reciprocity and thanksgiving is clear in what Winoma LaDuke, a member of the Mississippi Band of Anishinaabe, wrote for a *Greenpeace* quarterly publication:

> This means that when I harvest wild rice on my reservation in northern Minnesota or when we hunt deer, we always pray, offer tobacco . . . because we understand in our language all of those things are animate and have standing on their own. I always give thanks for them giving me their life, because I understand that I am totally reliant upon them to continue . . . my way of life on this land. It is part of our code of ethics to always give when we take, and when we take, we must only take what we need and leave the rest.

Tribal morality entails beliefs about what constitutes a virtuous character. Spiteful, selfish, angry, and violent people are neither harmonious nor happy nor other-regarding. There are many virtues and vices, and what is virtuous varies not only by society but also by considerations respecting age, sex, role, and status.[83] The virtues desired of fathers may differ in kind or substance from those of mothers, and those desired of warriors from those of peacemakers. Generally speaking, men and women of good character are loyal, courageous, patient, charitable, obedient, just, and wise. They are hospitable and generous, especially to kin. They are obedient to the rules of mutual obligation, observant of taboos, and respectful of tradition. They value wisdom and respect the wisdom of tribal elders and healers.

Justice is both an aspect of individual character and the ethos of a society. Simple ethnic societies did not have judicial systems and jails to maintain social control, but they did have mechanisms of containment, such as rituals, taboos, moral action guides, and social structures, that preserved social harmony and limited violence. When disputes and violations occurred, traditional justice sought to restore social harmony through forms of restitution that compensated the victims. Such procedures provided an alternative to violent forms of retaliation and enabled social healing to occur. When a person was accidentally or intentionally killed or injured, reparations were made. Typically, restitution required that the person responsible for the violation and his or her family, band, clan, or village compensate the victim's family and his or her band, clan, or village. Compensation might include payment of domestic animals or temporary or permanent banishment from the community. Anthropologist Kenneth Tollefson's remarks about the traditional justice system of the Tlingit, a Native American people of the Pacific Northwest, applies to other indigenous peoples as well: "'You don't pay your bill until you compensate the victim and satisfy tribal elders that you're rehabilitated.' It turns out restored people and a healed community."[84]

INDIGENOUS PEOPLES IN HISTORICAL TIMES

Our history of indigenous peoples in historical times is divided into two periods: (1) tribal peoples and premodern states and (2) tribal peoples and modern states. The premodern period began around 3000 B.C.E. with the emergence of centralized, urban states and ended in 1500 C.E. with the beginning of sustained contact of tribal nations with modern European states. The modern period covers the interaction of tribal peoples with modern states and the post–World War II struggle for self-determination.

TRIBAL PEOPLES AND PREMODERN STATES (3000 B.C.E.–1500 C.E.)

The emergence of the first literate societies in Mesopotamia around 3000 B.C.E. marks the chronological end of prehistory, but nonliterate societies did not disappear. During the premodern period, tribal peoples persisted along the edges of urban states in Africa, Asia, Europe, and America and existed relatively untouched by the influence of such states in Australia, the Arctic, Oceania, most of North America, and areas of South America and the Caribbean. Everywhere urban centers and state systems developed, however, they affected the lives of contiguous tribal peoples.

EUROPE   Prehistoric Europe was occupied by numerous tribes. Most of them spoke Indo-European languages (for example, Baltic, Celtic, Germanic, and Slavonic). By 3000 B.C.E., nearly all of Europe had made the transition to agriculture and was in the process of making the transition from stone to metal tools and weaponry. Copper tools were common by 3000 B.C.E., and the Bronze Age flourished by 2000 B.C.E. Iron was used in southeastern Europe by 1000 B.C.E. and most of the rest of Europe by 700 B.C.E. Social distinctions were more pronounced in the Late Neolithic and Bronze Age than among Europe's first farmers as chiefdom societies emerged—that is, societies that rank lineages and individuals on an inherited prestige ladder and in which the primary leader is a chief whose economic power is derived from his or her role as a distributor of goods.

The tribal peoples of Europe were dramatically changed by contact with the Roman Empire and the spread of Christianity. The Greeks referred to non-Greeks collectively as barbarians, and the Romans applied that epithet to European tribalists. Because the tribes left no written records, what we know about them comes from archaeology and Roman and Christian interpreters. We do not know what they called themselves, but the peoples of western Europe are commonly referred to as Celts or Gauls, those of northern Europe as Germans, those of eastern Europe as Slavs and those of the Baltic region as Balts. Each of these ethnic labels are labels for numerous tribes that differed from one another in language, social institutions, and culture.[85]

During the Bronze and Iron Ages, Europeans subsisted by farming supplemented by crafts and mining. Goods (for example, cattle, grain, tin, gold, and silver) were exchanged between villages and settlements over most of Europe. Chiefs and heads of clans were the principal leaders. There were religious categories as well. For example, Celtic religious leaders included druids (priests, teachers, and judges) and bards (poets). Male dominance was probably the norm, but grave goods and classical literary sources indicate that women also had wealth, high status, and power. Women worked at home and in the fields. They engaged in war as spectators, warriors, negotiators, and chiefs, and they functioned in religious roles as healers, prophets, and priests. As the Roman historian Tacitus observed of Germanic peoples, "They believe that there resides in women an element of holiness and a gift of prophecy; and so they do not scorn to ask advice or lightly disregard their replies." Reflecting Roman patriarchy, Tacitus regarded the leadership of women as indicative of Germanic "decline, I will not say below freedom, but even below decent slavery." [86]

The Celtic pantheon included Lugh, a guardian deity and patron of arts and crafts, whom the Romans conflated with their deity Mercury, the patron of merchants. On the continent, Lugh was associated with the Mother Goddess, Rosmerta. In the British Isles, the festival of Lughnasadh was an Irish harvest festival, and two of its principal sites were associated with fertility goddesses. The Sun Goddess, Sulis, was worshiped in Celtic Britain. The Romans identified Sulis with the traditions of Minerva, consort of Jupiter. Celtic traditions include a deity of the underworld who, in addition to creating storms and protecting cattle and crops, transported the dead to the otherworld.[87]

Odin (Wotan), was the chief deity of the Germanic pantheon. He was a god of war, poetic inspiration, and occult wisdom. Odin acquired occult wisdom by enduring ordeals, such as spearing himself to the World Tree (Yggdrasill) and exchanging one of his eyes for a drink from the spring at the base of the tree. Odin's son Thor was a guardian of ordinary people and was associated with rain and good crops. The goddess Frigg, the wife of Odin, knew the fate of all human beings. The Germanic pantheon included many other divinities, including Ull, the god of snow, and Loki, who fathered Hel (the goddess of death) and the World Serpent.[88]

The societies and religions of Europe's tribal peoples have vanished. Roman legions, commanded by Julius Caesar, conquered the Celtic and Germanic peoples of Gaul (58–50 B.C.E.) and, by Caesar's testimony, destroyed eight hundred towns, conquered over three hundred tribes, and enslaved and killed tens of thousands. Gaul, a region twice the size of Italy, became a Roman province, and the inhabitants were romanized by Roman institutions, law, language, and culture. However, Europe's indigenous peoples did not disappear. They established kingdoms beyond the boundaries of the Roman Empire, and when the empire weakened, they invaded and ultimately governed its western portion. In the period between the indigenous peoples' dominance by Rome and their dominance of Rome, tribal paganism gave way to Christianity. Between the fifth and eleventh centuries, the Irish, Franks, English, Germans, Danes, and Slavs were converted to Christianity. Only remnants of these folk traditions remain—as, for example, echoes of the Celtic celebration of Samhain in Halloween and All Saint's Day and traces of Wotan, Thor, and Frigg in the etymologies of *Wednesday, Thursday,* and *Friday.*

ASIA AND EURASIA   Simple agriculturalists and hunter-gatherers persisted throughout the premodern period in Asia and Eurasia. In the Indian subcontinent, tribal peoples interacted with the Mauryan (321–185 B.C.E.) and Gupta (320–540 C.E.) Empires and withstood invasions of pastoralists from Eurasia (the Huns) without losing their cultural identities. In the process, they came to occupy a recognized social status outside the Hindu caste structure. Eurasian nomads were the first to domesticate horses, using them as pack animals and for herding cattle. In time, they mastered the military use of horses and the production of metal tools and weapons.

During the time of Genghis Khan (1162–1227) and his grandson Kublai Khan (r. 1260–1294), the Mongols from the steppes of central Asia were transformed from a nomadic pastoral society to an imperial power encompassing China, Korea, Mongolia, Tibet, Persia, and Russia. The Mongols valued the heroic virtues of courage, honor, and loyalty and worshiped a variety of gods and goddesses, including their principal deity Tengri, the Eternal Sky. The most enduring tradition among this people has been *shamanism.* It was part of Eurasian religion long before there was a Mongol Empire. By the early modern period, even though most Mongolians had embraced Buddhism and fused elements of their traditional religion into it, traditional Mongol religion, including *shamanistic* practice (for example, healing, soul travel to the spirit world, and animal sacrifice), survived the dissolution of the empire and survives today among indigenous peoples in Siberia and Mongolia.[89]

AFRICA   Food production and metallurgy spread through northern Africa at roughly the same time as they did in Southwest Asia and somewhat later south of the Sahara. In Sudanic East Africa (the region between the Sahara and the equator), farming was established by 2000 B.C.E. and roughly 500 years later in Sudanic West Africa. Hunter-gatherers such as the Mbuti pygmies and the San (Bushmen) occupied the area south of the equator until the migration of tribes of Bantu-speaking farmers—beginning around 2000 B.C.E. in West Africa and ending in southern Africa during the fifteenth century C.E.—reduced their range and number. A West African Iron Age began around 500 B.C.E. and, together with increased agricultural production, development of crafts, and mining of gold, was accompanied by the transition from villages to chiefdoms to kingdoms. The emergence of African kingdoms and the migration of Bantu peoples resulted in the displacement of hunter-gatherers and the assimilation of farmers into national societies.

THE AMERICAS   Many changes occurred in the Americas in the premodern period. Sedentary agricultural villages were fully established in Mesoamerica by 1500 B.C.E. and slightly later in the Andean region. In North America, cultivation radiated out from the Ohio and Mississippi River valleys and from the farming cultures of the Southwest. The Hopewell culture (300 B.C.E.–700 C.E.) of the Ohio River valley was a farming-village society with elaborate earthworks and burial complexes with considerable grave goods. An elaborate chiefdom culture emerged in the Mississippi Valley (800–1600 C.E.) that included several large towns with ceremonial plazas; massive earthen temple mounds; and a hierarchy of priests, military leaders, heads of clans, and commoners. Squash and beans were cultivated in the southwestern part of North America around 1000 B.C.E., and the introduction of maize permitted sedentary village life by 300 B.C.E. Farmers in the area included the cliff-dwelling Anazasi and the Pueblo peoples (for example, the Acoma, Hopi, and Zuni). Between 1000 and 1500

C.E., hunting and gathering peoples (named the Apache and Navajo by the Spanish) migrated into the Southwest and settled into an uneasy coexistence with the Pueblo peoples.

OCEANIA   Humans were present in New Guinea (the first settled area of Melanesia) and Australia over forty thousand years ago. Indigenous Australians subsisted by hunting and gathering, but agriculture was present in New Guinea about nine thousand years ago. Around thirty-three thousand years ago, peoples settled on the islands of Melanesia now known as New Britain and New Wales and somewhat later in the Solomon Islands. Seagoing migrants arrived in the Santa Cruz Islands, New Caledonia, and Fiji by 1500 B.C.E. Parts of Polynesia (Samoa and Tonga) were inhabited in the same period because of migrations from Melanesia, but much of this far-flung area was settled later. Polynesians settled the Marquesas Islands and Easter Island around 400 C.E. and New Zealand around 1000 C.E. The Hawaiian Islands were initially settled around 400 C.E., and a second group of Polynesian immigrants arrived around 1000 C.E. Seagoing people from Southeast Asia arrived in Micronesia, the third region in insular Oceania, around 1000 B.C.E. in the Mariana Islands; Yap and Belau were settled 500 to 1,000 years later.

Generally speaking, the Neolithic societies of insular Oceania cultivated root crops, fished and hunted, lived in villages or homesteads, were accomplished seagoers, and were organized into chiefdom societies. Megalithic structures and massive stoneworks were common among the Neolithic cultures of Oceania and included temples, tombs, and large stone figures, including the gigantic human figures on Easter Island. Animal and human sacrifice were part of the religions of Polynesia and Melanesia, and ritual cannibalism occurred in some areas.

TRIBAL PEOPLES AND MODERN STATES (1500 TO THE PRESENT)

Many changes occurred in the situation of tribal peoples during the premodern period, but nothing that transpired in premodern times matched the dislocation of indigenous peoples that ensued from sustained contact with European states in modern times. By the outset of the twentieth century, those who followed ancient subsistence patterns survived only in the marginally desirable areas of Africa, the Americas, Asia, the Arctic, and Oceania. Tribal peoples have responded to dominant societies in various ways, but those that retain their identities today endure "as ethnic enclaves within the state, paying taxes and obeying common laws but preserving their own language, economic specialities, religions and philosophies."[90]

Between 1500 and 1880, most of Africa was governed by Africans, but by the end of the nineteenth century the colonizing and partitioning of Africa by European powers (Belgium, Britain, France, Germany, Italy, and Portugal) was in full swing. Direct contact between European and sub-Saharan African traders was established in the fifteenth century to the mutual advantage of European and African states. African commerce included ivory, precious metals, and humans. The exchange of slaves for goods was a source of wealth and prestige for African elites and their trading partners. The primary partners in the slave trade from outside sub-Saharan Africa were Islamic and European states. The latter needed labor to exploit the New World. Scholars estimate that 18 million Africans were sold in the Islamic trans-Saharan and Indian Ocean slave trade between 700 and 1905 C.E. and that 10 million enslaved Africans were brought to the Americas between 1500 and 1867. Roughly 427,000 of the latter were sold in the United States.[91]

European states began colonizing Oceania in the seventeenth century, and by 1900 most of insular Oceania (Micronesia, Melanesia, and Polynesia) was governed by colonial administrations. Micronesia was subject to Spanish rule in the late seventeenth century and to German domination in the late nineteenth century. British colonization of Aboriginal lands began in Australia in 1788 and in Tasmania in 1803. The Maori granted sovereignty of New Zealand to Great Britain in 1840. The Japanese occupied Micronesia from 1914 to the end of World War II. The first contact of

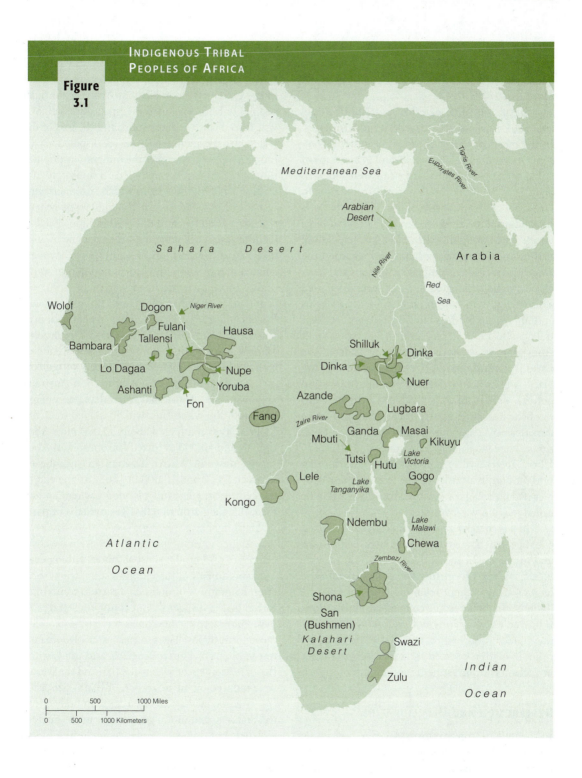

INDIGENOUS TRIBAL PEOPLES OF AFRICA

Figure 3.1

Hawaiians with Europeans occurred in 1778 with the arrival of a British expedition commanded by Capt. James Cook. The United States annexed Hawaii in 1898.

Simple ethnic societies were profoundly changed by sustained contact with modern states. In the most coercive contexts, state systems took control over the land, resources, and institutions of tribal societies. Soviet Russia depicted Siberian peoples as being "without culture" and sought to eradicate "all forms of traditional life in favor of a new Siberia in step with history."[92] Australians rejected the notion that the Aboriginal population had rights to their native lands and regarded the Aboriginals either as pests, like dingoes and kangaroos, to be eliminated or as subjects to be fully assimilated, that is, "observing the same customs and influenced by the same beliefs, as other Australians." In 1933, A. O. Neville, chief protector of Aborigines in Western Australia, articulated the nation's assimilation policy quite simply as "the blacks will have to go white."[93] Similar views and policies were invoked in the United States. Seen as obstacles to the march of civilization, Native Americans were subdued and forced onto reservations. They were subjects of concerted efforts to Christianize, civilize, and otherwise absorb them into the dominant culture. The view that oral peoples had no beliefs or practices that deserved to be called religion was common.

In less coercive contexts, state systems allowed tribal peoples some control over their institutions and resources. In India, the caste system provided a framework for fitting tribal peoples into the larger society without requiring their total assimilation.[94] In Africa, some colonial administrations followed a policy in which indigenous peoples maintained some control but acquiesced to Europeans in matters of trade and missionary activities in exchange for investments and military support.

DESTRUCTION AND DECULTURATION

In its most destructive form, the clash of simple ethnic and modern societies resulted in the death of millions of tribal peoples and the destruction of

entire societies and religious worldviews. In the Americas, European colonization sharply reduced the indigenous population through a combination of the extreme vulnerability of Native American peoples to European diseases (especially smallpox), war, forced labor, malnutrition, and the loss of the will to live. Although the figures are disputed, recent scholarship estimates that the indigenous population of the Americas numbered 75 million to 100 million in 1492, the year in which sustained contact with Europeans began. Roughly 90 percent of the population (67 million to 90 million) lived in Central and South America.[95] The decline in population was astronomical. Demographers have calculated that by 1650, the Indian population south of the United States declined by as much as 90 percent (a decline of 60 million to 81 million people). Recent studies place the number of people in pre-European North America at around 7 million to 10 million; in 1890, the indigenous population of Canada and the United States totaled 400,000.[96]

A similar depopulation occurred in Australia and Tasmania. Aboriginal Australians numbered over 300,000 when the British arrived in 1788. In 1930, they numbered about 30,000 pure Aboriginals and 40,000 of mixed European and Aboriginal descent. Native Tasmanians numbered between 5,000 and 10,000 in 1803. By the end of the century, the last full-blooded Tasmanian had died; there are around 6,000 Tasmanians of partly Aboriginal origin living today.

Aggression and violence are not exclusive characteristics of centralized urban states. Killing enemies was a mark of manhood in some tribal societies. Migrations of oral peoples were sometimes forced by the belligerence of contiguous oral peoples. For example, the Ojibwa forced the Sioux to move from their villages in the eastern woodlands to the plains of North America, and the territories of peaceful peoples like the San and the Mbuti were reduced by the migration of Bantu peoples.

Traditional peoples had a complex body of rituals, taboos, and moral guides to limit intratribal violence, but domestic violence, including blood feuds, killings, and rapes and disfigurations of women, was not uncommon and was endemic in

A group of Aboriginal people in traditional dress dance at a tribal ceremony in Arnheim Land, Australia (ca. 1960–1995).

some tribal societies. Some tribal societies practiced human sacrifice, and some engaged in ritual cannibalism. Compared with centralized state systems, however, violent tribal behaviors were limited in magnitude. The technology of violence has been "perfected" in the twentieth century: 10 million to 15 million combatants and noncombatants were killed in World War I, 55 million people died as a result of World War II, and over 70 million people were domestic victims of their own communist governments.

ASSIMILATION AND ACCULTURATION

Assimilation—the absorption of indigenous peoples into dominant states and cultures—has been the most persistent aim of modern states. This subtle and benign form of cultural genocide undergirded public policies and rested on assumptions that tribal societies and worldviews were hopelessly primitive and incompatible with modern life. Everywhere on earth, simple ethnic societies have been incorporated into the political structures of larger ones, and the religions of these societies have been displaced or are in danger of such a fate. Buddhist traditions have eclipsed Mongol and Tibetan folk religions. In Africa, there are approximately 350 million Christians, 295 million Muslims, and only 70 million who maintain their traditional faiths. Nearly all of the tribal religions of insular Oceania have been displaced by Christianity.

In pre-Columbian America there were more than nine hundred different languages and independent societies, each with distinctive religious traditions. Most of them have not survived. Today, most indigenous peoples of the Americas are Christian. According to one source, in the United States, Indians who follow traditional religions number less than 3 percent of the Native American population.[97] In 1982, Rosa Milisis, the last pure-blooded Yahgan—a Tierra del Fuegan people that numbered around three thousand in 1870—expressed her feelings about the destruction of her people: "If the missionaries had never come we would still be many. The air along this channel would be black from the smoke of our fires."[98]

Eclipses of local traditions are seldom total, however. Tribal traditions interact with the conquering culture, a process of **acculturation** (blending of cultures) that reshapes both. The Christian church has been enriched by the folk traditions of Celtic, Germanic, African, Native American, and Oceanic converts. Buddhist traditions in China, Tibet, Japan, and Korea have absorbed elements from the folk traditions of those areas.

ADAPTATION AND REVITALIZATION

Tribal peoples have responded to the assault on their religious traditions in a variety of ways. Some individuals have committed suicide. Most have converted. Others have sought to sustain and revive their traditions. One form the latter response has taken is the emergence of **revitalization movements.** Such movements have arisen when tribal peoples were destabilized by state systems and the imposition of dominant cultures. Scholars distinguish between revitalization movements that seek to restore traditional ways and those that accommodate and synthesize the old and the new. Table 3.1 lists some indigenous religious revitalization movements.

Restoration movements seek to restore traditional ways and expel alien elements. They often involve a **millenarian** message, proclaiming that with supernatural assistance restoration will soon occur, and an idealized life on earth will be established. The Native American Ghost Dance and the cargo cults of Melanesia are two such examples. The Ghost Dance movement was initiated in 1870 in Nevada by Wodziwob, a Northern Paiute who, during a trance, traveled to the spirit world, where he was informed that the ancestral dead would return and tribal ways would be reestablished. Whites were to be swallowed up and their goods left for those who followed Wodziwob. These events were to be ushered in through dancing and singing.

Wodziwob's movement lasted only a few years, but in late 1888 or January 1889, a message from the Great Spirit was revealed to the son of one of his assistants, the Paiute *shaman* Wovoka (1856–1932). During a trance, Wovoka traveled to the spirit world and was told that the living would be reunited with the dead. Wovoka proclaimed that a messianic figure would soon appear and return the dead to life. In this earthly paradise, the game would be restored and a lasting peace with the whites established. Humans were to hasten the change by dancing and by not drinking, fighting, or quarreling. The dance was performed in a circle and conducted over four to five consecutive nights.

Wovoka's message spread among the Plains Indians, who gave the ideology of the Ghost Dance a coloration of their own. In their version, the bison would return, the whites would disappear, and the dancers wore "ghost shirts" that they believed would magically protect them from the bullets of whites. The reaction of white authorities to the Ghost Dance movement was a factor in the massacre by U. S. soldiers of more than two hundred Lakota (Sioux) men, women, and children on December 29, 1890, at Wounded Knee Creek, South Dakota. The fear the movement engendered in the dominant culture contributed to federal regulations and state statutes that prohibited the performance of Native American ceremonies.

The Melanesian cargo cults were initiated by charismatic leaders who proclaimed that the material goods of Western culture, such as automobiles, canned foods, and tools, were produced supernaturally in some distant land and would be delivered through magico-religious means by airplane or ship to native peoples. The first of the cargo cults, the Vailala Madness, occurred in 1919 among the Orokaiva, a people of New Guinea. In a trance, a young man named Evara received a message that the dead would return in a ship filled with cargo. The response was electrifying. Many believed. Some were possessed by spirits and spoke in tongues. Miracles were reported. When the cargo never arrived, the movement languished and disappeared, only to be replaced by similar movements.

The cargo cults and Ghost Dance movement combined indigenous traditions and millenarian and messianic elements from Christianity. They also combined a desire for the material prosperity of westerners with a deep resentment of their oppressors and a fervent hope that these oppressors would, by some natural contrivance, disappear. Restoration movements have usually disintegrated or faded away in the face of the failure of the cargo or future age to arrive, as well as the lack of sufficient power to cleanse tribal communities from foreign influences and reestablish the old ways through force of arms and moral regeneration.

Like restoration movements, **accommodationist movements** are responses to the challenges

INDIGENOUS RELIGIOUS REVITALIZATION MOVEMENTS

Table 3.1

AFRICAN MOVEMENTS

Bwiti Church	movement among the Fang of Gabon to revitalize traditional religion
Church of the God of Our Ancestors	
	movement among the Fang of Gabon to revitalize traditional religion
Diola	cults in Senegal and Gambia inspired by the prophetess Alinesitoue
Mau Mau movement:	a 1950s revolutionary political movement with traditional religious elements among the Kikuyu of Kenya

OCEANIAN MOVEMENTS

Black Crusade	Australian Aboriginal synthesis of tradition and Christianity
Jinimim (Jesus)	Australian Aboriginal restoration movement
Moro movement	synthesis of Christianity and Solomon Islands indigenous religion
Mulunga	Australian Aboriginal restoration movement
Peli Association	synthesis of Melanesian traditional religion and Christianity
Yali movement	a cargo cult of Papua New Guinea

NATIVE AMERICAN (NORTH) MOVEMENTS

Longhouse religion	Iroquois movement founded by Handsome Lake in 1799
Native American Church	Pan-Indian peyotist church established in 1918
Pom Pom	derived from a cult established by the *shaman* Smohalla (ca. 1850)
Shaker Church	located in the Pacific Northwest; followers of prophet John Slocum
Yaqui Church	integration of Yaqui traditional religion and Roman Catholicism

NATIVE AMERICAN (CENTRAL AND SOUTH) MOVEMENTS

Candomble	Brazilian synthesis of African traditional religions and Christianity
Catimbo	Brazilian integration of African, Native American, and Christian traditions
Convince	Jamaican synthesis of African traditional religion and Christianity
Cumina	Jamaican synthesis of African traditional religion and Christian elements
Macumba	Brazilian synthesis of African, Native American, and Christian traditions
Santería	emerged in Cuba; integration of Yoruba religion and Christianity
Shango	integration of African traditional religions and elements of Christianity
Umbanda	popular Brazilian religion; synthesis of African, Native American, and Christian traditions
Vodou (Voodoo)	Haitian synthesis of African traditional religion and Christianity

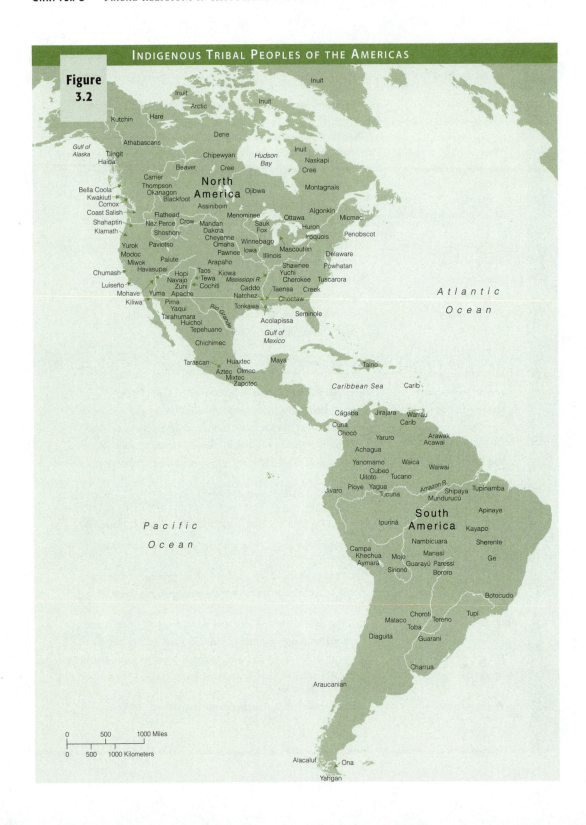

INDIGENOUS TRIBAL PEOPLES OF THE AMERICAS

Figure 3.2

that the dominant culture poses to traditional ways, but rather than seeking to restore the past, these movements involve an accommodation of the old and the new. Some accommodationist groups, such as the movement initiated by the Seneca prophet Handsome Lake (1735–1815), are rooted in a particular tribal community. The Handsome Lake Church remains an important center of traditional Iroquois culture. Other accommodationist groups are syncretic (integrate two or more religious traditions) and cross-cultural (do not function within the boundaries of a particular tribe) as, for example, the pantribal Native American Church. John Lame Deer spoke of religion's role in uniting Indians across the lines of tribal cultures: "It is a good thing for Indians to look upon all Indian religions as a common treasure house, as something that binds us together in our outlook toward nature, toward ourselves, making us one, no longer just Sioux, Cheyennes, Navajos, Pueblos, Iroquois, Haidas—but something much bigger, grander— *Indians*."[99]

The religious use of peyote, a nonaddictive cactus native to Mexico, is very old. A source of visions in pre-Columbian Mexico, peyote was first used in what is now the continental United States in the eighteenth century. By the 1880s, the "peyote way" had cut across traditional tribal lines and included Comanches, Kiowa, and other Native Americans. In a move to gain constitutional guarantees of religious liberty and legal status, the peyote movement was incorporated in the state of Oklahoma in 1918 as the Native American Church. In 1929, the Church numbered an estimated 13,300 adherents from approximately thirty tribes. Current membership is over 200,000. Officially known as the Native American Church of North America, it has incorporated many Christian elements, including the liturgical use of the *Bible* and association of the peyote spirit with Jesus. The blending of the peyote way and Christianity is evident in Lame Deer's observation that "in a way the peyote cult, as it is practiced by many Sioux, is a perfect marriage of Indian and Christian beliefs. That part is all right. We believe all religions are really the same—all part of the Great Spirit."[100]

Sometimes the forces of deculturation and assimilation are so coercive—as, for example, bringing 10 million Africans to the Americas as slaves without regard for tribal or family ties—that it is a wonder that any traditional elements survive. Nonetheless, African traditions persisted among the slaves and their descendants.[101] This was particularly true in regions where there were large concentrations of slaves and less so in the United States, where Africans were more dispersed. The traditions of the Yoruba, the Fon, and other West African peoples have been preserved, transformed, and combined with Roman Catholic and local folk traditions in syncretic movements such as Candomble in Brazil, Santería in Cuba, and Vodou in Haiti.

THE STRUGGLE FOR SELF-DETERMINATION

The years following World War II have been momentous ones for indigenous peoples as they have freed themselves from colonial status. Since 1945, indigenous peoples of Africa, Asia, insular Oceania, and the Philippines have achieved independence, and tribal peoples in those areas and elsewhere have gained ground in their struggle for political, economic, and cultural self-determination. In 1945, nearly all of Africa was colonized by European states; by 1980, the continent was free of colonial governments; and with the end of apartheid in 1991 in the Union of South Africa, indigenous peoples ruled everywhere on that continent. India and Pakistan became independent of the British in 1947; by 1954, the French had ceded all their claims in Indochina to Vietnam, Laos, and Cambodia. The Philippines achieved its independence from the United States in 1946. The peoples of insular Oceania are, with some exceptions, governed by indigenous rather than colonial governments.

The indigenous peoples who rule in the states that emerged from the shadow of Western colonialism after World War II are not tribalists. As noted, tribal nations are now ethnic groups within modern state systems rather than autonomous peoples. The population of most tribal nations con-

CHRONOLOGY OF TRIBAL RELIGIONS IN HISTORICAL TIMES

60	Boudica (Boadicea), a warrior chief of the Iceni tribe of ancient Britain, leads a revolt against the Romans; her army captures several Roman cities and military posts
CA. 400	First seagoing Polynesians reach Hawaiian Islands
CA. 650–1905	Islamic states trade in African slaves
900–1500	Rise of sub-Saharan African kingdoms
CA. 1492	Columbus lands in the Caribbean islands
1510–1865	European and Euro-American trade in African slaves
1531	The Blessed Virgin Mary appears to Juan Diego, an Indian peasant and Christian convert, and reveals that a church should be built near the spot; the Church of Our Lady of Guadalupe is constructed and becomes the most holy shrine in Mexico
CA. 1550	Formation of the Iroquois Confederacy (League of Five Nations)
1690	Pueblo revolt led by an Indian prophet briefly drives the Spanish from Arizona and New Mexico
1788	Establishment of the first British settlements in Australia
1797	Christian missionaries arrive in Tahiti and convert Chief Pomare II and his subjects
1799	During an illness, Seneca prophet Handsome Lake receives several dream messages from God that lead to the establishment of the Handsome Lake or Longhouse religion among the Iroquois
1803	Louisiana Purchase adds 828,000 square miles of mostly tribal lands to the United States
1819	King Liholiho and women of the Hawaiian royal family eat forbidden (taboo) foods in public and strike a blow against Hawaiian traditional religion

stitutes a small portion of the total population of the state or states that they are part of (for example, less than 1 percent in Brazil). However, there are states in which tribal peoples are the majority (around 63 percent in Bolivia) or a very large minority population (around 38 percent in Ecuador).

Although tribal nations remain on the margins of power in state systems, they have had success, especially in the final quarter of the twentieth century, in drawing attention to policies that adversely affect them and in advancing the cause of self-determination. The most fundamental issues involve self-rule, rights respecting the land and natural resources, and rights pertaining to culture and religious liberty. Self-governance, including jurisdiction and stewardship of the land and its resources, and cultural preservation are crucial to sustaining tribal identities as distinct peoples.

Advocates have pressed for the return of tribal lands, self-governance, and cultural integrity

1831	Nat Turner leads slave revolt in Jerusalem, Virginia
1838–1839	Trail of Tears: forced removal by the United States of Cherokees from their ancestral land in Georgia and relocation in Indian Territory; about 4,000 Cherokees die on the way
1876	Battle of the Little Big Horn: Sioux and Cheyenne defeat Col. George Custer and troops under his command
1880–1914	European industrial states partition Africa
1887	Dawes Act establishes a policy of individual, rather than communal, ownership of reservation lands in the United States
1888	Wovoka, a Paiute *shaman*, receives a revelation from God that triggers a revival of the Ghost Dance movement
1890	Massacre (Battle) of Wounded Knee, South Dakota: more than 200 Sioux men, women, and children are killed by U.S. troops
1945–1991	Independence of indigenous states in Africa, Asia, and most of Oceania and the end of Western colonialism
1969	N. Scott Momaday, a Kiowa, is awarded a Pulitzer Prize
1970	Blue Lake, a sacred place of the Tao Pueblo Indians of New Mexico, is restored to them by Congress
1978	American Indian Religious Freedom Act enacted by Congress
1988	Australian Aboriginals and Torres Strait Islanders take title to approximately 8 percent of Australian land.
1990	First Congress of (Soviet) Native Peoples held at the Kremlin
1993	U.N. International Year of the World's Indigenous People; Canadian territory of Nunavut created, to be governed by the aboriginal people of Canada; death of Oodgeroo Noonuccal (Kath Walker), the first Australian Aboriginal to have a book of poetry published

through courts, legislatures, international bodies, and other avenues of public policy and opinion. Progress has been made. The indigenous peoples of Scandinavia (the Saami) have been successful in establishing parliaments to administer their affairs in Finland (1973), Norway (1989), and Sweden (1993) and have secured the right to herd reindeer on public lands. In 1977, the Inuit filed claim to the Northwest Territories of Canada, and in 1993, by a vote of the people of Canada, they were grant-ed the authority to administer the northeastern portion of that vast region now known by the Inuit designation Nunavut (our land). In the United States, Native Americans have pressed for recognition of their legal claims to land. For example, in 1971 the Alaska Native Claims Settlement Act awarded the indigenous peoples of Alaska $962.5 million and control over 44 million acres of land in exchange for surrendering their claim to 331 million acres.

In South and Central America, the Pan-Mayan movement has been effective in securing the right of the indigenous peoples of Guatemala to maintain their identities. Colombia has adopted a constitution that grants traditional peoples control of areas within the country in which they are a majority, but legislation to implement self-governance has not been passed. Brazilian tribes have formed an umbrella group, known as the Union of Indigenous Nations, that has had some success in lobbying for constitutional protections of their ancestral lands. Enforcement has not been encouraging, however, because the economic potential of the rain forest has been irresistible.

Self-determination is a vexing, and not easily resolved, problem. Some states have vigorously resisted tribal self-rule. Postcolonial governments of sub-Saharan Africa have often viewed tribal identities as roadblocks to nation building and have sought to eradicate them through military force, single-party systems, and public education. Other state systems have granted tribal nations more control over their internal affairs. International bodies such as the United Nations and the International Labour Organisation have focused international concern on the rights of indigenous peoples and have urged states to recognize the desire of traditional peoples "to exercise control over their own institutions, ways of life, and economic development and to maintain and develop their identities, languages and religions, within the framework of the States in which they live."[102] Moderate indigenous leaders are comfortable with the latter statement, because they seek increased jurisdiction over tribal affairs within state systems. Militant movements, in contrast, argue that such statements perpetuate the authority of states over indigenous nations. These movements demand the right of tribal nations to determine their political status, a right that might lead to their establishment as independent states.

There have been noteworthy developments among tribal peoples in cultural integrity and preservation, as well as in economic self-determination. In 1968, the Navajo nation created the first tribally controlled college in the United States; today there are thirty tribal colleges serving twenty-five thousand students that prepare Native Americans and non–Native Americans for careers in a technological society and teach them about traditional cultures, languages, and worlds of meaning. Indigenous peoples have also established colleges and programs within existing universities in New Zealand, Canada, Greenland, and Scandinavia.

In the United States, gaming under Indian jurisdiction has been a source of prosperity and independence. Since the passage of the Indian Gaming Regulatory Act (1988), many of the more than five hundred federally recognized tribes have established gambling enterprises. In 1995, Indian gaming grossed nearly $30 billion. The income has provided capital for the creation of other tribally owned businesses and investments, the purchase of ancestral lands, and the establishment of entities that assist the revitalization of tribal identities (for example, museums, presses, and schools). The generation of jobs has helped ameliorate the high rate of unemployment on reservations. Programs that foster economic self-sufficiency and development are in place elsewhere.

A return to a preindustrial and preurban past is not possible. Industrialization, monetary economies, market systems, and modern technologies have replaced or are eroding traditional modes of subsistence. And though some traditionalists resist modernization, most of them have adapted to it. Tribal peoples are part of two worlds. They learn traditional ways and worlds of meaning from their elders and nontraditional ways and worlds of meaning in public schools and universities. They engage in traditional and nontraditional occupations. Some farm, manage herds, or hunt and fish. Some are clerics, clerks, doctors, entrepreneurs, laborers, lawyers, novelists, nurses, poets, politicians, scientists, and teachers. As one observer noted, "Native peoples fit 'traditional' and 'modern' together in their own unique cultural mix—not as living fossils, but as living links to our long-term human past and active participants in today's global village."[103]

CONTEMPORARY INDIGENOUS PEOPLES AND SPIRITUALITY

Tribal peoples and religions have not disappeared, nor are they likely to do so. They have managed to sustain themselves as vital and resilient communities and symbol systems within modern states. In fact, in the twentieth century, the population of indigenous peoples has increased. As noted earlier, the population of tribal ethnics who maintain elements of their traditional cultures and patterns of subsistence has been estimated at around 300 million, but the population is higher if they are defined broadly as peoples who have preserved their cultural identities within state systems. Over 90 percent of the population of sub-Saharan Africa is indigenous, and estimates of the number of tribal ethnics vary widely, from 25 million to 350 million of the region's 550 million population. The indigenous peoples of Asia and Siberia number over 200 million. In the United States, the Native American population has rebounded from 250,000 in 1900 to a census figure of 1.9 million in 1990. Estimates of the Indian population of South America range from 30 million to 40 million. The Aboriginal population of Australia has grown from roughly 30,000 in 1930 to over 225,000 today.

The challenges that traditional peoples and religions face are monumental. Jurisdiction over the land and resources essential to the social and cultural identities of tribal ethnics is unresolved. The gravitation of tribal ethnics to urban centers (over 65 percent of Indians in the United States live in urban areas) also poses a serious threat to the survival of tribal peoples as social and cultural entities. Urban life distances these peoples from their ancestral lands and traditional ways of life, facilitates marriage outside the tribe, and jeopardizes the extended family system.

Joblessness, alcoholism, drugs, poverty, disease, and domestic violence are other enemies. By one estimate, 19 million Africans have been infected by HIV, a problem of such epidemic proportions that the United Nations has estimated that by 2010, AIDS will reduce Africa's labor force by 25 percent. Collectively, Native Americans have the lowest standard of living and the highest rate of unemployment in the United States. Australian Aboriginal infant mortality is three to four times higher than the national average, and the Aboriginal life expectancy is fifty to sixty years, compared with seventy to eighty years for non-Aboriginals.

The problems are monumental, but there are also signs of hope for traditional peoples. One sign is the struggle of indigenous peoples for self-determination. Another is the role that tribal spirituality has played in preserving tribal identities, functioning as a bridge between tribal communities and providing a theological and ethical voice capable of speaking to nontribal peoples and communities of faith.

In the face of tremendous obstacles, indigenous peoples have preserved their tribal identities and traditions while assimilating many of the material and cultural features of the dominant society in which they are embedded. Those who have entered the arena of public discourse have revitalized and reinterpreted their traditions in the light of their experience in both worlds. As Native American scholar Vine Deloria, Jr., sees it, the ongoing vitality of tribal religion calls for a "total translation of tribal beliefs into contemporary terms" by indigenous peoples. Traditional spirituality must go through the fire of criticism, but there is little doubt in Deloria's mind that everyone has much to learn from tribal theologies.[104] Apologists, such as Deloria, argue eloquently for the moral and intellectual superiority of traditional religions.

The vitality of tribal spirituality is evident in four ways: (1) the persistence of tribal religions; (2) the integration of elements of primal spirituality, including morality and traditional medicine, into nontribal religions, modern medicine, and modern justice systems; (3) the emergence of syncretic religions that integrate traditional and nontraditional elements to form a new faith; and (4) the incorporation of tribal spirituality into popular culture. As anthropologist James Clifford observed:

> Throughout the world indigenous populations have had to reckon with the forces of "progress." . . . Many traditions, languages, cosmologies and values are lost . . . but much has simultaneously been invented and revived in complex, oppositional contexts. If the victims of progress and empire are weak, they are seldom passive. It used to be assumed, for example, that conversion to Christiantiy . . . would lead to the extinction of indigenous cultures rather than to their transformation. Something more ambiguous and historically complex has occurred, requiring that we perceive both the end of certain orders of diversity and the creation or translation of others.[105]

Contemporary tribal spirituality is a wondrous and sometimes disconcerting mix. African Christians and Muslims have integrated elements of traditional religions (for example, ancestral spirits, animal sacrifice, polygyny, clitoridectomies, traditional medicine, and circle dances) into their Christian and Islamic faiths. Segments within the Western scientific medical community and some traditionalists have taken steps toward a rapprochement. Traditional African healers have attended seminars to learn how to identify the symptoms of AIDS and to avoid methods that facilitate its spread (for example, sucking blood from patients to remove offending spirits or objects). It is reported that one-fourth of the medical schools in the United States now offer a course in traditional medicine, a practice that includes respect for the value of prayer in healing and applications from Chinese traditional medicine and tribal medicines. Technology and justice are other areas in which traditional and modern behaviors inter-

sect. Clients contact traditional healers by telephone, and professionals in Western justice systems and interested citizens are taking a look at the applicability of tribal justice to contemporary problems.

Progress has been made in religious freedom and respect for tribal religions. The American Indian Religious Freedom Act of 1978 recognized that the traditional religious practices of Native Americans are an "integral part of their culture . . . forming the basis of Indian identity and value systems" and hence are "indispensable and irreplaceable" in their lives. The act also affirmed that "it shall be the policy of the United States to protect and preserve" the inherent right of Native Americans "to believe, express, and exercise" their traditional religions.[106] Nonetheless, Native American religious practices continue to be curtailed. For example, the Native American Church and other indigenous groups that ingest peyote, as well as movements such as Santería that practice animal sacrifice, have been restricted by the law and mores of the dominant culture. There are also disputes about burial grounds, the display of skeletal remains in museums, and access to and control of sacred sites.[107]

Tribal religious traditions have not only survived but also appear to have the power and resiliency to sustain themselves in the forest of contemporary religions. Like all religions, those that have survived have changed over time, undergoing modifications in their symbolic universes to accommodate intrusive changes in their worlds. Once viewed as hopelessly backward and destined for extinction, tribal religions have touched a chord with contemporaries. In a world in which problems seem to defy rational solution, the common good appears to be fractured, and the planet itself is at risk, the rootedness of tribal spirituality in the earth and its conception of a living and spirit-filled cosmos speak to both tribal and nontribal peoples.

GLOSSARY OF TRIBAL RELIGIONS

accommodationist movement
    a religious revitalization group that seeks to integrate traditional ways and new cultural elements.

acculturation   adaptation to new cultural patterns; the blending of cultures.

assimilation   the process of being absorbed into; in this context, cultural assimilation.

axis mundi   a center or hub of the universe conceptualized such as a cosmic mountain or tree that connects the various worlds (heaven, earth, and the underworld).

berdache   a social device or process among several Native American peoples that permitted males to assume the roles of women (in behavior, dress, and occupation).

body soul   one of the elements of the perspective that human beings are composed of more than one soul or spirit. A body soul animates the body and is inseparable from it.

cultural diffusion   the spread of elements of material and linguistic culture within a cultural area or between geocultural areas; for example, the spread of iron technologies throughout the ancient Middle East.

deculturation   the destruction or disruption of the transmission of a culture; the displacement of one culture by another.

deus otiosis   literally, "God without work"; a label for the belief that the high or creator deity is disengaged from active contact with humans and therefore is not the object of cultic practice.

diffused monism   the argument that some tribal theologies conceive of God as many and yet one—that is, that all divinities and spirit beings are directly or indirectly dependent on the Supreme Being.

exorcism   a ritual healing involving the drawing or casting out of a malevolent spirit from the body of the afflicted.

fetish   an object imbued with sacred power and employed for human purposes.

foundational event   an event that signals a turning point in the life of a people.

free soul   a soul that can leave the body during sleep or a trance state and that survives the death of the body.

glossolalia   spirit-filled or spirit-induced speech. In Christianity, it is known as speaking in tongues.

indigenous society, indigenous religion
    a society or religion of peoples who subsist by hunting and gathering, simple agriculture, pastoralism, or some combination thereof. People in indigenous societies maintain some aspects of

their traditional culture within modern state systems. See **simple ethnic society, simple ethnic religion** and **tribal society, tribal religion.**

mana
a Melanesian word for an impersonal supernatural power or an object or person possessing such power.

millenarian
relating to a belief that the end of the world or the end of the present age is near.

pantheism
a belief that Divinity (God) permeates the entire universe.

parallel development
the independent evolution of elements of culture (for example, the independent development of corn agriculture throughout the Americas).

possession divination
divining the resolution to problems and healing by contact with spirit beings in a trance state in which the soul of the entranced travels to the spirit world or the body of the entranced is possessed by a spirit who speaks through the entranced (for example, necromancy and oracular and mediumistic possession).

primal religion
a term for the religion of an oral people.

reincarnation
the rebirth of the souls of the dead in a subsequent life form.

restoration movement
a movement that seeks to restore traditional ways and expel alien elements. A restoration movement often proclaims that with supernatural assistance, the old ways will be restored and an idealized life on earth will be established.

revitalization movement
a movement that seeks to preserve and revive religious traditions, either by the restoration of an idealized past and an explusion of alien elements or by accommodation with the dominant culture.

sacred space
a place set apart as sacred; for example, the center or navel of the cosmos, a place in which the sacred has been manifested (holy mountains, rivers, springs, or caves), or a place associated with foundational events (Christ's Crucifixion or Resurrection).

sacrifice
the ceremonial slaying of an animal or human being or the symbolic substitution of a nonblood offering or medium of exchange (for example, plants or cakes).

simple ethnic society, simple ethnic religion
the society or religion of peoples who subsist by hunting and gathering or simple agriculture. See **tribal society, tribal religion.**

spirit possession
the entering of spirits into other beings (for example, humans and animals) to speak or otherwise act through them.

Supreme Being   in tribal religions, often conceived of as the ultimate source of life. The Supreme Being is involved in creation either directly or by delegation of the work of creation to other spirit beings.

traditional society   narrowly defined, a preurban society (see **simple ethnic society, tribal society**); broadly defined, a society grounded in a religious system that emerged in a preindustrial, but not necessarily preurban, context. A traditional society is more sectarian (religious) than secular.

tribal society, tribal religion

    broadly conceived, a preurban and preliterate society that subsists by hunting and gathering or simple agriculture (preplow farming and pastoralism), and the religion of such a society. A tribe is a kinship group whose members trace themselves to real or fictive ancestors and who have a common language, religion, and culture.

trickster   a spirit being that combines benevolent and malevolent behaviors.

wisdom divination   healing; divining resolutions to problems; and discovering the significance of past, present, and future events by the interpretation, for example, of signs and dreams (for example, astrology, augury, and palmistry).

FOR FURTHER STUDY

Burenhult, Goran, ed. *Traditional Peoples Today: Continuity and Change in the Modern World.* Vol. 5 of *The Illustrated History of Humankind.* San Francisco: HarperSan Francisco, 1994.
> *An anthropological region-by-region overview of contemporary traditional peoples.*

Eliade, Mircea. *Australian Religion.* Ithaca, N.Y.: Cornell University Press, 1973.
> *A good place to begin a study of the traditions of Aboriginal Australians.*

Gill, Sam. *Beyond "The Primitive": The Religions of Nonliterate Peoples.* Englewood Cliffs, N.J.: Prentice-Hall, 1982.
> *A solid introduction to tribal religions, including art, symbolism, rituals, oral traditions, and revitalization movements.*

Graiule, Marcel. *Conversations with Ogotemmeli.* New York: Oxford University Press, 1965.
> *A plunge into the complex religious philosophy of a Dogon sage.*

Hultkrantz, Ake. *The Religions of the American Indians.* Translated by Monica Setterwall. Berkeley and Los Angeles: University of California Press, 1979.
> *An brief introduction to Native American religious concepts and practices*

Neihardt, John. *Black Elk Speaks: Being the Life Story of a Holy Man of the Oglala Sioux.* New York: Pocket Books, 1972.

    A classic text about the life and theology of Black Elk.

Ray, Benjamin. *African Religions.* Englewood Cliffs, N.J.: Prentice-Hall, 1976.

    An excellent overview of African traditional religions, including their divinities, myths, rites, sacred persons, evil, and human destiny.

Sullivan, Lawrence E. *Icanchu's Drum: An Orientation to the Meaning of South American Religions.* New York: Macmillan, 1988.

    A rich introduction to the religious worlds of the indigenous peoples of South America.

Vecsey, Christopher. *Imagine Ourselves Richly: Mythic Narratives of North American Indians.* San Francisco: HarperSan Francisco, 1991.

    A superb analysis of representative Native American myths.

READINGS

Reading 3.1   SYMBOLISM   John Lame Deer

Symbols are the lifeblood of communication and understanding. In the words of Sioux medicine man John Lame Deer, symbols "teach us the meaning of life." The symbolic universe—the world of meanings—of indigenous peoples is complex. In this universe, even ordinary things can have meaning; symbols have power to bring things about and to reveal and point to the visible world of spirit beings and values.

What does Lame Deer mean by his assertion that symbols are more than "just words, spoken or written in a book"? What do circles signify to the Sioux? How are stones used in divination? How are the different divinities (for example, the stone spirit, the thunder spirit, or the water spirit) related to the Great Spirit, Wakan Tanka? According to Lame Deer, life is a symbol to be lived. How is the symbolism of the number 4 acted out in the ritual life of the Sioux and the Native American Church? What was the great Spirit's role in the formation of men who acted like women? What special gift were the latter believed to possess? How does Lame Deer's viewpoint reflect a blending of cultures?

What do you see here, my friend? Just an ordinary old cooking pot, black with soot and full of dents.

It is standing on the fire on top of that old wood stove, and the water bubbles and moves the lid as the white steam rises to the ceiling. Inside the pot is boiling water, chunks of meat with bone and fat, plenty of potatoes.

It doesn't seem to have a message, that old pot, and I guess you didn't give it a thought. Except the soup smells good and reminds you that you are hungry. Maybe you are worried that this is dog stew. Well, don't worry. It's just beef—no fat puppy for a special ceremony. It's just an ordinary, everyday meal.

But I'm an Indian. I think about ordinary, common things like this pot. The bubbling water comes from the rain cloud. It represents the sky. The fire comes form the sun which warms us all—men, animals, trees. The meat stands for the four-legged creatures, our animal brothers, who gave of themselves so that we should live. The steam is living breath. It was water; now it goes up to the sky, becomes a cloud again. These things are sacred. Looking at that pot full of good soup, I am thinking how, in this simple manner, Wakan Tanka takes care of me. We Sioux spend a lot of time thinking about everyday things, which in our mind are mixed up with the spiritual. We see in the world around us many symbols that teach us the meaning of life. We have a saying that the white man sees so little, he must see with only one eye. We see a lot that you no longer notice. You could notice if you wanted to, but you are usually too busy. We Indians live in a world of symbols and images where the spiritual and the commonplace are one. To you symbols are just words, spoken or written in a book. To us they are part of nature, part of ourselves—the earth, the sun, the wind and the rain, stones, trees, animals, even little insects like ants and grasshoppers. We try to understand them not with the head but with the heart, and we need no more than a hint to give us the meaning. . . .

To our way of thinking, the Indians' symbol is the circle, the hoop. Nature wants things to be round. The bodies of human beings and animals have no corners. With us the circle stands for the togetherness of people who sit with one another around the campfire, relatives and friends united in peace while the pipe passes from hand to hand. The camp in which every tipi had its place was also a ring. The tipi was a ring in which people sat in a circle and all the families in the village were in turn circles within a larger circle, part of the larger hoop which was the seven campfires of the Sioux, representing one nation. The nation was only a part of the universe, in itself circular and made of the earth, which is round, of the sun, which is round, of the stars, which are round. The moon, the horizon, the rainbow— circles within circles within circles, with no beginning and no end.

To us, this is beautiful and fitting, symbol and reality at the same time, expressing the harmony of life and nature. Our circle is timeless, flowing; it is new life emerging from death—life winning out over death. . . .

From birth to death we Indians are enfolded in symbols as in a blanket. An infant's cradle board is covered with designs to ensure a happy, healthy life for the child. The moccasins of the dead have their soles beaded in a certain way to ease the journey to the hereafter. For the same reason, most of us have tattoos on our wrists—not like the tattoos of your sailors—daggers, hearts and nude girls—but just a name, a few letters or designs. The Owl Woman who guards the road to the spirit lodges looks at these tattoos and lets us pass. They are like a passport. Many Indians believe that if you don't have these signs on your body, that Ghost Woman won't let you through but will throw you over a cliff. In that case you don't have to roam the earth endlessly as a *wanagi*—a ghost. All you can do then is frighten people and whistle. Maybe its not so bad being a *wanagi*. It could even be fun. I don't know. But, as you see, I have my arms tattooed.

Every day in my life I see symbols in the shape of certain roots or branches. I read messages in the stones. I pay special attention to them, because I am a *Yuwipi* man and that is my work. But I am not the only one. Many Indians do this.

Inyan—the rocks—are holy. Every man needs a stone to help him. There are two kinds of pebbles that make good medicine. One is white like ice. The other is like ordinary stone, but it makes you pick it up and recognize it by its special shape. You ask stones for aid to find things which are lost or missing. Stones can give warning of an enemy, of approaching misfortune. The winds are symbolized by a raven and a small black stone the size of an egg. . . .

Nothing is so small and unimportant but it has a spirit given to it by Wakan Tanka. Tunkan is what you might call a stone god, but he is also part of the Great Spirit. The gods are separate beings, but they are all united in Wakan Tanka. It is hard to understand—something like the Holy Trinity. You can't explain it except by going back to the "circles within circles" idea, the spirit splitting itself up into stones, trees, tiny insects even, making them all *wakan* by his ever-presence. And in turn, all these myriad of things which make up the universe flowing back to their source, united in the one Grandfather Spirit.

Tunkan—the stone god—is the oldest spirit, we think, because he is the hardest. He stands for creation, you know, like the male part. Hard, upright, piercing—like the lance- and arrowheads fashioned from it in the old days.

Inyan Wasicun Wakan—the Holy White Stone Man—that's what we call Moses. He appeals to us. He goes up all alone to the top of his mountain like an Indian, to have his vision, be all alone with his God who talks to him through fire, bushes and rocks. Moses, coming back from the hill carrying stone tablets with things scratched on them—he would have made a good Indian medicine man.

Tunkan, the stone spirit; Wakinyan, the thunder spirit; Takuskanska, the moving spirit; Unktehi, the water spirit—they are all *wakan:* mysterious, wonderful, incomprehensible, holy. They are all part of the Great Mystery. These are our four great supernaturals, which brings us to yet another form of symbolism—the magic of numbers which we share with many other peoples.

Four is the number that is most *wakan,* most sacred. Four stands for Tatuye Topa—the four quarters of the earth. . . .

We Sioux speak of the four virtues a man should possess: bravery, generosity, endurance, wisdom. For a woman, these are bravery, generosity, truthfulness and the bearing of children.

We Sioux do everything by fours: We take four puffs when we smoke the peace pipe. Those of us who believe in the Native American Church take four times four spoons of peyote during a night of prayer. We pour water four times over the hot rocks in the sweat lodge. For four nights, we seek a vision during a *hanblechia.* Men abstain for four days and nights from the company of women before an important ceremony. The women in their turn stay away from the men's camp for four days when they are *isnati*—menstruating—or after giving birth. At least they used to. . . .

Words, too, are symbols and convey great powers, especially names. Not Charles, Dick and George. There's not much power in those. But Red Cloud, Black Elk, Whirlwind, Two Moons, Lame Deer—these names have a relationship to the Great Spirit. Each Indian name has a story behind it, a vision, a quest for dreams. We receive great gifts from the source of a name; it links us to nature, to the animal nations. It gives power. You can lean on a name, get strength from it. It is a special name for you and you alone—not a Dick, George, Charles kind of thing.

Each Indian name tells a story that remains hidden to outsiders unless it is explained to them. Take our famous chief Man-Afraid-of-His-Horse. It sounds funny in English. Man-Afraid once led the warriors in battle against the enemy who fled before him. The medicine men wanted to honor him and so they bestowed this name on him, which really means: He is so brave, so feared, that his enemies run away when merely seeing his horse, even if he is not on it. That is a powerful name. He had to live up to it.

Besides the names by which we were known, we Sioux also used to have a secret second name, which was never spoken aloud. This was our good-luck, life-long name. Sometimes the grandfather or a medicine man gave a child this secret name, but it was best to go to a *winkte* for it.

Winktes were men who dressed like women, looked like women and acted like women. They did so by their own choice or in obedience to a dream. They were not like other men, but the Great Spirit made them *winktes* and we accepted them as such. They were supposed to have the gift of prophecy, and the secret name a *winkte* gave a child was believed to be especially powerful and effective. In former days a father gave to a *winkte* a fine horse in return for such a name.

To a white man, symbols are just that: pleasant things to speculate about, to toy with in your mind. To us, they are much, much more. Life to us is a symbol to be lived.

Source: From John Fire/Lame Deer and Richard Erdoes, *Lame Deer: Seeker of Visions,* © 1972 by John Fire/Lame Deer and Richard Erdoes. Reprinted by permission of Simon & Schuster.

Reading 3.2 IN THE BEGINNING: A BAROTSE CREATION MYTH

Examine closely this creation myth of the Barotse people. It presents several common mythic motifs, including the belief that creation is the work of God, the notion of a divine couple, and a vision of an original paradise shattered by human aggression. Barotseland is now part of Zambia.

Is God's (Nyambi's) power limited or unlimited? How are male and female rooted in the divine? What events disrupted the primeval harmony and led to the separation of God and humankind? Where did the deities live before the separation? After the separation? How is the theme of human alienation from the divine related to the origin of suffering and death and to the human need for healing powers (medicine)? What does this story tell us about the important of divination?

In the beginning, Nyambi made all things. He made animals, fishes, birds. At that time he lived on earth with his wife, Nasilele. One of Nyambi's creatures was different from all the others. His name was Kamonu. Kamonu imitated Nyambi in everything Nyambi did. When Nyambi worked in wood, Kamonu worked in wood; when Nyambi forged iron Kamonu forged iron.

After a while Nyambi began to fear Kamonu.

Then one day Kamonu forged a spear and killed a male antelope, and he went on killing. Nyambi grew very angry at this.

"Man, you are acting badly," he said to Kamonu. "These are your brothers. Do not kill them."

Nyambi drove Kamonu out into another land. But after a while Kamonu returned. Nyambi allowed him to stay and gave him a garden to cultivate.

It happened that at night buffaloes wandered into Kamonu's garden and he speared them; after that, some elands, and he killed one. After some time Kamonu's dog died; then his pot broke; then his child died. When Kamonu went to Nyambi to tell him what had happened he found his dog and his pot and his child at Nyambi's.

Then Kamonu said to Nyambi, "Give me medicine so that I may keep my things." But Nyambi refused to give him medicine. After this, Nyambi met with his two counselors and said, "How shall we live since Kamonu knows too well the road hither?"

Nyambi tried various means to flee Kamonu. He removed himself and his court to an island across the river. But Kamonu made a raft of reeds and crossed over to Nyambi's island. Then Nyambi piled up a huge mountain and went to live on its peak. Still Nyambi could not get away from man. Kamonu found his way to him. In the meantime men were multiplying and spreading all over the earth.

Finally Nyambi sent birds to go look for a place for Litoma, god's town. But the birds failed to find a place. Nyambi sought council from a diviner. The diviner said, "Your life depends on Spider." And Spider went and found an abode for Nyambi and his court in the sky. Then Spider spun a thread from earth to the sky and Nyambi climbed up on the thread. Then the diviner advised Nyambi to put out Spider's eyes so that he could never see the way to heaven again and Nyambi did so.

After Nyambi disappeared into the sky Kamonu gathered some men around him and said, "Let us build a high tower and climb up to Nyambi." They cut down trees and put log on log, higher and higher toward the sky. But the weight was too great and the tower collapsed. So that Kamonu never found his way to Nyambi's home.

But every morning when the sun appeared, Kamonu greeted it, saying, "Here is our king. He has come." And all the other people greeted him shouting and clapping. At the time of the new moon men call on Nasilele, Nyambi's wife.

Source: E. W. Smith, *African Ideas of God* (London: Edinburgh House Press, 1950).

Reading 3.3   BEYOND THE DOME WE CALL THE SKY:
A SENECA MYTH OF ORIGINS

The Seneca, a Native American people indigenous to western New York, have several creation myths. This one introduces several motifs typical of Native American mythology. It speaks of a spirit world that existed before the visible world but that had much in common with the world of the Seneca, including chiefs, families, couples, ceremonies, lodges, tobacco, and bread. Identify the following mythic motifs: a primordial defilement and fall, a cosmic tree, fabulous spirit creatures, an earth diver, the origin of the earth, the birth of twins, the connection of the death of a goddess to the origin of domestic plants, the conflict between good and evil, a spiritual quest, the origin and naming of animals, the completion of creation, and the return of the Mother Goddess to the sky.

The Seneca were the largest of the original five nations in the Iroquois Confederacy (the League of Five Nations). They subsisted through a combination of gathering, hunting, fishing, and farming. Today most Seneca are Christians, but some follow a group that is an admixture of their traditional religion and Christianity (known as the Longhouse or Handsome Lake religion), which was inspired by the Seneca *shaman* and prophet Handsome Lake (ca. 1735–1815.) In a vision Handsome Lake was directed by messenger spirits sent by the Creator to revitalize traditional values and ceremonies and to urge the Iroquois to cooperate with one another and abstain from drinking, fighting, gambling, and adultery.

Beyond the dome we call the sky, there is another world. There in the most ancient of times was a fair country where lived the great chief of the up-above-world and his people, the celestial beings. This chief had a wife who was very aged in body, having survived many seasons.

In that upper world there were many things of which men of today know nothing. This world floated like a great cloud and journeyed where the great chief wished it to go. The crust of that world was not thick, but none of these men beings knew what was under the crust.

In the center of that world there grew a great tree that bore flowers and fruits and all the people lived from the fruits of the tree and were satisfied. Now, moreover, the tree bore a great blossom at its top, and it was luminous and lighted the world above, and wonderful perfume filled the air the people breathed. The rarest perfume of all was that which resembled the smoke of sacred tobacco and this was the incense greatly loved by the great chief. It grew from the leaves that sprouted from the roots of the tree.

The roots of the tree were white and ran in four directions. Far through the earth they ran, giving firm support to the tree. Around this tree the people gathered daily, for here the Great Chief had his lodge where he dwelt. Now, in a dream he was given a desire to take as his wife a certain maiden who was very fair to look upon. So, he took her as his wife, for when he had embraced her he found her most pleasing. When he had eaten the marriage bread he took her to his lodge, and to his surprise found that she was with child. This caused him great anger and he felt himself deceived, but the woman loved the child, which had been conceived by the potent breath of her lover when he had embraced her. He was greatly distressed, for this fair Mature Flowers was of the noblest family.

He, the Ancient One, fell into a troubled sleep and a dream commanded him to have the celestial tree uprooted as a punishment to his wife and as a relief for his troubled spirit. So on the morrow he announced to his wife that he had a dream and could not be satisfied until it had been divined. Thereupon she "discovered his word," and it was that the tree should be uprooted.

"Truly you have spoken," said Ancient One, "and now my mind shall be satisfied." And the woman, his wife, saw that there was trouble ahead for the sky world, but she too found pleasure in the uprooting of the tree, wishing to know what was beneath it. Yet did she know that to uproot the tree meant disaster for her, through the anger of Ancient One against her.

It so happened that the chief called all his people together and they endeavored to uproot the tree, it being deep-rooted and firm. Then did the chief grow even more angry, for Mature Flowers had cried out that calamity threatened and nobody would avert it. Then did the chief himself embrace the tree and with a mighty effort uprooted it, throwing it far away. His effort was tremendous, and in uprooting the tree he shook down fruits and leaves. Thereafter he went into his lodge and entered into the apartment where his wife, Mature Flowers, lay moaning that she too must be satisfied by a look into the hole. So the chief led her to the hole made by uprooting the tree.

He caused her to seat herself on the edge of the hole and peer downward. Again his anger returned against her, for she said nothing to indicate that she had been satisfied. Long she sat looking into the hole until the chief in rage drew her blanket over her head and pushed her with his foot, seeking to thrust her into the hole and be rid of her. As he did this she grasped the earth at her side and gathered in her fingers all manner of seeds that had fallen from the shaken tree. In her right hand she held the leaves of the plant that smelled like burning tobacco, for it grew from a root that had been broken off. Again the chief pushed the woman, whose curiosity had caused the destruction of the greatest blessing of the up-above-world. It was a mighty push, and despite her hold upon the plant and upon the ground, she fell into the hole.

Now, this hole had penetrated the crust of the upper world and when Mature Flowers fell she went far down out of sight and the chief could not see her in the depths of the darkness below. As she fell she beheld a beast that emitted fire from its head. It is said that as she passed by him he took out a small pot, a corn mortar, a pestle, a marrow bone, and an ear of corn and presented them to her, saying, "Because you have thus done, you shall eat by these things, for there is nothing below, and all who eat shall see me once and it will be the last."

Now it is difficult to know how this Fire Beast can be seen, for he is of the color of the wind and is of the color of anything that surrounds it, though some say he is pure white.

Hovering over the troubled waters below were other creatures, some like and some unlike those that were created afterward. It is said by the old people that in those times lived the spirits of the Wind, the Defending Face, the Thunder, and the Heavy Night. There were also what seemed to be ducks upon the water and these also saw the descending figure.

The creature-beings knew that a new body was coming to them and that here below there was no abiding place for her. They took council together and sought to devise a way to provide for her.

It was agreed that the duck-creatures should receive her on their interknit wings and lower her gently to the surface below. The great turtle from the under-world was to arise and make his broad back a resting place. It was as had been agreed and the woman came down upon the floating island.

Then did the creatures seek to make a world for the woman and one by one they dived to the bottom of the water seeking to find earth to plant upon the turtle's back. A duck dived but went so far that it breathed the water and came up dead. A pickerel went down and came back dead. Many creatures sought to find the bottom of the water but could not. At last the creature called Muskrat made the attempt and succeeded only in touching the bottom with his nose, but this was sufficient, for he was enabled to smear it [the mud] upon the shell and the earth immediately grew, and as the earth-substance increased so did the size of the turtle.

After a time the woman, who lay prone, aroused herself and released what was in her hands, dropping many seeds into the folds of her garment. Likewise she spread out the earth from the heaven world she had grasped and thus caused the seeds to spring into germination as they dropped from her dress.

The root of the tree that she had grasped she sunk into the soil where she had fallen and this too began to grow until it formed a tree with all manner of fruits and flowers and bore a luminous orb at its top by which the new world became illuminated.

Now in due season Mature Flowers lay beneath the tree and to her a daughter was born. She was then happy, for she had a companion. The girl grew rapidly until very soon she could run about. It was then the custom of Mature Flowers to say: "My daughter, run about the island and return telling me what you have seen."

Day by day the girl ran around the island and each time it became larger, making her trips longer and longer. She observed that the earth was carpeted with grass and that shrubs and trees were springing up everywhere. This she reported to her mother, who sat beneath the centrally situated great tree.

In one part of the island there was a tree on which grew a long vine and upon this vine the girl was accustomed to swing for amusement and her body moved to and fro giving her great delight. Then did her mother say, "My daughter, you laugh as if being embraced by a lover. Have you seen a man?"

"I have seen no one but you, my mother," answered the girl, "but when I swing I know someone is close to me and I feel my body embraced as if with strong arms. I feel thrilled and I tingle, which causes me to laugh."

Then did Mature Flowers look sad, and she said, "My daughter, I know not now what will befall us. You are married to Wind, and he will be the father of your children. There will be two boys."

In due season the voices of two boys were heard speaking, and the words of one were kind and he gave no trouble, but the words of the other were harsh and he desired to kill his mother. His skin was covered with warts and boils and he was inclined to cause great pain.

When the two boys were born, Elder One made his mother happy but when Warty One was born he pierced her through the arm pit and stood upon her dead body. So did the mother perish, and because of this Mature Flowers wept.

The boys required little care but instantly became able to care for themselves. After the mother's body had been arranged for burial, Mature Flowers saw the elder one, whom she called Good Mind, approach, and he said, "Grandmother, I wish to help you prepare the grave." So he helped his grandmother, who continually wept, and deposited the body of his mother in a grave. Then the grandmother said to her daughter, "O my daughter, you have departed and made the first path to the world from which I came bringing your life. When you reach that homeland make ready to receive many beings from this place below, for I think the path will be trodden by many."

Good Mind watched at the grave of his mother and watered the earth above it until the grass grew. He continued to watch until he saw strange buds coming out of the ground. Where the feet were the earth sprouted with a plant that became the stringed-potato; where her fingers lay sprang the beans; where her abdomen lay sprang the squash; where her breasts lay sprang the corn plant; and from the spot above her forehead sprang the tobacco plant.

Now the warty one was named Evil Mind, and he neglected his mother's grave and spent his time tearing up the land and seeking to do evil.

When the grandmother saw the plants springing from the grave of her daughter and cared for by Good Mind she was thankful and said, "By these things we shall hereafter live, and they shall be cooked in pots with fire, and the corn shall be your milk and sustain you. You shall make the corn grow in hills like breasts, for from the corn shall flow our living."

Then the grandmother, Mature Flowers, took Good Mind about the island and instructed him how to produce plants and trees. So he spoke to the earth and said, "Let a willow here come forth," and it came. In a like manner he made the oak, the chestnut, the beech, the hemlock, the spruce, the pine, the maple, the buttonball, the tulip, the elm, and many other trees that should become useful.

With a jealous stomach the Evil Mind followed behind and sought to destroy the good things but could not, so he spoke to the earth and said, "Briars come forth," and they came forth. Likewise he created poisonous plants and thorns upon bushes.

Upon a certain occasion Good Mind make inquiries of his grandmother, asking where his father dwelt. Then she said, "You shall now seek your father. He lives to the uttermost east and you shall go to the far eastern end of the island and go over the water until you behold a mountain rising from the sea. You shall walk up the mountain and there you will find your father seated upon the top."

Good Mind made the pilgrimage and came to the mountain. At the foot of the mountain he looked upward and called, "My father, where are you?" And a great voice sounded the words, "A son of mine shall cast the cliff from the mountain's edge to the summit of this peak." Good Mind grasped the cliff and with a mighty effort flung it to the mountain top. Again he cried, "My father, where are you?" The answer came, "A son of mine shall swim the cataract from the pool below to the top." Good Mind leaped into the falls and swam upward to the top where the water poured over. He stood there and cried again, "My father, where are you?" The voice answered, "A son of mine shall wrestle with the wind." So, there at the edge of a terrifying precipice, Good Mind grappled with Wind and the two wrestled, each endeavoring to throw the other over. It was a terrible battle and Wind tore great rocks from the mountain side and lashed the water below, but Good Mind overcame Wind, and he departed moaning in defeat. Once more Good Mind called, "My father, where are you?" In awesome tones the voice replied, "A son of mine shall endure the flame," and immediately a flame sprang out of the mountain side and enveloped Good Mind. It blinded him and tortured him with its cruel heat, but he threw aside its entwining arms and ran to the mountaintop where he beheld a being sitting in the midst of a blaze of light.

"I am your father," said the voice. "You are my son."

"I have come to receive power," said the son. "I wish to rule all things on the earth."

"You have power," answered the father. "You have conquered. I give to you the bags of life, the containers of living creatures that will bless the earth."

Thus did the father and son counsel together and the son learned many things that he should do.

Now the father said, "How did you come to find me, seeing I am secluded by many elements?"

Good Mind answered, "When I was about to start my journey, my grandmother gave me a flute and I blew upon it, making music. Now, when the music ceased the flute spoke to me, saying, 'This way shall you go,' and I continued to make music and the voice of the flute spoke to me."

Then did the father say, "Make music by the flute and listen, then shall you continue to know the right direction."

In course of time Good Mind went down the mountain and he waded the sea, taking with him the bags with which he had been presented. As he drew near the shore he became curious to know what was within, and he pinched one bag hoping to feel its contents. He felt a movement inside which increased until it became violent. The bag began to roll about on his back until he could scarcely hold it and a portion of the mouth of the bag slipped from his hand. Immediately the things inside began to jump out and fall into the water with a great splash, and they were water animals of different kinds. The other bag began to roll around on his back but he held on tightly until he could do so no more, when a portion of the mouth slipped and out flew many kinds of birds, some flying seaward and others inland toward the trees. Then as before the third bag began to roll about but he held on very tight, but it slipped and fell into the water and many kinds of swimming creatures rushed forth, fishes, crabs, and eels. The fourth bag then began to roll about, but he held on until he reached the land when he threw it down, and out rushed all the good land animals, of kinds he did not know. From the bird bag had come good insects, and from the fish bag had also come little turtles and clams.

When Good Mind came to his grandmother beneath the tree, she asked what he had brought, for she heard music in the trees and saw creatures scampering about. Thereupon Good Mind related what had happened, and the grandmother said, "We must now call all the animals and discover their names, and moreover we must so treat them that they will have fat."

So then she spoke, "Cavity be in the ground and be filled with oil." The pool of oil came, for Mature Flowers had the power of creating what she desired.

Good Mind then caught the animals one by one and brought them to his grandmother. She took a large furry animal and cast it into the pool and it swam very slowly across, licking up much oil. "This animal shall hereafter be known as bear and you shall be very fat." Next came another animal with much fur and it swam across and licked up the oil, and it was named buffalo. So in turn were named the elk, the moose, the badger, the woodchuck, and the raccoon, and all received much fat. Then came the beaver, the porcupine, and the skunk. Now Good Mind wished the deer to enter, but it was shy and bounded away, whereupon he took a small arrow and pierced its front leg, his aim being good. Then the deer came and swam across the pool and oil entered the wound and healed it. This oil of the deer's leg is a medicine for wounds to this day and if the eyes are anointed with it one may shoot straight.

Again other animals came and one by one they were named weasel, mink, otter, fisher, panther, lynx, wild cat, fox, wolf, big wolf, squirrel, chipmunk, mole, and many others.

And many animals that were not desired plunged into the pool of oil, and these Good Mind seized as they came out and he stripped them of their fat and pulled out their bodies long. So he did to the otter, fisher, weasel, and mink. So he did to the panther, wolf, big wolf, and fox, the lynx and the wildcat. Of these the fat to this day is not good tasting. But after a time Evil Mind secured a bag of creatures from the road to the cave and unloosed it, and evil things crawled into the pool and grew fat. So did the rattlesnake and great bugs and loathly worms.

Thus did Evil Mind secure many evil monsters and insects, and he enticed good animals into his traps and perverted them and gave them appetites for men-beings. He was delighted to see how fierce he could make the animals, and set them to quarreling.

He roamed about visiting the streams of pure water made by Good Mind and filling them with mud and slime, and he kicked rocks in the rivers and creeks to make passage difficult, and he planted nettles and thorns in the paths. Thus did he do to cause annoyance.

Now Good Mind sat with his grandmother beneath the tree of light and he spoke to her of the world and how he might improve it. "Alas," she said, "I believe that only one more task awaits me and then I shall go upon my path and follow your mother back to the world beyond the sky. It remains for me to call into being certain lights in the blackness above where Heavy Night presides."

So saying she threw the contents of a bag into the sky and it quickly became sprinkled with stars. And thus there came into being constellations, and of these we see the bear chase, the dancing brothers, the seated woman, the beaver skin, the belt, and many others.

Now it seems that Good Mind knew that there should be a luminous orb and, so it is said, he took his mother's face and flung it skyward and made the sun, and took his mother's breast and flinging it into the sky made the moon. So it is said, but there are other accounts of the creation of these lights. It is said that the first beings made them by going into the sky.

Shortly after the creation of the stars, the grandmother said to Good Mind, "I believe that the time has come when I should depart, for nearly all is finished here. There is a road from my feet and I have a song that I shall sing by which I shall know the path. There is one more matter that troubles me, for I see that your brother is jealous and will seek to kill you. Use great care that you overcome him and when you have done so confine him in the cave and send with him the evil spirit beasts, lest they injure men."

When morning came she had departed and her journey was toward the sky world.

Good Mind felt lonely and believed that his own mission was about at end. He had been in conflict with his brother, Evil Mind, and had sought, moreover, to overcome and to teach the Whirlwind and Wind, and the Fire Beast.

Soon Evil Mind came proposing a hunting trip and Good Mind went with him on the journey. When they had gone a certain distance Evil Mind said, "My elder brother, I perceive that you are about to call forth men-beings who shall live on the island that we here have inhabited. I propose to afflict them with disease and to make life difficult, for this is not their world but mine, and I shall do as I please to spoil it."

Then did Good Mind answer and say, "Truly I am about to make men-beings who shall live here when I depart, for I am going to follow the road skyward made first by my mother."

"This is good news," answered Evil Mind. "I propose that you then reveal unto me the word that has power over your life, that I may possess it and have power when you are gone."

Good Mind now saw that his brother wished to destroy him, and so he said, "It may happen that you will employ the cattail flag, whose sharp leaves will pierce me."

Good Mind then lay down and slumbered, but soon was awakened by Evil Mind who lashing him with cattail flags, and yelling loudly, "You shall die." Good Mind arose and asked his brother what he meant by lashing him and he answered, "I was seeking to awaken you from a dream, for you were speaking."

So, soon again the brother, Evil Mind, asked, "My brother, I wish to know the word that has power over you." And Good Mind perceiving his intention answered, "It may be that deerhorns will have power over me; they are sharp and hard."

Soon Good Mind slept again and was awakened by Evil Mind beating him with deerhorns, seeking to destroy him. They rushed inland to the foot of the tree and fought each other about it. Evil Mind was very fierce and rushed at his brother, thrusting the horns at him and trying to pierce his chest and his face or tear his abdomen. Finally, Good Mind disarmed him, saying, "Look what you have done to the tree where our grandmother used to care for us, and whose branches have supplied us with food. See how you have torn this tree and stripped it of its valuable products. This tree was designed to support the life of men-beings and now you have injured it. I must banish you to the region of the great cave and you shall have the name of Destroyer."

So saying he used his good power to overcome Evil Mind's evil power and thrust him into the mouth of the cave, and with him all manner of enchanted beasts. There he placed the white buffalo, the poison beaver, the poison otter, snakes, and many bewitched things that were evil. So there to this day abides Evil Mind, seeking to emerge, and his voice is heard giving orders.

Source: From Arthur C. Parker, *Seneca Myths and Folk Tales* (New York: Buffalo Historical Society, 1923), pp. 59–73.

Reading 3.4   A Conversation with Ogotemmêli:
A Dogon Creation Story   Marcel Griaule

The Dogon are a people of Mali, in Africa, who number around 300,000. They live in villages and subsist by farming, hunting, and crafts. Although many are Muslim or Christian, the majority still follow their traditional religions. The following conversation (one of many) with the Dogon sage Ogotemmêli (fl. 1946) was recorded by the French ethnographer Marcel Griaule (d. 1956).

The conversation with Ogotemmêli focuses on a Dogon understanding of the cosmos and how it came to be. Why is tobacco important to such a conversation? How did God (Amma) create the stars? What does God have to do with pottery? Describe the procedure involved in the creation of the earth. In what position is the earth feminine? Why did God seek intercourse with the earth? What initially blocked the satisfaction of this desire? Who was the first being born from the union of God and Earth? Why was the jackal a malicious spirit being? Who are the Nummo? What is their relationship to God? How did the Nummo finish the work of creation? What defilement did the jackal cause? Why were the first humans each created with male and female souls? What rituals were subsequently performed to divide humans into male or female? Why are these rituals performed today?

Ogotemmêli, seating himself on his threshold, scraped his stiff leather snuff-box, and put a pinch of yellow powder on his tongue.

"Tobacco," he said, "makes for right thinking."

So saying, he set to work to analyze the world system, for it was essential to begin with the dawn of all things. He rejected as a detail of no interest, the popular account of how the fourteen solar systems were formed from flat circular slabs of earth, one on top of the other. He was only prepared to speak of the serviceable solar system; he agreed to consider the stars, though they only played a secondary part. . . .

The stars came from pellets of earth flung out into space by the God Amma, the one God. He had created the sun and the moon by a more complicated process, which was not the first known to man but is the first attested invention of God: the art of pottery. The sun is, in a sense, a pot raised once for all to white heat and surrounded by a spiral of red copper with eight turns. The moon is the same shape, but its copper is white. It was heated only one quarter at a time. . . .

The God Amma, it appeared, took a lump of clay, squeezed it in his hand and flung it from him, as he had done with the stars. The clay spread and fell on the north, which is the top, and from there stretched out to the south, which is the bottom of the world, although the whole movement was horizontal. The earth lies flat, but the north is at the top. It extends east and west with separate members like a foetus in the womb. It is a body, that is to say, a thing with members branching out from a central mass. This body, lying flat, face upwards, in a line from north to south, is feminine. Its sexual organ is an anthill, and its clitoris a termite hill. Amma, being lonely and desirous of intercourse with this creature, approached it. That was the occasion of the first breach of the order of the universe.

Ogotemmêli ceased speaking. His hands crossed above his head, he sought to distinguish the different sounds coming from the courtyards and roofs. He had reached the point of the origin of troubles and of the primordial blunder of God.

"If they overheard me, I should be fined an ox!"

At God's approach, the termite hill rose up, barring the passage and displaying its masculinity. It was as strong as the organ of the stranger, and intercourse could not take place. But God is all-powerful. He cut down the termite hill, and had intercourse with the excised earth. But the original incident was destined to affect the course of things for ever; from this defective union, there was born, instead of the intended twins, a single being, the *Thos aureus* or jackal, symbol of the difficulties of God. Ogotemmêli's voice sank lower and lower. It was no longer a question of women's ears listening to what he was saying; other, non-material, ear-drums might vibrate to his important discourse. . . .

But, when he came to the beneficent acts of God, Ogotemmêli's voice again assumed its normal tone.

God had further intercourse with his earth-wife, and this time without mishaps of any kind, the excision of the offending member having removed the cause of the former disorder. Water, which is the divine seed, was thus able to enter the womb of the earth and the normal reproductive cycle resulted in the birth of twins. Two beings were thus formed. God created them like water. They were green in colour, half human beings and half serpents. From the head to the loins they were human: below that they were serpents. Their red eyes were wide open like human eyes, and their tongues were forked like the tongues of reptiles. Their arms were flexible and without joints. Their bodies were green and sleek all over, shining like the surface of water, and covered with short green hairs, a presage of vegetation and germination.

These spirits, called Nummo, were thus homogeneous products of God, of divine essence like himself, conceived without untoward incidents and developed normally in the womb of the earth. Their destiny took them to Heaven, where they received the instructions of their father. Not that God had to teach them speech, that indispensable necessity of all beings, as it is of the world-system; the Pair were born perfect and complete; they had eight members, and their number was eight, which is the symbol of speech.

They were also of the essence of God, since they were made of his seed, which is at once the ground, the form, and the substance of the life-force of the world, from which derives the motion and the persistence of created being. This force is water, and the Pair are present in all water: they *are* water, the water of the seas, of coasts, of torrents, of storms, and of the spoonfuls we drink.

Ogotemmêli used the terms "Water" and "Nummo" indiscriminately.

"Without Nummo," he said, "it is not even possible to create the earth, for the earth was moulded clay and it is from water (that is, from Nummo) that its life is derived."

"What life is there in the earth?" asked the European.

"The life-force of the earth is water. God moulded the earth with water. Blood too he made out of water. Even in a stone, there is this force, for there is moisture in everything."

"But if Nummo is water, it also produces copper. When the sky is overcast, the sun's rays may be seen materializing on the misty horizon. These rays, excreted by the spirits, are of copper and are light. They are water too, because they uphold the earth's moisture as it rises. The Pair excrete light, because they are also light." . . .

The Nummo, looking down from Heaven, saw their mother, the earth, naked and speechless, as a consequence no doubt of the original incident in her relations with the God Amma. It was necessary to put an end to this state of disorder. The Nummo accordingly came down to earth, bringing with them fibres pulled from plants already created in the heavenly regions. They took ten bunches of these fibres, corresponding to the number of their ten fingers, and made two strands of them, one for the front and one for behind. To this day masked men still wear these appendages hanging down to their feet in thick tendrils.

But the purpose of this garment was not merely modesty. It manifested on earth the first act in the ordering of the universe and the revelation of the helicoid sign in the form of an undulating broken line.

For the fibres fell in coils, symbol of tornadoes, of the windings of torrents, of eddies and whirlwinds, of the undulating movement of reptiles. They recall also the eight-fold spirals of the sun, which sucks up moisture. They were themselves a channel of moisture, impregnated as they were with the freshness of the celestial plants. They were full of the essence of Nummo: they *were* Nummo in motion, as shown in the undulating line, which can be prolonged to infinity.

When Nummo speaks, what comes from his mouth is a warm vapour which conveys, and itself constitutes, speech. This vapour, like all water, has sound, dies away in a helicoid line. The coiled fringes of the skirt were therefore the chosen vehicle for the words which the Spirit desired to reveal to the earth. He endued his hands with magic power by raising them to his lips while he plaited the skirt, so that the moisture of his words was imparted to the damp plaits, and the spiritual revelation was embodied in the technical instruction.

In these fibres full of water and words, placed over his mother's genitalia, Nummo is thus always present.

Thus clothed, the earth had a language, the first language of this world and the most primitive of all time. Its syntax was elementary, its verbs few, and its vocabulary without elegance. The words were breathed sounds scarcely differentiated from one another, but nevertheless vehicles. Such as it was, this ill-defined speech sufficed for the great works of the beginning of all things.

In the middle of a word Ogotemmêli gave a loud cry in answer to the hunter's halloo which the discreet Akundyo, priest of women dying in childbirth and of stillborn children, had called through the gap in the wall.

Akundyo first spat to one side, his eye riveted on the group of men. He was wearing a red Phrygian cap which covered his ears, with a raised point like a uraeus on the bridge of the nose in the fashion known as "the wind blows." His cheek-bones were prominent, and his teeth shone. He uttered a formal salutation to which the old man at once replied and the exchange of courtesies became more and more fulsome.

"God's curse," exclaimed Ogotemmêli, "on any in Lower Ogol who love you not!"

With growing emotion, Akundyo made shift to out-do the vigour of the imprecation.

"May God's curse rest on me," said the blind man at last, "if I love you not!"

The four men breathed again. They exchanged humorous comments on the meagerness of the game in the I valley. Eventually Akundyo took his leave of them, asserting in the slangy French of a native soldier that he was going to "look for porcupine," an animal much esteemed by these people.

The conversation reverted to the subject of speech. Its function was organization, and therefore it was good; nevertheless from the start it let loose disorder.

This was because the jackal, the deluded and deceitful son of God, desired to possess speech, and laid hands on the fibres in which language was embodied, that is to say, on his mother's skirt. His mother, the earth, resisted this incestuous action. She buried herself in her own womb, that is to say, in the anthill, disguised as an ant. But the jackal followed her. There was, it should be explained, no other woman in the world whom he could desire. The hole which the earth made in the anthill was never deep enough, and in the end she had to admit defeat. This prefigured the even-handed struggles between men and women, which, however, always end in the victory of the male.

The incestuous act was of great consequence. In the first place it endowed the jackal with the gift of speech so that ever afterwards he was able to reveal to diviners the designs of God.

It was also the cause of the flow of menstrual blood, which stained the fibres. The resulting defilement of the earth was incompatible with the reign of God. God rejected that spouse, and decided to create living beings directly. Modelling a womb in a damp clay, he placed it on the earth and covered it with a pellet flung out into space from heaven. He made a male organ in the same way and having put it on the ground, he flung out a sphere which stuck to it.

The two lumps forthwith took organic shape; their life began to develop. Members separated from the central core, bodies appeared, and a human pair arose out of the lumps of earth.

At this point the Nummo Pair appeared on the scene for the purpose of further action. The Nummo foresaw that the original rule of twin births was bound to disappear, and that errors might result comparable to those of the jackal, whose birth was single. For it was because of his solitary state that the first son of God acted as he did.

"The jackal was alone from birth," said Ogotemmêli, "and because of this he did more things than can be told."

The Spirit drew two outlines on the ground, one on top of the other, one male and the other female. The man stretched himself out on these two shadows of himself, and took both of them for his own. The same thing was done for the woman. Thus it came about that each human being from the first was endowed with two souls of different sex, or rather with two principles corresponding to two distinct persons. In the man the female soul was located in the prepuce; in the woman the male soul was in the clitoris.

But the foreknowledge of the Nummo no doubt revealed to him the disadvantages of this makeshift. Man's life was not capable of supporting both beings: each person would have to merge himself in the sex for which he appeared to be best fitted.

The Nummo accordingly circumcised the man, thus removing from him all the femininity of his prepuce. The prepuce, however, changed itself into an animal which is "neither a serpent nor an insect, but is classed with serpents." This animal is called a *nay*. It is said to be a sort of lizard, black and white like the pall which covers the dead. Its name also means "four," the female number, and "Sun," which is a female being. The *nay* symbolized the pain of circumcision and the need for the man to suffer in his sex as the woman does.

The man then had intercourse with the woman, who later bore the first two children of a series of eight, who were to become the ancestors of the Dogon people. In the moment of birth, the pain of parturition was concentrated in the woman's clitoris, which was excised by an invisible hand, detached itself and left her, and was changed into the form of a scorpion. The pouch and the sting symbolized the organ: the venom was the water and the blood of the pain.

Source: Marcel Griaule, *Conversations with Ogotemmêli.* 1965, London: Oxford University Press for the International African Institute. (London: Oxford University Press, 1970), pp. 16–23. Permission to reprint.

Reading 3.5   SEEKING A VISION: THE SIOUX VISION QUEST

George Sword (Long Knife)

Traditionally, humans have experienced the spirit world and discovered their destines through dreams and visions. In this selection, George Sword (Long Knife; fl. 1896)—a Lakota or western Sioux of the Ogalala tribe—describes the Sioux vision quest. Long Knife (Sword) was a healer associated with the Bear Medicine people (a society of Sioux healers), a performer of traditional ceremonies, and a teacher of Sioux theology and myths. He was a war chief and, later, a police officer and judge at the Pine Ridge Reservation. Sword (Long Knife) subsequently converted to Christianity and was a deacon for several years preceding his death.

Why are visions important? What steps does a seeker take to have a vision? How are pipes, tobacco, and *shaman* involved in spirit quests? What does one do if a vision is not received?

The following specialized terms are featured in this selection:

wakan being	a spirit being or god.
akicita	messengers of spirit.
Initi	a ceremonial lodge and sweat bath to make the body strong and pure; necessary preparation for visions and many other activities.
cansasa	"red wood," or dried willow or dogwood bark mixed with tobacco and smoked ceremonially. Like sweat baths, smoking was a preparation for visions. Tobacco played an important part in Sioux ceremonies and deliberations.
Wakan Tanka	the Great Spirit, which governs everything.
Taku Shanskan	"that which moves sky"; also identified as the Great Spirit.
Nagi Tanka	a spirit associated with the Great Spirit. For Sword, there were eight Great Spirits, but they could also be thought of as one Great Spirit. The latter is an example of a theology of one and the many discussed in Chapter 3.

It is the custom of all the Lakotas to seek a vision when they are to undertake some important thing or wish for something very earnestly. A vision is something told by a *wakan* being and it is told as if in a dream. The *wakan* beings are the superior beings, that is, they are superior to ordinary mankind. They know what is past and present and what will be. They can speak Lakota or any other language and they can use the sign language. Nearly all the superior beings have *akicita* and they send their communications by them. If one of these messengers gives a communication, it will be known from whom it comes because no two of the *Wakan* use the same *akicita*. There are four kinds of superior beings and each kind may give a communication. It may be known which kind it is that gives the communication by the kind of vision it is and by the messenger that gives it. When one seeks a vision and receives a communication he must obey as he is told to do. If he does not, all the superior beings will be against him.

If a boy or a young man wishes to know what he should do all his life, he should seek a vision. He may pray to a superior being to give it to him. Maybe that being will do so but maybe another will give him a vision and tell him what he should do and how he should live. There are many kinds of preparation for seeking a vision. If the vision is for something of little importance, there is not much to do before seeking it. The most important vision is of the sun. The preparation for that is made by dancing the Sun Dance.

Sometimes a vision is given without seeking it. Usually this is done only to the shamans and to old men or old women. If a man is alone and speaks to no one and neither eats nor drinks anything and thinks continually about the superior beings, he may have a vision. The usual way to seek a vision is to purify the body in an *Initi* by pouring water on hot stones and then go naked, only wrapped in a robe, to the top of a hill, and stay there without speaking to anyone of mankind or eating, or drinking, and thinking continually about the vision he wishes.

If one goes to [a] hill in this manner, he should remain there until he receives a vision or until he is nearly perished. His people should sing songs and pray to the superior being to give him a vision. They should give gifts and do nothing that would offend the superior being he is asking for a vision. When he comes to where he is to stay while fasting, he should prepare a place about as long as a man and about half as wide. He should take from this place all vegetation of every kind and all bugs and worms and everything that lives. He should have four charms made by a shaman and tied in little bundles about as big as the end of a finger. These should be fastened to the small ends of sprouts of the plum tree. These are spirit banners.

He should put a banner, first at the west side of the place he has prepared; then one at the north side; then one at the east side; then one at the south side. He should have a pipe and plenty of *cansasa* and tobacco mixed. He should then light his pipe and point the mouthpiece first toward the west and then toward the north and then toward the east and then toward the south. Then he should point it toward the sky and then toward the earth and then toward the sun. He should have some sweet-grass and very often he should burn some of this and some sage. If he does these things in the right way, he will surely receive a vision. If a little boy is seeking a vision, a man may stand far from him and do these things for him.

If he seeks a vision about a very important thing, he should have a shaman help him get ready for it and advise him about when he has had a communication. The shaman should make the *Initi* and do a ceremony while they are in it. When he comes from the hill, he and the shaman and as many others as he may invite should *ini* in the *Initi* and the shaman should do another ceremony. These things are all done to please the superior beings.

If one has a vision, he sees something. It may be like a man or it may be like an animal or a bird or an insect or anything that breathes, or it may be like a light of some kind or a cloud. He may see it come to him. Maybe it will come and he will not see it coming. It may speak to him or it may not speak. If it speaks to him, it may speak so that he will understand what it says, but maybe it will speak as the shamans speak. Maybe it will make only a noise. He should remember what it says and how it speaks. Maybe it will speak without his having a vision. If he sees something it is a vision. If he hears something it is a communication.

When a Lakota sees a vision, he should remain on the place he prepares until he receives either a vision or has a communication. He should stay there awaiting this as long as he is able and can live, if it need be for him to do so. If he concludes he is not to have a vision from the one he has asked, he may ask *Taku Skanskan* for a vision. If he does this, he should stand and offer smoke to *Wakan Tanka*. Then he should look toward the sky and offer smoke to *Nagi Tanka*. He should then bow with his face to the ground and look at nothing until he has a vision or a communication. When he can endure no longer to wait, he may go to his people.

When he goes to his people, if he has had a vision, he should go singing. If he has not had a vision, he should go silently and with his face covered.

Source: Reprinted from James R. Walker, *Lakota Belief and Ritual* (Lincoln: University of Nebraska Press, 1980), pp. 84–86. Edited by Raymond J. DeMallic and Elaine A. Johner by permission of the publisher. © 1980, 1991 by the University of Nebraska Press.

Reading 3.6   !KUNG HEALING   Marjorie Shostak

The !Kung are a people who subsist by hunting and gathering. The first part of this selection, which introduces !Kung healing and its relationship to the spirit world, is the voice and analysis of Marjorie Shostak, an American ethnologist. In the second part, the speaker is Nisa (fl. 1970s), a !Kung healer who speaks through Shostak about her healing and the manner in which she acquired her curative powers. Nisa's band lives in Botswana, on the northern edge of the Kalahari Desert.

!Kung healing is an example of possession divination and curing, which involves a trance state, soul travel to the spirit world, and a variety of curing techniques. What is a healer's "half-death"? What is the relationship of trance curing to the forming of healers through training and apprenticeship?

How did Nisa acquire the power to cure? Were drugs involved? What connection do hallucinogenic plants, such as mushrooms, peyote, and tobacco, have to experiences of the sacred? How can dancing contribute to trance states? What does the diviner's soul do in the spirit world? Does traditional curing require the consent and cooperation of spirit beings? What curing techniques did Nisa use?

[Marjorie Shostak:] The realm of the spiritual infuses all aspects of !Kung physical and social life, and is seen as a fundamental determinant in the delicate balance between life and death, sickness and health, rain and drought, abundance and scarcity. This realm is dominated by one major god in command of an entourage of lesser gods. Both the greater and lesser deities are modeled on humans, and their characteristics reflect the multitude of possibilities inherent in the human spirit. Sometimes they are kind, humane, and generous; at other times, whimsical, vindictive, or cruel. Their often erratic behavior is thought responsible for the unpredictability of human life and death.

One way the spirits affect humans is by shooting them with invisible arrows carrying disease, death, or misfortune. If the arrows can be warded off, illness will not take hold. If illness has already penetrated, the arrows must be removed to enable the sick person to recover. An ancestral spirit may exercise this power against the living if a person is not being treated well by others. If people argue with her frequently, if her husband shows how little he values her by carrying on blatant affairs, or if people refuse to cooperate or share with her, the spirit may conclude that no one cares whether or not she remains alive and may "take her into the sky."

Interceding with the spirits and drawing out their invisible arrows is the task of !Kung healers, men and women who possess the powerful healing force called *n/um*. *N/um* generally remains dormant in a healer until an effort is made to activate it. Although an occasional healer can accomplish this through solo singing or instrumental playing, the usual way of activating n/um is through the medicinal curing ceremony or trance dance. To the sound of undulating melodies sung by women, the healers dance around and around the fire, sometimes for hours. The music, the strenuous dancing, the smoke, the heat of the fire, and the healers' intense concentration cause their *n/um* to heat up. When it comes to a boil, trance is achieved.

At this moment, the *n/um* becomes available as a powerful healing force, to serve the entire community. In trance, a healer lays hands on and ritually cures everyone sitting around the fire. His hands flutter lightly beside each person's head or chest or wherever illness is evident; his body trembles; his breathing becomes deep and coarse; and he becomes coated with a thick sweat—also considered to be imbued with power. Whatever "badness" is discovered in the person is drawn into the healer's own body and met by the *n/um* coursing up his spinal column. The healer gives a mounting cry that culminates in a soul-wrenching shriek as the illness is catapulted out of his body and into the air.

While in trance, many healers see various gods and spirits sitting just outside the circle of firelight, enjoying the spectacle of the dance. Sometimes the spirits are recognizable—departed relatives and friends—at other times they are "just people." Whoever these beings are, healers in trance usually blame them for whatever misfortune is being experienced by the community. They are barraged by hurled objects, shouted at, and aggressively warned not to take any of the living back with them to the village of the spirits.

To cure a very serious illness, the most experienced healers may be called upon, for only they have enough knowledge to undertake the dangerous spiritual exploration that may be necessary to effect a cure. When they are in a trance, their souls are said to leave their bodies and to travel to the spirit world to discover the cause of the illness or the problem. An ancestral spirit or a god is usually found responsible and asked to reconsider. If the healer is persuasive and the spirit agrees, the sick person recovers. If the spirit is elusive or unsympathetic, a cure is not achieved. The healer may go to the principal god, but even this does not always work. As one healer put it, "Sometimes, when you speak with God, he says, 'I want this person to die and won't help you make him better.' At other times, God helps; the next morning, someone who has been lying on the ground, seriously ill, gets up and walks again."

These journeys are considered dangerous because while the healer's soul is absent his body is in "half-death." Akin to loss of consciousness, this state has been observed and verified by medical and scientific investigators. The power of other healers' *n/um* is all that is thought to protect the healer in this state from actual death. He receives lavish attention and care—his body is vigorously massaged, his skin is rubbed with sweat, and hands are laid on him. Only when consciousness returns—the signal that his soul has been reunited with his body—do the other healers cease their efforts.

The underlying causes of illness that healers discover while in trance seem to reflect an understanding of the role psychological factors may play in disease. The analysis a !Kung healer offered of a young woman's bout with malaria, for example, illustrated his awareness that her father's recent death might have been affecting her heath. The healer's soul made a journey to the world of the dead to find out why the woman was sick. He found the spirit of the woman's father sitting on the ground with the spirit of his daughter in his arms. He was holding her tenderly, rocking her and singing to her. The healer asked why his daughter was with him in the world of the dead and not in the land of the living. Her father explained that he had been desolate without her in the spirit world. He had brought her there so he could be with her again. The healer defended the daughter's right—and obligation—to remain alive: "Your daughter has so much work still to do in life—having children, providing for family and relatives, helping with grandchildren." After an impassioned debate, the healer convinced the spirit to give his daughter time to experience what life had still to offer and to grow old: "Then she'll join you." As the father reluctantly agreed, he loosened his grip on the young woman and her spirit returned to her body. A cure was thus effected, and her health restored.

N/um reflects the basically egalitarian nature of !Kung life. It is not reserved for a privileged few: nearly half the men and a third of the women have it. There is enough for everyone; it is infinitely divisible; and all can strive for it. Almost anyone who is willing to go through the rigors of apprenticeship can attain it. Not everyone wants to, however. Many apprentices become afraid or lack ambition and drop out. Others—though few in number—try but do not succeed. Although one can often strengthen one's *n/um* by working at it, its limit is said to be determined by God.

The usual way a young man receives *n/um* is from an experienced healer, often a close male relative, during the ceremonial medicine dance. The apprentice follows the healer around—dancing alone or with his arms wrapped tightly around the healer's waist—hour after hour, with only short rests, often from dusk until dawn. Each time the healer's trance state swells with sufficient intensity and power, he rubs the apprentice's body with his sweat, lays on hands, and snaps his fingers repeatedly against the apprentice's waist to shoot spiritual arrows—through which *n/um* is said to be transferred—into him. This process may be repeated several times during the night and may continue for a number of months or years—however long it takes the novice (typically in his late teens or early twenties) to become accomplished.

This apprenticeship involves a profound dependency on the teacher, which seems to help the novice drop his defenses, thereby making possible an altered state of consciousness—or, as the !Kung would view it, a heightened spiritual reality. The beginner often experiences extreme fluctuations in his emotional state as he learns to trance. At one moment, he may grab burning coals, throw himself into the fire, or run out into the bush and the night. He may cry, or rage against the group, or throw coals or hot sand at people, or break things around him. The next moment may find him whining plaintively, like a small child, begging for water or food; given it, he may spit it out on the ground. If the trance becomes too powerful, he may even be overcome and enter half-death, falling violently to the ground.

These actions do not really alarm others around him. Women sitting by the fire prevent him from burning himself and men run after him to bring him back from the bush. The other healers, especially his teacher, are responsible for ensuring that his soul returns to his body after he enters half-death and for helping him to learn to control the trance. Only when trance energy is harnessed can it be used for social good. Younger men, most dramatic and extreme in trance, are therefore usually less powerful as healers than are older men who have mastered the great forces released in trance.

One older man put it this way, "My *n/um* is so strong I can talk to people or even get up and put wood on the fire when I'm in trance." Healers like this one can also usually enter trance easily, almost at will, and depend minimally on external stimulation. For others, however, the weakening of the body that accompanies aging is reflected in a similar weakening of spiritual power. . . .

About one third of !Kung women are capable of entering trance, but only a small number of these learn to lay on hands and cure—without doubt, the most prestigious activity in !Kung spiritual life. The remainder do not channel their *n/um* into helping others, but seem to view the powerful state of trance as an end in itself. Many women express a desire to advance to higher spiritual planes, but most do not attempt it. Some claim this is because women are more afraid of pain than men are. (Intense physical pain is universally seen as closely associated with the !Kung trance.) But the erratic course by which girls and women receive *n/um* and the more limited opportunities available to them to practice their skills are more likely causes.

A girl's first exposure to altered states of consciousness may occur when she is as young as eight years old, when her mother feeds her small quantities of *gwa,* a purportedly psychoactive root. This training tapers off with the approach of motherhood, because *n/um* is thought harmful to fetuses and young children. If the woman's spiritual education, halted in its (as well as her) infancy, does resume, it is likely to be only when she is in her forties, after her last child has grown. By this time, male healers of the same age, having learned their skills when they were still young, physically strong, and more adaptable, have long since become accomplished.

Despite these obstacles, a handful of older !Kung women have always reached high levels of spiritual mastery. When they lay on hands, their *n/um* is considered as powerful and effective as that of men of comparable experience and accomplishment. The current interest in the women's dance is likely to encourage even more women to become actively involved. The few successful women healers are promoting this trend by initiating drum dances in villages they visit, by teaching women to trance, by transferring *n/um,* and by guiding others to lay on hands and cure.

[Nisa:] *N/um*—the power to heal—is a very good thing. This is a medicine very much like your medicine because it is strong. As your medicine helps people, our *n/um* helps people. But to heal with *n/um* means knowing how to trance. Because, it is in trance that the healing power sitting inside the healer's body—the *n/um*— starts to work. Both men and women learn how to cure with it, but not everyone wants to. Trance-medicine really hurts! As you begin to trance, the *n/um* slowly heats inside you and pulls at you. It rises until it grabs your insides and takes your thoughts away. Your mind and your senses leave and you don't think clearly. Things become strange and start to change. You can't listen to people or understand what they say. You look at them and they suddenly become very tiny. You think, "What's happening? Is God doing this?" All that is inside you is the *n/um;* that is all you can feel.

You touch people, laying on hands, curing those you touch. When you finish, other people hold you and blow around your head and your face. Suddenly your senses go "Phah!" and come back to you. You think, "Eh hey, there are people here," and you see again as you usually do.

My father had the power to cure people with trance medicine, with gemsbok-song trance medicine. Certain animals—gemsbok, eland, and giraffe—have trance songs named after them, songs long ago given by God. These songs were given to us to sing and to work with. That work is very important and good work; it is part of how we live.

It is the same with everything—even the animals of the bush. If a hunter is walking in the bush, and God wants to, God will tell him, "There's an animal lying dead over there for you to eat." The person is just walking, but soon sees an animal lying dead in the bush. He says, "What killed this? It must have been God wanting to give me a present." Then he skins it and eats it; that's the way he lives.

But if God hadn't wanted, even if the hunter had seen many animals, his arrows would never strike them. Because if God refuses to part with an animal, the man's arrows won't be able to kill it. Even if the animal is standing close beside him, his arrows will miss every time. Finally he gives up or the animal runs away. It is only when God's heart says that a person should kill something, be it a gemsbok or a giraffe, that he will have it to eat. He'll say, "What a huge giraffe! I, a person, have just killed a small something that is God's." Or it may be a big eland that his arrows strike.

That is God's way; that is how God does things and how it is for us as we live. Because God controls everything.

God is the power that made people. He is like a person, with a person's body and covered with beautiful clothes. He has a horse on which he puts people who are just learning to trance and becoming healers. God will have the person in trance ride to where he is, so God can see the new healer and talk to him.

There are two different ways of learning how to trance and of becoming a healer. Some people learn to trance and to heal only to drum-medicine songs. My mother knew how to trance to these, although she never learned to heal. There are other people who know how to trance and to heal to drum-medicine songs as well as to ceremony-dance songs. The *n/um* is the same in both. If a person is lying down, close to death, and someone beats out drum-medicine songs, a healer will enter a trance and cure the sick person until he is better. Both men and women have *n/um,* and their power is equal. Just as a man brings a sick person back to health, so does a woman bring a sick person back to health. . . .

N/um is powerful, but it is also very tricky. Sometimes it helps and sometimes it doesn't, because God doesn't always want a sick person to get better. Sometimes he tells a healer in trance, "Today I want this sick person. Tomorrow, too. But the next day, if you try to cure her, then I will help you. I will let you have her for a while." God watches the sick person, and the healer trances for her. Finally, God says, "All right, I only made her slightly sick. Now, she can get up." When she feels better, she thinks, "Oh, if this healer hadn't been here, I would have surely died. He's given me my life back again."

That's *n/um*—a very helpful thing!

I was a young woman when my mother and her younger sister started to teach me about drum-medicine. There is a root that helps you learn to trance, which they dug for me. My mother put it in my little leather pouch and said, "Now you will start learning this, because you are a young woman already." She had me keep it in my pouch for a few days. Then one day, she took it and pounded it along with some bulbs and some beans and cooked them together. It had a horrible taste and made by mouth feel foul. I threw some of it up. If she hadn't pounded it with the other foods, my stomach would have been much more upset and I would have thrown it all up; then it wouldn't have done anything for me. I drank it a number of times and threw up again and again. Finally I started to tremble. People rubbed my body as I sat there, feeling the effect getting stronger and stronger. My body shook harder and I started to cry. I cried while people touched me and helped me with what was happening to me.

Eventually, I learned how to break out of my self and trance. When the drum-medicine songs sounded, that's when I would start. Others would string beads and copper rings into my hair. As I began to trance, the women would say, "She's started to trance, now, so watch her carefully. Don't let her fall." They would take care of me, touching me and helping. If another woman was also in trance, she laid on hands and helped me. They rubbed oil on my face and I stood there—a lovely young woman, trembling in trance—until I was finished.

I loved when my mother taught me, and after I had learned, I was very happy to know it. Whenever I heard people beating out drum-medicine songs, I felt happy. Sometimes I even dug the root for myself and, if I felt like it, cooked and drank it. Others would ask for some, but if they hadn't learned how to trance, I'd say, "No, if I gave it to you, you might not handle it well." But once I really knew how to trance, I no longer drank the medicine; I only needed that in the beginning.

When my niece gets older, I'll dig some of the root for her, put it in her kaross for a few days, and then prepare it. She will learn how to drink it and to trance. I will stand beside her and teach her. . . .

Lately, though, I haven't wanted to cure anyone, even when they've asked. I've refused because of the pain. I sometimes become afraid of the way it pulls at my insides, over and over, pulling deep within me. The pain scares me. That's why I refuse. Also, sometimes after I cure someone, I get sick for a while. That happened not long ago when I cured my older brother's wife. The next day, I was sick. I thought, "I won't do that again. I cured her and now I'm sick!" Recently, Dau cured her again. I sat and sang the medicine songs for him. He asked me to help, but I said, "No, I was so sick the last time I almost died. Today, my medicine is not strong enough."

I am a master at trancing to drum-medicine songs. I lay hands on people and they usually get better. I know how to trick God from wanting to kill someone and how to have God give the person back to me. But I, myself, have never spoken directly to God nor have I seen or gone to where he lives. I am still very small when it comes to healing and I haven't made these trips. Others have, but young healers like myself haven't. Because I don't heal very often, only once in a while. I am a woman, and women don't do most of the healing. They fear the pain of the medicine inside them because it really hurts! I don't really know why women don't do more of it. Men just fear it less. It's really funny—women don't fear childbirth, but they fear medicine!

Source: Majorie Shostak, *Nisa: The Life and Words of a !Kung Woman* (New York: Vintage, 1983), pp. 291–295, 298–303. Reprinted by permission of the publisher from NISA: THE LIFE AND WORDS OF A !KUNG WOMAN by Marjorie Shostak, Cambridge, Mass.: Harvard University Press © 1981 by Marjorie Shostak.

Reading 3.7   CHIEF SEATTLE'S SPEECH OF 1854   Chief Seattle

Chief Seattle (ca. 1786–1866), the most prominent of the headmen of the Duwamish and Suquamish people of the Puget Sound area, delivered this speech in 1854 to the territorial governor Isaac Stevens and others assembled in front of Doc Maynard's store in Seattle, the city that bears his name. At that meeting, the governor notified the Duwamish and Suquamish of the U.S. government's intent to purchase their land for settlement by whites and to provide protection for them on reservations. Seattle's response is that of a proud visionary who believed that his people must accommodate the demands of the "Big Chief at Washington" whose people "are like the grass that covers vast prairies." Notes from the speech were taken by Henry Smith and Governor Stevens's translator, Benjamin Shaw. Smith's presumably embellished version of Seattle's remarks appeared thirty-three years later, a rendering of which is reprinted here.

What does Seattle's speech tell us about the relationship of tribal peoples to the land and to their ancestors? How did Seattle, a baptized Christian, juxtapose the Great Spirit of the Puget Sound people with the Christian God? Why does it appear to him that the Christian God is partial to "His paleface children"? What does he mean that Indians and whites have little in common and yet "may be brothers after all"?

Yonder sky that has wept tears of compassion upon my people for centuries untold, and which to us appears changeless and eternal, may change. Today is fair. Tomorrow it may be overcast with clouds. My words are like the stars that never change. Whatever Seattle says the great chief at Washington can rely upon with as much certainty as he can upon the return of the sun or the seasons. The White Chief says that Big Chief at Washington sends us greetings of friendship and goodwill. This is kind of him for we know he has little need of our friendship in return. His people are many. They are like the grass that covers vast prairies. My people are few. They resemble the scattering trees of a storm-swept plain. The great—and I presume—good White Chief sends us word that he wishes to buy our lands but is willing to allow us enough to live comfortably. This indeed appears just, even generous, for the Red Man no longer has rights that he need respect, and the offer may be wise also, as we are no longer in need of an extensive country.

There was a time when our people covered the land as the waves of a wind-ruffled sea covered its shell-paved floor, but that time long since passed away with the greatness of tribes that are now but a mournful memory. I will not dwell on, nor mourn over, our untimely decay, nor reproach my paleface brothers with hastening it, as we too may have been somewhat to blame.

Youth is impulsive. When our young men grow angry at some real or imaginary wrong, and disguise their faces with black paint, it denotes that their hearts are black, and that they are often cruel and relentless, and our old men and old women are unable to restrain them. Thus it has ever been. Thus it was when the white man first began to push our forefathers westward. But let us hope that the hostilities between us may never return. We would have everything to lose and nothing to gain. Revenge by young men is considered gain, even at the cost of their own lives, but old men who stay at home in times of war, and mothers who have sons to lose, know better.

Our good father at Washington—for I presume he is now our father as well as yours since King George has moved his boundaries further north—our great and good father, I say, sends us word that if we do as he desires he will protect us. His brave warriors will be to us a bristling wall of strength, and his wonderful ships of war will fill our harbors so that our ancient enemies far to the northward—the Hydas and Tsimpsians—will cease to frighten our women, children and old men. Then in reality will he be our father and we his children. But can that ever be? Your God is not our God! Your God loves your people and hates mine. He folds his strong protecting arms lovingly about the paleface and leads him by the hand as a father leads his infant son—but He has forsaken His red children—if they really are His. Our God, the Great Spirit, seems also to have forsaken us. Your God makes your people wax strong every day. Soon they will fill all the land. Our people are ebbing away like a rapidly receding tide that will never return. The white man's God cannot love our people or He would protect them. They seem to be orphans who can look nowhere for help. How then can we be brothers? How can your God become our God and renew our prosperity and awaken in us dreams of returning greatness? If we have a common heavenly father He must be partial—for He came to His paleface children. We never saw Him. He gave you laws but had no word for his red children whose teeming multitudes once filled this vast continent as stars fill the firmament. No; we are two distinct races with separate origins and separate destinies. There is little in common between us.

To us the ashes of our ancestors are sacred and their resting place is hallowed ground. You wander far from the graves of your ancestors and seemingly without regret. Your religion was written upon tablets of stone by the iron finger of your God so that you could not forget. The Red Man could never comprehend nor remember it. Our religion is the tradition of our ancestors—the dreams of our old men, given them in the solemn hours of night by the Great Spirit; and the visions of our sachems, and is written in the hearts of our people.

Your dead cease to love you and the land of their nativity as soon as they pass the portals of the tomb and wander way beyond the stars. They are soon forgotten and never return. Our dead never forget the beautiful world that gave them being. They still love its verdant valleys, its murmuring rivers, its magnificent mountains, sequestered vales and verdant-lined lakes and bays, and ever yearn in tender, fond affection over the lonely hearted living, and often return from the Happy Hunting Ground to visit, guide, console and comfort them.

Day and night cannot dwell together. The Red Man has ever fled the approach of the White Man, as the morning mist flees before the morning sun.

However, your proposition seems fair and I think that my people will accept it and will retire to the reservation you offer them. Then we will dwell in peace for the words of the Great White Chief seem to be the words of nature speaking to my people out of dense darkness.

It matters little where we pass the remnant of our days. They will not be many. The Indians' night promises to be dark. Not a single star of hope hovers above his horizon. Sad-voiced winds moan in the distance. Grim fate seems to be on the Red Man's trail, and wherever he goes he will hear the approaching footsteps of his fell destroyer and prepare stolidly to meet his doom, as does the wounded doe that hears the approaching footsteps of the hunter.

A few more moons. A few more winters—and not one of the descendants of the mighty hosts that once moved over this broad land or lived in happy homes, protected by the Great Spirit, will remain to mourn over the graves of a people— once more powerful and hopeful than yours. But why should I mourn at the untimely fate of my people? Tribe follows tribe, and nation follows nation, like the waves of the sea. It is the order of nature, and regret is useless. Your time of decay may be distant, but it will surely come, for even the White Man whose God walked and talked with him as friend with friend, cannot be exempt from the common destiny. We may be brothers after all. We will see.

We will ponder your proposition and when we decide we will let you know. But should we accept it, I here and now make this condition that we will not be denied the privilege without molestation of visiting at any time the tombs of our ancestors, friends and children. Every part of this soil is sacred in the estimation of my people. Every hillside, every valley, every plain and grove, has been hallowed by some sad or happy event in days long vanished. Even the rocks, which seem to be dumb and dead as they swelter in the sun along the silent shore, thrill with memories of stirring events connected with the lives of my people, and the very dust upon which you now stand responds more lovingly to their footsteps than to yours, because it is rich with the blood of our ancestors and our bare feet are conscious of the sympathetic touch. Our departed braves, fond mothers, glad, happy-hearted maidens, and even our little children who lived here and rejoiced here for a brief season, will love these somber solitudes and at eventide they greet shadowy returning spirits. And when the last Red Man shall have perished, and the memory of my tribe shall have become a myth among the White Men, these shores will swarm with the invisible dead of my tribe, and when your children's children think themselves alone in the field, the store, the shop, upon the highway, or in the silence of the pathless woods, they will not be alone. In all the earth there is no place dedicated to solitude. At night when the streets of your cities and villages are silent and you think them deserted, they will throng with the returning hosts that once filled them and still love this beautiful land. The White Man will never be alone.

Let him be just and deal kindly with my people, for the dead are now powerless. Dead did I say? There is no death, only a change of worlds.

Reading 3.8   SANTERÍA: A REVITALIZATION MOVEMENT   Joseph M. Murphy

Santería (the way of the saints) is a new religion that grew out of the experiences of African peoples (especially the Yoruba and baKonga, who were brought to Cuba as slaves) and free people of color who, by the mid-nineteenth century, constituted a significant portion of the Cuban population. Like other revitalization religious movements, it grew out of human suffering and cultural disorientation. Other new religions that emerged from the fusing of elements of West African traditional religions and Christianity include Vodou (Haiti), and Candomble (Brazil). Since the Cuban Revolution (1959), many Cubans who follow "the way of the saints" have migrated to the United States.

Santería preserved and recast traditional Yoruba religion, synthesizing elements of it with the religion of the dominant religious culture, Roman Catholicism. In the process, the traditional divinities *(orishas)* of the Yoruba took on some of the features of Catholic saints, and a new syncretic religion was formed that included African traditional and Christian elements. Communication and forms of exchange between the spirits and their devotees via a complex system of rituals are mediated by priests and priestesses and include sacrifice, divination, possession, and healing. The selection refers to *Ila-Ife,* the holy city of the Yoruba. In Yoruba mythology, the god Odudua (also known as Oduduwa) organized this city and founded the Yoruba kingdom.

What is *ashe?* How does dance relate to *ashe?* What is the relationship of the *orishas* to *ashe?* Identify some of the categories of *orishas.* How and for what purposes is divination performed? Why are sacrifices required? How are trance states induced? Why are *bembes* (drum and dance festivals) so important? What Santería practices do you think are most objectionable to outsiders in the United States and have led to legal troubles for Santeros (Santería devotees)?

> The sacred world of santería is motivated by *ashe. Ashe* is growth, the force toward completeness and divinity. The Belgian missionary Placide Tempels called this view of the world an ontology of dynamism, that is, a belief that the real world is one of pure movement. In fact, the real world is one not of objects at all but of forces in continual process. *Ashe* is the absolute ground of reality. But we must remember that it is a ground that moves and, so, no ground at all. To conceive this ground, in order to speak of it as something rather than nothing, *santeros* speak of Olodumare, the Owner of Heaven, the Owner of all Destinies. Olodumare is the object of *ashe,* the ultimate harmony and direction of all forces.
>
> As one enters more deeply into santería, one sees this vision of *ashe* with increasing clarity. All things that we are accustomed to call beings are, in reality, *caminos,* ways of *ashe* that can be liberated and channeled by those who understand

them. The person of wisdom, the true *santero*, learns to work with these forces. By words and actions, *ashe* can be awakened in what seem to be objects and people to bring about the fulfillment of their destinies. Stones, leaves, animals, and people are vibrations brought into harmony by *santeros* to further them on their road in the way of Olodumare.

Ashe is a current or flow, a "groove" that initiates can channel so that it carries them along their road in life. The prayers, rhythms, offerings, tabus of santería tune initiates into this flow. They are lifted out of the self-absorption and frustration of ordinary life into the world of power where everything is easy because all is *ashe,* all is destiny.

The *santero* reaches this world by movement. When I have attended santería ceremonies, I have been reminded of those old British anthropologists pronouncing on "savage" religion as "danced religion." For, in spite of themselves, they were right. What they did not know is the profound religious insight that African dancing reveals. Santería is a danced religion because dancing expresses the fundamental dynamism of *ashe.* Words, even a religious encyclopedia like Ifa [the art and path of divination], cannot express the mystery. The world is a dance. Its meaning lies in its constant movement. The dance is the expression of this mystery and more: it is its technology.

Ashe is liberated and channeled through dancing; the person and the community are brought to the source, the real world. In Eliade's terms, the dancers are brought back to the real time of the beginnings, the time of the myths when the *orishas* lived at *Ile-Ife.* The dancers become contemporaries of the gods.

The technology of santería dance may be neurobiological. Movement, rhythm, adrenaline, exhaustion, may trigger hypnotic states of mind that were imprinted in the brain during initiation. The insight that *santeros* bring to this explanation is the ontological claim of the religious—that the special states of mind brought on by dance reveal the world as it truly is, a world of unfiltered *ashe. Orisha* consciousness is true consciousness, and our ordinary view of the world is derived from it. . . .

Santeros in New York have told me that an *orisha* is *el dueño de tu cabeza,* the "lord of your head." This may mean little more than a deity above and beyond oneself, a lord in the medieval sense of one's social superior. Yet I am led to think that, if this deity is lord over one's "head," one's consciousness, then the language of consciousness is the most appropriate way to interpret the meaning of *orisha.* The lord of one's head is the personification of a higher, truer consciousness of the world. Through the images of deities, santería is presenting a precise and profound ontology of consciousness.

Santería teaches not only that *ashe* is dynamic but also that it can be channeled into types. There are innumerable kinds of *ashe* as there are innumerable kinds of people in the world. A monotheistic perspective sees these as "hypostases," "ministers," "intermediaries," manifestations," of one force. A polytheistic perspective recognizes intrinsic differences among our experiences of the world and sees these types representing the variety and possible ways of being in the world. While these experiences are theoretically infinite, there must be a limited number of types to be intelligible and useful as a typology of the sacred world. These are the *orishas,* the types of *ashe.*

Santeros have several overlapping ways of classifying the *orishas*. For example, *orishas* can be hot and cool. Shango, Ogun, and Babaluaye work through the fire of lightning, forge, and fever to heat up the *ashe* of the devotee in order to force change in the world. Osanyin, Inle, and Oshun cool through leaves, herbs, and fresh water, calming the hot head that impedes the devotee's vision of destiny.

There are also *orishas* of the sky and *orishas* of the earth. Obatala the sculptor and Orula the diviner work with Olodumare on high to shape and interpret our destinies. Nana and Babaluaye roam the earth choosing whom they will for illnesses, punishing or calling them to service.

There are *orishas* of the forest and *orishas* of the town. Osanyin is the lord of the forest, the genius of the wild leaves from which all the efficacy of santería ritual derives. Eleggua, Ogun, and Oshosi are hunters who walk together outside the boundaries of the community. They are fearless and fearsome because they know the secrets of an unknown world. Within the town are the royal *orishas*: Obatala, king of Ife; Shango, king of Oyo; and Ogun, kind of Ire. The royal *orishas* command the *ashe* of seniority, the power of connection to the world of the beginnings, Ile-Ife.

Finally, there is Eleggua and all the other *orishas*. Eleggua is the restless outsider betwixt and between worlds. He overturns order and, by doing so, reveals it. Ifa is the senior *orisha* of destiny and order, but Eleggua is the true *orisha* of divination because his randomness and unpredictability show the true order in the world. Out of the fall of shells and nuts, the order of our destinies becomes clear. Because Eleggua disrupts our lives, we learn the patterns that control them. *Santeros* say that Eleggua serves all the *orishas*, that each *orisha* has his or her own Eleggua. Without Eleggua and the disorder that he provokes, the *orishas* would all starve, for they would have no purpose. Human beings would have no need of them, and no sacrifices would be due them. Eleggua provides the dynamism that moves the road of life.

We have seen that santería expresses a religious ontology, that is, a belief about what is ultimately real. Reality is *ashe*, vital force, and all the objects of the world are in reality forces of *ashe* in relation to each other. The *orishas* are the major types of *ashe* expressed in the mythological language of personality and narrative. Myths, Eliade tells us, reveal how the real world works. The myths of the *orishas* are timeless stories that provide models for human beings to imitate in order to live in the real world. By imitating and repeating the timeless acts of the *orishas* in rituals, human beings can approach and align themselves with the real world of *ashe*.

Santería recognizes four principal ritual ways of approach to the world of the *orishas*: divination, sacrifice, trance and initiation.

All santería ritual begins with divination, and all divination begins with a devotee's problem. Since *santeros* are often poor, the most pressing problems are generally very practical ones involving health, money, and love. Without the money for private physicians, and finding little but insensitivity and misunderstanding in overworked public institutions, *santeros* trust the world of the *orishas* for help with health problems. This is not to say that it is only deprivation that forces *santeros* to turn to the *orishas*. *Santeros* say that modern medicine treats only the symptoms of more basic spiritual problems. . . .

It takes knowledge and insight to recognize the spiritual causes of ordinary problems, and it takes information to treat them. This is the realm of divination, the art of the awareness of destiny. Divination offers the means for interpreting the meaning of random events. With increasing subtlety and precision, Obi, *dilogun*, and Ifa divination open the devotee to the world of *ashe* by providing information. They offer models of divine action, stories of what the *orishas* and heroes did in Ile-Ife when they were faced with the same problem that querents face today. . . .

Nearly all the problems and situations that divination reveals are resolved or furthered by deepening the devotee's relationship with the *orishas*. There is no firmer way for the devotee to show this relationship than through the symbolism of shared food, that is, in sacrifice. Sacrifice *(ebo)* creates bonds between human beings and *orishas*. It is a gift that opens up the channels of *ashe* by exchange. In divination, the *orishas* speak to human beings, diagnosing their needs and opening their destinies to fulfillment. In sacrifice, human beings respond, giving back to the *orishas* the *ashe* that is the sustenance of life.

Though they are more powerful than human beings, the *orishas* are not omnipotent. Like all living things, they must be constantly nourished. A Yoruba proverb says that, without human beings, there would be no *orishas*. The *orishas* need the sacrifice and praise of human beings in order to continue to be effective.

Sacrifices can also be exchanges of another kind. The *orishas* can make terrible demands on their devotees, even to the point of threatening their lives. Sacrifices are gifts to propitiate the *orishas*, to give them the life that they need and to spare the devotee's own: *vida para vida,* say the *santeros,* life for life.

In a general sense, an *ebo* is any ceremony requested by an *orisha*, including purifying baths, feasts, or initiation ceremonies. More particularly, *ebos* are the offerings of foods requested by the *orishas* through divination. Each *orisha* has special foods that it enjoys. Yemaya, the ocean mother, prefers duck, turtle, and goat. Oshun, the lovely river maid, likes fine cakes and white hens. Ogun, the virile iron master, insists on red and white roosters. . . .

The theory behind all santería sacrifice is that the *orishas* consume the invisible *ashe* of the sacrifices that is instilled or, better, liberated from them through consecration, the sacred words of the *moyuba* dedication. A *santero* once told Lydia Cabrera, "La sangre para el Santo, la carne para el santero," "Blood for the saint, meat for the *santero*." The *ashe* of the sacrifices is consumed invisibly in vegetable sacrifices and through the blood of the animal in animal sacrifices, which is sprinkled or poured on the fundamental symbols of the *orishas*. The blood of animals consecrated to the *orishas* strengthens their powers: once again, *vida para vida,* "life for life." When the blood is poured on the "heads" of the *orishas*, the sacred stones, or the prepared heads of the initiates, the *orisha* is fed, and the devotee shares in the *orisha*'s *ashe*.

The most dramatic and intimate approach to the world of the *orishas* is the cultivation of a sacred state of consciousness induced by the drums and dances of the *bembe*. This consciousness, sometimes called trance or spirit possession by outsiders, collapses the sacred dialogue of divination and sacrifice into a single ritual encounter. In santería trance, the channels of *ashe* are fully open as human dancers merge with divine rhythms.

It is difficult to find an English word that will describe this sacred consciousness. "Trance" connotes an inferior, suggestible state of awareness, while "spirit possession" implies to most Westerners a demonic influence. Yet santería mediums claim to remember nothing of their activities when in this altered state of awareness, so the term "trance" is not entirely unfounded. And since their behavior is controlled by the *orisha*, "possession" convey something of the experience.

The basic problem rests on the understanding of this consciousness as religious. Santería presents an ontology of consciousness, the belief that certain states of awareness reveal the world as it truly is and that our ordinary awareness, while possessing its own validity, is dependent on this *orisha* consciousness.

If we recognize the limitations and possible misinterpretations of the word, "trance" is probably the easiest way to refer to this special awareness, especially if we remember that, for *santeros*, this "trance" is a special and genuine form of awareness. *Santeros* themselves speak of *bajar el santo,* "the saint descending," or *el santo montado,* "the saint mounted," which places emphasis on the activity of the *orisha* in descending on or mounting the head of the medium. The "mounting" activity of an *orisha* refers to the medium's role as a "horse" whose activities are directed by an *orisha* rider.

The most persistent misconception about trance is that it is frenzied or hysterical behavior. While the transition from ordinary to trance consciousness may involve some sudden, staggered movements among inexperienced mediums, once the *orisha* has fully mounted the medium his or her behavior becomes very precise indeed. The dances are tightly choreographed according to traditional models and are immediately recognizable to the congregation as reenactments of mythical themes.

Source: Joseph M. Murphy, *Santería: An African Religion in America* (Boston: Beacon Press, 1988), pp. 130–137. From *Santería* by Joseph M. Murphy. © 1988, 1993 by Beacon Press. Reprinted by permission of Beacon Press Boston.

CHAPTER 4

HINDUISM

One Sunday afternoon in Vrindaban, the son of my tailor invited me to come with him as he arranged for the performance of a ritual on behalf of his family. I knew that his father and his family were followers of some of the leading Vaishnava teachers in Vrindaban, the city on the Yamuna River in Uttar Pradesh that is the traditional site for the god Krishna's childhood and youth. So I was surprised when we walked away from the main temples that are the object of pilgrimage in Vrindaban toward an isolated shrine to Bhairava, a form of Shiva. There the priest of the shrine anointed the image, an almost formless stone, with vermilion paste, marked it with silver foil, and made the offerings of flowers and food brought by the tailor's son. As I shared in the food that had been offered, it was clear that more was going on in the religious life of this family than I had expected. They were certainly devotees of Krishna and followers of religious leaders who were also patrons of their business, but they were also related to Bhairava, whose anger had to be appeased and whose assistance sought. And one of the reasons for this religious journey, at least the reason I had been invited along, was to insure my future patronage for their clothing business.

A Hindu woman purifies herself in the holy waters of the Ganges River at Varanasi (Benares), one of India's most sacred cities

In Hinduism, there is always another layer, a deeper dimension, something else going on, which challenges the sympathetic observer. So much is going on, in fact, that one is tempted to narrow the vision and deal only with a part. However, the responsible study of Hinduism requires that we pay attention to these many layers, to the density of this tradition.

Hinduism, first of all, does not include several components of the common conception of a religion. There is no historical founder, no single scriptural text recognized by all, no single authoritative voice or organization or institution, no common creed for all who call themselves Hindu, and no single god or goddess or conception of divinity. There is a social order, *(dharma)*, a responsibility to sustain the world, but there is also a role for those who renounce society's benefits and burdens—ones who seek release, or **moksha.** Hinduism, a tradition that claims over 700 million adherents in India, seems full of paradoxes.

What metaphor, then, could point to the meaning of this tradition in Indian life? Some have suggested the ecology of a tropical jungle, whose luxuriant foliage seems totally out of control and perhaps frightening to an outsider but actually follows a very clear pattern of growth with which the local inhabitant is quite familiar and content. Others invite us to take a bewildering walk through the local bazaar, where in fact everything is available when one learns to look carefully and ask. Still others suggest that Hinduism as a system is just a map, a series of marks on paper, which do say something, but also nothing, about the land itself. Other natural images proposed are a river, which seems new every moment, draws everything into it, and rolls on as though there were no time, and a mountain, which provides the horizon of our perception but also leaves the observer dwarfed and humbled amidst the valley's fluid boundaries. Perhaps studying Hinduism is like looking at a tapestry from the back, wondering how all the "loose ends" do fit into a bigger picture. One image from Hinduism itself is that of the *mandala,* a circular geometric figure, like a maze, with several entrances, several rings or layers with new entries, and ultimately an arrival at the center, but with many possible ways of achieving it. There is not a single straight line, but everything is connected. That is Hinduism.

The responsible study of Hinduism also requires that we recognize that "Hinduism" as a religious system was an invention of the British colonial period, even though many Hindus, dealing wisely with their colonial rulers, adopted that definition for themselves as Hindus. In attempting to understand and govern their subjects, the British government officials tried to conceptualize the religious traditions of India by analogy with their own post-Reformation Christianity. A Protestant model of religious conversion, faith in particular doctrines, and emphasis on ethical virtues, but especially the notion of exclusive membership in a religious community—all of these features were expected in the religious traditions encountered in India.

One of the prime instruments of British colonial social control, the census of population conducted every ten years, required that people declare their religious identity. Those abstract categories took on a life of their own in describing exclusive communities with which the colonial administrators dealt. Those who studied the religions of India had commercial and political objectives in attempting to understand Indian languages, culture, and religions. Edward Said, professor of literature at Columbia University, has referred to this project of shaping the Other for colonial purposes of profit and control as "orientalism." Although his thesis is probably too sweeping, it would not be incorrect to say that because of British colonial policies, the religious identity of Hinduism and its boundaries with other traditions were drawn more sharply and artificially than was justified. A Hinduism was in fact constructed to serve colonial purposes, and many Indian subjects who wished to deal with the British colonial authorities found it not only convenient but also necessary to adopt the approved terms. In this fashion, many Indians adopted not only the name *Hindu* but also the colonial notion of a unified religious tradition called *Hinduism.* Students should bring a critical and suspicious eye to these all-too-convenient simplifications and look for what is not included in these concepts.

Scholars also played a role in the orientalist construction of Hinduism in their academic disciplines. Early colonial students of Indian cultures sought to master the languages of India. Because these scholars had been university trained in the Latin and Greek classics, they sought from their Indian teachers the "classics of the Indian tradition," thus focusing primarily on study and translation of certain Sanskrit texts that were available only to a relatively small cultural and literate elite. Whereas the work of producing grammars, dictionaries, and translations appears awesome, the study of vernacular texts, oral sources, and nonliterary material (music, architecture, and sculpture) received very secondary attention. Perhaps more important, colonial scholars took the norms of their study from the sciences and thus sought to make universally valid and rationally demonstrable statements. Critical inquiry seemed to demand detachment from the subject matter, whereas the nature of a traditional society is that one "stands within" a world shaped by that tradition.

Each of the individual experiences that make up Hinduism can stand for the whole tradition. Against the tendency to erect an overarching context-free system and to assign the individual event or experience a place within that pattern, Hinduism continually challenges observers by being relentlessly sensitive to the individual context. Around the corner from the Krishna temple where this author lived in the city of Vrindaban, Uttar Pradesh (traditional site of the god Krishna's childhood and youth), right on the daily path to the milk stall, was a small shrine to the goddess Durga. There was no official service and certainly no priest in control. Every day local women provided their own service, placing a garland of flowers before the goddess's image and pouring purifying water before her. Everything that is Hinduism is focused on that single, isolated, unorganized act of worship by a lay devotee. And it all could be focused on the group of men gathered around a sacred tree in the courtyard of the Krishna temple, singing the devotional songs associated with the leader, a *goswami,* who had founded that temple and discovered the deity image worshiped there. This ability of a particular devotional, ritual, or meditative activity to reflect the entire tradition is one of the richest and most difficult aspects of Hinduism.

Finally, Hinduism is a cumulative tradition: nothing, ancient or modern, is ever lost or forgotten. It constitutes a "cumulative memory" with amazing durability over time and density to its layers. Ultimately, those who inhabit the Hindu world or who come as appreciative tourists or earnest religious seekers acquire a sensibility for its connections and tensions, its paradoxes, its powerful energy.

HINDU BELIEFS

There is no single creed that all Hindus can accept. David R. Kinsley has suggested that the two practical criteria for "being Hindu" are "reverence for the *Vedas*" and "implicit acceptance of the social hierarchy known as the caste system."[1] Accepting the *Vedas,* the ancient texts of Hinduism, even if one cannot or does not care to read them, involves immersion in the whole cumulative development of Hinduism and its practical personal and social implications. David M. Knipe offers a more expansive description of a "typical Hindu" as "one who would accept karma and *samsara* in the belief system, uphold certain sacred texts and deities, honor ancestors with a continued lineage and with offerings, admit to class and caste status within a broader social system, express certain overt or symbolic ascetic practices such as fasts or vows, and consider important the pursuit of goals toward ultimate release."[2] However, being Hindu involves acceptance of a network of social relationships and the responsibility that comes from these relationships. Hinduism, therefore, is less a series of explicitly religious ideas and practices than complying with the behavioral implications of the social situation in which the individual participates.

DHARMA AND CASTE

The religious duty of a Hindu, then, is not a universal, generalized set of beliefs. Hindu religion, Hindu *dharma,* is specific to the situation of the particular individual or social group, establishing the religious identity of the individual through an expected pattern of social relationships and through the individual's fulfillment of responsibilities within this pattern. The classical model of social organization, the caste system, consisted of the four hierarchical divisions of society—Brahmans, rulers and warriors, merchants and farmers, and laborers—reflected in the Vedic creation myth and enshrined in the Hindu law books. The modern notion of caste, although still related in theory to the Vedic *varna,* or caste, system, applies to a vast system of local and regional occupational groups. These caste groups, called *jatis,* control interactions with people above and below the individual in caste hierarchy and enforce boundaries of purity that relate especially to the sharing of food and to suitability for marriage. One's personal and social religious duty, one's *dharma*, is determined primarily by birth into a particular social group. A large part of Hindu social behavior can be explained by strategies to maintain one's hierarchical status and to avoid pollution by those of lower social rank. With some exceptions, marriage is clearly expected "within one's own group." Matrimonial advertisements in Indian immigrant newspapers published in the United States include, among the qualities sought in prospective spouses, reference to caste, as well as to ethnic and regional, religious, professional, economic, and personal characteristics.

In contemporary India, caste plays a major role in economic advancement. Brahmans make up only about 3.5 percent of the population and other "forward," or upper, castes another 15 percent, yet these groups form the economic and sociocultural elite. At the other extreme, the "scheduled castes" ("untouchables," *harijans,* or **dalits**—specific caste groups listed or "scheduled" in the Indian Constitution) constitute about 15 percent and the "scheduled tribes" (tribal groups that were never incorporated into the caste system), about 7.5 percent. The category "other backward castes" includes most of the rest of the population—close to 50 percent. The reform structure recommended by an Indian government commission urged "reserving" 27 percent of government jobs and contracts and places in university and professional schools to advance the social and economic status of this latter group; these reservations were in addition to the 22.5 percent of places already reserved for scheduled castes and tribes.[3]

DHARMA, KARMA, SAMSARA, AND MOKSHA

A Hindu lecturer once told this author's class that if he could assume the process of rebirth, then he could make a coherent presentation of the entire Hindu worldview. This statement is only a slight oversimplification. A series of four mutually defining terms describe a "typical Hindu": *dharma,* *karma, samsara,* and *moksha*. These four concepts also play an important role in defining the core beliefs of Hinduism and as the basis for Hindu practice.

Each individual has a determined duty, or *dharma,* because of caste *(jati)* and stage in life, according to the **ashrama** system of student, householder, forest dweller, and renunciant **(sannyasin)**. Caste determines one's range of responsibility, the particular work *(karma)* with which one must be engaged. The results of action (also *karma)* determine the success of one's present life, as well as the status of one's rebirth. No divine intervention is implied in the system of *karmic* justice: "Each person is ultimately responsible for every action he or she performs. Every action has its moral consequences. According to the idea of karma, the present condition, character, and peculiar circumstances of a person are the result of his or her past deeds. A person is what he or she has done."[4]

The *dharma* of fulfilling social responsibilities makes some action *(karma)* necessary and, hence, the accumulation of the results of action, also *karma,* which determines the course of this life and the status of future rebirth. Rebirth, however, is by its nature a never-ending process. Birth as a human is the result of many prior exemplary lives, but it also bears the risk of failing to carry out *dharma* and thus regressing again to lower forms. This never-ending process of rebirth is called *samsara* and is regarded as a bondage that is ultimately meaningless. Consequently, although it is possible and, indeed, expected for individuals to seek wealth *(artha)* and pleasure *(kama)* in carrying out their *dharma,* the final goal of a life is to seek final release *(moksha)* from any future rebirth.

HINDU COSMOLOGY AND THE AGE OF KALI

The history of Hinduism's development shows many layers to the quest for release. Many of the Vedic creation myths show a deep sense that the material world and separate individuals are the result of a process that is terribly wrong. The origin of the world from a divine dismemberment does not suggest an understanding of creation as something beneficial or desirable, though perhaps it was inevitable or necessary. The cosmology developed in later texts called *puranas* describes a cyclical process that stretches out over vast periods of time, trillions of years, but a system that repeats itself over and over.

The notion of recurrent cyclical time is so fundamentally opposed to Western notions of unique individuality and, perhaps, eternal life—ideas that are sometimes taken for granted even by those who do not consciously "believe" them—that it requires some reflection for the implications of an endless circular process to sink in. Although it cannot be observed from the short span each person lives in this age, each person has existed countless times, and this process will simply continue without end, unless somehow some form of release can stop one's bondage in this process. To make matters worse, we are currently living through the worst of the four ages, or *yugas*, of this cycle. In this current age, the **Kali *yuga*,** religion and morality are in steep decline, people live comparatively short and miserable lives, and power is grasped by the worst elements in society. Observing inhumanity and suffering, one Hindu simply commented, "It's the Age of Kali." This rather fatalistic attitude does not encourage actions to transform society's ills, and some people in India have used it as the basis for renouncing involvement in social action and reform. And, because this is the Kali *yuga*, individuals can attain little of the high spiritual achievements that were expected in earlier ages. But, new religious paths have been provided to make realization possible even for people with little spiritual aptitude who are living in these evil times. So, paradoxically, the quest for liberation is actually easier for those willing to accept the opportunity.

PATHS TO RELEASE

Hinduism includes several answers to the question of how one can be freed from the bondage of *samsara*. The ancient philosophical treatises called *Upanishads* saw the recognition of the unity of the **atman** (the individual self) with **Brahman** (the underlying reality of all) as ending the illusion of

separate existence, which is the cause of rebirth. Systems of *yoga* taught practitioners to overcome desire by asserting control of the body and mind, realizing *samadhi*, a completely detached state of freedom. The *Bhagavad Gita,* perhaps the best-known Hindu text, emphasized two paths: the disciplined performance of duty without regard for the fruits of action, allowing the selfless performance of *karma* to effect release; and the offering of every action and the entire self to Krishna in love or **bhakti,** which assures that the devotee will escape rebirth and come to Krishna. The system of *dharma* itself included as the final stage of life *(ashrama)* the life of the renounced ascetic, the *sannyasin,* who has already died to self and hence is not reborn. Popular traditions promised that by the performance of certain vows or by the mere fact of dying in Benares, one could escape *samsara*. Ultimately, to be a Hindu is to accept in all of its practical implications the duty *(dharma)* of living one's life in accord with one's social class *(varna)* and one's stage in life *(ashrama),* as well as to pursue goals appropriate to them.

THE DIVINE PRESENCE

What is not included in this picture, all-encompassing as it may seem, is the pervasive sense of divine presence most Hindus share. This sense is not so much a matter of belief as an obvious fact of religious experience. The divine presence may be perceived as having a particular form or as going beyond the limits that are imposed by having a single form. Through the meditative practices of the *Upanishads,* a person experiences unity with Brahman, the One underlying Self without any limit of form. Hence, the ultimate reality, Brahman, is not a person; it may be without form, *nirguna.* In contrast, many devotees see the divine presence with form, *saguna*—the god or goddess in the image at a temple or household shrine or in a sacred tree along the riverbank. The notion of divine incarnation *(avatara)* asserts that God often takes form to be available to the love of the devotee. The divine is present in many forms, as god and goddess, in mountains and rivers, in popular devotions as much as elaborate rituals, and in the heart of the individual. Other devotees, the spiritual descendants of the poets Kabir and Ravidas, directed their love to a God who cannot be encompassed in form or, especially, in the social and religious organizations that temples and the priestly hierarchy involve. This form of devotion provides a religious basis for the criticism of caste privilege. However, whether one worships a deity image in a temple or surrenders to the One beyond form, the cultivated sensibility of how one's social responsibility intersects with divine presence in ordinary life is the basis for Hindu practice.

HINDU PRACTICE

It is possible for Hindus to hold quite diverse beliefs and to experience the divine presence in radically different ways while still fulfilling the *dharmic* duty associated with their caste and stage in life *(varna-ashrama-dharma),* which constitutes the practical expectations of Hindu life.

DHARMA IN EVERYDAY LIFE

No practices can be said to be universal for all Hindus. Instead, the context-specific character of this tradition again points to everyday experiences of life in family and society as the primary focus of Hindu practice: being yourself means playing your social role in the context of your family, according to the status of your caste and occupational group *(jati),* within the traditions proper to your linguistic region and its cultural heritage. Gerald Larson has pointed out that although being Hindu seems to have little to do with particular beliefs,

> Being religious for the Hindu, rather, has much more to do with behavior and action, or what is sometimes called "orthopraxy"—correct action. The Hindu has basic duties and responsibilities in terms of personal cleanliness (ritual bathing),

eating habits (what kind of food is to be eaten, who prepares it, and with whom it can be eaten), family relations (obligations to siblings and parents), marital practices (when and whom one can marry), regional associations (including caste associations), and the manner in which one can choose and interact with friends. In other words, Hindus are engaging in a kind of "religious" talk when they tell you about their family, their occupations, the regions in India from which they come, the groups to which they belong by birth or choice, the native languages they speak, and the sorts of food they eat. Moreover, as your Hindu friends describe all of this, you will be struck not only by how different their views and ideas can be, but also by the great range of differing duties and responsibilities that they follow depending upon the regions and groups from which they come. The rules are by no means the same for everyone. While you will come to realize that there are many ways of being "Hindu," you will also note an "all-pervasive sense of Indianness." This somewhat strange juxtaposition of radical diversity or tolerant pluralism along with an "all-pervasive sense of Indianness" is basically what it means to be a Hindu.[5]

Behind this pluralism is a very clear sense of what each individual person is expected to be and to do. As Larson shows, right action is fulfillment of one's personal religious duty, or *dharma,* determined concretely by one's social status and stage of life in pursuit of life's goals.

One of the prime examples of this regulated social behavior pertains to food exchange, something that is largely taken for granted in Western society. Because the caste system involves maintaining the purity of hierarchical relationships, and because eating together is, except for sexual relations in marriage, the most intimate sharing of life with others, the kind of food eaten (vegetarian or not, as well as the type and quality) and the relationships between the preparers and those consuming the food reinforce on a daily basis the social structure and boundaries of a person's life.[6]

Within the extended family and caste group (understood here as *jati*, the occupational subgroup to which one belongs), each individual has clearly defined and quite demanding responsibilities. Caste limits the bounds within which one must respond, but the obligations of this response are profound, extending to a great many individuals within the family group. Whereas Western society urges people to "love everyone," Hindu society emphasizes the individual's obligations to those within a particular caste—a group with defined social boundaries—while absolving him or her of responsibility to those outside. If all social groups fulfill their role, then all of society will find harmony and stability, not through the advancement of individuals but through the harmonious relations of groups. In this sense, caste is not so much hierarchical privilege but a heightened responsibility within a particular social group.

LIFE CYCLE RITUALS *(SAMSKARAS)*

Just as regulated social relationships constitute caste duty or *varna-dharma*, so proper passage through the stages of life *(ashrama-dharma)* is celebrated as a sacred event for many Hindus, particularly upper-caste men, through a series of rituals marking the passage from one stage of life to another. These rituals or sacraments, called **samskaras**, sacralize the movement from conception to birth, through childhood toward adulthood, by an intentional process of education, in commitment to marriage, until death ends this particular life and the body is cremated. The structure of *samskaras* is elaborate and is rarely followed completely, even by all who are eligible to do so. Prebirth *samskaras* express in ritual the meaning of conception, the quickening of a (male) child, and the symbolic parting of the mother's hair to assist the developing mind. The childhood rites sacralize birth, name giving, the child's first outing and first feeding, the first haircut, and the piercing of the ear. Education is recognized as a sacred initiation through rituals that mark first learning the alphabet, the start of formal education, commitment to a teacher, first shaving of the beard, and the end of studentship. The

upanayana ritual includes investiture with the sacred cord worn by upper-caste men. Marriage rituals are very elaborate, focusing on the seven steps taken together by husband and wife that formalize the marriage. Funeral rituals remove the pollution of death through the cremation of the corpse and the disposal of the ashes. Although this ideal pattern is drawn from the *Vedas* and accords with the *dharmic* code for householders *(Grihya Sutras)*, nevertheless it is clear that other non-Vedic rituals are performed for those excluded from the *samskaras* by caste or gender. Women's domestic rituals, without priestly blessing or written text, continue to celebrate and invoke divine blessings on the process of a woman's life.

The *samskaras* are primarily directed at supporting householder life; hence, they do not address the act of renunciation, the choice of becoming a wandering ascetic (a *sadhu* or *sannyasin*.) The pursuit of release, *moksha*, relieves one of all social obligations to others and shatters caste identity. A *sannyasin* has died to a former life. Adoption of a new name symbolizes the death of an old identity and initiation into a new one. India offers great tolerance to, and provides sufficient support for, the many who choose early or late in life to embrace the renounced state. Some live in religious retreats called *ashrams*, others in solitude by roadside shrines or in remote mountain caves, and still others in a constant state of pilgrimage to holy places. The sustaining of society, however, including the institution of renunciation, depends on the vast majority who continue to carry out their social roles. The visibility of *sadhus* does not detract from the fact that the stability of society depends on their being an exception.

GENDER ROLES

Indian society emphasizes the changed status that individuals possess at different periods of their lives. Unlike Western culture with its assertion of universal principles and rights, Indian culture is sensitive to an individual's changing context. *Dharma*, the life cycle, and the *samskaras* were described with attention on men. Women are to be respected for their family role but are subject to the "protection" of male relatives. The *Laws of Manu* (*Manu Smriti*, from 200 to 100 B.C.E.) describes the role of women:

> *Women must be honored and adorned by their fathers, brothers, husbands, and brothers-in-law who desire great good fortune.*
>
> *Where women, verily, are honored, there the gods rejoice; where, however, they are not honored, there all sacred rites prove fruitless.*
>
> *Where the female relations live in grief—that family soon perishes completely; where, however, they do not suffer from any grievance—that family always prospers. . . .*
>
> *Her father protects her in childhood, her husband protects her in youth, her sons protect her in old age— a woman does not deserve independence.*
>
> *The father who does not give away his daughter in marriage at the proper time is censurable; censurable is the husband who does not approach his wife in due season; and after the husband is dead, the son, verily, is censurable, who does not protect his mother.*
>
> *Even against the slightest provocations should women be particularly guarded; for unguarded they would bring grief to both the families.*
>
> *Regarding this as the highest dharma of all four classes, husbands, though weak, must strive to protect their wives.*
>
> *His own offspring, character, family, self, and dharma does one protect when he protects his wife scrupulously. . . .*
>
> *The husband should engage his wife in the collection and expenditure of his wealth, in cleanliness, in dharma, in cooking food for the family, and in looking after the necessities of the household. . . .*
>
> *Women destined to bear children, enjoying great good fortune, deserving of worship, the resplendent lights of homes on the one hand and divinities of good luck who reside in the houses on the other— between these there is no difference whatsoever.*[7]

Whereas the role of the man is maintaining caste purity, something his protection over women seeks to preserve, the blessing of the woman is to be "auspicious." To her husband and family she is like a goddess bringing the fruits of good fortune to sustain the family; to bear male children who continue the family line; and to secure the well-being of her husband and of his entire family, of which she becomes a member by marriage. Women possess tremendous but dangerous power *(shakti)*, which requires control by being focused on her domestic role as wife and mother—roles that confer on the woman considerable respect and power within the home. Women carry out this role in the tasks of daily life, including domestic religious rituals associated with food preparation, but also in special religious rituals of bathing, fasting, and pilgrimage—rituals that are combined in vows a woman performs to sustain the family.

In traditional settings, widowhood is seen as profoundly inauspicious, because the woman has "failed" to sustain her husband. In contemporary India, however, many widows maintain an honored place in their marital home, especially if they have sons. Others use widowhood as an opportunity to live their own lives, but often this decision is less a choice than the need to leave the husband's family, where another mouth to feed is not particularly welcome.

Marriage in Hinduism often reflects far more an expression of social responsibility than a source of personal fulfillment. Hence, in traditional settings, marriages were arranged by the respective families. A woman's suitability for marriage lies in her ability to carry out the role of wife within the husband's family, something that may have little to do with romance. Some Indians have defended the tradition of arranged marriages by saying that it is far easier to learn to love someone you are married to than to make a marriage with someone you love, and that parents know better than young people who would make a good marriage partner. They criticize the instability of marriage and of families in Western society and point to the relative infrequency of divorce in Indian society. It is true that the economic and social bonds involved in arranging a marriage are not lightly dissolved, unless it becomes very clear that this marriage was a mistake, something recognized not as a matter of unhappiness or lack of personal fulfillment but again in terms of the nonfulfillment of expected social roles.

A theatrical mask of the goddess Durga, who is renowned for slaying demons.

In practice, however, Indian youth have considerable say over prospective marriage partners, and women exercise substantial domestic power, often holding the only set of keys to the household. It is not uncommon, in Indian society as in any other, for a woman to be the real business mind of the family. Moreover, the economic value of an educated or skilled woman in advancing the status of the family can be very great. The work of a skilled seamstress, carried out on consignment in the home, could easily pay private school tuition for several children—girls as well as boys—thus effectively raising the status of the entire family in one generation. However, these practical accommodations and achievements cannot remove the structurally inferior position of women. According to some religious texts, worthy women must await their next rebirth as a man to achieve liberation. Such ideas, the work of men, are called into question by the tradition of women poet-saints, such as Mirabai (1498–1546), who rejected men as suitors and were wed to the deity, the only suitable spouse. In most cases, however, the changes in women's status in contemporary Hinduism are being accomplished not through abandoning marriage and family but through a carefully maintained tension that respects both

tradition and the challenging realities of the modern world.

A consideration of the religious practices of women turns attention toward "popular" religious traditions rather than toward the texts and institutions of the elite. Orientalism among scholars supported a tendency to identify the literary, elite "high traditions," which were preserved and directed by men, as "Hinduism" and to overlook oral and popular village traditions, often practiced by women with or without official sanction, or to regard them as aberrations from the norm. Some years ago, this author and another student had the opportunity to observe a *puja*—in this case, Durga puja, the ritual worship of the goddess Durga—being performed in a local home. The women of the household—spanning three generations—had depicted the goddess's image on the wall of the home. The youngest daughter, with considerable instruction from her grandmother and under the anxious watch of her mother, was offering light and prayer to Durga for the well-being of her family and for the success of her future marriage. The men of the family, despite the fact that this ritual was being performed primarily for their ultimate benefit, were quite amused that two male academics would be interested in such religious matters and tried to draw us away into discussions of education and computers. Nevertheless, village India is indeed the norm, and such popular Hinduism is the fundamental layer of religious life—even when we also look at India's vast religious literature, elaborate philosophical systems, or huge temple complexes. Women's religious expressions offer a privileged perspective on the significance of Hinduism.

YOGA

Hinduism recognizes the need for an individual process of intentional transformation through the following of a spiritual path *(marga)*. The general term for such a path is **yoga,** a system of spiritual discipline that unites the individual in a variety of ways. There are a great many *yogic* paths and a great many teachers and traditions, of which only a few general examples can be given. *Hatha yoga* provides physical and breathing exercises that are a requisite discipline for the other *yogas*. The classical *yoga* of Patañjali in the *Yoga Sutras* taught a progressive eightfold discipline and withdrawal into the self with the goal of achieving a complete focus of the self, called *samadhi*. *Karma yoga*, the *yoga* of work or action, involves the selfless performance of one's *dharma* without regard for the fruits of action, the practice that was taught to Arjuna by Krishna in the *Bhagavad Gita*. **Jñana** (knowlege) *yoga,* the *yoga* of knowledge that follows the heritage of the *Upanishads,* includes all the practices necessary to experience the understanding of the true self, the *purusha* or *atman,* through realizing the relationship of that self with Brahman, the underlying Self. The tradition of *bhakti yoga*, the yoga of devotion or love of God, encompasses an array of practices that bring about the surrender of the individual to a particular deity. These practices include chanting the divine name, imaginative entrance into the divine play *(lila),* service of a deity image, and simply living a life in which everything one is, has, and does is for the loving praise of God.

Common to all these various paths is the underlying assumption that to achieve full realization of personhood, one must engage in some process of spiritual transformation. Birth as a human is a rare privilege with great possibilities for spiritual growth toward release, perhaps in this very lifetime. Dedicated practice of some spiritual path is necessary to realize this potential.

Puja and Darshan

Perhaps the most visible form of Hindu religious practice involves the worship of a deity image *(puja),* a non-Vedic form of sacrifice with countless variants. The images worshiped may be any deity, god or goddess. The form may be iconic, with a clear shape or visible identity, such as the four-armed Vishnu or Shiva as the dancing lord *Nata-raja.* It may be aniconic, lacking any definite characteristics, such as the stone shaft of the Shiva *lingam,* which nevertheless is the presence of the god or goddess. The images may be permanent and be formed of wood, metal, or stone into which the divine presence is invited in a ceremony in which the image's eyes are opened. They also may be temporary and be formed of sand for a single ritual or shaped from clay for the worship of the goddess Durga and then dissolved in a nearby river.

Domestic worship may be simple, with a room or an alcove set aside as the *puja* room. The altar may display images of the particular deities worshiped by the families of both spouses, together with pictures of the family members' *gurus* and souvenir items brought back from pilgrimages. Such a shrine may receive intermittent worship by either spouse or by other family members only on festival days, or it may receive attentive daily service by family members with offerings of flowers and food, personal prayer and chanting, and the presentation of incense and light.

Worship in an established temple is far more elaborate. The service of the deities is carried out by priests with a daily program of worship, all of it meant to represent the attentive service of the deity, the god or goddess who has deigned to take this form to receive the loving service of his or her devotees. In a typical temple, the deity is awakened in early morning to the delight of those who have risen to have their sight purified by seeing the god first thing in the morning, their mouths and ears cleansed by giving and hearing praise, and their mind focused toward the god by this devotional service. In the course of the daily cycle, the deity will be bathed, clothed in fresh clothes, provided with abundant food at appropriate times, given midday rest, and finally prepared for sleep. The various daily or seasonal activities of the deity, such as Krishna's playful work as a cowherd, are remembered with particular fervor. Each period of worship includes the offering of light to the deity, a ritual called **arati,** with the light and warmth then shared with the assembled devotees. Offerings of food are returned to the priests and devotees as *prasada,* the Lord's grace, because the proper order has been followed by first giving all to God from whom it is returned. The water used to bathe the deity is given to the devotees to drink or is splashed over them; flower garlands given to the deity serve to adorn the devotees with God's graciousness.

Through all of this, in the simple home or the most famous shrine, the individual comes to see the deity in the image form. This seeing, called **darshan,** is mutual: the devotee sees the deity and is in turn seen by the deity. Devotional service constitutes the "real world," the play of the deity into which the individual devotee enters by worship, becoming a participant in the drama compared to which ordinary existence is just so much illusion. Nevertheless, devotional service does not replace the devotee's *dharma;* devotional service becomes the model for required activity carried out with selfless detachment.

FESTIVALS

Particular intensity is given to devotional emotions during festivals that honor the particular deities. These celebrations also cut across sectarian loyalties (for example, a **Vaishnava**—a worshiper of some form of Vishnu—will participate in the worship of the goddess Durga or in Shiva-ratri, nightlong worship of Shiva) and allow participation by social classes who might feel subtle exclusion within the temples. It is also in festivals that the many layers, depth, and density of religious practice become apparent.

One example is the springtime festival of Holi, which is celebrated with particular fervor in the Braj region of Uttar Pradesh (in north central India) and the neighboring state of Rajasthan. On one level this festival is a celebration of springtime warmth, the end of the cold season against which Indian homes and clothing provide scant protection, a release of pent-up emotion comparable to that greeting the first monsoon rains after five months of unmitigated heat. Holi is also the winter wheat harvest festival. The festival recalls in neighborhood bonfires ancient stories that are found in the *Vedas* and in the *Puranas* of the destruction of powers that threaten the social order. The lighting of these fires also becomes the occasion of seeking forgiveness within the neighborhood for the faults of the past year, putting aside enmity in fam-

ily and neighborhood, and beginning anew life in cooperation and fellowship. The members of the local community participate in one or more days of playful but intense splashing of one another with colored water and powder. Friends informed this author that the variety of colors and the amount of stains on white clothes was a sign of friendship—theirs in the splashing and the author's in the acceptance and the wearing of the colored clothing. But Holi is also a celebration of the love of Radha and Krishna, whose play of Holi is a prelude to their lovemaking. The devotional plays, called *ras-lila,* which are performed at this season invite the audience to become participants in the divine love-play. On the day of Holi itself, the loving divine couple are covered with layers of multihued flower petals. Radha and Krishna begin to play Holi, throwing handfuls of flower petals at one another and at the audience, who then join in the play of covering one another with the flowers.

There are other social dimensions to this festival. The neighboring towns of Barsana and Nandagaon ritually enact the conflicts emerging from generations of intermarriage between the towns. On the first day, the men of Nandagaon, who traditionally married the women of Barsana, arrive at the city wearing protective helmets and carrying leather shields. After much-needed pleas in the temple of Radha for her protection, the men attempt to make their way through the town. There they are met by richly dressed, masked women of Barsana who carry seven-foot staffs, with which they strike vigorously at both the men of Nandagaon (who seek to protect themselves with their shields) and any other unlucky men who come within range (who do not have benefit of shields). On the following day, the men of Barsana receive a similar welcome in Nandagaon.

Holi is an example of many springtime celebrations of temporary societal reversal. The masked women literally thrash the men, but they return to their previous (and unmasked) social roles after the festival. During the weeks that follow the official celebration of Holi, this ritualized conflict between men and women is enacted with vigor and enthusiasm in neighborhoods and bazaars throughout the region. And this regional character is but another layer of the Holi festival: it is a celebration of the land itself; of seasonal change and harvest; of the towns and neighborhoods; of forgiveness and social cohesion; of men and women and their complex social and sexual roles; of Radha and Krishna and their lovemaking; and of human play, which is participation in that divine play. Other regional festivals, such as the annual celebration of the marriage of Minakshi to Sundaresvara (Shiva) at Madurai or the Ratha-Yatra festival at the temple of Jagannatha in Puri, invoke similar levels of human and divine experience and involve the population in participatory social and religious transformation.

PILGRIMAGE

Thousands of people participate in regional festivals, but the process of pilgrimage itself is a more pervasive experience. Drawing on roots as old as the Indus Valley civilizations, pilgrims experience divine presence in rivers, on mountain peaks in the Himalaya, on the shores of the ocean, and just about everywhere else—in sacred trees and rocks, in places that remain sacred for reasons too deep for expression despite several overlays of later religious tradition. These places and objects are simply sacred, and pilgrims experience and acknowledge that holiness by the arduous journey as much as by the arrival.

In contemporary India, traditional pilgrims and *sadhus* (renunciants or ascetics) still come to shrines on foot, by horse carts, by motorized carts, and by crowded interstate buses and trains. Groups arrive carrying everything needed during the journey in order to avoid being at the mercy of local merchants in the pilgrimage towns, who exact a kind of "pilgrim's tax" in their prices. Alongside this traditional pilgrimage process, contemporary India has developed a kind of religious tourism that permits more affluent pilgrims to visit a number of holy sites by guided tour in air-conditioned buses. Figure 4.1 shows some of the sacred sites of Hinduism.

Still, the motives of pilgrimage remain much the same. A pilgrim comes to see (have *darshan* of) the god or goddess; each one comes with devotional feelings, and each comes unabashedly with very personal and practical needs. The songs of the Marathi saint Tukaram are still sung by pilgrims along the road to Vitobha 's shrine at Pandharpur. Millions of *sadhus* and ordinary people gather for the *kumbha-mela*, the vast assemblage of pilgrims every four years at sacred river sites in northern India. Varanasi (also called Benares), a city holy from prehistoric times and now uniquely sacred to Shiva, remains the destination of millions in life and, especially, in death. Death, and the body's cremation, on the banks of the Ganges at Varanasi brings freedom from rebirth.

HINDUISM AS EMOTIONAL TRANSFORMATION (RASA)

Underlying all of these religious activities, and especially the religious practice that is everyday life, is the process of acquiring and cultivating an emotional sensibility, or **rasa**—an aesthetic appreciation, a sensitivity to the structures of personal and social meaning that provide coherence amidst so much diversity and apparent chaos. Barbara Stoler Miller summed up Hinduism as "fundamentally a complex of attitudes and rituals integral to the routines of daily existence."[8] This fundamentally emotional attitude is a function of neither education nor elite social status. It is a cultivated consciousness—the availability of people to experience the world according to its natural and social dynamics, in the depth and diversity of the layers of religious experience that are only partially expressed in texts. It is this refined sensibility, acquired by Indian children in the course of their lives, that tantalizingly eludes the student and the scholar and emphasizes the element of multifaceted mystery to which Hinduism responds. Knipe provides a humbling anecdote:

> On the wall beside my desk is a photo taken many years ago of a darkly gnarled tree. From its branches hang half a dozen heavy burlap packages, blackened with mildew from the rains. Together they are an awesome, mysterious image. They provide no clue as to what they are,

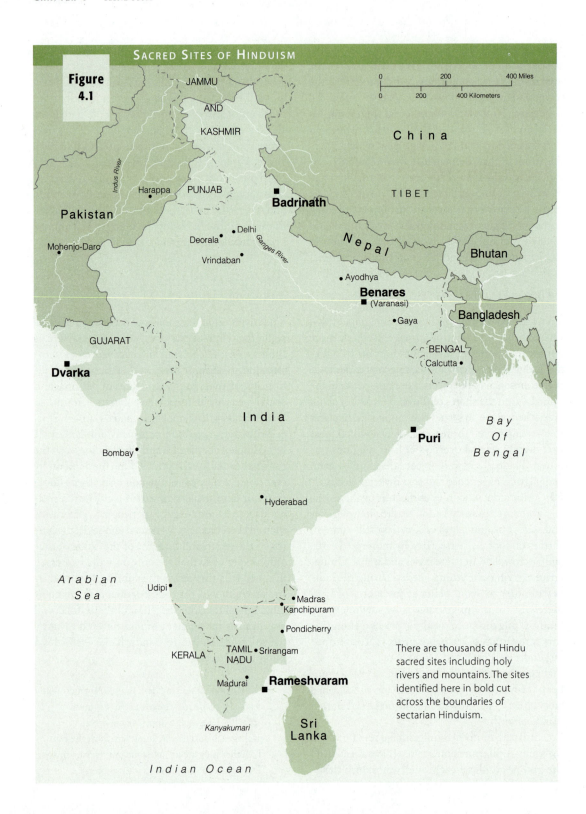

SACRED SITES OF HINDUISM

Figure 4.1

There are thousands of Hindu sacred sites including holy rivers and mountains. The sites identified here in bold cut across the boundaries of sectarian Hinduism.

although one suspects they may either be offerings to some local deity, ancestor, or power—named or nameless to the one who took the trouble to place them there—or bundles to draw attention of the evil eye and therefore protect the area. As for the photo, it hangs there as a reminder of how much of Hinduism I do not understand.[9]

HISTORY OF HINDUISM

The significance of the South Asian region in human development is not a new phenomenon. India has always been on land and sea trade routes. The mountain passes leading to India on the northwest have provided entry to both migrants and invaders. Persians and Greeks, Turks and Mongols, Afghanis and Jats—each played a role in the cultural development of India. Later it was the turn of European colonial powers: the Portuguese, Danish, French, Dutch, and English. To speak of Indian cultural history is to try to appreciate the contribution of each of these groups.

Similarly, the religious history of Indian culture includes a vast array of traditions, several of them native traditions that stand outside the boundaries of Hinduism, such as Buddhism, Jainism, or Sikhism. Other traditions were first brought from outside Indian culture: Christianity, the Parsi form of Persian Zoroastrianism, and Islam. Even the Vedic religion, which forms one foundation of Hinduism, arose from the interactions of groups emigrating into India more than three thousand years ago. Christians have lived in India for almost two thousand years. Although they make up only a little more than 2 percent of the national population, Indian Christians have played a significant cultural role in the south Indian state of Kerala, in which the proportion of Christians is 20 percent. Muslims have come to India by immigration and invasion for over a thousand years and have profoundly shaped the language and culture, especially in northern India. The cultural impact of religions is not dependent on numerical impor-

tance. The Parsi Zoroastrian community of Gujarat, whose ancestors emigrated from Persia several hundred years ago, has had an impact on the business and cultural life of India far out of proportion to its numbers. Among the heterodox movements in India, the Jains, who make up only 0.3 percent of the population, have exercised a powerful example of rigorous religious discipline, careful regulation of life for both monks and householders, and cultivation of radical nonviolence as a fundamental value in life. Jain religious thought has contributed to the global environmental and animal rights movements.

Without compromising its own distinct identity, each of these religions—especially Buddhism, Jainism, Sikhism, and Islam, but also the Parsi religion and Christianity—has had some impact on the development of contemporary Hinduism. Understanding the intersections of Hinduism with these other traditions provides the proper frame for understanding its historical development.

Some Hindus would argue there should be no historical treatment of Hinduism; it is *sanatana dharma,* the "eternal religious teaching." The Hindu scriptures are also considered to be eternal, with no author, human or divine, in a temporal sense. From another perspective, creation narratives in texts called *puranas* add an image of cycles of creation and destruction that occur over vast periods of time but that are an ever-recurring pattern, with no substantive change. A discussion of history in this cyclical context is very different from the linear mode of Western historical analysis. And yet some sense of the historical scope of Hinduism is necessary in the process of learning a new language that can describe the dynamics of Hindu religious life.

THE INDUS VALLEY CIVILIZATION (CA. 6500–1500 B.C.E.)

The starting point for the discussion of religion in India is older than civilization. The Indus Valley, located in the northwest corner of the South Asian subcontinent and part of contemporary Pakistan, is one of the sites where archaeologists have excavated evidence of the establishment, over the course of thousands of years, of stable herding and agricultural communities and the development of the technologies necessary to sustain such groups. Cultivation of cereal crops at some sites in this area dates from 6000 B.C.E. At around the same time as civilization developed in the Indus Valley, there were other tribal groups in various types of hunter-gatherer and stable agrarian settlements throughout the subcontinent. Tribal cultures in all of India continue to exist in the late twentieth century, despite the encroachment of modern civilization. Tribal peoples form one of the basic components of Indian civilization, even though they have always stood outside the religious and social structure of Hinduism.

By the second millennium B.C.E. there was a highly developed civilization, comparable to the civilizations of Egypt and Mesopotamia, in and around the Indus Valley, where the archaeological remains of urban societies at Mohenjo-Daro and Harappa have been discovered. These cities, which formed part of a larger social network of many villages and other cities, show a high level of social order and planning (see Chapter 2). Archaeological evidence reveals civic citadels that included places for bathing, suggesting the importance of ritual purification. Much of the attempt to understand the religious character of this civilization, however, remains speculation, because the inscriptions and seals that have been found there have not been deciphered. Figurines include many female images whose breasts and posture point to fertility worship. There are also images that suggest animal deities and the worship of sacred trees. One of the most intriguing of the seals appears to represent a horned male figure with erect phallus seated in a *yogic* position. The precise function and significance of these images remain unknown, but each image can be related to enduring elements in what became Hinduism: concern for ritual purity, image worship, goddesses and female energy, *yoga* practice, incorporation of sexuality into religion, and the worship of divine power in natural objects such as trees and rivers.

The Indus Valley culture declined and disappeared for reasons that remain speculative, per-

haps because of invasion or severe flooding, or as a result of changes in the climatic conditions necessary for their survival—the sorts of radical changes brought about even today by abrupt shifts in the course of rivers following the monsoon rains. Nevertheless, some aspects of this culture are so deeply rooted in the structure of Indian existence that they remain an important part of contemporary religion throughout South Asia.

VEDISM AND BRAHMANISM (1500–500 B.C.E.)

The middle of the second millennium B.C.E. has often been seen as marking a transition to a radically different form of religious belief and practice. According to theories that were adopted in the colonial period and accepted until quite recently, a new people began to migrate onto the Indian subcontinent and to subjugate many of the original inhabitants. These people, called the **Aryans,** or "noble ones," had much in common with many other groups who were migrating during that same period from central Asia into various parts of Europe and Asia; these groups shared languages of the Indo-European family and some similarities in their heavenly pantheon. These seminomadic immigrants who came into India over a period of several centuries were characterized by the Sanskrit language, an elaborate system of gods, a hierarchical social structure of classes (the origin of what later became the caste system) that established the superior status of the new arrivals over the aboriginal peoples, and a sacrificial system that was associated with a collection of hymns (the *Vedas*). This period is named for these Vedic texts (hence Vedism), but also for the centrality of a sacrificial system that required the services of a class of priests, the Brahmans (hence Brahmanism).

The Aryans began with small, impermanent village settlements; they used bricks for ritual altars but not for houses. Over time these individual settlements, ruled by local chieftains, became united into confederations with tribal kings, whose office suggests the origin of elaborate Vedic rituals of royal consecration. There was apparently a wide variation of forms of tribal leadership, including an assembly of all free men in the village, who would make decisions about important matters such as the appointment of a tribal leader. During the Indian movement for independence from Great Britain, the existence of such village councils was invoked by some nationalist leaders as the fundamental building block of Indian political life. The hierarchical social structure primarily established the supremacy of the Aryans over the indigenous peoples whom they were supplanting. Over a long period of time, the increasing need for ritual specialists to carry out the elaborate Vedic sacrifices made the priestly group a contender for superior status to that of tribal leaders.

Criticism of this "Aryan invasion" theory focuses on three objections: problems with oversimplifying the conflicting evidence of the archaeological record, the more flexible and overlapping character of religiosocial boundaries, and the colonial prejudice inherent in the theory—namely, that the basis of higher culture had to come from outside and from invaders, whether Aryans, Muslims, or the British. It is clear that there were widespread migrations, but not necessarily invasions, over such a long period that some "Aryan" qualities were indistinguishable from the "native" traditions. Thus, the range of religious influences throughout the subcontinent was far broader than the "either/or" quality of the Indus-Valley-versus-Aryan-invaders option. Vedic religious traditions and Brahmanical socioreligious structure arose in a complex and creative process within India rather than being imposed from outside. The notion of native or "indigenous" Aryans emphasizes the creativity and diversity of Indian prehistoric culture, with obvious implications for the assertion of Indian identity in the postcolonial era. Such criticism underscores the danger of oversimplified religious theories and calls for a more complex model of the development of Vedic myth and rituals and the Brahmanical social system. It is clear that over several hundred years, religious traditions emerged that differed significantly from those of the Indus Valley civilization. While scholars are struggling to develop an adequate theory to explain these devel-

opments, their clear legacy is found in the *Vedas,* in the sacrificial system, and in the Brahmanical social order.

THE *VEDAS* Although the *Vedas* seem to be a book, comparable to the scriptures of other traditions, their origin is described as **shruti,** "what is heard," affirming their immediate reception by holy men in the ancient past. Their power came from the immediacy of the sound of the Vedic hymns, and particularly from the sound of the prayers, or **mantras,** that are included in the *Vedas.* The *Vedas* were passed on for hundreds of years by being drilled into the memory of one priest by another. This form of education in sacred matters by rote memorization remains common throughout South Asia today. Indeed, Brahmans take their name from being reciters of *brahman,* a word for these Vedic prayers. As sacrifice became more elaborate and the roles in its performance more specialized, particular parts of the *Vedas* were restricted to *brahmans* who specialized in that part of the *Veda.* Utterance of the ritual sound was powerful in producing the intended result, and its misuse could have devastating consequences. Even when the *Vedas* were written down many centuries later, their primary power lay in their live recitation by one who had been initiated into their power. The notion of sitting down to read the *Vedas* as a sacred book of scripture could not be further from their actual context.

Because of increasing sacrificial complexity, the *Vedas* were collected and written down. There are four Vedic collections: the *Rig Veda,* over a thousand hymns that are concerned with sacrifice but that also contain many strands of mythic narrative in references made to various gods; the *Yajur Veda,* a sacrificial manual; the *Sama Veda,* a guide to the use of *mantras;* and the *Atharva Veda,* which includes details of domestic ritual, along with some early speculation about the deeper meaning and power of the sacrifice itself.

VEDIC DEITIES The Vedic hymns reflect an attitude of awe before the natural powers who control the cosmos and whose continued goodwill was essential for survival. The hundreds of divinities included Indra, a warrior atmospheric god, and Varuna, guardian of the heavenly sphere and sustainer of the cosmic order. One hymn to Varuna (*Rig Veda* 1:24) exalts his majesty and power, which is higher than other forces of nature. Varuna upholds all of creation and guides the order of the cosmos in a way beneficial to human beings. Students who are familiar with the *Psalms* of divine cosmic rule in the Hebrew *Bible* would recognize that despite some differences in imagery, the sense of divine rule and awesome majesty is the same. Some of the ambiguity in the relationship of humans to these deities is revealed in a hymn to Rudra (*Rig Veda* 2:33). This hymn is a plea for healing. Besides repeated praise of Rudra's saving power, there is an undercurrent of fear expressed in pleas that Rudra's arrow of destruction pass by, that his divine ire be diverted and that he slacken the drawn bow and grant mercy. This acceptance of a tension between contrasting, even apparently contradictory, qualities in gods is a distinctive characteristic of later Hinduism, manifested especially in the god Shiva and in the goddesses Kali and Durga. Other Vedic deities are concerned with the process of sacrifice itself: Agni, the god of the domestic sacrificial fire, carries the consumed offering to its intended object and thus insures the success of the sacrifice. Soma is both a god and the hallucinogenic drink used in many Vedic rituals, reflecting the goal of sacrifice to get beyond the limits of the present situation. Later Vedic hymns show an increasing concern with the underlying basis of all, with the "maker of all," Prajapati. However, the Vedic tradition is a polytheistic system in which many gods are worshiped, whereas the individual sacrifice is focused primarily on one particular deity whose response is sought.

SACRIFICE Sacrifice, the making of blood and nonblood offerings as worship to a particular deity, was central to Vedic religion. It functioned on the level of household ritual: the daily *agnihotra* involved the simple pouring of an offering of *ghee* (clarified butter) into the domestic hearth. But it

also encompassed complex sacrifices with profound societal and even cosmic significance, such as the Agnicayana, which involved the construction of an altar to Agni, or the Ashvamedha, a horse sacrifice celebrated to initiate the ruler. In the latter, before a king could assume rule, a horse was allowed to roam freely for a year. The territory that the horse traveled, unhindered, during that year was the extent of the new ruler's kingdom. Such a ritual process reflects both the realities of royal power and the dependence of a ruler on favorable cosmic forces.

In later hymns, the very process of sacrifice became the model by which the origin of everything was understood. Creation itself was pictured as the sacrifice of a primordial being. This sacrifice of dismemberment is the origin not only of the cosmos but also of human beings in four castes (priest, ruler, merchant/farmer, and servants), which are the basis for social relationships. A sense of creation that is primarily a dismemberment calls for a process of "re-membering," restoring the original unity by maintaining appropriate relations within the cosmic and social orders.

The importance of sacrifice as the power that sustains the cosmic order and controls human participation in it intensified concern with the proper performance of sacrificial ritual; failure to perform a sacrifice correctly could have devastating personal and cosmic consequences. A series of texts called *Brahmanas* gave very detailed instructions about performing sacrifices, but the very detail showed that sacrifice itself had eclipsed the Vedic gods in importance. Sacrifice itself, not the deity invoked, was the prime power of the universe. Each aspect of sacrificial ritual corresponded to some cosmic force; proper ritual performance connected the person sacrificing to those powers and brought about the outcome sought. Another collection of texts, called *Aranyakas* (forest meditations), amplified this symbolism of ritual process, making explicit the correspondences and connections between the person, the sacrifice, and cosmic power. These texts also sought to grasp by meditative experience the ground of cosmic power itself, the deepest foundation for all these connections: How does the individual person correspond to the reality that is the foundation of sacrifice and, indeed of everything?

THE UPANISHADS   The *Upanishads* are religious dialogues, composed over a period of several hundred years beginning about 900 B.C.E., which speculate about the correspondences between the individual self and the underlying support of all. The literary genre *upanishad* was sufficiently elastic to allow for hundreds of such texts, but thirteen have been traditionally accepted as "principal," largely because the great philosopher Shankara (eighth century C.E.) so regarded them. Many of the *Upanishads* explicitly involve a student in relation to the teacher, or *guru*. But whether this relationship is expressed or not, understanding the teaching found in these texts required a process of initiation that brought the student, under the guidance of the teacher, to the point of experiencing afresh the religious truth that is preserved in the *upanishad* text. Although the *Upanishads* are rightly regarded as one of India's greatest philosophical contributions to the world, their teaching was never merely intellectual or academic, but instead demanded a profound religious transformation: "Together [the *Aranyakas* and the *Upanishads*] constituted a reformation—a reassessment of the sacrificial worldview and a redirection of religious energies toward salvation by insight and knowledge rather than reliance upon ritual action alone."[10] Therefore, the teaching of the *Upanishads* is often referred to as **vedanta,** "the end of the *Vedas*." In other words, in the *Upanishads*, the religious process of the Vedic period reached its final development.

The *Upanishads* were an inquiry into the meaning of the individual self and its relationship to the underlying reality of all. When the inquiry was turned inward at the sacrificer, a different understanding of self emerged that distinguished the self, the *atman*, both from the body and from the individual identified by name and form. Although distinct from the body, the *atman* is subject to continuous rebirth in the cycle called

samsara, a prospect interpreted as a form of eternal bondage. Every action *(karma)* performed by an individual produces an effect (the *karmic* result, also called *karma*), which, like a seed, eventually bears fruit either in the present life or in a future life. *Karma* is not fate; rather one's current status is the direct result of one's own actions in this and previous lives, just as this morning's indigestion is the result of last night's indulgence in overeating. This process proceeds without cease unless one can achieve release, or *moksha*—liberation from the cycles of *samsara* or rebirth.

When inquiry was turned toward the ground of being, the underlying reality of all, the basis of sacrifice, earlier texts had pointed to the One, which existed before the gods. Among the many names applied to this One was the name Brahman. Much of the inquiry of the *Upanishads* explores the relationship between the individual self, *atman,* and this underlying One—this cosmic Self, Brahman. Some of the early *Upanishads* use various forms of argument to assert the identity of *atman* and Brahman. The teaching of the *Brihadaranyaka* led a person, by meditation, beyond the senses into the depths of the individual self to experience the way that Brahman is the true Self: beyond the waking state, beyond the dreaming state, beyond dreamless sleep, to Brahman—*"the Self that indwells all beings is within you."* Having realized that Self, there is no more sense of duality, nothing else whatever. Most important, there is no separate self to be reborn. One has achieved immortality, a deathless state, *moksha,* freedom from rebirth. The *Chandogya* looks at the external objects and points to a single underlying essence of everything: *"the subtle essence—this whole world has that essence for its Self; that is the Real; that is the Self."* The last phrase, *"that art thou"* (*tat tvam asi* in Sanskrit), is the recurrent theme of the *Upanishads*. The self is one with Brahman—you *are* that—like salt dissolved in water. Perception of duality or multiplicity is illusion, *maya,* or ignorance.[11]

In the early *Upanishads*, composed through the sixth century B.C.E., Brahman is not a personal god, nor can one talk of "loving" Brahman. The religious process of these *Upanishads* leads to a saving knowledge *(vidya)* that one's separate identity has been dissolved into Brahman; hence all illusion is destroyed and all reason for rebirth removed.

The *Katha Upanishad* provides a longer description of the individual's path to achieving liberation, *moksha*, immortality, the end of rebirth. This *upanishad* is a dialogue between a seeker named Naciketas and Yama, the god of death, about understanding the nature of the self. Yama tries to turn Naciketas from his quest and then tries to divert him with distractions. However, Naciketas rejects Yama's offers of material prosperity and sensual pleasures; death, after all, carries all these away. So, having failed in this diversion, Yama is constrained to instruct Naciketas about the true meaning of the self. By resisting the tendency to look outside the self for satisfaction, but looking instead within, Naciketas can come to see *"the Self, deep hidden in all things"* and so *"escape the jaws of death."* This Self, this Person, is the source of life: *"This in truth is That."* One who perceives this Self, in a meditative discrimination that goes beyond sense perception, goes beyond death and achieves immortality: *"Thence to Brahman one attains."*

Whereas these *Upanishads* proclaimed the oneness or nonduality **(advaita)** of self and Self, *atman* and Brahman, many later *Upanishads,* which continued to be written into the early centuries of the Common Era, struggled with the implications of this unity and sought ways that could balance the experience of unity with Brahman with some sense of separate individuality for the self. The fundamental insights of the *Upanishads* about the meaning of the self and release from rebirth by losing one's separate self in Brahman represent a major creative moment in human intellectual history. The insight about release from rebirth *(moksha)* through knowledge remains an enduring element of the Hindu tradition, but this path is generally limited to upper-caste males (those allowed to study the *Vedas*) and to those able to abandon ordinary life for a process of intellectual cultivation and meditative withdrawal that is incompatible with family and social responsibilities.

CLASSICAL INDIAN CIVILIZATION (500 B.C.E.–1000 C.E.)

The sixth century B.C.E. was a time of widespread cultural ferment in several centers of civilization across the globe. This period, sometimes referred to as the Axial Age, saw the start of philosophical speculation in Greece, major prophetic voices in Israel, Confucius and Lao-tzu in China, and major developments in the religious traditions of India.

HISTORICAL CONTEXT OF RELIGIOUS DEVELOP-MENTS

Indian cultural and political history, including the contemporary period, has been dominated by the geographical and cultural diversity of India's regions, a diversity that has undermined many attempts to unite and rule India. Events in the north, influenced by a succession of migrations and invasions, may have had little to do with the contemporaneous situation in the south, which was partially insulated from the immediate effects of the latest incursions. Southern India made extremely important contributions to what is regarded as Hinduism in the form of *puranas* (old stories) about Shiva and Vishnu and devotional poetry to these gods, elaboration of the notion of devotional love of God *(bhakti),* the growth of deity worship as the object of *bhakti,* and the construction of massive temple complexes as central places for expressing such devotion. These narratives and practices then made their way north into regions that were far more unstable. Indeed, the religious and social history of northern India for a millennium (600 B.C.E.–400 C.E.) is dominated by anti-Brahmanical movements, especially Buddhism, whose importance faded only when a pattern of devotional religious practice unrelated explicitly to the Vedic sacrifice or Brahmanical privilege was introduced from the south.

Invasions into the north (especially on the Ganges plain, which cuts across northern India) included those of the Persians (Cyrus, Darius, and Xerxes) in the fifth and sixth centuries B.C.E. and the Greeks under Alexander the Great of Macedonia in the fourth century. The Greek colonies that were established after Alexander's invasion later had a major influence on the development of Buddhist sculpture. However, the Mauryan Empire (321–184 B.C.E.) achieved a level of unification that was not equaled until the sixteenth century C.E. The most important of the Mauryans was Ashoka (r. 273–232 B.C.E.), who embraced Buddhism in response to his revulsion at the slaughter he had inflicted in battle. Ashoka's proclamation of laws on still-extant stone pillars and his efficient administration, together with the vast geographical extent of his reign, make this period particularly significant. The Buddhist wheel and the Ashokan lion's head from Ashoka's law pillars remain the national symbols of contemporary India.

After the end of the Mauryan Empire, the Sungas (184–70 B.C.E.) ruled, and small Greek kingdoms were formed in the north. In the south a succession of dynasties arose in the regions of Karnataka and Kerala, as well as in the Tamilnad cities of Madurai and Madras. The Gupta Empire (300–647 C.E.) is often regarded as an Indian golden age. During this period some of the richest developments in Sanskrit drama and poetry took place. In mathematics, the zero and algebra were introduced; significant discoveries in astronomy were also made. Following Gupta rule, there were more invasions by the Mongols and by a number of tribes, particularly the Jats and Rajputs, who established separate kingdoms and eventually became part of northern Indian culture.

Whereas northern India has been characterized by more contacts with other cultures through migration and invasion, southern India's history has been marked by the outflow of Indian civilization through trade. Thus, a "greater India" has been established not through conquest but through cultural adaptation.

HETERODOX AND ANTI-BRAHMANICAL MOVE-
MENTS   Against the background of the growth of regional kingdoms throughout northern India, several religious groups arose that challenged the supremacy of the *Vedas,* Brahmanical ritual and the caste system, and the Upanishadic religious goal of

moksha. The most important of these religions were Jainism, led by Vardhamana, called Mahavira, and Buddhism, founded by Siddhartha Gautama, called the Buddha, the Awakened One. Buddhism (see Chapter 5) played a major role in the religious and political life of India for over a thousand years and spread from India to Sri Lanka, China, Tibet, and all of Southeast Asia. Both Jainism and Buddhism exalted the ideal of ascetic renunciation of social ties and responsibilities; hence they challenged the whole basis of religious and social life. Because Jainism has remained a distinct religious influence in Indian culture especially through its radical advocacy of nonviolence, a brief description of Jainism and its teachings is offered in Appendix A.

EPICS
Partly in response to these heterodox challenges to the Brahmanical social and religious system, this period saw the development of a new kind of religious literature, called *smriti,* "what is remembered," in contrast to the *Vedas* or *shruti,* "what is heard." The *Vedas* remained the basis for religious and social life, even when those who invoked them could not read the texts themselves. But although the *smriti* literature lacks the immediacy and high authority of the *shruti*—what was directly heard and recorded by the ancient sages—it provided the structure for major religious developments that form the basis for contemporary Hinduism. (The major Hindu scriptures and other religious literature are listed in Table 4.1.)

Chief among the *smriti* are the two great Indian epics composed in Sanskrit, the *Mahabharata* and the *Ramayana,* which together form a "fifth *Veda,*" a text of religion and morality open to all without restriction as to caste. Because access to the *Vedas* was restricted to those upper-caste males who were initiated into their meaning, the stories of these epics became the vehicle of religious instruction for most people. As epic poems, these narratives were shaped by various storytellers over hundreds of years before being reduced to writing. Composition dates for the *Mahabharata* extend from the fifth century B.C.E. to the fifth century C.E., and for the *Ramayana* from the third century B.C.E. to the third century C.E.

MAJOR HINDU SCRIPTURES AND OTHER RELIGIOUS LITERATURE

Table 4.1

SHRUTI—THE FOUNDATIONAL SCRIPTURES

Vedic hymns	*Rig Veda*—the first of the Vedic collections (*samhitas*). These hymns, which were associated with the sacrifices, contain many fragments of mythic material about the gods and about the origin of the world. Later hymns (especially the tenth book) begin speculation about the underlying reality of all.
	Yajur Veda—a sacrificial manual.
	Sama Veda—a guide to the use of *mantras*.
	Atharva Veda—the fourth of the Vedic collections. Building on some of the speculation in the later hymns of the *Rig Veda*, the *Atharva Veda* goes further in trying to identify the underlying foundation of all reality.
Brahamanas	Ritual books connected with the *Vedas* that provide precise instructions on the correct performance of sacrificial ritual.
Aranyakas	"Forest-books"; an extension of the Vedic hymns, which develop the symbolic correspondences between the various elements of the sacrifice, the human person, and the underlying reality of everything.
Upanishads	A form of religious literature that was developed beginning about the seventh century B.C.E. The hundreds of *Upanishads* present a spectrum of views on the relation between the individual self and the ultimate reality, ranging from the dissolving of the self into identity with an impersonal Brahman to later theistic texts in which the individual recognizes the deity as the underlying reality of all (including oneself) but some real distinction remains between the deity, individual, and world.

SMRITI—LATER TEXTS WITH SCRIPTURAL AUTHORITY

Mahabharata	An Indian epic poem in which Krishna plays a part. This long narrative tells of a war between family members. The telling of the story highlights particular social and personal virtues and increases the role of Krishna, especially in the *Bhagavad Gita*.
Ramayana	The second major Hindu epic. It tells the story of Rama's quest for the throne that is rightly his and his battle to win back his wife, Sita, who has been abducted by the demon Ravana.
Dharma shastras	Law manuals that make explicit the responsibilities of religious duty, or *dharma*.
Bhagavad Gita	A late portion of the *Mahabharata* that is regarded by many Hindus as their most representative or comprehensive scripture. Literally, the title means "The Song of the Lord," Krishna's teaching to Arjuna.
Puranas	Literally, "old stories". These texts provide the basis for the various sectarian groups of contemporary Hinduism. The many *puranas* include origin stories and cosmology, legends of ancient kings, and much other traditional material, but the focus is on the particular sect's narratives, which are inserted into the framework.

Table 4.1

CONTINUED

OUTLINES OF TEACHINGS (*SUTRAS*) AND COMMENTARIES

Darshana Sutras	Outlines of the teachings of a particular philosophical or religious school that require elaboration by later commentators. For example, the *Vedanta Sutras* of Badarayana received major commentaries by Shankara (ca. 788–820) and by Ramanuja (1056–1137).
Commentaries	Commenting on the *sutra* texts is a creative shaping of the tradition. Shankara, Madhva (1238–1317), and Ramanuja represent discordant views of the *Vedanta Sutras*. Other Vaishnava theologians include Vallabha (1481–1533), Nimbarka (thirteenth century), and the followers of Caitanya (sixteenth century). The Kashmiri Shaiva theological tradition is represented by Abhinavagupta (ca. 1000).

THE LIVING AND EVOLVING TRADITION

Vernacular epics	More than translations, the Tamil *Ramayana* of Kamban and the Hindi *Ramcaritmanas* of Tulsidas represent a creative retelling of the epic in a different linguistic culture.
Vernacular devotional poetry	Includes the poetry of the Tamil Shaiva poets called Nayanmars (for example, Manikkavachakar, eighth century); the Tamil Vaishnava poets called Alvars (sixth to ninth centuries), the Kannada Shaiva poet Basavanna (c.a. 1106–1168), the Marathi Vaishnava poet Tukaram (1598–1649), the Hindi Vaishnavas Tulsidas (1532–1623), Surdas (sixteenth century), and Mirabai (sixteenth century), along with the nonsectarian poetry of Kabir (fifteenth century).

The *Mahabharata*, a text several times longer than the entire *Bible* or the *Iliad* and the *Odyssey* combined, is the complex and painfully honest story of a great war between branches of a family. It describes a conflict that is the story of India itself—indeed, of all humanity—in which the heroes sustain the moral order of *dharma* at a tremendous personal and ethical price. The various episodes of this story provided the material for further elaboration by poets and dramatists. The *Mahabharata* remains a living epic. When the narrative was recently produced for Indian television in more than ninety episodes, all business and social activity simply stopped for the duration of the broadcast. In contrast, Western students often read the Greek epics, the *Iliad* and the *Odyssey*, as part of an educational program; certain cultural values are contained in these texts, but they tell of gods no longer worshiped and of a social system that no longer exists. The narration of the *Mahabharata*, with its ethical dilemmas as much as its religious perspective, continues to be lived out in the lives and worship of contemporary Hindus.

The shorter *Ramayana*, attributed to the sage Valmiki, tells the story of Rama, the model of kingly virtue and the incarnation of Vishnu, who engages in a long struggle to rescue his wife, Sita, who has been seized by the demon Ravana. One of Rama's allies in this struggle is the monkey god Hanuman, one of the most beloved pan-Indian deities. Rama, Sita, and Hanuman are types, representing cultural values of king and husband, wife, and loyal ally. The *Ramayana* was adapted into Indian vernacular languages, notably into Tamil by

Kamban in the twelfth century and into Hindi by Tulsidas in the seventeenth century. These works are more than translations; they are new creative works that made the religious values of the *Ramayana* available to different cultures and in languages close to the people. The ideal of kingship presented in the *Ramayana* spread from India and was embraced throughout Southeast Asian countries, many of which have their own vernacular adaptations of the *Ramayana*. Thus, this text has exerted a profound influence on the social values of cultures that are not religiously Hindu but that formed part of "greater India" in cultural terms. Like the *Mahabharata*, the *Ramayana* was a great success on national television. Each year, throughout India, various episodes of the epic are performed to vast audiences as part of the celebration of Rama's victory, a festival that is not without political significance in contemporary India.

THE *BHAGAVAD GITA*   One late section of the *Mahabharata*, the *Bhagavad Gita* (the song of Lord Krishna), composed around the first century B.C.E., has become recognized as one of the most representative Hindu texts. Krishna, advisor to the epic's heroes and the incarnation *(avatara)* of Vishnu, explains to the prince Arjuna how it is possible for him to carry out his social duty (his *dharma* as a warrior) and also achieve *moksha* (release from the necessity of rebirth, or *samsara*, that arises from the effects, or *karma*, of actions performed). The *Gita* shows how one can continue carrying out one's social responsibility while achieving the highest religious goal. Hence it offers a path to liberation in the midst of social activity rather than through renunciation and monastic vows. The *Bhagavad Gita* also presents Lord Krishna as the proper object of selfless dedication, through devotional love, or *bhakti*. By performing his actions for Krishna, Arjuna can be freed from their effects; even more, anyone who dedicates to Krishna the simplest of offerings will be freed from the bondage to rebirth. Here is a path of release open to everyone, including members of low castes and women, but also a way that does not undo the social order or support those who abandon their responsibil-

ities. The *Gita* thus provides the basis for social and religious stability, sustaining the tensions between religious duty *(dharma)* and the quest for liberation *(moksha)*.

The context of the *Bhagavad Gita* is the climactic *Mahabharata* battle of Kurukshetra. Arjuna, one of the epic's heroes, is about to signal the start of the battle. Seeing his relatives and teachers on the opposing side, however, he stops, unwilling to engage in this battle because of the horrible results *(karma)*. Arjuna expresses (in Book 2) a willingness to become a renunciant, perhaps as a Buddhist monk, and so relinquish all social responsibility. Instead, Krishna urges him to carry out his social duty *(dharma)* and engage in the battle. In Book 3, Krishna shows Arjuna that actions are necessary to sustain the world; even he, Krishna, must act to prevent the world from falling apart (vv. 3–5, 24). The key virtue that Arjuna must bring to the battle—a necessary action that is his *dharma* as a warrior—is that of disciplined detachment from the results of action (vv. 8–14). All desire for success, all greed, must be rooted out. It is just as though Arjuna were watching the action happening without his being involved at all; he does not think, "I am the actor," but merely that nature's inert qualities or elements are acting on one another (vv. 18–19). Krishna says, *"As the ignorant act with attachment to actions, Arjuna, so wise men should act with detachment to preserve the world"* (v. 25).[12] Krishna then suggests another way for Arjuna to achieve detachment: through surrendering himself and all his actions to Krishna (v. 30). This book concludes with Krishna's explanation of why desire is so deeply rooted in the senses, and Arjuna is shown that the real battle is the one that he must wage against desire in his own heart (v. 43). This inner dimension of combat with desire was what made the *Bhagavad Gita* not a pro-war treatise but the foundation for Mohandas K. Gandhi's nonviolent struggle for Indian independence.

The first part of Book 9 teaches that Krishna is the underlying reality of all, the Brahman taught by the *Upanishads*. The *Bhagavad Gita* first accepts and then transforms the understanding of Brahman: Krishna is a personal form of Brahman; he has qualities and powers; he is approached with a loving knowledge; the devotee wants to continue this love as a separate individual; this path is open to all. The way in which the *Bhagavad Gita* accepts and transforms other layers of the cumulative tradition is one of the reasons for the popularity of the *Gita*. In this case, the path of knowledge of the *Upanishads*, which is often given a nondualist or *advaita* interpretation, is transformed into the basis for a loving knowledge of Krishna that combines the origin of all in God's own nature with the separation that is necessary for love to take place. This position, which has many varieties in Hinduism, is known as difference-in-nondifference *(bhedabheda)*.

The second part of Book 9 returns to the themes of surrender to Krishna and the path of love *(bhakti)*. Krishna makes clear that however humble the offering to him, *"a leaf or flower or fruit or water,"* he accepts the offering and the devotee. They will be freed from the bondage of actions and come to Krishna (vv. 26, 28). *"No one devoted to me is lost. If they rely on me, Arjuna, women, commoners, men of low rank, even men born in the womb of evil, reach the highest way"* (vv. 31–32). The summary advice of the *Gita* points to *bhakti*—devotional love and loving surrender—as the primary path to God:

> Whatever you do—what you take,
> what you offer, what you give,
> What penances you perform—
> Do it as an offering to me, Arjuna!
>
> Keep me in your mind and devotion,
> sacrifice to me, bow to me,
> discipline your self toward me,
> and you will reach me. (9:24, 34)

Although the teaching of the *Bhagavad Gita* widened the horizons of the Hindu tradition, the practical social implications of its teachings have been criticized as being anti-Buddhist rhetoric (opposing the abandonment of *dharmic* social roles) and for offering a semblance of religious equality to those *"born in the womb of evil"* without changing their social status or treatment at all.

HINDU SOCIAL STRUCTURE   Other texts composed during this period show the consolidation of a social structure that can be called Hindu (rather than Brahmanical). The *Dharma shastras* (treatises on religious duty), including the famous *Laws of Manu*, elaborated on the religiosocial duty *(dharma)* associated with one's caste *(varna)* and stage of life *(ashrama)*. These texts reflect the tension between the ideals of sustaining the world (which can be summed up in the word *dharma*) and the process of abandoning or renouncing it (seeking release, or *moksha*). The tension is not fully resolved; both paths are affirmed as valid. These texts accepted four appropriate goals for human life: attainment of success and acquiring wealth **(artha)**; enjoyment of pleasure, including sexual love **(kama)**; performance of socioreligious responsibilities *(dharma)*; and the achievement of release from rebirth *(moksha)*. The first three goals are necessary to sustain society, whereas the fourth, pursuit of release, transcends social responsibility.

The concrete realization of these goals takes place according to one's caste status and one's current stage of life. The four traditional castes, or *varnas*, are *brahmana* (priests and scholars), **kshatriya** (rulers and warriors), **vaishya** (merchants and artisans), and **shudra** (laborers and peasants). Rules regarding caste seek to control intercaste interaction, especially regarding food exchange and marriage, in order to maintain the ritually pure status of the higher castes. Practices such as vegetarianism and abstaining from inflicting pain **(ahimsa)** further separate the elite groups from others.

In the *ashrama* theory of life stages, each male Hindu passes successively through periods as a celibate student *(brahmachari)*, a married householder *(grihasta)*, a retiree dwelling in the forest *(vanaprastha)*, and a wandering renunciant *(sannyasin)*. In practice, most people, men and women, live out their lives as householders. This fourfold structure of life also provides a rationale for balancing *dharmic* responsibility for the world with the quest for release from rebirth. The vast majority of people raise a family and in turn are cared for in old age, and they must postpone the path of renunciation until a future birth. The *ashrama* theory of life stages shows that in an ideal society, all would have the opportunity to seek release in this lifetime.

Finally, these texts recommend the variety of paths *(marga)* to religious realization that are found in the *Bhagavad Gita.* Emphasis is placed on the three primary forms of *yoga* that can lead the practitioner to release: a path of disciplined meditation and knowledge of the divine *(jñana yoga),* performing action without attachment *(karma yoga),* and devoted service to a personal god *(bhakti yoga).* Knowledge of one's unity with Brahman leads to the complete dissolving of the separate self. Selfless performance of one's *dharma* removes the effects of past actions and frees the individual from rebirth. Loving service of God, often expressed by service to the Lord in the form of a deity image in a temple or at a home shrine, further develops the spirit of selfless service that will lead the devotee into continued love of God after death and not to further separation from the Lord in rebirth. The option to choose from these paths offers to the majority, who cannot abandon their families or business responsibilities, the possibility of religious fulfillment through selfless performance of their work or through loving service of God.

These attempts to explain and justify the Hindu social structure have been criticized both from within the tradition and from outside it. For example, those practicing *nirguni bhakti,* the love of God without any formal image, refuse to restrict access to God according to temple or priestly service. For these devotees, the love of God, especially among the lowest classes of society, completely transcends caste, status, gender, or wealth. Among the nonorthodox traditions, the Buddhists regarded arguments for performing *dharmic* responsibility (as in the *Bhagavad Gita*) as an attempt to legitimate a social structure that should not be defended.

PHILOSOPHICAL TRADITIONS The concern to provide a coherent intellectual defense against the challenges of Buddhists and Jains influenced the development of six major philosophical schools, each with its own core text *(sutra)* that received

many, and often divergent, commentaries (see Table 4.2). These systems provided basic philosophical tools of logic and cosmology (Nyaya and Vaisheshika), as well as an image of the structure of the universe (the Samkhya system, which provided a basis for the *Bhagavad Gita*'s teaching) and a program for disciplined detachment (Yoga). The fact that some of these schools were nontheistic did not prevent their teachings from being used by later devotional groups. Two of these traditions, the Mimamsa school of Vedic interpretation and the Vedanta school of Upanishadic analysis, have continued up to the present. Despite the rich intellectual tradition of these schools, however, the religious lives of the vast majority of believers may have been very little influenced by the works of these scholars.

Within Vedanta there arose three distinct schools. The school of nondualism *(advaita,* associated with Shankara, who lived in the eighth century) argued that there was no difference between the individual self and Brahman; all apparent difference was illusion or *maya,* which was to be removed in the attainment of *moksha.* Madhva's (thirteenth-century) school of dualism *(dvaita)* held that, on the contrary, the relation of the self to Brahman and to the world was one of radical duality and difference. The individual self is simply different and distinct from Brahman, other selves, and the world. The individual established a proper relation to the Lord by obedient service and loving worship. Ramanuja's (twelfth-century) qualified nondualism represented a middle position: although there is real difference between the self and God, nevertheless by love, the individual achieves union with the Lord. This school provided a theological basis for the devotional love *(bhakti)* that motivated the South Indian poet-saints.

Dualism is so typical of Western thought that it is rarely questioned. From its origins, however, Indian thought sought the unity (whether the impersonal Brahman or the power of a particular deity) that underlies the multiplicity that people see and are. Whereas the nondualist school *(advaita)* pushes this view to its logical extreme of absolute identity without difference, many Indian traditions allow for both identity and difference. These reli-

Table
4.2

THE SIX SCHOOLS OF HINDUISM

The "Six Schools" (each with distinctive *sutra* collections and commentaries) assume difference and multiplicity as the basis of reality, except for Vedanta, which probes the connection between the individual and the underlying reality or Brahman. Many of these systems were originally nontheistic, because their systems explain reality with no necessary link to any divine power. Despite this, Samkhya, Yoga, and Vedanta have been adapted to serve as the philosophical bases for theistic systems.

Samkhya	A dualist metaphysics that has played a very influential role in the development of Indian philosophies and religious systems (for example, as the basis for much of the teaching of the *Bhagavad Gita*)
Yoga	Follows much of the Samkhya system and provides a practice of discipline and liberation
Mimamsa	A system of Vedic interpretation and sacrificial performance that developed the methods of inquiry that served the development of Vedanta and other religious schools
Vaisheshika	An atomistic cosmology very similar to that of the earliest Greek philosophers
Nyaya	A system of logic that was developed along with Vaisheshika and that has exerted a major influence on all Indian thought
Vedanta	An inquiry into the *Vedas* and *Upanishads* about the nature of the self and Brahman and the relation between the two. The implications of Vedanta about the relation of the self and the world to Brahman were developed in three basic directions: assertion of identity with Brahman or nondualism (*advaita*); recognition of difference and multiplicity between self, others, world, and God (*dvaita*); and in many ways the most typical response, an experience and affirmation that self and Brahman (or self and a personal God) are both different and, in the most profound sense, one (*bhedabheda*). Each of these responses produced its own schools.

gious and philosophical schools are called *bheda-bheda,* because they combine both identity with the divine power (*abheda,* "no difference") and some individuality or separation of those who love the deity (*bheda,* "difference"). In popular analogies, it is said that a devotee wants to taste sugar, not become sugar; or that lovemaking would cease if the two lovers, even in their deepest union, became dissolved in one another. The sustained tension between identity and difference may be one of the deepest insights of Hindu thought.

SECTARIAN HINDUISM   In addition to the epics, there were many other stories about the popular deities, especially the incarnations, or *avataras,* of Vishnu; the forms of Shiva; and the manifestations of the goddess as Lakshmi, Durga, or Kali. Devotion to these deities led to the formation of sectarian Hinduism, with Vaishnavas, Shaivites, and Shaktas—those who worship, respectively, Vishnu, Shiva, and **Devi** (the Goddess). Each of these regionally and religiously diverse groups created and embellished its own *puranas,* which included stories of creation, legends of regional kings and heroes, and crucial sections that praised the sect's particular deity and described the devotional practices to be carried out. Such sectarian devotions found living exemplars in traditional lineages of poet-saints in South India, the Alvars praising Vishnu and the Nayanmars, Shiva. The stories of

Remnants of seven ancient stone-cut Hindu temples stand at Mahabalipuram, India (1982).

Vishnu, Shiva, and the Goddess illustrate the tremendous religious development that took place from the *Vedas* through the epics to the *puranas*.

Many temples were constructed to these deities through the patronage of various ruling families in the different regions of India. The temples became "*puranas* in stone" and "living *puranas*" both because of the many narratives carved into temple walls seen as the worshiper circumambulated the temple and also because the temples became a focus for devotional expressions in poetry and dance about the various divine figures. Thus, the deity was incarnate not only in the temple image but also in the experience of the devotees.

VISHNU   Vishnu is presented as the Lord of the Universe, the vanquisher of demons that threaten the proper religious and societal order of *dharma*. Indeed, Vishnu's primary role is to sustain a just *dharmic* society. He does this by descending in an appropriate form whenever *dharma* is threatened and when demons seem on the verge of defeating the good. These "descents," or *avataras,* make Vishnu manifest in various forms. Fish, tortoise, boar, dwarf, man-lion, Rama, and Krishna are some of the principal *avataras*. For example, as the dwarf Vamana, an *avatara* first described in the *Vedas,* Vishnu claimed from the demons only as much

territory as he could encompass in three steps; then he expanded himself to indeed encompass all—heaven, earth, and underworld—in those steps. In the epics, the divine role of Rama and Krishna was not overly emphasized (except in some episodes of the *Mahabharata*, such as the *Bhagavad Gita*), but in the *puranas* a full description is given of each of the *avataras*. Special emphasis was placed on the childhood and youth of Krishna, which became more and more fully elaborated in the *Harivamsha* (an appendix to the *Mahabharata*), the *Vishnu Purana,* and finally the *Bhagavata Purana.* The *Bhagavata Purana* included in its tenth book the stories of the childhood and adolescent play of Krishna, especially his amorous sports with the cowherd women of Vrindaban. These narratives changed the focus of Krishna devotion from awe-filled service of the Lord's majesty (as was prescribed in the *Bhagavad Gita*) to loving remembrance of his play, or *lila.* These *puranas* also incorporated cosmological forms *(vyuha)* of Vishnu through which he reveals the nature of the universe itself. Thus, whether one's concern was the loving presence of a playful child-God, his amorous play, or his creative activity in the cosmos, these *puranas* provided the basis for developing devotional sentiments and worship.

SHIVA The mythology of Shiva, rooted in ancient religious traditions that perhaps antedate even the *Vedas,* presents a divinity whose very nature is ambiguous. In the *Vedas,* Rudra-Shiva is an outsider, the lord of wild animals; he provides access to forgiveness, but also threatens destruction. It is this many-faced, ambiguous, and antithetical character that makes Shiva so complex as to reflect profoundly the tensions within human experience, especially human relations with the divine.

One of the most common images of Shiva is the Lord of the Dance, the *nata-raja.* In this image, Shiva leads a dance within a circle of flame, for all is being consumed. As he dances, he crushes a demon underfoot, for this dance is a victory over the forces of evil. But what a dance! Shiva possesses four arms (with the number of arms, what they hold, and the hand signs called *mudras* serving to identify the god and the meaning of the god). One arm holds the drum that gives the beat to human life, which summons everything to live fully. Another arm holds fire, for the dance of life is always also a dance that consumes, a dance of destruction. The other two hands sign "not to be afraid" and "come freely," a divine invitation to come join in the dance of life, which is both creation and destruction, both life and death. Both polar opposites are divine. Qualities and experiences that seem contradictory to humans are linked in Shiva.

Other apparent dualities sustained in Shiva are the erotic lover and the renouncer, the husband and the hermit, the male and the female. Another of the most common images of Shiva is the *lingam,* symbolizing in its shape the principle of male energy, but which here is joined with the *yoni,* the source of female energy. Still other images show Shiva as half male and half female, for in him all is joined, all oppositions are reconciled, and all energies are united. The North Indian city of Varanasi, or Benares, has been a pilgrimage site since the dawn of civilization. Varanasi is the city of Shiva, where the *lingam* is worshiped in the temple of Shiva as Vishva-natha, the Lord of the Universe, or simply the Lord of All. It is at Benares, alongside the Ganges, where people seek release at death or have their bodies brought to be cre-mated. Although much of the mythology and worship of Shiva seems to transcend reason, this tradition has given rise not only to devotional hymns but also to theological works, for the great theologian Shankara was a Shaivite, and worship of Shiva inspired the theological schools of **Shaiva** Siddhanta and Kashmiri Shaivism.

Shaiva poets show a passionate devotional love of Shiva. However the various dualities in Shiva are resolved on the ritual and theological planes, the devotional poems of the Kannada Virashaiva poet Basavanna clearly show his deep attachment to Shiva. Beyond his observance of any external ritual practice, Basavanna wants to be taken into the Lord's heart. Although he is ignorant of many things, he sings from the heart, the source of his deep love. He hands himself over to be the musical instrument of Shiva's praise, the Lord of the Meeting Rivers. Devotion to Shiva puts pilgrimage and temple worship, the multiplication of shrines and offerings, in a secondary place to the one thing necessary: the knowledge of Shiva that comes in loving surrender.

THE GODDESS Many of the early narratives of the Goddess saw her in various forms as consort or wife of particular gods—as Parvati with Shiva and Lakshmi with Vishnu. Worship of the Goddess separately, generically as Devi, is found everywhere in India and has an important place even when the largest temples appear to focus on male deities. In Vrindaban, there are shrines to Vrinda-devi (the Goddess of these groves) and Yamuna-devi (the Goddess of the Yamuna River). Even though so much emphasis is placed on Krishna there, no one can ignore the fact that the Goddess is an essential dimension of the matrix of divine power. Whereas the Goddess appears in many natural forms of earth, rivers, trees, and other plants, she is also represented in distinct deity images.

The goddess Durga is worshiped in a nine-day festival, Durga-puja, which celebrates her victory over a buffalo demon. None of the gods could subdue this foe, so they entrusted all their weapons to Durga, who succeeded. The victory shows her as the supreme power, because all the gods also became subject to her. Thus, she is uniquely able to help those who seek her help. The goddess Kali represents both aspects of maternal care, giving life in birth and receiving the dying. She is both maternally protecting and bloodthirsty. Kali continues to receive blood sacrifice in her temples. She subdued even Shiva; vanquishing him, she danced on his chest. Although the *puranas* concerning the Goddess were written by men, and most of the Goddess worship employs male priests, this many-faceted worship points to the centrality of the Goddess in her many forms in religious experience.

HINDU *TANTRAS*   Finally, this period saw the first *tantras*, texts that "claim to introduce techniques that lead directly to liberation without traditional practices and routines."[12] *Tantric* texts focused on attaining union with **shakti,** the Goddess or feminine principle. These traditions were seen as a heroic path seeking to emulate the union of Shiva with Shakti, the divine masculine power with the feminine. The *tantras* frequently used secret *yogic* techniques and erotic mysticism that went beyond societal norms.

THE MEDIEVAL PERIOD (MUSLIM INVASIONS TO 1757)

Within a century of the death of the prophet Muhammad in 632, there was a series of raids into northern India by various Muslim tribal groups, whose activity was characterized far more by being tribal groups in search of pillage than by their Muslim identity. After Mahmud of Ghazni's raids in the eleventh century, more permanent settlement became the norm. Large portions of India were ruled by the five dynasties of the Delhi Sultanate (1206–1526). However, the periods of stable rule from Delhi were punctuated with Rajput rule and by invasions by the Turks and by the Mongols under Timur (Tamerlane) during the fourteenth century.

The Mughal dynasty (1526–1858) brought a unity to northern India unequaled until the height of the British Raj (rule). The grandeur of Mughal architecture has never been excelled. Mughal rule

began with the arrival of Babur (r. 1526–1530) and continued through the two parts of the reign of his son Humayan (r. 1530–1540, 1545–1556). The high point of Mughal rule came with Akbar (r. 1556–1605), who combined military and administrative skill with a broad humanistic appreciation. Akbar welcomed representatives of many faiths, including Christian missionaries, to discussions of religion in his court, and he envisioned a religious worldview that could incorporate the best qualities of all beliefs. Akbar built the Red Fort at Agra and constructed a new capital nearby at Fetehpur Sikri, which has stood as a "ghost city" since its abandonment because of insufficient water. Akbar's son Jahangir (r. 1605–1627) and grandson Shah Jahan (r. 1624–1658) carried forward this ambitious building program, the former in Kashmir and the latter at Delhi and Agra. Delhi's Red Fort and the Jami Masjid, the largest mosque in India, were begun during Shah Jahan's rule. The Taj Mahal, built of white marble and inlaid stone on the Yamuna River at Agra as a tomb for Shah Jahan's favorite wife, is regarded as one of the wonders of the world.

Later Mughal rule was weakened by bloody struggles for succession and by rivalries within the ruling family. Shah Jahan was imprisoned for eight years (1658–1666) by his son Aurangzeb (r. 1658–1707). Aurangzeb is the most controversial of the Mughals, because he abandoned Akbar's tolerance of other faiths. Instead, he periodically embarked on iconoclastic expeditions, destroying temples and deity images or at least forcing devotees to remove their deities to safer territory. For example, he took the deity images from Keshavdev Temple in Mathura and placed them under the steps into the mosque in Agra. It is no surprise that the name of Aurangzeb still draws a hateful response from many contemporary Hindus.

Mughal rule was not without opposition, especially on the northern and western periphery from Marathas (especially under the famous Shivaji, who ruled from 1646 to 1680), Rajputs, Sikhs, and Jats. After Aurangzeb, Mughal rule was weakened by new invasions from Persia. Nevertheless, there was at least a figurehead Mughal ruler in Delhi until 1858, when the British deposed and exiled the last of them.

Although Muslim rule did reach South India, this was also the period of the Hindu Vijayana-gar empire, which ruled much of that region from the capital at Hampi from the fourteenth to six-teenth centuries. There was also the Ganapati dynasty in Orissa on the eastern central coast.

RESPONSES TO MUSLIM RULE: *DHARMIC ORTHO-DOXY* It would be difficult to imagine a greater contrast to classical Hinduism than the Islamic tra-dition, which brought a strict monotheism; rejec-tion of deity worship as idolatry; and a centralized view of religion with one scripture, one commu-nity, and the ideal of a single law for both the state and religious life. The mythological language of the Hindu epics and *puranas* stands in striking opposition to the historical revelation to Muham-mad by Allah.

Against the background of Mughal rule, the period prior to the British Raj saw a defensive response from the Hindu community's religious leaders that included strengthening the social coherence of the *dharmic* religious code, especial-ly through enforcing high-caste purity by the adop-tion of vegetarianism and opposition to cow slaughter.

Despite what appears to be simple contradic-tion, the actual interactions between the conquerors and their subjects were extremely complex and the boundaries between religious traditions far more porous than today. There was considerable com-mon ground between the Muslim Sufi saints and poets and the Hindu devotional poet-saints of northern and western India, and their experiences of divine grace and love of God were remarkably similar. Kabir (1440–1518) sang of God who was no respecter of caste or status and accepted anyone who brought love. It was in this context as well that Guru Nanak (1469–1539) proclaimed the Sikh path of loving submission to the transcendent One. (The Sikh path, distinct from both Hinduism and Islam, is treated in Appendix A.)

POET-SAINTS IN VERNACULAR LANGUAGES In response to the linguistic and cultural power of the Muslim rulers, there was a flowering of Hindu devotionalism in vernacular languages. In North India, the Hindi poets Surdas and Mirabai (both in the sixteenth century) and Ravidas (fifteenth century) personalized and reinforced a vital stream of devotion. Surdas places himself in the midst of the love play of Radha and Krishna as one of Radha's woman friends. Not only does she cele-brate the lovers' emotions but she also takes a role in advancing their intimacy, urging Radha to sat-isfy Krishna's passion. Mirabai will not let her in-laws or their guards keep her from Krishna, the true love of her life: "Why would I want anyone else?" Krishna's flute playing takes away all restraint. She yearns for the Lord to come quickly and quench her pain. Tulsidas's (1532–1623) Hindi ver-sion of the *Ramayana* gave a creative and accessi-ble interpretation to that epic.

In Bengal to the east, the mystic reformer Cai-tanya (1486–1533), revered as a divine incarnation by his followers, influenced the growth of Ben-gali literature—especially poetry and drama—among his followers. Their distinctive style of con-gregational devotional practice, based on the singing of the divine name *(kirtana)* and other sacred songs, provided a focus for religious activity that was not dependent on temple activity. Caitanya's followers helped to turn large parts of northern India, espe-cially the Braj region of Uttar Pradesh, into a liv-ing representation of the divine play, or *lila,* that was praised in their songs.

To the west, the Marathi saints Jñaneshvar (thirteenth century), Namdev (fourteenth centu-ry), Eknath (sixteenth century), and Tukaram (1598–1649) provided the devotional poetry that helped maintain local pilgrimage traditions. Many of these saints came from lower-caste groups and made their devotional activity a strong protest against the religious legitimation of social privilege.

The Marathi poet-saint Tukaram pictures him-self as the "dog of God," desperately looking for a home and finding it with his Lord. He drives away intruders and then comes back to be fed from the Lord's own hand, so pampered with affection that he is shameless and fearless in seeking God's favor. The intimacy of this relationship has nothing to do with status but only with the intensity of the love and with the close contact granted by the Lord to those who love so much.

As is clear in the case of these devotional poets, popular Hinduism continued to flourish during the period of Muslim rule virtually untouched by the tensions and machinations among the elite groups. However, it must be clear that many of the buildings that constitute the "wonder that was India" for the Western tourist imagination, such as the Red Fort in Delhi and the Taj Mahal in Agra, are monuments of Muslim rule. They are also reminders of the deep impact of Islam on India, which even after the partition of 1947 remains, after Indonesia, the country with the second largest Muslim population. It is partly as a result of later political conflict and the bloody rivalries of opposing religious communities that it is so difficult to present a unitary picture of South Asian religious history.

THE MODERN PERIOD
(COLONIAL RULE THROUGH 1947)

One significant political fact about India is that it was largely ruled by foreigners for most of the past millennium—first by the Delhi Sultans and the Mughals and then by the British (1757–1947).

THE RAJ IN INDIA   The British were not the first westerners to establish trading bases for the profitable spice trade in India. The Portuguese, Danish, and French had preceded them. Nevertheless, the chartering of the East India Company in 1600 began a relentless process of competition for commercial, and later political, domination of the subcontinent. The first British trading port was established at Surat in Gujarat in 1612. The East India Company factory at Hugli in Bengal was founded in 1651. During this period, the British and French acted out their continental rivalry in India. In 1757, at the Battle of Plassey, Robert

Clive defeated the Nawab of Bengal, thus beginning formal Company rule over Indian territory. Several wars were required for the British finally to defeat Tipu Sultan of Mysore in South India. The British gained control of Delhi and the figurehead Mughal emperor in 1801 and defeated the Marathas in 1803. But it was not until 1849 that they succeeded in defeating the Sikhs. The Mutiny of 1857 is regarded by Indians as their "first War of Independence." Although this rebellion was put down after considerable loss of life on both sides, it brought an end to East India Company control of India. With the establishment of the British Raj, or rule, in 1858, India became part of the British Empire, the last Mughal emperor was exiled, and the process toward forming a single nation called India began.

British scholars provided their own critical interpretations of Indian religions. A tremendous amount of scholarship was produced during the Raj, from translations of the sacred texts to grammars, dictionaries, gazetteers, and district guides. One effect of this scholarly effort was to produce a "canon" of Indian "classics," almost all of them originally in Sanskrit and often translated to conform with Western literary traditions. Popular and vernacular works, when they were treated at all, were given second place. Raj scholarship thus made Hindu texts available to Western (and Indian) readers, but at the same time obscured a major portion of Hindu literature and practice.

HINDU RESPONSES TO WESTERNIZATION   British rule challenged the power of Hindu religion and society by missionary activities and by demands for social reform. The introduction of Western education and the use of an alien language for the Anglo-Indian elite further challenged the validity of Indian culture. Of course, the vast majority of the Indian population who were not part of the English educational system were not troubled by colonial criticisms. A few Hindu leaders, though English educated, rejected outright the validity of Western culture and the criticism of the missionaries; instead, they wholeheartedly reaffirmed

Mohandas K. Gandhi, known as the Mahatma (great-souled one), was the leader of nonviolent civil disobedience in India's successful struggle for independence.

the traditional values of the "old order." One Bengali Vaishnava, Baba Premananda Bharati, came to the United States in 1902 to denounce the "white peril" that materialist Western culture posed to the more spiritual cultures of the East.

Four other types of Hindu response to the British presence in India took these challenges of modernity to heart: each put forward a "true" Hinduism that escaped or refuted the colonial criticisms. First, Ram Mohan Roy (1772–1833), impressed with the value of British education and the validity of British religious critique, used the Brahmo Samaj organization to argue for a nonidolatrous, monotheistic Hinduism based on the *Upanishads*. He hoped to combine the spiritual heritage of India with an assimilation of the power of modern science. Influenced by Christianity in trying to shape Hinduism as a universal theism, Roy criticized both idolatry and devotional practices in favor of that "true system of religion" that would bring knowledge of God and proper feelings for others without concern for "observances of diet and other matters of form."[14] The work of the Brahmo Samaj was continued by Keshub Chunder Sen (1838–1884) and Debendranath Tagore (1817–1905).

Swami Dayananda Sarasvati (1824–1883) founded the Arya Samaj, which asserted the ancient excellence of the Vedic tradition over against recent abuses. The *Vedas*, not the deity worship drawn from the epics and *puranas*, the *swami* said, constituted the real Hinduism. He was less impressed with the British than with the need of Indians to return to the glorious roots of their own culture, which were not subject to colonialism's complaints. To accomplish this goal, he adopted a more spiritual notion of sacrifice and a changed understanding of caste that denied the superiority of Brahmans. He opposed social abuses such as child marriage, not because they offended the modern mentality or the colonial sensibility but because they had no justification in authentic Hinduism.

A third approach was found in the lives of Swami Ramakrishna (1836–1886), a rather traditional Bengali devotee of the goddess Kali, and his disciple Swami Vivekananda (1863–1902), who attended the 1893 Parliament of Religions in Chicago. Vivekananda founded the Ramakrishna Mission to provide education and social service in India, as well as the Vedanta Society to bring the wisdom of Hinduism to the materialist and "pagan" West. This twofold structure presented Hinduism as a system of social service with a mission to the world. This missionary impulse in Hinduism rejected Christian religion outright and presented a form of Hinduism based on the *Upanishads* as the answer to the Western religious crisis. The movement of Hindu religious teachers to the West continues as a major influence in contemporary global religious culture.

A fourth approach to the British presence is found in Mohandas K. Gandhi (1869–1948), who professed a Hinduism that transcended traditional religious boundaries. Gandhi reinterpreted the

Bhagavad Gita as the basis for a nonviolent *(ahimsa)* struggle for Indian independence. He preached a system based on Hindu principles as the spiritual prerequisite for *svaraj,* a term he used for Indian home rule and, later, independence. He also worked for social change, especially a rejection of discrimination against untouchables, whom he called *harijans,* (children of God). Gandhi envisioned an India of decentralized village self-government with an identity that transcended religious affiliation. Unfortunately, the religious and political passions that were unleashed by the advent of Indian independence in 1947 did not reflect Gandhi's dream.

Continued criticism of traditional Hinduism by social scientists in India and the West poses the question of how an ancient tradition can modernize without losing its spiritual roots in its history and popular culture. The arguments for religious reform during the colonial period were only the opening act of a continuing debate over India's spiritual and material future.

THE MOVEMENT FOR INDEPENDENCE

The nineteenth and twentieth centuries were dominated by the Indian struggle for self-rule and independence from British rule. Colonial views of religion tended to "divide and rule" the members of various religious communities; census listings and separate electorates according to religion increased the competition between different groups. Many Hindu nationalist leaders united the rhetoric of religion with that of politics. Incidents of violence between different religious groups ("communal" violence) increased in number and severity. Many Muslim nationalists abandoned any hope of fair treatment for Muslims (about 24 percent of the population) within a united India and founded the Muslim League to campaign for a separate Muslim state, Pakistan. Although many nationalists, like Gandhi, still hoped for a single independent India, and some Muslims continued to work within the Indian National Congress, the levels of communal violence and the political activities of the Muslim League made partition seem the only possible solution.

THE POSTCOLONIAL EXPERIENCE (FROM 1947)

India's independence, then, was gained at the price not only of the country's partition but also of tremendous communal slaughter. Muslim-majority regions in the northwest and east became the Muslim state of Pakistan. Violence between members of the two religious communities in both countries caused more than a million deaths during the period immediately following partition. This type of violence is referred to as "communal" because of the absence of personal focus and the fact that the attack is motivated principally by one's membership in a particular religious community. The communal tensions between Hindus and Muslims throughout India (and between Hindus and Sikhs in the state of Punjab) remain a dominant, bloody theme. The issues of Hinduism and Indian identity, as well as the legal status of the Muslim-majority territory of Kashmir, are painful reminders of the unfinished character of Indian nationhood.

SECULARISM AND NATIONAL IDENTITY

The Constitution of India proclaims the nation a "sovereign socialist secular democratic republic." Jawaharlal Nehru, the first prime minister of India, advocated a nationhood that would embody democratic socialism and secularism. *Secular* meant a universal tolerance of religion and a government that could unite the country by transcending the interests of any religious group. The problem has been to achieve this goal in a society with a large Hindu majority and in a culture saturated with values and principles identifiable as Hindu. The revival of Hindu political identity, evidenced especially by the Bharatiya Janata Party, a Hindu political movement with nationwide impact, calls into question both Nehru's ideal of a secular state and Gandhi's dream of a tolerant multireligious nation. The challenge to the Indian constitutional system has been to confront legal problems that are by their nature religious in a society where at least 83 percent of the population are classified as Hindu. The necessity of laws regarding the status of "untouchables," who now call themselves *dalits* (oppressed people), and laws about dowries, divorce, and temple management make it impossible for the Indian government to avoid playing a role in the religious life of its people and, conversely, make it unthinkable that there should not be a Hindu political agenda.

Throughout its history, India has tolerated a regionalized and multilayered approach to society and to government. Many political scientists suggest that the Indian government may evolve into a loose confederation of regional states on a model far closer to Gandhian village council rule than to the centralized governments of Western nation-states. However, the present level of communal tension and violence, rendered international by strife between India and Pakistan as emerging nuclear powers, makes resolution of India's religious conflict a matter of life and death. Religious communalism also tends to divert and distort the most creative energies of the religious traditions themselves, thus weakening their ability to respond effectively to the challenges of human life and society.

CONTEMPORARY HINDUISM

The South Asian region, encompassing the Indian subcontinent and adjacent territory, includes Bangladesh, Bhutan, India, the Maldive Islands, Nepal, Pakistan, and Sri Lanka. India alone makes up almost 20 percent of the earth's population; the South Asian countries together make up more than a quarter of humanity. The density of the population in this region appears staggering by comparison with the United States. India has one-third the land area of the United States but four times the population. This means an Indian population density that is roughly twelve times that of the United States; for each American who sought employment and education, required food and transportation, and depended on the ecosystem for water and waste removal, there would be eleven more people competing for the same limited

resources. As testimony of the effectiveness of the improved seeds and cultivation techniques known as the "green revolution," India, despite variations in rainfall, has been a net food grain exporter for the last decade. The Indian middle class, with high aspirations for education and employment and for the material goods that signify prosperity and success, today numbers more than 200 million—close to the population of the United States. Multinational corporations rightly see India as a prime market for consumer products. Given current birthrates and the lack of an effective program for regulating family size, India's population will soon approach 1 billion people and, within about a decade, will surpass that of China. The resulting population density, the long-term effects of agricultural irrigation, and the aspirations of the middle class for "modern life" converge to place great stress on the environment.

In political and strategic terms, South Asia represents the intersection of the former Soviet Union (through Afghanistan) and China. India maintains the third largest military forces in the world. China, India, and Pakistan share active boundary disputes. Pakistan and India have engaged in three wars since 1947; India and China fought a brief border war in 1962. The issues at the root of these conflicts remain unresolved. This level of armed political tension exists between three states that either possess or are on the verge of acquiring nuclear weapons capability. For all these reasons, South Asia, and especially India, represents an important focus of contemporary economic and political history.

Wise advice counsels not discussing either religion or politics, but in contemporary India such avoidance is impossible. The significance one attributes to Hinduism is a political affirmation about the future of India. How does being Hindu relate to being Indian? Is "being Hindu" ("Hindutva") the meaning of Indian national identity? Although over 80 percent of India's population are Hindu, what of the 150 million citizens of India who are not Hindu? The search for answers to such questions is a matter of life and death that can cost

CHRONOLOGY OF HINDUISM

CA. 6500–1500	Prehistoric Indus Valley civilization
1500–1200	Aryan migrations into India
1200–900	Composition of the *Rig Veda*, hymns that provide the foundational scripture for Hindus
900–600	Composition of later *Vedas*, the *Brahmanas,* and the early *Upanishads*
600–200	Composition of later *Upanishads*
527	Death of Mahavira, founder of Jainism
483	Death of Shakyamuni, the Buddha
327–325	Invasion of India by Alexander the Great of Macedonia
321–184	Mauryan Empire
273–232	Ashoka rules as the first Buddhist emperor of India
500 B.C.E.–400 C.E.	Composition of *Mahabharata,* the epic that incorporates in its narrative extensive teachings on the meaning of religious duty (*dharma*)
500 B.C.E.–500 C.E.	Hindu lawbooks, development of six orthodox systems of philosophy/theology: Samkhya, Nyaya, Yoga, Vaisheshika, Purva-Mimamsa, and Vedanta
300 B.C.E.–300 C.E.	Composition of the *Ramayana,* the story of Rama, who provides a model for social relations and for the role of the enlightened ruler
200 B.C.E.–100 C.E.	Composition of that *Bhagavad Gita,* a late portion of the *Mahabharata,* which is the most important single scripture for many Hindus
300–647	Gupta Empire in India
500–900	The period of the Nayamnars, Tamil Shaiva poets who played an important role in the development of devotional traditions, along with the Alvars, Tamil Vaishnava poets who flourished slightly later (600–930)
788–820	Shankara, author of the major nondualist commentary on the *Vedanta Sutras*
850–1279	Chola rule in Tamil Nadu
1056–1137	Ramanuja, author of a major devotional commentary on the *Vedanta Sutras*

1175–1600	Rise of Muslim control in India by conquest of northwest regions
1238–1317	Madhva, founder of the dualist school of Vedanta
1336–1565	Vijayanagar kingdom in South India
1300–1500	Devotional movements flourish in North India, including Vallabha (1481–1530) in north central India and Caitanya (1486–1533) in Bengal and Orissa
1532–1623	Tulsidas, who composed the *Ramcaritmanas*, a Hindi version of the *Ramayana* that has wide popular appeal
1651	Foundation of East India Company factory at Hugli
1757	Battle of Plassey establishes British control of India
1722–1833	Ram Mohan Roy, leader of the Brahmo Samaj and advocate of a reformed Hinduism in response to modern Western thought
1836–1886	Swami Ramakrishna, Bengali saint who inspired Swami Vivekananda and others with his devotion to the goddess Kali
1858	Direct British rule of India begins
1863–1902	Swami Vivekananda, major Hindu missionary to the West
1893	Hindu participation at the Chicago Parliament of Religions marks the beginning of influence of Swami Vivekananda and the Vedanta Society in the United States
1861–1941	Rabindranath Tagore, poet, novelist, educator, and statesman who made a major contribution to Bengali culture in India and in Bangladesh
1869–1948	Mohandas K. Gandhi, who coordinated the nonviolent campaign for Indian independence
1917	Asian Exclusion Act limits Indian emigration to the United States
1947	Independence and partition of India
1960s	Numerous Hindu *gurus* travel to the West and gain followers there
1965	U.S. immigration law makes emigration from India easier
1970	Temple and Hindu community building begins to spread in the United States

thousands of lives in one frenzied outbreak of communal violence, such as that occasioned by the destruction in 1992 of an ancient mosque in Ayodhya, which many Hindus believed occupied the birthplace of the god Rama. Responsible study of Hinduism must confront the political implications of the views presented.

HINDUISM AS A "WORLD" RELIGION

Although Hinduism has served as a cultural model for all of South Asia and much of Southeast Asia, a current process of global expansion is transforming the Hindu tradition into a "world" religion and changing the Hindu focus from the specific context of India's geography and climate to a much more diverse cultural situation. Hinduism thrived by being context sensitive—by relating to this particular temple, this local tradition, this river, or this language group. Now the tradition is being transformed by being transplanted into a more generalized cultural context.

THE HINDU DIASPORA In the nineteenth and early twentieth centuries, a widespread emigration of businesspersons and laborers created a kind of Hindu diaspora not only in the traditional "greater India" of Southeast Asia but also in South Africa and the countries of central Africa, on the islands of the "West" Indies, and more recently, throughout the Persian Gulf states of Western Asia. Many of these emigrants assumed that they would return to India following a period of service. After independence, the absence of immigration barriers within the countries of the British Commonwealth led to the formation of large permanent Hindu communities in Great Britain and Canada (see Figure 4.2).

IMMIGRATION TO WESTERN COUNTRIES Changes in U.S. immigration laws in 1965 ended a half century of exclusionary policies toward Asians and initiated a continuing process of permanent migration by highly educated members of the professional, entrepreneurial, and managerial elite. In two generations, these immigrants have achieved notable success in education, scientific research, medicine, business, and politics. Although these nonresident Indians (NRIs) maintain family and business contacts in India and often seek to arrange appropriate marriages there, they have little interest in returning to India except as visitors.

Since 1970, considerable effort and expense have been directed toward the construction of temples in the United States, which serve not only as places of worship but also as community and cultural centers for training in Indian regional languages; Indian music and dance; and other aspects of Indian culture, including religion. These temples represent a kind of "congregational" Hinduism. Although some of this temple construction has been supported by religious groups in India, such as the Swaminarayan movement and the Shri Ventakeshvara temple in South India, many of these U.S. temples have a more ecumenical religious focus, combining Vaishnava, Shaiva, and Shakta elements and even including an image of Mahavira for Jain adherents. Despite these efforts, it is not clear what role these temples will play in the lives of succeeding generations of children who have grown up almost entirely outside the Hindu religiocultural context.

It is clear that U.S. colleges and universities are playing an increasing role in the religious acculturation of the children of South Asian immigrants. Prestigious chairs in South Asian studies have been established by Indian foundations and by immigrant donors at major state and private universities. Teachers of South Asian languages and religions have noted a significant increase in the number of second- and third-generation children of Indian immigrants whose basic religious education in Hinduism takes place in the context of a college education. In the United States, Hinduism has become a "religion" in a sense that is alien to India.

HINDU MISSIONARIES AND WESTERN CONVERTS During the last century, Hinduism has become a missionary religion. Various Hindu teachers have gone to Europe and especially to the United States, preaching forms of Hinduism as the cure for the perceived materialism of Western culture and for

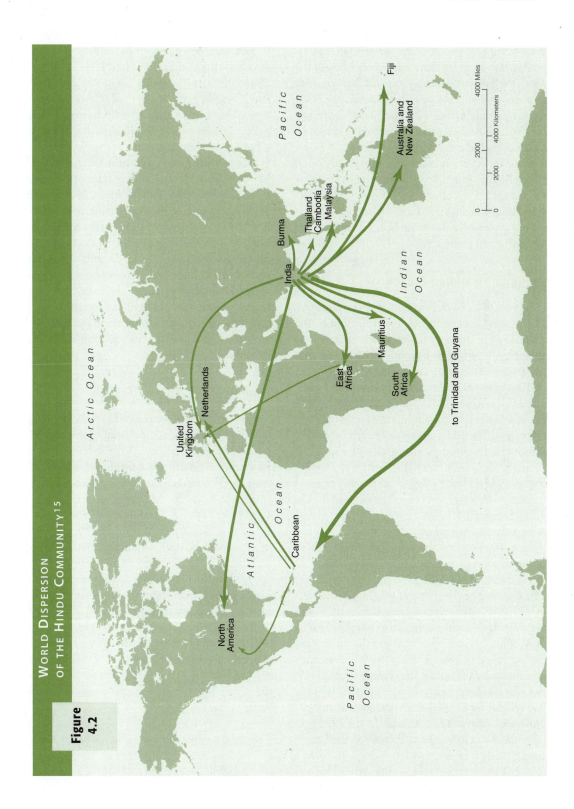

WORLD DISPERSION OF THE HINDU COMMUNITY[15]

Figure 4.2

WORLD DISPERSION OF THE HINDU COMMUNITY[15]

Figure 4.2

Arctic Ocean

Pacific Ocean

Fiji

Australia and New Zealand

Thailand
Cambodia
Malaysia

Burma

India

Indian Ocean

Mauritius

East Africa

South Africa

Netherlands

United Kingdom

Atlantic Ocean

Caribbean

to Trinidad and Guyana

Pacific Ocean

North America

4000 Miles
4000 Kilometers
2000
2000
0
0

the inability of "churchianity" to satisfy religious yearnings. Swami Vivekananda, who addressed the 1893 Parliament of Religions in Chicago and, through his disciples, established the Vedanta Society, is a prominent example. The lineages of teachers also include men and women; a wide variety of meditational and *yogic* styles; Vaishnava, Shaiva, and Shakta devotion; and a wide representation of regional variations. The phenomenon of westerners "converted" to Hinduism universalized a religious tradition that was formerly so closely connected to the religious geography and ecology of the Indian subcontinent.

HINDUISM IN INDIAN CULTURE

Hinduism in India faces a number of crucial issues. Most pressing is the unresolved question of the relation of Hinduism to Indian politics and national culture. The secular aspirations of Nehru that are enshrined in the Indian Constitution are being challenged by political movements that equate Hindutva (Hindu-ness) with Indian identity and that attempt to establish a religiously Hindu state embodying Ram-raj (the "rule of Rama," the ideal Hindu king) through electoral victories. The Bharatiya Janata Party (BJP, the Indian People's Party), with its Hindu religious agenda, has received legislative majorities in several large states in the Hindi heartland of north central India and seemed poised to win the national elections in 1991 until the assassination of Rajiv Gandhi brought a delay in the election process and a large sympathy vote in the states where voting was held subsequently. The question of the rights of religious minorities in a Hindu India had not been addressed. However, the destruction of the Babri Masjid mosque in Ayodhya in December 1992 and the subsequent rioting raised questions about the BJP's willingness or ability to contain the communal animosities that had been aroused by its political rhetoric and religiously focused activities, such as the pilgrimages organized across India. In the 1996 parliamentary elections, the BJP received the largest single block of seats, but its attempt to form a minority government was unsuccessful. However-

er, following new elections in 1998, the BJP gathered a coalition that permitted it to form a government under the leadership of Atal Bihari Vajpayee, but the party had to modify some of its own agenda in order to attract coalition partners. The political expression of Hindu identity in India will remain a developing issue.

In addition, the question of the status of Jammu and Kashmir, the only state of India with a Muslim majority, remains unresolved almost a half century after Indian independence. As a result of two wars between India and Pakistan over Kashmir, the political status of this state and its border remains a matter of bitter dispute between two countries that have large conventional armies and access to nuclear weapons. The issue of Kashmir reflects concerns about Hinduism and Islam in ways that regional separatist movements in the southern state of Tamilnad and in Sikh-dominated Punjab do not.

HINDUISM AND SOCIAL ISSUES

Secular modernity continues to challenge Hindu religious and social ideals in a number of ways. India's transition from a traditional to a modern society has insured that debate will continue about issues of caste, gender, ecology, and Hindu identity.

CASTE ISSUES   A fundamental conflict exists between the traditions of caste and the aspirations of a modern high-tech commercial state. The Indian Constitution outlawed untouchability and set up a system of "reserving" 22.5 percent of government jobs to compensate for discrimination against certain castes and tribes. In 1980, a government commission issued the Mandal report, which recommended a further reservation of 27 percent of government jobs for "other backward classes," who may form more than half the Indian population. Larson has described the "thrust" of this report as

> the claim that social and educational
> backwardness in India is not simply or even
> primarily a matter of economic inequity or

disparity, although economic factors may be symptomatic of backwardness. The main factor in understanding backwardness is the heritage of a hierarchical social order built largely on a religious understanding of caste whereby groups of people were systematically discriminated against on grounds of ritual impurity and rendered incapable of competing or functioning in a fair and equitable manner.[16]

Although attempts to implement the program recommended in the Mandal report contributed to the fall of the Indian government led by V. P. Singh in 1990, a form of job and program reservations on a national level was implemented in 1991.

GENDER ISSUES   Other social issues with religious as well as social relevance include a whole series of issues relating to the status and just treatment of women, such as dowry murders, selective abortion for gender selection, oppressive conditions of widowhood, sexual and physical harassment in the workplace, and unequal opportunities in education and employment. Far from being hidden or condoned, these issues are passionately discussed and vigorously criticized in the press. Legal remedies have been used to counteract the demands for dowries and to prevent medical tests to determine the gender of fetuses. The details of individual cases of women being threatened or slain over dowry demands are recounted with all the clarity of the crime-reporting genre, even though these charges are hard to prove in court.

India has a very active women's movement, representing a wide range of opinions about women's issues. Sophisticated journals advance the cause of feminism and bring critical reflection to bear on the role of women in the Indian tradition. The short story has become a powerful literary tool for the expression of women's experience and, especially, of their grievances. Support for just treatment is drawn both from secular thought and, especially, through the reinterpretation of the Indian religious heritage itself. For example, the goddess Kali has been interpreted in ways that make her a model for contemporary liberated Indian women and a sign of woman's redemptive action in society. Action to assert women's rights takes place among *dalit* (meaning "oppressed," a name preferred to *untouchable*) women in village India as much as among the educated elite in the cities. Courageous individual steps to achieve practical grassroots economic independence, to assert autonomy against a brutal or drunken husband, and to unite with other women for mutual support and agitation are frequent and have been celebrated throughout India as examples for others. Women have been in the vanguard defending the environment against deforestation and the construction of dams; this activity is explicitly tied to a reverence for Mother Earth and to the sacred bond between women and the creative power *(shakti)* of nature.

Such examples cannot erase the many instances in which women are abused, either individually or through the social system; however, Indian women are proud of their self-advocacy. And, on a sobering note, sociologists point out that women are far more likely to suffer violence from men in U.S. society than in India. It may well be that the self-assertion and mutual support of Indian women will serve to inspire their Western sisters.

ECOLOGICAL ISSUES   Another series of questions that link Hinduism and the future of India concern the natural environment, which has suffered from large hydroelectric projects; from the creation of industrial satellite cities; from land salinization from irrigation; from deforestation; and from an assortment of pollutants to land, air, and water. India's ability to tolerate environmental threats is limited by the density of its land usage, which is some twelve times more intense than that of the United States. Traditional Indian religion appreciated the beauty of nature, but the teaching of endlessly recurrent cyclical time provided little religious incentive to care for the environment. The challenge for ecological thought is to draw on the religio-aesthetic sensitivity to nature found in religious texts and devotional poetry in order to transform the present destructive relationship with the environment.

THE FUTURE OF *SANATANA DHARMA*

The prospect for Hinduism, however, transcends even the significant social and political problems we have just examined. Despite the challenges that cloud its immediate future, Hinduism has its millennia-old roots in India's lands, mountains, and rivers. It draws on the depths of religious experience from ancient Vedic *rishis* to contemporary religious leaders and brings together resources from the many layers of India's social and emotional heritage. Again and again, through the centuries, this multilayered tradition has drawn new meanings and direction from various aspects of its cumulative religious and cultural heritage. New saints and interpreters of tradition have come forward to give new focus to Hindu beliefs and practices. This has been particularly true at times of political conflict and shifts in social structure. Thus, our generation may see many new manifestations of Hinduism's vitality both on the Indian subcontinent and in the new "greater India" established by the global migrations of Hindus.

GLOSSARY OF HINDUISM

advaita	"not-two"; nondualism. The term describes the relation of identity, oneness, or nondifference *(abheda)* between the self *(atman)* and Brahman. It is applied to Advaita Vedanta, the religious system associated with the great teacher Shankara.
ahimsa	"not-hurting"; not causing pain to living beings. *Ahimsa* is the virtue that incorporates nonviolence with the broader avoidance of actions that by their nature cause pain to other living beings.
arati	a ritual of deity worship *(puja)* in which light and other offerings are made before a deity image
artha	wealth, success. One of the four goals *(purusharthas)* of human life.
Aryans	a name for invader-immigrant groups who entered the northwestern part of the Indian subcontinent from 1500 B.C.E. They brought with them the Vedic pantheon and sacrificial system that constitute one of the fundamental layers of Hinduism.
ashrama	a system of four stages in the (male) life cycle: *brahmachari* (celibate student), *grihasta* (householder), *vanaprastha* (forest dweller, person retired from active life), and *sannyasin* (renunciant, wandering ascetic).
atman	the individual self. In the Vedanta system based on the *Upanishads,* the individual self *(atman)* is experienced as one with the Self of the universe, the underlying reality of all, Brahman.
avatara	a "descent" of a deity, most often Vishnu, in some particular form (for example, Rama or Krishna).

bhakti	devotional attachment to God. *Bhakti* represents one of the paths to release; depending on one's perspective, it is either the highest path (*Bhagavad Gita* and later devotional literature) or a preparatory stage to deeper insight into ultimate reality or Brahman (the path of knowledge).
Brahman	the ultimate underlying Self of all, primarily described in the *Upanishads* and in the nondualist (Advaita) Vedanta. The term also applies to a *brahman* (often written *brahmin*), a member of the highest caste group of priest-scholars.
dalit	"oppressed peoples," the preferred name, with a distinct flavor of social protest, for previously "untouchable" castes (in Indian legal terms, "scheduled castes"), which avoids the paternalism of Mohandas K. Gandhi's term *harijans,* or "children of God."
darshan	from "to see." The term describes the situation of worship, especially of a deity image in which the devotee "sees" the deity and, in turn, is seen by the deity.
Devi	the Goddess. This general term points to the many manifestations in which the divine feminine appears in Indian culture.
dharma	religious duty, religious law; almost the Hindu equivalent of *religion.* *Dharma* is the order that holds the universe together. Fulfillment of one's part in the *dharmic* order involves primarily the carrying out of social responsibility within the bounds of one's caste and stage of life.
jati	caste. Although *varna* is the name for the traditional fourfold division of social classes, these regional occupational classes are the practical caste groupings in contemporary India.
jñana	knowledge. The path of knowledge, based on the Upanishadic goal of realizing one's unity with Brahman, leads to the dissolution of all illusion of a separate self and hence to the end of rebirth. Such a disciplined meditative quest is particularly appropriate to those who are *sannyasins.*
Kali *yuga*	the current age, the age of Kali (darkness, not the goddess). In each cycle of time, there is a progressive degradation from a golden to a silver to an iron age; finally there is an age where people are beasts, life is brutal, and religious knowledge is hard to acquire. Nevertheless, there is a benefit from birth in this age: an easier path, especially that of devotion, is now open to all.
kama	desire (especially sexual). Although the negative effects of desire are criticized in the *Bhagavad Gita,* *kama* (as Kama, the name of the god of love) is one of the accepted goals of life (with its own *sutra* of instructions, the *Kama Sutra*), but only for householders (those supporting society by raising families).
karma	work, action, the result of action; does *not* mean "fate." This multifaceted term points to the *yoga* of work whereby a person

who fulfills the duties of *dharma* will ordinarily acquire the fruits of action *(karma),* but these can be avoided if the individual acts with detachment and with no regard for the fruits of action. In this fashion, as outlined in the *Bhagavad Gita,* one can perform one's social responsibility and achieve release at the same time.

kshatriya	the second of the traditional fourfold caste *(varna)* division, which includes rulers and warriors.
lila	play. This concept points to God's activity—indeed, everything—as being playful rather than grimly purposeful. Humans are invited to appreciate and participate in this divine play.
mantra	sacred sound or prayer. These sacred words (often without direct translatable meaning) are repeated by devotees as a way to place themselves in the presence of the deity and to transform their own consciousness.
marga	path; here, a spiritual path. Although Hinduism accepts many paths to religious fulfillment, the most common are the paths of work *(karma-marga)* performed without regard for the fruits of action, knowledge *(jñana-marga)* of the self's union with Brahman, and devotional love *(bhakti-marga)* of a deity.
moksha	release or liberation. The fourth of the goals of human life, which involves the freedom from any further rebirth and release from the cycles of *samsara.*
puja	deity worship. This system of worship is distinct from the Vedic sacrificial system, or *yajña,* in that there is usually no actual animal sacrifice (worship of Kali is a notable exception) but the worshiper renders devotional service to the deity.
rasa	literally, "juice." This term refers to the highly refined aesthetic enjoyment by which a properly prepared person will savor ("taste") the religious moods of a particular divine *lila.* In many ways, participation in Hinduism calls for the cultivation of such a sensitivity.
samsara	the ongoing cycle of rebirth dependent on the actions performed in previous lives. This cycle is unending and hence meaningless, unless an individual breaks out of the bonds of action *(karma)* through achieving release or liberation *(moksha).*
samskara	traditional Hindu life cycle rituals that recognize the sacred character of the progressive steps of ordinary life.
sanatana dharma	"the eternal religion," a name traditionally given by Hindus to the religion that they practice.
sannyasin	a wandering ascetic; one who has entered the fourth stage of life *(ashrama).*
Shaiva	a worshiper of Shiva.

shakti	power, the energy of the divine feminine, in which devotees of the Goddess wish to participate.
shruti	a term that denotes the oral character of the *Vedas,* which were "heard" directly by the ancient *rishis.* The *shruti* are contrasted with the less immediate relationship of later holy texts (for example, the *Bhagavad Gita* or the various *puranas*), which are called *smriti,* "what is remembered."
shudra	the lowest caste in the fourfold caste structure; those who are to serve the three higher castes In addition, there were other groups that were not part of the caste structure at all ("outcastes" or tribal groups).
smriti	later holy texts that are characterized as less immediate in their reception than the *Vedas,* which were directly heard (hence *shruti*) by ancient *rishis.* These texts, including the epics, *Bhagavad Gita,* and *puranas,* were "remembered" (hence *smriti*).
Vaishnava	a worshiper of Vishnu or of one of his *avataras.*
vaishya	the third in the traditional fourfold caste system *(varna),* which includes artisans, farmers, and merchants.
varna	the traditional term for caste. It literally means "color" and recalls the hierarchical relationship between the lighter-skinned Aryans and the darker-skinned peoples they supplanted. The four *varna* are Brahman (priest), *kshatriya* (ruler, soldier), *vaishya* (farmer, artisan), and *shudra* (servant, manual laborer). The contemporary term for caste is *jati,* reflecting the current understanding of caste as membership by birth in a particular occupational group. Some attempt is made to link the many types and levels of *jatis* to the older structure of *varna.*
Veda	the fundamendal Hindu scripture. The term is applicable strictly to the four collections *(samhitas)* of Vedic hymns, but was extended to include the *Aranyakas, Brahmanas,* and *Upanishads.*
vedanta	the "end of the *Veda,*" referring to the doctrines that emerged from further reflection and commentary on the *Upanishads.* The term is especially used for the nondualist system (Advaita Vedanta) taught by Shankara.
yoga	a generic term for various systems of uniting aspects of the self, and uniting the self with the deity. The classical *Yoga Sutras of Patanjali* teach an eightfold process of restraint and interiorization leading to the realization of *samadhi.*
yuga	one of the ages in each cosmic cycle. The process of cosmic devolution passes from a golden to a silver to an iron age, from which comes the Kali *yuga,* the age of darkness and ignorance in which the world is now.

FOR FURTHER STUDY

Books and Articles

Basham, A. L. *The Wonder That Was India*. New York: Grove, 1959.
> *A classic presentation, complete with many illustrations, of the cultural background of Hindu India. The description, however, stops before the entrance of Muslims into Indian culture.*

Doniger [O'Flaherty], Wendy. *Asceticism and Eroticism in the Mythology of Siva*. London: Oxford University Press, 1973.
———. *The Rig Veda*. Baltimore: Penguin, 1988.
> *Two works, by one of the most effective translators of Hindu texts, that provide a rich selection of materials, that might well be used after a more general anthology, such as Ainslie T. Embree's.*

Eck, Diana. *Darsan: Seeing the Divine Image in India*. New York: Columbia University Press, 1987.
> *One of the most valuable introductions to the concrete quality of deity worship. This short work is also a very thorough initiation into the many ways in which the divine is present in the Hindu religious consciousness.*

Embree, Ainslie T., ed. *Sources of Indian Tradition*, 2d ed. Vol. 1, *From the Beginning to 1800*. New York: Columbia University Press, 1988.
> *An excellent anthology of texts with very clear introductory essays. Although this work covers all the religious traditions of India, the chronological and topical organization tends to overcompartmentalize these traditions. Nevertheless, the material in this volume (and its companion, edited by Stephen Hay, below) is basic to an understanding of Indian religions.*

Fuller, C. J. *The Camphor Flame: Popular Hinduism and Society in India*. Princeton, N.J.: Princeton University Press, 1992.

Gold, Ann G. *Fruitful Journeys: The Ways of Rajasthani Pilgrims*. Berkeley: University of California Press, 1988.
> *Two works, both anthropological studies, that show the depth and complexity of popular religion in India.*

Haberman, David L. *Journey through the Twelve Forests: An Encounter with Krishna*. New York: Oxford University Press, 1994.
> *A work based on the author's experience of making the pilgrimage around the sacred sites related to Krishna in the Braj region, which provides an introduction to the many layers of religious experience involved.*

Hay, Stephen, ed. *Sources of Indian Tradition*, 2d ed. Vol. 2, *Modern India and Pakistan*. New York: Columbia University Press, 1988.
> *Like the companion volume edited by Ainslie T. Embree (above), a selection of texts illustrating the encounter between Indian religions and Western culture, the movement for independence, and the tensions in contemporary India.*

Hiltebeitel, Alf. "Hinduism," in *The Religious Traditions of Asia*, edited by Joseph M. Kitagawa, pp. 3–40. New York: Macmillan, 1989.

> *A very brief but comprehensive view of the Hindu tradition by one of the outstanding critical scholars of classical Hinduism. The articles in this volume on other religious traditions of India give an excellent balance to the different traditions.*

Kinsley, David R. *Hindu Goddesses: Visions of the Divine Feminine in the Hindu Religious Tradition*. Berkeley: University of California Press, 1986.

———. *Hinduism: A Cultural Perspective*. 2d ed. Englewood Cliffs, N.J.: Prentice-Hall, 1993.

> *Very accessible treatments of Hindu deities and of the cultural dimensions that make up Hinduism. Kinsley's works can be helpful supplements to an introductory chapter like this one.*

Knipe, David M. *Hinduism: Experiments in the Sacred*. San Francisco: HarperCollins, 1991.

> *A short volume, intended as an introduction to Hinduism, that shows the author's search to find appropriate metaphors for various aspects of Hinduism.*

Larson, Gerald James. *India's Agony over Religion*. Albany, N.Y.: SUNY Press, 1995.

> *A work that deals with issues of nationalism and religious identity in contemporary India. Larson's historical treatment of several political issues with religious dimensions is especially helpful.*

Lopez, Donald S., ed. *Religions of India in Practice*. Princeton Readings in Religion. Princeton, N.J.: Princeton University Press, 1995.

> *A book with an extremely innovative method of treating the Hindu, Muslim, Jain, and Sikh traditions together and choosing texts that show the blurred boundaries between these religious traditions.*

Miller, Barbara Stoler, trans. *The Bhagavad Gita: Krishna's Counsel in Time of War*. New York: Bantam, 1986.

———. *The Love Song of the Dark Lord: Jayadeva's Gitagovinda*. New York: Columbia University Press, 1977.

> *Excellent translations of these texts. The* Gita *translation is particularly helpful because of consistency in translating technical words, whose equivalents are given in a glossary.*

Naipaul, V. S. *India: A Million Mutinies Now*. New York: Viking, 1990.

> *A novelist's perspective of both insider and outsider in a critical treatment of contemporary India written by a descendant of Indians who emigrated to Trinidad.*

CD-ROM Resources

Eck, Diana, and the Pluralism Project. *On Common Ground: World Religions in America*. New York: Columbia University Press, 1997.

> *A CD-ROM that provides perspectives on Hindus in the United States. The explanations about Hindu belief and practice are brief, but the audio and visual resources make this a very valuable teaching tool.*

READINGS

Reading 4.1   THE PRIMAL SACRIFICE: THE *RIG VEDA*

The Vedic hymns provide a number of images of the origin of the world and of human society. This particular hymn pictures the sacrifice of the cosmic person—Purusha—through which everything else came to be. The hymn points to the One—the single reality from which all came and which transcends all—but its tone of dismemberment shows a sense of devolution rather than evolution. However, it is from Purusha and this cosmic sacrifice that everything is sorted out, including the castes and their social roles. Multiplicity remains questionable; the One—unity, the cosmic Self—is primary.

This text describes the origin of the world and human society. How important is an "origin story" for self-understanding and for social stability? What are the images that establish the basic social relationships? What are the implications of these images for the transformation of individuals and society?

Thousand-headed Purusha, thousand-eyed, thousand-footed—he, having pervaded the earth on all sides, still extends ten fingers beyond it.

Purusha alone is all this—whatever has been and whatever is going to be. Further, he is the lord of immortality and also of what grows on account of food.

Such is his greatness; greater, indeed, than this is Purusha. All creatures constitute but one-quarter of him, his three-quarters are the immortal in heaven.

With his three-quarters did Purusha rise up; one-quarter of him again remains here. With it did he variously spread out on all sides over what eats and what eats not.

From him was Viraj (a cosmic source, perhaps the female principle) born, from Viraj then evolved Purusha. He, being born, projected himself behind the earth as also before it.

When the gods performed the sacrifice with Purusha as the oblation, then the spring was its clarified butter, the summer the sacrificial fuel, and the autumn the oblation.

The sacrificial victim, namely, Purusha, born at the very beginning, they sprinkled with sacred water upon the sacrificial grass. With him as oblation, the gods performed the sacrifice, and also the Sadhyas [a class of semidivine beings] and the rishis [ancient seers].

From that wholly offered sacrificial oblation were born the verses and the sacred chants; from it were born the meters; the sacrificial formula was born from it.

From it horses were born and also those animals who have double rows of (i.e., upper and lower) teeth; cows were born from it, from it were born goats and sheep.

When they divided Purusha, in how many different portions did they arrange him? What became of his mouth, what of his two arms? What were his two thighs and his two feet called?

His mouth became the brahman; his two arms were made into the rajanya; his two thighs the vaisyas; from his two feet the shudra was born.

The moon was born from the mind, from the eye the sun was born; from the mouth Indra and Agni, from the breath [prana] the wind [vayu] was born.

From the navel was the atmosphere created, from the head the heaven issued forth; from the two feet was born the earth and the quarters (the cardinal directions) from the ear. Thus did they fashion the worlds.

Seven were the enclosing sticks in this sacrifice, thrice seven were the fire-sticks made when the gods, performing the sacrifice, bound down Purusha the sacrificial victim.

With this sacrificial oblation did the gods offer the sacrifice. These were the first norms [dharma] *of sacrifice. These greatnesses reached to the sky wherein live the ancient Sadhyas and gods.*

Source: *Sources of Indian Tradition,* 2nd ed., Vol. 1, (New York: Columbia University Press, 1988), 18–19.

Reading 4.2 THE *KATHA UPANISHAD*

These lengthy selections from the *Katha Upanishad* are designed to show the dynamism of inquiry that underlies the *Upanishads.* Naciketas has won three boons from Yama, the god of death. Wisely, Naciketas decides not to ask for wealth, pleasure, or learning, but to ask about the self that transcends even death. It is the Self within him, which transcends the stages of sleep and which also transcends death. This is Brahman, the true essence of all. By knowing that One, a person achieves immortality.

This selection describes a process of self-understanding and transformation. Naciketas is led along a path to a new understanding of himself. What is the process at work here? Where has it led him? What has he put aside? What has he found? According to this text, what is the relationship between the individual and the Self within?

I. Naciketas speaks: "When a man is dead, this doubt remains: Some say, 'He is,' others again, 'He is not.' This I would know, by thee instructed,— this is the third of the boons I ask."

Yama speaks: "Of old the gods themselves this doubt assailed,—how hard it is to know! How subtle a matter! Choose another boon, Naciketas. Insist not overmuch, hold me excused in this."

Naciketas speaks: "Of old indeed the gods themselves this doubt assailed,—How hard it is to know! So, Death, hast thou declared. Thou alone canst tell it forth; none other is there like thee: No other boon is there equal to this in any way."

Yama speaks: "Choose sons and grandsons to live a hundred years; choose wealth in cattle, horses, elephants and gold; choose wide property in land, and thou thyself live out thy years as many as thou wilt. Or should you think this a boon at all equivalent, choose riches and long life; be one of the great ones of the land. I grant you enjoyment of all that you can desire! Whatever a person could possibly desire in this world, however hard to win, ask anything you wish at your good pleasure,—fair women, chariots, instruments of music. The like of these cannot be won by other people,—All these I give to you, Naciketas; ask me no further concerning death."

Naciketas speaks: "The days of a person's life, O Death, wear down the power of the senses. A life though lived entire is short indeed; keep then your chariots, keep your songs and dances! A person can never be satisfied with riches. When once we've seen you, how shall we win riches? We live only as long as you ordain; this, then, is the only boon I would claim. What mortal, grown old and wretched here below, could meet immortals, strangers to old age, know them, and still meditate on colors, pleasures, joys, finding some comfort in this life, however long. No, tell me what happens at the great departing!" (vv. 20–27)

II. Yama speaks: "You, Naciketas, have carefully considered all the objects of desire,—you have rejected them. You would not accept the garland of wealth in which so many a person has been submerged. Wisdom and unwisdom are far different, opposed, wide-separated. I see that it is wisdom that you are seeking; you are not distracted by manifold desire. Self-wise, puffed up with learning, some turn round and round imprisoned in unwisdom's realm. Rushing here and there, round they go, the fools, like the blind guided by the blind.

"No glimmering have such of human destiny. 'This world alone exists, there is no other,' so they think. Again and again they fall into my hands. Many there are who never come to hear of Him. Many, though hearing of Him, do not know Him. Blessed is the one who, skilled, proclaims Him, grasps Him. Blessed is the one who learns from one so skilled and knows Him!

"How difficult it is for a person, though meditating much, to know Him from the lips of the vulgar; yet unless another tells of Him, the way to Him is barred. For than all subtleties of reason He's more subtle,—Logic He defies. No reasoning or logic can attain to this Idea; let another preach it, then it is easily understood. And yet you have achieved it, for you are steadfast in truth. May there never be another like you, Naciketas, to question me about it.

"The winning of desires is the foundation of the world, the unending fruit of sacrifices: All this you have rejected, wise and steadfast. For you have seen that the foundation of all is Brahman.

"More subtle than the subtle, greater than the great, the Self is hidden in the heart of creatures here. A person without desire, all sorrow spent, beholds it, the majesty of the Self. Seated he strides afar, lying down he ranges everywhere: This God is joy and joylessness, —Who but I can understand him? In bodies bodiless; in things unstable abiding; the Self, the great Lord, all pervading,—Thinking on Him the wise knows no grief.

"This Self cannot be won by preaching, not by sacrifice or much Vedic lore heard; by those alone can He be won whom He elects: to them this Self reveals his own true form. Not those who have not ceased from doing wrong, not those who know no peace, no concentration, nor those whose minds are filled with restlessness, can grasps Him, wise and clever though they be. (vv. 3–9, 11, 20–24)

III. "Like light and shade there are two selves: one here on earth drinks the law of its own deeds; the other, though hidden in the secret places of the heart, dwells in the uttermost beyond,—So say the seers who know Brahman.

"Know this: the self is the owner of the chariot; the chariot is the body; soul is the body's charioteer, mind the reins that curb it. Senses, they say, are the chariot's steeds, their objects the road before. What, then, is the subject of experience? 'Self, sense and mind joined,' the wise say.

"Who knows not how to discriminate, with mind undisciplined all the while, cannot as the charioteer master the senses, which behave like vicious steeds untamed But one who does know how to discriminate, with mind controlled and disciplined, masters fully as charioteer the senses, which behave as well-trained steeds.

"The one who does not know how to discriminate, mindless, never pure, does not reach the highest state, but returns to this round of never-ending birth and death. But one who

does know how to discriminate, mindful, always pure, gains indeed that highest state from which one's never born again.

"*This is the Self, deep-hidden in all beings, the Self that does not shine forth: yet it can be seen by those who see subtle things by the soul, the noblest part of the person. Beyond the 'great,' abiding, endless, beginningless, soundless, intangible, It knows not form or taste or smell, eternal, changeless,—such It is, discern It! For only so can you escape the jaws of death.* (vv. 1, 3–8, 12, 15)

IV. "*The self-existent Lord bored holes facing the outside world; therefore a person looks outward, not into the self. A certain sage, in search of immortality, turned his eyes inward and saw the self within. Fools pursue desires outside themselves and fall into the snares of widespread death, but the wise, discerning immortality, seek not the stable here among unstable things. By what one knows of form and taste and smell, sound, touch and sexual union, by that same thing one knows: 'What of all this abides?' This in truth is That.*

"*By what one sees these both,—the state of sleep, the state of wakefulness, 'That is the self, the great, the lord,' so think the wise, without sorrow. Who knows this self, the living self so close at hand, Lord of what was and what is yet to be, does not shrink from him. This in truth is That.*

"*What we see here is also there beyond; what there, that too is here: Death beyond death does one incur who sees in this what seems to be diverse. Grasp this with your mind: In this there is no diversity at all. Death beyond death is the lot of those who see in this what seems to be diverse. The 'Person' abides within the self, Lord of what is and what is yet to be: No need to shrink from him. This in truth is That.*

"*This 'Person' like a smokeless flame, Lord of what was and what is yet to be: Today and tomorrow. This in truth is That.*

"*As rain that falls in craggy places loses itself, dispersed throughout the mountains, so does the person who sees things are diverse become dispersed in their pursuit. As pure water poured into pure water becomes as the pure water is, so too becomes the self of the silent sage who knows.*" (vv. 1–5, 10–12, 15)

V. "*When the embodied soul whose dwelling is the body dissolves and from the body is released, What then of this remains? This in truth is That.*

"*Neither by breathing in nor yet by breathing out does any one live; by something else they live on which the two breaths depend. I will declare to you the mystery of never-failing Brahman and of what the self becomes when it comes to the hour of death. Some to the womb return,— embodied souls, to receive another body; others pass into lifeless stone in accordance with their works.*

"*When all things sleep, this Person is awake, assessing all desires: That is the Pure, that Brahman, that the Immortal: in It all the worlds are established; beyond it none can pass. This in truth is That.*

"*As the one fire ensconced within the house takes on the forms of all that is in it, so the One Inmost Self of every being takes on their several forms, remaining without the while. As the one wind, once entered into a house, takes on the forms of all that is in it, so the One Inmost Self of every being takes on their several forms, remaining without the while. Just as the sun, the eye of all the world, is not defiled by the eye's outward blemishes, so the One Inmost Self of every being is not defiled by the suffering of the world,—but remains outside it. One and all-mastering is the Inmost Self of every being; he makes the one form*

*manifold: the wise who see Him as subsistent in their selves, taste everlasting joy,
—no others.*

*"Permanent among impermanents, conscious among the conscious, the One among the
many, Disposer of desires: the wise who see Him subsistent in their very selves, taste of
everlasting peace,—no others. 'That is this,' so the wise think concerning that all-highest
bliss which none can indicate. How, then, should I discern It? Does it shine of itself or but
reflect the brilliance? There the sun shines not, nor moon nor stars; these lightnings do not
shine there,—let alone this fire. All things shine with the shining of this light; this whole
world reflects its radiance."* (vv. 4–15)

*VI. "Could one but know it here and now before the body's breaking-up; falling from such
a state a person is doomed to bodily existence in the created worlds. Separately the senses
came to be, separately they rise and fall, separately they are produced,—so thinking, the
wise grieve no more. Higher than the senses is the mind, higher than the mind the soul,
higher than the soul the self, the 'great,' higher than this the Unmanifest. Higher than the
Unmanifest is the 'Person,' pervading all, untraceable, where once a creature knows Him,
that one is freed and goes to immortality. His form is not something that can be seen; no
one beholds Him with the eye; by heart and mind and soul is He conceived of: whoever
knows this becomes immortal.*

*"This Self cannot be comprehended by voice or mind or eye: How, then, can He be
understood, unless we say—HE IS? HE IS—so we must understand Him and as the true
essence of the absolute and relative; HE IS—when once we understand Him thus, the
nature of his essence is clearly shown forth. When all desires that shelter in the heart of a
mortal are cast aside, then a mortal puts on immortality,—thence to Brahman one
attains. When here and now the knots of doubt are cut out from the heart, a mortal puts
on immortality. Thus far the teaching goes."*

*So did Naciketas learn of this holy science by Death declared, and all the arts of Yoga:
Immaculate, immortal, to Brahman he won through; and so shall all who know what
appertains to Self.* (vv. 4–9, 12–15, 18)

Source: R. C. Zaehner, *Hindu Scriptures* (London: J. M. Dent, 1966), pp. 171–183.

Reading 4.3 SELECTIONS FROM THE *BRIHADARANYAKA*
AND *CHANDOGYA UPANISHADS*

These three short passages from the very long *Brihadaranyaka* and *Chandogya
Upanishads* show some of the key steps of the process of identifying the individual self
(the *atman*) with the underlying Self of all (Brahman). The two works show a
different direction of inquiry. The *Brihadaranyaka* looks into the self and sees that "the
Self that indwells all beings is within you." Like salt dissolved in water, there is no
semblance of duality. The *Chandogya* looks outside, identifies the essence of all, and
affirms that you are that *(Tat tvam asi)*. Like salt dissolved in water, the Self is
everywhere and the essence of everything. "That is the self. That thou art." The subtle
difference in the way the image of salt in water is used shows the different approaches
of the works.

These passages present some of the key phrases that are used to understand the relationship of the individual self *(atman)* with the ultimate underlying Self (Brahman). What is that relationship, and how is it described? What images are used to describe the nature of the Self?

Brihadaranyaka Upanishad 3:4.

Then Ushasta Cakrayana questioned him saying: "Yajñavalkya, explain to me that Brahman which is evident and not obscure, the Self which indwells all things."

"This Self that indwells all things is within you."

"But which one is it, Yajñavalkya, that indwells all things?"

"Who breathes in with the in-breath, he is the Self within you that indwells all things; who breathes out with the out-breath, he is the Self within you that indwells all things; who breathes along with your 'diffused breath,' he is the Self within you that indwells all things; who breathes along with your 'upper breath,' he is the Self within you that indwells all things: he is the Self within you that indwells all things."

Ushasta Cakrayana said: "Your teaching on this subject is exactly like that of a man who says: 'That is a cow, and that is a horse.' Explain to me that Brahman which is really evident and not obscure, the Self that indwells all things."

"This Self that indwells all things is within you."

"But which one is it, Yajñavalkya, that indwells all things?"

"How should you see the seer of seeing? How should you hear the hearer of hearing? How should you think of the thinker of thought? How should you understand the understander of understanding? This self that indwells all things is within you. What is other than that suffers." Then Ushasta Cakrayana held his peace.

Brihadaranyaka Upanishad 4:5

"As a mass of salt dissolved in water has neither a 'within' nor a 'without,' but is wholly a mass of taste, so too this Self has neither a 'within' nor a 'without,' but is wholly a mass of wisdom. Out of the elements do all contingent beings arise and along with them are they destroyed. After death there is no consciousness: this is what I say." Thus spake Yajñavalkya.

But Maitreyi said: "In this, you have thrown me into the utmost confusion. Indeed, I really do not understand this Self."

But he said: "There is surely nothing confusing in what I say. The Self is wholly indestructible; of its very nature it cannot be annihilated.

"For where there is any semblance of duality, there does one see another, there does one smell another, there does one taste another, there does one speak to another, there does one hear another, there does one think of another, there does one touch another, there does one understand another. But when all has become one's very Self, then with what should one see whom? With what should one smell whom? With what should one taste whom? With what should one speak to whom? With what should one hear whom? With what should one think of whom? With what should one touch whom? With what should one understand whom? With what should one understand the Self by whom one understands this whole universe?

"This Self—what can one say of it but, 'No, no!' It is impalpable, for it cannot be grasped; indestructible, for it cannot be destroyed; free from attachment, for it is not attached to anything, not bound. It does not quaver, nor can it be hurt.

"With what indeed should one understand the Understander?

"Maitreyi, now you have been told the full teaching. Of such is immortality."

So saying, Yajñavalkya took his leave.

Source: R. C. Zaehner, *Hindu Scriptures* (London: J. M. Dent, 1966), 50–51, 75.

Chandogya Upanishad 6:12–13

"Bring here a fig from there." "Here it is." "Break it." "It is broken." "What do you see there?" "These extremely fine seeds." "Of these, please break one." "It is broken." "What do you see there?" "Nothing at all." Then he said to Shvetaketu: "Indeed that subtle essence which you do not perceive—from that very essence does this great fig tree thus arise. Believe me, that which is the subtle essence—this whole world has that essence for its Self; that is the Real; that is the Truth; that is the Self; that thou art, Shvetaketu. [Tat tvam asi.]" "Still further instruct me." "So be it," he said.

"Having put this salt in the water, come to me in the morning." He did so. Then his father said to him: "That salt which you put in the water last evening—please bring it hither." Even having looked for it, he did not find it, for it was completely dissolved. "Please take a sip of water from this end," said the father. "How is it?" "Salt" "Take a sip from the middle," he said. "How is it?" "Salt" "Take a sip from that end," he said. "How is it?" "Salt." "Throw it away and come to me." Shvetaketu did so thinking to himself: "That salt, though unperceived, still persists in the water." Then Aruni said to him: "Truly, you do not perceive Being in this world; but it is, indeed, here only: That which is the subtle essence—this whole world has that essence for its Self. That is the Real. That is the Self. That art thou, Shvetaketu."

Source: *Sources of Indian Tradition*, 2nd ed., Vol. 1 (New York: Columbia University Press, 1988), 37–38.

Reading 4.4   *BHAGAVAD GITA* (BOOKS 3 AND 9)

The *Bhagavad Gita* is often regarded as the most universal of the Hindu scriptures. It incorporates aspects of many different schools of philosophy and religions and draws them into a synthesis. These two chapters of the *Gita* illustrate three of the important themes of the work. First, in Book 3, Krishna shows Arjuna how he can perform his assigned religiosocial duty *(dharma)* without accumulating more *karma* and being bound in the cycles of rebirth. The solution is a process of discipline *(yoga)* by which one remains unattached to the results of action. The *Gita* argues that one should not renounce action but should perform required action without attachment.

The second selection, Book 9, begins with Krishna's revelation that he is the underlying self of all, but in a way different from the impersonal Brahman of the *Upanishads*. He is the Lord of all sacrifices; everything belongs to him. Krishna then shows Arjuna that devotion to him is a sure path for everyone. Cultivation of devotional love and surrender to Krishna becomes the highest religious path.

The *Bhagavad Gita* presents several different models of religious practice and life. What are the religious ideals that are proposed in these two sections of the *Bhagavad*

Gita? How would the individual be transformed by putting into practice the principles of the *Gita?* What would be the social implications of applying the *Bhagavad Gita* as a model for life? What is your perception of Krishna as he speaks in the *Bhagavad Gita?* What does "loving Krishna" mean in this text?

BOOK THREE—THE DISCIPLINE OF ACTION

Arjuna

If you think understanding
is more powerful than action,
why, Krishna, do you urge me
to this horrific act?   1

You confuse my understanding
with a maze of words;
speak one certain truth
so that I may achieve what is good.   2

Lord Krishna

Earlier I taught the twofold
basis of good in this world—
for philosophers, disciplined knowledge;
for men of discipline, action.   3

A man cannot escape the force
of action by abstaining from actions;
he does not attain success
just by renunciation.   4

No one exists for even an instant
without performing action;
however unwilling, every being is forced
to act by the qualities of nature.   5

When his senses are controlled
but he keeps recalling
sense objects with his mind,
he is a self-deluded hypocrite.   6

When he controls his senses
with his mind and engages in the discipline
of action with his faculties of action,
detachment sets him apart.   7

Perform necessary action;
it is more powerful than inaction;
without action you even fail
to sustain your own body.   8

Action imprisons the world
unless it is done as sacrifice;
freed from attachment, Arjuna,
perform action as sacrifice!   9

When creating living beings and sacrifice,
Prajapati, the primordial creator, said:
"By sacrifice will you procreate!
Let it be your wish-granting cow!   10
Foster the gods with this,
and may they foster you;
by enriching one another,
you will achieve a higher good.   11
Enriched by sacrifice, the gods
will give you the delights you desire;
he is a thief who enjoys their gifts
without giving to them in return."   12

Good men eating the remnants
of sacrifice are free of any guilt,
but evil men who cook for themselves
eat the food of sin.   13

Creatures depend on food,
food comes from rain,
rain depends on sacrifice,
and sacrifice comes from action.   14

Action comes from the spirit of prayer,
whose source is OM, sound of the imperishable;
so the pervading infinite spirit
is ever present in rites of sacrifice.   15

He who fails to keep turning
the wheel here set in motion
wastes his life in sin,
addicted to the senses, Arjuna.   16

But when a man finds delight
within himself and feels inner joy
and pure contentment in himself,
there is nothing more to be done.   17

He has no stake here
in deeds done or undone,
nor does his purpose
depend on other creatures.   18

Always perform with detachment
any action you must do;
performing action with detachment,
one achieves supreme good.   19

Janaka and other ancient kings
attained perfection by action alone;
seeing the way to preserve
the world, you should act.   20

Whatever a leader does,
the ordinary people also do.
He sets the standard
for the world to follow.   21

In the three worlds,
there is nothing I must do,
nothing unattained to be attained,
yet I engage in action.   22

What if I did not engage
relentlessly in action?
Men retrace my path
at every turn, Arjuna.   23

These worlds would collapse
if I did not perform action;
I would create disorder in society,
living beings would be destroyed.   24

As the ignorant act with attachment
to actions, Arjuna,
so wise men should act with detachment
to preserve the world.   25

No wise man disturbs the understanding
of ignorant men attached to action;
he should inspire them,
performing all actions with discipline.   26

Actions are all effected
by the qualities of nature;
but deluded by individuality,
the self thinks, "I am the actor."   27

When he can discriminate
the actions of nature's qualities
and think, "The qualities depend
on other qualities," he is detached.   28

Those deluded by the qualities of nature
are attached to their actions;
a man who knows this should not upset
these dull men of partial knowledge.   29

Surrender all actions to me,
and fix your reason on your inner self;
without hope or possessiveness,
your fever subdued, fight the battle!   30

Men who always follow my thought,
trusting it without finding fault,
are freed
even by their actions.   31

But those who find fault
and fail to follow my thought,
know that they are lost fools,
deluded by every bit of knowledge.   32

Even a man of knowledge
behaves in accord with his own nature;
creatures all conform to nature;
what can one do to restrain them?   33

Attraction and hatred are poised
in the object of every sense experience;
a man must not fall prey
to these two brigands lurking on his path!   34

Your own duty done imperfectly
is better than another man's done well.
It is better to die in one's own duty;
another man's duty is perilous.   35

Arjuna

Krishna, what makes a person
commit evil
against his own will,
as if compelled by force?   36

Lord Krishna

It is desire and anger, arising
from nature's quality of passion;
know it here as the enemy,
voracious and very evil!   37

As fire is obscured by smoke
and a mirror by dirt,
as an embryo is veiled by its caul,
so is knowledge obscured by this.   38

Knowledge is obscured
by the wise man's eternal enemy,
which takes form as desire,
an insatiable fire, Arjuna.   39

The senses, mind, and understanding
are said to harbor desire;
with these desire obscures knowledge
and confounds the embodied self.   40

Therefore, first restrain
your senses, Arjuna,
then kill this evil
that ruins knowledge and judgment.   41

Men say that the senses are superior
to their objects, the mind superior to the senses,
understanding superior to the mind;
higher than understanding is the self. 42

Knowing the self beyond understanding,
sustain the self with the self.
Great Warrior, kill the enemy
menacing you in the form of desire! 43

BOOK NINE—THE SUBLIME MYSTERY

Lord Krishna

I will teach the deepest mystery
to you since you find no fault;
realizing it with knowledge and judgment,
you will be free from misfortune. 1

This science and mystery of kings
is the supreme purifier,
intuitive, true to duty,
joyous to perform, unchanging. 2

Without faith in sacred duty,
men fail to reach me, Arjuna;
they return to the cycle
of death and rebirth. 3

The whole universe is pervaded
by my unmanifest form;
all creatures exist in me,
but I do not exist in them. 4

Behold the power of my discipline;
those creatures are really not in me;
my self quickens creatures,
sustaining them without being in them. 5

Just as the wide-moving wind
is constantly present in space,
so all creatures exist in me;
understand it to be so! 6

As an eon ends, all creatures
fold into my nature, Arjuna;
and I create them again
as a new eon begins. 7

Gathering in my own nature,
again and again I freely create
this whole throng of creatures,
helpless in the force of my nature. 8

These actions do not bind me,
since I remain detached
in all my actions, Arjuna,
as if I stood apart from them.   9

Nature, with me as her inner eye,
bears animate and inanimate beings;
and by reason of this, Arjuna,
the universe continues to turn.   10

Deluded men despise me
in the human form I have assumed,
ignorant of my higher existence
as the great lord of creatures.   11

Reason warped, hope, action,
and knowledge wasted,
they fall prey to a seductive
fiendish, demonic nature.   12

In single-minded dedication, great souls
devote themselves to my divine nature,
knowing me as unchanging,
the origin of creatures.   13

Always glorifying me,
striving, firm in their vows,
paying me homage with devotion,
they worship me, always disciplined.   14

Sacrificing through knowledge,
others worship my universal presence
in its unity
and in its many different aspects.   15

I am the rite, the sacrifice,
the libation for the dead, the healing herb,
the sacred hymn, the clarified butter,
the fire, the oblation.   16

I am the universal father,
mother, granter, grandfather,
object of knowledge, purifier,
holy syllable OM, threefold sacred lore.   17

I am the way, sustainer, lord,
witness, shelter, refuge, friend,
source, dissolution, stability,
treasure, and unchanging seed.   18

I am heat that withholds
and sends down the rains;
I am immortality and death;
both being and non-being am I.   19

Men learned in sacred lore,
Soma drinkers, their sins absolved,
worship me with sacrifices,
seeking to win heaven.
reaching the holy world of Indra,
king of the gods,
they savor the heavenly delights
of the gods in the celestial sphere. 20

When they have long enjoyed
the world of heaven
and their merit is exhausted,
they enter the mortal world;
following the duties
ordained in sacred lore,
desiring desires,
they obtain what is transient. 21

Men who worship me,
thinking solely of me,
always disciplined,
win the reward I secure. 22

When devoted men sacrifice
to other deities with faith,
they sacrifice to me, Arjuna,
however aberrant the rites. 23

I am the enjoyer
and the lord of all sacrifices;
they do not know me in reality,
and so they fail. 24

Votaries of the gods go to the gods,
ancestor-worshippers go to the ancestors,
those who propitiate ghosts go to them,
and my worshippers go to me. 25

The leaf or flower or fruit or water
that he offers with devotion,
I take from the man of self-restraint
in response to his devotion. 26

Whatever you do—what you take,
what you offer, what you give,
what penances you perform—
do as an offering to me, Arjuna! 27

You will be freed from the bonds of action,
from the fruit of fortune and misfortune;
armed with the discipline of renunciation,
your self liberated, you will join me. 28

> I am impartial to all creatures,
> and no one is hateful or dear to me;
> but men devoted to me are in me,
> and I am within them.   29
>
> If he is devoted solely to me,
> even a violent criminal
> must be deemed a man of virtue,
> for his resolve is right.   30
>
> His spirit quickens to sacred duty,
> and he finds eternal peace;
> Arjuna, know that no one
> devoted to me is lost.   31
>
> If they rely on me, Arjuna,
> women, commoners, men of low rank,
> even men born in the womb of evil,
> reach the highest way.   32
>
> How easy it is then for holy priests
> and devoted royal sages—
> in this transient world of sorrow,
> devote yourself to me!   33
>
> Keep me in your mind and devotion,
> sacrifice to me, bow to me,
> discipline your self toward me,
> and you will reach me.   34

Source: Barbara Stoler Miller, trans., *The Bhagavad-Gita: Krishna's Counsel in Time of War* (New York: Bantam, 1986), pp. 41–47, 83–87.

Reading 4.5   VAISHNAVA DEVOTIONAL POETRY

The following selections present perspectives on the love of God and its effects in the lives of devotees and in society. What are the images that the authors use to describe the relationship of love between a person and God? What change has taken place in the lives of these individuals? How is the love of God, as described in these passages, different from the description in the *Bhagavad Gita?* What effect might it have on society if people relate to God in the way that is described in these passages?

TUKARAM

Tukaram (1598–1649), from the state of Maharastra, is a much-beloved poet-saint in the Marathi language. Here he shows the total loss of self and love of the Lord that is the basis of his style of devotion.

GOD'S OWN DOG

> I've come to Your door   1
> Like a dog looking for a home
> O Kind One
> Don't drive me away

I refuse to leave Your door
Don't force me out

I have no shame
I lick your feet

Says Tuka,
O Narayana
You look
So promising!

Once I chase someone   3
I chase him
Out of this world

Then I come back
To Your feet
And hide
Till you send me out
Again

The moment this dog
Smells a stranger
He scrambles
To attention

Says Tuka,
My Master's trained me hard
I am allowed to eat
Only out of his own
Hand

Pamper a dog   6
And it's spoilt for good
It'll loiter at your feet
And get in your way

That's how I've become
With You
Staying too damn close
All the time

I come wagging my tail
When You eat Your dinner

Says Tuka,
O Lord
I don't even notice
If You are annoyed!

Source: Tukaram, *Says Tuka,* trans. by Dilip Chitre (New Delhi: Penguin, 1991), pp. 86–87, 90.

SURDAS

Surdas (sixteenth century) wrote many Hindi songs about the birth and childhood of Krishna, but also about the Lord's love relationship with his beloved Radha. One of the motifs of Indian love poetry is the role of the friend of the beloved, who serves as a go-between and tries to inflame the passions of the couple and to quiet the anger of her friend. In this poem, Surdas takes the role of Radha's friend and reports to her about Krishna's response. Just as the man Surdas assumes this woman's role in his poem, so too the reader is expected to find a role in Krishna's love play.

> Ever since your name has entered Hari's ear
> It's been "Radha, oh Radha," an infinite mantra,
>   a formula chanted to a secret string of beads.
> Nightly he sits by the Jumna, in a grove
>   far from his friends and his happiness and home.
> He yearns for you. He has turned into a yogi:
>   constantly wakeful, whatever the hour.
> Sometimes he spreads himself a bed of tender leaves;
>   sometimes he recites your treasurehouse of fames;
> Sometimes he pledges silence: he closes his eyes
>   and meditates on every pleasure of your frame—
> His eyes the invocation, his heart the oblation,
>   his mutterings the food to feed
>   the priests who tend the fire.
> So has Syam's whole body wasted away.
>   Says Sur, let him see you. Fulfill his desire.

Source: *Songs of the Saints of India*, trans. by John Stratton Hawley and Mark Juergensmeyer (New York: Oxford University Press, 1988), p. 111.

MIRABAI

Mirabai (sixteenth century) is a North Indian Hindi devotional poet who extols Krishna, rather than the Rajput prince to whom she is married, as the true husband of her life. Krishna is the Mountain Lifter (an image from the *Bhagavata Purana*, in which he holds aloft Mount Govardhan). The sound of Krishna's flute, Murali, calls her thoughts away from her responsibilities to her family; instead, she yearns for Krishna.

> Life without Hari is no life, friend,
> And though my mother-in-law fights,
>   my sister-in-law teases,
>   the *rana* [the king, her father-in-law] is angered,
> A guard is stationed on a stool outside,
>   and a lock is mounted on the door,
> How can I abandon the love I have loved
>   in life after life?
> Mira's Lord is the clever Mountain Lifter:
>   Why would I want anyone else.

Murali sounds on the banks of the Jumna,
Murali snatches away my mind;
My senses cut loose from their moorings—
Dark waters, dark garments, dark Lord.
I listen close to the sounds of Murali
And my body withers away—
Lost thoughts, lost even the power to think.
    Mira's Lord, clever Mountain Lifter,
    Come quick, and snatch away my pain.

Source: *Songs of the Saints of India,* trans. by John Stratton Hawley and Mark Juergensmeyer (New York: Oxford University Press, 1988), pp. 134, 136. See also John Stratton Hawley, "Morality beyond Morality in the Lives of Three Hindu Saints," in *Saints and Virtues,* ed. John Stratton Hawley (Berkeley: University of California Press, 1987), pp. 55–59.

Reading 4.6 POEMS TO SHIVA Basavanna

Basavanna (ca. 1106–1168) was a devotee of Shiva in the Virashaiva movement in Karnataka, in South India. He places primary emphasis on the love of the Lord, not on religious institutions and the priestly caste. He refers to Shiva as the "Lord of the Meeting Rivers." His poetry shows the relationship between inner devotion for God and criticism of powerful religious elites.

What does the "love of God" mean in these passages? Compare this understanding of loving God with that in the readings about Vaishnava devotion to God. Why does Basavanna criticize religious institutions? What are the implications of criticizing religious practices in this fashion? Are these sentiments "antireligious"?

Feet will dance,   487
eyes will see,
tongue will sing,
and not find content.
What else, what else
shall I do?

I worship with my hands,
the heart is not content.
What else shall I do?

    Listen, my lord,
    it isn't enough.
    I have it in me
    to cleave thy belly
    and enter thee

O lord of the meeting rivers!   494
I don't know anything like time-beats and metre
nor the arithmetic of strings and drums;
I don't know the count of iamb and dactyl.

My lord of the meeting rivers,
as nothing will hurt you
I'll sing as I love.

Make of my body the beam of a lute   500
   of my head the sounding gourd
   of my nerves the strings
   of my fingers the plucking rods.

Clutch me close
   and play your thirty-two songs
   O lord of the meeting rivers!

The pot is a god. The winnowing   563
fan is a god. The stone in the
street is a god. The comb is a
god. The bowstring is also a
god. The bushel is a god and the
spouted cup is a god.

Gods, gods, there are so many
there's no place left
for a foot.

There is only
one god. He is our Lord
of the Meeting Rivers.

They plunge   581
wherever they see water.

They circumambulate
every tree they see.

How can they know you
O Lord
who adore
waters that run dry
trees that whither?

Source: *Speaking of Shiva,* trans. by A. K. Ramanujan (Baltimore: Penguin, 1973), pp. 82–85.

Reading 4.7   THE NEED FOR A MORE HUMANE MORALITY
AND A PURER MODE OF WORSHIP   Ram Mohan Roy

Ram Mohan Roy (1772–1833) used the nineteenth-century Hindu reform movement Brahmo Samaj as a vehicle to transform Hinduism in response to the criticisms brought by Western science and missionaries. He argued against idolatry and in favor of a monotheistic Hinduism that was based on the *Upanishads* and on his encounter with Western thought and with Christianity. What image of a "reformed" Hinduism did Roy propose? Compare this form of Hinduism with those of the Vaishnava and Shaiva devotional traditions. Roy argued against "idolatry." How might a Hindu who worships deity images respond?

> The advocates of idolatry and their misguided followers, over whose opinions prejudice and obstinacy prevail more than good sense and judgment, prefer custom and fashion to the authorities of their scriptures, and therefore continue, under the form of religious devotion, to practice a system which destroys, to the utmost degree, the natural texture of society, and prescribes crimes of the most heinous nature, which even the most savage nations would blush to commit, unless compelled by the utmost necessity. I am, however, not without a sanguine hope that, through Divine Providence and human exertions, they will sooner or later avail themselves of that true system of religion which leads its observers to a knowledge and love of God, and to a friendly inclination toward their fellow-creatures, impressing their hearts at the same time with humility and charity, accompanied by independence of mind and pure sincerity. Contrary to the code of idolatry, this system defines sin as evil thoughts proceeding from the heart, quite unconnected with observances as to diet and other matters of form. At any rate, it seems to me that I cannot better employ my time than in an endeavour to illustrate and maintain truth, and to render service to my fellow-laborers, confiding in the mercy of that Being to whom the motives of our actions and secrets of our hearts are well known.

> **Source:** *Sources of Indian Tradition,* 2d ed., Vol. 2, *Modern India and Pakistan* (New York: Columbia University Press, 1988), pp. 23–24.

Reading 4.8   RELIGION AND THE PRACTICE OF POLITICS
Mohandas K. Gandhi

These three passages show Mohandas K. Gandhi's (1896–1948) understanding that his own spiritual transformation was central to his mission in the public arena. They also illustrate how his sense of the power of divine truth *(satyagraha)* provides an incentive to social service: "To be true to such religion one has to lose oneself in continuous service of all life." In his "Talisman," he advised politicians to focus their concern on the needs of society's lowliest.

Gandhi's "Talisman" has often been cited as a model for public servants and politicians. Propose the strengths and weaknesses of this model of public service for a contemporary nation. Gandhi drew many of his principles from reflection on the *Bhagavad Gita.* What connections do you find between his understanding of public service and religion and the *Gita?*

MY MISSION (1924), RESPONDING TO A QUESTION ON THE RELATIONSHIP BETWEEN POLITICS AND RELIGION

I do not consider myself worthy to be mentioned in the same breath with the race of prophets. I am a humble seeker after truth. I am impatient to realize myself, to attain *moksha* in this very existence. My national service is part of my training for freeing my soul from the bondage of flesh. Thus considered, my service may be considered as purely selfish. I have no desire for the perishable kingdom of earth. I am striving for the kingdom of Heaven which is *moksha* . To attain my end it is not necessary for me to seek the shelter of a cave. I carry one around with me, if I would but know it. A cave-dweller can build castles in the air, whereas a dweller in a palace like Janak (the ideal of kingship as fulfilling the yoga of action) has no castles to build. The cave-dweller who hovers round the world on the wings of thought has no peace. A Janak, though living in the midst of "pomp and circumstance", may have peace that passeth understanding. For me the road to salvation lies through incessant toil in the service of my country and therethrough of humanity. I want to identify myself with everything that lives. In the language of the Gita I want to live at peace with both friend and foe. Though, therefore, a Mussulman or a Christian or a Hindu may despise me and hate me, I want to love him and serve him even as I would love my wife or son though they hate me. So my patriotism is for me a stage in my journey to the land of eternal freedom and peace. Thus it will be seen that for me there are no politics devoid of religion. They subserve religion. Politics bereft of religion is a death-trap because they kill the soul.

MY RELIGION (1935)

I have been asked by Sir S. Radhakrishnan to answer the following three questions:
  (1) What is your religion?
  (2) How are you led to it?
  (3) What is its bearing on social life?
  My religion is Hinduism which, for me, is religion of humanity and includes the best of all the religions known to me.

  I take it that the present tense in the second question has been purposely used instead of the past. I am being led to my religion through Truth and Non-violence, i.e., love in the broadest sense. I often describe my religion as religion of Truth. Of late, instead of saying God is Truth, I have been saying Truth is God, in order more fully to define my religion. I used at one time to know by heart the thousand names of God which a booklet in Hinduism gives in verse form and which perhaps tens of thousands recite every morning. But nowadays nothing so completely describes my God as Truth. Denial of God we have known. Denial of Truth we have not known. The most ignorant among mankind have some truth in them. We are all sparks of Truth. The sum total of these sparks is indescribable, as-yet-Unknown Truth, which is God. I am being daily led nearer to it by constant prayer.

  The bearing of this religion on social life is, or has to be, seen in one's daily social contact. To be true to such religion one has to lose oneself in continuous and continuing service of all life. Realization of Truth is impossible without a complete merging of oneself in and identification with the limitless ocean of life. Hence, for me, there is no escape from social service; there is no happiness on earth beyond or apart from it. Social service here must be taken to include every department of life. In this scheme there is nothing low, nothing high. For, all is one, though we *seem* to be many.

A TALISMAN (1947)

I will give you a talisman. Whenever you are in doubt, or when the self becomes too much with you, apply the following test. Recall the face of the poorest and the weakest man whom you may have seen, and ask yourself, if the step you contemplate is going to be of any use to him. Will he gain anything by it? Will it restore him to a control over his own life and destiny? In other words, will it lead to swaraj [self-rule] for the hungry and spiritually starving millions?

Then you will find your doubts and yourself melting away.

Source: K. Swaminathan and C. N. Patel, eds., *A Gandhi Reader* (Madras: Orient Longman, 1988), pp. 68–69, 124–125, 134–135.

Reading 4.9 THE HINDU VIEW OF LIFE Radhakrishnan

Sarvepalli Radhakrishnan (1888–1975), the first president of independent India, presented an argument in 1923 for the coherence of the Hindu way of understanding human life. In the selection, Radhakrishnan provides an explanation for the institution of caste in traditional Indian society, as well as in contemporary society. What does caste mean for him? What are the strengths and weaknesses of this argument? Compare the spirit of Gandhi's "Talisman" with Radhakrishnan's image of social responsibility.

Caste was the answer of Hinduism to the forces pressing on it from outside. It was the instrument by which Hinduism civilized the different tribes it took in. Any group of people appearing exclusive in any sense is a caste. Whenever a group represents a type a caste arises. If a heresy is born in the bosom of the mother faith and if it spreads and produces a new type, a new caste arises. The Hindu Society has differentiated as many types as can be reasonably differentiated, and is prepared to accept new ones as they arise. It stands for the ordered complexity, the harmonized multiplicity, the many in one which is a clue to the structure of the universe.

Today many brilliant writers are warning us of a world-conflict of races. . . . It is not my purpose here to deal with the practical difficulties in the way of any easy solution of the racial problem. They are great, but they can be solved only by the consciousness of the earth as one great family and an endeavor to express this reality in all our relationships. We must work for a world in which all races can blend and mingle, each retaining its special characteristics and developing whatever is best in it.

Very early in the history of Hinduism, the caste distinctions came to mean the various stratifications into which the Hindu society settled. The confusion between the tribal and the occupational is the cause of the perpetuation of the old exclusiveness of the tribal customs in the still stringent rules which govern the constitution of each caste. Caste on its social side is a product of human organization and not a mystery of divine appointment. It is an attempt to regulate society with a view to actual differences and ideal unity. The first reference to it is in the Purusha Sukta [see the text in Reading 4.1, "The Primal Sacrifice" from the *Rig Veda*], where the different sections of society are regarded as the limbs of the great self. Human society is an organic whole, the parts of which are naturally dependent in such a way that each part in fulfilling its distinctive function conditions the fulfillment of function by the rest. In this sense the whole is present in each part, while each part is indispensable to the whole. Every society consists of groups working for the fulfillment of the wants of the society. As the different groups work for a common end they are bound by a sense of unity and social brotherhood. The cultural and the spiritual, the military and the political, the economic classes and the unskilled workers constitute the four-fold caste organization. The different functions of the human life were clearly separated and their specific and complementary character was recognized. Each caste has its social purpose and function, its own code and tradition. It is a close corporation equipped with a certain traditional and independent organization, observing certain usages regarding food and marriage. Each group is free to pursue its own aims free from interference by others. The functions of the different castes were regarded as equally important to the well-being of the whole. The serenity of the teacher, the heroism of the warrior, the honesty of the business man, and the patience and energy of the worker all contribute to the social growth. Each has its own perfection.

The rules of caste bring about an adjustment of the different groups in society. The Brahmins were allowed freedom and leisure to develop the spiritual ideals and broadcast them. They were freed from the cares of existence, as gifts to them by others were encouraged and even enjoined. They are said to be above class interests and prejudices, and to possess a wide and impartial vision. They are not in bondage to the State, though they are consulted by the State. . . .

In spite of its attachment to the principle of non-violence, Hindu society made room for a group dedicated to the use of force, the Kshatriyas. As long as human nature is what it is, as long as society has not reached its highest level, we require the use of force. So long as society has individuals who are hostile to all order and peace, it has to develop controls to check the anti-social elements. . . .

The economic group of the Vaishyas were required to suppress greed and realize the moral responsibilities of wealth. Property is looked upon as an instrument of service. In the great days of Hinduism, the possessor of property regarded it as a social trust and undertook the education, the medical relief, the water supply and the amusements of the community. . . .

The unskilled workers and the peasants form the proletariat, the Shudras. These castes are the actual living members of the social body each centered in itself and working alongside one another in co-operation. . . .

The system of caste insists that the law of social life should not be cold and cruel competition, but harmony and co-operation. Society is not a field of rivalry between individuals. The castes are not allowed to compete with one another. A man born in a particular group is trained to its manner, and will find it extremely hard to adjust himself to a new way. Each man is said to have his own specific nature (svabhava) fitting him for his own specific function (svadharma), and changes of dharma or function are not encouraged. A sudden change of function when the nature is against its proper fulfillment may simply destroy the individuality of the being. We may wish to change or modify our particular mode of being, but we have not the power to effect. Nature cannot be hurried by our desires. The four castes represent men of thought, men of action, men of feeling, and others in whom none of these is highly developed. . . . The author of the *Bhagavadgita* believes that the divisions of caste are in accordance with each man's character and aptitude. . . . [Compare this perspective with the earlier readings from the *Bhagavad Gita.*]

The caste idea of vocation as service, with its traditions and spiritual aims, never encouraged the notion of work as a degrading servitude to be done grudgingly and purely from the economic motive. The perfecting of its specific function is the spiritual aim which each vocational group set to itself. The worker has the fulfillment of his being through and in his work. According to the *Bhagavadgita,* one attains perfection if one does one's duty in the proper spirit of non-attachment. . . .

While caste has resulted in much evil, there are some sound principles underlying it. Our attitude to those whom we are pleased to call primitive must be one of sympathy. The task of the civilized is to respect and foster the live impulses of backward communities and not destroy them. Society is an organism of different grades, and human activities differ in kind and significance. But each of them is of value so long as it serves the common end. Every type has its own nature which should be followed. No one can be at the same time a perfect saint, a perfect artist, and a perfect philosopher. Every definite type is limited by boundaries which deprive it of other possibilities. The worker should realize his potentialities through his work, and should perform it in a spirit of service to the common weal. Work is craftsmanship and service. Our class conflicts are due to the fact that a warm living sense of unity does bind together the different groups.

Source: S. Radhakrishnan, *The Hindu View of Life* (New York: Macmillan, 1962), pp. 75–90.

CHAPTER 5

BUDDHISM

Buddhism is a religion that is universal and nontheistic according to the classification scheme outlined in Chapter 1. Like other major religious traditions such as Christianity and Islam, Buddhism's founding can be traced back to a single charismatic figure (in this case, Shakyamuni Buddha). Buddhism, like Christianity and Islam, has also sought converts across the lines of kinship, nationality, and religious affiliation and attempted to weld them into a holy community on the basis of doctrine.

Where Buddhism differs sharply from these two, as well as from most other, major world religious traditions is in being nontheistic in most of its major manifestations. Although the founder of the religion, Shakyamuni Buddha (563–483 B.C.E.), claimed the realization of the ultimate truth, he did not identify himself as the special representative of a transcendent God. He was instead a human being who staked a claim for the "divine" birthright of every living being—the possibility of becoming a *buddha*. Shakyamuni, whose given name was Gautama, was born into the ruling family of the Shakya clan. From this clan is derived his name, which means "sage of the Shakyas." We usually refer to him by the name Gautama when we

A seated Buddha in a teaching position sculpted out of a rock formation on the grounds of the Lingyin Temple in Hangzhou, People's Republic of China (1983).

are talking about the period of his life before enlightenment and by the name Shakyamuni after his enlightenment.

The word *buddha* is a derived from the Sanskrit verbal root *budh*, which means "to awaken." Because Shakyamuni, upon his enlightenment, experienced a new level of awareness, comparable to the experience of awakening from a dream, he said, "I have awakened," or "I am Buddha." What the Buddha taught from that time forth he characterized as a method of awakening to reality. Thus, Buddhism has been from the outset a religion that proposes to teach a new worldview.

A common trait among religious teachings discussed in Chapter 1 is an emphasis on the experience of the sacred. If, in the context of Buddhism, we take *sacred* to be equivalent to *absolute truth*, then we can say that the experience of the sacred is indeed central to Buddhism. In Buddhism, as in many religions, this experience of the sacred is also closely related to the religion's *soteriology*—its accepted method for the attainment of liberation. Although Buddhism places emphasis on salvation to a degree at least equal to any of the great world religions, it is considered to be distinctive among these religions for the degree to which that salvation is connected to the practice of the "path" (Sanskrit **marga**). In most branches of Buddhism, the responsibility for liberation is placed on the efforts of the individual.

Buddhism is a tradition with a 2,500-year history that has passed through many cultures, each time having to adapt itself to preexistent religious worldviews. Therefore, even though Korean Son Buddhism, for example, shares many of its important basic concepts with Thai Theravada or Tibetan Gelukpa Buddhism, the external characteristics and the format of the practices of each of these versions of Buddhism often are noticeably different. The contexts of the philosophical discourses related to the origins of various sects are also notably different. For example, early Indian Buddhists were mainly concerned with establishing the metaphysical positions of Buddhism in the face of the arguments presented by competing Jain and Brahmanistic religions. In Tibet, Buddhism needed to be articulated through a radically different linguistic medium to a populace that had embraced native shamanistic paradigms for millennia. In Korea, meditation-oriented Buddhists were compelled to define their positions philosophically to competing Buddhist doctrinal schools, as well as to non-Buddhist Neo-Confucians. And if Buddhism ever achieves broad success in the modern West, it will have been obliged to do so through an adequate response to the modern, secular manifestations of philosophy, psychology, and natural science, as well as whatever remains of the Christian religious influence. Throughout the ages Buddhism has continually branched out into sects and subsects based on differences in interpretation of the *buddha-dharma* (teaching of the Buddha). Thus, though Buddhism must always teach a certain set of core concepts, such as compassion, unsatisfactoriness, emptiness, impermanence, and enlightenment, there will never be any such thing as a "singular" Buddhism.

BUDDHIST BELIEFS

In a religion as broad in scope as Buddhism, which has so many different doctrinal branches and cultural manifestations, it is not easy to name any single "belief" to which all Buddhists uniformly adhere. For example, the Buddhist belief system of lay practitioners in Thailand and Myanmar (formerly Burma) typically focuses on the accumulation of merit for a prosperous rebirth; the main belief of such a system is a personalized understanding of the concept of the law of cause and effect *(karma)*. **Pure Land** practitioners in Taiwan or Japan, in contrast, put all their trust in Amitabha Buddha, believing that chanting Amitabha's name will result in a rebirth in the Pure Land. This kind of conviction in the salvific powers of an external *buddha,* or *bodhisattva,* to remove personal suffering has strong similarities with the popular belief systems of such theistic religions as Christianity and Islam.

The fundamental doctrine that forms the basis for the practice of most scholarly and meditative forms of Buddhism is grounded in a "faith" or "conviction" (Sanskrit *sraddha,* Pali *saddha*) not in an external power but rather in one's own capacity to become a *buddha.* This is a faith that takes a deliberately interrogative stance in which the practitioners question their mistaken perceptions regarding themselves and existence. In Buddhist meditative schools, "mistaken views" are understood to completely dominate the consciousnesses of unenlightened people. A person is to have "confidence" in that which remains after rigorous self-questioning. This self-questioning mode, which was a key to Shakyamuni's success in attaining his awakening, is a central element in most subsequent Buddhist schools, and the doctrines that became the cornerstone of the Buddhist teaching would all be arrived at through rigorous, questioning analysis. Because Buddhist doctrine is regarded as being derived from Shakyamuni, we begin our discussion of Buddhist beliefs with an introduction to his life and enlightenment and then turn to his *dharma* (teachings).

FOUNDING FIGURE: SHAKYAMUNI BUDDHA

Although the account of the Buddha's life is probably based to some degree on actual occurrences, much of it should be understood as myth. To say it is mythical does not necessarily mean that the story is false, but that certain elements are exaggerated and emphasized in order to make specific points—points that the Buddhist tradition has deemed important for the transmission of its message.

Gautama's father, the ruler of the Shakya clan, was a man of considerable wealth and power. Having expected that his firstborn son would succeed him on the throne, he was somewhat unnerved to hear from fortune-tellers that his child-to-be possessed the strong inclination to become a religious leader. The father endeavored to thwart the prophecy by shielding his son from those difficulties of life that might cause him to reflect deeply, by keeping him entertained within the castle walls. Despite the fact that the father was somehow able to maintain this protected environment until the time of Gautama's young adulthood, Gautama, even as a small boy, was fond of long periods of spontaneous seated contemplation out in the palace grounds.

Eventually, after marriage and the birth of a son, Gautama reached the point where he could no longer tolerate his limited existence, and he pressed his father for permission to go out and experience the world that lay beyond the castle walls. At length his father agreed, but in an effort to preserve his son's innocence he sent his retainers out into the town in advance to clear away any possible disturbing sights. Despite these efforts, Gautama's father was unable to prevent him from witnessing, on three trips, three successive surprises: a crippled person, an aged person, and a funerary corpse. Shocked and disturbed by these three sights, Gautama questioned his father's men who accompanied him on these trips, and they were obliged to explain to him the realities of sickness, aging, and death.

Soon after these three encounters, Gautama had one more vitally important experience that would direct him on the way to his path: he saw a wandering monk who was striving to attain liberation. From this time forth, Gautama grew increasingly restless, to the point where he could no longer bear his life of empty satiety within the confines of his father's estate. One evening, he left his wife and young son in the care of his father's estate and slipped off into the forest to begin his quest for enlightenment.

The next six years of Gautama's life were a period of intense physical, mental, and spiritual struggle as he sought to attain liberation from the world of cyclic suffering. His efforts were directed through the various liberative methods of his time, such as concentration exercises, contemplation, self-restraint, and detachment from the world. He studied with several eminent teachers. Having been endowed with unusually strong religious abilities, he was a quick learner and was thus able to quickly master all that his teachers had to offer and to attain their level of advancement. But Gautama found himself repeatedly dissatisfied with the methods of salvation offered by these teachers. Although each of the paths that he followed during this period had developed his religious awareness in some way, none was able to satisfy him fully. He never felt that he had penetrated the truth.

The last path that he followed, that of Jainism, included fasting and other practices of extreme asceticism. The aim of Jainistic self-denial was to bring about liberation by forcing practitioners to detach themselves from all sorts of pleasures of the senses—pleasures of shelter, warm clothing, sex, taste, and the like. Fasting was also regarded as a powerful aid in achieving a rarefied spiritual condition conducive to the attainment of liberation. At the time of his eventual abandonment of this path, Gautama, along with a small band of disciples, had been fasting for a long period of time. Because of this extreme fasting, he had become physically emaciated, even on the verge of starving to death. He eventually realized the futility of these efforts, and when a young woman who was passing by offered him food and drink, he decided to accept. His disciples, disappointed by this show of weakness, left him. Now alone, Gautama reflected on his existence up to this point, including his

life of luxury at his father's estate and his agonized efforts toward the attainment of liberation. He finally concluded that neither extreme was capable of leading him to the truth that he was seeking. He then sat himself up against a tree and contemplated, determining with all his might not to leave this place until he had realized the truth for himself.

In his effort to perceive the ultimate reality of existence, Gautama sat for a week, absorbed in deep contemplation, looking deeper and deeper into the inner recesses of his mind and out to the various phenomena of the universe. At the end of the week, a major change occurred within his mind—a transition in consciousness so great that he compared it to awakening from a dream, and thus he would call himself Buddha, the "awakened one." After his awakening, Shakyamuni traveled to a religious festival in Benares, where he found his former companions at the Deer Park. It is here that he gave his famous first sermon, in which he outlined the basic tenets of his system. Most important among the doctrines of this sermon are his explanations of the Four Noble Truths, his refutation of the concept of an eternal soul, and his explanation of the key concepts of dependent co-origination and impermanence.

Discerning a change in Shakyamuni's demeanor, his former disciples were rapidly convinced by the power of his message. Thus, they once again followed him, now with a heightened sense of devotion. He continued to teach, and his mission grew in size and scope. During the course of his life, the body of Shakyamuni's dedicated followers was organized into a community of monks and nuns, called the *sangha.* Adherents of the Buddha's program of meditation and enlightenment could, if they liked, renounce the secular world, be ordained into the Buddhist order for the purpose of intensive self-discipline, and thus become active in the spreading of the Buddha's teaching to others. The organization of this clerical community necessitated the formulation of a code of discipline that prohibited excesses in all areas of human behavior, placing value on a moral lifestyle. Over the years, the code of discipline, or *vinaya,* would grow to a list of some 250 rules for monks and about 450 for nuns.

Shakyamuni Buddha is distinctive among some of the other major world religious leaders, such as Jesus and Muhammad, for the unusual length of his teaching career, traditionally reckoned at forty-nine years. When the time came for Shakyamuni to leave the world, his followers were faced with the challenging prospect of continuing their mission without their leader. So, as he approached advanced age, some of his disciples, concerned about the future of the mission, asked him how they were to carry on without him. To this query the Buddha had replied, "Follow my *dharma* [that is, teachings]."

PRE-BUDDHIST BELIEFS

As we have seen, Shakyamuni began his quest for enlightenment by pursuing some of the forms of world-renunciant ascetic practice and philosophy that were prevalent in northern India at the time. After leaving home, he spent some six years in an arduous quest for the truth. He had followed the instructions of his ascetic teachers assiduously yet was ultimately dissatisfied with what he attained. Finally giving up on all of these teachings, he started over from the beginning, questioning everything—all prior teachings, including his own habituated perceptions of reality. The most important belief he was forced to question was one that had been developing in Indian philosophical and religious circles for over a millennium and that was beginning to reach sophisticated levels of articulation around the time of his life. This was the belief that the entire manifest, changing, illusory world was supported by a substratal, unchanging, permanent reality called Brahman. Brahman, itself infinite and uncreated, was understood to be the basis upon which all individual beings, planets, world systems, and entire universes were born, destroyed, and reborn.

The metaphysics and cosmology that developed around the concept of Brahman gave rise to a general Indian scenario of existence in which all impermanent phenomena arose and disappeared in cycles. The shortest of these cycles were instantaneous, and the longest were incalculable eons in duration. During times of creation, whether during the birth of a world system or of a microbe, pieces of pure, eternal Brahman became encased in finite gross matter in a form called *atman*. This idea roughly includes the two English concepts of self and soul. Thus, humans had, as the basic reality of their being, this true self or soul. The body and mind attached to the *atman* were seen as impermanent and illusory. This process was understood to be cyclical, which means that the *atman* would cast off one body at death, to be reborn into another body in the future, a phenomenon known in the West as reincarnation.[1] Furthermore, the condition of continual rebirthing of the self into the human body was understood to be a negative experience—an experience of suffering, which humans are almost powerless to change. The self is trapped in a cycle of suffering and rebirth (called *samsara*), which is empowered by the inexorable law of cause and effect *(karma)*. The average human is born into this life totally unaware of his or her countless prior existences, or of the innumerable positive and negative activities that have led him or her to the present condition.

The term *karma* is derived from the Sanskrit root *kr*, which is related in origin and meaning to an English word with the same first consonant combination—cr*eate*. During the past generation, the word *karma* has been used in English, in a partial sense of its meaning, as a rough equivalent of *fate* or *reward*. In its original denotation, however (and, most important, in Buddhism), *karma* describes the fact that each being is continually creating, in each moment, its immediately future set of circumstances. This set of circumstances, in turn, is nothing other than one's true "self." Thus, *karma*, in early Indian metaphysics has active, here-and-now implications.

The self-liberation–oriented religions that were developing in India when Buddhism originated were seeking to reverse this cycle of ever-deepening entrapment in *samsara* through a variety of techniques, including meditation, detachment, and moral discipline. Shakyamuni had tried a number of these methods, without achieving full satisfaction. Thus, when he sat down under the tree of enlightenment determined to penetrate to the truth, it was precisely these prevalent views on human existence that he questioned. What he concluded, after much analysis, was that any concept of an eternal, changeless, and locatable self was ultimately implausible. Furthermore, it was exactly this realization of the untenability of the *atman* concept that constituted his enlightenment experience. But on what metaphysical grounds did Shakyamuni dare to proclaim such a revolutionary discovery? These principles would be outlined in his first reunion with his former colleagues, whom he found at a religious festival at the Deer Park in Benares. In this discourse, known as the *First Sermon,* Shakyamuni outlined his basic teachings.

THE FOUR NOBLE TRUTHS

The Buddha told his new audience that four important realizations were necessary to enter into an experience equivalent to his. These four realizations are called the **Four Noble Truths.** The First Noble Truth is the Noble Truth of Unsatisfactoriness (Sanskrit *duhkha,* also translated into English as "suffering"). This teaching of unsatisfactoriness is not intended to bring about a pessimistic attitude toward life itself but to make it known that life as it is perceived and handled by most people cannot but lead to dissatisfaction.

The most obvious form of unsatisfactoriness is ordinary suffering—the pain of everyday physical sickness and death. But there are a host of other kinds of dissatisfaction related to the fact that all things are impermanent. Although people experience relative pleasure and satisfaction all the time, these are temporary and conditional states. Therefore, we suffer when we are exposed to people, places, and things that we dislike, and we also suffer when we are separated from people, places, and things that we like. We suffer from not being able to gratify fully our desires. Also, no matter how lucky or skillful we are in arranging our life's circumstances, eventually all will be taken away by sickness, aging, and death. The Buddha also talked of a subtle form of unsatisfactoriness that comes from an unease at the core of our being stemming from not ever knowing exactly who or what we are—from not being able to identify our "self."

Because it is possible for the contemplation of the Noble Truth of Unsatisfactoriness to lead to the development of a pessimistic attitude, Buddhists place strong emphasis on the counterbalancing aspects of the religion's teaching—the Second, Third, and Fourth Noble Truths. The Second Noble Truth is called the Noble Truth of Arising (of suffering) (Sanskrit **samudaya**). This truth refers to the fact that suffering has a cause; it is not merely an inherent, unavoidable characteristic of existence. The mode of this arising, called *dependent co-origination,* is an important aspect of the Buddhist doctrine that we will discuss in detail later.

The Third Noble Truth is the Noble Truth of Cessation of Suffering (Sanskrit *nirodha*). After suffering arises, being impermanent, it must also disappear. This cessation can be interpreted in two ways. The first meaning is that a given individual, through a certain set of practices, may eliminate suffering permanently—may attain *nirvana.* But this individual and final attainment is only possible because of a more subtle meaning of cessation—that in fact all things cease every moment. It is only because all things cease from moment to moment that it is possible for all suffering to cease eventually.

The Fourth Noble Truth is the Noble Truth of the Way (Sanskrit *marga*). This is the path to enlightenment taken by Shakyamuni himself, and the path that he prescribed for his followers. The Noble Truth of the Way has eight parts and is thus called the **Eightfold Path.** Its components are (1) Right View, (2) Right Intention, (3) Right Speech, (4) Right Action, (5) Right Livelihood, (6) Right Effort, (7) Right Mindfulness, and (8) Right Concentration. These eight paths are not to be understood as sequential stages that gradually lead to the attainment of liberation. Rather, they are mutually contributing pieces to an overall enlightened lifestyle. Nonetheless, there is a rationale to their arrangement.

We can generally understand Right View as the possession of the right perspective regarding reality—in other words, a firm grasp of the meaning of the Four Noble Truths. It also implies having a religious experience of some sort, after which one has a much clearer idea of how things really are and what one needs to do to begin to align oneself with reality. In this sense, placing Right View first on the list means that proper orientation is necessary before embarking on any task. Right Intention (also translated as Right Thought or Right Understanding) means continuing to think and analyze correctly in accordance with the Right View—maintaining the correct intention to practice based on one's correct religious awareness. Right View and Right Intention are generally classified together under the rubric of *wisdom* and will be examined in more detail shortly.

The practices of Right Speech, Right Action, and Right Livelihood, grouped together under the rubric of *morality* or *discipline (shila)*, are usually seen contained in the doctrines of other major world religions in one form or another. Some kind of system of moral practice is at the heart of all the world's major religions, and practices of moral discipline were fully developed in many of the other religious schools of Shakyamuni's day. The fact that the kind and fair treatment of all other beings is simply the right way to act is common sense to any sincerely religious person. It is also difficult to attain the proper mental stability to carry out subtle meditation practice while one's life is disturbed by the turmoil caused by improper relationships with others. According to general Indian *karmic* theory, self-serving and inconsiderate actions increase one's *karmic* load and further blind one to the truth. Therefore, the Buddha emphasized morality as a foundation for practice. Right Speech implies such practices as not lying, not exaggerating, not slandering, not backstabbing, and not speaking in such a way as to cause a problem between other people. In this practice, as with the other moral practices, it is wise to recognize the harm negative words do to oneself as well as to others.

Right Action consists of not harming, not killing, not stealing, not committing adultery— desisting from all kinds of behavior that is injurious to others. Right Livelihood is closely connected to the prior two moral practices but places an emphasis on the fact that one should make his or her living in a way that is in harmony with the natural order. Thus, it is recommended that one not make a living as a panderer, thief, gambler, and the like. In Buddhist literature there are many volumes devoted to the detailed explanation of moral prohibitions.

The development of mental stability (concentration) is of vital importance, and the next three of the eight aspects of the path are labeled together as *concentration (samadhi)*. The first, Right Effort, refers to both the need for unflagging vigilance on the part of the practitioner to ward off delusory or entrapping thoughts and to the continuous effort required to maintain wholesome states of mind and ward off unwholesome states of mind.

Right Mindfulness refers to the development of the continuous awareness of bodily states, sensations, emotions, thoughts, and ideas that arise so that one can control extremes of thought, emotion, or physical sensation. Right Concentration *(dhyana)* is the development of the ability for single-minded concentration—the capacity to focus on a single object without wavering. A person who lacks concentration power will not be able to carry out the forms of contemplation that ultimately lead to the casting off of afflictions and the attainment of enlightenment.

If we reflect on these latter six aspects of the path (those contained under the categories of *morality* and *concentration*) and compare them with the other religious teachings that were present in Shakyamuni's world prior to his enlightenment, we will find nothing especially revolutionary contained within them. Many of the non-Buddhist sects that existed at Shakyamuni's time had teachings on morality similar to those expressed in Right Speech, Right Action, and Right Livelihood. There were also schools that based the attainment of liberation on the practice of some sort of program of concentration and meditation not unlike that found in the three components of Right Effort, Right Mindfulness, and Right Concentration. This being the case, how could Shakyamuni make the claim that his method was so radically different from, or superior to, the other paths that he had himself practiced? The answer to this question lies in a closer examination of the full implications of the Right View.

NO-SELF

In articulating the content of his realization to his early followers, Shakyamuni claimed that the reason the other religious paths were unable to achieve a level of liberation equal to that of Buddhism was because they contained a flaw in the foundation of their doctrines. This flaw, he said, was the concept of the possession by all living beings of a unitary, eternal, and immutable "self" or "soul" *(atman)*, upon which was imposed changing and impermanent mind and matter, and which served as the subject of reincarnation. This imagined soul was also the reason for, and the source of, the human being's notion of an ego, self, or "I." Through the course of his contemplation, Shakyamuni made his controversial refutation of this eternal soul based on two major tenets that became central to all subsequent Buddhist doctrine.

The first tenet was the understanding of the impermanence *(anitya)* of all existence. Before his awakening, Shakyamuni had been taught that although all of phenomenal existence was impermanent and illusory, the self was eternal, real, and changeless. Over his lifetime, however, through rational analysis and the insight of his meditation, he concluded that it was impossible for anything in the universe to be changeless. Shakyamuni asserted instead that all things change (arise and cease) from moment to moment and that it is not possible for anything in the universe to lie outside this process. This conclusion by the Buddha about the impermanence of all existence disallowed the possibility of any such thing as a separate, eternal, changeless soul. According to his understanding, it was not feasible for humans to be a composite of the changing and the changeless. (Where would the changing part end and the changeless part

begin?) Therefore, the doctrine of impermanence was one of the most important bases for the Buddha's declaration of his new and revolutionary position of no-self *(anatman)*.

Shakyamuni was not, however, denying the existence of the mind, emotions, or individual personality. He agreed that something transmigrated from life to life; whatever it was that transmigrated, however, no matter how subtle, had to be mutable like everything else in existence. This no-self stance was not only intended to refute the notion of *atman* as a metaphysical category; more important, it was directed at commonsense intuitions of "I-ness" or "ego." The Buddha maintained that most people possess deeply ingrained conceptions of an "I," upon which they base countless variations of like and dislike, resulting in suffering. But if this "I" is sought out in a thoroughgoing analysis, no location for it can be found. This difficulty in locating a subject leads us to the other important theoretical underpinning for the no-self theory: dependent co-origination.

DEPENDENT CO-ORIGINATION

Another reason that Shakyamuni considered such a thing as a centralized location for "self" to be an impossibility rose from his view of the way all things arise, subsist, and cease. This mode of existence is called, in Sanskrit, *pratitya-samutpada*, which is translated into English as **dependent co-origination.** The theory of dependent co-origination is fundamental for all forms of Buddhist philosophy, whether they be ancient or modern, and whether they be from any doctrinal branch or subbranch, or any cultural variation. According to Shakyamuni, the things of existence do not exist in a set, dualistic hierarchy of "real" and "unreal," such as is seen in other forms of Indian metaphysics (or, for example, in the metaphysics of Plato and his school). Shakyamuni denied the belief in a "higher" or "more real" substance present in living beings as eternal "self" surrounded by body/mind. Rather, he saw living beings as nothing other than a vast conglomeration of complex factors: physical matter and sensory, perceptive, emotional, and psychic forces joined in a marvelous combination. What non-Buddhists might call a *soul* or *ego,* Shakyamuni saw as a profound level of consciousness. Although this consciousness is hidden so deep as to seem unfathomable, it still has the characteristics of changeability, impermanence, and dependent co-origination—just like all the other things in our universe.

Although we are conditioned to see persons or objects as self-powered or self-determined, without a central "self" to power or determine something, there can be no such thing as true *total* self-determination. However, because "other things" are not really separate entities, determination also cannot be wholly attributed to an outside force or being. How, then, does determination of any kind occur? Again, by dependent co-origination. This means that although we are not *wholly* responsible for any single course of action we take in our lives, we also can never fully *avoid* responsibility.

To understand this idea, we might look at ourselves and try to see what constitutes us. Our original body at birth derives from both our parents, each of whom in turn derive from their parents, who are again derived from their parents, and so on ad infinitum. What we are in the present moment is a combination of that genealogy, drawn from infinite generations past, plus all the food, air, water, sunlight, and other environmental factors that have been present during our development in the present lifetime. Environment includes the whole gamut of emotional and intellectual input from our family, television, education, friends, enemies, and any other active source of input we have come across. Our present physical and mental makeup is none other than a combination of all these countless factors. Of course, from the Buddhist perspective, we have to add the influences of the deepest layer of our consciousness (called the *storehouse consciousness*), which has conditioned our current state of being with all the *karmic* impressions from a countless number of prior lifetimes. The implications of this huge amount of accumulated causes and conditions certainly cannot be cap-

tured in the meaning of a single word such as *Bob* or *Mary.* Therefore, in the Buddhist view, each living being is an extremely complex combination of factors, no single one of which is by itself determinative.

KARMA AND REBIRTH

Shakyamuni's refutation of the concept of the immutable soul made *karma* even more important in Buddhism, because without a separate, changeless substrate, there cannot be a place in existence where the law of cause and effect does not operate. All living beings are *nothing but karma.* The concepts of dependent co-origination and *karma* also become closely interlinked in Buddhism, because all formation (that is, dependent co-origination) happens in no other way than through the law of cause and effect. Humans, along with all other beings, are endlessly trapped in the sea of cyclical existence, called *samsara.* Each living being, existing as a cluster of numberless *karmas* from the timeless past, persists in the present as the manifestation of a vast, long-flowing river of *karma.*

Although on the one hand the fluidity of *karma* disallows for the existence of an immutable self, on the other hand it is *karma's* continuity of closely related causes and effects that allows for the appearance of distinctive and relatively constant features that might lead us to mistakenly assume the existence of an immutable self. Through the flow of *karma* continuity is maintained, because like causes bring about like results. For example, although we are continually creating our world anew, and we might be able to bring about minor changes in our mental and physical habits within the next few years, we cannot decide in the next moment to turn into a cat. Thus, the law of *karma* plays a total role in the development of what a living being will turn into in the future. Again, because there is no eternal, unchanging ego or self within living beings, each of us is *nothing but karma.* When people appear at birth with prominent natural inborn abilities, it is because these abilities have been cultivated through many lifetimes.

NIRVANA

The notion of the generation of beings through the modes of *karma* and dependent co-origination can be seen as a way of explaining the meaning of the Second Noble Truth, the Noble Truth of Arising. But given the Buddha's position that all is *karma*/dependent co-origination and nothing else, how is such a state as cessation *(nirvana)* or enlightenment explained? The meaning of *nirvana* is "cessation" *(nirodha)*, the annulment of all conditioned thoughts. Thus, *nirvana* is not the attainment of some worldly good or exalted state of consciousness but the cessation of conditioning itself. What sort of state is the cessation of conditioning? This is one of the most difficult aspects of Buddhism to understand.

Buddhist teachers assert that because *nirvana* is beyond all conditioning and causation, it is also beyond all mental and linguistic constructs and thus cannot be described through language. For this reason, they often answer questions about the nature of *nirvana* with metaphor or with silence. The difficulty of describing the state of *nirvana* is sometimes compared with a frog's attempt to explain its experience of dry land to a tadpole, which completely lacks the frame of reference to comprehend the frog's descriptions. We might say that *nirvana* is the cessation of all kinds of discriminations between subject and object. Because the normal waking consciousness of unenlightened people operates almost solely through such discriminations, there can be no framework with which to communicate the experience of *nirvana* to a person in the ordinary unenlightened consciousness. According to Shakyamuni, the only way to truly understand the meaning of *nirvana* is to experience it for oneself. Because of this, Buddhism, despite its profound philosophy, has always been a tradition rooted in direct experience.

FURTHER DEVELOPMENTS IN INDIAN BUDDHIST DOCTRINE: MAHAYANISM

What we have discussed so far are the basic doctrinal themes of early Indian Buddhism, roughly equivalent to that which is called Nikaya Buddhism.

Around the time of the start of the common era, a new Buddhist movement began to develop, which called itself **Mahayana,** meaning "great vehicle" (see also the extended discussion in the "History of Buddhism" section). The key characteristic of the Mahayana reform movement was its universalistic attitude—its stress on the fact that Buddhist beliefs and practice were intended for, and effective with, all sorts of people, not only monks and nuns living in monasteries. This new emphasis in Mahayana doctrine toward universalism was supported by some major reinterpretation of the earlier metaphysics.

NONDUALITY   A problem to which Mahayana philosophy was extremely sensitive was that of **duality.** Duality refers to all kinds of conceptual separations that occur in pairs in the discriminating human consciousness. Buddhism sees dichotomies such as creator/creature, divinity/human, life/death, and subject/object as basically erroneous, and therefore proposes to offer a method to correct these errors. In this vein the Buddhist notion of "ignorance," regarded as the most fundamental human problem, does not refer to a lack of knowledge about any specific fact. Rather, ignorance means that the person is trapped in the habitual condition of seeing things dualistically, which is in turn the root cause of entrapment within cyclic existence. When Shakyamuni had originally proposed his theory of no-self, he was trying to undo the dualism that had been created between the human and its "divinity"—the eternal soul. He was attempting to close the gap between ordinary suffering consciousness and enlightenment, and he saw the dualistic tendency as a barrier to this attainment.

Despite the fact that such concepts as dependent co-origination and no-self were intended to overcome dualistic tendencies in thinking, the fact that discrimination existed between the clergy and lay practitioners was evidence that dualistic patterns of thought still exercised strong influence within Buddhism. One of the major dichotomies was that of the distinction between the suffering realm of cyclic existence, which was associated with the outside world, and the pure world of enlightenment, which was associated with the *sangha* (the community of monks and nuns), and especially the *arhats* (pure, meditating monks who have eradicated all selfish tendencies and transcended the world of cyclic suffering). Mahayanists asserted that such a dichotomy was, according to the original Buddhist teaching, untenable. They proposed instead, through their rereading of the scriptures, that the nature of cyclic existence was equal to the nature of *nirvana*—that in essence, there was no difference between the two. This conclusion in turn led to the stance that at the absolute level there is no metaphysical distinction that could be shown between defilement and purity, and therefore those living the holy life in the monasteries have no reason to consider themselves superior to any lay practitioner. On what basis, however, could such nondualistic claims be made?

THE TEACHING OF EMPTINESS   The reformist position of equality was supported by a powerful new philosophical tool, which was a further extension of the concept of dependent co-origination. This tool was the principle of **emptiness** (Sanskrit *shunyata*), which is at once the most important and yet the most elusive notion to be grasped in understanding Mahayana Buddhism.

Through the concepts of no-self and dependent co-origination, Shakyamuni had attempted to refute the concept of an eternal and isolable self in living beings. In the minds of Mahayana thinkers, however, this interrogation of rigid thought constructs by the earlier Indian thinkers had not gone far enough. The Mahayanists pointed out that although Buddhist metaphysics had come up with a method for disproving the existence of a distinct and eternal ego, it seemed that Buddhists still believed in the self-sustained existence of the surrounding external objects—all those things that we perceive with our senses. The fact that these external objects were regarded as possessing their own intrinsic reality directly affected the way people conceptualized their world, so they still ended up getting stuck in dichotomies, such as subject/object, existence/nonexistence, and enlightened/unenlightened.

The Mahayana thinkers took note of the fact that the mistakenly conditioned human mind has a powerful tendency to attach to any kind of object, whether that object be sensory or conceptual, and to assign a rigid "reality-value" to it. It is precisely because of our habit of assigning reality (via naming) to all of the objects and concepts we come into contact with that we are able to function in the world. And in the realm of everyday activity we are going to need to agree that something has "good" or "evil" value. A serial killer must be recognized as a serial killer, and a saint must be recognized as a saint. On a simpler level, a table must be recognized as a table, and a chair as a chair. If we did not agree on these things, the world would be a mass of confusion.

From the standpoint of Buddhist emptiness, however, none of these designations has constant validity; each of them is ultimately arbitrary. We regard things as unitary, or as being self-existent, only because our consciousnesses are so easily trapped by the process of naming things. The four-legged, platformed object in my kitchen has been given the name *table*, but this designation is arbitrary—the object is not really a "table" for a number of reasons. First, it has more than a couple hundred other names applied to it in the various languages of the world, and none of these has any privilege of greater validity than the others. Second, the table does not have any single, unifying characteristic. Of course it needs to be flat, and it needs (usually) to have at least four legs to be functional. It also needs to fall within certain size constraints. A piece of furniture with four legs and a flat surface cannot be a table if the top of its flat surface is only 1 inch square—or if it is 1,000 miles square. For a single simple object, such as a table, we could go into a long list of factors that contribute to "tableness," but if we tried to find a single "essence" of tableness, we would fail. Therefore, what we have arbitrarily designated as a *table* is not really a table—it is a collection of causes and conditions that we have, for the sake of convenience, labeled a *table* and to which we have then unconsciously assigned a permanent reality-value. However, it is also not anything else but a table, and because it fits the conditions by which we normally define "tableness," we can, and should, call it a *table*. This kind of logic, which says "X is not X; therefore, it is called X," is the teaching pattern of one of the most widely studied Mahayana scriptures, the *Diamond Sutra*.

In a contrasting example from early Western philosophy, Plato stated in his *Republic* that beyond the physical form of a table, there is an eternal "form" or "idea" of table that exists in the realm of the intellect, that is more real, and that serves as a conceptual template for all tables. A Buddhist would disagree with this, claiming from the standpoint of dependent co-origination that any concept of a table would be, just like the physical table itself, dependently originated. The conceptual template of a table is as equally based on a person's experience with concrete tables as is the creation of an actual table based on a conceptual template.

In the same way, dependent co-origination/emptiness in Buddhism applies to all things: artificially created objects, animals, plants, molecules, atoms, concepts, emotions, worlds, and universes. None of these things possesses a singular locatable "self-nature." All exist only as the combination of various factors. Thus, in the Mahayana view, the two concepts of dependent co-origination and emptiness can be understood as two ways of talking about the same thing.

THE TWO TRUTHS AND EXPEDIENT MEANS As the preceding discussion has shown, Buddhism, especially in its scholarly and contemplative forms, is a religion that seems to deny reality-value to language. This being the case, we might justifiably wonder how any teaching is possible at all. This is a problem that teachers of Buddhist doctrine felt a pressing need to deal with, and they did so through the doctrine of Expedient Means and the Two Truth theory. **Expedient means** refers to the flexible usage of various strategies in teaching, even if such strategies are ultimately not true. This is comparable to the case where a parent lies to a child for the child's best interests. The **Two Truths** are

the absolute truth, which is beyond linguistic expression, and the relative truth, which occurs through the use of concepts and language. The main point made through these two closely related strategies is that despite the fact that the ultimate Buddhist reality is beyond all linguistic constructs, enlightened teachers must nonetheless attempt to use linguistic and other phenomenal methods to attempt to awaken unenlightened people, even if these methods lack ultimate validity. Buddhist teachers have the authority to construct whatever provisional teachings are necessary to gradually lead people to the point where they can accept and understand higher levels of truth, until ultimately they can make the leap to transcend all conceptual constructs and attain the "absolute truth." By contrast, the expedient methods are considered only "relative truths."

The popular metaphor of the raft is used to illustrate this point. When one needs to cross a river, one builds a raft to do so. But once one reaches the other side, having no more need for the raft, one discards it. As in this story, Buddhist teachers allow students relative truths but admonish them not to become attached to these truths as ultimate verities or to take them as the final experience. Within this framework, any Buddhist teaching (and certain non-Buddhist teachings) can be considered as correct up to a certain point. Ultimately, however, the concepts of the Four Noble Truths, dependent co-origination, and even emptiness must be regarded as provisional expedients—useful to a point but not capable of fully expressing the Buddhist enlightenment experience.

BUDDHIST PRACTICE

Because of the wide diffusion of Buddhism across cultures and times and the many sectarian interpretations, practices are extremely diverse and difficult to summarize in compact form. What practice consists of in Buddhism (as well as other religions) also differs according to the viewpoint of the beholder. Anthropologists and sociologists of religion want to know about everyday practices carried out by lay believers, as well as how such practices are related to, and interact with, local cultural norms. They may want to know, for example, what kinds of ceremonies and rituals the local Buddhist temple performs for its members. How does it handle weddings, funerals, royal coronations, and the like? What kind of prayer and ritual are lay believers encouraged to perform, either in the home or at the temple on Sunday meetings?

To function and survive as a major religious institution, Buddhism has had to be able to satisfy these kinds of needs in the various cultures it has penetrated over the course of its history. Adapting to local customs, monastic leaders have played the role of priests, fortune-tellers, charismatic *gurus,* family counselors, court advisors, and so on. From the start in India, local Buddhist temples became an integral part of local communities. The modern manifestations of this tendency can be clearly seen today in the Theravada Buddhist countries of Sri Lanka and Southeast Asia, where Buddhist temples and monasteries often function as community centers where people gather for the performance of ritual, instruction in the *dhamma* and meditation, and other activities.

Buddhist leaders themselves have also often become deeply involved in the affairs of government. This was especially the case in the ancient kingdoms and empires of premodern East Asia, when royal courts accepted and encouraged Buddhism as the official state religion. Leaders of the religious establishment replied in kind by offering their official religious sanction in the form of prayers for the safety and continuity of the royal house. Along with such privileges also came the occasional risk that the Buddhist establishment, or at least certain members of that establishment, might be used as scapegoats in the event something went wrong. Consequently, the Buddhist communities in most East Asian countries (north and south) also were the objects of occasional purges and repression.

RITUAL PRACTICES AND PRECEPTS

The most widely observable form of Buddhist practice is that of the rituals, ceremonies and festivals that are carried out by the Buddhist clergy, both within the temple and out in the local communities. The day-to-day living of monks, nuns, and trainees is in itself highly ritualized; the clergy generally follow a strictly set daily schedule of waking, eating, chanting, meditating, and so forth. This ritualistic lifestyle is further elaborated by the maintenance of precepts that are practiced with regularity throughout the Buddhist world.

The most basic set of moral regulations, which are practiced by both lay believers and the clergy, are the Five Precepts. The first precept is to refrain from killing living beings; the crime is to know that something is a living being, intend to kill it, attempt to do so, and succeed. The second is to refrain from taking what has not been given—in other words, not to steal. The third precept is to refrain from sexual misconduct, which concerns intercourse with an improper partner (another's spouse, someone betrothed, a member of the clergy, and so on), as well as unsuitable places and times for intercourse with one's own spouse. The fourth precept is to refrain from untrue speech. One should neither intentionally say what is untrue nor claim to know something that one does not know. The fifth precept is abstinence from drinking alcohol—mainly because its consumption engenders the tendency to commit other sins.

After these five, members of the clergy have five more precepts that are to be strictly observed. These are abstinence from the following: (1) eating after noon; (2) watching dancing, singing, and shows; (3) adorning oneself with garlands, perfumes, or ointments; (4) using a high bed; and (5) receiving gold and silver.

Beyond this regulated daily behavior, the daily lives of the members of the *sangha* are punctuated throughout the year by a number of ceremonies and festivals. One of the most commonly held rituals is that of ordination into the *sangha.* Men and women who are at least twenty years of age, and

A Japanese Buddhist monk meditating.

muni firmly believed that metaphysical speculation by itself could not bring about the full result of attaining liberation. He was thus noted for his reluctance to engage in empty debates with logicians who came to challenge his views on *karma*, reincarnation, no-self, and enlightenment, and many times he answered his questioners with silence. The main reason for the Buddha's reluctance was that he considered intellectual debate to be of limited use when it came to the matter of ending the suffering of sentient beings. Consequently, he preferred to characterize himself not as a philosopher but as a good doctor who had the remedy for the cure of the suffering of the world.

Another important aspect of the concept of *practice* in Buddhism is that it is often difficult to separate beliefs (or doctrine) and practice from each other. We recall that the first of the eight aspects of the Eightfold Path was called Right View. The practice of Right View means that one should assiduously apply the correct perception of reality in all aspects of one's life. The correct perception of reality is, in turn, all basic Buddhist beliefs, such as impermanence, no-self, dependent co-origination, and the like. In this sense, then, the category of Right View (thinking in accordance with reality) is one that bridges both the domain of belief and the domain of practice.

who have decided that they want to leave their worldly station in order to fully dedicate their lives to the practice of Buddhism in the monastic setting, may apply to the temple of their choice. Once the temple is satisfied with the sincerity of their intention and their capability of following the monastic life, they will be ordained in a ceremony in which their heads are shaved, they receive their robe, and they accept the ten precepts.

One of the most prominent of the yearly festivals that are held in the various sects is that of the celebration of the Buddha's birthday. This is an event that usually draws large participation from the lay community. Many of the other festivals held around the year in Buddhist countries are derived originally from local customs into which the Buddhist tradition has become integrated.

PRACTICE TOWARD LIBERATION

A stricter meaning of *practice* is the concrete training aimed at liberation, which is a thread that binds all forms of monastic Buddhism together. The stress on practice has always been paramount in Buddhism, and it was clear from the outset that Shakya-

THE THREE DISCIPLINES

Buddhist teachers have traditionally divided the Eightfold Path into three aspects, called the Three Disciplines. They are morality *(shila)*, concentration *(samadhi)*, and wisdom *(prajna)*. Within the discipline of morality are the three practices of Right Speech, Right Action, and Right Livelihood. Within the discipline of concentration are the three practices of Right Effort, Right Mindfulness, and Right Concentration. Within the discipline of wisdom are Right View and Right Intention. A proper balance of the Three Disciplines is considered necessary to attain enlightenment. A person practicing only morality and concentration will have a good conscience and strong attentiveness but, lacking the right wisdom, might be led down useless or harmful paths. Someone practicing concentration and wisdom but lacking a solid grounding in morality might become selfish and given to excesses of personal power and abuse of others. Someone practicing morality and wisdom might be ethically disciplined and knowledgeable about doctrine but, without the power of concentration, would lack the focus of energy necessary to carry himself or herself through to enlightenment.

Although all three disciplines are supposed to be practiced together, most texts list the three in an order of priority, with morality first, concentration second, and wisdom third. Morality is placed before concentration with the reasoning that one cannot really practice settled concentration while one's mind is continually agitated by the effects of morally discordant activities. Concentration is placed before wisdom because intellectual knowledge without the power of concentration is considered useless, possibly leading to a state of mental dissipation.

THE TWO ASPECTS OF MEDITATION

Once the practice of moral discipline is firmly in place in the practitioner's life, emphasis turns to wisdom and concentration, which combined together constitute the distinctive Buddhist approach to sitting meditation. Sitting meditation is a characteristic practice that can be seen in almost all forms of monastic Buddhism, regardless of culture or time period.

The schools of Buddhism that have focused on the practice of sitting meditation have traditionally distinguished between two major avenues of meditation, which are closely related to the character of the last two disciplines of the Three Disciplines, concentration and wisdom. Most Buddhist programs of meditation, regardless of sectarian orientation, start out beginners with the practice of a meditation called *stabilizing meditation,* or **shamatha.** This term is related in meaning to *samadhi,* referring to a state of mental calmness and stability wherein one can hold an object of concentration in one's mind for long periods of time. The object of concentration can vary, depending

upon the method of the particular teacher. It can be a visual or conceptual object, but often, especially in the beginning, it is simply one's own breathing process: one learns to train concentration by attempting to count breaths. This type of meditation is not uniquely Buddhist. Stabilizing meditation practices were carried out in India before the time of Shakyamuni and are still practiced today in a variety of non-Buddhist traditions throughout the world. The neophyte Buddhist meditator usually focuses exclusively on stabilizing meditation for at least several weeks, and as long as several months, until his or her ability to do focused concentration is well tuned.

What Buddhists consider distinctive about their meditation system is the combination of stabilizing meditation and a form of practice called *observational meditation.* Whereas stabilizing meditation is related to the concentration aspect of the path, observational meditation is associated with the wisdom aspect. After having cultivated stabilizing meditation to the degree that one can maintain steady concentration, this concentration is not taken as an end in itself but is used in the application of the contemplation of a Buddhist perception of reality, such as the Four Noble Truths, no-self, or dependent co-origination. In Mahayana Buddhist practice, one might carry out a meditation on emptiness or compassion. Because of this characteristic, we also might characterize observational meditation as a concentrated exercise in the usage of the Right View.

The practice of stabilizing meditation by itself is said to be capable of generating many positive effects: strong concentration, relaxation, confidence in the face of difficulty, stress release, and the promotion of general physical and mental health. But what Shakyamuni discovered through his own trial and error is that the effectiveness of stabilizing meditation has limitations. Although it can bring about positive mental and physical conditions, and even exalted spiritual states, by itself it cannot bring about complete enlightenment. In fact, if practiced with an incorrect attitude for too long, stabilizing meditation can even result in stubbornness and stupidity. It is for this reason that the practice of stabilizing meditation must eventually be combined with observational meditation, in order to incorporate the Buddhist wisdom, which is necessary to completely destroy all delusory views.

However, it is also considered wasteful, and even harmful, to remain engaged only in observational meditation. Mere intellectual understanding by itself is powerless in attaining enlightenment, because the power of the profound paradoxes contained in the Buddhist analytical formulas cannot be brought fully into play unless one has the strong concentration power necessary to hold these paradoxes before one's mind with total concentration for full periods of sitting—as long as an hour or more. Another danger of remaining engaged in only the intellectual study of these "right views" is that one might, in gaining an intellectual understanding of them, deceive oneself into believing that one has already fully actualized these understandings and reached a level of transformation. In this case progress stops, and one might even bring harm to others by supposing that one is now capable of acting as a spiritual guide.

Therefore, teachers of Buddhist meditation in most of its various cultural manifestations instruct their students in the balanced use of stabilizing meditation and observational meditation. The two techniques are to be used not only in a balanced manner over long periods of time but also in every individual sitting period. If, during sitting meditation, one holds too strongly to stabilizing meditation, one's mind may become dull and sink; conversely, if one depends too heavily on observational meditation, one's mind can become agitated and scattered. The meditator needs to stay aware and maintain a keen balance between the two kinds of meditation. The practices of stabilizing meditation and observational meditation are thus characterized as "two wings of a bird." If one or the other is lacking, the attainment of enlightenment is considered to be impossible.

WISDOM AND COMPASSION

The Mahayana movement, which emerged during the early centuries C.E., brought with it its new

hero (the **bodhisattva**) and its new metaphysical teaching (emptiness). The term *bodhisattva* literally means "enlightening being." It refers to a practitioner who has advanced far enough in practice to have achieved some level of enlightenment but has not yet reached Buddhahood. The special characteristic of the *bodhisattva* is his or her compassion, because he or she makes a vow not to enter *nirvana* until all sentient beings have been saved. Mahayana also outlined a new program of practice for its adherents in lieu of the Eightfold Path. This new program was composed of six parts, each called a *paramita* (perfected practice). The *paramita*s were understood to be "perfected" as long as they were engaged in from the standpoint of emptiness—that is, a position that transcends dualistic structures. The Six Perfections are (1) the Perfection of Giving, (2) the Perfection of Morality, (3) the Perfection of Patience, (4) the Perfection of Effort, (5) the Perfection of Concentration, and (6) the Perfection of Wisdom.

The Perfection of Giving involves the free donation of all of one's mental, physical, and spiritual assets without any thought of recompense. The Perfection of Morality reasserts the moral practices of the Eightfold Path, based further on the understanding that because all things are empty, objects of desire are also empty. The Perfection of Patience is concerned with facing the world and its ups and downs, its agreeable and disagreeable aspects, with equanimity. Seeing all things as equally empty, one is able to pass calmly through both praise and insult. The Perfection of Effort refers to a full development of the spirit of unflagging vigilance and striving in one's efforts toward all aspects of enlightened existence. The Perfection of Concentration refers to the full development of disciplined calming of the mental functions; it also can be called the Perfection of Stabilizing Meditation.

The sixth and most important perfection is the Perfection of Wisdom, or *prajnaparamita*. This is a wisdom that is able to penetrate to the true nature of all things based on the experience of emptiness. Actualizing the Perfection of Wisdom allows for the correct enactment of the other five perfections, because all of them, to truly be "perfect," need a correct experiential insight of emptiness at their base.

Of equal weight with wisdom in the *bodhisattva*'s path is compassion. A new emphasis on compassion by the Mahayana school does not necessarily mean that earlier Buddhist doctrine had completely neglected it, but it is clear that the architects of the new doctrine felt that the altruistic dimension of the religion had been ignored to the degree that it needed more emphasis. Thus, the most important single practice undertaken by the *bodhisattva* is the profound vow to dedicate his or her life to the uplifting of all sentient beings. This means that the *bodhisattva*, ideally, should be the person who goes without fear or regret into the most difficult of situations, giving of himself or herself without limit to others. Not caring about gain or loss, purity or defilement, the *bodhisattva* does not hide in a monastery in a meditative trance but instead goes "downtown" to the clamor of the world, interacting with and helping others selflessly. In this wider sense of the term *bodhisattva*, some Buddhists might even regard an energetic and selfless activist such as Mother Teresa as a *bodhisattva*, even though she was technically not a Buddhist.

In the development of the *bodhisattva*'s deep compassion, wisdom plays an integral part, because it is through the wisdom that understands emptiness that one becomes capable of overcoming one's egoistic tendencies and reaching out to others. The vision of all things as empty is what particularly allows the *bodhisattva* to practice the Perfection of Giving, because he or she is not attached to any possessions. The Perfections of Patience, Morality, and Effort are also only possible through a thoroughgoing vision of the emptiness of all things. Thus, compassion and wisdom go hand in hand, mutually enhancing each other.

ZEN: THE "MEDITATION" SCHOOL

The school that has become most widely known in the West for its practice of meditation is the Zen school. "Zen" is the Japanese pronunciation of a Chinese ideograph that means "meditation" and

that is transliterated **ch'an** in Chinese and *son* in Korean. The Zen schools in China, precursors to those in Korea and Japan, developed their strong practice orientation as a counterreaction to the overly scholastic tendencies that had become characteristic of the Chinese Buddhist schools. The originators of the Zen movement believed that an unbalanced emphasis on scriptural study was counterproductive to the original spirit of the Buddhist tradition, and that it tended to blur the importance of the original purpose of Buddhism—the attainment of enlightenment. Although many Zen monks were extremely literate and studious, writing poetry, essays, and commentaries, most Zen schools down to the present have continued to maintain a solid regimen of seated meditation at the core of their training.

The Zen monasteries in China had originally developed outside the large metropolitan centers without the government support that was offered to the large scriptural study centers. Zen monks needed to procure their own sustenance in the form of food, clothing, water, firewood, and other necessities. Thus, they developed a communal lifestyle inside the monastery with a strong work ethic. One of the first comprehensive codes of monastery operation was written down by the famous Chinese Zen master Pai-chang (749–814), who coined the famous Zen phrase "A day without work is a day without food." According to Pai-chang's biographical sketch, he insisted on doing his share of the gardening work well into his eighties. One time, when his disciples hid his tools in an effort to make him rest, he refused to eat, thus forcing them to allow him to keep making his contribution.

Over the years the Zen schools developed a standardized schedule of daily practice, which is followed to a great degree down to the present, even in newly established Western Zen monasteries. This schedule includes waking early (usually at 3 or 4 A.M.) for an initial scripture chanting and meditation session. After this, practitioners come together for a communal breakfast. The remainder of the day (depending upon the monastery, the season, and the practitioner's own role in the monastery) will be filled with work periods, meditation sessions, and occasional interviews with the master-teacher. The diet of monks and nuns is usually light and vegetarian, and the last meal of the day is lunch. Monks and nuns usually get to bed (after a final meditation session) around 9:00 P.M., leaving approximately six hours for sleep. The main point is the pursuit of a lifestyle centered on the attainment of enlightenment through meditation.

As in a number of other Buddhist meditational training systems, Zen schools usually conduct intensive meditation sessions at predetermined times during the year—for example, the summer meditation retreat, which usually lasts ninety days. During these intensive sessions, practitioners spend as much as twelve hours a day engaged in meditation practice. Therefore, those who enter the monastic system find themselves engaged in a life of difficult training with little comfort. Monks and nuns practicing in training monasteries in East Asia live with few clothes and sleep on wooden boards; they have only the barest amount of heat, even in the middle of winter.

The Zen school developed new forms of Buddhist meditation. Whereas earlier Chinese Zen meditation practice was characterized by the standard combination of stabilizing meditation and observational meditation, during the later T'ang (618–907) and early Sung (960–1127) dynasties, Zen teachers began to promote a new form of meditation that reflected the Chinese emphasis on simplicity, directness, and paradox. This new approach is now commonly referred to by the Japanese term **koan**. Koan, derived from the Chinese word meaning "public case," historically referred to a public hearing on a criminal or civil matter in which a magistrate was called to make a determination. The "public cases" of Zen tradition were stories about interactions in the past between legendary figures—usually famous teachers. Within the story of the interaction is contained the essence of a Buddhist problem of metaphysics or salvation, which the listener is to contemplate with full concentration with the intent of offering a solution. Unlike the solution of a mathematical problem or any other problem where one suddenly realizes the "answer," how-

ever, the "solution" to a *koan* is not a simple rational explanation. The gist of *koan* practice is in the process itself. That is to say, it is during the act of the unrelenting struggle to find the answer to the *koan* that the meditator undergoes a deep change in consciousness, which results in enlightenment. The actual linguistic formulations of the answer to a *koan* can be various. What is important is the personal realization within the mind and body of the meditator.

The best-known *koan* in East Asia is the *wu koan*, the first of the forty *koan* contained in the *koan* collection entitled the *Gateless Barrier*. In many Zen training systems, it is the first *koan* taught to students. (And in some systems, it is the first and last!) This *koan* is located within the story of the interaction between the famous Zen master Chao-chou and one of the monks who was studying with him at his monastery. In this story, the student, a monk who had already been practicing and studying Zen for a considerable time, had not yet attained enlightenment and was experiencing some doubts about the doctrine that all living beings contain the Buddha-nature (the capacity to become a *buddha*)—in other words, that all beings have enlightenment as the basic quality of their minds, and thus, actually bringing about the enlightened condition is just a matter of properly manifesting that originally enlightened mind. The student's doubts about this doctrine apparently came to a head at the time when a dog was passing by. The monk spontaneously asked his teacher, Chao-chou, "Does the dog also have the Buddha-nature?" With equal spontaneity, Chao-chou answered, *"Wu!"* which means "no," "not there," or "nonexistent."

There is a serious problem with this answer, because all of Mahayana Buddhist practice is based on the fact that *all living beings* possess the innate capacity to become a Buddha (Buddha-nature). This doctrine has been explicitly stated in a number of Mahayana scriptures. Such being the case, how could a renowned Buddhist master such as Chao-chou respond by saying, "no"? Or perhaps we should ask, What does Chao-chou's "no" actually indicate? A student who is assigned a *koan* is expected to investigate it not only during formal sitting meditation periods but also in all waking moments. Advanced students are expected to keep investigating the *koan* even during the deepest of sleep. Students who are training in a monastery environment also feel external pressure to penetrate the *koan* beyond the level of their own motivation for enlightenment, because they must periodically meet with the teacher of the monastery so that he or she may check their progress. The teacher, in turn, should be capable of discerning whether students' interpretations of the *koan* come from imitation of others, intellectual rationalization, or their own genuine realization. For this reason, regular personal interaction with a qualified teacher is considered extremely important in most branches of Zen.

MEDITATION IN SOUTHEAST ASIA

Zen is not the only branch of Buddhism that pursues an active program of meditation. In the **Theravada** Buddhist countries of Southeast Asia, such as Sri Lanka, Myanmar (formerly Burma), and Thailand, large numbers of the local lay population actively engage in meditation, and such practice has been in the culture long enough that engagement in meditation by laypersons is often accepted by society at large. Donald Swearer, in *The Buddhist World of Southeast Asia*, reports that participation in meditation sessions by lay practitioners is widespread and even seems to be on the increase.[2] The meditation practiced in these countries is not *koan* but rather various combinations of the stabilizing meditation and observational meditation described earlier.

Further, the definition of *practice* for many leaders of the Theravada community in these Southeast Asian countries extends far beyond that of personal meditation practice or even of providing services for the lay community in the form of performing rituals and religious instruction. Many members of the Southeast Asian Theravada Buddhist establishment have been involved deeply in their country's political, social, economic, and ecological struggles—as participants in what is loosely defined as "engaged Buddhism." The rationale

A Buddhist devotee prays and offers incense at the Dharma Bakti Chinese Temple, Jakarta, Indonesia (1995).

for such activity lies in the belief that the Buddhist principles of kindness, truth, harmony, and cooperation need to be manifested in the everyday world of human affairs. Thus, the presence of the Buddhist *sangha* in society, as well as the participation of lay society in the Buddhist *sangha,* is active and widespread. We will speak a bit more of this later.

It is probably safe to say that meditation-oriented Buddhism, whether it be South Asian *vipassana* (observational meditation) or East Asian Zen, has been widely regarded as the most "mainstream" of the forms of Buddhist liberative practice. But there are other currents of practice that have commanded the attention of large groups of followers in certain areas of Asia. Two of the most noteworthy of these are Esoteric Buddhism and Chanting Buddhism.

ESOTERIC BUDDHIST PRACTICE

Esoteric Buddhism is known by three terms: Vajrayana, Mantrayana, and Tantrayana, all of which are related to the others in meaning. The *yana* in each of these terms means "vehicle," as it does in Mahayana. *Vajra* means "diamondlike" or "indestructible," referring to the power of the Buddha's wisdom. *Mantra* means "magical spell," and *tantra* refers to the texts in which the *vajra* and *mantra* teachings are contained. Simply put, Esoteric Buddhism is a form of the religion that, rather than relying on the triple path of morality, concentration, and wisdom to achieve the goal of liberation, relies upon *yogic* and ritual practices that are intended to bring the body and psyche of the practitioner into alignment with some sort of supramundane force or deity. Through this alignment practitioners gain magical powers that can serve various purposes, including the enhancement of their vital energies and, most important, the ability to sever all conditioned connections with the mundane world and attain liberation.

Esotericism in Buddhism has always developed out of close interaction with elements of indigenous religion in the regions into which Buddhism entered. The earliest forms of Vajrayana, which developed in India starting from the third century C.E., show a very close relationship to similar trends in Hinduism at the time. Later on, when Tantrayana gained popularity in Tibet, it was also strongly influenced by local forms of Tibetan religion.

Esoteric Buddhism is divided into four categories: Action Tantras, Performance Tantras, Yoga Tantras, and Unsurpassed Yoga Tantras. In the Action and Performance Tantras, students are taught such practices as the study and visualization of *mandalas*, the recitation of *mantras*, and the performance of specialized body postures, all of which were intended to bring about the enhancement of personal power. In the Yoga Tantras, one also practices ritual, but it is specially designed ritual intended to bring forth a condition of unity with all the magical Buddhas of the Vajra-realm.

It is the fourth form, the Unsurpassed Yoga Tantras, that draw the greatest attention in terms of their apparent variance from the more standardized practices of Buddhism, such as morality and meditation. These practices seek to go directly against many of the established norms of the religion; they include practices of sexual *yoga* and direct efforts to negate moral/ethical conditioning, which practitioners do in the attempt to break through to enlightenment. Tantrayana, or Tantric Buddhism, received its greatest attention and development in Tibet, where it remains to the present one of the most influential currents in the religion. This form of Buddhism also had a significant degree of influence in Southeast Asia, as well as in Japan, where it is known as Shingon.

CHANTING: PURE LAND BUDDHIST PRACTICE

Another prominent form of Buddhism that departs from the meditation-centric form is that which is based primarily in chanting practice. In terms of actual practice in Northeast Asia, probably the most popular form of Buddhist devotion is chanting, such as the Pure Land sect's chanting of the name of Amitabha Buddha or the Nichiren sect's chanting of passages from the *Lotus Sutra*.

Pure Land Buddhism has its roots in a text called the *Pure Land Sutra*. This scripture tells a story about a Buddha of the distant past called Amitabha, the Buddha of the Pure Land or Western Paradise (a type of heaven into which people may be reborn). The *Pure Land Sutra* contains a description of what the Pure Land is like and a mention of who will be born there and how. Amitabha makes a number of vows toward the salvation of all sentient beings, the most important of which are his eighteenth and nineteenth vows. The eighteenth vow states that those who think of Buddha ten times will be reborn in the Pure Land. The nineteenth vow states that when a person dies who has practiced hard enough, Amitabha will come and take that person to the Pure Land. Various interpretations were made of these vows, but the general result was that chanting the name of a Buddha or *bodhisattva* became the common practice. People chant the name of Shakyamuni, Maitreya, and Avalokiteshvara, but the most popular is Amitabha.

Therefore, we can characterize Pure Land as a form of Buddhism that advocates the attainment of liberation, or the attainment of a rebirth in a Pure Land (a heaven), through the practice of the verbal or mental repetition of the name of Amitabha Buddha. Pure Land Buddhism is an interesting phenomenon because at first it may seem to deviate from the teachings of nonduality evident in Mahayana, and especially Zen, Buddhism. The attitudes taken by Pure Land practitioners toward Amitabha Buddha seem much closer to the devotional attitudes taken by Jews, Christians, and Muslims than to the characteristic Buddhist analytical/philosophical approach.

However, realistically speaking, we must acknowledge the difficulties of comprehending such a difficult teaching as that of Buddhist emptiness by the philosophically untrained mind. We can imagine how hard it must have been for everyday people, especially illiterate and uneducated people, to understand abstruse Buddhist philosophy during the period when Buddhism was introduced in East Asia. We might understand, then, how such a teaching as Pure Land could arise in response to this problem. If large segments of the population could not follow complex doctrinal formulas or were in a situation where it was neither practical nor desirable to enter a monastery and devote themselves single-mindedly to seated meditation, what kind of Buddhist teaching could they be offered? For these people, a teaching that revolves around the simple chanting of the name of Amitabha Buddha with a guarantee of a heavenly rebirth was a viable alternative.

Pure Land practice also has deeper underlying religious underpinnings in addition to mere simplicity of application. The early founders of the Pure Land school were philosophically sophisticated people with a deep religious consciousness who turned to Pure Land practice only after strenuous efforts at the attainment of enlightenment through other Buddhist methods. They experienced the degree to which the path toward liberation is fraught with subtle hindrances caused by egoism. As long as there is a consciousness of "self" actively trying to attain liberation, various impediments arising from egocentric consciousness tend to obstruct practice. This situation is understood in Pure Land theory as the impossibility of bringing oneself to salvation through "self-power." Pure Land adherents believe that because it is impossible for an ignorant, egoistic self to save

itself, it is necessary to depend on an "other power" to do this. Hence it is necessary for devotees to call upon Amitabha or some other powerful Buddha or *bodhisattva*.

HISTORY OF BUDDHISM

Buddhism is one of the most widespread of the world's religions in terms of the number of cultures that it has permeated. Originating in India in the sixth century C.E., Buddhism eventually spread to the north and northeast to central Asia, Tibet, China, Mongolia, Korea, and Japan. At the same time, it penetrated to the southeast, deeply influencing the cultures of Sri Lanka, Burma, Cambodia, Laos, and Vietnam. In the past century Buddhism has also made a significant impact in the Americas and Europe.

FORMATION OF THE BUDDHIST CANON

During the Buddha's life, no one made a written account of his sermons, so there were initially no records for the disciples to follow. This lack of material required the formation of councils to establish a canonical standard for the Buddha's teachings. At these councils, leaders attempted to reconstruct as best as possible the format and content of the Buddha's sermons, which they began to gather together in the form of "basket-collections" called *pitakas*.

The *pitaka*, purported to be the actual sermons of Shakyamuni, were labeled with the term *sutra* (Pali: *sutta*), which means "scripture." Thus, the sermon collection came to be known in Sanskrit as the *sutra-pitaka*. The rules of discipline for the monks and nuns were also written down and assembled in the "disciplines collection," or *vinaya-pitaka*. During the centuries after Shakyamuni's death, eminent Buddhist thinkers continued to express themselves in written commentaries on extant Buddhist *sutras* or in the form of their own original treatises. As time passed, these writings were gathered under the rubric of *abhidharma* (Pali: *abhidamma*), meaning "beyond the *dharma*" or "concerning the *dharma*." In its final form, then, the Buddhist canon was composed of three sections, or *pitaka:* the *vinaya-pitaka*, the *sutra-pitaka*, and the *abhidharma-pitaka.* Together, these three were named the **Tripitaka** (the Sankrit rendering of the term), or "three baskets." The *Tripitaka* remains down to the present the name for the authoritative canon for the Buddhist religion. However, there are a number of versions of the *Tripitaka*, such as the Pali *Tipitaka*, the Tibetan *Tripitaka*, and the Chinese (present version compiled in Japan) and Korean *Tripitakas*. Although there is considerable overlap between these canonical collections, each of them also contains a number of texts that are not found in the other versions. Table 5.1 identifies the major canonical collections of Buddhist scripture.

Moreover, because it is the aim of Buddhism to continue to enlighten all beings, the tradition considers it entirely possible for a new Buddha to appear in any age or culture. If such a person were to appear, his or her words might well be considered worthy of further inclusion into the *Tripitaka.* Therefore the Buddhist *Tripitaka* is called an *open canon,* meaning that theoretically it can still be added to. We should also note that the scriptures were not all compiled in writing soon after the Buddha's passing away. In fact, the Buddhist teachings probably developed as an oral tradition until the first century B.C.E. Thus, by the time they were finally compiled in written form, the contents of the canon had also been influenced by the various developments and transformations that had taken place within branches of Indian Buddhism for four to five centuries.

THE BIRTH OF MAHAYANA BUDDHISM

During the two to three centuries before and after the birth of Christ, Buddhism underwent a major sectarian break, as a segment of the *sangha* broke off to form a new faction that would eventually receive the name Mahayana, which means "great vehicle." Because Buddhist historical records from this period of time are scanty, we do not have detailed information about the actual process of this schism. The version of the story told from the Mahayanist side is that the Buddhist establishment had grown narrow and rigid in the scope of its mission. The general view of modern scholars is that a breach of understanding between the Buddhist clergy and influential lay practitioners had led to the exclusion of the lay practitioners from participation in many important activities. The *sangha* had become elitist in the sense that only the ordained clergy in the monasteries were considered capable of attaining *nirvana.*

As a reaction to these conditions, the new Mahayana school emphasized equality of all beings in the Buddha-nature, based on the new metaphysical concept called *shunyata*, usually translated into English as *emptiness* (see the discussion on pp. 298–299 in the "Buddhist Practice" section). The Mahayana group asserted that Buddhism should be for the purpose of the salvation of all sentient beings, not just a select few who were capable of renouncing the world for the sake of meditation. Because the Mahayanists viewed their own mission as universal, they helped to identify their own cause by labeling the previous tradition with the pejorative term **hinayana,** which means "small vehicle."

The writings of the Mahayana group stressed three main points in the development of the group's doctrine: a heightened sense of compassion; a deeper understanding of the "empty" character of existence, and the creation of a new exemplary practitioner named the *bodhisattva.* The *bodhisattva* contrasted with the **arhat,** the model practitioner of the earlier tradition. Before this time, the term *arhat* (worthy of respect) was applied to a person who had overcome all afflictions and had achieved *nirvana*—a pure, meditating monk or nun who had destroyed all of his or her evil and selfish tendencies. Such a person had done this by listening to the Buddha's sermons and by meditating on the Four Noble Truths.

According to the Mahayanists, however, the *arhat*'s enlightenment was based upon a selfish practice—a practice aimed primarily at self-purification. The *bodhisattva,* in contrast to the *arhat,* was said

Table 5.1

BUDDHIST SCRIPTURE: MAJOR CANONICAL COLLECTIONS

Pali Canon (*Tipitaka*)	Texts written in the vernacular Indian language of Pali, composed of three divisions: *vinaya* (discipline) *sutta* (scripture) *abhidhamma* (scholarly works) This was the canon used by Theravada Buddhists in Southeast Asia and Sri Lanka (see Table 5.2, "Major Buddhist Schools"). Based on the venerable Indian oral canon, the Pali canon was first transcribed in the early centuries C.E. and later translated into local languages such as Thai and Burmese.
Tibetan Canon	Texts mostly translated from Sanskrit, falling into two major divisions: *kanjur* (translations of the Buddha's words) *tenjur* (translations of the teachings) Translation of texts into Tibetan began as early as the eighth century C.E., but the canon was not fully completed until the fourteenth century.
Chinese Canon	Texts translated from Sanskrit (starting in the first century C.E.), along with texts later composed in Chinese. The Chinese canon consists of the twenty-four divisions of early Indian texts, later Indian Mahayana texts, and texts of the new Mahayana schools that developed in China. The Chinese edition, completed in 983 C.E., served as the basis for the later Korean and Japanese canons.
Korean Canon	The Korean edition of the Chinese canon, carved on woodblocks at Haeinsa Temple during the thirteenth century C.E. The Korean edition served as the basis for later East Asian editions of the canon.
Japanese (Taisho) Canon	Compiled between 1924 and 1935, during the Taisho Era, based primarily on the Korean canon. Bound in modern book format, the Japanese edition serves as the canonical standard for most scholarly work in modern East Asian Buddhism.
Digital Canons	The current conversion of all the Buddhist collections to digital format for distribution on the Internet and CD-ROM. These new digital versions of the canon allow students to find textual passages and make comparisons instantaneously. Thus, they are revolutionizing the methodologies of Buddhist textual studies.

to base his or her practice in the task of enlightening others through the teaching of nondiscrimination between the pure world of liberation *(nirvana)* and the defiled world of cyclical suffering *(samsara)*. To be considered a *bodhisattva*, a person needed not only to have reached a high level of mental attainment but also to have taken the vow not to enter *nirvana* until all sentient beings in the universe had been saved.

We describe this relationship between the concepts of *arhat* and *bodhisattva* not as an actual historical account of what happened but rather as the way that the developing Mahayana tradition (which would end up predominating in Tibet and East Asia) tells its own history. In fact, it is doubtful that such a black-and-white situation existed, although there was probably dissension in the Buddhist community and a need for change. But it must be understood that a Buddhist lineage that called itself *hinayana* never actually existed.

The Nikaya tradition, which encompasses most of the remaining (non-Mahayana) Indian sects during the two to three centuries before and after the birth of Christ, ended up being the other main division of Buddhism. Within this broad Nikaya grouping, one sect would end up predominant in future transmission. This sect was named Theravada (*thera* means "elders," and *vada* means "teaching" or "school"; thus, "school of the elders"). The Theravadin sects would later spread to Sri Lanka and Southeast Asia, where they thrive to the present day. Although the circumstances of the Mahayana split tend to identify the so-called *hinayana* groups with Nikaya or Theravada, such a correlation, especially done in a disparaging way, is not appropriate. Indeed, it has been the case throughout Buddhist history, and especially in recent times, that the Theravada lineages have often demonstrated a much more "universal" attitude in their practices than the so-called great vehicle traditions. For example, in Theravada countries such as Sri Lanka, Thailand, and Myanmar, monks are often noted for their unselfish involvement in regional development, community support programs, and environmental activism. By contrast, the so-called Mahayana traditions of Korea and Japan, especially in modern times, demonstrate relatively little community involvement or environmental activism. Table 5.2 lists the major Buddhist schools.

THE SPREAD AND DOCTRINAL DEVELOPMENT OF BUDDHISM IN INDIA

During the centuries after Shakyamuni's death, the Buddhist *sangha* continued to grow and develop, spreading throughout the Indian subcontinent and Sri Lanka. The Buddhist mission received a great boost during the third century B.C.E., when King Ashoka (273–232 B.C.E.), who was originally a cruel and violent man, mended his ways through a conversion to Buddhism. He subsequently worked with zeal to encourage the spread of Buddhism in India through the construction of temples, monasteries, and *stupas* (memorial monuments and pagodas).

During the remaining centuries before the Christian Era, Buddhism continued to develop in scope and sophistication within India, but it never made a significant expansion beyond Indian borders. It was not until the early centuries C.E. when the first important exportation of Buddhism would occur as missionaries first began to travel to China. Figure 5.1 shows the dispersion of Buddhism into East Asia.

In India during the early centuries C.E., the Theravada tradition continued to develop, eventually being exported with major impact into Sri Lanka and Southeast Asia. Also of great importance in India during the first few centuries of the new millennium were the two great Indian Mahayana schools of Madhyamika (middle way) and Yogachara (yoga practice), both of which made a major impact on the forms of Buddhism that later developed in Tibet and East Asia. It was within the writings of Madhyamika thinkers such as Nagarjuna (150–250) that the Buddhist concept of emptiness received its fully refined development. The Yogachara school, in contrast, worked out detailed explanations of the operations of the existent world: of consciousness, the law of cause and effect, and the methods of eradicating mistaken habituation—all extremely important for the development of later Mahayana philosophy. Also of considerable significance during the early centuries C.E. was the development of Tantric Buddhism, which first arose in connection with related *yogic* systems that were popular in India at the time.

Around the eighth to ninth centuries, however, Indian Buddhism would gradually die out, as the religious needs of the Indian people tended increasingly to be satisfied by early forms of Hinduism. Outside India, however, Buddhism experienced tremendous success.

TRANSMISSION TO CHINA

It is during the period of the emergence of the Mahayana movement that we see for the first time the concentrated exportation of Buddhism out of the Indian subcontinent. During the last centuries

Table 5.2

MAJOR BUDDHIST SCHOOLS

EARLY INDIA AND SOUTHEAST ASIA

Nikaya	The earliest schools of Indian Buddhism, based on the Buddha's fundamental teachings of the Four Noble Truths, dependent co-origination, etc. (often subsumed under the disparaging label *hinayana*, or "small vehicle," applied by a later movement that called itself Mahayana, or "great vehicle").
	Theravada: One of the most successful of the Nikaya schools, which later spread to Sri Lanka and Southeast Asia (also sometimes incorrectly labeled *hinayana*).
Mahasamghika (Great Assembly)	An Indian sect that stressed lay practice; believed to be a possible precursor of Mahayana.

INDIAN MAHAYANA (GREAT VEHICLE)

Madhyamika (Middle Way)	The first major Indian Mahayana school, founded by the famous philosopher Nagarjuna; attempted to clarify the subtle implications of the meaning of "emptiness."
Yogachara (Yoga Practice)	The second major Indian Mahayana school, also known as "consciousness-only"; taught that all of existence is none other than "mind".

TIBET

Gelukpa (Partisans of Virtue)	Also known as the Yellow Hat sect, the predominant school within Tibetan Buddhism and the school of the present Dalai Lama, His Holiness Tenzin Gyatso.

EAST ASIA AND VIETNAM

T'ien-t'ai (Ch'on-t'ae, Tendai)	One of the first new Buddhist schools to develop in China; attempted to harmonize doctrinal study and meditation practice.
Hua-yen (Hwaom, Kegon)	Philosophical school of East Asian Mahayana; taught the interpenetration of existence.
Pure Land	East Asian school that taught practitioners to seek rebirth in the Pure Land through chanting of the Buddha's name.
Ch'an (Son, Zen, Thien)	Best known in the West under the Japanese name Zen, the meditation-oriented East Asian school that deemphasized the academic study of Buddhism in favor of meditation practice.

B.C.E., Buddhism had begun to spread into central Asia. The traditional date of the first introduction of Buddhism into China is 148 C.E.. From this time forth, an increasing number of monks began to travel into China, and serious activity began in translating portions of the Buddhist canon into classical Chinese, the main written language for all of East Asia at the time.

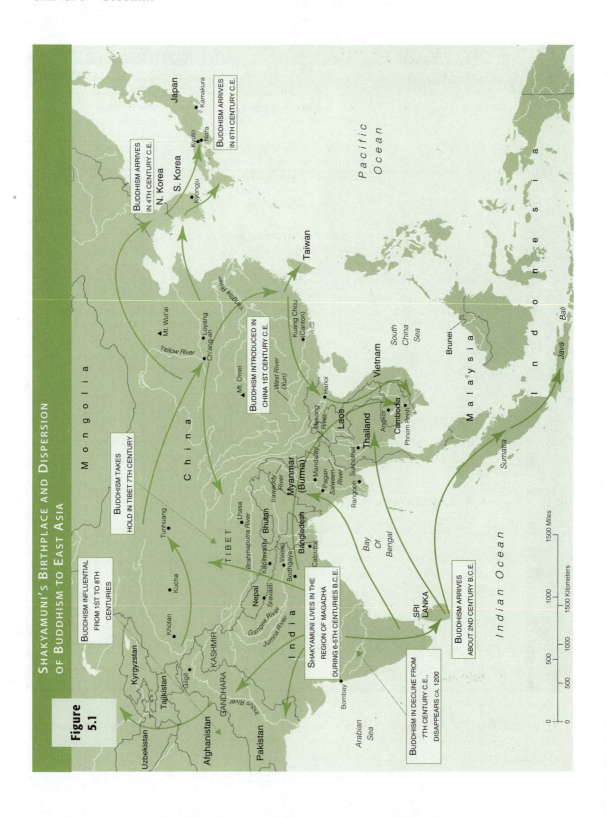

Figure 5.1

SHAKYAMUNI'S BIRTHPLACE AND DISPERSION OF BUDDHISM TO EAST ASIA

BUDDHISM ARRIVES IN 6TH CENTURY C.E.

BUDDHISM ARRIVES IN 4TH CENTURY C.E.

BUDDHISM INTRODUCED IN CHINA 1ST CENTURY C.E.

BUDDHISM TAKES HOLD IN TIBET 7TH CENTURY

BUDDHISM INFLUENTIAL FROM 1ST TO 8TH CENTURIES

SHAKYAMUNI LIVES IN THE REGION OF MAGADHA DURING 6-5TH CENTURIES B.C.E.

BUDDHISM IN DECLINE FROM 7TH CENTURY C.E., DISAPPEARS CA. 1200

BUDDHISM ARRIVES ABOUT 2ND CENTURY B.C.E.

Pacific Ocean

Indian Ocean

Japan — Kamakura, Kyoto, Nara

S. Korea, N. Korea — Kyongju

Taiwan

Mongolia

China — ▲ Mt. Wu'ai, Loyang, Ch'ang-an, Yellow River, Yangtze River

Kuang Chou (Canton)

▲ Mt. Omei, West River (Xun)

Hanoi, Vietnam, Laos, Mekong River, Thailand, Sukhothai, Angkor, Cambodia, Phnom Penh, Rangoon, Mandalay, Pagan, Salween River, Myanmar (Burma), Irrawaddy River

South China Sea

Brunei

Malaysia

Sumatra, Java, Bali — Indonesia

Tibet — Lhasa, Tunhuang

Bhutan, Bangladesh, Calcutta, Brahmaputra River, Kapilavastu, Vaisali, Bodhgaya, Sravasti, Nepal, Ganges River, Jumna River, India

Khotan, Kucha

Bay Of Bengal

SRI LANKA

Bombay

Arabian Sea

Kyrgyzstan, Tajikistan, Gilgit, KASHMIR, GANDHARA, Afghanistan, Pakistan, Uzbekistan, Indus River

1500 Miles

0   500   1000   1500 Kilometers
0   500   1000   1500 Miles

The indigenous religious/philosophical thought forms of East Asia (mainly Confucianism, Taoism, and various forms of shamanistic folk religion) provided a mixture of resistance against and attraction for, Buddhism. At the societal level, such Confucian sensibilities as perfect regard for family unit and lineage, loyalty to the state, and concrete this-worldliness made for opposition to "other-worldly" Buddhism. Indian and central Asian monks arrived in China bearing the distinct marks of Indian religious culture, including monk's robes, shaved heads, and the policy of renunciation of one's family ties—all offensive to the Confucian mind-set.

Nonetheless, several Mahayana schools eventually became highly successful in China and its cultural sphere. The reasons for this success are seen in two main ways by different groups of scholars. Specialists in the historical and political aspects of the transmission of Buddhism in China emphasize the degree to which the patronage of the emperors played a role in the firm establishment of the religion. During the reigns of kings and emperors who supported Buddhism, many temples were built, monks and nuns were ordained, and translations and other scholarly projects were financially supported. Those rulers believed that support of this powerful religion would bring *karmic* merit, resulting in future reward.

Philosophically oriented scholars, in contrast, focus on the metaphysical affinities observable between the native East Asian worldview and Indian Buddhism. Especially relevant are the philosophical concepts developed within the *I Ching* and in Taoist texts such as the *Tao Te Ching* and the *Chang-tzu* (see Chapter 6). These texts spoke of a universe that possessed a transparency and a nothingness *(wu)* not unlike the Buddhist notion of emptiness. These texts also presented an understanding of a universe linked as an organic whole, an interconnected world similar to that seen through the Buddhist concept of dependent co-origination. Finally, early Chinese traditions had a well-defined concept of humans as being perfectible into a level of sagehood, which was similar to the Buddhist concept of attainment of Buddhahood. For these reasons, Buddhism was philosophically attractive to Chinese intellectuals such as the Taoists, who were the first to welcome and attempt to understand Buddhist thought.

It took five or six centuries for the Buddhist religion and its sophisticated metaphysics to be fully understood and appreciated in China. During the earliest period of assimilation, Chinese and other East Asians were somewhat baffled by the diversity of doctrines among the numerous Buddhist sects, as well as by general Indian cultural concepts such as *karma* and reincarnation, which were also imported. To complicate matters further, it took a few centuries for all these difficult foreign metaphysical doctrines to be accurately translated from Indian and central Asian languages into the Chinese logographic language.

THE EAST ASIAN DOCTRINAL SCHOOLS

The early Buddhist sects that developed in East Asia tended to be rough models of Indian sects and to be based upon a particular stream of doctrine that was associated with a certain text or family of texts. Therefore, schools arose such as the Lotus Sutra school, the Nirvana Sutra school, the Three Treatise school (in India, the Madhyamika school), and the Dharma-characteristic school (in India, the Yogachara school). Another school founded in significant measure on Indian precedents was the True Word sect, which based its practice on Vajrayana/Tantrayana teachings and included the use of mystical spells, chants (called *mantra* or *dharani*), and other magical practices to obtain a "shortcut" salvation. Although it experienced a bit of initial popularity in China, the True Word school declined quickly in a couple of centuries, leading some scholars to speculate that the Chinese morality could not accept the sexually oriented *tantras*. This premise would make sense when we take note that Esoteric Buddhism also made little headway in Korea, the inhabitants of which have been known for an even stricter attitude in regard to sexual mores. The most successful East Asian manifestation of the True Word school would appear in the eighth century in Japan with the name Shingon, which survives to the present.

As Buddhism developed through the sixth and seventh centuries in China, the completeness of the assimilation of Buddhism was reflected in the formation of new East Asian schools that did not radically transform any of the fundamental Buddhist teachings but rather expressed these teachings in new ways to fit East Asian religious and philosophical intuitions.

One of the first major sects to be created in China was the T'ien-t'ai, which took the *Lotus Sutra* as the basis for its doctrinal positions. T'ien-t'ai developed a distinctive system of practice based largely upon the Indian techniques of stabilizing meditation and observational meditation. Later on, another influential scriptural sect, called Hua-yen, arose based on the teachings of the *Hua-yen Sutra*. This school was distinctive for its contemplation of a worldview of perfect interpenetration and nonobstruction. In addition to these major scripture-oriented schools, the sixth to eighth centuries in China witnessed the development of two more new sects, whose emphasis was to move away from scriptural study and into the direction of practice. These were the Meditation (Zen) and Pure Land schools.

THE MEDITATION (ZEN) SCHOOL

The founding of the Zen movement is traditionally attributed to an Indian monk named Bodhidharma, who is said to have arrived in China during the early sixth century for the express purpose of introducing a form of Buddhism that relied directly upon a "mind to mind transmission" from master to disciple rather than on the study of scriptures. The Zen schools record the transmission of the *dharma* through a succession of adepts encompassing several generations. Surrounding these adepts, who are called the "patriarchs" of the schools, are many legendary stories that were retold in the later tradition to characterize the school and to define its teaching methods.

The most famous of the later patriarchs, was the sixth patriarch, Hui-neng (638–713). An illiterate woodcutter who was the son of a poor widow, Hui-neng is said to have experienced a flash of illumination one day while overhearing a Buddhist monk chanting the *Diamond Sutra*. He subsequently traveled to the monastery of the current (fifth) patriarch, Hung-jen (601–674), where, despite his illiteracy and lack of training, he soon surpassed all the other monks in his understanding of the Mahayana teaching of nonduality. Because of Hui-neng's superior insight, the fifth patriarch, Hung-jen, eventually chose him as his successor. Although modern historians of Buddhism do not regard the entire story of Hui-neng as factual, it was continually retold to later generations of Zen students, along with the sermons attributed to Hui-neng, as a definitive source for the positions of the Zen school. The iconoclastic-meditative orientation of the Zen schools would be transmitted through the works of such famous masters as Lin-chi, Ma-tsu, Huang-po, Pai-chang, and Yun-men in China; Chinul and Pou in Korea; and Dogen and Ikkyu in Japan.

THE PURE LAND SCHOOL

The earliest development of Pure Land practices as a tradition is traced to T'an-luan (476–555), who was a student of Mahayana *sutras* and Buddha-nature theory. After a near-fatal sickness around the age of fifty, he met an eminent monk named Bodhiruci, who gave him some Pure Land writings. T'an-luan studied and simplified these writings and included his own instructions. Shan-tao (613–682) is the single most important figure in the development of Chinese Pure Land Buddhism. He did extensive research on, and emphasized the infinitude of the powers of, Amitabha. He wrote commentaries on Pure Land *sutras* and propagated the Pure Land teachings by setting recitations to hymns and then to music. He also called on practitioners to practice confession, and he encouraged the painting of Pure Land art. It is in great degree because of Shan-tao's influence that Pure Land Buddhism would end up becoming one of the most popular forms of Buddhism in East Asia. It would be transmitted to Korea, where its practices would be widely taught. However, Pure Land Buddhism enjoyed its greatest popularity in Japan, where it was revived in the form of the creation of new sects in the twelfth and thirteenth centuries.

Although the previously mentioned scripture-oriented schools, such as the Dharma-characteristic, Three Treatise, T'ien-t'ai, and Hua-yen schools, made a major impact on the Buddhist philosophical tone of East Asia, they were not able to maintain a strong identity as distinct sects. These doctrinal schools also suffered from extensive repression during the Buddhist purge of 841 to 845, from which they never recovered. Therefore, the most prominent surviving schools were the practice-oriented Zen and Pure Land schools. From about the tenth century, Buddhism received strong political and philosophical competition from Neo-Confucianism. Therefore, although it continued to survive as a major force in Chinese culture, Buddhism would never return to the prominence it held during its period of growth in the early portion of the millennium. In the twentieth century, with the arrival of communism as the state ideology, the influence of Buddhism in China was all but obliterated.

KOREA   The traditionally accepted date for the introduction of Buddhism to Korea is 372 C.E., when it came to the kingdom of Koguryo, closest of the three Korean kingdoms in proximity to China. During the next two centuries, Buddhism gradually grew and developed in the other two kingdoms, the kingdoms of Paekche and Silla, eventually becoming the major religious force in all three kingdoms. As was the case in China, Buddhism was not at first well understood, but it was accepted by the ruling class as the religion of a powerful god who could protect the country and throne from misfortune.

Because of the country's close geographical and cultural proximity to China, the development of Buddhism in Korea was strongly influenced by events in China. Therefore, the peninsula ended up having, with some variations, the same basic set of schools that had appeared in China. Although Pure Land practices were well known in Korea and were even advocated by major teachers, Pure Land never really developed into a distinct sect the way it did in other areas of East Asia. The Buddhism of Korea would be especially imbued with Hua-yen (Korean, Hwaom) thought, as two of Korea's

major early Buddhist leaders, Wonhyo (617–686) and Uisang (625–702), were deeply involved in Hua-yen philosophy and added their own significant contributions to its development. Wonhyo, the author of some 240 Buddhist works, was so influential in Korea that another school, the Dharma-nature school (closely related in doctrine to Hua-yen), was created based on his influence. From the ninth century onward, the predominant sect in Korean Buddhism was Zen, but a strain of Zen with a pronounced Hua-yen philosophical flavor.

The overall pattern, then, of the premodern history of Buddhism in Korea resembles somewhat that of China, in that Buddhism enjoyed a position of prestige and power among both royalty and commoners for over a millennium: from the middle of the Three Kingdoms (ca. 372–667) through the Unified Silla (667–918) and Koryo (918–1392) periods. But after the transition to the zealously Neo-Confucian Choson (Yi) dynasty (1392–1911), the Buddhist establishment was largely repressed.

JAPAN   Buddhism penetrated Japan a couple of centuries after its importation into Korea, through the influence of Korean monks who traveled across the narrow stretch of water between the two countries. The official date for the introduction of Buddhism to Japan is 552. As was the case in China and Korea before, much of the early impetus for the propagation of the new religion came from the fact that the newly ascended ruling family of the time understood the Buddhist religion as the magic of a powerful foreign god who could protect the kingdom from disaster. But before long, students of the religion began to fathom Buddhism's profundities, and eventually most of the same doctrinal schools began to develop in Japan as had appeared previously in China and Korea. As in China and Korea, much of the early period of Japanese Buddhist history is marked by the close involvement of court officials and eminent monks. As time passed, Japanese monks traveled in large numbers to China and Korea to receive direct teachings from the established Buddhist masters of those countries.

The Japanese Nara period (645–794) was, in general, a phase of importation of Chinese and Korean culture, and it was mainly during this time that Buddhism was introduced. The Nara period was followed by the Heian period, during which the predominant denominations were the T'ien-t'ai school (Japanese Tendai school) and the True Word school (Japanese Shingon school). Toward the end of the Heian period the forms of Buddhism that were to become most influential among the common people came into existence. These were the Pure Land school, the True Pure Land school, and the Nichiren school. Up to the present these three schools have made up the largest religious bloc in Japan.

Despite the popularity of these three "chanting schools" in Japan, the Japanese school of Buddhism that has become most well known in the West is Zen. The first teaching of Zen in Japan is attributed to Esai (1141–1215), but the most famous figure of medieval Japanese Zen is Dogen (1200–1253). From the time of Esai and Dogen down to the present, the Japanese Zen schools list a long string of famous teachers, whose influence has spread to the West.

TIBET Tibet is another major cultural region strongly influenced by Buddhism. Tibet bordered directly on India, and although the spread of Buddhism into that area was continuous, it was not until the seventh century that a solid Buddhist element had developed. Tibet was an isolated mountain country and also possessed a well-established native tradition in the Bon religion. Nonetheless, through the eighth and ninth centuries Buddhism grew in influence, and sects began to form as the *Tripitaka* was translated into the Tibetan language.

The eleventh century was a period of significant growth for Tibetan Buddhism through the influence of three major teachers of the period, Atisha (982–1054), Marpa (1012–1097), and Milarepa (1040–1123). The origins of Tibetan Buddhism's most well known sect, the Gelukpa (partisans of virtue), can be traced back to its influential teacher, Tsong-kha-pa (1357–1419). It was Tsong-kha-pa and his school that implemented the famous *geshe* training system, wherein monks study at a Buddhist monastic college until they attain the equivalent of a Ph.D. in Buddhist philosophy. To this day Gelukpa monks are trained in accordance with this *geshe* system, which accounts for the strong level of scholastic discipline for which this sect is famous.

Tsong-kha-pa's line is also associated with the development of a custom familiar to many modern people—the Dalai Lama system. The term *lama* means "spiritual guide" and is equivalent to the Sanskrit term *guru*. The Dalai Lama line started in the fifteenth century with the third successor in Tsong-kha-pa's line, his nephew Gendun Truppa, who was believed to be an incarnation of the great *bodhisattva* Avalokiteshvara. Since the time of this first Dalai Lama, the Dalai Lamas have been considered to be the ongoing reincarnation of Avalokiteshvara, who is repeatedly found as a baby born forty-nine days after the death of the prior incarnation. The present Dalai Lama is the fourteenth incarnation in this line.

In terms of doctrine and practice, Tibetan Buddhism has been developed primarily out of the three major streams that it inherited from India: Madhyamika, Yogachara, and Vajrayana. Developments of the latter school in Tibet have been especially pronounced, as the tendencies of indigenous Tibetan *shamanic* practice and thought provided much additional impetus to the Vajrayana tradition that had been developed by the Indians. Thus, Tibetan Buddhism is up to the present distinguished by its extensive use of *mantras*, ritual, and iconography, as well as its precise documentation of esoteric matters such as the passage of the spirit to its next destination after death.

SRI LANKA Because Sri Lanka lies in such close proximity to the Indian subcontinent, Buddhism reached this island country rather early. Some scholars believe that Buddhism may have arrived in Sri Lanka as early as the reign of King Ashoka (273–232 B.C.E.), but the earliest extant records indicate a presence of Buddhism at the beginning of the Christian Era. As would later be the case in Southeast Asia, Buddhism was imported along with a wide range of other Indian religious cultural manifestations, especially Hinduism. For approximately a thousand years, Buddhism enjoyed alternating periods of fortune and demise in Sri Lanka in relation to Brahmanistic teachings. By the tenth to eleventh centuries, however, Buddhism had worked itself into a position of relative prominence, with the representatives of a few major sects enjoying reasonable success. In the twelfth century, the great Singhalese king Parakkama-Bahu I undertook a reformation of the Buddhist *sangha*. After examining the three currently popular sects (a Mahayana sect, a Theravada sect and a mixed sect), he decided in 1165 to favor the Theravada sect and suppress the others. From this time, Theravada became the dominant sect in Sri Lanka.

BUDDHISM IN SOUTHEAST ASIA

The type and degree of Buddhist influence exerted on the Southeast Asian mainland are closely related to the overall cultural influences that came into play in this region, among which we can identify the two most important. The first is the Indian cultural influence, which subsumed the greater portion of Southeast Asia, including modern-day Myanmar, Cambodia, Thailand, and Laos. The second is the Chinese cultural influence, which includes most of modern-day Vietnam.

INDIANIZED SOUTHEAST ASIA   Before the beginning of the Christian Era, the political geography of Southeast Asia was not arranged in any way like the modern grouping of nation-states but was made up of a number of large tribal groups, such as the Mon, Khmer, Burmans, and Pagans. Most of these groups had attained a fairly sophisticated sociopolitical level with well-determined boundaries and kingships. But like the way that the Chinese culture permeated Korea and Japan, Indian culture strongly influenced the cultural characteristics of these Southeast Asian tribes. During the phase of indianization lasting from approximately the second to the ninth centuries, many aspects of Indian culture were borrowed, among the most important of which was religion. The

spread of Buddhism to this area, then, was somewhat different than in China and Tibet, where Buddhist missionaries apparently entered the new lands relatively separate from other types of Indian cultural influence. Thus, the importation of Buddhism into Tibet and East Asia brought with it relatively little overall Indian cultural transformation and relatively little in the way of non-Buddhist religious teachings. In most of Southeast Asia, however, there was a widespread importation of Indian culture, especially religious culture. Thus, Buddhism was brought together with various Hindu sects, such as Shiva and Vishnu worshipers, and other devotional groups. These imported traditions were further blended with indigenous religions to the point that any such thing as a "pure" form of Buddhism was for a long time almost unrecognizable.

During the eleventh century, however, this situation began to change. Under the leadership of Anoratha, a king of an area of upper Burma who became a devout Theravada Buddhist, the religion was aggressively propagated. The Burmese at that time had been keeping fairly close ties with Sri Lanka and were strongly influenced by Sri Lankan culture, especially its religion. Monks from Burma who traveled to Sri Lanka found Theravada Buddhism being promoted as the "true faith" with an aggressiveness that had not been the case before. This situation influenced Buddhist centers throughout Southeast Asia. Under Anoratha's orders, monks were sent to Sri Lanka to study Theravada Buddhism and bring back scriptures and commentaries.

The development of Theravada dominance in the Southeast Asian cultural sphere is also connected with the arrival of the Tai-speaking people from southern China. The Tai began to migrate into Southeast Asia around 900, bringing with them their own culture, which was neither Indianized nor Sinicized (influenced by China). The Tai, not unlike the Mongols in China, ended up achieving political dominance in the region while at the same time being culturally swallowed up by the peoples they conquered. The new Tai state of Sukhothai that developed in the early part of

CHRONOLOGY OF BUDDHISM

563	Commonly accepted date of Shakyamuni's birth
483	Death of Shakyamuni; followed by the convening of the first council
CA. 280	Convening of the second council; beginning of the schism between Theravada and Mahasamghika schools
273	Ascension of King Ashoka, which resulted in the spread of Buddhism throughout the Indian subcontinent; transmission of Buddhism into Sri Lanka
CA. 200	Beginning of the lay movement toward *stupa* worship
CA. 100	Full establishment of Nikaya Buddhism
CA. 100	Spread of Mahayana movement, with the extensive composition of early Mahayana scriptures; beginning of transmission of Buddhism into China
CA. 150	Mahayana movement becomes firmly established; Nagarjuna and his followers develop Madhyamika philosophy
350	Beginning of the Yogachara philosophical movement
372	Official transmission of Buddhism to Korea
CA. 400	The pilgrim Fa-hsien travels to India and Sri Lanka
401	The famous translator Kumarajiva arrives in China

the thirteenth century rejected the blended religious condition that was characteristic of the prior Burman civilization and embraced the energetic Theravada movement. From the end of the thirteenth century through the middle of the fourteenth century, the kings of Sukhothai supported the efforts of missionary monks to establish orthodox Theravada Buddhism. Generally speaking, then, from the time of the eleventh through the twelfth centuries, monks in Southeast Asia began to promote Theravada Buddhism with increasing vigor. By the early fifteenth century, the vast majority of people living in what is today Myanmar, Thailand, Cambodia, and Laos had become adherents

of Theravada Buddhism. This remains true to the present day.

SINICIZED SOUTHEAST ASIA: VIETNAM   As a culture of the Southeast Asian peninsula, the Vietnamese are closely related to their neighbors genetically and culturally. But unlike the people of Myanmar, Laos, Cambodia, and Thailand, since about 111 B.C.E. the Vietnamese have been, except for a few minor periods of independence, a population within the Chinese Empire. Hence, their religious outlook has been deeply influenced by Chinese traditions. This means that the forms of Buddhism that have penetrated Vietnamese soci-

CA. 550	Early development of the Pure Land and Ch'an movements in China
552	Official transmission of Buddhism from Korea (Silla) to Japan
589	Unification of China under Sui-T'ang; establishment of T'ien-tai and San-lun studies
CA. 600	Beginning of spread of Buddhism to Tibet; spread of Esoteric Buddhism in India
CA. 629	Hsuan-tsang travels to study Yogachara in India
650	Development of Esoteric Buddhism in India; Chinese Pure Land Buddhism becomes fully established; flowering of doctrinal Buddhist studies in China and Korea
750	Spread of Buddhism to Indonesia and Java
CA. 800	Growth of Tendai and Shingon in Japan
1000	Maturation of Ch'an school in China; spread of Theravada Buddhism to Southeast Asia
CA. 1100	Construction of Angkor Wat in Cambodia
CA. 1200	Decline and eventual disappearance of Buddhism in India
CA. 1250	Transmission of Tibetan Buddhism to Mongolia
CA. 1900	Beginning of study of Buddhism in the West
CA. 1960	Widespread establishment of Buddhist centers in the West

ety have been those of East Asian Mahayana, the most successful of which over the long term have been Zen and Pure Land. But being under Chinese influence, the Vietnamese, like the Koreans and Japanese, were also profoundly affected by the other dominant streams of Chinese philosophy, most notably Confucianism and Taoism. Furthermore, as in China, these two religions also had a transformative effect on the nature of Chinese Mahayana Buddhism itself, in the sense that religious activity would be focused not so much on a quest for salvation (as is characteristic of Theravada) as on the achievement of harmony in the present world.

CONTEMPORARY BUDDHISM

Buddhism reached its peak in terms of overall global penetration between the eighth and sixteenth centuries C.E., when it held considerable influence in most Asian countries. Since this peak period there has been an overall decline in the global influence of Buddhism, although the religion has continued to maintain a considerable presence in some geographical regions and has attained some new growth in the West.

THE TRADITIONAL BUDDHIST CULTURES

The first country in which Buddhism underwent a major decline was India, where it was gradually eclipsed by various forms of Brahmanistic religion, such as Hinduism, as well as by the importation of Islam from the West. Buddhism was able to maintain a foothold in southern India until the seventeenth century. After that time the religion all but disappeared from the mainland, although Theravada forms survived well in neighboring Sri Lanka, where Buddhism has been a predominant religion for two millennia, maintaining its significant influence in both upper and lower classes. The religion lost some of its power in Sri Lanka during the first influx of European Christian culture during the seventeenth and eighteenth centuries, but in recent times it has regained a considerable degree of popularity. Today many young people come to Theravada centers for societal rituals, as well as for instruction in meditation. Theravada Buddhism also continues to thrive in the Southeast Asian countries of Myanmar, Thailand, Laos, and Cambodia. The characteristics of the Theravada Buddhism that flourished in this region are interesting, as well as instructive about the nature of the religious tradition of Buddhism as a whole.

In Northeast Asia (China, Korea, and Japan), Mahayana Buddhism was originally studied and practiced by members of the elite classes, and it was promoted by rulers. It was not until the development of "new" forms of Mahayana—namely, Zen and especially Pure Land—that Buddhism in any sense became a religion for the masses. Even in later history, Zen would end up being a practice associated with religious adepts, leaving only Pure Land and other various blends of Buddhism and folk religions popularly practiced. This course of Buddhism in Northeast Asia suggests that the status of Buddhism as a profound religion of dedicated practice toward the attaining of salvation has actually only applied to a limited, elite circle of world-renunciant practitioners.

The transformation of Theravada Buddhism in Southeast Asia is analogous in some ways to the occurrences in the north. Whereas Theravada Buddhism was originally understood to be a religion for *arhats,* in Southeast Asia it has become highly integrated into the lives of the common people. But this fact does not mean that farmers in the countryside of Sri Lanka, Myanmar, Laos, Thailand, and Cambodia spend all their free time in seated meditation or the study of scriptures. Typically, they come to a local temple for charitable community activities and prayer and believe deeply in the law of *karma.* In fact, among the common people in Southeast Asian Theravada societies, understanding the law of *karma* and the other more apprehensible aspects of the Buddhist teaching (such as keeping the moral precepts and practicing charity), along with a significant mixture of folk beliefs, has become the main characteristic of religious life. Charles Keyes, one of the leading experts on Buddhism and society in Southeast Asia, says the following: "Most people in Theravada societies have not and do not focus on the attainment of nirvana as their religious goal. Rather, they have sought and still seek to attain a reduction in suffering, first in this life and next in a future existence, postponing the quest for total cessation of suffering to a remote future many lifetimes away. In historical terms, it is clear that in the process of becoming a popular religion, Buddhism ceased to be a religion of universal salvation."[3]

Nonetheless, in terms of influence and number of actual participants, it is in the Theravada countries of Sri Lanka, Myanmar, Thailand, Cambodia, and Laos that Buddhism retains its greatest vitality. As noted earlier, among the lay community there is widespread participation in monastery-sponsored meditation sessions.

In these areas, Buddhism is not limited to monastically defined religious cultivation. For better or worse, the Buddhist establishment is usually involved in some fashion in the political arena, and politicians are usually sufficiently aware of the influence of the Buddhist world to pay it due attention in their own attempts at gaining or maintaining their power bases. Recent leaders such as U Nu and Aung San Suu Kyi of Myanmar, S. W. R. D. Bandaranaike of Sri Lanka, and Prince Norodom Sihanouk of Cambodia have been deeply involved with Buddhism in one form or another, whether it be as the main source for their spiritual convictions or merely as a way of garnering support for their power base.

Members of the monastic communities in these countries have also tended to be deeply involved in societal and ecological issues in modern times. In Thailand, for example, the noted monk Phra Khru Sakorn distinguished himself (starting in 1962) by taking the role of economic and spiritual renovator of his entire region. He worked toward the correction of ecological problems; initiated numerous community development projects; and generally acted as a catalyst and coordinator among teachers, heads of villages, local administrators, and the police. By 1984, he had raised hundreds of thousands of dollars to establish a foundation for community development. Sakorn also worked hard at the same time to develop the spiritual life of the people of the region by promoting meditation at the *wat* (monastery) and through the school, as well as by stressing the relevance of the Buddha's teaching for self-awareness and peace.[4] Beyond Sakorn, the Southeast Asian countries have a long list of Buddhist leaders who have been deeply engaged in efforts to improve society and protect the natural environment in their areas.

VIETNAM   Vietnam lies in close proximity to its Southeast Asian neighbors, and the relative health of the Vietnamese *sangha* and the nature of its involvement in societal and political affairs show pronounced similarities to the countries just mentioned. But there are differences. First, whereas most of the Southeast Asian countries received the influence of southern Indian and Sri Lankan Theravada Buddhism, Vietnam was permeated by major forms of Chinese Buddhism. Remaining especially popular in Vietnam over the centuries have been the Vietnamese versions of Zen and Pure Land Buddhism. As in other areas of Asia, in Vietnam from the eighteenth to the twentieth centuries, Buddhism has had to contend with Western cultural forms and religious traditions. Furthermore, as a general rule, religious traditions do not fare

well under the auspices of a communist-led government, and the Buddhist tradition of Vietnam has been no exception. Nonetheless, it seems that the religion was able to survive fairly well. Although reports from Vietnam in the earliest part of the post–Vietnam War period (after 1975) indicated strong repression and harassment from the communist-dominated government, it is clear from recent events that Buddhism is in a period of resurgence as a cultural force.

CHINA   Chinese Buddhism never received any major challenge in the form of a foreign religion such as Christianity or Islam. However, the emergence of communism after World War II resulted in a significant weakening of the religion. Communist ideology by and large opposed the Buddhist teachings (more because they were "religious" than because of particular issues of Buddhist doctrine), and a number of communist movements have sought the destruction of Buddhism as a force in Chinese society. This destruction, however, has never been complete, and the number of Buddhist clergy on the mainland has been steadily increasing in recent years to the extent that the number of Buddhist clergy is now estimated to be in the hundreds of thousands.

TAIWAN   In stark contrast to the People's Republic of China, Taiwan, which escaped the communist transformation, maintains one of the strongest Buddhist traditions of the Northeast Asian Mahayana stream, most influential being the two schools of Zen and Pure Land. Although the present Taiwanese government generally does not actively support Buddhist studies or other Buddhist-related endeavors, meditation and Pure Land practice among the populace is fairly common. One of the most well known Buddhist centers in Taiwan is the large and prosperous temple Fo Guang Shan, the main headquarters of which is in southern Taiwan but which also maintains a large office in Taipei that serves as a center for many advanced Buddhist studies projects. Fo Guang Shan has recently published one of the largest Buddhist dictionaries in the East Asian region and has supported a number of significant academic Buddhist conferences.

TIBET   Tibetans, who have been predominantly Buddhist for more than a millennium, have suffered greatly at the hands of the communist Chinese government. During Buddhism's period as the dominant religious tradition in Tibet, its doctrine, ritual, music, art, and medicine thoroughly permeated Tibetan culture. In 1950, the government of the People's Republic of China began to move into Tibet and gradually took control. In the wake of a brief and unsuccessful uprising in 1959, the Fourteenth Dalai Lama, along with some 100,000 Tibetans, escaped to India, where they have been receiving political sanctuary up to the present. Since 1959, the Chinese government has embarked on a wholesale attempt to systematically eradicate Tibetan, and especially Tibetan Buddhist, culture through the destruction of monasteries, universities, and ethnic collections. The Chinese government has also encouraged the emigration of its own people into Tibet in an effort to sinicize the Tibetan homeland. Tibet has recently been reopened for limited access to foreigners, and visitors report that despite the widespread destruction of Tibetan Buddhist culture, monasteries with practicing monks remain, and a large portion of Tibetan people still maintain their Buddhist faith. The Fourteenth Dalai Lama, His Holiness Tenzin Gyatso, with his general goal of world peace, has worked unstintingly for the halt of the Chinese government assault on Tibetan culture and the liberation of his country from the bondage of the People's Republic of China. However, his efforts have continued to meet with stubborn resistance from the Chinese government.

SOUTH KOREA   Since the end of the Japanese occupation of Korea in 1945, there has been a resurgence of Buddhism, but this growth has also been tempered by the increasing influence of Western material culture and of Christianity. Christianity has developed in South Korea to the point where it holds a following roughly equal to that of Buddhism. The rise in popularity of Christianity has brought with it an unhealthy measure of extremism, as Buddhist monks and nuns, monasteries, and Buddhist cultural treasures have recently been subject to wanton, and sometimes violent, attacks by Christian groups.

Nonetheless, the Son (Zen) Buddhist tradition remaining in South Korea is relatively healthy compared with that of its Northeast Asian neighbors China and Japan. Son Buddhism retains a distinct atmosphere of genuine religious and philosophical inquiry in South Korea, and in recent years there has been lively intellectual debate in both monastic and academic circles on the issue of sudden and gradual enlightenment. At the center of this debate, advocating a radical position of sudden enlightenment/sudden practice, was the Reverend Songch'ol, the head of the major Son order in South Korea, the Chogye. Songch'ol's death in November 1993 was a major media event, highlighting the influence of this charismatic leader who was noted for his great self-discipline, as well as for brutal straightforwardness in dealing with practitioners and politicians alike.

The South Korean Son Chogye school presently has a large number of mountain monasteries in which both South Koreans and foreigners are actively engaged in strict meditation practice. These centers also have a significant lay support base, mostly made up of women. In current South Korean society, Buddhism has largely become associated with movements involved in the maintenance of traditional artifacts and values, whereas Christianity is commonly associated with change and westernization.

JAPAN   Since the purge of Christianity at the hands of the Tokugawa Shoguns during the early part of the seventeenth century, Japanese Buddhism has never had to face the competition of another major world religion, nor has it experienced sustained and rigorous government repression. Therefore, at least on an institutional level, Japan has remained as purely Buddhist as some of the Southeast Asian countries. Surviving today are the major Zen sects, the major Pure Land sects, and the various manifestations of Nichiren Buddhism. Mainly because of the growth of materialism and secularism, however, the number of modern people who carry out a lifestyle of devoted practice within these traditions is negligible. Very few people of middle age or younger in present-day Japan have any knowledge of Buddhism whatsoever.

Of greater importance on the current Japanese religious scene are a number of new religions. The largest and most well known of the modern popular Buddhism-based religions in Japan is the Soka Gakkai sect, which has its roots in Nichiren Buddhism. This sect, which focuses its practice on the recitation of the title of the *Lotus Sutra,* involves itself in various political agendas, some of which have received negative attention in the Japanese media. Beyond Soka Gakkai are a growing number of smaller, Buddhist-influenced new religious sects.

THE WEST: THE NEW BUDDHIST FRONTIER

Knowledge of Buddhism gradually reached the Americas and Europe at the end of the nineteenth century. The twentieth century, especially the past thirty years, has seen the establishment of Western representatives of almost all the major surviving Asian Buddhist traditions, including the various branches of Tibetan Buddhism, Southeast Asian Theravada, and East Asian Zen and Pure Land. Buddhism in the United States, a country that still experiences fairly widespread immigration, is bifurcated into two general groups: the "ethnic" Buddhist centers run by and for the immigrants from Asian countries (including Thailand, Myanmar, Vietnam, Tibet, Japan, South Korea, Taiwan, and China) and the Buddhist centers run by and for Americans who are embracing Buddhism as a new tradition. Sometimes there is communication and cooperation between these two groups, but often there is not.

North American Buddhism began to develop in the latter half of this century, mostly through the efforts of intellectuals with a strong interest in meditation. It is not surprising, therefore, that the initial adoption of Buddhism by North Americans was dominated by sects that specialized in the teaching of meditation practice. Since the late 1920s, when the Japanese Zen Buddhist scholar D. T. Suzuki published his *Essays in Zen Buddhism,* Zen has gradually spread throughout the United States and Canada. As far as the East Asian meditational schools are concerned, to date, the strongest influence in the West has continued to be from certain forms of Japanese Zen. Numerous Zen monasteries and meditation centers have sprung up and are spreading throughout the United States. Some of the larger ones, in California, New York, and Hawaii, are led by eminent homegrown American Zen masters. A smaller, but steadily growing, number of Korean Son and Chinese Ch'an temples are also appearing throughout the country. By far the largest concentration of these temples can be found in urban areas in California and New York, where these monasteries are supported by South Korean and Chinese immigrants.

Also of considerable size as a Buddhist group in the United States are the Tibetan organizations, with all four major Tibetan sects having ample representation. The Gelukpa (the Dalai Lama's group) have a large monastery in New Jersey and centers in various other locations around the country. The Dalai Lama's boundless energy, which carries him all over the world as an ambassador of world peace, has contributed greatly to the popularity of Buddhism as a whole in the West.

No doubt the largest single vehicle for the transmission of information about Buddhism in the past few decades has been the university classroom. During the 1960s and 1970s, Buddhist studies courses and programs began cropping up in major universities within departments of religious studies and Asian cultural studies. This trend has increased to the point where even the smallest colleges around the country offer courses in Buddhism, along with courses in other Asian religions such as Hinduism, Confucianism, and Taoism. An ever-widening number of major universities also offer advanced degree opportunities in Buddhist studies.

GENDER ISSUES

As in other major world religions, women have been viewed as marginal in the development and main-

Byodo-In Buddhist Temple in Koolay Mountains, Oahu, Hawaii (ca. 1983–1985).

tenance of the Buddhist tradition. Similarly, it must be kept in mind that whatever practices and doctrines the religion assumes for itself are to a great extent culturally determined. The fact that women have traditionally been forced to play a subordinate role in Buddhism has much to do with the fact that they have also been subject to a similar subservient role in the host societies in general.

Nonetheless, direct prejudice against women can be observed in the earliest Buddhist doctrine, for it is recorded that the Buddha originally intended to deny women access to the *sangha* based on the belief that their presence would bring about problems related to improper sexual activity—the blame for which was always placed on women. For this reason, when women were accepted into the *sangha*, the number of regulations placed on their behavior was almost double that placed on the male members. The Buddhist sects that subsequently formed in all areas of Asia (areas with strongly male centered societal power systems) have been mostly male centered. Throughout the long history of the Buddhist tradition, the major monastic teachers, writers, and textual commentators have been

almost exclusively male—a situation that continues to the present day.

If we examine the actual life of the *sangha* itself and the *sangha*'s interaction with the lay community, however, we can observe throughout all the East Asian countries (both Southeast Asia and Northeast Asia) a common tendency for most community support to be from women. It is, in the majority of situations, women who donate their money and volunteer their services to the local temples. The exact nature of this situation differs, of course, according to the sect and the geographical region. In major Taiwanese Buddhist institutions, for example, the day-to-day monastery activities are run almost completely by nuns, who are in turn amply assisted by female lay acolytes. In terms of *sangha* membership, the number of women far exceeds that of men. Charles B. Jones, a specialist in Taiwanese Buddhism, reports from his research that nuns in Taiwan currently outnumber monks about three to one and furthermore are far less likely to renounce their vows and return to lay life. Jones comments: "Although one may adduce many sociological reasons for this, the most common explanation that I received from Chinese Buddhists themselves was that women are 'more religiously inclined' than men. It was also interesting to observe that nuns generally receive greater respect than monks for the superiority of their commitment and rigor of their practice."[5]

Localized belief in many Asian countries generally holds that women are in some ways more naturally "in tune" with Buddhist principles than are men—a position quite distinct from that seen in the earliest canonical sources. Charles Keyes has asserted that at the popular village level, women are depicted as more sensitive to the problem of suffering produced by attachment and therefore naturally embody more positive Buddhist values than do men. Because in this perspective, the natural state of men inclines toward immoral acts, males are required to enter the monastery to be trained in virtues that are naturally embodied in women.[6] This attitude can be seen as one rationalization of why women are generally not permitted to be ordained as nuns in Southeast Asian Theravada systems—even though they play a powerful role in their status as lay members.

The Buddhist tradition thus sends conflicting messages on the issue of women. Even today, despite the fact that women make up a significant portion (in some cases a majority) of the devoted monastic and lay practitioners (including those in the growing U.S. Asian ethnic Buddhist communities), the Buddhist textual tradition rarely acknowledges the vital role played by women. This paradox in turn offers the strong possibility that the current pronounced-but-unacknowledged role of women in the Buddhist community is a phenomenon that is not dramatically different from that in the earlier, classical periods of the religion in East Asia. Women have long played a major role in the actual day-to-day handling of the affairs of the temple and lay community, but because of male domination of the literary dimension of the religion, such activity has gone largely unrecorded.

In the modern West, where Buddhism is now growing as a small sprout replanted in a wholly new cultural environment, women are becoming more visible in their roles as teachers, writers, and administrators than they had been in the Asian versions of their traditions. Nonetheless, the majority of the people in these positions of authority are still men. In terms of cultural experiment, it will be interesting to see what direction the nature of the Buddhist community takes as it continues to develop and grow in its new environment.

BUDDHISM AND THE DIGITAL AGE

One of the most interesting contemporary developments in Buddhism, which is showing itself in both the monastic and academic worlds, is the rapid adaptation of computerized media such as CD-ROM and the Internet for the dissemination of Buddhist-related information.

THE ELECTRONIC BUDDHIST TEXT INITIATIVE (EBTI)   The first important step in the digitalization of Buddhist information is the Electronic Buddhist Text Initiative (EBTI), a consortium of individuals and organizations around the globe who have been working toward the digitization of all forms of Buddhist-related data. This includes canonical texts, scholarly articles, images of art, and architecture. One of the distinctive aspects of the Buddhist religion as compared with the other major world religious traditions is the unusually large volume of its canonical texts. The various Southeast Asian versions of the Theravada canon and the Northeast Asian versions of the Chinese/Korean/Japanese canon are all huge collections made up of hundreds of thick volumes of tiny printed characters. This circumstance has made them especially difficult to handle in storage and to use as reference materials. The advent of computerized input and storage has therefore been attractive to Buddhist scholars and missionary organizations that seek to make the study and transmission of Buddhist textual materials more efficient. In response to these new digital possibilities, in the 1990s electronic Buddhist textual input projects began to spring up at academic and religious centers around the globe, and new projects are appearing all the time. (See Appendix C for a listing of these Web sites.)

THE INTERNET AND THE WORLD WIDE WEB

Another vitally important step in the digitization of Buddhist studies has been the rapidly increasing use of the Internet. At present there are numerous E-mail discussion groups with all kinds of sub-specializations in the transmission of information about Buddhism. These groups fall mainly into the two categories of practice and scholarly orientation, but these lines are often blurred. A couple of the most prominent Buddhist studies lists are Buddha-L and ZenBuddhism, which serve as important sources for scholarly information about Buddhism in the English-speaking world. Many Buddhist scholars who have Internet access subscribe to lists such as these. There many other variations in list character and orientation. Some lists specialize in Tibetan issues; others focus on the study and practice of Zen. The character of the interchange through these media has become quite interesting, because participants may include Zen masters, Buddhist scholars, lay practitioners, and complete beginners—all of them communicating on an equal basis through the E-mail medium.

BUDDHISM INTO THE TWENTY-FIRST CENTURY

Despite the small promising developments in terms of adaptation to new technologies, Buddhism in its status as an active, thriving religion stands at a crossroads as it enters the twenty-first century. Originally a religion that developed in a radically different culture at a radically different time in the development of human culture, Buddhist teachings were designed to fit a certain type of consciousness—a distinct view of reality in which the culture felt the need to place strong focus on religious matters. Far from feeling themselves to be masters of the universe, the peoples of the ancient cultures felt themselves to be at its mercy. And religion, in whatever form, was considered the primary way for humans to have any influence on maintaining the world order. Because of this perception, participation in the religious life within the culture, at one level or another, was taken for granted.

It is also true that when Buddhism was exported to new cultures, it was able to adapt incredibly well, especially in cultures with no major organized religion that dealt with the matters of life and the hereafter in the systematic manner of Buddhism. Therefore, Buddhism was deeply embraced by Tibetans, Sri Lankans, Chinese, Koreans, Japanese, Burmese, Cambodians, Vietnamese, and others. But once again, although there was much adaptation to dramatically different worldviews, these recipient cultures were nonetheless, like India, basically cultures that held a deep respect for the unknown powers of the universe and of the human spirit. For these cultures, the acceptance of Buddhism was an integration of new beliefs into a worldview that was already basically religious.

What is significant now is that at no previous time in recorded history have we known of a human community that was as secularly and materially oriented as the world we live in today. Can Buddhism (and, indeed, the other major religious traditions) survive in the present environment? Buddhism has almost completely disappeared from India. The Chinese government, after effectively eliminating the influence of the religion within its own borders, has continued in its efforts to limit the religion's influence in Tibet. In Korea, Buddhism continues to lose its adherents to Christianity. In Japan, the religion is all but moribund beyond its role for handling funerals and as a museum artifact. Only in Southeast Asia does the influence of Buddhism seem to maintain anything like conspicuous strength.

To survive and grow, Buddhism will have to find a way to either regain strength in the cultures of its origin or make significant headway in the West. Can we consider the latter possibility as a serious one? As westerners, we certainly find it a most interesting question. Statistics show that after making initial headway during the 1960s and 1970s, the growth of Buddhism in the West has stagnated to the point that the number of adherents in the United States, for instance, has remained at less than a million for the past few decades. Will Buddhism remain as a fringe religion for a certain segment of the intelligentsia, or does it have the potential of someday becoming "mainstream"? On the one hand, the persistence of the materialistic and secular tendencies in our culture and in our educational systems would seem to indicate great difficulties for the growth of a widespread spirituality of any kind, let alone such a foreign and esoteric tradition as Buddhism. On the other hand, however, there is a growing disillusionment with many established norms that is brought about by failures of the promises of the natural sciences and technology—failures that lead more and more people to reflect on their own spiritual values and beliefs. Buddhism, especially in its purely critical-philosophical format, offers no contradictions with the established truths of modern science; it demands, rather than up-front faith in the unknown, an open and inquiring attitude. What will the future hold for the Buddhist tradition? Only time will tell.

GLOSSARY OF BUDDHISM

anatman "no-self"; the important basic doctrine taught by the Buddha that the actual existence of sentient beings is not in the form of a distinct, eternal ego/soul but is dependently co-originated.

anitya "impermanence"; one of the most important characterics of existence in Buddhism. Along with *duhkha* and *anatman*, *anitya* is one of the three basic components of Buddhist teaching.

arhat literally, "worthy of respect"; a sage who has overcome all personal afflictions and has attained *nirvana*.

atman "eternal soul" or "self"; a key doctrine of pre-Buddhist Brahmanistic thought that was refuted by the Buddha.

bodhisattva the model practitioner of Mahayana, who at an advanced stage of practice enlightens others while continuing to enlighten himself or herself. The *bodhisattva* takes a vow not to enter *nirvana* until all other sentient beings have been relieved of suffering.

ch'an the Chinese transliteration of the Sanskrit term *dhyana*, which means "meditation"; also a general term for an East Asian sectarian movement that placed emphasis on meditation practice as opposed to scriptural study. (In Korean, *son*, in Japanese, *zen*).

dependent co-origination
  the fundamental understanding of existence shared by all Buddhist sects, which sees all entities in the universe as existing only in dependence on all other entities.

dharma in earlier Indian thought, a term that referred to the order of the universe. In Buddhism, the term has a related meaning in that it implies the "truth" of the universe, as it really it. By extension, *dharma* comes to mean the Buddha's description of reality, or his "teaching." Another extension of the meaning of the term *dharma* can be seen in the writings of the Consciousness-only masters, where *dharma* comes to refer to the components, or "elements," of reality.

dhyana	a Sanskrit term for "meditation."
duality	the condition brought about when the unenlightened mind makes hard and fast distinctions between apparent opposites, such as subject and object, or enlightenment and nonenlightenment. The ignorant mind cannot but function through duality and further engender the view of duality.
Eightfold Path	the *marga*, the Fourth Noble Truth taught by Shakyamuni Buddha. It consists of Right View, Right Intention, Right Speech, Right Action, Right Livelihood, Right Effort, Right Mindfulness, and Right Concentration.
emptiness	*(shunyata)* "voidness"; the understanding that all things in existence are lacking in an inherent, eternal nature. Emptiness is one of the most important concepts in Mahayana philosophy.
expedient means	*(upaya-Kaushalya)* the strategy of instruction wherein it is considered acceptable to teach views of reality that are less than true, as long as they have a clearly defined place in eventually leading to the ultimate truth.
Four Noble Truths	four aspects of existence revealed by the Buddha at his first sermon: *duhkha* (suffering), *samudaya* (arising of suffering), *nirodha* (cession of suffering), and *marga* (path to the cessation of suffering).
hinayana	"small vehicle"; a disparaging term coined by members of the Mahayana movement to indicate what was conceived as the inferiority of the teachings of their predecessors.
karma	the law of perfect continuity between cause and effect. It refers to the creation of causes, as well as to the reception of the effects of these causes.
koan	in Japanese, "public case"; a paradoxical story, usually about an ancient adept. Practitioners in many Zen schools are assigned *koan* as an object of meditation for the attainment of enlightenment (in Chinese, *k'ung-an*; in Korean, *kong'an*).
lama	"spiritual guide" or *guru*; a term used in Tibetan Buddhism to refer to an enlightened teacher.
Mahayana	"great vehicle"; a reform movement that arose in India around the turn of the millennium. Members of the Mahayana movement claimed to teach a more universalistic version of the Buddhist doctrine. It was primarily the Mahayana schools that spread to Tibet and Northeast Asia.

marga	"path," "way," "method," the Fourth Noble Truth, which is roughly equivalent in meaning to the Chinese *tao*.
nirvana	the cessation of all *karmic* habituation. In Buddhism it is equivalent to liberation *(moksha)* and enlightenment *(bodhi)*.
prajna	"wisdom"; one of the three disciplines of the path. In Mahayana Buddhism, *prajna* refers especially to the wisdom that cognizes emptiness.
Pure Land	a paradise in which practitioners believe that they will be reborn as a result of practices devoted to Amitabha or some other great saint. The most important of these practices is the recitation of Amitabha's name.
samadhi	a condition of one-pointed concentration, usually attainable only after long and strenuous practice of meditation.
samsara	literally, "flowing together"; the delusory world of cyclic existence in which unenlightened beings are trapped. Buddhist practices aim to liberate one from entrapment in *samsara*.
samudaya	the Noble Truth of Arising (of suffering). This is the Third Noble Truth, which teaches how all things arise in dependence upon each other.
sangha	the community or order of the Buddhist clergy; in a larger sense, all Buddhist practitioners.
shamatha	calm abiding, or stabilizing meditation; a form of meditation practice in which the meditator focuses on a single object without any thought movement.
shila	precepts, or discipline of moral practice; one of the three disciplines of the Eightfold Path and one of the Six Perfections.
Theravada	the most prominent early orthodox school of Indian Buddhism, which still flourishes in Sri Lanka and most of Southeast Asia.
Tripitaka	"three baskets"; the three collections of *vinaya, sutra,* and *abhidharma* that make up the Buddhist canon.
Two Truths	the relative truth and absolute truth; two ways of seeing reality and teaching in Buddhism.
vinaya	the code of discipline for monks and nuns. The *vinaya* writings make up one of three parts of the Buddhist canon.
vipassana	observational meditation; a form of Buddhist meditation in which practitioners use their Buddhist doctrinal training to try to see reality as it is.
wu	"no," "nothing," or "nothingness." Originally a technical term in Taoism, in Buddhism it becomes one of the terms that refers to *shunyata* (in Korean and Japanese, *mu*). It is also the key phase of a popular *koan*.

FOR FURTHER STUDY

Aitken, Robert. *Taking the Path of Zen.* Berkeley, Calif.: North Point Press, 1982.
  An accessible, well-written introduction to Zen Buddhism by one of the leading Western Zen masters.

Buswell, Robert E. *The Zen Monastic Experience.* Princeton, N.J.: Princeton University Press, 1992.
  An insider's view into the actual life of practicing monks and nuns based on the author's rich experience as a monk in South Korea.

Chang, Garma C. C. *The Buddhist Teaching of Totality: The Philosophy of Hwa Yen Buddhism.* University Park, Pa.: Pennsylvania University Press, 1971.
  A book that contains the most lucid explanation of the Buddhist concept of emptiness available anywhere.

Ch'en, Kenneth. *Buddhism in China: A Historical Survey.* Princeton, N.J.: Princeton University Press, 1964.
  A complete and detailed text on the history of Chinese Buddhism

Gyatso, Tenzin. *Kindness, Clarity and Insight.* Translated and edited by Jeffrey Hopkins. Ithaca, N.Y.: Snow Lion, 1984.
  A collection of the Dalai Lama's sermons. Mahayana Buddhist teachings are explained in easy language for newcomers to Buddhism

———. *The Meaning of Life from a Buddhist Perspective.* Boston: Wisdom Publications, 1992.
  A readable introduction to the basic Buddhist ideas such as dependent co-origination, impermanence, and no-self.

Harvey, Peter. *An Introduction to Buddhism.* Cambridge, England: Cambridge University Press, 1990.
  Heavy on detail, but a solid introduction to Buddhism, especially its Theravada manifestations.

Robinson, Richard, and Willard Johnson. *The Buddhist Religion: A Historical Introduction.* Belmont, Calif.: Wadsworth, 1997.
  A popular text for college introductory Buddhist courses that provides the historical background for all branches of Buddhism.

Swearer, Donald K. *The Buddhist World of Southeast Asia.* Albany, N.Y.: SUNY Press, 1995.
  The best introduction available to Southeast Asian Buddhism.

Walpola, Rahula. *What the Buddha Taught.* New York: Grove, 1974.
  A well-written and accessible introduction to basic Buddhist concepts written by a Theravada scholar-monk.

READINGS

Reading 5.1   *THE MAJJHIMA-NIKAYA:*

QUESTIONS WHICH LEND NOT TO EDIFICATION

Buddhism has always shown a strong tendency to characterize the role of the Buddha not as a metaphysician, logician, or mystic but as a skillful doctor who has the right cure for every disease. This characterization of the Buddha was especially pronounced in many of the earlier Indian texts, which often told of situations in which the Buddha was challenged by contemporary philosophers. In these cases he is usually depicted as answering either briefly and cryptically or not at all. In the following passage, from the *Majjhima-Nikaya* 63:13, sermon 1, the Buddha receives a series of questions from the elder Malunkyaputta about life and death, reincarnation, and so forth. The Buddha does not answer these questions but instead chides Malunkyaputta for not realizing what is important and for not realizing exactly the purpose for which the Buddha has appeared in the world. He then relates one of the most famous teaching stories in Buddhism: the parable of the arrow. What can we say about the original Buddhist attitude toward philosophizing expressed in this passage? What can we say, in view of this passage, that the "religious life" is dependent on?

Thus I have heard:

On a certain occasion The Blessed One was dwelling at Savatthi in Jetavana monastery in Anathapindika's Park. Now it happened to the venerable Malunkyaputta, being in seclusion and plunged in meditation, that a consideration presented itself to his mind, as follows:—

"These theories which The Blessed One has left unelucidated, has set aside and rejected—that the world is eternal, that the world is not eternal, that the world is finite, that the world is infinite, that the soul and the body are identical, that the soul is one thing and the body another, that the saint exists after death, that the saint does not exist after death, that the saint both exists and does not exist after death, that the saint neither exists nor does not exist after death—these The Blessed One does not elucidate to me. And the fact that The Blessed One does not elucidate them to me does not please me nor suit me. Therefore I will draw near to The Blessed One and inquire of him concerning this matter. If The Blessed One will elucidate to me, either that the world is eternal, or that the world is not eternal, or that the world is finite, or that the world is infinite, or that the soul and the body are identical, or that the soul is one thing and the body another, or that the saint exists after death, or that the saint does not exist after death, or that the saint both exists and does not exist after death, or that the saint neither exists nor does not exist after death, in that case will I lead the religious life under The Blessed One. If the Blessed One will not elucidate . . . [these things], in that case I will abandon religious training and return to the lower life of a layman."

[Malunkyaputta, gaining a chance to speak to the Buddha, related these questions, demanding a reply to each. He repeated this whole series and finished by saying the following:]

". . . If The Blessed One does not know either that the saint both exists and does not exist after death, or that the saint neither exists nor does not exist after death, the only

upright thing for one, who does not know, or who has not that insight, is to say, 'I do not know; I have not that insight.'

[The Buddha replied:]

"Pray, Malunkyaputta, did I ever say to you, 'Come Malunkyaputta and lead the religious life under me, and I will elucidate to you either that the world is eternal, or that the world is not eternal, . . . or that the saint neither exists nor does not exist after death'?"

"Nay, verily, Reverend Sir."

"Or did you ever say to me, 'Reverend Sir, I will lead the religious life under The Blessed One, on condition that The Blessed One elucidate to me either that the world is eternal, or that the world is not eternal, . . . or that the saint neither exists nor does not exist after death'?"

"Nay, verily, Reverend Sir."

"So you acknowledge, Malunkyaputta, that I have not said to you, 'Come Malunkyaputta, lead the religious life under me and I will elucidate to you either that the world is eternal, or that the world is not eternal, . . . or that the saint neither exists nor does not exist after death; and again that you have not said to me, 'Reverend Sir, I will lead the religious life under The Blessed One, on condition that The Blessed One elucidate to me either that the world is eternal, or that the world is not eternal, . . . or that the saint neither exists nor does not exist after death.' That being the case, vain man, whom are you so angrily denouncing?

"Malunkyaputta, anyone who should say, 'I will not lead the religious life under The Blessed One until The Blessed One shall elucidate to me either that the world is eternal, or that the world is not eternal, . . . or that the saint neither exists nor does not exist after death;—that person would die, Malunkyaputta, before the Tathagata [that is, the Buddha] had ever elucidated this to him.

"It is as if, Malunkyaputta, a man had been wounded by an arrow thickly smeared with poison, and his friends and companions, his relatives and kinsfolk, were to procure for him a physician; and the sick man were to say, 'I will not have this arrow taken out until I have learned whether the man who wounded me belonged to the warrior caste, or to the Brahman caste, or to the farmer caste, or to the menial caste.'

"Or again, he were to say, 'I will not have this arrow taken out until I have learned the name of the man who wounded me, and to what clan he belongs.'

"Or again, he were to say, 'I will not have this arrow taken out until I have learned whether the man who wounded me was tall, short, or of the middle height.'

"Or again, he were to say, 'I will not have this arrow taken out until I have learned whether the man who wounded me was black, dusky, or of yellow skin.'

"Or again, he were to say, 'I will not have this arrow taken out until I have learned whether the man who wounded me was from this or that village, town, or city.'

"Or again, he were to say, 'I will not have this arrow taken out until I have learned whether the bow which wounded me was a capa, or a kodanda.'

"Or again, he were to say, 'I will not have this arrow taken out until I have learned whether the bow-string which wounded me was made from swallow-wort, or bamboo, or sinew, or maruva, or from milk-weed.' . . .

[The Buddha continues with several more such examples:]

"That man would die, Malunkyaputta, without ever having learned this. In exactly the same way, Malunkyaputta, any one who should say, 'I will not lead the religious life under The Blessed One until The Blessed One shall elucidate to me either that the world is eternal, or that the world is not eternal, . . . or that the saint neither exists nor does not exist after death;—that person would die, Malunkyaputta, before the Tathagata ever elucidated this to him.

"The religious life, Malunkyaputta, does not depend on the dogma that the world is eternal; nor does the religious life, Malunkyaputta, depend upon the dogma that the world is not eternal. Whether the dogma obtain, Malunkyaputta, that the world is eternal, or that the world is not eternal, there still remain birth, old age, death, sorrow, lamentation, misery, grief, and despair, for the extinction of which in the present life I am prescribing. . . .

"And what, Malunkyaputta, have I elucidated? Misery, Malunkyaputta, have I elucidated; the origin of misery have I elucidated; the cessation of misery have I elucidated; and the path leading to the cessation of misery I have elucidated. And why, Malunkyaputta, have I elucidated this? Because, Malunkyaputta, this does profit, has to do with the fundamentals of religion, and tends to aversion, absence of passion, cessation, quiescence, knowledge, supreme wisdom, and Nirvana; therefore I have elucidated it. Accordingly, Malunkyaputta, bear in mind what it is that I have not elucidated, and what it is that I have elucidated. . . ."

Source: Henry Clarke Warren, *Buddhism in Translations* (New York: Atheneum, 1986), pp. 117–122. ©1986 by the President and Fellows of Harvard College. Reprinted by permission of Harvard University Press.

Reading 5.2   CONTEMPLATION OF THE IMPURITY OF THE BODY:
VISUDDHI-MAGGA

One of the earliest forms of Buddhist meditation focused on the transience and the impurity of the human body. It is generally speaking, a relatively introductory sort of contemplation. What effect do you think this contemplation is intended to have on a practitioner?

For even as the body when dead is repulsive, so is it also when alive; but on account of the concealment afforded by an adventitious adornment, its repulsiveness escapes notice. The body is in reality a collection of over three hundred bones, and is framed into a whole by means of one hundred and eighty joints. It is held together by nine hundred tendons, and overlaid by nine hundred muscles, and has an outside envelope of moist cuticle covered by an epidermis full of pores, through which there is an incessant oozing and trickling, as if from a kettle of fat. It is a prey to vermin, the seat of disease, and subject to all manner of miseries. Through its nine apertures it is always discharging matter, like a ripe boil. Matter is secreted from the two eyes, wax from the ears, snot from the nostrils, and from the mouth issue food, bile, phlegm, and blood, and from the two lower orifices of the body, feces and urine, while from the ninety-nine thousand pores of the skin an unclean sweat exudes attracting black flies and other insects.

Source: Henry Clarke Warren, *Buddhism in Translations* (New York: Atheneum, 1986), pp. 298. ©1986 by the President and Fellows of Harvard College. Reprinted by permission of Harvard University Press.

Reading 5.3 REALIZING THE FOUR NOBLE TRUTHS

The Four Noble Truths were heard for the first time in the Buddha's first sermon, which was delivered to his five former fellow practitioners, who would become his first disciples. These Four Truths—Suffering, the Origination of Suffering, the Cessation of Suffering, and the Way—form the core of Indian Buddhist teaching. They were also studied in all later forms of Buddhism as it spread to different cultures. Anyone who wants to understand the Buddhist message should start by studying the Four Noble Truths. After reading this selection, do you think that the Noble Truth of Suffering represents an accurate characterization of human existence? If so, why? If not, why not?

Thus have I heard: Once, when the Blessed One was dwelling in Benares, at the Deer Park in Rsivadana, he spoke to the "Fortunate Five," the group of elders who were his first disciples.

"Monks," he said, "for one who has wandered forth, there are two extremes. What two? On the one hand, there is attachment to sensual pleasures; this is vulgar, common, ignoble, purposeless, not conducive to a chaste and studious life, to disgust with the world, to aversion from passion, to cessation, monkhood, enlightenment, or nirvana. On the other hand, there is addiction to exhausting the self through asceticism; this is suffering ignoble, and purposeless. Monks, for one who has wandered forth, these are the two extremes. Staying with the Tathagata's Noble Doctrine and Discipline, away from both of these extremes, is the middle course, fully realized [by the Buddha], bringing about insight, and conducive to tranquillity, disgust with the world, aversion from passion, cessation, monkhood, enlightenment, and nirvana. . . .

"Furthermore, monks, there are Four Noble Truths. What four? The Noble Truth of suffering, the Noble Truth of the origination of suffering, the Noble Truth of the cessation of suffering, and the Noble Truth of the way leading to the cessation of suffering.

"Now, monks, what is the Noble Truth of suffering? Just this: Birth is suffering, old age is suffering, sickness is suffering, death is suffering. Involvement with what is unpleasant is suffering. Separation from what is pleasant is suffering. Also, not getting what one wants and strives for is suffering. And form is suffering, feeling is suffering, perception is suffering, karmic constituents are suffering, consciousness is suffering; in sum, these five agglomerations (skandhas), which are the basis of clinging to existence, are suffering. This, monks, is the Noble Truth of suffering.

"And what is the [second] Noble Truth of the origination of suffering? It is the thirst for further existence, which comes along with pleasure and passion and brings passing enjoyment here and there. This, monks, is the Noble Truth of the origination of suffering.

"And what is the [third] Noble Truth of the cessation of suffering? It is this: the destruction without remainder of this very thirst for further existence, which comes along with pleasure and passion, bringing passing enjoyment here and there. It is without passion. It is cessation, forsaking, abandoning, renunciation. This, monks, is the Noble Truth of the cessation of suffering.

"And what is the Noble Truth of the way leading to the cessation of suffering? Just this: the Eightfold Noble Path, consisting of right views, right intention, right effort, right action, right livelihood, right speech, right mindfulness, right meditation. This, monks, is the Noble Truth of the way leading to the cessation of suffering.

"This is suffering. . . . This is the origination of suffering. . . . This is the cessation of suffering. . . . This is the way that leads to the cessation of suffering.' . . . monks, from these basic mental realizations, according to doctrines that were not handed down from previous teachers, there were produced in me knowledge, insight, understanding, enlightenment, intelligence, and wisdom; illumination became manifest.

"This Noble Truth of suffering is to be thoroughly known. . . . This origination of suffering is to be given up. . . . This Noble Truth of the cessation of suffering is to be realized. . . . This Noble Truth of the leading to the cessation of suffering is to be cultivated': monks, from this basic mental realization, according to doctrines that were not handed down from previous teachers, there were produced in me knowledge, insight, understanding, enlightenment, intelligence, and wisdom; illumination became manifest.

"This Noble Truth of suffering has come to be known thoroughly. . . . This origination of suffering has been given up. . . . This Noble Truth of the cessation of suffering has been realized. . . . This Noble Truth of the way leading to the cessation of suffering has been actualized; monks, from this basic mental realization, according to doctrines that were not handed down from previous teachers, there were produced in me knowledge, insight, understanding, enlightenment, intelligence, and wisdom; illumination became manifest.

"And monks, as long as I did not perceive, with right wisdom, these Four Noble Truths as they are, thrice-turned and in their twelve aspects, I could not claim to have fully attained unsurpassed complete enlightenment, nor would there be produced knowledge in me, nor would I have realized certain emancipation of the mind. But since, monks, I did perceive, with right wisdom, these Four Noble Truths as they are, thrice-turned and in their twelve aspects, I know I have fully attained unsurpassed complete enlightenment. Knowledge was produced in me, and I did realize certain emancipation of the mind, liberation through wisdom."

Thus the Buddha spoke while he was residing in Benares, at the Deer Park in Rsivadana. And hearing this explanation, the Venerable Ajnata Kaundinya's understanding was awakened, and he attained the perfectly pure, pristine, unstained Dharma-eye into the nature of things.

Source: John S. Strong, *The Experience of Buddhism: Sources and Interpretations* (Belmont, Calif.: Wadsworth, 1997), pp. 32–33; translated from Emile Senart, ed., *Mahavastu,* vol. 3 (Paris: Imprimerie Nationale, 1897), pp. 330–334.

Reading 5.4   EXPEDIENT MEANS: THREE PARABLES FROM THE *LOTUS SUTRA*

The *Lotus Sutra* is one of the most famous scriptures in Mahayana Buddhism for its explanation of the usage of expedient means (flexible teaching techniques for leading people to enlightenment). Because people are unable at first to appreciate the full import of the Buddha's message, he leads them gradually through expedient methods. The first parable shows how Buddhahood is the original endowment of humans, who are often incapable of directly appreciating it. Therefore, they must be led gradually. In the second passage, the Buddha tells the story of his career as a Buddha in a previous era and concludes with a parable that illustrates a main theme of the *Lotus Sutra.* In the third parable, enlightenment is compared to a hidden jewel secretly sewn into a man's coat. Teaching by parable has always been a major part of instruction in all religions, not just Buddhism. Can you find any parallels between these parables and those taught by other religious traditions?

A. THE LONG-LOST SON

A father and son parted company while the son was still a very young man. In the course of time the father became very rich, while the son sank into the depths of poverty and beggary. Once, during the course of his wanderings, he happened to come to the palatial home of his father. The father, at once recognizing him, had him brought into his presence. This only frightened the poor man, and the father let him go. Then he sent two men to ask the beggar whether he wished to do menial labor on the rich man's estate. The beggar consented, and worked this way for many years. One day the rich man told the beggar that in view of his many years of honest and conscientious service he would reward him with the charge of all of his possessions. After several years more had passed, the rich man gathered his entire household and clan and told them that the beggar was his son, from whom he had been parted many years before, and that he was now reclaiming him and declaring him heir to all of his possessions. When the beggar heard this, he was amazed, thinking that he had received something quite unexpected.

B. THE CONJURED CITY

A guide was leading a group of travelers to a spot where a treasure lay buried. On the way the travelers wearied, and some spoke of turning back. The guide accordingly conjured up an apparent city on the way, and successfully urged his companions to rest and refresh themselves there. When they had done so, they went on and reached the spot where the treasure was concealed. Then the guide told them that the city they had seen a while back had been an illusory city, and not a real one, which he had conjured up for the purpose of conquering their discouragement.

C. THE HIDDEN JEWEL

At that time, the five hundred arhats, having received a prophecy [of future salvation] in the Buddha's presence, danced for joy, then, rising from their seats, went into the Buddha's presence, where with head bowed they did obeisance to his feet, repented of their transgressions, and reproached themselves, saying: "O World-Honored One! We have been constantly having this thought, saying to ourselves, 'We have already gained the ultimate passage into extinction.' Now that at last we understand it, we know we have been like ignoramuses. What is the reason? We should have gained the Thus Come One's wisdom, yet we were content with petty knowledge. We are to be likened to the following case: There is a man who arrives at the house of a close friend, where he gets drunk on wine, then lies down. At that time, his friend, having official business, is on the point of going away, when he sews a priceless jewel into the interior of the first man's garment and departs, leaving it with him. The first man, laid out drunk, is unaware of anything. When he has recovered, he sets out on his travels, then reaches another country, where he devotes every effort to the quest for food and clothing. He suffers such hardship, that he is content with however little he may get. Then his friend, encountering him by chance, speaks these words to him: 'Alas, sir! How can you have come to this for the sake of mere food and clothing? Once I, wishing to afford you comfort and joy, as well as the natural satisfaction of your five desires, in such-and-such a year, on a certain day of a certain month, sewed a priceless jewel into the inside of your garment. Yet you, not knowing of it, have suffered pain and grief in quest of a livelihood. How foolish you have been!...

Source: Leon Hurvitz, trans., *Scripture of the Lotus Blossom of the Fine Dharma* (New York, Columbia University Press, ©1976), pp. xi–xii, 164–165. Reprinted by permission of the publisher.

Reading 5.5 *THE HEART SUTRA*

The *Heart Sutra* is probably the most popular single scripture in all of Mahayana Buddhism. In this short text, the great *bodhisattva* Avalokiteshvara (he who observes the sounds of the world) teaches the great *arhat* Shariputra that all of the major concepts of earlier Buddhism are nothing in the context of the teaching of emptiness and that the only real way to enlightenment is through the Perfection of Wisdom *(prajnaparamita)*. A critical line in this text says, "With nothing to attain, the bodhisattva depends on *prajnaparamita*." Why is it that the *bodhisattva* has nothing to attain? What does it mean to "depend upon *prajnaparamita*"?

> *Avalokiteshvara Bodhisattva, when practicing the deep perfection of wisdom*
> *Perceived that all five skandhas are empty,*
> *And was saved from suffering and distress.*
> *[He said:]*
> *"Shariputra, form is not different from emptiness*
> *Emptiness is not different from form.*
> *Form is exactly emptiness, emptiness is exactly form.*
> *The same is true of sensations, perceptions, impulses and consciousness.*
> *Shariputra, the characteristic of all the things in the world is emptiness;*
> *They do not appear or disappear, are not tainted or pure,*
> *Do not increase or decrease.*
> *Therefore in emptiness, no form,*
> *No feelings, perception, impulses, consciousness.*
> *No eyes, no ears, no nose, no tongue, no body, no mind.*
> *No color, no sound, no smell, no taste, no touch, no object of mind;*
> *No realm of eyes and so forth until no realm of mind-consciousness.*
> *No ignorance and also no extinction of it, and so forth until*
> *No old-age-and-death and also no extinction of them.*
> *No suffering, no arising, no cessation, no path.*
> *No knowing and also no attainment.*
> *With nothing to attain, the bodhisattva depends on* prajnaparamita
> *And his mind is no hindrance.*
> *Without any hindrance no fears exist;*
> *Far apart from every perverted view he dwells in Nirvana.*
> *In the three worlds all Buddhas depend on* prajnaparamita
> *And attain Supreme Correct Enlightenment.*
> *Therefore know the* prajnaparamita
> *Is the great transcendent mantra, is the great bright mantra,*
> *Is the utmost mantra, is the supreme mantra,*
> *Which is able to relieve all suffering;*
> *It is true and not false.*
> *So proclaim the* prajnaparamita *mantra*
> *Proclaim the mantra, saying:*
> Gate, gate, paragate, parasamgate! Bodhi! Svaha! . . ."

Source: Charles Muller, trans., *Taisho*, Vol. 8, no. 249, p. 846.

Reading 5.6   *THE AWAKENING OF MAHAYANA FAITH:* STABILIZING MEDITATION AND OBSERVATIONAL MEDITATION ATTRIBUTED TO ASHVOGHOSHA

Many people consider the *Awakening of Mahayana Faith* to be the single most important text for the understanding of Northeast Asian Mahayana Buddhism. It is especially important for its explanation of the dynamics of the impure and pure aspects of the human mind and how one may overcome the impure part and attain enlightenment. The later sections of the *Awakening of Mahayana Faith* also provide concrete guidelines for practice. The following section is excerpted from the discussion of using stabilizing and observational meditation. After reading it, can you briefly characterize the relationship between stabilizing meditation and observational meditation? Why is it important that they be practiced in conjuction with each other?

If you only practice stabilizing meditation, your mind will sink and you will be likely to experience laziness. Lacking enjoyment of the cultivation of wholesome activities, you drift far away from Great Compassion. In this case, you need to practice observational meditation. In the practice of observational mediation you should observe that all the conditioned dharmas of the natural world are not graspable for any sustained period of time, as they change and dissipate. All mental functions arise and cease from moment to moment, and thus there is suffering. You should observe all former mental formations from the past to be like the fading images of a dream. You should observe presently experienced mental formations to be like a flash of lightning. You should observe the mental formations of the future which are yet to come to be like a cloud which suddenly arises. You should observe all of those in the world who possess a body to be impure, filled with various defilements, such that there is not one who can experience joy.

You should think like this: Due to their permeation by ignorance, the minds of all sentient beings from beginningless generations past are made to arise and cease, and have been made to undergo great suffering of body and mind. In the present they experience a multitude of pressures. The suffering of the future also will know no limit. Unable to detach or free themselves from this condition, the condition of sentient beings is quite pitiable.

To engage in this kind of contemplation, you must arouse all of your courage and make the Great Vow for enlightenment, saying: "I vow to free my mind from discrimination, so that I may penetrate the ten directions with the practice of all kinds of meritorious virtues, penetrating to the future with countless expedient methods designed to relieve all sentient beings from suffering and affliction, allowing them to attain the absolute bliss of Nirvana." If you arouse this kind of vow, you will act according to your ability at all times and in all places performing all good acts. You will never abandon practice and you will not become lazy. Except while sitting in meditation where you single-mindedly practice stabilization, in all other things you should clearly observe what is to be done and what is not to be done.

In all actions, whether moving or standing still, whether lying down or arising, you should always practice both stabilizing meditation and observational meditation together. That is to say, although you contemplate upon the non-arising of all things of the world in their nature, you still contemplate upon the fact that everything arises through the combination of cause and conditions, and that the karma of good and bad actions, and the retribution of suffering and pleasure are neither lost nor destroyed. Although you contemplate upon the good and evil karmic retribution arising from cause and conditions, you also contemplate upon the fact that their nature is unobtainable.

If you practice stabilizing meditation, you can eliminate the attachment of ordinary people to the world and will be able to forsake the timid view of the practitioners of lesser attainment. If you practice observational meditation you are able to eliminate the fallacy of the narrow, inferior minds of lower-level practitioners which do not arouse great compassion. You will furthermore be far removed from the state of ordinary people who do not cultivate their good roots. Because of this, the two practices of stabilizing meditation and observational meditation complement each other, and are never separated. If you do not practice both stabilizing meditation and observational meditation, you will never enter into the path of wisdom.

Source: Charles Muller, trans., *Taisho*, vol. 32, no. 1666, pp. 582c–583a.

Reading 5.7   *THE SUTRA OF PERFECT ENLIGHTENMENT:* CONTEMPLATION OF IMPURITY AND HOW TO FIND A QUALIFIED TEACHER

The *Sutra of Perfect Enlightenment* is one of the most popular scriptures in the East Asian Mahayana meditative traditions. In the modern-day Korean Chogye school, it is part of the standard scriptural curriculum in the monastery schools. The main reasons for its popularity are its concise presentation of important Buddhist soteriological and metaphysical matters, along with its clear discussion of concrete aspects of meditation practice. The following two selections are from, respectively, the third and tenth chapters of the *sutra*. The selection from the third chapter is the beginning part of a long guided meditation that starts with an early Indian–style contemplation on no-self and the fundamental impurity of the physical body. The selection from the tenth chapter deals with the issue of selecting a qualified teacher, who must show that he is free from attachment to certain aspects of the path, which are called "maladies." Reading 5.2 also contained a passage that dealt with the impurity of the body. Can you see any important differences in perspective between that passage and the first selection here? In reading the second selection here, can you identify the main points that Buddhist practitioners should keep in mind in looking for a dependable teacher?

A. THE CONTEMPLATION OF IMPURITY

Good sons, newly awakened bodhisattvas and sentient beings of the degenerate age who yearn for the pure enlightened mind of the Buddha must correct their thoughts and rid themselves of all illusions, first relying on the Buddha's practice of stabilizing meditation. Firmly established in moral discipline and living in harmony with like-minded students, then practicing silent sitting in a quiet room, they should uninterruptedly be mindful of the following:

This present body is a synthesis of the Four Elements. Hair, nails, teeth, skin, flesh, bones, marrow, brains and pigment all return to Earth. Saliva, mucus, pus, blood, sputum, scum, phlegm, tears, semen, urine and feces all return to Water. Heat returns to

Fire, and movement returns to Wind. When the Four Elements have been separated, where can the false body exist? Now you know that this body ultimately has no substance. It appears as a synthesis, but in reality it is like an illusion conjured by a magician. When these four factors temporarily combine, the Six Senses Faculties falsely appear; through the internal and external matching of the Six Faculties and Four Elements, there is the deluded apprehension of conditioned energy. Within this conglomeration, there seem to be marks of this conditioned energy, which is provisionally called "mind." Good sons, if this false mind does not have its Six Objects, it cannot exist. If the Four Elements are separated, there are no objects to be experienced. At this point, the cognized objects each disperse and vanish, and ultimately there is no dependently arisen mind to be seen.

Good sons, since the illusory body of this sentient being vanishes, the illusory mind also vanishes. Since the illusory mind vanishes, illusory objects also vanish. Since illusory objects vanish, illusory vanishing also vanishes. Since illusory vanishing vanishes, non-illusion does not vanish. It is like polishing a mirror: when the filth is gone its brightness naturally appears. Good sons, you should understand both body and mind to be illusory filth. When the defiled aspects are permanently extinguished, the entire universe becomes pure.

Good sons, it is like a pure mani-*pearl which reflects as all kinds of colors, depending upon its surroundings. The foolish see that pearl as really having these colors. Good sons, it is the same with the pure nature of Perfect Enlightenment: it appears in people's bodies and minds, according to their individual type. Yet these fools say that pure Enlightenment really has body and mind. It is only because these people are unable to free themselves from illusory appearances that I call body and mind "illusory filth." The one who opposes and removes illusory filth is called the "bodhisattva." When filth is gone, its opposition is removed; then there is no opposition, no filth, nor anything to be named.*

B. THE GENUINE TEACHER WHO IS FREE FROM THE FOUR MALADIES

Good Sons, sentient beings of the degenerate age must arouse "great mind" and seek Genuine Teachers. Those who want to practice should seek out only someone with correct insight, whose thoughts do not abide in characteristics, who is not attached to the realms of lower level practitioners, and whose mind is constantly pure even while manifesting the world's afflictions.

Even while pointing out your various faults, he praises your practices of purity, and prevents you from breaking the precepts. If you find this kind of person, you can attain Unsurpassed Correct Universal True Enlightenment. Sentient beings of the degenerate age who meet this kind of person should make offerings to him, not sparing body or life, even as far as holding on to property, wife, children and retainers. This Genuine Teacher constantly demonstrates purity throughout the four postures [of walking, standing, sitting, and lying down]. Although he points out all of your errors and weak points, his mind lacks pride. Good Sons, if you do not arouse any negative feelings toward this Good Friend, you will ultimately be able to accomplish Correct Enlightenment. Your mind-flower will blossom, illuminating the worlds of the ten directions.

Good Sons, the subtle doctrine that is actualized by this Genuine Teacher should be free from the Four Maladies. What are the Four Maladies? The first is the malady of "contrivance." Say, for example, there is someone who says "based on my original mind I shall carry out various practices" and wants to achieve Perfect Enlightenment. Since the nature of Perfect Enlightenment is not something which can be attained by contrivance, it is called a "malady."

The second is the "naturalist" malady. Say, for example, there is someone who says "We should presently neither cut off samsara *nor seek* nirvana. Samsara *and* nirvana *actually lack any conception of arising and ceasing. We should just natually go along with the various natures of reality" and wants to achieve Perfect Enlightenment. Since the nature of Perfect Enlightenment does not come about through accepting things as they are, this is called a "malady."*

The third is the "stopping" malady. Say, for example, there is someone who says "from my present thought, I shall permanently stop all thoughts and thus apprehend the cessation and equanimity of all natures" and wants to achieve Perfect Enlightenment. Since the nature of Perfect Enlightenment is not met through the stopping of thoughts, it is called a "malady."

The fourth is the "annihilation" malady. Say, for example, there is someone who says "I will now permanently annihilate all defilements. Body and mind are ultimately empty, lacking anything. How much more should all the false realms of the sense organs and their objects be permanently erased" and seeks Perfect Enlightenment. Since the characteristic of the nature of Perfect Enlightenment is not annihilation, it is called a "malady."

When you are free from the Four Maladies you will be aware of purity. The making of this observation is called "correct insight." Any other insight is called "mistaken insight."

Good Sons, sentient beings of the degenerate age should exhaust their energies in making offerings to Good Buddhist Friends and serving Genuine Teachers. If the Genuine Teacher becomes close and familiar with you, you should not be proud. If he is distant, you should not be resentful. The states of unpleasantness and pleasantness are just like the empty sky. Fully realize that body and mind are ultimately equalized and that you share the same essence with all sentient beings without difference. If you practice in this way you will enter Perfect Enlightenment.

Source: Charles Muller, trans., *Taisho*, vol. 17, no. 842, pp. 914b–914c.

Reading 5.8   How to Contemplate: The *Mu Koan*

This is the commentary attached to the *Mu Koan* (*Wu k'ang-an* in Chinese), which explains to practitioners the attitude that they should take in attempting to contemplate the *koan*. It is from the text called the *Gateless Barrier*, a collection of forty *koans*, the first of which is the *Mu Koan*. This commentary features a discussion between the Zen master Chao-chou and his student, which was introduced in the "Buddhist Practice" section in the discussion of Zen Buddhism. Can you identify any way in which this approach to Buddhist practice seems different than that described in some of the other readings? What do you think *Mu* refers to here?

For the practice of Zen, it is essential that you pass through the barrier set up by the ancestral teachers. For subtle realization, it is of utmost important that you cut off the mind road. If you do not pass the barrier of the ancestors, if you do not cut off the mind road, then you are a ghost clinging to bushes and grasses. What is the barrier of the ancestral teachers? It is just this one word Mu, the one barrier of our faith. We call it the "Gateless Barrier of the Zen sect." When you pass through this barrier, you will not only interview Chao-chou [an ancient Chinese Zen master] intimately, you will walk hand in hand with all the ancestral teachers in the successive generations of our lineage, the hair of your eyebrows entangled with theirs, seeing with the same eyes, hearing with the same ears. So then, make your body a whole mass of doubt, and with your 360 bones and joints, and your 84,000 hair follicles, concentrate on this one word Mu. Day and night, keep digging into it. Don't consider it to be nothingness. Don't think in terms of "has" or "has not." It is like a red-hot iron ball. You try to vomit it out, but you cannot. Gradually, you purify yourself, eliminating mistaken knowledge and attitudes you have held from the past. Inside and outside become one. You are like a dumb person who has had a dream. You know it for yourself alone. Suddenly Mu breaks open. The heavens are astonished and the earth is shaken. It is as though you snatch away the great sword of General Kuan. When you meet the Buddha, you kill the Buddha. [Note: This phrase should not be taken literally. It is a way of telling the practitioner to get rid of all mistaken conceptions regarding enlightenment.] When you meet Bodhidharma, you kill Bodhidharma. At the very cliff-edge of birth-and death, you find the Great Freedom. In the six worlds and in the four modes of birth, you find a samadhi *of frolic and play. So, how should you work with it? Exhaust all your life-energy on this one word Mu. If you do not falter, then it's done. A single spark lights your dharma-candle.*

Source: Robert Aitken, *Taking the Path of Zen* (Berkeley: North Point Press, 1982), pp. 95–96.

CHAPTER 6

TAOISM

Chinese religion encompasses a great many indigenous and imported traditions. Religions indigenous to China include Confucianism, Taoism, the state cult of China, and the folk (popular) religion of China. Traditions from outside China have also been part of the Chinese religious landscape. Of these influences, Buddhism has been most pervasive; emissaries of Buddhism first arrived in China during the first century of the common era. Islam has been influential in China, especially among peoples living west of the Great Wall in Chinese central Asia and in southwestern China; estimates of the number of Muslims in China today range from 15 million to 50 million. Zoroastrianism, Manichaeism, Nestorian Christianity, and Judaism played small parts in Chinese religious history before disappearing. Roman Catholic and Protestant missionaries brought their forms of Christianity to China, and both traditions have survived. The number of Christians in contemporary China is a subject of debate, but it is likely that Christians number no more than 4 percent of China's 1.2 billion population.

Taoism and Confucianism are the subjects of Chapters 6 and 7, but to understand them we need to discuss early Chinese religion and identify those features of ancient folk religion that continued over the centuries

The Dragon and Tiger Pagodas, along the shores of Lotus Lake in Kaohsiung, Taiwan, feature twin pagodas that form the central temple. Worshipers at the Taoist temple enter through the mouths of a larger-than-life dragon and tiger (1991).

to be part of everyday Chinese life. As we proceed, we must be aware that for most Chinese, religion is not a separate compartment of life; in many ways it is integrated into family life, government, medicine, and other aspects of everyday existence that readers may think of as being separate from religion.[1] Moreover, it is not uncommon for a person to participate in the activities of some combination of folk religion, Taoism, Buddhism, and Confucianism.

The most important theme in Chinese religion is the pursuit of harmony. From ancient times, the Chinese have seen heaven, earth, and human beings as integrally or organically related. An event in one realm affects the other two realms; hence, for example, sin or misbehavior has cosmic implications. Even the dead are affected by the actions of the living, and the ancestor, in turn, may influence the lives of the living. In the context of this worldview, human actions—whether good or bad, whether in special rituals or in everyday activities—are crucial. Crops fail or flourish, dynasties rise or fall, depending in part upon whether human beings are performing well.

TAOIST BELIEFS

We begin our investigation of Taoist beliefs by drawing from the Taoist classic *Tao Te Ching*, the text traditionally attributed to the sage Lao-tzu of the sixth century B.C.E. Many Western scholars have taken the philosophical classic work of Lao-tzu as their sole or primary source for Taoist belief. But as we discuss the Taoist conception of the cosmos, divinities, humankind, human destiny, and government, we draw on a variety of sources.

COSMOS: THE TAO

The **Tao (Dao)*** is the mysterious source and ordering principle underlying all that is. Even though Taoists perceive right conduct as action that "follows the Tao," the Tao gives no commands and

---

*The older and still widely used system for romanizing Chinese characters is the Wade-Giles system. In 1958 the People's Republic of China adopted a different system, called Pinyin. We employ the Wade-Giles system, but we add the Pinyin spelling in parentheses where it may be helpful—in cases such as Mao Tse Tung (Mao Ze-dong), Peking (Beijing), *jen (ren)*, and Tao (Dao).

makes no judgments. The Tao is the source of the gods and is therefore a more fundamental reality than divine beings. *The Tao Te Ching* refers to the Tao in these terms:

> *It can be regarded as the mother*
>   *of Heaven and Earth*
> *I do not yet know its name:*
> *I "style" it "the Way" [Tao].*
> *Were I forced to give it a name,*
>   *I would call it "the Great."*
> *We call it the mysterious female—*
>
> . . . .
>
> *Subtle yet everlasting! It seems to exist.*
> *In being used, it is not exhausted.*[2]

Taoists experience the Tao as female, because it is the source and because it sustains and nurtures; it is not a master. The workings of the Tao can be suggested through an analogy to an uncultivated, unattended field. The varieties of wildflowers that grow there represent the myriad of particular beings or things in the universe. The field may appear to be barren in winter, but in the spring we discover that it was, in reality, a very fecund womb. The field nurtures the flowers by supplying nutrients, but we do not see this nurturing work. The field appears to take no action, and it takes no credit.[3] Even though this account is oversimplified, it provides a model for understanding Taoist thought and practice. The Tao is like a mother, not a father, and a commentary to the *Tao Te Ching* says, "Practice non-action and meekness, keep to what is female, never make the first move."[4]

The Tao is the source of everything, as we have said. But how does the Tao produce the world? Taoists refer to this creation process as self-generation or gestation. In a sense, the Tao "grows itself" into the universe, and so the world is the body of the Tao. This universal body is also called the body of Lao-tzu—a vast cosmic Lao-tzu. A Taoist text explains that Lao-tzu's left eye became the sun, his right eye the moon, his head the K'un-lun mountain, his beard the planets, and his bowels the snakes.[5] Taoists explain that the cosmic Lao-tzu is an androgynous being who is identical with his mother, traditionally called Mother Li: "It must be understood that he himself transformed his vacuous body into Mother Li's form, and then returned into his own womb; it was not that there was really a Mother Li's womb. In reality this is not so."[6] The creation of the world, then, is the gestation of the Tao into a vast cosmic body that is really a single organism—the cosmic, androgynous Lao-tzu. We turn now to a step-by-step account of the gestation process.

THE GESTATION OF THE COSMOS   The growth or evolution of the Tao proceeded by coagulation or congealment, expansion, division, and combination until it evolved into the "ten thousand things"—the Chinese term for the totality of beings and things. In the beginning there was the Tao, or rather Tao in a condition of primal chaos *(hun-t'un)*. A Taoist scripture (the *Huai-nan-tzu*) puts it thus: *"When Heaven and Earth were not yet shaped, It [the Tao] was amorphous, vague . . . a blur; call it therefore 'the Primal Beginning.'"*[7] Another text calls

this chaos a "primordial undifferentiated mass."[8] This mass seethed and churned until in its center was formed a "drop" of primordial breath *(ch'i)*. We follow one version of Taoist numerology in tracing the order of gestation (see Table 6.1).[9]

Tao itself can be called "Zero," because it is neither negative nor positive but is "pure potential," or *ling*. The *ch'i*, the primordial energy, can be called "the One"; all that is, comes from this *ch'i* (this breath of life). The myriad of things solidify out of, or dissolve into, this primal energy. Each human being has this *ch'i*, and Taoist practice is based on how humans nurture their vital breath.

The *Tao Te Ching* states the process in abbreviated form as follows:

> *The Way [Tao] gave birth to the One;*
> *The One gave birth to the Two;*
> *The Two gave birth to the Three;*
> *And the Three gave birth to the ten thousand things.*
> (Chap. 42)

The Taoists interpret "the Two" to be *yin* and *yang*. Although not limited by the doctrines of the ancient *yin/yang* cosmology, Taoists agree with the basic notion that *ch'i* parcels itself out—that is, divides itself—into patterns of energy that are bipolar complements of one another (for example, dark and light). Every thing and every event can be understood as *yin*, *yang*, or some combination of the two. *Yin* patterns of energy are associated with the following qualities/realities: dark, cool, wet, obscure, female, passive, earth, and death. *Yang*, by contrast, is associated with light, warm, dry, bright, male, active, heaven, and life. *Yin* energy tends to drift to low levels, whereas the *yang* tends to rise to the heavens.

The purpose of Taoist practice is to learn how to control *ch'i* so as to ally oneself with the *yang* pattern of light-male-heaven. To do this, the complementarity of *yin* and *yang* must be understood. Without *yin* patterns like dark-female-earth, the *yang* patterns could not exist. Indeed, Taoist practice involves cultivation of the *yin* quality of femaleness because it is the female/*yin* energies that nurture and vitalize the male/*yang* energies. Thus, Taoism embraces the *yin* in order to attain

STAGES OF COSMIC GESTATION

Table 6.1

0	Tao as primal chaos
1	Primordial breath or energy (*ch'i*)
2	*Yin* and *yang*
3	Heaven, earth, and humanity
4	The four seasons
5	The five directions (four directions plus the center)
.	
.	
.	
10,000	The totality of beings and things

the *yang*. We can see why Taoism has what one Sinologist has called a "peculiar esteem for the female."[10]

Yin and *yang* interact in such a way as to evolve "the Three"—heaven, earth, and humanity. The many heavens or celestial realms were formed first; then their residents (the gods) were formed, and then the universe. The gods are personal manifestations of the Tao. In terms of spiritual potential, human beings are located between heaven and earth, for we can be the most potent of all beings on earth. Although the conditions of human life usually "wear out" our *ch'i* (vital energy), we can learn to reverse this process. We have the choice to expend our energies or to capitalize on them so as to save ourselves. What is more, human activities strongly influence the whole cosmos, and our behavior can destroy or renew its harmony. Hence, the major type of Taoist ritual, the *chiao*, can be called the rite of cosmic renewal. The fate of the universe depends on human behavior.

The fourth stage of gestation is the initiation of a basic structure within nature—the four seasons. Four is thus associated with succession or alteration and is temporal. Five is more oriented to spatial disposition and relations among particular physical forces: five stands for the five directions (the four directions, plus the center) and the five "elements" or phases, known to the ancients as

metal, wood, fire, water, and earth. Each direction corresponds to an element—for example, south corresponds to fire. The fifth stage of the gestation of the cosmos involves the dispersal of energy in all directions, and it sets up a cycle of relationships among the physical forces that operate therein: wood is said to give birth to fire, fire to earth, earth to metal, and metal to water. An opposite cycle operates by controlling or conquering: metal conquers wood (with an axe), fire conquers metal, water conquers fire, earth conquers water (by damming), and wood conquers earth (by growth).

The end of Table 6.1, "10,000: the totality of beings and things," indicates that the gestation process produces the entire cosmos and all life forms. The number 10,000 is a symbolic way to say "things beyond number."

BRINGING THINGS TOGETHER: CORRESPONDENCE IN THE MACROCOSM AND MICROCOSM Taoists see each person or being in the universe as a **microcosm**—that is, a replica of the larger system. Thus, the universe as a whole is a **macrocosm**—a system that mirrors the structure of any of its constituent parts. For example, the planets are related to one another in the same way that the internal organs of a person are related to one another. The network of correspondences that informs the Taoist vision of reality, shown in Table 6.2, is not merely sym-

COSMIC CONNECTIONS

Table 6.2

Body Part	Government	Gods	Directions	Five Elements (phases or modes)	Colors	Seasons	Planets
Kidneys	Officials	Chuang-hsu	North	Water	Black	Winter	Mercury
Lungs	Officials	Shao-hao	West	Metal	White	Autumn	Venus
Spleen	Officials	Huang-ti	Center	Earth	Yellow	Middle four months	Saturn
Heart	Ruler	Shen Nung	South	Fire	Red	Summer	Mars
Liver	Generals (military)	Fu Hsi	East	Wood	Green or blue	Spring	Jupiter

Source: Based on Michael Saso, *Taoism and the Rite of Cosmic Renewal* (Pullman: Washington State University Press, 1972), p.53 ff. Saso is drawing mainly from the *Huai-nan-tzu*.

bolic or metaphorical; the connections are real. These correspondences may seem unlikely or unexpected to the unenlightened, but the adept or priest sees them as the keys to well-being and immortality. To use a rough analogy, we may be surprised to discover that our drinking glass is resonating with the sounds of a musical instrument being played quite some distance away in another house. We may find it hard to believe that there are overtones from this glass and that they in turn set up a series of vibrations elsewhere. The average person is oblivious to the full range of physical and spiritual correspondences. Whereas the correspondence of heart-ruler-south-fire-red-summer (Table 6.2) may strike a chord for us, other series may not; when the high priest performs the *chiao* (rite of cosmic renewal), he calls forth the green energy of the precious heaven of charity to enter his liver.

The notion of the human person as a microcosm of the universe is crucial. Our four limbs correspond to the four seasons, our joy to the wind, our anger to the rain, our taking to cold, and our giving to heat. Powerful divinities who correspond to aspects of our person may be called down or materialize so as to revitalize us. Thus, there are *correspondences* that operate in *microcosms* and that can *cause* transformations.

Our understanding of the Taoist view of the cosmos can shed light on Taoist practice and on other elements of Chinese culture. The techniques of inner alchemy, with their emphasis on *ch'i* and channeling *ch'i* to body organs, are based on the whole system we have just explored. The ritual techniques of the priest in revitalizing the community are a dramatic reinvigoration of the "worn-out" *ch'i*. The martial art/exercise form **T'ai-chi ch'uan** is based on much of the cosmology just described. Finally, Chinese medicine overlaps with Taoist views of the body to a great extent; historically, we know that many Taoists were physicians.

DIVINITIES

Taoists recognize the existence of four major types of spiritual beings: gods, immortals, ancestor spirits, and demons. Taoists believe that the gods are the most powerful of these entities and the only beings who can grant salvation to humans. However, as has been discussed, the gods are not the creators of the universe; the Tao is the source from which all is generated.

Ancestor spirits may be benevolent or demonic. The Chinese term **shen** is often used to mean "benevolent ancestor" but can refer to any

A group of people practice T'ai-chi ch'uan next to an outer wall of the Forbidden City in Peking (Beijing), People's Republic of China.

benevolent spiritual being. If a person dies in an especially violent or unjust way, his or her spirit may become demonic. The "hungry ghosts" of Chinese lore are the "mildly evil" spirits of uncared-for ancestors—those not shown homage by their surviving offspring. The term *kuei* is used to refer to such malevolent spirits. The exorcism of demons has traditionally been a function of the Taoist priest. This function is invaluable, because most illnesses and tragedies are partly caused by the *kuei*.

Taoists distinguish their pantheon of gods from those of the folk religion in three ways: potency, origin, and residence. The gods of Taoism either are supremely powerful (the most powerful of all beings) or are messengers or appointees of these higher gods. According to the Taoists, the gods of folk religion were once human beings who are believed to have risen to divine status, whereas the Taoist gods were never human but are special divine

manifestations of the Tao. Finally, Taoists believe that the gods of folk religion reside either in the posterior (lower) heavens or on earth, whereas the Taoist gods reside in the anterior (higher) heavens or "stellar" realms. "Residence" in the anterior heavens does not mean the gods cannot also be present elsewhere, but it does indicate a significant degree of power and position. These distinctions can be seen in practice when the Taoists remove the scrolls depicting folk gods from the local village temples and replace them with depictions of Taoist gods before performing ceremonies.

Taoists do not worship the gods of folk religion, but some Taoist gods are worshiped in the folk religion. From the tenth century onward, the **Jade Emperor (Yu-huang)** has been a supreme god in the Taoist pantheon and also a supreme deity in folk religion. Many of the popular gods report to the Jade Emperor; the immensely popular god of Chinese folk religion Tsao Chun, Lord of the Stove, is believed to station himself near the stove or hearth (the symbolic center of the household) and periodically report the moral and spiritual record of the family to the Jade Emperor.

The term *Jade Emperor* is actually a title, not a name. Strictly speaking, a deity occupies a post or position and, especially in the lower reaches of the celestial bureaucracy, may change positions. The Taoist writer Yen Tung describes the pantheon as a hierarchized administration closely imitating the Chinese imperial bureaucracy.[11] Terms like *emperor, department, official, marshal, general,* and even *soldier* are commonly used in referring to the gods, their roles, and their relationships. The military aspect (generals and soldiers) is essential because of the myriad of demons whose evil ways must be overcome upon orders from the higher members of the Taoist pantheon.

The three highest gods of Taoism are the **Three Pure Ones.** The Pure Ones are called Worthies or Lords; they are the Lord of Heaven, Lord of Earth, and Lord of Humanity, corresponding to the three basic forms of *ch'i* in the macrocosm. The Primordial Heavenly Worthy (Yuan-shih t'ien-tsun) is Lord of Heaven, and his sphere of influence in the microcosm of the human body is the head. The Numinous (or Pure Potential) Treasure Heavenly Worthy (Ling-pao t'ien-tsun) is Lord of Earth, and his sphere of influence in the body is the heart or chest. The third member of the triad is the Heavenly Worthy of the Way and Its Power (Tao-te t'ien-tsun), who is the Lord of Humanity. His microcosmic power is seated in the abdomen of each person. This third worthy is none other than Lord Lao, the deity who incarnated into a human form as the sage Lao-tzu. Thus, Lao-tzu is a multidimensional being who exists in many forms on different levels: he is the cosmos, he is one of the three high gods, and he is the human sage to whom the *Tao Te Ching* is attributed.

According to most Taoists, the Jade Emperor is the executor of orders from the Three Pure Ones. He confers duties, advancements, and demotions in the vast spiritual bureaucracy and functions like a minister of ministries. As his name indicates, he is regarded as an emperor and is portrayed in imperial regalia. The Jade Emperor wears a long, dragon-embroidered robe and sits on a throne. He wears an emperor's headgear—a mortarboard with pendants of colored pearls hanging from the front and back. In his hands he holds the imperial ceremonial tablet. The extent of his reign includes the ministries of Work, of Time, of Fire, of Thunder and Wind, of the Five Peaks, of Literature, of War, of Epidemics, of Exorcisms, of Medicine, and much more.

The mysterious beings called **immortals** were once mere humans who have attained a transcendent condition through Taoist practice. The immortals, however, display more independence and spontaneity than the other members of the Taoist spiritual hierarchy. One early text refers to these amazing beings as follows: *"Far away on Mount Ku lives a holy man. His flesh and skin are like ice and snow; he is as gentle as a young girl. He eats none of the five grains, but takes deep draughts of the wind and drinks the dew. He rides on clouds and mounts a flying dragon and wanders beyond the four seas."*[12] Such "holy men" came to be called immortals, and they became the Taoist ideal of human perfection. They are not disembodied souls but rather beings who possess a refined or etherealized body that links their physical and spiritual dimensions.

The fully developed Taoist belief in the immortals goes far beyond the concept expressed in the passage just quoted. Some immortals live "amid the stars" and participate in the celestial bureaucracy; these are the heavenly immortals. The terrestrial immortals usually wander among the mountains and secret caverns of the world. In addition to the incredible powers already mentioned (feeling no heat or cold and riding on the clouds), the immortals can change their shapes, become invisible, or appear as hermaphrodites. But when they are among mortals, they are inclined to maintain a mundane appearance and, as the Taoist saying goes, "remain hidden among the people." Although some of their activities are whimsical, the immortals sometimes perform the serious and important function of revealing scriptures, such as the *Mao Shan* revelations, to be discussed in "History of Taoism" later in this chapter. Many of the actions of the immortals show unconditional benevolence toward humans.

The chief of the immortals is Chung-li Ch'uan. He is said to have lived under the Chou dynasty (1122–221 B.C.E.) and to have obtained the secrets of the elixir of life and the power of transmutation. According to the traditional story, Chung-li Ch'uan married a young and beautiful wife and settled in the country. One day Chung-li came upon a young woman fanning a grave mound. She told Chung-li that her late husband had asked her not to remarry until the dirt on his grave was dry. Chung-li took her fan, invoked spirits to help, and hit the tomb with the fan. Suddenly the soil became completely dry. The young woman ran away happily to find her admirer, leaving Chung-li with the fan.

The story might have ended there if Chung-li's wife had not found the fan in Chung-li's room. On hearing the story, she was angry at the young widow, saying she herself would never behave so. This gave Chung-li an idea. He put himself into a special condition with a powerful spell and pretended to be dead, while at the same time taking the shape of a handsome young man. In the form of this young man he made love to the supposed widow, who in two days agreed to marry him. The young man told her he needed the brain of her late husband to make a powerful potion, so the widow opened the coffin. Her former husband suddenly came to life, and her lover disappeared. She was so ashamed she hung herself. Chung-li set the house on fire, taking with him only the fan and a copy of the *Tao Te Ching*.[13]

THE NATURE AND DESTINY OF HUMANS

Not everyone can become immortal in the special sense just defined, but all humans possess the primal energy *(ch'i)* that can enable them to attain salvation. Humans are a microcosm of the universe; like the universe or macrocosm, they are manifestations of that original eternal energy—the One.

Within a human, this One is variously called the *real self,* the *real one,* the *immortal embryo,* or the *divine ch'i of Lao-tzu.*

Even though each human possesses this spiritual essence, many people are unable or unwilling to realize it or make use of it. Human nature also includes destructive elements that can cause physical and spiritual decline. The body contains Three Worms or Three Corpses, which incite the person to lust and gluttony and try to bring about early death. On certain designated days and nights, the Three Worms leave the sleeping body and rise to heaven to report on sins so that the person's life will be shortened. To control the Three Worms, one should keep a cereal-free diet, for they feed on cereals; one should also stay awake on the designated days and nights so that the Three Worms cannot leave the body to report to heaven. Taoist techniques and rituals, as well as virtuous deeds, are also effective in controlling these negative forces. Taoists also believe that demons may lodge themselves in a person, especially when the person's positive *ch'i* is weakened by misdeeds.

Many Taoists believe that in addition to the spiritual essence called the One, each human body contains some thirty-six thousand gods, whose powers may be used to counter the negative forces just mentioned. This belief in internal gods follows from the view that the body is a microcosm of the universe: just as the macrocosm contains a myriad of gods, so does each human body. These gods feed upon the purest nutrients—saliva and breath; they detest wine and meat. Finally, the presence of the Three Pure Ones themselves can be invoked to invigorate the person and ward off evil energies; the Three Pure Ones can exert their influence in their microcosmic correlates in the head, the heart, and the abdomen.

Compared with earlier Chinese notions of human destiny, Taoist belief concerning the afterlife is more appealing to many people. The ancient belief in Shang times was that only aristocrats would attain heaven after death. In the age of classic philosophy, the philosopher Chuang-tzu offered no clear promise of continued conscious existence after death but only the concept of death as transformation of energy. But Taoism developed a belief in eternal conscious existence after death. Taoism offers to all, regardless of social class, a promise of an afterlife in one of many heavens. It is a conditional promise, however: in this life one must perform good deeds, repent of sins, and either use individual spiritual techniques or participate in collective ceremonies. In some cases, the efforts and faith of mourners and Taoist priests may even effect the rescue of a soul from hell. Records from the third century C.E. refer to rescue attempts for ancestors as far back as nine generations.[14] Depending on a number of factors, then, Taoists believe in a range of possible destinies. One might suffer punishments by demons in hell without hope of rescue, or one might linger in this world, hovering over one's grave, or one might become a demon. A more pleasant outcome would be continued existence in this world near the ancestral tablets, nourished by filial survivors. Life in the many Taoist heavens is blissful and can even involve advancement to a higher position (office) or to a higher heaven. Finally, a few individuals may become immortals and exercise the activities and freedoms enjoyed by those unique beings.

Taoism did not initially include rewards for goodness and punishment for evil in the afterlife, but with the influence of Buddhism, concepts of rebirth, *karma,* and heaven and hell were woven into Taoism. Taoists began to develop concepts of an afterlife in which sinners must either be reborn or be condemned to suffer for their sins in a hell located under certain mountains.

GOVERNMENT AND THE IDEAL STATE

According to the *Tao Te Ching,* the best ruler or government leader is the person who knows and follows the Tao: the ruler should not impose on the people but play a passive role. The existence of such a leader is *"hardly noticed by the people";* the leader takes the feelings and opinions of the people as his own (Chap. 49). If the government tries to impose many strict laws, it will only cause resentment and crime; if the government favors skill and profit, competition and robbers will abound; if it stresses morality, the people act artificially.

The *Tao Te Ching* summarizes this concept of government and the ideal state in Chapter 80:

> 1 *Let the country be small and people few—*
> 2 *Bring it about that there are weapons for "tens"*
> *and "hundreds," yet let no one use them;*
> 3 *Have the people regard death gravely and put*
> *migrating far from their minds.*
> 4 *Though they might have boats and carriages, no*
> *one will ride them.*
> 5 *Though they might have armor and spears, no one*
> *will display them.*
> 6 *Have the people return to knotting cords and using*
> *them.*
> 7 *They will relish their food,*
> 8 *Regard their clothing as beautiful,*
> 9 *Delight in their customs,*
> 10 *And feel safe and secure in their homes.*
> 11 *Neighboring states might overlook one another,*
> 12 *And the sounds of chickens and dogs might be*
> *overheard,*
> 13 *Yet the people will arrive at old age and death*
> *with no comings and goings between them.*[15]

The ideal leader does not wish for expansion but favors simplicity: little or no use of technology or sophistication, few and simple desires, and a self-possessed state. The ambiguity of the original text admits both a nonmilitary and a military translation in lines 2 and 5, so other translations read, for example, *utensils* instead of *weapons.*[16] Elsewhere, the *Tao Te Ching* admonishes the ruler to use weapons with great restraint (Chap. 31). Overall, Chapter 60 contains the best single-line statement of Lao-tzu's general approach to this subject: *"Ruling a large state is like cooking a small fish."* Too much handling and stirring will spoil it.

Taoist belief evolved into what has been called a "fusion" or compromise between the sort of view found in Lao-tzu's teachings and the Legalist philosophy of government. Legalism called for a strictly enforced complex of laws governing every aspect of life and a leader who ruled with an iron hand;

the ruler could use any method he deemed necessary to insure obedience and order. Perhaps the term *Lao-tzu/Legalist compromise* better describes Taoist belief, because the mature Taoist view departs somewhat from both the classic Lao-tzu teachings and those of Legalism. It is a compromise between authoritarian rulership and the passive approach associated with the Lao-tzu book. The compromise position is not opposed to strong leadership. The ruler is the source of commands, and he insists that government officials perform their duties and enforce the laws. In the mature Taoist view, the ruler is a prominent symbol of the kind of regularity and order the laws provide so that, for example, the people "feel safe and secure in their homes." This regularity or order is perceived as the way (Tao) of nature.

The legal system and the order it provides is not imposed by the ruler according to his personal likes and dislikes. Because the ruler is never to impose upon the people through artifice or deception, some scholars have called the policy "noninterventionalism," in contrast to the arbitrary methods of Legalism.[17]

The discussion of the history of Taoism will show that prominent Taoist leaders have supported a powerful imperial order that was not averse to expansion. This is a radical departure from the teachings of the *Tao Te Ching*. Taoists have cooperated with dynasties that wielded enormous political and military power. The Taoists have often sought authorization by some level of government and have in turn supported what they have perceived as legitimate government. Yet the Taoist ideal of the sage ruler remains, as does the belief that one day an ideal state will emerge to establish a "grand tranquility." The Taoist *Mao Shan* revelations of the fourth century C.E. teach that the *"Sage who is to come"* will one day descend and establish the reign of Great Peace. Although a given government in the present age may not be perfect, it can be legitimate. In the future a perfect government will bring about a perfect or grand harmony. In sum, the mature Taoist political teachings constitute what may be called a tempered utopianism.

TAOIST PRACTICE

To understand Taoist practice, we need to be aware of the difference between the Tao-min (the masses or average persons) and the **Tao-shih** (the Taoist priest and/or the **adept**). The Tao-min are expected to follow certain relatively simple ethical and spiritual directives and to rely on the priests. The people rely on the priests to manage their relation to spiritual forces. Although a priest may also be an adept, the latter need not be ordained. An adept is a person who practices techniques of longevity and immortality as a recluse or monk.

This section begins with the description and analysis of the priest's ritual functions, featuring the cosmic renewal ceremony and exorcism. Then follows an account of techniques used by Taoist adepts. The perspective of the common people (Tao-min) will enter into our analysis of ritual and also into the final topic of this section, values for daily living.

TAOIST RITUAL: THE *CHIAO*

To the majority of Taoists, nothing brings together and embodies Taoist beliefs more powerfully than Taoist rituals. For them, ritual is the quintessential religious act. Taoist rituals may be conducted in a home or in a temple. The major types of ritual are the *chiao* (the offering or rite of cosmic renewal) and the *chai* (literally, "fast"), a ceremony with a more specific purpose than the *chiao*. An example of *chai* is the ritual that effects the rescue of an ancestor's soul from hell. Broadly speaking, the following ceremonies can also be counted as *chai:* confession of sins, weddings, exorcisms, and funerals.

It has been rightly observed that no cultural group enjoys a familial or communal observance more than the Chinese. The traditional Chinese calendar calls for sacrifices to the god of the soil in the twelfth lunar month, various new year celebrations in the first month, observance of the "three days of origin" (the fifteenth day of the first, seventh, and tenth months—the three poles around which the year is constructed), celebration of the birthday of the god of the soil (February 2), and the celebration of Lao-tzu's birthday (February 16).

The traditional festivals and other occasions such as the completion of a new temple may be celebrated by the performance of a *chiao* (offering by a Taoist priest). In most cases, it is the local community that requires the priest to perform the *chiao*, which consists of a variety of rituals over a four- or five-day period. The purpose of the entire program is to honor the deities and petition their blessings. Because the efficacy of the *chiao* means that humanity and nature are restored to harmony and vigor, it can be called the "rite of cosmic renewal."

The *chiao* engages the whole person, including all five senses—hearing, seeing, smelling, tasting, and touching. The sounds include the chanting and singing of the high priest and his entourage of assistants. These chanters are sometimes accompanied by several oboes, drums, and cymbals. The ritual is punctuated periodically by exploding firecrackers, as, for example, when the high priest dispatches a set of petitions to the celestial realm. Outside the temple, two or three theater groups are competing, each with microphones turned up full blast. Amid these sounds and those of the crowd are arm-banded officials hawking "stock" in the community and announcing the names of contributors as their names are written on a huge bulletin board.[18]

The visual power of the *chiao* is no less impressive than its sounds. Thousands of colorful lanterns and flags decorate the front of the temple. Placards of calligraphy, as well as drawings and paintings, are displayed. The clerical robes are rich in color and symbolism. The priests' movements are sometimes slow and sometimes rapid, but always stately—somewhat like an operatic performance. Occasionally the priests' assistants or a local medium may engage in less reserved and more (popularly) dramatic activities, such as gymnastic movements or ecstatic shaking movements. Parts of this panoply

of visual imagery are seen through wafts and billows of smoke—smoke from burning paper money, incense, firecrackers, and the many candles that adorn the altars.

Outside the temple, the mounds of food seem almost to spill from the tables—2-foot-deep containers of rice, snow peas, cabbages, carrots, broccoli, cauliflower, bean curd, and vegetable and rice balls. At the end of the chiao, fruit, breads, and cakes also appear with wine and varieties of meats. Most visible among the celebrative foods are huge pigs slit from throat to tail with a green orange in the mouth and a stick of incense in the orange. Their pink bodies have been covered with red stamps, and their intestines have been draped over their backs.

With the exception of the performing entourage of priests, their assistants, and a few representatives of the community, most of the participants enjoy being jostled about in a throng in front of the temple. In a sense, the whole community comes to feel like one body. There are also feasts in each household; hospitality is never more abundant, because all relations and friends are expected to pay a visit and partake of the special foods.

On the first morning, an elaborate ritual dispatches a myriad of messages to the celestial realm. These messages are written documents that have been prepared by the priests and the community representatives. The dispatch of messages (announcements, expressions of gratitude, petitions, and the general request for the renewal of relationships with the gods and the cosmos) must be performed in the right way by the right person. Like other important matters, it should be enacted by people who have connections and who can go through proper channels. The high priest must first use his expertise to transform his body into the cosmic body of Lao-tzu. The first step in this process is purification of himself and the altar. The priest sings, *"In order to get rid of all that is perverse and filthy . . . we must first invite respectfully the perfect officers who destroy filth . . . and transform this place of ordinary men into a land of immortals."* The transformation can then begin. The priest says, *"My Cinnabar Field* [in this case a reference to the lower belly] *opens up for communication. The ten thousand spirits unite; the body depends on the tranquility of its spirits.* "Transformation proceeds by visualization techniques and is based on a series of correspondences in accord with the microcosm-macrocosm concept: *"My left eye becomes the sun, and my right the moon. . . . Respectfully I request the green energy of the precious heaven of charity to enter my liver."*[19] The priest visualizes the moon 9 inches from his face. With the word *enter*, the priest makes an exaggerated sound of inhaling.

After the transformation, the priest is in a position to summon the gods and dispatch the community's messages. He announces his name and rank. There follows a flurry of gongs and music by a two-string violin and a mandolin. The high priest then stands on a table in front of the temple to issue a general summons to the celestial realm. The summons has been written out and signed by the high priest; it is issued in the name of Chang Tao-ling, the founder of the largest Taoist sect, the Celestial Masters. The priest folds the summons in a cone shape and sets it aflame. He holds it until it is nearly burned and then blows the remains out into the air.

Once the summons is thus transmitted to heaven, the community's messages are burned on a wok in front of the temple. A profusion of firecrackers are exploded as the smoke rises. A blast of music ends this portion of the *chiao*. The whole dispatch (also called the "announcement") takes about one and a half hours and constitutes only about one-twenty-fifth of the *chiao*. Included among the many other rituals performed in the *chiao* are the flag-raising ceremony (to attract the attention of the gods), the floating of water lamps (to summon souls from the hells to the Universal Salvation feast), and scripture recitation.

These Taoist practices illustrate how Taoism unites the community through its liturgies. They also show why it is called a theistic religion. Although the priest never loses sight of the importance of the Tao as pure impersonal Absolute, the community focuses on the gods. Thus, Taoism has both theistic and nontheistic elements.

THE RITE OF EXORCISM

The importance of exorcism in Chinese tradition derives from the common belief that many sicknesses and behavior disorders are caused by demons. Demons *(kuei)* range from mildly troublesome ghosts to vicious spirits who can readily destroy the person possessed. In any case, because the gods are more powerful than the demons, one who can invoke the powers of the gods is needed: a Taoist priest. Not all exorcistic functions involve a victim who suffers from seizures, and not all exorcisms involve complex and lengthy liturgies. In some cases the priest may simply write out a charm in the name of a powerful god. The charm may read: "I, Jade Emperor, hereby order the evil and crooked forces causing this illness to leave immediately. This order has the power to smash and drive away all demons." The priest reads this charm aloud and then burns it so that its message is carried to the heavens in the smoke.

Stronger or more vicious demons must be exorcised by the full-scale rite. To be able to perform such a ritual, the priest must conduct a special meditation on the occasion of the first thunderstorm in the spring. At the first thunderstorm clap, he rises and faces the direction from which the sound of thunder is coming. He then envisages twelve earthly powers as embodied in the twelve joints of each hand. Next, the priest holds his breath and circulates the primordial breath through the corresponding twelve organs of his body. Finally, he envisages the power of the thunder and lightning entering seven of these organs, thereby investing himself with their power. Thus empowered, a priest can perform the full rite of exorcism.[20]

In an exorcism, the priest invokes the powers of the gods by calling their esoteric names and by special *mudras* (hand positions). The power, or *ch'i*, stored in the priest's body is here called upon to breathe out the names of the deities. The climax of the exorcism occurs as the Taoist breathes on the head of the patient and thus focuses insurmountable power to exorcise the demon. The actual presence of the deities vanquishes the demon. The ritual ends with the priest's bowing before the altar

A Taoist priest. The photograph was taken at the base of Luofu Shan, Kwangtung province, People's Republic of China (ca. 1980s–1990s).

and mentally restoring the gods to their positions in the cosmos.[21]

TECHNIQUES OF LONGEVITY AND IMMORTALITY

Up to this point the discussion of Taoist practice has described some of the ways in which the priest uses special powers in ministering to the people. We now turn to a discussion of individual techniques to promote one's own longevity and immortality. These techniques are used by specialists (Tao-shih)—priests or adepts. For such Taoists, the following saying holds true: "My destiny is in me, it is not in Heaven."[22] We will see that this is an operational principle indicating the importance of personal responsibility and the ability to animate personal, even bodily, energies.

However, the saying in no way denies the importance of cosmic forces; the point is to be able to focus these forces in oneself. From the varieties of Taoist methods, three examples are considered here: embryonic breathing, holding the Ones, and Taoist *yoga*.

These methods are neither isolationist nor selfish; none of them is completely effective if the practitioner does not live a moral life and perform acts of virtue. Spiritual techniques and moral virtues complement each other and have equal importance. One of greatest early writers on such techniques, Ko Hung (fourth century C.E.), makes the point quite clearly: "Those who do not carry out acts of virtue and are satisfied only to practice magical procedures will never obtain Life Eternal."[23] The sorts of good deeds the Taoist adept is to perform include feeding the poor (especially orphans), maintaining roads and bridges, and protecting people from illness and misfortune.

Examples of virtuous acts by Taoist adepts abound in Chinese literature. The *History of the Later Han* documents many cases, as does T'ang literature. The outstanding figure in the T'ang was the wonder worker Yeh Fa-shan (631–720 C.E.), whose altruistic actions were said to have stimulated many to follow his example.[24] These points about ethical virtues are worth stressing, because some modern writers have tended to emphasize Confucian ethics and ignore Taoist ethics. The truth is that virtuous action plays a major role in Taoist teaching. This fact will become more obvious later, when we discuss the obligations of ordinary people (nonadepts).

The various techniques of longevity and immortality can be practiced in different combinations, depending on the needs of the individual. In any case, Taoists recommend that one undertake such exercises under the guidance of an experienced and trusted teacher. With this background, we now turn to the first of the spiritual disciplines to be considered, embryonic breathing.

EMBRYONIC BREATHING *Embryonic* refers to the spiritual center below the navel—the center containing the spiritual embryo. To perform **embryonic**

breathing one lies down in a dark room, closes one's eyes, and concentrates on a point 1 inch below the navel. Breathing will naturally become slow. The tongue is arched back against the roof of the mouth to stimulate the flow of saliva. One swallows saliva along with the breath. One simply breathes in and swallows saliva and air at the same time, then exhales. Saliva and breath are the purest nourishment.

After a while the center of concentration, the embryo, becomes warm. When this happens one allows the center of concentration to become a circle that gradually becomes larger and larger until its circumference coincides with one's feet and head. This is not a "technique" in the sense that it works mechanically and guarantees results. However, at this point one may feel a bliss or joy that pervades one's whole being. The passing of the euphoria can occur just as unexpectedly as its coming.[25]

HOLDING THE ONES   A more complex Taoist technique, called **holding the Ones,** incorporates many elements of the Taoist tradition into one exercise: the macrocosm-microcosm metaphysics, the Three Pure Ones, the calendar, a stellar constellation, Taoist views of human nature, and much more. Students of religion find the method interesting because many aspects of the technique have parallels in Hindu *yoga* and Buddhist meditation. Revealed as a part of the great *Mao Shan* scriptures (380 C.E.), this technique is said to "give eternal life" and enable the adept to achieve amazing feats: *"You can transform your body into all things, you can go through water and fire, you can tie up tigers and leopards, and you can control demons and spirits."*[26]

To begin, at midnight, just as the spring season begins, one sits upright, faces east, exhales nine times, and swallows saliva thirty-five times. One envisions the seven stars of the Big Dipper and brings them down to a position directly above the head. Now if the practitioner is able to meditate on the Three Ones (the Venerable Lords), they will appear in the bowl of the Big Dipper accompanied by their three ministers; each Lord has a thousand chariots and ten thousand horsemen.

This breathtaking vision is not the purpose of the technique, however. Taoist texts warn against being transfixed by such a vision and "merely gazing" at the Ones: *"Ill-fated persons, their will is not firm! Or if it is firm, it cannot endure. They know the names of the Ones but cannot hold them. Or if they can hold them, they cannot be resolute. They boast and bluster but cannot constantly hold [the Ones]. Therefore the Three Ones depart, and then the truth breath disappears."*[27]

A person possessed of full powers of concentration will now resolutely proceed to breathe in deeply three times, allowing the Venerable Lords to enter through the mouth. They proceed to their residences—the cinnabar fields between the two eyebrows, the heart, and 3 inches below the navel. The Pure One who resides in the lowest field is called "the Child"; he and his minister are dressed in yellow robes and look like newborn infants. They dwell in a palace that, in earthly measurements, is 1 inch square.

The formal meditation session ends with a short recitation; a typical session lasts about forty minutes. But holding the Ones during a formal session is neither the highest achievement nor the greatest challenge. The adept must learn to hold the Ones at all times: *"Eating and drinking, think of the Ones. Happy and rejoicing, thinking of the Ones. Sad and grieving, think of the Ones. . . . Traveling by carriage or on horseback, think of the Ones."*[28]

Although this sounds incredibly difficult, and it is indeed difficult, the paradox is that the state of mind that is capable of holding the Ones is a "simple and open mind." Advanced adepts refer to the ideal as a kind of original or natural mind; the Chinese term for this is *p'u,* often translated as "an uncarved block." Plans and worldliness are in a sense artificial. Our minds are usually so filled with plans and worldly concerns that our original, pure mind is cluttered or clouded. So habitual are our distractions that great effort is required to concentrate. But when we succeed in getting through the clutter, what we find is a natural, pure awareness.

TAOIST YOGA   The Chinese term *tao-yin shen-t'i* literally means "stretching and contracting the body." Some writers translate this as *gymnastics;*

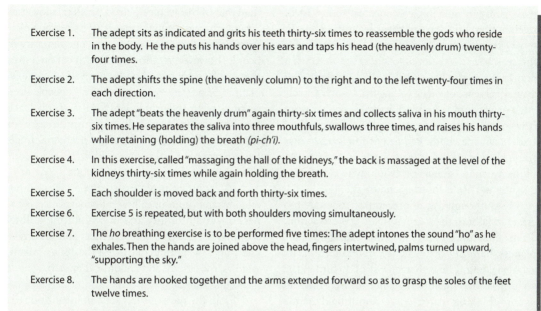

Exercise 1.	The adept sits as indicated and grits his teeth thirty-six times to reassemble the gods who reside in the body. He the puts his hands over his ears and taps his head (the heavenly drum) twenty-four times.
Exercise 2.	The adept shifts the spine (the heavenly column) to the right and to the left twenty-four times in each direction.
Exercise 3.	The adept "beats the heavenly drum" again thirty-six times and collects saliva in his mouth thirty-six times. He separates the saliva into three mouthfuls, swallows three times, and raises his hands while retaining (holding) the breath *(pi-ch'i)*.
Exercise 4.	In this exercise, called "massaging the hall of the kidneys," the back is massaged at the level of the kidneys thirty-six times while again holding the breath.
Exercise 5.	Each shoulder is moved back and forth thirty-six times.
Exercise 6.	Exercise 5 is repeated, but with both shoulders moving simultaneously.
Exercise 7.	The *ho* breathing exercise is to be performed five times: The adept intones the sound "ho" as he exhales. Then the hands are joined above the head, fingers intertwined, palms turned upward, "supporting the sky."
Exercise 8.	The hands are hooked together and the arms extended forward so as to grasp the soles of the feet twelve times.

Figure 6.1 Taoist Yoga

Source: Adapted from Henri Maspero, *Taoism and Chinese Religion,* trans. Frank A. Kierman, Jr. (Amherst: University of Massachusetts Press, 1981), pp. 542 ff.

others call it *yoga*. We use the term **yoga** here to refer to a system of movements and stretches designed to facilitate physical and spiritual health. Taoists believe these methods will tone up the body and clear it of obstacles; these obstacles can be physical or spiritual. Once the organism is cleared of obstacles, the *ch'i* (the vital breath) can flow through it smoothly The system outlined in Figure 6.1 is attributed to Chung-li and was written down, with drawings, on a stone wall by Master Lu (Tung-pin). This system was in use at least by the twelfth century C.E. and continues to be practiced today.[29] The eight exercises can be performed by both men and women.

VALUES FOR DAILY LIVING: TAOIST ETHICS

Taoist ethics involves living by two fundamental principles—*wu-wei* (nonaction) and *te* (virtue)—

and performing specific good works in a wide range of social and environmental contexts. The concept that informs all Taoist action is **wu-wei**, literally, "nonaction." The Taoist ideal of *wu-wei* does not always mean refraining from action, however. It means refraining from phony, forced, and blatantly aggressive action and refraining from willful, selfish action. When one is functioning in *wu-wei* fashion, all is accomplished as though no action were being taken.

Wu-wei might be called a natural or spontaneous way of functioning. For the Taoist, it is a way of being and acting in accord with one's Tao-nature. It is based on profound intuition of the interrelatedness and the interaction of all things. When one acts out of this understanding, one's actions have the character of *wu-wei*.

Many, perhaps most, people do not base their actions on such intuition. Their minds are filled with words, images, jingles, concepts, and codes of right action, but none of these is subtle enough to put them in touch with their Tao-nature. For this reason they feel "out of touch." They need what one Taoist writer has called "belly knowledge"—a gut-level sense of what is going on.[30] Such knowledge or wisdom is no mere impulse or emotion; it is contact with that embryo, that divine *ch'i* of Lao-tzu in one's body. People need to learn to distinguish this *ch'i*, or at least draw on the powers of those beings (human or divine) who can distinguish it and use it for the good of all.

Even though lists of precepts or codes are too crude to fathom the true nature of *wu-wei* action, Taoist literature includes such lists calling for suppleness, humility, benevolence, quietude, and the art of yielding. These characteristics do hint at the style of *wu-wei* functioning, but they may mislead us into thinking that *wu-wei* cannot be dynamic or powerful. Taoists teach that *wu-wei* carries a kind of power called *te (de),* which may be translated as "virtue," "power," or "effectiveness." Because the *te* of something comes from its Tao-nature, the *te* is its most natural aptitude. The Taoist ideal is thus an internally based ethics, not an externally imposed one. In this light, we can understand such Taoist statements as *"the highest virtue is not virtuous"* and *"when the Way [Tao] is lost, only then do we have virtue"* (*Tao Te Ching,* chap. 38).

Te is not a mere inner feeling, however. Like the power of water, *te* can overcome great obstacles or get around them by seeking a natural course. Taoists often refer to the water course in illustrating *te* and *wu-wei:* water is adaptive and soft, yet it wields tremendous power. *Te* is neither brute force nor total passivity. The great Taoist sage Chuang-tzu told this story to illustrate its effectiveness: There was a butcher whose cleaver did not get dull during twenty years of work. Pressed for his secret, he replied, "Between the bones of every joint there is always some space, otherwise there could be no movement. By seeking out this space and passing through it, my cleaver lays wide the bones without touching them."

A deep understanding of *wu-wei* and *te* may require a more contemplative or simpler lifestyle

than that of the average person. In all religious traditions, there is a small minority who prefer a contemplative or mystical approach. The majority of people, however, require specific ethical directives that can be understood without mystical contemplation. To put the matter another way, people need to know what the principles of *wu-wei* and *te* call for specifically: Is there an obligation to care for orphans and widows? Must one protect animals from harm? Is filial piety required? Let us consider some of these specific questions.

Taoist ethics is not unlike the ethics of other religious traditions in calling for benevolence, compassion, and humility and in prohibiting killing, stealing, and lying. Taoist teachers and texts regularly urge the faithful to care for the poor, orphans, widows, the elderly, and children; they warn against greed and idle talk.

From the days of the Taoist political and religious leader Chang Lu (third century C.E.), Taoist teachers have found strong altruistic directives in the *Tao Te Ching*. The sage is said to accept the needs and interests of others as his or her own (Chap. 49). Loving kindness *(tz'u)* is seen as the principal treasure in life (Chap. 67). Chapter 81 of the *Tao Te Ching* closes the gap between the needs of others and one's own needs by saying, *"The more one gives to others, the more one is enriched."*

Taoism is unusual among the world religions in laying considerable stress on the protection of the environment (including animals). This theme was present early on.[31] When emperors wished to please Taoist masters with gifts, they often bestowed large wildlife preserves upon them. Masters Ssu-ma Ch'eng-chen and Li Han-Kuang were thus honored, and "those who consumed meat" could not obtain access to the latter's holy mountain. Historians like J. Russell Kirkland have documented many cases of Taoist masters promoting environmental concerns and urging the establishment of imperial wildlife preserves. According to one high Confucian official, many Taoist masters "took the accomplishments of yin and the rescue of creatures as their priorities."[32] The *T'ai-Shang Kan-Ying P'ien (The Treatise of the Exalted One on Response and Retribution),* an extremely popular Taoist text, urges compassion for all creatures, saying, *"Even the multifarious insects, herbs and trees should not be injured."* In decrying the actions of evildoers, this same text identifies the following activities as evil: *"[They] shoot the flying, chase the running, expose the hiding, surprise nestlings, close up entrance holes, upset nests, injure the pregnant, and break the egg."*[33]

It is in popular texts like the *Response and Retribution* that we find the Taoist ethics to which vast numbers of Chinese people have been exposed since Sung dynasty times. *Response and Retribution* begins by explaining that poverty, illness, and other calamities inevitably befall a person who performs immoral actions. If at death an unatoned offense is left, "evil luck" will be transferred to one's children and grandchildren. The text includes a condensed form of Confucian ethics in this line: *"Be faithful, filial, friendly, and brotherly."*[34]

A major theme or thread that runs though Taoist practice for both the priests/adepts and laypersons is the value placed on altruistic actions—actions one performs for the benefit of others. Although all forms of Taoism prescribe self-perfection, benevolence is also prescribed. Indeed, altruism is often indicated as a necessary condition for self-perfection.

HISTORY OF TAOISM

The Chinese have tended to see their history in terms of dynasties—periods of rule by sovereigns in one line of descent (Table 6.3). In feudal China (Chou dynasty, 1122–221 B.C.E.), society was stratified into a hierarchical system. The emperor was the unifying figure over all, but the nobles or lords maintained semi-independent jurisdiction over their own territories.[35] *Imperial China,* as we use the term, refers to postfeudal China, beginning with the first complete unification of China during the Ch'in dynasty (221–206 B.C.E.) and ending in 1912 with the establishment of a republic. The feudal lords lost most of their power to the

emperor in imperial China and were gradually replaced by appointed officials. The importance of this imperial unity is indicated by etymology: we get our word *China* from the name of the dynasty that first achieved this unity, the Ch'in.

Except for some periods of disunion, the imperial system continued into modern times. The turbulence of the nineteenth and twentieth centuries resulted in the collapse of the imperial system and the establishment of a republic. The collapse was caused in part by the influence of the modern industrialized West, but other factors include the corruption of the last dynasty and the Japanese invasion of China. The new republic was overwhelmed by the Japanese invasion and by the struggle for power among communists, Western powers, Japanese imperialists, and Nationalist (Kuomintang) forces. With the victory of the Chinese communists in 1949, China became a unified communist nation called the People's Republic of China.

Because folk religion is such an important and enduring feature of Chinese religion, the discussion of the history of Taoism begins with the manifestations of folk religion in prehistoric and early dynastic China. The ancient folk religion permeated all aspects of life for many centuries before Taoism, Confucianism, and Buddhism emerged in Chinese history. Folk religion can be defined as those beliefs and practices typical of everyday life that are passed on orally from generation to generation but that do not constitute an official cult. Elements of ancient China's folk tradition, such as ancestor veneration and divination, were later incorporated into Taoism, Confucianism, and Buddhism, and the relationship was reciprocal: elements from these three traditions also found their way into folk religion.

RELIGION IN PREHISTORIC CHINA

The archaeological record indicates that by 5000 B.C.E. there were numerous tribal groups living in China. Religious activities included those associated with the dead and the hereafter. The dead were buried in segregated cemeteries, apparently according to kinship, and the wine goblets and pig

MAJOR DYNASTIES AND PERIODS OF CHINESE HISTORY		
Prehistoric China	?–1600 B.C.E.	
Shang dynasty	1600–1122 B.C.E.	
Chou dynasty	1122–221 B.C.E.	
(Warring States Period	403–221 B.C.E.)	
Ch'in dynasty	221–206 B.C.E.	
Han dynasty	206 B.C.E.–220 C.E.	
Period of disunion	220–589 C.E.	
Sui dynasty	589–618 C.E.	
T'ang dynasty	618–906 C.E.	
Period of disunion (Five Dynasties Period)	906–960 C.E.	Imperial China
Sung dynasty	960–1279 C.E.	
Yuan dynasty	1279–1368 C.E.	
Ming dynasty	1368–1644 C.E.	
Ch'ing dynasty	1644–1911 C.E.	
Republic	1912–1948 C.E.	
People's Republic of China (communist)	1949 C.E.–PRESENT	

Table 6.3

jaws found at the sites would perhaps indicate a farewell feast. There was evidently a regard for the social rank of the deceased, because grave offerings vary in quantity and quality; these items include tools, pottery vessels, jade ornaments, dogs, and in some cases, human beings. Bodies and faces were often painted with red ocher, a symbol of life. Some of the grave offerings were intended, it seems, for use in the afterlife.

FOLK RELIGION IN THE SHANG DYNASTY (1600–1122 B.C.E.)
The Shang dynasty is the first clearly identifiable Chinese state. It emerged along the Yellow River in north-central China about 500 miles from the present city of Peking (Beijing). Archaeological digs at the sites of large fortified towns have uncovered beautiful bronze sacrificial vessels and divination bones with inscriptions. Evidently, the Shang had developed expertise in metalworking and were literate in proto-Chinese.

Because most of the people in Shang times were involved in agriculture, the principal crops being wheat and millet, Shang folk religion was in large part animated by agricultural concerns. In the settled agricultural society, harmony between the earth and human beings was of the essence. The farmland was dotted with villages and an occasional market city. Heaven and earth were seen as teeming with a variety of spirits, both benevolent ones (shen) and malevolent ones (kuei), and all were involved in reciprocal relationships. The millet crop depended on the local water spirit, who depended on, or required sacrifices by, humans, who in turn depended on many things, including the millet. The Shang people offered jade, fermented liquors, cattle, sheep, dogs, and (occasionally) human beings to the spirits. In awe of the mysterious unity and order of the universe as a whole, the Shang made special sacrifices to earth itself and to **Shang-ti,** the Supreme Ruler of Heaven.

Besides sacrifices, another means of communicating with the spirits was divination. Some hundred thousand oracle bones and shells uncovered from Shang times tell us how the people obtained information from, or ascertained the will of, natural and ancestral spirits. The diviner would smooth off the surface of a cattle bone or tortoise shell and make a series of depressions on the surface. A question was inscribed on the reverse side. The bone was then exposed to heat, causing cracks to appear. These cracks were read by the diviner and interpreted as answers to the questions or petitions.

According to a leading Chinese authority, most of the sacrifices and oracular questions were directed to the spirits of the ancestors: "'To serve the dead as if they were living'—we can say that the piety of the [Shang] people did reach that degree."[36] Indeed, Chinese tradition has it that the dead are still living, and their descendants must establish harmonious relations with them.

Consistent with the integral or organic worldview of the early Chinese religion, death was not seen as a separation of two radically different entities such as matter and spirit. A person was viewed as a psychophysical whole composed throughout of *ch'i* (vital substance or breath), which can exist in different modes and densities. The psychic energy or "soul" of a dead person followed the body into the grave or descended to the "Yellow Springs," a netherworld under the earth. The spirits of aristocrats also included a more celestial "soul," which went to join the court of heaven. Neither heaven nor the Yellow Springs was a "world apart," as the ancestors interacted with their descendants.

The concern for ancestors is linked to family solidarity in general. Loyalty to family members— that is, the extended family—has been an exalted virtue in China, and the respect due to a parent or grandparent increases with age. The forebear's real power begins with death, however. As a spirit, the deceased person can have greater influence than before. In addition to their influence on crops, relationships, and politics, the ancestors can mediate between humans and other beings such as nature spirits, deities, and even great deities like Shang-ti. An ancestor whose presence is revered and whose good offices are coveted can be a blessing to a family. An unattended ancestor can wreak havoc.

Shang-ti, whom we have referred to as the Supreme Ruler of Heaven, was believed to be the divine ancestor of the ruling Shang family. He was revered as a personal being who granted blessings and dealt out punishments. But there is no hint that Shang-ti was seen as the creator of the universe. He was consulted on crucial matters by the king and his diviners. A divine ancestor of the rulers, Shang-ti's blessings were absolutely essential for both the rulers and the society as a whole.

The rulers' ancestral devotions constituted a state religion. The king was the chief priest and diviner of the realm, performing rites on behalf of all the people. A Chinese state cult—a system of rites and shrines designated and maintained by the ruling dynasty and its appointed officials— persisted from the Shang dynasty to the end of dynastic China in 1911.

FOLK RELIGION AND PHILOSOPHY IN THE CHOU DYNASTY (1122–221 B.C.E.)
Shang oracle bones refer to a people called Chou who lived in the area of modern Shensi province. Although the Chou were at first culturally and technologically inferior to the Shang, by the eleventh century they were challenging the Shang for supremacy and conquered them by 1122. After the conquest, Chou rulers preserved the higher culture of the Shang and, perhaps as a precaution, offered sacrifices for the ancestors of the deposed Shang rulers for several hundred years. Four enduring elements of Chou culture are important in understanding the later development of Taoism: the Mandate of Heaven, the stratification of humans and gods, the cosmology, and divination.

The Mandate of Heaven   To justify the overthrow of the Shang, the new rulers invoked a unique idea called *t'ien ming* (Mandate of Heaven). The classic phrase in the *Book of Odes* to explain the ascendancy of the Chou is "Chou is an old people but its charge is new." The concept is that a virtuous family may be charged or obligated by Heaven to rule. It is a special relationship based on merit, not birth. If rulers become cruel or corrupt, Heaven (conceived of as a deity or as the divine ordering of the universe) gives the mandate to another family. Thus, Heaven and earth are properly linked, and the emperor is fit for performing special religious ceremonies on behalf of the people. This general idea has gripped the Chinese imagination ever since; Confucius revitalized it, and it has been invoked throughout Chinese history.

Because of his association with Heaven, the emperor was called T'ien Tzu, or Son of Heaven. The emperors worshiped Heaven on behalf of all the people at regular annual ceremonies. This practice is an antecedent of the grand and solemn ceremonies of state religion conducted for centuries on the beautiful marble terraces of the Altar of Heaven south of Peking.

The term **T'ien** (literally, "Heaven") was at first used in alternation with Shang-ti, but eventually it took precedence over the latter. T'ien was evidently a divine power rather like Shang-ti but was never identified as the ancestor of the rulers. (Again, mandate was to be by merit, not lineage.) Although *T'ien* sometimes referred to a personal being, as in "T'ien presides over the celestial court," it was often used as an impersonal designation for the divine ordering forces in the universe. In common usage, *Shang-ti* and *T'ien* were often synonymous.

The Stratification of Humans and Gods

Chou society was hierarchical and thoroughly stratified in a kind of feudal arrangement. Under the emperor were vassal lords, who had under them governors of the provinces or states. The governors had under them officers, who had under them subalterns, who had under them petty officers, who had under them menials, who had under them menials' helpers. The spirit forces, gods, and ancestors were similarly organized, from T'ien at the top (mirroring the position of the Chou emperor) to Hou Chi, divine ancestor and lord of millet, to gods in charge of streams, to those in charge of privies. The celestial bureaucracy and the earthly one were mirror images of each other.

Ancestral rituals continued as in Shang times; the worship of nature gods was emphasized, because the Chou was also a settled agricultural society. Earth worship was focused on sacred earth mounds located at the imperial capital, in each state capital, and in at least some of the villages. Chou rituals were elaborate, dramatic performances with music and dancing. They concluded with enormous feasts in which great amounts of wine were consumed.

It would be hard to overemphasize the importance of these ancient practices as precedents for later developments in Chinese religion. Tradition sets out a deep-rooted pattern of faith: social and spiritual propriety calls for careful attention to a person's qualifications or role. A major cosmic or celestial force, for instance, is not to be addressed by an ordinary persons, and T'ien is to be addressed only by the true Son of Heaven, the emperor. Although feudalism was to be dealt a lethal blow by the succeeding dynasty, the Chinese senses of stratification and propriety lingered on; both Taoism and Confucianism were affected by them.

Proper stratification was also based on gender roles. Patriarchal China has counted the family line through male ancestors, and the official power in a household rested with the father or grandfather. Female infanticide was not uncommon, because a female child could not maintain the family heritage or amass wealth. A woman was valuable primarily insofar as she could produce sons for her husband's family. Double-standard sexual codes were everywhere in force, especially among the rich and powerful; for example, men could have concubines, but strict chastity was required of women. Although this hierarchy placed women well below men, the position of males as leaders and the importance of avoiding shame have tended to mitigate the suppression of women. If a woman showed her bruises to other women or complained that her husband was shirking his duties, he might lose face and shame his parents and ancestors.

Ancient Chinese Cosmology

Sensitivity to the ways of nature is no doubt the source of what has come to be called the *yin/yang* cosmology. It was probably part of the Chinese worldview before the

Figure 6.2 The *Yin/Yang* Symbol

Chou dynasty, but it was fairly clearly articulated by then. According to this way of experiencing things, every object, event, or situation is an interaction between two energy modes, called *yin* and *yang*. *Yin* was originally characterized as "covered as by clouds," dark, cool, wet, hidden, female. *Yang* was light, warm, dry, open, male. These pairs of apparent opposites interact and complement each other; life is a process of balancing or harmonizing such opposites.

Figure 6.2 shows the *yin/yang* symbol, called the T'ai-chi t'u, Diagram of the Great Ultimate. Although this symbol did not appear until the eleventh or twelfth century C.E., it can serve to illustrate the ancient teaching. The symbol contains a dynamic cyclic symmetry. The two dots show that each time one of two opposite energy modes reaches its extreme, it contains in itself the seed of its opposite. Each reverts to the other at its extremity, and thus a balancing process occurs. "The yang returns cyclically to its beginning; the yin attains its maximum and gives place to the yang."[37] Thus, when winter has reached its extreme, it then begins to change into summer.

Yin and *yang* are complementary. Light allows dark, or rather makes dark, appear as dark, and vice versa. The two cannot exist separately. Neither is defined in itself as good or bad. "Goodness" is a proper balance of *yin* and *yang*, and an imbalance is bad.

Another aspect of the ancient Chinese cosmology was the so-called five elements teaching. The five elements are modes of activity, not static substances. They are woodlike, fiery, earthen, metallic, watery. From the point of view of the *yin/yang* cosmology, they are particular modes of *yin/yang* interaction. The *yin/yang* and five elements theories probably first emerged separately and were later combined.

According to the Han dynasty scholars (206 B.C.E.–220 C.E.), the ancients viewed the five basic elements or modes as giving rise to one another in succession as follows: wood produces fire, fire produces earth, earth produces metal, and metal produces water. They came to be seen in various systems of correspondences. These systems were worked out by the scholar Tung Chung-Shu (ca. 179–104 B.C.E.) as follows: wood corresponds to the season of spring, which prevails in the east and correlates with the color green; fire corresponds to summer, which prevails in the south and correlates with red; earth corresponds to the center, which assists the four seasons; metal corresponds to autumn, which prevails in the west and correlates with white; water corresponds to winter, which prevails in the north and correlates with black.

The unity in which all things fit together is the Tao (Dao). It is even more fundamental than *yin/yang* and the five modes. The Tao is the basic reality behind or within appearances and is the ultimate ordering principle in the world.

Divination The *yin/yang* cosmology, the idea of the Tao, and the concept of harmony are integral aspects of the well-known book of divination, the *I Ching (Book of Changes)*. Derived in part from Shang methods of divination, the earliest versions of the *I Ching* emerged in Chou times. In its present form the book contains an amalgam of interpretive insights added over the centuries. It is designed to aid people in making decisions in a world of change.[38]

The *I Ching* is consulted when one needs to make a decision; typically, the person using the book will ask a question, such as, Should I accept this job offer from that company? The process of consultation involves throwing yarrow (milfoil) stalks or coins. The coin tosses (or pattern of stalks) are then "read"—that is, they are assigned a meaning in terms of a set of broken *(yin)* and unbroken *(yang)* lines. When coins are used, three coins are thrown six times to generate a hexagram, for example:

One then reads the *I Ching* passage that explains the meaning of that particular hexagram. This passage is believed to be the answer to the question that has been posed. Because *yin/yang* energy patterns are the fundamental structure of the universe (the basic manifestations of Tao), it is no surprise that one's course of action must depend on how *yin* and *yang* are interacting. The *I Ching* commentaries or "answers" are somewhat vague and ambiguous or suggestive. Some modern interpreters of the consultation process view the commentaries as the stimulus to intuition, aiding a person in getting beyond the limits of purely rational decision making.[39]

In addition to *I Ching* divination, there are divination blocks, planchette methods, and many other varieties. Although in ancient times kings and aristocrats may have employed divination more than peasants did, the practice became an enduring, widespread part of Chinese folk religion. One could use divination to decide such matters as when to take a trip or examination, plant a crop, or get married. Divination has also been employed as a means of communicating with the gods—especially to consult their will in regard to difficult decisions. The process of divination can be understood as a kind of therapeutic ritual, relieving stress and giving a person confidence in following the course of action indicated.[40]

Many of the features of Shang-Chou folk religion have endured; they run at deep levels of Chinese culture. The notion of life as integrated and harmonious remains to this day, and along with it the ideas of Tao, *yin/yang*, the five elements, and the cosmos as a series of correspondences. Among the common people the belief in a multiplicity of good and bad spirits, including the spirits of the ancestors, has endured. The importance of kinship and ancestor worship is likewise an integral aspect of Chinese culture, as is a tendency to view the earthly and celestial realms as hierarchical. Ancestors and other spirits have been perceived as engaging in reciprocal relationships with humans. Benevolent spirits can be expected to respond with favors when worshiped, but ghosts and demons may at most be propitiated. Finally, various forms of divination have continued as common practices among Chinese people for two millennia.

CLASSICAL CHINESE THOUGHT

The feudal system of Chou times began to decline as early as 750 B.C.E., and by the fifth century B.C.E. China entered a long period of civil wars called the Warring States Period (403–221 B.C.E.) As is usually the case in periods of political and social change, philosophers emerged to offer solutions. Because the occasion of these cogitations was political and social chaos, thinkers addressed the issue of rulership. Among the many "schools" of philosophy that emerged in this age of One Hundred Philosophers, the most noteworthy were the Moist, Confucian, Legalist, and Taoist.

The categorization of thinkers and the labeling of these "schools" of thought occurred after the age of the philosophers; later scholars rather arbitrarily named the schools and grouped the thinkers and writers into them. It was probably not until the first century B.C.E. that the term *Tao-school (Tao-chia)* was used as a label for the writings attributed to the two figures Lao-tzu and Chuang-tzu.

Mo-tzu is, in many ways, an enigmatic figure in the history of Chinese thought. Rarely does a philosopher emerge, as he did, from among the peasants. What was even more unusual in ancient

China was Mo-tzu's rejection of all social hierarchies, including the feudal system; he called for universal love—"love for all equally."

Moism enjoyed considerable popularity during the late Chou years; but by 221 B.C.E., the school was all but dead, and it has never been revived. Perhaps its basic teaching of universal love was fundamentally opposed to Chinese culture. What is more characteristically Chinese—or what came to be a leading philosophy in China—is the Confucian teaching of "love with distinctions." The Confucian sage Mencius criticized Moism in this way: "Mo's principle is—'To love all equally'—but this does not acknowledge the peculiar affection due to a father. To acknowledge neither king nor father is to be in the state of a beast."[41]

While recognizing T'ien (Heaven) as the ultimate source of truth and order, Confucius put his emphasis on human relations: *"Devote yourself earnestly to the duties due to men, and respect spiritual beings but keep them at a distance."*[42] Confucius called for bolstering the family, thinking that love starts with one's parents. Rejecting, the Moist approach, Confucian philosophers argue that human beings need structure and a set of traditional rules in order to learn to love; this calls for an extensive system of social rituals and a network of government bureaucracies.

Legalism (also known as Authoritarianism) makes a strong, if somewhat harsh, claim to realism: because human beings are basically selfish and materialistic, a complex of clearly defined laws must be rigorously enforced to maintain order. No notion of universal love or family training will suffice. Legalism was embraced by the Ch'in dynasty (221–206 B.C.E.)

In the age of the philosophers (ca. 500–220 B.C.E.), the "Taoist school" was no more than a tiny group of philosophers who studied texts associated with Lao-tzu and Chuang-tzu; there was no Taoism as an organized system of worship at that time. Although the founding of Taoism as a religion came centuries later, its teaching was profoundly influenced by Lao-tzu, Chuang-tzu, and the texts associated with them.

LAO-TZU AND THE *TAO TE CHING*   Who was Lao-tzu? He has been viewed as a sage, as an oft-reincarnated personage, as a god, and as the energy of the cosmos. According to popular tradition, he was conceived by a shooting star, carried in the womb for sixty-two years, and born in about 556 B.C.E., with a long white beard. He was called Lao-tzu, meaning "Old Master." (The second Chinese ideograph in Lao-tzu's name can also be translated as "boy," making his name Old Boy.) It is said he was keeper of the archives for the court of Chou. At the age of 160, Lao-tzu, disgusted with the corruption and wars of the time, climbed on a water buffalo and rode westward toward the wilderness area that is now Tibet. At Hankao Pass on Chungnan Shan, the gatekeeper, Yin Hsi, pleaded with him: "You are about to withdraw yourself from sight. I pray you to compose a book for me." Within three days, Lao-tzu wrote the 5,000-character book called *Tao* (way) *Te* (power) *Ching* (book), or *Te-Tao Ching* in the versions discovered in the Ma

An artist's depiction of the Chinese philosopher Lao-tzu.

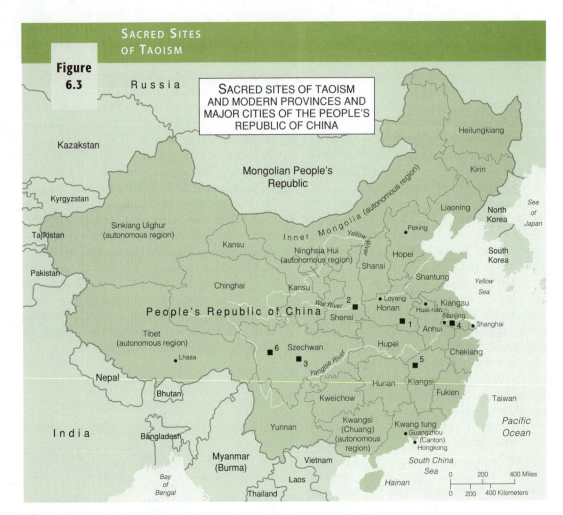

SACRED SITES OF TAOISM

Figure 6.3

SACRED SITES OF TAOISM AND MODERN PROVINCES AND MAJOR CITIES OF THE PEOPLE'S REPUBLIC OF CHINA

(1) Home of Lao-tzu—according to tradition, home of Lao-tzu in the ancient state of Chu; (2) revelation of Tao Te Ching at Chung-nan Shan (mountain)—popular tradition claims Chung-nan Shan as the site of the revelation of the Tao Te Ching by Lao-tzu to the gatekeeper Yin Hsi; (3) founding of the Celestial Masters—the site of the origin of the Celestial Masters movement in the second century C.E.; (4) Mao Shan—Taoist pilgrimage site and area where the Mao Shan revelations were received and written in the fourth century C.E.; (5) Long-hu Shan (Dragon and Tiger Mountain)—Taoist pilgrimage; holy mountain and center for the Celestial Masters and Chen-i sects; (6) Ch'ingchen Shan in Chengdu—Taoist pilgrimage site; location of temples and monastery of the Ch'uan-chen order.

Wang Tui dig in 1973.[43] (Figure 6.3 is a map showing Chung-nan Shan, along with other sacred sites of Taoism.)

The *Tao Te Ching (Dao De Jing)* begins with this statement about the Tao: *"The Tao that can be named is not the true Tao"* (Chap. 1). Lao-tzu is referring to the ancient notion of Tao that was touched on earlier, but he is saying that it is too mysterious, too great (infinite) to be described or conceptualized. This Tao is the ultimate ordering reality lying behind and within all things. Tao is not a creator or personal deity, but it is the source of all, because it issues into the myriad of things, including humanity. Lao-tzu's central concern is that individuals experience the Tao and learn to let their lives flow in harmony with it.

As a solution to the political and social chaos of the Warring States Period, the *Tao Te Ching* recommends that rulers learn to attune themselves with the Tao, for short of that experience, an understanding of life and all its difficulties is impossible. Without such an experience, the Moist idea of "universal love" is useless. The Legalist notion of many detailed laws rigorously enforced is too structured and too aggressive: *"When one desires to take over the empire and act on it (interfere with it), I see that he will not succeed"* (*Tao Te Ching*, chap. 29). The classic Confucian ideal of a system of rules tied to a hierarchy of roles is too structured and unnatural, according to Lao-tzu. The Taoists put more emphasis on the cosmic basis of their views than did the other three schools.

Among Lao-tzu's values, the most fundamental is *wu wei* (literally "nonaction"). *Wu-wei* means refraining from overly aggressive action; one is better off moving with the flow of things. A life based on *wu-wei* is a life of spontaneity, simplicity, naturalness, tranquility, and virtue (even filial piety will come naturally if one has tapped into one's Tao-nature).

The *Tao Te Ching* teaches that because the Tao is the way in which all opposition and otherness is ultimately unified, people can live in a *wu-wei* fashion—they can let their lives flow. Unfortunately, however, they do not always see or experience this unity:

People through finding something beautiful
Think something else unbeautiful,

. . . .

Life and death, though stemming from each other,
Seem in conflict. (Chap. 2)

Lao-tzu's book describes how people make life uncomfortable, even dreadful, by failing to see the unity of opposites. The person who sees to the core of life, however, *"makes no distinction between left and right"* (Chap. 34).

Although the world appears to be an interplay of distinct opposites, like north and south, in reality the opposites are interdependent unities. Reality as a whole is a unity, and the way that this whole evolves is the Tao. Tao is the source of everything, both within us and in the world.

This concept of the complementarity of opposites can be understood as a reinterpretation and refinement of a principle underlying the ancient *yin/yang* cosmology. Tao as the-way-the-whole-of-reality-evolves is a regular and ceaseless alternation of things or experiences we call opposites: they go together as alternate modes in a single whole. Thus, periods of quietude alternate with periods of excitement. More than this, as prolonged quietude is likely to instill a yearning for excitement, just so, the ascension of one pole or opposite implies its diminution. The relationship might be called *bipolar complementarity.*[44]

The *Tao Te Ching* touches on two topics that we will return to later: meditation and the goal of immortality:

[The sage] blocks up his holes,
Closes his doors,
Softens the glare,
Settles the dust. (Chap. 56)

A life lived in the fashion of *wu-wei* and punctuated by meditation may lead to immortality—or so some interpreters have read this line from Chapter 16:

Being in accord with the Tao,
he is everlasting.

CHUANG-TZU Whereas the *Tao Te Ching* offers advice to rulers, the book attributed to Chuang-tzu (simply called *Chuang-tzu*) is less concerned with government.[45] Focused mainly on the individual path to liberation, the *Chuang-tzu* includes a variety of styles that have made it a classic of Chinese literature. Its brilliant essays, its occasional analyses, and its witty anecdotes have perplexed, amused, and delighted Chinese readers for two millennia. Quite unlike the poetic verses of the *Tao Te Ching*, the *Chuang-tzu* introduces the techniques of analytic philosophy and uses them to show how words, concepts, and even logic finally turn against themselves in search of the truth. Direct experience alone, not concepts or words, is the means to understanding and, ultimately, to spiritual liberation.

Chuang-tzu teaches that death is not to be avoided or feared. In the same vein, he even makes fun of the coveted Chinese ideal of longevity. "Long" life is a relative quality and not necessarily natural for everyone. He even seems to suggest that the desire for immortality with continued personal identity is not compatible with faith in the Tao: *"You were born in a human form, and you find joy in it. Yet there are ten thousand other forms endlessly transforming that are equally good, and the joys in these are untold."* And again, Chuang-tzu says, *"Great is the Maker [Tao]! What will He use you for now? Where will he send you? Will he make you into a rat's gizzard or a snake's leg?"*[46]

These passages suggest the idea that upon death, one's energy will be transformed into another form, from thence into another, and so on, *ad infinitum*. We might call this a "recycled energy" view of the afterlife. However, many people prefer the notion of an afterlife in which they have the kind of self-consciousness, individual identity, and memory we enjoy as humans.

One of the puzzling aspects of the *Chuang-tzu* is that it does not attempt to present a systematic, consistent philosophy. Some passages in the *Chuang-tzu* suggest that humans may transcend normal and natural limits: *"Having transcended the distinction of past and present, [the Taoist begins] to enter the land where there is no life or death."*

We can readily see how passages such as the preceding and the following were interpreted as recommending the quest for superhuman powers and the quest for immortality: *"The perfect man is spiritual. Though the great swamp burns, he will not feel the heat. Though the great rivers freeze, he will not feel the cold. Though thunder-bolts split the mountains and gales shake the sea, he will have no fear. Such a man can ride the clouds and mist, mount the sun and moon, and wander beyond the four seas. Life and death do not affect him."*[47]

Passages such as these later became scriptural bases for Taoist belief in immortality. The *Tao Te Ching* (the Lao-tzu book) and the *Chuang-tzu* came to be included among the holy scriptures of Taoism. Some scholars question whether we can attribute these texts to Lao-tzu and Chuang-tzu; indeed, both books may be composites of several unknown authors or editors. Nonetheless, they are clearly powerful texts.

EARLY TAOIST TEACHINGS Before discussing the establishment of Taoism as an organized religion in 142 C.E., more needs to be said about the connection between early Taoist thought and religious Taoism. The founders of religious Taoism were particularly indebted to four texts: the *Tao Te Ching*, the *Chuang-tzu*, the Huang-Lao texts, and the *Huai-nan-tzu*. They drew freely from these early Taoist texts and interpreted them in the light of their own insights and revelations. The dates of the composition of these texts are in dispute, but all four were in circulation during the Han dynasty prior to the founding of Taoism.

The teachings of the *Tao Te Ching* about how the Tao is manifested are terse; they seem to cry out for explanation and elaboration:

> The Tao gave birth to the One
> The One gave birth to the Two
> The Two gave birth to the Three
> And the Three gave birth to the
> Ten thousand things. (Chap. 42)

Passages such as these later became the framework for elaborate Taoist cosmologies, numerologies, and theologies. The Lao-tzu book *(Tao Te Ching)* does not refer to any god, but later Taoist texts contain a pantheon of gods. Indeed, Lao-tzu himself came to be viewed as a god. Taoists found inspiration from the *Tao Te Ching* and *Chuang-tzu* teachings on *wu–wei*, virtue, compassion, and rulership. They also derived their spiritual techniques (for example, meditation) from certain suggestive passages in these texts, and the belief in "perfected men," or wonder workers with superhuman powers is based in part on Chuang-tzu's references to them. The belief in immortality is also based partly on passages in these earlier philosophic works.

Another set of early Taoist teachings was contained in the Huang-Lao texts. The term *Huang* (yellow) is a reference to the legendary Yellow Emperor of remote antiquity; *Lao* refers to Lao-tzu. The Huang-Lao writings were not available to modern historians until 1973, when four silk manuscripts were discovered in south-central China in a tomb sealed in 168 B.C.E. Although the Huang-Lao teachings may have included much more than a theory of government, the four manuscripts we now have focus mainly on the question of how to rule. They present an ideal way of governing that is a fusion of Legalism and the views on government in the *Tao Te Ching*.[48]

As we have seen, Legalism represented strong, aggressive, authoritarian rule, whereas Lao-tzu had called for *wu–wei*, a kind of passive approach. How can such apparently opposite views be combined? Huang-Lao doctrine teaches that laws and regulations, if not in excess, are appropriate. The ruler is the sole source of authority and law throughout the empire, but the ruler must base his understanding on meditative awareness of the Tao. The sovereign should not arbitrarily impose laws upon the people; he should provide those laws that the actual situation calls for. Strong leadership is appropriate (an aspect of Legalism), yet the ruler's actions are to be based on knowledge of the Tao (Lao-tzu's view), not personal likes or dislikes. Thus, Huang-Lao teachings provide a Taoist ontology, or theory of being, as a foundation for Legalism. To put it another way, Huang-Lao offers a spiritual rationale for, and places some limits on, government. In the ideal state, the government maintains a definite set of laws, and the resulting regularity or order in the realm is experienced as the way (Tao) of nature.

Many early Taoist teachings are articulated in the fascinating encyclopedic book *Huai-nan-tzu*, compiled and edited by the philosopher-poet Liu An (180?–122 B.C.E.), who was governor or "king" of the province of Huai-nan. Liu An assembled some of the greatest thinkers of the time at his court, especially those with Taoist leanings.[49] The result was a compendium of thoughts on government, cosmology, methods of self-cultivation, and theology. Liu An presented the book to the Han imperial court in 139 B.C.E.

The cosmological vision in the *Huai-nan-tzu* is a development of the ancient *yin/yang*–five elements theory discussed previously. The three guiding principles are correspondence, microcosm-macrocosm, and causation. For example, the human body *corresponds* to the cosmos (heaven and earth), and correlations are drawn between specific parts of each—for example, blood and breath correspond to wind and rain *(Huai-nan-tzu,* 3b-1). The basic structure of the relationships is that of *microcosm-macrocosm;* our breath functions in our body (microcosm) as the rain functions in the universe (macrocosm). Corresponding items influence or *cause changes* in each other: *"Man's control over his breath is connected to the heavens above. Cruel punishment means violent winds; useless vain laws bring blight and pestilence; gross slaughter causes the earth of the country to be scorched"* *(Huai-nan-tzu,* 4b-2).

The techniques of self-cultivation in the *Huai-nan-tzu* are based on what we might call a "medical model": People (as psychophysical wholes) need to be restored to a healthy condition. The body is to be returned to its original purity and power—perhaps even to a superhuman condition.[50] The techniques include *yoga,* dietary rules, use of vegetal and alchemic drugs, and breath control. The text often groups physicians and spiritual healers together, because both proceed according to a broadly conceived medical model.[51]

THE FORMATION OF RELIGIOUS TAOISM

The imperial age in China began in 221 B.C.E. with the ascendancy of the harsh, but unifying power of the Legalistic Ch'in dynasty (221–206 B.C.E.). The Ch'in virtually destroyed the feudal system, although the preference for some kind of hierarchical social system remained. The repressive Ch'in rulers tried to silence all criticism; they decreed that all books in private collections be burned except those dealing with medicine, divination, agriculture, and Legalism. As one historian put it, "the golden age of Chinese philosophy was over."[52]

Rebellions led to the end of the Ch'in reign after two decades. More humane, or at least less authoritarian, was the Han dynasty, which ruled China for the next 426 years (206 B.C.E.–220 C.E.). In the age of the Han, Confucianism became established as the official philosophy, and only the Confucian classics were studied at the imperial academy. But this fact did not inhibit the development of other faiths. Toward the end of the Han, Buddhist missionaries from India began to teach in China, and Taoism was founded as an organized religion. The realm was relatively prosperous and peaceful during the first three Han centuries and is remembered as a kind of golden age; many Chinese refer to their ethnic group as Han-ren—people of the Han.

THE RELIGIOUS MILIEU OF THE LATE HAN

DYNASTY   The spiritual preoccupations of the Ch'in-Han years included the quest for immortality. The first Ch'in emperor, Ch'in Shih huang-ti (221–210 B.C.E.), engaged in this quest, sending out groups of young people across the China Sea to look for P'eng-lai, the island of the immortals. They sought a psychophysical immortality, not the immortality of an eternal soul. The attempt was to make the whole person immortal by transforming its substance. Methods included special exercises, diets, ingestion of herbs or alchemic mixtures such as those containing cinnabar (mercuric sulfide), and even esoteric sexual techniques. One could also petition the immortals or a deity for assistance.

By the first century C.E., Lao-tzu was referred to as an immortal, and by 165 C.E. inscriptions described him as a deity. The Yellow Emperor (Huang-ti), a legendary hero and sage of ancient China (ca. 2800 B.C.E.), was transformed into the patron deity of immortality, a personified saving deity. Emperor Wu worshiped T'ai I, "the Great Supreme One," and he revived the ancient *chiao*, or sacrifices, at the winter solstice. The emperor toured the realm, sacrificing at various shrines to express his piety and solidify his power.

Another significant element of the Han spiritual and political atmosphere of the times was a kind of messianism—the expectation of a blessed age in which heaven would send a divinely appointed leader to save humankind from the "evils of the age." The evils of the age included the confusion and crime resulting from internal dissension as the Han Empire began to crumble. One second-century text even claimed that Lao-tzu would manifest himself and "shake the Han rule." This messianic spirit was inordinately strong in the second century C.E.

Finally, the spiritual landscape included mediums who could allow a deity or spirit to possess them and whose spiritual functions were virtually unlimited, including invoking the gods, dancing for rain, and exorcising harmful forces. Despite the incredible proliferation of spiritual ideals and practices in the Han, not just any medical/spiritual wonder worker was allowed to carry on his or her activities. Government officials made sporadic attempts to suppress spirit mediums and to control blood sacrifices. These attempts began in about 100 B.C.E. and have continued throughout the history of Chinese religion.

INSTITUTIONALIZED TAOISM: CHANG TAO-LING

AND THE CELESTIAL MASTERS   The use of texts such as the *Tao Te Ching*, homage to deities, messianism, healing techniques, and many other elements—some as old as China, some apparently new—were brought together in the second century C.E. in a new religious dispensation that many Taoists regard as the foundation of institutionalized Taoism. Centered in the organization called the Way of the Celestial Masters, Taoism was no longer a collection of unorganized scholars and poets who studied certain spiritual or philosophical texts. Neither was it a mere technique to foster longevity or immortality. Nor was Taoism to be identified with popular religion, because from its inception it identified itself in antithesis to "unauthorized worship."

In the mountains of western China, in what is now Szechwan province, there arose a Taoist movement that endures today. It is said that in 142 C.E., the deified Lao-tzu, T'ai-shang Lao-chun, Lord Lao the Most High, revealed a new pattern of faith to Chang Tao-ling (a reputed spiritual seer and healer, 34?–156? C.E.). Lord Lao revealed to Chang his "orthodox and sole doctrine of authority of the covenant." Later, Chang is said to have ascended on high to receive the title T'ien-shih—Heavenly or Celestial Master. The organization founded by Chang was called T'ien-shih Tao, or the Way of the Celestial Masters. The term *t'ienshih* undoubtedly called to mind the ancient Chinese notions of *t'ien ming* (mandate of heaven) and *t'ien-tzu* (son of heaven). This was not mere coincidence: the Way of the Celestial Masters was a religious and political substitute for the crumbling Han administration. Under Chang Tao-ling's descendants, the organization had religious and political control. It was what we might call a **Taocracy,** or rule of Tao.

In contrast to the unstructured and diffused folk religion, the Way of the Celestial Masters had a strict and complex hierarchy. Henceforth—after this New Advent of Lord Lao—the world was to be ruled by three Heavens, each of which was presided over by a celestial official. In turn, the faithful were to gather for major congregational meetings and liturgies three times a year. As the solar year had twenty-four phases, the original Celestial Masters Taocracy consisted of twenty-four dioceses spread throughout northern Szechwan and southern Shensi provinces. Each diocese was headed by a **libationer** (one who makes an offering) and twenty-four officials. A *Code of the Dioceses* lays out the following structure for the organization: "[It is to consist] of 24 dioceses, each having 24 officials, each official having a different function. To each function belong 240 armies [made up of] 2,400 generals, 24,000 officers, and 240,000 soldiers. There are 24 male and 24 female officials, 24 male and female functions."[53]

The reader should pause over the significance of this system in which the Chinese organic worldview is evident. The earthly hierarchy corresponds to the cosmic; it is a microcosm. The stratified bureaucracy was modeled after the Han system of local administration. But what is wholly unique for the time is the role given to women. In part because of cosmological considerations (the place of *yin*), there were female officials and libationers in the movement. Despite its authoritarian hierarchy, the Celestial Masters movement was surprisingly egalitarian; it openly welcomed women and minorities, including tribal groups in the region. At the grassroots level the movement met the needs of any and all, even the stranger who stopped for free food at the wayside inns run by the movement. Thus, the Celestial Masters appealed to all segments of Chinese society—from the upper-class elite who sought temporal power in the Taocracy to the lowly peasant.

Another aspect of this religious revolution was that participation began by a voluntary decision. Whereas folk religion was a "natural" part of Chinese culture, requiring no explicit decision or conversion, the Celestial Masters set itself apart by requiring a definite decision by the individual and adherence to the rules of the organization. Only certain deities and spirits were to be worshiped, and only at specified times. Even ancestor worship was regulated. Celestial Masters ceremonies were performed by a hereditary, ordained priesthood; the frenzied performances of local spirit mediums were allowed only under the supervision of the libationer. Blood sacrifices were to be banished. Liturgy and scriptures came to be written in classical or literary Chinese, whereas most of the popular religion expressed itself orally in colloquial language. Considerations such as these have led some leading scholars to call Taoism "China's own indigenous higher religion."[54]

The Celestial Masters movement amplified the ancient medical model for spiritual methods by attributing disease and tragedy to sins committed by the individual or by his or her ancestors. Because everyone sins in some way, and because everyone feels threatened by sickness or tragedy, a movement claiming power to overcome such adversities has a universal appeal. No doubt the age-old Chinese ideal of longevity contributed to the success of the movement. Chang Tao-ling and his priests and officials claimed divinely ordained authority to assist confessed and repentant sinners as individuals and through elevated community rituals. For an individual possessed by a demon, the libationer could draw up a written talisman, a charm against evil. This document was burned, and the ashes, mixed with water, were swallowed by the demon's victim.

On the occasion of the special congregational meeting in the tenth month, each household contributed five bushels of "faith rice" *(hsin-mi)* to the Heavenly Granary—hence the other name of the movement, the Five Pecks of Rice Way (Wu Tou Mi Tao). The family registry was to be brought up to date at that time and duly reported to the Celestial Masters officials. The economic and political bonds in this Taocracy were held in place by the libationers, who administered justice as they saw it, literally building links within the realm by imposing roadwork as punishment for minor infractions.

Powerful liturgies have always been at the core of the Way of the Celestial Masters. These ceremonies express and establish bonds that are both "vertical" and "horizontal." The libationer exteriorizes spirits from his or her own body, and these spirits in turn bear messages carried upward in the flame and smoke of the incense burner to the appropriate bureau of the three Heavens; at the same time, such ceremonies provoke feelings of oneness in the community, because they are performed on behalf of the group. Moreover, this same libationer functions as a teacher of social ethics, teaching that works that benefit family and community can insure immunity from disease because they are in the spirit of the Tao. Although the Way of the Celestial Masters would eventually cease to function as the sole or dominant political entity governing large portions of China, it has always had a utopian potential—claiming the ability to authorize cosmic, spiritual, economic, social, and even political bonds for the well-being of the people.

The founder of the Celestial Masters, Chang Tao-ling, was succeeded by his son, Chang Heng, and he in turn by his son, Chang Lu. The outstanding contributions of the third Celestial Master, grandson of the founder, were his tireless emphasis on moral conduct and his political compromise with the future leaders of the Wei dynasty. In works attributed to Chang Lu, the faithful are urged to moral conduct: *"Who practices the Tao and does not infringe the commandments will be profound as the Tao itself; Heaven and Earth are like the Tao, kind to the good, unkind to the wicked; therefore people must accumulate good works so that their spirit can communicate with Heaven."*[55]

In 215 C.E., Chang Lu submitted to the authority of the Han warlord Ts'ao Ts'ao, who six years later founded the Wei dynasty in the north. Ts'ao Ts'ao rewarded Chang with honors, gave him a fiefdom, and married his son to Chang's daughter. Chang lived at the court of Wei for many years, as did his mother, who is said to have been an important priestess at the court.[56] Chang's submission resulted in official recognition of the Celestial Masters by the state. The Celestial Masters, in turn, expressed spiritual approbation of the Wei's mandate to replace the Han and urged the faithful to obey the "pure government of the Wei." The flexible ideology employed by Chang Lu and his successors called for cooperation with a "worthy dynasty"; the Celestial Masters were to act as intermediaries between temporal powers and spiritual powers. Only when a responsible ruler was not on the throne would the Celestial Masters assume temporal guidance of the people simply to hold the power in trust for the next virtuous leader.

Abetted by this ability to compromise with secular power, Chang's movement spread to northern China by the end of the third century and, by the end of the fourth century, to all of China. The Celestial Masters condemned the more militant

Taoist groups that had also emerged during this period, labeling them "perverse ways." The following is the story of one such militant movement.

THE YELLOW TURBANS

By 184 C.E. there was little hope for the declining Han dynasty. In that year the great Yellow Turban Rebellion broke out in eastern China. The leader of the movement, Chang Chueh, proclaimed that a new "Yellow Heaven" mandate was to replace the Han dynasty mandate; his followers wore yellow turbans as a symbol of their destiny. The official name of the organization, the Way of Great Peace (T'ai P'ing Tao), was inspired by a version of a scripture called the *Classic of Great Peace (T'ai P'ing Ching)*. The history of this text is obscure, because a variety of different works were given this same title and because a number of different movements claimed to be based upon it. The scripture retained today in the Taoist canon is probably not the text used by the Yellow Turbans.[57]

The Way of Great Peace is best understood as a political and religious movement that developed as a parallel to the Celestial Masters but was not connected to it. Worshiping a deity called Huang-lao Chun, the Yellow Turbans took control of eight provinces in eastern China in 184 C.E. Within ten months the imperial forces had crushed the rebellion, but remnants of the movement continued to emerge from time to time, often associated with a messianic figure called Li Hung. The last recorded Li Hung was executed in 1112.

Like the Celestial Masters, the Yellow Turbans viewed illness as being a result of sin and saw confession and repentance as being prerequisites for healing. Dramatic ceremonies were performed to effect the necessary rectifications and renewals in relation to divine and cosmic forces. Thus, the similarities between the Way of Great Peace and the Celestial Masters are numerous. In addition, both movements were utopian, but the Way of Great Peace was more militant and more eschatological—zealously striving for the new age and prepared to risk large-scale violence in pursuit of its uncompromising revolutionary ideals. In this emphasis on violence and the end of the world, the

Yellow Turbans must be distinguished from the Celestial Masters. The Yellow Turbans no longer exist, but the Way of the Celestial Masters has endured. Table 6.4 lists these two and other important Taoist movements and sects.

TAOISM IN SOUTH CHINA

Taoism continued to develop as it spread throughout China during the period of disunion from 220 to 589 C.E.. Into Southeast China came many followers of the Celestial Masters, driven there by invasions of non-Chinese tribes. The result was an unprecedented period of religious effervescence and synthesis, including the revelations of two great bodies of scripture and the systemization of these materials by Taoist masters.

To set the stage for these events, we first introduce the eclectic scholar and writer Ko Hung. In his major work, the *Pao-p'u-tzu (He Who Holds to Simplicity)*, completed in 317 C.E., Ko Hung expounded a wide variety of technical means to immortality. These included dietetics (for example, eating mushrooms and avoiding alcohol and grains), gymnastics, and the conservation of vital fluids through special sexual techniques. Such methods were generally viewed as techniques to promote longevity and as preliminaries for transformation into an immortal. Ko Hung's work was nearly completed when the Celestial Masters tradition entered South China. His comprehensive summary of southern spiritual preoccupations is significant because it is these techniques that came to be synthesized with, and transformed into, a form of Taoism different from the Celestial Masters tradition of the second century.

Many aristocratic families of the south joined the Celestial Masters movement, following the practices and beliefs described earlier. But southern additions to the old Celestial Masters liturgies were inevitable. For example, the following phrase was added at the conclusion of a set of prayers: *"Thurifer-emissary [Incense bearer] Lords Dragon and Tiger of left and right, may there suddenly be in this oratory [chapel] the Mushroom, Liquefied Gold, Essence of Cinnabar and all transcended powers intermingling*

IMPORTANT MOVEMENTS AND SECTS IN THE HISTORY OF TAOISM

Table 6.4

One Hundred Philosophers (ca. 600–300 B.C.E.)	An age of philosophical inquiry in China during which many philosophical schools emerged, including Confucianism, Legalism, Moism, and Taoism.
(Way of) the Celestial Masters (founded 142 C.E.)	The oldest of the surviving Taoist sects, founded by Chang Tao-ling, a seer regarded as a great healer and model of devotion.
Yellow Turbans (184 C.E.)	A political and religious movement aimed at achieving T'ai P'ing (Great Peace); not to be confused with the nineteenth-century movement that also called itself T'ai P'ing. Although the Yellow Turban movement included some Taoist elements, it was rejected by leading Taoists such as the Celestial Masters.
Pure Conversation (200–400 C.E.)	An extended philosophical debate among leading intellectuals, including Taoists, usually involving arguments among defenders of spontaneous naturalism and defenders of conservative morality.
Orthodox Unity (founded twelfth century C.E.)	A modification of Celestial Masters Taoism; also called the Chen-i sect.
Perfect Realization (founded twelfth century C.E.)	The Perfect Realization or Ch'uan-chen sect, founded by Wang Che, an eccentric Taoist priest with a strong Confucian education and considerable experience in the practice of Buddhism. Perfect Realization Taoism was the first Taoist sect with a monastic base and has survived to the present day.

before the flame of this incense-burner."[58] With this addition, the incense burner did not merely issue billows of incense to speed the prayers heavenward; it was assimilated to the alchemist's furnace.

Alchemy has always linked heating and transmuting metals with a belief in healing, spiritual powers, and even immortality; some Chinese alchemists recommended ingestion of certain "refined" metals and minerals to enhance spirituality and produce immortality. Alchemy was sometimes combined with the Celestial Masters tradition, but it should not be viewed as an essential part of Taoism. As far as we know, Chang Tao-ling and his immediate successors did not use alchemic methods, and Taoism has often flourished without alchemy. Furthermore, later Taoists developed an "inner alchemy" *(nei-tan),* in which the (outer) metals were replaced or symbolized by the functions of body organs. Thus, for example, inner alchemy

claimed that the heart supplies all the spiritual powers accredited to mercury by outer alchemy. In any case, we know that some Taoist adepts have practiced some form of alchemy, whether inner or outer, from the fourth century onward.

In the latter half of the fourth century, two new bodies of Taoist scriptures effected a brilliant synthesis of the Way of the Celestial Masters, the indigenous traditions of the southeast, and (to some extent) Buddhism. The first of these revelations was received by a visionary named Yang Hsi, who was in the service of the Hsu family, members of the same clan as Ko Hung. During a six-year period, Yang Hsi experienced visions of "perfected immortals from the heaven of **Shang Ch'ing.**" These revelations made up an extensive literature dealing primarily with meditation and private practice, featuring the recitation of powerful sacred texts and techniques of visualization. The revelations included a messianic theme reminiscent of the earlier Taoist movements: the present unjust order was to be replaced by a new Taoist imperium. Yang and the Hsus retired to the sacred mountain Mao Shan (near Nanking) to complete their study of immortality. The texts were called the *Shang Ch'ing* or *Mao Shan* revelations.

Another member of Ko Hung's clan, Ko Ch'ao fu, began composing a text called the *Classic of the Sacred Jewel (Ling Pao Ching)* in 397 C.E., which he claimed had first been revealed to his ancestor early in the third century. The central theme of the *Ling Pao Ching* was that the Tao is personified in celestial worthies, its primordial and uncreated manifestations. This scripture called for two types of liturgies: the *chiao* and the *chai*. The *chiao* are elaborate collective liturgies performed in outdoor arenas that last for a day and a night or for three, five, or seven days and require six officiants. The *chai* are less elaborate rituals focused on a more specific goal, such as exorcism, and therefore attended by only a segment of the community. The liturgies of the Celestial Masters, along with a number of Buddhist concepts and ceremonial practices, were absorbed into the new system. Because many of the Taoist rituals of today derive directly from these liturgies, versions of them are described in detail in the "Taoist Practice" section of this chapter. Suffice it to say that these powerful ceremonies became immensely popular—so much so that many subsequent liturgies down to the present day are adaptations of the *Ling Pao* legacy.

Just as the period of One Hundred Philosophers occurred in a time of political uncertainty, the collapse of the Han dynasty in 220 C.E. stimulated philosophical inquiry and debate. The debates—called Pure Conversation—usually involved arguments between defenders of spontaneous naturalism and defenders of conservative morality.[59] These discussions were part of the intellectual and cultural background of two of the greatest Taoist masters of all time: Lu Hsiu-ching, who systematized the *Ling Pao* texts, and T'ao Hung-ching, who edited the *Mao Shan* scriptures.

Lu Hsiu-ching (406–477) and other leading Taoists complacently accepted the regional supremacy of the Liu-Sung dynasty (despite the messianic impulse of the *Mao Shan* scriptures) and set about codifying scriptural materials. After editing the *Ling Pao* texts, Lu put together the first semblance of a Taoist canon, consisting of the *Mao Shan* texts, the *Ling Pao* texts, and some southern occult and exorcist literature extant before the Celestial Masters had migrated to the south. (Table 6.5 lists some of the major works in the Taoist canon.) Because the teachings and liturgies of the Celestial Masters were absorbed into these texts, these new developments can be viewed as extensions of the Celestial Masters tradition.

Another renowned Taoist master of the south was T'ao Hung-ching (456–536), editor of the *Mao Shan* texts and famous calligrapher and poet. T'ao was also very well versed in Buddhism and monastic life, and he suggested the celibate life as an alternative lifestyle for Taoists.

STATE TAOISM IN NORTH CHINA

Northern Taoism enjoyed the favor of the regional political rulers for long periods during the centuries of disunion. Just as Chang Lu had functioned as supporter and advisor of the new Wei rulers in his time (third century C.E.), two centuries later the great Taoist scholar and Celestial Master K'ou Ch'ien-chih (d. 448) cooperated with the Wei emperor and tacitly accepted the emperor's claim to be the representative of Lord Lao on earth. K'ou received a revelation from Lord Lao himself, warning Taoists against militant messianism and calling for the discontinuance of the Celestial Masters' practice of collecting rice and taxes from the people. Such reforms were pleasing to the emperor. K'ou was given the title Erudite of Transcendent Beings and put in charge of all religious affairs in the territory, which was referred to as a Taoist Kingdom on Earth. He joined with the government in inveighing against "heterodox cults with mediums and sorcerers." In 444 and 446 the emperor proscribed both the unauthorized mediums and Buddhism. Although K'ou was not opposed to Buddhism, he supported the edicts.

Table 6.5

TAOIST SCRIPTURE

The *Tao Tsang*, the full Taoist canon, consists of over one thousand volumes. The following are a few examples of a literature to which materials were being added as late as the seventeenth century C.E.

I Ching (ca. 800 B.C.E.)	An ancient book of divination based on the *yin/yang* cosmology. Cherished by Taoists, Confucians, and folk religionists, the *I Ching (Book of Changes)* includes an amalgam of interpretive insights gathered over the centuries.
Tao Te Ching (ca. 500 B.C.E.)	A short book of Taoist philosophy in semipoetic form that includes teachings on Tao, *wu-wei*, simplicity, and government attributed to Lao-tzu.
Chuang-tzu (ca. 300 B.C.E.)	Elaboration of Taoist philosophy in anecdotes and essays; attributed to Chuang-tzu.
Pao-p'u-tzu (317 B.C.E.)	A compendium of techniques of immortality and Taoist alchemy.
Huai-nan-tzu (ca. 140 B.C.E.)	An encyclopedic collection of Taoist teachings on cosmology, theology, government, and self-culture (e.g., diet and breath control).
Mao Shan revelations (ca. 380 C.E.)	Teachings about meditation; the texts contain a messianic theme.
Ling Pao revelations (ca. 400 C.E.)	Teachings that develop the theme of celestial worthies who personify the Tao; also present ritual materials to be used in the *chiao* and *chai*.

As Taoism was closely allied with the state religion in terms of ideology and rituals in the territory of Wei, we may call it **state Taoism** or Taocracy. Later, in T'ang times (618–906), the alliances between Taoism and the state were less close, but the emperors claimed that Lao-tzu was their ancestor and required knowledge of Taoist texts, along with Confucian classics, for civil service employment. Taoists, for the most part, were on good terms with subsequent dynasties as well, occasionally performing specific rites at court.

THE GOLDEN AGE OF THE T'ANG DYNASTY (618–906 C.E.)

The three centuries of T'ang dynasty rule was a period of unification and cultural consolidation. So impressive was Chinese society that one leading Western scholar has called T'ang China the greatest civilization in the world at the time.[60]

In many ways it was a period of conservatism; no new Taoist revelations or movements occurred.

The T'ang rulers claimed Lao-tzu as their royal ancestor and viewed the realm as Taocratic. As attested by Japanese Buddhist pilgrims who traveled across China in those years, Mao Shan Taoism was flourishing. Both Confucian and Taoist texts were the bases of civil service examinations.

Buddhism reached the zenith of its development and popularity during the T'ang dynasty, and Taoist hostility toward this "foreign" religion came to a head. Reinforced by irritation over Buddhist monasteries' accumulation of precious metals and tax-exempt land, Emperor Wu-tsung (r. 840–846), an ardent Taoist, issued decrees that led to the destruction of 4,600 Buddhist monasteries and 40,000 temples and shrines, as well as the return of 260,500 monks and nuns to lay life. However, this suppression was ended in 846 by Wu-tsung's successor, and in time Buddhism regained its position of strength alongside Taoism and Confucianism.

Chinese folk religion continued with irrepressible vitality straight down to contemporary times despite periodic attempts by the state, the Taoists, and the Confucians to suppress and control it. We have seen that the official view of the Taoists was that folk religion lacked spiritual and political authorization, yet Taoism absorbed some elements of folk religion, such as rites of exorcism. Taoist priests even recommended that their followers engage in ancestor worship and worship of the god of the soil, both perennial activities of folk religion.[61]

NEW TAOIST MOVEMENTS IN THE SUNG (960–1279 C.E.) AND YUAN (1279–1368 C.E.) DYNASTIES

Because of increased economic growth, large numbers of schools, and innovations in philosophy and religion, historians refer to the Sung (Song) period as the "beginning of early modern China."[62] The period saw the emergence of new Taoist movements and official recognition of Taoism by the royal court. Taoism lost royal favor in the subsequent Yuan dynasty, gained it again in the Ming, and lost it in Ch'ing times.

The Taoists coveted official recognition by various levels of government, especially the imperial court. The Sung emperors favored the Taoists with gifts and titles, allying themselves with the Taoists and declaring their rule to be a Taocracy. Emperor Hui-tsung (r. 1101–1126), a devout believer, even achieved the first printing of the Taoist canon, the **Tao Tsang**, in 1120 C.E..

Shortly after the printing of these scriptures, a new religious ferment began to occur. Partial causes of this ferment were the threat of foreign invasions and the influence of Buddhism. Many new Taoist sects arose, and an old sect, the Celestial Masters, was slightly modified. Given historical hindsight, we know that only two of these movements contributed significantly to modern Taoism: the Orthodox Unity (Chen-i) organization (a modification of the Celestial Masters) and the Perfect Realization (Ch'uan-chen) sect.

During this period the lineage of the Celestial Masters originating with Chang Tao-ling was officially recognized at Lung-hu Shan (Dragon and Tiger Mountain), in the province of Kiangsi. The thirtieth Celestial Master, Chang Chi-hsien, is credited with the renovation of the old Way of the Celestial Masters, including the introduction of new liturgical material into the movement, known after 1126 as the Chen-i or Orthodox Unity sect.

Whereas the Orthodox Unity organization was a new form of an old movement, the Ch'uan-chen (Perfect Realization) sect was a completely new combination of several older religious currents. This fascinating sect brought together such Taoist currents as inner alchemy, *Mao Shan* techniques, and interpretations of the philosophy of the *Tao Te Ching*. From Confucianism it drew its ethical impulse, as is evidenced by its use of the Confucian *Hsiao Ching (Classic of Filial Piety)*. Its monastic ideal and meditation technique were drawn from Ch'an Buddhism.

The founder of Ch'uan-chen was an eccentric recluse by the name of Wang Che (1113–1170). Wang was the son of a great Shensi province landowner. Confucian educated, Wang had practiced Buddhism for a time before turning to Taoism and receiving ordination as a priest. Wang Che was visited by several mysterious immortals in 1160; this visit prompted him to dig a grave (which he called the "tomb of a living corpse") and to live in it for three years. For the next four years he lived in a thatched hut, but in 1167 he suddenly burned down the hut and departed for Shantung to begin seeking followers. One of Wang Che's seven disciples spent six years under a bridge; he neither spoke nor moved and ate only when people gave him something. A second disciple, Wang Ch'u-i (1142–1217), was known as an exorcist and master of herbal medicine who spent his nights in a cave standing on one foot so as not to fall asleep.[63]

The Ch'uan-chen sect was the first major Taoist organization with a monastic base, although it enjoyed a large lay following as well. The movement gained considerable favor politically, but the political winds blew against the Taoists under the Yuan (Mongol) rulers (1279–1368). Taoist-Buddhist debates were held at court in 1281; the emperor Kublai Khan declared the Buddhists to be the winners, and portions of the Taoist scriptures were burned. Yuan rulers tended to favor the Buddhists, but the Chen-i and Ch'uan-chen sects of Taoism continued to thrive. Taoist spirituality and metaphysics were incorporated into Neo-Confucianism (to be discussed in Chapter 7). Under Taoist influence, the deities of folk religion came to be organized in a celestial hierarchy presided over by a deity called the Jade Emperor, who holds a prominent position in both the Taoist and folk pantheons. During the Yuan dynasty, Islam spread from central Asia to all of China.

THE MING DYNASTY (1368-1644 C.E.)

During Ming times, Taoist organizations enjoyed a close cooperative relationship with the ruling dynasty. Perfect Realization Taoism (Ch'uan-chen) continued to flourish in Ming times, but the Orthodox Unity (Chen-i) organization, with the Celestial Master as its head, enjoyed more imperial support. The Celestial Master occupied a government post overseeing all Taoist affairs and all forms of folk religions as well. The Ming emperor and the Taoists attempted to control folk religion through the office of the Celestial Master. Although the control of Chinese folk religion is virtually impossible, the concept of the Taoist as an elite administrator of spiritual affairs has been an ideal of Taoist organizations since the second century C.E. The key image here is that of a "superior controller of gods and demons." The Celestial Masters composed hymns for the court and conducted some of the court rituals, thus effecting a partial fusion with state religion. The forty-third Celestial Master was appointed by the emperor to compile a new, comprehensive Taoist canon, an arduous task completed in 1445. The Ming emperor T'ai-tsu proclaimed that each of the San-Chiao (Three Teachings)—Taoism, Buddhism, and Confucianism—had an important role to play; this explicit official sanction stimulated syncretic tendencies that had been at work for centuries.

THE CH'ING DYNASTY (1644–1911 C.E.) AND THE REPUBLIC (1912–1948 C.E.)

The Ch'ing (Manchu) rulers were patrons of Confucianism in the area of public policies, and they also lent considerable support to Buddhism. Even though the Ming's special relationship with the Celestial Masters was terminated by the Ch'ing, the Chen-i and Ch'uan-chen organizations continued to be active without court support during Ch'ing times.

Western influence began to mount exponentially during the Ch'ing dynasty. A small Christian community had been established in the sixteenth century by the Jesuits, but Western commercial interests had a greater impact. By the mid-nineteenth century, the British were forcibly maintaining profitable trade through Canton despite the Chinese government's objection to the British sale of opium. The resulting Opium War was one of the first in a series of military and political losses that humiliated the Chinese and reduced their sovereignty.

The most unusual innovation in Ch'ing religion was the curious phenomenon called the T'ai-p'ing T'ien-kuo, or Celestial Kingdom of Great Peace and Prosperity—a millennial movement that combined Christian and Chinese religious motifs. The founder of this "Taiping" movement was Hung Hsin-ch'uan (1814-1864), a would-be Confucian who failed the civil service exams several times. Hung had been given Christian tracts for the first time in 1836, and he was deeply moved by them. After failing his exams in 1837, he claimed to have had a vision in which it was conveyed to him that he was the younger brother of Jesus Christ. Hung had been sent as the new messiah to rule a theocracy. There was to be a new kingdom on earth— a society based on the *Ten Commandments*, equality of the sexes, and property held in common.

In addition to Hung's own specialized interpretations of selected aspects of Christianity, he included a version of the Chinese notion of the mandate of heaven. Hung himself took on the title of Celestial King; he was to rule in place of the Ch'ing. The movement preached filial piety as a cardinal virtue but otherwise rejected Confucianism's hierarchical social teachings. From Taoist ideology, Hung adopted the concept of a struggle against demonic forces. However, the leading Taoist organizations did not support Hung's movement. The Taipings condemned many Chinese religious practices such as the veneration of ancestors, the worship of Buddhas, the worship of Taoist deities, and the worship of the gods of folk religion. As the movement became more militant, the Taipings destroyed images and temples wherever they went. Teaching, organizing, and inspiring peasants and artisans—especially the poor and disillusioned—Hung's movement formed a massive army that eventually involved all of China in civil war. The Taipings took control of Nanking in 1852.

The Taipings were finally crushed by a combination of Chinese and Western forces in 1864; their great dream of peace had cost 20 million lives. In the end, however, the Taipings were an anomaly. One leading Sinologist has said that Taiping teachings and practices "had no positive effect on the history of Chinese religions after this time, while all the indigenous traditions resumed and rebuilt."[64] The Taiping movement, a unique combination of various religious themes marshaled into the form of a powerful rebellion, was perhaps an indication of the need for radical change in Chinese civilization.

The initial Chinese reaction to increasing Western impact had been to reject the influence of the foreign "barbarians." Many intellectuals, however, suggested a compromise capsulized in the slogan "Chinese substance, Western function." Basic values were to be Chinese, but Western technology was to be accepted and used. The Three Teachings (Taoism, Confucianism, and Buddhism) concept officially sanctioned in the Ming continued in the form of syncretic books on morality.

Chinese resentment of foreign influence culminated in the Boxer Rebellion in 1900, in which foreign cultural and commercial elements, including Christian missionaries, were violently attacked. To understand the extent of the resentment and humiliation experienced by the Chinese at the turn

of the century, we need to realize that Chinese civilization had been an immensely long-lived culture accustomed to perceiving itself as superior to all others.

Outright rejection of foreign ways changed to a kind of compromise in the early twentieth century as the Ch'ing government began to crumble from internal decay, military uprisings, and foreign pressure. In 1912, the imperial system was abandoned in favor of a republican form of government. The significance of this change cannot be overestimated. For two thousand years, changes in government had meant a change in dynasties, but now, with the attempt to institute a republican government, the entire imperial system and its state religion were to be abandoned. Chinese cities were shaken by struggles for power as the nation tried to effect the transformation; the republican government was at times a fictional entity. A New Culture Movement proclaimed widely that traditional Chinese culture must be abandoned along with the imperial form of government. Chinese intellectuals traveled abroad and studied foreign philosophies, including Marxism. The hope for a new, united, sovereign China was fraught with confusion and conflict. A student demonstration on May 4, 1919, in T'ien-an Men (Tiananmen) square in Peking (Beijing) came to symbolize the frustrations and hopes of the youth.

In 1928, the Kuomintang or Nationalist Party established a modicum of unity and order, but four years later the Japanese invaded China. The conclusion of World War II did not bring peace and order to China: in 1945 the Nationalist government confronted a powerful communist movement that had been growing steadily since the 1920s. The Nationalists and communists engaged in open military conflict from 1947 to 1949, when the communists, under Mao Tse Tung (Mao Ze-dong), defeated the Nationalists. Following basic Marxist doctrine, Mao Tse Tung introduced policies that suppressed all religion. Although the Nationalist government, in exile on the island of Taiwan, allowed religious activity to flourish, the People's Republic of China on the mainland took a firm stance against religion.

CHRONOLOGY OF TAOISM

CA. 1500	Divination with oracle bones; worship of nature spirits
1000	*I Ching* in use; *yin/yang* cosmology developed
CA. 500	*Tao Te Ching* written, attributed to Lao-tzu
CA. 300	*Chuang-tzu* written, attributed to Chuang-tzu
CA. 150 B.C.E.	Further development of Taoist thought
142 C.E.	Revelation to Chang Tao-ling, founder of the Celestial Masters
CA. 275	Taoist Pure Conversation movement
CA. 317	Ko Hung writes *Pao-p'u-tzu*
CA. 380	*Mao Shan* revelations
CA. 400	*Ling Pao Ching* revelations

THE PEOPLE'S REPUBLIC OF CHINA: 1949 TO THE PRESENT

Great and glorious celebrations accompanied Mao Tse Tung's proclamation of a communist victory and the institution of the People's Republic of China (PRC) in 1949. From the perspective of China's religious traditions, the advent of the People's Republic of China signaled not glory but a period of ridicule, persecution, and suppression. Following Marxist doctrine, Mao declared Chinese religion to be "feudal superstition." It was not the first attempt that government had made to control religion in China, but it was the most thorough. One of Mao's reports on the progress of the revolution gives us a sense of his forceful style in attacking religion:

> "The gods? They may quite deserve our worship. But if we had no peasant association but only Emperor Kuan and the Goddess of Mercy, could we have knocked down the local bullies and bad gentry? The gods and goddesses are indeed pitiful, worshipped for hundreds of years, they

have not knocked down for you a single one of the bad gentry!

> "Now you want to have your rent reduced. I would like to ask: How will you go about it? Believe in the gods, or believe in the peasant association?" These words of mine made the peasants roar with laughter.[65]

In the period called the Cultural Revolution (1966–1976), the suppression of religion became more direct and violent. Religious artifacts were destroyed, scriptures were burned, and clergy were defrocked. During this time the fervor of communism and the veneration of Chairman Mao became so intense that many observers began to echo a theory about communism that had been held from Karl Marx's own time (ca. 1880): perhaps communism itself is a religion or a quasi religion. The evidence for such a notion is striking indeed if we look at what happened in China: Mao was seen by his followers as a Moses-like figure leading the communist forces on the Long March to eventual vic-

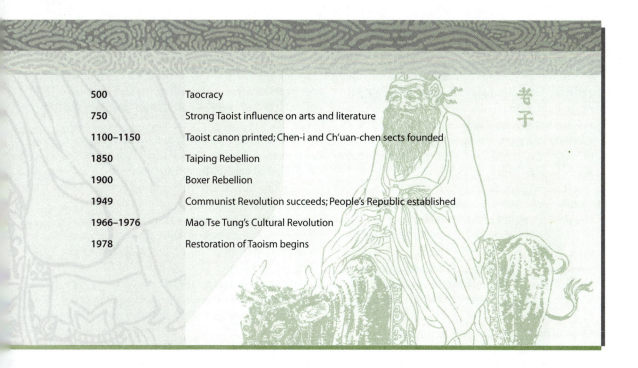

500	Taocracy
750	Strong Taoist influence on arts and literature
1100–1150	Taoist canon printed; Chen-i and Ch'uan-chen sects founded
1850	Taiping Rebellion
1900	Boxer Rebellion
1949	Communist Revolution succeeds; People's Republic established
1966–1976	Mao Tse Tung's Cultural Revolution
1978	Restoration of Taoism begins

tory. Mao's book was said to be "the sun in our heart, the root of our life, the source of all strength."[66] If Mao's writings functioned like scripture, so the practices he required were like religious rituals: people were to confess their sins against the revolution and vow their obedience before portraits of Chairman Mao. Meals of wild herbs were eaten to recall the bitter days before the liberation. For a time, Maoism functioned as the state religion.

No political program is static, however. Communist practice evolves and changes. With the death of Mao in 1976, his cult disappeared. Article 36 of the PRC Constitution of 1982 states that citizens "enjoy freedom of religious belief." It states further that the state protects "legitimate" religious activities.[67] The vague word *legitimate* has been interpreted in increasingly liberal ways. As early as 1978, new policies resulted in the building or rebuilding of Taoist temples and monasteries, and a revitalization and restoration process is continuing and increasing—a topic that will be explored in the next section.

CONTEMPORARY TAOISM

Taoism is experiencing a revival today. Although this restoration is genuine and the growth is real, the number of Taoist priests, monks, and nuns is small and is, of course, far less than before the revolution of 1949.

An example of this revitalization process is the Taoist activity in the Minnan region of southeastern Fujien province in eastern China. In January 1986, a four-day *chiao* was performed in a small village near Changchou by twelve Chen-i Taoist priests, six musicians, and four assistants.[68] This was the first *chiao* to be celebrated in that village since 1949; such firsts are not uncommon in China today.

As in the days before the revolution, almost everyone in the community was involved in the preparations for the *chiao* over a ten-month period. The only exception were Communist Party members. Party members dare not show support for any religious activity, even when everyone else in the community is openly participating. They fear that their own belief in communism might be questioned if they were to lend support to a religious activity. Although religious activity is now permitted, the official objections to religious festivals runs as follows: (1) Religious festivals lead to excessive economic waste; (2) such events disturb public security; and (3) "spiritual charlatans and witch-women" extort money from the people.

The inscription at the entrance to the new temple near Changchou reads: "If anyone dares to violate the grounds of this temple, such a man will become ill and such a woman will encounter disaster."[69] The idea of illness or disaster as a result of wrong action is common in Chinese culture, so the inscription cannot be interpreted as a blatant political warning against future attempts at suppression. However, the inscription is public notice that the Chinese people are again staking out sacred grounds after decades of destruction. The villagers do not understand the full meaning of the Taoist rituals, but they understand that they are methods or techniques of salvation, and they understand that their performance is a restoration of traditional religious practice.

The *chiao* for this temple was nonetheless somewhat abridged; it was less elaborate than the *chiaos* the elders remember, and this *chiao* lasted only four days, whereas the ideal is five days. Many of the Taoist liturgical manuscripts and accoutrements such as robes, paintings, and other materials were destroyed during the Cultural Revolution; it takes time to reestablish religious tradition. However, most of the villagers were quite satisfied with the *chiao*. It was followed by visits by the Taoist priests to each household in the community.

There are numerous reports of the reopening of over a hundred Taoist monasteries throughout the country. Estimates of the numbers of monks and nuns range from three thousand to fifteen thousand. In addition to the usual problems of the accuracy and meaning of statistics in China, we should realize that monastic life has never been the main focus of the Taoist religion. Moreover, none of the statistics includes the number of Taoist priests who

marry and live at home. There are reports of the openings or reopenings of Taoist temples, but the statistics can be very deceptive, because many village temples, such as the one near Changchou, are not exclusively Taoist. The village community builds the temple and uses it for a variety of religious and nonreligious purposes. For example, it may be used for **T'ai-chi ch'uan**—the system of breathing and movement valued as a martial art, a dance form, and physical and spiritual hygiene.

Noteworthy among presently operating Taoist centers are those in Peking, Shanghai, Chengdu, and Wuhan. The Baiyun (White Cloud) Taoist temple and monastery in Peking is in full operation (having been reopened in 1984), and Taoist liturgies mark special days. North of Shanghai stands a temple reopened in 1982. Chen-i priests perform liturgies there today, including a ceremony on the occasion of the birthday of the Buddhist *bodhisattva* Kuan-yin; the name given her by Taoism is **Chihangdaoren** (Taoist sage of the boat of compassion).

Taoist mountain centers today are places of pilgrimage and tourism. One example is the Taoist mountain Ch'ingchen Shan in Chengdu. Priests report that an average of one thousand people per day visit the temple and monastery, which are affiliated with the Ch'uan-chen order.

Taoist performance of the liturgy of merit (also called the "attack on hell" or "mass for the dead" by Western scholars) sometimes occurs in semisecrecy today. There is hesitance about the acceptability of this ritual; it is dramatic, employs mediums, and may be called "superstitious" by Communist Party members. As late as 1985, a Western scholar witnessed the liturgy of merit performed in Wuhan "in a secluded area, almost in secret."[70]

The last example should temper our generally positive evaluation of the future of Taoism. Although a restoration of Taoism is taking place in the People's Republic of China, some obstacles exist. Government policies today guarantee religious freedom but discourage "superstitious activities."[71] It is not clear what is meant by this last phrase. Another problem faced by Taoists is the government's insistence that monks engage in "productive work":

"Work in the fields . . . is a good way for Taoists to support themselves and contribute to the country's socialist economic construction."[72] This requirement reduces the time and energy that can go into spiritual education, contemplation, and religious services to the community.

A very interesting indicator of how Taoism interrelates with other elements in contemporary China is the role of women. We have seen that Chinese tradition has held women in a position of inferiority; infanticide, arranged marriages, and foot binding are the legacy of ancient Chinese attitudes. But we also observed that Taoists have in some ways liberated women by accepting them as spiritual adepts, nuns, and even priests. Modern, secular reform movements have also promoted human rights for both women and men, and the communists are attempting to protect women from

infanticide and arranged marriages. However, the communist opposition to what they perceive as "superstition" tends to inhibit the open practice of female Taoist adepts (so-called witch-women). Overall, the resurgence of Taoism in China should continue and with it, gradual amelioration of conditions for women.

Although years of suppression have left their mark, the gradual liberalization of government policies since 1978 and the restoration of Taoism is evident. Although the numbers of priests, monks, and nuns are relatively small, there is clearly hope for increased vitality and growth in the future. Taoism has shown remarkable resilience in being able to endure the years of suppression. Today, in addition to its uninhibited continuance in Taiwan and Singapore, we can say that Taoism is alive and well in the People's Republic of China.

GLOSSARY OF TAOISM

adept
: one who is highly proficient in a spiritual discipline, often involving special physical postures or breathing techniques. Usually, a person who practices techniques of immortality is a recluse, monk, or nun.

alchemy
: a reputed spiritual science that links the heating and transmuting of metals with belief in healing powers and even immortality.

chai
: a Taoist rite, usually less elaborate than the *chiao;* many *chai* are rituals for the salvation of the dead.

ch'i
: vital breath or energy.

chiao
: a Taoist rite of cosmic renewal; an elaborate four- or five-day series of rituals performed by Taoist priests.

Chihangdaoren
: literally, "Taoist sage of the boat of compassion"; a compassionate female Taoist immortal; known in Buddhism as the *bodhisattva* Kuan-yin.

embryonic breathing
: a Taoist spiritual practice focusing on the abdomen and involving special breathing methods.

holding the Ones
: a complex *Mao Shan* technique designed to draw down the Three Pure Ones into one's body.

immortal	a being who, formerly human, has attained a transcendent condition and possesses a refined, etherealized body. Becoming an immortal is the Taoist ideal of perfection.
Jade Emperor	(Yu-huang) a Chinese deity viewed by Taoists as the executor of orders from the Three Pure Ones.
kuei	a malevolent spirit; the demonic spirit of a person who has died in an especially violent or unjust way; the spirit of an ancestor who has not been shown proper homage. All such spirits can cause difficulty for living humans and may have to be exorcised by a Taoist priest.
libationer	one who makes an offering; usually a Taoist priest of the Celestial Masters or Chen-i sect.
macrocosm	the scheme of things entire; "the big picture." In Taoist thought, the elements and structure of the macrocosm are believed to be mirrored in the microcosm, and causal relationships hold between macrocosm and microcosm.
microcosm	a relatively small object or system, such as a human body; a system that mirrors and is causally related to the macrocosm.
Shang Ch'ing	the name of the heaven from which the *Mao Shan* revelations were brought by perfected immortals.
Shang-ti	the Supreme Ruler in Heaven.
shen	a benevolent spirit, deity, or ancestor; broadly, the spirit component of life.
state Taoism	see **Taocracy.**
Tai-chi ch'uan	literally, "supreme, ultimate fist"; a slow movement/dance process based in part on Taoist principles; also viewed as a martial art.
Tao (Dao)	the way of the universe; the source and ordering principle of all that is; the ultimate sacred reality.
Tao Tsang	the Taoist canon.
Taocracy	state Taoism; a society governed by Taoist principles.
Tao-shih	a Taoist priest or adept.
te (de)	the Taoist term for "virtue" or "power"; natural effectiveness.
Three Pure Ones	the three highest gods in the Taoist pantheon. Also called Lords or Worthies, they are the Lord of Heaven, Lord of Earth, and Lord of Humanity.
T'ien	literally, "heaven"; a supreme divine power, sometimes conceived of in personal terms and sometimes in impersonal terms.
wu–wei	the Taoist ideal mode of functioning in a flowing, unforced way.
yang	the male, bright, positive force in the universe.
yin	the female, dark, negative force in the universe.
yoga	a system of movements and stretches designed to facilitate physical and spiritual health.

FOR FURTHER STUDY

Chan, Wing-Tsit. *A Source Book in Chinese Philosophy*. Princeton, N.J.: Princeton University Press, 1963.

> *An anthology of selections from the basic texts of Chinese philosophy, with excellent introductions and commentary by an outstanding twentieth-century scholar.*

Cleary, Thomas. *Immortal Sisters: Secrets of Taoist Women*. Boston: Shambhala, 1989.

> *One of the few studies of female adepts in the Taoist tradition.*

DeBary, William Theodore, comp. *Sources of Chinese Tradition*. New York: Columbia University Press, 1960.

> *A comprehensive collection of important texts to give the reader a good overview of Chinese tradition from its origins to the twentieth century. Unlike Chan's anthology, DeBary's work is not limited to philosophical texts.*

Girardot, Norman J. *Myth and Meaning in Early Taoism: The Theme of Chaos*. Berkeley and Los Angeles: University of California Press, 1983.

> *A somewhat technical work on the specified theme.*

Henricks, Robert G. *Lao-tzu, Te-Tao Ching*. New York: Ballantine, 1989.

> *A recent, highly respected translation with very useful commentaries.*

Lagerway, John. *Taoist Ritual in Chinese Society and History*. New York: Macmillan, 1987.

> *A work that presents the details of Taoist ritual along with relevant aspects of the metaphysics of religious Taoism.*

Needham, Joseph. *Science and Civilization in China*. Cambridge, England: Cambridge University Press, 1954.

> *A multivolume work that includes a vast amount of material on all aspects of Chinese civilization.*

Pas, Julian, ed. *The Turning of the Tide: Religion in China Today*. London and New York: Oxford University Press, 1990.

> *A very readable account of the revival of religion in China in the 1970s and 1980s.*

Thompson, Laurence G. *Chinese Religion: An Introduction*. 4th ed. Belmont, CA.: Wadsworth, 1989.

> *A relatively short book (184 pages)that is a good general introduction to the subject.*

Watson, Burton, trans. *Chuang Tzu: Basic Writings*. New York: Columbia University Press, 1968.

> *A highly respected and readable translation of the work attributed to an early Taoist philosopher.*

Yang, C. K. *Religion in Chinese Society*. Los Angeles: University of California Press, 1961.

> *Probably the best general work from a sociological perspective.*

READINGS

Reading 6.1   CHINESE DIVINATION: *I CHING*   John Blofeld

One of the classics of Chinese religious literature, the *I Ching,* or *Book of Changes,* is perhaps the oldest extant Chinese book. The heart of the *I Ching* is a set of sixty-four hexagrams—patterns of *yin* and *yang* lines. The hexagrams and the commentaries on them are designed to help a person divine the future and determine a proper course of action. What follows is the description of one eminent English author's description of his consultation of the *I Ching;* next are presented the texts of the two hexagrams he discusses. Why are combinations of *yin* and *yang* thought to indicate something about how things will turn out? Do you think the person consulting the *I Ching* must use faith and intuition to derive an answer from the book? Explain.

My interest in the *I Ching* was fully awakened towards the end of 1962 at about the time when hostilities between India and mainland China commenced in the Tibetan border region. Before long, the newspapers in Bangkok (where I live) were prophesying that the Chinese armies would continue their rapid advance, swoop down onto the plains of India and perhaps occupy some major cities there before India's friends could come to her defence. The contrary view was never expressed in the newspapers that came to my notice. As I had been very happy both in China and India and felt a keen affection for both peoples, I was deeply disturbed; finally, in a spirit of sincere enquiry, I consulted the *Book of Change.* The answer was so contrary to other people's predictions that I decided to write it down word for word. I do not have the record by me now; but, as far as I remember, my interpretation, which was closely based upon the actual wording of the book, ran something like this, though it was considerably longer and more detailed. An army in the hills (the Chinese) was looking down upon the marshy plain below (India). If its leaders were wise, they would halt their attack at the very moment when everything was going well for them, refrain from advancing further and perhaps withdraw in some places. A week or two later this is precisely what happened. Moreover, the *I Ching* had given reasons for this advice, namely that the lines of communication were already too long for safety; that the opponent (India) was likely to receive powerful support from its friends; that the moral value of calling a halt before any necessity for it became generally apparent would be greater in the long run than fresh military gains; and several other reasons which I cannot now recall. I remember that every one of them was later adduced in newspaper articles to explain the unexpected behaviour of the Chinese and I vividly recall the astonishment of my friends when I showed them what I had written down in advance of the newspapers. It could of course be claimed that a good deal of the accuracy of my answer was due to my particular interpretation of the actual words below the two hexagrams and the two moving lines involved; but, as I had not at all expected the Chinese to call a halt or reasoned out the possible reasons for their doing so, it is hard to see how I could made myself the dupe of autosuggestion.

The following is a reconstruction from memory of the way in which I obtained these results. The response consisted of Hexagram 48 plus . . . Hexagram 63 (which results when those lines "move" and thus become their own opposites).

Hexagram 48 signifies a well. My knowledge of the Indo-Tibetan borderlands, where the mighty Himalayas slope sharply down to the dead flat plain of north India, led me promptly to equate India with the well and to think of the Chinese as looking down into it from above. Of the two component trigrams, one has "bland" or "mild" among its meanings, while the other means "water." Taking water, the contents of the well, to be the people of India, I found it easy to think of bland or mild as representing their declared policy of non-violence and neutrality. Thus, the significance of these two trigrams convinced me that I had been right to suppose that the well represented India (or the whole of that country except for the Himalayan border region). The Text attached to that hexagram contained three ideas which seemed to me appropriate to the situation. That the well suffers no increase or decrease suggested that India would lose no territory lying south of the mountainous frontier region; the rope's being too short suggested that the Chinese could not safely extend their lines of communication further than they had already done; otherwise, their "pitcher" would be broken, i.e., they would suffer a serious reverse or defeat. . . .

The main Text and Commentary of Hexagram 63 reinforced the conclusions I had reached. "Success in small matters" suggested that the Chinese would not forfeit their local gains in the Himalayan region. The reward promised for persistence in a *righteous* course appeared enigmatic until I remembered that the Chinese had never accorded recognition to the McMahon Line; thus they could argue (and certainly believed) that they had a legal claim to certain border areas, to which past Chinese governments had also laid claim; whereas there could be no shadow of legality to back up an advance into the Indian plains (i.e. down into the well). The last sentence of the main Commentary attached to this hexagram states: "It is clear that good fortune will accompany the start; but, ultimately, affairs will be halted amidst disorder because the way peters out." The last four words of this passage are often taken to mean: "thenceforth, heaven's blessing is (or will be) withdrawn." In other words, for the Chinese to advance into the plains with no moral claim whatsoever to support them would be to court disaster. Thus, in a nutshell, the whole response conveyed to me the idea that the Chinese would gain local successes, but that there were tactical, strategic and moral reasons for supposing that no further advance could be made with impunity.

HEXAGRAM 48: CHING, A WELL

Component trigrams:
Below: SUN, wind, wood, bland, mild.
Above: K'AN, water, a pit.

Text

A Well. A city may be moved, but not a well. A well suffers from no decrease and no increase; but often, when the people come to draw water there, the rope is too short or the pitcher gets broken before reaching the water—misfortune!

Commentary on the Text

Where (the pitchers are put) into the water to draw it up—such is a well. That a well gives nourishment without suffering depletion and that a city may be moved, but not a well, are both implied by the firm line in the centre (of the upper trigram). The rope's being too short indicates failure to achieve results; the breaking of the pitcher presages a positive misfortune.

Symbol

This hexagram symbolizes water over wood. The Superior Man encourages the people with advice and assistance.

HEXAGRAM 63: CHI CHI, AFTER COMPLETION

The component trigrams:
Below: LI, fire, brilliance, beauty.
Above: K'AN water, a pit.

Text

After Completion—success in small matters! Persistence in a righteous course brings reward. Good fortune at the start; disorder in the end!

Commentary on the Text

This hexagram presages success in small matters. That right persistence will be rewarded is indicated by the correctness and suitable arrangement of the firm and yielding lines. Since the yielding (line 2) is central (to the lower trigram), it is clear that good fortune will accompany the start; but, ultimately, affairs will be halted amid disorder because the way peters out.

Symbol

This hexagram symbolizes water above fire. The Superior Man deals with trouble by careful thought and by taking advance precautions.

Source: *I Ching,* trans. and ed. John Blofeld (New York: Dutton, 1968), pp. 27–29, 179–180, 208.

Reading 6.2   THE FOUNDER'S WORDS: *TAO TE CHING*

The passages selected here reveal some of the most important teachings of the Lao-tzu text, *Tao Te Ching.* The translation used is a standard translation by a highly respected scho1ar; however, there are other reputable translations that offer significantly different renderings. Questions of how to translate and interpret the Lao-tzu text continue to be debated by scholars today.

The last three passages selected—from Chapters 33, 16, and 50—may appear to refer to meditation techniques (Chap. 16, lines 1 and 2) and an afterlife (Chap. 33, last line, and Chap. 50, last line). However, the apparent reference to meditation is vague. As for the afterlife: highly acclaimed translation by Robert G. Henricks based on the oldest scrolls (see For Further Study) does not read Lao-tzu as referring to an afterlife. After reading this selection, can you state and explain five important points Lao-tzu makes about the Tao in these passages? Based on what Lao-tzu says here, what is the ideal person like—that is, what image or vision of the ideal person do the passages create?

> The Tao (Way) that can be told of is not the eternal Tao;
> The name that can be named is not the eternal name.
> The Nameless is the origin of Heaven and Earth;
> The Named is the mother of all things.
> Therefore let there always be non-being so we may see their subtlety,
> And let there always be being so we may see their outcome.
> The two are the same,
> But after they are produced, they have different names.
> They both may be called deep and profound (hsuan).
> Deeper and more profound,
> The door of all subtleties! (Chap. 1)

> To hold and fill to overflowing
>   Is not as good as to stop in time.
> Sharpen a sword-edge to its very sharpest,
>   And the (edge) will not last long.
> When gold and jade fill your hall.
>   You will not be able to keep them.
> To be proud with honor and wealth
>   Is to cause one's own downfall.
> Withdraw as soon as your work is done.
> Such is Heaven's Way. (Chap. 9)

> Attain complete vacuity,
> Maintain steadfast quietude.
> All things come into being,
> And I see thereby their return.
> All things flourish,
> But each one returns to its root.
> This return to its root means tranquillity.
> It is called returning to its destiny.
> To return to destiny is called the eternal (Tao).
> To know the eternal is called enlightenment.
> Not to know the eternal is to act blindly and so to result in disaster.
> He who knows the eternal is all-embracing.
> Being all-embracing, he is impartial.
> Being impartial, he is kingly (universal). (Chap. 16)

The best (rulers) are those whose existence is (merely)
known by the people.
The next best are those who are loved and praised.
The next are those who are feared.
And the next are those who are despised.
It is only when one does not have enough faith in others
that others will have no faith in him.
[The great rulers] value their words highly.
They accomplish their task; they complete their work.
Nevertheless their people say that they simply follow Nature (Tzu-jan). (Chap. 17)

When the great Tao declined,
The doctrines of humanity (jen) and righteousness (i) arose.
When knowledge and wisdom appeared,
There emerged great hypocrisy.
When the six family relationships are not in harmony,
There will be the advocacy of filial piety and deep love to children.
When a country is in disorder,
There will be praise of loyal ministers. (Chap 18)

Abandon sageliness and discard wisdom;
Then the people will benefit a hundredfold.
Abandon humanity and discard righteousness;
Then the people will return to filial piety and deep love.
Abandon skill and discard profit;
Then there will be no thieves or robbers.
However, these three things are ornament (wen) and not adequate.
Therefore let people hold on to these:
   Manifest plainness,
   Embrace simplicity,
   Reduce selfishness,
   Have few desires. (Chap. 19)

There was something undifferentiated and yet complete.
Which existed before heaven and earth.
Soundless and formless, it depends on nothing and does not change.
It operates everywhere and is free from danger.
It may be considered the mother of the universe.
I do not know its name; I call it Tao.
If forced to give it a name, I shall call it Great.
Now being great means functioning everywhere.
Functioning everywhere means far-reaching.
Being far-reaching means returning to the original point.
Therefore Tao is great.
Heaven is great.
Earth is great.
And the king is also great.
There are four great things in the universe, and the king is one of them.

Man models himself after Earth.
Earth models itself after Heaven.
Heaven models itself after Tao.
And Tao models itself after Nature. (Chap. 25)

He who knows others is wise;
He who knows himself is enlightened.
He who conquers others has physical strength.
He who conquers himself is strong.
He who is contented is rich.
He who acts with vigor has will.
He who does not lose his place (with Tao) will endure.
He who dies but does not really perish enjoys long life. (Chap. 33)

Reversion is the action of Tao.
Weakness is the function of Tao.
All things in the world come from being.
And being comes from non-being. (Chap. 40)

The softest things in the world overcome the hardest things in the world.
Non-being penetrates that in which there is no space.
Through this I know the advantage of taking no action.
Few in the world can understand teaching without words
and the advantage of taking no action. (Chap. 43)

One may know the world without going out of doors.
One may see the Way of Heaven without looking through the windows.
The further one goes, the less one knows.
Therefore the sage knows without going about,
Understands without seeing,
And accomplishes without any action. (Chap. 47)

Man comes into life and goes out to death.
Three out of ten are companions of life.
Three out of ten are companions of death.
And three out of ten in their lives lead from activity to death.
And for what reason?
Because of man's intensive striving after life.
I have heard that one who is a good preserver of his life will
not meet tigers or wild buffalos,
And in fighting will not try to escape from weapons of war.
The wild buffalo cannot butt its horns against him,
The tiger cannot fasten its claws in him,
And weapons of war cannot thrust their blades into him.
And for what reason?
Because in him there is no room for death. (Chap. 50)

Source: Wing-Tsit Chan's translation in his *Source Book in Chinese Philosophy* (Princeton, N.J.: Princeton University Press, 1963). Renewed © 1963 by Princeton University Press. Reprinted by permission.

Reading 6.3 THE MYSTIC PHILOSOPHER: *CHUANG-TZU*

Chuang-tzu was a mystic philosopher whose estimated dates are 399 to 295 B.C.E. In terms of humor, style, lucidity, and imagination, the *Chuang-tzu* may well be the best piece of literature Chinese religion has produced. It is included in the Taoist canon. The last two passages selected here may be Chuang-tzu's reference to the techniques and miraculous feats of the immortals. The last line seems to prefigure the role of the Taoist priest. According to Chuang-tzu, from what things or attitudes do we need to be liberated? How does Chuang-tzu use humor in these passages?

> *Suppose you and I have had an argument. If you have beaten me instead of my beating you, then are you necessarily right and am I necessarily wrong? If I have beaten you instead of your beating me, then am I necessarily right and are you necessarily wrong? Is one of us right and the other wrong? Are both of us right or are both of us wrong? If you and I don't know the answer, then other people are bound to be even more in the dark. Whom shall we get to decide what is right? Shall we get someone who agrees with you to decide? But if he already agrees with you, how can he decide fairly? Shall we get someone who agrees with me? But if he already agrees with me, how can he decide? Shall we get someone who disagrees with both of us? But if he already disagrees with both of us, how can he decide? Shall we get someone who agrees with both of us? But if he already agrees with both of us, how can he decide? Obviously, then, neither you nor I nor anyone else can know the answer. Shall we wait for still another person?*
>
> *"But waiting for one shifting voice [to pass judgment on] another is the same as waiting for none of them. Harmonize them all with the Heavenly Equality, leave them to their endless changes, and so live out your years. What do I mean by harmonizing them with the Heavenly Equality? Right is not right; so is not so. If right were really right, it would differ so clearly from not right that there would be no need for argument. If so were really so, it would differ so clearly from not so that there would be no need for argument. Forget the years; forget distinctions. Leap into the boundless and make it your home!"*
>
> *Master Ssu, Master Yü, Master Li, and Master Lai were all four talking together. "Who can look upon inaction as his head, on life as his back, and on death as his rump?" they said. "Who knows that life and death, existence and annihilation, are all a single body? I will be his friend!"*
>
> *The four men looked at each other and smiled. There was no disagreement in their hearts and so the four of them became friends.*
>
> *All at once Master Yü fell ill. Master Ssu went to ask how he was. "Amazing!" said Master Yü. "The Creator is making me all crookedy like this! My back sticks up like a hunchback and my vital organs are on top of me. My chin is hidden in my navel, my shoulders are up above my head, and my pigtail points at the sky. It must be some dislocation of the yin and yang!"*
>
> *Yet he seemed calm at heart and unconcerned. Dragging himself haltingly to the well, he looked at his reflection and said, "My, my! So the Creator is making me all crookedy like this!"*
>
> *"Do you resent it?" asked Master Ssu.*

"Why no, what would I resent? If the process continues, perhaps in time he'll transform my left arm into a rooster. In that case I'll keep watch on the night. Or perhaps in time he'll transform my right arm into a crossbow pellet and I'll shoot down an owl for roasting. Or perhaps in time he'll transform my buttocks into cartwheels. Then, with my spirit for a horse, I'll climb up and go for a ride. What need will I ever have for a carriage again?

"I received life because the time had come; I will lose it because the order of things passes on. Be content with this time and dwell in this order and then neither sorrow nor joy can touch you. In ancient times this was called the 'freeing of the bound.' There are those who cannot free themselves, because they are bound by things. But nothing can ever win against Heaven—that's the way it's always been. What would I have to resent?

Carpenter Shih went to Ch'i and, when he got to Crooked Shaft, he saw a serrate oak standing by the village shrine. It was broad enough to shelter several thousand oxen and measured a hundred spans around, towering above the hills. The lowest branches were eighty feet from the ground, and a dozen or so of them could have been made into boats. There were so many sightseers that the place looked like a fair, but the carpenter didn't even glance around and went on his way without stopping. His apprentice stood staring for a long time and then ran after Carpenter Shih and said, "Since I first took up my ax and followed you, Master, I have never seen timber as beautiful as this. But you don't even bother to look, and go right on without stopping. Why is that?"

"Forget it—say no more!" said the carpenter. "It's a worthless tree! Make boats out of it and they'd sink; make coffins and they'd rot in no time. Use it for doors and it would sweat sap like pine; use it for posts and the worms would eat them up. It's not a timber tree—there's nothing it can be used for. That's how it got to be that old!"...

. . . The morning mushroom knows nothing of twilight and dawn; the summer cicada knows nothing of spring and autumn. They are the short-lived. South of Ch'u there is a caterpillar which counts five hundred years as one spring and five hundred years as one autumn. Long, long ago there was a great rose of Sharon that counted eight thousand years as one spring and eight thousand years as one autumn. They are the long-lived. Yet P'eng-tsu alone is famous today for having lived a long time, and everybody tries to ape him. Isn't it pitiful!

Once Chuang Chou [Chuang-tzu] dreamt he was a butterfly, a butterfly flitting and fluttering around, happy with himself and doing as he pleased. He didn't know he was Chuang Chou. Suddenly he woke up and there he was, solid and unmistakable Chuang Chou. But he didn't know if he was Chuang Chou who had dreamt he was a butterfly, or a butterfly dreaming he was Chuang Chou. Between Chuang Chou and a butterfly there must be some distinction! This is called the Transformation of Things.

The emperor of the South Sea was called Shu [Brief], the emperor of the North Sea was called Hu [Sudden], and the emperor of the central region was called Hun-tun [Chaos]. Shu and Hu from time to time came together for a meeting in the territory of Hun-tun, and Hun-tun treated them very generously. Shu and Hu discussed how they could repay his kindness. "All men," they said, "have seven openings so they can see, hear, eat, and breathe. But Hun-tun alone doesn't have any. Let's trying boring him some!"

Every day they bored another hole, and on the seventh day Hun-tun died.

Master Lieh Tzu said to the Barrier Keeper Yin, "The Perfect Man can walk under water without choking, can tread on fire without being burned, and can travel above the ten thousand things without being frightened. May I ask how he manages this?"

The Barrier Keeper Yin replied, "This is because he guards the pure breath. . . ."

. . . There is a Holy Man living on faraway Ku-she Mountain, with skin like ice and snow, and gentle and shy like a young girl. He doesn't eat the five grains but sucks the wind, and drinks the dew, climbs up on the clouds and mist, rides a flying dragon, and wanders beyond the four seas. By concentrating his spirit, he can protect creatures from sickness and plague and make the harvest plentiful.

Source: Burton Watson, trans., *Chuang-tzu: Basic Writings* (New York: Columbia University Press, 1968). © 1968 by Columbia University Press. Reprinted with permission of the publisher.

Reading 6.4 THE POWER OF THE PRECIOUS NAMES: "THE HEAVEN-HONORED ONE OF THE PRIMAL BEGINNINGS SPEAKS THE SCRIPTURE OF THE PRECIOUS NAMES OF THE THREE CONTROLLERS"

The following is a brief extract from the liturgical tradition of the Celestial Masters sect of Taoism. The words are chanted by the priest. The term "Heaven-Honored One" refers to one of the Three Pure Ones. The "Three Controllers" are the celestial officials who rank below the Three Pure Ones and supervise the three realms: heaven, earth, and waters. Buddhist influence is detectable in the formula "At that time," which is an imitation of the Mahayana Buddhist *sutra* opening, and in the word *Dharma*, a Buddhist term that means "teaching." Can you imagine that people listening to these words might have a powerful religious experience? Can you explain why?

At that time

The Heaven-Honored One of the Primal Beginnings was in the Palace of the Eight Scenic Views in the Grand Heaven together with the Spirit Kings of all the Heavens, the [deities of] sun and moon, stars and constellations, the Superior Saints and High Venerables—an infinite crowd of Holy Ones; and He spoke the unsurpassed and perfectly true and wonderful Dharma.

There was a True Man named Great Immortal Transcendent Bare Legs who left his place and came out [of the crowd]. He raised his clasped hands to his forehead in salutation, and prostrated himself, saying to the Heaven-Honored One: The people of the world below all suffer distress, whether it be from water or fire, weapons or disease. The devils and bogies who produce [these calamities] ensnare them in Heaven and net them in Earth, and everyone suffers distress. How can they be saved?

The Heaven-Honored One replied: All the spiritual beings and immortal transcendents who have attained the Tao are protected by the Three Controllers (San Kuan). Men born in the lower region, if only they hold to the Precious Names of the Three

Controllers, will be able to eliminate distress, to do away with it entirely. I now communicate to you [the Precious Names]. Disseminate them in the world below. Those among men who take care to recite them will get blessings without limit, and all their troubles will be mitigated. Then He spoke the Precious Names:

> *In the North Pole [Star], mysterious and lofty,*
>   *Courtyard of the Purple Invisible Emperor—*
> *In the [subterranean] prisons of Mt. T'ai,*
>   *And in the pure cold Watery Country—*
> *Ruling the Three Realms*
>   *And governing the myriad spirits—*
> *The Three Primordials collate the Registers [of life and death]*
>   *Whereby the good and the evil are divided.*

> *Observe fasting and abstinence and ceremonially chant,*
> *And do not fail to carry out every vow,*
> *[Thereby] dispersing calamities and dispelling [the karmic results of] sins*
> *And bringing down blessings and extending life.*

> *[In accordance with] the perfectly true and wonderful Tao,*
>   *Whose merits are boundless,*
> *They have made the Great Vow of Commiseration*
>   *And have the Great Compassion of the Great Saints.*

> *The First Primordial, of First Rank,*
>   *Controller of Heaven who confers blessings,*
>   *Great Emperor of Purple Invisibility;*
> *The Second Primordial, of Second Rank,*
>   *Controller of Earth who saves from sin,*
>   *Great Emperor of Pure Vacuity;*
> *The Third Primordial, of Third Rank,*
>   *Controller of the Waters who does away with distress,*
>   *Great Emperor of the Grotto of Yin;*
> *The Ch'ien Primordial, of Fourth Rank,*
>   *Controller of Fire, who investigates and compares [human conduct],*
>   *Great Emperor of the Grotto of Yang;*
> *Three Primordial Lords,*
> *Three Hundred and Sixty Responding Heaven-Honored Ones,*
> *Feminine-youths True Men—*
>   *[These] will investigate and compare [human] officials.*

At that time
The great Immortal Transcendent Bare Legs together with the Spirit Kings of all the Heavens and the great crowd of True Men and Immortal Transcendents, hearing the Precious Names, greatly rejoiced. They saluted, bowing their heads, and retired. Receiving [the Precious Names] with faith, they carried out [the instructions of the Heaven-Honored One of the Primal Beginnings].

Source: Laurence G. Thompson, *Chinese Religion: An Introduction,* 4th ed. (Belmont, CA.: Wadsworth, 1989). Reprinted by permission of the publisher.

Reading 6.5 THE JADE EMPEROR'S BIRTHDAY Peter Goullart

The following autobiographical selection allows readers to savor the atmosphere of a festival celebrated in a Taoist monastery. The time is somewhere in the 1920s or 1930s, when the author, Peter Goullart, a European Taoist, was living in China. The occasion is the birthday of the Jade Emperor, sovereign of heaven. What does this reading tell you about how Taoism can accommodate many different kinds of needs and function as an integral part of Chinese culture? Based on your own image of a monastery, does this festival seem inappropriate? From what sources did you form your idea or image of a monastery?

It was already dark when Abbot Lichun called for us and led us to the top of the monastery to enable us to see the climax of the festival. From the little upper terrace it looked as if the whole immense structure was on fire. Long tongues of flame shot from the great incense burners in front of the Jade Emperor's Hall as more and more incense sticks and joss paper were thrown in by hundreds of worshippers. Masses of paper money and paper representations of earthly objects, offerings for the gods and the departed, were burning in huge heaps, sending sparks into the night sky, and smoke rose in dense columns. There was the sound of drums and bells and the deafening hubbub of milling crowds. Thousands of red candles burned in the halls and galleries before the different deities, and the waves of heat and the smell of incense were carried upwards on the breeze. Priests in red vestments began a slow dance on the terrace of the main hall, each holding a red paper lantern in the shape of a lotus flower. There was a clashing of cymbals, a wail of trumpets and flutes and the tinkling of innumerable little bells.

The procession now turned down into the subterranean passages under the monastery. It was dark and suffocatingly hot here from so many burning candles, but the people happily jostled along together. Unescorted ladies got a few winks from some braves in smart hats but they did not seem to mind, and some merry widows purposely walked close to Koueifo and myself, pressing themselves close against us in the recesses of the cave. Now and then, I noticed, some couples quietly drifted into narrow and unlighted branch passages. Soon we emerged on to an open platform outside the monastery, where the priests sang and danced a short compline and then dispersed.

We were asked to join in the dinner which was provided for the pilgrims and guests staying at the Upper Tower of Literature. It was a sumptuous feast as befitted the dignity of a reception at the Jade Emperor's Court. Of course, the ingredients were all donations from the villagers, pooled together, and the wine, decanted from a battery of jars standing by the wall, flowed freely.

Due to a lack of tables and space, we were seated together with local farmers and rubbed elbows with people sitting at surrounding tables. There was little room, but everybody was in good humour and nobody complained. There were dishes of live and cooked shrimps, turtles and eels roasted with garlic and ham, chickens and ducks and traditional roast pork. In this Chengyi Taoist establishment there was no ban on meat and wine and its superb chefs utilized everything which was good to eat or to drink. . . .

There was a noise of similar festivities coming from other sections of the monastery. The crops had been bountiful and the weather good. All these people were gathered not to pray to the gods for any favour but in gratitude for the continued flow of the good things of life, for the virility of their lovers and the apparent constancy of their husbands, the fruitfulness of their wives and the goodly number of their offspring. The concubines thanked the gods for the possibility of a child from their old and seemingly sterile masters, a blessing which might be realized after their visit to the monastery. The sing-song girls were grateful for the secrets of a new bliss which they would carry to their jaded patrons.

In this upsurge of joy and content, amidst these simple pleasures of eating and drinking, I felt that all sense of time and reality had disappeared. I looked at Abbot Lichun; he appeared carefree and gay and his face was pink. Lifting his cup he toasted all of us.

"Drink, drink!" he exclaimed. "A happy moment of life, like tonight, which may never be recaptured again, is pure meditation according to our Taoistic concept," and he emptied the cup. We all followed suit.

After the tables had been cleared, some people produced mahjongg chips and Koueifo joined a group. I retired, but outside the gambling, music and laughter continued until the small hours.

Source: Peter Goullart, *The Monastery of Jade Mountain* (London: John Murray, 1961).

Reading 6.6   WOMEN'S SPIRITUALITY: *IMMORTAL SISTERS*

Taoists have attached significance to female energy as perceived in the very nature of the Tao itself, in Lao-tzu as androgynous divinity, and in the activities of women in the early Celestial Masters movement. Females number among the immortals. The first passage here is a short piece, "Cutting Off the Dragon," by the female immortal Sun Bu-er (b. 1124 C.E.). Sun Bu-er began a single-minded practice of inner alchemy (Taoist meditation) at age fifty-one, after raising three children. She and her husband were both disciples of Wang Che, founder of Chuan-chen Taoism. The second passage is a part of a modern work (1899) of unknown authorship, "Spiritual Alchemy for Women," written for Cao Chenji, an outstanding female Taoist practitioner of the time. Note that the excerpt ends with an important difference in meditation technique: women are to focus attention on the sternum between the breasts, whereas men focus in the abdomen. What are the ways these passages teach women to use consciousness (attention) to effect spiritual change? Based on the various references to female energy here and elsewhere in this chapter, can one say Taoism attaches more significance to female energy than do most religions?

SUN BU-ER'S *FOURTEEN VERSES:* CUTTING OFF THE DRAGON
(FOR WOMEN ONLY)

1. When stillness climaxes, it can produce movement;
2. Yin and yang mold each other.
3. Grab the jade tiger in the wind,

4. Catch the golden bird in the moon.
5. Keep your eyes on the incubation process,
6. Keep your mind on the course of following and reversing.
7. When the magpie bridges are crossed,
8. The alchemical energy returns to the furnace.

Commentary [following the twentieth-century scholar Chen Yingning]:

The phrase "cutting off the dragon" refers to the voluntary stopping of the menstrual flow. As male adepts are to learn to refrain from emitting semen, so women are to stop their flow. The first 2 lines recall the complementarity of yin and yang. Line 3 urges us to recognize primal energy (jade tiger) in our breath (the wind). The golden bird in line 4 is spirit; it is to be known in the moment of no-thought (moon). Lines 5 and 6 refer to our spiritual embryo and its nourishment. The magpie bridges (line 7) are in the forehead and at the base of the spine; once the ch'i or alchemical energy (line 8) has circulated it returns to the center of the torso (the furnace).

SPIRITUAL ALCHEMY FOR WOMEN

In the science of essence and life, men and women are the same—there is no discrimination. In sum, what is important is perfect sincerity and profound singlemindedness. An ancient document says, "Only perfect sincerity in the world is capable of ruling." A classic says, "The perfection of singlemindedness is that whereby one may heed the order of life."

In general, what is most essential at the beginning of this study is self-refinement. Self-refinement is a matter of mind and breathing resting on each other. This means that the mind rests on the breathing and the breathing rests on the mind.

What is most important in this is harmony. Harmony is in balance, balance is in harmony. Are they one or two? The union of balance and harmony is called the go-between.

With the harmonious attunement of the go-between, there is mutual love between mind and breathing; there is mutual attraction, mutual inspiration, mutual expiration. Continuing uninterrupted, do not forget, yet do not force.

Lao-tzu said, "The singleminded energy is most supple, able to be like an infant." This is the perfection of true harmony.

The Master of the Jade Moon, a spiritual alchemist, said, "When husband and wife meet in old age, their feelings are naturally affectionate."

A classic says, "Tie them into one whole, mix them in one place, make them into one piece, force them in one furnace."

The same classic also says, "Cow and bull go along with each other, sun and moon are in the same place; positive and negative charges merge, metal and fire commingle."

The reality behind all of these sayings is spirit and energy being together, which means mind and breathing being together.

Spirit is essence, energy is life. This is what is meant by the classic saying, "The root of essence is rooted in mind; the stem of life stems from breathing."

It is necessary to know that creative evolution only takes place when spirit and energy are joined into one. The joining of the two into one is the reversion of the two modes—yin and yang—back into one totality.

This is called the twin cultivation of essence and life.

The twin cultivation of essence and life is a matter of keeping the mind and breathing together, not letting them separate even for a moment.

Therefore an ancient alchemist said that "firing the medicine to produce the elixir" means driving energy by spirit, thereby attaining the Tao.

In daily practice it is essential to embrace the breathing steadily with the mind and embrace the mind steadily with the breathing. When you have done this for a time, once you reach even balance you naturally become very stable and concentrated. You plunge into a profound trance where there is no sky and no earth, where you forget about everything, including your own body.

This stage is the experience referred to by the classic saying, "Knowing the white, keep the black, and illumination of spirit will come of itself." You seem to feel body and mind revitalized and supple, with unusual buoyancy and well being.

One alchemist said that in this state you are like someone without the power of speech eating honey, unable to tell of its sweetness.

Another alchemist said, "Almost imperceptible, the first transformation of yin and yang—heaven and earth, full of living energy, suddenly revolve. Therein is a bit of fine scenery—how can this work be put into words?"

This time is what is known as "the one primordial energy coming from the void of space."

As one alchemist said, "The winter solstice is midnight, where you find the celestial mind has no change, where creative energy first stirs, before myriad things are born."

This is what is referred to in alchemical texts as Living Midnight.

One alchemist said of this, "Gather energy quickly when winter comes."

Another said, "Gathering means gathering without trying to gather, which means splitting open the primordial indefinite."

This "splitting open the primordial indefinite" refers to the time of ultimate emptiness and perfect quietude. To empty oneself to the ultimate extent and preserve quietude to perfection is known as returning to *Earth,* the spiritually receptive mode.

Earth the receptive is associated with the southwest: It is known as "the region where the medicine is produced," "the land of primordial nondifferentiation," and "the opening of the Mysterious Female."

An alchemist called Seeker of the Fundamental said, "If you want to look for the primordial seed of realization, you must seek out undifferentiated wholeness to set up the foundation."

Understanding Reality, the classic of spiritual alchemy, says, "If you want to attain the immortality of the open spirit, you must set the foundation on the Mysterious Female. Once the foundation is set up, the open spirit does not die. Then how can the person die?"

The aforementioned self-refinement, setting up the foundation, and gathering the great primal medicine, are all the same for men and women. Therefore it is said, "The great Way does not make a distinction between men and women; yin and yang, in their various combinations, are all the same." After this I'll talk more about temporal difference.

In his *Secret of Feminine Alchemy*, Liu I-ming says, "There is a true secret about starting practice. The operation is as different for men and women as sky from sea. The principle for men is refinement of energy, the expedient for women is refinement of the body."

Men begin practice with the attention in the lower abdomen, just below the navel. Women start work with the attention between the breasts.

Reading 6.7 TAOIST MEDITATION IN MOTION: T'AI-CHI CH'UAN

T'ai-chi ch'uan is valued for its contributions to physical, mental, and spiritual health. It is also a martial art, but its slow dance-like forms are quite unlike those of the faster, "harder" fighting arts. T'ai chi masters explain that the slow movements help one learn balance and control; when the situation requires it, one will act quickly. The smooth, circular motions are designed to create a blend or harmony with the actions of an opponent. Some martial arts develop intense power that can be used to attack or retaliate, but T'ai chi teaches self-control, adaptivity, and harmony. After reading this selection, explain and illustrate the Taoist notion that in combat—and in every moment of our lives—harmony, lightness, and agility are the keys to success. Based on the foregoing account of T'ai-chi ch'uan, does it seem plusible to you that it promotes physical and mental health?

Most westerners have seen video clips of Chinese people performing what appears to be slow-motion exercise in the park at dawn. These movement forms are a version of T'ai-chi or T'ai-chi ch'uan. *T'ai-chi* means "Supreme Ultimate," and *ch'uan* means "fist." The practice of T'ai-chi ch'uan is said to promote physical, mental, and spiritual well-being. It has elements of exercise, dance, meditation, *yoga*, and the martial arts.

Although the historical origins of Tai'-chi are obscure, the influence of Taoism is obvious, as can be seen in the words of T'ai-chi master Al Chung-liang Huang:

> Think of the contrasting energies moving together and in unison, in harmony, interlocking, like a white fish and a black fish mating. If you identify with only one side of the duality, then you become unbalanced. . . . Movements and stillness become one. One is not a static point. One is moving one, one is changing one, one is everything. One is also that stillness suspended, flowing, settling, in motion.[73]

Huang dubs T'ai-chi the "perfect and unobstructed flow of *ch'i* [vital breath or energy] through the body."

Many T'ai-chi movements are modeled after those of animals. Tradition has it that early masters watched a snake and stork fighting and incorporated their postures and movements into their art. The poise and balance of T'ai-chi are understood as the harmony of *yin* and *yang;* it is the poise and balance manifested by *wu-wei.* The Tao is experienced as immanent, but most T'ai-chi masters keep their students focused on the precise physical movements rather than on abstract concepts like "Tao" or "Supreme Ultimate."

T'ai-chi masters emphasize that T'ai-chi is a way of life, not just an exercise or martial art. The physical "prowess," if it can be called that, is more a matter of adaptability than aggressive force. In combat, the T'ai-chi practitioner is advised to "yield at your opponent's slightest pressure and adhere to him at his slightest retreat."[74] In life, as in combat, lightness and agility are the keys to effectiveness and success. Instead of muscling our way through, we should live life in the fashion of dancers harmonizing with music and with our whole environment.

CHAPTER 7

CONFUCIANISM

Portrait of Confucius (K'ung fu-tzu).

Chapter 1 indicated that Confucianism is a complex ethnic, nontheistic religion. Like Taoism, it is native to China. Its influence has been pervasive in Chinese life, as well as in Korea, Japan, and Vietnam. Confucianism meshes well with other traditions; thus, a person who practices Buddhism, for example, does not thereby cease to be Confucian.

The very words and concepts we have used in the Western world in studying Confucianism betray the fact that in the past we have seriously distorted the tradition to be explored in this chapter. The word *Confucius* is a romanized version of the name and title **K'ung fu-tzu,** that is, Master K'ung (Kong fu-zi in the Pinyin system).* There is no Chinese term that corresponds to the English word *Confucianism* (a label coined in Europe as recently as the eighteenth century). The most common Chinese way of referring to teachers who have followed and elaborated the principles of Master K'ung is *ju (ru)* or *ju-hsueh* (literati or scholars); the teachings

---

*The older and still widely used system for romanizing Chinese characters is the Wade-Giles system. In 1958 the People's Republic of China adopted a different system, called Pinyin. We employ the Wade-Giles system, but we add the Pinyin spelling in parentheses where it may be helpful— in cases such as Mao Tse Tung (Mao Ze-dong), Peking (Beijing), *Jen (ren),* and Tao (Dao).

and doctrines may be called *ju-chiao* (teachings of the scholars). The meanings and nuances of these Chinese terms are quite different from westernized terms like *Confucianism*. We cannot avoid these English words, but we need to rectify their meanings. Ironically, it was Master K'ung himself who said that learning must begin with the "rectification of names."[1]

It is an exaggeration to speak of "Confucian China" if that label implies that Confucianism is equivalent to Chinese civilization. Chapters 5 and 6 described the important roles that Buddhism and Taoism have played in China. However, Confucianism did play a special role; it is that role that we now investigate.

CONFUCIAN BELIEFS

Truly fulfilling human existence is the main theme and goal of Confucianism. Believing that this fulfillment was experienced in its purest form by the supremely virtuous sages of ancient times, Confucianism perpetuates and revitalizes the teachings of these sages. The tradition is said to have been successfully practiced for more than one hundred generations—even down into modern times.

Following the sages of old, Confucianism accepts the basic organic worldview of ancient Chinese culture. Principles of order and rectitude are seen as ingrained in the universe, and proper behavior corresponds to patterns present throughout the universe. These proper behavior patterns, called *li*, are the conventions—etiquette, social propriety, morals, laws, and rites—that can bring about harmony between Heaven and earth. **Heaven** is understood as the supreme spiritual power and source of all truth. Confucianism calls for the conventionalization or ritualization of life in order to establish this Heaven-earth harmony.

Because the passage of tradition from elder to younger is crucial, Confucianism emphasizes the practice of filial piety, reverence for ancestors, and modeling the community on the family. The ruler-subject relationship is correlated to the father-son relationship, and past-present is correlated to ancestor-descendant.

The good society can be achieved through neither unrestrained individualism nor forceful legalistic means. Confucianism focuses forthrightly on sincere and earnest moral effort on the part of the individual; the faithful daily performance of respectful acts, over time, produces truly human-hearted (loving) people, and that, in turn, produces a good society. Our sacred duty is not to strive for an afterlife or to ponder the nature of deity; it is to enact the principles of Heaven in everyday life. Confucian leaders are thus not priests but **literati** *(ju)*—scholars who are steeped in the Confucian classics and deeply concerned with education. The literati aim at individual moral perfection so as to serve society as models and administrators.

FOUNDING FIGURE: CONFUCIUS

We thus begin our study of Confucian beliefs with the central figure, Master K'ung, or Confucius (551 –479 B.C.E.), the sage who said, *"He who by rean-imating the old can gain knowledge of the new is fit to be a teacher"* (*Analects* 2:11).

One Western encyclopedic reference to the life of Confucius calls it "starkly undramatic . . . in contrast to its tremendous importance."[2] A Chinese expression has it that Confucius's life was "plain and real." There is truth in these impressions of the man, but they should not obscure ways in which Master K'ung was charismatic and, in his time, radical. In what follows we explore both the apparently "undramatic" and the awe-inspiring aspects of his life.

Confucius was born in the town of Ch'u-fu (Qufu) in the small feudal state of Lu (Shantung province). (See Figure 7.1 for the location of Ch'u-fu and other sacred sites of Confucianism.) His family name was K'ung and his personal name Ch'iu, but he came to be referred to as K'ung fu-tzu (Master K'ung). Early Jesuit missionaries rendered the name-title as Confucius. He was born into plain and humble circumstances; his ancestors were members of the aristocracy who had become virtually poverty-stricken commoners by the time of his birth. His father died when he was only three. Confucius recalled that he set his heart upon learning when he was fifteen. He studied the "six arts"— ritual, music, archery, charioteering, calligraphy, and arithmetic—as well as history and poetry. He was married at a relatively early age and had three children. Little is known of the marriage, though some biographers believe it was not a very successful one.

Confucius's desire to obtain a good political post was never fulfilled. He was too virtuous to be a part of the political corruption that was commonplace. Some historians believe Confucius served as minister of justice in the state of Lu, but in any case his tenure was very short-lived.

Master K'ung was not the founder of Confucianism in the sense that Shakyamuni Buddha was the founder of Buddhism and Christ the founder of Christianity. Despite important continuities with their inherited religious traditions, both Buddha and Christ came to be seen as founders of traditions that detached themselves from the older religions and became independent traditions. Not so with Confucius; Confucians have always seen Confucius as a transmitter of tradition, though he was not without originality.

The foregoing account of Confucius's life may seem "undramatic," yet such an impression of Confucius fails to take into account that he was a charismatic teacher who earned the attention and respect of thousands of students. His vocation turned out to be that of a teacher. He was called "the wooden bell of China," one who awakens the people— a role comparable to Socrates' role as the gadfly of Athens. Confucius had the courage to openly challenge the corrupt and autocratic leaders of the time. In the words of one leading Sinologist, "he was unforgivably honest."[3] When asked by a powerful official how to cope with a crime wave, Master K'ung pointed out that if the official himself were not so covetous, the people would be so honest that they could not be induced to steal, even for a reward. Rejecting the political status quo, he argued for the selection of leaders by merit, not birth; he was also known as the first teacher in China who wanted to make education available to all men, not just the elite. Radical, forthright, and outspoken in his devotion to truth and justice, Confucius inspired a group of students who would not, and could not, let the way of the Master be buried with him. The tradition they perpetuated became a pillar of Chinese civilization.

Confucius had a passion for a kind of nobility that modern peoples have all but forgotten. One key to being a noble person, according to Confucian teaching, is having great respect for the best aspects of the traditions we inherit from the past. This means that we must learn what tradition teaches us, and this requires discipline and humility. It means we must not assume that we know what is best for us without consulting the ancients.

Figure 7.1

IMPORTANT SITES OF CONFUCIANISM

SACRED SITES OF CONFUCIANISM AND MODERN PROVINCES AND MAJOR CITIES OF THE PEOPLE'S REPUBLIC OF CHINA

(1) Ch'u-fu (Qufu)—Confucius's birthplace, a pilgrimage site; (2a) Peking—site of the Temple of Heaven, location of imperial ceremonies performed on behalf of the nation; (2b) Peking—location of T'ien-an Men (Tiananmen) square (where in 169 and 1989 C.E. large numbers of students were killed by police); (3) Mount T'ai and (4) Mount Wu T'ai—holy mountains valued by all three major religions of China; sites where officials offered prayers on behalf of the people; (5) and (6)— Korea and Japan, which have been strongly influenced by Confucianism.

It means that modernity must not be assumed to be best, superior, or even feasible.

A glimpse of the nobility of Confucius comes through accounts of his reactions to his many critics. Once a bystander called, "Great indeed is Confucius! He knows about everything and has made

no name in anything." Confucius then remarked to his followers in mock dismay, "Now what shall I take up? Charioteering? Archery?" Confucius was doing the work that he believed was most important for the situation in which he lived. If this made no name for him, no matter. Book 1, section 1, of the *Analects* advises, *"To remain unsoured even though one's merits are unrecognized by others, is that not after all what is expected of a gentleman?"*

Confucius was down to earth. His followers tell us, *"The Master did not speak of marvels, feats of strength, irregular happenings, and spirits"* (*Analects* 7:20). He adapted the ancient traditions so as to shift the focus from the divine to the human: *"Till you have learnt to serve men, how can you serve spirits?"* (*Analects* 11:11). As we shall see, he focused on this life, not the next, even in his attitude toward ancestor worship: one world at a time. This "practicalness" of Chinese thought has often been noted; Confucius is part cause of this practical tendency. He was not a prophet, not a mystic, and definitely not given to metaphysical speculation.

The *Analects* gives us only a few impressions of Confucius's personality. He was not without emotions; he says that once he was so moved by observing a dance that he did not notice he was eating during the following three days (*Analects* 7:13). He apparently drank wine but says he was "never overcome with wine." Although he was a scholar, he was not bookish or stuffy. We know almost nothing about his attitudes toward women, but the following remark is suggestive: *"The Master said, 'Women and people of low birth are very hard to deal with. If you are friendly with them, they get out of hand, and if you keep your distance, they resent it,"* (*Analects* 17:25). This attitude is very common in the Confucian classics, as summarized by Richard Guisso in *Woman in China:* "The female was inferior by nature. She was dark as the moon and changeable as water, jealous, narrow-minded, and insinuating. She was indiscreet, unintelligent, and dominated by emotion. Her beauty was a snare for the unwary male, the ruination of states.[4]

Confucius was markedly selective in his response to the sixth-century (B.C.E.) culture into which he was born. He strongly affirmed much of the social ethics he inherited from the past, but he deemphasized belief in gods and the afterlife. Did he thus found a tradition that is more a social philosophy than a religion?

There are, we believe, good grounds for regarding Confucianism as a nontheistic religion. Confucius believed in a transcendent reality, which he referred to as Heaven, and he believed that Heaven gave him his teaching and protected him (*Analects* 7:23). For Confucius's own views, we rely mainly on his disciples' collection of sayings, called *Analects*. For Confucians generally, **Heaven** is "a supreme spiritual presence, a great moral power, and the source of all."[5] Most Confucians do not think of Heaven as a personal being, but it is clearly an exalted sacred reality.

Another unmistakable religious aspect of Confucianism is the promotion of the Confucian cult and the worship of ancestors. Although the literati do not claim that Confucius is a god or dwell upon the supernatural aspects of ancestor worship, they have strongly advocated ancestor worship and have even tolerated the deification of Master K'ung. Ceremonies in honor of Confucius and ancestors involve offerings, prayers, and kowtows (kneeling and touching the forehead on the ground), and they are performed before altars in the home or in a temple. Thus, despite the literati's specialized interpretations of these actions, they are religious in the most obvious sense of the term.

Finally, Confucians view performance of social duties and behaviors *(li)* as sacred ceremonies. The Chinese character for *li* is a combination of the character for "worship" and the character for "sacrificial vessel." The religious overtones here are not merely etymological; the *li* are perceived as sacred ceremonies based on the teachings of Heaven. Caring for an elder parent and paying tax to a legitimate political authority are, in this sense, sacred rites.

MANIFESTATIONS OF THE ULTIMATE

Confucius believed that the way of Heaven is manifest in this world: it can be observed in the records of the virtuous lives of ancient sages and in the conduct of some people living today. The way of Heaven is also evident in a unique way to sincere scholars who seek the truth through study. Above all, the nature of the ultimate reality can be perceived in the performance of traditional, respectful ceremonies *(li)*, such as the veneration of ancestors. Confucians argue that these are not speculations; these claims can be tested in experience. When we understand or act on the way of Heaven, we experience harmony. When we comprehend the way and when we act on *li* (conventional, respectful norms), something "clicks." There is harmony in us and harmony between Heaven and earth. Beyond this, Confucius himself had very little to say about metaphysical questions.

A more comprehensive metaphysics was developed in a text attributed to Confucius's grandson, Master Tzu Ssu. This text, the *Doctrine of the Mean (Chung Yung)*, states that the truths handed down from the ancient emperors Yao and Shun *"harmonize with the divine order which governs the revolutions of the seasons in the Heaven above and ... fit in with the moral design which is to be seen in physical nature upon the Earth below.*[6] The ultimate is ingrained in physical nature, as well as in human nature: *"The Way (Tao) cannot be separated from us for a moment."* Our fundamental nature, before particular feelings like joy and sorrow arise, is **equilibrium,** or the mean. This equilibrium is *"the great foundation of the world, and harmony its universal path."* In this way, the *Doctrine of the Mean* teaches a metaphysics that traces fundamental links between the universe, moral order, and human nature.[7] Basically, it comes down to saying that the fundamental truths are ingrained in our hearts, in traditional ethical codes, and in the physical universe as well.

Confucians like Tung Chung-Shu (second century B.C.E.) and Yang Hsiung (first century C.E.) emphasized the organic structure of reality. Tung combined the ancient *yin/yang* cosmology with the concept of the five elements, both inherited from ancient Chinese philosophy. *Yin* (the cosmic energy patterns that are passive and dark) and *yang* (patterns that are active and light) are the basic structuring energies of the whole universe. Tung viewed the five elements (woody, fiery, earthen, metallic, and watery elements) as the fundamental types of realities formed by the interaction of *yin* and *yang*. For example, in this view, wood is the result of a unique combination of *yin* and *yang*. In addition, the constant movement of *yin* and *yang*

creates changes, as when wood changes by fire to earth. The other scholar, Yang Hsiung, attempted a synthesis of Taoism and Confucianism **(Taoist Confucianism).**[8] Like the Taoists, he saw the Tao as the Supremely Profound Principle by which all things emerge. As a Confucian, he emphasized codes of ethics that he viewed as emerging from the activity of the Tao. In terminology and content, Yang prefigured the more thoroughgoing metaphysical synthesis of the movement called Neo-Confucianism, a movement whose emergence we trace in detail in the "History of Confucianism" section later in the chapter.

The worldview of most modern literati is some variation of the Neo-Confucian vision of Chu Hsi, the great twelfth-century philosopher who synthesized many major Chinese philosophical movements. His worldview may be displayed as shown in Table 7.1. The **principle** of a thing is its source—that which makes it that thing and not something else. For example, by their respective principles, a boat travels on the water, and a truck travels on a road. The principle is not the material stuff of the thing; the materiality of a thing—its *ch'i*—is its physical actuality. This concept may sound like a very abstract dualism, but principle and material forces are always interfused. Neither exists separate from the other. The broken line between principle and material force *(ch'i)* in Table 7.1 shows that all things and humans are a combination of the two. Neither principle nor *ch'i* is the creator of the world.

There also exists an overarchng principle called the **Great Ultimate (T'ai Chi).** The Great Ultimate has no physical form, but it is existent in reality-as-a-whole and in each thing individually. The Great Ultimate is to individual things as the moon is to its reflection in many rivers. Just as the moon is manifest in various bodies of water, so the Great Ultimate is manifest in the world. In being manifest, the Great Ultimate is not broken up and distributed among the manifestations; each manifests the Great Ultimate in its totality.[9]

It follows that humans are manifestations of the Great Ultimate. But as we have pointed out, humans are a combination of principle and *ch'i*.

Table 7.1

CHU HSI'S WORLDVIEW		
Basic Types of Reality	**Characteristics**	**Related Stages of Human Existence**
Principle [a]	Incorporeal-eternal-unchanging (the essence of a thing)	4. Transcendent ↑ 3. Moral
Ch'i (material force or energy-matter)	Corporeal-transitory-changeable	2. Utilitarian ↑ 1. Natural

T'ai Chi (Great Ultimate)

a. To avoid confusion, we have avoided the use of the Chinese word here because it transliterates with the same spelling as terms that have very different meanings (*li*).

Particular differences among people come from varying proportions and densities of *ch'i.* Thus, people whose *ch'i* is turbid will be inclined toward laziness and vice; they should exert special efforts to improve their moral knowledge and ability. In this light we can understand Chu Hsi's notion that within the limits of natural abilities and training, humans are capable of moral and spiritual progress. At first their unreflective pursuit of physical drives *(ch'i)* dominates their lives (Table 7.1, Stage 1), but eventually they become more calculating and "utilitarian" (Stage 2) in the pursuit of selfish desires, including the desire for wealth and status. If they mature further, they fully comprehend the principles of things, especially the principle of moral rectitude. At this Stage 3, they transcend selfishness and begin to act out of altruism. Although the mature person never loses this altruistic attitude, the knowledge of principles leads in the last stage (Stage 4) to a comprehensive knowledge of the fundamental structure of reality—the Great Ultimate. The mystic vision of the Great Ultimate is the highest form of knowledge and well-being.

THE NATURE AND DESTINY OF HUMANS

For a more in-depth examination of human nature as seen from the Confucian perspective, let us begin with the views of the Confucian sage who was sec-

ond only to Confucius himself: Mencius (371–289 B.C.E.). Here is a portion of his classic argument to demonstrate the original goodness of human nature:

All men have a sense of compassion for others. . . . What I mean by all men having a sense of compassion is that if, for instance, a child is suddenly seen to be on the point of falling into a well, everybody without exception will have a sense of distress. It is not by reason of any close intimacy with the parent of the child, nor by reason of a desire for the praise of neighbors and friends, nor by reason of disliking to be known as the kind of man (who is not moved by compassion). From this point of view we observe that it is inhuman to have no sense of shame over wickedness, inhuman to have no sense of modesty and the need for yielding place to a better man, inhuman not to distinguish right and wrong.[10]

Although Confucius had no more than implied that human nature is good, Mencius explicitly affirms our innate goodness. Likening this original good nature to an ever-present seed or root that will grow and flourish when nurtured, Mencius strongly emphasizes social and educational environment. People differ in their ability to express their good nature. A bad environment can prohibit the development of goodness, although a few **superior persons** *(chung-tzu)* are said to be destined by

Heaven to succeed in developing their good nature. In any case, all humans need to exert their will to follow their innate good nature.

A minority Confucian position on this issue is Hsun-tzu's (third century B.C.E.) view that human nature is evil. He asks, "What would happen if all law and authority were done away with?"[11] If people were not threatened by punishment for anti-social acts, how would they behave? Why are rules necessary? Because human nature is basically evil. For Hsun-tzu, righteousness is purely a matter of training.

Although the controversy seems difficult to solve, there is a cluster of agreed-upon Confucian principles: With proper training, humans can develop good moral qualities, and a good society can be created. Strenuous and sincere effort is required on the part of everyone—especially on the part of parents, government leaders, and the literati. Humans are perfectible or corruptible, depending upon proper training and sincere effort.

JEN: THE VIRTUE OF HUMAN-HEARTEDNESS
Humans are perfectible in the sense that they can achieve the virtue of *jen (ren)*. It is the will of Heaven that they strive to achieve this virtue—the virtue of human-heartedness or loving respect. *Jen* (the approximate pronunciation is like the sound of the English word *run*) is represented in Chinese by an ideograph 仁, constructed from two simpler ideographs; the left side, 亻, represents "person," and the right side, 二, represents "two." It has been translated into English as *human-heartedness, goodness, man-to-manness, love,* and similar terms. As the ideograph shows, it is a quality that has to do with the problems of relating to other people. Its meaning is close to "the art of dealing with others." In the *Analects,* Confucius associates *jen* with understanding reciprocity—the realization that relations with others are two-way streets. Hence he teaches, "Do not do to others that which you would not have them do to you." The ultimate concern of the person who possesses *jen* is the good of humans, not just himself or herself.

Jen is not to be identified with a feeling or emotion of affection. It is closer to an ability or way

of being. It involves the whole person, including a kind of intellectual input, because reciprocity is a fact that must be understood quite apart from our feelings about it. In terms of the pillars of Western culture, *jen* is a type of virtue in Aristotle's sense of the term. It is not something that comes and goes as emotions do. The virtue of *jen* is an active, rather than a passive, approach. We do not "fall in *jen*" as we "fall in love."

The Confucian approach to human relations uncovers an oddity about the phrase *fall in love.* If love is something we fall into, it is something we can fall out of, too. But do we not want to say that true love is an active commitment to a person, not just a passive "undergoing" of emotions that overwhelm us? (Confucius speaks disapprovingly of a man who is *"at the mercy of his desires"* [*Analects* 5:10].) Jesus commanded love; but if love can be commanded, it must be an active rather than a passive approach. It does not just happen to us; we must will it. So it appears that true love is not what we are talking about when we speak of falling in love. The key point that Confucianism teaches us here is that the highest form of relating to another person—call it *jen* or true love—is an active approach, a quality or virtue or act of will.

LI: THE FORMATION OF HUMAN-HEARTEDNESS THROUGH RITUAL
Given that most people would want to attain such a high virtue as *jen* and given that all people should try to attain it, Confucian logic leads us to this question: What is the best method for achieving *jen*? The unique Confucian answer to this question is "through the practice of *li*." The term *li,* which can be tentatively translated as "ritual," refers to traditional ceremonies and formal patterns of conduct. *Li* originally referred to ceremonies in which religious offerings were made. Although the term was extended from narrowly defined religious rites to include all formal conducts that structure interpersonal activities, the term never lost the sense of sacredness or sacrifice. *Li* includes matters of etiquette, religious ceremonies and observations, family traditions, moral rules, and laws. Western readers might think of some of these activities as religious and some as

secular, but in Confucianism they are all sacred ceremonies.[12] Participation in a family gathering for Thanksgiving would count as an American form of *li*. Confucianism would emphasize the social function rather than the theological meaning associated with such an observance. The gathering for a family meal on this holiday can renew relationships and increase cooperative spirit and unity. Even an atheist should seize this opportunity to sustain or improve family bonds.

Let us take a simple example to illustrate the Confucian understanding of *li* and to explain its power. If I am introduced to another person (in the United States), I participate in the *li* of a handshake. This is the traditional way to respond to the introduction situation with dignity and respect. I should not hesitate in following this *li*, because that might suggest insincerity. My motive should be the desire to express respect and amiability, for that is what this *li* is designed to express; *li* are vehicles for conveying respect. If I fail to see it this way, and if I fail to perform the *li* with the appropriate attitude of reverence, it is my loss. The *li* are also concrete ways to *learn* respect: the practice of *li* can lead to the internalization of its meaning. Thus, these ceremonies have the power to develop and express socially beneficial attitudes.

Confucians see *li* as powerful guiding structures, but their power does not consist primarily in the use of legal measures to enforce or prohibit actions. In fact, most *li,* such as the personal care of one's aging parents, are social rules or moral obligations, not legal obligations.

Because these morally obligatory behaviors may or may not coincide with genuine inner concern, *li* may be seen by some as mere show or mere external performances. But Confucian belief counters this objection to *li* in several ways. First, the Confucian ideal is that *li* should be performed with genuine goodwill; for example, a benevolent act should flow from benevolence. But even when the ideal inner condition is lacking, benevolent acts are of great value. A drowning girl benefits from being saved, no matter what the motive of the person who saved her. Individuals and society as a whole need the benefit and the order that the myriad of

li provide. Finally, Confucians believe that the repeated performance of actions in accord with *li* has the power to change the inner life of the person who performs them. The performance of *li* leads to the achievement of *jen*.

Another way to understand the power of *li* is through the function of tradition. *Li* is by nature traditional. One does not invent or create "new *li*." Traditional behaviors are easily understood because they are well established in the culture; their meaning has been passed along and refined over time. The *li* can bridge generation gaps by deferring to the elders. Such deference is appropriate because the oldest members of society are those who are least able to accept a new order. Yet we should hasten to add that although *li* does not undergo radical change, it can be adapted to new conditions and undergo partial and gradual evolution.

In sum, then, given the potential for goodness in human nature, the *li* provide the structure or vehicle for our moral development and for the creation of the good society.

CONFUCIAN PRACTICE

No tradition has emphasized practice more than Confucianism, and the kind of practice it has emphasized has been ethical conduct (rather than other sorts of practice such as prayer or meditation). As we have seen, the vehicle that carries out this conduct is *li*. Our discussion begins with family *li*, the most important. Other types of *li* include the Confucian cult and state religion. Confucian practice also includes the conduct of government—the virtues of citizens and officials. Last, and least (involving only a few individuals), we discuss the various personal disciplines undertaken by the literati.

FAMILY *LI*

The key *li* are family *li*. This situation is clear from the fact that of the **Five Great Relationships** in

Confucian practice (father-son, elder brother-younger brother, husband-wife, elder-junior, ruler-subject), three are family relationships. Therefore, when it comes to conduct, Confucianism begins at home. In the *Analects* (1:2) Confucius is recorded as saying, *"Surely the proper behavior towards parents and elder brothers is the trunk of* jen.*"* There is even a Confucian saying to the effect that when there is harmony in the home, there will be order in the nation; and when there is order in the nation, there is peace in the world. This saying does not mean that Confucius had no philosophy of government; it does mean that he thought government policies, no matter how great, will not make a good society unless family members conduct themselves properly toward one another.

MARRIAGE Marriage must be stable and realistic, and it must represent an agreement between the two families (not just between the husband and wife). Romance is unstable. What good is stability, however? Stability in a marriage provides the absolutely essential requirement for learning how to deal with other people: daily interaction in all dimensions of life over a long period of time. Husband and wife must relate to each other day and night physically and mentally/psychologically. They must share space, money, joy, sorrow, sickness, health, and so on. The regularity of this interaction is what trains and tests in a way that nothing else can do. Reasoning about human-heartedness, meditating on it, asking God for it—none of these is a substitute for the actual rubbing of elbows in day-to-day family life. Relations with friends, associates, and fellow workers are only partial relationships and therefore are not as important in developing *jen*. I may be able to conduct myself well when with a friend, but such a relationship does not go deep enough or "wide" enough: we do not share money, home, food, the illnesses of grandparents, or the legal obligations that family members do. When it comes down to it, only family relationships provide a thorough training ground for developing *jen*. Therefore, absolute loyalty to spouse and other family members is required by Confucian *li*.

The "realism" of Confucian marriage can be understood by repeating that romance is not the basis for marriage. The Confucian approach surprises a person raised with the notion of a romantic basis for marriage. In the *Book of Mencius* (3A:4.8), we find a remarkable statement of the most important qualities in several important types of relationships. Note where "affection" is of prime importance and where "distance" is of prime importance: Between father and son there is affection; between ruler and minister there is integrity; between husband and wife there is proper distance; between elder and junior there is proper precedence; between friends there is faithfulness. Thus, the key to a sound marriage relationship is not closeness or emotion but rather the willingness to perform the *li* of marriage.

Marriage has a considerable formal aspect. The specific details of the *li* vary from culture to culture. Most cultures traditionally assign the role of provider and stern exemplar of virtue to the husband/father and assign to the wife/mother the role of obedient homemaker and nurturer. A set of duties go with each role. The Confucian injunction is to perform these duties religiously. Happiness will result, but only as a by-product. Happiness is not something the individual can obtain by directly seeking it: *"The Good Man rests content with Goodness; he that is merely wise pursues Goodness in the belief that it pays to do so"* (*Analects* 4:2).

The formalism of Confucian marriage and the Confucian approach to life in general is sometimes criticized as lacking in spontaneity. Chapter 18 of the *Tao Te Ching* (a Taoist text) criticizes it as being external, forced, and hypocritical. But the Confucian question remains: What is realistic in a marriage? If being "spontaneous" means acting on the emotion of the moment, one would have a hopelessly erratic marriage, if any marriage at all—the husband and wife would be together off and on, depending on the emotion. If "spontaneous" means acting as a whole person (emotion, intellect, and spirit) without any conflict, such wholeness is a quality of only a few advanced persons called *sages* in the Chinese tradition. So "spontaneity" does not appear to be a good answer to the question of what is realistic in a marriage. The Confucian way calls for exerting the will to perform the correct *li*. It is not hypocritical if the person understands that external behavior patterns can lead to inner conditions like *jen*.

The traditional Chinese marriage and family system was valued greatly and supported by Confucius, though he did not explicitly preach about the value of the specific details. A marriage should be an agreement between two families. Because true love *(jen)* is learned, not fallen into, a young couple is not expected to "be in love" at the time of the marriage ceremony. They are expected, rather, to be prepared to learn to love by committing themselves to practice marriage *li*. Here, as elsewhere, Confucianism does not value "individual choice"—especially in the case of a young person just entering upon marriage.

"Marry one who has not betrayed her own kin, and you may safely present her to your ancestor" (*Analects* 1:3). Before a person is married, he or she is already a part of the web of important family relationships. For example, the groom-to-be has an ongoing relationship with his mother, father, brothers, sisters, and grandparents. The marriage should not disrupt these relationships but rather should harmonize with them. Hence, the parents and grandparents must play a major role in the selection of the marriage partner.

The web of relationships just mentioned includes the extended family, not just the nuclear family. This web helps each person develop the ability to deal with a variety of age types. Let us cite just one example: grandparent-grandchild relations. When a significant ongoing relationship of this type exists, old people do not get out of touch with the youngest people, and the youngest people must learn to deal with the oldest people.

If one marries into a Confucian-style extended family, one carries on close supportive relationships with many family members, not just one's spouse. This point is especially important in view of the claim by some modern social psychologists that marriages break up more readily when the couple have few or no long-term, close, supportive nonsexual relationships. The romantic mystique

makes one believe that one's beloved can satisfy all one's needs, but in the long run one realizes that this is a myth.

We have referred to the primary role of women as homemaker and nurturer. Traditionally a woman assumed this role when she married into the extended family of her husband. From this point she was brought under the authority of her husband's household. She was expected to behave in a filial way toward her in-laws, and the completion of these filial obligations called for giving birth to a son, who would be her husband's heir. As Mencius said, *"There are three ways in which one may be unfilial, of which the worst is to have no heir"* (*Book of Mencius* 4A:26.1). The following are proverbs from Chinese folklore: "Raising a daughter is like weeding another man's field" and "The best daughter isn't worth a splay-footed son."[13] The Confucian gender-based hierarchy of relationships placed such an emphasis on having a male heir that a woman's value was measured primarily by her ability to give birth to sons for extending her husband's family line.

THE PARENT-CHILD RELATIONSHIP   A crucial family relationship is child to parent: *"Whilst thy father and mother are living, do not wander afar. If thou must travel, hold a set course"* (*Analects* 4:19). Of course, one must see that one's parents are fed. But *"even dogs and horses are cared for to that extent. If there is no feeling of respect, wherein lies the difference?"* (2:7). Obedience is called for under the term **filial piety (hsiao)**—respect for parents and family elders. However, in *Analects* 4:18 it is indicated that one may discuss matters with parents and show a difference of opinion with them.

The significance of the Confucian view of the parent-child relationship may not be understood by readers who have learned to emphasize individualism and the marital (spouse-spouse) relationship. In traditional Chinese culture, the most fundamental and important relationship throughout life is the bond between parent and child. Unlike the love of one's spouse, it is based on birth (a biological bond). When a person reaches the point of marriage, the relationship with his or her

Paper offerings are burnt as a way of sending them to departed ancestors at a Confucian temple in Tainan, Taiwan (1993).

of some Americans; that such institutions are even needed would be cause for great shame to a Confucian. A Confucian would assume that the children would themselves administer this care and support, physically, in person.

Confucian views on these matters are clearly put in perspective by the modern Chinese novelist and philosopher Lin Yutang. Filial piety and respect for age are not, of course, isolated virtues but are facets of a way of life woven together by the logic of the Confucian vision: "If one cannot tolerate one's own parents when they are old and comparatively helpless, parents who have done so much for us, whom else can one tolerate in the home? One has to learn self-restraint anyway, or even marriage will go on the rocks. And how can the personal service and devotion and adoration of loving children ever be replaced by the best of hotel waiters?"[16] Writers like Lin Yutang can help us see some striking differences among societies; to a Confucian, these matters are of great moral and spiritual significance as well.

ANCESTOR WORSHIP Ancestor worship, in the broad sense of the term, includes funerary rites, mourning, worship at the family altar in the home, worship in the family or community temple, and periodic cleaning and sacrifices at graves. The most common form of rites are those for the deceased parent of the head of the household.

The classic statement to explain the reason for ancestor worship is that of the *Book of Rites (Li Chi)* section 8: *"[It is to] express gratitude toward the originators and recall the beginnings."* *Analects* 2:5 shows that in Confucius's mind, filial piety and ancestor worship tie in together: *"The Master said, 'While [the parents] are living, serve them with* li; *when they die, bury them with* li; *sacrifice to them with* li.'" In other words, ancestor worship is really a part of filial piety; it is filial piety in relation to one's deceased elders. One should *"render the same service to the dead as to the living—to the absent as to the present."*[17]

Numerous observers of Chinese culture have called ancestor worship the "essential religion" of

parents is already about twenty years old; therefore, a new nonblood bond cannot take precedence over it.[14] The relationship to a parent is the oldest relationship in a person's life.

The parent-child bond thrives on a sense of dependence, based at first on the obvious needs of the infant. A fascinating study of such relationships in modern Japan shows that this most important bond even becomes a model for other relationships, such as the relationship between employer and employee. The dynamics of this sort of dependence have been traced through the various stages of life by the prominent twentieth-century Japanese psychiatrist Takeo Doi in *The Anatomy of Dependence*.[15] Despite a degree of westernization, Japanese culture is more influenced by Confucianism than by individualism.

Nowhere has a culture shown more respect for age than in Confucian China. The traditional way to compliment a man on hearing he had turned forty was to say, "Really? You seem more like a man of fifty." The institutions in the United States for "senior citizens," such as centers for recreation and nursing, might be a matter of pride in the minds

China because of its universal importance from ancient to modern times.[18] From peasant to emperor, all classes of people have participated in these rites. Although Confucianism, Taoism, and Buddhism may have been in or out of favor with a given dynasty, no dynasty tried to suppress ancestor worship. The government, the literati, and the Taoist organizations may have tried to suppress some forms of folk religion, but ancestor worship was never targeted as problematic, least of all by the Confucians. The literati adopted and promoted ancestor worship, and they were looked upon as the official interpreters of the *li* of ancestor worship.

Setting aside the matter of interpretation for just a moment, we should note here that ancestor worship is, in many ways, a mirror image of social relations among the living. Those who died at an advanced age received the most elaborate rites (just as the oldest living family members receive the most respect); male ancestors received more sacrifices than female, and authority figures more than followers. Those who died unmarried or under the age of twelve received simple ceremonies or none at all. Finally, just as special service is due to one's own parents and not to others' parents, so *"sacrifice to spirits which are not those of one's own dead is [mere] flattery"* (*Analects* 1:24).

As interpreters of ancestor worship, many literati have set aside metaphysical implications (concerning the soul and the afterlife) and focused on the social and psychological value for the living. For them, ancestor worship is a "human practice," while for the common people "[it is] serving of the spirits."[19] However, a good portion of the literati have retained the supernatural aspects of these rites, following passages in the classic authority on rites, the *Li Chi*. The person performing the rites is said to commune with the spirits:

> On the day of the sacrifice, when he enters the apartment [of the temple], he will seem to see [the deceased] in the place [where his spirit-tablet is]. After he has moved about [to perform his operations], and is leaving the door, he will be arrested by

> seeming to hear the sound of his [the deceased's] movements, and will sigh as he seems to hear the sound. . . .
>
> . . . Still and grave, absorbed in what he is doing, he will seem to be unable to sustain the burden, and in danger of letting it fall. . . . In this his heart reaches the height of filial piety and reverence. . . . Thus he manifests his mind and thought, and in his dreamy state of mind seeks to commune with the dead in their spiritual state, if peradventure they could indeed do so.[20]

The skeptical phrases in the *Li Chi* (*"seeming to hear," "if peradventure they could indeed do so,"* and so on) exemplify the openness and tolerance of the tradition. Both a supernatural and a nonsupernatural understanding of the rites are acceptable. Even if the head of a household does not see *li* as communion with spirits, he rarely interferes with the views of family members who do.

Ancestor worship has at least four important functions in the practice of Confucianism. First, participation in the *li* of ancestor worship tends to cultivate moral values, especially filial piety and associated feelings. Reverence for those who provided life, security, and well-being to us is both expressed and instilled by the ceremonies. Here again is the Confucian formula that *li* leads to *jen*. The *li* of ancestor worship can cultivate *jen* (human-heartedness) in relation to the living.

A second function of ancestor worship is the healthful and proper channeling of natural feelings of grief, longing, and guilt. Whether rational or irrational, whether based on belief in spirits or not, many people feel a need to "pay their respects" to their deceased parent or grandparent, even many years following the death. Feelings may vary from remorse, attachment, loss, or desire to communicate with the forebear, or a combination of these. Being able to express these feelings in socially appropriate ways in words and actions can bring relief and satisfaction to the worshiper. Ancestor worship provides a definite and socially recognized vehicle for the periodic catharsis of such feelings.

Some readers may feel that the extensive *li* summarized here involve an undue preoccupation or obsession with death and the deceased. However, some psychologists argue that the much more abbreviated practices that are common in the United States today involve an obsessive and unsuccessful attempt to deny the reality of death and the loss of family members. It may be that grieving and paying respects are processes that take a long time and warrant periodic ceremonies for their expression.

The third role of ancestor worship in Confucian practice is the unification of the living family. Chinese sociologist C. K. Yang maintains that discontinuance of these rites tends to weaken family ties.[21] The periodic sacrifices and ceremonial cleaning of the graves (**ch'ing ming** ceremony) literally bring the family together around a common source and a common bond. This unity of the family, in turn, strengthens the lives of all its members through an intricate web of support systems.

A final function of ancestor worship concerns its connection to marriage and the bearing of children. Having a family is, among other things, a way of providing future services for older family members both in life and after death. In a sense, one provides for the future, including the afterlife, by having and rearing a devoted family.

Before describing some of these *li* in specific terms, we must recall the integrated nature of Chinese religion. Ancestor worship is not exclusively Confucian; it is also part of folk religion, and it may involve the services of both Taoist and Buddhist clergy as well.

Immediately after the corpse is placed in the main room of the house, it is washed by family members and clothed with grave clothes ("longevity clothes"). The person's rice bowl is broken, and a three-day vigil begins with a focus on a photograph of the deceased. The family members leave their hair unkempt. At various specific times, wailing and lamentation are prescribed.

The funeral and mourning procedures are elaborate and extend over long periods of time, as is appropriate in Confucian tradition: "Far from being an isolated event in the lives of the family members, a harrowing experience best gotten over as quickly as is decently possible so that the family life may get back to normal, the funeral and the subsequent mourning are protracted, momentous, and integrally a part of the normal flow of that family life."[22] A Taoist or Buddhist priest will preside at the funeral and at the numerous observances during the first seven weeks of mourning. Traditionally, the mourning period extends over three years: *"Only after a child is three years old does it leave its parents' arms; and [thus it is that] the three-year mourning is observed everywhere under Heaven"* (*Analects* 17:21).

The family household altar usually contains a spirit tablet, in which the soul of the deceased resides, as well as images of or tablets for other ancestors, deities, and revered individuals such as Confucius. On the table in front of the altar are placed two incense burners, two candles, and a vase of flowers. Food and beverage items are offered here periodically. Many families light a stick of incense at the altar every morning before breakfast. Special offerings are made in July during the ancestor festival.

A grave may or may not be located in a cemetery, but for the traditional devout family the grave site has a positive, active feeling. The atmosphere on the occasion of grave cleaning is pleasant and sometimes even boisterous, including the crackling of firecrackers, which are said to ward off evil spirits.

THE CULT OF CONFUCIUS

The ritual veneration of Master K'ung (Confucius) is part of Confucian practice and was also a function of Chinese state religion for nearly two millennia. These observances are not the exaltation of Confucius as a bloodline ancestor but the veneration of a great sage whose temples bear the inscription "The Most Holy Ancient Sage, the Prince of Culture." Although the literati do not teach that Confucius was divine, the sacrifices in his honor are almost identical to those of a deity cult. The temples themselves resemble those dedicated to gods, and the ceremonies include incense, candles, kowtows, and formal prayers. In the same building or satellite buildings, the patron god of literature and the divine creator of writing are worshiped, thus reinforcing the association with divinity and reinforcing the link between Confucianism and education. The "hymn to Confucius" exalts the sage with these opening lines:

> Great is Confucius
> He perceives things and knows them
>   Before the time;
> He is in the same order with
>   Heaven and Earth.
> The teacher of ten thousand ages.[23]

For long stretches in the history of imperial China, Confucian temples were maintained by law "in every prefecture, sub-prefecture, district, and in every market town throughout the empire."[24] Sacrifices were offered there by the literati. These ceremonies were one part of Chinese state religion. The other ceremonies of state religion, such as the worship of the god of grain, were also formulated and interpreted by the literati. Thus, the literati have been the principal maintainers and performers of the *li* of state religion.

The literati felt obligated to make special contributions toward a good society and a good government. It was expected that people of all walks of life would practice family *li* (including respect for the aged and ancestor worship) and reverence Confucius. But the literati undertook at least two further public obligations—those of functionaries of state religion (performing ceremonial sacrifices) and those of government officials (such as director or clerk in one of the vast array of ministries). Following Master K'ung, the literati have desired to enact good government, not just theorize about it.

GOVERNMENT AND PUBLIC VIRTUE

The Confucian view of good government is based solidly upon the practice of the moral virtues. Political and economic structures can only supplement moral virtue; they cannot be the primary means to the good society. Above all else, a good leader must be a good person; whatever political or economic strategies the leader may have are of secondary importance. The leader should be chosen on the basis of moral integrity, not because of inheritance, wealth, connections, or strategy platforms.

Confucianism is alone among the world's great religious philosophies in emphasizing the careful and correct use of language, especially for those who aspire to political office. In the *Analects*, Confucius called for the *"correction of language"* as the *"first measure"* in establishing the good society (13:11). The point is interesting in view of the vast communications technology that dominates political appeals today and because of the amounts of rhetoric and hype involved in politics. Among other linguistic virtues, the Confucian leader will avoid, rather than take advantage of, the ambiguity and vagueness of many of the words used in political arenas.

The practice of good government will thus proceed through the example of the leader's behavior, to policies that bolster the family (the foundation of society), to systems of land distribution and other resource distribution to avoid injustice. The people are expected to obey the leaders, but only insofar as the leaders display moral integrity. The Readings section at the end of the chapter includes more detailed statements of these aspects of the Confucian teachings regarding government.

THE LITERATI

In Confucianism, to attain the ideal (to be a *chung-tzu*, or superior person), one must develop what might be called "personal culture." As will be discussed in the "History of Confucianism" section, the personal culture of the literati is a special emphasis of Neo-Confucianism. (Table 7.2 lists the major Confucian scholars.)

First, in addition to basic book learning, the literati must study the "nature of things" to attain the knowledge of the fundamental principles of reality. Second, an attitude of seriousness is required

MAJOR CONFUCIAN SCHOLARS (LITERATI)

Table

7.2

Confucius (sixth century B.C.E.)	Founder of the Confucian tradition. Confucius saw himself as a transmitter of wisdom from the past.
Mencius (fourth century B.C.E.)	Elaborator of the teachings of Confucius. Mencius argued that human nature is basically good.
Hsun-tzu (third century B.C.E.)	Confucian scholar who held that human nature is basically bad.
Tung Chung-Shu (second century B.C.E.)	The most influential Confucian scholar in the Han years. Tung synthesized Confucian ethics and ancient metaphysics. He persuaded the emperor to require Confucian teachings as the core curriculum at all levels of education.
Han Yu (ninth century C.E.)	Outspoken scholar who criticized Buddhism and Taoism but employed some of their ideas in his syncretic system of thought.
Ch'eng Hao and Ch'eng I (twelfth century C.E.)	Neo-Confucian literati who based their thought on the concept of principle.
Chu Hsi (twelfth century C.E.)	The most prominent Neo-Confucian philosopher. Chu Hsi was very influential as an author and as an editor of the *Five Classics* and the *Four Books*.
Wang Yang-ming (sixteenth century C.E.)	Second only to Chu Hsi among Neo-Confucians, Wang distinguished himself in government, the military, and academic circles.

so that they can concentrate and allow the "original good mind" to perceive the truth. Third, they must rectify the mind/heart *(hsin)*. The untranslatable Chinese word *hsin* conveys some aspects of intellection and some aspects of emotion or will. The final goal of this rectification process is the experience of oneness or harmony with the Great Ultimate. Fourth, many modern literati practice a form of meditation. Confucians are critical of any form of meditation that attempts to transcend sensation or thought; they advocate sitting quietly in self-examination. Wang Yang-ming explains it as follows:

> In teaching people, don't insist on a particular one-sided Way. In the beginning, one's mind is like a restless monkey and his feelings are like a galloping horse. They cannot be tied down. His thoughts and deliberations mostly tend to the side of selfish human desires. At that point, teach him to sit in meditation and to stop those thoughts and deliberations. Wait a long time till

his mind becomes somewhat settled. If, however, at this time he merely remains quiet in a vacuum, like dry wood and dead ashes, it is also useless. Rather, he must be taught self-examination and self-mastery. There is no letup in this work. It is like getting rid of robbers and thieves. There must be the determination to wipe them out thoroughly and completely. Before things happen, each and every selfish desire for sex, wealth, and fame must be discovered. The root of the trouble must be pulled up and thrown away so that it will never sprout again.[25]

The third and fourth aspects of personal culture (rectifying the mind/heart and meditation) prepare the literati for worldly duties and protect them from identifying their whole happiness with the success of the Confucian project to create a good society. The calm induced by meditation and the sense of oneness with the Great Ultimate can help a person cope with failures and with the evils of this world.

HISTORY OF CONFUCIANISM

Confucius died in 479 B.C.E. at the age of seventy-three. Although we know neither the exact circumstances nor the cause of death, we can gather from *Analects* 9:12 that there were no "special stewards" in attandance, for such would befit a wealthy lord. Mencius tells us the Master K'ung's disciples mourned his death for three years and then became teachers or ministers of feudal lords. They gathered together the material that ultimately became the *Analects*. This was presumably, the beginning of the Confucian school, and some of the disciples founded institutions devoted to spreading the teachings of the master. However, the decline of the Chou feudal system and the rise of different schools of thought impeded the spread of Confucian teaching.

EARLY CONFUCIANISM (479–206 B.C.E.)

Although the Confucian school was only one among several competing schools of thought, the Confucians survived both the Warring States Period (403–221 B.C.E.) and the book burning and cruel autocracy of the Ch'in dynasty, the first dynasty to unify China (in 221 B.C.E.). (Table 6.3 in Chapter 6 lists the major dynasties and periods of Chinese history.) What is especially remarkable about the survival of Confucianism is that the Confucians held a number of "unsafe" doctrines, such as the view that rulers should be chosen by merit rather than heredity. As A. C. Graham has pointed out, it was a view that could not safely be put in writing.[26] Yet the Confucians did put it in writing, attributing it to the ancient sage-kings and to K'ung fu-tzu himself.

The rejection of the principle of hereditary rule is contained in the legend of the sage-kings of antiquity:

> *Yao and Shun were worthy rulers who both took the worthiest for successor instead of giving the throne to their own descendants; . . . they in establishing officials were sure to make them stand square. The rulers of the present all desire not to lose the throne for future generations, and give it to their own descendants, but in establishing officials are unable to make them stand square, because they throw them into disorder by desire which is partial. Why is that? Their desires reach far ahead but all they know is the near.*[27]

> *When the Great Way prevailed there was impartiality throughout the world. They chose the worthy and capable, studied to be trustworthy and cultivated harmony. Therefore they did not treat only their own parents as parents, their own sons as sons. They enabled the old to live out their term, the able-bodied to have employment, the young to be reared; they pitied the widow, orphan, childless and sick, and provided nurture for all.*[28]

These sage-king figures functioned as idealized images to which Confucians would continually refer. Despite the importance of family loyalty, the virtuous leader does not confuse it with sound political judgment. According to the legend, Yao and Shun were virtuous sage-kings who exercised correct judgment, but another ancient king, Yu, failed when he turned the throne over to his son.

During the fifth to third centuries B.C.E., the rejection of hereditary and highly autocratic rule would have to count as a kind of political heresy. So controversial was Confucius's concept of succession by merit that even two of his outstanding advocates, Mencius and Hsun-tzu, hesitated to support it. However, once included in the *Analects* and other writings, it came to stand as a milestone in Confucian political theory.

MENCIUS During the first two and a half centuries after Confucius died, his teachings enjoyed only moderate success. The greatest advocate of Confucian teachings in this period was Mencius (Meng-tzu, 371–289 B.C.E.), who is said to have studied under Confucius's grandson. Mencius's life was the same as the life of Confucius in many essential elements. Like Confucius, Mencius saw his mission as that of bringing society back to the classical ideals. Like Confucius, he traveled for at least ten years to offer advice to rulers for reform. Like

Confucius, he was more successful as a scholar and teacher than as a politician.

Mencius's views are based on Confucius's thought, but Mencius was more thorough and systematic. In holding that human nature is basically good, Mencius went beyond Confucius. He argued that a person who sees a child about to fall into a well will, without exception, have a feeling of alarm and distress and a desire to rescue the child. These feelings are instantaneous and not prompted by desire for reward.

Mencius's emphasis on the goodness of human nature did not lead him to set aside Confucius's insistence on traditional social obligations. Like Confucius, he emphasized obligations to, and love of, family members. Mencius was emphatic in teaching that rulers are obligated to help provide the material means for life to all citizens and to adhere to a land distribution system to insure fair distribution. Citizens have the right to revolt against a ruler who fails to live up to such obligations.

DOCTRINE OF THE MEAN

One of the key documents to emerge during this period was the *Doctrine of the Mean (Chung Yung)*. Confucian tradition attributes it to Confucius's grandson and regards it as a major authoritative text. As such, the *Doctrine of the Mean* has played a significant role throughout the history of Confucianism. This significance has all too often been ignored. When generalizers say, for example, that Confucianism or early Confucianism is nothing more than a set of ethical principles, they are ignoring Confucian teachings like those of the *Mean:*

> How abundant is the display of power of spiritual beings! They form the substance of all things and nothing can be without them. . . .
>
> The way of the superior man functions everywhere and yet is hidden. Men and women of simple intelligence can share its knowledge and yet in its utmost reaches there is something that even the sage does not know.[29]

The *Doctrine of the Mean* goes on to say that this Way (Tao) is so great that nothing in the world can contain it but is so small that nothing in the world can split it. Further, *"the operations of Heaven have neither sound nor smell."*[30]

Followers of the Confucian path of faith have found in this text a religious and metaphysical basis for their strong ethical philosophy. The *Mean* has a kind of universal appeal, and it is no surprise that Taoists and Buddhists wrote lengthy commentaries on it. Although Confucius's disciples complained that Master K'ung refused to speak about metaphysics (*Analects* 5:12), this does not mean that he had none. In the Chinese context, it is safe to assume that Master K'ung accepted the basic organic interrelational Chinese worldview that was discussed in Chapter 6. There are touches of it in Meng-tzu (Mencius), and we shall see how it was presupposed or explicitly developed by later followers of the Confucian way.

HSUN-TZU

Another outstanding Confucian scholar of the time was Hsun-tzu (Xun-zi), who flourished from 298 to 238 B.C.E. Unlike Meng-tzu, Hsun-tzu held that humans are basically bad. Hsun-tzu's "realism" called for training people away from their innate evil tendencies. In regard to this issue of human nature, it is interesting to look back at the neutral statements of Confucius: *"By nature men are pretty much alike; it is learning and practice that set them apart"* (*Analects* 17:2).

Given the hindsight of history, we can see that Meng-tzu's view of human nature won out, and Hsun-tzu's short-term popularity changed over time to a position of secondary importance. Hsun-tzu's is one branch of Confucian thought, representing a kind of realism about human weaknesses and an emphasis on laws as a way to control them.

Hsun-tzu emphasized laws, but he did so for moral reasons. He believed in the function of moral training as a crucial method for the betterment of society. However, as the violent struggles among regional warlords reached their climax in 221 B.C.E., the dominant social philosophy was **Legalism,** not the teachings of Confucianism. The leading advocate of Legalism was Han Fei-tzu, a one-time student of Hsun-tzu. Legalism called for a ruthlessly autocratic power structure with laws governing virtually every aspect of life.

SUPPRESSION OF CONFUCIANISM UNDER CH'IN RULE In 221 B.C.E., the Ch'in leaders defeated the other competing states and united China. In 213, Shih huang-ti, who called himself the "First Emperor," ordered the burning of Confucian books and ordained severe punishments for all who "appeal to the past to condemn the present." He made it a capital offense to discuss Confucian books. Such thoroughgoing attempts at "cultural revolution" are rare in the history of China, the latest attempt being the communist one in 1966.

It seems that the First Emperor of imperial China was not able to bring off his cultural revolution completely, however. When he wanted to have stones inscribed with eloquent proclamations of his glory, he consulted with Confucian scholars (literati). Again, in 219 B.C.E., he demanded the help of seventy literati from the provinces of Ch'i and Lu in preparing for the imperial sacrifice to Heaven on Mount T'ai. He always kept a team of seventy Confucian scholars for educational purposes. These are early signs indicating that the Confucians were to play a special role in Chinese history. The Confucian scholars were highly literate educators steeped in tradition. Even the arrogant Ch'in emperor could not dispense with them, precisely because he wanted to unite the Chinese people under his power. The fundamental truth of the matter was well put by Graham: "[China has] a unique capacity for political and cultural integration which has been inseparable from the sense of continuing tradition."[31] Because the literati had been the guardians of Chinese civilization, it became impossible to treat them as just another competing school.

CONFUCIANISM IN THE HAN DYNASTY (206 B.C.E.–220 C.E.)

The Chinese people did not take kindly to the harsh ways of Ch'in rule. Rebellion and civil wars ensued, and in 206 B.C.E. a new dynasty—the Han—began its four-hundred-year reign. Although the Han leaders used much of the legal structure that was already in place, the new government was also influenced by Taoism. Under this less authoritarian regime, the early Han years brought release from regimentation, and the Confucian scriptures were dug out from the walls where they had been hidden.

The process of Confucianization was very gradual. The now famous exchange between the Han emperor Kao-tzu and a Confucian scholar, Chia I, in 196 B.C.E. prefigures later developments. Chia I repeatedly extolled moral virtues and the study of Confucian texts in the presence of the emperor. The emperor became impatient and exclaimed, "I have conquered my empire on horseback and I am going to rule my empire on horseback." To his surprise, the scholar had a ready reply: "Your Majesty, one may conquer an empire on horseback but one may never rule an empire on horseback." We don't know whether this exchange attracted Kao-tzu to Confucianism, but on his tour of the country the next year, he offered the *ta-chi* (grand sacrifice) to the tomb of K'ung fu-tzu. This was the first time any government official had sacrificed to Confucius.

TUNG CHUNG-SHU The most influential Confucian in the Han years was Tung Chung-Shu (179–104 B.C.E.), who distinguished himself as a scholar, writer, professor, and statesman. On all accounts Tung was "a Confucian," but we should not suppose that the different philosophical and religious schools of thought worked out their views into separate and totally distinct positions. As we shall see, Tung borrowed from, and shared with, many other schools, especially with Taoism and even with folk religion.

Tung brought together the ancient *yin/yang* cosmology, the notion of the five elements of activity (woody, fiery, earthen, metallic, and watery elements), the organic whole worldview, and the concept of the **mandate of heaven** (divine sanction for rulers). The universe is a set of corresponding series of elements in which the mutual responsiveness of Heaven and humanity is but one example. Even colors, sounds, directions, and seasons are related in a network of correspondences. Tung believed that the hierarchy of social order was justified as a correspondence with natural phenomena. The mandate of heaven can be understood, then, as an alliance or correspondence between heavenly principles and the policies of the emperor. If the ruler failed to rule with wisdom and virtue, Heaven would respond by causing social disharmony and economic disaster. Even earthquakes were viewed as portents—signs of the cosmic response to human actions.

In 136 B.C.E., Tung persuaded the Han emperor Wu Ti that in the long run the unity and stability of the empire would depend upon imperial preference for one from among the many divergent philosophical schools of the time. Tung claimed that the government statutes were in a state of confusion and that the people did not know what to cling to. Wu Ti perceived the wisdom of the idea of a Confucian state ideology and officially proclaimed Confucianism as such. This notion of state ideology did not imply that all other religions and philosophies were prohibited; Wu Ti himself was politically a Legalist and a practitioner of various Taoist techniques of immortality. It meant rather that the *Wu Ching (Five Classics)* were to become the core curriculum for all levels of education.

THE FIVE CLASSICS (WU CHING)   We have referred to Master K'ung and those who followed him as transmitters of "ancient or classical wisdom." The literature containing this wisdom is called the *Wu Ching*, or *Five Classics*. The first three works listed in Table 7.3 were definitely in existence before Master K'ung, and parts of the remaining two classics were probably pre-Confucian also. However, as transmitters, the Confucians were not mere recorders of "dead letters." All of these materials were continually reedited, and commentaries were added so that fresh applications of the teachings could be made. There were also additions to the *Five Classics* during Han times, as is the case with parts of the *Doctrine of the Mean*. This latter text, the *Mean*, was extracted from one of the *Five Classics*, the *Book of Rites*. The *Mean* was given independent status as one of the *Four Books* (see Table 7.3); additions and commentaries were published with the original text. Studying the *Five Classics*, then, is a process of reanimation of ancient insights so that contemporary people may apply them.

While giving a strong sense of identification with ancient tradition, the study of the *Classics* is supposed to prepare the present generation for the challenges of the day.[32]

The *Book of Changes (I Ching* or *Yi Jing)* is perhaps the most widely known and respected Chinese book. The *Book of Changes* expresses the ancient metaphysical vision, combined with divinatory art, numerology, and ethical insight. It was in existence by at least 674 B.C.E.,[33] and probably centuries before. Confucian tradition holds (without solid evidence) that Master K'ung wrote the ten commentaries *("Ten Wings")* of the *I Ching*; but the book and its teachings are no more the exclusive property of Confucianism than the concept of Tao is the special possession of the Taoists.

The *Book of History (Shu Ching)* is also called the *Book of Documents*. This pre-Confucian text expresses a political vision. The *Shu* purports to be a historical record of words and deeds of ancient rulers like the sages to whom we have already referred: Yao, Shun, and Yu. The following brief excerpt shows how metaphysics, religion, and ethics are tied together in the *Shu:*

> The works of Heaven, it is man who carries them out on its behalf. Heaven arranges the existing rules [of family relations], we carefully regulate our five rules and the five modes of amply practicing them. Heaven regulates the existing rites [pertaining to the king, the higher feudatories, the lower feudatories, the ministers and the dignitaries, the officers and commoners] and their five constant norms. Together we reverence [them], concordantly we respect them, [then there is] harmony and correctness.[34]

The *Book of Poetry (Shih Ching)*, a collection of Chou dynasty song lyrics traditionally said to have been selected and edited by Master K'ung, shows that feelings or emotions were given their due in antiquity. The *Shih* expresses a poetic vision of the good life. Here is an expression of feelings of fulfillment on completion of ancestral sacrifices:

> The musicians go in to perform.
> And give their soothing aid at the sacred blessing.

Table 7.3

CONFUCIAN SCRIPTURE

The *Five Classics* and the *Four Books* are the traditional authoritative texts of Confucianism.

THE *FIVE CLASSICS* (*WU CHING*)

With the exception of the *Spring and Autumn Annals*, all of the *Five Classics* were written or compiled in some form by about the eighth century B.C.E.

Book of Changes (I Ching or Yi Jing)	A book of divination that expresses the ancient metaphysical vision combined with numerology and ethical insight.
Book of History (Shu Ching)	A text that expresses a political vision, tying together metaphysics, religion, and ethics.
Book of Poetry (Shih Ching)	A poetic vision of the good life, consisting of Chou dynasty song lyrics.
Book of Rites (Li Chi)	A social vision that states and explains the myriad of *li* (traditional, respectful behavioral rules).
Spring and Autumn Annals (Ch'un-ch'iu)	A text that expresses an historical vision of events in the province of Lu from the eighth through the fifth centuries B.C.E.

THE *FOUR BOOKS*

Analects (Lun Yu)	Selected sayings attributed to Confucius. The style is terse, with cryptic fragments.
Doctrine of the Mean (Chung Yung)	A chapter extracted from the *Book of Rites* (see above). The *Mean* pursues the theme of moral humanity in a moral universe.
Great Learning (Ta Hsueh)	A short chapter extracted from the *Book of Rites* (see above). Its theme is the ordering of society through individual self-cultivation.
Book of Mencius (Meng-tzu)	The writings of Mencius (ca. 371–289 B.C.E.). Mencius elaborates on and extends the teachings of Confucius.

Your viands [tasty dishes] are set forth;
There is no dissatisfaction, but all feel happy.
They drink [wine] to the full;
Great and small, they bow their heads, saying
The Spirits enjoyed your spirits and viands.[35]

The *Book of Rites (Li Chi)* is impossible to date with accuracy, but the ideal social vision portrayed by the *li* is unmistakably Confucian. This text was in the process of being written and edited from the eighth century (or perhaps earlier) through the second century B.C.E. Among its chapters are works that were later extracted and treated separately, such as the *Doctrine of the Mean* and the *Great Learning*. In a brief phrase, the social vision of the *Book of Rites* is a community of trust. Crucial to the understanding of the *Book of Rites* (or *Book of Rituals*) is the realization that "rite" or "ritual" in the Confucian context is a much broader concept than most Westerners are accustomed to. Roughly speaking, the term *li* refers to any formal and proper behavior. Thus, the behaviors described here are to be regarded as sacred rites: Having gotten up at the first crowing of the cock and when properly dressed, children should

> go to their parents and parents-in-law. On getting to where they are, with bated breath and gentle voice, they should ask if their clothes are (too) warm or (too) cold, whether they are ill or pained, or uncomfortable in any part; and if they be so, they should proceed reverently to stroke and scratch the place. . . .
>
> . . . In bringing in the basin for them to wash, the younger will carry the stand and the elder the water; they will beg to be allowed to pour out the water, and when the washing is concluded, they will hand the towel.[36]

The *Spring and Autumn Annals (Ch'un-ch'iu)*, a record of events in the province of Lu from the eighth through the fifth centuries B.C.E., constitutes a historical vision giving its readers a collective memory and communal identity. Confucian tradition has it that K'ung fu-tzu edited the material and added commentaries expressing his opinions about the events. The commentaries to the *Ch'un-ch'iu* have come to be attached to the text regularly; the following excerpt is from the commentary called *Tso Chuan*. Confucian thought as a whole includes both positive and negative (or skeptical) attitudes about portents (omens). This passage is on the skeptical side, but the *Ch'un-ch'iu* sometimes expresses belief in natural signs as rewards or punishments.

> There appeared a comet in Ch'i, and the marquis gave orders for a deprecatory sacrifice [to appease Heaven by admitting his own faults]. Kan Tzu said to him, "It is of no use; you will only practice a delusion. There is no uncertainty in the ways of Heaven; it does not waver in its purposes:—why should you offer a deprecatory sacrifice? Moreover, there is a broom-star in the sky;—it is for the removal of dirt. If your lordship have nothing about your conduct that can be so described, what have you to deprecate? If you have, what will be diminished by your deprecation? . . . Let your lordship do nothing

contrary to virtue, and from all quarters the States will come to you;—why should you be troubled about a comet? . . . If the conduct be evil and disorderly, the people are sure to fall away, and nothing that priests and historiographers can do will mend the evil." The marquis was pleased, and stopped the sacrifice.[37]

THE "TRIUMPH" OF CONFUCIANISM The gradual Confucianization of politics and education during the Han years resulted in what has been called the triumph of Confucianism. A Han emperor had already declared Confucianism to be the state ideology. In 136 B.C.E., Emperor Wu Ti set up at court five chairs of philosophy—one for each of the *Five Classics*—and brought in five great Confucian scholars to teach students in this new imperial university. Other materials, such as Taoist texts, were excluded. Eventually the difficult tests covering the *Classics* became civil service examinations for gaining a position in the government. A student aspiring to public office had to know the *Classics* and their Confucian interpretation. In this way the literati began to control politics and edge Han policies over from Legalism toward Confucianism.

From the later Han years onward, the literati's function tended to go beyond scholarship. The Confucians were gaining prestige through their education, and their education in turn gave them political position and power. Many modern writers now use the term *literati* to refer to a Confucian scholar-official. In the Han, most of the literati belonged to a new kind of landowning gentry who had largely replaced the old aristocracy. Their tasks were three: (1) to master and transmit the great tradition embodied in the *Five Classics*, (2) to live a virtuous—that is, a noble—life, and (3) to serve the sovereign in his Heaven-appointed duty in establishing a harmony between Heaven and earth.

As government officials, the literati oversaw the educational network; they also performed rituals in the court and on the local level. Their involvement with education concerned much more than the *Five Classics*; the literati administered the teaching of all subjects, including history, calligraphy, mathematics, and even music. An example of the role of ritual is the **Ming T'ang phenomenon—**

A person bows before the Confucian temple in Ch'u-fu (Qufu), the birthplace of Confucius, Shantung province, People's Republic of China.

the building of "halls of light" (also called "calendar houses") throughout the realm for the worship of ancestors and all the major deities. The emperor himself performed some of these rites, but for the most part it was the task of the literati to carry out this vital function.

We have preferred not to call Confucianism the state religion, because the term is appropriate as a label for a religious function that is distinct from Confucianism. Chinese state religion may be defined as the state-sponsored rituals and associated places of ritual where natural powers, deities, ancestors, and the souls of great men are worshiped. The purposes of the rituals have always been to establish harmony between Heaven and earth and to increase or maintain the prestige and power of the government.

Chinese state religion antedates the acceptance of the Confucian *Five Classics* as state ideology (ca. 136 B.C.E.). Many of the sacrifices and deities worshiped derive from Shang dynasty times. Also, it appears that in some territories, such as the state of Wei during the period of disunion from 220 to 589 C.E., Taoist priests sometimes held important roles in the performance of government ritual. Thus, Confucianism and state religion are distinct, but there has often been a significant overlap between the two: from about 100 B.C.E. until the

beginning of the twentieth century, the literati were usually the ones who codified and performed the rituals of the state religion.

The literati's support of rituals included special emphasis on ancestor worship and ceremonies in honor of Confucius. By 58 C.E., all government schools were required to make sacrifices to Confucius, and eventually each of the two thousand counties had a state-supported temple dedicated to him. The Master's birthplace in Ch'u-fu became a national shrine. In 175 C.E., the *Five Classics* were engraved in stone to avoid scribal loss or error. All of this stands as clear evidence of the triumph of Confucianism, and with it came the elevation of Master K'ung to the position of the most important man in the history of China. He was even revered as a saint or deity.

THE DECLINE OF THE HAN DYNASTY Although leading scholars such as Tung Chung-Shu never explicitly endorsed the deification of Master K'ung, Tung's followers treated Confucius as semidivine. On the popular level, a wealth of stories began to be told about the Master's life. A unicorn was said to have appeared before his birth, and two dragons appeared when he was born. He reportedly could see hundreds of years into the future and predict events with complete accuracy. There developed out of

Tung's philosophy a movement (called New Text, because its scholars used the simplified script adopted during Ch'in times) emphasizing supernaturalism: belief in omens, spirits, and the worship of Confucius. The Han rulers favored this New Text movement, but many literati criticized it fiercely.

The variety of approaches and perspectives among the literati during the last two Han centuries is remarkable. Yang Hsiung (53 B.C.E.–18 C.E.) wrote cosmology along Taoist lines. Chen Hsun (127–200 C.E.) was a literalistic commentator; he tended to stay with the letter of the texts, refusing to take any points as metaphorical or merely suggestive. Wang Chung (27 C.E.–100 C.E.) was a skeptic who tried to discredit belief in the spirits of the dead, belief in portents, and belief in the divinity of the Master. The extreme skepticism of the Wang Chungs has been tempered by gentler approaches, so in the main the literati have not been antisupernaturalistic.

The four hundred years of Han rule had brought prosperity and stability, but the signs of Han demise were already evident by 150 C.E. Incompetent rulership and a faction-ridden bureaucracy resulted in dissension and outright insurrection. The Celestial Masters had set up an independent Taoist state in Szechwan. By 184 the massive Yellow Turban Rebellion exploded in East China. The would-be literati studying at the imperial university rose in protest against the government in 169, in T'ien-an Men (Tiananmen) square, and (paralleling events in 1989) thousands of them were killed. To make matters worse, barbarians invaded from the north as Han control began to wane. China was now thrown into a period of disunion from 220 to 589 C.E.—years dominated by civil wars and invasions.

The confusion and misery of the times created an opportunity for Indian Buddhist missionaries to gain a hearing in China beginning about 100 C.E. Despite the fact that the Chinese were used to dismissing all foreigners as "barbarians," the times were right for a fresh alternative. Sidestepping Chinese institutions, Buddhism made its appeal on a more private level. Early Chinese Buddhism was centered in the monastic order—a full-time celibate community independent of the family and the state. Buddhism attracted those who saw only an uncertain future in a chaotic time. A well-educated Buddhist clergy brought a sophisticated metaphysics and meditation techniques that appealed to the upper classes.

The Confucian response to Buddhism was to reject it as otherworldly and destructive to essential family values. The literati charged that the Buddhist belief in transmigration detracted from concern for this present life. They pointed out that the unavoidable and most important problem is out in broad daylight: how to live this life well and in accord with moral principle. The Buddhists, they said, spoke of hidden, marvelous things beyond the senses and ignored everyday moral problems. Such criticisms did not apply to all Chinese Buddhist sects equally well, but we can see why it made for good polemic. Eventually, as the patterns of Buddhist faith unfolded into a major dimension of Chinese religion, the literati came to appreciate and freely employ Buddhist metaphysical and psychological insights.

CONFUCIANISM IN THE PERIOD OF DISUNION (220–589 C.E.)

The increasing vitality of Buddhism and Taoism in the period of disunion is sometimes said to mark a "decline" in Confucianism, but such blanket terms obscure the historical realities. It is true that the literati enjoyed less political prominence and produced no fresh philosophical perspectives in these years. Some states, such as the northern Wei kingdom, established Taoist offices at court. However, the vitality of a tradition at a given time is not necessarily to be measured by the presence of prominent, innovative philosophers. Nor should it be measured by identifying certain practices or institutions as uniquely or explicitly "Confucian."

We can see the vitality of Confucianism during the period of disunion in several important aspects of Chinese life. Despite the diminished influence of Confucian political methods, Confucianism flourished in the form of family rules, lineage organizations, and clan cooperatives. On the level of community and family life, Confucianism was the common practice. In the area of literature, the literati continued to study and write commentaries on the *Five Classics,* history, and ritual. The *Five Classics* remained the "foundation of all literate culture."[38]

Confucianism was also embodied in the Ming-T'ang ritual houses previously mentioned. These buildings were usually not referred to as "Confucian" by Chinese writers, and foreign historians may have been even less aware of their relation to Confucianism. But the Ming-T'ang houses were first mentioned in the Confucian *Five Classics,* and the geometric cosmology on which their construction was based was typically Confucian (derived in part from Tung Chung-Shu). The ancestral rituals performed in the Ming-T'ang houses were based on Confucian values and conducted by the emperor or the literati. The Confucian ritualization of life continued in the Ming-T'ang houses and in other aspects of life amid the disunity and turbulence of this period.

THE EMERGENCE OF NEO-CONFUCIANISM

Confucianism began to assert itself with new vigor during the T'ang dynasty years (618–906 C.E.) and blossomed into Neo-Confucianism amid the cultural splendor of the Sung (960–1279 C.E.). Buddhism tended to dominate in art and philosophy in the golden age of the T'ang, but mastery of the new Confucian edition of the *Five Classics* with commentaries was still a prerequisite for political success.

At the beginning of the ninth century, several literati vigorously defended Confucianism, gave it a clearer sense of identity, and indicated the directions along which Neo-Confucianism would develop. The outstanding figure among them, Han Yu, was forthright indeed, as we can see from the following episode in relation to Emperor Hsien Tsung:

It seems that in 819 C.E. the emperor was preparing a great pageant to welcome a relic of the Buddha—allegedly a finger bone. Buddhist monks were to march to the palace in public procession carrying the precious relic. Han Yu wrote

an eloquent and potent petition to the emperor. In this famous letter, Han Yu was not satisfied simply to rehearse the timeworn Confucian arguments that the Buddhist way was barbarian, that cultural achievements had been achieved in China without Buddhism, and that Buddhist monks deserted the family and the state. He reminded the ruler that the founder of the T'ang had contemplated exterminating Buddhism because Shakyamuni, who could not speak Chinese, wore outlandish clothes and had no conception of the sacred ties that bind ruler and subject or father and son. Foolish ministers had prevented the ouster of Buddhism in the past, but now, Han Yu boldly asserted, let the present emperor send the noxious, putrid bone to the executioner so that he might burn it—and if the Buddha became angry at such an action, let the blame be upon him, Han Yu, as being alone responsible.

For such audacious statements, the scholar nearly lost his life; he was banished to an official post in the far south of the empire. However, Han Yu's message began to gain ground throughout China. The literati were saying, "Chinese tradition is *our* tradition, not the tradition of the Buddhists and not the tradition of the Taoists. *We* are the guardians of Chinese civilization." Han Yu was indeed a great master of Chinese literary tradition, and his attacks on the Buddhists and Taoists were based on copious quotations from the *Doctrine of the Mean,* the *Great Learning* (a standard Confucian text on creating a good society through self-cultivation), and the *Book of Changes.*

Another extremely important move made by Han Yu was his insistence on the orthodox line of transmission *(tao t'ung)* for the literati. This concept of transmission refers to the idea of the passage of Confucian doctrine without error from Confucius to Mencius and through other sages down through history. In a dogmatic fashion, Han Yu rejected Hsun-tzu and Yang Hsiung, and he virtually ignored other Confucians, such as Tung Chung-Shu. Neo-Confucians came to accept Han Yu's notion of an orthodox transmission, and it has influenced Chinese and Western historians to this day. When it is said that after Mencius (371–289

B.C.E.) there were no true Confucians for about a thousand years, this is a Neo-Confucian rewriting of history and not necessarily the way it was.

Han Yu and his friend Li Ao gave the literati a new sense of identity: the literati had a clearer notion of being a distinct school of thought and practice—clearer, at least, than their predecessors. At the same time, they were definitely influenced by Buddhism and Taoism. This influence is most obvious in the case of Li Ao, who emphasized "recovering one's nature" and "having no thought"—notions that he evidently got from Ch'an (Zen) Buddhism.[39] This phenomenon turned out to be a key feature of Neo-Confucianism: while absorbing and adopting certain elements from Buddhism and Taoism, the literati were aware of their own special identity and sometimes strongly criticized these other traditions.

After the fall of the T'ang, the first Sung ruler called on the literati to help establish stability; on their recommendation, the emperor dropped the Buddhist and Taoist texts from the school curriculum and reinstated the Confucian *Five Classics*. The literati had won this round in the "battle of the books." Again they capitalized on their capacity as experts useful to government. But they now faced several challenges. There were threats of Mongol invasions, for one thing. The Buddhist tradition was offering deep and highly sophisticated philosophical analyses, salvation promises, and the compassion and merit available to humans through *bodhisattvas*. There was also the intriguing, poetic, imaginative, and magical appeal of Taoism.

The Sung literati developed a new and more systematic theory of knowledge and reality. They placed more attention on self-cultivation and meditation, and sagehood *(sheng-jen)* took on a more spiritual dimension. The Neo-Confucian sage was to be the ultimate development of true humanity, one whose every "thought and action flowed in effortless harmony with the Cosmic Tao."[40] Self-realization came to be emphasized by Neo-Confucian literati. Sagehood was in some ways comparable to the competing images of the Buddhist *bodhisattvas* and the True Men of Tao. Yet

it was not a new concept for Confucianism, for "inner sageliness and outer kingliness" is the classic phrase to characterize the ideal person.

The great northern Sung literati who developed the core of Neo-Confucian thought were not ivory-tower philosophers but men of action in the world who came to hold civil or military offices. Most of them went through Buddhist and Taoist phases in their early years and then set themselves to the task of building the Neo-Confucian philosophical system. Chou Tun-I (1017–1073) obtained a Diagram of the Great Ultimate (T'ai-chi T'u) from a Taoist priest and made it the basis of his cosmology and moral philosophy. Chou's students, the brothers Ch'eng Hao and Ch'eng I, were the first to base their thought entirely on the concept of principle. In Ch'eng I's thought there is clearly a Buddhist strain, as can be seen in one of his statements about how principle functions:

> Empty and tranquil, and without any sign,
> And yet all things are luxuriantly present.[41]

The greatest Neo-Confucian of them all was Chu Hsi (1130–1200). He synthesized the work of other Sung literati and, in so doing, crafted Neo-Confucian teachings into the most comprehensive and systematic vision in the history of Confucian tradition. He set out to base Confucian ethics on an absolute metaphysical base, and in this he was indirectly influenced by Buddhism. From Chou Tun-I, he adopted the notion of the Great Ultimate—a concept that bears Taoist influence. The Great (or Supreme) Ultimate structures reality through *yin/yang* and the five modes of being; from these modes emerge the myriad of things, including humanity. This Great Ultimate is the sum total of all principles. By *principle* Chu Hsi meant the essence of a thing; principles are incorporeal, eternal, and unchanging. Chu Hsi was following the Ch'eng brothers in his use of the concept of principle, hence one of the names of his philosophy— the Ch'eng-Chu school.

In addition to study, philosophical reflection, and sustained moral effort, Chu Hsi recommended a type of meditation he called *silent-sitting*, which he distinguished from Buddhist meditation technique: "Silent-sitting is not the Buddhist type of [meditation] which requires the cessation of all processes of thinking. Mine is to help aim our mind so that it will not be distracted by conflicting streams of thought. When our mind is calm and undisturbed, concentration is a matter of course."[42] One who excels in study, moral effort, and silent-sitting may become a sage; such a person has attained knowledge, virtue, spirituality, and the ability to act in this world for the betterment of humankind.

Chu Hsi's success was phenomenal. With some exceptions, his views dominated Chinese thought from 1200 until 1905. Chu Hsi published what he termed the *Four Books* to accompany the *Five Classics* as required readings for public education. The *Four Books* are the *Analects* (*Lun Yu*, the sayings of Confucius), the *Great Learning (Ta Hsueh)*, the *Doctrine of the Mean (Chung Yung)*, and the *Book of Mencius (Meng-tzu)*. All these materials were edited with commentary by Chu Hsi and were the basis of the questions on the civil service exams. Again confirming the claim that the Confucians were educators *par excellence*, Chu Hsi's curriculum was comprehensive, including mathematics, physical exercise, calligraphy, and so on. Finally, Chu Hsi was successful in gaining wide acceptance of Han Yu's notion of an "orthodox line of transmission" for the literati. The result has been to spotlight K'ung fu-tzu, Meng-tzu, Chou Tun-I, the Ch'engs, and Chu Hsi.

Informed and inspired by Ch'eng-Chu philosophy, the Neo-Confucians could offer striking interpretations and refutations of Buddhist and Taoist teachings. The literati claimed that the Buddhists were world denying and life denying because Buddhism warned against clinging to this life and its experiences. They argued that the Taoists tended toward self-preservation and nonparticipation on the one hand or magico-religious penance on the other. Neo-Confucianism affirmed this world and this life; it advocated improving the quality of life for all. Rather than nonparticipation or life denial, Neo-Confucianism uttered an emphatic yes to life.

CONFUCIANISM IN PREMODERN AND MODERN CHINA (1279–1948 C.E.)

During the Yuan (1279–1368), Ming (1368–1644), and Ch'ing (1644–1911) dynasties, Neo-Confucianism was a strong, if not dominant, force pervading Chinese society. We shall investigate how it faced the challenges of those times and discuss Western influence on China as it began to be strongly felt from the nineteenth century onward. Obvious signs of the decline of Neo-Confucianism were evident by 1912, when China changed from a dynastic to a republican form of government. With the communist takeover in 1949, all traditional Chinese religions were suppressed.

The Yuan dynasty ascended in 1279. China under Mongol rule did not progress to a higher level of intellectual sophistication; the Yuan rulers did not value scholarship as much as their predecessors. Yet because of the usefulness of the literati in government, the Great Khan appointed a Confucian scholar, Hsu Heng, president of the Imperial Academy. Hsu Heng took a practical approach and presented Neo-Confucianism to Yuan rulers in a much simplified form, focusing on Chu Hsi's *Elementary Education (Hsiao Hsueh)* and the *Four Books*. Evidently he was successful, because in 1313 the Mongol ruler promulgated an official edict making the *Four Books* and the *Five Classics* the basic texts for the civil service exams. The edict remained in force until 1905.

The notion of teaching and practicing Confucianism in a practical way (with fewer behavioral rules and less metaphysical speculation) became a theme for many literati in these centuries. During the Ming dynasty (1368–1644), China was pervaded by syncretism as the first Ming emperor proclaimed the importance of each of the "three teachings"—Confucianism, Taoism, and Buddhism. This meant, for example, that all were to show due respect for the Taoist priests who performed court ceremonies for the emperor. It also meant that anyone wishing a government position had to master Confucian literature. It even involved the creation of a syncretic religious sect by

Confucian scholar Lin Chao-en (1517–1598). Lin explicitly combined the teachings of Confucianism, Taoism, and Buddhism. Explicit and implicit syncretism and various modes of mutual influence were especially common in the Ming years. We mention just two more examples: It was not uncommon for the literati to practice some form of Buddhism or Taoism. Buddhists, in turn, absorbed Confucianism; for example, the Buddhist monk Yun-ch'i Chu-hung published morality books into which he incorporated Confucian values. Folk religion was also combined with the "three teachings" in multifarious ways, and Chinese state religion continued right down into the twentieth century (to 1911).

The outstanding Confucian thinker of the day was Wang Yang-ming (1492–1529), the greatest Neo-Confucian after Chu Hsi. In harmony with the practical theme referred to earlier, Wang tended to eschew speculative metaphysics and was indeed a man of action, serving many years as a government official and military leader. Wang taught that knowledge and action are one: a person who knows the duty of filial piety, for example, will fulfill his or her duty, and only in these actions will he or she attain genuine understanding. Like Chu Hsi, Wang believed in the pervasive power of principle; but for Wang, principle and the mind were one. Wang was the outstanding advocate of this emphasis on the mind, the most important minority position among Neo-Confucians. According to Wang, apart from the mind, neither law nor objects exists. This is a form of philosophical idealism (the view that mental events are the fundamental realities), but because understanding comes only through action, it may be called "dynamic idealism." Wang Yang-ming's main thrust was moral education and moral action.

Two striking examples of the Confucianization of other Asian societies—Korea and Japan—deserve mention here. The Yi (Choson) dynasty in Korea was thoroughly Confucian in court policies and elite culture. Even today the vitality of Confucian tradition is widely felt in South Korea as manifest in political behavior, legal practice, ancestral veneration, and village schools.

Although not as thorough as the Confucianization of Korea, the role of Confucianism in Japan has been very strong—a point lost on many westerners who may know of only Japanese Shinto and Buddhism. As early as the seventh century C.E., the Japanese prince Shotoku compared Japanese religion to a tree: Shinto is the root, Confucianism the trunk and branches, and Buddhism the flowers and fruits.[43] In the seventeenth century the Tokugawa rulers saw to a more thorough Confucianization, and its legacy is still in evidence today. It can even be argued that Japanese companies are operated on the model of the Confucian family, including the key virtues of loyalty on the part of the workers and benevolent paternalism on the part of the executives. Princeton University professor of sociology Gilbert Rozman goes so far as to claim that modern Japanese Confucianism is superior to that of China: "Japan's greater success in modernization can be attributed partially to the greater ability to harness Confucian traditions to modern need."[44]

The last Chinese dynasty, the Ch'ing (1644–1911), was still quite Confucian; the dominant influences, though somewhat diminished, were the philosophies of Chu Hsi and Wang Yang-ming. But there was also a reaction against Neo-Confucianism on the part of some Confucians who called themselves the School of Han Learning. Placing strong emphasis on a kind of realism, literati such as Yen Yuan and Tai Chen argued that principle cannot be understood by intellectual speculation or intuition but rather through objective, critical, and analytical observation of things.

As Western influence gradually increased in the nineteenth century, the dominant Chinese response was well summarized in the motto "Chinese studies for substance, Western studies for function"; in the face of Western economic and military superiority, many literati called for adherence to Confucian views of humanity and society (substance) while also accepting Western technology (function):

What we then have to learn from the barbarians (Western foreigners) is only one thing, solid ships and effective guns. . . .

If we let Chinese ethics and famous [Confucian] teachings serve as an original foundation, and let them be supplemented by the methods used by the various nations for the attainment of prosperity and strength, would it not be the best of all procedures?[45]

Chinese views of westernization were not all opportunistic or mere reactions to Western encroachment. If we look at the question of the wisdom of westernization from the perspective of many leading Neo-Confucians, westernization can be seen as being motivated by ancient Confucian goals.[46] The perennial goals of Confucianism include national oneness, order, and economic well-being—the peoples' livelihood, not mere greed or desire for a high standard of living. Because of these concerns, the literati were frustrated and saddened by their nation's shortage of wealth and power. Some of them reasoned that a more thorough westernization, not merely Western technology, might be a way to achieve China's ancient goals. In any case, the literati could not simply turn within and attain self-fulfillment while the mass of peasants suffered; in a sense, "inner sageliness" calls for success in "outer kingliness." Such was the literati's predicament.

Chinese philosophers and political leaders considered a wide range of options. Should they attempt a return to Han Confucian teachings or continue to apply the Neo-Confucianism of Chu Hsi and Wang Yang-ming? Should they accept the individualistic ethic and political ideology of the West, or should they consider the communist ideology of the Marxists? Some literati forthrightly advocated the importation of Western technology and methods of political participation, but they rejected Western individualism in favor of their own concept of the self that is guided by moral obligation. Although freedom of the individual is not a priority for Confucians, this does not mean the denial of self-assertion. Confucianism values interdependence but does not advocate hierarchy and dependence in a way that suppresses the individual's moral integrity.[47]

Elderly men in traditional attire talking at a Confucian ceremony in Seoul, South Korea (1989).

Foreign influence and political changes accelerated toward the end of the nineteenth century, leaving the Ch'ing government behind the times. By 1899, China had fought and lost short wars with Japan, France, and Britain and it had lost territory or political influence to Russia, Germany, France, and Japan. A wave of antiforeign sentiment spread throughout China and took the form of open rebellion—the Boxer Rebellion. The Ch'ing rulers, caught in the middle of this turmoil, decided to abolish the civil service exam system in 1905 in favor of a Western system of education. This decision was a serious defeat for the literati because the traditional education system had been a major function of Confucianism and a means of instilling Confucian values. With the establishment of the

CHRONOLOGY OF CONFUCIANISM

ANCIENT PAST	Legendary kings Yao and Shun exemplify virtue
551	Birth of Confucius
371	Birth of Mencius
136 B.C.E.	Emperor Wu Ti establishes the Confucian *Five Classics* as the basis for civil service examinations
PERIOD OF DISUNION (220–589)	
	Community and family life is based on Confucian rules

Republic in 1912, the official sacrifice to Confucius and Heaven was terminated. The tide had now turned in favor of Western forms of education and government.

The first several decades of the twentieth century brought widespread turbulence to Chinese cities, resulting in the destruction or occupation of thousands of temples. Anti-Confucian rhetoric was common. In the 1920s filial piety was often condemned as "a big factory for the manufacture of obedient students." Confucius-bashers declared Confucianism unfit for modernity and raised the cry, "Destroy the old curiosity shop of Confucius!" However, in 1939, just at the beginning of World War II, a leading Chinese philosopher, Fung Yu-lan, published a widely respected reconstruction of the Ch'eng-Chu school of Neo-Confucianism.[48] Even after World War II, China was still torn by strife; the Nationalists (Kuomintang) battled Mao Tse Tung's communist movement in civil war from 1945 to 1949.

Before discussing the People's Republic of China, we offer a brief account of one of the last public ceremonies honoring Confucius before the victory of communist forces in 1949. For about thirty years (1949–1978), Confucianism would be severely suppressed by the new communist government.

On Confucius's birthday, which fell on August 27, 1948, fairly elaborate ceremonies in Shanghai were conducted by the mayor, K. C. Wu, a Protestant Christian. The hall was decorated in traditional manner, incense was burning before the altar, and after a presentation everyone bowed before the Confucian tablet.[49] Essentially the same ceremony was performed in Canton in 1949, even though the communist armies were about to enter the province of Kwang tung. There were lectures on Confucianism sponsored by many cultural and educational organizations, and there was a commemorative bulletin in honor of the 2,500th birthday of Confucius.[50]

THE PEOPLE'S REPUBLIC OF CHINA (1949 C.E. TO THE PRESENT)

Beginning in 1949, official Chinese communist pronouncements boldly criticized Confucianism for impeding progress by clinging to the past, for being feudalistic and autocratic, and for placing family loyalties above the well-being of all. Flurries of conferences repeated these attacks in 1963 and as the communist Cultural Revolution began in 1966. Portraits of Confucius were carried through the streets of Canton bearing the caption "I am an ox, a demon, a snake, and a devil."[51] The Red Guards even defaced Confucius's tomb in Ch'u-fu (Qufu) in Shantung

800–1100	Emergence of Neo-Confucianism; literati such as Han Yu, Ch'eng Hao, and Ch'eng I flourish
1130	Birth of Chu Hsi, the foremost Neo-Confucian philosopher
1492	Birth of Wang Yang-ming, a major Neo-Confucian philosopher
1600–1700	Japanese leaders Confucianize Japan
1949–1978	Communists suppress Confucianism, along with all other religions
1978 TO PRESENT	Partial revival of Confucianism and all other religions

province—the ultimate desecration in the Chinese context. Among communist intellectuals, Confucianism was viewed as more detrimental to society by those who defined it as a religion; those who saw it as a mere philosophy or system of ethics held it in less contempt. This point is worth noting because it may be a partial determinant of the fate of Confucianism in Communist China.

In 1978 the political climate changed as more moderate leadership allowed the formation of Confucian study societies. By 1985, official pronouncements stated that Confucius was "neither a god nor a devil." Intellectuals such as Tu Wei Ming of Harvard have been impressed by the increase in Confucian studies in China—"[research and study] with a dynamism unprecedented since the May Fourth Movement of 1919."[52]

Also telling are the ritual celebrations of Confucius's birthday at the site of his tomb in the town where he was born (Ch'u-fu). These signs of renewed respect for Confucius began again in 1986, after thirty-seven years of communist suppression. The ceremonies are performed with great pageantry in the old Confucian temple, a vast complex of buildings on the site where the original buildings were constructed in the fifth century B.C.E. Drums, music, incense, and offerings express renewed devotion to Master K'ung.[53]

CONTEMPORARY CONFUCIANISM

Can the literati take the lead in revitalizing Confucian tradition after some thirty or forty years of disruption? Is Confucianism dead? These will be our leading questions as we examine the problems and prospects of Confucianism. Even if Confucianism is not dead, does its life consist only as a subject of study and a set of memorial ceremonies?

Sociologist C. K. Yang has argued that the tradition cannot be effective today because of its "stifling ritualism, its authoritarianism, and its association with a monarchical social order."[54] Some other scholars disagree, pointing out that Confucianism can adapt its social rituals and reanimate its concept of interdependence in opposition to both dependence and individualism.[55] Confucian texts do not clearly call for slavish devotion to authority figures; however, they clearly deny the validity of individualism. In condemning individualism, Confucianism is in agreement with communist theory, and the government has publicly recognized the validity of Confucianism on this score. Both the Confucians and the communists see an emphasis on individual rights as an invitation to selfishness. Chinese communists have also affirmed that filial piety (respectful behavior toward, and caring for, parents and elders) can be a socially valid practice, because it relieves the state of an obligation that is more appropriate to the family. The prospect that Confucianism may be adapted to the needs of today and the future seems to depend in part on its nontheistic social philosophy. Its focus is primarily upon society, not upon Heaven or the divine. Therefore, a syncretism with atheistic communism is a real possibility.

The question of the adaptability of Confucianism today can be explored by considering the role of women. We have already seen that Confucian ethics relegated women to an inferior position; a good woman was docile and subordinate. Confucianism tended to restrict women more than did Buddhism or Taoism (the latter including the importance of *yin* energy in its metaphysics and being less concerned with strict social order than was Confucianism). Confucians were not in the forefront of the reform movements of the nineteenth century; the communists continued the modernization process in 1950 by outlawing arranged marriages, female infanticide, and other practices that demeaned women.

The future of Confucianism depends on its ability to adapt to modern reform movements regarding women's rights and other social issues. We believe the matter comes down to this question: Can the great themes and goals of the tradition, such as achieving *jen,* be pursued by adapting and changing the *li* to fit the modern world? The Confucian emphasis on moral integrity over acquisitiveness and the goal of loving respect are worthy indeed, but what social policies and behaviors *(li)* will be acceptable in a modern communist society and at the same time actually effect these ends? We cannot answer the question today because the policies of the People's Republic of China are still evolving, but we hope we have at least raised the question that holds the key to the future of the tradition.

GLOSSARY OF CONFUCIANISM

ch'ing ming   a ceremony associated with cleaning the graves of the ancestors.

equilibrium   the fundamental nature of humans; the condition before joy, sorrow, and the other emotions arise; in the broadest sense, the foundation of the world. The Chinese term is often translated as *mean*.

filial piety *(hsiao)*   respect for parents and all elders; one of the most important foundational virtues of human society.

Five Great Relationships
    the father-son, elder brother–younger brother, husband-wife, elder-junior, and ruler-subject relationships; the basic relationships upon which society is built.

Great Ultimate (T'ai Chi)
    the Neo-Confucian concept of the overarching principle or principle of principles. The Great Ultimate is present in reality-as-a-whole and in each individual thing.

Heaven   the great spiritual power from which all truth and moral principle derives. The term is sometimes used to refer to a power with personal traits, but most literati think of Heaven as an impersonal spiritual power.

jen (ren)   the cardinal virtue of the superior person: the virtue of loving respect. Other translations include *human-heartedness, goodness,* and *altruistic love.*

ju (ru)   literati; Confucian scholar.

K'ung fu-tzu   Confucius.

Legalism   a non-Confucian philosophy of governing that called for autocratic rule and many specific laws that were to be strictly enforced.

li   traditional, respectful behavior patterns or rules; propriety.

literati *(ju)*   Confucian scholars; sometimes viewed as scholar-officials because of the role of the literati in government.

mandate of heaven   divine sanction of rulers. Confucians believe the sanction is based solely on merit.

Ming T'ang phenomenon
    the construction and use of halls or houses for the worship of ancestors and major deities; "halls of light."

principle   that which makes a thing what it is; essence. Principle is a key concept in Neo-Confucian philosophy.

superior person *(chung-tzu)*

> a noble person defined by moral character; the ideal person in the *Analects* and other texts.

Taoist Confucianism

> a small movement stemming from the attempt by scholars such as Yang Hsiung (53 B.C.E.–18 C.E.) to base Confucian ethics on Taoist cosmology. Yang taught that following the Tao (the way of nature) will lead one to practice the Confucian virtues of loyalty and filial piety.

For Further Study

Chan, Wing-tsit. *A Source Book in Chinese Philosophy*. Princeton, N.J.: Princeton University Press, 1963.

> *An excellent collection of readings and commentary by a first-rate scholar.*

DeBary, William Theodore, comp. *Sources of Chinese Tradition*. New York: Columbia University Press, 1960.

> *A comprehensive anthology that includes scriptures, philosophy, and some more popular literature.*

Fingarette, Herbert. *Confucius: The Secular As Sacred*. New York: Harper & Row, 1972.

> *An insightful philosophical reflection on Confucius's teachings.*

Fung, Yu-lan. *A Short History of Chinese Philosophy*. Edited by Derk Bodde. New York: Free Press, 1966.

> *A great modern scholar's history, published in the period of suppression.*

Graham, A. C. *Disputers of the Tao: Philosophical Arguments in Ancient China*. Lasalle, Ill.: Open Court, 1989.

> *A helpful study for advanced students.*

Pas, Julian, ed. *The Turning of the Tide: Religion in China Today*. London and New York: Oxford University Press, 1990.

> *An excellent collection of articles about the revival of Chinese religion.*

Thompson, Laurence G. *Chinese Religion: An Introduction*. 4th ed. Belmont, Calif.: Wadsworth, 1989.

> *Although subtitled "An Introduction," a good connecting link between* Patterns of Faith *and advanced studies. The book is remarkably readable for a sophisticated piece of work.*

———. *The Chinese Way in Religion*. Belmont Calif.: Wadsworth, 1973.

> *A companion to the previous book, the* Way *is an anthology of writings that may be difficult for some readers.*

Waley, Arthur, trans. and annotator. *The Analects of Confucius.* New York: Random House, n.d.

>*A very readable translation.*

Yang, C. K. *Religion in Chinese Society.* Los Angeles: University of California Press, 1961.

>*Still one of the best sociological studies of Chinese religion.*

READINGS

Reading 7.1   THE FOUNDER'S WORDS: *ANALECTS OF CONFUCIUS*

The Chinese title of the book excerpted here is *Lun Yu*, meaning "selected sayings." It was written down one or two generations after Confucius, and it probably contains sections that are not from Confucius himself. However, as the best single direct source of information about Confucius and his teachings, it now stands as a basic sourcebook for that body of teachings. Authenticity debates aside, the *Analects* has the ring of a true book of wisdom. Based on "Glimpses of Confucius" (see the Reading), how would you describe Confucius in modern terms; that is, how would you describe him to someone living today? Based on Reading 7.1, explain what Confucius envisages as the ideal society. What would it be like?

GLIMPSES OF CONFUCIUS

Confucius said, "At fifteen my mind was set on learning. At thirty my character had been formed. At forty I had no more perplexities. At fifty I knew the Mandate of Heaven (T'ien-ming). At sixty I was at ease with whatever I heard. At seventy I could follow my heart's desire without transgressing moral principles." (2:4)

The guardian of the frontier-mound at I (on the border of the state of Wei) asked to be presented to the Master, saying, No gentleman arriving at this frontier has ever yet failed to accord me an interview. The Master's followers presented him. On going out the man said, Sirs, you must not be disheartened by his failure. It is now a very long while since the Way prevailed in the world. I feel sure that Heaven intends to use your Master as a wooden bell. (3:24)

Tzu-kung said, Our Master's views concerning culture and the outward insignia of goodness, we are permitted to hear; but about Man's nature and the ways of Heaven he will not tell us anything at all. (5:12)

If at a meal the Master found himself seated next to someone who was in mourning, he did not eat his fill. When he had wailed at a funeral, during the rest of the day he did not sing. (7:9)

THE VIRTUES

The Master said, In serving his father and mother a man may gently remonstrate with them. But if he sees that he has failed to change their opinion, he should resume an attitude of deference and not thwart them; he may feel discouraged, but not resentful. (4:18)

The Master said, I have never yet seen anyone whose desire to build up his moral power was as strong as sexual desire. (9:17)

Yen Hui asked about Goodness [jen]. The Master said, (quoting from "an old record"), "He who can himself submit to ritual is Good." If (a ruler) could for one day "himself submit to ritual," everyone under Heaven would respond to his Goodness. For Goodness is something that must have its source in the ruler himself; it cannot be got from others.

Yen Hui said, I beg to ask for the more detailed items of this (submission to ritual). The Master said, To look at nothing in defiance of ritual, to listen to nothing in defiance of ritual, to speak of nothing in defiance of ritual, never to stir hand or foot in defiance of ritual. Yen Hui said, I know that I am not clever; but this is a saying that, with your permission, I shall try to put into practice. (12:1)

Jan Jung asked about Goodness. The Master said, Behave when away from home as through you were in the presence of an important guest. Deal with the common people as though you were officiating at an important sacrifice. Do not do to others what you would not like yourself. Then there will be no feelings of opposition to you, whether it is the affairs of a State that you are handling or the affairs of a Family.

Jan Yung said, I know that I am not clever; but this is a saying that, with your permission, I shall try to put into practice. (12:2)

Ssu-ma Niu asked about Goodness. The Master said, The Good (jen) man is chary of speech. Ssu-ma Niu said, So that is what is meant by Goodness—to be chary of speech? The Master said, Seeing that the doing of it is so difficult, how can one be otherwise than chary of talking about it? (12:3)

TYPES OF MEN

Tzu-kung asked about the true gentleman. The Master said, He does not preach what he practises till he has practised what he preaches. (2:13)

Master K'ung said, Highest are those who are born wise. Next are those who become wise by learning. After them come those who have to toil painfully in order to acquire learning. Finally, to the lowest class of the common people belong those who toil painfully without ever managing to learn. (16:9)

The Master said, A gentleman, in his plans, thinks of the Way; he does not think how he is going to make a living. Even farming sometimes entails times of shortage; and even learning may incidentally lead to high pay. But a gentleman's anxieties concern the progress of the Way; he has no anxiety concerning poverty. (15.31)

The Master said, It is wrong for a gentleman to have knowledge of menial matters and proper that he should be entrusted with great responsibilities. It is wrong for a small man to be entrusted with great responsibilities, but proper that he should have a knowledge of menial matters. (15:33)

GOVERNMENT

Tzu-kung asked about government. The Master said, sufficient food, sufficient weapons, and the confidence of the common people. Tzu-kung said, Suppose you had no choice but to dispense with one of these three, which would you forgo? The Master said, Weapons. Tzu-kung said, Suppose you were forced to dispense with one of the two that were left, which would you forgo? The Master said, Food. For from of old death has been the lot of all men; but a people that no longer trusts its ruler is lost indeed. (12:7)

Tzu-lu said, If the prince of Wei were waiting for you to come and administer his country for him, what would be your first measure? The Master said, It would certainly be to correct language. Tzu-lu said, Can I have heard you aright? Surely what you say has nothing to do with the matter. Why should language be corrected? The Master said, How boorish you are! A gentleman, when things he does not understand are mentioned, should maintain an attitude of reserve. If language is incorrect, then what is said does not concord with what was meant; and if what is said does not concord with what was meant, what is to be done cannot be effected. If what is to be done cannot be effected, then rites and music will not flourish. If rites and music do not flourish, then mutilations and lesser punishments will go astray. And if mutilations and lesser punishments go astray, then the people have nowhere to put hand or foot.

Therefore the gentleman uses only such language as is proper for speech, and only speaks of what it would be proper to carry into effect. The gentleman, in what he says, leaves nothing to mere chance. (13:3)

The Master said, "Only if the right sort of people had charge of a country for a hundred years would it become really possible to stop cruelty and do away with slaughter." How true the saying is! (13:11)

Source: Arthur Waley, trans. and annotator, *The Analects of Confucius* (Winchester, Mass.: Allen & Unwin, 1983).

Reading 7.2 THE SECOND GREAT CONFUCIAN: MENCIUS

As a writer and adept arguer, Mencius (371–289 B.C.E.) was responsible for maintaining a place for Confucius's teachings at a time when many voices vied for a hearing. More than that, Mencius added a number of important points to Confucius's teachings (for example, the doctrine of the innate goodness of humanity). He held firmly to Confucius's stress on the primacy of the family, as can be seen in the passage on filial piety presented here. Mencius is again a follower of Confucius in tying his well-field system strictly to a two-class system: gentlemen and countrymen. (The shape of this land division system resembles the Chinese character for "well," and it is therefore so named.) Do the first two passages (on human nature and humane government) contradict each other by saying that human beings are good and then saying that people may fall into depravity? Based on the tone and content of these passages, do you think rulers would have resented Mencius's counsel?

HUMAN NATURE

Mencius said: "All men have a sense of commiseration. The ancient kings had this commiserating heart and hence a commiserating government. When a commiserating government is conducted from a commiserating heart, one can rule the whole empire as if one were turning it on one's palm. Why I say all men have a sense of commiseration is this: Here is a man who suddenly notices a child about to fall into a well. Invariably he will feel a sense of alarm and compassion. And this is not for the purpose of gaining the favor of the child's parents, or seeking the approbation of his neighbors and friends, or for fear of blame should he fail to rescue it. Thus we see that no man is without a sense of compassion, or a sense of shame, or a sense of courtesy, or a sense of right and wrong. The sense of compassion is the beginning of humanity; the sense of shame is the beginning of righteousness; the sense of courtesy is the beginning of decorum; the sense of right and wrong is the beginning of wisdom. . . ."

HUMANE GOVERNMENT

Mencius said to King Hsuan of Ch'i: . . . "Only the true scholar is capable of maintaining, without certain means of livelihood, a steadfast heart. As for the multitude, if they have no certain means of livelihood, they surely cannot maintain a steadfast heart. Without a steadfast heart, they are likely to abandon themselves to any and all manner of depravity. If you wait till they have lapsed into crime and then mete out punishment, it is like placing traps for the people. If a humane ruler is on the throne how can he permit such a thing as placing traps for the people? Therefore, when an intelligent ruler regulates the livelihood of the people, he makes sure that they will have enough to serve their parents on the one hand and to support their wives and children on the other, so that in good years all may eat their fill and in bad years no one need die of starvation. Thus only will he urge them to walk the path of virtue, and the people will follow him effortlessly. But as the people's livelihood is ordered at present, they do not have enough to serve their parents on the one hand or to support their wives and children on the other. Even in good years life is one long struggle and in bad years death becomes all but inevitable. Such being the case, they are only anxiously trying to stay alive. What leisure have they for cultivating decorum and righteousness? . . ."

THE WELL-FIELD SYSTEM

Duke Wen of T'eng sent Pi Chan to Mencius to learn about the well-field land system. Mencius said: "Now that your prince has made up his mind to put through a humane measure in government and has appointed you to carry it out, you must do your best. At the bottom of all humane government, we might say, lies the system of land division and demarcation. When the land system is not in proper operation, then the well-field farms are not equally distributed among the farmers or the grain for salaries equitably apportioned among the ministers. So a wicked lord or a corrupt magistrate usually lets the land system fall into disuse. When the land system is in proper operation, on the other hand, the distribution of land and the apportioning of salaries can be settled where you sit.

"Although T'eng is a small state, yet there must be those who are gentlemen and those who are countrymen. Without the gentlemen there would be none to rule the countrymen; without the countrymen there would be none to feed the gentlemen.

"In the surrounding country let the land tax be fixed at one part in nine to be paid according to the well-field group plan, while within the limits of the state capital let it be one in ten to be paid individually. For all officers, from the chief ministers down, there should be sacrificial land, in lots of fifty mu *[*mu = one-sixth acre*]. For all extra-quota men in a household there should be additional land, in lots of twenty-five* mu. *Whether in burying the dead or in house-moving, a family does not go beyond the district. Within the district those whose farms belong to the same well-field unit befriend one another in their going out and coming in, practice mutual aid in their self-defense, and uphold one another in sickness. Thus the people learn to live in affection and harmony.*

"Each well-field unit is one li [li = one-third mile] square and contains nine hundred mu of land. The center lot is the public field. The eight households each own a hundred-mu farm and collaborate in cultivating the public field. When the public field has been properly attended, then they may attend to their own work. This is how the countrymen are taught their status.

"The above are the main features of the system. As to adapting to your present circumstances, it is up to you and your prince." (3A:3, 13–20)

THE RIGHT TO REVOLUTION

King Hsuan of Ch'i asked: "Is it not true that T'ang banished Chieh and that King Wu smote Chou?" Mencius replied: "It is so stated in the records." The king asked: "May a subject, then, slay his sovereign?" Mencius replied: "He who outrages humanity is a scoundrel; he who outrages righteousness is a scourge. A scourge or a scoundrel is a despised creature [and no longer a king]. I have heard that a despised creature called Chou was put to death, but I have not heard anything about the murdering of a sovereign." (1B:8)

DEFENSE OF FILIAL PIETY

Now that sage-kings are no longer with us, the feudal lords yield to their lusts and idle scholars indulge in senseless disputation. The words of Yang Chu and Mo Ti fill the land, and the talk of the land is either Yang Chu or Mo Ti. Yang is for individualism, which does not recognize the sovereign; Mo is for universal love, which does not recognize parents. To be without sovereign or parent is to be a beast. (3B:9)

Mencius said: "Of services which is the greatest? The service of parents is the greatest. Of charges which is the greatest? The charge of oneself is the greatest. Not failing to keep oneself and thus being able to serve one's parents—this I have heard of. Failing to keep oneself and yet being able to serve one's parents—this I have not heard of." (4A:19)

Mencius said: "There are three things which are unfilial, and the greatest of them is to have no posterity." (4A:26)

Mencius said: "The substance of humanity is to serve one's parents; the basis of righteousness is to obey one's elder brothers." (4A:27)

Source: William Theodore DeBary, comp., *Sources of Chinese Tradition* (New York: Columbia University Press, 1960). Reprinted by permission of Columbia University Press.

Reading 7.3   THE GREAT ULTIMATE OF CHU HSI: THE *CHU TZU CH'UAN-SHU*

The twelfth-century Confucian philosopher Chu His (1130–1200 C.E.) added a complete metaphysics to Confucian ethics, thus making Confucianism a more complete philosophy. We see in the following passage that Chu Hsi is dealing in his own way with traditional Chinese notions like Tao, *yin/yang,* and Heaven and earth. Chu Hsi is the key thinker of the Neo-Confucian movement. Based on this reading, how would you compare or contrast the concept of the Great Ultimate with the Taoist concept of Tao, or with the Judeo-Christian concept of God? How is it that the Great Ultimate can be a single reality and yet be present in the many things of the world?

Question: The Great Ultimate is not a thing existing in a chaotic state before the formation of Heaven and earth, but a general name for the principles of Heaven and earth and the myriad things. Is that correct?

Answer: The Great Ultimate is merely the principle of Heaven and earth and the myriad things. With respect to Heaven and earth, there is the Great Ultimate in them. With respect to the myriad things, there is the Great Ultimate in each and every one of them. Before Heaven and earth existed, there was assuredly this principle. It is the principle that through movement generates the yang. It is also this principle that through tranquillity generates the yin. [49:8b–9a]

Question: [In your commentary on Chou Tun-yi's *T'ung shu*], you said: "Principle is a single, concrete entity, and the myriad things partake of it as their reality. Hence each of the myriad things possesses in it a Great Ultimate." According to this theory, does the Great Ultimate not split up into parts?

Answer: Fundamentally there is only one Great Ultimate, yet each of the myriad things has been endowed with it and each in itself possesses the Great Ultimate in its entirety. This is similar to the fact that there is only one moon in the sky but when its light is scattered upon rivers and lakes, it can be seen everywhere. It cannot be said that the moon has been split. [49:10b–11a]

The Great Ultimate is not spatially conditioned; it has neither corporeal form nor body. There is no spot where it may be placed. When it is considered in the state before activity begins, this state is nothing but tranquillity, Now activity, tranquillity, yin and yang are all within the realm of corporeality. However, activity is after all the activity of the Great Ultimate and tranquillity is also its tranquillity, although activity and tranquillity themselves are not the Great Ultimate. This is why Master Chou Tun-yi spoke only of that state as Non-ultimate. While the state before activity begins cannot be spoken of as the Great Ultimate, nevertheless the principle of pleasure, anger, sorrow, and joy are already inherent in it. Pleasure and joy belong to yang and anger and sorrow belong to yin. In the initial stage the four are not manifested, but their principles are already there. As contrasted with the state after activity begins, it may be called the Great Ultimate. But still it is difficult to say. All this is but a vague description. The truth must be genuinely and earnestly realized by each individual himself. [49:11a–b]

Someone asked about the Great Ultimate.

Answer: The Great Ultimate is simply the principle of the highest good. Each and every person has in him the Great Ultimate and each and every thing has in it the Great Ultimate. What Master Chou called the Great Ultimate is an appellation for all virtues and the highest good in Heaven and earth, man and things. [49:11b]

The Great Ultimate is similar to the top of a house or the zenith of the sky, beyond which point there is no more. It is the ultimate of principle. Yang is active and yin is tranquil. In these it is not the Great Ultimate that acts or remains tranquil. It is simply that there are the principles of activity and tranquillity. Principle is not visible; it becomes visible through yin and yang. Principle attaches itself to yin and yang as a man sits astride a horse. As soon as yin and yang produce the five agents, they are confined and fixed by physical nature and are thus differentiated into individual things each with its nature. But the Great Ultimate is in all of them. [49:13a]

Source: *Chu Tzu Ch'uan-shu,* trans. Wing-Tsit Chan, in Wing-Tsit Chan, *A Source Book in Chinese Philosophy* (Princeton, N.J.: Princeton University Press, 1963). Renewed ©1963. Reprinted by permission.

Reading 7.4   THE RELEVANCE OF CONFUCIANISM TODAY   Herbert Fingarette

Can Confucianism be relevant to a person living in the West twenty-five centuries after Confucius? And is Confucianism really a religious path? These two questions deserve answers, and the following passage attempts to provide those answers. If Herbert Fingarette is correct, Confucianism is indeed a universal religion. Try to give an example of *li* and explain how it is "magical" in Fingarette's sense.

When I began to read Confucius, I found him to be a prosaic and parochial moralizer; his collected sayings, the *Analects,* seemed to me an archaic irrelevance. Later, and with increasing force, I found him a thinker with profound insight and with an imaginative vision of man equal in its grandeur to any I know. Increasingly, I have become convinced that Confucius can be a teacher to us today—a major teacher, not one who merely gives us a slightly exotic perspective on the ideas already current. He tells us things not being said elsewhere; things needing to be said. He has a new lesson to teach.

The remarks which follow are aimed at revealing the magic power which Confucius saw, quite correctly, as the very essence of human virtue. It is finally by way of the magical that we can also arrive at the best vantage point for seeing the holiness in human existence which Confucius saw as central. In the twentieth century this central role of the holy in Confucius's teaching has been largely ignored because we have failed to grasp the existential point of that teaching.

By "magic" I mean the power of a specific person to accomplish his will directly and effortlessly through ritual, gesture and incantation. The user of magic does not work by strategies and devices as means toward an end; he does not use coercion or physical forces. There are no pragmatically developed and tested strategies or tactics. He simply wills the end in the proper ritual setting and with the proper ritual gesture and word; without further effort on his part, the deed is accomplished. Confucius's words at times strongly suggest some fundamental magical power as central to this way.

Confucius saw, and tried to call to our attention, that the truly, distinctively human powers have, characteristically, a magical quality. His task, therefore, required, in effect, that he reveal what is already so familiar and universal as to be unnoticed. What is necessary in such cases is that one come upon this "obvious" dimension of our existence in a new way, in the right way. Where can one find such a new path to this familiar area, one which provides a new and revealing perspective? Confucius found the path: we go by way of the notion of *li.*

One has to labor long and hard to learn *li.* The word in its root meaning is close to "holy ritual," "sacred ceremony." Characteristic of Confucius's teaching is the use of the language and imagery of *li* as a medium within which to talk about the entire body of the *mores,* or more precisely, of the authentic tradition and reasonable conventions of society. Confucius taught that the ability to act according to *li* and the will to submit to *li* are essential to that perfect and peculiarly human virtue or power which can be man's. Confucius thus does two things here: he calls our attention to the entire body of tradition and convention, and he calls upon us to see all this by means of a metaphor, through the imagery of sacred ceremony, holy rite.

The (spiritually) noble man is one who has labored at the alchemy of fusing social forms *(li)* and raw personal existence in such a way that they transmuted into a way of being which realizes *te*, the distinctively human virtue or power.

The novel and creative insight of Confucius was to see this aspect of human existence, its form as learned tradition and convention, in terms of a particular revelatory image: *li*, i.e., "holy rite," "sacred ceremony," in the usual meaning of the term prior to Confucius.

In general, what Confucius brings out in connection with the workings of ceremony is not only its distinctively human character, its linguistic and magical character, but also its moral and religious character. Here, finally, we must recall and place at the focus of our analysis the fact that for Confucius it is the imagery of Holy Ceremony that unifies and infuses all these dimensions of human existence. Perhaps a modern Westerner would be tempted to speak of the "intelligent practice of learned conventions and language." This has a fashionably value-free, "scientific" ring. Indeed the contemporary analytical philosophers tend to speak this way and to be suitably common-sensical and restrained in their style. But this quite fails to accomplish what Confucius's central image did.

The image of Holy Rite as a metaphor of human existence brings foremost to our attention the dimension of the holy in man's existence. There are several dimensions of Holy Rite which culminate in its holiness. Rite brings out forcefully not only the harmony and beauty of social forms, the inherent and ultimate dignity of human intercourse; it brings out also the moral perfection implicit in achieving one's ends by dealing with others as beings of equal dignity, as free coparticipants in *li*. Furthermore, to act by ceremony is to be completely open to the other; for ceremony is public, shared, transparent; to act otherwise is to be secret, obscure and devious, or merely tyrannically coercive. It is in this beautiful and dignified, shared and open participation with others who are ultimately like oneself (12:2) that man realizes himself. Thus perfect community of men—the Confucian analogue to Christian brotherhood—becomes an inextricable part, the chief aspect, of Divine worship—again an analogy with the central Law taught by Jesus.

Confucius wanted to teach us, as a corollary, that sacred ceremony in its narrower, root meaning is not a totally mysterious appeasement of spirits external to human and earthly life. Spirit is no longer an external being influenced by the ceremony; it is that that is expressed and comes most alive in the ceremony. Instead of being diversion of attention from the human realm to another transcendent realm, the overtly holy ceremony is to be seen as the central symbol, both expressive of and participating in the holy as a dimension of all truly human existence. Explicitly Holy Rite is thus a luminous point of concentration in the greater and ideally all-inclusive ceremonial harmony of the perfectly humane civilization of the *Tao*, or ideal Way. Human life in its entirety finally appears as one vast, spontaneous and holy Rite: the community of man. This, for Confucius, was indeed an "ultimate concern"; it was, he said, again and again, the only thing that mattered, more than the individual's life itself. (*Analects* 3:17; 4:5, 6, 8)

Source: Herbert Fingarette, *Confucius: The Secular As Sacred* (New York: Harper & Row, 1972). ©1972 by Herbert Fingarette. Reprinted by permission of HarperCollins Publishers, Inc.

Reading 7.5   CONFUCIANISM AND THE FUTURE OF CHINA   Tu Wei Ming

This excerpt takes a penetrating look at the potential of Confucianism in China. How can Confucianism function in synthesis with Western technology and socialist ideology? We feel the author, Harvard University professor Tu Wei Ming, raises the right questions in the right way. Ming begins by noting that there is a revival of religion in China today. Does Ming's concept of Confucianism fit what you learned in this chapter? What is the predicament faced by Confucian scholars in attempting to revive Confucianism or Confucian thought today?

CONFUCIANISM AND THE SOCIALIST IDEOLOGY

The sound and sight of these apparently religious activities does not mean that the political leadership in the People's Republic of China, by allowing a certain measure of religious freedom is no longer concerned about the Marxist-Leninist stance on ideological purity. For me, the intriguing question is, given that the majority of the Chinese intellectuals do not seek membership in any organized religion, in what sense are they religious? The Chinese Christians, Muslims, Buddhists and Taoists do not present us with serious theoretical problems. The conceptual apparatus at our disposal can be properly employed to understand comparatively and historically their ways of life in a secular state. The religiosity of the Chinese intellectual who is still profoundly influenced by the spiritual self-definition of the Confucian scholar, presents a serious challenge to us. It impels us to broaden our ordinary notions of being religious and reexamine our deeply held convictions that the secular cannot be sacred.

The common impression that Chinese are eclectic, practical, utilitarian and even worldly in their approach to religion has been enhanced by recent anthropological studies of popular beliefs in Taiwan. A field worker was surprised and somewhat amused to learn that a temple manager of a local cult near Taipei periodically reassigns seats of honor to a host of gods according to their performance. A god who fails to answer legitimate requests after proper prayers have been said and rituals observed is likely to be demoted, and moved from the top shelf to the bottom. This reminds us that in traditional China the earth god could be reprimanded, indeed removed by the magistrate, if he consistently failed to bring seasonable rains to the land. However, the Chinese ritual expert past and present knows that the imposition of human will and judgment on the supernatural order is always a grave matter. One rarely takes such action and when one does, it is accompanied by elaborate expiatory sacrifices. The temple manager, I surmise, knows what he is doing and knows the right way of doing it according to the rules of the local cult. His seemingly frivolous behavior is predicated on a deep-rooted Confucian belief: the human heart-and-mind has privileged access to the biddings of Heaven. By implication, the Confucian also believes that that which is truly human will necessarily be approved by the gods. Since one of the Confucian dicta insists that "Heaven sees as the people see and Heaven hears as the people hear," the will of Heaven is not only knowable but can very well be realized through the communal enterprise of human hearts and minds.

Being religious, in this sense, entails both a personal dialogical response to the transcendent and a communal act. The transcendent so conceived can simply mean that which is beyond. Understandably, filial love, social responsibility, party loyalty, and patriotism can all evoke strong "religious" sentiments in China. The Chinese intellectuals' preoccupation with China's modernization renders the collective endeavor to build a "modern socialist civilizational state with a chinese character" a "sacred" mission. In this perspective, the deification (or demonization) of Chairman Mao during the Cultural Revolution was not simply an historical accident. Nor was the acceptance of Marxist-Leninism as the revolutionary ideology which was deemed particularly fitting for saving China from perpetual backwardness and constant humiliation a simple strategic maneuver of the Chinese Communist Party. The tragic fate of China as a civilizational state and the sufferings of the Chinese people since the Opium War have made "saving the nation" an "ultimate concern" of the Chinese intelligentsia. The holocausts that the Chinese have endured have left deep scars on the Chinese soul but they have also engendered a collective consciousness unprecedented in Chinese history.

China has been blessed with the longest continuous cultural heritage in human history, as a good many Chinese scholars on both sides of the Taiwan Straits are fond of reminding their foreign audiences, but her memory of the recent past is painfully short. In the Chinese scheme of things, it is virtually impossible to imagine that a university has continuously operated as long as Harvard for example. They could not imagine that a school which was founded in the Ming dynasty (1368–1644), such as the famous Donglin Academy at Wuxi on the lower Yangzi River, could have survived the collapse of the Ming, the Manchu conquest, the Opium War, the Taiping Rebellion, the Boxer Uprising, the disintegration of the Qing dynasty, the internecine struggles among the warlords, the Northern Expedition, the Japanese aggression, the conflict between the Communists and the Nationalists, and the Cultural Revolution. The oldest modern institute of higher learning in China today, Peking University, can claim no more than ten years of uninterrupted existence.

Understandably, as the Chinese intellectuals re-emerge from the suffering and humiliation of the Cultural Revolution, their quest for personal dignity, communal participation and universal relevance evokes a new sense of urgency for the establishment of a corporate critical self-awareness which necessarily involves tapping the spiritual resources of their own indigenous traditions. The revival of Confucian studies both as an academic pursuit and as a cultural renaissance is a natural consequence of this collective intellectual concern. A recent bibliography on Confucius alone lists more than five hundred authors who published more than a thousand books and articles on the ancient sage in the last decade.

Ironically, however, an overwhelming sense of the weight of the feudal past still haunts the Chinese intellectual community. The intellectuals (including college students and professionals), the majority of whom are dedicated to reform, often consider the more than two thousand years of political culture in which authority features prominently as the regulator and arbiter of every conceivable arena of life the real enemy of modernization. To them, this old habit of the mind is ubiquitous:

statism, bureaucratism, nepotism, conservatism, and uniformism are either its blatant or insidious expressions. The recognition that this aspect of "feudalism" may have already become an integral part of the "psycho-cultural" construct of the Chinese has made many intellectuals staunch anti-traditionalists and, by implication, anti-Confucians.

The conflicting image of Confucianism as a humanist tradition that still defines the Chinese intellectual and as the feudal past that cannot be expunged from the collective consciousness of the Chinese people helps us to understand a dimension of Chinese religiosity which is most intriguing to the outside observer.

The vice president of the Chinese Academy of Social Sciences, Zhao Fusan, notes in a recent article, that the ideological scene in China for the next decade will be characterized by three major forces: Marxist-Leninist socialism, bourgeois capitalism and Confucian humanism. He hopes for a happy synthesis of (1) a revitalized Marxist-Leninism which will continue as the ideological foundation for building a socialist civilizational state, (2) the introduction of Western science, technology, market mechanism, industrial management, and even some measures of liberal democratic thought to ensure China's modernity and (3) the continuation of Confucian moral values to provide the modern socialist civilizational state with a distinct Chinese character. Unfortunately, in light of the crisis of faith in China in the post-Mao era, it is extremely difficult to prevent Marxist-Leninism from degenerating into dogmatic formalism. Likewise, Confucian humanism faces overwhelming odds in freeing itself from the perception that it is synonymous with "feudalism," and Western ideas have a hard time escaping the damnation of being labeled as spiritual pollutants.

The challenge for the Chinese intellectuals is complex indeed. Can they develop a communal critical self-consciousness nourished by the spiritual resources of the past and informed by the practical necessities of the present? The deification of Mao and the unquestioned loyalty to the Party clearly indicate that mass mobilization of energy (the communal act) for serving the state as the embodiment of the people (the transcendent) can be dangerously dehumanizing. An eclectic, practical, utilitarian and worldly approach to nation-building without probing the deep meaning of human existence may help China to be strong and wealthy in the short run but it cannot answer the basic question, for what purpose? Similarly, allowing organized religions limited freedom of expression without fundamentally restructuring the overall pattern of symbolic control, which is still dominated by the rhetoric of class struggle, dictatorship of the proletariat, democratic centralism and continuous revolution, may result in destructive tension between the faith communities and the secular state. In some quarters, such as Tibet and Inner Mongolia, the situation is explosive.

The Chinese belief that Heaven is not capricious or unknowable and that, through the cultivation of one's heart-and-mind, one can realize not only one's human nature but also the will of Heaven suggests a faith in the intrinsic worth of being human individually and communally. To Confucian intellectuals, the human condition here and now provides the basis for ultimate self-transformation. We are engaged, indeed embedded, in our humanness not by default but by choice. To know who we are is not merely to know that we are fated culturally and historically to be human in a particular sense; it is also to act communally and to respond faithfully and dialogically to a calling that is forever beyond our limited conception of humanity. To be fully human, which is tantamount to this Confucian meaning of being religious, is to engage ourselves in ultimate self-transformation as a faithful dialogical response to the transcendent and as a communal act. The question remains: is this enough to safeguard the dignity of the person, the authenticity of the fiduciary community and the truth and reality of the transcendent?

PLURALISM AND THE COMMON CREED.

The upsurge of activity in organized religions is a reflection of China's open-door policy. As this policy continues, pluralism both as an ideological stance and as an experienced reality seems inevitable. The perceived danger of the vulgarization of culture, the disintegration of society (especially the family) and the destabilizing influence on the political structure, as the result of intensified contact with the outside world, will have an effect on the ability of the reformers to sustain high-level support in the ruling minority as well as among the people. The voice of the intelligentsia (the scholars, writers, journalists and those who are characterized as workers in the theoretical fields who are charged with the responsibility of fixing the superstructure) will be critical in setting up the agenda for and adjudicating unavoidable conflicts in determining the priority of values in China's changing, indeed restless ideological landscape. Whether or not a new common creed will actually emerge, as the result of a confluence of many potentially contradictory streams of thought, the quest for a common creed despite pluralist tendencies will continue. This seems to me profoundly meaningful for students of religion. After all, the necessity for working toward a common creed in this pluralistic world of ours is urgent. The Chinese attempt is at least heuristically suggestive.

Source: Tu Wei Ming, "The Religious Situation in the People's Republic of China Today: A Personal Reflection," in *Religion in Today's World*, ed. Frank Whaling (Edinburgh: T & T Clark, 1987), pp. 285–291. Reprinted by permission of T & T Clark, Ltd.

CHAPTER 8

JUDAISM

A good starting point for the study of Judaism, the religion of the Jews, is the issue of Jewish identity. Who are the Jews? Hebrews, Israelites, and Jews are their oldest, most enduring names. The word *Hebrew* comes from a root that means "to cross over" and may have been derived from *Habiru,* a general term for nomadic groups living on the edges of urban centers in ancient Egypt and Mesopotamia. The Hebrews included a group known as Israelites, a name derived from the patriarch Jacob (Israel) and his twelve sons. In the biblical narrative, God changed Jacob's name to Israel because he had *"striven with God and with men and* [had] *prevailed"* (*Gen.* 32:28). The word *Jew* is derived from the Latin *Judaeus,* a transliteration of the Hebrew term *Yehudi,* which means "one who lives in Judah," the kingdom named after the fourth of Israel's sons. Initially, the term *Jew (Judaeus)* was a Greek and Roman designation for those who identified with the traditions of ancient Israel, but by the beginning of the common era it had become a form of Jewish self-identification.

What distinguishes Jews from non-Jews? The term *Jew* does not primarily designate a nationality; that is, Jews are not all citizens of modern Israel. The worldwide Jewish population is around 16 million; around

A synagogue in the Plaza Lavalle, Buenos Aires, Argentina. Note the star of David above the door. (ca. 1988–1995).

4.6 million Jews live in Israel, and 6 million live in North America (see Figure 8.1). Further, Israeli citizenship does not make one a Jew, as many Israelis (around 20 percent) are not Jewish. Most Jews who live outside of Israel have a deep attachment to Israel but are loyal citizens of other states. Jewishness is not simply a religious classification. Some Jews think of themselves as religious, and some do not; for example, the majority of Israeli Jews are secular and nonobservant. Traditionalists believe that trust in God and obedience to the divine commands are central to Jewishness and Judaism. For others, Jewishness is rooted in an identification with the Jewish people and culture rather than in God and observance of God's commands.

Who are the Jews? They are an ethnic community with a heritage that binds them together in spite of their diversity.

JUDAIC BELIEFS

There is no doctrine to which all religious Jews subscribe and no institution to which all of them belong. In a sense, because of the diversity of Judaic beliefs, it is easier to say what Jews do not believe than to identify a set of beliefs that they all share. Devout Jews do not accept the worldviews of non-Jewish religions; thus, they do not believe that Jesus is the **Messiah,** the expected redeemer of the Jewish people. As one **rabbi** (the title of an ordained Jewish leader) put it, the possibility that Jews who believe that Jesus is the Messiah are still Jews is "as impossible as Kosher pork."[1] Our treatment of Judaic belief is divided into sections on God, *Torah,* Israel, the nature and destiny of humans, and evil.

GOD

Although there are no creeds to which all Jews subscribe, Jews are not entirely bereft of doctrinal formulas. Two credos—the ***Shema*** (a daily prayer recit-

ed by observant Jews) and the thirteen principles of belief formulated by the renowned philosopher Moses Maimonides (1135–1204 C.E.)—contain the basic doctrines of classical Jewish theology. The *Shema* (Hebrew for "hear") begins with the proclamation *"Hear O Israel! The LORD is our God, the LORD alone. You shall love the LORD your God with all your heart and with all your soul and with all your might"* (*Deut.* 6:4–5). The thirteen principles aver that there is only one God, that "God is one," and that only God is worthy of worship. Affirmation of God's indivisible oneness repudiates the Christian doctrine of a trinitarian deity (God as Father, Son, and Holy Spirit).

In classical Judaic theology, God is both transcendent (beyond) and immanent (within). As transcendent, the Holy One is eternal, incomparable, immutable, incorporeal, omniscient, and omnipotent. God's incorporeality reflects the biblical teaching that *"man may not see Me and live"* and the the-

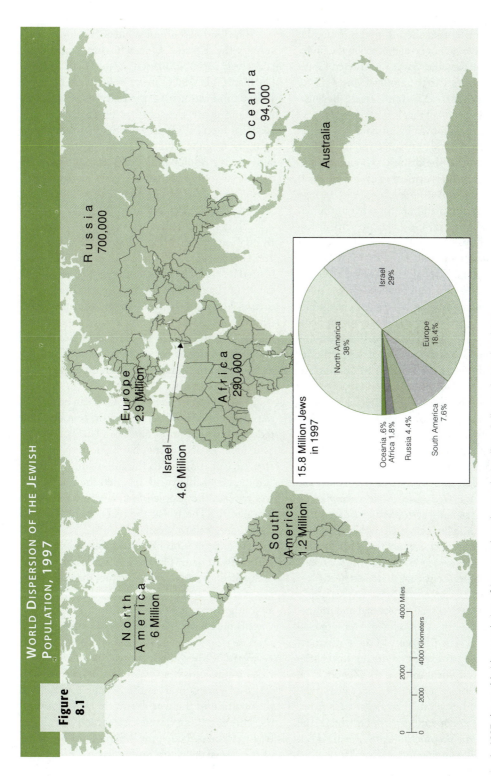

Figure 8.1

WORLD DISPERSION OF THE JEWISH POPULATION, 1997

North America 6 Million

South America 1.2 Million

Europe 2.9 Million

Israel 4.6 Million

Africa 290,000

Russia 700,000

Oceania 94,000

Australia

15.8 Million Jews in 1997

- North America 38%
- Israel 29%
- Europe 18.4%
- South America 7.6%
- Russia 4.4%
- Africa 1.8%
- Oceania .6%

In 1997, the worldwide population of Jews numbered around 16 million. Collectively, Israel and Asia, including Greater Russia, have a population of around 4.7 million Jews. The Jewish population of Europe includes the Ukraine.

Source: Data from the *1998 Britannica Book of the Year: Events of 1997* (Chicago: Encyclopaedia Britannica, 1998).

ological contention that the infinite, immutable, and unsurpassable cannot be embodied in the finite, mutable, and surpassable. Sages interpreted God's self-revelation *("I Am")* to the prophet Moses (*Exod.* 3:14) to mean that God is Being Itself. Because Being Itself transcends all that is finite, God is incapable of being fully known by humans.

As immanent, God's attentive and indwelling presence (called the **Shekhinah**) fills heaven and earth. The Shekhinah is evident in events in which the divine will is revealed—for example, in the revelation of God's commandments on Mount Sinai. The rabbis taught that God was present in the Temple (the house of the Lord), in the study of *Torah* (divine law, scripture), in prayer, and in benevolent and just acts. They also believed that God's presence could be obscured by murder and injustice. Judaic sources provide expansive conceptions of God's immanence. In a commentary on the book of *Exodus,* the commentator responded to the question, "Why did God speak to Moses from a thornbush?" by declaring that it was to teach that "no place is devoid of God's presence, not even a thornbush."[2] When the Rabbi of Kotzk was asked, "Where is the dwelling of God?" he replied that "God dwells wherever man lets him in."[3]

The problem of reconciling God's transcendence and immanence is evident in King Solomon's prayer at the dedication of the Temple. When the king asked, *"Does God really dwell with man on earth?"* he understood the foolishness of assuming that God could be contained within the Temple: *"Even the heavens to their uttermost reaches cannot contain You; how much less this House that I have built!"* But Solomon's entreaty that God heeds *"the prayers that Your servant offers toward this place"* also reflects the conviction that the eternal and unlimited are present within the finite and temporal (*2 Chron.* 6:18–20). The paradox of God's otherness and nearness is aptly expressed in the thirteenth-century Jewish mystical treatise the **Zohar:** "The Blessed Holy One . . . is hidden, concealed, transcendent, beyond, beyond." The *Zohar* adds, however, that there are openings through which "the Blessed Holy One becomes known . . . were it not so, no one could commune with Him."[4]

The God of traditional Judaic theology is personal—the Eternal One who hears and sees, addresses, and is addressed. *Ehyeh* (I am or I will be), that is, YHWH (Yahweh)—is the divine name. By the third century B.C.E., respect for God's holy name prompted the substitution of Adonai (the LORD) for YHWH in worship. Orthodox Jews continue to show reverence for the divine name by substituting Adonai for YHWH and by using the term G–d in printed matter. Divine attributes such as *Almighty, Everlasting, Shalom* (Peace), and the *Merciful One* are also synonyms of *God.*

The Holy One has been primarily addressed through male metaphors. God is "He who spoke and the world was" and "King of the universe, blessed be He." There are female metaphors as well. *Isaiah* 66:13 portrays Yahweh as a mother comforting her child. In **Kabbalism** (a form of Jewish mysticism), the Shekhinah (God's indwelling presence) is the female aspect of God. Some contemporary liturgies substitute female images such as "Queen of the universe, blessed be She" for more traditional ones.

The personal character of God can be illuminated by the attributes of creator, revealer, and redeemer, whose importance can hardly be overestimated. Jacob Neusner has reduced the mythic structure of Judaism to the following narrative: "God created the world, revealed the Torah, and will redeem the people of Israel—to whom God revealed the Torah—at the end of time through the sending of the Messiah."[5]

As creator, God brings the world into being and renews it daily. The cosmos is creation—an act of intelligence and purpose—rather than the product of chance and mindless forces. The world and all living things are God's creation. The book of *Genesis* proclaims the goodness of creation: *"God saw everything that he had made, and behold, it was very good."* Other Judaic sources on creation provide insights into what matters most. A commentary on *Genesis* observes that six things preceded the creation of the world: two things (*Torah* and the Throne of Glory) were created, and four things (the patriarchs, Israel, the Temple, and the name of the Messiah) were contemplated.[6] Belief that mercy and justice are fundamental to the relationship between God and humankind and to human relationships is enunciated in a Kabbalist creation myth: "First the Holy One, Blessed be He, tried to create the world according to the measure of Mercy, but it fell apart. Then He tried to create it according to the measure of Justice but that, too, fell apart. What did he do? He took an equal measure of Mercy and Justice. The result is our world."[7]

As revealer, the Holy One makes known the divine will. God's commands were revealed to Moses, who received them on behalf of the people. God commissioned prophets to warn against injustice and idolatry and to speak of repentance and reconciliation. Rabbis taught that God is present in studying, in doing God's instructions, in praying, and in acting justly and mercifully. Philosopher Franz Rosenzweig (1886–1929) believed that God is known in those moments of love that overcome human loneliness and that such experiences lead to the love of God and the commands to love our neighbors.

As redeemer, God is the deliverer of humans. Obedience to God's *Torah* (law; see the next section) undergirds Israel's corporate and individual well-being, and disobedience leads to alienation, brokenness, and exile. The Holy One gives Israel into the hands of her enemies but also delivers her from them. The message that Israel's tribulations were punishment for her sins was balanced by the promise that her sins were pardoned. Central to the rabbinic conception of redemption is the belief that the observance of God's *Torah* liberates, heals, makes whole, and saves. The *Torah* is so central to redemption that a **midrash** (commentary) on the book of *Ruth* has God declare that had Israel "not accepted My *Torah,* I should have caused the world to revert to void and destruction."[8]

Redemption involves repentance, a turning to God and away from sin. In the words of the philosopher Martin Buber (1878–1965), turning to God "is capable of renewing a man from within and changing his position in God's world. . . . turning . . . means that by a reversal of his whole being, a man who had been lost in the maze of selfishness . . . finds a way to God."[9] The power of

repentance is so great that a midrash on the Hebrew scripture *Leviticus* pictures Cain as telling Adam that he had repented slaying his brother Abel and had been pardoned.[10] No human or society is entirely innocent; all stand in need of expressing contrition, making reparation for wrongdoing, and changing their behavior.

Jews have traditionally thought of God as a divine person, but there are impersonal ideas of God as well. The philosopher Baruch Spinoza (1632–1677) rejected belief in a personal deity. In his philosophy, God does not answer prayer or intervene in the world; the world is God, and both nature and thought are attributes of God. Rabbi Mordecai Kaplan (1881–1983) conceived of God as a cosmic process that makes for the interdependence of all things and the worthwhileness of life. God is the totality of the forces and relationships "which are forever making a cosmos out of chaos."[11]

TORAH

Torah literally means "divine law," but here we are interested in *Torah* as scripture, and we return to it as God's law in the "Judaic Practice" section. What makes up the *Torah?* In its primary sense, *Torah* is God's revelation to Moses embodied in the **Pentateuch,** the first five books of Hebrew scripture (*Genesis, Exodus, Leviticus, Numbers,* and *Deuteronomy*). In another sense, the *Torah* includes the entire Hebrew scripture, a collection of books that Jews refer to as the *Bible* or the **Tanakh** and that Christians refer to as the *Old Testament. Ta*na*kh* is an acronym derived from the three primary divisions of Hebraic scripture: *T* for *Torah* (or the *Pentateuch*), *N* for *Nevi'im* (the prophetic books), and *K* for *Kethuvim* (the writings).

In a wider sense, the *Torah* includes the *Tanakh* and the **Talmud** (a collection of Jewish law and teaching). In its most encompassing meaning, the *Torah* includes the entire spectrum of Judaic teaching. In the latter sense, the *Torah* is God's revelation to Moses, but it is also God's indirect revelation to subsequent sages and rabbis who have participated, or are participating, in this revelation

Table 8.1

HEBREW SCRIPTURE *(TORAH)*

Hebrew scripture is organized here under the collective category of *Torah* and its two principal subdivisions, written and oral. Together, the oral and written *Torah* constitute God's instructions to Israel and humankind.

WRITTEN *TORAH* (*TANAKH*, HEBREW *BIBLE*)

The *Tanakh*, or written *Torah*, has three primary divisions: *Torah*, *Nevi'im*, and *Kethuvim*. The first division, known as *Torah* (the written law given to Moses on Mount Sinai), is composed of the five books of Moses (also called *Humash* or *Pentateuch*) and is considered more authoritative than the other divisions of the *Tanakh*. (The *Torah* scroll is the holiest object in a synagogue.)

Torah *(law; Pentateuch)*	Nevi'im *(prophets)*	Kethuvim *(writings)*
Genesis	*Joshua*	*Psalms*
Exodus	*Judges*	*Proverbs*
Leviticus	*Samuel*	*Job*
Numbers	*Kings*	*The Song of Songs*
Deuteronomy	*Isaiah*	*Ruth*
	Jeremiah	*Lamentations*
	Ezekiel	*Ecclesiastes*
	The Twelve (regarded as	*Esther*
	a single book): *Hosea, Joel, Amos,*	*Daniel*
	Obadiah, Jonah, Micah, Nahum,	*Ezra*
	Habakkuk, Zephaniah, Haggai,	*Nehemiah*
	Zechariah, Malachi	*Chronicles*

ORAL *TORAH* (*MISHNAH*)

The oral *Torah*, or *Mishnah*, was revealed to Moses on Mount Sinai and handed down over the generations from Moses to Joshua to the prophets to the sages to the Pharisees and to the rabbis from Hillel to Judah, the patriarch who, in conjunction with other rabbis, edited and codified the oral tradition into a written text around 200 C.E. Over the next four centuries, the *Mishnah* was supplemented by a codification of post-Mishnaic commentary (*Gemara*); the result was the combined text known as the *Talmud* (*Mishnah* plus *Gemara*).

through reason and reflection. Table 8.1 outlines the organization of Hebrew scripture.

The *Pentateuch* is the foundational layer of the *Torah* and the first to take on the aura of scriptural authority. The process of weaving together and editing Israel's oral and literary traditions to form the *Pentateuch* was completed by 400 B.C.E. By 200 B.C.E., Israel's priests and sages regarded the prophetic books as scripture. In the final quar-ter of the first century C.E., a third body of literature (the writings) was added, and Hebrew scripture, the first layer of *Torah*, was henceforth closed.

The second layer of Torah is the *Talmud*, the body of Judaic law and literature that Neusner has called "the single most influential document in the history of Judaism."[12] Just as Christians read the *Old Testament* in the light of the *New Testament*, Jews read the *Tanakh*, the first layer of *Torah*, in the light of the *Talmud*. The *Talmud* is composed of *Mishnah* and *Gemara*. Traditional Judaists believe that both an oral and written *Torah* (law) was revealed to Moses on Mount Sinai. In their view, the written *Torah* is embodied in the *Pentateuch*, and the oral *Torah* is embodied in the **Mishnah**. The oral *Torah* is believed to have been passed down over the centuries by human recitation and was codified and written down around the end of the second century C.E. **Gemara** is a body of post-Mishnaic rabbinic literature that further interprets and expands Mishnaic law and articulates Judaic values. There are other layers of *Torah*, including commentaries on biblical and talmudic texts and summations of Judaic law, but the *Tanakh* and the *Talmud* are foundational to all subsequent texts.

The *Mishnah* reflects the practical need of the rabbis to make legal decisions and interpretations that clarify and amplify the commands of the written *Torah*. The *Mishnah*'s 6 divisions ("Seeds," "Set Feasts," "Women," "Damages," "Holy Things," and "Purifications") are subdivided into 63 tractates (books) and 523 chapters. The entire text is somewhat shorter than the *Tanakh*. The first division, "Seeds," addresses agricultural laws. "Set Feasts" contains laws respecting the Sabbath, daily worship, festivals, and fast days. "Women" covers marriage contracts, divorce, adultery, rape, and other subjects. "Damages" includes laws respecting property rights, courts, criminal law, real estate, and inheritance, as well as a tractate on ethics. "Holy Things" focuses on laws covering the Temple and sacrifice. The concluding section, "Purifications," covers rules associated with types of pollution and the means of ritual purification.

There are two *Talmuds:* Palestinian and Babylonian. The former was compiled in Palestine around 400 C.E., and the latter in Babylonia between 400 and 600 C.E. Neither was ever completed, but the Babylonian *Talmud* is the most complete and authoritative. The *Mishnah* is the same in both. The Palestinian (Jerusalem) *Talmud* contains approximately 750,000 words and includes commentary on thirty-nine of the *Mishnah*'s tractates, usually in the form of a paragraph of *Mishnah* followed by rabbinic explanation. The Babylonian *Talmud* contains around 2.5 million words, of which roughly two-thirds are legal matters and one-third are stories, ethics, and midrash. Its commentaries on thirty-seven of the sixty-three Mishnaic tractates summarize essential points through a chain of questions and answers, objections and rejoinders.

Traditional Judaic theology assumes that the oral and written *Torah* revealed at Sinai is eternal, immutable truth. God is said to have created the world with the *Torah* (analogous to an architect's blueprint) and for the *Torah*. Jews turn to it over and over again. For example, over the course of each liturgical year, the *Pentateuch* is read during Sabbath services from the first passage of *Genesis* to the concluding passage of *Deuteronomy*. *Torah* scrolls must contain no errors, and if the *Torah* is incorrectly read or recited in public worship, participants are obliged to correct the mistake so no one will leave the service with a corrupted version of the Hebrew text.

Whether it is regarded as immutable truth or a divinely inspired human creation, scripture requires interpretation. Judaic interpreters have found numerous layers of meaning, including literal, metaphorical, allegorical (hidden), legal, and moral meanings. A talmudic story illustrates the importance of the act of interpretation: Rabbi Eliezar urged other rabbis to assent to his position on a legal matter by asking heaven to support his interpretation. Heaven responded; canal water flowed backward, other miracles followed, and finally a heavenly voice concurred with Eliezar. The rabbis were not convinced. One cited a passage in *Deuteronomy:* "It [Torah] *is not in heaven.*" Another rabbi explained that the *Torah* was given at Sinai; thus, "*we pay no attention to a heavenly voice. For already from Mount Sinai the Torah said, 'By a majority you are to decide.'*"[13] In other words, human deliberation, rather than miracles and heavenly voices, decides legal issues.

When science and *Torah* disagree, many Orthodox Jews side with scripture, because they believe it embodies immutable truth, whereas "scientific theories are always being revised and rejected."[14] In the traditional Judaic calendar, the year 1

(3761 B.C.E. in the common dating) begins with God's creation of Adam and Eve on the sixth day, a calculation of time that traditionalists believe is consistent with scripture. Jews who have accommodated their faith to science believe that the origin stories in *Genesis* are mythological and figurative. These stories are profound (for example, creation is good, and humans are created in the image of God), but they are not factually descriptive (for example, the world was not literally created in seven days, and Eve was not created from Adam's rib). In addition to noting challenges posed by the natural sciences, biblical critics (a category that includes Jewish scholars) deny that Moses authored the *Pentateuch*. In their view, the *Pentateuch* is composed of several strands of tradition.[15]

ISRAEL

Israel, understood as both a land (Eretz Israel) and a people (Beth Israel), is a cornerstone of Judaic belief. Peoplehood and land are part of God's covenant with Abraham, the father of the Jews: *"And I will maintain My covenant between Me and you, and your offspring to come, as an everlasting covenant"* and give *"to you and your offspring to come, all the land of Canaan, as an everlasting possession"* (*Gen.* 17:17). Israel's election is reiterated in God's covenant with Moses: *"If you will obey Me faithfully and keep My covenant, you shall be My treasured possession among all the peoples. Indeed, all the earth is Mine, but you shall be to Me a kingdom of priests and a holy nation"* (*Exod.* 19:5-6).

Israel's favored position is puzzling. Why would God treasure one people among all the peoples and nations? Is this simply a case of ethnocentrism? Clearly, belief in Israel's election is a means of validating claim to the land of Canaan, but what of the claims of other peoples, such as the ancient Canaanites and the modern Palestinians? Jews have been troubled by the doctrine of election and have struggled to reconcile it with their vision of God's justice. A commentary on *Exodus* playfully interprets Israel's election as happening by default: God is depicted as offering the gift of *Torah* to several peoples, each of whom insists on

hearing the divine commands before consenting to obey them. Upon hearing God's law, the various peoples refuse to covenant with God. The Jews, in contrast, agree to obey God's commands without first hearing them (*Exod.* 24:7). The prophet Isaiah saw Israel's chosen status as a means of deliverance, *"a light of nations . . . rescuing those who sit in darkness"* (*Isa.* 42:6–7). Consistent with Isaiah's images, some contemporary Jews have regarded Israel's election as a witness to monotheism among the peoples of the world, a light that bore fruit in Christianity, Islam, and other traditions.

Some Jews reject the doctrine of election as incompatible with divine or human justice. Secular Jews dissociate Israel as a land and a people from the belief in divine election; they maintain that Israel is a creation by Jews and for Jews. Feminists such as Judith Plaskow reject the notion of a chosen people on the grounds that it is rooted in systems that subjugated Jewish women, devalued non-Jews, and served as a justification for injustices to both groups. A great many Jews would agree that Beth Israel is about peoplehood, not about divine favor.

THE NATURE AND DESTINY OF HUMANS

Humans are of incalculable value in Judaism. They are created in the likeness of God and are the culmination of creation. The philosopher Philo of Alexandria (ca. 20 B.C.E.–50 C.E.) taught that "each single individual in himself, when he is law-abiding and obedient to God, is equal in value to a whole nation . . . even to the whole world."[16] The *Mishnah* expressed a similar sentiment: *"All mankind was created from a single ancestor to teach us that whoever takes a single life it is as though he destroyed a whole world, and whoever sustains a single life it is as though he sustained a whole world."*[17] Compared with God's unsurpassable power and glory, humans are remarkably frail and flawed. They are often faithless, quarrelsome, and rapacious, yet God has made them little less than God and has given them dominion over the works of creation. A midrash of *Isaiah* 43:12 suggests that Israel has such a prominent role in the divine scheme that "when you are my witnesses, I am God, and when you are not my witnesses, I am [as it were] not God."[18]

Humans are an expression of the goodness of creation, but as beings who have been blessed by freedom of choice, they are capable of both good and evil. In a commentary on *Deuteronomy*, God is pictured as saying, "I created within you the impulse to evil, but I created the Torah as a medicine. So long as you occupy yourselves with the Torah, the impulse to evil will not dominate you. But if you do not occupy yourselves with the Torah, you will be delivered in the power of the impulse to evil."[19] Right behavior entails knowledge of divine law; thus, the study of God's *Torah* is itself a divine command and part of the "joy of observing the law." Righteousness is a necessary condition of salvation, but even the most righteous person needs God's grace: *"Surely there is not a righteous man on earth who does good and never sins"* (*Eccles.* 7:20). The *Mishnah* teaches that fasting and prayer atone for sins against God, but transgressions against humans can only be forgiven by making amends.

Judaism does not focus on the world to come or teach that the soul's liberation from the body is the ultimate human goal. This world has inestimable value. Creation is good. Human sexuality and marriage are divine blessings. Asceticism, in the sense of prolonged and repeated fasting and renunciations of sex and marriage, is rare in the history of Judaism. Such practices are at odds with God's law; marriage and procreation are commanded. Permitted pleasures such as wine, lawful intercourse, food, dance, and music are of such value that a talmudic passage declares that *"a man will have to give account in the judgment day of every good thing which he might have enjoyed and did not."*[20] Reflection about the questions God will ask human beings at the final judgment provides a feel for the worldly and moral focus of Judaism. The rabbis taught that humans will be asked whether they have treated others fairly, whether they have set aside regular periods for the study of *Torah,* and whether they have brought children into the world. Only then will God inquire whether they have looked forward to redemption.

Doctrines later incorporated into Judaic theology, such as the world to come, the resurrection of the body, and the Messiah, are not in the *Pentateuch*. Abraham and Moses, the central figures of the *Pentateuch* and ancient Israelite religion, covenanted with God without reference to a world to come. The dead were believed to "live" in Sheol, a shadowy land of spirits. Later, in conjunction with the destruction of the Jewish kingdoms, Jews looked to the future as the context in which God would redeem them. Prophets promised the coming of the Messiah and the establishment of a messianic age here on earth. Belief in life after death and in rewards and punishment in the hereafter was also articulated. For example, *Isaiah* promises that *"the dead shall live, their bodies shall rise,"* and *Daniel* speaks of a resurrection of the dead in which the righteous rise to everlasting life and the wicked to everlasting contempt.

The Judaism of the talmidic rabbis shared the beliefs about "last things" that emerged in the late biblical period, including the belief that the Messiah will come and the dead will be revived. The rabbis taught that human existence was lived in two worlds—this world and the next. Both worlds are precious, but righteous living in this world is preparation for the world to come: *"This World is like a vestibule to the World to Come. Prepare yourself in the vestibule, so that you may be admitted into the banquet hall."*[21] Judaic tradition does not conclude that only Jews will be saved; for example, a talmudic passage teaches that *"the righteous of all nations have a place in the world to come."*

Rabbinic theology speaks of humans as having bodies and souls, but it does not regard them as mutually exclusive. The *Talmud* teaches that *"the soul fills the whole body"* and that body and soul are not separable. Faith in the resurrection of the dead entails the conviction that at the end of time, after the Messiah has come, God will raise the dead as whole persons and judge them according to their deeds. The righteous are to be rewarded in Paradise and the wicked punished in Gehinnom (hell). In some Judaic theologies, belief in the resurrection of the body at the end of time gave way to the belief that the soul survived death and the body perished; accordingly, the souls of the deceased went directly to Paradise or to hell.[22] Many Jews believe eternal punishment is incompatible with God's justice and compassion.

Jewish mystical traditions provide an alternative to the view that humans live one life in two worlds. In Kabbalism, for example, human souls are regarded as divine sparks that resulted from a cosmic accident that shattered God's original design of creation. Life is a process of restoring creation *(tikkun)*. Souls are captives in their bodies until they can achieve perfection. Souls of the pious can escape being reborn, but most souls repeat the cycle of death and rebirth many times and may be reborn in human bodies or in animals, plants, or inanimate objects. The Other Side (sometimes personified as Satan) thwarts the completion of *tikkun* and will not be completely overcome until the final redemption. An alternative position to traditional or mystical teachings about the afterlife is taken by Jews who reject belief in personal immortality and think of immortality in terms of the survival of Israel as a nation and a people.

EVIL

The rabbis recognized that all humans suffer: "There is no man in the world to whom suffering does not come."[23] But undeserved suffering—the suffering of the righteous—is central to the Judaic understanding of evil. Trust in God's goodness and trust in the triumph of good over evil are fundamental assumptions. In a perfectly just world, those who do good ought to prosper, and those who do evil ought to be punished; human experience, however, invalidates this assumption. At least in the short run, good does not always triumph over evil; as Job observed, the wicked grow mighty in power, see their children established, and die in peace (*Job* 21:7–13). The problem of reconciling God's goodness with the existence of evil is implicit in *Jeremiah* 12:1: *"Why does the way of the guilty prosper? Why are the workers of treachery at ease?"*

Personified evil is not an important feature of Judaic theology and adds little in the way of resolving the problem of undeserved suffering in a world created by a good God. In religions such as Zoroastrianism and Christianity, evil is personified as a figure who is abetted in evildoing by demons and malevolent human beings. Belief in Satan or the devil as God's adversary, and as the tempter who enticed the first couple, Adam and Eve, to sin, are part of Christian, rather than Judaic, theology. There is no explicit reference to the devil in Hebrew scripture. Satan appears there, but not as the evil prince of this world. Likewise, talmudic thought did not resolve the problem of good and evil by pitting God against a personified cosmic enemy. However, in popular Judaic lore, the evil impulse was personified as Sammael or Satan, the evil one who directs the forces of evil against God and the righteous.

Moses Maimonides denied the existence of evil as either an independent force or as a personified cosmic being. In his philosophical theology, God does not create evil. Creation is good; thus, evil is the absence of good. Evil is evident when something lacks that which is proper to it. For example, an unconsummated marriage is incomplete in the same way that an unfinished building is. The failure to realize one's potential for *shalom* (peace and wholeness) is an example of the absence of good.

Why is there evil in a world created by a righteous God? In classical Judaic theology, evil is the consequence of sin. There are several interpretations of *sin*. In one perspective, sin is incompleteness or fragmentation. In another, sin is alienation from God and consequently from others, from self, and from nature. But the primary sense of *sin* is willful disobedience of God's commands. God demands righteousness, purity, and faithfulness; sin is injustice, pollution, and faithlessness.

Basic to the Judaic conception of sin is the conviction that humans were created free—that is, capable of distinguishing between good and evil and responsible for their choices. God foresees everything, yet inexplicably, "freedom of choice is granted." Human freedom provides a means of exonerating God from the charge that the Blessed

One is responsible for evil. Humans are responsible for evil; their afflictions are the result of sin. Injustice and infidelity bring disaster. Righteousness and faithfulness bring prosperity, progeny, and good health. *"The LORD will not let the righteous go hungry, but He denies the wicked what they crave"* (*Prov.* 10:2). A similar chord is struck in a talmudic passage: *"There is no death without sin, and no affliction without transgression."*[24]

The problem of reconciling faith in God's goodness with the existence of evil was intensified for Jews by the destruction of the kingdom of Judah (586 B.C.E.) and by being exiled in Babylon. Yahweh's covenant with King David promised the everlasting continuity of the Davidic dynasty, but Judah's defeat and the subsequent end of the dynastic line forced Jews to seek an explanation for what seemed to be a broken promise. The prophets maintained that Israel's sin (idolatry and injustice) broke the covenant. This judgment was tempered by the promise that a Jewish remnant would survive and a Messiah would come and restore the nation. The prophet Hosea used the imagery of marriage: God had not granted Israel a divorce; reconciliation was possible. The prophet Zechariah depicted God as going into exile with the captives and as returning from exile with them: *"Thus said the LORD of Hosts: I will rescue My people from the lands of the east and from the lands of the west, and I will bring them home to dwell in Jerusalem. They shall be My people, and I will be their God—in truth and sincerity"* (*Zech.* 8:7–8).

Belief that Israel's fall was punishment for her sins did not satisfy everyone. When the Syrian King Antiochus IV (in the second century B.C.E.) demanded that the Jews embrace paganism, it was obvious that the most righteous of God's servants suffered and were sometimes martyred precisely because they refused to disobey God's commands. In such a context, the traditional explanation was no longer convincing. Alternative solutions were offered. The author of *Ecclesiastes* suggested that human existence is intrinsically unsatisfactory and counseled humans to expect little from life. The book of *Job* rejected the notion that all human suffering is punishment for sin; it suggested that no

satisfactory explanation of evil is possible, because humans lack the vantage point to understand God's providential rule.

If human afflictions are not simply the consequence of sin, then what purposes do they serve in a world created by a righteous God? Some interpreters regarded the suffering of the righteous as redemptive. The prophet Isaiah saw Israel as God's suffering servant who would be given as a light of nations *"that My salvation may reach to the end of the earth"* (*Isa.* 49:6). Thus, the suffering of the righteous "brings salvation to the world" and was evidence of God's love rather than of divine punishment. Rabbis took comfort in the view that God had gone into exile in Babylon with the remnants of Israel—that God, in a sense, suffered with them. They looked to the messianic age and the world to come for the triumph of righteousness and the reward of the righteous.

The capacity of the Jewish faith to make suffering sufferable has been repeatedly demonstrated over the course of time, but the **Holocaust**— the extermination of 6 million Jews by the Nazis during World War II—has shaken traditional Judaic belief. *Night,* the story of Elie Wiesel's personal struggle to survive in a Nazi death camp, contains stark images of the horror of the Holocaust and the struggle to have faith in God in a context in which the prayers of the pious were unanswered and innocent children perished. Wiesel described a rabbi in the death camp at Buna who came to the painful conclusion that "God is no longer with us." The rabbi confessed that no one has the right to say such things, as humans are unable to understand the ways of God, but the horror of the death camp led him to declare, "How can I believe, how could anyone believe, in this merciful God?"[25]

Jews have interpreted the Holocaust's meaning in a variety of ways. Some have reiterated traditional theodicy (a justification of the goodness and justice of God in the face of evil and human suffering): the destruction of European Jewry was punishment for not keeping God's law. Another theodicy sees divine providence bringing good out of the Holocaust through the creation of modern

Israel and the mending of the Jewish people. Emil Fackenheim argues that all claims that God acted or will act in history lose their force unless there is some way to affirm "God's relationship to the holocaust."[26] The recovery of the Jewish people, including the creation of modern Israel, enables contemporary Jews to believe that their experience is still linked to the redemptive presence of God. Fackenheim rejects the idea that the victims were being punished for their failure to obey God's instructions (roughly 1 million were children). It is in remembering the Holocaust and resisting evil that God's presence can be "seen" and through which a reorientation toward the future is possible.

For theologian Richard Rubenstein, however, the God of classical Judaism is dead. It is impossible to reconcile belief in God or the goodness of humans with "the unprecedented magnitude of violence in the twentieth century"—a century of Nazism; Stalinism; Maoism; and the unholy fires of Auschwitz, Dresden, and Hiroshima.[27] Belief in an omnipotent and omniscient God who loves us as good parents love their children is no longer possible; modern Jews "live after the Death of God" and must look for meaning in the Jewish people as a community of faith.

Other voices agree that the traditional conception of God is no longer viable and attempt to reimagine God. In one reconstruction, God is vulnerable and surpassable (by God) rather than perfect and immutable. God is in the world and suffers with those who unjustly suffer. An event Wiesel describes in *Night* can serve as a metaphor for God's identification with those who suffer and of God's vulnerability, even to the death of God. Wiesel relates that two men and a very well liked boy were hanged for resisting the Nazis. During the hanging, Wiesel heard a voice ask, "Where is God? Where is He?" The adults died quickly, but the child took more than thirty agonizing minutes to die. Again Wiesel heard the man's voice asking, "Where is God now?" A voice from within Wiesel replied, "Where is He? Here He is—He is hanging here on this gallows."[28]

JUDAIC PRACTICE

In Judaism, practice (following or doing God's instructions) is more important than doctrinal correctness.[29] Talmudic wisdom depicted God as saying that it is better for his children to forget him than to fail to keep his instructions, for by observing *Torah* they will come to him. *Torah* matters so much that the rabbis pictured God as studying and obeying it, as well as creating the world with and for *Torah*. Judaic practice is treated here under the categories of *Torah*, gender roles, and worship and ritual.

TORAH AS HALAKAH AND MITZVOT

We have considered the *Torah* as scripture. Here, we focus on *Torah* as *halakah* (law) and *mitzvah* (command). *Halakah* literally means "to go" or "to walk" in the sense of how life is to be lived. **Halakah** refers to the Judaic legal system—the entire body of Judaic law and observance—but it can also denote a particular law or legal decision. It includes the written and oral *Torah* and the elaboration of the Mosaic law as interpreted and ruled on by talmudic and post-talmudic sages. As Neusner has observed, *halakah* "is full of normative, prescriptive rules about what one must do and refrain from doing in every situation of life and at every moment of the day."[30]

Because the *Torah* required elaboration and application to changing conditions, Israel's sages prepared "a fence around Torah" in the form of legal measures that clarified Judaic practice. For example, a *Mishnah* tractate clarifies the command that it is not permissible to work on **Shabbat (Sabbath)** by identifying thirty-nine classes of work that are forbidden, including sowing, reaping, weaving, baking, writing, slaughtering, and putting out or lighting fires. *Halakah* is continuously being interpreted and applied in rabbinic courts, and decisions respecting Shabbat have been required to cover modern modes of transportation and communication.

Mitzvah means "divine commandment" and, in popular usage, "good deeds." To obey a *mitzvah* is a good deed, and to break one is a transgression. According to rabbinic tradition, there are 613 *mitzvot* (commands) in the *Pentateuch,* as well as additional *mitzvot* in the *Talmud.* The 613 biblical *mitzvot* are divided into 248 positive and 365 negative commands.[31] Positive *mitzvot* include directives to love your neighbor and to praise God after eating. Negative commands include prohibitions on refusing charity to the poor and destroying fruit trees, even in a time of war. Each *mitzvah* is derived from a passage in the *Torah.* For example, the command to marry and procreate is derived from the following verse: *"and God said to them, 'Be fertile and increase'"* (*Gen.* 1:28). Talmudic *mitzvot,* like biblical *mitzvot,* are believed to be divinely inspired, and they include, for example, prescriptions to wash one's hands before eating and to study *halakah.*

Many *mitzvot* are no longer observed. Roughly one-third of the 613 biblical *mitzvot* are related to priests and services in the Temple in Jerusalem. For example, prior to the destruction of the Second Temple (70 C.E.), two male yearling lambs, whole and without blemish, were offered to Yahweh daily. On Sabbath and other special days, additional animals were sacrificed. High standards of purity were required of priests. They were commanded to be without blemish (free of diseases such as leprosy) and to avoid contact with polluting things (for example, bodily discharges and dead bodies). Because the Temple and the priesthood no longer exist, most of the *mitzvot* applicable to them, including animal sacrifice, are no longer observed.

Reflecting the divisions in modern Judaism, Jews are divided on the issue of whether all *mitzvot* are binding. Orthodox Jews believe that *Torah* is divinely revealed and eternally binding. Reform and Reconstructionist Jews teach that Judaism is an evolving tradition and must be adapted to the needs of each generation and reexamined in the light of modern science and social practice. They accept the moral law as binding but argue

that the purity and dietary codes are no longer obligatory.

Orthodox and Hasidic Jews observe what are sometimes referred to as the "Laws of Family Purity." Women are considered unclean because of their body discharge during their menses and seven days following it. During their unclean period, women are excluded from public worship, and intercourse is prohibited (*Lev.* 18:19). Like the menstrual flow, semen is polluting (for a day), and garments or persons in contact with it must be purified. Human impurities are removed by a ritual bath.

Jewish law distinguishes between ritually clean (fit) and unclean (unfit) foods. Kosher *(kashrut)* laws govern those birds, fishes, and mammals that observant Jews are permitted to eat and those that are not permitted (*Lev.* 11:1–47; *Deut.* 14:3–20). These laws also provide rules for the slaughter of animals and their preparation. According to God's law, Jews are permitted to eat cud-chewing animals that have cloven hooves, such as oxen, sheep, and goats; animals lacking one of those features, such as camels, rabbits, and pigs, are not to be eaten or touched. Sea life with fins and scales are kosher, but crustaceous animals, such as crabs and shrimp, are not. Scavenger birds and permitted animals with defects (such as spotted lungs) are also unfit to eat.

Moral action is commanded. The prophets and rabbis taught that obedience to God's moral commands and deeds of love were preferable to sacrifice. Many of the 613 biblical *mitzvot* are moral directives: You shall honor your parents. You shall not murder, commit adultery, steal, bear false witness, or covet what belongs to your neighbor. You shall leave some of your harvest for the poor (*Lev.* 23:22). You shall not oppress the widow or orphan, accept bribes, defraud, deny charity to the poor, or decide capital cases by a majority of one. Because of the value of life, prohibitions, such as those respecting Shabbat, can be suspended in order to save life.

Justice and mercy are attributes of God and primary Judaic virtues. Jews are to love and pursue peace and to love all humankind and lead them to *Torah*. Rabbinic tradition taught that Jews are to imitate God. Like the Holy One, they are to walk in righteousness and speak uprightly. As God clothed Adam and Eve and comforted the mourning, Jews are to clothe the naked and comfort the mourning. In the view of Rabbi Akiva ben Josef (ca. 50–ca. 135 C.E.), a revered scholar and sage whose teaching and personality are prominent in the *Mishnah,* the failure to do so is analogous to murder. Jews have continued the ethical legacy of Judaism by engaging in the struggle for civil rights, economic justice, and racial equality. By themselves, humans cannot complete the task of perfecting the world, but they are not *"free to desist from it"* (*Avot* 2:19).

Israel's teachers taught that all *mitzvot* should be obeyed, but they also identified basic ones under which all *mitzvot* could be subsumed. The prophet Micah reduced the 613 *mitzvot* to three: *"what does the LORD require of you but to do justice, and to love goodness, and to walk modestly with your God"* (*Mic.* 6:8b). Hillel the Elder (ca. 40 B.C.E.–10 C.E.) taught that the Golden Rule is the basic principle underlying God's law: *"What is hateful to yourself, do not do to your neighbor. This is the whole Torah; the rest is commentary. Go and study"* (*Shabbat* 31a).

Classical Judaic ethics is an ethic of obedience: *"As a dove is saved by its wings, so Israel is saved by mitzvot, by fulfilling God's commandments"* (*Berakhot* 53b).[32] But the absoluteness of *Torah* is tempered by the view that revelation is an ongoing process and by reinterpretations of *Torah* to fit changing conditions and values.

GENDER ROLES

Traditionally, women have been subordinate to men in Judaic practice. In the biblical period (1900 B.C.E.–70 C.E.), women were primarily under the control of their fathers and husbands. They were bearers of children, and barrenness was seen as an affliction; for example, Sarah responded to "her failure" to conceive by arranging for her husband, Abraham, to father a child with her servant, Hagar. Women were excluded from the priesthood because their discharge of blood during menses and birthing

made them impure—forty days of uncleanness for giving birth to a boy and eighty days for a girl (*Lev.*15). During their uncleanness, they were prohibited from touching holy things or attending Temple services. Subordination of women was tempered, however, by the affection and loyalty that bound husbands, wives, and families together.

Sexual fidelity was important for both sexes, but the conduct demanded of women—premarital virginity and faithfulness in marriage—was more restrictive than that required of men. If the token of virginity—vaginal blood following the consummation of the marriage—was not evident, the bride could be stoned to death (*Deut.* 22:13–21). Should a husband's charge against his bride be unfounded, he was fined, whipped, and not permitted to divorce her. Laws respecting adultery and rape protected male interests. Both kinds of laws were intended to insure that a husband's sons were his own and, in cases of rape, to compensate the father of the victim. Adultery involved intercourse with another man's wife; a married male who had intercourse with a nonmarried woman was not guilty of adultery. A rapist was required to marry his victim and pay a fine to her father, and he was not permitted to divorce her (*Deut.* 22:28–29). Put in the starkest terms, the victim was required to marry her assailant.

Biblical narratives are primarily male centered. Only males covenanted with God and bore the sign of the covenant (circumcision). Women spoke to God and, on some occasions, for God, but for the most part men acted as intermediaries between God and the people. Nevertheless, there are powerful biblical women. A talmudic tractate noted that forty-eight prophets and seven *"prophetesses [Sarah, Miriam, Deborah, Hannah, Abigail, Huldah, and Esther] prophesied to Israel."* *Proverbs* observed that a good wife is *"more precious than jewels"* and commended them not only for domestic virtues but for buying fields and profiting on sales as well.

Male domination continued during the rabbinic period (70–1789 C.E.). Women were excluded from the rabbinate on the grounds that their periodic pollution (discharges from menstruation and birthing) and domestic duties excluded them from performing rabbinic duties. Rabbinic law extended the time of menstrual uncleanness and the prohibition against intercourse between husband and wife for seven days beyond the seven days associated with menstrual flow. Even more devastating for women was the teaching that the formal study of God's saving *Torah* was a *mitzvah* from which women were excused. Maimonides reiterated the talmudic view that study of scripture was a male duty and added a rationale that devalued the intelligence of women: "The Sages have warned us that a man shall not teach his daughter Torah, as the majority of women have not a mind adequate for its study."[33]

Both sexes were required, with some exceptions, to observe all negative commandments. Positive ordinances were another matter. Men were obligated, with some exceptions, to keep all positive ordinances, but women were exempted from most that involved a set time. Both sexes were to keep Shabbat (a specific time command), but women were not required to observe commands that conflicted with their domestic responsibilities. Men were to recite morning, afternoon, and evening prayers (a time-specific ordinance) and to study *Torah* (a nontime-specific ordinance), commands from which women were exempted and, in practice, excluded.

Exempting women from the obligation to study and pray left synagogue worship and formal study of scripture to men. As Judith Hauptman observed, "Balancing this loss of opportunity is a parallel trend in the opposite direction. Certain commands in the course of time became labeled 'women's commandments,' because it was women who became responsible for fulfilling them. Men left domestic observance of the dietary laws to their wives."[34] A result of this distinction was the conviction that the wife is the priest of the home and that the table around which her family gathers is her altar, as she is the one who makes sure that the kosher rules are observed. Domination of the public sphere by men provides the context for one of the morning blessings recited by Orthodox adult males: "Blessed be God, King of the universe, for not making me a woman." Apologists explain that the blessing is not intended to imply that women are inferior; it is an expression of gratitude for maleness and for the opportunity of the males to fulfill more *mitzvot* than those required of women.

Although rabbinic law limited the public role of women, it provided protections for them that went beyond those of the biblical period. Biblical injunctions excluded daughters from inheriting property unless there were no surviving sons, but the rabbis found a way around this exclusion; they permitted fathers to give a gift of property to their daughters, who then deferred taking possession of the gift until after their father died. A woman's consent was required before a bethrothal could take place, and a marriage document *(ketubah)* outlining the husband's financial obligation to his wife in the event of his death or a divorce was signed before the marriage took place. The *ketubah* is an important protection, because in rabbinic law, the wife's assets are managed by her husband, and anything she earns belongs to him.

Divorce is a male prerogative; a wife cannot obtain a religious divorce *(get)* without her husband's consent, whereas a husband can get a divorce without his wife's consent. Although a husband's consent is required to end a marriage, rabbis devised a way for Jewish courts to coerce a husband to "voluntarily" divorce his wife when the wife insists on a divorce. Nevertheless, husbands can "chain" their wives to them for years, making it impossible for them to remarry in a religious ceremony.

Statutes respecting a husband's sexual obligations to his wife assume that women, as well as men, feel sexual desire. The rabbis recognized that licit sexual relations entail more than procreation; they involve tenderness and gratification and should not be forced. Talmudic *halakah* directs husbands to be concerned with their wife's pleasure and obligates them to respond to her sexual desire on a regular basis. Frequency of sexual obligation is linked to profession; for example, scholars are obligated once a week, preferably on Sabbath, and "laborers twice a week."[35]

Talmudic texts both praise and malign women. Sexuality is a divine blessing and is necessary for the fulfillment and continuation of life, yet women were depicted as the source of temptation. Hillel the Elder lamented that more women meant more witchcraft and more lust (*Avot* 2:7). Philo identified statesmanship as the sphere of men and household management as the sphere of women, a division of labor he believed was rooted in their respective natures. Philo associated males with reason, strength, and good and women with feelings, weakness, and "everything vile."[36]

Women also received accolades. Rabbi Akiva professed that whatever he had achieved belonged to his wife. A talmudic passage declares that *"any man who has no wife lives without joy, without blessing, and without goodness"* (*Yevamot* 62b). Women were commended for freeing their husbands from activities that would distract from the study of *Torah* and were rarely praised for their scholarship, but Rabbi Meir's wife, Bruria, was commended for her mastery of *halakah*. When her husband prayed that all sinners would perish, Bruria pointed out that scripture (*Ps.* 104) "meant that all sin should disappear, not all sinners."

Religiously sanctioned patriarchy is gradually breaking down. In contrast to traditional practice, women have been admitted to the rabbinate in the Reform, Conservative, and Reconstructionist branches of Judaism. Women also serve as cantors and read from the *Torah* scroll at services in these three traditions.

JEWISH WORSHIP AND RITUAL

Jewish identity as individuals and a community has been and is shaped, nurtured, and preserved through worship. Dietary observances, the practice of circumcision, the celebration of holy days, and Sabbath observance have bound Jews together in contexts where the dominant culture has sought to assimilate them. The activities of each day are sanctified through the observance of *mitzvot*. As it is written, *"May all your actions be for the sake of Heaven"* (*Avot* 2:12). At the center of classical Judaic worship is God and the people whom God has blessed with a holy book *(Torah)* and a holy day (Shabbat). The prayer book *(Siddur)* contains the liturgy for worship in the synagogue; it is primarily directed at giving thanks and praise to God. In Morris Adler's words, "Ritual is the language of religion. It brings into our daily life the invisible world of the spirit and the unseen presence of God."[37] Our study of Judaic worship and ceremonies focuses on calendrical and life cycle rites.

CALENDRICAL RITES   Jewish worship includes a full spectrum of calendrical rites, including daily worship, Shabbat observance, and special festivals. Prayer is a daily obligation and part of all worship. Adult Jewish males are directed to pray three times each day (morning, afternoon, and evening), either at home or in the synagogue, as well as at other times, such as before and after eating. Congregational prayer in the synagogue requires a minimum of ten adult males to form a quorum *(minyan)* for the purpose of congregational worship or business. Reform Judaism permits adults of either sex to form a *minyan*. Obligatory prayers are repeated each day, but they do not preclude prayers of the heart. Morning and evening prayers entail recitation of the *Shema* (*Deut.* 6:4–9, 11:13–21; *Num.* 15:37–41) and benedictions praising, petitioning, and thanking God. A shortened *Shema* (*Deut.* 6:4–9) is recited before going to sleep:

> Hear O Israel! The LORD is our God, the LORD alone. You shall love the LORD your God with all your heart and with all your soul and with all your might. Take to heart these instructions with which I charge you this day. Impress them upon your children. Recite them when you stay at home and when you are away, when you lie down and when you get up. Bind them as a sign on your hand and let them serve as a symbol on your forehead; inscribe them on the doorposts of your house and on your gates.

Shabbat is a day of rest and *shalom* commemorating the seventh day of creation. God blessed the seventh day and made it holy, and he commanded Israel to remember and sanctify it. Shabbat is practiced here and now, but it is a foretaste of the world to come. In the words of the theologian Abraham Heschel (1907–1972), "The essence of the world to come is Sabbath eternal, and the seventh day in time is an example of eternity."[38]

A family in northern California lights a *menorah* during Chanukah (ca. 1996).

Shabbat is from Friday at sundown to Saturday at sundown. Its observance is such a fundamental *mitzvah* that rabbis declared that if all Jews kept it, the Messiah would come. Observances begin in the home with the lighting of candles, usually by the mother of the household, who also invokes God's blessing on her house. The Sabbath meal is preceded by blessings recited or sung over a cup of wine *(kiddush)* and two loaves of special bread *(hallah)*. Shabbat worship in the synagogue begins with a call to worship and recitation of the *Shema;* its high point is reading from the *Torah* scroll. *Havdalah*, a ceremony performed in the home on Saturday evening, marks the end of Shabbat and the beginning of the new week.

The Jewish calendar includes several festivals or holidays. The twelve-month lunar year begins with **Rosh Hashanah** (the New Year) on the first day of Tishri (September–October). **Yom Kippur** (Day of Atonement) falls on the final day of a ten-day period of penitence that begins with Rosh Hashanah. **Sukkot** (Festival of Booths) is an annual eight-day fall festival (beginning five days after Yom Kippur); it entails thanksgiving for nature's fruits and remembering the forty-year sojourn of the Israelites in the Sinai wilderness. Sukkot is rounded off by **Simchat Torah,** the joyous celebration of the completion of the annual reading of the *Torah*. **Chanukah (Hanukkah)** is an eight-day festival (November–December) commemorating the victory of the Maccabees over the Syrians and the rededication (165 B.C.E.) of the Temple in Jerusalem. **Purim** celebrates the deliverance of Jews from a Persian oppressor as narrated in the book of Esther. **Pesach (Passover)** is an eight-day festival celebrating the Exodus of the Israelites from Egypt (March–April). **Shavuot** (Pentecost) commemorates the giving of God's commandments at Sinai; it occurs seven weeks after Passover. Originally Sukkot, Pesach, and Shavuot were agricultural festivals that required a pilgrimage to the Temple in Jerusalem and ritual sacrifice. After the destruction of the Temple (70 C.E.), the rabbis transformed these holidays into occasions for remembering momentous events in the life of the community.

Lieutenant Cadet Marc Moyer blows the *shofar*, an ancient instrument made of a hollow ram's horn and used in conjunction with the observance of Rosh Hashanah (the Jewish New Year), West Point, New York (Jewish New Year 5746 [1985]).

Rosh Hashanah (literally, "head of the year") is the first day of the High Holidays, collectively referred to as the Ten Days of Penitence. It is the day when God remembers and judges human deeds (determines the destiny of humans for the New Year). Human contrition, prayer, and acts of atonement may influence God's judgment, and penitents may be inscribed in the Book of Life for a good year. Rosh Hashanah is a time of rest and prayer punctuated by blowing the *shofar* (ram's horn). One prayer petitions God to grant humans and their children mercy, cause hate and oppression to vanish from the earth, and "inscribe us for blessing in the book of life." On the eve of the Day of Remembrance (another name for Rosh Hashanah), families celebrate the new year at dinner. A ritual is performed, and wine is shared by the family. Apples or some other fruit dipped in honey is eaten to symbolize the hope that the new year will be sweet. Synagogue services include a reading from the *Torah*, prayers, a homily, and blowing the *shofar*.

Yom Kippur concludes the Ten Days of Penitence with a day of reconciliation and restoration between humans and God and among humans. It is a day to seek forgiveness from God and from those who have been sinned against and, in atoning for sin, being restored to wholeness before God

and with others. Judaic tradition teaches that sins against humans can be atoned for only by seeking pardon from the offended party and, whenever possible, by righting the wrong. Yom Kippur is a day of fasting, abstentions, and worship. Perhaps the most memorable part of Yom Kippur services is the recitation of the *Kol Nidre* (all vows). It is a prayer asking God to forgive Israel (collectively and individually) for breaking any vows to God in the new year that they might be unable—through no fault of their own—to fulfill.

Pesach remembers God's liberation of the Israelites from bondage in Egypt. Perhaps its most profound feature is the **Seder** (order of worship) conducted in Jewish homes on the first night or first two nights of the celebration. The Passover Seder is intended to fix the significance of the **Exodus** of the Israelites out of Egypt in the minds of the participants. In the words of one rabbi: "The food we eat, the songs we sing, the stories we tell, the ritual we conduct, all are designed to help us relive that Exodus experience, to feel the lot of the oppressed, to feel the sting of slavery."[39] After a family and their guests have gathered around the table, the Seder begins with a benediction over wine giving thanks to God for the Holy Sabbath and for Passover, "the season of our freedom." The main body of the liturgy is the retelling of the liberation of the Israelites from bondage in Egypt. The story is retold in response to four questions, usually asked by the children present:

> "Why is this night different from all other nights?"
> "Why on this night do we eat bitter herbs?"
> "Why on this night do we dip them in salt water and haroseth?"
> "Why on this night do we hold this seder service?"[40]

Afterward, the meal is eaten, and the Seder is concluded with a benediction.

LIFE CYCLE RITES   Life cycle rites are performed in conjunction with birth, the onset of adulthood, marriage, and death. Circumcision initiates male infants into the Abrahamic covenant. It is performed on the eighth day after birth by a *mohel* (circumciser) with family members and other witnesses present. At the onset of puberty, around the age of thirteen, a male ritually becomes a "son of the commandments" *(bar mitzvah).* In less traditional forms of Judaism, an analogous rite permits a female to become a "daughter of the commandments" *(bat mitzvah).* The ceremony signals that the young person knows something of Judaic tradition and is ready to assume responsibility for keeping God's commands. It is performed as part of the synagogue service where, for the first time, the young adult pronounces a benediction and reads from the *Torah* scroll in a congregational setting.

Jewish weddings normally begin with the entry of the groom, escorted by his father and father-in-law, and the bride, escorted by her mother and mother-in-law. Bride and groom meet under a canopy supported by four rods symbolizing that the couple shall live under one roof. Sanctification of the marriage begins with blessings over a cup of wine (the cup of betrothal). Rings are exchanged, and the contract detailing the couple's obligations is read and signed before witnesses. The rabbi blesses a second cup of wine (the cup of marriage), which the bride and grooom share. At the conclusion of the ceremony, the husband breaks a glass under his

A young woman reads from a *Torah* scroll at her *bat mitzvah* (Maryland, 1994).

foot as a reminder of the destruction of the Temple; thus, even during a joyous celebration, there is grieving for the suffering endured by Israel.

Funerary rites mark the transition from being to nonbeing. If possible, the dying person recites—in the presence of family—the following: "May it be Your will to heal me. Yet if You have decreed that I shall die of this affliction, May my death atone for all sins and transgressions which I have committed before You. Shelter me in the shadow of Your wings. Grant me a share in the world to come."[41] The rite concludes with the recitation of the *Shema.* Eulogies are common. At the grave, God's justice is proclaimed, and a mourners' prayer is recited that praises God and hopes for the messianic age and the resurrection of the dead. During the following week, the family may observe other signs of grief; they may stay at home, sit on low stools, keep candles lit, recite prayers, cut their hair, and cover mirrors. In subsequent years, memorial services may be held on the anniversary of the day of death.

Judaic practice constitutes the melody or personality of Judaism. It involves obeying God's law, doing good deeds, keeping Shabbat, and participating in the ritual life of the Jewish community.

HISTORY OF JUDAISM

It is impossible to separate Judaism from its history; in Judith Plaskow's words, "The Jewish present is rooted in Jewish history."[42] Our four-thousand-year history of Judaism is divided into the biblical, rabbinic, and modern periods.

THE BIBLICAL PERIOD (1900 B.C.E.–70 C.E.)

Our narrative of the biblical period follows the divisions of traditional biblical historiography, even though their reliability is disputed. Scripture has been the primary source for Judaic and Christian histories of the biblical period, but studies of peoples who interacted with the Israelites provide a more accurate and balanced picture. The biblical period includes events that have been foundational to Judaism: God's covenant with Israel, the Exodus, and the revelation of God's *Torah* at Mount Sinai.

AGE OF THE PATRIARCHS (1900–1600 B.C.E.)

In the Judaic tradition, the Jewish thread in the fabric of the human story begins with Abraham and Sarah, who are regarded by Jews, Christians, and Muslims as the father and mother of the Jewish people. Abraham's and Sarah's lineage constituted a Hebrew-speaking branch of the Semitic linguistic family of West Asia. Some Semites were agriculturalists. Others, such as Abraham and Sarah and their descendants (the patriarchs Isaac and Jacob and his twelve sons), were seminomadic pastoralists. Scholars disagree on whether the stories of the patriarchs are chiefly historical or legendary. The biblical stories about them are not corroborated by nonbiblical sources and likely include both legendary and historical elements.

The story of Abraham and Sarah contains five enduring features of traditional Judaism: monotheism, covenant, peoplehood, a holy land, and circumcision. Traditionally, Jews have averred that Abraham was humankind's first monotheist, but some scholars question the historicity of such a claim. Some trace monotheism to Moses (ca. thirteenth century B.C.E.). Others believe that Judaic monotheism was not articulated until the sixth century B.C.E. (see *Isa.* 45:5–7, 46:1–13).

The contention that Judaic monotheism emerged after Abraham and Moses is reinforced by recent scholarly assessments of the relationship of the Israelites and the Canaanites, another Semitic people. Hebrew scripture depicts the Canaanites and Israelites as having very different cultures and theologies, but nonbiblical evidence and a closer reading of scripture suggest that prior to the onset of the Hebraic monarchy (1000 B.C.E.), the Canaanites and Israelites were closely related cultures. Their theological affinity is reflected in the *el* ending of Israel (El was a major Canaanite deity), in biblical passages that suggest that El preceded Yahweh as an Israelite name for God, and in the biblical identification of El with Yahweh. Hints of polytheism in early Israelite religion are evident in the convergence of Yahweh and the Canaanite deities El and Baal, as well as in the possibility that Baal's consort, the goddess Asherah, was part of an Israelite pantheon.[43]

God's covenant with Abraham entailed that the Hebrews were chosen by God and promised a holy land. It began with a directive and a promise: Abraham was to leave his father's house in Mesopotamia and travel to the land of Canaan, and God would bless him and make his descendants a great nation. God pledged an *"everlasting covenant"* to be God to Abraham and his descendants and to give them *"all the land of Canaan, for an everlasting possession."* The Abrahamic covenant set forth the obligations of the Hebrews to be blameless and to practice circumcision: *"You shall circumcise the flesh of your foreskin, and that shall be the sign of the covenant between Me and you. And throughout the generations, every male among you shall be circumcised at the age of eight days"* (*Gen.* 17:2–12).

MOSES, THE EXODUS, AND THE MOSAIC COVENANT

Following the deaths of Abraham and Isaac, the biblical account of their descendants shifts from the land of Canaan to Egypt. After being sold into slavery by his brothers, Joseph (Jacob's eleventh son) rose to prominence in Egypt. During a famine in Canaan, Joseph's brothers traveled to Egypt to buy grain. After reconciling with Joseph, the brothers and their elderly father brought their flocks to Egypt, where they settled and prospered. Possibly, their welcome in Egypt and Joseph's position as an advisor to the king occurred during the period that the Hyksos, another Semitic people from West Asia, ruled Egypt (1676–1566 B.C.E.). Expulsion of the Hyksos and reestablishment of indigenous Egyptian rule were accompanied by the oppression of alien minorities, including the Israelites, who were reduced to the status of slaves.

It was in this setting that Moses, the foundational Judaic lawgiver and leader, made his appearance. There are no references in Egyptian records to any of the biblical episodes associated with Moses, but scholars usually place Moses' story in the reign of Ramses II (1290–1224 B.C.E.). According to the narrative in *Exodus*, when Moses' mother could no longer protect him from the king's decree of death for male Hebrew infants, she put him in a basket and placed it in the Nile. A daughter of the king rescued the child and named him Moses (an Egyptian name). Moses was reared in the king's household as a free man familiar with the ways of the Egyptians rather than those of his people. One day he observed an Egyptian beating an Israelite and in anger killed the Egyptian. Discovering that his crime had been witnessed, Moses fled to the land of Midian, where he married Zipporah, a daughter of Jethro.

While Moses was tending the flock of his father-in-law, an angel of the Lord appeared to him *"in a blazing fire out of a bush . . . yet the bush was not consumed."* When Moses had turned aside to look, God spoke to him: *"I have marked the plight of My people in Egypt. . . . I have come down to rescue them from the Egyptians and to bring them out of that land to a good and spacious land, a land flowing with milk and honey, the region of the Canaanites"* (Exod. 3:7–8). God continued, *"I will send you to Pharaoh and you shall free My people, the Israelites, from Egypt."* Moses was reluctant to undertake such a task; in whose name was he to speak? God said to Moses, *"Thus shall you say to the Israelites, 'Ehyeh* [I Am]

sent me to you.'" And God said further to Moses, *"Thus shall you speak to the Israelites: The LORD* [God's personal name YHWH, perhaps pronounced "Yahweh" and translated here as "the LORD"], *the God [El] of your fathers, the God of Abraham, the God of Isaac, and the God of Jacob has sent me to you: This shall be My name forever"* (Exod. 3:14–15).

Moses and his brother Aaron supplicated the pharaoh to let God's people go. The pharaoh responded by increasing the hardships of the Israelites. Subsequently, the Egyptians were struck by ten calamities, concluding with the death of all first-born of the Egyptian people and their cattle. The grieving king relented and bid the Israelites to go. The liberated slaves were led on their Exodus from Egypt by Yahweh, who went before them by day in a pillar of cloud and by night in a pillar of fire. The pharaoh changed his mind and pursued the Israelites with his army and six hundred chariots. When the Israelites arrived at the Red Sea—or, as some scholars believe, the Sea of Reeds—they were trapped between the sea and the pursuing Egyptians. Why, they lamented to Moses, did you bring us out of Egypt? It would have been better to serve the Egyptians *"than to die in the wilderness."* Then a miracle occurred. The sea was parted, allowing the Israelites to escape. When the pharaoh's army pursued them, the sea closed over the Egyptians and drowned them. The Israelite women celebrated by dancing to the song of Moses' sister, the prophet Miriam: *"Sing to the LORD, for He has triumphed gloriously; Horse and driver He has hurled into the sea"* (Exod. 15:21).

Tradition has it that the Israelites sojourned for forty years in the wilderness of Sinai before crossing the river Jordan into the land of Canaan. During this period, they came together at Mount Sinai (the mountain of God) as a people bound to a covenant that governed their relations with God and one another. In the *Exodus* narrative, God called Moses to the mountaintop and revealed the commandments to him, which were engraved on tablets of stone and later kept in the Ark of the Covenant, a rectangular acacia wood box adorned in gold. There is no consensus on what laws were disclosed at Sinai. Were they the *Ten Command-ments* (*Exod.* 20:2–17), or did they include other legal codes associated with Moses, such as the covenant code (*Exod.* 20:22–23:33), the deutero-nomic code (*Deut.* 12–26), and the priestly code (*Leviticus)?* Whatever transpired, the revelation at Sinai was of such magnitude that all Jewish law codes have been legitimated by it.

The Exodus from Egypt and God's covenant with Moses and the Israelites at Mount Sinai are enduring features of Judaism. The message of the Exodus is twofold: human freedom (*"for you were a slave in the land of Egypt"*) and divine deliverance (*"see the salvation of the LORD, which he will work for you today"*). The miracle at the sea and God's revelation at Sinai express the conviction that Yah-weh's promise to Moses and the Israelites was to be with them to instruct, judge, commission, sanc-tify, and save. Jews commemorate the Exodus event through Passover observances and the Mosaic covenant forged at Sinai through faithfulness to God's commands. The importance of the two events for religious Jews can hardly be overstat-ed. By obeying *Torah* (God's instructions) and reen-acting the meaning of the Exodus, generations of Jews have been shaped by these root experiences.[44]

THE CONQUEST OF CANAAN (CA. 1220–1020 B.C.E.)

At the outset of Israel's conquest of Canaan, the land and its peoples occupied a buffer area between the empires of the Egyptians and the Hittites.[45] Scripture provides conflicting accounts of what transpired. In *Joshua,* the conquest of Canaan was completed in the lifetime of Joshua, a leader whom God commissioned as Moses' suc-cessor. After numerous delays on their way from Sinai to Canaan, the Israelites crossed the river Jor-dan into Canaan and defeated the Canaanites and other peoples in battle. Only one setback occurred, a defeat at Ai. In contrast, in *Judges,* the conquest took around two hundred years and involved numerous Israelite defeats.

The theologies of the two books are similar: in both, Israel's faithfulness to Yahweh is reward-ed, and disobedience is punished. In *Joshua,* it is expressed in the story of the defeat at Ai, which

was seen as punishment for the sin of Achan, who, in disobeying God's command to destroy the booty taken in the battle of Jericho, hid some of it. The pollution of Israel was removed by stoning Achan and his family to death. In *Judges,* it is evident in stories that repeat a cycle in which Israel sins (covenants with the Canaanites and worships at their altars) and is punished (given into the hands of its enemies), followed by God's raising up of "judges" or "deliverers," such as Gideon and Deb-orah, who free the Israelites from their enemies. But whenever a judge died, *"they would again act basely"* and worship other gods.

THE RISE AND FALL OF ISRAEL'S KINGDOMS (1020–587 B.C.E.)

During the conquest of Canaan, the Israelites were a loose confederation of tribes and clans. There was no priestly hierar-chy; male heads of clans and families performed the ritual sacrifices. There were several local altars, and a central sanctuary in Shiloh that housed the Ark of the Covenant. Israel's shift to a monarchy and priesthood occurred in a context in which the people had made the transition from pastoralists to agriculturalists. In biblical historiography, the period of Israel's kingdoms is divided into the Unit-ed Kingdom (1020–922 B.C.E.) and the Divided Kingdom. During the latter period there were two Israelite kingdoms: Israel, the northern kingdom, (922–722 B.C.E.) and Judah, the southern kingdom (922–587 B.C.E.).

The hold of Israel's tribes on the land was pre-carious; they were threatened to the east by the Ammonites and to the west by the Philistines, a people from Crete who had dislodged the Canaan-ites along the Palestine coast. The *Bible* depicts the Israelites as beset by tribal rivalries and external enemies and clamoring for a monarchy. Prodded by the people, Samuel, a priest and seer, reluctantly anointed Saul as Israel's king, the first of the three kings (Saul, David, and Solomon) of a united Israel. The anointing symbolized that the authority of Israel's kings was derived from God, but they were neither divine kings nor above the law.

Saul's reign (1020–1000 B.C.E.) was never secure or lavish. He held court in a tent and had neither harem nor palace. Most of his reign was spent fighting the Philistines and other adversaries. Saul had domestic opposition as well. When Saul, in defiance of God's will, did not utterly destroy the possessions of a conquered people and kill their king, Samuel broke with Saul. He pronounced that Saul's kingship had been taken from him and anointed David, the son of Jesse, as king. The kingdom was soon divided between Saul's supporters and those of David. Saul's reign ended with his army defeated by the Philistines and his own death, along with three of his sons.

After Saul's death, David's tribe, called Judah, conferred the kingship on David, who ruled in Hebron while Saul's surviving son, Ishbosheth, ruled in the north. A war between David and Ishbosheth ended in the latter's death, and David was made king of a united Israel (see Figure 8.2). David (r. 1000–961 B.C.E.) solidified his rule by making Jerusalem the capital (a more accessible point between north and south) and by bringing the Ark of the Covenant to Jerusalem. Campaigns against the Philistines forced them to retreat to their coastal cities. David's reign appeared so blessed that Nathan prophesied that his *"throne shall be established forever"* (*2 Sam.* 7:16).

David, Israel's greatest king, was succeeded on the throne by his son Solomon (r. 961–922 B.C.E.), Israel's most renowned sage. Solomon imported craftspeople and conscripted Israelites to labor on the fortification of Israelite cities and the building of the king's palace and the Temple of the Lord in Jerusalem. Solomon's palace was the scene of a lavish courtly life, including a harem of wives and concubines; at the Temple's dedication, 22,000 oxen and 120,000 sheep were reportedly sacrificed (*2 Chron.* 7:5).

After Solomon's death, the kingdom was torn apart by civil war. Seeds of discontent had been sown during "wise" Solomon's reign; his building projects were funded by heavy taxes, obligatory labor, and indebtedness to other states. Resentment was intense, especially in the north. Solomon's successor, his eldest son Rehoboam, rejected the petition of tribal elders for a redress of their grievances. The northerners revolted and made Jeroboam

(r. 922–901 B.C.E.) king of their new kingdom, called Israel. Following the prosperity and stability that marked the reign of Jeroboam II (786–746 B.C.E.), problems arose that led to Israel's destruction by the Assyrians. The Assyrian campaign ended with the fall of Samaria, Israel's capital, in 722 B.C.E. The population was decimated; many were killed, and thousands were relocated in other parts of the Assyrian Empire.

Judah, the southern kingdom, barely survived the Assyrian threat. In 701, the Assyrians laid siege to several Judean cities, including Jerusalem, and though Jerusalem was not surrendered, Judah subsequently existed under Assyrian rule. King Manasseh (r. 687–642 B.C.E.) ruled as a vassal to Assyria; he oppressed Yahwists and encouraged the worship of pagan deities. Unlike his grandfather, Manasseh, King Josiah (r. 640–609 B.C.E.) was a devout Yahwist. In 622, the priest Hilkiah discovered a temple scroll containing the Mosaic covenant. (Scholars believe the scroll was later integrated with other sources to form *Deuteronomy*.) The scroll was read to Josiah, who was deeply moved by it. After its words were authenticated by the prophetess Huldah, the king had the Mosaic covenant read to the people and implemented a reform based on its strictures. Yahwists warred against polytheism and idolatry. Pagan shrines were closed, and cult objects associated with Baal, Asherah, and other pagan deities were destroyed. Sacrifices were henceforth performed exclusively in the Jerusalem Temple, and worship outside of Jerusalem focused on Yahweh and the scroll of the Mosaic covenant. In 609, Josiah, Yahweh's champion, died from wounds suffered in battle with the Egyptians.

The Assyrians and Judeans were conquered by a new power, the Chaldeans (neo-Babylonians). In 598, King Jehoiachin surrendered Jerusalem to the Chaldean king, Nebuchadnezzar II (r. 605–562 B.C.E.). Jehoiachin and many other Jews were deported to Babylon, and Zedekiah was installed as a vassal king. In 589, Zedekiah heeded the advice of the prophet Hananiah and rebelled. The Chaldeans invaded and besieged Jerusalem. The city fell in 587; it and the Temple were plundered

Figure 8.2

and destroyed by fire. Another group of deportees was exiled; one group included Zedekiah, who was forced to witness the execution of his sons before being blinded and taken in chains to Babylon. Other Jews relocated in Egypt.

THE PROPHETS   During the time of the Israelite kingdoms, prophets helped the people interpret the politics of their kings and the destruction of their kingdoms. The prophets depicted in *Samuel* and *Kings* included ecstatics who prophesied in trance states and seers, such as Samuel, who divined the future and communicated God's answers to people's petitions. The classic form of biblical prophecy was exemplified by figures who saw themselves as the "tongues" (messengers) of Yahweh. They prefaced their proclamations by phrases such as "Thus said the Lord" and communicated through dramatic acts as well. For example, Jeremiah wore a wooden yoke around his neck as a sign that Judah should accept the rule of Babylon. It is not surprising that these "troublers of Israel" were usually rebuffed by the priestly and courtly establishments.

Prophetic theology saw God as the Lord of human events and determiner of the fate of nations. Obedience to God—devotion and just behavior—leads to well-being. Disobedience to God—idolatry and injustice—leads to punishment. Amos warned that God's judgment would press upon those *"who defraud the poor, who rob the needy."* Why, the prophet Hosea asked, were the Israelites beset by enemies? *"Because there is no honesty and no goodness/And no obedience to God in the land."* The prophets taught that just behavior is preferable to sacrifice: *"For I desire goodness, not sacrifice; Obedience to God, rather than burnt offerings"* (*Hos.* 6:6). God commands us to *"seek good, and not evil, that you may live"* and to *"let justice well up like water, righteousness like an ever-flowing stream"* (*Amos* 5:14, 24).

Figure 8.2   At its maximum, the authority of David and Solomon was said to have extended northward to the Euphrates (1 *Kings* 4:24; Hebrew text 5:4). During the reign of Solomon's son, the realm was split into a northern kingdom (Israel) and a southern kingdom (Judah).

The prophetic message was not one of unremitting judgment and punishment. There was hope; a remnant of Israel would survive and be reestablished in the land. Hosea tempered God's judgment with a message of reconciliation. Israel has played the harlot, but God has not divorced her. God will woo her back, and she will be transformed. Jeremiah proclaimed that God's love is an *"everlasting love"* and envisioned a *"new covenant with the house of Israel and the house of Judah"* in which God's law would be written in their hearts.

A breathtaking note of deliverance was struck by Isaiah of Babylon, an anonymous prophet who prophesied during the Exile of the Jews in Babylon and whose message is contained in *Isaiah 40–55.* (Biblical critics believe that the book of *Isaiah* is a composite of two or three prophets.) Isaiah of Babylon begins with words of comfort. God has not forgotten the people: *"Fear not, for I am with you. Be not frightened, for I am your God"* (*Isa.* 41:10). Deliverance from exile is near; on their return to Zion, the mountains and hills shall be leveled and the crooked made straight. The new exodus will endure: *"My triumph shall endure forever, My salvation through all the ages"* (*Isa.* 51:8b).

Some prophets proclaimed that God would send a Messiah—literally, an "anointed one"—who would deliver the Israelites from their enemies and usher in a new age. Messianic prophecies surfaced with Isaiah of Jerusalem (742–701 B.C.E.), the prophet of *Isaiah* 1–39. This Isaiah announced that Yahweh would anoint a new king descended from the seed of Jesse, a king who would sit upon the throne of David *"that it may be firmly established in justice and in equity now and evermore"* (*Isa.* 9:6). When the messianic age arrives, the deaf shall hear, the blind shall see, and nations *"shall beat their swords into plowshares and their spears into pruning hooks; Nation shall not take up sword against nation; They shall never again know war"* (*Isa.* 2:4). The idea of the Messiah was associated with the anointing of Israel's kings, and although most messianic passages imply that the Messiah is a person (an idealized king akin to David), it is plausible to argue that Israel is God's servant.

EXILE AND RESTORATION The Chaldean conquest dealt a mortal blow to the remaining kingdom. Jerusalem (Zion) was no more, and many Jews were deported to Babylon. *Psalm* 137:1–4 speaks of the desolation of the exiles during the period known as the Exile:

> *By the rivers of Babylon,*
> *there we sat, sat and wept,*
> *as we thought of Zion.*
> *There on the poplars*
> *we hung up our lyres,*
> *for our captors asked us there for songs,*
> *our tormentors, for amusement,*
> *"Sing us one of the songs of Zion"*
> *How can we sing a song of the LORD*
> *on alien soil?*

The exiles interacted with the Chaldeans but remained a separate people. Sabbath observance, dietary and purity rules, and disapproval of intermarriage contributed to the preservation of their identity. In the absence of the Temple, the Jewish exiles met in assemblies (precursors of synagogues) and focused on God's laws, including the copying and editing of the *Pentateuch*, and on their survival as a community of memory.

In 539 B.C.E., Babylon was defeated by the Persians. Soon thereafter, the founder of the Persian Empire, Cyrus the Great, permitted the descendants of the exiles to return home (an act referred to as the Restoration). Cyrus granted permission to reconstruct the Temple and returned the holy things the Babylonians had looted from it. Some Jews stayed in Babylon, where they had prospered, but others, fueled by prophecies of restoration, returned home to Judah, a land inhabited by the Samaritans (descendants of Assyrian deportees and Jewish peasants) and other peoples.

In 515 B.C.E., a new Temple (known as the Second Temple) was dedicated. Afterward, a priestly class, whose members traced their lineage to Aaron, presided over special festivals, daily worship, and animal and cereal sacrifices. Three agricultural feasts required Jews to make annual pilgrimages to the Temple, and each feast was accompanied by sacrifice. The Temple and sacrifice were central to Judaism after the Exile until the destruction of the Second Temple in 70 C.E. Sages and scribes copied, edited, and interpreted scripture and provided leadership in nontemple assemblies. Prophets did not disappear, but their voices were secondary to the leadership of priests and sages.

In 458 B.C.E., Ezra, a priest and scribe from Babylonia, returned to Jerusalem with a mandate from the Persian king, Artaxerxes (464–428 B.C.E.), to instruct the Jews in the "laws of their own God." Ezra was learned in *Torah* and appears to have brought a codified *Torah* from Babylon. In 444 B.C.E., he read the law of Moses to an assembly of Jerusalemites, who pledged fidelity to it. Ezra was instrumental in the reshaping of older Israelite traditions and in weaving them into postexilic Judaism. Ezra's opposition to marriage with non-Jews contributed to the "set-apartness" of the Jews.

Greeks and Syrians succeeded the Persians as masters of Palestine. In 332 B.C.E., Alexander the Great conquered Judea (the Greek transliteration of *Judah*). After Alexander's death in 323, his empire was divided into separate spheres governed by his generals. Ptolemy ruled in Egypt and Palestine, and Seleucus ruled in Syria. In 198 B.C.E., King Antiochus III (251–197 B.C.E.), a descendant of Seleucus, took Jerusalem and imposed Greek culture on the Jews. Jason, a Jewish high priest under King Antiochus IV (175–164 B.C.E.), attempted to integrate Hellenism and Hebraism; for example, he established a gymnasium near the Temple in which Jews, following the example of the Greeks, exercised naked. Pious Jews were appalled. Street fights broke out between Hellenizers and Yahwists. Antiochus responded by forbidding *Torah* study, circumcision, and Sabbath observance.

In 167 B.C.E., Antiochus decreed that the Jews embrace paganism. Pagan images were placed in the Temple, and sacrifices of unclean animals were conducted. Outraged Yahwists revolted. Mattathias, a priest of Hasmonean lineage, killed a Jew who was sacrificing to Zeus and a Syrian officer who urged Mattathias to worship a pagan deity. Mattathias and his five sons initiated a rebellion against the Syrians. After Mattathias's death, his son Judas took command of the rebels. Following a lengthy war known as the Maccabean revolt, in which Judas and three of his brothers were killed, Syria acknowledged Judea's independence. Simon, the surviving brother, was appointed high priest and king by the people. Simon's son, John Hyrcanus, conquered most of Palestine and Idumea and forced the Idumeans to convert to Judaism. By 70 B.C.E., Queen Salome Alexandra ruled a Jewish kingdom nearly as large as that of David and Solomon. Following her death, feuding between factions ended in 63 B.C.E. with Judea as a vassal state under Roman rule.

JUDAIC THOUGHT IN THE LATE BIBLICAL PERIOD

Diverse strands of Judaic thought emerged after the Exile. Beliefs that marriage with non-Jews was polluting and that Israel's enemies were God's enemies were challenged in the books of *Ruth* and *Jonah*. Ruth, a Moabite woman married to a Jew, was depicted as a pious widow whose love cut across ethnic barriers. By countering Jonah's desire that God destroy the Assyrians with God's forgiveness of them, the book of *Jonah* viewed Israel's enemies in a different light. Diversity of thought is also evident in *Ecclesiastes,* a text traditionally ascribed to King Solomon but probably the work of an anonymous sage. Its biblically atypical theology teaches that all human endeavors are transitory, a chasing after the wind. Nothing ultimately satisfies. Life is capricious and unjust; the battle does not always go to the strong or the race to the swiftest. When humans die, they will not rise again. God has put a desire for the eternal in humans but has made them so that this desire can never be satisfied. The sage advises us to limit our expectations. Moments of enjoyment are the most satisfying *"for the only good a man can have under the sun is to eat and drink and enjoy himself"* (*Eccles.* 8:15).

In spite of opposition to alien influences, Jews incorporated Persian and Greek elements and reworked them to give them a Judaic flavor. Postexilic Judaism appears to have been influenced by the Persian religion Zoroastrianism, which conceived of the world as a battleground between the forces of good and evil, culminating in the triumph of good and the reward of the righteous in Paradise. Whatever the origin of these ideas, they were part of Judaic belief in the late biblical period. Hebraic literature with apocalyptic (end of the world) themes appeared that reiterated prophetic beliefs about God's justice but also revealed what had been hidden. In the short run, the righteous suffer and the wicked prosper, but ultimately good will triumph over evil, the just will be rewarded, and the wicked will be punished. Justice will prevail—if not in this world, then in the next. One apocalypse, the book of *Daniel,* offered hope to those who suffered under Antiochus IV. As God had brought low the Chaldeans and Persians, he would destroy Antiochus and deliver Israel. A messianic figure was coming who would inaugurate God's everlasting kingdom (*Dan.* 7:13). The righteous would be delivered, and many *"that sleep in the dust of the earth will awake, some to eternal life, others to . . . everlasting abhorrence"* (*Dan.* 12:2).

Greek influences were evident in a number of ways. During the third century B.C.E., **diaspora** Jews (those living outside of Palestine, a phenomenon initially triggered by the Babylonian Exile) translated scripture into Greek, a translation known as the *Septuagint.* Philo of Alexandria integrated biblical theology with elements borrowed from the philosophical schools of Platonism and Stoicism. For Philo, the God of Hebrew scripture is the Mind of the universe. As transcendent, God is unnameable and incomprehensible. As immanent, God is the indwelling reason that pervades the cosmos and is present in the human mind. Wisdom is the intermediary between God's transcendent being and the world. Plato's influence is evident in Philo's view that life is a pilgrimage of the soul to God and that God created the world from preexistent forms. Against skeptics, Philo argued that just as works of art require a designer to account for them, the interdependence and harmony of nature require a Maker. [46]

JEWS UNDER ROMAN RULE (63 B.C.E.–135 C.E.)

As noted, the Maccabean revolt led to the establishment of a Jewish state ruled by the Hasmonean dynasty, but a civil war ended in 63 B.C.E. with

Judea as a vassal of Rome. During the reign of Augustus (27 B.C.E.–14 C.E.), the Jewish population numbered around 5 million, roughly 1 million of whom lived in Palestine.[47] Relations between Jews and Romans periodically turned violent. When the Parthians (a people who reestablished the Persian Empire) invaded Syria, Hasmonean loyalists turned against their Roman overseers. In 38 B.C.E., Roman legions invaded Judea and killed many Jews, including the last Hasmonean heir to the throne. Herod (r. 37–4 B.C.E.), a convert to Judaism, was appointed king of Judea by the Roman Senate.

For the most part, the Romans tolerated the religious convictions of Jews and did not require them to worship the gods of Rome or attend pagan ceremonies. The **Sanhedrin** (a council of elders) was recognized as a court of Jewish law; it set festival dates on the basis of the new moon and tried civil and religious cases involving Jews. Interaction, however, entailed animosity as well as respect. Jews dealt with non-Jews, whom they called Gentiles, in the public sphere but avoided private interaction with them. The food, homes, and temples of Gentiles were regarded as polluting. Many Romans accommodated their Jewish neighbors and found their faith attractive, but others were offended by their "set-apartness." The Roman historian Tacitus (ca. 55–ca. 120 C.E.) groused that "things sacred with us, with them have no sanctity, while they allow what with us is forbidden." He charged Jews with adopting the practice of circumcision "as a mark of difference from other men" and concluded that "the Jewish religion is tasteless and mean."[48]

Tacitus's view was probably atypical, but tensions between Jews and Romans were real.[49] When Roman authorities permitted pagans to build an altar in Yavneh, a city within Judea, Jews responded by tearing it down. An angry Caligula (r. 37–41 C.E.) ordered a statue of the Roman deity Jupiter adorned with the emperor's facial features placed in the Temple in Jerusalem. A Jewish delegation communicated to officials that they were prepared to die rather than violate God's laws. Jewish historian Flavius Josephus (ca. 37–100 C.E.) reported that the envoys "threw themselves down upon their faces, and stretched out their throats, and said they were ready to be slain."[50] Desecration of the Second Temple and civil war were averted by a Roman officer's murder of Caligula.

In the Roman Era there were many Jewish factions. The most influential, the Sadducees and Pharisees, originated during the time of the Seleucids. Sadducees were an aristocratic group of priests, merchants, and landowners who accepted the *Pentateuch* as the whole *Torah* and rejected the claim that an oral, as well as a written, *Torah* had been revealed at Sinai. Sadducees rejected belief in the resurrection of the body, the world to come, and the Messiah, noting that they were not in the *Pentateuch*. The Sadducees stressed that temple sacrifice and interpretation of *Torah* were priestly functions.

Pharisees came from the ranks of scribes and pious laity. Out of devotion, they did not speak God's personal name, YHWH, substituting in its place Adonai (LORD) or other forms of address. Pharisees believed that an oral, as well as a written, *Torah* had been revealed to Moses and handed down from generation to generation and that the former contained the promise of the resurrection of the dead and the world to come. Pharisees stressed the study of *Torah* and established houses of learning, or **synagogues,** which would later become places of worship as well. The most distinguished Pharisee was Hillel the Elder, who as leader of the Sanhedrin enacted reforms to protect the poor and to open the synagogues to a wider range of people. On one occasion a proselyte challenged Hillel: *"If you can teach me the whole Torah while I stand on one foot, you can make me a Jew."* Hillel responded, *"What is hateful to you, do not do to your neighbor. This is the whole Torah; the rest is commentary. Go and study."*[51] In another context, the sage spoke of the importance of our obligations to ourselves and to others: *"If I am not for myself, who will be for me? And if I am only for myself, what am I? If not now, when?"*[52]

Other Jewish factions included the Essenes, the Zealots, the followers of John the Baptist, and the Jesus movement. The group referred to as the Essenes by Josephus and identified by many scholars as the community associated with the Dead Sea Scrolls responded to what they saw as a corruption of the Temple and priesthood by creating a purified community in the desert. Whereas the communitarian Essenes separated themselves from pagans and defiled Jews, the Zealots urged revolt against their oppressors. In response to a Roman census taken in 6 C.E., Judas the Galilean led an insurrection under the slogan "No God but Yahweh, no tax but to the temple, no friend but the Zealot." His passion for liberty and opposition to Roman taxes ended in the crucifixion of two thousand Jews.

Palestine abounded in charismatic leaders. Convinced that the kingdom of heaven was at hand and that God's wrath would fall upon the unrepentant, John the Baptist preached a message of repentance and baptism. Jesus of Nazareth was an itinerant preacher and healer during the administration of Pontius Pilate (26–36 C.E.); his disciples taught that he was the Messiah and the Son of God and that his death on the cross atoned for all. Another charismatic, Theudas (ca. 40 C.E.), convinced others to follow him to the river Jordan, which he believed would part and let them through. The Romans beheaded Theudas and killed and imprisoned many of his followers.

After a period of tranquility under Rome's vassal King Herod Agrippa, the cauldron that was Judea boiled over into war. Zealots urged revolt against Rome and found followers among a people oppressed by taxes. Messianists proclaimed that the Messiah was coming and the messianic age was near. The first war with Rome (66–73 C.E.) began with a Sabbath day violation in Caesarea; a riot ensued, resulting in the death of pagans and Jews. The conflict shifted to Jerusalem, where the procurator of Judea insisted that those who had insulted him be punished. When the offenders were not identified by Jewish authorities, Roman troops were brought into action, and 3,600 Jerusalemites were killed. Zealots captured the desert fortress at Masada and killed its defenders. In Jerusalem, Jews gained the advantage, and the Roman garrison prepared to leave. After laying aside their arms, they were slaughtered.

After defeats left most of Palestine in Jewish hands, the Romans reasserted control. In March 70 C.E., the siege of Jerusalem began. In August, the Second Temple was looted and destroyed by fire. Jerusalem was leveled and its inhabitants killed or enslaved. Masada was the last bastion of Jewish resistance to fall. The Zealots elected to commit suicide rather than surrender the fortress; the dead included 960 men, women, and children; the survivors numbered two women and five children. Josephus's history includes the final exhortation of Eleazar, the leader of the Masada community: "Since we, long ago . . . resolved never to be servants to the Romans, nor to any other than to God Himself . . . the time is now come that obliges us to make that resolution true in practice. . . . Let us make haste to die bravely."[53]

Conflicts between Jews and Romans continued amid expectations that a Messiah would come and restore Judah. In 131 C.E., Hadrian (r. 117–138) issued an edict against mutilations, including circumcision, and established a Roman colony in Jerusalem with a shrine of Jupiter on the site of the destroyed Temple. Another war resulted (132–135 C.E.). Led by a figure who was given the messianic title bar Kochba (son of the star), the Jewish rebels made the Romans withdraw from Jerusalem and briefly reestablished a Jewish state; by late 134 or early 135, however, they were forced to abandon Jerusalem. Hadrian issued an order forbidding Sabbath observance and public reading of the *Torah*. In the summer of 135 C.E., bar Kochba, whom Rabbi Akiva (ca. 50–135) had hailed as the Messiah, was killed and his army defeated. Jews who survived the war were excluded on penalty of death from entering Jerusalem except on the anniversary of the destruction of Solomon's temple. Antoninus Pius (r. 138–161) set aside Hadrian's edicts against Judaism, but by that time the Jewish population in Palestine probably numbered no more than five thousand.[54]

THE RABBINIC PERIOD (70–1789 C.E.)

The period of rabbinic Judaism began with the destruction of the Temple by the Romans in 70

C.E. and ended with the emancipation of European Jews in 1789 from constraints that excluded them from public life. It is referred to as rabbinic because leadership was chiefly provided by rabbis. In the rabbinic period, there was no Temple, no priesthood, no animal sacrifice, and no Jewish state. Nearly all Jews lived outside Palestine; only a marginal existence was possible for them in their holy land, which was ruled for over two thousand years (63 B.C.E.–1948 C.E.) by Romans, Christians, and Muslims. Rabbinic Judaism emerged as a response to wars with Rome that decimated Palestinian Jewry and destroyed their spiritual center, the Temple. In spite of the devastation, Jews did not disappear; they recentered themselves in the study of, and devotion to, God's instructions. Like the biblical period, the rabbinic period is a foundational one in which new texts and new directions emerged.

THE RABBIS AT YAVNEH

During the first war with Rome, the sage Johanan ben Zakkai left Jerusalem and sought asylum from the Romans. Dispatched to a refugee camp at Yavneh in northern Palestine, Johanan assembled a group of sages and students to study *Torah.* The academy at Yavneh included a new Sanhedrin that ruled on spiritual and secular matters. The sages were called *rabbi,* a title indicating ordination by peers and competence to teach the *Torah,* make legal decisions, and serve in the religious court. Under Johanan and his successor Gamaliel II, rabbis made decisions by majority vote on the law and, after considerable discussion, added the third and final body of literature (the *Kethuvim,* or "writings") to Hebrew scripture.

The rabbis at Yavneh set an example that has endured. After the Second Temple was destroyed, the priesthood and animal sacrifice disappeared. Judaism was henceforth centered in the studying and doing of God's instructions, the *Torah* of Moses. Prayer, study, and other forms of worship in homes and synagogues replaced the Temple. When Rabbi Joshua lamented that atonement for sin through sacrifice was no longer possible, Rabbi Johanan responded, "We have a means of making atonement. And what is it? It is deeds of love."[55]

THE FORMATION OF THE *MISHNAH* AND *TALMUD* (CA. 200–600 C.E.)

After the second Roman war rained destruction on Judea, a remnant from Yavneh led by Rabbi Simeon ben Gamaliel reestablished the academy and Sanhedrin in Galilee. Simeon's son, Judah the Patriarch (ca. 170–217), succeeded him as head of the Sanhedrin. With the assistance of the Sanhedrin, Judah edited and codified the *Mishnah,* a body of oral tradition that the rabbis believed was revealed to Moses at Mount Sinai and passed down through the centuries by recitation. In codifying the *Mishnah,* Judah relied on the legal opinions of sages from Hillel the Elder to himself. The *Mishnah* that emerged is a written body of Jewish law applying Mosaic law to prayer, agriculture, festivals, Sabbath, women, marriage, divorce, property, sacrifice, dietary rules, and other subjects. The *Mishnah's* authority rests on the conviction that God revealed it to Moses, who delivered it to Joshua, who passed it to the prophets, who gave it to the sages of the Great Assembly, who gave it to the Pharisees, who delivered it to the Tannaim (the rabbis from Hillel to Judah).

Following the codification of the *Mishnah,* rabbis in Palestine and Babylonia continued the task of memorizing, interpreting, and compiling traditions that were not in the *Mishnah.* Some of these traditions were included in the *Gemara,* a body of literature containing amplifications of the *Mishnah* by rabbis following the Tannaim. *Mishnah* plus *Gemara* equals the *Talmud.* As noted, there are two *Talmuds,* one compiled in Palestine around 400 C.E. and one in Babylonia around 500. The *Talmuds* can be thought of as a discussion extending over generations of sages and rabbis from the schools of Hillel and Shammai to Judah the Patriarch to the rabbis of Palestine and Babylon. Modern students of *Talmud-Torah* continue this dialogue.

Rabbis of the talmudic period produced other literature, including collections of commentaries expounding the meaning of scripture. An example from the *Mekhilta,* a commentary of *Exodus,* will suffice. *Exodus* 20:2 indicates that the *Torah* was revealed at Sinai, which prompted the exegete to ask, "Why was the Torah not given in the land of Israel?" The rhetorical question is answered: "In order that the nations of the world should not have the excuse, for saying, 'Because it was given in Israel's land, therefore we have not accepted it.'" In probing the meaning of the text, the commentator notes other possibilities why the *Torah* was revealed at Sinai: "To avoid causing dissension among the tribes. Else one might have said, 'In my territory the Torah was given.'" Therefore, the exegete concluded, "The Torah was given in the desert, publicly and openly, in a place belonging to no one. . . . so also are the words of the Torah free to all who come into the world."[56]

TALMUDIC TEACHING An emphasis on justice and mercy was characteristic of rabbinic ethics from the beginning. Johanan's mentor Hillel the Elder admonished Jews to *"be of the disciples of Aaron, loving peace and pursuing peace, loving all men and leading them to Torah."*[57] Hillel's concern for the vulnerable was shared by Rabbi Akiva, who taught that *"whosoever neglects the duty of visiting the sick is guilty of shedding blood."*[58] Akiva once reduced the essence of *Torah* to *Leviticus* 19:18: *"You shall love your neighbor as yourself."* Talmudic teaching moderated the conception of Yahweh as a deity who commanded the Israelites to utterly destroy the Canaanites by depicting the Holy One as suffering when any aspect of creation is destroyed. In contrast to the biblical account of Israel's celebration of the drowning of the Egyptians in the Red Sea, the rabbis taught that God commanded the angels not to rejoice: *"My children lie drowned at the sea, and you would sing?"*[59]

Talmudic rabbis were cautious about messianic claims, as indicated by remarks attributed to Johanan: "If you are holding a sapling in your hand and someone says to you the Messiah is here, plant the sapling first and then welcome the Messiah."[60] The rabbis did not reject belief in the Messiah but modified it to fit their emphasis on *Torah*.[61] In accord with the prophets, the rabbis taught that the Messiah would come from the house of David, but they molded his royal persona into that of sage and priest. They reaffirmed the hope of a messianic age but grounded its advent in obedience to God's instructions; they taught, for example, that the Mes-

siah would come if all Jews kept a single Sabbath. The rabbis had cause to be wary of messianic movements, because they sometimes led to Israel's destruction. A rabbi asked rhetorically, *"Why was the second Temple destroyed?"* And he answered, *"because of groundless hatred."*[62] Roman factions were at odds with the Jews, and zealous segments of the Jewish community despised Roman rule. In place of such antipathies, the rabbis sought to substitute goodwill: *"We support the poor of the pagans along with the poor of Israel, and visit the sick of the pagans along with the sick of Israel, and bury the dead of the pagans along with the dead of Israel, in the interests of peace."*[63]

THE INTERACTION OF JEWS AND CHRISTIANS FROM 50 TO 1000 C.E. Although Jesus of Nazareth and his disciples were Jews, the *New Testament* pictures their relations with other Jewish factions as strained and sometimes violent. After Jesus' crucifixion by Roman authorities, tensions between Christians and Jews resulted in the deaths of his followers Stephen and James and the imprisonment of Peter and Paul. By the time the Romans destroyed the Second Temple, the Jesus movement had made the transition from that of a Jewish sect to a community with a majority of non-Jews. Animosity and competition between Jews and Christians continued. In the eighties, a rabbinic edict closed the synagogues to Christians and urged Jews to have no interaction with them. Christian antipathy was evident in the *New Testament's* depiction of Jews as doing the will of their *"father the devil"* (*John* 8:44) and as *"Christ killers"* whose blood guilt was handed down from generation to generation (*Matt.* 27:25), charges that fueled centuries of Christian **anti-Semitism** (hostility to Jews).

Anti-Jewish and anti-Judaism sentiments in the *New Testament* were reinforced by early Church fathers. In his *Eight Orations against the Jews*, the patriarch of Constantinople Saint John Chrysostom (ca. 347–407), vilified Jews as thieves and animals who lived "by the rule of debauchery and inordinate gluttony. Only one thing they understand: to gorge themselves and to get drunk." Saint Augustine's (354-430) judgment reflects the ambiguous status of Jews in Christian theology. Augustine observed that although Jews deserved harsh punishment for the crucifixion of Jesus, God permitted them to survive as witnesses to the truth of Christianity. As enemies of the gospel, Jews were justifiably constrained, but as recipients of God's grace, they should be permitted to do those things conceded by law without injury.

Conversion of the emperor Constantine (306–337) to Christianity was momentous for both Christians and Jews. Christians exchanged their status as an illegal and persecuted religious minority to that of a group favored by the Roman emperor. Jewish fortunes took a turn for the worse. Legislation in the fourth century prohibited conversions to Judaism and intermarriage of Jews and Christians. In the following century, an imperial edict excluded Jews from posts that would place them in a position to judge matters related to Christians.

In 395, the emperor Theodosius divided the Christianized Roman Empire between his two sons. The eastern part of the Roman (Byzantine) Empire endured until 1453, when it fell to the Ottomans, a Muslim dynasty centered in Turkey. The western part of the empire was centered in Rome. In the fourth and fifth centuries, it was invaded by Germanic tribes. With the Roman Empire in the west replaced by Germanic states, the period known as the Middle Ages (476–1492) began. Conversion of the "barbarians" to Christ was harmful to the Jews. For example, before the king of Spain converted to Christianity (587), his subjects—whether pagans, Jews or Christians—were relatively equal before the law. Afterward, Jews were forcibly converted.

JEWS AND MUSLIMS FROM MUHAMMAD TO 1453 C.E.   In the Middle East a new force, Islam, emerged that deeply affected Jewish life. While western Europe suffered a period of decline after the fall of Rome (476–800), Arab peoples experienced a period of remarkable vitality. The prophet Muhammad (ca. 570–632) united the tribes of Arabia into a single community obedient to God's will as revealed in the *Quran*. His successors completed the conquest of Arabia; wrested Syria, Iraq,

Palestine, and Egypt from the Byzantine Empire; and defeated the Persian (Iranian) Empire. By the 700s, North Africa and the Iberian Peninsula (Portugal and Spain) had fallen to the Muslims.

Jews, Christians, and Zoroastrians were granted the status of protected minorities under the supremacy of the Islamic state. As monotheists, they were afforded religious toleration and protection of life and property, but their activities were restricted. They paid a special tax and could not make converts, build new churches or synagogues, or carry weapons. Although such restrictions were not always enforced, the protected faiths suffered heavy losses. The state religions of Byzantium (Christian) and Persia (Zoroastrian) changed from privileged majorities to tolerated minorities, a change of status accompanied by conversions of many Christians and Zoroastrians to Islam. By 800, roughly 90 percent of the Jewish population lived under Muslim rule and, in spite of restrictions and periodic oppression, experienced periods of prosperity and achievement. The most notable Jewish centers were in Babylonia, Spain, and Egypt.

During the Abbasid caliphate (750–1258), an Islamic dynasty centered in Baghdad, the Jews of Babylonia experienced a period of vitality. The Abbasids acknowledged the authority of their academies and the office of the exilarch, the leader who, with the presidents of the academies at Sura and Pumbeditha, governed Babylonian Jews. Leaders of these academies held the title of *gaon* (excellency). The most renowned *gaon* of the period was Saadia (882–942) of Sura, who translated the *Bible* from Hebrew to Arabic and wrote handbooks on Jewish law. Saadia's theology was influenced by Hellenistic and Islamic philosophy. He taught that revealed truths are available to everyone through "reliable tradition" but also believed they can be corroborated through reason. Saadia argued that the *Torah* is worthy of belief because it is right rather than because of the miracles Moses performed. Against the doctrine of predestination, he reasoned that it was contradictory for God to give us commands and yet predetermine our actions.[64]

The Damascus-centered Umayyad caliphate (661–750) conquered Christian Spain between 711 and 715; a remnant remained until Grenada, the last outpost of Muslim rule, surrendered in 1492. Under the Umayyads, Spanish Jews known as **Sephardim** (a term derived from the Hebrew word for Spain) experienced a golden age (ca. 950–1146) of prosperity, influence, and creativity and were the largest population of Jews outside Babylonia. Sephardic sages translated the Greek classics and Muslim scholarship into Latin and integrated Greek and Hebraic wisdom. One of these sages, Judah Halevy (1075–1141), had reservations about Greek philosophy. He contrasted the God of Israel with the impersonal God of the philosophers. God delivered the Israelites from bondage in Egypt and revealed the divine will at Sinai, whereas reason conceives of a supreme being that accounts for the origin of motion, a conception that fails to speak of divine love and justice. Therefore, Halevy intoned, "Let not the wisdom of the Greeks beguile thee."[65] Nonetheless, he believed that divine revelation *(Torah)* was not at odds with reason but was a gift that surpassed the achievements of human intellect.

The Sephardic Golden Age ended in 1146 with the arrival in Spain of the Almohades, a Muslim dynasty from Morocco that forcibly converted Jews and closed their synagogues and academies. Many Jews, including the family of medieval Judaism's most renowned figure, Moses Maimonides, fled Spain. The latter's travels led to Alexandria, Egypt, a relatively stable haven for Jews until Mongol invasions and Turkish rule destabilized the Jewish communities of the Middle East. Praised as the most distinguished Jew since Moses, Maimonides' influence rests on his philosophical classic *The Guide of the Perplexed*, his digest of talmudic and post-talmudic *halakah*, the *Mishnah Torah*, and his *Commentary on the Mishnah*.

Maimonides was convinced that religion and philosophy point to the same truth. His proofs of God's existence were influenced by Aristotle and anticipated those of Saint Thomas Aquinas (1225–1274). Maimonides argued that because an infinite regress of causes is impossible, there must exist an Uncaused Cause (God) that created the world. He reasoned that the contingent character of things necessitates the existence of a necessary and eternal Being "who brought every existing thing into being."[66] Like the talmudic sages, Maimonides stressed the obligation to study *Torah*, a duty rooted in the biblical injunction to teach God's commands to your children (*Deut.* 6:7). He urged excommunication of Jewish communities that neglected educating the young, because "the world is only maintained by the breath of school children."[67]

CHRISTIAN ANTI-SEMITISM IN MEDIEVAL EUROPE (1000–1500 C.E.)

By the time of the emperor Charlemagne (742–814), Jewish communities existed in northern France and western Germany. Jews referred to those regions as Ashkenaz, and eventually the term **Ashkenazim** referred to Jews whose culture originated from areas of Europe north of Italy and Spain. The most beloved Ashkenazi of medieval Europe was Rashi, an acronym for Rabbi Solomon ben Isaac (ca. 1040–1105), whose commentaries continue to be important to biblical and talmudic studies.

The road to religious toleration in the West has been a tortuous one. Christian monarchs envisioned a state united by Christianity, and clerics declared that outside the Church there was no salvation. Jews were appalled by the deification of Jesus and critical of Church institutions such as monasticism and celibacy. For the most part, they sought accommodation, but they also wrote tracts that exacerbated the ill will of Christians. On the other side, Christians blamed Jews for the death of Christ and were frustrated by their refusal to accept Jesus as Messiah and Lord. However, they affirmed with Saint Paul that God's covenant with Israel was irrevocable.

Christian anti-Semitism was fed by events in the Holy Land, economic woes, and the plague. In 1009, the Church of the Holy Sepulcher in Jerusalem was destroyed by fire, and French Jews were rumored to have urged Muslims to burn it. Soon thereafter, the Jews of Limoges and Mainz were given the option of expulsion or conversion. Itinerant Christian preachers urged people to prepare for Christ's imminent return by fasts, mortifications of the flesh, and liberation of holy shrines from the Muslims. In 1095, Pope Urban II called for a crusade to free the Holy Sepulcher in Jerusalem after Muslims had closed the city to Christian pilgrims. On the way to Jerusalem, crusaders vented their wrath on victims close at hand. Jews in Rouen who refused baptism were murdered. As rumors circulated that Jews were collaborating with Muslims, more Jews were baptized or martyred.

The antipathy that Christians felt toward Jews was complicated by indebtedness, poverty, and hunger. Most Jews were artisans or tradespeople, but some achieved prominence as moneylenders. Because the Church prohibited charging interest on loans, Christian monarchs, nobles, and merchants turned to Jews for the service. Monarchs and prelates often protected Jews, but they were not entirely motivated by justice and compassion. Jews were economic assets. Monarchs borrowed from them to finance their armies and projects; in return, Jews were protected as the "king's persons." In a context in which poverty, hunger, and abuse were intractable features of the lives of the lower classes and in which many of the nobility borrowed heavily from Jews, the latter became objects of the people's disaffection. The "king's persons" were not permitted to arm themselves, and the protection of kings and prelates was not sufficient to shield them from indebted nobles and oppressed peasants.

As economic conditions worsened, attacks on Jews increased. Jews were alleged to have committed heinous crimes. They were charged with killing Christians to obtain blood for the unleavened bread of the Passover observance (Jews allegedly needed the blood of their victims to maintain their human form), with desecrating the Host (the body of Christ present in the consecrated bread of Holy Communion), and with poisoning Christians. Although authorities such as Pope Innocent IV (1253–1254) repudiated the charge of ritualistic cannibalism, "blood libels" (the charge that Jews killed Christians to obtain their blood) were relatively common (the first case was reported in 1144 in Norwich, England) and were usually followed by the execution of Jews and the confiscation of their property. The first of several episodes of "desecration of the Host" (inflicting pain on the embodied Christ) occurred in Germany in 1243 and ended with several Jews being burned to death.

Jews, especially physicians, were accused of plotting to poison Christians. The most preposterous of the calumnies was the charge that Jews caused the plague. The bubonic plague, or Black Death, broke out in Europe in 1347; it was caused by a bacillus transmitted to humans by fleas carried by infected rats. By the time the plague had run its course, 15 million to 20 million Europeans had died. Christians asked what caused the plague and answered that it was punishment for their sin or the work of Satan. Others pointed to a more tangible scapegoat: Jews had poisoned the wells. Massacres of Jews began in Germany in 1348 and spread elsewhere. Thousands were killed or committed suicide even as Pope Clement VI (1342–1352) tried to curb the madness by pointing out that the plague killed Jews as well as Christians.

Jews were increasingly forced to live in separate areas (known as ghettos), and they could not hold public office or marry Christians. In 1215, the Fourth Lateran Council demanded that Jews and Muslims wear clothes and badges to set them apart from Christians. Eventually the hatred culminated in the expulsion of Jews from most of western Europe. Jews were expelled from England in 1290. In 1240, the *Talmud* was publicly tried and condemned in Paris, and in 1306, Jews were banished from France. In Spain, Jews who converted to Christianity were accused of secretly practicing Judaism. The Spanish Inquisition (instituted in 1480 to counteract heresy) ferreted out "secret" Jews and Muslims, as well as heretics and witches. Thousands were killed. In 1492, Judaism was banned in Spain. Many Jews resettled in Portugal. Pressured by Spain, the Portuguese monarch expelled them in 1496 but then, in order not to lose valuable subjects, changed his mind and ordered Jewish children baptized and their parents converted in 1497.

Jews responded to the persecution in different ways. Some converted. Some committed suicide rather than embrace Christianity. Others moved to areas where they were welcome. Some viewed the tribulations as a sign of the advent of the Messiah or found solace in mystical traditions that spoke of being joined to God in this world or the next. Sometimes the victims blamed themselves, rationalizing that they were being punished for their sins. In the midst of the crisis, Jews continued to study *Torah,* observe Sabbath, perform daily liturgies, celebrate holy days, and remember the martyrs who died rather than profane God's holy name.

JEWS IN THE MIDDLE EAST (1500–1750 C.E.)

Many Sephardic and Ashkenazic refugees gravitated to the Muslim Middle East, where the Ottomans, a Turkish dynasty, allowed them to pursue their religious and economic interests. Scarred by their experiences in Christian Europe, the mixture of refugees and indigenous Jews emphasized the messianic and mystical aspects of their heritage. The initial phase of Jewish mysticism (100 B.C.E.–1000 C.E.) stressed the ascent of the soul from the terrestial to the celestial realms, whence it "sees" God and is revealed the secrets of the highest heaven.

The second phase of Jewish mysticism, Kabbalism, originated in twelfth-century Europe. Kabbalists distinguish between God's unknowable essence *(Ein Sof)* and God's self-revelation *(Sefirot)* as a being to whom prayer and worship is directed. God's ten Sefirot include the Divine Will, Wisdom, Understanding, Love, Power, Beauty, Endurance, Majesty, Foundation (of all active forces in God), and Shekhinah (the Divine Presence and female aspect of God that is the intermediary between the divine and nondivine worlds).[68] Creation began at that moment in which the Sefirot emerged out of the divine essence: "A blinding spark flashed within the Concealed of the concealed." This divine light "has never been fully revealed, but it plays a vital role in the world, renewing every day the act of Creation!"[69]

Kabbalists spoke of evil as the "other side" engaged in a struggle with the righteous and the Divine Presence for domination. The human soul is a spark of divinity; each soul is originally both masculine and feminine but, in the descent into the material world, is separated into female or male. At death, souls return to the realms of the seven heavens or, if not sufficiently purified, are reincarnated in another body. The ultimate activity of the soul is to participate in the repair of the cosmic disharmony that resulted from the sin of Adam or, as the mystic Isaac Luria (1534–1570) believed, from a cosmic accident. Luria taught that an accident during creation—rather than Adam's sin—resulted in the imprisonment of the divine sparks in husks of evil. God, like humankind, was fragmented by the scattering of the divine sparks and can be restored only by the return of souls to God; thus, humans assist God in restoring the cosmos.

Mystics were often messianists. Luria and his students hoped for the coming of the Messiah and taught that the task of repairing the world aided the coming of the messianic age. Jews were a people set apart by law and custom, living under the jurisdiction of peoples who alternated between welcoming and abusing them. In such a milieu, Shabbatai Zevi (1626–1676) appeared and bewitched Jews from the Middle East to eastern Europe. Born in Smyrna and ordained at age eighteen, Zevi was a quixotic figure; in emulation of the prophet Hosea, he married a prostitute and, on another occasion, announced that the commandments had been abolished. In 1665, Rabbi Nathan of Gaza informed Zevi that he was the Messiah. In May, the public was informed. Local rabbis denounced Zevi's pretensions and banished him from Jerusalem. Rabbi Nathan predicted that the Messiah would restore the world in 1666. A messianic fervor spread over Europe, prompting some Jews to sell their property in preparation for the day of redemption. In February 1666, Turkish officials imprisoned Zevi; in September, he was tried and convicted. Given the choice between conversion to Islam or death, Zevi converted, and the messianic fervor subsided.

JEWS IN EUROPE (1500–1750 C.E.)

After initially urging people to deal kindly with Jews, Martin Luther (1483–1546) turned against them. In a pamphlet entitled "Against the Jews and Their Lies," Luther urged Protestant princes to burn synagogues and destroy *Talmuds.* After the Treaty of

Westphalia (1648) brought Europe respite from wars between Catholics and Protestants, Jews began to resettle in England, France, and other countries from whence they had been expelled. Most Sephardic survivors of Christian persecution fled from Christian to Muslim centers, but the majority of Ashkenazic refugees moved to Poland and Lithuania. By 1648, the Jews of Poland were the largest of the diaspora communities. The Jews of eastern Europe lived in separate villages known as *shtetls* (little towns); however, the tranquility of their villages was periodically shattered by *pogroms*, officially sanctioned violence against Jews.

Hasidism, another form of Jewish mysticism, originated in these settlements in Poland. The first Hasidic master was Israel ben Eleazer (1700–1760), also known as the Baal Shem Tov (master of the divine name). According to his disciples, the Baal Shem Tov taught the core Hasidic beliefs: God is mystically present in all things; there is joy in all aspects of life; one must follow a "righteous man"; and one must study *Torah*.

Modern Judaism (1789 to the Present)

The genesis of modern Judaism occurred in the context of the emergence of modern Western nation-states, a time in which economic, intellectual, and political revolutions changed how people thought and lived. Within this context, restrictions that formerly excluded European Jews from public life were abolished. Our treatment of modern Judaism is divided into five main subdivisions: the Enlightenment, the emancipation of the Jews, modern forms of Judaism, modern anti-Semitism and the Holocaust, and modern Israel. Like the biblical and rabbinic periods, the modern period is one in which Jewish traditions were refashioned and new models created.

The Enlightenment: Precursor to Jewish Emancipation
The Enlightenment of eighteenth-century Europe was preceded in the seventeenth century by a revolution in thought that constituted a shift from medieval to modern. Whereas the medieval worldview saw the world as a collection of things that God had ordered according to their nature, the modern worldview saw the world as a mechanical or clocklike universe functioning according to the laws of nature.

The shift in perspective had its casualties, as is evident in the stories of two seventeenth-century European Jews: Uriel da Costa (ca. 1590–1640) and Baruch Spinoza (1632–1677). Costa was born to a family of Portuguese *conversos* (new Christians) who had converted from Judaism. Dissatisfied with Christianity, he converted back to Judaism and escaped with his family to Amsterdam. After publishing his contention that the immortality of the soul was not a biblical doctrine, Costa was excommunicated (expelled) by the Sephardic community of Amsterdam. Repentant, he returned to the synagogue, only to be excommunicated again for questioning the divine origin of Mosaic law, which he argued "contained many things contrary to natural law; and God, the creator of nature, cannot possibly have contradicted himself, which would have been the case had he given to men a rule of obedience contrary to that first law."[70] Shunned by the Jewish community, he asked to return. As part of his penance, he submitted to thirty-nine lashes and prostrated himself on the threshold of the synagogue. Tormented beyond endurance, Costa committed suicide. Baruch Spinoza, perhaps the first modern Jewish thinker to leave Judaism without becoming a Christian, was excommunicated on July 27, 1656, for "abominable heresies." Doubting that Moses authored the *Pentateuch* and convinced that the *Bible* was a human creation, Spinoza also rejected the belief that God is a divine person.

During the eighteenth century, enlightened thinkers sought the liberation of humankind from obsolete institutions and religious fanaticism. Liberal solutions were freedom of speech, religious tolerance, and constitutional limitations on the power of government. The aims of the Enlightenment were perceived to be at odds with the segregation of Jews. Reformers called for the removal of restrictions that prevented Jews from participation in public life. Moses Mendelssohn (1729–1786) advised that the way out of the ghetto required the dual burden of maintaining "the religion of your fathers" and openness to non-Jewish knowledge. Mendelssohn and other leaders of the Jewish *haskalah* (enlightenment) sought to transform ghetto dwellers into citizens who would preserve their identities as Jews. Accommodation with new modes of thinking and doing was articulated in the slogan "A Jew at home, a man outside."[71]

EMANCIPATION OF THE JEWS (1789–1880 C.E.)

At the turn of the eighteenth century, around 500,000 Jews lived in central Europe, and over 1 million in eastern Europe. Restrictive laws forced most of them to live in communities set apart from their Christian neighbors. The first steps to emancipation were taken in the 1780s by Hapsburg emperor Joseph II (1741–1790), who abolished the Jewish badge and restrictions on places of residence and vocations.

The French Revolution also brought emancipation. On August 26, 1789, the French National Assembly adopted the "Declaration of the Rights of Man and Citizen." Article One declared that "men are born and remain free and equal in rights," but it was not until September 1791 that the status of Jews was clarified by the Assembly: French citizenship was available to every qualified male. Restrictions limiting Jewish activities were annulled, but the privileges granted them as an autonomous community were also revoked. Removal of the legal barriers excluding Jews from public life proceeded slowly in the German states. Nevertheless, when a united Germany was established in 1871, it included provisions for Jewish emancipation.

Emancipation was never fully realized in eastern Europe. Polish Jews had a range of economic opportunities and a sizable middle class. Russian Jews were confined by imperial law to an area known as the Pale of Settlement, but reforms in the 1870s permitted privileged Jews to live outside the Pale and to enter public schools and universities. Forms of social exclusion were relatively common in the United States, but Jewish citizenship was not a problem. In an address to the Jewish congregation at Newport, Rhode Island, in 1790, President George Washington assured his audience that

they possessed "liberty of conscience and immunities of citizenship."[72]

The catch-22 of emancipation was the assumption that in achieving full political rights, Jews would cease to be Jews. Belief that there was a conflict between the rights of Jews as individual citizens and as members of an ethnic community is evident in a remark made before the French Assembly in September 1789: "To the Jews as citizens, everything, to the Jews as a nation, nothing."[73] In the confederation of Germanic states, Jewish emancipationist Gabriel Riesser argued that Jews were not a separate nation but rather a religious group, and that their religion did not keep them from being good Germans. Nevertheless, the notion persisted that Jewish identification with the "house of Israel" diluted their patriotism.

Conversion to Christianity provided a way out of the ghetto before political emancipation was achieved. German poet Heinrich Heine (1797–1856) embraced Lutheranism so he could earn his doctorate and pursue his career. British statesman Benjamin Disraeli (1804–1881) was baptized an Anglican. Heinrich Marx, the father of Karl Marx, converted to Lutheranism to retain his position as a lawyer. Heine and Disraeli never lost their affection for their Jewish heritage, but Karl Marx despised it: "Money is the jealous one God of Israel, beside which no other God may stand." The aim of "the emancipation of the Jews is the emancipation of humanity from Judaism."[74]

MODERN FORMS OF JUDAISM

The Enlightenment and removal of legal barriers to Jewish participation in public life in western Europe elicited new forms of Judaism. Reform Judaism emerged in nineteenth-century Germany as a self-conscious effort to accommodate Judaism to modern life. Repelled by traditional rabbinic Judaism with its Hebrew liturgy and strict observance of *halakah*, founders of the Reform movement, such as Rabbi Abraham Geiger (1810–1874) in Germany and the German immigrant to the United States Rabbi Isaac Mayer Wise (1819–1900), repudiated the claim that the *Torah* was a timeless revelation that served as an ideal pattern for human existence;

instead, divine revelation was seen as progressive and Judaism as evolving. Only those religious directives compatible with modern life and "in accord with the postulates of reason" were to be maintained.[75] The reformers attempted to resolve the problem of the relationship of Jews to Israel as a people by arguing that Judaism was a religion based on conviction rather than an ethnic-national way of life. As evidence that they were loyal Germans or Americans, they rejected the notion of a return to Palestine and the expectation of the Messiah. In contrast to traditional practice, the main elements of Reform liturgy were in the vernacular rather than in Hebrew, rabbis gave sermons and congregations participated in the service through responsive readings, and men and women worshiped together.

Reform Judaism triggered a reaction. Two new forms of Judaism resulted: Orthodox and Conservative Judaism. Orthodox Judaism is the label for those Jews who maintain that the oral and written *Torah* is the binding standard of Jewish life. In opposition to Reform principles, champions of Orthodoxy, such as Rabbi Samson R. Hirsch (1808–1888), reiterated the belief that God's revelation to Moses cannot be doubted and that the *Torah* is an eternal, unchanging revelation. For Orthodox Jews, the essence of Judaism is the observance of the Lord's commands. Sabbath day observance excludes working, writing, answering the phone, preparing foods, riding in a car or public conveyance, and a host of other activities. Women are separated from men during worship in the synagogue and are excluded from the rabbinate. Services are in Hebrew, and dietary and purity rules are carefully observed.

Orthodox Jews aver the thirteen principles of faith articulated by Maimonides. These principles affirm that the *Torah* is true and will not be changed, that God rewards good and punishes evil, that the Messiah will come, and that the dead will eventually be revived. Orthodox theology is remarkably at odds with the principles of Reform Judaism articulated in the Pittsburgh Platform of 1885. The latter rejected the notion that *halakah* is universally binding and replaced belief in a personal Messiah with belief in a messianic age of truth, justice,

and peace that must be achieved by all humankind. The Pittsburgh Platform also rejected beliefs in heavenly rewards and punishment in hell and replaced the doctrine of the resurrection of the body with the immortality of the soul. In contrast, Orthodox Jews maintained that the inherited tradition cannot change because "it derived from God's will at Sinai and was eternal and supernatural, not historical and man-made."[76] They also rejected the Reform view that Judaism is a religion and reaffirmed their faith in the ingathering of Jews in Zion (Israel). In Rabbi Hirsch's words, Jews constituted a people who, though it "carries the Torah with it in all the lands of its dispersion, will never find its table and lamp except in the Holy Land."[77]

Conservative Judaism took a centrist position. Like Reform and Orthodox Judaism, it germinated first among German Jews and subsequently bloomed in the United States. Conservatives were convinced that in rejecting much of Jewish tradition, the reformers had thrown the "baby out with the bathwater." Rabbi Zacharias Frankel of Dresden (1801–1875) insisted that Hebrew was the essential language of Jewish worship, and Conservatives have regarded it as indispensable to Jewish learning. Conservative Jews agree with the Reform contention that *Torah* is an ongoing rather than static entity, but they also insist that *halakah* continues to have a claim on their lives. In their view, Judaism cannot survive without the Hebrew language, a fidelity to Jewish law, and a respect for Jewish traditions.

New Judaisms have emerged in the twentieth century. Rabbi Mordecai Kaplan (1881–1983) was instrumental in the formation of Reconstructionist Judaism, a movement native to the United States that emerged between the two world wars as a response to the other Judaisms and modernity. Kaplan saw Judaism as an evolving religious organism of the Jewish people and linked salvation to experiences of the worthwhileness of life. Rabbi Sherwin Wine established the Society for Humanistic Judaism in the United States in 1969. It provides an association for nontheist Jews to celebrate and preserve Jewish identity and culture consistent with a humanistic understanding of life. The soci-

	CONTEMPORARY JUDAISMS
Table 8.2	
Conservative Judaism	Conservative Judaism originated in Germany as a response to the Reform movement and was officially established in the United States in 1886. Conservative Jews stress the importance of the Hebrew language and the adaptation of *halakah* to modern life. The United Synagogue is the national organization of Conservative congregations. Conservative Judaism is the second largest body of religious Jews in the United States.
Hasidism	Hasidism was established in eastern Europe in the eighteenth century; it is composed of several independent Hasidic movements, including the Lubavitchers, Belzers, Bobovers, and Satmarers. Hasids combine careful observance of *halakah* with pietism, mysticism, and charismatic leadership.
Humanistic Judaism	The Society for Humanistic Judaism was established in the United States in 1969 to provide nontheist Jews with a group consistent with Jewish identity and culture and humanistic values. It is affiliated with the International Federation of Secular Humanistic Judaism.
Orthodox Judaism	Orthodox Judaism was established in Europe in the nineteenth century as a response to the Reform movement. Orthodox Jews believe that the *Torah* is eternally binding. Orthodox Judaism is the third largest segment of religious Jews in the United States.
Reconstructionist Judaism	Reconstructionist Judaism was established in the United States in the twentieth century. Reconstructionists conceive of Judaism as an "evolving civilization" and, like Reform Jews, reject the Orthodox belief that the *Torah* (divine law) is eternally binding. Its institutional affiliation is the Federation of Reconstructionist Congregations.
Reform Judaism	Reform Judaism was established in nineteenth-century Germany and is the largest organized body of religious Jews in the United States. Reform Jews believe that Jewish law and thought are progressive rather than immutable. Reform congregations are affiliated internationally with the World Union for Progressive Judaism and in the United States with the Union of American Hebrew Congregations.
Secular Judaism	A label for nontheist Jews who wish to recenter Judaism in the Jewish people and Israel rather than in God and the *Torah*; it is a perspective and not an organization.

ety is affiliated with the International Federation of Secular Humanistic Judaism (1986). Table 8.2 summarizes various forms of contemporary Judaism.

MODERN ANTI-SEMITISM AND THE HOLOCAUST

Enlightened Jews and Gentiles assumed that as the Enlightenment spread, anti-Jewish words and deeds would disappear. Instead, there was a resurgence of anti-Semitism. It was fed by Christian anti-Jew-ishness, but it also took the form of racial anti-Semitism, the conviction that Jews were biologically corrupt. Hatred of Jews led to the Holocaust, the murder of approximately 6 million European Jews by Adolf Hitler (1889–1945), the driving force behind Nazi racial anti-Semitism, and his collaborators. Hitler informed leaders of the German churches that he intended to do to Jews what the Church had been attempting for centuries—annihilate them. Christians had only intermittently pursued forced conversions of Jews, but as Jews have pointed out, the aim of conversion has been their annihilation as Jews: "racial anti-Semitism and traditional Christianity . . . were moved by a common impulse directed either to the conversion or to the extermination of Jews."[78]

Causes of modern anti-Semitism are complex. The immediate cause of the resurfacing of hostility toward Jews was a combination of economic distress, social change, and movements that blamed the social upheavals of the nineteenth century on democratic and economic liberalism. As beneficiaries of social change and as Europe's most conspicuous minority, Jews provided critics with a symbol of liberal, capitalist society. They lived in urban centers and found opportunities for advancement in the businesses, professions, and financial institutions of the period. Liberalism's advocacy of democracy and economic individualism (capitalism) had its critics. Socialists decried the inequalities fostered by capitalist societies. Fascists promised a new order based on devotion to the state, blamed Jews for the loss of status by groups that had suffered most from social change, and accused liberalism of being a facade for Jewish domination. Christians of various persuasions, including those who embraced liberalism, were troubled by what they regarded as the selfishness, materialism, and injustices of the new social order. In 1864, Pius IX issued an encyclical delineating "the principal errors of our time." The *Syllabus of Errors* pronounced that it was wrong to believe that "the Roman Pontiff . . . ought to . . . come to terms with progress, liberalism and modern civilization."[79]

If the scapegoating Jews for the woes of society by antiliberal forces was an immediate cause of the resurgence of anti-Semitism, the root causes were centuries of Christian anti-Semitism and the human tendency to "dislike the unlike." Fear and hatred of what is different is a relatively common human response, and anti-Jewishness has fed on perceptions of Jews as the alien other. Jews are a people set apart by their ethnicity; this "otherness" has contributed to anti-Semitism, but it does not morally justify it. Christians repeated the ancient calumnies: Jews throughout the generations were

guilty of the blood of Christ and, as bearers of the brand of Cain, were condemned to wander the earth. Politicians found that denunciations of Jews helped advance their agendas. In the 1890s, Karl Lueger constructed the first political party in Europe that gained power on the issue of Jewish influence by enlisting the antiliberal and anti-Jewish sentiment of Viennese Catholics. The widely distributed *Protocols of the Elders of Zion* first appeared in Russia (1905) as a tsarist effort to discredit democratic liberalism. The fictitious tract purported to be a record of a series of secret meetings in which Jewish leaders discussed their hold over the European economy and press and depicted alcoholism and freedom of speech as techniques to corrupt and confuse Gentiles and to insure eventual Jewish domination.

A distinctive feature of modern anti-Semitism is the characterization of Jews as an inferior and subversive race. Racial anti-Semitism grew out of a late-nineteenth-century proclivity for dividing humans into so-called subspecies with distinctive psychological and physical characteristics. Two of the most fateful were Aryan and Semitic, categories that were to loom large in Nazi racial theory. "Semitic types" were characterized as materialistic, egotistic, skillful in trade and finance, and lacking in courage and cultural creativity. "Aryan types" were depicted as life affirming, heroic, and creative. In 1881, Karl Duhring (1833–1921) pronounced that Jews were a biological, as well as a cultural, threat to Germans. He argued that the danger was even more insidious when the "Jewish type" embraced Christianity: "A Jewish question would still exist, even if every Jew were to turn his back on his religion and join one of our major churches. . . . It is precisely the baptized Jews who infiltrate furthest, unhindered in all sectors of society and political life."[80]

A devastating example of how deeply anti-Semitism was ingrained in European culture was the Dreyfus affair. In 1894, Capt. Alfred Dreyfus (1859–1935), the only Jewish officer on the General Staff of the French army, was falsely convicted of treason. The trial elicited a storm of anti-Semitic propaganda. Dreyfus's innocence was eventually vindicated, but the outpouring of anti-Jewish sentiment evoked the conviction in journalist and playwright Theodor Herzl (1806–1904) that Jews were not safe in the nations of modern, enlightened Europe. As a spectator at Dreyfus's trial, Herzl wrote: "The Dreyfus case contains more than a miscarriage of justice: it contains the wish of the vast majority in France to damn one Jew and through him all Jews."[81]

Zionism **Zionism**, the movement to establish a Jewish homeland, grew out of the failures of emancipation and the revival of anti-Semitism. Convinced that anti-Semitism was rooted in an irrational fear of the stranger, Leon Pinsker (1821–1891) reasoned that because Jews had no nation of their own, they were always perceived as aliens whose economic successes elicited resentment and whose powerlessness made them ideal victims. As a solution, Pinsker called on Jews to establish a homeland. Perhaps the most influential Zionist was Theodor Herzl, a liberal Jew already mentioned in the context of the Dreyfus affair who had little interest in Judaism and was only marginally familiar with Jewish history and culture. In response to the Dreyfus affair, Herzl urged Jews to establish their own state. He was instrumental in organizing the first Zionist Congress, which was held in Basel, Switzerland, in August 1897 and which sought an international charter for a Jewish homeland.

Zionists promoted immigration to Palestine. In 1881, Jews in Israel numbered approximately 24,000; over half lived in Jerusalem, and nearly all were devout traditionalists. Between 1904 and 1914, around 40,000 Zionists immigrated to Palestine; the majority were socialists committed to working the land and creating a classless society. By 1914, there were approximately 85,000 Jews in Palestine and forty-three agricultural settlements, including the first cooperative farming community *(kibbutz)*. At the urging of the president of the World Zionist Organization, Chaim Weizmann (1874–1952), British Foreign Secretary Arthur James Balfour sent a letter in 1917 to the British Zionist organization indicating that his government favored the establishment of a Jewish homeland in Palestine. In the 1920s, the Balfour Declaration was approved by the League of Nations, and Great Britain was given a mandate to govern Palestine and prepare Arabs and Jews for independence. In 1939, with the Jewish population of Palestine at roughly 500,000, the British nullified the Balfour Declaration and limited future Jewish immigration to 75,000.

Jews were divided on what kind of homeland they wanted. Religious Jews wanted one that reflected the rabbinic conviction that "the Jewish people is a people only for the sake of its Torah."[82] Zionists favored a democratic, secular state and urged Jews to be liberated from tradition and submissive piety and to cultivate physical exertion, self-initiated action, and delight in nature and the "wholeness of life."[83] Socialist Zionists believed that the state should be socialist as well as secular and democratic. Their ideal of a classless community was embodied in the *kibbutz.*

Zionists such as Ahad Ha-Am (Asher Ginsberg, 1856–1927) saw the movement as another form of Judaism, a secular Judaism with the Jewish culture and the land of Israel serving as its spiritual center. Love of Zion, Ahad Ha-Am wrote, "is not merely part of Judaism . . . it is the whole of Judaism." Secular Judaists resolved the issue of identity by insisting that Jews are Jews by birth and heritage rather than by obedience to God. In Ahad Ha-Am's words, "Why are we Jews? How strange the very question! . . . Ask the tree why it grows! . . . It is within us. . . . It has an existence and a constancy of its own, like a mother's love for her children, like a man's love of his homeland."[84]

The Rise of Fascism and Racial Anti-Semitism

The triumph of fascist governments in Germany and Italy and the influence of fascist movements elsewhere came on the heels of the havoc visited on Europe by World War I and the economic dislocation and political crises that followed. Fascists found support among the victimized and alienated by promising them economic and spiritual recovery through a strong single-party government led by a charismatic leader. They glorified unquestioned loyalty to the state through slogans such as

"Nothing against the state, nothing outside the state."[85] Jews were blamed for the ills of modern societies. Nazis defamed them as biologically degenerate and propagandized that the survival of Western civilization depended on the triumph of "Aryans" over the corrupt forces of international Jewry. Jews were denounced as economic parasites who, in collusion with liberals, pacifists, and Freemasons, had caused Germany to lose the war and as those responsible for the war reparations required of Germany by the Treaty of Versailles. Wedding anticommunism to anti-Semitism, Nazi diatribes depicted communism as part of the Jewish conspiracy to achieve world domination.

Repression of Jews quickly followed the consolidation of power by Hitler's party in the German Reichstag (parliament) and his appointment as chancellor in 1933. Those classified as "non-Aryans" were barred from positions in the civil service, the schools, and the legal and medical professions. Aryan and Jewish intermarriage and sexual relations were henceforth crimes against "German blood and honor." Anyone with a Jewish grandparent was defined as a Jew. The assassination of a German diplomat in Paris by a Jew triggered the *pogrom* known as Kristallnacht (night of the breaking glass). On November 9–10, 1938, Jewish homes, businesses, and synagogues were looted and burned and their windows broken. Many of the roughly 550,000 German Jews were beaten, some were murdered, and thousands were arrested. By 1939, thousands had fled Germany. Relocation was difficult because of British limits on immigration to Palestine and the refusal of other nations to admit more than a trickle of Jewish refugees.

The Holocaust   The Holocaust (a term connoting a burnt sacrificial offering) and Shoah (annihilation) are terms for the Third Reich's murder of roughly 6 million Jews between 1938 and Germany's surrender in World War II in 1945. The Holocaust was the logical outcome of Nazi racism: the "final solution" to the Jewish problem was to be their eradication; there was to be no new generation of Jews. The Nazis nearly achieved their grotesque aim; out of a prewar European Jewish population of 9.2 million, roughly 3.1 million survived. A comparable number of non-Jews (Slavs, gypsies, homosexuals, and others demonized by the German state) also perished. Nazi propaganda described the genocide euphemistically as evacuation, resettlement, and final solution. Gestapo chief Heinrich Himmler commiserated with his colleagues on the difficulty of remaining "decent" while "bravely" annihilating the Jews. Minister of Propaganda Joseph Goebbels wrote in his diary that "one must not allow sentimentality to prevail . . . [in the] life and death struggle between the Aryan race and the Jewish bacillus."[86]

Plans for the mass murder of the Jews were completed in 1942. The Nazis already had some experience with genocide; in the late 1930s, they had instituted a program to eliminate insane and "racially defective" (physically handicapped) Germans. From 70,000 to 100,000 people were gassed, but outraged Germans forced the closure of the program. There was no such public outrage on behalf of the Jews. Camps that facilitated the mass murders of approximately 4 million Jews were built in Germany and Poland. Dachau, near Munich, was the prototype; 80 percent of its estimated 40,000 victims were Jews. In Poland, carbon monoxide poisoning took the lives of around 600,000 Jews at Belze, and roughly 800,000 were gassed at Treblinka. Approximately 3 million Jews and Gentiles were murdered, usually by hydrogen cyanide, at Auschwitz.[87]

The Third Reich's goal of genocide was complicated by its need for labor to support the war effort. The latter was met by enslaving Slavs and those Jews whom mobile killing units had not already murdered. Unlike most death camps, Auschwitz also served as a slave labor camp. New arrivals were separated into groups of those who were immediately gassed because they were of no use to the Nazis and those who were forced to work until they dropped or were no longer of value. But, as theologian Richard Rubenstein noted, "the motive of economic utility was never strong enough to overrule the decision to kill the Jews."[88] Several of the victims were subjects of experiments for scientific, military, and pharmaceutical purposes.

Several were sterilized as part of the "master race's" effort to develop a method of sterilization that would terminate the descent lines of racial undesirables. Even the dead provided grist for the Nazi war effort: gold fillings and women's hair were harvested from the corpses.

Victims did not all go quietly to the gas chambers. The Warsaw ghetto revolt by Polish Jews took weeks to subdue. Two hundred inmates engineered an escape from Treblinka. Some Jews joined the resistance or fought on the side of the Soviets. Although the number of Jews who were rescued is dwarfed by the number of those who were victims, thousands were saved by "righteous Gentiles" as well as by Jewish organizations. Danish Christians smuggled over six thousand Danish Jews to neutral Sweden. Swedish diplomat Raoul Wallenberg helped save Hungarian Jews. The Bulgarian parliament and Orthodox Church refused to deliver fifty thousand Bulgarian Jews to the Nazis and threatened civil disobedience against any attempt at their deportation.[89]

MODERN ISRAEL (1948 TO THE PRESENT) The state of Israel was created on May 14, 1948, the fruit of Zionist efforts to establish a Jewish nation and the reaction of Europeans and Americans to the horror of the Holocaust. In the Balfour Declaration of 1917, Great Britain supported establishment of a Jewish homeland in Palestine and acknowledged the rights of non-Jewish Palestinians. After World War I, the League of Nations gave the British jurisdiction over Palestine. For a time the British remained committed to the Balfour Declaration, but in response to conflicts between Arabs and Jews, they restricted Jewish immigration and land purchases in Palestine in 1939. In 1945, as World War II was winding down, an Arab League was formed to prevent a Jewish state. At the war's conclusion, Britain continued to restrict Jewish immigration and prevented Holocaust survivors housed in Displaced Persons (World War II refugee) camps in Europe from settling in Palestine.

Tensions escalated into a Jewish War of Independence (1947–1949). Jewish resistance was initially directed against British rule; over three hundred British officials and many Arabs were killed. Britain turned Palestine over to the United Nations, which on November 19, 1947, voted in favor of partitioning it between Jews and Arabs. War between Palestinian Arabs and Jews followed. On May 14, 1948, Jewish leaders in Tel Aviv proclaimed the independence of Israel. Subsequently, Israel was attacked by the armies of Egypt, Jordan, Lebanon, Syria, and Iraq. A truce in February 1949 left Israel with 8,400 square miles of Palestine. Egypt controlled the Gaza Strip, and Jordan took possession of East Jerusalem and the West Bank of the Jordan River. Roughly 750,000 Palestinian Arabs were displaced by the war.

Arab countries such as Yemen, Iraq, and Libya expelled their Jewish populations, dramatically increasing the number of Jews in Israel. At the outset of the War of Independence, Jews numbered around 630,000. By 1951, the "ingathering of the exiles" from Displaced Persons camps and Arab countries swelled the Jewish population to 1.2 million. Palestinians and Arab nations refused to acknowledge the right of Israel to exist and vowed "to throw the Jews into the sea." In 1964, Palestinian refugees formed the Palestine Liberation Organization (PLO).

In June 1967, the Six-Day War between Israel and neighboring Arab countries reshaped the territory of Israel and enhanced Jewish solidarity both within Israel and around the world. Israel took East Jerusalem and the West Bank from Jordan, the Golan Heights from Syria, and the Gaza Strip and Sinai Peninsula from Egypt. Roughly 1.3 million Arabs living in the area captured during the Six-Day War came under Israeli jurisdiction and complicated the problem of the internal security of Israel. The Security Council of the United Nations passed Resolution 242, which demanded that Israel withdraw from the occupied territories. It also recognized the right of all nations in the area to security within their borders and called for a resolution of the Palestinian refugee problem. The PLO refused to recognize Israel's right to exist and, with assistance from Arab states, turned to terrorism as a means of resistance.

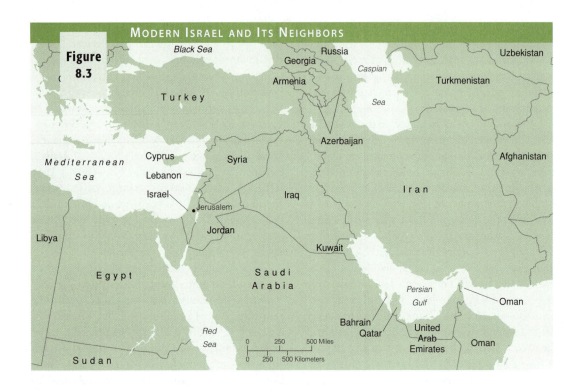

MODERN ISRAEL AND ITS NEIGHBORS

Figure 8.3

Black Sea
Russia
Georgia
Caspian
Uzbekistan
Armenia
Turkmenistan
Turkey
Azerbaijan
Sea
Mediterranean Sea
Cyprus
Syria
Afghanistan
Lebanon
Israel
Iraq
Iran
Jerusalem
Libya
Jordan
Kuwait
Egypt
Saudi Arabia
Persian Gulf
Oman
Red Sea
Bahrain
Qatar
United Arab Emirates
Oman
Sudan

0   250   500 Miles
0   250   500 Kilometers

Religion is one of the ingredients in the conflict. Most Arabs are Muslims. Some Jews insist that Muslims should not reside in Israel and that giving some of Israel away would be a sin. Ultra-Orthodox Jews believe they are obligated to rebuild the Temple in preparation for the Messiah's coming, but the Temple Mount is also home to the Al Aqsa Mosque and the Dome of the Rock, which Muslims proclaim they will defend "to their last drop of blood."[90]

Israeli Jews are threatened from without by hostile Islamic states and from within by angry Palestinians. They are enraged by Palestinian terrorism and fearful that Palestinians are committed to their extermination. Uncompromising Jews insist the occupied territories are part of Israel and that none of them should be given away; moderate voices agree to the creation of a Palestinian state in exchange for the security of Israel. Meanwhile, Palestinians are enraged by being displaced in their own land. They are vehemently opposed to Israel's settlements and confiscation of Palestinian land in the occupied territories. Opposition involves episodic violence and other forms of resistance, such as boycotting Israeli goods. Uncompromising Palestinians refuse to recognize the right of Israel to exist, call for the destruction of the Zionist state, and equate Zionism with racism. Moderate voices, including the leadership of the PLO, acknowledge Israel's existence but demand the formation of a Palestinian state out of the occupied territories.

No resolution is in sight, but some progress has been made. An Egyptian-Israeli treaty signed in 1979 provided for the gradual withdrawal of Israel from the Sinai Peninsula, and the latter was fully returned to Egypt in 1982. An accord between Israel and the PLO was reached in 1993 that provided for Palestinian self-government in much of the West Bank and Gaza Strip and promised negotiations on the status of Jerusalem. A peace treaty with Jordan was reached in 1994, but negotiations with Syria involving the Golan Heights and other security matters are unresolved, as are many other issues. Figure 8.3 shows a map of modern Israel and its neighbors.

The ingathering of Jews has continued. By the 1970s there were nearly 3 million Israeli Jews, almost equally divided between Ashkenazim and Sephardim. Since then, a new wave of Jewish immigrants from Russia, plus modest numbers from Ethiopia and elsewhere, have helped raise the number of Israeli Jews to 4.6 million. Nonetheless, some Jews fear they will eventually be a minority in Israel.

CONTEMPORARY JUDAISM

Contemporary Judaism exists in what some observers refer to as a postmodern age in which the worldview of the Enlightenment has unraveled and the authority of science has been questioned. Postmodernism involves the recognition that there are many communities of faith and philosophies, including scientific ones, each with their own truth claims. In such a context, *Torah* becomes *a* scripture rather than *the* scripture and Judaism one option among many. The story of contemporary Judaism is inseparable from the Holocaust, the issue of Jewish identity, and the relationship of Jews to Israel and the Palestinians.

THE HOLOCAUST IN CONTEMPORARY JUDAISM

One of the legacies of the Holocaust is the reinforcement of Jewish distrust of non-Jews. Jews see in the state of Israel the possibility of their survival as a people in a hostile world. As long as a Jewish state exists, they believe there is a sanctuary for Jews. Prior to the rise of Nazi anti-Semitism, many Jews were anti-Zionist, but the Holocaust ended nearly all Jewish opposition to the establishment of a Jewish state.

Jews have resolved that "never again" will they be passive victims. For many, the Holocaust invalidated the rabbinic teaching that it is morally prefer-

able to be killed than to kill. Jews must defend themselves, and a powerful Jewish state embodies this resolve. To be passive in the face of evil or to abandon Jewish culture is, according to Emil Fackenheim, to abet the Nazi plan for the extermination of the Jews.[91] To engrave the lessons and horror of the Holocaust in one's consciousness is a step toward the repair of the world and a refusal to let it ever happen again. Remembering occurs on several fronts. There is an annual day of Holocaust remembrance. The names of Holocaust victims and those of groups and individuals who, in rescuing Jews, exemplified the teaching that those who save a single life save a whole world. Centers such as the Simon Wiesenthal Center for Holocaust Studies in Los Angeles and the national Holocaust Museum in Washington, D.C., educate the public about the Holocaust and contemporary manifestations of anti-Semitism.

In response to the Holocaust, there have been gut-wrenching reexaminations of Christian anti-Semitism. The Roman Catholic Church has removed references to Jewish blood guilt from church texts and has acknowledged the enduring legitimacy of God's covenant with the Jews. In 1980, the German Evangelical Conference declared that it believed in the permanent election of the Jewish people, a dramatic shift from its 1948 judgment that "the terrible Jewish suffering in the Holocaust was a divine visitation and a call to Jews to cease their rejection and ongoing crucifixion of Christ." During the last decade of the twentieth century, several Christian denominations and service organizations, such as the International Red Cross, have acknowledged their complicity in the Holocaust. However, Christian anti-Semitism has not disappeared.

THE ISSUE OF JEWISH IDENTITY

One of the issues in contemporary Judaism is that of Jewish identity. The Enlightenment and emancipation brought fragmentation. Rabbinic Judaism fragmented into many Judaisms, including those that affirm theism and the obligatory character of *halakah,* those that are seeking new

CHRONOLOGY OF JUDAISM

		Traditional Calendar Years from Creation
3761	Creation of Adam	Day one
1250	Exodus of Israelites from Egypt	2448
1020–922	United Kingdom: Saul, David and Solomon	2881–2964
722	Fall of the Kingdom of Israel to Assyria	3205
597–538	Exile in Babylon	3338–3390
587	First Jerusalem Temple destroyed	3338
515 B.C.E.	Second Temple completed	3408
70 C.E.	Destruction of Jerusalem and the Second Temple by the Romans	3828
CA. 200	*Mishnah* codified by Judah the Patriarch	3979
CA. 400	Palestinian (Jerusalem) *Talmud*	4128
CA. 500	Babylonian *Talmud*	4260
638	Conquest of Jerusalem by Muslims	4398

ways of imagining God and stress the moral aspect of *halakah,* and those that have abandoned theism and redefine Judaism as being centered in the Jewish people, culture, and Israel. In addition, divisions gounded in older, premodern traditions (Ashkenazic and Sephardic traditions and that of the Black Jews of Ethiopia) continue to muddle the identity issue.

Conflicts among Jews are particularly tense in Israel, where secular and non-Orthodox religious Jews clash with Orthodox Jews over what is permitted under Israeli law. Secularists oppose restrictions that would close theaters or soccer matches on the Shabbat. Opposing parties clash over the jurisdiction of religious courts in matters of marriage and divorce. Currently, Israeli Jews can marry

or divorce only in accord with Orthodox *halakah;* civil marriage and divorce are not an option. Constraints on non-Orthodox Jews are very real. For example, a childless widow cannot marry without the consent of her deceased husband's brother, and a woman cannot obtain a divorce without her husband's consent.

In Israel, the question "Who is a Jew?" is related to citizenship. Diaspora Jews can emigrate to Israel with full citizenship under the law of the "right of return." The "right of return" guarantees anyone who has at least one Jewish grandparent the right to citizenship. Israeli law follows Orthodox rabbinic law in recognizing persons as Jews if they were born of a Jewish mother or were converted to Judaism. Immigrants who have Jewish

		Traditional Calendar Years from Creation
1096	First Crusade; Jews massacred in Rhineland	4856
1242	Christians ritually burn *Talmuds* in Paris	5002
1290	Expulsion of all Jews from England	5136
1306	Expulsion of all Jews from France	5155
1492	Expulsion of all Jews from Spain	5252
1791	Jews receive full citizenship in France	5651
1897	First Zionist Congress (Basel, Switzerland)	5657
1938	Every synagogue in Germany destroyed	5698
1942	Plan to eliminate all Jews is adopted by the German government	5702
1942–1944	Nazi extermination camps in full operation	5702–5704
1943	Warsaw ghetto revolt	5703
1945	World War II ends	5705
1948	State of Israel is created	5708

fathers but do not have Jewish mothers are regarded as converts. Orthodox Jews are seeking to amend the "right of return" law so that it would recognize only conversions authenticated by Orthodox rabbis, an action that would deny Jews with only a Jewish grandfather or father the "right of return." Reform Judaism, the largest body of religious Jews worldwide, has ruled that either patrilineal or matrilineal descent makes one a Jew, a decision condemned by Orthodox and Conservative bodies and one that has no legal standing in Israel.

Conversion of non-Jews and ordination of homosexuals are also areas of disagreement. Jews have usually not sought converts, but rabbinic authorities can be cited in favor of doing so. Because birth is the primary mode of entry into the Jewish community, assimilation is a threat to the survival of religious and cultural ways of being Jewish. Assimilation is particularly acute in the United States, where roughly half of all Jewish marriages involve intermarriage, and over 60 percent of the children of such marriages are not raised as Jews. The threat of assimilation and the gradual disappearance of Jews as Jews have sparked Jewish opposition to intermarriage and fueled the debate as to whether Jews should seek converts. Traditionally, homosexuality has been regarded as a sin, but Jews at odds with the command that forbids homosexuality (*Lev.* 18:22) have found grounds to nullify it in a tradition of selective obedience. Some branches of Judaism have been responsive to gay men and lesbians, and

Reconstructionist and Reform Judaism have legitimated their ordination.

Equally challenging are issues raised by what Judith Plaskow refers to as *feminist Judaism*, a movement that may transform postmodern Judaism. Feminist Judaism shares feminism's commitment to the well-being of women and their liberation from patriarchy. Like other theistic feminists, Judaic feminists argue that when exclusively male metaphors and pronouns for God are used, men are seen as superior and women as inferior. As Rita Gross has observed, "if we do not mean that God is male when we use masculine pronouns and imagery," there can be no adequate reason for not "using female imagery and pronouns as well."[92] Judaic feminists are reshaping tradition by seeking to transform Judaic thought and practice to address the needs of women. They point out that the experiences of women are missing from biblical and rabbinic Judaism. As Cynthia Ozick noted, " 'Thou shalt not lessen the humanity of women' is missing from the Torah."[93]

ISRAEL, JEWS, AND PALESTINIANS

One of the most divisive issues facing Israeli and diaspora Jews is the Palestinian problem. Critics point out that the treatment of non-Jewish residents of the occupied territories (for example, closing schools, expropriating Palestinian land, and destroying homes) is at odds with Judaic ethics and the democratic principles that helped form the state of Israel. Israel has a right to exist, but that right does not supersede the rights of Palestinians. Jews everywhere are caught between a vision of Israel as a democratic state that respects the rights of Jews and non-Jews alike and the reality of Israel's national security needs. It is a dilemma of the Jewish soul.

Who is a Jew? A Jew is a person bonded to other Jews by language and culture and who, like the patriarch Jacob, struggles with God and the meaning and future of the Jewish people and the land of Israel.

GLOSSARY OF JUDAISM

anti-Semitism a hatred of Jews and Judaism.

Ashkenazi (pl. Ashkenazim)
 a name for central and eastern European Jews descended from medieval German Jews.

bar mitzvah literally, "son of the commandments"; a Judaic initiation rite marking the transition of a boy (usually at age thirteen) to religious maturity.

bat mitzvah literally, "daughter of the commandments"; a Judaic initiation rite marking the transition of a girl (usually at age twelve) to religious maturity.

Chanukah (Hanukkah)
 literally, "dedication"; a Jewish festival commemorating the rededication of the Temple at Jerusalem in 165 B.C.E. Chanukah, also known as the Festival of Lights, is observed in November–December.

diaspora	(1) the dispersion of the Jews beginning with deportations associated with the fall of Israel (722 B.C.E.) and Judah (598 B.C.E.) and later under Roman rule; (2) Jews living outside Palestine; (3) people separated from their homeland.
Exodus	(1) the "going out" of Egypt; (2) the second book of the *Pentateuch.*
Gemara	literally, "completion"; rabbinic interpretation of *Mishnah. Mishnah* and *Gemara* form the *Talmud.*
halakah	"to go," in the sense of the way things should be done; Judaic law and legal system.
Hasidism	a mystical strand of Judaism that stresses the mystical presence of God in all things, joy in all aspects of life, and the leadership of "righteous men." The origins of modern Hasidic Judaism are traced to Israel ben Eleazer (ca. 1700–1760), a healer and mystic from South Poland. Rabbi Israel is referred to as the Baal Shem Tov (master of the divine name) or as the Besht, an acronym of Baal Shem Tov. Contemporary Hasidism is divided into several groups centered around their respective *rebbe,* a Yiddish word for *rabbi* (teacher or master).
Holocaust	"burnt offering." The Holocaust refers to Jewish victims of the Nazis' genocidal anti-Semitism. *Shoah* is another term for the Holocaust.
Kabbalism	a general term for various forms of Jewish mysticism. Moses de Leon (d. 1305) and Isaac Luria (1534–1572) are representative Kabbalists.
kashrut	that which is permitted or fit (kosher); Jewish dietary laws regulating the choice, preparation, and eating of food and drink.
kibbutz	a communal settlement initiated by Zionists prior to the establishment of Israel (1948) and important to the life of the nation after independence.
Messiah	"anointed one"; the expectation that God's anointed will at some point in the future usher in a messianic age.
midrash	"inquiry"; (1) rabbinic literature involving exegesis and commentary of biblical texts; (2) a name for collections of midrash, such as the *Sifre Deuteronomy.*
minyan	"number." Ten adults is the number required to form a quorum for Judaic worship. Traditionally, ten adult males are required, but nonorthodox traditions count adult women. Ten families are required to start a congregation.
Mishnah	oral law collected and codified by Judah the Prince (ca. 200 C.E.). It includes six major divisions and sixty-three books (tractates) covering agriculture, Sabbath, holidays, marriage, divorce, property, damages, and court procedures.

mitzvah (pl. *mitzvot*)

divine commands and, in popular usage, good deeds. Rabbinic Judaism identified 613 biblical commands, plus additional talmudic injunctions.

Pentateuch the *Torah;* "the book of the five scrolls": *Genesis, Exodus, Leviticus, Numbers,* and *Deuteronomy.*

Pesach (Passover) the festival of freedom commemorating the Exodus of the Israelites from Egypt. It is an eight-day festival in Orthodox and Conservative Judaism and a seven-day festival in Reform Judaism.

Purim a holiday commemorating the deliverance of Persian Jews from destruction in the fifth century B.C.E. Purim is based on the narrative in *Esther.*

rabbi the principal title of the leaders of Judaism from the first century C.E. to the present; it indicates ordination by peers and the authority to teach and interpret Judaic law.

Rosh Hashanah "head of the year"; the Jewish New Year (falls in September and October) and the first day of the Ten Days of Penitence; known as the Day of Remembrance.

Sanhedrin the chief Jewish legal, political, and religious council in Roman Palestine.

Seder "order"; the order of worship performed in association with the family dinner on the first night or first two nights of the Passover festival.

Sephardic (pl. Sephardim)

Jews of Iberian descent, including those who fled to North Africa from Spain and Portugal. By extension, it includes Middle Eastern Jews.

Shabbat (Sabbath) Jews are commanded (in the fourth of the *Ten Commandments*) to keep Shabbat. It is the seventh day of the week and a reminder of the seventh day of creation. Shabbat is a day of rest and *shalom* marked by worship and abstaining from work. It begins at sundown on Friday and concludes with Havdalah after sundown on Saturday.

Shavuot "weeks"; also known as Pentecost. The Feast of Weeks falls in May–June, fifty days after Passover. Shavuot commemorates the revelation of *Torah* at Mount Sinai and celebrates the fruitfulness of the earth. In biblical times, it was one of three festivals (with Sukkot and Pesach) that required men to make a pilgrimage to Jerusalem.

Shekhinah a talmudic term for the indwelling presence of God in the world. In Kabbalism, God's indwelling presence is the female aspect of God's being.

Shema	a prayer recited in daily services. Referred to as a summation of Judaic belief, it includes three passages from *Torah* (*Deut.* 6:4–9, 11:13–21; *Num.* 15:37–41).
Simchat Torah	"rejoicing of the Law"; a festival day following Sukkot on which the annual *Torah* reading cycle is completed (*Deut.* 33:1–29) and the new cycle is begun (*Gen.* 1:1–2:3).
Sukkot	"booths"; the Festival of Booths is a fall harvest festival commemorating the sojourn of the Israelites in the Sinai wilderness.
synagogue	literally "assembly"; a Jewish house of study and worship.
Talmud	"learning"; a compendium of Judaic law and tradition composed of *Mishnah* and *Gemara.* There are two *Talmuds:* the Palestinian (Jerusalem) and the Babylonian. The latter is more authoritative.
Tanakh	an acronym for the three major divisions of the Hebrew *Bible*: *Torah* (the law), *Nevi'im* (the prophets), and *Kethuvim* (the writings).
tikkun	"mending"; in Judaism, the task of joining God in the healing, mending, or restoration of the world.
Torah	"instruction"; the divine revelation of the law at Sinai; the *Pentateuch* and, by extension, the Hebrew *Bible,* the oral law *(Mishnah),* and the entire body of Judaic teaching.
Yom Kippur	Day of Atonement; the last day of the Ten Days of Penitence; the most solemn day in the Jewish calendar.
Zionism	a movement that began in the late nineteenth century to establish a Jewish state as a response to the failure of emancipation and to anti-Semitism.
Zohar	a mystical treatise written by the Sephardic Kabbalist Moses de Leon (d. 1305).

FOR FURTHER STUDY

Encyclopedia Judaica. 16 vols. New York: Macmillan, 1971.
> *A primary resource for matters related to Judaica.*

Neusner, Jacob, trans. *Mishnah: A New Translation.* New Haven, Conn.: Yale University Press, 1988.
> *A very readable English translation of the* Mishnah *with introductory and explanatory notes.*

————. *The Way of Torah: An Introduction to Judaism.* 5th ed. Belmont, Calif.: Wadsworth, 1993.
> *Perhaps the best single-volume introduction to Judaism.*

Pirke Avot: Torah from Our Sages. Translated and commentary by Jacob Neusner. Chappaqua, N.Y.: Rossel, 1984.
> *The* Avot *is a popular and highly readable* Mishnah *tractate and an excellent introduction to Judaic values.*

Plaskow, Judith. *Standing Again at Sinai: Judaism from a Feminist Perspective.* San Francisco: HarperCollins, 1991.
> *A historical overview and challenging critique of Judaic thought and practice from a feminist perspective.*

Roth, John, and Michael Berenbaum, eds. *Holocaust: Religious and Philosophical Implications.* New York: Paragon House, 1989.
> *A collection of essays that provide a solid introduction to the Holocaust and its implications.*

Seltzer, Robert M. *Jewish People, Jewish Thought: The Jewish Experience in History.* New York: Macmillan, 1980.
> *A comprehensive and thoughtful introduction to the history of Judaism and, especially, to Judaic philosophical theology.*

The Talmud: Selected Writings. Translated by Ben Zion Bokser. New York: Paulist Press, 1989.
> *A good resource to begin a sampling of talmudic texts.*

Tanakh: The Holy Scriptures: According to the Traditional Hebrew Text. Philadelphia: Jewish Publication Society, 1985.
> *A good choice for those seeking an English translation of the Hebrew* Bible *by Jewish scholars. The quotations from Hebrew scripture in Chapter 8 are from this source.*

READINGS

Reading 8.1   "WHEN GOD BEGAN TO CREATE . . ." *GENESIS* 1:1–2:4A

Genesis, the name of the first book of the *Pentateuch*, means "beginning." It is an apt title, as the narrative is about God's creation of the cosmos and of all life forms. *Genesis* 1:1–2:4a is about God's creation of the world, culminating in the creation of humans on the sixth day and a day of rest on the seventh day. It includes several important theological themes: the world and all living things are God's creation, creation is good, humans (male and female) are made in the image of God, sexuality is a blessing, and creation was completed on the seventh day.

Does the text suggest that the first human was androgynous (*Gen.* 1:27)? What do you make of the suggestion that humans were initially vegetarians (1:29)? Notice that after God created humans and blessed their reproductivity, God directed them to *"fill the earth and master it"* and to rule all nonhuman living things (1:26, 28). How do you interpret human "dominion" over nature? How many times does the creation narrative declare that what God has created is good? Shabbat observances are a fundamental feature of Judaic practice. How is Shabbat grounded in the creation story?

1When God began to create heaven and earth—2the earth being unformed and void, with darkness over the surface of the deep and a wind from God sweeping over the water—3God said, "Let there be light"; and there was light. 4God saw that the light was good, and God separated the light from the darkness. 5God called the light Day, and the darkness He called Night. And there was evening and there was morning, a first day.

6God said, "Let there be an expanse in the midst of the water, that it may separate water from water." 7God made the expanse, and it separated the water which was below the expanse from the water which was above the expanse. And it was so. 8God called the expanse Sky. And there was evening and there was morning, a second day.

9God said, "Let the water below the sky be gathered into one area, that the dry land may appear." And it was so. 10God called the dry land Earth, and the gathering of waters He called Seas. And God saw that this was good. 11And God said, "Let the earth sprout vegetation: seed-bearing plants, fruit trees of every kind on earth that bear fruit with the seed in it." And it was so. 12The earth brought forth vegetation: seed-bearing plants of every kind, and trees of every kind bearing fruit with the seed in it. And God saw that this was good. 13And there was evening and there was morning, a third day.

14God said, "Let there be lights in the expanse of the sky to separate day from night; they shall serve as signs for the set times—the days and the years; 15and they shall serve as lights in the expanse of the sky to shine upon the earth." And it was so. 16God made the two great lights, the greater light to dominate the day and the lesser light to dominate the night, and the stars. 17And God set them in the expanse of the sky to shine upon the earth, 18to dominate the day and the night, and to separate light from darkness. And God saw that this was good. 19And there was evening and there was morning, a fourth day.

20God said, "Let the waters bring forth swarms of living creatures, and birds that fly above the earth across the expanse of the sky." 21God created the great sea monsters, and all the living creatures of every kind that creep, which the waters brought forth in swarms, and all the winged birds of every kind. And God saw that this was good. [22]God blessed them, saying, "Be fertile and increase, fill the waters in the seas, and let the birds increase on the earth." [23]And there was evening and there was morning, a fifth day.

[24]God said, "Let the earth bring forth every kind of living creature: cattle, creeping things, and wild beasts of every kind." And it was so. [25]God made wild beasts of every kind and cattle of every kind, and all kinds of creeping things of the earth. And God saw that this was good. [26]And God said, "Let us make man in our image, after our likeness. They shall rule the fish of the sea, the birds of the sky, the cattle, the whole earth, and all the creeping things that creep on earth." [27]And God created man in His image, in the image of God He created him; male and female He created them. [28]God blessed them and God said to them, "Be fertile and increase, fill the earth and master it; and rule the fish of the sea, the birds of the sky, and all the living things that creep on earth."

[29]God said, "See I give you every seed-bearing plant that is upon all the earth, and every tree that has seed-bearing fruit; they shall be yours for food. [30]And to all the animals on land, to all the birds of the sky, and to everything that creeps on earth, in which there is the breath of life, [I give] all the green plants for food." And it was so. [31]And God saw all that He had made, and found it very good. And there was evening and there was morning, the sixth day.

[2]The heaven and the earth were finished, and all their array. [2]On the seventh day God finished the work that He had been doing, and He ceased on the seventh day from all the work that He had done. [3]And God blessed the seventh day and declared it holy, because on it God ceased from all the work of creation that He had done. [4]Such is the story of heaven and earth when they were created.

Source: *Tanakh: The Holy Scriptures: According to the Traditional Hebrew Text* (Philadelphia: Jewish Publication Society, 1985). Reprinted by permission.

Reading 8.2   A SECOND ACCOUNT OF CREATION: *GENESIS* 2:4B–3:24

Genesis 1:1–2:4a is followed by a second account of creation (*Gen.* 2:4b–3:24), which differs in style and details. How are we to account for their differences? One resolution assumes that both accounts have the same author (Moses) and that the former (*Gen.* 1:1–2:4a) paints creation in broad, majestic brushstrokes and that the latter (*Gen.* 2:4b–3:24) elaborates on the story in a more folksy fashion.

Another resolution—known as the Documentary Hypothesis of the *Pentateuch*—rejects the notion that both creation stories were written by a single author (Moses) in favor of the view that they originated in different times and contexts and that later editors wove them into a continuous narrative. According to the Documentary Hypothesis, the *Pentateuch* includes four main strands: the Yahwist, the Elohist, the Priestly, and the Deuteronomist. The traditions were composed centuries apart; for example *Gen.* 1:1–2:4a (from the Priestly strand) dates from the sixth century B.C.E., and Gen 2:4b–3:24 (from the Yahwist strand) dates from the ninth century B.C.E.

One reason scholars arrived at the idea of multiple strands is the striking differences between the two creation accounts (*Gen.* 1:1–2:4a and *Gen.* 2:4b–3:24). There are, for example, different versions of the order of creation. In the Priestly narrative, humans are created after plants and animals, but in the Yahwist story, the first man (Adam) is formed before the flora of the earth and the birds and animals were created. In the Priestly creation story, man (male and female) is created in God's image, but in the Yahwist narrative, Adam is formed from dust of the earth, and the first woman is made from Adam's rib and is named Eve by Adam.

Here are some questions to ponder about *Gen.* 2:4b–3:24: What is implied by God's declaration that *"It is not good that the man should be alone; I will make a fitting helper for him"*? Does this verse imply subordination or partnering? The first woman is created after the animals and from man's side. What does coming last in the order of creation signify? What led to the expulsion of Adam and Eve from the garden? Note that after the fall, the man is to rule over his wife. Is this God's will, or does it reflect a male shaping of the text and a means of validating male dominance?

When the Lord God made earth and heaven—[5]*when no shrub of the field was yet on earth and no grasses of the field had yet sprouted, because the Lord God had not sent rain upon the earth and there was no man to till the soil,* [6]*but a flow would well up from the ground and water the whole surface of the earth—*[7]*the Lord God formed man from the dust of the earth. He blew into his nostrils the breath of life, and man became a living being.*

[8]*The Lord God planted a garden in Eden, in the east, and placed there the man whom He had formed.* [9]*And from the ground the Lord God caused to grow every tree that was pleasing to the sight and good for food, with the tree of life in the middle of the garden, and the tree of knowledge of good and bad.*

[10]*A river issues from Eden to water the garden, and it then divides and becomes four branches.* [11]*The name of the first is Pishon, the one that winds through the whole land of Havilah, where the gold is. (*[12]*The gold of that land is good; bdellium is there, and lapis lazuli.)* [13]*The name of the second river is Gihon, the one that winds through the whole land of Cush.* [14]*The name of the third river is Tigris, the one that flows east of Asshur. And the fourth river is the Euphrates.*

[15]*The Lord God took the man and placed him in the garden of Eden, to till it and tend it.* [16]*And the Lord God commanded the man, saying "Of every tree of the garden you are free to eat;* [17]*but as for the tree of knowledge of good and bad, you must not eat of it; for as soon as you eat of it, you shall die."*

[18]*The Lord God said, "It is not good for man to be alone; I will make a fitting helper for him."* [19]*And the Lord God formed out of the earth all the wild beasts and all the birds of the sky, and brought them to the man to see what he would call them; and whatever the man called each living creature, that would be its name.* [20]*And the man gave names to all the cattle and to the birds of the sky and to all the wild beasts; but for Adam no fitting helper was found.* [21]*So the Lord God cast a deep sleep upon the man; and while he slept, He took one of his ribs and closed up the flesh at that spot.* [22]*And the Lord God fashioned the rib that He had taken from the man into a woman; and He brought her to the man.* [23]*Then the man said,*

> *"This one at last*
> *Is bone of my bones*
> *And flesh of my flesh.*
> *This one shall be called Woman,*
> *For from man was she taken."*

^{24}Hence a man leaves his father and mother and clings to his wife, so that they become one flesh.

^{25}The two of them were naked, the man and his wife, yet they felt no shame. $^{3\,1}$Now the serpent was the shrewdest of all the wild beasts that the Lord God had made. He said to the woman, "Did God really say: You shall not eat of any tree of the garden?" ^{2}The woman replied to the serpent, "We may eat of the fruit of the other trees of the garden. ^{3}It is only about fruit of the tree in the middle of the garden that God said: 'You shall not eat of it or touch it, lest you die.'" ^{4}And the serpent said to the woman, "You are not going to die, ^{5}but God knows that as soon as you eat of it your eyes will be opened and you will be like divine beings who know good and bad." ^{6}When the woman saw that the tree was good for eating and a delight to the eyes, and that the tree was desirable as a source of wisdom, she took of its fruit and ate. She also gave some to her husband, and he ate. ^{7}Then the eyes of both of them were opened and they perceived that they were naked; and they sewed together fig leaves and made themselves loincloths.

^{8}They heard the sound of the Lord God moving about in the garden at the breezy time of day; and the man and his wife hid from the Lord God among the trees of the garden. ^{9}The Lord God called out to the man and said to him, "Where are you?" ^{10}He replied, "I heard the sound of You in the garden, and I was afraid because I was naked, so I hid." ^{11}Then He asked, "Who told you that you were naked? Did you eat of the tree from which I had forbidden you to eat?" ^{12}The man said, "The woman You put at my side—she gave me of the tree, and I ate." ^{13}And the Lord God said to the woman, "What is this you have done!" The woman replied, "The serpent duped me, and I ate." ^{14}Then the Lord God said to the serpent,

> "Because you did this,
> More cursed shall you be
> Than all cattle
> And all the wild beasts:
> On your belly shall you crawl
> And dirt shall you eat
> All the days of your life.
> ^{15}I will put enmity
> Between you and the woman.
> And between your offspring and hers;
> They shall strike at your head,
> And you shall strike at their heel."

^{16}And to the woman He said,

> "I will make most severe
> Your pangs in childbearing;
> In pain shall you bear children.
> Yet your urge shall be for your husband,
> And he shall rule over you."

^{17}To Adam He said, "Because you did as your wife said and ate of the tree about which I commanded you, 'You shall not eat of it,'

Cursed be the ground because of you;
By toil shall you eat of it
All the days of your life:
¹⁸Thorns and thistles shall it sprout for you.
But your food shall be the grasses of the field;
¹⁹By the sweat of your brow
Shall you get bread to eat,
Until you return to the ground—
For from it you were taken.
For dust you are,
And to dust you shall return."

²⁰The man named his wife Eve, because she was the mother of all the living. ²¹And the Lord God made garments of skins for Adam and his wife, and clothed them.

²²And the Lord God said, "Now that the man has become like one of us, knowing good and bad, what if he should stretch out his hand and take also from the tree of life and eat, and live forever!" ²³So the Lord God banished him from the garden of Eden, to till the soil from which he was taken. ²⁴He drove the man out, and stationed east of the garden of Eden the cherubim and the fiery ever-turning sword, to guard the way to the tree of life.

Source: *Tanakh: The Holy Scriptures: According to the Traditional Hebrew Text* (Philadelphia: Jewish Publication Society, 1985). Reprinted by permission.

Reading 8.3   THE COMING OF LILITH   Judith Plaskow

Read this selection in conjunction with Readings 8.1 and 8.2. In the Judaic tradition, there is a legend that Adam had a wife before Eve. Lilith, the first woman God created, left Adam and disappeared into the night, whence she became a night demon. In "The Coming of Lilith," Judith Plaskow, a professor of religious studies and feminist, reshapes the older myth so that Lilith, in concert with Eve, discovers the power of sisterhood.

In Plaskow's transformation of the myth, what leads to the separation of Adam and Lilith? How did Adam perceive the role of Eve? Why was Eve troubled by the relationship of God and Adam? Why did Lilith return? How did Adam attempt to keep her away? How was Eve's experience of Lilith different from the stories Adam told about her? What did Eve and Lilith learn from their relationship? Why were God and Adam perplexed and apprehensive? In what sense is Plaskow's story of Lilith a story about deliverance? What (or who) is the enemy?

In the beginning, the Lord God formed Adam and Lilith from the dust of the ground and breathed into their nostrils the breath of life. Created from the same source, both having been formed from the ground, they were equal in all ways. Adam, being man, didn't like this situation, and he looked for ways to change it. He said, "I'll have my figs now, Lilith," ordering her to wait on him, and he tried to leave to her the daily tasks of life in the garden. But Lilith wasn't one to take any nonsense; she picked herself up, uttered God's holy name, and flew away. "Well now, Lord," complained Adam, "that uppity woman you sent me has gone and deserted me." The Lord, inclined to be sympathetic, sent his messengers after Lilith, telling her to shape up and return to Adam or face dire punishment. She, however, preferring anything to living with Adam, decided to stay where she was. And so God, after more careful consideration this time, caused a deep sleep to fall on Adam and out of one of his ribs created for him a second companion, Eve.

For a time, Eve and Adam had a good thing going. Adam was happy now, and Eve, though she occasionally sensed capacities within herself that remained undeveloped, was basically satisfied with the role of Adam's wife and helper. The only thing that really disturbed her was the excluding closeness of the relationship between Adam and God. Adam and God just seemed to have more in common, both being men, and Adam came to identify with God more and more. After a while, that made God a bit uncomfortable too, and he started going over in his mind whether he may not have made a mistake letting Adam talk him into banishing Lilith and creating Eve, seeing the power that gave Adam.

Meanwhile Lilith, all alone, attempted from time to time to rejoin the human community in the garden. After her first fruitless attempt to breach its walls, Adam worked hard to build them stronger, even getting Eve to help him. He told her fearsome stories of the demon Lilith who threatens women in childbirth and steals children from their cradles in the middle of the night. The second time Lilith came, she stormed the garden's main gate, and a great battle ensued between her and Adam in which she was finally defeated. This time, however, before Lilith got away, Eve got a glimpse of her and saw she was a woman like herself.

After this encounter, seeds of curiosity and doubt began to grow in Eve's mind. Was Lilith indeed just another woman? Adam had said she was a demon. Another woman! The very idea attracted Eve. She had never seen another creature like herself before. And how beautiful and strong Lilith looked! How bravely she had fought! Slowly, slowly, Eve began to think about the limits of her own life within the garden.

One day, after many months of strange and disturbing thoughts, Eve, wandering around the edge of the garden, noticed a young apple tree she and Adam had planted, and saw that one of its branches stretched over the garden wall. Spontaneously, she tried to climb it, and struggling to the top, swung herself over the wall.

She did not wander long on the other side before she met the one she had come to find, for Lilith was waiting. At first sight of her, Eve remembered the tales of Adam and was frightened, but Lilith understood and greeted her kindly. "Who are you?" they asked each other, "What is your story?" And they sat and spoke together, of the past and then of the future. They talked for many hours, not once, but many times. They taught each other many things, and told each other stories, and laughed together, and cried, over and over, till the bond of sisterhood grew between them.

Meanwhile, back in the garden, Adam was puzzled by Eve's comings and goings, and disturbed by what he sensed to be her new attitude toward him. He talked to God about it, and God, having his own problems with Adam and a somewhat broader perspective, was able to help out a little—but he was confused, too. Something had failed to go according to plan. As in the days of Abraham, he needed counsel from his children. "I am who I am," thought God, "but I must become who I will become."

And God and Adam were expectant and afraid the day Eve and Lilith returned to the garden, bursting with possibilities, ready to rebuild it together.

Source: Judith Plaskow, "The Coming of Lilith: Toward a Feminist Theology," in *Womanspirit Rising: A Feminist Reader in Religion,* ed. Carol P. Christ and Judith Plaskow (San Francisco: Harper & Row, 1979), pp. 198–207. ©1979 by Carol P. Christ and Judith Plaskow. Reprinted by permission of HarperCollins Publishers, Inc.

Reading 8.4   THE ABRAHAMIC COVENANT: *GENESIS* 17:1–14

There are several covenants in the *Pentateuch;* the Abrahamic covenant is reproduced here first (Reading 8.4), followed by the Mosaic covenant (Reading 8.5) There are two accounts of God's covenant with Abraham (*Gen.* 15:18–21 and *Gen.* 17:1–14). The former is from the Yahwist and Elohist traditions, and the latter, printed here, is part of the Priestly strand (see Reading 8.2). El Shaddai (*Gen.* 17:1) was probably the name of a Canaanite deity, as well as one of the names of the Hebrew God. Abram is a variant form of Abraham and is the patriarch's name in the older traditions. Here it is changed to Abraham.

What is significant about the renaming? What does God promise Abraham? What does the covenant require of Abraham and his descendants? What is the sign of the covenant?

17When Abram was ninety-nine years old, the Lord appeared to Abram and said to him. "I am El Shaddai. Walk in My ways and be blameless. 2I will establish My covenant between Me and you, and I will make you exceedingly numerous."

3Abram threw himself on his face; and God spoke to him further, 4"As for Me, this is My covenant with you: You shall be the father of a multitude of nations. 5And you shall no longer be called Abram, but your name shall be Abraham, for I make you the father of a multitude of nations. 6I will make you exceedingly fertile, and make nations of you; and kings shall come forth from you. 7I will maintain My covenant between Me and you, and your offspring to come, as an everlasting covenant throughout the ages, to be God to you and to your offspring to come. 8I assign the land you sojourn in to you and your offspring to come, all the land of Canaan, as an everlasting holding. I will be their God."

9God further said to Abraham, "As for you, you and your offspring to come throughout the ages shall keep My covenant. 10Such shall be the covenant between Me and you and your offspring to follow which you shall keep: every male among you shall be circumcised. 11You shall circumcise the flesh of your foreskin, and that shall be the sign of the covenant between Me and you. 12And throughout the generations, every male among you shall be circumcised at the age of eight days. As for the homeborn slave and the one bought from an outsider who is not of your offspring, 13they must be circumcised, homeborn and purchased alike. Thus shall My covenant be marked in your flesh as an everlasting pact. 14And if any male who is uncircumcised fails to circumcise the flesh of his foreskin, that person shall be cut off from his kin; he has broken My covenant."

Source: *Tanakh: The Holy Scriptures: According to the Traditional Hebrew Text* (Philadelphia: Jewish Publication Society, 1985). Reprinted by permission.

Reading 8.5   THE MOSAIC COVENANT: *EXODUS* 19:1–20:14

Speaking of the Mosaic covenant, one commentator observed that it repudiates the notion that history is meaningless, just as *Genesis* denies that the cosmos is the result of random chance. The Mosaic covenant shifts from a vow to a person (the covenant with Abraham) to a vow binding God and his chosen people: God promised that *"if you will obey Me faithfully and keep My covenant, you shall be My treasured possession among all the peoples."* The people of Israel committed themselves to obey God's commands: *"All that the Lord has spoken we will do!"* (*Exod.* 19:5, 8).

What is meant by the *"house of Jacob"*? What does the phrase *"kingdom of priests"* mean? Does the kingdom of priests include women? What phrases undergird the doctrine of Israel's election as a chosen people? What taboos must the Israelites observe in preparation for the disclosure at Mount Sinai? Judaic feminists are particularly critical of Moses' injunction *"do not go near a woman"* (19:15). Does this imply that women were not part of God's covenant with Israel?

Scholars disagree as to the content of the revelation, but tradition points to what is commonly referred to as the *Ten Commandments* (the *Decalogue*) as the core of the Mosaic covenant. Notice that the commandments (*Exod.* 20:2–14) are not numbered; Christian and Judaic traditions number them differently. Scripture indicates that the commandments were inscribed on tablets and placed in the Ark of the Covenant (*Deut.* 10:5). Both the ark and the tablets are presumably irretrievably lost.

The first four commandments deal with humankind's relationship to God. The remaining six govern the interaction of humans. Does the command to *"have no other gods besides Me"* imply that the Israelites recognized other gods? How has the command respecting sculptured images affected Judaic art? What blessing is granted those who honor their parents? Notice that the command is "You shall not murder" rather than "You shall not kill." What is the difference? Which of the commands are relatively universal moral codes, and which are culturally specific and not easily universalized? The *Ten Commandments* are reiterated with some variations in *Deuteronomy* 5:6–18; identify some of the differences.

> 19 On the third new moon after the Israelites had gone forth from the land of Egypt, on that very day, they entered the wilderness of Sinai. 2 Having journeyed from Rephidim, they entered the wilderness of Sinai and encamped in the wilderness. Israel encamped there in front of the mountain, 3 and Moses went up to God. The Lord called to him from the mountain, saying, "Thus shall you say to the house of Jacob and declare to the children of Israel: 4 'You have seen what I did to the Egyptians, how I bore you on eagles' wings and brought you to me. 5 Now then, if you will obey Me faithfully and keep My covenant, you shall be My treasured possession among all the peoples. Indeed, all the earth is Mine, 6 but you shall be to Me a kingdom of priests and a holy nation.' These are the words that you shall speak to the children of Israel."
>
>   7 Moses came and summoned the elders of the people and put before them all that the Lord had commanded him. 8 All the people answered as one, saying, "All that the Lord has spoken we will do!" And Moses brought back the people's words to the Lord. 9 And the Lord said to Moses, "I will come to you in a thick cloud, in order that the people may hear when I speak with you and so trust you ever after." Then Moses reported the people's words to the Lord, 10 and the Lord said to Moses, "Go to the people and warn them to stay pure

today and tomorrow. Let them wash their clothes. ¹¹Let them be ready for the third day; for on the third day the Lord will come down, in the sight of all the people, on Mount Sinai. ¹²You shall set bounds for the people round about, saying, 'Beware of going up the mountain or touching the border of it. Whoever touches the mountain shall be put to death: ¹³no hand shall touch him, but he shall be either stoned or shot; beast or man, he shall not live.' When the ram's horn sounds a long blast, they may go up on the mountain."

¹⁴Moses came down from the mountain to the people and warned the people to stay pure, and they washed their clothes. ¹⁵And he said to the people, "Be ready for the third day: do not go near a woman."

¹⁶On the third day, as morning dawned, there was thunder, and lightning, and a dense cloud upon the mountain, and a very loud blast of the horn; and all the people who were in the camp trembled. ¹⁷Moses led the people out of the camp toward God, and they took their places at the foot of the mountain.

¹⁸Now Mount Sinai was all in smoke, for the Lord had come down upon it in fire; the smoke rose like the smoke of a kiln, and the whole mountain trembled violently. ¹⁹The blare of the horn grew louder and louder. As Moses spoke, God answered him in thunder. ²⁰The Lord came down upon Mount Sinai, on the top of the mountain, and the Lord called Moses to the top of the mountain and Moses went up. ²¹The Lord said to Moses, "Go down, warn the people not to break through to the Lord to gaze, lest many of them perish. ²²The priests also, who come near the Lord, must stay pure, lest the Lord break out against them." ²³But Moses said to the Lord, "The people cannot come up to Mount Sinai, for You warned us saying, 'Set bounds about the mountain and sanctify it.'" ²⁴So the Lord said to him, "Go down, and come back together with Aaron; but let not the priests or the people break through to come up to the Lord, lest He break out against them." ²⁵And Moses went down to the people and spoke to them.

²⁰God spoke all these words, saying:

²I the Lord am your God who brought you out of the land of Egypt, the house of bondage: ³You shall have no other gods besides Me.

⁴You shall not make for yourself a sculptured image, or any likeness of what is in the heavens above, or on the earth below, or in the waters under the earth. ⁵You shall not bow down to them or serve them. For I the Lord your God am an impassioned God, visiting the guilt of the parents upon the children, upon the third and upon the fourth generations of those who reject Me, ⁶but showing kindness to the thousandth generation of those who love Me and keep My commandments.

⁷You shall not swear falsely by the name of the Lord your God; for the Lord will not clear one who swears falsely by His name.

⁸Remember the sabbath day and keep it holy. ⁹Six days you shall labor and do all your work, ¹⁰but the seventh day is a sabbath of the Lord your God: you shall not do any work—you, your son or daughter, your male or female slave, or your cattle, or the stranger who is within your settlements. ¹¹For in six days the Lord made heaven and earth and sea, and all that is in them, and He rested on the seventh day; therefore the Lord blessed the sabbath day and hallowed it.

¹²Honor your father and your mother, that you may long endure on the land that the Lord your God is assigning to you.

¹³You shall not murder.

You shall not commit adultery.

You shall not steal.

You shall not bear false witness against your neighbor.

14You shall not covet your neighbor's house: you shall not covet your neighbor's wife, or his male or female slave, or his ox or his ass, or anything that is your neighbor's.

Source: *Tanakh: The Holy Scriptures: According to the Traditional Hebrew Text* (Philadelphia: Jewish Publication Society, 1985). Reprinted by permission.

Reading 8.6   The Law of Holiness: *Leviticus* 19

Leviticus, the third of the five books of Moses, contains Priestly traditions. It includes laws respecting sacrifice, diet, pollution, sexual relations, priests, the observance of sabbatical years (every seven years) for the land to rest, and the observance of Jubilee years (every fifty years) for the redistribution of wealth and property. Leviticus points to the sanctification of all aspects of life through ritual and moral action. *Leviticus* 19 includes each of the *Ten Commandments.* Can you identify them? What provisions are made to care for the poor? What directives are given respecting divination and ghosts? In what contexts does the command to love others as you love yourself occur (see 19:18, 34)?

19The Lord spoke to Moses, saying 2Speak to the whole Israelite community and say to them:

You shall be holy, for I, the Lord your God, am holy.

3You shall each revere his mother and his father, and keep My sabbaths: I the LORD am your God.

4Do not turn to idols or make molten gods for yourselves: I the Lord am your God.

5When you sacrifice an offering of well-being to the Lord, sacrifice it so that it may be accepted on your behalf. 6It shall be eaten on the day you sacrifice it, or on the day following; but what is left by the third day must be consumed in fire. 7If it should be eaten on the third day, it is an offensive thing, it will not be acceptable. 8And he who eats of it shall bear his guilt, for he has profaned what is sacred to the Lord; that person shall be cut off from his kin.

9When you reap the harvest of your land, you shall not reap all the way to the edges of your field, or gather the gleanings of your harvest. 10You shall not pick your vineyard bare, or gather the fallen fruit of your vineyard; you shall leave them for the poor and the stranger: I the Lord am your God.

11You shall not steal; you shall not deal deceitfully or falsely with one another. 12You shall not swear falsely by My name, profaning the name of your God: I am the Lord.

13You shall not defraud your fellow. You shall not commit robbery. The wages of a laborer shall not remain with you until morning.

14You shall not insult the deaf, or place a stumbling block before the blind. You shall fear your God: I am the Lord.

15You shall not render an unfair decision: do not favor the poor or show deference to the rich; judge your kinsman fairly. 16Do not deal basely with your countrymen. Do not profit by the blood of your fellow: I am the Lord.

[17]You shall not hate your kinsfolk in your heart. Reprove your kinsman but incur no guilt because of him. [18]You shall not take vengeance or bear a grudge against your countrymen. Love your fellow as yourself: I am the Lord.

[19]You shall observe My laws.

You shall not let your cattle mate with a different kind; you shall not sow your field with two kinds of seed; you shall not put on cloth from a mixture of two kinds of material.

[20]If a man has carnal relations with a woman who is a slave and has been designated for another man, but has not been redeemed or given her freedom, there shall be an indemnity; they shall not, however, be put to death, since she has not been freed. [21]But he must bring to the entrance of the Tent of Meeting, as his guilt offering to the Lord, a ram of guilt offering. [22]With the ram of guilt offering the priest shall make expiation for him before the Lord for the sin that he committed; and the sin that he committed will be forgiven him.

[23]When you enter the land and plant any tree for food, you shall regard its fruit as forbidden. Three years it shall be forbidden for you, not to be eaten. [24]In the fourth year all its fruit shall be set aside for jubilation before the Lord; [25]and only in the fifth year may you use its fruit—that its yield to you may be increased: I the Lord am your God.

[26]You shall not eat anything with its blood. You shall not practice divination or soothsaying. [27]You shall not round off the side-growth on your head, or destroy the side-growth of your beard. [28]You shall not make gashes in your flesh for the dead, or incise any marks on yourselves: I am the Lord.

[29]Do not degrade your daughter and make her a harlot, lest the land fall into harlotry and the land be filled with depravity. [30]You shall keep My sabbaths and venerate My sanctuary: I am the Lord.

[31]Do not turn to ghosts and do not inquire of familiar spirits, to be defiled by them: I the Lord am your God.

[32]You shall rise before the aged and show deference to the old; you shall fear your God: I am the Lord.

[33]When a stranger resides with you in your land, you shall not wrong him. [34]The stranger who resides with you shall be to you as one of your citizens; you shall love him as yourself, for you were strangers in the land of Egypt: I am the Lord your God.

[35]You shall not falsify measures of length, weights, or capacity. [36]You shall have an honest balance, honest weights, an honest ephah, and an honest hin.

I the Lord am your God who freed you from the land of Egypt. [37]You shall faithfully observe all My laws and all My rules: I am the Lord.

Source: *Tanakh: The Holy Scriptures: According to the Traditional Hebrew Text (*Philadelphia: Jewish Publication Society, 1985). Reprinted by permission.

Reading 8.7 A SUMMATION OF THE COMMANDMENTS: THE *TALMUD*

In this selection from the *Babylonian Talmud Tractate Makkot*, Rabbi Similai attempts to reduce the Mosaic commands from 613 to an essential core that expresses the heart of the law. What method of proof does Rabbi Similai use to reduce the commands from 613 to 11 to 6 to 3 to 2 to 1? How would you respond if you were asked to reduce the commandments to a single principle? There are variant lists of the 613 commands; if you are interested in such a listing, see the *Encyclopedia Judaica* (cited in this chapter's For Further Study section.)

> *R. Similai expounded: Six hundred and thirteen commandments were communicated to Moses at Sinai, three hundred and sixty-five negative ones, corresponding to the number of days in a solar calendar year, and two hundred and forty-eight positive ones, corresponding to the number of joints in the human body. David came and reduced them to eleven. Thus it is written: "A Psalm of David. Lord, who shall sojourn in Your tabernacle, who shall dwell on Your holy mountain? (1) He who walks uprightly, and (2) acts righteously, and (3) speaks the truth in his heart; (4) who hears no slander on his tongue, (5) who does no evil to his fellow, (6) nor takes up a reproach against his neighbor, (7) in whose eyes a vile person is despised, (8) but he honors those who fear the Lord. (9) He swears to his own heart and does not change. (10) He does not put out his money on interest, (11) nor does he take a bribe against the innocent. He who does these things will never be moved" (Ps 15).*
>
> *Isaiah came and reduced them to six. Thus it is written: "(1) He who walks righteously, and (2) speaks uprightly, (3) who despises the gain of oppression, (4) who withdraws his hands from holding a bribe, (5) who stops his ears from hearing of blood, and (6) shuts his eyes from looking on evil. He shall dwell on high" (Is 33:15–16).*
>
> *Micah came and reduced them to three. Thus it is written: "It has been told you, O man, what is good and what the Lord requires of you: only (1) to do justly, (2) to love mercy, and (3) to walk humbly with your God" (Mi 6:8).*
>
> *Isaiah came again and reduced them to two. Thus it is written: (1) "Keep justice and (2) do righteousness" (Is 56:1).*
>
> *Amos came and reduced them to one. Thus it is said: "Thus has the Lord spoken to the House of Israel: 'Seek me and live'" (Am 5:4). R. Nahman b. Isaac challenged this. Perhaps "seek me" means by observing all the prescriptions in the Torah. But it was Habakuk who reduced them to one. Thus it is said: "The righteous shall live by his faith" (Hb 2:4).*

Source: *The Talmud: Selected Writings,* trans. Ben Zion Bokser (New York: Paulist Press, 1989), pp. 214–215. ©1989 by Baruch M. Bokser. Used by permission of Paulist Press.

Reading 8.8 Trying a Capital Case: The *Talmud*

The *Torah* recognizes that there are contexts in which taking a life is the moral and divinely commanded course of action. Hebrew scripture commands capital punishment for various crimes, including adultery, blasphemy, striking or cursing a parent, kidnapping, premeditated murder, and idolatry. Justice requires that no one be put to death on the testimony of a single witness. In the formative period of rabbinic Judaism, rabbis placed further restrictions on cases involving the death penalty. For example, in the *Mishnah Tractate Sanhedrin,* commercial cases require three judges, whereas capital cases require twenty-three. Capital cases require a majority of one (twelve of twenty-three) for acquittal but a majority of two for conviction. *Sanhedrin* 4:5 instructs witnesses on the grave difference between commercial and capital cases: "*In the case of a trial for property cases, a person pays money and achieves atonement for himself. In capital cases [the accused's] blood and the blood of all those who were destined to be born from him [who was wrongfully convicted] are held against him [who testifies falsely] to the end of time."*

Instruction of witnesses continues with the teaching that humankind was created from a single ancestor *"to teach you that whoever destroys a single Israelite soul is deemed by Scripture as if he had destroyed a whole world. And whoever saves a single Israelite soul is deemed by Scripture as if he had saved a whole world."* Some translators make this teaching inclusive by dropping *Israelite.*

The reluctance of rabbis to condemn a person to death is evident in the judgment that *"A sanhedrin which imposes the death penalty once in seven years is called murderous"* (*Tractate Makkot* 1:10). Rabbis Akiva and Tarfon observed that were they to serve on the Sanhedrin, *"no one would ever be put to death,"* to which Rabbi Gamaliel objected that an unwillingness to execute persons convicted of capital crimes *"would multiply the number of murderers in Israel"* (*Makkot* 1:10).

The selections here show how the *Mishnah* limited the biblical command that *"a rebellious and incorrigible son"* shall be put to death (*Deut.* 21:18–21). The injunction was limited by the ruling that both parents had to agree on the subject and was effectively nullified by the judgment that parental agreement required that both parents resemble each other in voice, height, and appearance. Consequently, *"there never was a 'rebellious son' and there never will be."* Although the rabbis effectively nullified God's command to put to death a rebellious and incorrigible son, how does their reasoning reflect their profound respect for God's commands? How does their reasoning reflect a difference in perspective from that of the command?

The selections on the "rebellious and incorrigible son" are from both components of the *Talmud: Mishnah* and *Gemara.* The first selection is from the *Mishnah Sanhedrin,* a tractate within the "Division of Damages." The second selection is *Gemara* (a commentary on the text in the *Sanhedrin*). Generally speaking, when the *Mishnah* presents *halakah* without identifying the rabbis involved by name, such *halakah* are meant to be regarded as the decision of the majority. When there is a lack of consensus on a subject, judgments are recorded and identified with specific rabbis.

Mishnah Tractate Sanhedrin 8:1–5 sets out the legal decisions and opinions respecting *Deuteronomy* 21:18–21:

> *If a man has a stubborn and rebellious son, who does not obey the voice of his father or the voice of his mother and, though they chastise him, he will not give heed to them, then his father and his mother shall take hold of him and bring him to the elders of the city at the gate of the place where he lives and they shall say to the elders of the city, "This our son is stubborn and rebellious, he will not obey our voice, he is a glutton and a drunkard." Then all the men of the city shall stone him to death with stones, so shall you purge the evil from your midst; and all Israel shall hear and be afraid.*

Mishnah Tractate Sanhedrin 8:1A–F
(words not italicized are from *Deut.* 21:18–21)

A. A rebellious and incorrigible son . . .

B. *At what point [does a child] become liable to be declared a rebellious and incorrigible son?*

C. *From the point at which he will produce two pubic hairs, until the 'beard' is full. . . .*

E. *As it is said,* "If a man has a son *(Deut. 21:18)—(1) a son, not a daughter; (2) a son, not an adult man.*

F. *And a minor is exempt, since he has not yet entered the the scope of the commandments.*

*Mishnah Tractate Sanhedrin 8:4*A–N
(words not italicized are from *Deut.* 21:18–21)

A. *[If] his father wanted [to put him to judgment as a rebellious and incorrigible son] but his mother did not want to do so,*

B. *[if] his father did not want and his mother did want [to put him to judgment],*

C. *he is not declared a rebellious and incorrigible son—*

D. *until both of them want [to put him to judgment],*

E. *R. Judah says, "If his mother was unworthy of his father, he is not declared to be a rebellious and incorrigible son."*

F. *[If] one of them was (1) maimed in the hand, (2) lame, (3) dumb, (4) blind, or (5) deaf,*

G. *he is not declared a rebellious and incorrigible son,*

H. *since it is said,* Then his father and his mother will lay hold of him *(Deut. 21:20)—so they are not (1) maimed in their hands;*

I. and bring him out—*(2)so they are not lame;*

J. and they shall say—*(3) so they are not dumb;*

K. "This is our son"—*(4) so they are not blind;*

L. "He will not obey our voice"?—*(5) so they are not deaf.*

Source: Jacob Neusner, trans., *Mishnah: A New Translation* (New Haven, Conn.: Yale University Press, 1988), pp. 599–601. Reprinted by permission of the publisher.

Tractate Sanhedrin 71A: *Gemara* ON THE *Mishnah Tractate Sanhedrin* 8:4

It has been taught similarly: R. Judah said: If his father is not like his mother in voice, in appearance, and in height he is not treated as "a stubborn and rebellious son." What is the reason for this? The verse states [in the charge brought against him]: "He will not listen to our voice" (Deut. 18:20)—since there has to be a similarity in voice, there also has to be a similarity in appearance and height. With whom does the following teaching accord: There never was a "rebellious son" and there were never will be. Why then was it written in the Torah? To give us the benefit of study."

Source: Reprinted from *The Talmud: Selected Writings;* translated by Ben Zion Bokser. ©1989 by Baruch M. Bokser. Used by permission of Paulist Press.

Reading 8.9   SELECTIONS FROM THE *MISHNAH TRACTATE AVOT*

The *Tractate Avot* is the most popular of the *Mishnah's* tractates. Unlike the other tractates, which are largely *halakah,* the *Avot* is a collection of the sayings of sages from Hillel and Shammai to the generation of Judah the Patriarch and perhaps a generation thereafter. Although attributed to Judah, the *Avot* was codified after the *Mishnah* of Judah, sometime around 250 to 275 C.E. The *Avot* is part of the *Mishnah's* fourth division, the "Division of Damages." The excerpt from the *Avot* includes all of Chapter 1 plus selections from other chapters. It begins with the teaching of an unbroken chain of authority from Moses to the rabbis. What purpose does the chain of authority serve? How are women characterized? What does the world rest on?

CHAPTER 1

1. Moses received the Torah at Sinai. He conveyed it to Joshua: Joshua to the elders; the elders to the prophets; and the prophets transmitted it to the men of the Great Assembly. The latter emphasized three principles: Be deliberate in judgment; raise up many disciples; and make a fence to safeguard the Torah.

2. Simeon the Just was of the last survivors of the Great Assembly. He used to say: The world rests on three foundations: the Torah: the divine service; and the practices of lovingkindness between man and man.

3. Antigonus of Soho received the tradition from him. He was accustomed to say: Be not like servants who serve their master because of the expected reward, but be like those who serve a master without expecting a reward; and let the fear of God be upon you.

4. Yose ben Yoezer of Zeredah and Yose ben Yohanan of Jerusalem received the tradition from them. Yose ben Yoezer of Zeredah said: Let your house be a gathering place for wise men; sit attentively at their feet, and drink of their words of wisdom with eagerness.

5. Yose ben Yohanan of Jerusalem said: Let your home be a place of hospitality to strangers; and make the poor welcome in your household; and do not indulge in gossip with women. This applies even with one's own wife, and surely so with another man's wife. The sages generalized from this: He who engages in profuse gossiping with women causes evil for himself and neglects the study of the Torah, and he will bring upon himself retributions in the hereafter.

6. Joshua ben Perahya and Nittai the Arbelite received the tradition from them. Joshua ben Perahya said: Get yourself a teacher; and acquire for yourself a companion; and judge all people favorably.

7. Nittai the Arbelite said: Avoid an evil neighbor; do not associate with the wicked; and do not surrender your faith in divine retribution.

8. Judah ben Tabbai and Simeon ben Shatah received the traditions from them. Judah ben Tabbai said: Let not the judge play the part of the counselor; when two litigants stand before you, suspect both of being in the wrong; and when they leave after submitting to the court's decree, regard them both as guiltless.

9. Simeon ben Shatah said: Search the witnesses thoroughly and be cautious with your own words lest you give them an opening to false testimony.

10. Shemaya and Abtalyon received the traditions from them. Shemaya said: love work; hate domineering over others; and do not seek the intimacy of public officials.

11. Abtalyon said: Sages, be precise in your teachings. You may suffer exile to a place where heresy is rampant, and your inexact language may lead your disciples astray, and they will lose their faith, thus leading to a desecration of the divine name.

12. Hillel and Shammai received the tradition from them. Hillel said: Be of the disciples of Aaron. Love peace and pursue peace; love your fellow creatures and bring them near to the Torah.

13. He also said: He who strives to exalt his name will in the end destroy his name; he who does not increase his knowledge decreases it; he who does not study has undermined his right to life; and he who makes unworthy use of the crown of the Torah will perish.

14. He also said: If I am not for myself who will be? But if I am for myself only, what am I? And if not now, when?

15. Shammai said: Set a fixed time for the study of the Torah; say little and do much; and greet every person with a cheerful countenance.

16. Rabban Gamaliel said: Provide yourself with a teacher, and extricate yourself from doubt; and do not habitually contribute your tithes by rough estimates.

17. Simeon his son said: All my life I was raised among scholars and I found that no virtue becomes a man more than silence; what is more essential is not study but practice; and in the wake of many words is sin.

18. Rabban Simeon ben Gamaliel said: The world rests on three foundations: truth, justice, and peace. As it is written (Zech 8:16): "You shall administer truth, justice and peace within your gates."

Source: Reprinted from *The Talmud: Selected Writings;* translated by Ben Zion Bokser. ©1989 by Brauch M. Bokser. Used by permission of Paulist Press.

CHAPTER 9

CHRISTIANITY

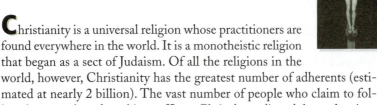

Christianity is a universal religion whose practitioners are found everywhere in the world. It is a monotheistic religion that began as a sect of Judaism. Of all the religions in the world, however, Christianity has the greatest number of adherents (estimated at nearly 2 billion). The vast number of people who claim to follow the example and teachings of Jesus Christ have aligned themselves into many different groupings, the major ones being Roman Catholic Christians, Protestant Christians, and Orthodox Christians. These groupings represent significant disagreements among believers on many important issues, and we study the historical and theological forces that caused these divisions to occur and that still play a part today.

For all the disagreement, however, Christians are united in the belief in the importance of the person and role of Jesus Christ. In every age and in every setting where Christianity is found, there stands at the center a profound and enduring commitment to the person of Jesus Christ, who the Christian scriptures say *"is the same today as he was yesterday and as he will be forever"* (*Heb.* 13:8). He is the Christ, the Savior, the Son of God, the Good Shepherd, the Light of the World, the Resurrection and the Life. (In fact, there are more than twenty-seven different titles given to him in

Christ on the Cross *by Diego Rodriguez de Velazquez, seventeenth century at the Museo del Prado, Madrid, Spain. Jesus' crucifixion and subsequent resurrection are defining events of Christianity.*

the pages of the uniquely Christian part of the *Bible* known as the *New Testament*.) Thus, when we begin to study Christianity, we must begin with what we know of the life of Jesus and his message.

Saint Paul, an apostle to the Gentiles (non-Jews) in the first century of the common era, said of Jesus that he was *"the image of the invisible God, the first born of all creation. . . . He is before all things, and in him all things hold together. . . . For in him all the fullness of God was pleased to dwell"* (*Col.* 1:15–19). There is no more concise statement of the Christian faithful's understanding of the person and importance of Jesus. He is before time and in time and beyond time. He is the central figure of all history, and his life and work make understanding the meaning of the human journey possible. He is the God-man who healed the sick yet himself was broken on the hard wood of a Roman cross; he conquered death and yet broke bread with the lowly and outcast. For Christians, he is the mystery of God come near. He is the Anointed One, the Christ (the Messiah).

CHRISTIAN BELIEFS

In this section we explore Christianity's fundamental beliefs about God, the cosmos, the nature and destiny of humans, and evil. While respecting the rich diversity in belief systems within the Christian religion, it is still possible to make statements about these issues with which most Christians can identify. First and foremost is their focus on the founder of Christianity, Jesus of Nazareth.

FOUNDING FIGURE: JESUS OF NAZARETH

We can trace Christianity's beginnings to the birth of Jesus at a particular moment in time (somewhere between 4 B.C.E. and 6 to 9 C.E.), and to a particular geographical locale (what we call today the Middle East). There is evidence from Roman and Jewish sources attesting to the existence of the person Jesus, who lived, preached, and died at the hands of adversaries. And we have a long, well-

documented record of his followers' belief, beginning with his contemporaries, that this Jesus overcame death. It was this event, the Resurrection, that scholars point to as the beginning of the religion, which took its name, *Christos*, from the Greek translation of the Hebrew word for "Messiah" and was first used at Antioch between 40 and 44 C.E.

As we will examine in detail in the "History of Christianity" section, there is considerable controversy over the actual circumstances of Jesus' life. What, then, can we learn, even minimally, about Jesus' life and work from the testimony of his followers? The *gospels*, writings attributed to Jesus' disciples, present us with a general outline of the course of Jesus' life as viewed against the backdrop of his day and world. Jesus was a Jew, born into a Jewish family that lived in a town called Nazareth, located in a region of Israel known as Galilee in the central highlands.[1] The *Gospels* agree that Mary was the mother of Jesus and that Joseph was her husband. However, they do not agree, or are silent, on the particulars of Jesus' birth. *Matthew* (1:18–2:23) and *Luke* (2:1–52) provide accounts of the birth of Jesus that differ in significant detail but that concur in the belief that Jesus was conceived not by Joseph but by *"the power of the Holy Spirit."* Christians have long been in disagreement over the exact meaning of the phrase, though it is generally regarded to mean that Jesus did not have a human "father." *Mark* (the earliest written *Gospel*) says nothing about Jesus' birth, and the *Prologue* in *John* (1:1–18) professes Jesus to be the preexistent Logos, or Word of God, who became human in the fullness of time.

Did Jesus have sisters and brothers? *Mark* 6:3 and *Matthew* 13:56 give names for his brothers and mention his sisters. Again, there is disagreement on this point. Many Christians hold to the perpetual virginity of Mary—that she was a virgin both before and after the birth of Jesus, and hence that those called "brothers and sisters" must actually be cousins or dependent children of Joseph from an earlier marriage. Little else is said of the family save the isolated verse in *Mark* that reports that Jesus' family tried to prevent him from continuing his preaching by seizing him and taking him home because they thought he was *"beside himself"* (3:21).

None of the *Gospels* offer anything remotely resembling a chronology of events from the time of Jesus' birth to the beginning of his public life at age thirty (according to *Luke* 3:23). We know nothing about his childhood, family life, or adolescence. *Luke,* the only one to comment on the time, simply says that Jesus *"increased in wisdom and in stature, and in favor with God and man"* (2:52).

Again, *Luke* offers the fifteenth year of Tiberius Caesar (27 or 29 C.E.) as the beginning of Jesus' public life. (Figure 9.1 shows a map of Palestine at the time.) All the *Gospels* agree that Jesus' ministry as an itinerant preacher began after he was baptized by John. John was regarded by the early Christians as more than a prophet. He was the one who was to come before the Messiah and announce his coming. The evangelists are very careful to portray John as "lesser" than Jesus and to put into his mouth the testimony of the Church that Jesus is *"the Lamb of God who takes away the sins of the world"* (*John* 1:29, 39).

Jesus came after John, but he did not follow John or imitate John. He did not continue John's baptizing. He differed from John in significant ways. John was an ascetic who dressed in animal skins and a leather belt, ate scant food, and shunned towns and cities. He was a man of the desert. Jesus was notorious for his table fellowship, eating and drinking so much that he was often accused of gluttony and drunkenness (*Mark* 2:18–20; *Luke* 7:33–35), and he was very much at home in towns and villages. The desert, for him, was a retreat and refuge.

What is amazing is that Jesus did not fit the depiction of the Messiah, a heavenly judge who would bring fire, as foretold by John the Baptist. Jesus was a human preaching mercy and repentance. His tongue was Aramaic. We do not know if he spoke Greek, the language of commerce and administration. There is no trace of any influence on Jesus of Greek philosophy, thought patterns, or lifestyle.

All the *Gospels* agree that Jesus gathered about him an inner circle of friends (apostles), who accompanied him in his travels. He taught in the synagogues, in the fields, on the hillsides, and by the shore. And the apostles were with him.

The ministry of Jesus was marked by several distinctive features. First, his message "Repent, the kingdom of God is at hand" was a call for a profound transformation of the whole person. The Greek *New Testament* uses the word *metanoia*, or "change of heart," a conversion from the ways of pride and hard-heartedness to humility and compassion. Unlike John, who preached "repentance" for fear of judgment, Jesus' message, although no less urgent, was of a different stripe. Always, Jesus proclaimed that this change was possible because God is infinitely loving and merciful.

Second, the *Gospels* say that Jesus taught complex religious ideas by means of **parables,** stories designed to bring the listener to a moral or theological insight, thus making them accessible to his mostly illiterate audiences. He emphasized in his

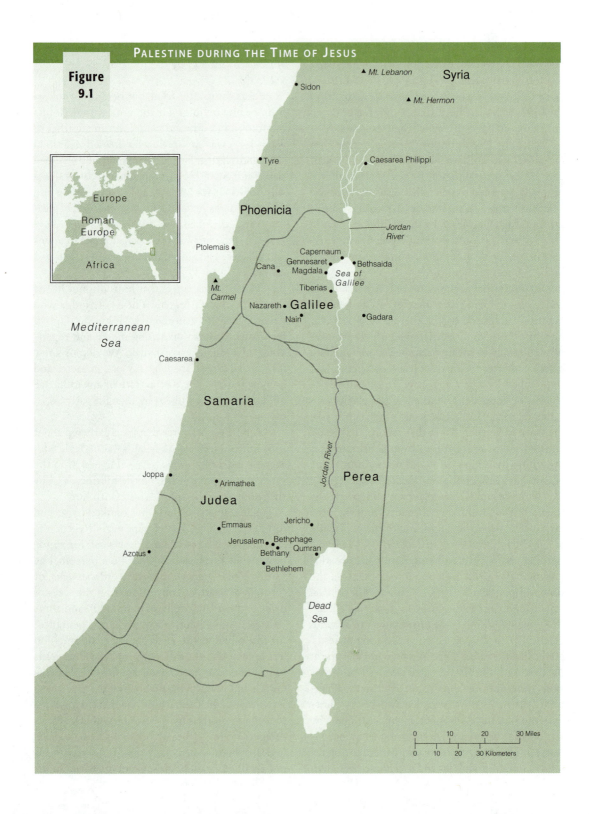

PALESTINE DURING THE TIME OF JESUS

Figure 9.1

teachings that simplicity of heart and childlike humility and trust are the virtues that God requires. One does not need to be a scholar or even respectable by the world's measure to understand and live the way God asks people to live.

Third, the writers of the *Gospels* picture Jesus as frequently in disagreement and confrontation with some of the Jewish religious authorities of his day, the scribes and Pharisees, over the role and interpretation of the law of Moses. Unlike the teachers of his day, Jesus spoke about the law with an authority that impressed and infuriated many who heard him. Jesus is portrayed acting as one who was absolutely convinced that he had a special, intimate relationship with the God of Israel. So convinced was he of this special relationship that in prayer, he addressed God with the familial Abba (daddy). He is often depicted as putting his own teaching above the law on such issues as the meaning of the Sabbath (*Mark* 2:23 and 3:1ff), divorce (*Matt.* 5:31), and love of enemies (*Matt.* 5:38–42), using the formula *"You have heard it said . . . but I say to you. . . ."* He chastised the legalists and purists for being self-righteous and arrogant in their belief that following the letter of the law was the same thing as being moral. Jesus respected the law of Moses but refused to let it be the final arbiter of morality. The heart of Judaic law was to love God with one's whole heart, mind, and soul and to love one's neighbor as oneself, even if the neighbor were an enemy.

Fourth, the biblical Jesus performed cures and wonders that amazed those who witnessed them, including healings of the physical body from diseases, restoration of lost senses, exorcism, and resuscitations of the seemingly dead. He often claimed that his marvelous works proclaimed his sovereignty over the power of sin and evil (*Mark* 2:1–12; *Luke* 5:18–26). His miracles announced that the reign of God had begun. The kingdom was near, and his miracles were signs of its reality.

Fifth, in sharp contrast to the piety of many Jews, Jesus is pictured as preferring the company of the marginalized and outcasts of his day: sinners, the sick, the poor, and the sincere Gentiles. These people were aware of their true situation in life: they were in need of grace and mercy. The outcasts understood that they had no claim on God. Their sin, sickness, poverty, race, or religion made absolutely no difference to God, who regarded a person's worth and dignity by virtue of his love for them, not their ability to do anything for him. Ultimately, in associating with the sinners, Jesus was proclaiming that God's love and mercy are pure gifts that cannot be earned, won, or even deserved, and that they are given to all.

Sixth, Jesus' teaching was extended to all, regardless of sex. In a time when women had no legal rights and were often placed in roles of subservience, Jesus' example taught respect for women. Jesus rejected the double standard of morality prevalent in his day, going as far as to condemn men if they merely lusted after a woman in their thoughts. He also affirmed the dignity of marriage.

Finally, Jesus' moral teaching was more than a collection of do's and don'ts. He taught what theologian Charles Curran has termed a *radical ethic,*[2] calling his follows to a life in union with God and neighbor. The followers of Jesus, Curran says, can find no excuse (not even worship at the altar or love of their families) that takes priority over their loving concern and forgiveness of neighbors. In other words, the radical aspect of Jesus' teachings is that he called people to love others just as God loved, no matter what.

The decisive turning point in Jesus' life was the decision to go to Jerusalem to present his message. According to the *Gospels*, there he met with apparent success with the people but won the animosity of the Jewish religious establishment. All the *Gospels* agree that on the night before he died, Jesus celebrated a ritual meal, a Passover, with his closest friends. His actions of offering them bread and wine and giving thanks were well-known and common Jewish practices, but Jesus gave to them a new significance when he commanded his followers to repeat his gestures in memory of him. Doubtless, this Last Supper is a reflection of the early Christians' liturgical practices retrojected into the Passion narratives (those sections of the four *Gospels* that give accounts of the last three days of Jesus' life, from the time of his betrayal to his death).

However, this Last Supper must have been based on something very deep in the community's memory of Jesus for all the *Gospels* to devote so much attention to its detail. Today, many Christians refer to this meal Jesus shared as a **Eucharist.**

Soon afterward, Jesus was taken by his opponents and brought before the **Sanhedrin,** the supreme Jewish priestly authority in Jerusalem, which condemned him for blasphemy and turned him over to the Romans for trial and execution. It is possible that the Jewish leaders had a political motive as well in delivering him to the Romans. They might have feared that a pretender-messiah would bring upon Jerusalem a swift and brutal military response from Roman troops. Some scholars hold that the *Gospels* overemphasize the responsibility of the Jews for Jesus' death and minimize the Romans' participation. The intent, it is theorized, would be to allay any Roman suspicions that the Christian Church might be politically subversive to the Roman emperor. Accordingly, **Pontius Pilate,** the symbol of Roman power in Judea, is depicted as a reluctant participant in Jesus' death.[3] In any event, the Romans must have interpreted Jesus as a zealot, a revolutionary threat to the rule of Caesar, for he was tried and convicted for being an enemy of Caesar, an offense that warranted capital punishment, crucifixion. No Jewish heretic ever died on a Roman cross for **blasphemy,** speech or action deemed insulting to God. Rome would never find that a capital offense. However, to keep the peace with the Jewish leaders, Pilate might have "accommodated" them by translating the religious crime into a political one.

All the *Gospels* agree that Jesus was taken down from the cross and laid in a tomb. They all attest, and take great care to report, that he was, indeed, dead; his side had been lanced with a sword before the body was removed from the cross. Later—one day in *John,* and three days in *Matthew, Mark,* and *Luke*—some of his followers and friends saw Jesus. None of the *Gospels* claims that there were eyewitnesses to the event of Jesus' leaving the tomb. It is proclaimed by all the *Gospels* but never explained: Jesus is risen from the dead. Belief in the Resurrection of Jesus of Nazareth is the cornerstone of Christian faith and of the notion of a Supreme Being who is three divinities in one.

GOD

Christianity is unique among the world's religions in its conception of God as a Trinity. Unlike mystical religions, which emphasize the immanence of God, and unlike other monotheistic religions, which emphasize the transcendence of God, Christianity proclaims God to be both utterly beyond and yet, paradoxically, intimately near. As the "History of Christianity" section will trace, the doctrine of the Trinity emerged slowly over centuries of profound and passionate theological controversy. No simple explanation exists for this belief that lies at the very heart of the nature of God. God is a being who humbles intellects and before whom all language can only be analogous. The doctrine of the **Trinity** proclaims that God, a personal being—a being with whom one can have a relationship—is, at the same time and without contradiction, one and plural. God's nature is dynamic, and this nature expresses itself. The traditional language uses the words *Father, Son,* and *Holy Spirit* as names for the Godhead. Christians have attributed the act of creation to the Father, the first person of the Trinity; redemption to the Son, the second person; and comfort and inspiration to the Holy Spirit, the third person.

Obviously, these words and the very concept of the Trinity are not, in any sense, scientifically descriptive. They are not analytical. That is, they do not pretend that God is an entity that has "parts" that can be reduced to simpler parts and examined. They are always analogous. They are more like similes than metaphors. Having said the words, we do not "understand" any more of God. Christians profess, not explain, that God is not an object that is known in the same way other persons or things are known. God is "apprehended" only indirectly and, most profoundly, in faith. God could be, and is, called Mother, Lover, and Friend. These are comparisons for a being and a land of relationship with that being.

Some of the greatest Christian theologians have speculated about the nature of God. Augustine of Hippo (354–430 C.E.), in his *De trinitate,* is an example. Here, borrowing from Aristotle, Augustine depicted God as the "First Principle," the cause of all truth and goodness, "above whom, outside of whom, and without whom nothing exists." For him, God is pure love and truth. Thomas Aquinas (ca. 1225–1274), again using Aristotle's thought, offered Five Proofs (arguments) for the existence of God. In the *Summa Theologiae,* he argued that God is the "Unmoved Mover" who is responsible for everything that has motion; God is the "First Cause" that is the source of all change in the universe; God is the only "Necessary Being" upon whom all other beings are contingent; God is the "Standard of Excellence" who is the measure of all things; and God is the "Reason and Harmony" in the design behind the cosmos.

Paul Tillich (1886–1965) spoke of God as the "Ground of Being." For Tillich, faith, the "ultimate concern," stands facing the vastness of reality that is God. God is the very foundation on which every created thing stands and from which it draws its existence—whether it (God) is noticed or not, named or anonymous. Because God is, humans can be.[4]

Another group of theologians, known as process theologians, conceive of God as a being in the process of development through God's interaction with a changing world that is still evolving. For these thinkers, Jesus is a disclosure in a particular historical event of what God has been doing from the beginning, being creative with humans and demonstrating that love is more important than coercion in changing human hearts. The process theologians reject any notion of God's having a substance *(oosios)* as being a relic of an outdated metaphysic. God is love in action. God is "event."[5]

These sketches do not exhaust the variety of Christian beliefs about God. But at this point, it is clear why Christians value the gift of Jesus Christ, who is believed to be Immanuel, "God with us." For Christians, Jesus is God who became flesh. He is God incarnate. He is the ultimate revelation of the Father. Jesus shows us who God is and what God is like. Throughout the Christian scripture, the role of Jesus as the one who can speak with authority about God is pointed to again and again: *"He who sees me sees him who sent me"* (*John* 13:45). The Son is like the Father, so to know Christ is to know the Father. Jesus is the personality of the Father made known.

Most astounding of all Christ's revelations is that the most precise image for the God of heaven and earth, and the best way to address God in prayer, is by the use of the word *Abba,* "Daddy." The Creator is like a loving and kind parent. Christian theologians have written volumes about the attributes of God, but when Jesus was asked about who the Father was, he told stories and parables so nontechnical and free of jargon that even a child could follow him: What is this God like? God is like the Father who forgives his prodigal (wayward) son without being asked for forgiveness (*Luke* 15). God is like the man who owned a vineyard and paid his workers according to his generosity, not their merit (*Matt.* 20:1–16)

Perhaps John said it best: *"God is love"* (1 *John* 4:8). Christians celebrate this absolute and unconditional love of God revealed in the Passion and Resurrection of Jesus. This is what love does; it gives of itself: *"In this is love, not that we loved God but that He loved us and sent his son to be the expiation for our sins"* (1 *John* 4:10).

THE COSMOS

A traditional Christian belief is that the universe was brought into creation as the result of a deliberate, purposeful act of an all-powerful maker who created it *ex nihilo* (from nothing). Whereas some Fundamentalist Christians argue that God's creation precludes evolution, many other Christians allow for scientific explanations as the "how" of creation. The traditional belief specifies only that God is the ultimate source of what is.

This concept of God's being Creator and hence distinct from creation can be contrasted with such notions as pantheism and dualism. The former holds that God and the material universe are identical: that God is nature. The latter maintains that

God and matter are distinct and unrelated. The Christian view is more of a monism—that all that exists has a single, ultimate source but that God is not created.

A constant theme throughout the centuries has been the belief that creation "will end," that it is not eternal. Again, differences in theology abound among Christians. Fundamentalist Christians, taking *Revelation* to be a prediction of actual events to come, believe that the earth will undergo testing and trial; do battle with the Beast, Satan; and experience a time of rapture before Jesus returns to judge the living and the dead. Other Christian theologians dispute this understanding and use of *Revelation*. They hold, again with great diversity among them, that *Revelation* is a symbolic account of the early Church's struggle with the Roman Empire, which tried to destroy it, and that what the book points to is the ultimate victory of good over evil. Further, they hold that God never destroys what he creates—that God only perfects what he makes. In this scheme, the "end of time" is the perfection of creation and the fulfillment of the biblical promise of a New Jerusalem.

What is this end of time like? Theories vary from utopian imaginings to agnostic disclaimers. Both Fundamentalists and mainline Christians agree that the created order is moving toward an Omega Point, a decisive moment when its history and future will be centered in Christ.

THE NATURE AND DESTINY OF HUMANS

There are several questions hidden inside the question, What is a human? For example, What is different about me from all the other creatures that inhabit the earth? or Where am I going? and ultimately, What is life all about? Addressing the question of the nature and destiny of humans is asking the "question of questions" that has intrigued believers and nonbelievers for centuries. The way we answer shapes our thinking and acting in this world.

Christian anthropology presents a rich and complex understanding of humans. To appreciate this view, we must make it distinct from other kinds of anthropology. *Scientific anthropology* studies humans as animals; *cultural anthropology* studies them as creators of human civilizations and art; *philosophical anthropology* makes inquiries into the ontological structures that constitute humans. *Christian anthropology*, a subject of *religious anthropology*, views humans through the belief system of Christian faith—using scripture and theology (informed by all the other sciences) to speak about the ultimate questions.

Christian anthropology features five main doctrinal areas: (1) theocentricity, (2) anthrocentricity, (3) the doctrine of original sin, (4) the doctrine of grace, and (5) belief in immortality. We will explore each in turn.

THEOCENTRICITY In the *Bible*, God created humans in the divine image. **Theocentricity** means that the cosmos is God *(theos)* centered, not human *(anthropos)* centered. The key concept here is that humans are created; they are not God. Christianity accepts the Jewish position that leaves no doubt that humans are creatures, not the Creator. God is the Supreme Being, the ultimate source of goodness and power. Humans were created by God in an act of divine favor and generosity. God did not have to create this universe and populate it. Protestant theologian Jurgen Moltmann maintains that creation was God's "play"—it did not spring from necessity, but from pleasure.[6]

ANTHROCENTRICITY Although humans are creatures, they are special creatures. *Genesis* states that humans were not created with the animals and that the world was made for them. A literal reading tends toward the conclusion that humans are the masters of the world and entitled to use everything in it for their benefit; another reading, however, would conclude that humans have been entrusted with the good keeping and conservation of creation. They have a responsibility to be good stewards of the planet and to live in harmony with all its inhabitants, both human and nonhuman. *Psalm* 8 expresses this **anthrocentricity** beautifully:

When I look at thy heavens, the work of thy
fingers, the moon and the stars which thou hast
made; what is man that thou are mindful of him,
and the son of man that thou dost care for him?
Yet thou hast made him little less than God,
and dost crown him with glory and honor.
Thou hast given him dominion over the works of thy
   hands;
thou hast put all things under his feet. (3–6)

ORIGINAL SIN   The Christian view of human nature is complex. Yes, humans are special, but humans are also flawed. One aspect of Christian anthropology elevates humans, but another soberly challenges humans to remember that they are sinners in need of redemption. As Martin Luther (1483–1546) expressed it, each human is *simul iustus et peccator* (at the same time justified and a sinner). As far back as Paul, Christianity has taught that there is a state of sin in which humans have been held since the Fall—**original sin.** This sin of the first humans, Adam and Eve, was expressed in the creation account as the illicit taking of the forbidden fruit in the Garden of Eden. In *Romans* (5:12–21), Paul maintains that *"through one man [Adam] sin entered the world."*

The fathers of the Church taught the solidarity of the human race with Adam. Augustine maintained that Adam's guilt was transmitted to his descendants by **concupiscence** (sexual desire). Aquinas modified this understanding by saying that original sin is transmitted not as the personal fault of Adam but as the "state of human nature." The Reformers, Luther and John Calvin, equated original sin with "birth sin" *(Augsburg Confession)* and "hereditary evil" *(Westminister Confession).* The Anglicans spoke of it as "the fault and corruption of the nature of every man that naturally is engendered of the offspring of Adam" *(Thirty-nine Articles).*

It is important to translate the theological jargon here. What the Christian tradition has said is that all members of the human race are born into a condition that they have inherited from their ancestors. For the Catholics, the human condition means that human nature is wounded; it has a tendency to be motivated by desire for worldly things and to be stimulated by the senses. The human heart is, by nature, divided between the things of God and the things of this world. For the Protestants, the human condition is the abiding state of moral rebellion. In other words, Christians are saying that all humans are in need of salvation from themselves, and that work is God's work through Christ.

Contemporary Christian theologians largely repudiate the classical theories. They object to the presupposition of monogenism (the belief that the entire human race came from one set of parents) and the assumption that there was ever an "original condition" of human perfection from which to "fall." The modern interpretation does not speak of an original sin that is inherited, but rather of the state or condition of the world into which every human being is born, a world in which individual humans have contributed their own personal sins. This collective "sin of the world" is an environment and a momentum in human events that is impossible for humans alone to redress. Every individual needs redemption; every human must take responsibility for his or her share of the human condition. In this light, baptism is an initiation into the community of faith that supports a person in his or her journey through life.

GRACE   In considering human nature, Christianity draws on Augustine's theology of grace that was developed in his controversy with Pelagianism. Pelagius (ca. 354–418) maintained that humans are capable of achieving eternal life without any special divine assistance. A variation on the theme, offered by John Cassian (360–435), was semi-Pelagianism, which holds that humans can make at least initial steps toward salvation by their own efforts.

Augustine argued that because of original sin, humans are powerless to save themselves. Indeed, so destructive is original sin that humans cannot even do good deeds without God's **grace** (*gratia* means "gift")—God's favor. Grace, said Augustine, is absolutely gratuitous: humans can do nothing to earn it or deserve it. Grace is not earned by good deeds; good deeds are possible only because of grace.

This classic doctrine argues that grace transforms humans into participants in God's own righteousness, but contemporary theologians understand grace as a relationship between individuals and God. To be in a "state of grace" is to have a relationship with God.[7] Grace is the self-communication of God to his children. Sin is seen as the deliberate breaking of the relationship or the turning away from it. To sin is to reject God. Yet even when humans sin, God continues to love. Paul wrote that *"where sin increased, grace abounded all the more"* (*Rom.* 5:20).

BELIEF IN IMMORTALITY
Belief in a life beyond this one is in no way unique to Christianity, as we have seen. Still, Christianity is rooted in a confidence embedded in a hope of resurrection. As Paul wrote: *"But in fact Christ has been raised from the dead, the first fruits of those who have fallen asleep. For as in Adam all die, so also in Christ shall all be made alive"* (*1 Cor.* 15:20–21). Christian hope anticipates the highest destiny for humans: to be with God forever, a life of abiding union with God.

Christianity holds that the person is a unity of body and spirit. A human is an incorporated spirit. In death, there is a separation or suspension of that unity, but there will be a time when the person, body and spirit, are united and will live in eternity. Conceptions of the afterlife vary widely among theologians, and there is tension between contemporary and traditional language expressing those conceptions. Traditional Christian theology depicts the afterlife as a reward or punishment, heaven or hell. Heaven is interpreted as a "place," though few dare to describe it in detail. Rather, it is stressed that "in heaven" the just are rewarded for their virtuous life on earth by the "beatific vision," the actual seeing of God face to face in all glory. Hell is depicted as a "place" of torment for unrepentant sinners. The nature of the torments is often described imaginatively, drawing on the symbolic aspect of fire as a purifying and punishing agent. Roman Catholics hold to a belief in **Purgatory** as a temporary place of punishment and suffer-

ing for those who die in the grace of God but who are not totally free of sin or the punishment associated with it.

Contemporary Christian theologians reframe these concepts. Heaven is a state of union with God. Biblical imagery is employed to describe it: *"heavenly Jerusalem," "heavenly banquet,"* and *"kingdom of God."* Modern thinkers are agnostic on the details and reluctant to speculate in flights of theological fancy. Eschatology, the study of final things, is a serious focus, but theologians are reserved in their speculations. Hell is seen not as a punishment for sin but as the consequence of a person's continued and ultimate rejection of God exercised through the use of free will, which God respects. Hell, then, is a separation from God imposed on the hard-hearted by themselves, not by God. God desires the salvation of all. The existence of hell, then, is not contrary to God's justice or God's love, because God forces no one to virtue. Within a range, people are free and responsible for their moral choices. Some theologians (Clement of Alexandria, Origen, Gregory of Nyssa, and Friedrich Schleiermacher) have taught (contrary to Augustine's view and traditional doctrine) that ultimately, all creatures (angels, devils, and humans) will share salvation.

EVIL

The Christian religion professes its confidence that Christ's victory over sin and death is a victory all can share. It is a victory that has been guaranteed in eternity. For now, the victory is incomplete. Evil and suffering are very much part of the human condition. The fact of evil in the world seems self-evident (natural disasters that kill innocent people, diseases, wars, brutal murders, Nazi death camps, spoiling of the environment, racism, sexism, homophobia, and so on). That this evil is often collective and at the same time very personal is also evident. The definition, source, and meaning of evil, however, are far more difficult to understand. Mature Christian faith is not embraced until the believer has confronted and struggled with the "problem of evil."

Plato (428–348 B.C.E.) said that evil is the absence of good. The Stoics defined evil as the harvest of unreason and lack of self-control. Augustine explained that nature is good (not perfect, as God is, but good), and that goodness can be either increased or diminished. Good diminished is evil. Many hold that evil is a spiritual force, Satan (Hebrew for "adversary"), working in opposition to God in this world. Many Christians recognize evil as a real power, personal or not, that works against the good.

It was Epicurus (341–270 B.C.E.) who gave shape to the question of evil developed by philosophers and theologians after him, most notably by David Hume (1711–1776) in his *Dialogues Concerning Natural Religion*. As stated, the "problem" of evil arises from the paradox resulting from belief in an all powerful, all-good, and all-loving God and the human experience of evil. If God is all good and all powerful, then why does evil exist? Either there is no God, or God is not what is believed of him. Is he willing to prevent evil, but not able to do so? Then God is impotent. Is God able to prevent evil but unwilling to do so? Then he is malevolent. For if God were both willing and able, then evil would not exist.

The defense of God, known as **theodicy** in orthodox Christianity, has been to deny the paradox. That is, Christians affirm all the terms in the premises (God is all good, and evil exists) but deny the conclusion. They argue that God can exist with evil and still be all good and all powerful. Theodicies like these abound. The following are a representative sampling.[8]

THE FREE WILL DEFENSE   Advocates of the free will defense categorize evil into "moral evil" and "natural evil." Moral evil results from the abuse of the free will that God gave to every human. Brutal murders, terrorist attacks, and child abuse are understood as products of sin prompted by either the devil or human weakness. Hence, humans are responsible. They make decisions either for good or against it, sometimes unreflectively but more often very deliberately. Humans create evil when they act either unjustly or unlovingly—when they

disrespect the rights or dignity of others—and God, respecting this freedom, is committed to bringing good out of evil, not to preventing it.

Natural evil (diseases, disasters, and the like) is dealt with in one of several ways. Some would deny that these events are, indeed, evil at all. They are evidence that God has placed humans in an unfinished universe, a universe still in process. Such disasters are promptings from God to promote charity and concern for others—to make the world a better place. A more traditional Augustinian view would hold that these events are punishments for sin and that if innocent people are hurt, God will reward them in the next life.

A variation on the free will defense is offered by contemporary philosopher of religion John Hick. In his *Evil and the God of Love* (1966), Hick departs from the traditional view. Drawing on the thinking of Irenaeus (120–202 C.E.), he views Adam not as a fully mature free agent rebelling against God but as a moral child who must learn to distinguish right from wrong through trial and error. The Fall is humanity's first step in the direction of knowledge of good and evil—moral maturity. God still works with humanity to bring from undeveloped life a state of self-realization in divine or spiritual love. This earthly existence is seen as a place where souls are made. Life is a soul-making process. Evil prompts good, to which, inevitably, it must lead.

COSMIC DUALISM   Christian dualists argue that evil is a product of human will, but they disagree about whose will is ultimately responsible. Evil is traceable to the power of darkness (Lucifer, Satan), who is the mortal opponent of the Supreme Being. The devil was created good and free but for some reason turned away from God. The evil one will always be evil and will always work to destroy the good by tempting weak human nature. This temptation is a distortion of the truth. Evil presents choices in a false light, and this is why people choose lesser goods over greater goods on the most flimsy of motives that, at the time, seem so substantial. Although the power of evil is stated not to be equal to the power of God, it is often presented that way.

COSMOGENESIS In the *Activation of Energy*, Catholic theologian Pierre Teilhard de Chardin (1881–1955) outlines a theory that sees the world in a process of continual creation. Teilhard de Chardin holds that what many consider to be evil is really "crisis," and that crisis is a sign of hope, not despair; crisis makes obvious the struggle between good and evil. He argues that world crisis is at the root of the change of humankind, the transformation of consciousness. The developed nuclei of civilizations have multiplied and packed themselves closer together, have forced themselves against one another so much that an overall unity (psychic and economic) is inevitable. In this drive toward unity from plurality, there will be conflict, war, food shortages, health problems, and nervous strain. He views these problems as secondary effects, as by-products of the process of a world consciousness in evolution.

Teilhard de Chardin sees pain and perversity, if contributing to the evolution of consciousness, as dynamic factors that are vindicated and transformed. Suffering can produce spiritual energy and involve humans in the betterment of those around them. The more human humans become, the more serious becomes the problem of evil, evil that has to be borne. There is no spiritual progress without paying a mysterious tribute of tears, blood, and sin. Thus, for Teilhard de Chardin, evil and suffering (in all its forms) are no more than the natural consequences of the movement by which humans were brought into being and by which they will be perfected.

To conclude this section, it must be noted that nowhere in the Christian religion is there any promise of a life without suffering, and nowhere is there a simple answer given for why we suffer. Tradition holds that evil is real and a part of the scheme of things. Evil is not the good in disguise. In the *Gospels,* Jesus is neither unusually sensitive nor insensitive to evil. Suffering cannot be avoided. It affects the just and the unjust alike. In Christ, God participates in the suffering of all. The cross stands as a testimony to that participation. Christian scripture admonishes that those who suffer are blessed, and Christians are exhorted by Jesus: *"In the world you have tribulation; but be of good cheer. I have overcome the world"* (*John* 16:33).

CHRISTIAN PRACTICE

How are Christians called to live their lives? What are the norms for their judging right and wrong? Is morality objective or subjective? These are the kinds of questions we address in this section.

THE MORAL LIFE

To be a Christian, a believer must take seriously the example of Jesus. The Christian is called to follow that example with a humble and sincere heart. The scriptural command is clear: *"What I command you is to love one another"* (*John* 15:17). This love is not romantic emotion; it is the very imitation of Christ: *"A man can have no greater love than to lay down his life for his friends"* (*John* 15:13). Christians are called to love beyond friendship. In the *Sermon on the Mount,* the compilation of the core of Jesus' ethical teaching, we find the dictum: *"Love your enemies, do good to those who hate you"* (*Luke* 6:27). In other words, the moral life is to love the way Christ loved.

The Christian is called to take this love into every aspect and activity of life. There can be no pious and dutiful worship of God on Sunday to the exclusion of loving others during the week. Jesus referred to such people who live double lives as hypocrites. No matter how much a person prays, fasts, and gives alms to the poor, no matter what kind of external actions are shown to the world, morality and the moral life, Jesus said, is centered in the heart.

Christians believe that to live the moral life is to live in response to God's love. Because Christians are convinced that God loves them—warts and all—they are able to love others the same way. This is what distinguishes authentic morality from mere conformity to religious convention or from psychological needs for acceptance and approval.

Authentic morality is rooted in the personal experience of God's love and mercy for sinners. For Christians, it is being convinced that they are forgiven and loved by God that empowers them to turn the other cheek, walk the extra mile, and do good to those who hate them. Simple obedience to moral codes can never move a person to that kind of love.

A Christian is called to understand that God loves everyone unconditionally. God loves an Adolf Hitler as much as a Francis of Assisi. (There well may be a difference, though, in how much each of these men loved God.) That is what it means to say that God is "perfect love." It is, as the Greeks called it, a form of the highest kind of love, *agape.* It is irrevocable. God puts no conditions on love. It is not a reward or an exchange, but pure gift. As a Christian hymn put it, "There is a wideness in God's mercy."

Christian morality is a call to perfection: *"You must be perfect as your Heavenly father is perfect"* (*Matt.* 5:48). Note that it is a call to love with the wideness of God's love, not a call to perfectionism, which only leads to self-righteousness. The radical demand to be perfect can be understood as the goal of a life dedicated to the imitation of Christ's love. It can also be seen as a challenge to move beyond any easy or cheap standard of love with which the Christian has grown comfortable. As Dietrich Bonhoeffer (1906–1945) said, there is a cost to discipleship: "When Jesus calls a man, he calls him to come and die."[9]

Christians believe in the existence of the moral conscience. This is not Sigmund Freud's superego nor a "little voice" of God in one's head. Conscience is at the center and most secret core of a person. It is what summons a person to do good or avoid evil. Contemporary theologian Timothy O'Connell suggests that conscience be understood on three levels.[10] On the first level, conscience is a fundamental sense of value and personal responsibility. We may disagree on what is right and wrong, but we agree that there is a difference. The second level is a moral judgment that something is morally good or bad. On this level, it must be realized that the conscience is not an infallible

guide. It is always limited by our culture, the age in which we live, personal upbringing, and lack of knowledge. For this reason, conscience must be open to information from sources outside itself. The third level is reached with the decision itself. This is the very doing of what we see to be right, even if that decision brings us into disagreement and conflict with religious or civil authority. The true test of conscience is that its decisions do not cause harm (though they may cause difficulties) to others, and its decisions leave the moral agent with a genuine peace.

Christian moral theologians vary widely in the ways they explain the moral life. Rather than enumerate these differences, it is more to our purpose to note their agreement. All agree that human dignity resides in the freedom God has given humans to make moral choices. Humans are, in varying degrees, responsible for their actions.

In sum, morality is the character and content of the Christian life. It is more than obedience to a set of rules. It is a way of life based on the example of Christ and the law of love. It is not an appendage to the obligation to worship. It is not operative only in sexual matters. It is the effort to love as Christ loved—aware of one's limitations and need for strength and mercy. Paul called the Christians of his day "saints," not because they were perfect but because they were seeking moral perfection. Thomas Merton (1915–1968) defined *saints* as "sinners who don't quit," those who never get discouraged by their own failings because they trust God's great goodness and mercy. To be a moral person is to be a friend of God. To be a Christian moral person is to be a friend of God in the imitation of Christ.

What do Christians do? How do they practice their religion? Given the differences in beliefs and culture, a safe generalization is to say that Christians feel called to live their entire lives as a response to God's love for them. It would be a distorted view to see worship and prayer divorced from everyday morality. Ideally, these aspects inform and influence one another. Having offered this generalization, let us look at the particulars. For Christians, religious practice can be divided into three basic categories: worship, prayer, and good works.

WORSHIP

Christians regard the first and third commandments of Moses as clear expressions of the need to recognize the existence of God, to give God honor and homage, to thank God, and to present before God their personal and communal needs. When these homages are performed together, it is called *liturgy,* or "order of worship." In essence, all worship is public prayer.

The concept of the Sabbath as a day set aside for rest and remembrance of God was an ancient tradition among the Jews. Christians adopted and adapted the Sabbath to the Lord's Day and changed it from Saturday—according to *Genesis,* the seventh day of the week, on which God rested after six days of creation—to Sunday, honoring the day of the week Jesus rose from the dead. (Some Christians, such as the Seventh-day Adventists, still worship on the seventh day). Among all but a few Christians, the activities of the Sabbath consist of participating in a religious service of about one hour's duration. This is a noticeable dilution and reduction of Sabbath ritual, which in the past forbade shopping, work, frivolous entertainment, or any kind of gambling.

In some Reformation and Evangelical churches, worship centers around the reading of scriptures and a sermon preached by a minister or pastor. The minister and laypersons lead the congregation through the liturgy, which has been established by custom and tradition in each denomination. A typical service runs something like this: an opening hymn, a call to prayer or an invocation, the reading of lessons (selections from both the *Old Testament* and the *New Testament*), another hymn, a sermon on the lessons, an opportunity for reflection and quiet prayer, a collection of donations for the upkeep of the church, a public prayer for the needs of the community (called a Prayer of the Faithful), the recitation of the Lord's Prayer (the "Our Father"), a final prayer, and a closing hymn. Following the service, many Christian congregations gather in the church hall for light refreshment and socialization, and sometimes for church committee work.

In contrast to Reform and Evangelical churches, the celebration of the Lord's Day (and every day of the year) by Roman Catholics, Episcopalians, and Lutherans centers on the Eucharist. The word, taken from the Greek, means "thanksgiving by remembering." Although there are significant differences underlying these "communion meals," they have enough in common to be grouped together. The ritual is divided into two parts: a Liturgy of the Word and a Liturgy of the Altar. The first part is very similar to the entire service of worship found in most Protestant churches. The second part begins with an offertory of bread and wine that, it is believed, will be transformed by faith into the body and blood of Jesus. Through the office of the ordained priest or pastor, the elements of bread and wine mysteriously become the "real presence" of Jesus during the words of consecration. Whatever it means to say that "Jesus is there" is what these Christians believe. (The theological explanations of exactly how that happens differ markedly from denomination to denomination.) At an appointed time, the members of the congregation come to a minister to "receive communion" (either in the form of a wafer or piece of bread alone or in combination with a sip of consecrated wine). These Christians believe that Jesus, at the Last Supper, commanded that his follows have such a meal in memory of him.

The Fourth Lateran Council (1215 C.E.), a Roman Catholic council, accepted the theology of transubstantiation to proclaim the mystery of what happens at the consecration of bread and wine in the Eucharist. Using Aristotelian categories, the council said that Jesus Christ is truly present under the appearances of bread and wine. That is, the accidental properties (color, taste, and shape) of bread and wine remain, but the substance of bread and wine are changed into the substance of the body and blood of Christ. Catholics held that the mass (the Eucharist) was the "unbloody sacrifice," the reenactment of Jesus' death on the cross that was repeated because of his command given at the

Last Supper: *"Do this in memory of me"* (*Luke* 22:19). (Luther modified transubstantiation to consubstantiation, meaning that Jesus was present *with* the bread and wine—there being no change in their accidents or substance.)

One of the ways in which the living Christ is encountered is through participation in "sacred actions," call **sacraments.** In these liturgical (ritual) ceremonies, it is believed, the faithful meet Christ, share his life, and are made holy. The sacramentals are "sacred signs, actions but not ceremonies instituted by the Church that remind the practitioner of Christ's presence in the Church. An example of a sacramental is the making of the sign of the cross with blessed water, or "holy water."

There are, of course, abundant variations on the theme of worship ritual. For example, one denomination, the Quakers, gather at the eleventh hour each Sunday and "sit in silence" waiting for the Holy Spirit to inspire members to stand and address a brief message to the others. There is no officiating clergy, no communal prayers, and no communion. At the end of the meeting each shakes the hand of the person on either side. The Greek Orthodox surround their worship with elements of mystery: incense is used throughout the liturgy; during the solemn moments of consecration, the priest goes behind a screen to utter the sacred words of the service. In many charismatic churches, the worship service is a spontaneous prayer service in which passages of scripture are read by members prompted to do so. There is singing, talking in tongues, and prophecies. There are prayers for healing and witnessing to what God is believed to have brought about in people's lives. And, in the electronic era, some worship by staying home and watching any of the "televangelists" who broadcast their services across the airwaves.

PRAYER

Traditional definitions of *prayer* abound. Prayer means humbly coming into God's presence. It is the lifting of the heart and mind to God. It is the opening of the human heart to intimate communion with the loving God. Prayer is said to be the result of a divine prompting of grace, a silent call from God that initiates conversation. In response, the individual praises God (adoration), expresses love, thanks God, and asks God for particular needs or forgiveness. This conversation can be vocal or silent (mental). Prayer can be accomplished alone or with others.

These traditional definitions, however, do make critical distinctions that must be grasped if prayer is to be understood. There is a difference between saying prayers and praying. Saying prayers involves the recitation of words written by others or using words of one's own. But praying is different. Praying is giving time to God and God alone. It is a devoted, conscious, concentrated "being with" God. It was defined by fourth-century monks as "sweet repose," a silent absorption in God. Prayer is a communion, a common union of the divine and the human in an act of openness one to the other. Prayer is the voice of the heart.

GOOD WORKS

There are things that Christians "do" that are motivated by their faith, and therefore, they are "religious" acts in intention. Christianity has never seen its activity limited to the vertical (God-human) plane. It has always had a vigorous commitment to imitate the example of Christ by being in the everyday world and being of service to everyday people, believers or otherwise.

For example, Christian churches found and staff orphanages, hospitals, homes for battered women, hospices for the dying, centers for AIDS patients, soup kitchens and shelters for the homeless, thrift stores for the poor, halfway houses for former convicts, and homes for the mentally retarded. They collect monies for food and services to the poor around the world. (Many leave their native lands to administer these programs.) In some places (Latin America, for example), some Christians help organize "base communities" for the spiritual, economic, and political welfare of the people. In other places they are at the forefront of social justice issues, and they have struggled for human rights throughout history. Countless schools, colleges, and universities are run under the auspices of Christian churches.

The Christian gospel demands service to friend and foe alike. Jesus is recorded to have taught, *"Truly, I say to you, as you did it to one of the least of these my brethren, you did it to me"* (*Matt.* 25:40). And in the parable of the Good Samaritan (*Luke* 10:25–37), Jesus made it clear that love of neighbor meant being willing to assist anyone who is in need, even at a cost. So important is the commandment to love the neighbor that John wrote, *"If anyone says 'I love God' and hates his brother, he is a liar; for he who does not love his brother whom he has seen cannot love God whom he has not seen"* (*1 John* 4:20).

HISTORY OF CHRISTIANITY

Besides the testimony of the *Gospels*, what do we really know about Jesus of Nazareth, the founding figure of Christianity, from the historical record? For centuries, Christians accepted the *Gospels* at face value, reading them as either biographies or journalistic accounts of the everyday life of Jesus. (Many Christians today still do so.) But with the beginning of the modern era—specifically at the end of the nineteenth and the beginning of the twentieth centuries—historical questions began to surface that would not go away. If the *Gospels* were complete records of Jesus' life and work, then, scholars wondered, why was so much detail left out? For example, why is there no physical description of Jesus? Why is there no mention of the early influences on his life? Why is there nothing said about the "invisible years," from approximately age twelve to age thirty? Why are no specifics given about the important people in his life? Why do the evangelists differ in the order of events and in the details of the same events they recount? Why is the chronology so vague, with movement from event to event indicated with little more sense of time than a "Then Jesus went on from there . . ." or "Now when Jesus came into the district . . ."? And why

do the majority of the pages of each of the *Gospels* focus on the last three days of Jesus' life? One scholar, Martin Kahler (1835–1912), described the *Gospels* as "passion narratives with an extended introduction."

THE SOURCES AND THEIR INTERPRETATION

The hunger for details about Jesus that would stand up to the critical standards of the scientific study of history gave rise to what became known as the "quest for the historical Jesus." The phrase has come to stand for the attempt by historians and some biblical scholars (both Protestant and Catholic) to discover the personality and career of Jesus of Nazareth as a figure in human history by the application of such biblical critical research tools developed in the late nineteenth and early twentieth centuries as source, form, and redaction criticism. **Source criticism** studies the texts of the *Gospels* and asks, From what materials were they constructed? **Form criticism** asks, Can we get behind the written documents to the events that created them? **Redaction criticism** asks, How did the writers of the *Gospels* bring together the sources that they had at their disposal? Before examining these approaches more closely, we must start with the surviving written documents, Jewish and Roman, as well as Christian.[11]

JEWISH SOURCES   In his *Jewish Antiquities,* the historian Flavius Josephus (ca. 37–100 C.E.) mentions James, who was stoned to death in 62 C.E., as "the brother of Jesus, the so-called Christ." In the eighteenth book of this work is the famous *Testimonium Flavianum,* the alleged testimony of the author to the Christ. Most scholars now agree that the passage was revised by a later Christian editor and no longer exists in its original form. Still, it seems unjustified to regard the entire piece as a Christian insertion. In it Josephus spoke of Jesus as a wise teacher and wonder-worker who was denounced to Pontius Pilate, a Roman official, by the Jewish authorities because of his messianic claims and who was crucified on Pilate's orders: "Now there was about this time Jesus, a wise man, if it be lawful to call him a man, for he was a doer of wonderful works—a teacher of such men as receive the truth with pleasure. He drew over to him both many of the Jews and many of the Gentiles. He was the Christ."[12]

In addition to the account by Josephus, there are a few obscure passages in the Hebrew *Talmud* that mention Jesus is as a miracle worker, sorcerer, and heretical teacher who was hanged on the feast of Passover.[13]

ROMAN SOURCES   Roman historian Cornelius Tacitus (ca. 55–120 C.E.), in his *Annals* 15:44, mentions the persecution of Christians by Nero. Tacitus traces the name *Christians* to the founder of the sect, Christ, who was crucified on orders of Pilate under the emperor Tiberius. This passage contains one of the earliest witnesses in non-Christian literature to the Crucifixion.

According to Gaius Suetonius (70–145 C.E.), historian and biographer, the emperor Claudius (41–54 C.E.) banished the Jews from Rome because they "constantly made disturbances at the instigation of Chrestus."[14] Chrestus no doubt means Christ, and Suetonius was referring to civil disturbances arising from Jewish-Christian tensions in the city.

Pliny the Younger (ca. 61–114 C.E.), jurist and writer, served as governor of Bithynia (modern Turkey) from the year 100 until his death. In a letter to the emperor Trajan (112 C.E.), Pliny asked for instructions about treating those accused of being Christians and described their beliefs and mores. Pliny mentioned that Christians sung a hymn to Christ as to God.[15]

CHRISTIAN SOURCES   Jewish and Roman references reveal little historical knowledge of the person Jesus, but they leave no doubt as to his existence. The most important source of our knowledge about Jesus is the ***New Testament,*** and specifically the *Gospels* attributed by tradition to Matthew, Mark, Luke, and John. The nature of these books (composed between 60 and 100 C.E.) is disputed among Christians, but it is safe to say that all agree that they are the closest thing Chris-

tians have to the words and actions of Jesus, however edited and theologically interpreted. Here, more than any other place, must we look for an understanding of Jesus' thought and teaching, a sense of the kind of person he was, as well as his purposes. Table 9.1 describes the writings that make up Christian scripture.

Modern biblical criticism has directed considered attention to what is called the "synoptic problem" or the "synoptic question," which arises from the substantial agreement in content and the numerous and striking differences in detail existing among the *Gospels* of Matthew, Mark, and Luke when they are lined up and compared (in a "synopisis"). These three **synoptic** *Gospels* are quite different from John's in many ways: theology, structure, imagery, and presentation of the person of Jesus. How can this be explained?

The conclusion of scholars such as Julius Wellhausen, Albert Schweitzer, Rudolf Bultmann, C. H. Dodd, Oscar Cullmann, Joachim Jeremias, Raymond E. Brown, Norman Perrin, and others is clearly summarized in the words of the eminent Lutheran scholar Günther Bornkamm, who said: "It is difficult to arrive at a precise historical knowledge of Jesus' life, and certainly of any 'biography' because of the nature of the sources—the New Testament. . . . No one is any longer in a position to write a 'life of Jesus.' So much of the presentation of Jesus found in the gospels reflects the confession [of faith] of the early church in his lordship—stirred by their experience of him after the resurrection. Thus, finding the 'bare facts' of history, of biography, is difficult if not futile."[16] In other words, the **historical-critical school** of biblical scholars contends that the Jesus we meet in the *Gospels* is not Jesus himself but rather what Jesus *meant* to those who, after the Resurrection, believed in him and spread his message. It is the firm consensus of these researchers that the *Gospels* were never designed to be life histories of a famous man and that they make no attempt to present adequate data for a biography.

Biblical critics believe that the *Gospels* were written years after the death of Jesus with material that was shaped by the preaching and teaching

CHRISTIAN SCRIPTURE

Table 9.1

The Christian *Bible* common to all Christian denominations (over 22,000 independent groups) is composed of two testaments, the *Old Testament* and the *New Testament*. However, the *Bible* shared by the majority of Christians (Roman Catholic and Eastern Orthodox) includes a third set of books, collectively known as the *Apocrypha*. Some Christian denominations have additional scriptures, such as the *Book of Mormon* of the Church of Jesus Christ of Latter-day Saints. The Christian *Old Testament* includes all of the books of the *Tanakh*, or Hebrew Bible. The *New Testament* includes four gospels (*Matthew, Mark, Luke,* and *John*), a history of the early Church (*Acts of the Apostles*), 21 letters, and an apocalypse (*Revelation*) disclosing God's will for the future.

Old Testament (39 books)	New Testament (27 books)	The Apocrypha (12–17 books)
See Table 8.1, "Hebrew Scripture (Torah)," in Chapter 8.	Matthew	*Tobit, Judith, Wisdom of Solomon, Ecclesiasticus, Baruch, Susanna, Maccabees, Esdras,* etc.
	Mark	
Genesis	Luke	
Exodus	John	The number and positioning
Leviticus	*Acts of the Apostles*	of the books vary:
Numbers	Romans	Orthodox and Catholic *Bibles*
Deuteronomy	*1, 2 Corinthians*	place the apocryphal or
Joshua	Galatians	deuterocanonical books in
Judges	Ephesians	the *Old Testament*.
Ruth	Philippians	Protestants place them
I, II Samuel	Colossians	between the *Old Testament*
I, II Kings	*1, 2 Thessalonians*	and the *New Testament*.
I, II Chronicles	*1, 2 Timothy*	
Ezra	Titus	
Nehemiah	Philemon	
Esther	Hebrews	
Job	James	
Psalms	*1, 2 Peter*	
Proverbs	*1, 2, 3 John*	
Ecclesiastes	Jude	
Song of Solomon	Revelation	
Isaiah		
Jeremiah		
Lamentations		
Ezekiel		
Daniel		
Hosea		
Joel		
Amos		
Obadiah		
Jonah		
Micah		
Nahum		
Habakkuk		
Zephaniah		
Haggai		
Zechariah		
Malachi		

of the **apostles,** who all were eyewitnesses to Jesus' public life. Each of the *Gospels* was written with a different theological perspective on the significance of Jesus. Each was addressed to a specific audience (Gentiles, Jewish Christians, and so on) that had particular questions about Jesus. Further, the scholars hold that the evangelists were writing from the vantage point of the Resurrection, and thus they mingled narration of fact with post-Resurrection interpretation of fact.

This is not to say that the *Gospels,* as sources of information on Jesus, cannot stand up to historical investigation. They can, and they have done so. The scholars are saying that the *Gospels* are designed to be read as testimonies of faith in Jesus and that they contain material that has been "organized" by the apostles and early Church. The material is rooted in the Church's knowledge and experience of Jesus. The *Gospels* are unique forms of literature—certainly not fiction, but, not pure history either. They are a proclamation (*gospel* means "good news") and instruction, announcement, and witness all at the same time.

The work of the historical-critical school has its critics. Scholars such as T. W. Manson attempt to refute the more radical versions of form criticism by maintaining that the synoptic *Gospels* can be shown to contain substantial amounts of basically eyewitness material.[17] Scandinavian scholar Birger Gerhardsson accepts the contention of form critics that the *Gospel* tradition passed through a period of oral transmission, but he insists that the Christian community exercised careful control over the development of the oral tradition, and so it is trustworthy.[18] Finally, there are Christians who identify themselves as Fundamentalists, who believe in the verbal **inerrancy** of scripture and reject the premise and methods of the historical-critical approach.

Can there ever be a reconciliation between the skepticism of the scholars and the biblical fundamentalism of some believers? That is for each Christian to decide. It is instructive, however, to remember the position of Rudolf Bultmann, who maintained that the fact that the quest for the historical Jesus was methodologically doomed to failure was unimportant. Christians live by faith in Christ, said Bultmann, and they have more than adequate proof that Jesus was a person belonging to history, not just a symbol or a mythical figure. For Bultmann and for Christians throughout the centuries, the "Jesus of History" is the "Christ of Faith."[19]

THE APOSTOLIC AGE (CA. 33–100 C.E.)

The time from about 33 to 100 C.E. was formative in the development of Christianity from a sect within Judaism to a cross-cultural religious movement. It coincided with the preaching and organizational activity of the original apostles and Paul of Tarsus, as well as their immediate successors. There are few sources for this period except the *Acts of the Apostles* and the letters of Paul. However, these documents provide adequate information for a general sense of what happened after Jesus was no longer on the scene.

The Christian scriptures frankly record how, after Jesus was taken prisoner, his apostles deserted him, scattered, and went into hiding *"for fear of the Jews"* (*John* 20:19). But after they experienced Jesus as living, a radical change came over the apostles. After **Pentecost** and the manifestation of the Holy Spirit in their lives, they left their hiding places behind locked doors and began to proclaim their faith in Jesus publicly, even if it meant risking abuse and harassment. Peter, who had denied Jesus three times, is shown as exemplifying this new courage; he is portrayed in *Acts* as the leader of the community and the first one to preach a sermon in Jerusalem (2:14–37). Christian tradition designates the period from Pentecost (ca. 33 C.E.; the Christian feast day remembering when the Holy Spirit filled the hearts and minds of the followers of Jesus with courage to publicly proclaim his message) to the close of the first century as the Apostolic Age.

At this time, the Christian community was located in Jerusalem. The witnessing of the apostles to Jesus (the public confessing of their faith in

Jesus) won many followers to the faith. The leadership of the Church was in the hands of the apostles; James and Peter were especially prominent in the pages of *Acts*. Women played an important role in the life of the early Christian community. Paul (in *Rom.* 16:1; *1 Tim.* 3–11) makes note of the qualifications and work of deaconesses and mentions one, Phoebe, by name. They were ordained by bishops and were to devote themselves to the care of the sick and poor. They were to instruct other women in preparation for acceptance into the Church, and they were to assist at the baptism of women.

At first, the followers of Jesus did not see themselves as members of a new religion. (Many expected Jesus' imminent return to earth, when he would definitively establish his kingdom.) Rather, they regarded themselves as a sect within Jewish Pharisaism (which accepted the notion of resurrection) that accepted Jesus as the Messiah. They continued to pray in the Temple (*Acts* 3) and observe Jewish law. In addition to whatever it meant to be "Jewish," the Christians met in one another's homes to celebrate *agapes* (love feasts) and to remember Jesus' Passion (*1 Cor.* 11:17ff).

Those in Jerusalem who opposed Jesus, however, were just as opposed to his followers. Tension between "traditional" Jews and "Jewish Christians" mounted until a persecution erupted. Stephen, a deacon in the early Church, was accused of disrespect for the Jewish law and was killed. Before he died, he is attributed with a speech (*Acts* 7) that clearly represented the earliest preaching of the converts to Christianity from Judaism. In it Stephen denied any holiness to the law, the Temple, or sacrificial ritual. This, of course, was blasphemy, and Stephen was stoned to death.[20] Many Christians fled to regions outside Jerusalem, thus giving rise to early missionary activity. Those Jewish Christians who remained behind insisted that they were children of the "true Israel," but the centrality they gave to Jesus in their lives made reconciliation with normative Judaism impossible.

In the post-Resurrection Church several persons and events were of great significance. First, Paul of Tarsus was a fervent, dedicated Pharisee and a participant in the killing of Stephen (*Acts* 8:1) and early persecutions. Sometime between 34 and 36 C.E., on his way to Damascus to continue his activity against the Christians, Paul had a vision of the risen Jesus that completely reoriented his life (*Acts* 9:1–19; 22; 4–16; 26:9–18). Paul moved from being a persecutor and adversary to being a proclaimer and builder of Christian communities. His activity left a permanent mark on what we know today as Christianity.

Second, a decision was made about 40 C.E. at Antioch, a center of Christianity outside Israel, that had consequences for the history of Christianity and the world. It was agreed by the leaders of the Church there that the gospel should be preached to Gentiles (non-Jews), as well as to Jews. Paul and Barnabas were chosen to lead this mission. On several journeys, they traveled extensively through Asia Minor to Greece and Rome.

Paul's approach to spreading the gospel was direct. He went first to the Jewish synagogues—and they were numerous throughout the Roman Empire—and proclaimed the message that Jesus had been crucified and had risen. If he was not well received (and most often he was not), he went to street corners and marketplaces to talk to any who would listen.[21] Paul won many converts.

The Greek converts came into Christianity in growing numbers. When it became evident that they were outnumbering Jewish Christians, the early Church experienced its first internal crisis. Jewish Christians—who thought themselves Jewish and who had harbored anti-Gentile hostility since the Roman occupation of Israel in 63 B.C.E.—demanded that all the converts be circumcised and that they observe the law of Moses in order to be eligible for membership in the fellowship of Jesus. These demands were not well received, and tension between the two factions was ongoing.

Third, in 51 C.E., Christians in Jerusalem met in council to address the acrimony between the two groups (*Acts* 15). Here an uneasy compromise was struck. Converts were free from the need for circumcision and many ceremonial requirements of the law, but they were to maintain standards of moral conduct and observe dietary rules. This was the beginning of the end for Jewish Christianity. By force of argument and personality, Paul—who was present at the council—was responsible for the ultimate break between Christianity and Judaism. He stripped Christianity of its Jewish character and universalized it. In his letter to the Christians at Galatia, he wrote: *"For as many of you as were baptized into Christ have put on Christ. There is neither Jew nor Greek, there is neither slave nor free, there is neither male nor female; for you are all one in Christ Jesus"* (*Gal.* 3:27–28).

In Paul's letter to the Romans, which represents his most mature thought on the issue of the Christian's relationship to the law, he proclaimed that the law of Moses was no longer valid or necessary for those who found Christ. Christ, not observance of the law, is the source of salvation (*Rom.* 7:4 and *passim*). In what was perhaps his most revealing self-disclosure, Paul personalized the new direction of his life without the law of Moses to guide him:

> But whatever gain I had, I counted as loss for the sake of Christ. Indeed I count everything as loss because of the surpassing worth of knowing Christ Jesus my Lord. For his sake I have suffered the loss of all things, and count them as refuse, in order that I may gain Christ and be found in him, not having a righteousness of my own, based on the law, but that which is through faith in Christ, the righteousness from God that depends on faith; that I may know him and the power of his resurrection, and may share in his sufferings, becoming like him in his death, that, if possible, I may attain the resurrection from the dead. (*Phil.* 3:7–11)

With the adaptation of Jesus to Greek culture, an extremely complex and intricate process,[22] the doors were open to universal evangelization. The gospel spread with great success through the Roman world. In the wake of the onrush of Greek Christianity and continued conflict between Jews and Christians, Jewish Christianity was doomed. *Torah*-following Christians, once dominant in the Jerusalem church before 70 C.E., survived as a tiny minority, the Ebionites (the poor or needy), until the Middle Ages, and then vanished.[23]

A sad legacy of this formative period, and one that remained embedded in Christianity throughout its history, was **anti-Semitism.** The gentile Christians never forgot the early persecutions. They blamed the Jews, as a race, for the death of Jesus (*Matt.* 27:25–27; *Acts* 5:28), and they saw the Jews as a stiff-necked people clinging to a religion whose centerpiece, the law of Moses, they regarded as obsolete and deficient—unable to bring people to righteousness.[24]

Finally, Christianity spread through the Roman Empire so quickly that by the end of the first century there was no place under Roman rule that had not heard the name Jesus. What accounted for this phenomenal expansion? Historians generally point to four causes: (1) The Roman Empire had an extensive, well-maintained, and safe network of roads and highways that allowed missionaries easy access to population centers. (2) The military might of Rome guaranteed the Pax Romana, a period free of the major conflicts and wars that always disrupt travel and distract attention from everyday activities. (3) There was a spiritual hunger in the people that had been nourished by the traditional nature or national religions. These religions were in decline, and Christianity offered an alternative. (4) In the early years of Christianity there was no reliance on professional religious leaders or clergy. Each Christian was a priest and missionary. Each Christian took responsibility for spreading the faith.[25]

THE SECOND CENTURY C.E. TO THE MIDDLE AGES (100–476 C.E.)

This section looks ahead to the important event of the emperor Constantine's embrace of Christianity and the consequences of this official recognition. It explores this period of expansion and looks at the major Christological controversies (passionate theological disputes about the nature of Jesus) that precipitated seven **ecumenical** (churchwide) **councils.** These assemblies of bishops took their names from the places where they were convened: Nicaea (in modern Turkey, 325), Constantinople I (modern Istanbul, 381), Ephesus (in modern Turkey,

431), Chalcedon (in Turkey, 451), Constantinople II and III (553 and 680), and Nicaea II (787).[26]

These councils were important because Christianity was shaping and formulating its doctrinal positions on the person of Jesus in response to challenges of accepted, if unformulated, understandings of the faithful. The resolution of the theological controversies resulted in a cohesive presentation of doctrine. These formulations and terms were conditioned by the vocabulary and mind-set of the bishops of that period. We can see how the institutionalization of Christianity required far more intellectual clarification than was given in the simple message Jesus preached in Galilee.

At the end of the Apostolic Age and the turn of the first century, there were no sudden transformations in the life of the growing Church.[27] Starting with the second century, we have better sources to draw on for our knowledge of the times. The second century was a time of external and internal struggle against the persecutions of Romans and the forces of **heresy.** Within the community it was a time of clarification and consolidation.

The Roman statesman Pliny the Younger called Christianity a "contagious superstition," and Christians were viewed with suspicion for multiple reasons. They were charged with atheism because they did not respect the Roman emperor as a god and refused to burn incense in his honor. They had no altars, images, or temples where they worshiped. Trajan blamed them for the fact that the Roman temples stood empty and sacrifices to the traditional gods had been abandoned. Caesars criticized Christians for not being willing to defend the empire by serving in the army. Christians, it was believed, participated in private rituals that included cannibalism and human sacrifice. (Obviously, the Romans mistook the symbolism of a eucharistic meal for a literal depiction of communion rites.)

During the second century, Roman Christians began to take preeminence among Christians living in centers of Christianity outside Rome. Certainly this was because the apostles Peter and Paul were believed to have been martyred in Rome and because Rome was the capital of the empire and

was itself a very important city. All roads did lead to Rome.

During this period as well, a general structure for governance of the Church emerged. Leadership was an **episcopacy,** that is, a form of government with supervision by presbyters or elders under a president (a "bishop of bishops"). This structure could be found in all places where the Church existed. The president of the Roman Church, the bishop of Rome, enjoyed a preeminence that would eventually develop into the role of **pope.**[28] Starting with Pope Damascus (366–384), a body of thought developed about the role of the bishop of Rome. Damascus was the first to refer to Rome as the **Apostolic See,** and he was the first to address the other bishops as *sons*—rather than *brothers.* His successor, Pope Siricius (384–399), was the first to use the *decretal*—a letter of instruction modeled on the emperor's decree—in which he claimed that his authority was supreme. But it was Pope Leo I (440–461) and Pope Gelasius (492–496) who really established the role that the pope would play throughout the Middle Ages.

Finally, it was during the second century that the idea of standardizing those books that would be regarded as Christian scripture was born. As early as 150 C.E., lists (or canons) of authoritative sources of doctrine were drawn up—though they were not finalized until centuries later. There were three criteria for inclusion of a work in the canon: (1) the work was deemed to have been written by an apostle or close associate, (2) it was accepted by the Church at large as authoritative, and (3) its contents were edifying. Because of these standards, many books were rejected and have become known as "apocryphal," such as the *Gospel According to Thomas,* the *Gospel of Peter,* the *Gospel of Mary Magdelene,* and the *Acts of Paul.*

The third century C.E. was a time of persecution and martyrdom for Christians, but by 320 in the following century Christians were safe from persecution, and the Church had a "most-favored status" within the Roman Empire. In 202 C.E., the emperor Septimus Severus issued an edict forbidding Christians to make any more converts. In 250, Decius demanded that each Roman citizen signify loyalty to him by publicly burning incense. In 255, the emperor Valerian published an edict ordering the removal of all Christian bishops from their sees and forbidding Christians to worship. After Valerian's death in 261, the persecutions ceased, and the Church was left to go its way until the final, and most severe, persecution by Diocletian (r. 285–305), beginning in 303. Churches were destroyed, copies of scriptures were burned, Christians in the military were forced to recant their faith or be discharged, clergy were imprisoned, and many were executed. Subsequent edicts from the emperor required pagan temples to be rebuilt and all citizens to be present at (and to participate in) public sacrifices to the traditional Roman gods.

By 310, however, none of these measures had succeeded in discouraging the new religion, and by 313, the emperor Constantine (r. 313–337) issued the edict of Milan, which recognized the rights of persons, including Christians, to worship as they would. During various times of his reign, Christian churches were both tolerated and favored.[29]

Did Constantine convert to Christianity? The question is not easily answered. He certainly favored the Christian Church, but he also protected the freedom of worship of his pagan subjects, who made up more than half his empire. Constantine rebuilt destroyed churches; ordered basilicas erected over the shrines of Peter and Paul; financed new copies of scriptures to replace those burned in earlier persecutions; and gave his wife's mansion in Rome, the Lateran palace, to be used as an episcopal residence. He supported Church charities, prohibited magic and fortune-telling, and humanized the laws of the empire for what appear to be Christian motives (for example, an edict of 316 forbids the branding of criminals on the face because "man is made in the image and likeness of God"). Constantine also declared Sunday a day of rest throughout the empire, but this could have been motivated by his respect for the traditional solar religion of his day. It seems that Constantine saw no implicit contradiction between his pagan religion and Christianity—at least not at first.

Did Constantine personally embrace the new religion? He was not baptized until shortly before his death, but this was not an uncommon practice at that time. Constantine's personal attitude toward Christianity seems to have been a mixture of awe and practical politics. The Christians were a growing force and influence in the empire. Once converted exclusively from the ranks of the poor, by the fourth century, members of the Church came from the military and the middle classes, along with large numbers of women from the upper classes. Christians regarded Constantine as a "New David"—a God-given ruler whose role included involvement with the affairs of the Church. Constantine did more than end persecution; he acted to promote and preserve the unity of the Church when it was threatened, as he came to see that the fate of the Church affected the empire and vice versa.

A profound and widespread conflict faced Constantine and the Church with the **Arian controversy.** Arius (ca. 250–336) was born in North Africa (Libya) and ordained a priest in Alexandria, Egypt. In 320 he taught that Jesus was not God. Jesus was "made," created. ("The Son had a beginning; there was a time when he was not.") Arius said that Jesus derived his being from the Father, and hence was subordinated to the Father and in no way eternal. Yes, Jesus was more than just a man, but he was called God in name only. Arius wanted to protect the oneness of God by denying any divinity to Jesus. He reasoned that if the Father of Jesus is God and Jesus is God, then there is not one God, but two. That, he said, could not be.

Arius himself was not an important figure in the struggle. When his teaching began to draw fire, Arius appealed to others for help, most notably Eusebius of Nicomedia (d. ca. 342), who had influence with Constantine. Eusebius spearheaded the fight and made it his own. Through his efforts, Arianism quickly spread throughout the empire.

The emperor first tried to settle the dispute by silencing both sides. The tactic failed. Then Constantine called for, and personally presided over, a council of three hundred bishops (only four from the West) that met at Nicaea in the summer of 325. At the insistence of Athanasius of Alexandria (ca. 296–373), a creed (a formalized belief) was written that asserted that Jesus Christ was "true god of true god, begotten not made, consubstantial *[homoousious]* with the Father." This **Nicene Creed,** based on a Syrian baptismal creed, affirmed Jesus as the Son of God, equal in divinity with the Father, out of whose being he proceeded and whose nature he shared. The Nicene Creed was proclaimed to be the faith of the Church, and all but two bishops signed it. Arius's teachings were condemned, he was exiled, and his books were burned.

The council did not resolve the issue; it intensified it. For more than fifty years, discord and hostility raged through the primarily Greek-speaking eastern regions of the Church and occasionally spilled over into the Latin-speaking western segment of the Church centered in Rome. The creed was not well received, and it was out of favor with most clergy and laity of the time. Rival creeds were drafted by various factions, who were careful to avoid the word *homoousious,* because it was not found in scripture. Constantine himself was unsympathetic to the Nicene formula, having been swayed toward Arianism by Eusebius. When Constantine died in 337, the empire was divided among his three sons. They were not cordial to one another, and political strife was added to an empire already badly shaken by religious divisions.

Although the major players in the story were primarily from the East, the ramifications of the schism shook the entire Church for a century. More important, in responding to the Arians, Constantine would define and focus the role of the emperor in relation to the Church. He called ecumenical (churchwide) councils to settle doctrinal disputes; he would not get involved in the actual theological debates but did work to enforce the decrees of these councils. Unity of the empire, more than theological orthodoxy, was Constantine's goal.

The next doctrinal crisis to confront the Church was the issue of the relationship between the divine and human natures of Christ. Although there existed no systematic scriptural presentation of the issue, it was generally believed that Jesus was truly God (meaning that whatever traits were assigned to God had to be assigned to Jesus) and truly human (meaning that whatever traits were said to be human, except sin, had to be assigned to Jesus). After the First Council of Constantinople (381), two groups in the Church raised questions about the relationship between Christ's two distinct natures. Together, the Nestorians and the Monophysites were responsible for provoking the need for further clarification.

Nestorius (d. ca. 451) was a Syrian priest renowned for his exciting preaching. In 428, when the See of Constantinople became vacant, Theodosius II (408–450) dismissed local candidates for the position in favor of Nestorius. The latter was a vigorous opponent of anyone who used the term Theotokos (God-bearer) in reference to Mary, the mother of Jesus, around whom there was a growing popular devotion. Nestorius and his followers, believing that this word indicated a compromise of the full humanity of Jesus, favored the term Christokos, thus protecting, he thought, the two natures of Jesus.

Nestorius's opponents secured the help of Cyril of Alexandria (d. 444), who championed their cause. But the Nestorians charged that Cyril's position led to **Monophysitism,** the belief that the human nature of Jesus was absorbed by the divine nature, hence becoming minimalized, if not totally discounted. To settle the dispute, Theodosius II called the Council of Ephesus in 431. The council was marked by rancor, bitter debate, and invective. Cyril and his allies succeeded in condemning Nestorius's position, excommunicating him, and reaffirming the Nicene Creed. The Syrian and Palestinian bishops, supporters of Nestorius, were outraged and left the council and the Church in schism.

Once again, the pattern was repeated. Controversy threatened the empire, the emperor convened a council, doctrinal positions were agreed upon, those not happy with the formulation bolted from the community, and controversy intensified. In this case, the doctrinal controversy over the nature of Jesus was not laid to rest until the Council of Chalcedon in 451. The emperor Marcian (r. 450–457) called for and attended this assembly of more than five hundred bishops (all but four from the East). On the surface, the reason for the

Exterior of the Coptic monastery of Saint Anthony, near Zafaranah, Egypt (1993).

conclave was to address the teachings of Eutyches (378–454), a monk of Constantinople who denied that the humanity of Jesus was equal with his divinity. In reality, however, this debate was only a continuation of the one between Nestorius and Cyril that had not subsided since Ephesus. Eutyches merely brought Cyril's position to its most logical conclusion: Jesus had only one nature, and that was divine. An extreme form of Monophysitism is **Docetism** (*doketis*, or "semblance"), the theory that Christ only appeared to be human, which was earlier advanced by the Gnostics and condemned by the Apologists and Nicaea.

At Chalcedon, Cyril's position was identified as indeed Monophysite and was condemned. The council issued a "definition" of the Church's belief in Jesus that was eventually accepted as the orthodox definition in both the East and the West. Reaffirming previous councils, the Council of Chalcedon declared that Christ is one person *(prosopon)*; recognizable in two distinct natures; without confusion, change, separation, or division. These natures are united (not absorbed, conjuncted, or subordinated) while leaving the properties of each nature intact. In this way the Council of Chalcedon arrived at Christianity's definitive understanding of who Jesus was—some five hundred years after he died.

True to the pattern of history, the council provoked discontent and further division. Now it was the Egyptian bishops who left the fold, taking the Nubian and Ethiopian churches with them. To this day, their descendants, the Coptic Christians, are still separated from the rest of the Christian churches that accepted Chalcedon. The doctrinal quarrel was never healed.

Relations between East and West declined after the Council of Chalcedon for several reasons. First, Rome claimed universal jurisdiction over the Church and supreme rule of the bishop of Rome. The East preferred the system in which control of the Church was under the direction of a council of five bishops from the major Christian centers. Rome never accepted this scheme. Second, political, theological, and ecclesiastical differences further separated the two churches—especially the East's insistence on venerating images (icons). At the Second Council of Nicaea (787), the Eastern churches proclaimed that the love given to these pictures of Jesus and Mary was a "relative" love—"absolute" love being reserved for God alone. But the West was never comfortable with such practices. Third, the differences in language (the West used Latin; the East, Greek) and culture made communication difficult. Language and culture were also responsible for very different liturgies— forms of worship and prayers—in the two churches. Fourth, the sorry and bitter rivalry between Pope Leo IX (1002–1054) and the patriarch of Constantinople, Michael Cerularius (d. 1058), led to the eventual and permanent division of the churches. The leaders exchanged excommunications in 1054, marking the beginning of the Great Schism, which has never ended, even though Pope Paul VI (1897–1978) and Patriarch Athenagoras (1886–1972) simultaneously nullified the excommunications in 1965—some nine hundred years later.

Having examined the theological disputes that gave form to orthodox Christian doctrine (for example, the Trinity and the divine and human natures of Christ), we return to the political history of the Church in imperial Rome. To more effectively govern such a large empire, Diocletian (in 286) divided the Roman Empire into two administrative districts (east and west), each administered by an emperor. In 324, Constantine united the empire under his rule and founded a new capital, Constantinople (formerly Byzantium), in the empire's eastern portion. Following Constantine's death (337), the empire, as noted previously, was again divided. Later in the century, Theodosius I ruled in the east (379–392) and subsequently ruled a united empire (392–395). Theodosius I was an ardent champion of the Church; he prohibited the worship of pagan gods (392) and effectively established Christianity as the religion of the Roman state. The division of the Catholic (universal) Church into separate entities—the Roman Catholic Church centered in the Latin-speaking west and the Eastern Orthodox churches centered in the Greek-speaking east—reflects the cultural and linguistic divisions present in the Rome Empire.

After the death of Theodosius I in 395, the Roman Empire was divided between his sons and was never reunited. In 410, Rome, a city whose population had been ravaged by plague and diminished politically by Constantinople, was sacked by the Visigoths, a Germanic people led by King Alaric (ca. 370–410). Like other Germanic peoples, the Visigoths were Christian, albeit Arian. The defeat

of Rome had little impact on that city, because shortly after their victory the Visigoths resettled in southern France (Gaul) and Spain. The sacking of Rome and the invasion of Italy caused psychological consternation throughout the empire. Many Christians read in the event the coming apocalypse. Pagans were convinced that the traditional gods were working revenge on the Christians for causing them to be abandoned.

In response to that event and other reversals, Augustine wrote the *City of God.* Along with Augustine's 500 sermons, 100 books, and 240 letters, this magnificent work is a testimony to Christian faith in a time of trial. Augustine argued that the temporal organization (the "city of man") and the spiritual reality of the Church (the "city of God") were intertwined. The fall of Rome indicated that the city of man was doomed, but the Church, no matter how depressed it might seem, would not be defeated. The Church's ultimate destiny was safe. In the long run, Augustine said, transformation takes place through adversity.

THE MIDDLE AGES (476–CA. 1500 C.E.)

Historians call the period from the fall of the Western Roman Empire (476) to the beginning of the Renaissance (ca. 1500) the Middle Ages. Once regarded as a sterile and dark age, it is now appreciated as one of the most creative times in human history. Although it is true that the political and cultural institutions of the old Greco-Roman world largely disappeared, Christianity survived; in fact, it thrived. To address the important events in this entire age, we focus our attention on three points of reference: (1) the rise, decline, and reform of monasticism; (2) the phenomenal advance of Islam and Christianity's response to it; and (3) the institutional life of the Church, particularly the sacramental system.

MONASTICISM   As we have seen from the study of other religions, asceticism and monasticism are not unique to Christianity. The origins of these practices lie in the Eastern world for Christianity, as well as for other religions.[30]

Jesus certainly left no example of renunciation of the world for his followers to imitate. Although it is true that he did not marry, it is not recorded that he imposed celibacy on his followers. Paul, however, was more ambiguous on the subject. He opposed rejection of marriage if it was based on a Gnostic dualism, but he freely allowed it, and even encouraged it, if celibacy made preparation for the immanent return of Christ easier (*1 Cor. 7*).

Christians were slow to adopt **asceticism,** the renunciation of physical pleasures and the practice of other forms of self-denial. There always have been individuals who lived apart from society and who left the cities for the wilderness, but initially this was not a generally accepted lifestyle among most early Christians. Asceticism took hold of the Christian imagination in the late third and early fourth centuries in Egypt and in the fifth century in France.[31] It should be noted that the ascetic movement attracted many kinds of personalities. Sprinkled among the pious were the dropouts, the irresponsible, criminal elements hiding out, and neurotic masochists. Furthermore, it should be noted that in the East, monks took part in the political struggles of their bishops. They were often called upon to act as foot soldiers, in addition to harassing heretics and destroying pagan temples.

Antony of Egypt (251?–356) is recognized by all to be the first Christian ascetic of note. Antony was an illiterate peasant, sincere in his desire to follow his Lord. His biographer claims that Antony became a hermit because he took literally the gospel message: *"If you would be perfect, go and sell all your possessions, give to the poor, and come follow me"* (*Luke* 18:22). For Antony and the many who would come after him, the world (that is, other people) was a distraction or a hindrance to holiness. These hermit ascetics required, so they believed, a purer form of Christianity than what they found practiced in the churches. Their purpose was to leave behind everything and everyone of this world that tempted them away from totally following Christ. By identifying themselves with the sufferings of Christ, they hoped to reach union with God.[32] They utilized the Neoplatonic ideal of "the flight of the alone to the alone" to describe what they were doing.

What did Antony do? He "went into the desert" (*anachoresis,* "to live the life of a solitary"). He lived in a cave or under the open sky, worked with his hands, prayed through the night, and practiced rigorous feats of self-mortification. He sought *apatheias,* or "tranquillity."

Contemporary reactions to Antony are instructive. To the ordinary Christian of his time, Antony was eccentric but nonetheless holy for that. Pilgrims from the cities would venture into the desert to visit him and seek his counsel with the phrase "Speak to me a word, Father, that I may live." It was assumed that he was close to God. Many followed his example. Origen (ca. 185–264), a biblical scholar, theologian, and spiritual writer, thought that ascetics like Antony were the spiritual elites. Local bishops, in contrast, had a different evaluation. They viewed the act of turning one's back on the world, of living alone, of making one's own salvation the chief priority as individualistic and privatistic. They saw such "holy loneliness" as a contradiction to the example of Jesus. They were quick to point out that by separating themselves from the community, the hermits also separated themselves from the eucharistic liturgy—something that was supposed to be a cherished gift for the Christian. Following Antony, asceticism developed in different forms.

Groupings of Hermits In lower Egypt, for example, those who came to the desert to be trained by a holy man built cells in caves near his neighborhood. Each lived and prayed alone, but they came together occasionally for common prayer or instruction. Such arrangements still exist today in the Egyptian desert of Scete, west of the Nile Delta.

Communities of Ascetics Around 320, Pachomius (ca. 290–346) founded a way of life known today as cenobitism (common way of life), which would become the framework for all monastic movements that came after him. He drafted a rule, or constitution, of 194 articles that organized the daily life (work, prayer, worship, and discipline) of anchorites (hermits), who occupied separate dwellings but otherwise lived as a fellowship under a spiritual superior. His first success was at Tabennisi, near the Nile in Upper Egypt. Before he died, Pachomius founded nine other monasteries for men. His sister, Mary, founded two convents—monastic communities for women—the first in 340.

Basilian Communities   Basil of Caesarea (330–379) was himself a hermit for a time in Syria and Egypt. When he became a bishop later in life, Basil developed a new conception of **monasticism.** Totally opposed to hermit and cenobitic life, he wanted to integrate monastic groups into the life of the local church and place them under the authority of the bishop. The ascetic movement, he said, had a social purpose: it was to be of benefit to the neighbor. His rule conceived of asceticism as a means to help individuals be of perfect service to God through fellowship in community and under obedience to authority. Basil's work spread to other Eastern regions, including Palestine, Cyprus, and Syria, and it is the rule of Eastern Orthodox monasteries to this day.

Convents of Religious Women   The history of monasticism is almost always written as a catalog of the deeds of males, but the vocation was equally open to women. When Antony began his work, he left his younger sister in charge of a "convent of virgins" dedicated to community life. Macrina, the elder sister of Basil of Caesarea, embraced monasticism *before* he did and influenced Basil's decision to become a monk. Women had places of authority in their own religious communities by Church law. The oldest reference to an abbess, or convent leader, is dated to 514 in Rome. An abbess had almost all the same duties as an abbot, the leader of a monastery. She would dress in a miter (bishop's hat), receive homage from local clergy, and have the final word on religious practice in her domain. (Abbesses must have wanted equality of functions with their male counterparts, because Pope Innocent III [1198–1216] had to officially forbid them to hear the confessions of their nuns.)

Monasteries in the West   Athanasius of Alexandria wrote a biography of Antony that was the most influential vehicle for bringing asceticism to the attention of the West, but it was not the only one. Sulpicius Severus (ca. 360–420), a French historian, was deeply moved by the life and preaching of Martin of Tours (d. 397), who had founded a monastery, the first in the West, in 360. He wrote a biography of Martin that won immediate notice and popularity. Martin's example caught on, even though much of Severus's account was little more than pious overexaggeration.

In about 415 in Marseilles, John Cassian (360–435) founded two monasteries, and there he wrote two influential books: *Institutes* and *Conferences*. The former set out ordinary rules for monastic life that he had learned from being a monk in Bethlehem. The latter recounted conversations he had with great figures of Eastern monasticism.

From these predecessors monasticism spread. In Milan, Ambrose (ca. 339–397) founded a monastery. In North Africa, Augustine of Hippo gathered a celibate community about him in a monastery devoted to serving the poor and to study. This community would later become the model for the "cathedral school" that eventually evolved into the European university. In Ireland, Patrick (ca. 390–460) founded monasteries. But by far the greatest influence on Western monasticism came from Benedict of Nursia (ca. 480–545).

Little is known of Benedict save that he was educated in Rome, was scandalized by the decadence there, and retreated to a life as a hermit at Subiaco, in northern Italy. He was never ordained a priest, nor did he intend to form a religious order. Yet Benedict's view of the monastic life and the rule he established for it became the definitive model for all monastic communities in the Western world, and Benedict's version of monasticism is credited as being one of the proudest achievements of Western Christianity.

People were attracted to Benedict. He founded twelve monasteries of twelve monks, each with its own abbot, whom he appointed. At Monte Cassino (midway between Rome and Naples), where he remained until his death, he founded a much larger community. The monks at Benedict's monasteries were not clergy. They were simple peasants—so simple that they had to be taught to read so that they could use the scriptures. Benedict called upon monks to live a life of simplicity and moderate self-discipline (seen as rigorous by modern standards, perhaps), to be a part of a spiritual family under the guidance of the abbot, whose absolute authority was always tempered by mercy.

The aim of Benedict's Rule was to aid monks to live in the presence of God and to win salvation by their actions: work and prayer. To free themselves to do this wholeheartedly, the members took vows of poverty, chastity, and obedience. They also took a promise of stability—never to leave the monastery. This last vow was of tremendous importance, because it guaranteed continuity to the life of each monastery.

The monks' day followed a predictable rhythm of hours of prayer (*nocturnes, lauds, prime, terce, none, vespers,* and *compline*) interspersed by hours of private meditation and physical labor. They took all their simple meals together; slept in dormitory quarters; and sung the mass, or Eucharist, together in the community chapel.

When Monte Cassino was destroyed by the Lombards around 585, the monks fled to the protection of Pope Gregory I (540–604), himself once a monk. Gregory ordered them to start monasteries elsewhere. They did, and the Benedictines, as they were called, became the first religious congregation in the West.

Monasteries sprang up all over medieval Europe. Because Benedict's Rule guaranteed a standardized, stable, ordered community life, rulers were eager to donate lands and financial support to begin monasteries; they saw that these institutions did not exist just for the benefit of the monks.[33] The monasteries served political and social, as well as religious, purposes. First, the monks prayed for their ruler and benefactors. This kind of support was most appreciated, as demonstrated by this excerpt from a letter from one nameless medieval prince to another:

Look carefully at the things which are provided for you by trained monks living in monasteries under a Rule: strenuous is the warfare which these castellans of Christ wage against the Devil; innumerable are the benefits of their struggle. Who can recount the vigils, hymns, psalms, prayers, alms and daily offerings of masses with floods of tears, which the monks perform? These followers of Christ give themselves up wholly to these employments, crucifying themselves that they may please God. . . . And so, noble earl, I advise you to build such a castle in your country.[34]

Second, the monasteries served a family function. They provided a place for the "lesser" children of the nobility—those who could not inherit or marry. Children of nobles were given to monasteries *(oblati)* to be educated and trained for an honorable profession. Parents endowed these institutions handsomely. Third, given the structure of penance for sins as practiced in the Middle Ages, monks could do penance for wealthy sinners, and the monastery would be given a financial reward for such service. In the thinking of the day, payment of the debt to heaven for sin—not who needed to pay it—was the important thing.

The Benedictine monasteries reached their peak at the Abbey of Cluny, France, in the eleventh century. Cluny was described as a perfect community. Here all the best of the monastic movement flowered: service to the poor, service to learning, preservation of culture, and giving glory to God through liturgy. But as beautiful as it could be, the monastic institution could not avoid corruption. By the end of the early Middle Ages, the uniformity, zeal, and high purposes of the ascetic life were dissipated. Spiritual and economic factors contributed to the undoing. Spiritually, the penitential activity on behalf of benefactors diverted attention away from the original purpose people had for entering the monastery—to find God. Economically, as times changed, the feudal system could no longer afford to endow and support monasteries with huge cash grants and donations. Instead, benefactors gave monasteries "scattered rights" (to fish and collect tolls, rents, and taxes), which required monks to leave the monasteries to administer them. The more they were outside the monastery doing this worldly business, the more the spiritual aspect of their vocation diminished and their spiritual practices relaxed.

Popes and monastic reformers knew that something was wrong, but they could devise no cure. By the end of the eleventh century, those seeking a spiritual life looked elsewhere. Other religious orders sprang up, and the Benedictine monopoly on religious life ended. Some of the newer orders were monastic reform movements, such as the Cistercians or the Augustinians. Some were preaching orders, such as the Dominicans. Some, such as the Franciscans, devoted themselves to working with the poor, and others, such as the Jesuits, to teaching and missionary work. These orders provided a disciplined rule and a mandate to live the gospel virtues. Throughout the Middle Ages, their work fitted into the evolving social patterns of western Europe. They produced saints and scholars too numerous to catalog, though the founders warrant special notice: Bernard of Clairvaux (1090–1153), Dominic de Guzman (1170–1221), Francis of Assisi (1162–1226), and Ignatius of Loyola (1495?–1556).

THE INFLUENCE OF ISLAM   The significance and consequences of Islam for medieval Christianity were profound. The lives of both the Orthodox East and the Catholic West were more profoundly affected by this new religion than by the invasion of Slavs in the East and Germanic peoples in the West. After all, the "barbarian" invaders offered no competing religious systems to the Christian religion, but Islam quickly won the hearts and minds of many. By the seventh century, Syria, Egypt, North Africa, and Persia, once Christian strongholds, were now populated by converts to the emerging religion. Minarets atop mosques became as prevalent, if not more so, than crosses atop basilicas and cathedrals. By the eighth century, Islam had stretched into Spain and southern France. Islamic society was not only religiously successful but also the most prosperous in the early Middle Ages.

Christianity was put on the defensive. Early boundaries to the expansion were set when Charles Martel checked the Arab advance in 732 at Tours, France, before it reached the heart of Europe. In the East, a boundary was established when the Muslims were unable to take Constantinople. But what of the lands "lost" to the Muslims? Particularly, what was to be done about the loss of the holy lands that held the sacred shrines of Christianity?

In 1095, Pope Urban II (ca. 1042–1099) appealed for aid to win back Jerusalem and save Constantinople, which was threatened by Islam's armies.[35] Urban called for a Christian response to Islam's *jihad* (armed struggle against those who resist the faith). Western princes enthusiastically embraced the Crusades—Holy Wars, military pilgrimages blessed by the Church—to recover and retain the Holy Land. Crusaders were given incentives to volunteer: tax exemptions while they were away, **indulgences** (remission of punishment in Purgatory) for past sins, and the hope of attaining the status of martyrdom in the event of their death. (These were the same rewards that Islamic leaders offered their soldiers.)

Little that was Christian could be discerned in the brutal manner in which these campaigns were conducted and the ways in which the peoples of the East (both Jews and Muslims) were treated. The Crusaders even ravished their allies, the people of Constantinople, in a rape of that city in 1204 that still lives in infamy and contributed to the separation of Eastern and Western Christians.

Historically, the Crusades can be divided into three periods—1095–1204, 1204–1291 and 1291–1464—but this division is misleading. It is more comprehensive to see the Crusades as a series of continuous waves of Western Christian expansionism after years of being on the defensive from both invaders and Muslims. Judged as military campaigns, however, the Crusades were more failures than successes. The Holy Land was returned to Christian control for only a brief time. One positive result of the Crusades, however, was something

The Gothic Cathedral of Notre Dame towers above the surrounding rooftops of Chartres, France. The imposing edifice was rebuilt in the Gothic style between 1194 and 1260 and stands as one of the most famous Gothic structures in the world.

unplanned. The West came in touch with the rich Arab culture that had been saving and restoring the ancient learning of Greece. The works of Aristotle and others that became available to the returning Crusaders would eventually give impetus to the cultural explosion of the Renaissance.

THE SACRAMENTAL SYSTEM   The Christian faithful truly believed that Jesus had conquered death and lived in his church. During the Middle Ages, theologians gave more attention to doctrines about the sacraments. As late as the time of Hugh of Saint Victor (d. 1142), it was believed that there were as many as thirty sacraments. Peter Lombard (ca. 1100–1160) drastically revised this view, and in his *Sentences* he made a critical distinction between numerous sacramentals and seven sacraments.

Lombard's system defined *sacraments* as "outward signs of grace and channels of grace"—points where the divine and human intersect. The Fourth Lateran Council accepted this schema as doctrine, and Thomas Aquinas further codified it in his *Summa Theologiae*. The seven sacraments are best seen in groupings: baptism, Eucharist, and confirmation (the sacraments of initiation); penance and extreme unction, now termed the sacraments of the sick (the sacraments of healing); and marriage and orders (the sacraments of vocation). Baptism, confirmation, and orders were unrepeatable.

It is to be noted, of course, that the Protestant reformers had significantly different views on sacraments. For them, baptism and Eucharist were certainly differentiated from the other five because they were specifically mentioned in the *New Testament* as instituted by Christ himself, not by the followers of Christ. But this is a story left to a later section.

THE LATER MIDDLE AGES AND THE GREAT SCHISM
By the end of the thirteenth century, feudalism and the papacy were about to be altered. These alterations would drastically change Christianity in the West. A money economy and the growth of towns altered feudalism by creating new forms of wealth and reviving commerce. These economic transformations, in turn, would change the political, social, and economic patterns of the Middle Ages. The authority of the papacy, once dependent on the weak, decentralized feudal power structure, was to be challenged by rising monarchs who ruled nations.

In the thirteenth century, Western Christianity demonstrated little tolerance for doctrinal pluralism. If an individual disagreed with established religious teaching and practice, he or she was usually branded a heretic. Pope Innocent III (1198–1216) was the first pope to link heresy with the civil crime of treason. He and his successors Honorius

III (1216–1227), Gregory IX (1227–1241), and Innocent IV (1243–1254) waged a consistent campaign to identify and prosecute those who were "lightly suspect," "vehemently suspect," or "violently suspect" of such crimes. The Church court that conducted the investigations and trials of suspects was known as the Inquisition, but the term is usually applied to the elaborate process of detecting and punishing those who deviated from orthodox belief. Many innocent people were ruined in the attempt to impose religious uniformity. Some were condemned and handed over to civil authority to be put to death.

When Pope Boniface VIII (1234–1303) and King Philip IV of France had a dispute over taxation of the French clergy, the pope issued a papal bull, or mandate. In 1302, *Unam sanctam,* in which he declared that there was only "one, holy, catholic and apostolic church," and that the pope was the supreme head of it. He maintained that anyone who rejected his authority put himself or herself outside church, and that would mean neither "salvation nor remission of sins." Boniface declared that the temporal authorities were subject to the spiritual authority of the pope of Rome.

A year later, Boniface died and was succeeded by Clement V (1305–1314). Clement moved the papal court from Rome to Avignon, France (five miles south of Lyons). For sixty-eight years and the reign of eight popes, Avignon, not Rome, was the center of Western Christianity. The papal court was lavish and extravagant, which scandalized the faithful. Because of the efforts of Catherine of Siena (1347–1380), the last Avignon pope, Gregory XI (1370–1378), agreed to return to Rome.

Upon Gregory's death, a Roman faction put great pressure on the cardinals to elect an Italian pope. Urban VI (1318–1389) was elected and was eager to reform. However, because he was overbearing in his dealings with the powerful French cardinals and because he was, apparently, mentally deranged, Urban provoked a serious division in the curia (upper bureaucracy). The sixteen French cardinals went back to Avignon and declared Urban's election invalid. They elected Clement VII (1378–1394), and he established a second papal court at Avignon. Now there were two popes—each with his own college of cardinals. Confusion reigned. Urban and Clement exchanged excommunications, and the rulers of nations chose to support one or the other pope for political reasons. Europe was split into two camps. When Urban and Clement died, both had successors.

The schism was a religious and political disaster, and the unity of Western Christianity was lost for a long time. Reformers within the Church urged repair of the damage. In 1409, a council for that purpose met in Pisa and rejected the claims of both the Avignon and Roman popes. The council elected Alexander V (1339–1410). The two other popes rejected the authority of this council and refused to step down. Now there were three popes.

In 1414 at Constance, another council was held that deposed all three popes and elected Martin V (1368–1431), who returned to Rome and ended the schism. In the interim, the papacy had been badly shaken, and respect for it had been lost. Later councils (Pavia, 1424; Basel, 1431; and Florence, 1439) proved ineffective in reforming papal and clerical politics and practices. Christian unity in the West was destroyed little by little. Without doubt, however, the foundation of its demise was laid by nationalism, Renaissance humanism, and internal power conflicts.

THE RENAISSANCE (1400–1600 C.E.)

The cultural flowering known as the Renaissance in Italy affected the style of the papacy. Material wealth, learning, and **humanism** ended any pretense to the era of medieval asceticism. Renaissance popes imitated the courts of Renaissance princes. Nicholas V (1397–1455) and his successors, especially Alexander VI (1492–1503) and Julius II (r. 1503–1513), used church revenues to acquire libraries, sponsor artists such as Michaelangelo and Raphael, commission buildings by architects such as Bramante, and in general beautify Rome.

A source of this papal wealth was the practice of simony—the selling and buying of holy things (prayers, relics, ecclesiastical offices, and indulgences). Although this practice was clearly condemned by both councils and popes, its use was widespread during the Church's history, and it was the immediate cause of what has come to be known as the Protestant Reformation.

THE PROTESTANT REFORMATION (CA. 1517–1648 C.E.)

It is clear that everyone wanted reform, but how and what to reform was not clear. When Church people spoke of reform, they were almost always thinking of administrative, legal, or moral reformation—hardly ever doctrinal reformation. They thought that the popes were corrupt or wasteful. Few thought that their doctrinal teaching was erroneous. And because the clergy were very often corrupt and uneducated, anticlericalism was rampant among the faithful of the sixteenth century. So low had the reputation of the clergy sunk that the Dutch theologian Erasmus (1466–1536) remarked that a layperson was insulted if he or she were mistaken for a cleric, nun, priest, or monk. The sixteenth-century Christians looked backward, to the early Church, for a model and standard of Church life.

In addition to humanism and anticlericalism, purely secular and political instigations for reform were also present. Princes resented the popes' interference in local issues and loss of revenues to support papal causes.

Of the many voices of protest within the church prior to Martin Luther (1483–1546), we mention only a few. The English reformer John Wycliffe (ca. 1330–1384) foreshadowed much of what later reformers would say. Wycliffe held that the pope was not infallible and denied the doctrine of transubstantiation. Further, he denied the need for sacramental confession, and he called for a married clergy. Most notably, Wycliffe held that the scriptures were the sole criteria of doctrine and, to that end, encouraged their translation into the language of the people.

Wycliffe influenced the Czech scholar John Hus (1372–1415), who echoed his mentor in demanding reform. Hus called for communion under both bread and wine, an end to the secular wealth of the Church, and punishment for simony.

The ideas of both Wycliffe and Hus were condemned by the Council of Florence (1414–1417), and Hus burned at the stake for his positions. But the idea of reform could not be crushed. Reformers who held clerical offices within the Church were calling for change, too. The Dominican preacher Savanarola (1454–1498) is an example. Well regarded as a sincere, fervent ascetic, he won attention for his passionate denunciation of the immorality of the people of Florence—including the clergy. Savanarola actually organized a reform movement within the city that he hoped would serve as a model for reform elsewhere. His severity, however, made him enemies, and he was hanged as a schismatic (a person separated from the church by his or her beliefs). Martin Luther was fourteen years old at the time.

Born in Erfurt, Germany, Luther was the son of a peasant family. In 1505, while returning from a visit to his parents, he was frightened by a thunderbolt, which triggered a religious experience in him. In return for safety, he promised God to become a monk. Luther kept his promise by entering the Augustinian monastery in his hometown.[36] In 1508, he was assigned to teach at Wittenberg, the new university founded by Frederick of Saxony. Here, as he was developing his lectures, he became obsessed with the question of justification: How does God judge us? In wrath or mercy? Luther found his answer in Paul's *Letter to the Romans:* *"For in it [the gospel] the righteousness of God is revealed through faith for faith; as it is written, 'He who through faith is righteous shall live'"* (1:17). According to Luther, God loves sinners and judges in mercy. God's love and mercy are total gifts; through faith alone we live and are saved. Salvation comes through belief in God's mercy. Our moral deeds, Luther claimed, earn us no merit. Roman Catholics responded by pointing to *James* 2:17: *"Faith by itself, if it has no works, is dead"*.

Lecturing on justification by faith, Luther became very popular with the students. In 1516, he had become so critical of his Roman Catholic training that he felt impelled to preach against another controversial theological position of Rome: indulgences. It was here that he became the center of a storm that changed Christianity. The match that ignited the Reformation was just this question of indulgences.[37] Prince Albert of Brandenburg was named archbishop of Magdeburg and bishop of Halberstadt in return for a large donation to Pope Leo X's cause of rebuilding a basilica, Saint Peter's, in Rome. By Church law, the elevation of Albert was illegal for several reasons. First, it was simony (selling holy things or offices). Second, Albert was seven years younger than Church law required for a bishop. And third, he had absolutely no theological training. Albert borrowed monies from the Fugger banking house to pay his debt to Leo, but he could not borrow enough. Leo then agreed to grant indulgences for those who contributed to the building of Saint Peter's. The pope and the prince agreed that one-half the funds raised by the indulgences would go to Leo and one-half to Albert for his debt.

A Dominican priest, John Tetzel, was commissioned to preach the indulgence. Tetzel was energetic in his cause, but also very commercial in his framing of the theology of the indulgence. Although it was standard practice that those seeking an indulgence must first go to penance, confess sin, and make a sincere intention not to sin again, Tetzel preached that a simple money payment was sufficient to deliver a soul from the punishment due to past sins. And more, Tetzel preached that a person could have an indulgence applied to a soul already suffering in Purgatory. This, he said, was backed up by the power and authority of the pope, to whom Jesus gave the "keys of the kingdom"—the authority to make rulings on earth that would have consequences in heaven with unfailing effect.

Luther, and many other Catholics, vociferously objected. In February 1517, he began to preach against the indulgence. To provoke debate on the issue, he posted a list of ninety-five theses (arguments) on the doors of the university church at Wittenberg. Within ten days, Luther's arguments spread throughout Germany and were even translated into several other languages. They were welcomed by the humanists, who were anticlerical; the nationalists, who were anti-Italian; and those who were looking for a rallying cry against

the abuse of papal power. Luther had no intention of making a break with Rome over the issue; he was protesting a particular practice that offended his theological sensibilities.

A pamphlet war began. Luther was directly challenging the power of Rome. The Dominicans took up the cause of the indulgence. Tetzel, an unlearned and overly flamboyant man, answered Luther, poorly, with 122 "antitheses." Luther's own order, the Augustinians, took up his side. When the pope was informed of the debate, he regarded it at first as no more than a "monks' squabble." But the squabble did not exhaust itself. Leo, in a concessional, publicly "clarified" some of the excessive claims made by Tetzel and others on behalf of papal power. But by this time it was too late. Luther was calling the pope the "Antichrist," and the pope was calling Luther the "child of Satan."

In October 1518, the German bishops convened a diet (a legislative body and regional gathering of bishops convoked to deal with ecclesiastical matters) at Augsburg and invited Luther to attend under guarantee of safe passage. There he refused to recant his objections to both the preaching of the indulgence and the authority given to justify it. In the following year, Luther debated the reowned theologian Johann Eck at Leipzig, and there the political and ecclesiastical fortunes of Luther changed. Eck got Luther to admit that John Hus (a condemned heretic in the eyes of Rome) was a good Christian and that the councils that had condemned him were in error. Thus, Luther went on record as rejecting the authority of the pope and the councils, substituting *sola scriptura* (by scripture alone) as an authority. Luther insisted that faith alone saved. No pope, no council could change that.

Contemporary observers of the debate recorded that from then on, Luther began to "play to the gallery."[38] He preached open revolt and even suggested that it would be entirely in order to "wash our hands in the blood" of cardinals and popes. For Luther, the Church had become "the sink of the Roman Sodom." In 1520, Leo issued the bull *Exsurge Domini,* in which he condemned forty-one of Luther's theses and ordered him to recant within sixty days or be excommunicated. Luther's response was to publicly burn the bull. From this moment on, there was no turning back for either the pope or Luther.

Later that year, Luther wrote *Letters to the Christian Nobility*, in which he attacked the institution of the papacy and advocated a German national church. In 1520, he also wrote *The Babylon Captivity of the Church*, in which he claimed that there were only three sacraments (baptism, the Lord's Supper, and penance), rejected transubstantiation (although he did hold that Jesus was consubstantially present with the bread and wine), and rejected the concept of the mass as a sacrifice.

In 1521, Charles V called the Diet of Worms. There Luther again defended his positions and on April 18 made his final refusal to rescind any of them. In May of that year his teachings were formally condemned by Rome. Under the protection of Prince Frederick, Luther retired to safety to write a condemnation of monastic vows and to translate the *New Testament* into German. He would complete a translation of the Hebrew scriptures by 1534. Over 200,000 copies of Luther's *Bible* were sold in a twelve-year period, making it the biggest seller of its day (assisted, of course, by the invention of the printing press).

Luther did not start out to create a new religion or a separate church, but his attacks on the Catholicism of his day were more than broadsides against superficial abuses. With the help of theologian Philip Melanchton (1497–1560), Luther presented the *Augsburg Confession* to Charles V in 1530. In this document, the essential doctrines of Lutheranism stand in clear contrast to those of Catholicism. In addition to what has already been said, Luther rejected belief in Purgatory, the cult of saints, any special devotion to Mary, monasticism, fasts, and celibacy for the clergy. (Luther himself married a former nun, Catherine von Bora, and had six children with her.)

The differences between Luther's position and that of Rome were enormous. His movement emphasized justification by faith; the authority of scripture and, consequently, a diminution of the role of sacraments (Luther ultimately concluded

that there were only two: baptism and Eucharist); and a married clergy. Inspired by Luther's break from long-standing conventions, German peasants revolted against their masters. Luther, eager to distance himself from these rebels, preached that the peasants' revolt should be crushed with all cruelty, if necessary. In his pamphlet *Against Thieves, Murderous Hordes of Peasants,* Luther called on princes to use their God-given power to end the rebellion. This stance turned the peasants away from Lutheranism and toward more radical reformers. Luther's reputation suffered because of the stance he took in this work, as it later did because of his vitriolic tracts against Jews.

THE REFORMATION SPREADS   In 1526, the Lutheran princes who had left the Roman Church gathered at the Diet of Speyer to call for reform. Here they "protested" the abuse of papal authority and became known as Protestants. From Germany, the protest spread throughout Europe.

Two reformers, Ulrich Zwingli (1484–1531) and John Calvin (1507–1564), brought the Reformation to Switzerland. Zwingli was a priest and an idealist whose break with Rome happened gradually. Beginning with his lectures on the *New Testament* in Zurich in 1519, Zwingli eventually arrived at the position that the *Gospels* were the sole basis for truth. From this theological starting point, he rejected the teaching authority of the popes and bishops, as well as much of what they taught. He attacked belief in the existence of Purgatory, the practice of praying to saints, monasticism, celibacy (he married in 1524), and the saying of the Eucharist as anything other than a symbolic meal. For a time, he even forbade the celebration of the mass in Zurich, his center of operations. It was in Zurich that Zwingli also removed all images and pictures from the churches—a custom that is still followed in most Protestant churches.

John Calvin, a French-born reformer and theologian, claimed to have had a religious experience in 1533 in which God mandated that he restore the Church to its original purity. Because of a persecution against "free thinkers" by King Francis I of France, Calvin fled to Switzerland in 1535. He

CHRONOLOGY OF CHRISTIANITY

CA. 4	Birth of Jesus
33	Crucifixion of Jesus
CA. 35	Conversion of Paul
CA. 40	Decision by Church at Antioch to preach the gospel to Gentiles
51	Council of Jerusalem
CA. 60–100	Writing of canonical *Gospels*
150	Earliest lists of Christian scriptures compiled
202	Emperor Septimus Severus forbids Christians to evangelize
313	Edict of Milan
325	Council of Nicaea
381	Council of Constantinople I
430	Death of Augustine of Hippo
451	Council of Chalcedon
CA. 520	Rule of Benedict
800	Charlemagne; Holy Roman Empire
1054	Great Schism: Eastern and Western Christian Churches separate

remained there until he died, making the reformation of the Church and state his life's work.

In his *Institutes of the Christian Religion* (1536–1539), regarded by many as the supreme authority for non-Lutheran Protestantism, Calvin accepted most of Luther's reforms but went beyond them, too. Most significant was his teaching on absolute predestination. According to this view, before the dawn of time or the creation of humans, God in his infinite wisdom and justice predestined (predetermined) some of his creatures to salvation and others to damnation. In other words, Calvin was rejecting the idea of the universal saving will of God—that God wanted all to be saved in the death and Resurrection of Christ. But in Calvin's

view, based on scripture (*Dan.* 12:1; *Matt.* 20:23; *John* 10:29; *Rom.* 8:28–30) and the theological tradition of Augustine, Christ died only for the "elect." This very controversial theological opinion was modified by later Calvinists, but it demonstrates the radical nature of the reformer's thinking.

From Switzerland, the Reformation spread to France and the Low Countries, where Melchior Hoffmann (ca. 1495–1543) declared his country to be the New Jerusalem to which Christ would soon return to reward the faithful and condemn the infidels. The Reformation crossed the channel to England as Henry VIII (1491–1547) broke from the Roman authority yet still maintained much of the doctrine and ritual of the Roman Church.

1095	First Crusade
1232	Inquisition begins
1274	Death of Thomas Aquinas
1305–1371	Avignon papacy
1384	Death of John Wycliffe
1415	Death of John Hus
1517	Martin Luther's ninety-five theses
1519	Ulrich Zwingli in Zurich
1536–1539	John Calvin's *Institutes of the Christian Religion*
1540	English Reformation
1545–1563	Council of Trent; Counter-Reformation
1642	Death of Galileo Galilei
1791	Death of John Wesley
1869–1870	First Vatican Council
1910	*The Fundamentals* published in the United States
1962–1965	Vatican Council II
1989	Christians celebrate Christmas in all communist bloc countries

John Knox (1513–1572) brought Calvinism to Scotland after taking refuge in the Protestant city of Geneva, which he considered "the most perfect school of Christ."

THE COUNTER-REFORMATION, OR ROMAN CATHOLIC REFORMATION   The term *Counter-Reformation* must be understood with qualification if it is to be understood at all. Many within Roman Catholicism itself saw the abuses that the reformers saw and worked to make changes. Ignatius of Loyola (1491–1556), Francis de Sales (1567–1622), and Charles Borromeo (1538–1584) all recognized that the renewal of the institution of the Roman Church required a personal self-renewal, and to that end these men founded religious orders dedicated to spirituality, learning, and working with the poor.

However, there is no doubt that the Roman Church, as an institution, felt impelled to respond to the doctrinal challenges presented by the Protestants. It did this by extending and sanctioning the authority of the Inquisition (by papal mandate of Pope Paul III in 1542), by instituting the Index of Forbidden Books (by mandate of Pope Paul IV in 1557), and by the three sessions of the Council of Trent (1545–1547, 1551–1552, and 1562–1563). Taken together, this collection of responses, both individually and collectively, is known as the Counter-Reformation, or Catholic Reformation.

The consequences of this movement still affect world Christianity today.

Specifically, the Council of Trent condemned the practice of simony and the selling of indulgences. It established seminaries for the proper moral and theological training of the clergy. It reformed the role of the bishop, restricting his jurisdiction and specifying his obligations. Although the council did not formally condemn Luther, it reasserted the position that doctrines of faith rest on scripture and tradition, hence reaffirming the teaching authority of the popes. It took issue with each of the reformers' theological programs, particularly Luther's *sola fides* (faith alone) doctrine and the more radical reformers' denial of the presence of Christ in the mass. The Council of Trent also fixed the number of sacraments at seven.

CHRISTIANITY SINCE THE SIXTEENTH CENTURY C.E.

It is not disputed that the Reformation and Counter-Reformation left an indelible stamp on the history of Christianity. During the years 1517 to 1555, religious wars shattered Western Christianity, and it never regained religious unity. Relations between Protestants and Catholics remained frozen in suspicion, distrust, and acrimony until the last third of the twentieth century, when an ecumenical spirit opened up a season of rapprochement. But even today, that attitude has not produced any significant reunification of the churches. The consequences of the sixteenth century are still with us and continue to affect relations between the churches—and indeed every aspect of modern life and thought wherever Christians live and work.[39] We can only touch on a few of the many aspects of the period since the sixteenth century.

Second-generation reformers and counter-reformers took their differences to the New World. European Christians migrated as no earlier people ever had, and as they did, they colonized and indoctrinated their converts with the biases and theological prejudices of earlier centuries.[40]

The seventeenth century saw the birth of the modern secular culture. In this theater of operations—in which the state owed allegiance to no church—Protestants and Catholics needed to learn how to coexist and to learn tolerance and respect for pluralism in theological tastes, personal devotional preferences, and ascetic disciplines. In the emerging modern state, as today, economic, military, and nationalist self-interest—not religious doctrines—dictated national policy. In response to the war-making tendency of the state, "pacifist churches" gave witness to the radical ethic of Jesus: the Society of Friends (Quakers), Moravians, Church of the Brethren, and the Mennonites. Catholics, as a church, were not identified with peace movements.

The new sciences forced both Protestants and Catholics to recognize the limits of the authority of scripture. Copernicus and his descendants made it clear that the scriptures might have authority to speak about what is necessary for salvation, but scripture cannot offer authoritative explanations for the phenomenal world. After Galileo Galilei (1564–1642), Rome made easier accommodations with the natural sciences, seeing them, as did mainline Protestants, as discovering and explaining—not inventing—the wonders of creation.

The eighteenth century, firmly under the influence of the Enlightenment, saw the development of new social and cultural movements. Clearly, Protestantism (much more than Roman Catholicism, with its hierarchical and clerical structure) gave impetus to democracy and capitalism. In America, for example, the ideas found in the Declaration of Independence and the Constitution were commonplace in Protestant pulpits long before the Revolutionary War. The notion of respect for conscience was soon protected by law.

The eighteenth century saw greater and greater numbers of Christians, but they were also more divided. Roman Catholicism, with its emphasis on centralized authority, tended to avoid fragmentation. Protestantism was exactly the opposite. Protestant denominations proliferated because, for one thing, there was no single conforming norm or insti-

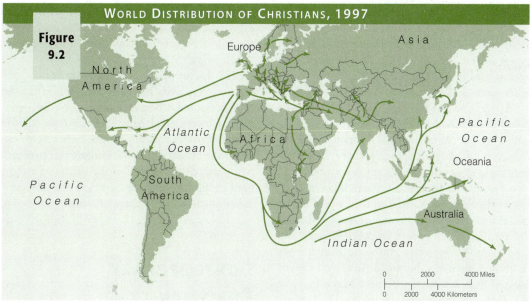

WORLD DISTRIBUTION OF CHRISTIANS, 1997

Figure 9.2

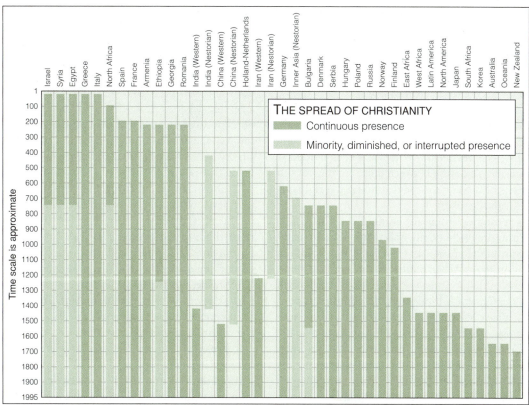

THE SPREAD OF CHRISTIANITY

Continuous presence

Minority, diminished, or interrupted presence

Sources: Adapted from Ward J. Fellows, *Religions East and West* (San Diego: Harcourt, Brace, 1998). Partially adapted from Johathan Z. Smith, *Dictionary of Religion* (San Francisco: HarperCollins, 1995) © by The American Academy of Religion, p. 508.

tution that bound believers together. Illustrative of this diversity was the **Great Awakening** of the 1730s and 1740s. This period was marked by religious fervor. Preachers stirred audiences with accounts of human sinfulness and the need for redemption and conversion. John Wesley (1703–1791) and Charles Wesley (1707–1788) began a popular, pietistic movement called Methodism, which became the largest single Christian denomination in the English-speaking world. Its adherents came from other Protestant denominations.

The nineteenth century was marked by reaction to the French Revolution and the rise of industrialization. These forces fomented social and political turmoil, which in turn provoked "liberal" and "conservative" responses. Revolutions took place in France, Germany, Italy, and Austria-Hungary. Liberal Protestants (the Broad Church Party of Anglicanism, for example) and the Modernists in Roman Catholicism gave support to the ideals of respect for individual freedom and the power of reason over the authority of tradition. These liberal movements, of course, provoked conservative reactions. Perhaps these are best illustrated by Pope Pius IX's (1846–1878) *Syllabus of Errors* (1864), which condemned the Modernists' ideas, and the First Vatican Council (1869–1870), which reaffirmed the controversial doctrine of papal infallibility. The nineteenth century has been described as the battleground between those arguing for the rights of God and those defending the rights of individual persons.[41]

Another important event of the nineteenth century must be noted, and that is the intensification of the missionary movement. From the very beginning of Christianity, spreading the "good news" of Jesus Christ was regarded as a basic task of the Church. Throughout the centuries, Christians have left their home countries to teach others about Jesus. The nineteenth century is noteworthy for the extent of this effort. It has been estimated that Catholicism increased its numbers by 8 million in this era. The Reformation churches were active as well. One Protestant theologian spoke of the nineteenth century as the Great Century" because of its range of missionary activity. No

corner of the earth has been excluded from the efforts of those seeking to take the gospel into the world. Figure 9.2 shows the world dispersion of Christianity today.

In the twentieth century, we may note, this missionary activity has been regarded by many—Christians and others—as not necessarily a good thing. Citing the link between Christianity and the colonial powers of Europe, these critics have evaluated the efforts of the missionaries as "paternalistic" and "disrespectful" of the beliefs of indigenous peoples. Indeed, the twentieth century was to usher in considerable changes of its own.

CONTEMPORARY CHRISTIANITY

Religions are organic. They are not cast in concrete but are written on the human heart and imagination. Religions are alive. Just as all living things develop or perish, so too do religions. There is considerable debate over whether religions change or not, but no one argues that they are forever in the same shape or relation to the world. Our earlier survey of the history of Christianity has clearly made that point.

Christianity is a thriving and vibrant religion as it heads toward the twenty-first century. It has not merely survived its passage through time; it has flourished. In the United States alone there are more than 900 Christian churches, sects, cults, societies, or missions. (In 1800, there were only 201.) Worldwide, there are more Christians than members of any other single religion. And Christianity is found on every continent. Table 9.2 identifies the major divisions of Christianity.

Because it is in the mainstream of life, Christianity is influenced and modified by the global and cultural settings in which it is found. It does not exist in a vacuum, nor is its theology unaffected by the times in which it lives. This section identifies some of the controversies that enliven the religion

A Bantu Christian is baptized in Johannesburg, South Africa (ca. 1950).

and some of the challenges to it. Three of the important events on the twentieth-century Christian landscape are (1) Fundamentalism, (2) the important changes in Catholicism brought about by Vatican Council II, and (3) the encounter of Christianity with other religions.

THE RISE OF FUNDAMENTALISM

In 1910, a group of Protestant Christians who were unhappy with biblical criticism and the conclusions it was drawing wrote a pamphlet entitled *The Fundamentals.* Those who ascribed to the doctrines set forth in its contents, who were members of many different sects and denominations, were known as **Fundamentalists.** These Christians believed that they were defending the *Bible* against the attacks of the godless. Fundamentalists emphasized strict obedience to, and belief in, the absolute answers for all of life's questions found in the *Bible.* For them, the *Bible* was inerrant (without error). The *Bible* was dictated, they believed, word for word by God to a human, who was, in their view, only a secretary. Christian belief, they maintained, was not based on science and did not require science to validate or support it.

Although the Fundamentalists have been around since the turn of the century, their numbers have grown dramatically since the 1950s. Today, more than 60 million persons identify themselves as belonging to or holding to a Fundamentalist Christian church or worldview. It is important to note that **Fundamentalism** is not a specific branch of Christianity but rather a way of viewing the sources of beliefs, moral code, and expectations of life within a faith in Jesus Christ. Christian Fundamentalists are more visible in the Protestant churches.

VATICAN COUNCIL II AND THE REVITALIZATION OF PUBLIC WORSHIP

Pope John XXIII (1958–1963) convoked a council of Catholic bishops to meet at the Vatican in 1959. This was the second time a council had been held at the Vatican; hence these famous proceedings were dubbed Vatican Council II. The pope's purpose was to renew the religious life of Catholics; he brought up to date the Church's teaching, discipline, religious practices, organizations, and most important, its relationships with non-Catholic Christians and people of other religions.

Table
9.2

MAJOR DIVISIONS OF CHRISTIANITY

	Roman Catholic	Eastern Orthodox	Protestant[a]
Beginnings	Traces its origins to Jesus and the apostles	Traces its origins to Jesus and the apostles; officially broke with Rome in 1054	Gradual development since 1517
Distribution	Found universally	Found universally, but mostly in Eastern Europe	Found universally
Leadership	Hierarchical; pope is the spiritual and organizational head of the church; bishops and priests are "set part" by ordination to serve the "People of God"	Hierarchical; patriarch of Constantinople holds honorary primacy over eleven national churches; the national churches are independent in internal administration; bishops and priests are "set apart" by ordination	Has no one head or spokesperson; each denomination elects its own leaders or body of leaders; varying degrees of commitment to theology of ordination; most democratic in structure of the three divisions
Teaching Authority	Vested in the papacy and the authority of ecumenical councils	Highest outward authority vested in the dogmatic definitions of the seven ecumenical councils (none recognized as such after 787); Roman pontiff recognized as "first among equals"	Based on historic formulations of faith (creeds or confessions)
Sacraments	Accepts seven	Accepts seven	Depending on the denomination, accepts one (Quakers), two (most), or seven (Episcopalians)
Role of Mary	Regarded as Mother of Christ, preeminent among the saints; honored, not adored; immaculate conception (conceived without original sin), virgin birth, and assumption into heaven accepted as dogmas; church encourages devotions and prayer to Mary as "intercessor" and "advocate"	Regarded as the Theotokos (the God-bearer); venerated by iconography; church accepts perpetual virginity and assumption but not immaculate conception; devotions and prayer to Mary as "intercessor" are encouraged	Reformers stressed the humility of Mary, respected her as mother of Jesus, but attacked any glorification of her or special role assigned to her in salvation; virtually no devotion to Mary in any Protestant denomination

	Roman Catholic	Eastern Orthodox	Protestant[a]
Table 9.2 CONTINUED			
Membership, worldwide	1,040 billion, or over 59% of all Christians	223 million, or 11% of all Christians	702 million, or 36% of all Christians
Membership, United States	60 million, or 23% of the U.S. population	6 million, or about 2.4% of the U.S. population	123 million, or 45% of the U.S. population

a. *Protestant* is used here as a label for very diverse groups (around 22,000 independent, living denominations or movements), including the Reformation churches (e.g., Anglican-Episcopal, Congregational, Lutheran, Reformed, Presbyterian, Mennonite, Quaker, Baptist, Amish, and Hutterite) and post-Reformation churches (e.g., Methodist, Moravian, Disciples of Christ, African Methodist, and Seventh-day Adventist; Pentecostal churches, such as the Assemblies of God, Church of God, Church of God in Christ, and Women's Aglow Fellowship; and Evangelical-Fundamentalist churches, such as Churches of Christ, Calvary Chapel, and Promise Keepers). The label includes indigenous churches in Africa and Asia, as well as churches that depart from classical Christian doctrine (e.g., Unitarian-Universalist, Mormonism, Christian Science, Jehovah's Witnesses, Unity, and Religious Science). The categories Roman Catholic, Eastern Orthodox, and Protestant do not include 105 million Christians who are unaffiliated with a church.

From 1962 to 1965, bishops from all the countries of the world deliberated on such issues as the role of the pope in relation to the bishops, affirming an ancient understanding that the pope works in collegiality (fraternity) with the bishops—not like a prince "ruling over" them. The bishops revitalized the public worship of Catholics and mandated that the mass be celebrated in the native languages of the people, not just in Latin. In two major documents, "The Pastoral Constitution of the Church in the Modern World" and the "Dogmatic Constitution of the Church," the bishops redefined the Church as the "People of God" and a "Pilgrim People" who were called by God to join all persons of goodwill to make the kingdom of God on earth. In a key document on religious freedom, they declared that God speaks most profoundly to the conscience of humans and that in matters religious, each person must be free to come to God as he or she feels called. If we recall the assumptions of the Inquisition, it is easier to gain a perspective on the momentous nature of this pronouncement for Catholics.

More than any specific document it produced, Vatican II expressed to the world the sincere desire of the Catholic Church to enter into a new relationship with it and, especially, with people of other religions. When John died, Paul VI (1963–1978) continued the work and direction of the council. Without a doubt, this council expressed many of the theological currents that had been alive within Roman Catholicism for years but that had never before been articulated at the level of "official teaching."[42]

COMPETING WORLDVIEWS

Perhaps the most encompassing controversy within all religions, and certainly within Christianity, is the tension that exists between competing worldviews (philosophies that enable people to understand where they are in the scheme of things and that help people make meaning out of life). These basic assumptions about the world are often transferred to religion. Within Christianity are two camps: those who hold a classical worldview and those who hold a historical-critical one. These worldviews often get simplistically reduced to labels such as *conservative* and *liberal*, but they bespeak something more profound. Each worldview is, in effect, a set of assumptions about the world and how it ought to be.

The classical theologians within Christianity hold that Christianity is the embodiment of absolute truth, that it must teach today what it taught in the past, that the *Bible* is inerrant in all things, that morality can be taught by the deductive application of universal rules to specific cases, that obedience to authority is the primary virtue of the faithful, and that neither time nor human experience changes religious truth.

Those who hold the historical-critical worldview disagree. They assert that we live bounded by time and that our perception and grasp of truth are always conditioned by our epistemologies (ways of knowing). Truth may be objective and absolute, but we never know it purely. We always interpret it, and hence color it. As the human race learns more about life, it must incorporate the new data into its understanding of itself and the world and into the struggles of real people. Hence, moral norms are conditioned, and human experience is valued at least as much as traditional teaching. The primary virtue of the faithful is obedience not to authority but to the truth.

ISSUES OF GENDER AND SEXUAL MINORITIES

From this basic disagreement, other issues arise. What is the role of women in the Christian religion? What is the basic understanding of womanhood? Is it as the traditional "helpmate," or is it as a more contemporary "equal in all things"? Some denominations (for example, Episcopalian, Presbyterian, Methodist, and Moravian) ordain women and afford them opportunities for visible leadership roles. The Catholics, the Greek Orthodox, and many Protestant denominations do not ordain women and, while claiming to respect the dignity of women, do not permit them access to the ranks of those who have real power in the Church. This crisis has not been happily solved.

What is the Church's position on sexual minorities? This issue reflects the kinds of disagreements that exist over the role of traditional teaching versus new information from the sciences,

over the method and meaning of scripture, and over the role Christians are called to play in fighting prejudice. A few mainline churches do ordain gay and lesbian clergy—even publicly acknowledged ones—but only if they promise not to advocate their sexual preference. Many Christians are prominent in the forefront of opposition to any civil legislation that would give the appearance of accepting gay and lesbian lifestyles. Many gay men and lesbians have left the Christian churches because they feel that they are not welcomed for who they are.

THE RELATIONSHIP OF THE CHURCH TO THE POOR AND OPPRESSED

Should the Church actively participate in the changing of oppressive political and social structures that keep people poor and assault their rights and dignity as person? Or should the Church be more concerned with the spiritual welfare of people, leaving to Caesar things that are Caesar's? "Liberation theology" is a movement begun in the early 1960s among thinkers within Roman Catholicism and many black churches that wishes to interpret social, political, and economic structures in light of radical prophetic and gospel demands to extend justice to all, especially the poor and disenfranchised.[43]

WHAT IS PERMISSIBLE DISSENT?

On both doctrinal and moral issues, every church is faced with disagreement from within. Because of biomedical technology, issues have arisen that have left the churches without time-honored positions to help the faithful deal with them: organ transplants, reproductive technologies, and genetic engineering are a few. What of those who differ with the churches on specific questions, such as birth control, the divinity of Christ, abortion, or the infallibility of the pope? To date, religious authority in Roman Catholicism has been more active in restricting dissent than in Protestantism, yet in many local Protestant churches great pains are taken to insure doctrinal purity—even if that forces dissenters to leave and found another gathering.

In the concluding verse of *Matthew* (28:20), Jesus tells his apostles to observe all *"that I have commanded you; and lo, I am with you always, to the close of the age."* For two thousand years the Christian Church has understood itself to be the body of Christ on earth charged with the authority to preach, teach, and remind the human race that God is very much alive and in its midst. Christians of all denominations, despite their many profound differences, are united in the belief that the Jesus they proclaim is the Lord of history, the Son of God, the Promised One, whose life is of infinite value and whose message of mercy and forgiveness of sins is a reason for hope and gratitude, a gratitude that should impel them to love the world the way he did and does.

GLOSSARY OF CHRISTIANITY

agape	the common religious meal in use in the early Church and in close relationship to the eucharistic meals; also, the Greek term for "love," used in the *New Testament* to mean "unconditional love."
anthrocentricity	a view of the universe that puts humans and their experiences as the most important concerns.
anti-Semitism	hostility or discrimination against Jews.
apostle	from a Greek word meaning "to send forth." In the *New Testament* it designates one of the twelve men who were called by Jesus into his inner circle of confidants and disciples. It also means one who is an ambassador, delegate, or messenger; someone who announces, proclaims, or spreads the "good news" of Jesus' teaching.
Apostolic See	a term referring to the office of the papacy or the official title of any individual pope.
Arian controversy	a theological disagreement among Christians of the fourth century C.E. over the question of the nature of Jesus. Followers of Arius (ca. 250–336) claimed that Jesus was entirely human, and hence not divine. This view was rejected by the Christian Church at the Council of Nicaea in 325.
asceticism	practices of self-mortification and self-denial utilized by many adherents of Christianity over the centuries as a way to establish control over desires arising from human appetites.
blasphemy	speech, thought, or action that expresses contempt for God or the sacred.

concupiscence	according to Ausgustine of Hippo, the inherent flaw in human nature due to original sin. Because of it, human willpower is corrupted and easily tempted by stimulation of the senses. Concupiscence is also defined as the inordinate desire for temporal things.
Docetism	the early heresy that denied the humanity of Christ in favor of the view that Jesus was fully God only appearing to be in a human form.
ecumenical council	a gathering or meeting of bishops from around the world to decide on matters of religious doctrine or practice.
episcopacy	a form of church government in which authority resides with those who are in a hierarchy of leaders.
Eucharist	literally, "thanksgiving by remembering"; a specific ritual, the central act of worship in the Roman, Greek Orthodox, and some Protestant churches in which it is believed that Jesus is made present in a unique way; also known as the mass or Holy Communion. During the Roman Catholic and Orthodox Catholic Eucharist, a consecration takes place: the act of faith transforms bread and wine into the body and blood of Christ.
form criticism	the tool of biblical scholarship that attempts to discover the origin and history of particular passages of the *Bible*. Examples of *New Testament* forms are parables, sayings about the law, and legends.
Fundamentalism, Fundamentalist	
	a belief system and way of understanding the Christian faith and life that puts particular emphasis on the words of the *Bible* and its place in directing one's passage through life. A Fundamentalist is an adherent of this belief system or someone who rejects any of the tools of biblical criticism or interpretation, such as form or source criticism.
Gospel	a book of the *New Testament*, Literally, the word *gospel* means "good news" and refers to the Christian beliefs that God sent a savior and that redemption is available for all.
grace	in Christian theology, the supernatural assistance of God given to humans in order to make them sanctified; the self-communication of God to an individual that enables a person to realize sanctity.
Great Awakening	the time in U.S. history when a religious fervor swept the land. Revivals and revivalists stirred the audiences with vivid accounts of human sinfulness and the need for redemption. Many claimed that they had conversion experiences at these meetings and that their lives were forever changed.
heresy	the denial of a defined doctrine of faith.

historical-critical school
> a way of interpreting scripture by using the tools of scientific study of history with an eye for historically verifiable information.

humanism
> basically, the love and respect of all things human and made by humans; valuing the human more than the mechanical. Traditionally *humanism* refers to the intense interest in things human demonstrated by the Greeks and Renaissance thinkers.

indulgence
> the remission by the Church of the temporal punishment spent in Purgatory due to sin.

inerrancy
> the belief that the *Bible* is of God and cannot be in error, because God, through the inspiration of the biblical authors by the Holy Spirit, is the author.

monasticism
> a form of Christian living in which individuals separate themselves from an ordinary lifestyle in the world in order to concentrate on spiritual matters. Monasticism took many different forms over the centuries, from individuals living as hermits, to individuals living within a community of hermits, to individuals living a community life structured around work and prayer.

Monophysitism
> the belief that in Christ there is a single, divine nature.

New Testament
> a term referring to the books exclusive to the Christian scriptures in contradistinction to the *Old Testament* or Jewish scriptures. The *New Testament* includes twenty-seven books—four gospels, one history, twenty-one letters, and one piece of apocalyptic literature.

Nicene Creed
> formulated at the Council of Nicaea in 325, a statement of faith that enumerates specific Christian beliefs about the nature of God and the Church.

original sin
> in Christian theology, the state of sin in which humans have been held captive since the Fall. Some theologians describe it as the loss of sanctifying grace. The scriptural foundation of the doctrine is a verse from *Paul*: *"through one man [Adam] sin entered the world,"* so that *"by the trespass of the one the many died."*

parable
> a short tale told by Jesus to set forth aspects of his teaching about what God is like (for example, the parable of the Prodigal Son), the nature of the kingdom of God (for example, the parable of the Mustard Seed), or morality (for example, the parable of the Last Judgment). Using parables was a distinctive feature of Jesus' teaching; scholars agree there are between thirty and forty in the *New Testament*.

Pentecost
> literally "fiftieth day"; a Jewish harvest feast adapted by Christians to commemorate the day the Holy Spirit is believed to have descended upon the apostles to embolden them to proclaim their faith in public.

Pontius Pilate	the governor of Judea fom 25 to 35 C.E., under whom Jesus was executed.
pope	the title for the bishop of Rome. In Roman Catholicism, the pope is the supreme authority of the Church and its spiritual leader.
Purgatory	according to Roman Catholic teaching, the place or state of punishment for those who have died not totally free of sin. The souls in Purgatory are believed to eventually gain heaven and its joys. It is a temporary station. Protestants do not accept the belief in Purgatory, but the Eastern Orthodox churches do.
redaction criticism	the most recent tool of biblical scholarship, which examines the theological ideas of the editors (reactors) of the *Gospels* as we have them today.
sacraments	ritual ceremonies or sacred actions in which the faithful meet Christ, share his life, and are made holy. Christians differ on the number of sacraments. Some theologians describe the sacraments as celebrations of key human experiences from life to death.
Sanhedrin	literally, the "group of seventy-one." The Sanhedrin was the supreme Jewish authority in Jerusalem that was dominated by the priestly aristocracy but that also included scribes and Pharisees. The *New Testament* records that this body condemned Jesus for blasphemy before turning him over to Roman authorities for execution.
source criticism	the study of the materials or sources for the *Bible* in its present form; for example, identifying Paul's passage on love in *1 Corinthians* 13 as a song used in early Christian liturgy.
synoptic *Gospel*	the *Gospels* of *Matthew, Mark,* and *Luke.* Present theory holds that *Mark* was written first and used as the framework for both *Matthew* and *Luke,* hence the correspondences in the texts.
theocentricity	the view that God and the things of God are at the center of the universe and that all other things are oriented toward the holy.
theodicy	literally "the justification of God"; the attempt by some theologians to defend God's omnipotence and goodness in the face of the evil and suffering in the world.
Trinity	the Christian doctrine that expresses the belief that the one God exists in three persons and one substance; that is, that God— dynamic, united, and whole—is also, at the same time, a community.

FOR FURTHER STUDY

Several excellent modern translations of the *Bible* are available:

Good News Bible. New York: American Bible Society, 1976.

Jerusalem Bible. Garden City, N.Y.: Doubleday, 1966.

King James Bible. New York: American Bible Society, 1952.

New English Bible with Apocrypha. New York: Oxford University Press, 1970.

The New Testament in Modern English. Translated by J. B. Phillips. New York: Macmillan, 1970.

Chadwick, Henry. *The Early Church.* New York: Penguin, 1967.
   A clear and concise compendium of information on the first three centuries of Christianity.

Cross, F. L., ed. *The Oxford Dictionary of the Christian Church.* 2d ed. New York: Oxford University Press, 1978.
   A desk reference book containing articles on every notable name or term associated with the Christian religion.

Fiorenza, Elisabeth. *Invitation to the Book of Revelation.* Garden City, N.Y.: Doubleday, 1981.
   A helpful guide into the complex theology and imagery of the last book of the Bible.

Jeremias, Joachim. *Jerusalem in the Time of Jesus.* Philadelphia: Fortress, 1975.
   A very readable treatment of the culture, politics, economics, geography, demographics, and religious customs during the time of Jesus.

Kelly, J. N. D. *Early Christian Doctrines.* New York: Harper & Row, 1978.
   A collection of every major piece of theology written during the first five centuries, along with commentary.

Marty, Martin. *Protestantism.* New York: Holt, Rinehart & Winston, 1972.
   A summary of the major features of the major Protestant denominations.

McBrien, Richard. *Catholicism.* Oak Grove, Minn.: Winston Press, 1972.
   An exhaustive introduction to every aspect of the Catholic religion, which was originally written for college students.

Perkins, Pheme. *Love Commands in the New Testament.* New York: Paulist Press, 1982.
   A leading biblical scholar's study of the question of ethics in the New Testament through the examination of Jesus' directives to his disciples.

Ware, Timothy. *The Orthodox Church.* New York: Penguin, 1964.
   Essential reading for those wishing a nontechnical background on the history and distinct features of the Eastern churches.

Weaver, Mary Jo. *An Introduction to Christianity.* Belmont, Calif.: Wadsworth, 1991.
   A readable and accessible overview of the Christian faith.

READINGS

Reading 9.1   THE OLDEST NON-CHRISTIAN ACCOUNT OF JESUS:

TESTIMONIUM FLAVIANUM   Flavius Josephus

Flavius Josephus, the first-century Jewish historian, is the first non-Christian source to attest to the historical existence of Jesus, in his *Jewish Antiquities*. In a now-renowned passage in Chapter 18, the text (ca. 94 C.E.) makes a reference to Jesus. Scholars believe that the original passage was edited by a later Christian. What about the passage is curious? What grounds would there be to support a claim that the text was "doctored" at some point?

> Now, there was about this time Jesus, a wise man, if it be lawful to call him a man, for he was a doer of wonderful works—a teacher of such men as receive the truth with pleasure. He drew over to him both many of the Jews, and many of the Gentiles. He was [the] Christ; and when Pilate, at the suggestion of the principal men amongst us, had condemned him to the cross, those that loved him at the first did not forsake him, for he appeared to them alive again the third day, as the divine prophets had foretold these and ten thousand other wonderful things concerning him; and the tribe of Christians, so named from him, are not extinct at this day.

> **Source:** S. Zeitlin, *Josephus on Jesus* (Philadelphia: John Knox Press, 1931).

Reading 9.2   THE ACCOUNT OF THE EMPTY TOMB:

MATTHEW, MARK, AND LUKE

In 1776, J. J. Griesbach published the *Gospels* of *Matthew, Mark*, and *Luke* in a three-column format. This was a way to study the interdependence of the first three *Gospels*. This method became known as the synoptic method (from the Greek word *synopsis*, which means "a seeing together"). The fact that the texts differed significantly in several important details gave rise to what biblical scholars called the "synoptic problem." What are the major differences in the texts? How do you account for them?

MATTHEW 28:1–8	*MARK* 16:1–8	*LUKE* 24:1–19
¹Now after the sabbath, toward the dawn of the first day of the week, Mary Magdalene and the other Mary went to the sepulcher.	*¹And when the sabbath was past, Mary Magdalene, and Mary the mother of James, and Salome, bought spices, so that they might go and anoint him. ²And very early on the first day of the week they went to the tomb when the sun had risen.*	*¹But on the first day of the week, at early dawn, they went to the tomb, taking the spices which they had prepared.*

MATTHEW 28:1–8	MARK 16:1–8	LUKE 24:1–19

2And behold, there was a great earthquake; for an angel of the Lord descended from heaven and came and rolled back the stone, and sat upon it. 3His appearance was like lightening, and his raiment white as snow. 4And for fear of him the guards trembled and became like dead men.

3And they were saying to one another, "Who will roll away the stone for us from the door of the tomb?" 4And looking up, they saw that the stone was rolled back; for it was very large. 5And entering the tomb,

2 And they found the stone rolled away from the tomb, 3 but when they went in they did not find the body. 4While they were perplexed about this, behold, two men stood by them in dazzling apparel; 5and as they were frightened and bowed their faces to the ground, the men said to them, "Why do you seek the living among the dead?

they saw a young man sitting on the right side, dressed in a white robe; and they were amazed. 6And he said to them, "Do not be amazed; you seek Jesus of Nazareth, who was crucified. He has risen, he is not here; see the place where they laid him. 7But go, tell his disciples and Peter that he is going

5But the angel said to the women, "Do not be afraid; for I know that you seek Jesus who was crucified. 6He is not here; for he has risen, as he said. Come, see the place where he lay. 7Then go quickly and tell his disciples that he has risen from the dead, and behold, he is going before you to Galilee; there you will see him. Lo, I have told you."

6remember how he told you while he was still in Galilee, 7that the Son of man must be delivered into the hands of sinful men, and be crucified, and on the third day rise." 8And they remembered his words, 9and returning from the tomb they told all this to the eleven and to all the rest.

8So they departed quickly from the tomb with fear and great joy, and ran to tell his disciples.

before you to Galilee; there you will see him, as he told you." 8And they went out and fled from the tomb, and they said nothing to anyone, for they were afraid.

Source: *King James Bible,* rev. ed. (New York: American Bible Society, 1952).

Reading 9.3   AN EARLY PRAYER: FROM THE *DIDACHE*

As best as can be determined, the *Didache* was a Christian manual on morals and Church practices probably written sometime in the first century C.E.. Quite possibly, this prayer was said at a community *agape,* or eucharistic meal just before communion. Its author is unknown. Notice the different titles by which God is addressed, the theme of gratitude, and the refrain that ends each stanza. What do you think of the criteria used for admission to receive Holy Communion? Do they seem to imply exclusivity? Have you ever been invited to take part in a communion service at a church other than your own?

[Instruction to the community]: Let no one eat and drink of your Eucharist but those baptized in the name of the Lord; to this, too, the saying of the Lord is applicable: Do not give to dogs what is sacred. After you have taken your fill of food, give thanks as follows:

We give thee thanks, O Holy Father, for thy holy name which thou hast enshrined in our hearts, and for the knowledge and faith and immortality which thou hast made known to us through Jesus, the Servant. To thee be the glory for evermore.

Thou, Lord Almighty, hast created all things for the sake of thy name and hast given food and drink for men to enjoy, that they may give thanks to thee; but to us thou hast vouchsafed spiritual food and drink and eternal life through Jesus, thy Servant. Above all, we give thee thanks because thou art mighty. To thee be the glory for evermore.

Remember, O Lord, the Church: deliver her from all evil, perfect her in thy love, and from the winds assemble her, the sanctified, in thy kingdom which thou hast prepared for her. For thine is the power and the glory for evermore.

May grace come to thee, and this world pass away! Hosanna to the God of David!

If anyone is holy, let him advance; if anyone is not, let him be converted. Maranatha [Aramaic word for either "The Lord has come" or "Come, O Lord"].

Amen

Source: R. H. Connolly, "The Didache in Relation to the Epistle of Barnabas," *Journal of Theological Studies* 33 (1932): 237–253.

Reading 9.4   THE NICENE CREED

In 325 C.E., three hundred bishops met at the Council of Nicaea to settle the theological controversy raised by Arius concerning the nature of Jesus. The Arians had claimed that Jesus was a good man but was in no way divine. The bishops rejected that claim and, using a baptismal creed from the Palestine church as a beginning point, crafted this document, the earliest official universal statement of the Christian Church on the nature of God, and particularly the nature of Jesus. Notice that the creed is not an explanation but a proclamation of beliefs. Do you see the "divisions" in the creed as in any way assigning "tasks" to the Father, Son, and Holy Spirit? If so, what are those things assigned to them?

We believe in one God, the Father Almighty, maker of heaven and earth, and of all things visible and invisible. And in one Lord Jesus Christ, the only begotten Son of God, begotten from his Father before all ages, Light from Light, true God from true God, begotten not made, of one substance with the Father, through whom all things were made. Who for us men and our salvation, came down from heaven, and was made flesh from the Holy Spirit and the Virgin Mary, and was made man, and was crucified for us under Pontius Pilate. He suffered and was buried, and the third day he rose again according to the scriptures and ascended into heaven, and sits on the right hand of God the Father. And he shall come again in glory to judge both the living and the dead; his kingdom shall have no end. And in the Holy Spirit, the Lord and Giver of life, who proceeds from the Father, who with the . Father and the Son together is worshipped and glorified, who spoke by the prophets. And in one, holy, catholic, and apostolic church. We confess one baptism for the remission of sins; we look for the resurrection of the dead and the life of the world to come. Amen.

Reading 9.5   LIVING IN TWO CITIES: *THE CITY OF GOD*
Augustine of Hippo

Augustine of Hippo (354–430 C.E.) is regarded as one of Christianity's greatest theologians. His thinking has left its mark on almost every Christian doctrine. He lived during the time known as the Fall of the Roman Empire (410), and he wrote *The City of God* from 413 to 426 to explain the temporal reversals that befell the Christian Church, which was so identified with the empire since the Edict of Milan (313). The "city" is the Church, Christ's kingdom on earth, living amid the secular world, the earthly city of men. Notice how Augustine begins with a stark contrast of the two "cities" and then moves on to a defense of the Christian Church against those who took sanctuary in its holy places to avoid being slaughtered by the barbarians and who now blame it for the fall of the empire. He claims that the blessings and evils of life come to the good and evil alike, but that those with faith in Jesus Christ will endure and triumph. The following excerpt is the Preface and Chapter One of Book 1.

What evils of Augustine's day are still found in our day? What is the major difference in church-state relationships in the United States versus the ancient Roman Empire?

> The glorious City of God is my theme in this work which you, my dearest son [really Augustine's friend] Marcellinus, suggested, and which is due to you by my promise. I have undertaken its defense against those who prefer their own gods to the Founder of this city [God], a city surpassingly glorious, whether we view it as it still lives by faith in this fleeting course of time, and sojourns as a stranger in the midst of the ungodly, or as it shall dwell in the fixed stability of its eternal seat, which it now with patience waits for, expecting until "righteousness shall return unto judgment," and it obtain, by virtue of its excellence, final victory and perfect peace. A great work this, and an arduous one; but God is my helper.
>
> I am aware what ability is requisite to persuade the proud how great is the virtue of humility, which raises us, not by a quite human arrogance, but by a divine grace,

above all earthly dignities that totter on this shifting scene. For the King and Founder of this city of which we speak, has in scripture uttered to His people a dictum of the divine law in these words: "God resists the proud, but gives grace unto the humble." But this, which is God's prerogative, the inflated ambition of a proud spirit also affects, and dearly loves this be numbered among its attributes to "show pity to the humbled soul, and crush the sons of pride." And therefore, as the plan of this work we have undertaken requires, and as the occasion offers, we must speak also of the earthly city, which though it be mistress of the nations, is itself ruled by its lust of rule.

For to this earthly city belong the enemies against whom I have to defend the city of God. Many of them, indeed, being reclaimed from their ungodly error, have become sufficiently credible citizens of this city [the Church]; but many are so inflamed with hatred against it, and are so ungrateful to its Redeemer for His signal benefits, as to forget that they would now be unable to utter a single word to its prejudice had they not found its sacred places as they fled from the enemy's steel, that life in which they now boast themselves.

Are not those very Romans, who were spared by the barbarians through their respect for Christ, become enemies to the name of Christ? The reliquaries [burial places] of the martyrs and the churches of the apostles bear witness to this; for in the sack of the city they were open sanctuary for all who fled to them, whether Christian or pagan. To their very threshold the blood-thirsty enemy raged; there his murderous fury owned a limit. To that place did such of the enemy as had pity convey those to whom they had given quarter [mercy] lest any less mercifully disposed might fall upon them. And, indeed, when even those murderers who everywhere else showed themselves pitiless came to those spots where that was forbidden which the license of war permitted in every other place, their furious rage for slaughter was bridled, and their eagerness to take prisoners was quenched.

Thus escaped multitudes who now reproach the Christian religion, and impute to Christ the ills that have befallen their city; but the preservation of their own life—a boon which they owe to the respect entertained for Christ by the barbarians—they attribute not to our Christ, but to their own good luck. They ought rather, had they any right perceptions, to attribute the severities and hardships inflicted by their enemies, to that divine providence which is wont to reform the depraved manners of men by chastisement, and which exercises with similar afflictions the righteous and praiseworthy, either translating them when they have passed through the trial to a better world, or detaining them still on earth for ulterior purposes.

And they ought to attribute it to the spirit of these Christian times, that, contrary to the custom of war, these blood-thirsty barbarians spared them, and spared them for Christ's sake, whether this mercy was actually shown in [disordered] places, or in those places specially dedicated to Christ's name, and of which the very largest were selected as sanctuaries, that full scope might thus be given to the expansive compassion which desired that a large multitude might find shelter there.

Therefore ought they to give God thanks, and with sincere confession, flee for refuge to His name, that so they may escape the punishment of eternal fire—they who with lying lips took upon them this name that they might escape the punishment of present destruction. For of those whom you see insolently and shamelessly insulting the servants of Christ, there are numbers who would not have escaped that destruction and slaughter had they not pretended that they themselves were Christ's servants. Yet now, in ungrateful pride and most impious madness, and at the risk of being punished in everlasting darkness, they perversely oppose that name under which they fraudulently protected themselves for the sake of enjoying the light of this brief life.

Reading 9.6 LIVING THE MONASTIC LIFE: EXCERPTS FROM *RULE*
Benedict of Nursia

From the third century of Christianity onward, many Christians have felt called to leave the everyday world, with all its distractions from the spiritual life, and create an alternative environment in which they can concentrate more fully on the things of God. This impulse gave rise to what became known as the monastic movement, communities established to foster and develop a concentrated attention on prayer and spiritual activity and to serve as a place where care-weary visitors from the world could come to be refreshed. After the Protestant Reformation, beginning in 1517, the monastic alternative was preserved primarily by Roman and Orthodox Catholics only, and many in these religions to this day live the monastic life. The structure, or blueprint, for the organization of the monastic life was established by Benedict of Nursia (480–545). In his *Rule,* or comprehensive directives for the spiritual and administrative life of a monastery, Benedict drew on the work of previous monastic figures, such as Basil, John Cassian, Antony of Egypt, and Augustine of Hippo. As close as we can determine, the *Rule* was written about 540 for Benedict's monastery in Monte Cassino, Italy. What kinds of responsibilities does Benedict place on the abbot? What are his suggestions for effective leadership?

CHAPTER TWO: THE QUALITIES OF THE ABBOT

To be qualified to govern a monastery an abbot should always remember what he is called [*Abba* = Father] and carry out his high calling in his everyday life. In a monastery he is Christ's representative, called by His name: "You have received the spirit of the adoption of sons, whereby we cry, Abba, Father" [*Rom.* 8:15]. The abbot should not command, teach, or demand anything contrary to the way of the Lord. But his orders and teaching ought to be tempered by Divine justice.

The abbot should always remember that he will be held accountable on Judgement Day for his teaching and the obedience of his charges. The abbot must be led to understand that any lack of good in his monks will be held as his fault.

However, he shall be held innocent in the Lord's judgement if he has done all within his power to overcome the corruptness and disobedience of his monks. Through his diligence and care he may say with the prophet; "I have not hidden your righteousness in my heart; I have declared Your truth and Your salvation; but they have despised me and turned away" [*Ps.* 40:10]. In the end death shall be given as a just punishment to those who have not responded to his care.

When a man is made abbot he should rule his monks by two principles: first, he should show them by deeds, more than by words, what is good and holy. To those who understand, he may expound verbally the Lord's directions: but to the stubborn and dull, he must exhibit the Divine commandments by his actions in his everyday life. If, by chance, he has taught his charges anything contrary to the law of God, he ought to clarify in his deeds that such things should not be done. For in his preaching he may be carried away and become a castaway, believing his own untrue words. If he has thus sinned, God shall not have to say to him: "Why do you declare my precepts and take my testament in your mouth/you have hated discipline and cast my speeches behind you" [*Ps.* 50:16–17]. And "You who saw the splinter in your brother's eye, saw not the plank in your own" [*Matt.* 7:3].

The abbot shall not make distinctions among the people in the monastery. No one shall be loved more than others, except those who are found more obedient or observant in his faith. Unless there is good cause, the freeman should not be compared to the serf. If the abbot, after taking counsel with himself, finds such cause he may place the monk where he wishes in the order of precedence; otherwise let everyone stay in his own place for "whether bond or free we are all one in Christ" [*Rom.* 2:11] and are equal in the service of the Lord; with God there is no respecter of individuals. Only if we are found to excel in good works and humility are we preferred in the eyes of God as individuals. The abbot should love all equally, and let all be under the same standard of discipline according to that which each deserves.

In his instruction the abbot should always observe the apostolic rule: "Reprove, entreat, rebuke" [*1 Tim.* 4:2]. As the occasion requires he should mix encouragement with reproof. He should show the sternness of a master and the love and affection of a father. He must reprove the unruly and undisciplined with severity, but he should exhort the obedient and patient for their betterment. We warn him to reprove and punish the slothful and stubborn. He should not ignore the sins of offenders: But as soon as they appear and grow, he must root them out, remembering Heli, the priest of silo [found in *1 Kings* 2:4]. He should verbally reprove the more virtuous and intelligent once or twice; but the stubborn, the proud, the disobedient and hard hearted should be punished with whips, even at the first signs of sin. "For the fool is not corrected by words" [*Prov.* 29:19]. And "Strike your son with rod and you shall deliver his soul from death" [*Prov.* 23:14].

The abbot must always remember what he is and be mindful of his calling; he should know that the greater his trust, the greater his responsibility. He should recognize the difficulty of his position—to care for and guide the spiritual development of many different characters. One must be led by friendliness, another by sharp rebukes, another by persuasion. The abbot must adapt himself to cope with individuality so that no member of the community leaves and he may celebrate the monastery's growth.

Most important, the abbot must not undervalue or overlook the salvation of his charges. Thus, he must always remember his task is the guidance of souls (for which he will be held accountable) and he must put aside the worldly, transitory, and petty things. And if he complains of less abundant earthly goods, he ought to remember: "Seek first the kingdom of God, and His justice, and all things shall be given to you" [*Matt.* 6:33]. And "Nothing is wanting to them who fear God" [*Ps.* 34:10].

He must prepare himself to account for the souls in his care; for on Judgement Day he will have to account for all his monks' souls, as well as his own, no matter how many. By fearing God's future questioning, he will be concerned for his charges as he is for himself. He will be cleansed of vice by helping others through admonition and correction.

Reading 9.7 WHAT IS A SACRAMENT? *SUMMA THEOLOGIAE*

Thomas Aquinas

In Question 60 of his *Summa Theologiae,* Thomas Aquinas (1225–1274), the greatest systematic theologian of Christendom, offered a theological reflection on the meaning of a sacrament. This selection comes from the third part of the *Summa Theologiae,* dated around 1271 and named "Of Christ as the Way of Man to God." The influence of Thomas's thinking on the sacraments influences the Christian Church to this day, though Catholics more than Protestants are more likely to quote him today. Notice Thomas's method of raising objections to his own points and then answering them. Note also his recognition of his sources. Does Thomas's anticipation of objections to his own position seem intellectually honest? Is there any unasked question that might be avoided?

QUESTION 60 WHAT IS A SACRAMENT?

After considering those things that concern the mystery of the incarnate Word, we must consider the sacraments of the Church which derive their efficacy from the Word incarnate Himself. First we shall consider the sacraments in general; secondly, we shall consider specially each sacrament.

Concerning the first our consideration will be fivefold: (1) What is a sacrament? (2) Of the necessity of the sacraments. (3) Of the effects of the sacraments. (4) Of their cause. (5) Of their number.

Under the first heading there are eight points of inquiry: (1) Whether a sacrament is a kind of sign? (2) Whether every sign of a sacred thing is a sacrament? (3) Whether a sacrament is a sign of one thing only, or of several? (4) Whether a sacrament is a sign that is something sensible? (5) Whether some determinate sensible thing is required for a sacrament? (6) Whether signification expressed by words is necessary for a sacrament ? (7) Whether determinate words are required? (8) Whether anything may be added to or subtracted from these words?

FIRST ARTICLE
Whether a Sacrament Is a Kind of Sign?

We proceed thus to the First Article:—

Objection. 1. It seems that a sacrament is not a kind of sign. For sacrament appears to be derived from *sacring (sacrando);* just as medicament, from *medicando (healing).* But this seems to be of the nature of a cause rather than of a sign. Therefore a sacrament is a kind of cause rather than a kind of sign.

Obj. 2. Futher, sacrament seems to signify something hidden, according to Tob. xii. 7: *It is good to hide the secret (sacramentum) of a king;* and Ephes. iii. 9: *What is the dispensation of the mystery (sacramenti) which hath been hidden from eternity in God.* But that which is hidden, seems foreign to the nature of a sign; for *a sign is that which conveys something else to the mind, besides the species which it impresses on the senses,* as Ausgustine explains (*De Doctr. Christ.* ii). Therefore it seems that a sacrament is not a kind of sign.

Obj. 3. Futher, an oath is sometimes called a sacrament: for it is written in the Decretals (*caus.* xxii, *qu.* 5): *Children who hve not attained the use of reason must not be obliged to swear: and whoever has foresworn himself once, must no more be a witness, nor be allowed to take a sacrament,* i.e. an oath. But an oath is not a kind of sign, therefore it seems that a sacrament is not a kind of sign.

On the contrary, Augustine says (*De Civ. Dei* x): *The visible sacrifice is the sacrament, i.e. the sacred sign, of the invisible sacrifice.*

I answer that, All things that are ordained to one, even in different ways, can be denominated from it: thus, from health which is in an animal, not only is the animal said to be healthy through being the subject of health: but medicine also is said to be healthy through producing health; diet through preserving it; and urine, through being a sign of health. Consequently, a thing may be called a *sacrament,* either from having a certain hidden sanctity, and in this sense a sacrament is a *sacred secret;* or from having some relationship to this sanctity, which relationship may be that of a cause, or of a sign or of any other relation. But now we are speaking of sacraments in a special sense, as implying the habitude of sign: and in this way a sacrament is a kind of sign.

Reply Obj. 1. Because medicine is an efficient cause of health, consequently whatever things are denominated from medicine are to be referred to some first active cause: so that a medicament implies a certain causality. But sanctity from which a sacrament is denominated, is not there taken as an efficient cause, but rather as a formal or final cause. Therefore it does not follow that a sacrament need always imply causality.

Reply Obj. 2. This argument considers sacrament in the sense of a *sacred secret.* Now not only God's but also the king's, secret, is said to be sacred and to be a sacrament: because according to the ancients, whatever it was unlawful to lay violent hands on was said to be holy or sacrosanct, such as the city walls, and persons of high rank. Consequently those secrets, whether Divine or human, which it is unlawful to violate by making them known to anybody whatever, are called *sacred secrets or sacraments.*

Reply Obj. 3. Even an oath has a certain relation to sacred things, in so far as it consists in calling a sacred thing to witness. And in this sense it is called a sacrament: not in the sense in which we speak of sacraments, now; the word *sacrament* being thus used not equivocally but analogically, i.e. by reason of a different relation to the one thing, viz. something sacred.

SECOND ARTICLE
Whether Every Sign of a Holy Thing Is a Sacrament?

We proceed thus to the Second Article:—

Objection 1. It seems that not every sign of a sacred thing is a sacrament. For all sensible creatures are signs of sacred things; according to Rom. i. 20: *The invisible things of God are clearly seen being understood by the things that are made.* And yet all sensible things cannot be called sacraments. Therefore not every sign of a sacred thing is a sacrament.

Obj. 2. Further, whatever was done under the Old Law was a figure of Christ Who is the *Holy of Holies* (Dan. ix. 24), according to 1 Cor. x. 11: *All (these) things happened to them in figure;* and Col. ii. 17: *Which are a shadow of things to come, but the body is Christ's.* And yet not all that was done by the Fathers of the Old Testament, not even all the ceremonies of the Law, were sacraments, but only in certain special cases, as stated in the Second Part (I–II, Q. 101, A. 4). Therefore it seems that not every sign of a sacred thing is a sacrament.

Obj. 3. Further, even in the New Testament many things are done in sign of some sacred thing; yet they are not called sacraments; such as sprinkling with holy water, the consecration of an altar, and such like. Therefore not every sign of a sacred thing is a sacrament.

On the contrary, A definition is convertible with the thing defined. Now some define a sacrament as being *the sign of a sacred thing;* moreover, this is clear from the passage quoted above (A. 1) from Augustine. Therefore it seems that every sign of a sacred thing is a sacrament.

I answer that, Signs are given to men, to whom it is proper to discover the unknown by means of the known. Consequently a sacrament properly so called is that which is the sign of some sacred thing pertaining to man; so that properly speaking a sacrament, as considered by us now, is defined as being the *sign of a holy thing so far as it makes men holy.*

Reply Obj. 1. Sensible creatures signify something holy, viz. Divine wisdom and goodness inasmuch as these are holy in themselves; but not inasmuch as we are made holy by them. Therefore they cannot be called sacraments as we understand sacraments now.

Reply Obj. 2. Some things pertaining to the Old Testament signified the holiness of Christ considered as holy in Himself. Others signified His holiness considered as the cause of our holiness; thus the sacrifice of the Paschal Lamb signified Christ's Sacrifice whereby we are made holy: and such like are properly styled sacraments of the Old Law.

Reply Obj. 3. Names are given to things considered in reference to their end and state of completeness. Now a disposition is not an end, whereas perfection is. Consequently things that signify disposition to holiness are not called sacraments, and with regard to these the objection is verified: only those are called sacraments which signify the perfection of holiness in man.

THIRD ARTICLE

Whether a Sacrament Is a Sign of One Thing Only?

We proceed thus to the Third Article:—

Objection 1. It seems that a sacrament is a sign of one thing only. For that which signifies many things is an ambiguous sign, and consequently occasions deception: this is clearly seen in equivocal words. But all deception should be removed from the Christian religion, according to Col. ii. 8: *Beware lest any man cheat you by philosophy and vain deceit.* Therefore it seems that a sacrament is not a sign of several things.

Obj. 2. Further, as stated above (A. 2), a sacrament signifies a holy thing in so far as it makes man holy. But there is only one cause of man's holiness, viz. the blood of Christ; according to Heb. xiii. 12: *Jesus, that He might sanctify the people by His own blood, suffered without the gate.* Therefore it seems that a sacrament does not signify several things.

Obj. 3. Further, it has been said above (A. 2, *ad* 3) that a sacrament signifies properly the very end of sanctification. Now the end of sanctification is eternal life, according to Rom. vi. 22: *You have your fruit unto sanctification, and the end life everlasting.* Therefore it seems that the sacraments signify one thing only, viz. eternal life.

On the contrary, In the Sacrament of the Altar, two things are signified, viz. Christ's true body, and Christ's mystical body; as Augustine says *(Liber Sent. Prosper.).*

I answer that, As stated above (A. 2) a sacrament properly speaking is that which is ordained to signify our sanctification. In which three things may be considered; viz. the very cause of our sanctification, which is Christ's passion; the form of our sanctification, which is grace and the virtues; and the ultimate end of our sanctification, which is eternal life. And all these are signified by the sacraments.

Reading 9.8   AGAINST INDULGENCES: *NINETY-FIVE THESES, OR DISPUTATION ON THE POWER AND EFFICACY OF INDULGENCES*

Martin Luther

In 1517, an Augustinian monk from Germany, Martin Luther (1483–1546), profoundly altered the shape and direction of Christianity forever. He disagreed with Pope Leo X's granting indulgences to people who contributed to the renovation of Saint Peter's basilica in Rome. An indulgence was a kind of "spiritual pardon" from punishment that one had to endure in the next life because of sins committed in this life. The pope claimed he was given this power by Christ, who is reported in Matthew's *Gospel* to have said to Peter, the first pope, *"I will give you the keys to the kingdom of heaven, and whatever you bind on earth shall be bound in heaven, and whatever you loose on earth shall be loosed in heaven"* (*Matt.* 16:19). Luther made his objections public by posting them on the door of the university chapel in Wittenberg and inviting debate. In challenging indulgences, Luther was really challenging the authority of the office of the papacy, and that challenge is what precipitated the

Protestant Reformation. To what authority does Luther primarily appeal—reason, scripture, or the teachings of Roman pontiffs? How does Luther's objection seem very "modern"?

Out of love and zeal for truth and the desire to bring it to light, the following theses will be publicly discussed at Wittenberg under the chairmanship of the reverend father Martin Luther, Master of Arts and Sacred Theology and regularly appointed Lecturer on these subjects at that place. He requests that those who cannot be present to debate orally with us will do so by letter.

In the Name of Our Lord Jesus Christ. Amen.

1. When our Lord and Master Jesus Christ said, "Repent" [Matt. 4:17], he willed the entire life of believers to be one of repentance.

2. This word cannot be understood as referring to the sacrament of penance, that is, confession and satisfaction, as administered by the clergy.

3. Yet it does not mean solely inner repentance; such inner repentance is worthless unless it produces various outward mortifications of the flesh.

4. The penalty of sin remains as long as the hatred of self, that is, true inner repentance, until our entrance into the kingdom of heaven.

5. The pope neither desires nor is able to remit any penalties except those imposed by his own authority or that of the canons.

6. The pope cannot remit any guilt, except by declaring and showing that it has been remitted by God; or, to be sure, by remitting guilt in cases reserved to his judgment. If his right to grant remission in these cases were disregarded, the guilt would certainly remain unforgiven.

7. God remits guilt to no one unless at the same time he humbles him in all things and makes him submissive to his vicar, the priest.

8. The penitential canons are imposed only on the living, and, according to the canons themselves, nothing should be imposed on the dying.

9. Therefore the Holy Spirit through the pope is kind to us insofar as the pope in his decrees always makes exception of the article of death and of necessity.

10. Those priests act ignorantly and wickedly who, in the case of the dying, reserve canonical penalties for purgatory.

11. Those tares of changing the canonical penalty to the penalty of purgatory were evidently sown while the bishops slept [Matt. 13:25].

12. In former times canonical penalties were imposed, not after, but before absolution, as tests of true contrition.

13. The dying are freed by death from all penalties, are already dead as far as the canon laws are concerned, and have a right to be released from them.

14. Imperfect piety or love on the part of the dying person necessarily brings with it great fear; and the smaller the love, the greater the fear.

15. This fear or horror is sufficient in itself, to say nothing of other things, to constitute the penalty of purgatory, since it is very near the horror of despair.

16. Hell, purgatory, and heaven seem to differ the same as despair, fear, and assurance of salvation.

17. It seems as though for the souls in purgatory fear should necessarily decrease and love increase.

18. Furthermore, it does not seem proved, either by reason or Scripture, that souls in purgatory are outside the state of merit, that is, unable to grow in love.

19. Nor does it seem proved that souls in purgatory, at least not all of them, are certain and assured of their own salvation, even if we ourselves may be entirely certain of it.

20. Therefore the pope, when he uses the words "plenary remission of all penalties," does not actually mean "all penalties," but only those imposed by himself.

21. Thus those indulgence preachers are in error who say that a man is absolved from every penalty and saved by papal indulgences.

22. As a matter of fact, the pope remits to souls in purgatory no penalty which, according to canon law, they should have paid in this life.

23. If remission of all penalties whatsoever could be granted to anyone at all, certainly it would be granted only to the most perfect, that is, to very few.

24. For this reason most people are necessarily deceived by that indiscriminate and high-sounding promise of release from penalty.

25. That power which the pope has in general over purgatory corresponds to the power which any bishop or curate has in a particular way in his own diocese or parish.

26. The pope does very well when he grants remission to souls in purgatory, not by the power of the keys, which he does not have, but by way of intercession for them.

27. They preach only human doctrines who say that as soon as the money clinks into the money chest, the soul flies out of purgatory.

28. It is certain that when money clinks in the money chest, greed and avarice can be increased; but when the church intercedes, the result is in the hands of God alone.

29. Who knows whether all souls in purgatory wish to be redeemed, since we have exceptions in St. Severinus and St. Paschal, as related in a legend.

30. No one is sure of the integrity of his own contrition, much less of having received plenary remission.

31. The man who actually buys indulgences is as rare as he who is really penitent; indeed, he is exceedingly rare.

32. Those who believe that they can be certain of their salvation because they have indulgence letters will be eternally damned, together with their teachers.

33. Men must especially be on their guard against those who say that the pope's pardons are that inestimable gift of God by which man is reconciled to him.

34. For the graces of indulgences are concerned only with the penalties of sacramental satisfaction established by man.

35. They who teach that contrition is not necessary on the part of those who intend to buy souls out of purgatory or to buy confessional privileges preach unchristian doctrine.

36. Any truly repentant Christian has a right to full remission of penalty and guilt, even without indulgence letters.

Reading 9.9 REPLY TO LUTHER: *EXSURGE DOMINE* Pope Leo X

What follows are several of the particulars contained in Pope Leo X's (1475–1521) excommunication of Martin Luther for teaching forty-one propositions that were judged "heretical or scandalous or false or offensive to pious ears." It should be noted that the pope did *not* condemn the other fifty-four of Luther's theses, which served as a reminder that Catholics, too, recognized the need for reform. This papal encyclical (letter), or bull, was issued in June 1520. Luther publicly burned it at Wittenberg in December of that year. What do all the pope's objections have in common? What is the purpose of avoiding debate with Luther on those points?

ERRORS OF MARTIN LUTHER CONDEMNED BY POPE LEO X

17. The treasures of the Church from which the Pope gives indulgences are not the merits of Christ and the saints.

18. Indulgences are a pious fraud on the faithful and a remission from good works; they are among those things that are lawful, but not those that are expedient.

19. Indulgences, for those who really gain them, do not signify the remission of the punishment for actual sins due to the divine justice.

20. They are led astray who believe that indulgences are salutary and spiritually fruitful.

21. Indulgences are necessary only for public crimes (and are properly conceded only to the hardened and impatient.

22. For six kinds of men indulgences are neither necessary nor useful, viz: the dead and the dying, the infirm, the lawfully hindered, those who have not committed crimes, those who have committed crimes but not public ones, those who lead a better life.

PROPOSITIONS OF LUTHER CONDEMNED BY POPE LEO X (1520)

1. It is an heretical but widespread opinion that the sacraments of the New Law give justifying grace to those who set no obstacle in the way.

2. To deny that sin remains in a child after baptism is to spurn both Paul and Christ.

3. Even if there is no actual sin, the *fomes peccati* hinders a soul leaving the body from entering into heaven.

31. The just man sins in every good work.

32. A good work however well done is a venial sin.

36. After sin, free will is just nominal; and when a man does his best he sins mortally.

Reading 9.10 THE PROTESTANT DECLARATION: FROM THE *AUGSBURG*
   CONFESSION Martin Luther and Philip Melanchton

In 1530, Martin Luther (1483–1546), with the assistance of theologian Philip Melanchton (1497–1560), presented Charles V of the Holy Roman Empire (1500–1558) the *Augsburg Confession*. In this document, whose Preface and Articles of Faith are presented here, the essential doctrines of Lutheranism stand in clear contrast with those of Catholicism. The *Confession* is accepted by most reformed Christian denominations. How does this *Confession* compare with the Nicene Creed? How does it differ?

PREFACE

(1) Most serene, most mighty, invincible Emperor, most gracious Lord:

A short time ago Your Imperial Majesty graciously summoned a diet of the empire to convene here in Augsburg. In the summons Your Majesty indicated an earnest desire to deliberate concerning matters pertaining to the Turk, that traditional foe of ours and of the Christian religion, and how with continuing help he might effectively be resisted. (2) The desire was also expressed for deliberation on what might be done about the dissension concerning our holy faith and the Christian religion, and to this end it was proposed to employ all diligence amicably and charitably to hear, understand, and weigh the judgments, opinions, and beliefs of the several parties among us, to unite the same in agreement on one Christian truth, (3) to put aside whatever may not have been rightly interpreted or treated by either side in the writings of either party, (4) to have all of us embrace and adhere to a single, true religion and live together in unity and in one fellowship and church, even as we are all enlisted under one Christ. (5) Inasmuch as we, the undersigned elector and princes and our associates, have been summoned for these purposes, together with other electors, princes, and estates, we have complied with the command and can say without boasting that we were among the first to arrive.

(6) In connection with the matter pertaining to the faith and in conformity with the imperial summons, Your Imperial Majesty also graciously and earnestly requested that each of the electors, princes, and estates should commit to writing and present, in German and Latin, his judgments, opinions, and beliefs with reference to the said errors, dissensions, and abuses. (7) Accordingly, after due deliberation and counsel, it was decided last Wednesday that, in keeping with Your Majesty's wish, we should present our case in German and Latin today (Friday). (8) Wherefore, in dutiful obedience to Your Imperial Majesty, we offer and present a confession of our pastors' and preachers' teaching and of our own faith, setting forth how and in what manner, on the basis of the Holy Scriptures, these things are preached, taught, communicated, and embraced in our lands, principalities, dominions, cities, and territories.

(9) If the other electors, princes, and estates also submit a similar written statement of their judgments and opinions, in Latin and German, (10) we are prepared, in obedience to Your Imperial Majesty, our most gracious lord, to discuss with them and their associates, in so far as this can honorably be done, such practical and equitable ways as may restore unity. Thus the matters at issue between us may be presented in writing on both sides, they may be discussed amicably and charitably, our differences may be reconciled, and we may be united in one, true religion, (11) even as we are all under one Christ and should confess and contend for Christ. All of this is in accord with Your Imperial Majesty's aforementioned summons. That it may be done according to divine truth we invoke almighty God in deepest humility and implore him to bestow his grace to this end. Amen.

(12) If, however, our lords, friends, and associates who represent the electors, princes, and estates of the other party do not comply with the procedure intended by Your Imperial Majesty's summons, if no amicable and charitable negotiations take place between us, (13) and if no results are attained, nevertheless we on our part shall not omit doing anything, in so far as God and conscience allow, that may serve the cause of Christian unity. (14) Of this Your Imperial Majesty, our aforementioned friends (the electors, princes, and estates), and every lover of the Christian religion who is concerned about these questions will be graciously and sufficiently assured from what follows in the confession which we and our associates submit.

ARTICLE OF FAITH AND DOCTRINE

1. God

(1) Our churches teach with great unanimity that the decree of the Council of Nicaea concerning the unity of the divine essence and concerning the three persons is true and should be believed without any doubting. (2) That is to say, there is one divine essence, which is called and which is God, eternal, incorporeal, indivisible, of infinite power, wisdom, and goodness, the maker and preserver of all things, visible and invisible. (3) Yet there are three persons, of the same essence and power, who are also coeternal: the Father, the Son, and the Holy Spirit. (4) And the term "person" is used, as the ancient Fathers employed it in this connection, to signify not a part or a quality in another but that which subsists of itself.

(5) Our churches condemn all heresies which have sprung up against this article, such as that of the Manichaeans, who posited two principles, one good and the other evil, and also those of the Valentinians, Arians, Eunomians, Mohammedans, and all others like these.

(6) They also condemn the Samosatenes, old and new, who contend that there is only one person and craftily and impiously argue that the Word and the Holy Spirit are not distinct persons since "Word" signifies a spoken word and "Spirit" signifies a movement which is produced in things.

2. Original Sin

(1) Our churches also teach that since the fall of Adam all men who are propagated according to nature are born in sin. That is to say, they are without fear of God, are without trust in God, and are concupiscent. (2) And this disease or vice of origin is truly sin, which even now damns and brings eternal death on those who are not born again through Baptism and the Holy Spirit.

(3) Our churches condemn the Pelagians and others who deny that the vice of origin is sin and who obscure the glory of Christ's merit and benefits by contending that man can be justified before God by his own strength and reason.

3. The Son of God

(1) Our churches also teach that the Word—that is, the Son of God—took on man's nature in the womb of the blessed virgin Mary. (2) So there are two natures,

divine and human, inseparably conjoined in the unity of his person, one Christ, true God and true man, who was born of the virgin Mary, truly suffered, was crucified, dead, and buried, (3) that he might reconcile the Father to us and be a sacrifice not only for original guilt but also for all actual sins of men. (4) He also descended into hell, and on the third day truly rose again. Afterward he ascended into heaven to sit on the right hand of the Father, forever reign and have dominion over all creatures, and sanctify those who believe in him (5) by sending the Holy Spirit into their hearts to rule, comfort, and quicken them and defend them against the devil and the power of sin. (6) The same Christ will openly come again to judge the living and the dead, etc., according to the Apostles' Creed.

4. Justification

(1) Our churches also teach that men cannot be justified before God by their own strength, merits, or works but are freely justified for Christ's sake through faith (2) when they believe that they are received into favor and that their sins are forgiven on account of Christ, who by his death made satisfaction for our sins. (3) This faith God imputes for righteousness in his sight (Rom. 3, 4).

5. The Ministry of the Church

(1) In order that we may obtain this faith, the ministry of teaching the Gospel and administering the sacraments was instituted. (2) For through the Word and the sacraments, as through instruments, the Holy Spirit is given, and the Holy Spirit produces faith, where and when it pleases God, in those who hear the Gospel. (3) That is to say, it is not on account of our own merits but on account of Christ that God justifies those who believe that they are received into favor for Christ's sake. Gal. 3:14, "That we might receive the promise of the Spirit through faith."

(4) Our churches condemn the Anabaptists and others who think that the Holy Spirit comes to men without the external Word, through their own preparations and works.

6. The New Obedience

(1) Our churches also teach that this faith is bound to bring forth good fruits and that it is necessary to do the good works commanded by God. We must do so because it is God's will and not because we rely on such works to merit justification before God, (2) for forgiveness of sins and justification are apprehended by faith, as Christ himself also testifies, "When you have done all these things, say, 'We are unprofitable servants'" (Luke 17:10). (3) The same is also taught by the Fathers of the ancient church, for Ambrose says, "It is ordained of God that whoever believes in Christ shall be saved, not through works but through faith alone, and he shall receive forgiveness of sins by grace."

7. The Church

(1) Our churches also teach that one holy church is to continue forever. The church is the assembly of saints in which the Gospel is taught purely and the sacraments

are administered rightly. (2) For the true unity of the church it is enough to agree concerning the teaching of the Gospel and the administration of the sacraments. (3) It is not necessary that human traditions or rites and ceremonies, instituted by men, should be alike everywhere. (4) It is as Paul says, "One faith, one baptism, one God and Father of all," etc. (Eph. 4:5, 6).

8. What is the Church?

(1) Properly speaking, the church is the assembly of saints and true believers. However, since in this life many hypocrites and evil persons are mingled with believers, it is allowable to use the sacraments even when they are administered by evil men, according to the saying of Christ, "The scribes and Pharisees sit on Moses' seat," etc. (Matt. 23:2). (2) Both the sacraments and the Word are effectual by reason of the institution and commandment of Christ even if they are administered by evil men.

(3) Our churches condemn the Donatists and others like them who have denied that the ministry of evil men may be used in the church and who have thought the ministry of evil men to be unprofitable and without effect.

9. Baptism

(1) Our churches teach that Baptism is necessary for salvation, that the grace of God is offered through Baptism, (2) and that children should be baptized, for being offered to God through Baptism they are received into his grace.

(3) Our churches condemn the Anabaptists who reject the Baptism of children and declare that children are saved without Baptism.

10. Lord's Supper

(1) Our churches teach that the body and blood of Christ are truly present and are distributed to those who eat in the Supper of the Lord. (2) They disapprove of those who teach otherwise.

11. Confession

(1) Our churches teach that private absolution should be retained in the churches. However, in confession an enumeration of all sins is not necessary, (2) for this is not possible according to the Psalm, "Who can discern his errors?" (Ps. 19:12).

12. Repentance

(1) Our churches teach that those who have fallen after Baptism can receive forgiveness of sins whenever they are converted, (2) and that the church ought to impart absolution to those who return to repentance. (3) Properly speaking, repentance consists of these two parts: (4) one is contrition, that is, terror smiting the conscience with a knowledge of sin, (5) and the other is faith, which is born of the Gospel, or of absolution, believes that sins are forgiven for Christ's sake, comforts the conscience, and delivers it from terror. (6) Then good works, which are the fruits of repentance, are bound to follow.

CHAPTER 10

ISLAM

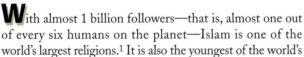

A muezzin calls Muslims to prayer from a mosque in Tehran, Iran.

With almost 1 billion followers—that is, almost one out of every six humans on the planet—Islam is one of the world's largest religions.[1] It is also the youngest of the world's great religious traditions. Although other, newer religions are considered world religions by some scholars, Islam is still by far the largest and most widespread religion to arise in the last 1,400 years. Furthermore, after a 200-year period of decline, the twentieth century has witnessed a resurgence of Islam, in part as a reaction against what is perceived as the dominance of a materialistic and idolatrous Western culture.

Although Islam did originate in a specific region—what is now Saudi Arabia—it certainly has become a universal religion, geographically and culturally. Islam is a dominant force not only in the Near East but also in Africa, Asia, the republics of the former Soviet Union, Europe, and the Americas. And as it is not geographically limited, neither is Islam culturally limited. Some **Muslims** (members of the community of Islam) are Arabs, but most are non-Arabs.[2] In fact, Southeast Asia—especially Indonesia and Malaysia—has the largest proportion of the world's Muslim population. Muslims are Arab, European, American, Asian and East Indian. Because of its size and its geographical and cultural extent, the

Islamic tradition has an effect on contemporary political events and is one of the major influences in the world today.[3]

Before making the journey through the beliefs, the practices, and the history of this universal religion, one must first be clear about the status of Islam and its founding figure, Muhammad. The Arabic root of the word *Islam* means "submission" and the peace that is attained in submission to the one God, Allah; one who submits to Allah is called a *Muslim*. Muhammad is important as the one who speaks for God, the prophet whose revelations, administration, and leadership catapulted the religion of Allah into the world scene. To call Islam "Mohammadenism," however, is a mistake and is offensive to Muslims. The religion is not based on the person Muhammad. Muhammad is not a god, nor is Muhammad the son of God. Islam equals submission to Allah. In fact, Islam's monotheism is so crucial that the greatest offense possible for a Muslim is idolatry. For Islam, idolatry means mistaking something or someone other than Allah as transcendent, divine, the one God.

ISLAMIC BELIEFS

Although Islam, as we will see, has had a complex and fluid history, it is nonetheless possible to recognize what the philosopher Ludwig Wittgenstein called "family resemblances" of ideas within this tradition. That is, at some point in the complicated story of the tradition, Muslims will recognize themselves as related, as sharing similar ideas. Clearly, the members of any family do not share an absolute identity, but enough similarities exist in the family of religious ideas to claim that there is a resemblance.

Even more than this, however, these family resemblances of ideas can be organized into what historian of religion Ninian Smart has called a "world view."[4] He argues that religions have not only a history but also a coherent structure that forms a set of beliefs. The beliefs or ideas of a religion cohere in a way that makes some sense, and this coherence provides an intellectual structure for believers, thus creating a way to view the world in all its richness.

A philosopher of religion, Ronald Cavanagh, sorts religious beliefs into the following categories: numinological, soteriological, anthropological, sociological, and cosmological beliefs.[5] Numinological beliefs answer the question, "What is the nature of the sacred?" Soteriological beliefs answer the question, "What is the nature of salvation?" Anthropological beliefs respond to the question, "What does it mean to be truly human?" Sociological beliefs focus on the question, "How should society be organized?" And finally, cosmological beliefs respond to the question, "What is the nature of the world?" Islam's worldview—its coherent system of beliefs—includes all of Cavanagh's categories, and this discussion of Islamic belief will use his categories as a structure.

First, the life of Islam's founding figure, Muhammad, is presented. Second, reflection on the *Quran,* the revelation to Muhammad, leads to a description of the nature of the sacred and what kind of knowledge or experience means salvation for a Muslim. Thus, a discussion of Allah is necessary, followed by a brief examination of beliefs about the nature of the world. Finally, from this basis, Muslim beliefs about the nature and destiny of humans and the end of the world are investigated. This investigation completes the discussion of the belief structure of Islam, the worldview created by the religion of submission to Allah.

FOUNDING FIGURE: MUHAMMAD

The history of Islam proper begins with the prophet Muhammad. The **Quran,** the sacred text of Islam, is not much assistance when it comes to the life of the Prophet. Much of the information about Muhammad comes from the **hadith,** a body of originally oral traditions from the first generation of Islam. (Table 10.1 describes the *Quran* and *hadith* in more detail.) However, these traditions are not universally accepted by Muslims. Another source of information about Muhammad is a set of biographies of the Prophet from the first centuries of Islam.[6] From these sources, a sketch of the life of Muhammad, the prophet of Allah, can be reconstructed.

The exact date is not known, but the consensus of scholarship is that Muhammad was born around 570 C.E.. His father, a member of the Quraysh tribe of the Hashimite clan, died before he was born. His mother, Amina, died when Muhammad was a small boy. His grandfather reared him until Muhammad was six years old. After his grandfather's death, the boy who was to become the prophet of Allah was nurtured by an uncle, Abu Talib. This relationship was to prove crucial for the Prophet later in his life. Abu Talib, though he never converted to Islam, remained a staunch supporter of Muhammad when he experienced fierce opposition to his message in Mecca.[7]

The life of an orphan during this period was certainly difficult. In fact, the tradition affirms that Muhammad had no formal education; he was illiterate. During his adolescence, Muhammad worked as a shepherd near the city of Mecca, in the west-central part of the Arabian peninsula. Certain benefits came to Muhammad from such an occupation. For one thing, he was steeped from this early age in a traditional Arabian way of life that included a sensitivity to language and a facility in the necessary survival skills for a harsh climate.

The details of the time between the Prophet's birth and marriage are sketchy at best. As a young adult, Muhammad went to work for Khadija, a widow with a caravan business who was about fifteen years his senior. They were married in approximately 595 C.E. and had several children. But only one, their daughter Fatima, survived Muhammad. Although later Muhammad had several other wives, he had no other wife during his marriage to Khadija, and by all accounts, theirs was a strong and satisfying relationship.

When Muhammad was about forty years old—around 610—the revelations that would eventually become the *Quran* began. Muhammad often retreated to caves around Mecca to practice private religious meditation. In a cave on Mount Hira during the Islamic month of Ramadan, the angel Gabriel—the angel of revelation—told Muhammad to "recite." From this Arabic verb, the name *Quran* is derived: *"Recite: In the Name of thy Lord who created, created Man of a blood-clot. Recite: And thy Lord is the Most Generous, who taught by the Pen, taught Man that he knew not."*[8] That initial experience has come to be known as "the Night of Power and Excellence," but the revelations continued throughout Muhammad's life. These were important, but often painful, experiences. Muhammad often experienced discomfort during the revelations, which some have called ecstatic seizures. Others have claimed that the revelations to Muhammad were epileptic seizures. However, such a claim ignores the phenomenon of ecstatic

ISLAMIC SCRIPTURE

Table 10.1

The *Quran*	In the Islamic tradition, the *Quran* is the word of God (Allah) speaking to every human in every time, place, and condition. The *Quran* (literally, "recitation") was recited by the angel Gabriel from a heavenly tablet (the "mother of the book") to the prophet Muhammad, who recited it to his followers. After the Prophet's death, his followers compiled God's revelation into a book of 114 *suras* (chapters).
The *Hadith*	The *hadith* (literally, "tradition") is an account or report of what the prophet Muhammad said or did, or of what a companion of his said or did. The *hadith* (Muhammad's speech and example) is second to the *Quran* (God's speech) in importance in Muslim piety and Islamic law. There is no single, definitive book of *hadith* that all Muslims share, but several collections of *hadith* have the aura of authority.

revelation—revelations in trancelike or extraordinary states—that appears in various religious traditions across cultures and across the centuries.

At the time of the revelations, Muhammad was inspired, excited, and moved. But accompanying these moments were lingering doubts about his own sanity. Unsure whether the revelations were authentic, Muhammad consulted a *hanif* (believer in one God, or monotheist), who assured both Muhammad and Khadija that Muhammad was not possessed by the evil *jinn* (spirits capable of assuming human and animal shapes); the experience was consistent with that of other prophets. After this time of doubt and self-questioning, Muhammad came to see himself as the prophet of Allah.

The main message of these revelations to Muhammad was that the polytheism and lack of a transcendent morality in the culture of Mecca were wrong. **Allah** was the one true God, and Muhammad was the prophet of Allah. Allah was the God of judgment; one's behavior affected how one was to be judged. Initial support for this dramatic message came from Khadija, who is considered the first convert to Islam. Then a few family members and friends converted; other converts came from primarily the poor and the young in Mecca. The movement, however, was slow in its initial growth. The first four years brought only about forty conversions.

The message of ethical monotheism was perceived as a threat by the religious and economic leaders of Mecca. Such a reaction is understandable in view of the fact that the veneration of gods and spirits in Mecca made the city the destination of people from the entire Arabian peninsula. To say that these images, spirits, and gods were not real or not powerful could be perceived as a threat to the city's economic welfare. The Quraysh tribe was especially upset by this message. They opposed Muhammad's claim to be a prophet not only because of the threat to the 360 deities that made Mecca prosperous but also because the title Prophet implied leadership over the city, thus compromising their power. In addition, the Prophet emphasized social justice, always a threat to the *status quo* of vested economic interests because it suggests that the resources controlled by a few powerful people should be shared and redistributed among the entire population.

Even in the midst of this forceful opposition, the revelations to Muhammad continued. The Quraysh continued to taunt and disturb the small, newly forming religious group, but Muhammad and his followers were protected by his uncle, Abu Talib. For a time, Muhammad was restricted to a small sector of Mecca. Some early followers left Mecca to find refuge elsewhere. The difficulties of the situation did not subside. Khadija, Muhammad's wife, died in 619; five weeks after her death, Abu Talib, Muhammad's uncle and protector, also died. Muhammad no longer had a defender, and the forces opposing him continued and even increased their threats.

In 620, however, a series of events set into motion a new, much more positive direction and, in effect, a destiny for the religion of Islam. In this year, six people came from Yathrib to talk to Muhammad. Yathrib, a city about 270 miles north of Mecca, was in disarray and beset by warring clan factions. It needed an impartial arbitrator to solve its social problems. These early visitors had heard about Muhammad and his revelations, and they wanted to see if he could be the answer to their problems. The next year, another group of twelve people from Yathrib came to visit Muhammad. As a result of those meetings, an invitation was extended for Muhammad to be the leader of that city.

In 622, Muhammad, avoiding an assassination plot by members of the Quraysh, slipped out of Mecca and traveled to Yathrib. This event is so crucial in Islam that the Muslim calendar begins with this "flight" from Mecca, called the *hijra*. The convention to designate years in the Muslim calendar is A.H., the abbreviation for the Latin Anno Hegira (the year of the *hijra*).

In Yathrib, Muhammad served in the roles of mediator, arbitrator, and legislator all at the same time. He was a leader creating a space in which the religious values revealed to him by Allah ordered society. Much of the secret of his success lay in the continuing revelations and in the external, visible proof of the authenticity of those revelations. Many people converted. After consolidating power, Muhammad was given almost unrestricted authority over the city, now named Medina, the city of the Prophet (Medina al-Nabi). During this time the first place of worship, or mosque, was established. Furthermore, the practices that would eventually become the Five Pillars of Islam, such as daily prayer and almsgiving, were instituted during the Medinan years.

However, tension still remained between the cities of Mecca and Medina. This tension escalated into war with the Battle of Badr in 624 C.E., in which Muslims from Medina defeated the Meccans. This victory was a great stimulus for Islam in Medina. In 627, approximately ten thousand Meccans attacked Medina. Although there was no decisive winner in the battle, this, too, was considered a victory for the Medinans, because the Muslims were not totally destroyed. The Meccans withdrew, realizing that Muhammad could not be eliminated.

The following years saw a peace treaty, and Muslims arranged a pilgrimage to Mecca. After solidifying his strength both economically and militarily in Medina, Muhammad triumphantly returned to Mecca in 630, declaring amnesty for his opposition. When it came to the issue of Allah, however, Muhammad drew the line. He worshiped at the **Kaba,** the sacred site in the middle of Mecca, and gave the order to destroy the idols and images that were so offensive to the strict monotheism of Islam. From now on, Allah alone was to be worshiped. With this act, Muhammad became virtually the only leader of the Arabian peoples. When Muhammad died two years later, in 632, the religion of Islam was well on the way to becoming a world-changing force.

THE *QURAN*

The accepted spelling of the sacred text for Muslims is *Quran*. Sometimes the older spelling *Koran* is used; sometimes an apostrophe is inserted—*Qur'an*—to indicate the Arabic glottal stop between the syllables. The more recent spelling has been adopted here, however, because it is closer to the Arabic pronunciation.

Because the *Quran* is a record of divine speech to Muhammad, the language of revelation, Arabic, is crucial. The Arabic of the *Quran* is viewed as beyond imitation. For devout Muslims, moreover, the *Quran* is impossible to translate into other languages. Islam considers translations of the *Quran* very rough approximations of the actual *Quran*. The translations are not the scripture itself, so the written *Quran* exists only in Arabic. Because of this belief, Arabic is the common language of Muslims throughout the world, constituting a bond of unity within the Muslim community from Russia to Canada to Egypt to Malaysia.

The argument that the *Quran* cannot be translated is open to debate within the academic study of religion, but the claim that the force and poetry of the Arabic language is central to the *Quran* cannot be denied. Because the style of the revelation was oral speech, the written version has all the qualities of a speech event. There is repetition and a sense of immediacy; the language transmits a rhythm and a force. The Arabic of the *Quran* is, ultimately, the language within which Muslims find ethics, morality, responsibility, and hope for the future.

Three stages in the origins and growth of the *Quran* can be identified. The first stage is the revelation received by the prophet Muhammad, lasting over a period of about twenty years. The next stage is Muhammad's oral transmission of these revelations to his followers. Some of the revelations were written down, but many were preserved in the memory of Muhammad's followers. The third and final state is the more systematic recording of the revelations. After Muhammad's death, his revelations were collected and preserved under the second *caliph*, Umar, thus creating the written *Quran*. (A **caliph** was a leader of Islam after Muhammad's death.) In the initial years after Muhammad's death, however, different versions of the written *Quran* arose. Out of four competing versions or collections, an authorized version was chosen during the period 644 to 656 C.E., under the caliph Uthman.

Within Judaism and Christianity, various critical techniques have been used by people of many perspectives to address the sources and development of textual traditions in scripture. Islam, in contrast, claims that the *Quran* is the word of Allah—eternal, absolute, unchangeable, and undistorted. Further, the *Quran* is the final revelation to humanity. Muhammad is considered the "seal" of the prophets, an idea initiated by Abu Bakr, who asserted that there are no other prophets after Muhammad and his divine revelation. The *Quran* was revealed to Muhammad, who was the mouthpiece for God, and the reve-

lation has been transmitted unchanged since the initial years of Islam.

The use of the *Quran* in the religious life of a Muslim is ritually prescribed. It is customary to wash—symbolizing purification—before using the *Quran* in any way. The *Quran* is never to touch the floor, and if there is a stack of books, it is always on top. Although many Muslims read the *Quran* every day, it is customary to read it all the way through during the holy month of Ramadan. Many Muslims memorize parts of the *Quran*. Moreover, it is a special mark of piety to memorize the entire *Quran*. The title **hafiz** is given to a person who has committed the entire *Quran* to memory. The *Quran* also is used to ward off evil curses by both *jinn* and humans; the last two chapters are explicitly used to repel evil supernatural powers. However it is used, the *Quran* remains the revelation of Allah, the source of structure for the life of a Muslim.

There are 114 **suras** in the *Quran*. Although *sura* is sometimes translated "chapter," a *sura* is not necessarily a coherent literary unit. The *suras* are not organized topically or chronologically. Except for the first *sura*, they are arranged in order of decreasing length. Initial readers of the *Quran* who assume a topical or chronological order to the *suras* are quickly disappointed or even frustrated. The *suras* are organized into approximately 6,000 verses, or **ayas**. The longest *sura* contains 287 *ayas;* the shortest contains three. Modern scholarly translations of the *Quran* have often tried to organize the *suras* differently—topically, historically, divided by Muhammad's Meccan and Medinan revelations, or by interest. According to Islamic scholar Caesar E. Farhah, "None, however, are entirely faithful to the letter of the original because of certain idiosyncrasies of the Arabic language which the most literate of Arab philologists can not always render with exactitude."[9] This judgment reinforces the Muslim assertion of the transcendence and the authoritative definiteness of the Arabic *Quran*.

ALLAH

The *Quran* provides the foundation for the rest of the Muslim worldview. At its center is belief in Allah. Islam is, in a word, monotheistic. It acknowledges one God, and only one God—Allah. Allah is all powerful, merciful, compassionate, just, the Lord of the Universe. The belief in one God sets Islam apart from its historic predecessors on the Arabian peninsula. That belief is, furthermore, the cutting edge of the distinction between Islam and every other religion, even other monotheisms. Islam claims a certain value and authority for the other "religions of the Book," Christianity and Judaism. But according to Islam, these traditions have not maintained the purity and integrity of the monotheism that is the basis of faith. The claim that Jesus is in some way divine compromises Christian claims to be monotheistic. And the tendency in the tradition of Judaism to fall into "idol worship"—acknowledged, for example, in the biblical incident of the worship of the Golden Calf while Moses was receiving the law—constitutes a violation of monotheism as well. The *Quran* perhaps says it best:

> Say: 'He is God, One,
> God, the Everlasting Refuge,
> who has not begotten, and has not been begotten,
> and equal to Him is not any one.[10]

The worst offense in Islam is idolatry, or **shirk.** To guard against idolatry, the fundamental practice of Islam, the recitation of the creed that "there is no god but Allah; Muhammad is the Prophet of Allah" affirms monotheism and rejects polytheism. This statement of faith is described in more detail later in this chapter in the "Islamic Practices" section. *Shirk* is regarded so seriously that Islamic art has been influenced directly by this belief. Human images—even realistic images of any kind—are relatively rare in Islamic art. Because a danger exists that the image might be mistaken for Allah, any image can be idolatry. Artistic expression, therefore, has tended to focus on geometric patterns rather than on the realistic reproduction of images. This same issue arises in Judaism's interpretation of the commandment against graven images, in Christianity's iconoclast controversy, and even in the differences between Protestant and Catholic versions of the faith.

Characteristics of Allah are majesty and the ability to inspire awe. Allah is present everywhere (omnipresent), all knowing (omniscient), and all powerful (omnipotent):

> Surely your Lord is God, who created the heavens
> and the earth in six days—
> then sat Himself upon the Throne
> covering the day with the night
> it pursues urgently—
> and the sun, and the moon, and the stars
> subservient, by His command.
> Verily, His are the creation and the command.
> Blessed be God,
> the Lord of all Being.[11]

But Allah is not merely power. Allah embodies absolute justice and mercy as well: *"Surely thy Lord is wide in His forgiveness. Very well He knows you, when He produced you from the earth, and when you were yet unborn in your mothers' wombs; therefore hold not yourselves purified; God knows very well him who is godfearing."*[12]

Another way to describe the divine, Allah, is to articulate what he is not. This is *via negativa,* "the way of the negative," that is also found in other religious traditions—for example, Hinduism and Christianity—as they attempt to describe the divine: "God is not a formed body; nor a measurable substance; neither does He resemble bodies, either in their being measurable or divisible. Neither is he a substance, nor do substances exist in him; neither is he an accidental form, nor do accidentals exist in him."[13] But neither the *via positiva* (the way of articulating attributes of Allah) nor the *via negativa* (the way of saying what he is not) is sufficient. Islam combines both approaches to the divine by attributing ninety-nine names to Allah. In spite of that large number, however, the one-hundredth name is unknown; Allah is beyond naming. There are positive ways to describe Allah—ninety-nine names. But in the end, the believer is left with mystery—the unnamed name.[14]

Although the monotheism of Islam is uncompromising, it includes a variety of supernatural, heavenly figures. Angels are the messengers of Allah. The angel Gabriel was instrumental in the revelation of the *Quran* to Muhammad. Further, angels side with the fighters of Islam as they war against the unfaithful. Another sort of heavenly beings are the *jinn*, beings halfway between humans and angels. Some are good and some are bad. The leader of the latter category is Iblis, who looks very much like the Satan figure in the *Bible*'s Job. Iblis acts as tempter and lawyer against humans and, according to tradition, was responsible for the fall of Adam. But nothing regarding these supernatural realities compromises the strict monotheism of Islam. As the *Quran* puts it, *"Is there a god with God? Nay, but they are a people who assign Him equals!"*[15]

Cosmology

Islam believes that Allah created the world, including the heavens and celestial bodies. Allah is the transcendent Creator, not only of the celestial level of the universe, but of the earthly plane as well. The providence and power of Allah are reflected in the bounteous creation, wonderfully designed. Islamic cosmology affirms that the world is real and the world is good. Thus, the study of the natural world by means of mathematics, astronomy, chemistry, or any of the natural sciences is held as a form of appreciating the creation of Allah.

However, the world, the cosmos, is not eternal. It was created; it is not Allah. Islam, unlike some religious traditions, does not, for the most part, identify cosmos and divinity. Pantheism, although a part of the history of Islam, is not the norm. There is no incarnation in Islam, no material form that becomes Allah. If nature is not transcendent, then the world is made for people to savor. Food and drink—with the exception of alcohol—are to be enjoyed. Sex and procreation are good. Wealth, property, and possessions are good so long as they do not keep others in a state of need. The world of the senses can even be seen as a preview of the heavenly conditions that await faithful Muslims if they are judged properly. In any case, the beliefs about Allah and humanity are much more of a concern for Islam than is cosmology.

THE NATURE AND DESTINY OF HUMANS

Humankind is regarded as the crown of creation, entrusted by Allah with management of the whole created order. Yet humanity is also seen as weak, prone to disbelief in Allah and to disobedience to his will. Humanity's weakness is pride. Humans often do not realize their limitations and view themselves as self-sufficient. Islam contains the story of Adam and Eve, which symbolizes both the high and low points of this picture of human nature. In this story, humans are above all the creatures in nature, because they have the moral responsibility to live according to the will of Allah. Further, Islam acknowledges the sin of Adam and Eve, but there is no concept of "original sin," as in some parts of Christianity, where the original act of sin is passed on to all people. For Islam, sin, the error of humanity, is not to submit to the will of Allah.

If God is sovereign and rules over human life, then the philosophical issue is that of reconciling human freedom with divine control and power. It is the issue of predestination. As will be seen in the "History of Islam" section, some Muslims are predestinarians, some acknowledge human freedom, and some maintain a middle position. The *Quran* lends authority to those who lean toward predestination: *"Surely we have created everything in measure."*[16] *"Magnify the Name of thy Lord the Most High, who created and shaped."*[17] *"Naught shall visit us but what God has prescribed for us."*[18] Furthermore, the sayings attributed to Muhammad also lend evidence to support the predestination claim. However, the apparent contradictions of such a position can have profound psychological consequences. That is, if everything is preordained, then the notion of individual responsibility for actions in the world is less convincing. The ability to choose, even if that choice is wrong, is often held as a necessary component of a fully developed consciousness. So perhaps Allah has determined his will but has hidden that information. Periodically, then, there are messengers to make this divine intention clear and available for human choice. Thus, freedom and determinism are held in tension in Islam: "the omnipotence of God does not prevent man from enjoying freedom of will."[19] A frequently uttered phrase in Islam is *Insh allah,* or "as God wills." The one thing held in common, though, is that Allah allows humans the freedom to choose certain actions, and on those actions judgment will be passed. The tension between freedom and determinism is built into the heart of Islam.

Whether a believer sides with a predetermined worldview or one that emphasizes more human freedom, human life is a struggle. Remaining faithful is also a struggle that requires exertion. The term for this struggle or exertion in Islam is **jihad.** Often this term is translated "holy war," but *jihad* is a more nuanced term whose basic meaning is "struggle," including all struggles of the faith against those forces that would destroy the faith of Islam. *Jihad* is dealt with in more detail later in this chapter.

THE END OF THE WORLD

Divine judgment, one of the basic beliefs of Islam, is integrally related to the concept of Allah, as well as to concepts about human responsibility. There will come a time, an end, when everyone will be judged by Allah. Islam and the *Quran* reflect various components of the eschatology (the roots of this word mean "talk of the end time") found in Judaism, Christianity, and Zoroastrianism (the dualistic religion of Persia). These traditions share a concern with the end of time or the future. In Islamic belief, when a person dies, the body returns to the earth. The soul, however, goes into a state of sleep until resurrection day. This is the day when, by the power of Allah, souls and bodies reunite, and those resurrected will be judged.

Regarding rewards and punishment, the Quranic images of heaven and hell are appropriate to the Arabian desert. Heaven has abundant water and shade. Hell is filled with salty water, smoke, and fierce desert winds:

The Companions of the Right (O Companions of the Right!) mid thornless lote-trees and serried acacias, and spreading shade and outpoured waters, and fruits abounding unfailing, unforbidden, and upraised couches. . . . The Companions of the Left (O Companions of the Left!) mid burning winds and

boiling waters and the shadow of a smoking blaze neither cool, neither goodly.[20]

THE CAVANAGH MODEL OF BELIEFS

In addition to the five categories of religious beliefs presented earlier, Cavanagh has also created a model for organizing the range of complex beliefs within a tradition. Religions, he argues, can be seen as having three fundamental elements or components. Although these might not be acknowledged in the creeds of the traditions, they can nonetheless be analyzed from the perspective of the academic study of religion. The first element or belief is that humans are confronted with an essential *problem.* Second, Cavanagh argues that each religion posits a *goal,* an essential ideal, a place or time when the essential problem is overcome. Third, he argues that religions posit a *mode of transformation,* a way of transforming the essential problem and overcoming its influence.

If Cavanagh's model is valid, then the belief system of Islam can be analyzed in this way: The essential problem confronting humans is the tendency not to view Allah as the God. This can be labeled *shirk*—idolatry or polytheism. The essential ideal, or goal, in Islam is total and complete surrender and submission to the will of Allah. Finally, Islam's mode of transformation includes the beliefs articulated here, as well as the practices and activities that remind Muslims of Allah. It is fitting, then, that the next section of this chapter focus on those practices that embody the belief structure of Islam.

ISLAMIC PRACTICE

The complex and multifaceted Islamic religious practices include the Five Pillars of Islam; life cycle rituals; the veneration of "saints"; feasts and festivals; and the moral emphasis of Islam, including practices associated specifically with the practice of *jihad* and women.

THE FIVE PILLARS OF ISLAM

If Islam is the religion of submission to the one, true God—Allah—then the specific practices of Islam are related to that submission. The primary obligations for the life of submission for a Muslim are called the **Five Pillars of Islam.** Recitation of the creed, daily prayer, fasting, giving alms, and a pilgrimage to Mecca constitute the Five Pillars. Although not precisely detailed in the *Quran*, these prescriptions are amplified in the traditions that followed the original revelation to Muhammad. Taken together, these five obligations create and continually renew a life focused upon the principal beliefs of Islam. Orthodoxy (right belief) becomes orthopraxis (right action) though the Five Pillars.

In his classic text *The Sacred Canopy*, sociologist Peter Berger argues that every religion functions as a canopy or tent.[21] As such, the religion covers and protects a religious community from outside or so-called evil forces. The religion also creates an identity for the community within the boundaries of that tent. Of all the religious traditions around the world, Islam fits most clearly into Berger's image. Islam claims that Five Pillars of religious practice create and protect the lives of the faithful. If any of these pillars is removed or weakened, then the identity of the Muslim and the reality of Islam are put into question.

THE FIRST PILLAR: PROFESSION OF FAITH

The first of the Five Pillars holding up the sacred canopy of Islam is the creed—the profession of faith (see Table 10.2). In contrast to formulas from other traditions, Islam's creed, called Shahada, is simple and straightforward: "There is no God but Allah; Muhammad is the Prophet of Allah." This is indeed a creed, or belief, but it is also a practice, an action of faith. Utterance of this creed, publicly and with full knowledge of its implications, constitutes entrance into the community of faith. This creed affirms the strict monotheism of Islam—there is no God but Allah—while it places Muhammad as a messenger, a prophet, rather than a deity or even a quasi-deity.

Yvonne Y. Haddad describes the emphasis of this creed as not merely the unity of God but rather the "unicity" of God. It is an "unequivocal denial of any divinity or lordship of anything or anyone except God and the rejection of all alternate claims of sovereignty. He alone is God; there is none other beside him."[22] Moreover, Muhammad is the Prophet, the one who seals the prophecy that had come before. Islam does not reject the prophetic tradition of Abraham, Moses, and Jesus, but it argues that prophecy is completed and sealed with the revelations to Muhammad. Thus, "there is no God but Allah; Muhammad is the Prophet of Allah."

In practice, the creed is whispered in the ear when a person is born and then again when that person dies. Thus, it effectively brackets the life of a Muslim, creating the expectation of divine guidance through this life and the reminder of judgment in the life beyond.

THE SECOND PILLAR: RITUAL PRAYER

The confession of faith is repeated often during the course of each day, but a more structured practice serves as a reminder of the requirements of submission to Allah. The second of the Five Pillars of Islam is ritual prayer, or *salat*. This requirement gives a distinct and orderly structure to the Muslim's daily routine. Five specific times during the day, life is given a direction and filled with a sense of holiness that connects a Muslim not only to the community of other Muslims but with the power and presence of Allah as well. At sunrise, noon, midafternoon, sunset, and nightfall, the community is called to prayer. Traditionally this has been the function of the **muezzin,** the official caller, but knowledge of the proper time is sufficient to call a Muslim to prayer. Furthermore, although the mosque is a preferred place of prayer, any place—every place—is the appropriate place to worship Allah. Prayer is performed facing the direction of Mecca. Thus, the act of ritual prayer orients a Muslim to the center of the religious universe. This ritual, when it is done five times a day, becomes a powerful reminder of the direction and orientation of the faith. It is not surprising, then, that the most important part of a

Table 10.2	THE FIVE PILLARS OF ISLAM	
	1. Shahada	"Witness"; the creedal statement of the Five Pillars:"There is no God but Allah; Muhammad is the Prophet of Allah."
	2. *salat*	The obligatory Muslim prayer service held five times daily.
	3. Ramadan	The holy month of fasting during the daylight hours.
	4. *zakat*	The obligation of charity or almsgiving. Usually equal to 2.5 percent of accumulated wealth.
	5. *hajj*	The pilgrimage to Mecca.

mosque is the ***mihrab,*** the wall niche that serves as a pointer to Mecca.

Prayer includes specific physical action. Standing, kneeling, bowing, and prostrating oneself before Allah submits one to the power and wisdom of God. Touching the forehead to the ground—an extremely vulnerable position for humans—represents absolute submission. The need to approach the divine with respect and purity is symbolized by ***wudu,*** the ritual cleansing that involves washing—with water and sometimes with sand—the hands, mouth, nostrils, face, lower arms, head, ears, neck, and feet. Further, shoes must be removed, and the worshiper must be properly clothed. Prayer, therefore, demands an attitude of respect even as it embodies submission.

Friday at noon is the time for the prayer to occur within community. Although this practice is not prescribed, it is the time when the community is bound together and feels a sense of unity. During this time, an ***imam*** (religious leader) leads the service, which includes recitations from the *Quran,* a sermon espousing Muslim doctrine, and prayer. The community is gathered with no distinction of race, nationality, or social status. Women, however, customarily remain behind screens or worship separately from men. In their homes, women sometimes pray in the same rooms as men.

THE THIRD PILLAR: RAMADAN   In addition to the statement of belief and repeated ritual action in prayer, Islam includes as one of the Five Pillars a fast during the month of Ramadan. Two reasons set apart Ramadan as a special month. First,

it is the time when Muhammad received his first revelations. Second, during this month there occurred the Battle of Badr, the successful encounter of Muhammad's Medinan forces over the Meccans in 624 C.E. Because the Islamic calender is lunar rather than solar, Ramadan is not a month fixed in one season. It gradually rotates during the seasons so that one year the ***sawm***—the fast—may be in the winter, and another year it may be in the heat of summer. No matter what the season of Ramadan, from the time that one can distinguish a white thread from a black thread in the morning until the setting of the sun, Muslims must refrain from food, drink, and sexual activity for the duration of the month. This custom serves at least two functions: it helps remind the Muslim of certain passions that can run wild, and it reminds the Muslim of what it is like to be poor.

There exists a variety of interpretations of this practice, depending on local custom and individual piety. Some Muslims take the fast so seriously that they try to refrain from swallowing their own saliva. Others take the nights of Ramadan as opportunities for feasting. Special acts of devotion also distinguish Ramadan. Additional prayers and a rereading of the *Quran* are often components of the sacred month. Certain persons are exempted from the fast: women during pregnancy, small children, and people who are sick. But this yearly ritual reminding Muslims of their identity is certainly a central pillar in Islam's sacred canopy.

THE FOURTH PILLAR: ALMSGIVING   The fourth of the Five Pillars of Islam is *zakat,* or almsgiving.

Akrima Sabri (center), the *mufti* of Jerusalem, prays with his family during Ramadan, the Muslim holy month of fasting. The *mufti* is both the religious and political leader of the Palestinian community (1995).

Muslims are obligated to contribute a portion of their wealth to those who are more needy. Whereas some religions speak of a tithe, a tenth of a person's income, the *zakat* requires one-fortieth, or 2.5 percent, of wealth—net worth, if you will. In Islamic states, this contribution is often collected by the government and therefore appears to outsiders to be a tax. In non-Muslim countries, the *zakat* is collected by the religious community. Whether perceived as a tax or a tithe, the obligation to give alms serves to level the economic wealth of the community and to bind one Muslim to another in solidarity.

The notion of almsgiving also has restrictions. The money collected should not be used for building projects or for burying the dead, even though these are important acts of charity. Furthermore, alms should not be used to take care of immediate family—children, spouse, or parents. According to the *Quran*, alms are to be given to those who are poor and needy, to those who are traveling, and to slaves for their ransom.[23] This pillar of Islam suggests that wealth is not evil. Rather, Allah directs people to share and distribute wealth to those who

may not be as fortunate. Also, this act should not embarrass the person receiving the gift or inflate the pride of the giver. Thus, some contemporary Muslims prefer to use the term *wealth sharing* instead of *almsgiving*.

THE FIFTH PILLAR: PILGRIMAGE TO MECCA The final pillar in the sacred canopy of Islam is the *hajj*, the pilgrimage to Mecca and its environs.[24] Once in a lifetime, if at all possible, every Muslim is expected to journey to Mecca on the *hajj*. Although pilgrimage had been a key element of religious practices prior to the time of Muhammad, Islam has preserved the key elements and purified any reference to what could be considered polytheism. The *hajj* is performed in the twelfth month of the Muslim lunar calender. Men, women, and children can go on the pilgrimage, but men predominate. Pilgrims approach Mecca stripped of all external evidence of distinction or separation, wearing two pieces of seamless white cloth. On the *hajj*, Muslims are one; equality and egalitarianism are the rule. Pilgrims must abstain from food and drink during the day, they must not engage in sexual intercourse, and their hair and nails must not be cut.

There are several components to the *hajj*. When pilgrims reach Mecca, they circumambulate the Kaba, a cube-shaped building at the center of the sanctuary. Pilgrims are to walk seven times around the Kaba, with the first act of each circuit being the touching or kissing of the Black Stone in the corner of the Kaba. According to tradition, this stone was delivered to Abraham by the angel Gabriel; white originally, the stone was turned black by the sins of humanity. Because stones were commonly held to be deities in the animistic prehistory of Islam, one wonders why this stone has been preserved in one of the key practices of Islam. One interesting interpretation is that kissing or touching the stone is merely the will of Allah and that one of the great teachings of the rite is precisely that it is not open to any rational interpretation.

Once the circumambulation has been completed, pilgrims perform the ritual of running between two hills near the Kaba. As with the Black Stone, this element of the *hajj* connects the Muslim tradition with Abraham. Because Abraham was unable to bear a son with his wife, Sarah, she gave him the woman Hagar to produce an heir. The product of that union was Ishmael. Later, Sarah convinced Abraham to expel Hagar and Ishmael. Tradition claims that they wandered in the wilderness until they came to Mecca. Dying of thirst, Hagar ran between the two hills imploring divine assistance, and the well of Zamzam was Allah's miraculous response. Much like water from the Jordan River is a focus for some Christians, the water of the well of Zamzam is thus much sought after by pilgrims.

The *hajj* ends at Arafat, a plain fourteen miles from Mecca. Here the rite of standing—*wuquf*—means that all stand before God in unity and in awe of the divine presence. Just before his death, Muhammad addressed his followers on a hill next to this plain, where it was revealed to him that Islam was completed. The rite of standing lasts from noon until sundown.

On the way back to Mecca, the pilgrims on the *hajj* throw stones at three pillars. This act is usually interpreted as a symbolic resistance of evil, but it is also a commemoration of Abraham's escape from Satan when he was tempted to resist the divine command to sacrifice his son.

Every Muslim is obligated to make the *hajj*, but not all are able. In fact, most will not make the *hajj*, but scorn falls only on those who have the ability and time and still do not undertake the pilgrimage. The *hajj* is, without question, a moving experience. For example, Malcolm X, a leader of portions of the African American community in the United States in the 1960s, came back from the *hajj*, with a new message, a message of reconciliation. Moreover, when Muslims return from the pilgrimage, they may have the title *hajj* attached to their names. As with other religious traditions, the changing of a name signifies the changing of status and, in fact, a change of identity.

The preceding rituals are crucial for Islam. However, the everyday religious practices of Muslims encompass more than the Five Pillars. Berger's image of the sacred canopy also includes its fabric, which is woven of individual strands or threads. In a religion, these threads are those minor, commonplace factors that may vary from place to place but that are nevertheless vital to the whole. If the threads are removed or altered in sufficient number, the canopy will develop gaps and holes that will allow both evil to enter into the community and the community to pour into the rest of the profane world. Islam creates a tightly woven fabric with three categories of religious practice: rituals to accompany the life cycle, veneration of "saints," and feasts and festivals.

LIFE CYCLE RITUALS

Every religion has rites of passage, and Islam is no exception. These rituals correspond to periods of life that, barring premature death, are experienced by everyone: birth, puberty, adulthood, and finally death. Because these are not the pillars of the faith, Islamic rites of passage very from country to country and from generation to generation, but

The Great Holy Mosque in Mecca is Islam's shrine. Thousands pack the courtyard during the annual pilgrimage. In the courtyard of the Great Mosque is the Kaba, a small stone building that contains Islam's Black Stone, believed by the faithful to have been given to Abraham by Gabriel. Since the time of Muhammad, the Kaba has been the chief object of pilgrimage of the Islamic world. The Kaba represents the direction to which Muslims turn in praying.

they remain important to the faith that creates the identify of a Muslim.

The birth of a child is certainly a major event in the life of a person, a family, or a religious tradition. Islam affirms that an identity for the new human must be acknowledged and created; thus, a day of naming typically occurs the seventh day after birth. This ritual of bestowing a name is often combined with the sacrifice of an animal and the shaving of a portion of the child's hair. Naming, however, is important not only for a newborn child. Upon conversion to Islam, most new Muslims also take an Islamic name. Muhammad Ali (formerly Cassius Clay) and Kareem Abdul Jabbar (formerly Lew Alcindor) are two examples of Muslim converts from the world of U.S. sports. Malcolm Little was converted to Islam and changed his name to El-Hajj Malik El-Shabazz. He is known in U.S. history as Malcom X.

Puberty is another time of transition. Rites vary dramatically, but circumcision is a widely held symbol of male identity. Circumcision is often done at infancy or at about age seven, but sometimes it is reserved for puberty. The scarring or removal of the clitoris in girls is sometimes performed. This, however, is purely a cultural, not a specifically Islamic, ritual. A complete recitation of the *Quran*, a ritual of coming of age, also is associated with

puberty. There is a parallel here with the Jewish tradition of the *bar mitzvah* and *bat mitzvah*. In that tradition, as in Islam, the adolescent's entrance into the religious community is accompanied by a public recitation or a reading of the scripture.

Marriage, traditionally, is arranged by the parents of the bride and groom, but a woman can refuse a match, express preferences, or both. After a choice of mate has been made, there are severe restrictions on a couple's association before marriage. Usually during this period, males associate with other males, and females with other females. The engaged couple may spend time together, but this is usually in the presence of other responsible adults. Based on the *Quran*, men may have up to four wives. The key provision here, however, is that all wives be treated equally; because this is difficult, monogamy is the norm. Women can have only one husband at a time. The marriage ceremony is primarily contractual, but often a passage from the *Quran* is recited and a speech is delivered. The real celebration for this rite of passage begins after the formal ceremony. The form of the marriage ceremony varies from place to place, but the celebration usually includes food, further recitation of the *Quran*, and dancing.

The final rite of passage is death. If someone is dying, the thirty-sixth *sura* of the *Quran* is recited:

Is man not aware that We created him from a little germ? Yet he openly disputes Our power. He answers back with arguments, and forgets His own creation. He asks: "Who will give life to rotten bones?" Say: "He who created them at first will give them life again: He has knowledge of every creature; He who gives you from the green tree a fire with which to light your fuel." Has He who created the heavens and the earth no power to create their like? That He surely has. He is the all-knowing Creator. When He decrees a thing He need only say: "Be," and it is. Glory be to Him who has control of all things. To him you shall return.[25]

After death, there is final ritual cleansing; no embalming is permitted. The body is wrapped in a plain white grave cloth. No coffin in required, and usually the body is buried the same day as death, with the head turned toward Mecca; even in death, Islam provides for the proper orientation in the world. In the case of the death of a martyr, the body does not need final cleansing, because the wounds and death constitute the necessary purifications before Allah. Martyrs include those who die in battle defending Islam, pilgrims who die while making the *hajj,* or persons who die while reciting the *Quran.*

The rituals that accompany the life cycle are important, even if not absolutely consistent across the wide spectrum of Islam. As U.S. Islamic scholar Frederick M. Denny puts it, "All humans typically are born, develop, mature, pass through a marriageable phase when reproduction is a possibility, grow old and die. All societies have rites marking these transitions. Islam puts its special stamp on each of these natural passages and thus consecrates them to God."[26]

Veneration of "Saints"

The quotation marks surrounding the word *saints* in the heading of this section should serve as a caution. Although popular Islam does indeed include something that looks like the veneration of saints in the Christian tradition, the *Quran* does not speak of saints as such. Instead, it speaks of a **wali,** often

translated as "friend." God is one; no saint could detract from the oneness of Allah. In the lives of Muslims, however, certain persons have often been considered specially blessed with power. This power is often seen as transportable—the power can be bestowed on others. This veneration primarily happens after a person's death, and his or her memory takes on a life of its own.

In Egypt, the greatest Muslim saint is Sayyid Ahmad al-Badawi, who lived in the thirteenth century.[27] At various times during the year, there are major celebrations for this saint that are sometimes linked with non-Muslim beliefs, even including magical charms to make women fertile.[28] Islam was brought to Java in the fifteenth and sixteenth centuries, according to tradition, by nine men, called the *wali songo,* or the "nine saints."[29] Ritual traditions and celebrations also have grown up around these figures.

The previous two examples come from Sunni Islam. But another Muslim group, Shiite Islam, also has a rich tradition of powerful persons. Often the burial places of these saints are crucial to belief. Thus, Shiite Muslims make a pilgrimage to Karbala, the burial place of the martyr Husayn, and to Najaf, where the grave of Ali, the first *imam,* is found. Figure 10.1 shows some sacred sites of Islam.

In addition to being associated with specific sacred places, the power of "saints" is also connected to specific rituals. The tenth day of the month of Muharram, the anniversary of the martyrdom of Husayn in Karbala in 680 C.E., is the date of the commemorative passion play *ta ziya,* "consolation," which recounts the crucial events of the history of Shiite Islam and interprets them.[30] Husayn is the paradigm of the righteous person whose suffering is used by God to redeem the faithful, the Shiites. The "martyrdom of Husayn and the ritual repetitions of it by means of the ta ziya sacred drama are finally not tragic at all; rather they are a persistent showing forth of victorious faith in God's ultimate vindication."[31] Thus, the veneration of saints provides Islam with an opportunity to express much emotion and demonstrate the fervor of the faith.

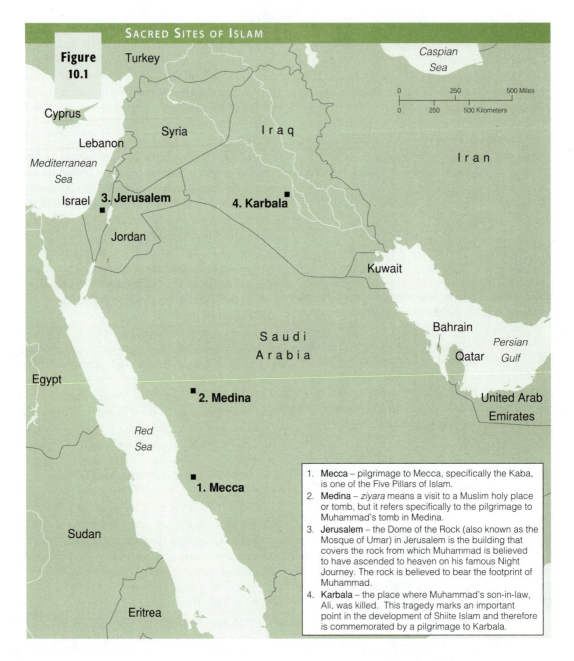

SACRED SITES OF ISLAM

Figure 10.1

1. **Mecca** – pilgrimage to Mecca, specifically the Kaba, is one of the Five Pillars of Islam.
2. **Medina** – *ziyara* means a visit to a Muslim holy place or tomb, but it refers specifically to the pilgrimage to Muhammad's tomb in Medina.
3. **Jerusalem** – the Dome of the Rock (also known as the Mosque of Umar) in Jerusalem is the building that covers the rock from which Muhammad is believed to have ascended to heaven on his famous Night Journey. The rock is believed to bear the footprint of Muhammad.
4. **Karbala** – the place where Muhammad's son-in-law, Ali, was killed. This tragedy marks an important point in the development of Shiite Islam and therefore is commemorated by a pilgrimage to Karbala.

FEASTS AND FESTIVALS

Id al-Adha, the Feast of Sacrifice or the Great Feast, is the most important feast in the Muslim year. It occurs on the day when those on the *hajj,* the pilgrimage to Mecca, have returned halfway and make a feast by sacrificing an animal. This act commemorates the time when Abraham was commanded by God to sacrifice his son. Although this son is not named, it is assumed in Islam that the son is Ishmael. (In the Jewish tradition, the son to be sacrificed is Isaac.) Because Abraham was faithful, God provided a ram as a substitute sacrifice. On this date in the Muslim year, the head of each household is to kill an animal and give a feast. Some of the food is to be eaten within the family, some is to be given to neighbors and friends, and some is to be given to the poor. The celebration extends over three days and includes family visits. The feast is not a requirement but rather an important tradition. It is, however, often difficult to observe in areas where Islam is a minority tradition.

Id al-Fitr, the Feast of Breaking Fast, is the second most important holiday in Islam. It occurs at the end of the fast of Ramadan, on the first day of the month of Shawwal. After the prolonged fast, which necessarily and intentionally disturbs the day-to-day routine of people, normal life returns. This feast may last for three days and is characterized by special *salat,* special almsgiving, visiting, and exchanging greetings.

The first day of the month of Muharram is the first day of the Islamic year and is therefore celebrated as the festival of the New Year. It marks the date of the *hijra*—the flight of Muhammad from Mecca to Medina. It is important to note that the orientation of time in the Muslim world is not centered on the Night of Power, when Muhammad first received God's revelation, or on the birthday of Muhammad. Rather, the forming of a single Muslim community—accomplished by the *hijra*—is the focal point of time. The beginning of the year is a day of piety, but there are no special services. Prayer at the mosque at dawn, however, is considered especially good. In Shiite Islam, this first day of the new year begins the period of mourning in remembrance of the martyrdom of Hysayn. In Sunni Islam, it is more a day of blessing.

The observance of the Prophet's birthday is not in the *Quran* or the traditions of Muhammad. It began, rather, in the twelfth century. Any celebration of Muhammad's birthday, therefore, is purely a function of local custom. In Morocco, for example, the day includes a procession of people carrying wax figures. It is normally celebrated on the twelfth day of the third month of the Muslim year. *Suras* of the *Quran* that speak of the life of the Prophet

are chanted. Extremely conservative Muslims, however, do not celebrate Muhammad's birthday, because they consider it a modern invention. Furthermore, they contend that there is a danger implicit in such a birthday celebration: the danger of focusing worship toward a person rather than toward Allah.

The festival of the Prophet's Heavenly Journey is traditionally celebrated on the eve of the twenty-seventh day of the month of Rajab. Based on the *Quran* (as related in *sura* 17), this festival celebrates the time when Muhammad ascended to heaven. More specifically, Muhammad was carried through the sky from Mecca to Jerusalem, and the angel Gabriel then carried him to heaven. The Dome of the Rock, a mosque in the Old City of Jerusalem, is situated on the rock where, tradition has it, Muhammad ascended through the seven heavens, through seven degrees of separation between mundane existence and Allah. At the "uttermost limit" in this journey, God commanded that men pray fifty times a day. Eventually, this requirement was lowered to five times of prayer each day. The festival of the Prophet's Heavenly Journey features devotional reading of popular accounts of the heavenly journey.

The image of the sacred canopy provides at least one more element by which the practices of the Islamic religious tradition can be analyzed. The threads of the fabric, and even the pillars themselves, can be imagined to be colored or permeated with a certain attitude or tendency. In Islamic practice, the element that colors all other practices is the emphasis on morality.

THE MORAL LIFE

The moral obligations that color all the activities of Islam consist basically of selflessness as a form of gratitude toward God.[32] Gratitude constitutes an element of love for Allah. Obedience, kindness, consideration for others, chastity and restraint, justice, and equality are key categories of the Muslim morality. An overarching principle for morality is to submit to Allah, to serve God as if he were pre-

The Dome of the Rock, one of Islam's holiest sites, on the Temple Mount, Jerusalem, Israel, was built in the seventh century C.E. by Abdel-el-Malik.

sent with you. Belief in Allah, belief in judgment based on one's actions, and belief that Allah is merciful and compassionate form the basis for Muslim morality.

Further, there is a connection between individual and social morality. Making one's own character pure is a necessary factor in making the character of society pure. Thus, the life of every Muslim is always lived within the context of the community of the faithful. Moderation rules the moral life of individual Muslims. Some practices held to be acceptable within much of Western culture—gambling and the consumption of alcohol—are avoided. Muslims envision a universal "brotherhood of man," with the mission to establish true social and economic justice. With this universal moral emphasis, Islam expects its message to be heard around the world. Also, because Islam makes no distinction between religious and secular elements, all facets of life fall within the realm of Islamic morality.

Sharia, Islamic law, in spite of being complex and extensive, has resulted in the standardizing of practices concerning prayer, marriage, divorce, inheritance, burial, almsgiving, and fasting. Although there have often been periods of exact legalism, the law creates what its name, Sharia,

means—guidance, the path leading to life. A five-fold classification of acts allows for flexible guidance in all aspects of life. First, some acts are *required* of all Muslims. Some acts, in contrast, are strictly *forbidden.* Both of these sorts of acts are associated with punishment—punishment for doing something forbidden and punishment for failing to accomplish something required. An example of a required act is prayer; a forbidden act is drinking alcohol. Furthermore, some actions are *recommended;* these acts are rewarded. One example would be saying extra prayers beyond those required. Some acts are *disapproved* but not forbidden or punished. Finally, some acts are classified as *indifferent* and are neither rewarded nor punished. It is in the last two classifications—disapproved and indifferent—where disagreement in interpretation of the law arises. However, the desire to determine the moral force of action in the world transcends the differences in interpretation. The standardization of the Sharia is to see all of life as a moral arena. Two examples of the moral coloring or universal morality in Islam can be found in the practice of *jihad* and in the role of women.

THE PRACTICE OF *JIHAD* The issue of *jihad* is complex and sensitive because of misrepresentation by non-Muslims and Muslims alike. Non-Muslims often have focused on the military context of the *jihad*—the holy war—to the exclusion of the broader notion of the term. In contrast, some Muslims have denied that there is any military or violent interpretation of *jihad*. Although this may be a theological assertion, the claim ignores an obvious component of the history of Islam. The militant, militaristic interpretation of *jihad* does have justification. To die on the battlefield in the name of Allah makes one a martyr and guarantees entrance to Paradise. Allah grants security to those who fight aggression:

> *Assuredly God will defend those*
> *who believe; surely God loves not any*
> *   ungrateful traitor*
> *Leave is given to those who fight because*
> *they were wronged—surely God is able*
> *   to help them—* [33]

However, the idea of engaging in a battle for faith has limits and is conceived in moderation. In fact, the *Quran* itself provides for the militaristic *jihad* only as a last resort, and some argue that the term refers only to self-defense.[34] In the early Islamic community, *jihad* meant the use of force in the form of a holy war. The intent was not to force conversion on anyone; this was forbidden by the *Quran*. The object of *jihad* was rather to gain political control over societies and run them in accordance with the principles of Islam.

To focus only on this aspect of *jihad*, however, is to miss the crucial coloring of the practice for the entire tradition of Islam. *Jihad* means "struggle" and "exertion"; thus, it is an expression of submission to Allah. One must struggle, constantly, against those forces that try to mitigate the power and the majesty of Allah. In the Sufi tradition of Islam, there is a distinction between a greater and a lesser holy war. The lesser holy war is the violent, military struggle against the "other," whoever the other may be. But there is a greater holy war—a greater *jihad*—and that is the conquest of oneself and the tendency to place blame on others. Therefore, *jihad* is both a belief and a practice in Islam. The interpretations vary, but *jihad* is included in this section because it is best seen as a practice that colors all the other practices of Islam.

GENDER ROLES   The role of women in the practices of Islam deserves special attention. It has been argued that contemporary Muslim women suffer discrimination and persecution because of the traditions of Islam. This is a complicated assertion that will be taken up again at the end of this chapter. Contextually, practices focusing on women must be subject to a less critical judgment. In pre-Islamic Arabia, for example, infanticide was common. More specifically, female infanticide was frequent, because male children were valued more than females. Females were objects of ownership. Further, in that historical period, a man could divorce a woman for any reason—or no reason—whereas a woman could not initiate such a break in a relationship. With Muhammad's revelations and administration, the status of women improved considerably. There was to be no female infanticide. Polygyny—having more than one wife—was allowed, up to four wives. This was a benefit to the women if the man was killed early in life, which was often the case. Moreover, divorced women were allowed to keep their dowries. Thus, in a sense, the status of women improved with the advent of Islam.

In terms of specific practices, women are exempt from the requirements for prayer during menstruation and after childbirth. There are exemptions for women during Ramadan, the month of fasting, for menstruation, pregnancy, or illness, but the obligation is expected to be made up at a later date. Women can make the *hajj*, the pilgrimage to Mecca, but they are to be accompanied by their husband or a male relative. Islam does not dissolve distinctions or profess absolute equality with no divisions between sexes. Men have authority over women because Allah had made one sex superior to the other. Good women are obedient, but women also have dominant roles in raising children and in running the family. The *Quran* presents a basic equality of women and men, but this does not mean that their functions in society should be the same. The special treatment received by women is another element of the practices of Islam that colors the entire tradition.

HISTORY OF ISLAM

This section on the history of Islam begins with both a warning and an admission. The warning is that when establishing an order of things—here, an order in history—there always will be something missing, something left out. Perception, even historical perception, is selective. This rendition of the history of Islam is no exception; it is incomplete and selective. The selection may even appear strange to some observers. That is the warning. But any attempt at ordering demands a "sharp eye" and an "articulate language."[35] This is the admission: This particular telling of the history of Islam focuses its eye primarily on two categories—political history and intellectual history. Thus, it neglects many different categories, such as art, from which the story of Islam could be told. Further, the language of articulation for this story is recursive. That is, each section of the history of Islam comments on political history as well as intellectual history, and the two keep modulating back and forth, weaving their threads together. Therefore, this "sharp eye" focusing here on the two categories of politics and thought attempts to create an "articulate language" through which the history of Islam can be understood.

ARABIA BEFORE MUHAMMAD

To understand the history of Islam, one must first be acquainted with the geographical setting of its place of origin. The story of Islam begins in Arabia, a peninsula with an extremely varied geography. Some scattered, relatively infrequent oases and some fertile areas on the coasts are overshadowed by enormous deserts and vast areas of barren land. In fact, scholars speak of three Arabias: the "rocky Arabia" (*Arabia petra*) on the western boundaries near Sinai and Jordan; the immense desert, extend-

ing over much of the central part of the peninsula, often called the "vacant quarter"; and "happy Arabia" (*Arabia felix*), which is fertile and productive. The southern part of *Arabia felix*, the west central part of the Arabian peninsula, which includes Mecca, was important historically and culturally as a link in the trade between India and the cultures of the Mediterranean. Natural boundaries such as oceans, seas, and deserts have led to the peninsula's metaphoric designation as the "Arabian island," but it is a large "island." Arabia consists of approximately 1 million square miles.[36] Although any absolute notion of geographical determinism—the theory that geographical realities necessarily determine cultural characteristics—must be rejected as an explanation for cultural and religious realities, it is nonetheless important to understand how this geographical setting influenced the originating events, as well as the historical expansion, of Islam.

Because of its geography, there were only a few cities, such as Mecca, in Arabia prior to the advent of Islam. The social groups in Arabia moved frequently to find food and water. In such a nomadic framework, the crucial social organizations were the tribe and the clan. Although it may seem strange to a twentieth-century U.S. culture steeped in the values of individual rights, the individual in this Arabian context only became important as a part of the tribe. Blood ties rather than law were the links among people. Furthermore, tribal identities were more important than loyalties to specific geographical regions. In the final analysis, survival depended on the strength of the tribe. There was some economic interdependence, with herders, farmers, and merchants intertwined, but pre-Islamic Arabian culture is best labeled as nomadic, independent, and tribal.

The religious situation of pre-Islamic Arabia was woven together with all of life, inseparable from what can be labeled within a modern Western perspective as "other" facets of life. The first element of this "enchanted universe" of Arabian religious culture on the eve of Islam is polytheism. Each population center had specific and special local gods and/or goddesses. Mecca had three goddesses: Al-Lat (a mother goddess), Manat (fate), and Al-Uzza (power). All were daughters of Allah, who was seen as a distant, creator God and who was revered by the Quraysh, Muhammad's tribe. There were also *jinn,* spiritual creatures that could be invisible or visible, sometimes assuming human form and even having sexual relations with humans. (In English, the term *genie* is taken from the singular form of the Arabic *jinn.*) The *jinn* could be friendly or demonic. A subset of the demonic *jinn,* the ghouls, often robbed graves, desiring decaying human flesh.

In addition to polytheism and a well-populated spiritual universe, animism—in which religious forces are identified with and found in natural objects—was a part of the religious life of the Arabian peninsula. Mecca emerged as a key site for such animistic religion because of a large meteoric stone that had become an object of veneration. The enclosure around the stone, called the Kaba, was filled with other images and objects, thereby solidifying its central role as the dwelling place of spirits. Pilgrimages to religious sanctuaries were allowed by warring tribes during extensive periods of truce, and Mecca was an important destination for such pilgrims because of the 360 spirits or gods that were thought to dwell there.

Besides indigenous religious practices, Christianity and Judaism also figure in the religious culture of pre-Islamic Arabia. Although there was a Jewish presence in Arabia for centuries, it was not until the second century of the common era that Jews become an important force in the area. They had a strong presence in the city of Yathrib, which would later become important for the prophet Muhammad. The influence of Christianity was at the periphery of Arabia. Byzantine Christianity was a presence in the cities around the Arabian "island," but the intense divisions within the Byzantine Empire, coupled with its often cruel treatment of Arabs, mitigated any influence. However both Judaism and Christianity contributed to the idea of monotheism, a distinct idea in the incredible spiritual pluralism of Arabia. A person who was a monotheist within the pluralism of early Arabian religion was called a *hanif.* Muhammad was

to come into contact with such monotheists, who were to influence him greatly.[37]

EARLY HISTORY OF ISLAM (632–750 C.E.)

During the first hundred years after Muhammad's death, Islam spread dramatically across the globe. Was this a result of premeditated calculation, a plan to convert the world? Medieval Christians often said that the expansion was an evil impulse. Devout Muslims sometimes say it was by invitation. Neither assertion tells the whole story. One reason for the quick expansion was that the Arab peoples experienced unity for the first time under Muhammad. Furthermore, other empires in the region—Persian and Byzantine—were weakened by both internal and external forces. Therefore, there are historical, political, religious, and social factors to consider in the growth of Islam. In this retelling of the story, each era within the history of Islam first will be examined from a political and social perspective, and then in terms of religious and philosophical ideas. This division does not imply that these two facets of history are separate in reality. However, for the sake of clarity and convenience, it is a useful model.

THE FOUR "RIGHTLY GUIDED" CALIPHS (632–661 C.E.)

With the death of Muhammad, Islam reached a watershed. Because Muhammad had designated no successor, his death left a vacuum in the religious and political leadership of the still new religion. The struggle over succession proved—and still proves—to be a major source of conflict within Islam itself. One way of establishing succession was through the bloodlines emanating from Muhammad; another way was choosing from a select group the person who possessed certain qualifications for leadership without regard for blood relationship. This division plays a role in the political history of Islam, and it also plays a role in the history of religious ideas, as will be seen shortly. Nevertheless, the majority of Muslims view this early era of the first four *caliphs*—called "Rightly

Guided"—as the normative period. It provides the idealized past to which Muslims have looked back for inspiration and guidance, a time to be remembered and emulated.[38]

The first leader after Muhammad was chosen based on the perspective that focused on leadership. Abu Bakr became the first *caliph* (literally "successor"). He was not a blood relative of Muhammad; rather, he was Muhammad's father-in-law, the father of Muhammad's wife, Aisha. Abu Bakr was one of the first converts to Islam and remained a faithful follower of Muhammad his entire life. Although Abu Bakr's rule lasted only from 632 to 634 C.E., it was nonetheless important. First, he was able to consolidate control and power even among various groups within Islam. Second, Abu Bakr took the message of Islam to the rest of the world, moving his large army out of southwestern Arabia into Syria. But he was not able to witness the full expansion of Islam. Abu Bakr died less than two years after becoming the leader of the religion professing surrender to Allah.

For the next ten years, from 634 to 644, Umar was *caliph* during an extremely favorable time for Islam. Both the Persian (Sassanid) and Byzantine Empires were exhausted after years of conflict. The repressive Christian Byzantine Empire fostered the hatred and resentment of other Christians, some of whom were considered heretics. These Christians who were labeled heretics by fellow Christians found themselves in a curious position. Although they might claim that Islam was wrong theologically, Islam did create a much more tolerable political situation than the one instituted by the Christian Byzantines. A Muslim historian describes the reaction of Christians in Syria: "We like your rule and justice far better than the state of oppression and tyranny under which we have been living."[39] In this way, Islam was able to expand into areas formerly controlled by Christian empires.

The Persian Empire proved to be more difficult for the Muslim conquest. The population was non-Semitic, so there was not an immediate cultural bond. Further, the empire's predominant religion was Zoroastrianism, a dualistic religion that has its roots in Persia. During Umar's rule, however, the power of the Byzantines (in Syria and Egypt) was sapped, and the Sassanids (in Iraq and Iran) also fell from power. What are now Syria, Iraq, Iran, and Egypt became Muslim, and the expansion of Islam proceeded quickly.

After a servant stabbed Umar with a poisoned dagger, Uthman was chosen to succeed as *caliph* (644–656). Uthman belonged to the Umayyad, a clan of the Quraysh tribe that had been late converts to Islam. Even though Uthman was not, as were many of his tribe, an early opponent of Islam, and even though he was an early believer and convert, some of the original faithful did not trust him and started to subvert his leadership. Ali, first cousin and son-in-law (husband of Fatima) to the Prophet, hoped to succeed. Eventually, Uthman had little support. The end of his reign came as he was accused of treachery and was assassinated by those formerly loyal to his leadership.

Ali, the fourth "Rightly Guided" Caliph, ruled from 656 to 661, but his reign never had universal acceptance. In an effort to solidify power and put down his enemies, Ali moved his capital to Kufa in Iraq, thereby shifting the center of politics of Islam away from the Arabian peninsula. A power struggle ensued between Ali and the powerful Umayyad governor of Syria, who wanted Ali to hand over the assassins of Uthman for punishment. Ali attempted to crush the Syrian Muslims through military action, but with victory almost within his grasp, Ali submitted the issue to arbitration. This decision proved to be a fatal mistake.

Because of the decision to let arbitration settle the dispute, a group in Ali's army, known as Kharijites (seceders), declared war on both Ali and his Umayyad opponent. From the perspective of the Kharijites, Ali had failed by letting humans settle the disputes; the issue should have been settled

Islam was established in the Americas in the early 1800s and in Western Europe in the twentieth century.

Sources: Adapted from Ward J. Fellows, *Religions East and West* (San Diego: Harcourt, Brace, 1998). Partially adapted from Jonathan Z. Smith, *Dictionary of Religion* (San Francisco: HarperCollins, 1995) © by The American Academy of Religion, p. 508.

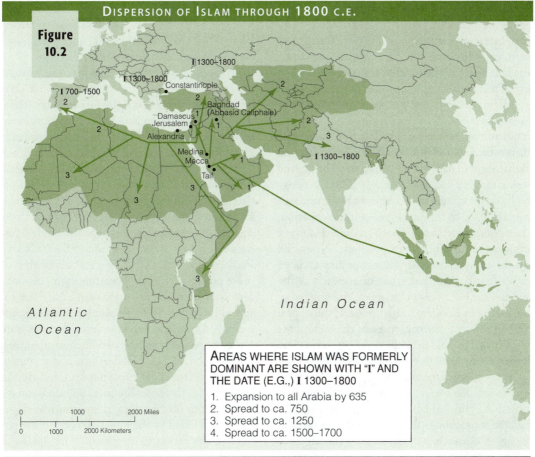

DISPERSION OF ISLAM THROUGH 1800 C.E.

Figure 10.2

I 1300–1800

I 1300–1800

Constantinople

I 700–1500

2

2

2

Baghdad
(Abbasid Caliphate)

Damascus 1
Jerusalem
Alexandria

2

2

1

2

3

I 1300–1800

Medina
Mecca
Taif

1

1

3

3

1

3

3

3

4

Indian Ocean

*Atlantic
Ocean*

0   1000   2000 Miles

0   1000   2000 Kilometers

AREAS WHERE ISLAM WAS FORMERLY
DOMINANT ARE SHOWN WITH "I" AND
THE DATE (E.G.,) **I** 1300–1800

1. Expansion to all Arabia by 635
2. Spread to ca. 750
3. Spread to ca. 1250
4. Spread to ca. 1500–1700

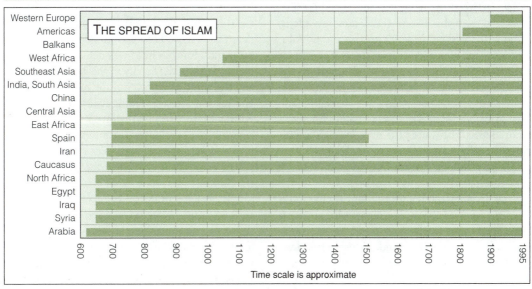

THE SPREAD OF ISLAM

Western Europe
Americas
Balkans
West Africa
Southeast Asia
India, South Asia
China
Central Asia
East Africa
Spain
Iran
Caucasus
North Africa
Egypt
Iraq
Syria
Arabia

600   700   800   900   1000   1100   1200   1300   1400   1500   1600   1700   1800   1900   1995

Time scale is approximate

by God on the battlefield. Succession in the leadership for Islam for this group had nothing to do with heredity; piety and morality were the qualifications for leadership of the faith. Ali put down the first revolt by the seceders but in 661 was slain by a Kharijite as he was going to a mosque in Kufa.

With this political and social picture of this early period drawn, one can distinguish the beginnings of an intellectual history, a history of conflicts over ideas and theology. The amazingly rapid expansion of Islam during this period brought a new situation: Muslims not united by the geography or the culture of the Arabian peninsula (see Figure 10.2). In this pluralistic cultural situation, the applicability of the *Quran* to each and every ethical situation became a problem. When the *Quran* was not absolutely clear regarding an issue or a situation, the first court of appeal was the *sunna*—the behavior or practice of Muhammad or the traditions associated with his life. If this appeal was insufficient, the consensus of the community, or *ijma*, was held to be the deciding factor. And if this was not enough, then the method was to find an analogy, or *qiyas*, based on the principles of the *Quran* and the community. That is, when a new situation or ethical question arose, it was seen to be "like" a situation in the *Quran* or the *sunna*, even though it was not exactly the same. An analogy was drawn between the new situation and the tradition, and from that likeness, that analogy, a legal judgment could be made. With this methodology for solving ethical dilemmas, the Sunni or Sunnite branch of Islam—those who follow the *sunna*—was formed. In this approach, Islam makes no clear distinction between faith or religion and law. Thus, the word for "law" in Islam, Sharia, is translated as "the way or the path," which constitutes the religion of submission to Allah.

The pluralism that confronted Islam was not only internal; it was external as well. Because the *Quran* includes references to biblical characters from the Jewish and the Christian traditions, there developed a special relationship with these groups. Called People of the Book under Muslim rule, Jews and Christians often were required to pay a special tax and were barred from military service. Religious practices were also restricted to some degree. Still, there remained a fundamental underlying respect for these groups. The same could not be said, however, for polytheists and so-called pagans.

Opposed to the Sunni tradition in Islam is another major stream that arose during this early period in the expansionist history of Islam. After the murder of the *caliph* Ali, his followers, eventually called **Shiites,** claimed that it was the divine right of the family of Muhammad to rule. When leadership is decided by other factors, they argued, disaster is imminent. By his marriage to Fatima, daughter of Muhammad and Khadija, Ali was a kinsman of the Prophet and therefore the true source of the leadership within Islam. Shiite Muslims claim that authority is granted in this way. Furthermore, such authority is invested with even more power within the community by passions associated withe assassination of Ali and, later, his son Husayn. Ali was assassinated because some perceived him too weak to lead. But his son, Husayn, was the grandson of Muhammad himself and, as such, claimed leadership. The people of what is now Iraq called Husayn to lead, and Husayn accepted. However, at Karbala (680 C.E.), on his journey from Medina, he and his family were surprised and killed by the forces of Yazid, his opponent in the struggle for power. The deaths of Husayn and his family are the source of the passion for legitimate authority among Shiites. Their death took days. Husayn's family died before his eyes, and Husayn's head was delivered as a trophy to Yazid. Thus, the loyalty to this line of succession and the emotional power of the martyrdom of Ali and his son Husayn distinguish the Shiite strand within Islam. Sunni Muslims, in contrast, focus leadership more on the consensus of the community and on reasoned argument concerning matters of faith. (Table 10.3 describes the Sunnis and the Shiites.)

In its long and extremely complicated history, the Shiite version of Islam has developed some distinctive theologies and a variety of religious subgroups. Probably out of its reverence for Ali, Shiite Islam came to regard the community leader, the *imam,* as an infallible being who was the only one

Table 10.3	**MAJOR ISLAMIC GROUPS: SUNNIS AND SHIITES**	
	The two most important divisions in Islam are the Sunnis (derived from the term *sunna*, or "tradition") and the Shiites (derived from the term *shia*, or "faction"). Sunnis are by far the largest group, making up approximately 85 percent of Islam, whereas the Shiites make up between 10 and 15 percent. The division originated from a controversy about the successors of Muhammad; over time, however, it has widened to include beliefs, as well as practices. The split has been reflected in recent political and even military conflicts in the Middle East.	
	Sunni (or Sunnite) Islam	Argues that the true successors to Muhammad do not need to be descended from the immediate family of Muhammad; legitimate succession does not need to be transmitted through heredity. Sunni Islam emphasizes tradition in religious life, the way the Prophet and his followers lived. Thus, the *Quran* is the fundamental authority, along with the *hadith* and the consensus of the community. Sunni Islam has developed an entire way of life that includes religion, law, politics, and all of culture. Saudi Arabia, including Mecca, is the center of power for Sunni Islam.
	Shiite Islam	Argues that the true successors to Muhammad descend directly from Muhammad's family, that Ali and his sons were the rightful heirs to the leadership of Islam but were killed by those distorting and misusing power in the decades after Muhammad's death. Even though they are a minority, Shiite Muslims believe that a spiritual power of these true successors is transmitted to a series of *imams*. Although there is disagreement within this faction on the number of *imams* and their exact progression, most Shiites assume that the spiritual power of the *imams* works through and guides Shiite leaders. Some assume that the last *imam* will return to restore true Islam and inaugurate a new age in world history. Most Shiites are found in Iran, although minority groups exist throughout those countries with significant Muslim populations.

who knew the hidden and true meaning of the *Quran*. One group of Shiites recognizes twelve *imams* in their history, the last of whom disappeared (the technical term for this disappearance is *occultation*) in the late 870s. It is believed that his return as the **Mahdi,** (the divinely guided one) will inaugurate a period of righteousness prior to the last judgment. Until he returns, all law and doctrine are interpreted by scholars or **mujtahids,** who are believed to be under his guidance. The Twelvers, as those who recognize twelve *imams* are called, constitute the majority of Shiite Muslims.

A smaller subgroup within Shiite Islam is the Ismailis. The distinguishing feature of this group originates in the identity of the seventh in the series of *imams*. The main body of Shiites accept Musa as the seventh *imam,* but the Ismaili recognize instead his brother, Ismail. Since Ismail's disappearance, they have awaited his return and hence are usually called Seveners, instead of Twelvers. The seven *imams* recognized by the Ismailis are, in a sense, higher in excellence than the Prophet, because they receive their teachings directly from God himself. Although other divisions exist within Shiite Islam, the distinction between the Seveners and the Twelvers is the most dramatic.

Because divine knowledge was mediated through the infallible teachings of an *imam,* the Shiites believe, in contrast to the Sunnis, that all knowledge derived from fallible, human sources is worthless. It is not what the community thinks, but rather what the *imam* proclaims, that is authoritative. This position effectively narrows the scope for toleration of divergent views. Another major difference from Sunni Islam was the emergence of a "passion history" among the Shiites, comparable in many ways to the Christian Passion plays about the life of Jesus. The violent death in 680 C.E. of Ali's son, Husayn, is celebrated annually with plays, orations, and processions. The influence of this emphasis on passion history is also felt in the veneration in which Muslims hold Ali and his family and in the respect that they show for his descendants. (An earlier section of this chapter focused on the veneration of "saints" related to this emotional attachment.)

The total Shiite movement makes up probably less than 15 percent of the Islamic world. The greatest concentration is in Iran, where over 80 percent of the population is Shiite. It is within Iran and between Iran and other Muslim nations that the conflict between the Shiites and the Sunnis has become explosive in the late twentieth century. Thus, the early period in Islam's history provides perhaps the major theological distinction in the religion even today—that between Shiite and Sunni. The history of Islamic expansion continued, however, with those who followed the first four *caliphs*, the Umayyad dynasty.

THE UMAYYAD DYNASTY (661–750 C.E.)

The century of the Umayyad dynasty was a difficult time. The geographical expansion of Islam had outrun its institutional development, and the problems of regional competition and internal division complicated the spreading of the faith. The Kharijites, those seceders who eventually assassinated Ali, were more than ready to fight against what they believed were impurities infiltrating into Islam. Nonetheless, this century was a remarkable time. Islam expanded across all of North Africa, extended through the Iberian Peninsula, crossed the Pyrenees, and approached central France. If it were not for a decisive battle in 732 C.E., when Charles Martel defeated Muslim forces in France and forced

them back into what is now Spain, it is arguable that all of Europe would have become Muslim. The century after the Prophet's death—from 632 to 732—saw the widest expansion of Islam in the Western world. At its zenith, this Islamic Empire was larger than the Roman Empire.

In Spain, Islam created an Iberian-Islamic culture that was the principal center of learning throughout this period and even beyond. Umayyads ruled in Spain until the eleventh century. It was during this time, the so-called Dark Ages in Europe, that Muslim scholarship became the vehicle by which the classical ideas of Greece were preserved and eventually transmitted to Christian Europe. It was also during this period that the first independent schools of Islamic law were organized. Although these four schools flourished and received their most extensive development in a period of Muslim history to be discussed shortly (the Abbasid caliphate), they nonetheless began to take shape during the Umayyad period. The establishment of these schools led to an organization of the ethical and legal basis of Islam. A brief description of these schools will identify the various strands of Muslim hermeneutics, the theory of interpretation that has both legal and theological components in Islam.

Of the four schools, the Hanafite school was the freest in its use of speculation about the law. This school was founded by Abu Hanifa, whose method included, first, Quranic consultation (ignoring the *hadith*, by and large) and second, analogy. The question asked when a dispute over interpretation arose was, How could the Quranic principle be applied in this particular geographical area, namely Iraq, based on the principle of analogy? If the analogy ran against the public good or general principles of justice, Abu Hanifa resorted to reasoned justice, using his personal, rational perspective to take the public good into consideration. For example, the punishment for theft in the *Quran* is cutting off the hand of the thief. Because that principle, when taken literally, does not translate well to benefit the social situation in Iraq, the analogy from other portions of the *Quran* leads to the conclusion that a more effective punishment would be imprisonment.

A second approach to Islamic law during this period, the Malikite school, was founded by Malik ibn-Anas of Medina. This school supported the tradition of Medina as the cradle and the first capital of Islam. It approached disputes within laws and rituals by combining both the *Quran* and the *hadith.* When difficulties in consistency arose between the *Quran* and the *hadith,* the Malikite bias was to decide the issue based on the consensus of opinion, or *ijma,* that prevailed in Medina.

The Shafiite school, the third of the four schools, was founded by al-Shafii, a descendant of the Quraysh tribe. His approach identified four sources of law: the *Quran,* the practice of Muhammad as discerned through the *hadith,* the consensus of the community, and analogy through reasoning. This school gave equal weight to all four components, but when there was a conflict, it might even prefer the *hadith* over the *Quran.* In this sense, the Shafiite schools is more liberal than some of the other approaches to the law, but it is clear in its rejection of any unwarranted speculation. Perhaps the major influence of this school was its standardization of the vocabulary and the approach to Islamic law.

The Hanbalite school, the most conservative of the four, adheres to the letter of the *Quran* with only a minor, secondary recognition of the *hadith.* This approach is the dominant approach to the law today in Saudi Arabia.[40]

THE ABBASID CALIPHATE (750–1258 C.E.)

Among the enemies of the Umayyads were the Abbasids, the descendants of Muhammad's uncle, al-Abbas. The Umayyads were increasingly condemned for not adhering to Islamic law. Because there were multiple perspectives on the law itself, this charge could be raised at any time. The Umayyad Empire was also experiencing internal tensions between Arab Muslims and non-Arab Muslims. Specifically, Iranian Muslims, who were rightfully proud of their own Persian history, resented being treated as second-class Muslims because they were not Arabs. They especially resented the taxes they had to pay—taxes from which Arab

Muslims were exempt. In 750 C.E., a revolution almost wiped out the Umayyads; thus, the Abbasid caliphate was created, with the label *caliphate* implying a return to the perceived proper succession of Islam.

During this period in the history of Islam, the political center of the religion moved from Medina to Baghdad. For half a millennium, the Abbasid caliphate ruled Islam. Because of the expansion that had occurred during the first century of Islam, the Abbasids inherited a culturally plural empire united by religion. It is this period that saw the encouragement, albeit often frustrated, of a cultural synthesis between the various Muslim groups.

The attempt at universalism, however, was short-lived. By 850, the Islamic Empire was more fragmented than unified. During the latter part of the Abbasid caliphate, there were competing spheres of influence. One center of power was Spain; another was Iran; and still others lay in Egypt, North Africa, and Syria. Late in the tenth century, the Abbasid *caliphs* of Baghdad confronted a people from the steppes of Europe, the Seljuq Turks. These people converted to Islam but nonetheless soon ended the rule of Iranian Muslims. They also seized power in Syria and Palestine. In fact, the differences between these Muslim Seljuqs and the Christians concerning access to Jerusalem and its holy shrines led to the Christian Crusades late in the eleventh century. In 1099, Jerusalem was captured by the Christians. It was retaken by Muslim forces in 1187 under the leadership of Salah-al-Din, known as Saladin to non-Muslims.

Political and military history, however, are only part of the "sharp eye" of this chapter's historical ordering of Islam; intellectual and philosophical history play their part as well. A key group during this period in Muslim history were the Mutazilites. First arising in the Umayyad caliphate, these ardent defenders of the faith desired converts from non-Arab cultures, such as Greek, Jewish, Christian, and Zoroastrian cultures. The Mutazilites were some of the first to engage in **kalam**—reasoned argument in defense of the faith; thus, they can be considered analogous to the apologists for the faith found in other traditions. The key assumption of this group was that the faith grounded on the *Quran* could be subject to rational testing. Reason and faith, therefore, were not mutually exclusive. The Mutazilites were influential through the tenth century.

Whereas the Mutazilites were comfortable using reason in an Islamic context, this period of Islamic history also gives witness to those who moved even more comfortably in the realm of rationalistic Greek thought. These were the *falasafa,* or "philosophers." The key idea was to state the faith of Islam in philosophical terms, thus gaining the full support of reason. Ibn-Sina (Persian, d. 1037) and ibn-Rushd (Spanish, d. 1198)—known in the West as, respectively, Avicenna and Averroes—are two examples of philosophers who brought together the concepts of Greek philosophy and the tradition of Islam. Ironically, however, the turning of the trend of Islamic thought away from its focus on reason came when more conservative members of the faith used reason to argue against a rationalistic approach to the faith. The key thinker here was al-Ashari.

The ideas of the Mutazilites bothered al-Ashari, who was born at the end of the ninth century. Although trained by the Mutazilites, he ultimately rejected their position because it placed human limits on the power of God by inflating the power of reason. This was, for al-Ashari, simply human arrogance, pride, or *hubris.* Opposed to this inflated view of humanity, al-Ashari proclaimed that God determines everything, even those deeds defined in human terms as "evil." Al-Ashari regarded God as the immediate and direct cause of every occurrence. Therefore, he rejected the notion of God as a First Cause who steps out of the creative, causal process and lets things happen. Further, al-Ashari rejected the idea of natural law, which was popular among some of the philosophers, substituting for it a concept of "divine habits." For example, he argued that although flames are usually perceived as hot and snow is usually perceived as cold, these attributes are constantly recreated by Allah out of "habit." A so-called miracle happens when Allah suspends his habits. Al-Ashari's the-ology claimed that every moment of time, every act, every thought, and every separate thing or event is directly created by God.

If one takes al-Ashari's line of thinking to its logical, rational conclusion, then a reasonable claim would be that nothing has any real existence other than God. So it can be argued that al-Ashari's theology of divine omnipotence, predestination, and determinism is more rigorous than anything comparable from Judaism or Christianity. Further, al-Ashari taught that God creates belief in the Muslim and disbelief in the infidel and that any perception of human decision is, in fact, an illusion. His philosophy, harmonizing with the ancient cultural tendency toward fatalism, became the established theological truth throughout most of the Muslim world.[41]

Neither philosophy nor the reasoned rejection of philosophy exhausts the depth and variety of this period of Islam. In many traditions, groups appear who are not satisfied with the outward observances and rituals or the abstract philosophy of their religion; Islam is no exception. During the eighth century, beginning about a hundred years after the death of Muhammad, one group of Muslims wanted a religion based on inner experience, a religion that renounced the luxuries of the world and devoted itself purely to obedience to God. Initially, they did not want any of the external trappings of a socialized religion. These Muslims became known as Sufis, probably from their garments made of *suf,* "wool."

As a sect of Islam, **Sufism** evolved through three phases. First was the phase of asceticism, the rejection of worldliness. The believers' coarse woolen garments symbolized the denial of physical desires. Second was an emphasis on ecstasy, the desire for communion with God. Last came the cognitive dimension, in which the believer sought a higher knowledge than that granted to the average Muslim. At a later stage in the development of Sufism—by the twelfth century—forms of communal organization were developed that were not unlike Christian forms of monasticism.

One of the most articulate voices of Sufism during the Middle Ages was ibn-Arabi, whose mysticism is widely documented and continues to be an inspiration for Muslims. For ibn-Arabi, the profession of faith—"there is no God but God"—means that there is absolutely no reality except God. God is an absolute transcendence and unity, the One underlying the multiplicity of forms of external existence.[42] To describe this experience, ibn-Arabi uses an image. Creation, he says, was the mirror in which the One perceived his own beauty and wisdom. As the mirror returns the gaze, so, too, does creation mirror the face of the Creator. Thus, ibn-Arabi's philosophy is a monism; reality is one thing and one thing only. In this monism, humanity has a special place. Humans have the power to experience the secret of the one and the many, multiplicity and unity. Everyone, potentially, can experience this oneness. But only those who realize the unity experientially truly "know" the unity. The goal of this Sufi mystic is to experience the singular essence underneath the buzzing confusion of particular, isolatable events. In this experience, there is, in effect, an extinguishing of what later will be called the *ego*. After this experience of unity beyond the limits of the ego, the mystic can then return to this world. For ibn-Arabi, Muhammad is thus the perfect human, a divine manifestation who experienced the unity and then dwelled in the world to help others experience that unity of being. Sufi or Islamic mysticism parallels the experience of mystics in other religious traditions, such as Buddhism, Hinduism, and Christianity.[43]

Regarding the interpretation of the sacred text, ibn-Arabi recognized that the *Quran* has many levels of truth. The *Quran* acknowledges Jesus as a prophet. Traditionally, however, his prophecy is eclipsed by the revelation to Muhammad. From the perspective of ibn-Arabi, the only difficulty with the Christian portrayal of Jesus as the Christ is that Christians have limited that manifestation of unity to only one person rather than extending it to all humans. As can easily be imaged, ibn-Arabi's ideas were attacked by traditionalists as blasphemy. Even within the Sufi tradition, he had his critics. Ibn-Arabi could speak of an identity between Creator and creation, whereas Sufi tradi-

tionalists maintained a distinction between the Creator and the created.

As the example of ibn-Arabi demonstrates, the mystical element dominant in Sufism creates a constant tension with more formal, traditional forms of Islam. The idea that the believer could experience a "union" with Allah borders on idolatry at best. Sometimes Sufis were considered heretics for such language. After asserting "I am the True," the Sufi al-Hallaj was mutilated and executed. His prosecutors assumed that al-Hallaj was committing blasphemy by asserting that he was Allah, the True.

Sufism remained a parallel development within Sunni Islam until the eleventh century, when the theologian al-Ghazali made a formal attempt to merge the doctrines of mysticism with the orthodox consensus of the community. His message to other theologians was that unless there was a "science of the heart" for all believers, the doctrines of Islam would be nothing more than outward formalities devoid of any inner life or meaning.

Al-Ghazali, who lived in twelfth-century Baghdad, was highly regarded as a theologian and as an authority on Islamic law. As a theologian, he represented the scholastic approach to religion, an approach that contrasted dramatically with that of the Sufis. But al-Ghazali's scholastic approach was transformed when he experienced a spiritual crisis. The crisis developed out of the self-realization that the real motivation for his religious studies was his hope of personal reputation and fame. Realizing his pride and yet still serious in his search for God, al-Ghazali could not continue in his faith as before. He left his position at the university in Baghdad and went to live as the Sufi mystics did—in humility. When he returned years later, al-Ghazali was able to include Sufism in the mainstream of Muslim orthodoxy. In his writings, al-Ghazali demonstrates the essential harmony between the rational scholastic theology of al-Ashari on the one hand and Sufi teachings on the other. Because of al-Ghazali's great influence, a community consensus formed on the acceptability of Sufism within Islam; consequently, Sufism did not become a separate religious tradition.[44]

THE MOGUL AND THE OTTOMAN EMPIRES (1290–1924 C.E.)

A problem even greater than the pluralism within Muslim thought was the external threat that emerged during the Middle Ages when nomadic Mongols from central Asia swept into Baghdad in the middle of the thirteenth century C.E.. The Mongols were eventually turned back, but not before creating a political vacuum that could not be filled. This void, in turn, created an unstable Muslim world that lasted until the sixteenth century. At this time, two great Muslim empires formed, filling the political vacuum. The Moguls ruled over India, and the Ottoman Turks controlled an area including West Asia, North Africa, and eastern Europe.

Muslim warriors had entered India toward the end of the tenth century. They occupied the Punjab and eventually set up the sultanate of Delhi in 1206, which controlled northern India. The first Muslim invaders of India pursued a harsh policy toward the local population. Because Buddhists and Hindus were not People of the Book, there was little concern for their shrines or religions. Buddhism never recovered from this Muslim persecution. Hinduism survived by creating new forms of devotion; in time, greater tolerance was granted to the Hindu population. During this period, however, there were also many conversions to Islam. Some converts came from the lower castes of Hinduism, and conversion immediately improved their lot in life dramatically.

THE MOGUL EMPIRE (1526–1858 C.E.)

Early in the sixteenth century, Babur (1483–1530 C.E.), who claimed to be a descendant of Genghis Khan, invaded India, sweeping aside the sultan of Delhi's troops. Thus, he became the ruler of northern India and, in 1526, the founder of the Mogul or Mongol Empire. This empire peaked faster and declined more rapidly than the Ottoman Empire. Still, it created a culture that left a permanent mark on the Indian subcontinent.

Akbar, Babur's grandson, ruled from 1556 to 1605. He extended the territory of the Mogul Empire; most of India, including Kashmir in the north and much of the Deccan region in the south, was brought under Muslim rule. In this expansion, Akbar never forced Hindus to become Muslims. His enlightened policy was that unity was possible only when there was a perspective that took into consideration the well-being of all the people of the area, not just the good of the few who professed to a certain religion. Controverting traditional, orthodox Islam, Akbar declared universal religious toleration. He even induced some scholars of his time to support an infallibility decree that gave him almost unlimited power to dismantle anything that got in the way of a unified empire. Akbar argued that a syncretic religion was needed—the Divine Faith—to unify the empire with a sort of civil religion. The attempt did not attain converts, but politically and socially the Mogul Empire was strong.

Jahangir, Akbar's son (1605–1625), extended Muslim territory in the south of India. Following him, Shah Jahan (1628–1658) restored Islam as the state religion. Shah Jahan's reign is regarded as the golden age of Mogul art. In fact, the Taj Mahal was built in Agra as a monument to one of his wives. But his son, Aurangzeb, imprisoned Shah Jahan when he was ill and assumed power.

Aurangzeb (1658–1707) had grand visions that saw the Mogul Empire becoming larger than ever. However, he also reintroduced the system of discrimination among religions, making sure that Islam was the religion at the pinnacle of the hierarchy. Aurangzeb's punishment for non-Muslims, a poll tax, went beyond what the law required. There were forced conversions to Islam, and Hindu temples were destroyed. Finally, in 1675, a Sikh *guru*—Tegh Bahadur (1621–1675), the ninth Sikh *guru*—was executed for refusing to convert to Islam. (*Sikh* means "disciple," "student," "seeker of truth," specifically the followers of Guru Nanak.) This execution was a turning point for the Sikh community, which aggressively resisted injustice and vigorously opposed Islam. (See the discussion of Sikhism in Appendix A.) The end result of the conflict between Islam and other religious communities was a weaker, rather than a stronger, empire.

The Mogul Empire declined quickly. Corruption among officials, oppression of the people, widespread revolts, and invaders from Iran were only part of the problem. When the Sikhs seized power in the Punjab, quasi-independent states were created where once there had been an empire. In the eighteenth century, Britain and France battled over interests in India. The British won and, after the Seven Years' War, became the strongest power in the region, thereby taking control of the Mogul Empire.

THE OTTOMAN EMPIRE (1290–1294 C.E.)

During the thirteenth century, the Ottoman Turks increased in influence and seized power in Asia Minor, the territory that is now Turkey.[45] This strength in one geographical location provided enough impetus for Islam to move into Europe. In 1453, Constantinople fell to the Ottomans, ending the long reign of the Christian Byzantine Empire. Within the next hundred years, the Muslims had moved into Russia and the Balkans, and they had approached Vienna. Further, the Ottoman Empire reintegrated the areas previously controlled by Muslims: the Arabian peninsula, the lands around the Mediterranean, and North Africa. By the end of the sixteenth century, the Ottoman form of Islam had assimilated the Umayyad and Abbasid dynasties. Thus, the Ottoman rule deserves the title *empire*. With its capital in Istanbul (formerly Constantinople), the Ottoman Empire, in effect, replaced the Christian Byzantine influence. There was, indeed, a strong central government and military, but the key to Ottoman success was its synthesis of religious and political authority.

Suleiman II, the Magnificent (1520–1566), led the Ottoman Empire to its zenith. Under Suleiman, the Ottomans conquered Belgrade, the island of Rhodes, and finally the kingdom of Hungary. He launched a campaign against Austria, the defender of the western flank of Christian Europe. But Suleiman failed in this attempt and turned his efforts toward the east. Mesopotamia, Egypt, and southern Arabia were eventually brought into the fold. In a curious way, Suleiman contributed to the success of the Protestant Reformation in Europe in the sixteenth century. With powerful Muslim forces constituting an external threat, the Holy Roman Emperor was unable to take effective action against the leaders of the Reformation—Martin Luther and, eventually, the German Protestant princes.

The decline of the Ottoman Empire began in 1683, when Muslim forces failed once again to take Vienna. In the resulting treaty of Karlowitz, Hungary was given to Austria. The treaty may have been a symptom, but what was the cause of the decline? First, the rise of European naval power severely limited Ottoman military options. Furthermore, the colonization of the New World broadened European horizons. An influx of gold led to inflation and, thus, to poverty. All during the seventeenth and eighteenth centuries, the Ottomans tried to make an old system work. In 1770, however, almost total defeat by the Russian fleet led to the realization that some borrowing from the West was necessary. This realization, however, was a case of "too little, too late, too slowly." The first reforms came in the early part of the nineteenth century. By then, however, the Industrial Revolution had increased Europe's power and had further accelerated the rate of change occurring in that region. Ottoman reforms had difficulty keeping up with the rapid transformations taking place in Europe.[46]

Just as the Ottoman rulers were finally convinced of the need to respond to the modern world, another challenge was forming in what is now Saudi Arabia—a challenge that can be seen as a reactionary movement in response to the developments of the modern Western world. Muhammad ibn-Abd al-Wahhab (1703–1792) was creating a militant and puritanical form of Islam, a form that would pervade the entire Islamic world. Wahhab's was a reform movement. He sought to revive and spread a pure, original form of Islam by following the plain sense of the *Quran* and the *sunna*. Esoteric, rationalistic, convoluted interpretations of the *Quran*, Wahhab maintained, merely hid the power of Allah's revelations. The basic tenet of the Wahhabi movement was a militant, radical monotheism that fought any and every manifestation of idolatry, immorality, and innovation.

This reform movement also protested against the Sufi tradition within Islam. The key issue was

A small boy stands with a crowd of Muslim women as they pray in Cirebon, Java. The women recently returned from a pilgrimage to Mecca (1980s–1990s).

the distinction between Creator and creation. According to the Wahhabis, the Sufis had so blurred the line between the two that creation and Creator were identified, producing a sort of pantheism—blasphemy from the perspective of a radial ethical monotheism as perceived by the Wahhabis. Sufism was too esoteric; it did not adhere to the plain sense of the *Quran*. Because this plain sense emphasized the transcendence and power of Allah, any mystical identification with the divine was idolatry.

The key to the Wahhabi reform movement was literal sense of the *Quran*. This became the canon, the yardstick by which all thought and action were judged. Thus, the reform movement was, in a sense, merely a reconversion to the Islam of the originating period of the faith. The forming of the Wahhabi community led to a purification of Islam. Artifacts such as tombs and shrines, or anything that could be seen as a focus for polytheism, were destroyed. Religious training was rigorous. Conduct in public was severely regulated. In this process, the Wahhabi movement created a very disciplined community with military, economic, religious, and

social functions; in fact, the present tradition of government in Saudi Arabia is a consequence of the Wahhabi reforms.

The Wahhabi reform movement became a direct challenge to the power and authority of the Ottomans. After an initial expansion of the Wahhabis, the Ottoman Empire regained much political control, but the movement inspired other revivalist movements. When it appears that the world is falling apart and the center cannot hold, reform and revival movements provide a source of new commitment, energy, and hope for the tradition.

ISLAM AFTER THE OTTOMAN EMPIRE

The nineteenth century was the zenith of Western European colonialism. British, Dutch, French, Italian, and even Russian interests infringed upon areas influenced by Islam. Throughout the entire century, the Ottoman Empire was pressured by external forces and internal divisions. Turkish control of the Balkans was lessened. The last effective ruler of the Ottoman Empire, Abd-al-Hamid II

(1876–1909 C.E.), attempted to reassert control and power but met resistance in his efforts from separatist Arabs who, from the puritan perspective of the Wahhabi movement, thought they were viewing a perverted version of Islam.

After the Ottoman Empire entered World War I on the side of Germany and Austria-Hungary, Arab leaders were enlisted by the Allies to help fight against the Ottomans, with the promise of autonomy for Arab Muslim states after the war was over. When the war ended, however, the ambiguity of those agreements did not lead to the power and control that the Muslims had hoped for. In the end, the Arabs controlled only the Arabian peninsula; the Western powers established mandates over much of the rest of the Arab world. France was given Syria and Lebanon. Britain had Palestine, Transjordan, and Iraq. This agreement had been made among the Western powers long before the end of the war, and it included a provision, responding to the Zionism of the era, for a Jewish homeland.

Arab nationalism remained an issue during the period between the world wars. As a function of this nationalism, the Palestine question became a major focus. The Balfour Declaration of 1917 (named after Britain's foreign secretary, Arthur Balfour), just as ambiguous as the treaties made previously with the Arabs, pledged to facilitate a Jewish national homeland at the same time that it precluded anything that would compromise the rights of the the non-Jewish communities existing in Palestine. Because of this political maneuvering, the mandate system put into place after World War I became a symbol of Western contempt for everything Islamic and Arab.

A different sort of nationalism, one with a secular emphasis, arose in Turkey after the war. Mustafa Kemal (1881–1939) created a modern, secular Turkish state that represented, in part, an attempt to free society from the influence of religion, specifically Islam. Kemal's attack on the institution and symbols of traditional Islam was little short of total war. Religious law was largely replaced by secular law. The adoption of a Latin alphabet aided learning but hampered traditional Islamic studies. Organized Sufism was eliminated from public life, and mosques were maintained by the government. Moreover, there was an effort to substitute Turkish for the Arabic of the *Quran*. In 1928, all references to Islam were removed from the constitution of the Turkish Republic. Islam was therefore disestablished in that country.

Turkish revolution was viewed with mixed feelings in Islam. The issue of accommodation to the West became a concern. Not adapting to the modern period had led to the collapse of the Ottoman Empire. At the same time, adapting to the modern world compromised the morality and the religion of Islam. This ongoing tension within Islam will be investigated further at the end of this chapter.

By the beginning of World War II, Western imperialism was beginning to decline. After the war, in regions dominated by Islam, the nationalist struggle took on religious overtones—the legacy of ancient Islamic militancy. After World War II, several Muslim nations gained political independence. Pakistan was established as a separate state in 1947 and, in 1971, Bangladesh. The militant revivalism of Islam can be viewed as a reaction to the westernization of the world. In theory, the new puritanism of such revivalism does not mean the rejection of science, technology, and modern innovations in politics and economics. But this sort of puritanism does have political consequences, because all efforts at modernization have to conform to the enduring absolutes of the purified, original religion of Islam.

Islam also has influence in Southeast Asia and Indonesia. The Wahhabi movement described earlier extended into central Java, where the folk elements of the indigenous Javanese religion were the targets of Wahhabi puritanism. The tension still exists between an inclusive, nationalistic framework for Indonesia and more exclusive elements. The five principles upon which Indonesia organizes itself—belief in God, nationalism, democracy, humanitarianism, and social justice—square with the beliefs of Islam. However, the first element, belief in God, is deliberately interpreted broadly to include other religious perspectives. This inclusiveness continues to be an issue with reform-minded Muslims.

CHRONOLOGY OF ISLAM

CA. 570	Birth of Muhammad
CA. 595	Marriage of Muhammad to Khadija
610	Beginning of the revelations of the *Quran*
622	*Hijra*: emigration of Muhammad from Mecca to Medina
624	Battle of Badr
630	Muhammad's conquest of Mecca and dedication of the Kaba to Islam
632	Muhammad dies
632–661	Period of the "Rightly Guided" Caliphs
661	Assassination of Ali; rise of Umayyad rule from Damascus
680	Massacre of Husayn and his followers at Karbala
732	Charles Martel turns back Muslim advance at Tours and Poitiers

CONTEMPORARY ISLAM

How does one begin to describe the chaotic and turbulent latter half of the twentieth century in contemporary Islam? This is the era of the "war to end all wars," the atomic bomb, the Cold War, the space race, Vietnam, civil rights, the rise and then the fall of the Berlin Wall, AIDS, and global problems with the environment. Throughout this tumult, a name has risen for the spirit of this period, a name that somehow binds this increasingly complex and complicated experience: *postmodernism*.

ISLAM AND OTHER RELIGIONS IN THE POSTMODERN WORLD

The term *postmodernism* is rooted in some notion of, and even reaction to, the so-called modern period, which we date roughly from the sixteenth cen-

tury through 1914. This is the era when the scientific method began to control the worldview of the West, determining, to a large extent, what is real for humans and how humans can know that reality. The modern period, moreover, is a period that includes the Enlightenment (the age of rationalism), as well as the period of optimism in the human project that was the nineteenth century. Overall, the modern period exhibited a tendency to control and manipulate both nature and other peoples, because that is how it was thought the better world of the future would be created. However, the unified, stable, controllable world of the modern period no longer exists. The postmodern world is plural, multiple, historical, and polyvalent, with fluid boundaries of reality, self, and society continually negotiated. Islam must confront this contemporary world.[47]

Because Allah has sent Muhammad and revealed the *Quran*, it is obvious in Islam that all people should be Muslims. Those who commit

750	Fall of the Umayyads; beginning of the Abbasid caliphate	
LATE 870s	"Disappearance" of the twelfth *imam*	
935	Al-Ashari dies	
1099	Crusaders conquer Jerusalem	
1165	Ibn-Arabi born	
1258	Fall of the Abbasid caliphate	
CA. 1290–1924	Major Islamic empires: Ottomans, Moguls	
1453	Turks conquer Constantinople, renaming it Istanbul	
1700s	Rise of the Wahhabi reform movement	
1900s	Rise of Islamic nation-states	
1947	Establishment of Pakistan as a separate Muslim state	
1979	Ayatollah Khomeini returns to Iran from exile to lead an Islamic revolution	

shirk, idolaters and polytheists, do not have proper knowledge of Allah and should convert immediately. The relationship with People of the Book—Jews, Christians, and Zoroastrians—is more complicated. These people have received knowledge of God through a progressive series of revelations, including those to Abraham, Moses, and Jesus. This knowledge, however, is incomplete. Muhammad is the seal of the prophets, both in the sense of being the last prophet and being the one to culminate a long tradition of prophecy in the monotheistic traditions. Jews and Christians are wrong in their compromised monotheism; Muhammad is the one who brings the correction to the beliefs of Christians and Jews. The People of the Book can be tolerated, but the force of the tradition is toward conversion. Islam is, basically, a universal missionary religion that seeks converts from all people, everywhere.

The issue here, then, is the status of Islam and other religions on a planet where the diversity of religious beliefs and practices is astounding. Prior to the twentieth century and its technological advances in transportation and communication, the distance between cultures and religions could be measured in miles and experienced by crossing a sea or a mountain range. Now, however, those boundaries are no longer daunting or even important. Worldwide communication is instantaneous. Information about other peoples, other cultures, and other religions is available to anyone who accepts the technology. The clash of religions previously, as during the Crusades, was the clash between two camps, two traditions. Now, however, the pluralism of the global village means that each religion must live side by side with many different traditions. The issue for Islam is what to do in such a situation, especially when several missionary traditions compete within the same culture.

Another way to express this conflict is by the notion of tolerance. If Islam is tolerant of other traditions in the global village, is there a limit to this tolerance? Or can tolerance even include tolerance for the intolerant? To put this another way, can Islam live within shouting distance of cultures that are openly atheistic or polytheistic? Of course, Islam's response will manifest itself differently in different cultural contexts. This question remains to be addressed by Islam in the last decade of the twentieth century.

ISLAM IN THE UNITED STATES

Another variation on the same theme facing Islam in a postmodern period is the status of Islam in the United States. Whereas Islam is a majority religious tradition in many countries around the globe, it is still a minority tradition in the United States. As such, it has had to struggle against the majority traditions for acceptability or even for the space to exist. Sociologists have used two terms for the processes of a minority religion existing within the context of another religious majority. The first term, *resistance*, signifies that the minority tradition resists the majority and fights for its own identity, its integrity. The other term, *accommodation*, suggests that the minority tradition accommodates, or adjusts to, the new cultural milieu. Resistance is seen in the United States when there is a struggle to practice prayer at the appropriate times in the workplace. Accommodation is seen as events are structured at U.S. mosques to correspond with Sunday School on the Christian Sabbath. The combination of accommodation and resistance that will be taken by Islam in the United States is still being negotiated.

Another issue for Islam in the United States is its relation to African Americans. At times, in spite of its idealism welcoming all, Islam engaged in the slave trade. In the twentieth century, however, Muslims have made efforts to win converts in Africa and the United States. Elijah Muhammad began the Black Muslim movement in the United States as an alternative to Christianity with its oppressive white majority, teaching that white people were devils. Malcolm X, formerly Malcolm Little, initially adhered to these separatist policies. Malcolm X broke with the Black Muslims, how-

ever, after his experience of the universal brotherhood and sisterhood of humanity that he experienced on the *hajj*. After that experience, he fought against racism and held up Islam as the religion of universality, in which all races are equal.

In 1975, Elijah Muhammad died, and W. D. Muhammad, his son, took control of the Nation of Islam. Under his leadership, this group moved closer to the position of the late Malcolm X and the group he founded, the Muslim Mosque, Inc. People who were dissatisfied with the approach of the moderated and transformed Nation of Islam came together around Louis Farrakhan in a movement to return to the separatist views and policies of the old Nation of Islam. Farrakhan's followers continue to be an outspoken minority among U.S. Muslims. The struggle between the more moderate and the more inflammatory expressions of the tradition will determine how successful Islam is in making inroads in the African American community.

GENDER ISSUES

In Muhammad's time, women were viewed and treated more equally than in other cultures. In many ways, Islam should be considered a liberation movement for women. Women could not be treated as property, and women finally had a say in the marriage relationship. These factors alone constituted a radical improvement for the conditions of women in the time of Muhammad and the *Quran*. Having said this, however, it must also be noted that women and men were acknowledged as being different, with different responsibilities and roles. As we have seen, a woman's first responsibility was in the home and a man's, in the public eye.

What is the status of women in the contemporary context? When many cultures profess—maybe not living out this profession but at least paying lip service to it—that men and women have equal rights and responsibilities, how is Islam to react or respond? Some nations, such as Egypt and Syria, have given women considerable freedom and equality in education and participation in public life. Other nations, however, have more restrictive responses. Saudi Arabia has preferred to keep women in public view and in roles close to those of early Islam. Iran, under Ayatollah Khomeini, placed women in **purdah** (the practice of veiling and covering their faces and bodies), reversing some of the trends that had developed during the tenure of the shah of Iran. Malaysian women are allowed to attend universities in the same classes with men, but their dress and conduct are closely regulated to prevent easy social interaction with males. The question of female spiritual leaders has not become a burning issue; that is an idea too radical for most Muslims to consider at this point. However, it may well be under consideration in the coming years.

In her book *The Veil and the Male Elite: A Feminist Interpretation of Women's Rights in Islam*, Fatima Mernissi asks that question: Can a woman be a leader of Muslims? Her response, from within the tradition of Islam, is one that would be upsetting to many Muslims:

> When I finished writing this book, I had come to understand one thing: if women's rights are a problem for some modern Muslim men, it is neither because of the Koran nor the Prophet, nor the Islamic tradition, but simply because those rights conflict with the interest of a male elite. The elite faction is trying to convince us that their egoistic, highly subjective, and mediocre view of culture and society has a sacred bias. But if there is one thing that the women and men of the late twentieth century who have an awareness and enjoyment of history can be sure of, it is that Islam was not sent from heaven to foster egotism and mediocrity.[48]

Mernissi argues, based on the *hadith*, that the only way to describe the place of the female is as equal to the male. Any hierarchy or inequality is perpetuated by misreading and manipulating the traditions. There has been, from her perspective, a violent misrepresentation of Muhammad: "To what extent can one do violence to the sacred texts? Not only have the sacred texts always been manipulated, but manipulation of them is a structural characteristic of the practice of power in Muslim societies. Since all power, from the seventh century on, was only legitimated by religion, political forces

and economic interest pushed for the fabrication of false traditions."[49] Mernissi is undertaking a daunting task, but one that finds her imagining the possibilities of liberation for women in Islam.

Mernissi's claim is a radical one, but such a reexamination of the tradition is precisely what women from many religions are doing. How Islam reacts to, or participates in, this reexamination will be a central concern within the next decade.

ISLAMIC "FUNDAMENTALISM"

The quotation marks around *fundamentalism* are intended to warn the reader that there is a problem with the term. Many Muslims argue that to use *fundamentalism* to describe any segment of Islam is to use a Protestant Christian term to label Islam in a derogatory, negative way. Having acknowledged that this is a common idea, the term is used here, nonetheless, because it is convenient and, arguably, accurate. First, "Fundamentalism" as a label did indeed arise in the late nineteenth and early twentieth centuries in U.S. Protestantism to describe a reaction against the Darwinism and theological liberalism of the late nineteenth century. In resisting these trends, certain Protestant groups identified five "fundamentals of faith"— items of belief that would easily identify a true Christian from one who was not. One of the five fundamentals was the infallible, inerrant, literal truth of the Christian scriptures. To take this historical root, the term *fundamentalism* is not literally applicable to Islam. Further, because there is no formal creedal structure in Islam, the idea that there wold be certain fundamental beliefs to distinguish a Muslim from a non-Muslim is also inaccurate.

Fundamentalism can also be defined, however, so that "its direct meaning is assumed to indicate a certain intellectual stance that claims to derive political principles from a timeless, divine text."[50] With such a definition, Youssef M. Choueiri can include revivalism, reformism, and radicalism in the same social and political analysis of Islam. It is here that a contemporary political issue confronting Islam appears. When the *Quran* is held to be a timeless, unaltered text—not unlike the way Christian Fundamentalists describe the *Bible*—and when the text is the basis of political organization, clashes can occur within Islamic society. This is a problem in some Muslim countries where revivalism and reform are demanding that society return to the basics of Islam and jettison anything that has found its way in from another culture or another tradition. It is more of a problem, however, where Islam is not a majority religion. There the revivalism and the reform can be seen as a threat to the dominant culture. This problem often occurs in the United States, as well as in other countries around the world.

Another way to use the term *fundamentalism* is the way suggested by Frederick Denny, who argues that some Muslims express themselves politically in their revival and reform movements. Others who can be called fundamentalists express themselves through various forms of communication, such as preaching, teaching, and the media. Finally, a third group of so-called fundamentalists consists of Muslims who wish to live out and transmit a pure version of the faith every day. Here *fundamentalist* would equal *devout Muslim*.[51] In any case, the issue that remains is how the purified version of Islam, based on the eternal and divinely inspired *Quran* and applied to all of society, should be articulated and dealt with in the postmodern world.[52]

After almost two centuries of decline, Islam is thriving in the postmodern world. It is a major force in terms of world religion, politics, and culture. Clifford Geertz warns us, however, that before anyone can overlay a certain category or system of classification upon a culture that claims to be Muslim, one must wait. Islam must be observed before it can be defined.[53] This chapter has attempted not to define Islam but to describe enough of the tradition so that it will appear as neither foreign nor an immediate threat, but rather as a living, breathing religion that inspires hundred of millions of people all over the planet.

GLOSSARY OF ISLAM

Allah	God. The term has no plural; it refers to the one true God of Islam.
aya	often translated as "verse"; a subdivision of a *sura* of the *Quran*.
caliph	literally, "successor"; the title of a leader of Islam after Muhammad's death.
falasafa	literally, "philosophers"; thinkers, such as Avicenna and Averroes, who desired to bring together the concepts of Greek philosophy and the tradition of Islam.
Five Pillars of Islam	the specific and primary obligations for the life of submission for a Muslim. These obligations include Shahada, the creed; *salat*, ritual prayer; *zakat*, almsgiving; Ramadan, the holy month of fasting; and the *hajj*, the pilgrimage to Mecca.
hadith	the body of tradition concerning the actions and sayings of Muhammad.
hafiz	the honorific title given to one who has memorized the *Quran*.
hanif	a believer in one God.
hijra	"withdrawal"; the migration or flight of Muhammad from Mecca to Medina in 622 C.E.
Id al-Adha	the Feast of Sacrifice, or the Great Feast, commemorating Abraham's sacrifice of the ram.
Id al-Fitr	the Feast of Breaking Fast, which marks the end of Ramadan.
ijma	consensus of the community.
imam	a religious leader.
jihad	exertion; struggle in the name of the faith; holy war.
jinn	spirits capable of assuming human and animal shapes.
Kaba	the cube-shaped structure in the sanctuary in Mecca. The Kaba is the center of the Muslim world.
kalam	reasoned argument in defense of the faith.
Mahdi	the divinely guided one who will return and inaugurate a period of righteousness prior to the last judgment.
mihrab	the place in a mosque that serves as a pointer to Mecca.
muezzin	the one to call Muslims to prayer
mujtahid	a scholar believed to be under the guidance of the Mahdi.
Muslim	one who submits to Allah; a member of the community of Islam.
purdah	the practice of veiling and covering the faces and bodies of women.

qiyas	an analogy; a method of determining the meaning of the *Quran*.
Quran	the sacred text of Islam.
sawm	ritual fasting that occurs in the holy month of Ramadan.
Sharia	the right way of living set forth in the *Quran*.
Shiite	a follower of the leadership of Ali.
shirk	idolatry; polytheism; association; mistaking something other than Allah as God.
Sufism	a mystical sect of Islam dating from the eighth century.
sunna	the behavior or practice of Muhammad or the traditions associated with his life.
Sunni (also Sunnite)	one who follows the *sunna*.
sura	a section of the *Quran*; often translated as "chapter."
wali	friend; saint.
wudu	ritual cleansing prior to prayer.
wuquf	the rite of standing during the *hajj*.

For Further Study

Ahmed, Akbar. *Postmodernism and Islam: Predicament and Promise.* New York: Routledge, 1992.
>   *A recent attempt to locate Islam within a postmodern perspective.*

Ahmed, Leila. *Women and Gender in Islam.* New Haven, Conn.: Yale University Press, 1992.
>   *A recent scholarly view of the social conditions, historical background, and attitudes about women in Islam.*

Arbery, A. J., trans. *The Koran Interpreted.* New York: Macmillan, 1955.
>   *A translation that attempts to combine scholarly accuracy with literary quality.*

Armstrong, Karen. *Muhammad: A Biography of the Prophet.* San Francisco: HarperSanFrancisco, 1992.
>   *A recent biography of Muhammad.*

Choueiri, Youssef M. *Islamic Fundamentalism.* Boston: Twayne, 1990.
>   *Redefines fundamentalism and places it in a broader perspective than is often used.*

Cleary, Thomas, trans. and presenter. *The Essential Koran: The Heart of Islam.* San Francisco: HarperSanFrancisco, 1993.
>   *A translation that focuses on the literary quality of the* Quran.

Esposito, John L. *Islam: The Straight Path.* New York: Oxford University Press, 1998.
>   *An excellent—and recently updated—introduction to the tradition, as well as the impact of religion on politics and society in the Muslim world.*

Farah, Caesar E. *Islam.* 4th ed. New York: Baron's Educational Series, 1987.
>   *A text that traces the history of Islam, focusing on Muhammad, the* Quran, *beliefs, and contemporary expressions of the faith.*

Guillaume, Alfred. *Islam.* New York; Penguin, 1954.
>   *Although dated, still considered a solid introduction to the general study of Islam.*

Mernissi, *Fatima. The Veil and the Male Elite: A Feminist Interpretation of Women's Rights in Islam.* Translated by Mary Jo Lakeland. New York: Addison-Wesley, 1991.
>   *A modern feminist interpretation.*

Rahman, Fazlur. *Islam and Modernity: Transformation of an Intellectual Tradition.* Chicago: University of Chicago Press, 1984.
>   *A scholarly look at "Islamic intellectualism" with a focus on hermeneutics— interpretation of the* Quran—*drawing on the thought of Hans-Georg Gadamer.*

Watt, W. Montgomery. *Muhammad: Prophet and Statesman.* New York: Oxford University Galaxy Press, 1974.
>   *A combination and abridgment of the previous* Muhammad at Mecca *and* Muhammad at Medina.

READINGS

Reading 10.1   The "Lord's Prayer" of Islam: *Quran, Sura* 1

This selection from the *Quran* can be considered the "Lord's Prayer" of Islam. Even though the *suras* in the *Quran* are arranged according to length, this short chapter is placed first. These are the first words a casual reader of the *Quran* might encounter, and these are the words that also focus the faith of the devout Muslim. What does this short passage say about God? What does it say about the obligations of a Muslim?

In the Name of God, the Merciful, the Compassionate

Praise belongs to God, the Lord of all Being,
the All-merciful, the All-compassionate,
  the Master of the Day of Doom

Thee only we serve; to Thee alone we pray for succour.
  Guide us in the straight path,
the path of those whom Thou hast blessed,
not of those against whom Thou art wrathful,
  nor of those who are astray.

Source: A. J. Arberry, trans., *The Koran Interpreted,* vol. 1 (New York: Macmillan, 1955), p. 29. © 1955 by George Allen and Unwin Ltd. Reprinted with permission from Simon & Schuster.

Reading 10.2   ON GOD: THE *QURAN*

The following excerpts from the *Quran* focus on various aspects of Allah: transcendence, compassion, power, majesty, and judgment. These selections are best read as companion pieces for the "Islamic Beliefs" section of the chapter. Especially relevant are the sections on God and eschatology. What images are invoked by the description of Allah? What characteristics of Allah are his most powerful?

God
there is no God but He, the
Living, the Everlasting.
Slumber seizes Him not, neither sleep;
  to Him belongs
all that is in the heavens and the earth
Who is there that shall intercede with Him
  save by His leave?
He knows what lies before them
  and what is after them,
and they comprehend not anything of His knowledge
  save such as He wills.
His Throne comprises the heavens and earth;

the preserving of them oppresses Him not;
He is the All-high, the All-glorious.
No compulsion is there in religion.
Rectitude has become clear from error.
So whosoever disbelieves in idols
and believes in God, has laid hold of
the most firm handle, unbreaking; God is
*   All-hearing, All-knowing.*
God is the protector of the believers;
He brings them forth from the shadows
*   into the light.*
And the unbelievers—their protectors are idols, that bring them
forth from the light into the shadows;
those are the inhabitants of the Fire,
*   therein dwelling forever. (II, 256–259)*

*   That then is God your Lord;*
*   there is no god but He,*
*   the Creator of everything.*
*   So Serve Him,*
for He is Guardian over everything.
The eyes attain Him not, but He attains the eyes;
He is the All-subtle, the All-aware. (VI, 102, 103)

He who created the heavens and earth, and sent down for you
*   out of heaven water;*
and We caused to grow therewith gardens full of loveliness
*   whose trees you could never grow.*
*   Is there a god with God?*
Nay, but they are a people who assign to Him equals!
*   He who made the earth a fixed place*
*   and set amidst it rivers*
*   and appointed it firm mountains*
*   and placed a partition between the two seas.*
*   Is there a god with God?*
Nay, but the most of them have no knowledge.
He who answers the constrained, when he calls unto Him,
*   and removes the evil*
*   and appoints you to be successors in the earth.*
*   Is there a god with God?*
Little indeed do you remember.
He who guides you in the shadows of the land and the sea
*   and looses the winds,*
*   bearing good tidings before His mercy.*
*   Is there a god with God?*
Little indeed do you remember.

He who guides you in the shadows of the land and the sea
　and looses the winds,
　　bearing good tidings before His mercy.
　　Is there a god with God?
High exalted be God, above that which they associate!
Who originates creation, then brings it back again,
　and provides you out of heaven and earth,
　　Is there a god with God? (XXVII, 61–65)

God is He that looses the winds, that stirs up clouds,
and He spreads them in heaven how He will, and shatters them;
　then thou seest the rain issuing out of the midst of them,
　and when he smites with it whomsoever of His servants
　He will, lo, they rejoice,
although before it was sent down on them before that
　they had been in despair.
　So behold the marks of God's mercy.
　how He quickens the earth after it
　was dead, and He is powerful
　over everything.
But if We loose a wind, and they see it growing yellow,
　they remain after the unbelievers.
　Thou shalt not make the dead to hear,
　neither shalt thou make the deaf to hear the call
　when they turn about, retreating.
　Thou shalt not guide the blind out of their error
　neither shalt thou make any to hear
　except for such as believe in Our signs, and so surrender.
God is He that created you of weakness, then He appointed
after weakness strength, then after strength he appointed
weakness and grey hairs; He creates what He will, and
　He is the All-knowing, the All-powerful. (XXX, 47–54)

God knows the Unseen in the heavens and the earth;
　He knows the thoughts within the breasts.
It is He who appointed you viceroys in the earth.
So whosoever disbelieves, his unbelief shall be
charged against him; their unbelief increases
the disbelievers only in hate in God's sight;
their unbelief increases the disbelievers only in loss.
Say: "Have you considered your associates on whom
you call, apart from God? Show what they have
created in the earth; or have they a partnership
in the heavens?" Or have We given them a Book,
so that they are upon a clear sign from it?
Nay, but the evildoers promise one another

naught but delusion.
God holds the heavens and the earth, lest they remove;
did they remove, none would hold them after Him.
Surely He is All-clement, All-forgiving. (XXXV, 36–39)

In the Name of God, the Merciful, the Compassionate
All that is in the heavens and the earth magnifies God;
*   He is the All-mighty, the All-wise.*
To Him belongs the Kingdom of the heavens and the earth;
He gives life, and He makes to die, and He is powerful
*   Over everything.*
He is the First and the Last, the Outward and the Inward;
*   He has knowledge of everything.*
It is He that created the heavens and the earth in six days
*   then seated Himself upon the Throne.*
He knows what penetrates into the earth
*   and what comes forth from it,*
what comes down from heaven, and what goes up into it.
*   He is with you wherever you are; and God sees*
*   the things you do.*
To Him belongs the Kingdom of the heavens and the earth;
*   and unto Him all matters are returned,*
*   He makes the night to enter into the day*
*   and makes the day to enter into the night*
*   He knows the thoughts within the breasts. (LVII, 1–5)*
Hast thou not seen that God knows whatsoever is in the heavens, and whatsoever is
in the earth? Three men conspire not secretly together, but He is the fourth of them,
neither five men, but He is the sixth of them, neither fewer than that, neither more,
but He is with them, wherever they may be; then He shall tell them what they have
done, on the Day of Resurrection. Surely God has knowledge of everything.
(LVIII 7, 8)

*   He is God.*
*   There is no God but He.*
He is the knower of the unseen and the Visible;
He is the All-merciful, the All-compassionate.
*   He is God;*
*   There is no God but He.*
He is the King, the All-holy, the All-peaceable.
*   the All-faithful, the All-preserver,*
*   the All-mighty, the All-compeller,*
*   the All-sublime.*
Glory be to God, above that they associate!
*   He is God;*
*   the Creator, the Maker, the Shaper.*
*   To Him belong the Names Most Beautiful.*

> *All that is in the heavens and the earth magnifies Him;*
> *He is the All-mighty, the All-wise. (LIX 23–25)*

Source: A. J. Arberry, trans., *The Koran Interpreted* (New York: Macmillan, 1955), vol. 1, pp. 65, 66, 161; vol. 2, pp. 81, 82, 110, 111, 142, 258, 264, 270. © 1955 by George Allen and Unwin Ltd. Reprinted with permission from Simon & Schuster.

Reading 10.3   ON PIETY AND SOCIAL JUSTICE: THE *QURAN*

The following selections from the *Quran* deal not so much with theology or belief but with action in the world. Action can be individual or social; it can be an act of worship or an act of generosity and justice to another. According to the *Quran*, all these acts are rooted in submission to Allah. If the attitude is submission, then the peace of Allah will follow. This set of readings is a good companion to the chapter's discussion of the religious practices of Islam and the status of women. What do these passages demand of faithful Muslims? What is the status of women, according to these passages?

> *It is not piety, that you turn your faces*
> *   to the East and to the West.*
> *   True piety is this:*
> *to believe in God, and the Last Day,*
> *the angels, the Book, and the Prophets,*
> *to give of one's substance, however, cherished,*
> *   to kinsmen, and orphans,*
> *the needy, the traveller, beggars,*
> *   and to ransom the slave,*
> *to perform the prayer, to pay the alms.*
> *And they who fulfil their covenant*
> *when they have engaged in a covenant,*
> *   and endure with fortitude*
> *   misfortune, hardship and peril,*
> *these are they who are true in their faith,*
> *these are the truly godfearing.*
>
> . . . .
>
> *O believers, prescribed for you is*
> *the Fast, even as it was prescribed for*
> *those that were before you—haply you*
> *   will be godfearing—*
> *for days numbered; and if any of you*
> *be sick, or if he be on a journey,*
> *then a number of other days; and for those*
> *who are able to fast, a redemption*
> *by feeding a poor man. Yet better*
> *it is for him who volunteers good,*
> *and that you should fast is better for you,*

if you but know;
the month of Ramadan, wherein the Koran
was sent down to be a guidance
to the people, and as clear signs
of the Guidance and the Salvation
So let those of you, who are present
at the month, fast it; and if any of you
be sick, or if he be on a journey,
then a number of other days; God desires
ease for you, and desires not hardship
for you; and that you fulfil the number, and
magnify God that He has guided you, and haply
    you will be thankful.

And when My servants question thee
concerning Me—I am near to answer
the call of the caller, when he calls
to Me; so let them respond to Me,
and let them believe in Me; happy so
    they will go aright.

Permitted to you, upon the night of
the Fast, is to go in to your wives;
they are a vestment for you, and you are
a vestment for them. God knows that you have been
betraying yourselves, and has turned to you
and pardoned you. So now lie with them,
and seek what God has prescribed for you.
And eat and drink, until the white thread
shows clearly to you from the black thread
at the dawn; then complete the Fast
unto the night, and do not lie with them
while you cleave to the mosques. Those are
God's bounds; keep well within them. So God
makes clear His signs to men; haply they
    will be godfearing.

Consume not your goods between you
in vanity; neither proffer it
to the judges, that you may sinfully
consume a portion of other men's goods,
    and that wittingly.

WOMEN

In the Name of God, the Merciful, the Compassionate

Mankind, fear your Lord, who created you
of a single soul, and from it created

its mate, and from the pair of them scattered
abroad many men and women; and fear God
by whom you demand of another,
and the wombs; surely God ever
    watches over you.

Give the orphans their property, and do not
exchange the corrupt for the good; and devour
not their property with your property; surely
    that is a great crime.
If you fear that you will not act justly
towards the orphans, marry such women
as seem good to you, two, three, four;
but if you fear you will not be equitable,
then only one, or what your right hands own;
so it is likelier you will not be partial.
And give the women their dowries as a gift
spontaneous; but if they are pleased
to offer you any of it, consume it
    with wholesome appetite.
But do not give to fools their property
that God has assigned to you to manage;
provide for them and clothe them out of it,
and speak to them honorable words.
Test well the orphans, until they reach
the age of marrying; then, if you perceive
in them right judgment, deliver to them
their property; consume it not wastefully
    and hastily
ere they are grown. If any man is rich,
let him be abstinent; if poor, let him
    consume in reason.
And when you deliver to them their property,
take witnesses over them; God suffices
    for a reckoner.

THE BELIEVERS

In the Name of God, the Merciful, the Compassionate

    Prosperous are the believers
    who in their prayers are humble
    and from idle talk turn away
    and at almsgiving are active
    and guard their private parts
    save from their wives and what their right hands own
        then being not blameworthy
        (but whosoever seeks after more than that,

> *those are the transgressors)*
> *and who preserve their trusts*
>   *and their covenant*
> *and who observe their prayers.*
> *Those are the inheritors*
> *who shall inherit Paradise*
> *therein dwelling forever.*

Source: A. J. Arberry, trans., *The Koran Interpreted* (New York: Macmillan, 1955), vol. 1, pp. 50–53, 100–101; vol. 2, p. 37. © 1955 by George Allen and Unwin Ltd. Reprinted with permission from Simon & Schuster.

Reading 10.4   ON CHRISTIANS AND JEWS: THE *QURAN*

The following passages from the *Quran* describe the relationship between the People of the Book—Muslims, Christians, and Jews. The dominant themes are the uncompromising monotheism of Islam and the status of Islam's message as supreme, a message that supersedes previous revelations. What would Christians and Jews think about the themes in these passages? What would adherents of other religions think?

> *People of the Book, now there has come to you*
> *Our Messenger, making clear to you many things*
> *you have been concealing of the Book,*
> *and effacing many things. There has come*
> *to you from God a light, and a Book Manifest*
> *whereby God guides whosoever follows*
> *His good pleasure in the ways of peace,*
> *and brings them forth from the shadows into*
> *the light by His leave; and He guides them*
>   *to a straight path.*
>   *They are unbelievers*
> *who say, "God is the Messiah, Mary's son."*
> *Say: "Who then shall overrule God in any way*
> *if He desires to destroy the Messiah,*
> *Mary's son, and his mother, and all those*
>   *who are on earth?"*
> *For to God belongs the kingdom of the heavens*
> *and of the earth, and all that is between them,*
> *creating what He will. God is powerful*
>   *over everything.*
>
>   *Say the Jews and Christians,*
> *"We are the sons of God, and His beloved ones."*
> *Say: "Why then does He chastise you for your sins?*
> *No; you are mortals, of His creating;*
> *He forgives whom He will, and He chastises*
>   *whom He will."*

For to God belongs the kingdom of the heavens
and of the earth, and all that is between them;
 to Him is the homecoming.

People of the Book, now there has come to you
Our Messenger, making things clear to you,
upon an interval between the Messengers
lest you should say, "There has not come to us
any bearer of good tidings, neither any warner."
Indeed, there has come to you a bearer of
good tidings and a warner; God is powerful
 over everything.

· · · · · · · · · · · ·

  They are unbelievers
who say, "God is the Third of Three."
 No god is there but
  One God.
It they refrain not from what they say, there
shall afflict those of them that disbelieve
 a painful chastisement.
Will they not turn to God and pray His forgiveness?
God is All-forgiving, All-compassionate.

The Messiah, son of Mary, was only
a Messenger; Messengers before him
passed away; his mother was a just woman;
they both ate food. Behold, how We make clear
the signs to them; then behold, how they
 perverted are!

Say: "Do you serve, apart from God,
that which cannot hurt or profit you? God is
 the All-hearing, the All-knowing."
Say: "People of the Book, go not beyond the
bounds in your religion, other than the truth,
and follow not the caprices of a people
who went astray before, and led astray
many, and now again have gone astray
 from the right way."
Cursed were the unbelievers of the Children
of Israel by the tongue of David, and
Jesus, Mary's son; that, for their rebelling
 and their transgression.
They forbade not one another any dishonour
that they committed; surely evil were
 the things they did.
The seest many of them making unbelievers

their friends. Evil is that they have forwarded
to their account, that God is angered
against them, and in the chastisement they
  shall dwell forever.
Yet had they believed in God and the Prophet
and what has been sent down to him, they would
not have taken them as friends; but many of them
  are ungodly.
Thou wilt surely find the most hostile
of men to the believers are the Jews
and the idolaters; and thou wilt surely find
the nearest of them in love to the believers
are those who say "We are Christians"; that,
because some of them are priests and monks, and
  they wax not proud,
and when they hear what has been sent down
to the Messenger, thou seest their eyes
overflow with tears because of the truth
they recognize. They say, "Our Lord,
we believe; so do Thou write us down
  among the witnesses.
Why should we not believe in God and the
truth that has come to us, and be eager
that our Lord should admit us with
  the righteous people?"
And God rewards them for what they say
with gardens underneath which rivers flow,
  therein dwelling forever;
that is the recompense of the good-doers.
But those who disbelieve, and cry lies
to Our signs—they are the inhabitants of
  Hell.

Source: A. J. Arberry, trans., *The Koran Interpreted*, vol. 1 (New York: Macmillan 1955), pp. 130–131, 140–141. © 1955 by George Allen and Unwin Ltd. Reprinted with permission from Simon & Schuster.

Reading 10.5   SUFI POETRY   Jalal al-Din

The mystical experience of Sufism demands expression, but not in ordinary language. Poetry and symbolism become the vehicle for religious expression. The thirteenth-century poet Jalal al-Din Rumi uses the language of love to express religious truth. The following selections are brief, but as with all poetry, their language is dense, meaningful, and highly symbolic. Why is the language of love used to communicate ultimate truth? Does the poetic language help or hinder the communication of religious truth?

When God appears to His ardent lover, the lover is absorbed in Him, and not so much as a hair of the lover remains. True lovers are as shadows, and when the sun shines in glory the shadows vanish away. He is a true lover of God to whom God says "I am thine, and thou are mine."

Hail to thee, then O LOVE, sweet madness!
Thou who healest all our infirmities!
Who art the physician of our pride and self-conceit!
Who art our Plato and our Galen!
Love exalts our earthly bodies to heaven,
And makes the very hills to dance with joy!
O lover, 'twas love that gave life to Mount Sinai,
When "it quaked, and Moses fell down in a swoon."

Did my Beloved only tough me with his lips,
I too, like the flute, would burst out in melody.

Source: N. H. Doe and Belle M. Walker, eds., *The Persian Poets* (New York: Thomas Y. Crowell, 1901), pp. 216, 207–209.

Reading 10.6   MAKING THE *HAJJ:* MALCOLM X AFTER MECCA   Malcolm X

Although Islam has its origins in Saudi Arabia, it is nonetheless a universal religion. One expression of Islam in the United States is the Nation of Islam, or the so-called Black Muslims. Malcolm X (1925–1965), whose birth name was Malcolm Little, is one of the best-known representatives of Islam among African Americans. He was one of the most effective organizers of the Nation of Islam, which often taught that white people were devils and the source of evil in the world. However, because of differences with the organization, Malcolm left the Nation of Islam in 1964. That same year, he made the pilgrimage to Mecca—the *hajj.* It was during the *hajj* that he experienced the true community of all humanity and realized that all white people were not, by definition, racist. To symbolize his continuing conversion, Malcolm X changed his name to El-Hajj Malik El-Shabazz and, upon his return to the United States, became a rigorous opponent of racism. But his work was cut short. Malcolm X was assassinated in Harlem, New York, in 1965. This selection is Malcolm X's personal account of his religious transformation experienced on the *hajj.*

What created Malcom X's transforming experience of "brotherhood"? How does Malcolm X link that experience of "brotherhood" to the American experience?

About twenty of us Muslims who had finished the Hajj were sitting in a huge tent on Mount Arafat. As a Muslim from America, I was the center of attention. They asked me what about the Hajj had impressed me the most. One of the several who spoke English asked; they translated my answers for the others. My answer to that question was not the one they expected, but it drove home my point.

I said, "The *brotherhood!* The people of all races, colors, from all over the world coming together as *one!* It has proved to me the power of the One God."

It may have been out of taste, but that gave me an opportunity, and I used it, to preach them a quick little sermon on America's racism, and its evils.

I could tell the impact of this upon them. They had been aware that the plight of the black man in America was "bad," but they had not been aware that it was inhuman, that it was a psychological castration. These people from elsewhere around the world were shocked. As Muslims, they had a very tender heart for all unfortunates, and very sensitive feelings for truth and justice. And in everything I said to them, as long as we talked, they were aware of the yardstick that I was using to measure everything—that to me the earth's most explosive and pernicious evil is racism, the inability of God's creatures to live as One, especially in the Western World.

I have reflected since that the letter I finally sat down to compose had been subconsciously shaping itself in my mind.

The *color-blindness* of the Muslim world's religious society and the *color-blindness* of the Muslim world's human society: these two influences had each day been making a greater impact, and an increasing persuasion against my previous way of thinking.

The first letter was, of course, to my wife, Betty. I never had a moment's question that Betty, after initial amazement, would change her thinking to join mine. I had known a thousand reassurances that Betty's faith in me was total. I knew that she would see what I had seen—that in the land of Muhammad and the land of Abraham, I had been blessed by Allah with a new insight into the true religion of Islam, and a better understanding of America's entire racial dilemma.

After the letter to my wife, I wrote next essentially the same letter to my sister Ella. And I knew where Ella would stand. She had been saving to make the pilgrimage to Mecca herself.

I wrote to Dr. Shawarbi, whose belief in my sincerity had enabled me to get a passport to Mecca.

All through the night, I copied similar long letters for others who were very close to me. Among them was Elijah Muhammad's son Wallace Muhammad, who had expressed to me his conviction that the only possible salvation for the Nation of Islam would be its accepting and projecting a better understanding of Orthodox Islam.

And I wrote to my loyal assistants at my newly formed Muslim Mosque, Inc., in Harlem, with a note appended, asking that my letter be duplicated and distributed to the press.

I knew that when my letter became public knowledge back in America, many would be astounded—loved ones, friends, and enemies alike. And no less astounded would be millions whom I did not know—who had gained during my twelve years with Elijah Muhammad a "hate" image of Malcolm X.

Even I was myself astounded. But there was precedent in my life for this letter. My whole life had been a chronology of—*changes.*

Here is what I wrote . . . from my heart:

"Never have I witnessed such sincere hospitality and the overwhelming spirit of true brotherhood as is practiced by people of all colors and races here in this Ancient Holy Land, the home of Abraham, Muhammad, and all the other prophets of the Holy Scriptures. For the past week, I have been utterly speechless and spellbound by the graciousness I see displayed all around me by people *of all colors.*

I have been blessed to visit the Holy City of Mecca. I have made my seven circuits around the Ka'ba, led by a young *Mutawaf* named Muhammad. I drank water from the well of Zem Zem. I ran seven times back and forth between the hills of Mt. Al-Safa and Al-Marwah. I have prayed in the ancient city of Mina, and I have prayed on Mt. Arafat.

There were tens of thousands of pilgrims, from all over the world. They were of all colors, from blue-eyed blonds to black-skinned Africans. But we were all participating in the same ritual, displaying a spirit of unity and brotherhood that my experiences in America had led me to believe could never exist between the white and the non-white.

America needs to understand Islam, because this is the one religion that erases from its society the race problem. Throughout my travels in the Muslim world, I have met, talked to, and even eaten with people who in America would have been considered "white"—but the "white" attitude was removed from their minds by the religion of Islam. I have never before seen *sincere* and *true* brotherhood practiced by all colors together, irrespective of their color.

You may be shocked by these words coming from me. But on this pilgrimage, what I have seen, and experienced, has forced me to *re-arrange* much of my thought-patterns previously held, and to *toss aside* some of my previous conclusions. This was not too difficult for me. Despite my firm convictions, I have been always a man who tried to face facts, and to accept the reality of life as new experience and new knowledge unfolds it. I have always kept an open mind, which is necessary to the flexibility that must go hand in hand with every form of intelligent search for truth.

During the past eleven days here in the Muslim world, I have eaten from the same plate, drunk from the same glass, and slept in the same bed (or on the same rug)—while praying to the *same God*—with fellow Muslims, whose eyes were the bluest of the blue, whose hair was the blondest of blond, and whose skin was the whitest of white. And in the *words* and in the *actions* and in the *deeds* of the "white" Muslims, I felt the same sincerity that I felt among the black African Muslims of Nigeria, Sudan, and Ghana.

We were *truly* all the same (brothers)—because their belief in one God had removed the "white" from their *minds,* the "white" from their *behavior,* and the "white" from their *attitude.*

I could see from this, that perhaps if white Americans could accept the Oneness of God, then perhaps, too, they could accept *in reality* the Oneness of Man—and cease to measure and hinder, and harm others in terms of their "differences" in color.

With racism plaguing America like an incurable cancer, the so-called "Christian" white American heart should be more receptive to a proven solution to such a destructive problem. Perhaps it could be in time to save America from imminent disaster—the same destruction brought upon Germany by racism that eventually destroyed the Germans themselves.

Each hour here in the Holy Land enables me to have greater spiritual insights into what is happening in America between black and white. The American Negro never can be blamed for his racial animosities—he is only reacting to four hundred years of the conscious racism of the American whites. But as racism leads America up the suicide path, I do believe, from the experiences that I have had with them, that the whites of the younger generation, in the colleges and universities, will see the handwriting on the wall and many of them will turn to the *spiritual* path of *truth*—the *only* way left to America to ward off the disaster that racism inevitably must lead to.

Never have I been so highly honored. Never have I been made to feel more humble and unworthy. Who would believe the blessings that have been heaped upon an *American Negro?* A few nights ago, a man who would be called in America a "white" man, a United Nations diplomat, am ambassador, a companion of kings, gave me *his* hotel suite, *his* bed. By this man, His Excellency Prince Faisal, who rules this Holy Land, was made aware of my presence here in Jedda. The very next morning, Prince Faisal's son, in person, informed me that by the will and decree of his esteemed father, I was to be a State Guest.

The Deputy Chief of Protocol himself took me before the Hajj Court. His Holiness Sheikh Muhammad Harkon himself okayed my visit to Mecca. His Holiness gave me two books on Islam, with his personal seal and autograph, and he told me that he prayed that I would be a successful preacher of Islam in America. A car, a driver, and a guide, have been placed at my disposal, making it possible for me to travel about this Holy Land almost at will. The government provides air-conditioned quarters and servants in each city that I visit. Never would I have even thought of dreaming that I would ever be a recipient of such honors—honors that in America would be bestowed upon a King—not a Negro.

All praise is due to Allah, the Lord of all the Worlds.

Sincerely,

El-Hajj Malik El-Shabazz (Malcolm X).

Source: Malcolm X, *The Autobiography of Malcolm X,* with the assistance of Alex Haley (New York: Grove , 1965), pp. 343–347. © 1964 by Alex Haley and Malcolm X. © 1965 by Alex Haley and Betty Shabazz. Reprinted by permission of Random House, Inc.

MILLENNIAL RELIGIONS

The publication of this textbook coincides with the eve of a new millennium. The timing is significant both from a cultural perspective and from the perspective of religious studies. In Western culture, reaching the thousand-year mark traditionally heralds religious fringe movements and prophecies of the end of the world. From a cultural perspective, such prophecies are abundant in movies, on television, and in tabloid headlines. In addition to the entertainment industry, there has been a surge of interest among scholars in visions of the end. Boston University has even created a Center for Millennial Studies as a clearinghouse for the rapidly increasing mountain of scholarly information on such phenomena. It is telling that the advent of the new historical period marked in thousands of years is causing significant problems for computer networks across the world. Decades ago, the writers of the computer codes used by popular programs did not take into consideration the fact that the change in dates from 1999 to 2000 might be misunderstood by some computers as being the change from 1999 to 1900. This major problem for computers—called Y2K for "year 2000"—is also a problem for the humans and institutions that depend so much on the special, esoteric information dispensed by computers, our culture's icons of salvation.

The turn of this century, the dawn of a new thousand period—a new millennium—is thus an issue in both the world's cultures and computerized information systems. But the millennium holds a special interest for students of religious studies as well. The world's religious traditions described in this textbook also deal with "saving information," albeit not usually found in digital form. Although there are significant differences between and among the religions of the world, they share, at one level, the assumption that some sort of knowledge or experience is special or extraordinary for humans, and that ignoring this special, extraordinary knowledge or experience has an impact, often profound, on the individual or group. Not practicing the Five Pillars of Islam, not keeping Jewish dietary and moral laws, not respecting the Five Great Relationships in Confucianism—all have negative implications for believers of these religions. The message is similar to the message to the computer programmers facing the Y2K millennium problem: ignore that special information at your own risk. Moreover, religious traditions often regard the dawn of a new century or a new millennium or a new cycle of time, however that is conceived across the centuries or across cultures, as a time of special revelation of the sacred. One thread linking together all the traditions examined in this text, therefore, is this: the new time of the millennium—with its imagined end—can be revelatory of that saving, special information.

A millennial focus is usually associated with those religious traditions with a linear perspective on time and history. According to these traditions, history and the world began at a certain point in time and will come to some sort of an end at another specific point. The end is often presaged by messianic figures who announce some new time when life will be transformed. A famous prophecy from the Jewish tradition is found in *Isaiah* 2:4: humans *"shall beat their swords into plowshares and their spears into pruning hooks; nation shall not lift up sword against nation, neither shall they learn war anymore."* In the Christian tradition, Jesus is seen as the Messiah, the anointed one, who came and who will return again. Among the various versions of Christian millennialism, one says that a thousand years of peace will be the precursor of the return of Christ. Another version envisions the present era coming to a violent, cataclysmic end with the Second Coming of Christ, who will then reign for a thousand years. Dualism—the battle between the cosmic forces of good and evil—is a frequent feature of Christian millennialism: in the last judgment, the righteous will be rewarded, and the evil will be punished.

Millennialism is not limited to only so-called Western religions, however. When their cultures seemed on the verge of extinction, Native American groups produced prophets who told of a new age of restoration and healing. In the late nineteenth century, the Ghost Dance religion taught that the dance should be performed by the living to restore the dead and to bring about a revival of the Native American culture. On the other side of the world, Hindus anticipate that the Age of Kali, or Kali *yuga*, the worst of times, will be followed by the return of Satya *yuga*, the initial golden age in a cosmic cycle when there will be unity and when the castes will perform their roles without oppression or envy; in short, this will be a time when *dharma* will again rule over evil. New forms of Japanese religion, such as the Omoto religion (described in Appendix B, on Shinto), emerged in the nineteenth century because of the perceived inability of traditional religions to deal with the growing poverty and the instability at the end of the Tokugawa Era. Contemporary new religions making headlines because of their millennial, apocalyptic tendencies include, for example, the Branch Davidians, the Aum Shinrikyo movement, and the group called Heaven's Gate.

Besides being a powerful contemporary cultural and religious force, millennialism might even be considered a major theme of American religion. Harold Bloom, literary and culture critic who wrote *The American Religion* and its sequel, *Omens of Millennium,* asserts that several themes unite to form a uniquely American experience of religion, including angelology, a "quasi-predictive element in

dreams, the 'near-death experience,' and the approach of the Millennium."[1] Thus, millennialism is an issue in the contemporary United States as much as it is in cultures and religions around the world and across the centuries. Students of religious studies who ignore this issue risk misunderstanding a powerful force in human culture, past and present.

THE PHENOMENON OF MILLENNIALISM

The phenomenon of millennialism needs to be understood, first, in the context of established and new religions, categories described in Chapter 1 of this text. If you remember, *established religions* have lasted over time, surviving the death of foundational figures. *Dominant established religions* have a stake in the well-being of society, whereas *minority established religions* are on the margins of society in terms of power and influence. *New religions,* in contrast, span the lives of their foundational figures and initial disciples. If the group continues to exist, grow, and thrive, new religions become established religions. New religions are manifestations of social change, responses to other traditions, and products of cultural anxieties. Specifically, new religions can be stimulated by conquest, colonization, dramatic climatic change, or specific historical incidents. Therefore, in this context, the end of a millennium constitutes one of those historical incidents that promotes the creation of a new religious expression.

In a narrow sense, the term *millennialism* refers to the beliefs of people who live in daily anticipation of the advent of the "Millennium" described in the Christian *New Testament,* specifically in the book of *Revelation.* But in a broader context, **millennialism** refers to a belief "that the end of the world is at hand and that in its wake will appear a New World, inexhaustibly fertile, harmonious, sanctified, and just."[2] Along with the belief in an imminent end to human history, most millennial movements are characterized by behavior considered outside the norm of society. Sometimes this behavior involves retreating from society or the world; sometimes it involves violence toward others or suicide to hasten the end. Sometimes it involves extreme attitudes related to sexual behavior.

Millennialism often arises in extreme social situations—for example, with economic deprivation or when security is threatened. The feeling and sense that the end is near is much more real and tangible when the social order is collapsing, when the cohesion that would provide social stability is nonexistent. A rash of suicides followed the crash of the U.S. stock market in 1929, when economic deprivation and a perceived threat to security and stability led to a literalizing of the end of an individual's life through suicide. Socially, the mass suicides and death of 913 people at the Reverend James Jones's People's Temple in Guyana can be directly attributed to the threat perceived by the visit of a California congressman. Furthermore, the vision of an end that purifies injustice and restores wholeness, goodness, and truth is an appealing vision when society is "on the brink." In his book *Dr. Strangegod,* Ira Chernus argues that our society's ability to imagine a nuclear exchange between the superpowers was a result of a sense of a society falling apart, a society in need of total purification—here, purification through the fire of thousands of nuclear weapons. So millennialism need not be confined to periods of time when the centuries or millennia come to a close. The millennium can be interpreted as the symptom of, as well as the cure for, a society that is falling apart.

Millennialism is apocalyptic; the term **apocalypse** comes from the Greek term for "revealing" and means the portent or revelation of impending doom. Thus, millennialism associates some sort of revelation with the vision of an end-time. These assurances can come from a returning savior figure or, more recently, from extraterrestrial beings, and they often include promises of restoration for a remnant group or area. Images of the end of time and the concomitant revelations are extremely varied. Throughout the history of millennialism, however, is exhibited "a basic human urge to align great events—even terrible ones—with the numerical configuration of a divine plan."[3] Although the millennium is associated with a specific date—1000 or 2000, for example—it can occur any time. And the reading of the various scriptural and cultural signs presaging the end have produced years that are not round numbers—1260, 1367, 1688, and 2033, for instance. In this numerological aspect of millennialism, there appears to be some comfort in the calculations and the connections of events with mathematical certainty.

TWENTIETH-CENTURY MILLENNIAL GROUPS

Twentieth-century millennial groups exemplify the characteristics just described. The following descriptions of a few specific groups—which are by no means a complete listing—illuminate the special spirit of millennialism.

RASTAFARIANISM

In the late nineteenth century, a millennial prophecy was delivered in Jamaica. Alexander Bedward, a prophet-healer in Kingston, saw a future holocaust where all white people would be killed, and black people would be inheritors of the true new world. The predicted date passed, and Bedward was considered insane. A more generalized vision was put forth in the 1930s by Marcus Garvey, who prophesied that blacks would rebuild a great civilization in Africa. This prediction was thought to be realized when Ras Tafari of Ethiopia was crowned as Emperor Haile Selassie. Although Selassie's reign did nothing for the liberation of Jamaicans, a new religion developed around the millennial ideals of Bedward and Garvey. In the Rastafarian belief system, a revival of the "Way of the Ancients" opposed to the symbols of oppression—the United States, Britain, and the Christian Church—symbolizes the dying of an old order and a rebirth of the new. The movement developed a distinctive form of language, dress, and hairstyle (dreadlocks). Further, the ritual element of the tradition included a new form of music, called *reggae,* and the adoption of *ganja* (marijuana) as a sacramental agent for healing and meditation. Although the tradition has modulated from its initial millennial prophecies, Rastafarianism continues to be a distinctive twentieth-century millennial movement.

JEHOVAH'S WITNESSES

Another millennial movement of the late nineteenth and early twentieth centuries is that of the Jehovah's Witnesses. This tradition imagines a world of peace and harmony of all races, but only after most of the human race is destroyed. For the remaining true Christians, there will be life with God for 144,000 saints; for the rest, there will be a reunion with loved ones in an earthly paradise. The founder of Jehovah's Witnesses, Charles Taze Russell, predicted that the cataclysmic events of this change would occur in 1914. When 1914 passed, the prophecy was adjusted to refer to the time when Jesus began to rule in heaven. Followers of this tradition encourage the interpretation of the Christian *Bible* as the prophecy of the millennium and advocate leaving the ideologies of political and false religions. Although almost a century has passed since the predicted date of the apocalypse, Jehovah's Witnesses remain a visible force not only on the U.S. religious scene but also worldwide, especially in Mexico and Russia. In fact, the tradition of Jehovah's Witnesses now qualifies as a minority established religion rather than a new religion, because it is several generations past its charismatic founder and because its members are so dispersed. This group illustrates how a new religion founded on millennial principles can begin the process of assimilation into the mainstream of religious expression.

THE CHRISTIAN IDENTITY MOVEMENT

The label "Christian Identity" refers not to an official organization but rather to a conglomeration of churches, study groups, political organizations, and World Wide Web sites all tied together by shared beliefs. It is their beliefs that qualify this movement as millennial and also as a potential threat to the dominant culture. "At its core lie three convictions: first, that white 'Aryans' are direct descendants of the biblical tribes of Israel; second, that Jews are the biological descendants of Satan, having their origin in Satan's seduction of Eve in the garden of Eden; and third, that the Last Days, when history reaches its consummation, are about to begin."[4]

The third and millennial characteristic of the group is important in that the end of human history is seen in racial terms as the final struggle between white Aryans and those who are impure and, therefore, inferior. Enemies of the Aryans include Jews and all "inferior" peoples, who must be destroyed before the millennium can be actualized. The corollary of this belief has justified violent confrontation with governments, which the movement regards as the official representative of the impure. One example of such a confrontation occurred in Missouri in the early 1980s, when a Christian Identity group called the Covenant, Sword and Arm of the Lord established a fortified community, conducted paramilitary training, and published guerrilla warfare manuals. The group disbanded in 1985, after being raided by federal authorities.

An element of belief for many Christian millennialists is the **tribulation,** a period of violence and conflict prior to the end. This period will not have to be endured, however, because of a related belief in the **Rapture,** the lifting up of the saved when the tribulation begins. But the Christian Identity movement is often considered posttribulationist—that is, pure, true Christians will have to endure the violence and trauma of the tribulation until the Second Coming of Christ. Add to this their racial beliefs, and the violence of the tribulation for Christian Identity adherents is a racial war.[5]

AUM SHINRIKYO

The Aum Shinrikyo group came to widespread public awareness in 1995. This Japanese millennial group was led by Shoko Asahara, who taught that only he and his followers should control history. Although the notion of the end of time is less prevalent in Japanese culture than in the Western world, Aum Shinrikyo demonstrated the great potential for killing innocent nonmembers of a group by its release of the deadly nerve gas sarin on the Tokyo subway system. What religious convictions prompted such a drastic act? The answers are not clear. But all the ingredients for violent action based on millennial expectations are included in Aum Shinrikyo: a charismatic leader, revelations of a utopian existence, predictions of disaster, feelings of persecution from the authorities of mainstream society, authoritarian control of a social group, and finally, drastic measures to insure the survival of a righteous remnant.

The Hindu god Shiva was this syncretic group's primary deity. A revelation from Shiva led Asahara to view himself as "a messianic figure who was to lead his followers in the establishment of an ideal society referred to as the Kingdom of Shambhala."[6] The publications of this group evince an ever-increasing concern with the end-time and a transformation in attitude toward the end. An early emphasis was on the prevention of a major catastrophe, predicted for 1999, by the focus of believers' positive energy. This prevention and implied optimism, however, gave way to a more fatalistic attitude: the end is near, the battle is unavoidable, but the survival of a select few will insure the survival of civilization in a purified state. The last incarnation of the group was especially concerned with its own survival, a self-sufficient sustainable survival. Asahara became more and more authoritarian and viewed himself as a key figure in an unfolding cosmic drama. Caught in a timetable of "precarious prophecies," Asahara had "locked the religion into a scenario from which it had little way out unless something drastic happened in . . . 1995, which Asahara had marked out as the year when the slide to destruction would begin."[7] This pattern is repeated, with variations in the details, in other millennial religions.

The violence of the Aum was not initially random, but directed toward members of the group itself, in part to preserve the unity of the group. To hold a dissenting idea or act outside the norms of the group would put at risk the survival of the select few. And one way to enforce conformity within a social group is punishment. Apparently, the punishment included death. According to police reports, thirty-three Aum followers are believed to have been killed between October 1988 and March 1995, with another twenty-one followers reported missing. After the release of the nerve gas in the Tokyo subway system, Aum members were arrested, and Asahara was accused of murder. Although some members of this group have been convicted of murder and sentenced to life in prison, current members of this group—membership numbered in the thousands in both Japan and Russia—are still active and are raising millions of dollars.

THE BRANCH DAVIDIANS

David Koresh had an orthodox Seventh-day Adventist background. But his specific revelations led to his associating with, and leadership of, a group of Branch Davidians, a preexisting Adventist sect. Koresh's group built an enclave at a site near Waco, Texas. In 1993, after a lengthy impasse in negotiations following a violent encounter between federal officials and members of the group, federal officials attacked the community. During that attack, cult members set the compound on fire, thus leading to the deaths of more than seventy people, including Koresh.

Before his death, Koresh had developed an amazingly intricate apocalyptic theology. It was not unique, however; it demonstrated continuity with the ideas of his Davidian predecessors. When Koresh told Federal Bureau of Investigation (FBI) negotiators that he had been taken into the heavens by angelic beings in a flying saucer, this was not necessarily the ravings of a lunatic. His predecessors in the Davidian tradition had stated their belief in flying saucers and connected this phenomenon to Jewish history. Further, his community lived constantly with the expectation of the end, and Koresh's own language constantly emphasized the inevitability of an apocalyptic struggle between the forces of good and the forces of evil. It is this dualism that helps explain the events near Waco in 1993. The assault on the Davidian compound fit in with the dualism of good and evil; from Koresh's perspective, the forces of evil were assaulting the forces of good. "The Davidians' millenarian beliefs are the most important single factor in the drama of Waco; and the authorities' ignorance of these beliefs, which bordered on a determination to ignore them, explains why so many lives were lost."[8]

In one sense, the Davidian millennial group exemplified one feature of belief in end-time—that of self-fulfilling prophecy. If you believe the end is near, then your actions may not be tempered by so-called normal restraints of society. And if violence is available as an option for the necessary cleansing that would insure salvation, then physical survival of the individual or group is not the primary concern. The end is predicted, violence is necessary, the battle is engaged—the prophecies of the end are brought about by the situation created by the prophecies of the end.

THE ORDER OF THE SOLAR TEMPLE

The Order of the Solar Temple, based in France and French-speaking Canada, was a modern manifestation of a long-standing occult tradition associated with the Knights Templar, a medieval order suppressed by the Catholic Church. The modern version was founded in 1980 and emphasized ornate ritual activity. The leader, Luc Jouret, a charismatic young doctor, was fixated on the idea of an approaching ecological disaster. He coupled this with New Age predictions of the emergence of a new kind of human life in the Age of Aquarius, which would begin after two thousand years of darkness. The apocalyptic vision of the Solar Temple was that of the book of *Revelation* interpreted as an ecological crisis. In this crisis, fire would indeed consume the world. But there was a com-

ponent of purification to this fire as well. "The apocalyptic fire would serve to purify the Order's elect, who were in fact the reincarnated Knights Templar. They would then begin a journey across space to the star Sirius, where they would become Christlike solar beings."[9]

The apocalyptic fiery end, however, was literally the end of the group itself. The end began for this group with the ritual murder of a couple and their young son in Canada. The child was the Antichrist, they decreed, and needed to be eliminated. After a series of events that is still not clear, the entire community in Switzerland—all the members of the entire inner circle of the group—were ritually killed (nineteen members were found shot in the head) and/or committed group suicide by detonating incendiary devices, thereby creating fires that consumed all the members of the group. Although the exact scenario remains ambiguous, this behavior is consistent with that of other millennial groups that have participated in their own apocalypse.

HEAVEN'S GATE

A group that had little, if any, biblical prophetic base, Heaven's Gate was formed by two people, Marshall Applewhite and Bonnie Lu Nettles, also known as "Bo" and "Peep." Twelve years after Peep's death, Applewhite talked his followers into committing suicide. They were willing to shed their bodies in order to ride comet Hale-Bopp to a new level of existence called Heaven's Gate while the rest of the human race degenerated.

The context for this millennial group is not biblical, nor is it an offshoot of established traditions. Rather, the context can be called **New Age.** In contemporary culture, the New Age sensibility is not specific but diffuse, ranging from divination to palmistry to astrology to astral travel. Sources of New Age thought are those minority traditions in Western culture that have served as an undercurrent beneath the established, majority religions and philosophy, such as Gnosticism, alchemy, Neoplatonism, and Hermeticism.[10] One of the constants in this array of historical sources, however, is the assumption of a hierarchy in the universe in which spirit and matter are intertwined, and human and cosmos are brought together by transcendent forces and/or intermediaries: "Underlying it all is a belief that the universe is fundamentally mental, that it operates more like an immense mind than a gigantic machine. Thus, most basic is sheer, infinite, impersonal consciousness; it expresses itself in both law and descending ranks of consciousness—the 'Great Chain of Being'—from gods or angels to humankind and below, the whole integrated by 'correspondences' or special relationships between various parts of the system."[11] No consensus exists in New Age doctrine or ritual, but millennialism is related to the hierarchical concept of the universe: There will be an end to this present level of existence, a lower level sloughed off to allow a higher level of existence to show forth. In this kind of hierarchical millennialism, visions of the end tend to be nonconfrontational, with little question of punishment of the unsaved. The focus is on the group of the chosen few and its journey upward in the hierarchy of existence.

When Applewhite and his followers committed suicide near San Diego in 1997, the initial press reports from the coroner's office estimated that tracing the identities would take weeks, if not months. The process was completed in hours, however, because the members of the group had placed passports and other identification in their pockets precisely to make their identification possible and easy. What ideas were at the base of such cooperation with authorities, even after death? In an unpublished presentation of 1993,[12] Applewhite's own words describe a move to a higher level, a level prepared and facilitated by a crew—the "Admiral" and his "Captain"—from a "UFO":

> Let's call the physical space or area in the literal Heavens where their "Headquarters" is, the "NEXT LEVEL," in place of the descriptive phrase—the Evolutionary Level Above Human. Also, let's call the "space races" (what some humans refer to as space aliens), which are not associated with the NEXT LEVEL or its Headquarters, "Luciferians," for they are all

offshoot civilizations from the period in history (prior to the present civilization) when one-third of the "heavenly creatures" became renegades from Headquarters—went out on their own and reverted to lower behavior and interests which placed them in opposition to Headquarters. By now you realize that we are saying that the "NEXT LEVEL" and "Headquarters" represent the only true Kingdom of God—a many-membered Kingdom which physically exists in the Heavens and is the only place from which souls, life, and all creating originates.

There is assumed a hierarchy of the universe, and representatives of the higher level are said to have descended in order to assist the raising of others to the "next level." Further, this next level is the source and destiny of life—the Kingdom. Present existence must end in order for the next level to be experienced:

> Now their last task is to once again offer what they have accomplished to others who might get their change started. However, as was the case 2000 years ago, and all times previously that the NEXT LEVEL has had Representatives relate to humans, those individuals who believe these "midwives" and start their grafting to them as members and Representatives of the only true Kingdom of God, will not have to worry about the planet's approaching recycling.

With its emphasis on the transformation of existence, the Heaven's Gate creed shows less concern than other cult manifestos for ecological disasters of the eventual end of life on the planet: if the next level transcends the present worry, and the end is near, then the end is the beginning of a life at a new level of a hierarchical reality.

MILLENNIALISM AS A FOCUS FOR RELIGIOUS STUDIES

What are some of the implications of millennialism for the study of religions? As a category, millennialism can serve as an important entry into the study of religion, and it can launch an investigation that extends beyond the scope of this book. The material on millennialism, specifically, raises issues in the sociology of religion, psychology of religion, and **hermeneutics**, the theory of interpretation. Information on millennialism provides a focus for opening up perspectives and methods of study—productive avenues for analyzing any religious tradition.

SOCIOLOGY OF RELIGION

Although millennialism is a theme in our larger culture, it takes on incredible power and energy when embodied within a single social group. The subdiscipline in sociology called the **sociology of knowledge** helps us to understand this phenomenon. The sociology of knowledge model argues that what counts as knowledge and what counts as the relevant modes of gaining knowledge are constructed by the social group. One group knows something—that it is the chosen people, for example—because the group's epistemic (knowledge) structures create that reality. In applying this model to religions, we see that the tradition provides reality and knowledge, but this reality often clashes with other realities, other social groups, and other religions. In the example just mentioned, one chosen group may clash with another group that also thinks it is the chosen people. Millennialism is an area of religious studies that can lead to an appreciation of the value of categories of sociology as an aid in understanding such conflicts.

One example will suffice. What is unsettling about the Christian Identity movement, from a sociological perspective, is the clash of the "dominant" culture with the so-called deviant culture. This phenomenon is not new or dramatic, but this millennial movement illustrates the sociological concept known as **deviance amplification.** Briefly, deviance amplification describes a situation where culture and subculture fit a certain pattern: initial deviance, punitive reaction, increased alienation; intensified deviance, increased punitive reaction,

increased alienation; and so on. This explanatory theory helps understand both culture and subculture. Michael Barkun states that deviance amplification "is precisely the process described . . . for Christian Identity, in which withdrawal, hostility toward minorities, and a sense of being besieged stimulate the responses from governmental and private organizations that are most likely to reinforce the original behavior. By the same token, just as the process, seen from the perspective of the deviant group, increases the likelihood of more deviant behavior, so the process of reinforcement exists on the other side."[13] Thus, the process continues as the culture is reinforced in its sanctions by the increased deviance of the subgroup—in this case, Christian Identity.

How can society break free of the vicious circle? Deviance *deamplification* can occur when sanctions become so severe that the deviant group cannot function or when the sanctions are no longer applied. Deamplification occurs at the end of the spectrum of severity of sanctions. For example, the Covenant, Sword and Arm of the Lord, mentioned previously in this Epilogue, was a relatively small collection of paramilitary survivalists in Arkansas. On April 19, 1985, the group's leader, James Ellison, was arrested after a three-day standoff. Inside the group's compound were illegal weapons, land mines, cyanide, a rocket launcher, and an armored car. Ellison and six other members of the group were indicted on weapons and racketeering charges; the group was effectively shut down.[14] Such a confrontation, with the severity of the sanctions clearly identified, can end the cycle. Although there is no guarantee of the end of the escalating cycle, amplification of deviance will almost always occur when the sanctions are ambiguous and when the culture at large is still perceived to be a threat.

PSYCHOLOGY AND RELIGION

The second field of study for which millennialism serves as an entry point is the psychology of religion. Perhaps the best representative of the cross-fertilization of the two fields is the work of psychologist Robert J. Lifton. Lifton has used extreme situations as the basis for much of his psychological research, including work with survivors of the atomic bombing of Hiroshima, survivors of the experiments of the Nazi doctors during the Holocaust, and veterans of the war in Vietnam. When he interviewed survivors of the atomic bombing of Hiroshima, Lifton was struck by images of the end of the world.[15] Initial feelings of individual death and ending in Hiroshima were complemented by "the sense that the whole world was dying."[16] These words are reminiscent of language used to describe the experience of the plague in Europe in the fourteenth century. The words also relate to those Lifton heard in interviews of the survivors of a smaller disaster in Buffalo Creek, West Virginia, where a flood killed 125 people and left 500 homeless in 1972: "While interviewing survivors, I was struck by many resemblances to the patterns I found in Hiroshima. . . . [As] a 'total disaster' in the sense of the complete destruction of a finite area, it produced its own end-of-the-world imagery."[17] After connecting Hiroshima and Buffalo Creek with the experience of schizophrenia, Lifton concludes that there are three levels of experience related to a sense of the end of the world: an external event, the shared theological imagery of the end, and internal derangement or disintegration in the individual.

From Lifton's psychoanalytic perspective, what is at stake is **desymbolization,** a state of mind in which the individual experiences himself or herself as a thing, thereby losing a sense of integrity, integration, and self. Further, in such experiences or imaginings of the end, there is a **totalization of attitudes,** in part a result of a fear of being annihilated. That is, if the image of the end is present, a psychological response to such a threat would be the "totalizing" or absolutizing of the threat—the creation of an absolute enemy, an evil force that needs to be dealt with absolutely and totally. A final psychological category that Lifton contributes to an analysis of millennialism is that of psychic numbing. For Lifton, psychic numbing is a common experience in extreme situations, from Hiroshima to Buffalo Creek to the death camps in World

War II to recent attempts to avoid dealing with nuclear proliferation. *Psychic numbing* describes the loss of feeling function when a person is confronted with extreme experiences. The psyche "shuts down" in order to get through, much like the physical body numbs itself at the initial shock of trauma.

Lifton uses psychological categories to analyze images of the end of the world, even if these endings are local and even if the world at large continues. He asks: "How is millennial imagery related to death equivalents, such as separation, stasis, and disintegration? What further questions can one raise about the millennial imagery of clinical syndromes, including schizophrenia?"[18] Lifton's work is a response to this question. This psychological process of dealing with the end and images of the end, however, should not be considered negative; death and destruction are connected with rebirth and regeneration. Millennial imagery is complex; it includes images of death or annihilation along with images of renewal and revitalization.[19] The problem, however, is interpretation and emphasis. If a vision of the end of the world is literalized and associated with a specific prediction of the end at a particular time, then in the modern world, millennialism can be extremely dangerous. If a millennial expectation is coupled with the ability to use nuclear weapons on anything more than a limited scale, then the vision of the end is literalized into omnicide. And if a protracted nuclear apocalypse destroys life on the planet, then the images of rebirth and renewal, always a part of the psychology of millennialism, are moot. One modern millennial perspective reported in 1982 in the *Boston Globe* was embodied in the belief that "any who oppose the nuclear arms race are in fact guilty of opposing God's will, since they would be standing in the way of the End, which . . . would be an expression of the purpose of God!"[20]

HERMENEUTICS

Hermeneutics is the study of the process of interpretation, usually (but not limited to) the interpretation of texts. For example, when the United States Supreme Court hears a case, the process deals with the interpretation of the laws of the land. When biblical scholars look at an ancient text with new questions, with new lenses, they are involved with interpretation. Although he addresses the psychological implications of millennialism, David L. Miller, a theorist in the relationship between theology and culture, also raises perhaps the most pressing and relevant issue—hermeneutics. Miller recounts the various attempts to reckon the timing of the end of the world and then comes to a conclusion:

> There has been, of course, no end to counting among these people who, chiliastically speaking, "count." Justin Martyr, who lived in the second century, expected the end, as he said, "soon." Hippolytus imagined it would come a little later, in 500 C.E., and Augustine put the date at 1000. Because of the 1260 days mentioned in John's Apocalypse (12: 6), the year 1260 was a favorite. Others made other calculations concerning the incalculable: 1365, 1367, 1660, 1688, 1715, 1730, 1774. In 1827 the Plymouth Brethren said it would happen any day. The Mormons, Latter Day Saints, began their predictions in 1830. They were followed by William Miller who picked 1834, and then 1844, and then gave up counting. But the Seventh Day Adventist movement continued his number business. Nor need I say here that since the two World Wars, numerous others have joined the counting: 1984, 2000, 2001, and so on.[21]

After this litany, what is the point for the readers of this text? Miller answers that question in the context of a meditation on the "chiliast complex." The word *chilias* means "one thousand" in Greek; **chiliasm,** then, is the theory that Christ will reign for a thousand years before the final consummation of all things. But an analysis of those who count and enumerate the dates of the end, like the litany above, includes other themes: a miraculous salvation of the chosen people, a battle between good and evil, a purification that may include death, and some sort of living even after the end. Something is even more important to Miller, however: "The point to this recital of names and ever-pressing final

dates is to note yet another motif crucial to the chiliast complex: *literalism*."[22] Thus, the emphasis on the end of the world and then trying to reckon the exact date raise the key issue of interpretation—specifically, literalism.

Literalism is a style of interpretation that assigns some plain, ordinary, or so-called literal meaning to a referent in a text. In the creation story recounted in the first chapter of the Hebrew scripture *Genesis*, God is said to have created the world in six days. A literal reading of that text would take *day* to be a normal, everyday twenty-four-hour period. Similarly, if a text states that the end of the world is "close at hand," then it is precisely that, not some far-off future event. So many millennial groups have used so many schemes and formulas to calculate the end—the end that never came quite at the right time in the right way—that the very project is put into question. By extension, the project of literal interpretation of any textual tradition is also put into question. This is an issue of the first order.

What are the assumptions of a literal approach? The text or source has to be seen as authoritative, to be in need of application to contemporary experience, and ultimately, to be decipherable. For example, the signs of the end are in the *Bible,* and with the right numeric key, the end can be known. But the plethora of millennial groups illustrates the postmodern situation: there is no stable center that can be agreed upon. One group has one key; one group has another. And there can be no truck between two literal interpretations of the end. If one reading has the world ending next Tuesday and the other, next Thursday, both of those readings cannot be correct from a literal perspective. At least one will be proved wrong—and maybe both.

Literal readings, then, provide the setting for conflicts between interpretations. And here is the rub. If millennialism raises the issue of literalism along with the inevitable consequence of conflict between literal interpretations, then perhaps millennialism will enable students of religion to think about interpretation, including the varieties of interpretation beyond the literal, while at the same time giving voice to one of the ways that people have interpreted texts—literally. Miller says it this way: "The chiliast paradox . . . is that literal and metaphoric belong together. And the proper dialect of this paradox involves a movement from literal to mythic, *not the reverse.*"[23]

Further, what appears at first blush to be misguided—counting the days until the end of the world, say—becomes instructive in two ways. First, as Miller points out, "we all need images of the literal, ways to imagine what is happening when we go literal, as inevitably we will do, from time to time, having sensed some potential end."[24] Millennialism can give a face or an image both to endings and to a literal mode of interpretation. But second, the literal can be included in a metaphoric reading in which the end of the world is not a once and future event but rather a continual psychological process and sociological event: "the literal, then, is one of our lively metaphors."[25] Reflection on interpretation brought about by the study of millennial religions may moderate the condemnation of literalism from a pluralist perspective along with the condemnation of pluralism from a literal perspective. Reflection on millennialism may show us the middle path.

ENDS AND BEGINNINGS

Millennialism is a cultural phenomenon, as well as a religious phenomenon. As a religious element, the sensing of the end has been a common characteristic of many religions for thousands of years. As a cultural phenomenon, the expectation of an ending and a purified existence after the end is included in modern secular culture, even if it is merely embodied in the rhetoric of an election campaign. Furthermore, contemporary millennial groups exemplify the common themes and threads that unite the various manifestations of religion around the globe, thereby constituting a theme uniting the study of world religions. Finally, using millennial religion as an impetus or focus can launch inquiry in a number of fruitful directions, including the sociology of religion, the psychology of religion, and interpretation theory. The end, therefore, is really the beginning. May this reflection on the end speed your journey into and through religious studies.

GLOSSARY OF MILLENNIALISM

apocalypse   Jewish and Christian literature of revelations that make known the features of a heavenly or future time or world, or in general, things hidden from present knowledge; often associated with catastrophic events (for example, the end of the world).

chiliasm   another name for *millennialism;* the theory that Christ will reign for a thousand years before the final consummation of all things.

desymbolization   according to Robert J. Lifton, a state of mind in which the individual experiences himself or herself as a thing, thereby losing a sense of integrity, integration, and self.

deviance amplification
     in social theory, the explanation for situations when a subgroup confronts a dominant culture in an ever-increasing cycle of deviance on the part of the subgroup that is reinforced by the sanctions and threat of the dominant culture.

hermeneutics   the theory of interpretation, usually (but not necessarily) the interpretations of texts such as scriptures, literature, and law.

literalism   a form of interpretation that asserts that the meaning of a text is its plain, obvious meaning; distinct from metaphoric, symbolic, or allegorical forms of interpretation, which emphasize other levels of meaning in addition to the plain or obvious.

millennialism   the Christian belief in the thousand-year reign of Christ on earth. Premillennialists believe that the millennial will be preceded by Christ's Second Coming. Broadly conceived, millennialism refers to Christian and non-Christian beliefs in the imminent end of the present age and the ushering in of a paradisal age.

New Age   relating to a diverse set of ideas and organizations united by their enthusiasm for the creation of a new era of enlightenment and harmony. New Age teachings are characterized by an emphasis on monism, relativism, individual autonomy, and the rejection of the emphasis on sin as the cause of evil in the world.

Rapture   the action in which believers will be "caught up" to meet Christ in the air at his Second Coming.

sociology of knowledge
     the academic subdiscipline devoted to the study of how societies create and perpetuate structures of reality. Karl Mannheim, Peter Berger, and Thomas Luckmann are prominent theorists associated with this subdiscipline.

totalization of attitudes

> according to Robert J. Lifton, the psychic process whereby a single event, idea, or person becomes the controlling factor in all of existence; the making absolute of one contingent component of existence.

tribulation

> a component of Christian millennialism that describes the period of violence, conflict, and destruction prior to the end of the world.

FOR FURTHER STUDY

Andrews, Valerie, Robert Bosnak, and Karen Walter Goodwin, eds. *Facing Apocalypse.* Dallas: Spring Publications, 1987.

> *A collection of essays dealing with images of the end of the world from a psychoanalytic and literary perspective.*

Melton, J. Gordon. *Encyclopedia of American Religions.* 5th ed. Detroit: Gale, 1996.

> *An encyclopedia of religious organizations in the United States. Although it does not focus on millennialism specifically, there are numerous entries associated with the concept.*

Robbins, Thomas, and Susan J. Palmer, eds. *Millennium, Messiahs, and Mayhem: Contemporary Apocalyptic Movements.* New York: Routledge, 1997.

> *A collection of essays focusing on not only religious movements but secular groups as well. Further, the last section deals specifically with violence and confrontation between millennial groups and the general culture.*

Thompson, Damian. *The End of Time: Faith and Fear in the Shadow of the Millennium.* Hanover, N.H.: University of New England Press, 1996.

> *An excellent overview of millennialism giving both a history of the concept and an analysis of contemporary millennial religious movements.*

Zellner, William W. *Counter Cultures: A Sociological Approach.* New York: St. Martin, 1995.

> *Deals with a variety of subgroups from a sociological perspective. Although this text is not specifically millennial in orientation, many of the groups described exhibit one or more of the characteristics of millennial religions.*

JAINISM AND SIKHISM

The description of Hinduism in Chapter 4 showed it as a complex interweaving of traditions that draws on the religious richness and diversity of India. However, an exclusive focus on Hinduism obscures the religious power of the many regional and linguistic cultures of India that nurtured these traditions. To place the traditions included in Hinduism within their proper context, some mention needs to be made of Buddhism's origin in India and its development in India for almost two thousand years. Although Buddhism as a separate tradition was almost absent from India for a thousand years, there is renewed Buddhist influence in contemporary India through the establishment of shrines by Buddhists from other nations; through the visible presence of Tibetan Buddhists in exile; and through the efforts of Dr. B. R. Ambedkar to urge the "untouchables," or *Dalits*, to reject the Hindu social system outright and to convert to Buddhism.

Mention of the rich thousand-year history of Islam on the Indian subcontinent is also necessary. Even after the Partition of India in 1947, Muslims made up about 10 percent of the Indian populace; in terms of population, India today is the second largest Muslim nation. Before Pakistan became a separate nation, there were cultural and social contexts in art and music, in secular and devotional poetry, in architecture and statescraft, in which the boundaries between religious traditions were far less fixed or were consciously crossed. This was particularly true in villages where Hindus and Muslims freely participated in each others' lives and rituals.

Buddhism and Islam are appropriately treated as world religions in their own right. But many other Indian religious traditions, some highly developed and others closely related to village and tribal life, continue to make a great contribution to the religious dynamics of India. Two examples are examined here: Jainism, which emerged as a contemporary of Buddhism in the sixth century B.C.E., and Sikhism, which was begun by Guru Nanak in the fifteenth century C.E.

JAINISM

The Jain tradition has maintained its independent status among Indian religions for over 2,500 years. There are specifically Jain elements and also ways in which Jains participate in the wider religious environment of India. Jainism illustrates how a religious group can exert influence to an extent totally out of proportion to its numerical size.

JAIN BELIEFS

The name *Jain* denotes those who follow a *jina,* one who has been victorious over the obstacles to liberation. Jainism calls for a life of discipline, self-denial, and renunciation, leading to liberation. Historically, the tradition opposed the caste system and refused to accept the authority of the *Vedas* or the necessity of traditional ritual activity in temples. Unlike Buddhists, Jains affirm the substantiality of individual selves, as *jivas,* or sentient beings. Unlike Vedantic Hindus, Jains see this self as a material soul caught by the more gross aspects of matter. Even in its liberated omniscient state, the *jiva* is not merely spirit, like the *atman,* but subtle matter. Many Jains believe in the eternity of the world, including individual sentient beings; hence, there is no need for a creator, or any role for divine power.

The individual sentient being, or *jiva*, whether monk or householder, is held back from a pure, detached, omniscient, blissful state by the bondage of gross matter that adheres to the soul, obscuring and weighing it down. This *karmic* burden must be removed for the self to be free, and it is the responsibility of the individual to achieve this liberation. Jains accept the notions of *karma*, action and its effects, and the process of rebirth based upon one's previous *karma*. One must start the path to liberation by avoiding the acquisition of more *karma*, especially through acts that cause pain to other sentient beings or that focus on passionate attachments. Then, by a life of discipline and insight, one must remove the previous accumulation of *karma* to achieve liberation. The bondage of the individual is reflected in the parable of the well, which tries to shock believers into an attitude of detachment from material pleasure:

> *A certain man, much oppressed by the woes of poverty, left his own home, and set out for another country. He passed through the land, with its villages, cities, and harbors, and after a few days he lost his way. And he came to a forest, thick with trees and full of wild beasts. There, while he was stumbling over the rugged paths, a prey to thirst and hunger, he saw a mad elephant, fiercely trumpeting, charging him with upraised tusk. At the same time there appeared before him a most evil demoness, holding a sharp sword, dreadful in face and form, laughing with loud and shrill laughter. Seeing them he trembled in all his limbs with deathly fear, and looked in all directions. There, to the east of him, he saw a great banyan tree. And he ran quickly, and reached the mighty tree. But his spirits fell, for it was so high that even the birds could not fly over it. And he could not climb its high unscalable trunk. All his limbs trembled with terrible fear, until, looking round, he saw nearby an old well covered with grass. Afraid of death, craving to live if only for a moment longer, he flung himself into the well at the foot of the*

> *banyan tree. A clump of reeds grew from its deep wall, and to this he clung. While below him he saw terrible snakes, enraged at the sound of his falling; and at the very bottom, known from the hiss of its breath, was a black and mighty python with mouth agape, its body thick as the trunk of a heavenly elephant, with terrible red eyes. He thought, "My life will only last as long as these reeds hold fast," and he raised his head; and there, on the clump of reeds, he saw two large mice, one white, one black, their sharp teeth ever gnawing at the roots of the reed-clump. Then up came the wild elephant, and, enraged the more at not catching him, charged time and again at the trunk of the banyan tree. At the shock of his charge a honeycomb on a large branch which hung over the old well, shook loose and fell. The man's whole body was stung by a swarm of angry bees, but, just by chance, a drop of honey fell on his head, rolled down his brow, and somehow reached his lips, and gave him a moment's sweetness. He longed for other drops, and he thought nothing of the python, the snakes, the elephant, the mice, the well, or the bees, in his excited craving for yet more drops of honey.*

> *This parable is powerful to clear the minds of those on the way to freedom. Now hear its sure interpretation. The man is the soul, his wandering in the forest the four types of existence (divine, human, animal and hellish). The elephant is death, the demoness old age. The banyan tree is salvation, where there is no fear of death, the elephant, but which no sensual man can climb. The well is human life, the snakes are passions, which so overcome a man that he does not know what he should do. The tuft of reed is a man's allotted span, during which the soul exists embodied; the mice that steadily gnaw it are the dark and bright fortnights. The stinging bees are manifold diseases which torment a man until he has not a moment's joy. The awful python is hell, seizing the man bemused by sensual pleasure, fallen in which the soul suffers pains by the thousand. The drops of honey are trivial pleasures, terrible at the last. How can a wise man want them, in the midst of such peril and hardship?*[1]

The extreme level of discipline that Jainism requires arises from its very wide understanding of the term *sentient being*, which goes far beyond humans and animals. *Jivas*, with different levels of consciousness from five senses down to one sense, exist in plants, in the "physical" elements themselves, in earth, in water, and in fire. Even vegetarians, then, cause pain to some sentient beings; almost any activity, such as the lighting of a fire, will cause pain to some level of sentient beings, and thus bring more *karmic* bondage on the self. This extension of the meaning of *sentient being* demands much personal discipline and attentiveness to avoid causing pain, not so much out of compassion for the suffering of others as because of the ill effects to the one causing pain.

JAIN PRACTICE

The Jain path, then, is not a system of compassion but a heroic striving for freedom. Jain monks and nuns take vows to abstain from causing injury, from speaking falsely, from taking what is not freely given, from unchaste behavior, and from attachment to material wealth. Monks and nuns have a clear responsibility to assist and guide laypeople toward liberation. Although Jain laypeople do not take on the full force of these vows, householders are expected to observe lesser vows of noninjury, truthfulness, and charitable support of the monastic community.

The Jain tradition has consistently raised the standard of *ahimsa*, or nonviolence, as an important aspect of Indian culture. Jain monks wear a mask to avoid causing hurt in breathing and carefully sweep their meditation spot to remove as many sentient beings as possible from harm's way. The intake of food and water is reduced to a minimum, and in the end many monks and nuns undertake the "last fast" to cultivate lack of attachment and freedom from all occasions of causing pain. The "fast unto death" remains an option for Jains at the close of life. Christopher Chapple describes one such event in the course of his research in India:

> [My hosts] informed me that a nun downstairs had taken the vow to fast unto death (santara or sallekhana) twenty nine days prior, and that I

would be allowed to see her. And then plans changed again. Acharya Tulsi [leader of this particular lineage of Jains] would come to bless her imminently. So we rushed downstairs and, sure enough, the three top Thereapanthi leaders were arrayed in front of this tiny octogenarian nun. Acharya Tulsi invited me to sit next to him directly in front of her as he spoke of her situation and blessed her. He pointed out that she had a great deal of courage and was able to do this because she had no desire for life or death. He emphasized her bravery. He blessed her with the Managalcara chant and spoke of the momentousness of the occasion and locale: the first major assembly in the building had been held the prior November; this was the first fast unto death to be held there; he was present; and the "Jaina professor" [Chapple] was present, all the way from America. The nun said that she had waited until he could be there to declare the fast; most often nuns and munis (monks) die when they are on the road, and pass on without benefit of seeing their preceptor. She expressed gratitude and happiness at seeing him clearly. Acharya Tulsi declared what a joyous event this was, and how unlike a Western style death or a death where life is prolonged by injections and technology. I was told by Mr. Gandhi [his guide] that she had earlier been told that a "second surgery" would be required. Though I am not certain of her condition, this is in keeping with the Jaina tradition which only allows persons to undertake the final fast for whom death is imminent. The woman's daughter, also a Jaina nun, was by her side. The woman's physician was also present. It was a moving, profound, and challenging experience.[2]

HISTORY OF JAINISM

The present Jain tradition can be traced to Vardhamana (599–527 B.C.E.), who is called Mahavira, "the Great Hero." Mahavira is regarded as the last of twenty-four religious heroes who forged a path toward spiritual liberation from bondage;

hence, these figures are called Tirthankaras—those who have made a path or ford and thus have found a way to the other side of the bondage in which all persons are caught. Mahavira's biography is similar to that of his contemporary Siddhartha Gautama, the Buddha: dissatisfaction with householder life, leave-taking to seek release, long practice of asceticism, a breakthrough of realization, and then a life spent teaching others the path.

From the start, there has been a distinction between the world renouncers—the monks and nuns—and the householders who support the monastic orders but do not take the "great vows." This long-standing harmonious relationship between monastics and lay disciples has been an essential factor in the endurance of Jainism. Another fundamental division within Jainism occurred in the first centuries: a division between those monks who wore white robes (the Shvetambara) and those who wandered naked or "sky-clad" (the Digambara). Although both groups hold many teachings in common, this separation—and disagreement on issues as important as the basic scriptural canon—continues to the present day. Jainism was favored and sustained by many royal patrons over the centuries; wealthy followers supported the construction of temples and shrines that rival those of Buddhists, Shaivas, and Vaishnavas. But even without such benefactors, the dynamic relationship between the Jain laity and monastics provided the basis for ongoing reform movements and for the revitalization of Jain orders and institutions.

CONTEMPORARY JAINISM

Jain influence remains strongest in the western Indian states of Gujarat (where Mohandas Gandhi was raised) and Rajasthan, as well as in the state of Karnataka. Although Jains as a group are numerically small (about 4 million) within India's vast population, they have exercised a powerful example of rigorous religious discipline, careful regulation of life for both monks and householders, and cultivation of radical nonviolence as a fundamental value in life. The Jain principle of *ahimsa*, or

nonviolence, was embraced by Gandhi as a principle of personal and social transformation during the Indian movement for independence. This ideal of nonviolent social change, celebrated more in the breach than in the observance, remains a profound challenge to the Indian political process. Jainism's attitude toward nature has contributed to the global environmental and animal rights movements. Sound ecological attitudes emerge from Jain religious principles: the recognition that humans are part of a single ecosystem, that they reap the *karmic* results of destructive behavior in that shared environment, and that their enlightened self-interest calls for a disciplined lifestyle so as to minimize the further accumulation of damage. Finally, the Jain approach to death by a final fast that crowns a life of disciplined awareness calls into question both the indefinite prolonging of life by technological means and the search for simple ways to "end life" without the lifelong spiritual development that is an essential element of the Jain path.

SIKHISM

The foundational *gurus* of Sikhism in the sixteenth century drew from the depths of all Indian religious experience, especially from the devotional traditions in North India, which transcended the religious boundaries of Hindu *bhakti* or Sufi (Islamic) mysticism. The *gurus* were also influenced by the traditions of devotional religious poets called Sants and by *yogic* groups called Naths, who seem to go beyond any sort of explicit religious affiliation. A sense of going beyond, or even of breaking down, traditional religious boundaries is at the heart of Sikhism. Thus, the Sikh scriptures include "non-Sikh" saints and poets, individuals traditionally identified as Hindu or Muslim. Nevertheless, the Sikh path remains distinct from both Hinduism and Islam as a new creative focus of the religious energies of India. The vitality of the Sikh path illustrates the power of religious creativity to transform individual lives and to establish a new social structure.

SIKH BELIEFS

Sikhism is, first of all, the community of those who are *sikhs*, disciples of the line of ten *gurus*, beginning with Guru Nanak, who lived in the Punjab region of northwestern India from 1469 to 1539. Sikhism arose from Guru Nanak's transformative religious experience, which led him to affirm surrender to the One, the formless and transcendent God, and so to reject both caste divisions and the competing religious identities of Hindu and Muslim. His devotional songs, compiled by Arjun Dev, the fifth *guru*, in the *Adi Granth*, along with poems of the other *gurus* and various other saints, affirm the singularity of God as the One, who, though without form, pervades and supports all. To God one owes absolute submission in love. These loving feelings are fostered and expressed in communal singing of devotional songs *(kirtan)* rather than through temple ritual or asceticism.

Guru Nanak's religious experience was first a repudiation of other religious traditions—their shrines, asceticism, prophets and incarnations, practices, and scriptures. After his transformation, he is reported to have said, "There is no Hindu; there is no Muslim." His fundamental experience of God is found in the opening verses of *Japji*, the composition by guru Nanak with which the Sikh scripture *Adi Granth* begins:

> *There is one God,*
> *Eternal truth is His Name;*
> *Maker of all things,*
> *Fearing nothing and at enmity with nothing,*
> *Timeless is His Image;*
> *Not begotten, being of His own Being:*
> *By the grace of the Guru, made known to men.*
>
> *As he was in the beginning: The Truth,*
> *So throughout the ages,*
> *He has ever been: The Truth,*
> *So even now He is Truth immanent,*
> *So for ever and ever he shall be truth eternal.*[3]

The one, formless God is known through the grace of the *guru*. The One, without form of image or incarnation, is the Truth, residing in all creation but especially in the depths of the human heart. It is by devotion, by loving surrender, by this self-forgetting *bhakti*, that the disciple achieves the goal of realizing God—that is, coming to be filled with the divine Name, which brings with it full realization of Truth, as well as all the fruits of prayer and detachment, which are sought in vain through ritual and asceticism. The power of the divine Name, made known by the *guru* in the heart of the disciple, replaces asceticism and ritualism as the privileged path to realization. This is a theme common to many schools of North Indian devotion to the formless One. The encounter with the formless God takes place in community, in the congregational singing of devotional songs that bring the experience of the divine Name. This congregational worship is a distinctive characteristic of the Sikh community; the One God, formless, is experienced through a community that enters into the devotional songs that, compiled into the *Guru Granth Sahib*, become the abiding *guru*.

Another distinctive characteristic of the Sikh community is the rejection of caste hierarchy and socioreligious separation. This fellowship of all people is symbolized by the shared kitchen (the *guru's langar*), from which all eat together, thus expressing unity and equality among Sikhs through the "common table." In U.S. society, where fast food characterizes much social interaction, the great significance given to sharing food may seem obscure. In Indian society, however, the sharing of food reflects a relationship of intimacy that is generally impossible because of caste and religious divisions. Thus, in Sikhism, the experience of a formless God who transcends all images and ritual becomes the foundation for a community that goes beyond the usual social boundaries. Eating together means that all of the social, class, and religious divisions have been put aside because of the transcending character of devotion to the One God who goes beyond all forms of society and religion.

SIKH PRACTICE

The basic Sikh practices parallel the principles of faith. The first practice is the personal surrender to the One, formless God, through participation in the communal singing *(kirtan)* of sacred songs from the *Guru Granth Sahib* ("the revered Book which is Guru" the *Adi Granth*). Loving attention to the Name of God overcomes worldly desire and enters into the depths of the heart as the principle of life that is present everywhere. The community assists in this process by the support of the congregation's song and rhythm.

The sharing of food together reflects the deep sense of fellowship that is the basis of Sikh life. The congregational encounter with the One God who is Truth becomes the norm for all behavior: living in accord with the Truth in surrender to God, in the depths of one's heart, and in all one's relations with others. This dynamic observance of Truth—a life of truthfulness—becomes the foundation for all right living. To be other than truthful in all one's dealings would be to betray the religious and communal experience of the Sikh religion.

Obviously, then, this faithful observance of the Truth is not primarily a solitary activity. Guru Nanak and the other Sikh *gurus* rejected the path of renunciation central to other Indian religions. Sikhism is thus not a religion for the *sannyasin*, or world renouncer, but for the householder, for those involved in family life and the world of commerce and government. The Sikh role in the world is one of activism, perhaps even a militant quest for social change. This world-transforming attitude is partly responsible for the fact that Sikhs have played a disproportionate role in the Indian circles of business, finance, defense, and government. The distinctive appearance of Sikh men—especially their wearing the turban and unshorn hair—insures that they are a very visible presence both in Indian society and throughout the Indian diaspora.

HISTORY OF SIKHISM

The growth and set apartness of the Sikh community led to the founding of the city of Amritsar in the Punjab; the building of its Golden Temple by the fourth *guru,* Ram Das; and eventually, conflict with the Mogul rulers, war, and martyrdom. The history of the later *gurus* is closely connected with military and political struggles in northern India, and it is almost entirely a painful story. The tenth and last *guru*, Gobind Singh, who died in 1708, established the Khalsa fellowship, a special level of religious commitment symbolized by wearing the signs of unshorn hair, a dagger, military-style shorts, a steel bracelet, and a comb. He also added to the *Adi Granth* and declared it the *Guru Granth Sahib,* the living *Guru* in the midst of the community, into which the members enter through their devotional celebration of the collected songs.

The Sikhs continued to play a role in the struggles for military control of northern India. Ranjit Singh (1780–1839) was one of the last opponents to the consolidation of British power during the early nineteenth century. Following their defeat, Sikhs found a place in the native troops organized by the British, but they cultivated a distinct spirit of religious and cultural identity. The memory of their independent kingdom echoes in the political aspirations and militant rhetoric of contemporary Sikh nationalism.

CONTEMPORARY SIKHISM

Sikhs make up about 2 percent of the Indian population, but they also play a significant role in the Indian diaspora throughout Europe and especially the United States. Nevertheless, Sikhism is in many ways identified with the regional culture of the Punjab, where the Sikh population is concentrated. The Punjab was divided in the 1947 partition that produced the states of India and Pakistan, and Sikhs have struggled to find a cultural and religious identity within independent India. Agitation for Sikh regional autonomy within the Indian Punjab state or for an independent Khalistan, a separate Sikh state, continues to fan flames of violence in this region. Many Sikh political leaders have been slain on all sides, while the Indian government has sought an advantageous political solution. Political maneuvers seem only to have fanned the flames of regional separatism and to have increased the internecine death toll among various Sikh factions. Even the Golden Temple in Amritsar, the most sacred Sikh shrine, became a pawn in the battle when it was occupied in 1984 by Sikh nationalists who turned the complex into a fortification. The Indian Army's subsequent invasion of the Golden Temple, which caused more than a thousand deaths and widespread destruction in the shrine, brought on the assassination of Indian Prime Minister Indira Gandhi by her Sikh bodyguards and, in turn, the slaughter of thousands of Sikhs in Delhi and throughout northern India.

In its founding, the Sikh tradition addressed its audience by drawing on all of the available resources within Indian culture, adopting a wide spectrum of poet-saints, religious vocabulary, and shared cultural assumptions and attitudes. However, present ethnic and nationalist pressures and resistant repression make realization of the Sikh ideal of a single transcendent God and a universal community of disciples much harder to achieve.

SHINTO

Shinto is the term used to designate the formalized version of native Japanese religion. Rooted in ancient Japanese culture and strong to this day, Shinto is an ethnic religion practiced, for the most part, by Japanese people. The Japanese Ministry of Cultural Affairs reports that about 90 percent of the population of Japan is affiliated with the religion through Shinto organizations and community shrines. However, surveys that ask people if they are Shinto "believers" result in much lower figures, some as low as 4 percent of the population.[1] The study of Japanese religion challenges us to consider whether definitions of religion in terms of beliefs are adequate. In Japan, religion is not so much a set of beliefs as it is a matter of participation, activities, rituals, a feeling of reverence, or a sense of belonging.

Most Japanese participate at some level in two or more of the five religious currents that have endured throughout Japanese written history (from the sixth century C.E.): Shinto, Buddhism, Confucianism, Taoism, and folk religion. This religious pluralism is possible because allegiance is rarely exclusive. For example, reverence for the *kami* (the term for gods or spirits in Shinto) does not mean one cannot also practice Buddhism.[2] A favorite anecdote to explain the Japanese approach to religion has it that an old man told the people that Japanese religion is like a medical prescription—the pill that, in the main, consists of Shinto, Buddhism, and Confucianism. Someone drew a circle, half of which was marked "Shinto" and two quarter-segments of which were labeled "Confucianism" and "Buddhism." "Is it like this?" the people asked. The old man smiled: "You won't find medicine like that anywhere. In a real pill all the ingredients are thoroughly blended so as to be indis-

tinguishable. Otherwise it would taste bad in the mouth and feel bad in the stomach."[3]

Whereas Buddhism, Confucianism, and Taoism were imported from China, Shinto originated in Japan and was given its name and a degree of structure or organization in order to distinguish it from the foreign religions. The category of "folk religion" generally refers to beliefs and practices and oral traditions and customs that exist outside organized religion. In Japan these may be indigenous beliefs and practices that have not been formally incorporated into Shinto, or they may be unofficial expressions and adaptations of imported religions like Buddhism. In addition to the pluralistic and nonexclusivistic perspective that permits the Japanese people to participate in different religions, each of these religions has borrowed beliefs and practices from the others and blended them with its own. For example, Shinto mythology adopted Taoist *yin/yang* cosmology to explain the process of creation. Therefore, we cannot say that Shinto is a *purely* native religious tradition. From very early times, Chinese and Korean influences began to be incorporated into what we now call Shinto. By the same token, outside religions, such as Buddhism, have been adapted to fit Japanese culture. Thus, Shinto is a distinct religion, but it must be seen as a dimension or strand within the mesh of the whole cord: religion in Japan.

SHINTO BELIEFS

In general, Shinto does not involve a claim to the absolute truth, nor does it claim to have exclusive possession of the truth; it does not proclaim itself as superior to all other religions. For example, belief in the *kami* does not mean a person cannot also believe in Buddhas or other beings as well. An exception to this characteristic nonexclusiveness was Restoration Shinto, as we will see in the "History of Shinto" section.

Another general characteristic of Shinto belief is its highly integrated worldview. Although reference may be made to the "afterlife" or the "*kami* of heaven," such realities are inextricably interconnected with this world. Mortals, *kami,* and nature form a triangle of close interrelationships. Even the ancestors are not "departed" to a distant realm; their spirits are believed to exist in close relation with our world.

The classic definitional statement about *kami* is the following by Norinaga Motoori (1730–1801):

> The word kami refers, in the most general sense, to all divine beings of heaven and earth that appear in the classics. More particularly, the kami are the spirits that abide in and are worshipped at the shrines. In principle human beings, birds, animals, trees, plants, mountains, oceans—all may be *kami.* According to ancient usage, whatever seemed strikingly impressive, possessed the quality of excellence, or inspired a feeling of awe are called *kami.*[4]

Thus, the term *kami* is broad enough to include good and evil *kami,* and even Buddhas and *bodhisattvas.* Although the universe is teeming with different types of *kami,* Shintoists believe that these beings establish cosmic harmony overall. *Kami* are often associated with impressive natural settings, and shrines are often built at such sites. The old groves surrounding the Ise Shrine (near Nagoya) and the Meiji Shrine (Tokyo) are especially impressive.

Although some Shinto scholars have tried to correlate the manifold *kami* reverenced throughout Japan with those mentioned in the ancient chronicles of Japan (*Kojiki* and *Nihonshoki*), the notion of organizing or limiting the number and types of *kami* runs counter to the spirit of Shinto. How many *kami* are there? "Eight hundred myri-ad" is a standard answer; this is to say, "innumerable." The polytheism of Shinto is inexhaustible.

In a more philosophical vein, Shinto thought includes the subtle notion of *kannagara,* which means "in accord with the *kami*" or "so-of-itself." In its pure condition, when it is not categorized by the human mind, reality is pure or natural. The experience of *kannagara* is said to be deeply moving and is linked to the Japanese love of nature. Although Japanese Zen Buddhists have often been credited with expressing love of nature in *haiku* poetry and landscape gardens, the sources of the Japanese sensitivity to nature are as much derived from Shinto as they are from Zen.[5]

The Japanese sense of the sacred in nature is based in part on the immanence of the *kami.* Shintoists believe the *kami,* even the *kami* of heaven, are present within the forces and qualities of the world. They are the inner power of nature. *Kami* are the forces that bestow and promote all life, growth, and creativity.

Ancient texts describe the creation of Japan as follows: In the beginning was primal chaos—a "chaotic mass like an egg," which then separated into heaven (male) and earth (female). From this fertile source emerged the *kami*—seven generations worth—culminating in the marriage of Izanagi (a male *kami*) and Izanami (a female *kami*). They created the Japanese islands by thrusting the "jewel-spear of heaven" from the bridge of heaven into the briny waters below. Then they stepped down upon the islands, came together, and Izanami bore many *kami.* The sun goddess Amaterasu descended from this couple. She sent her grandson Ni-ni-gi to rule the Japanese islands, and it is from this unbroken line that the emperors are descended. The Japanese people are descended from the *kami* who reside on these islands.

One of the recurring themes of these mythological accounts is the *kami*'s preference for light, life, and purity and their abhorrence of death, pollution, and impurity. The view of death as defilement, an indigenous perspective from ancient times, was absorbed into Shinto. It is for this reason that the Buddhist priests, not the Shinto priests, perform almost all the funeral ceremonies in Japan today. Although here is no definite Shinto teaching about the afterlife, it is tacitly understood that after a number of periodic memorials, a dead person joins the company of ancestors as a kind of *kami*.

Shinto ethics is based on the perception of the two types of energies just mentioned: purity (including light, life, sincerity, and honesty) and impurity or pollution (including defilement, sickness, death, error, disasters, and selfishness). Humans, who are not hindered by any innate or original sinfulness, are capable of purity. Shinto offers no lists of moral do's or don'ts but urges the attainment of *makoto*—sincerity or a cleansed state of mind. The scholar Kitabatake quotes Shinto texts that call for a "bright, red heart and not a dirty, black heart."[6] He explains that this way of purity means discarding one's own desires and keeping oneself clear in any situation. Impurity hinders the flow of life and blessings from the *kami*. The phrase "discarding one's own desires" indicates the priority of the group or nation over the individual—a teaching that is central to Confucianism as well.

SHINTO PRACTICE

Shinto practice often takes place at a shrine. The entrance to the shrine area is marked by a *torii*, a gateway consisting of two pillars with two crossbeams at the top. The *torii* often straddle the road or walkway leading up to them, informing those who pass through that they are entering the realm of the holy and the presence of the *kami*. Along the path to the shrine building may be several *torii*, or even hundreds of them. Private individuals, organizations, or companies may donate a *torii*. As one approaches the outer hall of the shrine, called the *haiden*, there is a large basin for ablutions: worshipers pour water over their hands and wash out their mouths. The atmosphere is pure, simple, clean, and tranquil (unless it is a special occasion or festival time). The outer hall is used to direct prayers to the *kami* hall or inner hall *(honden)*. The worshiper bows, rings a bell, claps to get the atten-

tion of the *kami*, drops a coin in the offering box, and prays, sometimes leaving a prayer written on a piece of paper or a wooden tablet. The inner hall contains the presence of the enshrined *kami* symbolized by a sacred object such as a mirror or sword. Worshipers do not enter the inner hall.

There are at least eighty thousand registered shrines and many "wayside" shrines maintained locally. Some shrines, such as the Ise Shrine (south of Nagoya), the Meiji Shrine (in Tokyo), and the Yasukuni Shrine (in Tokyo), are for explicitly national concerns, such as the protection of the nation and prayers for war dead.

The major Shinto celebrations during the calendar year include New Year's Day, January 1; Adult's Day, January 15 (to honor and bless twenty-year-olds); Girl's Day, March 3; Spring Festival, March 21 (prayers for a good crop and the success of various industries); Boy's Day, May 5; Shichi-go-san, November 15 (meaning "seven-five-three," for children of those ages); and Labor Thanksgiving Day, November 23 (celebrated throughout Japan as Labor Day; traditional offerings made by the emperor). There are no weekly services at shrines, but the calendar year and lives of individuals are punctuated periodically by Shinto observances at shrines or in the home. Prayers for fertility and the child's "first outing" bring the family to the local shrine. Eighty percent of Japanese marriages are conducted by a Shinto priest. Any experience of crisis, special concern, or gratitude may call for prayers to the *kami*. Only 10 percent of the funerals are Shinto rituals, the Buddhists having largely taken over this rite; however, Shinto rites are conducted upon the death of the emperor. There are many other events, including each shrine's "annual festival." We describe here in some detail the New Year's celebration and an annual festival, presented from a participant's perspective.

The New Year's celebration is the most important celebration of the year; it is a national holiday; a time for family togetherness and relaxation; and a religious event with themes of regeneration, purification, and renewal. Most people clean house and pay up their debts before the old year ends. Tradition calls for everyone to return to their parents' or grandparents' household, so many people leave the cities for a few days. In the home, special foods such as a dried fish and *omochi* (a sticky rice cake) are prepared, and special offerings are made to the ancestors.

Families visit a shrine at midnight on December 31, during the day on January 1, or both. On New Year's Eve, large numbers gather at the *torii* or near the outer hall. The Shinto priests turn on the sound for the television broadcast of the bell of Chionin, a famous Buddhist temple in Kyoto where the great bell tolls 108 times just before midnight. The number 108 symbolizes ills, unhappiness, and evil passions, and the tolling symbolically eradicates them one by one. Now all approach the outer hall *(haiden)*, toss coins into the offertory box, clap their hands, and pray.

The shrine compound is crowded, and most people have purchased a *hamaya* (evil-destroying arrow), a symbolic arrow that will be placed in the home as a protective talisman to drive away bad luck. People read their divination slips aloud with family and friends in a lighthearted manner. These slips are tied onto the trees or fences in the shrine precincts so that the bad luck predicted will blow away or the good luck predicted will be shared. In the main hall, the priest chants sacred Shinto prayers to the accompaniment of shrine music played by assistants while shrine maidens wearing traditional red skirts and white blouses perform *kagura*, sacred dances to please the *kami* and transfer the *kami*'s benevolence to the people.

The shrine precincts will be filled with people from New Year's Day, until January 4. Individuals and small groups frequent the shrine on January 2 and 3 to make special petitions or offer special prayers of thanksgiving. The shrine grounds may retain a festive appearance until mid-January, when even the poster stands announcing the donations of individuals or organizations are taken down. Last year's "worn-out" talismans brought to the shrine by the people, along with decorations that cannot be reused, are burned in a purificatory rite. The pollution and hindrances of the past year are now dispensed with, and the spirits of the people are renewed.

The annual festival begins with the priest's performing two functions: purification and offering. Vested in white silk, the priest sprinkles salt and waves a wand and an evergreen branch to purify the shrine and the people gathered in the outer hall. To make the offering, extremely slow and solemn movements are used in opening the doors of the inner sanctuary, where the symbol of the *kami* is kept. The offerings typically consist of rice, rice wine, vegetables, fruit, seafood, and salt. Red meat and fowl are rarely presented. The priest then intones prayers of thanks and asks for continued blessings.

The annual festival culminates in a carnival-like atmosphere with all manner of booths and entertainment. These festivities may begin with the *kagura* dance, but then, as the *sake* (rice wine) flows more freely than at New Year's, activities include *sumo* wrestling, pageants, martial arts demonstrations, dances by workers from a local company, and much more.

A striking aspect of the Shinto annual festival is the carrying of a mobile shrine containing the *kami* symbol through the streets by boisterous young men. Normally, the people go to visit the *kami* at the shrine, but on this occasion the *kami* goes to visit the people in the streets. The structure is carried on poles and is often heavy and hard to control. It is carried on the shoulders of young men, who zigzag through the streets shouting, "Washo, washo." This scene stands in great contrast to the solemnity of other aspects of the festival. Shinto scholars are fully aware of its rightful place in the festival. A Shinto reference work states: "Generally the ceremonies of the *matsuri* [festival] are made up of solemn rituals, followed by celebrations of wild, frantic joy."[7] Clearly, the unrestrained activities of the festivals provide an important psychological release function, a catharsis.

Shinto practice is not limited to the shrine. Earlier mention was made of talismans to drive away or absorb bad luck; these are purchased at the shrine for use in the household. The household altar is called a *kamidana* (literally, "god shelf"). Surveys indicate that about 60 percent of Japanese homes have a *kamidana*, and about the same percentage have a *butsudan* (Buddhist altar).[8] In addition to the talismans and other items linking the household to shrines, the *kamidana* may also contain memorial tablets of wood or paper inscribed with the name of an ancestor, of a patron deity of the household or of some other deity. Talismans from a well-known national shrine may occupy a central place in the *kamidana*. The rituals are usually very simple: the placing of offerings (such as rice, water, and salt) on the shelf and a brief prayer. Special occasions or crises may call for offerings of *sake*.

Japanese businesses may place a talisman or a *kamidana* in the workplace. One Western researcher even saw a *kamidana* on the wall amid the technological equipment on the overnight ferry between the southern island of Kyushu and Kobe. He was told that offerings were made every day.[9] Businesses may also organize visits to a shrine dedicated to good fortune in business. In the 1980s, sixty-seven Osaka firms dealing with shares, equities, and securities began to organize annual visits of their employees to the Fushimi Inari Shrine in Kyoto. Some companies have built their own shrines: Toyota built its shrine close by the company's head office in the town of Toyota, near Nagoya. Shiseido, a leading cosmetics firm, has built a shrine on the roof of its headquarters in the Ginza area of Tokyo. Company-related rites are performed before this shrine, which is open to the public during the Ginza festival in October.

Two more examples help illustrate how pervasive the presence of Shinto is in the midst of modern Japanese urban life. An individual, but more often an organization such as a school or company, will call upon a Shinto priest to purify and bless a new car, van, or truck to insure against accidents. A talisman reflector is then affixed to the back bumper. Finally, talismanic telephone cards, which include the name of the shrine, the name of the guardian deity, and a brief prayer, are increasingly popular. This combination of ancient religious objects with modern technology symbolizes the continuing vitality of Shinto—its shrines, its talismans, and above all, the sense of dependence on the *kami*.

HISTORY OF SHINTO

After a brief account of prehistoric religion, we describe the development of Japan's principal religious traditions up to the beginning of the Meiji Era (1868). Finally, we discuss Shinto in the modern period, including the incredible proliferation of new religions in Japan.

PREHISTORIC RELIGION IN JAPAN (10,000 B.C.E.–794 C.E.)

It is difficult to reconstruct prehistoric beliefs, but it appears that the religious aspects of Japanese prehistoric culture included reverence for the dead, sacred objects, concerns about fertility, and reverence for *kami*. The Japanese people have always shown a reverent concern for the dead, and special types of burial in prehistoric times indicate this concern. One ancient practice was to cover the body with red ocher and stones. From very early times, the Japanese concern for personal cleanliness was linked to a dread of death as pollution. Funerals were held as soon as possible, and bathing was essential for the survivors after mourning. Although Shinto did not exist as a separate religion in ancient times, this perception of death as an unclean state was to become a Shinto perspective.

Phallic symbols of stone and small clay figurines, including explicitly female figures dating from prehistory, point to a link between religion, fertility, and female *kami*. The fertility of the earth was important, and as rice cultivation developed, religious ceremonies were performed to gain the blessings of the *kami* for each phase of rice production.

What appear to have been sacred objects have been recovered in archaeological digs, often in the tombs of prominent ancestors. The three most important objects for later times are comma-shaped jewels, swords and mirrors, a set of which eventually became the sacred regalia of the emperor. These objects, especially the mirror, are still used today in Shinto shrines to represent or embody the *kami* enshrined there.

The evidence indicates that women had considerable religious and political power in prehistoric Japan. Early Chinese records tell of powerful Japanese female *shamans* who could channel the will of the *kami,* making the divine will known to the people. Some of these women were also rulers. One was the ruler Pimiko, who was attended by more than a thousand female servants. There was also a tradition of the princess-priestesses, who were relatives of clan chieftains. These women would be consecrated and live apart to maintain purity. They would go into trances, possessed by the clan *kami,* and deliver advice to the chieftains.

In prehistoric Japan, society was organized into clans or tribes, each of which paid reverence to a clan *kami (ujigami).* The clan chief was, in practice, also a priest figure. Although the concept of *kami* was not clearly defined, many *kami* were associated with particularly impressive natural settings, such as a waterfall or mountain. By the fourth century C.E., a group of clans called Yamoto, progenitors of the present imperial line, gained political ascendancy. Their religious justification for establishing their imperial throne was the claim that their chieftains were descendants of the *kami* Amaterasu, the sun goddess. Along with this belief in the mystic origins of the imperial throne, elements of prehistoric Japanese folk religion that were later incorporated into formalized Shinto include the importance of the *kami,* veneration of ancestors, and the sense of death as pollution.

INTRODUCTION OF CHINESE RELIGIOUS TRADITIONS AND THE FORMATION OF SHINTO

In the sixth century C.E., the Japanese imported and began to adapt many aspects of Chinese civilization: the Chinese writing system, Confucianism, Buddhism, Taoism, and many aspects of material culture as well. With the introduction of foreign religions came the need to distinguish and label the old traditional ways. Buddhism called itself "the way of the Buddha," or Butsudo, so the traditional Japanese folk religion set itself apart by using the counterpart term "the way of the *kami,*" or Shin-

to (*shin* means "*kami,*" and *to* or *do* means "way"). The introduction of writing brought to an end the prehistoric period, and the introduction of new ways of believing and doing resulted in the formation of Shinto as a distinct entity.

The adaptation of new Chinese religions was masterminded by Prince Shotoku (573–621 C.E.). Although he attempted to maintain a balance among Buddhism, Shinto, and Confucianism, Shotoku favored Buddhism because, as an imported religion, it was not the special possession of any contentious chieftain. Thus, Shotoku consolidated the power of the state. His famous Seventeen Article Constitution was mainly Confucian in inspiration, but it also cited Buddhism. The continued Confucian influence tended to reduce the role of females as spiritual or political authorities, because it favored males as authority figures. Confucianism became the main resource from which Japanese social ethics has been drawn.

The political leaders who succeeded Shotoku continued to include Shinto ceremonies among the court rites. The emperor Temmu ordered the production of the *Kojiki,* a collection of ancient myths and historical information, published in 712. It was supplemented in 720 by the *Nihonshoki* (also called *Nihongi*). Together, these works constitute the earliest Shinto literature; they include a cosmology and an account of the descent of the imperial line from the sun goddess. No doubt these scriptures reflect both political and religious motives for unifying Japan. The creation story in the *Nihonshoki* incorporates the Chinese concepts of *yin* and *yang* and weaves these principles together with the Japanese *kami* and love of nature. In addition to the divine descent of the imperial line and the creation of the Japanese islands, these Shinto texts describe the creation of the Japanese people as descended from *kami.* Thus, they sanctify the homeland, its people, and its leadership.

Although these themes are developed and elaborated throughout history, we may say that the formation of Shinto out of prehistoric folk traditions was completed with the production of the *Nihonshoki* and *Kojiki,* because these texts include most of the major teachings and practices and because they designate Shinto as the original Japanese religion. The production of officially sanctioned scriptures raised Shinto to the level of the imported Chinese religions. Shinto now had a scripture and a clearer identity.

DEVELOPMENT OF JAPAN'S PRINCIPAL RELIGIOUS TRADITIONS (794–1868 C.E.)

During the next ten centuries, Shinto was overshadowed by Buddhism as Japanese society shifted from imperial rule to a feudal system that came to be governed by a military dictator *(shogun)*. But the indigenous faith maintained considerable strength in the countryside and in the form of periodic Shinto ceremonies performed as state functions. Shinto developed philosophically by using Buddhist concepts, and the Shinto pantheon, already rich, was elaborated to include Buddhas and *bodhisattvas*. In short, Shinto learned how to live with Buddhism. Toward the end of this medieval period, the *shogun*'s rule became unstable, and political change was in the offing. As early as 1350, the seeds of Restoration Shinto were being sown. Among its principles were the revival of Shinto and the restoration of imperial rule. This movement, along with other factors, launched Shinto into a position of great influence in modern times.

The Heian period (794–1185 C.E.) saw the flowering of classical Japanese culture and imperial court society. The emperor shared political power with powerful aristocratic families who combined Buddhist, Shinto, Confucian, and Taoist practices. Rulers and aristocrats tended to favor Buddhism over Shinto. In the Heian and subsequent periods of the medieval era, the major sects of Japanese Buddhism were established: Shingon, Tendai, Zen, Nichiren, and Pure Land. Buddhist temples were built throughout the land, and the Great Buddha statue of Nara (built 752 C.E.) stood as a symbol of Buddhist influence.

Buddhists introduced the concepts of "original substance" and "manifest traces" to show that the Buddhas are the basic or fundamental reality and the *kami* are lesser realities (manifest traces of the Buddhas). Eventually, Shinto scholars enjoyed

some success in arguing for the opposite relationship, viewing the *kami* as the fundamental realities. The relations among Shinto and the imported faiths from China, as we have seen, were often a matter of borrowing and blending. One new form of Shinto, called Two Parts or Dual Shinto (Ryobu Shinto), correlated *kami* and Buddhas, For example, Amaterasu, paired with the Sun Buddha; in later times these two came to be equated. In some cases popular divinities, such as Hachiman (spirit of the emperor Ojin), were revered as both Shinto *kami* and Buddhist *bodhisattvas*.[10]

Many westerners have learned about medieval Japan through novels and films featuring *samurai* sword fighters. During the feudal period (late twelfth century to late nineteenth century), the warrior *(bushi)* class dominated Japanese society. Their code *(bushido)* was a combination of the virtues of all the major religions of Japan. For the most part; the emperor was bereft of power, some emperors even became Buddhist monks and withdrew from the world.

By the fourteenth century, a movement began to purify Shinto of its Buddhist overlay and to establish the indigenous religion as superior. Perhaps stimulated by the belief that the national *kami* had helped drive away the Mongols in 1274 and 1281 through a storm or divine wind *(kamikaze)*,[11] this movement promoted the national character of Shinto. Shinto scholar Chikafusa Kitabatake (1293–1354) defended the traditional concept of the divine descent of the imperial line. A very influential Shinto spokesman for what later came to be called Restoration Shinto was Kanetomo Yoshida (1435–1511), who pursued the same themes and claimed that "all foreign doctrines are offshoots of Shinto."[12]

Warring factions created civil strife for long periods in feudal times, but in 1603 the Tokugawa family was able to unify the country under its strong military control and initiate a 250-year reign of peace. The Tokugawas used conservative Confucian and Neo-Confucian ethical and political principles to maintain order, and they used the Buddhist temples as a structure through which to control the populace. Each family was required to belong to a Buddhist temple and to record births and deaths in the temple registry. Christian missionaries had entered Japan in 1549, but the Tokugawas believed that Christianity and trade with the West would disrupt political and economic stability in Japan. Consequently, the *shoguns* prohibited Christianity from 1613 to 1858 and severely limited foreign trade and other forms of contact with outsiders—hence the saying that the *shoguns* wanted to make Japan a "hermit nation."

The Tokugawa emphasis on national unity and pride provided a fertile ground for the cultivation of what came to be known as Restoration Shinto. Shinto scholars argued that Japan should be purged of all foreign religions—especially Christianity and Buddhism. They proclaimed the themes of divine descent of the emperor and the Japanese people and the superiority of Japan and Shinto. They called for the restoration of the emperor to his "proper role" of leadership. The most influential spokesman among the Restoration Shintoists was Norinaga Motoori (1730-1801), who argued that Shinto surpassed all religions and encompassed all religions. He declared that Shakyamuni (Buddha) and Confucius are *kami* and that their "ways" are branch roads of the wide Way of Kami.[13]

SHINTO IN MODERN JAPAN (1868–1945 C.E.)

The modern period of Japanese history began with the Meiji government reforms that resulted in Japan's entry into the world of modern nation-states. From 1868 to 1945, however, ancient imperial institutions and concepts, such as the emperor's divinity and the ancient creation myth, were revived and combined with modern policies. In this section we discuss the modern period through 1945. The postwar period (1945 to the present) will be treated in the last part of this appendix, "Contemporary Shinto."

The Meiji Restoration of 1868 was a pivotal point in Japanese history. The end of the Tokugawa period meant the end of isolation, the end of feudalism, the end of the *samurai* era, and the end of Buddhist patronage. The Meiji government restored to the emperor his title of head of state with a constitution and legislative body under him. Japan was opened up to foreign trade, and the government set out to modernize Japan at a rapid pace.

The Constitution of 1889 was drawn up in accord with the principles of Restoration Shinto: Article I read: "The Empire of Japan shall be reigned over and governed by a line of Emperors unbroken for ages eternal." Article III stated: "The Emperor is sacred and inviolable." Shinto became the state religion, but the Meiji reformers also wanted to institute the right of freedom of religion into modern Japan. To make Shinto the national religion but maintain "freedom of religion," the government declared that there would be Shrine Shinto and Sect Shinto. Shrine Shinto was state Shinto, the national religion. However, the government proclaimed that this Shrine Shinto or state Shinto was not a religion. The priests were instructed not to conduct unmistakably religious ceremonies such as funerals; they could perform rituals intended to establish the "national morality." (These latter rites were said to be religious in form but not in intent.) The government's term for "shrine" was *jinja*, which means "*kami* house" or "*kami* shrine." "Shrine" Shinto or state Shinto was only "nonreligious" in the terminology of the government.

The government then singled out thirteen groups that had developed as sects of Shinto; these they labeled "Sect Shinto" and categorized as religious. These groups could not use the term *shrine* but were to call their buildings *kyokai*, a term usually translated as "church." Sect Shinto received no state support. Along with Buddhism, Christianity, and all other religions, Sect Shinto was "free" because it was not regulated or supported by the state.

Most of the Shinto sects were based on the experience of a charismatic leader who was given authority by a Shinto deity viewed as a monotheistic supreme being. Some of these sects, such as Kurozumikyo and Tenrikyo, were founded toward the end of the Tokugawa Era. The founder of Kurozumikyo believed himself to be possessed by the sun *kami* Amaterasu, whom he identified as the infinite deity. Tenrikyo (heavenly wisdom teaching) became one of the most popular sects, claiming 2.5 million members today. The founder, Miki Nakamura (1798–1887), was regarded as a living *kami.* Supplementing the ancient Shinto myth, her scripture reveals the exact spot where Izanagi and Izanami began the creation process.

The religious ideology of Restoration Shinto was put into practice in the Meiji Era, with one major exception: although Restoration Shinto scholars wished to rid Japan of all influence from foreign religions, Japan could not be purged of all foreign religions. Buddhism, Confucianism, and some aspects of Taoism were already inextricably woven into Japanese culture. Also, it would have been politically impossible to proscribe Christianity, the religion of many of Japan's modern trade partners. Because the Japanese government was increasingly controlled by the military, Shinto was used to promote not only nationalism but militarism and empire building as well, sweeping the nation into war. Perhaps this movement can be called Shinto nationalism and militarism, but as Daniel Holtom and H. Byron Earhart have pointed out, most Japanese Buddhists and Japanese Christians also supported the government's actions.[14]

Because some postwar Western writers have alleged that Shinto caused Japanese militarism, we need to clarify the nature and role of Shinto. Shinto mythology clearly links Shinto tradition with the national identity, but it is not clear that the *Kojiki* or any classic Shinto text fosters militarism.[15] It is also important to recall, as we have seen, that Shinto is not equivalent to state Shinto. We need to see state Shinto in the context of the overall history of Shinto. Finally, let us consider that in general, there were probably three different perspectives among the Japanese people in the period when state Shinto flourished: the perspectives of government administrators, the shrine priests, and the people at large. Although almost everyone was loyal to the imperialistic cause, the government administrators may have been concerned mainly with ideological control of the people, the shrine priests may have had in mind ritual and theological concerns,

and the people may have looked for simple blessings of their homes and welfare.

CONTEMPORARY SHINTO

After World War II, Allied occupation forces disestablished state Shinto, the national religion that the Japanese government had claimed was not a religion. Since 1945, Shinto has received neither supervision nor subsidies from the government.[16] The emperor officially renounced his divinity; his religious activities, such as those rituals performed at the Ise Shrine, were to be viewed as private rites. The new constitution insured complete religious freedom.

Thus disestablished, Shinto lost some of its popular support for a time. When people lamented the destruction of the war, they tended to blame Shinto. But as we have shown already, Shinto had been meeting fundamental spiritual needs for at least a thousand years before it was used by the government as a state religion. Shinto was not long in decline after 1945. In 1946, most of the shrines that had been controlled by the government as state shrines were organized into the Association of Shinto Shrines; they have been supported since then by private donations.

The Association of Shinto Shrines is a vital organization today with a branch office in each prefecture, and beneath it are ranked subbranches attached to member shrines. The association carries out the education of believers, the training of priests, and the development of shrines. It also publishes statements of Shinto objectives or principles such as the following;

1. To express gratitude for divine favor and the benefits of ancestors, and with a bright, pure, sincere mind to devote ourselves to the shrine rites and festivals.

2. To serve society and others and . . . to endeavor to improve and consolidate the world.

3. To identify our minds with the Emperor's mind and, in loving and being friendly with one another, to pray for the country's prosperity and for peaceful co-existence and co-prosperity for the people of the world.[17]

Clearly, the association is concerned that Shinto not be seen as a narrowly ethnic religion: Principles 2 and 3 express concern for all peoples. Principle 3 does not uphold the emperor as divine, but it does maintain that the emperor is the symbolic head of the nation and of Shinto.

THE NEW RELIGIONS

A remarkable feature of the contemporary religious landscape in Japan is the proliferation of the so-called New Religions. The emergence of relatively new forms of Japanese religion actually began in the early nineteenth century with the founding of Shinto sects, as previously discussed. Kurozumikyo (founded in 1814) and Tenrikyo (founded in 1838) are examples of "Old New Religions" that arose in the context of the perceived inability of the traditional religions to deal with the growing poverty and instability at the end of the Tokugawa Era. Another group of New Religions stems from the ecstatic experiences of a peasant woman, Nao Deguchi, in the 1890s. She and her son-in-law founded the Omoto (great source) religion, which later inspired the founders of other New Religions. The influence of Western spiritualism on the Omoto religions is apparent. A third group of New Religions may be called the Nichiren Group, because they are offshoots of Nichiren Buddhism. Soka Gakkai (Value Creation Society, founded in 1937) is the most popular and aggressive of these movements.

These three types of New Religions are flourishing today, along with many additional religions that defy categorization. Two examples of religions founded after World War II are PL Kyodan (Perfect Liberty Fellowship, founded in 1946) and Tensho Kotai Jingukyo (or Odorukyo, the "Dancing Religion," founded in 1946). PL Kyodan has an aesthetic theme, emphasizing that life is art. The Dancing Religion is a highly syncretic religion founded by a farm woman, Sayo Kitamura, who, as a "living *kami*," taught followers to shout the Buddhist *Lotus Sutra* and transcend their egos in the ecstasy of an ego-annihilating dance. In the 1980s there came another great wave of New Religions, labeled the "New New Religions" by many observers. Byakko Shinkokai (popularly called the Peace Religion) portrays Japan as the holy center from which peace will emanate to the rest of the world, whereas Oyama Nezunomikoto Shinshikyokai combines the Shinto theme of purification with a strong emphasis on spiritual healing.

Many characteristics of the New Religions and New New Religions are not really new. For example, some New Religions regard their founders as a living *kami;* this is a contemporary use of an old Shinto concept. A quality of these religions that is new, however, is the sense of entering an accessible, very close, caring community that in many New Religions is largely focused on laypeople, not clergy. To some Japanese, Shrine Shinto and Buddhism have seemed to be too formal and too traditional to meet the need for community created by a rapidly changing urban lifestyle. Religions that met the needs of traditional village communities gave people a sense of belonging, but that scenario has long since been eroded away by urbanization.

It appears, however, that traditional or Shrine Shinto is indeed in step with modern, urbanized society by being involved in what may be called company-communities. The term *company-community* refers to the sense of family that exists among employees in many Japanese companies. This social unit may in part fill the gap created by urbanization. Employees feel a strong sense of loyalty to the company, their employer, and fellow workers. Companies provide many benefits, including housing, social activities, and even visits to a Shinto shrine. In earlier times, society was organized by clans *(uji)* in traditional village communities, and a clan prayed to the clan *kami (ujigami)*. Although not a strict parallel, we now see Shinto involved in somewhat similar patterns: the company-community may have a *kamidana* at the workplace, build its own shrine, visit a shrine dedicated to business success, participate as a group in a shrine festival taking place near the company facilities, and so forth.

Shinto has regained a strong position in Japanese society today. It still gives the Japanese people a way to focus the sense of sacredness experienced in relation to innumerable spirits, natural phenomena, historical figures, ancestors, and national identity. It continues to be a vehicle for people to express gratitude or to express desire for positive outcomes, such as healthy pregnancy and childbirth. In Japan today, most people are "born Shinto and die Buddhist." The Japanese still turn to the *kami* in times of crisis, concern, or thanksgiving. Most pregnant women pray to the *kami* for a safe birth, and the child will be taken for blessings at the shrine on its "first outing" (hence the phrase "born Shinto").

GENDER ISSUES

If contemporary life and modernization are thought to call for giving many more leadership roles to women, then neither Shinto nor Japanese society in general is modernizing rapidly. In ancient times, women often functioned as *shamans* and political leaders, but Confucianism and Neo-Confucianism promoted the concept of women as subordinate and inferior. For the most part, women have not functioned as leaders in Shinto; today about 7 percent of Shinto priests are women.[18] The shrine maidens have continued to perform the *kagura* sacred dance and to assist in shrine activities, sometimes giving tourists the impression that they play

a leadership role. But the clearest indications of females in authority positions in Japanese religion today are found in the New Religions (as in Tenrikyo and others) and in the increasing numbers of female *shamans* in folk religion.

THE FUTURE OF SHINTO

Will Shinto remain strong despite continuing urbanization, modernization, and the appeal of the New Religions? Some studies indicate that fewer households have *kamidanas* today than ten years ago and that in some areas of the country, participation in Shinto festivals is decreasing. The overall picture, however, does not indicate that Shinto is declining. Shinto is not out of step with contemporary society in Japan. Participation in Shinto observances such as New Year's activities at shrines, blessings for children (Shichi-go-san, or "seven-five-three," blessings), and the purchase of talismans (including telephone card talismans) are increasing.[19] Most marriage ceremonies are conducted by Shinto priests, although today the clothing style may be "Christian-white," and the ritual and banquet may take place in a privately owned, modern marriage hall equipped to present laser light shows.

Whether the concern is marriage, entering a good university, safety in travel, or success in business, Shinto is intimately involved in modern life when the people turn to the *kami* for protection or blessings. The Japanese people are known for determination and "doing all one can." When it comes to doing all one can to meet important needs, more often than not, this includes praying to the *kami*.

APPENDIX C

WORLD WIDE WEB RESOURCES

META-INDEXES AND COMPARATIVE RELIGION DIRECTORIES

http://religion.rutgers.edu/links/vrindex.html

"Virtual Religion Index: Links for Research on Religion": An index designed as a tool that highlights important contents of religion-related Web sites to speed research. Hyperlinks are provided not only to home pages but also to major subsites, directories, and documents within the field of religion.

The site includes information regarding U.S. religions, ancient Near Eastern studies, anthropology and sociology of religion, archaeology and religious art, biblical studies, Buddhist tradition, Christian tradition, comparative religion, confessional agencies, East Asian studies, ethics and moral values, Greco-Roman studies, Hindu tradition, Islam, Jewish studies, philosophy and theology, and psychology of religion. This site is a good starting point for the academic study of religion on the Internet. Maintained by M. H. Smith, Associate Professor of Religion, Rutgers University

http://www.freenet.edmonton.ab.ca/~cstier/ religion/toc.htm

"A Guide to the Best Religious Studies Resources on the Internet": A subject guide "whose purpose is to provide useful links to Internet resources in Religious Studies that are of value to the undergraduate student in Religious Studies. This subject guide is intended to cover the most useful

resources related to each of the world's major religious traditions: Buddhism, Christianity, Hinduism, Islam, Judaism, and the Chinese and Japanese religions" (Confucianism, Taoism, and Shinto). The guide also provides limited coverage of some smaller, nontraditional forms of religion, such as Paganism and New Age spirituality. Maintained by Cory Stier, Edmonton Public Library; Gary Werber, a Cybrarian for the City of Calgary; and Boyd Blackwell, a graduate of the Masters of Library and Information Studies program at the University of Alberta.

http://web.bu.edu/STH/Library/contents.html

"Religion and Philosophy Resources on the Internet": Annotated listings for general religion, Asian religions, Christianity, Islam, Judaism, and philosophy. Maintained by David Suiter, Public Services Librarian, Boston University School of Theology.

http://www.wlu.ca/~wwwrandc/ internet_links.html

"Religious Studies Internet Links": A lengthy and well-organized listing that includes current news, course syllabi, software, images, multimedia resources, departments, and societies, as well as listings for the major religions. Maintained by Adrien Desjardins, Wilfrid Laurier University.

http://scholar.cc.emory.edu/

"TELA" (Scholars Press): The official Web site of Scholars Press and other sponsoring societies, which include the American Academy of Religion, the Society of Biblical Literature, the American Philological Association, the American Schools of Oriental Research, and the American Society of Papyrologists. This is an essential site for the student of religion.

SPECIFIC TRADITIONS

BUDDHISM

http://coombs.anu.edu.au/WWWVL-Buddhism.html

An outstanding database with information, electronic texts, and links on every imaginable aspect of Buddhism.

http://www.mahidol.ac.th/budsir

Web site of the Thailand Pali Text Project at Mahidol University, Thailand.

http://www.iijnwt.or.jp/iriz/irizhtml/irizhome.htm

Web site of the Zen Text Input at Hanazono University, Japan.

http://www.sol.nuri.net/~hederein/indexing.html

Site of the Korean Canon Input Project, carried out by Haeinsa monastery, South Korea. The Haeinsa monastery has also announced the release of the full Korean canon on a single CD-ROM, the first completed task of such scope.

http://www.acmuller.gol.com/ebti.htm

A site that accesses, along with many other Buddhist texts, the Electronic Buddhist Text Initiative (EBTI), a gathering of the major Buddhist on-line text projects organized by Lewis Lancaster of the University of California at Berkeley. Maintained by Charles Muller, Toyo Gakuen University, Japan.

CHRISTIANITY

http://www.iclnet.org/pub/resources/christian-history.html

"Early Christian Texts": An excellent resource for the study of Christianity in the patristic and medieval periods. The site contains the full-text versions of creeds, texts, and writings of the early Church fathers.

http://www.gospelcom.net/bible?version=RSV

"TheBible Gateway": Translations of the *Bible* in several languages.

CONFUCIANISM AND TAOISM

http://www-personal.monash.edu.au/~sab/index.html

"Chinese Philosophy Page": An extensive page dealing with Chinese philosophy. The intention is to provide all the information available on the Internet about Chinese philosophy and related subjects at a single site (a daunting task).

http://www.clas.ufl.edu/users/gthursby/taoism/

"Taoism WWW Virtual Library": Perhaps the most comprehensive source for World Wide Web information on Taoism.

http://www.acmuller.gol.com/index.html

A listing of many of the important sources for Buddhism, Confucianism, and Taoism. Maintained by Charles Muller, Toyo Gakuen University.

HINDUISM

http://www.hindunet.org

A general directory listing links to many facets of Hinduism, including language, arts, temples, and organizatiaons.

http://www.acusd.edu/theo/ref-gen.shtml
http://www.columbia.edu/cu/libraries/index/area/sarai/

Two sites—one maintained at the University of San Diego and the other, at Columbia University—with a long history of consistent updating with technology. They also provide numerous links to other resources.

http://www.ncb.gov.sg/nhb/alam/

An incredible resource for exploring Hinduism, Buddhism, and the character of the various empires in India through artistic portrayals.

http://www.cco.caltech.edu/~vidya/advaita/

"The Advaita Vedanta Home Page": Attempts to provide a structured introduction to the philosophy of Advaita Vedanta. Sections include an introduction, philosophy, philosophers, and history. Maintained by S. Vidyasankar.

ISLAM

http://wings.buffalo.edu/student-life/sa/muslim/isl/texts.html

An extensive number of links to hypertext versions of the *Quran* (in several languages), sound files of recitations of the *Quran,* and commentaries.

http://www.unn.ac.uk/societies/islamic/index.html

A site that is maintained by members of the Muslim community and therefore embodies a per-

spective from within the tradition of Islam. The site provides extensive information about the beliefs, history, and culture of Islam.

JUDAISM

http://www.shamash.org/trb/judaism.html

A directory with access to a variety of Jewish resources, both academic and general.

http://world.std.com/~alevin/jewishfeminist.html

A site for resources on Judaism, with specific interest in Jewish feminism.

MISCELLANEOUS

http://www.nativeweb.org/

"Indigenous Peoples on the Web": A collective project of many peoples. The intent of the site is to provide a cyber-community for the earth's indigenous peoples. This site combines high technology and ancient visions and wisdom traditions.

http://www.as.wvu.edu/coll03/relst/www/link.htm

"American Religion Links": A clearinghouse for over a hundred hypertext links related to U.S. religions or U.S. religious history. Although not specifically targeted to world religions, the context of the U.S. experience is such that there are sufficient connections with many of the traditions discussed in *Patterns of Religion.*

NOTES

PREFACE

1. Data on religious adherents in the Preface are from the *1998 Britannica Book of the Year: Events of 1997* (Chicago: Encyclopaedia Britannica, 1998), p. 314.

CHAPTER 1

1. Statistics on religious adherents in Chapter 1 are from the *1998 Britannica Book of the Year: Events of 1997* (Chicago: Encyclopaedia Britannica, 1998), p. 314.

2. Wilfred Cantwell Smith, *The Meaning and End of Religion* (New York: New American Library, 1964), p. 22 and chap. 3.

3. Ibid., pp. 23–29.

4. Ibid., pp. 85–89.

5. Ibid., pp. 90–96; and *The Koran Interpreted*, trans. A. J. Arberry (New York: Macmillan), 5.5, 3:19.

6. Wilfred Cantwell Smith, *Meaning and End of Religion,* chap. 3.

7. Ibid., p. 119.

8. Jonathan Z. Smith, *Imagining Religion: From Babylon to Jonestown* (Chicago: University of Chicago Press, 1982), pp. 2–4.

9. W. Richard Comstock, "Toward Open Definitions of Religion," *Journal of the American Academy of Religion* 52, no. 3 (1984): 505.

10. Edward Burnett Tylor, *Primitive Culture,* vol. 1 (New York: Gordon Press, 1974), p. 383.

11. Melford E. Spiro, "Religion: Problems of Definition and Explanation," in *Anthropological Approaches to the Study of Religion,* ed. Michael Banton (London: Tavistock Publications, 1966), p. 94.

12. Richard Gombrich, *Theravada Buddhism* (London: Routledge & Kegan Paul, 1988), chap. 7.

13. Reported in *The Guardian* (London), September 16, 1990.

14. Rudolf Otto, *The Idea of the Holy,* trans. John W. Harvey (New York: Oxford University Press, 1958), pp. 12–19.

15. Mircea Eliade, *Patterns in Comparative Religion,* trans. Rosemary Sheed (New York: World, 1963), p. 1.

16. Paul Tillich, "The Significance of the History of Religions for the Systematic Theologian," in *The History of Religions,* vol. 1, ed. Joseph M. Kitagawa (Chicago: University of Chicago Press, 1967), pp. 147–148.

17. Zenkei Shibayama, *A Flower Does Not Talk: Zen Essays* (Rutland, Vt.: Charles Tuttle, 1970), p. 16.

18. Spiro, "Religion," p. 89 .

19. Jonathan Z. Smith, *Imagining Religion,* p. 1.

20. Gerardus van der Leeuw, *Religion in Essence and Manifestation,* vol. 2, trans. J. E. Turner (New York: Harper & Row, 1963), pt. 5.

21. John Cobb, "Feminism and Process Thought: A Two-Way Relationship," in *Feminism and Process Thought,* ed. Sheila Greene Davaney (New York: Edwin Mellon, 1981), p. 42.

22. Jonathan Z. Smith, *Imagining Religion,* p. 4.

23. Ibid., p. 4

24. Emile Durkheim, *The Elementary Forms of the Religious Life,* trans. J. W. Swain (New York: Macmillan, 1965), p. 62.

25. Clifford Geertz, "Religion as a Cultural System," in *Anthropological Approaches to the Study of*

Religion, ed. Michael Banton (London: Tavistock Publications, 1966), p. 19.

26. George Lindbeck, *The Nature of Doctrine: Religion and Theology in a Postliberal Age* (Philadelphia: Westminster Press, 1984), p. 32.

27. Ibid., p. 51.

28. Hans J. Mol, *Identity and the Sacred* (New York: Free Press, 1976), p. 9.

29. Comstock, "Toward Open Definitions of Religion," p. 502.

30. E. A. Burtt, ed., *The Teachings of the Compassionate Buddha* (New York: New American Library, 1955), p. 113.

31. See Rosemary Ruether, *Sexism and God-Talk* (New York: Crossroad, 1983).

32. Wayne Proudfoot, *Religious Experience* (Berkeley: University of California Press, 1985), p. 108.

33. Otto, *Idea of the Holy*, pp. 6–11.

34. *Apocalyptic Spirituality*, ed. and trans. Bernard McGinn (New York: Paulist Press, 1979), p. 112.

35. Kitarō Nishida, *The Intelligibility and the Philosophy of Nothingness*, trans. Robert Schinzinger (Tokyo: Maruzen, 1958), p. 130.

36. Joachim Wach, *Types of Religious Experience: Christian and Non-Christian* (Chicago: University of Chicago Press, 1970), p. 32.

37. Richard Erdoes and John Fire/Lame Deer, *Lame Deer: Sioux Medicine Man* (London: Quartet Books, 1980), pp. 262–263.

38. Rodney Stark, "A Taxonomy of Religious Experience," *Journal for the Scientific Study of Religion* 5 (1965): 97–116.

39. van der Leeuw, *Religion in Essence and Manifestation*, vol. 2, pp. 681–682.

40. *Basic Writings of St. Thomas Aquinas*, vol. 1, trans. Anton Pegis (New York: Random House, 1945), p. 97.

41. E. E. Evans-Pritchard, *Nuer Religion* (Oxford: Oxford University Press, 1977), pp. 127, 134, 140.

42. *Selected Poems and Letters of Emily Dickinson*, ed. Robert N. Linscott (Garden City, N.Y.: Doubleday Anchor, 1959), p. 307.

43. Isaac Bashevis Singer, *Naftali the Storyteller and His Horse, Sus* (New York: Farrar, Straus & Giroux, 1973), pp. 18–21.

44. Jonathan Z. Smith, *To Take Place: Toward Theory in Ritual* (Chicago: University of Chicago Press, 1987), p. 109.

45. In Jonathan Z. Smith, *Imagining Religion*, p. 9.

46. *Heb.* 9:22.

47. René Girard, *Violence and the Sacred*, trans. Patrick Gregory (Baltimore, Md.: Johns Hopkins University Press, 1977), p. 23.

48. Jonathan Z. Smith, *Imagining Religion*, pp. 5–7.

49. Anne Llewellyn Barstow, *Witchcraze: A New History of the European Witch Hunts* (San Francisco: HarperCollins, 1994), pp. 19–25.

50. Wilfred Cantwell Smith, "Non-Western Studies: The Religious Approach," in *Religion in the State University*, p. 51.

51. "Seeking Christian Interiority: An Interview with Louis Dupre," *The Christian Century*, July 16–23, 1997, p. 655.

52. Louis Dumont, *Essays on Individualism* (Chicago: University of Chicago Press, 1986), p. 279.

53. *The Poems of Emily Dickinson*, vol. 1, ed. Thomas H. Johnson (Cambridge, Mass.: The Belknap Press, Harvard University Press, 1974), pp. 254–255. © 1951, 1955, 1979, 1983 by the President and Fellows of Harvard College. Reprinted by permission of the publishers and the Trustees of Amherst College.

54. Robert Bellah et al., *Habits of the Heart: Individualism and Commitment in American Life* (New York: Harper & Row, 1985), pp. 221ff.

55. "Seeking Christian Interiority," p. 655.

56. See David Tracy, "On the Origins of Philosophy of Religion," in *Myth and Philosophy*, ed. Frank Reynolds and David Tracy (New York: SUNY Press, 1990), n. 15, p. 30.

57. Durkheim, *Elementary Forms of the Religious Life*, pp. 464–466.

58. Ibid., p. 469.

59. Karl Marx, *Early Writings*, trans. T. B. Bottomore (London: Watts, 1963), pp. 43–44.

60. Sigmund Freud, *Totem and Taboo* (New York: Random House, 1944), p. 183.

61. Ibid., p. 202.

62. Ibid., p. 190.

63. Eliade, *Patterns in Comparative Religion*, p. 459.

64. van der Leeuw, *Religion in Essence and Manifestation*, vol. 2, p. 591.

65. *All Men Seek God* (Kansas City, Mo.: Hallmark Cards, 1968), pp. 43–44.

66. John Hick, *God and the Universe of Faiths* (London: Macmillan, 1973), p. 139.

67. *Analects* 7.20, in *The Sayings of Confucius,* trans. James R. Ware (New York: Mentor Books, 1955), p. 53.

CHAPTER 2

1. Margaret Ehrenberg, *Women in Prehistory* (London: British Museum Publications, 1989), p. 16.

2. On language, see Bernard Campbell, *Humankind Emerging,* 5th ed. (San Francisco: HarperCollins, 1988), chap. 13.

3. Stephen Jay Gould, *The Mismeasure of Man* (New York: Norton, 1981), p. 324.

4. Helen E. Fisher, *Anatomy of Love: The Natural History of Monogamy, Adultery, and Divorce* (New York: Norton, 1992), pp. 196–197.

5. Ibid., pp. 184–185.

6. For heritable social behaviors, see Fisher, *Anatomy of Love*, pp. 254–255.

7. Gould, *The Mismeasure of Man,* chap. 2.

8. See Campbell, *Humankind Emerging,* pp. 472–481; and Goran Burenhult, ed., *The First Humans: Human Origins and History to 10,000 B.C.* (San Francisco: HarperSan Francisco, 1993), pp. 97–121.

9. On the agricultural revolution see *The New Encyclopaedia Britannica,* vol. 26, s.v. "Prehistoric Peoples and Cultures," pp. 45–61; and Goran Burenhult, ed., *People of the Stone Age: Hunter-Gatherers and Early Farmers* (San Francisco: HarperSan Francisco, 1993).

10. Ehrenberg, *Women in Prehistory,* pp. 70, 95.

11. Ibid., p. 81.

12. Mircea Eliade, *A History of Religious Ideas: From the Stone Age to the Eleusinian Mysteries,* vol. 1, trans. Willard R. Trask (Chicago: University of Chicago Press, l978), p. 5.

13. Marija Gimbutas, *The Encyclopedia of Religion,* vol. 9 (New York: Macmillan, 1987), s.v. "Megalithic Religion," p. 343.

14. Ibid., p. 341.

15. See Marija Gimbutas, *The Goddesses and Gods of Old Europe* (London: Thames and Hudson, 1981).

16. Eliade, *History of Religious Ideas,* vol. 1, p. 19.

17. Campbell, *Humankind Emerging,* pp. 422–425.

18. Gordon Childe, *What Happened in History* (Baltimore: Penguin, 1965), chap. 2, 3.

19. Walter J. Ong, *The Presence of the Word: Some Prolegomena for Cultural and Religious History* (New Haven, Conn.: Yale University Press, 1967), pp. 166–169.

20. George Hart, *Egyptian Myths* (London: British Museum Publications, 1990), p. 13.

21. Henrietta McCall, *Mesopotamian Myths* (London: British Museum Publications, 1995), p. 52.

22. Yves Bonnefoy, comp., *Greek and Egyptian Mythologies,* trans. under direction of Wendy Doniger (Chicago: University of Chicago Press, 1992), pp. 66–78.

23. Karl Taube, *Aztec and Maya Myths* (London: British Museum Publications, 1995), pp. 33–37.

24. Miguel Leon-Portilla, ed., *Native Mesoamerican Spirituality* (New York: Paulist Press, 1980), pp. 28–29.

25. Walter Burkert, *Greek Religion,* trans. John Raffan (Cambridge, Mass.: Harvard University Press, 1985), p. 216.

26. Leonard H. Lesko, "Egyptian Religion," in *Religions of Antiquity,* ed., Robert M. Seltzer (New York: Macmillan, 1989), pp. 40–41, 50.

27. Philip Wheelwright, ed., *The Presocratics* (New York: Odyssey Press, 1966), p. 32.

28. Miguel Leon-Portilla, *Aztec Thought and Culture: A Study of the Ancient Nahuatl Mind* (Norman: University of Oklahoma Press, 1963), p. 31.

29. Burkert, *Greek Religion,* p. 307.

30. Wheelwright, *Presocratics,* p. 33.

31. Ibid., p. 33.

32. Ibid., p. 33.

33. Ibid., p. 240.

34. Evan Zuesse, *Ritual Cosmos: The Sanctification of Life in African Religions* (Athens: Ohio University Press, 1979), pp. 118–120.

35. Hart, *Egyptian Myths*, pp. 22–28.

36. Lesko, "Egyptian Religion," p. 40.

37. James B. Pritchard, ed., *The Ancient Near East: An Anthology of Texts and Pictures*, vol. 1 (Princeton, N.J.: Princeton University Press, 1958), p. 36.

38. *Popol Vuh: The Mayan Book of the Dawn of Life*, trans. Dennis Tedlock (New York: Touchstone, 1996), pt. 1, 4.

39. Edward Tripp, *Dictionary of Classical Mythology* (London: Collins, 1970), p. 199.

40. *Gilgamesh* (New York: New American Library, 1970), p. 79.

41. Pritchard, *Ancient Near East*, vol. 2, pp. 138–140.

42. Ibid., vol. 1, p. 64.

43. Stephen Quirke, *Ancient Egyptian Religion* (London: British Museum Press, 1992), p. 162.

44. Gherardo Gnoli, "Zoroastrianism," in *Religions of Antiquity*, ed. Robert M. Seltzer (New York: Macmillan, 1989), p. 138.

45. Burkert, *Greek Religion*, pp. 159–161.

46. Thomas M. Finn, *From Death to Rebirth: Ritual and Conversion in Antiquity* (New York: Paulist Press, 1997), pp. 80–83.

47. Leon-Portilla, *Aztec Thought and Culture*, p. 136.

48. Leon-Portilla, *Native Mesoamerican Spirituality*, p. 37.

49. Pritchard, *Ancient Near East*, vol. 2, p. 140.

50. John A. Wilson, *Before Philosophy* (Baltimore: Penguin, 1968), pp. 117–118.

51. Lesko, "Egyptian Religion," p. 40.

52. "The Book of the Dead," trans. E. A. W. Budge, in *Sacred Books and Early Literature of the East*, vol. 2 (New York: Parke, Austin, and Lipscomb, 1917), pp. 257–258.

53. *The New Encyclopaedia Britannica*, vol. 26, s.v. "rites and ceremonies," p. 794.

54. Alberto R. W. Green, *The Role of Human Sacrifice in the Ancient Near East* (Missoula: Univresity of Montana: Scholars Press, 1975), pp. 189–203.

55. Gould, *Mismeasure of Man*, pp. 56–57.

56. Ibid., p. 41.

57. Ibid., p. 104.

58. Claude Levi-Strauss, *The Savage Mind* (Chicago: University of Chicago Press, 1966), pp. 14–15.

59. Emile Durkheim, *The Elementary Forms of the Religious Life* (New York: Free Press, l965), p. 20.

60. J. Samuel Preuss, *Explaining Religion: Criticism and Theory from Bodin to Freud* (New Haven, Conn.: Yale University Press, 1987), p. xvii.

61. Lawrence E. Sullivan, *Icanchu's Drum: An Orientation to Meaning in South American Religions* (New York: Macmillan, 1988), p. 2.

62. Marija Gimbutas, *The Language of the Goddess* (San Francisco: HarperCollins, 1991) p. 316.

63. Merlin Stone, *When God Was a Woman* (New York: Dial Press, 1976), p. 1.

64. Gimbutas, *Language of the Goddess*, p. 321.

65. Joan B. Townsend, "The Goddess: Fact, Fallacy and Revitalization Movement," in *Goddesses in Religions and Modern Debate*, ed. Larry Hurtado (Atlanta: Scholars Press, 1990), pp. 189–193.

66. Ibid., p. 194.

67. *Myth, Religion, and Mother Right: Selected Writings of J. J. Bachofen*, trans. Ralph Manheim (Princeto, N.J.: Princeton University Press, 1992), p. 79.

68. Ibid., p. 109.

69. See Marvin Harris, *Cows, Pigs, Wars and Witches: The Riddles of Culture* (New York: Vintage, 1974), p. 73; and Fisher, *Anatomy of Love*, p. 217.

70. Riane Eisler, *The Chalice and the Blade: Our History, Our Future* (San Francisco: HarperSanFrancisco, 1987), p. 14.

71. Ehrenberg, *Women in Prehistory*, p. 94.

72. Townsend, "The Goddess," p. 183.

73. Ehrenberg, *Women in Prehistory*, pp. 99–106.

74. Bonnie S. Anderson and Judith P. Zinsser, *A History of Their Own: Women in Europe from Prehistory to the Present*, vol. 1 (New York: Harper & Row, 1988), p. 5.

75. Bruce Bower, "Whys of War," *Los Angeles Times*, February 18, 1991; and Fisher, *Anatomy of Love*, p. 352.

76. Fisher, *Anatomy of Love*, pp. 286–287; and Harris, *Cows, Pigs, Wars and Witches*, p. 92.

77. Harris, *Cows, Pigs, Wars and Witches*, p. 67.

78. Marija Gimbutas, *The Early Civilization of Europe,* monograph Los Angeles: UCLA 1980, chap. 2; and Eisler, *The Chalice and the Blade,* pp. 17–27.

79. Eisler, *The Chalice and the Blade,* p. 31.

80. Townsend, "The Goddess," pp. 193–196.

81. See Colin Renfrew, *Archaeology and Language: The Puzzle of Indo-European Origins* (New York: Cambridge University Press, 1990).

CHAPTER 3

1. *1995 Britannica Book of the Year: Events of 1994* (Chicago: Encyclopaedia Britannica, 1995), p. 275.

2. *The New Encyclopedia Britannica,* 15th ed., vol. 7, p. 169.

3. John (Fire) Lame Deer and Richard Erdoes, *Lame Deer: Sioux Medicine Man* (London: Quartet Books, 1980), pp. 250, 253.

4. John V. Taylor, *The Primal Vision: Christian Presence amid African Religion* (London: SCM Press, 1963), p. 71.

5. From Pam McAllister, ed., *Reweaving the Web of Life,* quoted in *The 1985 War Resisters League Peace Calender,* vol. 30 (New York).

6. Lame Deer and Erdoes, *Lame Deer,* p. 244.

7. In Sam D. Gill, *Native American Religions* (Belmont, Calif.: Wadsworth, 1982), pp. 42–43.

8. In T. C. McLuhan, *Touch the Earth: A Self-Portrait of Indian Existence* (New York: Dutton, 1971), p. 176.

9. W. Richard West, Jr., "Reflections on the Quincentenary," *Redlands* 70, no. 2, (Spring 1993): 18.

10. Leslie Marmon Silko, *Ceremony* (New York: Penguin, 1986), p. 2.

11. *Geronimo: His Own Story,* ed. S. M. Barrett (New York: Ballantine, 1971), p. 77.

12. John Mbiti, *African Religions and Philosophy* (New York: Praeger, 1969), p. 2.

13. Godfrey Lienhardt, *Divinity and Experience: The Religion of the Dinka* (London: Oxford University Press, 1961), pp. 15–25.

14. Duane Champagne, *American Indian Societies: Strategies and Conditions of Political and Cultural Survival* (Cambridge, Mass.: Cultural Survival, 1989), pp. 101–102.

15. Wayne Suttles, *Katzie Ethnographic Notes: The Faith of a Coast Salish Indian* (Victoria: British Columbia Provincial Museum, 1955), p. 39.

16. In Gerardus van der Leeuw, *Religion in Essence and Manifestation,* vol. 1 (New York: Harper Torchbooks, 1963), p. 24.

17. Joseph Epes Brown, *The Sacred Pipe: Black Elk's Account of the Seven Rites of the Oglala Sioux* (New York: Penguin, 1981), pp. 5–6.

18. Mbiti, *African Religions and Philosophy,* p. 31.

19. James R. Walker, *Lakota Belief and Ritual* (Lincoln: University of Nebraska Press, 1980), p. 75.

20. Geoffrey Parrinder, *Religion in Africa* (Baltimore: Penguin, 1969), p. 41.

21. John Middleton, *Lugbara Religion* (London: Oxford University Press, 1960), p. 253.

22. McLuhan, T*ouch the Earth,* p. 23.

23. van der Leeuw, *Religion in Essence and Manifestion,* vol. 1, p. 65.

24. Ake Hultkrantz, *The Religions of the American Indians,* trans. Monica Setterwall (Berkeley and Los Angeles: University of California Press, 1980), p. 54.

25 John Neihardt, *Black Elk Speaks: Being the Life Story of a Holy Man of the Oglala Sioux* (New York: Pocket Books, 1972), p. 2.

26. Middleton, *Lugbara Religion,* p. 25.

27. Elisabeth Tooker, ed., *Native North American Spirituality of the Eastern Woodlands* (New York: Paulist Press, 1979), pp. 22–29.

28. Bolaji Idowu, *African Traditional Religion* (London: SCM Press, 1973), pp. 135–136.

29. Lienhardt, *Divinity and Experience,* p. 56.

30. John D. Loftin, *Religion and Hopi Life in the Twentieth Century* (Bloomington: Indiana University Press, 1991), p. 15.

31. Brown, *Sacred Pipe,* p. xx.

32. E. E. Evans-Pritchard, *Nuer Religion* (Oxford: Clarendon Press, 1956), p. 52.

33. Ibid., p. 120.

34. Ibid., p. 49.

35. Clyde Holler, "Lakota Religion and Tragedy: The Theology of Black Elk Speaks," *Journal of the American Academy of Religion*, March 1984, p. 30n.

36. Evan Zuesse, *Ritual Cosmos: The Sanctification of Life in African Religions* (Athens: Ohio University Press, 1979), p. 110.

37. Ibid., p. 110.

38. Lee Sackett, "Aboriginal Australia," in *Traditional Peoples Today: Continuity and Change in the Modern World*, vol. 5 of *The Illustrated History of Humankind*, ed. Goran Burenhult (San Francisco: HarperSan Francisco, 1994) p. 82.

39. Ibid.

40. Christopher Vecsey, I*magine Ourselves Richly: Mythic Narratives of North American Indians* (San Francisco: HarperSan Francisco, 1991), pp 94–117; and Tooker, *Native North American Spirituality*, pp. 33–47.

41. Vecsey, *Imagine Ourselves Richly*, p. 99.

42. Ibid.

43. Ibid., p. 100.

44. Zuesse, *Ritual Cosmos*, p. 110.

45. On Hopi prophecy, see Loftin, *Religion and Hopi Life*, and Vecsey, *Imagine Ourselves Richly*, pp. 34–63.

46. R. I. Page, *Norse Myths* (London: British Museum Publications, 1990); and *Encyclopedia of Religion*, vol. 5 (New York: Macmillan, 1987), s.v. "Germanic religion," pp. 520–536.

47. Lawrence E. Sullivan, *Icanchu's Drum: An Orientation to the Meaning of South American Religions* (New York: Macmillan, 1988), p. 112.

48. Frank Waters, *The Book of the Hopi* (New York: Ballantine, 1963), p. 3. For an analysis of the Hopi myth, see Vecsey, *Imagine Ourselves Richly*, pp. 34–63.

49. Waters, *Book of the Hopi*, pp. 8, 13, 16.

50. In Vine Deloria, Jr., *God Is Red* (New York: Delta Books, 1973), p. 176.

51. Neihardt, *Black Elk Speaks*, p. 176.

52. Loftin, *Religion and Hopi Life*, p. 4.

53. Ibid., p. 10

54. Hultkrantz, *Religions of the American Indians*, chap. 9.

55. Taylor, *Primal Vision*, p. 48.

56. Evans-Pritchard, *Nuer Religion*, p. 144.

57. Deloria, *God Is Red*, p. 177.

58. Neihardt, *Black Elk Speaks*, p. 116.

59. Evans-Pritchard, *Nuer Religion*, p. 148.

60. Benjamin Ray, *African Religions* (Englewood Cliffs, N.J.: Prentice-Hall, 1976), p. 17.

61. Jonathan Z. Smith, *Imagining Religion: From Babylon to Jonestown* (Chicago: University of Chicago Press, 1982), p. 63.

62. Walker, *Lakota Belief and Ritual*, p. 75.

63. Lienhardt, *Divinity and Experience*, p. 157.

64. For the Hainuwele myth, see Barbara C. Sproul, *Primal Myths: Creating the World* (London: Rider, 1980), pp. 327–330.

65. Mbiti, *African Religions and Philosophy*, p. 116.

66. Walker, *Lakota Belief and Ritual*, p. 79.

67. Suttles, *Katzie Ethnographic Notes*, p. 68.

68. Ibid., p. 67

69. Ray, *African Religions*, p. 106.

70. I. M. Lewis, *Ecstatic Religion* (New York: Penguin Books, 1975), p. 70.

71. Nick Williams, "Rain Forest and Its Medical Secrets Shrinking Fast," *Los Angeles Times*, April 11, 1988, sec. 2, p. 4.

72. Lienhardt, *Divinity and Experience*, p. 296.

73. Taylor, *Primal Vision*, p. 35.

74. Mbiti, *African Religions and Philosophy*, pp. 108–109.

75. Peter J. Paris, *The Spirituality of African Peoples* (Minneapolis: Fortress, 1995), p. 77.

76. Mary Crow Dog and Richard Erdoes, *Lakota Woman* (New York: Harper Perennial, 1991), p. 13.

77. Paris, *Spirituality of African Peoples*, p. 79.

78. Gontran de Poncins, *Kabloona* (Chicago: Time-Life Books, 1980), p. 263.

79. Ibid., p. 277.

80. David Little and Sumner B. Twiss, *Comparative Religious Ethics: A New Method* (San Francisco: Harper & Row, 1978), pp. 40–41, 108.

81. Suzanne Slesin and Emily Gwathimey, comp., *Amen: Prayers and Blessings from Around the World* (New York: Viking Studio Books, Penguin Group).

82. In Loftin, *Religion and Hopi Life*, p. 9.

83. For a discussion of virtue in traditional African morality and its continuity with African American morality, see Paris, *Spirituality of African Peoples*.

84. In Louis Sahagun, "Banishment Tests Not Only Criminals but Their Tribe As Well," *Los Angeles Times*, June 21, 1995, p. A5.

85. Colin Renfrew, *Archaeology and Language: The Puzzle of Indo-European Origins* (New York: Cambridge University Press, 1990), chap. 9.

86. Quoted in Margaret Ehrenberg, *Women in Prehistory* (London: British Museum Publications, 1989), pp. 155–156.

87. Renfrew, *Archaeology and Language*, chap. 9; and *Encyclopedia of Religion*, vol. 3, s.v. "Celtic Religion," pp. 148–166.

88. *Encyclopedia of Religion*, vol. 5, s.v. "Germanic religion," pp. 520–536.

89. *Continuity and Change in the Modern World*, vol. 5 of *The Illustrated History of Humankind*, ed. Goran Burenhult (San Francisco: HarperSan Francisco, 1994), *Encyclopedia of Religion*, vol. 10, pp. 54–57.

90. Marvin Harris, "Foreward," in *Traditional Peoples Today: Continuity and Change in the Modern World*, vol. 5 of *The Illustrated History of Humankind*, ed. Goran Burenhult (San Francisco: HarperSan Francisco, 1994), p. 9.

91. *The New Encyclopedia Britannica*, 15th ed., vol. 27, p. 290.

92. Bruce Grant and Susan Rowley, "Northern Peoples: 1200 to the Present," in *Traditional Peoples Today: Continuity and Change in the Modern World*, vol. 5 of *The Illustrated History of Humankind*, ed. Goran Burenhult (San Francisco: HarperSan Francisco, 1994), p. 153.

93. Sackett, "Aboriginal Australia," p. 86. Also see Keith D. Suter and Kaye Stearman, *Aboriginal Australians*, report no. 35 (London: Minority Rights Group, 1988).

94. E. Pendleton Banks, "Traditional Peoples of the Asian Continent: 1200 to the Present," in *Traditional Peoples Today: Continuity and Change in the Modern World*, vol. 5 of *The Illustrated History of Humankind*, ed. Goran Burenhult (San Francisco: HarperSan Francisco, 1994), p. 49.

95. Henry F. Dobyns, *Native American Historical Demography* (Bloomington: Indiana University Press, 1976), p. 1.

96. Frederick Hoxie, "Traditional Peoples of North America," in *Traditional Peoples Today: Continuity and Change in the Modern World*, vol. 5 of *The Illustrated History of Humankind*, ed. Goran Burenhult (San Francisco: HarperSan Francisco, 1994), p. 188.

97. Figures based on "Religion: World Religious Statistics," in *1995 Britannica Book of the Year: Events of 1994*, (Chicago: Encyclopaedia Brittanica, 1995), p. 275, and the 1990 census of 1.9 million Native Americans.

98. *Los Angeles Times*, April 4, 1982, sec. 1A, p. 5.

99. Lame Deer and Erdoes, *Lame Deer*, p. 217.

100. Ibid., p. 216.

101. Albert Raboteau, *Slave Religion: The "Invisible Institution" in the Antebellum South* (New York: Oxford University Press, 1978), pp. 4–42.

102. S. James Anaya, "Indigenous Peoples in International Law," *Cultural Survival Quarterly*, Summer 1997, p. 59.

103. David Hurst Thomas, "Preface," in *Traditional Peoples Today: Continuity and Change in the Modern World*, vol. 5 of *The Illustrated History of Humankind*, ed. Goran Burenhult (San Francisco: HarperSan Francisco, 1994), p. 11.

104. Deloria, *God Is Red*, chap. 15, 16.

105. In West, "Reflections on the Quincentenary," p. 17.

106. Robert S. Michaelsen, "The Significance of the American Indian Religious Freedom Act of 1978," *Journal of the Amer can Academy of Religion* 52, no. 1 (March 1984): 114–115.

107. See Christopher Vecsey, ed., *Handbook of American Indian Religious Freedom* (New York: Crossroad Publishing, 1991).

CHAPTER 4

1. David R. Kinsley, *Hinduism: A Cultural Perspective*, 2d ed. (Englewood Cliffs, N.J.: Prentice-Hall, 1993), p. 53.

2. David M. Knipe, "Hinduism: Experiments in the Sacred," in *Religious Traditions of the World*, ed. H. Byron Earhart (San Francisco: HarperCollins, 1993), p. 806.

3. Gerald James Larson, *India's Agony over Religion* (Albany, N.Y.: SUNY Press, 1995), pp. 10, 261–262.

4. Kinsley, *Hinduism*, p. 85.

5. Gerald James Larson, "Hinduism in India and in America," in *World Religions in America: An Introduction*, ed. Jacob Neusner (Louisville: Westminster/John Knox, 1994), pp. 178–179.

6. For a full description of the pattern of "food interaction" in Indian culture, see the series of essays edited by Ravindra Khare, *The Eternal Food: Gastronomic Ideas and Experiences of Hindus and Buddhists* (Albany, N.Y.: SUNY Press, 1992).

7. *Manu Smriti (The Laws of Manu)*, 3:55–57; 9:3–7, 11, 26, in Ainslie T. Embree, ed., *Sources of Indian Tradition*, 2d ed., vol. 1, *From the Beginning to 1800* (New York: Columbia University Press, 1988), pp. 228–229.

8. Barbara Stoler Miller, "The Imaginative Universe of Indian Literature," in *Masterworks of Asian Literature in Contemporary Perspective* (New York: Columbia University Press, 1994), p. 10.

9. Knipe, "Hinduism," p. 833.

10. Ibid., p. 751.

11. Citations from the *Bribadaranyoka* and *Katha Upanishads* are taken from R. C. Zachner, tr., *Hindu Scriptures* (London: J. M. Dent, 1966). Citations from the *Chandogya Upanishad* are taken from *Sources of Indian Tradition*, 2nd ed., vol. 1 (New York: Columbia University Press, 1988).

12. Citations of the *Bhagavad Gita* are taken from the translation by Barbara Stein Miller, *The Bhagavad-Gita: Krishna's Counsel in Time of War* (New York: Boston, 1986).

13. Kinsley, *Hinduism*, p. 21.

14. From Stephen Hoy, ed., *Sources of Indian Tradition*, 2nd ed., vol. 2, Modern India and Pakistan (New York: Columbia University Press, 1988), p. 24.

15. Adapted from Kim Knott, *Hinduism: A Very Short Introduction* (New York: Oxford University Press, 1998), p. 96.

16. Larson, *India's Agony over Religion*, pp. 262–263.

CHAPTER 5

1. What we are describing here is an oversimplification of this process. Also, there were a number of differing theories concerning death and rebirth. But this general treatment suffices to present the philosophical environment in which the Buddha developed his theories.

2. See Donald K. Swearer, *The Buddhist World of Southeast Asia* (Albany, N.Y.: SUNY Press, 1995), pp. 141-145 on meditation in the lay community.

3. Charles Keyes, *The Golden Peninsula: Culture and Adaptation in Mainland Southeast Asia* (New York: Macmillan, 1977), p. 90.

4. Swearer, *The Buddhist World*, pp. 120-123.

5. Charles B. Jones, "Buddhism in Taiwan: A Historical Survey" (Ph.D. diss., University of Virginia, 1996), pp. 272-276.

6. Charles Keyes, "Mother or Mistress but Never a Monk: Buddhist Notions of Gender in Rural Thailand," *American Ethnologist* 11, no. 2 (May 1984): 223-241, as cited in Swearer, Donald K. *The Buddhist World of Southeast Asia* (Albany, SUNY Press), 1995.

CHAPTER 6

1. See Chapter 1 for a fuller explanation of traditional religion as holistic, pervasive, and integrative.

2. Robert G. Henricks, *Lao-tzu, Te-Tao Ching* (New York: Ballantine, 1989), chap. 25, 26. We use Henricks's translation for all subsequent quotations from the *Tao Te Ching*.

3. Ibid., pp. xx ff.

4. Kristofer Schipper, "The Taoist Body," in *History of Religions*, vol. 17, 1978, p. 364.

5. Ibid., p. 359.

6. Ibid., p. 363.

7. A. C. Graham, *Disputers of the Tao* (LaSalle, Ill.: Open Court, 1989), p. 332.

8. Michael Saso, *Taoism and the Rite of Cosmic Renewal* (Pullman: Washington State University Press, 1972), p. 10.

9. Based on John Lagerway, *Taoist Ritual in Chinese Society and History* (New York: Macmillan, 1987), and Saso, *Taoism and the Rite of Cosmic Renewal.*

10. Laurence G. Thompson, *Chinese Religion: An Introduction*, 4th ed (Belmont, Calif.: Wadsworth, 1989), p. 156.

11. Henri Maspero, *Taoism and Chinese Religion*, trans. Frank A. Kierman, Jr. (Amherst: University of Massachusetts Press, 1981), pp. 361–362.

12. Gia-fu Feng and Jane English, trans., *Chuang-tsu: Inner Chapters* (New York: Vintage, 1974), p. 12.

13. For a fuller account of Chung-li Ch'uan and the other immortals, see C. A. S. Williams, *Encyclopedia of Chinese Symbolism and Art Motives* (New York: Julian Press, 1960).

14. Maspero, *Taoism and Chinese Religion*, p. 388.

15. Henricks, *Lao-tzu*, p. 36.

16. For a discussion of this issue, see Ibid., p. 156.

17. Benjamin I. Schwartz, *The World of Thought in Ancient China* (Cambridge, Mass.: Belknap Press of Harvard University Press, 1985).

18. Lagerway, *Taoist Ritual*, pp. 50–51.

19. Ibid., pp. 70, 71.

20. Michael Saso, "Orthodoxy and Heterodoxy in Taoist Ritual," in *Religion and Ritual in Chinese Society,* ed. Arthur P. Wolf (Stanford, Calif.: Books Demand, 1974), pp. 331 ff.

21. Ibid., pp. 333–335.

22. Quoted in Maspero, *Taoism and Chinese Religion,* p. 298.

23. Ibid., p. 321.

24. J. Russell Kirkland, "The Roots of Altruism in the Taoist Tradition," *Journal of the American Academy of Religion* 54, no. 1 (1989): 67

25. For more detailed accounts of this and other Taoist methods, see Holmes Welch, *Parting of the Way* (Boston: Beacon Press, 1957).

26. Paul Anderson, trans., *The Method of Holding the Ones: A Taoist Manual of Meditation of the 4th Century a.d.* (Atlantic Highlands, N.J.: 1980), p. 6.

27. Ibid., pp. 41–42.

28. Ibid., p. 42.

29. Maspero, *Taoism and Chinese Religion,* pp. 542 ff.

30. Norman J. Girardot, *Myth and Meaning in Early Taoism: The Theme of Chaos* (Berkeley and Los Angeles: University of California Press, 1983), p. 25.

31. Schipper, "Taoist Body," p. 378.

32. Kirkland, "The Roots of Altruism," p. 73.

33. *T'ai-Shang Kan-Ying P'ien (Treatise of the Exalted One on Response and Retribution),* trans. Taitaro Suzuki and Paul Carus (LaSalle, Ill.: Open Court, 1944), pp. 53, 56.

34. Ibid., p. 52.

35. John Fairbank et al., *East Asia: Tradition and Transformation* (Boston: Houghton Mifflin, 1978), p. 31.

36. Tung Tso-pin, *An Interpretation of Ancient Chinese Civilization* (Taipei: Chinese Association of the United Nations, 1952), p. 19; quotation from *Chung Yung (Doctrine of the Mean)* 9.

37. Statement made by Kuei Ku Tzu, fourth century B.C.E.; quoted in Joseph Needham, *Science and Civilization in China*, vol. 4 (Cambridge, England: Cambridge University Press, 1954), p. 6.

38. The Chinese ideograph for *I* in the title *I Ching* originally referred to a chameleon, a lizard with a striking way of dealing with changes. A chameleon has independently moveable eyeballs and can change the color of its skin. The *Ching* in the title means "volume" or "classic."

39. Khigh Dhiegh, *The Eleventh Wing: An Exposition of the Dynamics of I Ching for Now* (New York: Dell, 1973).

40. C. K. Yang, *Religion in Chinese Society* (Berkeley and Los Angeles: University of California Press, 1961), pp. 107, 261.

41. Graham, *Disputers of the Tao*, p. 87.

42. Lun Yu, *Confucian Analects* 6:20, in *A Source Book in Chinese Philosophy,* trans. and comp. Wing-tsit Chan (Princeton, N.J.: Princeton University Press, 1963), p. 30.

43. Henricks, *Lao-tzu.*

44. Andrew H. Plaks, *Archetype and Allegory in the Dream of the Red Chamber* (Princeton, N.J.: Princeton University Press, 1976), chap. 3.

45. *Chuang-tsu* does deal with the question of good government in chapters 5 and 28.

46. Feng and English, *Chuang-tsu,* pp. 123, 131.

47. Ibid., pp. 126, 40.

48. Tu Wei-ming, "The 'Thought of Huang-Lao': A Reflection on the Lao Tzu and Huang Ti Texts in the Silk Manuscripts of Ma-wang-tui," *Journal of Asian Studies* 39, no. 1 (1979): 95–110.

49. For a brief account of the life of Liu An, see *Encyclopedia of Religion,* vol. 9, ed. Mircea Eliade (New York: Macmillan, 1987), s.v. "Liu An."

50. Girardot, *Myth and Meaning in Early Taoism,* p. 42.

51. Michael Loewe, *Chinese Ideas of Life and Death* (London: Allen and Unwin, 1982), p. 107.

52. Here we draw upon an excellent historical survey by Daniel L. Overmyer, "Chinese Religion: An Overview," in *Encyclopedia of Religion,* vol. 3, ed. Mircea Eliade (New York: Macmillan, 1987), pp. 257b–289a.

53. Schipper, "Taoist Body," p. 375.

54. *New Encyclopaedia Britannica,* Macropaedia, vol. 28, s.v. Michel Strickmann, "Taoism, History of."

55. John Lagerway, "Taoism," in *Encyclopedia of Religion,* ed. Mircea Eliade (New York: Macmillan, 1987), p. 307.

56. Schipper, "Taoist Body," p. 375.

57. Mark Kaltenmark on the *T'ai P'ing Ching* in *Facets of Taoism,* ed. Holmes Welch and Anna Seidel (New Haven, Conn.: Yale University Press, 1979), p. 49.

58. Michel Strickmann, "On the Alchemy of T'ao Hung-ching," in *Facets of Taoism,* ed. Holmes Welch and Anna Seidel (New Haven, Conn.: Yale University Press, 1979), p. 169.

59. Liu I-Ch'ing, with commentary by Liu Chun, *Shih-shuo Hsin-yu (A New Account of Tales of the World),* trans. with introduction and notes by Richard B. Mather (Minneapolis: University of Minnesota Press, 1976).

60. Thompson, *Chinese Religion,* p. xviii.

61. Rolf A. Stein, "Religious Taoism and Popular Religion from the Second to Seventh Centuries," in *Facets of Taoism,* ed. Holmes Welch and Anna Seidel (New Haven, Conn.: Yale University Press, 1979), pp. 53–81.

62. Fairbank et al., *East Asia,* pp. 116 ff.

63. Lagerway, "Taoism," p. 314.

64. Overmyer, "Chinese Religion," p. 286.

65. William Theodore DeBary, *Sources of Chinese Tradition* (New York: Columbia University Press, 1960), pp. 875–876.

66. Robert J. Lifton, *Revolutionary Immortality: Mao Tse-tung and the Chinese Cultural Revolution* (New York: Random House, 1968), p. 73.

67. Donald E. MacInnis, *Religion in China Today: Policy and Practice* (Maryknoll, N.Y.: Orbis Books, 1989).

68. Kenneth Dean, "Revival of Religion Practices in Fujian: A Case Study" in Julian Pas, ed., *The Turning of the Tide: Religion in China Today*

(London and New York: Oxford Unversity Press, 1990), pp. 51–77.

69. Ibid., p. 55.

70. Julian Pas, ed., *The Turning of the Tide: Religion in China Today* (London and New York: Oxford University Press, 1979), p. 161.

71. MacInnis, *Religion in China Today,* p. 8.

72. Ibid., p. 213.

73. Al Chung-liang Huang, *Embrace Tiger, Return to Mountain* (Moab, Utah: Real People Press, 1973), pp. 12, 185.

74. Cheng Man-ch'ing and Robert W. Smith, *T'ai-chi* (Rutland, Vt.: Charles E. Tuttle, 1967) p. 109.

CHAPTER 7

1. Wing-Tsit Chan, *A Source Book in Chinese Philosophy* (Princeton, N.J.: Princeton University Press, 1963), p. 40.

2. *New Encyclopaedia Britannica,* vol. 16, p. 654.

3. Laurence G. Thompson, "Confucianism as a Way of Ultimate Transformation" (unpublished manuscript, University of Southern California), p. 4.

4. Richard Guisso, "Thunder over the Lake: The Five Classics and the Perception of Women in Early China," in *Women in China*, ed. Richard Guisso et al. (New York: Philo, 1981), p. 59.

5. For an excellent discussion of the Confucian concept of Heaven in its historical context, see *Encyclopedia of Religion*, vol. 4, ed. Mircea Eliade (New York: Macmillan, 1987), p. 17.

6. Ku Hung Ming, *The Conduct of Life: A Translation of the Doctrine of the Mean*, Wisdom of the East series (London: John Murray, 1906), p. 53.

7. Chan, *Source Book in Chinese Philosophy*, p. 98.

8. Ibid., pp. 289 ff.

9. *Encyclopedia of Religion*, vol. 4, p. 27.

10. E.R. Hughes, *Chinese Philosophy in Classical Times* (London: J. M. Dent & Sons, 1941), pp. 100–104.

11. Chan, *Source Book in Chinese Philosophy*, p. 131.

12. Herbert Fingarette, *Confucius: The Secular As Sacred* (New York: Harper & Row, 1972).

13. "Splay-footed" refers to feet that are abnormally flat and turned outward; hence, they are awkward and unsuitable. This proverb and the practice of foot binding for women indicate how the condition of one's feet symbolically represented the Confucian system of roles.

14. However, as we have pointed out, traditional Chinese culture dictates that a woman comes under the authority of her husband's family when she marries. Her new obligations mitigate her ability to attend to her own parents.

15. Takeo Doi, *The Anatomy of Dependence* (New York: Kodansha International, 1973).

16. Lin Yutang, *The Importance of Living* (1931; reprint, Cutchogue, N.Y.: Buccaneer Books, 1991), p. 200.

17. Statement from the *Ta-tai Li Chi* [Book of rites of the elder tai], quoted in Fung Yu-lan, *History of Chinese Philosophy* (Princeton, N.J.: Princeton University Press, 1952), p. 345.

18. C. K. Yang, *Religion in Chinese Society* (Los Angeles: University of California Press, 1961), p. 53.

19. Statements by Hsun-tzu quoted in ibid., p. 48.

20. Ibid., p. 50

21. Ibid., p. 52

22. Laurence G. Thompson, *Chinese Religion: An Introduction*, 4th ed. (Belmont, Calif.: Wadsworth, 1989), p. 51.

23. Laurence G. Thompson, *The Chinese Way in Religion* (Belmont, Calif.: Wadsworth, 1973), p. 152.

24. Ibid., p. 146.

25. Wang Yang-ming, *Instructions for Practical Living*, as cited in Thompson, "Confucianism as a Way of Ultimate Transformation."

26. A. C. Graham, *Disputers of the Tao: Philosophical Arguments in Ancient China* (Lasalle, Ill.: Open Court, 1989), p. 293.

27. *Spring and Autumn Annals*, as cited in ibid., p. 298.

28. *Book of Rites*, as cited in ibid., p. 298.

29. *Encyclopedia of Religion*, vol. 4, p. 19.

30. Ibid., p. 19.

31. Graham, *Disputers of the Tao*, p. 4.

32. As we will discover in Chapter 8, these themes— love of learning and the reanimation of ancient tradition—are strongly emphasized in Judaism. Other striking similarities, such as the emphasis on ethics and the stability of the family, will also become evident.

33. Graham, *Disputers of the Tao*, p. 359.

34. Thompson, *Chinese Way in Religion*, p. 7.

35. Ibid., p. 11.

36. James Legge, ed. and trans., *The Sacred Books of China*, pt. 2, *The Liki* (Oxford: Clarendon Press, 1895), pp. 449–451.

37. Thompson, *Chinese Way in Religion*, p. 16.

38. *New Encyclopaedia Britannica*, Macropaedia, vol. 16, p. 658.

39. Some scholars believe that Li Ao drew these notions from Confucian sources, not from Buddhist ones. For example, the *Book of Mencius* 2A:2 seems to advocate the experience of having no thought. In any case, no one denies that Li Ao was influenced by Buddhism, at least in terms of his interests and emphases. See Chan, *Source Book in Chinese Philosophy*, for a detailed account of these matters.

40. Thompson, *Chinese Religion*, p. 107.

41. Attributed to Ch'eng I by Chu Hsi in his *Chinssu Lu* (Reflections on things at hand) 1:32, in Chan, *Source Book in Chinese Philosophy*.

42. Gung-hsing Wang, *The Chinese Mind* (New York: John Day, 1946), p. 139.

43. Masahara Anesaki, *History of Japanese Religion* (Rutland, Vt.: Charles E. Tuttle, 1963), p. 8.

44. Gilbert Rozman, ed., *The East Asian Region: Confucian Heritage and Its Modern Adaptation* (Princeton, N.J.: Princeton University Press, 1991), p. 199. On the general question of the continuing influence of Confucianism in Japan today, the noted scholar Edwin Reischauer has written, "Almost no one considers himself a Confucianist today, but in a sense all Japanese are." *The Japanese* (Cambridge, Mass.: Harvard University Press, 1977), p. 214.

45. Statements made by the scholar Feng Gui-fen, quoted in Ssu-yu Teng et al., *China's Response to the West* (Cambridge, Mass.: Harvard University Press, 1954), pp. 52, 53.

46. Thomas A. Metzger, *Escape from Predicament* (New York: Columbia University Press, 1977), pp. 17, 214–215.

47. Ibid., pp. 192–197.

48. Yu-lan Fung, *The New Rational Philosophy (Hsin li-hsueh)*, 1939.

49. Reported in the *Shanghai Ta Kung Pao*, August 28, 1948.

50. Reported in *Asia*, October 1949.

51. Richard Bush, *Religion in Communist China* (Nashville, Tenn.: Abington, 1970), p. 377.

52. Tu Wei Ming, "The Religious Situation in the People's Republic of China Today: A Personal Reflection," in *Religion in Today's World*, ed. Frank Whaling (Edinburgh: T & T Clark, 1987), p. 279.

53. Paula Swart and Barry Till, "A Revival of Confucian Ceremonies in China," in *The Turning of the Tide: Religion in China Today*, ed. Julian Pas (London and New York: Oxford University Press, 1990), pp. 210 ff.

54. Yang, *Religion in Chinese Society*, p. 357.

55. Metzger, *Escape from Predicament*, p. 197.

CHAPTER 8

1. Russell Chandler, "Traditional Jews on Attack to Shelter Flock from Messianics' Influence," *Los Angeles Times*, October 19, 1985, pt. 2, p. 4.

2. *Exodus Rabbah* 2:5.

3. Martin Buber, *The Way of Man* (New York: Citadel, 1970), pp. 40–41.

4. *Zohar: The Book of Enlightenment*, trans. Daniel C. Matt (New York: Paulist Press, 1983), pp. 65–66.

5. Jacob Neusner, *The Way of Torah: An Introduction to Judaism*, 3d ed. (Belmont, Calif.: Wadsworth, 1979), p. 30.

6. Robert M. Seltzer, *Jewish People, Jewish Thought: The Jewish Experience in History* (New York: Macmillan, 1980), p. 279.

7. Herbert Weiner, *9½ Mystics: The Kabbala Today* (New York: Holt, Rinehart & Winston, 1969).

8. Seltzer, *Jewish People*, p. 285.

9. Buber, *Way of Man*, p. 32.

10. Seltzer, *Jewish People*, p. 295.

11. Ibid., p. 751.

12. Jacob Neusner, *Invitation to Talmud: A Teaching Book* (New York: Harper & Row, 1973), p. 1.

13. Seltzer, *Jewish People*, p. 284.

14. Liz Harris, "Holy Days," *New Yorker*, September 23, 1985, p. 89.

15. See Richard E. Friedman, *Who Wrote the Bible?* (Englewood Cliffs, N.J.: Prentice-Hall, 1987).

16. *Philo of Alexandria*, trans. David Winston (New York: Paulist Press, 1981), p. 276.

17. *Mishnah Tractate Sanhedrin* 4:9.

18. Seltzer, *Jewish People*, p. 286.

19. *Sifre Deuteronomy* 45.

20. *Jerusalem Talmud Kiddushin* 4:12.

21. *Avot* 4:16.

22. See Cecil Roth and Geoffrey Wigoder, eds., *The New Standard Jewish Encyclopedia* (New York: Doubleday, 1970), pp. 958, 1619.

23. *Genesis Rabbah* 92:1.

24. *Babylonian Talmud Tractate Shabbat* 55a.

25. Elie Wiesel, *Night* (New York: Bantam, 1982), p. 73.

26. Emil Fackenheim, *God's Presence in History* (New York: Harper & Row, 1970), p. 31.

27. Richard Rubenstein, *The Cunning of History: The Holocaust and the American Future* (New York: Harper & Row, 1978), p. 7.

28. Wiesel, *Night*, pp. 61–62.

29. Seltzer, *Jewish People*, pp. 295–297.

30. Neusner, *Way of Torah*, p. 51.

31. For a list of the 613 *mitzvot*, see *The Encyclopaedia Judaica*, vol. 5 (Jerusalem: Keter Publishing House, 1972).

32. Joel Gereboff, "Jewish Bioethics: Redefining the Field," *Religious Studies Review* 8, no. 4 (1982): 316–324.

33. Jacob Minkin, *The World of Moses Maimonides* (New York: Thomas Yoseloff, 1957), p. 258.

34. Judith Hauptman, "Images of Women in the Talmud," in *Religion and Sexism*, ed. Rosemary Reuther (New York: Simon & Schuster, 1974), pp. 184–212.

35. Judith Plaskow, *Standing Again at Sinai: Judaism from a Feminist Perspective* (San Francisco: HarperCollins, 1991), pp. 180–181.

36. *Philo of Alexandria*, p. 280.

37. In the Reform prayer book *Likrat Shabbat*, comp. and trans. Rabbi Sidney Greenberg (Bridgeport, Conn.: Prayer Book Press, 1975), p. 85.

38. Abraham Heschel, *The Sabbath* (New York: Farrar, Strauss & Young, 1951), p. 74.

39. Rabbi Hillel Cohn, remarks at a community Seder at Congregation Emanu El, San Bernardino, California, April 14, 1987.

40. Abraham Millgram, *Jewish Worship* (Philadelphia: Jewish Publishing Society of America, 1971), pp. 307–309.

41. Ibid.

42. Plaskow, *Standing Again at Sinai*, p. 30.

43. For the convergence of Israelite and Canaanite theologies, see Mark S. Smith, *The Early History of God* (San Francisco: HarperCollins, 1990).

44. Fackenheim, *God's Presence in History*, pp. 14–16.

45. For the view that the Israelites were Canaanite peasants, see Norman K. Gottwald, *The Tribes of Yahweh* (Maryknoll, N.Y.: Orbis Books, 1979).

46. *Philo of Alexandria*, pp. 124–125.

47. Chaim Potok, *Wanderings: History of the Jews* (New York: Fawcett Crest, 1978), p. 263.

48. Tacitus, *The Histories*, trans. A. J. Church and W. J. Brodribb (Chicago: Encyclopaedia Britannica, 1954), pp. 295–296.

49. See John Gager, *The Origins of Anti-Semitism: Attitudes toward Judaism in Pagan and Christian Antiquity* (New York: Oxford University Press, 1983).

50. *The Works of Josephus*, trans. William Whiston (London: Routledge & Sons), p. 546.

51. *Babylonian Talmud Tractate Shabbat* 31a.

52. *Pirke Avot* 1:14.

53. *Works of Josephus*, pp. 901–993.

54. Abba Eban, *Heritage: Civilization and the Jews* (New York: Summit Books, 1984), p. 100.

55. Potok, *Wanderings*, p. 296.

56. Salo W. Baron and Joseph L. Blau, *Judaism: Postbiblical and Talmudic Period* (Indianapolis: Bobbs-Merrill, 1954), p. 124.

57. *Pirke Avot* 1:12.

58. Simon Noveck, *Great Jewish Personalities in Ancient and Medieval Times* (New York: Farrar, Straus, & Cudahy, 1959), p. 138.

59. *Babylonian Talmud Tractate Megillah* 10b.

60. Potok, *Wanderings*, p. 295.

61. Neusner, *Way of Torah*, pp. 14–15.

62. *The Talmud: Selecting Writings*, trans. Ben Zion Bokser (New York: Paulist Press, 1989), p. 100.

63. Potok, *Wanderings*, p. 275.

64. Seltzer, *Jewish People*, pp. 377–381.

65. Noveck, *Great Jewish Personalities*, p. 194.

66. Minkin, *World of Moses Maimonides*, p. 160.

67. Ibid., p. 286.

68. Seltzer, *Jewish People*, p. 430.

69. *Zohar*, p. 430.

70. Seltzer, *Jewish People*, p. 549.

71. Jacob Neusner, *Death and Rebirth of Judaism: The Impact of Christianity, Secularism, and the Holocaust on Jewish Faith* (New York: Basic Books, 1987), p. 9.

72. Eban, *Heritage*, p. 268.

73. Neusner, *Death and Rebirth of Judaism*, p. 9.

74. From "The Jewish Question," in T. Z. Lavine, *From Socrates to Sartre* (New York: Bantam, 1984), pp. 276–277.

75. Nathan Glazer, *American Judaism* (Chicago: University of Chicago Press, 1972), p. 42.

76. Neusner, *Death and Rebirth of Judaism*, p. 116.

77. Ibid., p. 138.

78. Gager, *Origins of Anti-Semitism*, p. 22.

79. Mortimer Chambers et al., *The Western Experience since 1600*, 4th ed. (New York: Knopf, 1987), pp. 938–940.

80. Eban, *Heritage*, pp. 296–297.

81. Ibid., p. 254.

82. Neusner, *Death and Rebirth of Judaism*, p. 271.

83. Seltzer, *Jewish People,* pp. 703–705.

84. David Hardan, ed., *Sources of Contemporary Jewish Thought* (Jerusalem: World Zionist Organization, 1970), pp. 53–54.

85. Chambers, *Western Experience*, p. 1059.

86. Seltzer, *Jewish People,* p. 668.

87. Lucy S. Dawidowicz, "Thinking about the Six Million: Facts, Figures, Perspectives," in *Holocaust: Religious and Philosophical Implications,* eds. John Roth and Michael Berenbaum (New York: Paragon House, 1989).

88. Richard L. Rubenstein, *Cunning of History*, p. 41.

89. Harold M. Schulweis, "Remembering the Rescuers: The Post-Holocaust Agenda," *Christian Century,* December 7, 1988, pp. 1126–1128.

90. Daniel Williams, "Controversy over Land for Palestinians Becomes Religion Issue," *Los Angeles Times*, November 11, 1989, p. B6.

91. See the concluding chapter of Fackenheim, *God's Presence in History*.

92. Plaskow, *Standing Again at Sinai*, p. 136.

93. Ibid., p. 5.

CHAPTER 9

1. Günther Bornkamm notes that the assertion that Jesus was Aryan, hence not Jewish, was stated for the first time by H. St. Chamberlain in *Foundations of the Nineteenth Century, v*ol. 1, in 1910. This theory was accepted in Germany by the Third Reich and elsewhere. It is not necessary to refute the point. The Jewishness of Jesus is self-evident to all but the anti-Semite. See Bornkamm, *Jesus of Nazareth* (New York: Harper & Row, 1959), p. 199, n. 2. Also see John Rousseau and Rami Arav, *Jesus and His World* (Minneapolis: Fortress, 1995).

2. See Charles Curran, *A New Look at Christian Morality* (Notre Dame, Ind.: Fides Press, 1970), pp. 1–25. See also Gerard Sloyan, *The Crucifixion of Jesus* (Minneapolis: Fortress, 1995).

3. See Thomas Bokenkotter, *A Concise History of the Catholic Church* (Garden City, N.Y.: Image, 1966), pp. 22–23.

4. See Paul Tillich, *The Courage to Be* (New York: Scribner, 1952).

5. The seminal works on process thought are A. N. Whitehead, *Religion in the Making* (Cambridge, England: Cambridge University Press, 1926), and his Gifford Lectures of 1929 entitled *Process and Reality.* For other titles, see C. Hartshorne, *Man's Vision of God and the Logic of Theism* (New York: Sheed & Ward, 1941); John Cobb, *A Christian Natural Theology* (New York: Augsburg, 1966); and S. M. Ogden, *The Reality of God and Other Essays* (New York: SCM Press, 1967).

6. See Jurgen Moltmann, *Theology of Hope* (New York: Harper & Row, 1967). See also Thomas V. Morris, ed., *God and the Philosophers* (New York: Oxford University Press, 1994).

7. See Piet Fransen, *The Life of Grace* (New York: Crossroads, 1975).

8. The reader is directed to Stephen Davis, ed., *Encountering Evil* (Atlanta: John Knox Press, 1981); and Paul Woodreuff et al., eds. *Facing Evil* (LaSalle, Ill.: Open Court, 1988). See also Elaine Pagels, *The Origin of Satan* (New York: Random House, 1995).

9. See Diederich Bonhoeffer, *The Cost of Discipleship* (New York: Macmillan, 1951).

10. Timothy O'Connell, *Principles for a Catholic Morality* (New York: Seabury, 1978).

11. The definitive work on the secular and Jewish sources is C. K. Barrett, *The New Testament Background: Selected Documents* (New York: Harper & Row, 1956).

12. See the *Testimonium Flavianum* in Stephen Davies, *The First Three Centuries* (Garden City, N.Y.: Doubleday, 1970).

13. See R. Travers Herford, *Christianity in Talmud and Midrash* (London, 1903); C. G. Montefore and H. Lowe, eds., *A Rabbinic Anthology* (London, 1938); and Louis I. Newman, ed., *The Talmudic Anthology* (New York: Behrman House, 1945), pp. 72–74.

14. See Robert Graves, ed., *Suetonius' Lives of the Caesars* (London: Penguin Classics, 1957).

15. See J. Stevens, ed., *The New Eusebius: Documents Illustrative of the History of the Church to A.D. 337* (London: Society for the Promotion of Christian Knowledge, 1957).

16. Julius Wellhausen, *The Composition of the Hexateuchs and the Historical Books of the Old Testament* (Berlin: 1885); see also his commentaries on the *Gospels* (none are available in translation); Albert Schweitzer, *The Quest for the Historical Jesus* (London: A. & C. Black, 1952); Rudolf Bultmann, *Jesus and the Word* (New York: Scribner, 1934); C. H. Dodd, *The Interpretation of the Fourth Gospel* (Cambridge, England: Cambridge University Press, 1953); Oscar Cullman, "Out of Season Remarks on the 'Historical Jesus' of the Bultmann School," *Union Seminary Quarterly Review* 16 (January 1961): 131–148; Joachim Jeremias, *The Problem of the Historical Jesus,* vol. 13, Facet Books, Biblical Series (Philadelphia: Fortress, 1964); Raymond E. Brown, *The Gospel According to John,* in *The Anchor Bible* (Garden City, N.Y.: Doubleday, 1966); Norman Perrin, *Rediscovering the Teaching of Jesus* (New York: Harper & Row, 1967); and Bornkamm, *Jesus of Nazareth,* pp. 14–15.

17. T. W. Manson, *The Teaching of Jesus,* 2d ed, (Cambridge, England: Cambridge University Press, 1935).

18. Birger Gerhardsson, *Memory and Manuscript: Oral Tradition and Written Transmission in Rabbinic Judaism and Early Christianity* (Copenhagen: Ejnar Munksgaard, 1961).

19. See, Rudolf Bultman, "The Primitive Christian Kerygma and the Historical Jesus," in *The Historical and the Kerygmatic Christ,* ed. Carl E. Braaten and Roy A. Harrisville (New York: Abingdon, 1964). See also John Dominic Crossan, *Jesus: A Revolutionary Biography* (San Francisco: Harper, 1994).

20. John L. McKenzie, *Dictionary of the Bible* (Chicago: Bruce, 1965), pp. 846–847.

21. See Massey Shepherd, "The Rise of Christianity," in *A Short History of Christianity,* ed. Archibald Baker (Chicago: University of Chicago Press, 1940), pp. 10–11.

22. See Werner Jaeger, *Early Christianity and Greek Paideia* (Cambridge, Mass.: Harvard University Press, 1965); John H. Randall, *Hellenistic Ways of Deliverance and the Making of the Christian Synthesis* (New York: Columbia University Press, 1970); and James Shiel, *Greek Thought and the Rise of Christianity* (New York: Barnes & Noble, 1968).

23. Stephen Reynolds, *The Christian Religious Tradition* (Encino, Calif.: Dickenson, 1977), pp. 20–21.

24. See Samuel Sandmel, *We Jews and Jesus* (New York: Oxford University Press, 1965), pp. 6–8. See also Peter Richardson, ed., *Anti-Judaism in Early Christianity* (Waterloo, Ont.: Wilfred Laurer, 1986); and John Dominic Crossan, *Who Killed Jesus?* (San Francisco: Harper, 1995).

25. Adolph von Harnack, *The Mission and Expansion of Christianity in the First Three Centuries* (New York: Harper, 1961), pp. 147–198.

26. Roman Catholics reckon fourteen other councils as possessing ecumenical character and authority. These took place after the schism between East and West in 1054.

27. Readers are referred to For Further Study for histories of this period. No condensation can do justice to the richness and complexity of the data.

28. See Edwin Hatch, *The Organization of the Early Christian Churches* (New York: B. Franklin, 1972).

29. See Andras Alfordi, *The Conversion of Constantine and Pagan Rome* (Oxford, England: Clarendon Press, 1948); Norman Baynes, *Constantine the Great and the Christian Church* (London: Oxford University Press, 1972); and Robert M. Grant, *Augustus to Constantine* (New York: Scribner, 1970).

30. See Jean Danielou and Henri Marrou, *The Christian Centuries,* vol. 1 (New York: Paulist Press, 1964), pp. 269–279.

31. See Michael A. Smith, "Christian Ascetics and Monks," in *Eerdman's Handbook of Christianity,* ed. Tom Dowly (Grand Rapids, Mich.: Eerdmans, 1977), pp. 204–216.

32. See Danielou and Marrou, *Christian Centuries,* pp. 268–277.

33. R. W. Southern, *Western Society and the Church in the Middle Ages* (London: Penguin, 1970), pp. 218–223.

34. As quoted in Ibid., p. 225.

35. For an excellent, comprehensive, and readable survey of the Crusades, see John McManners, ed., *The Oxford Illustrated History of Christianity* (New York: Oxford University Press, 1990), pp. 163–232.

36. See Erik Erikson, *Young Man Luther* (New York: Norton, 1958).

37. For classical treatments of the Reformation, see Charles Beard, *Martin Luther and the Reformation in Germany* (London: Philip Green, 1896); B. J. Kidd, ed., *Documents Illustrative of the Continental Reformation* (1911); Preserved Smith, *The Life and Letters of Martn Luther* (New York: Houghton Mifflin, 1911); and R. H. Bainton, *The Reformation of the Sixteenth Century* (Kansas, 1952).

38. R. H. Bainton, *Here I Stand* (New York: Abington, 1930).

39. See Carter Lindberg, "The Late Middle Ages and the Reformations of the 16th Century," in *Christianity: A Social and Cultural History,* ed. Howard Kee (New York: Macmillan, 1991), pp. 257–425.

40. See James H. Nichols, *The History of Chrtstianity, 1650 to 1950* (New York: Ronald Knox Press, 1956).

41. Jean-Loup Seban, "European Christianity Confronts the Modern Age," in *Christianity: A Social and Cultural History,* ed. Howard Kee (New York: Macmillan, 1991), pp. 425–601.

42. See Walter M. Abbott, ed., *The Documents of Vatican II* (Baltimore: America Press, 1966). For a compendium on Catholic social teaching since the council, see Joseph Gremillion, ed., *The Gospel of Peace and Justice* (Maryknoll, N.Y.: Orbis Books, 1976).

43. See Leonardo and Clovis Boff, *Introducing Liberation Theology* (Maryknoll, N.Y.: Orbis Books, 1989); and Deane Ferm, *Profiles in Liberation: 36 Portraits of Third World Theologians* (Mystic, Conn.: Twenty-third Publication, 1988).

CHAPTER 10

1. Estimates regarding the number of Muslims in the world vary from 600 million to well over 1 billion. The figure of 900 million to 950 million is a rough but fair approximation.

2. Bruce Lawrence, *Defenders of God: The Fundamentalist Revolt against the Modern Age* (New York: Harper & Row, 1989), p. 16.

3. Walter Truett Anderson, *Reality Isn't What It Used To Be* (San Francisco: Harper San Francisco, 1990), p. 243. Anderson calls Islam one of the six "meta-stories" used to organize experience in a postmodern world.

4. Ninian Smart, *Worldviews: Crosscultural Explorations of Human Beliefs* (New York: Scribner, 1983).

5. William Hall, Richard Pilgrim, and Ronald Cavanagh, *Religion: An Introduction* (New York: Harper & Row, 1985), pp. 98–99.

6. Because of this gap in time, some secular authors challenge the historicity of the details of the biographies.

7. Fazlur Rahman, *Islam* (New York: Doubleday, 1968), p. 1.

8. *Quran* 96:1–5, in A. J. Arberry, trans., *The Koran Interpreted,* vol. 2 (New York: Macmillan, 1955) , p. 344.

9. Caesar E. Farhah, *Islam,* 4th ed. (New York: Barron's Educational Series, 1987), p. 102.

10. *Quran* 112, in Arberry, *Koran Interpreted,* vol. 2, p. 353.

11. *Quran* 7:54, in Arberry, *Koran Interpreted,* vol. 1, pp. 177–178.

12. *Quran* 53:32–33, in Arberry, *Koran Interpreted,* vol. 2, p. 245.

13. Quoted in Farhah, *Islam,* p. 108.

14. This notion parallels the first chapter of the *Tao Te Ching* in Chinese Taoism, where it is asserted that the Tao that can be named is not the true Tao.

15. *Quran* 27:60, in Arberry, *Koran Interpreted,* vol. 2, p. 82.

16. *Quran* 54:49, in Arberry, *Koran Interpreted,* vol. 2, pp. 249–250.

17. *Quran* 87:2–3, in Arberry, *Koran Interpreted,* vol. 2, p. 335.

18. *Quran* 9:51, in Arberry, *Koran Interpreted,* vol. 1, p. 213.

19. Farhah, *Islam,* p. 123

20. *Quran* 56:1–56, in Arberry, *Koran Interpreted,* vol. 2, pp. 254–255.

21. Peter Berger, *The Sacred Canopy* (New York: Doubleday, 1967).

22. Yvonne Y. Haddad, "Islam: 'The Religion of God,'" *Christianity and Crisis,* November 15, 1982, p. 355.

23. *Quran* 9:60, vol. 1, p. 214.

24. *Quran* 2:193–194, vol. 1, pp. 54–55.

25. *Quran* 36:75 ff, in Arberry, *Koran Interpreted,* vol. 2, pp. 148 ff.

26. Frederick M. Denny, *Islam* (New York: HarperCollins, 1987), p. 90.

27. Ibid., p. 90.

28. Annemarie Schimmel, *Islam: An Introduction* (Albany: State University of New York Press, 1992), pp. 122–123.

29. Denny, *Islam,* p. 93.

30. Ibid., pp. 96–97.

31. Ibid., p. 97.

32. Farhah, *Islam,* pp. 125 ff.

33. *Quran,* 22:40–42 in Arberry, *Koran Interpreted,* vol. 2, p. 32.

34. *Quran,* 2:186, vol. 1., p. 53; 2:190, vol. 1, p. 54.

35. The categories of "sharp eye" and "articulate language" come from Michel Foucault, *The Order of Things: An Archaeology of the Human Sciences* (New York: Vintage, 1970) pp. xv–xix.

36. Arno Peters, *The New Cartography* (New York: Friendship Press, 1983). This text on maps and their influence on perspective is a revealing look at European views of the rest of the world. Using nineteenth-century European projections, Arabia looks small compared with Scandinavia or Greenland, for example. However, Arabia's 3.5 million square kilometers is much larger than Scandinavia's 1.1 million square kilometers and Greenland's 2.1 million square kilometers. Although Peters's projection may look strange at first, this new view of the world does justice to the actual size of the "Arabian island."

37. Alfred Guillaume, *Islam* (New York: Penguin, 1954); and Farhah, *Islam.* Both of these texts provide a wealth of information on the cultural context of Arabia prior to Muhammad.

38. John L. Esposito, *Islam: The Straight Path* (New York: Oxford University Press, 1998), p. 36.

39. In Philip K. Hitti, *History of the Arabs* (New York: Macmillan, 1937), p. 153.

40. Farhah, *Islam,* pp. 195–201.

41. Richard J. McCarthy, ed., *The Theology of Al-Ashari* (Beirut, 1953), esp. pp. 33–37, 63–67.

42. The capitalized form of *One* often is used to describe the ineffable, mysterious unity in mystical forms of religious expression.

43. Annmarie Schimmel, "Islamic Mysticism," in *Encyclopaedia Britannica,* 15th ed. (Chicago: Encyclopaedia Britannica, 1973–1974), vol., 9, p. 946.

44. W. Montgomery Watt, trans., *The Faith and Practice of al-Ghazali* (London: Allen & Unwin, 1953), pp. 54–59.

45. The term *Ottoman* probably comes from Osman (d. 1326), who founded the dynasty.

46. Schimmel, *Islam,* pp. 19–29.

47. Akbar Ahmed, *Postmodernism and Islam: Predicament and Promise* (New York: Routledge, 1992); and Michael W. Fisher and Mehdi Abedi, *Debating Muslims: Cultural Dialogues in Postmodernity and Tradition* (Madison: University of Wisconsin Press, 1990) are two relatively recent works that address this notion of the postmodern.

48. Fatima Mernissi, *The Veil and the Male Elite: A Feminist Interpretation of Women's Rights in Islam,* trans. Mary Jo Lakeland (New York: Addison-Wesley, 1991), p. ix.

49. Ibid., pp. 8–9.

50. Youssef M. Choueiri, *Islamic Fundamentalism* (Boston: Twayne, 1990), p. 9.

51. Denny, *Islam*, p. 118.

52. For an analysis of this phenomenon in the context of several expressions of fundamentalism, see Lawrence, *Defenders of God.*

53. Clifford Geertz, *Islam Observed: Religious Developments in Morocco and Indonesia* (New Haven, Conn.: Yale University Press, 1968).

EPILOGUE

1. Harold Bloom, *Omens of Millennium: The Gnosis of Angels, Dreams, and Resurrection* (New York: Riverhead, 1996), p. 2.

2. *American Encyclopedia of Religion,* cited in Damian Thompson, *The End of Time: Faith and Fear in the Shadow of the Millennium* (Hanover, N.H.: University of New England Press, 1996), p. xii.

3. Thompson, *End of Time,* p. 30.

4. Michael Barkun, "Millenarians and Violence: The Case of the Christian Identity Movement," in *Millennium, Messiahs, and Mayhem: Contemporary Apocalyptic Movements,* ed. Thomas Robbins and Susan J. Palmer (New York: Routledge, 1997), pp. 247–248.

5. Barkun, "Millenarians and Violence," pp. 249–251.

6. Mark R. Mullins, "Aum Shinrikyo as an Apocalyptic Movement," in *Millennium, Messiahs, and Mayhem: Contemporary Apocalyptic Movements,* ed. Thomas Robbins and Susan J. Palmer (New York: Routledge, 1997) p. 316.

7. Mullins, "Aum Shinrikyo," p. 320.

8. Thompson, *End of Time,* p. 296.

9. Ibid., p. 219.

10. Robert S. Ellwood and Harry B. Partin, *Religious and Spiritual Groups in Modern America* (Englewood Cliffs, N.J.: Prentice-Hall, 1988), pp. 30–73. Chapter 2 of this text describes, in detail, this undercurrent of religious sensibilities.

11. Ibid., pp. 31–32.

12. Many of the group's ideas were presented on its Web site. Although this site was taken off the World Wide Web, mirror sites have preserved the material. The quotations included here can be found at the following URL: http://www.washingtonpost.com/wp-srv/national/longterm/documents/heavensgate/data/5-3etret.htm

13. Barkun, "Millenarians and Violence," p. 257.

14. William W. Zellner, *Counter Cultures: A Sociological Analysis* (New York: St. Martin, 1995), p. 53.

15. Robert J. Lifton, *The Future of Immortality* (New York: Basic Books, 1987), p. 148.

16. Robert J. Lifton, "The Image of 'The End of the World': A Psychohistorical View," in *Facing Apocalypse,* ed. Valerie Andrews, Robert Bosnak, and Karen Walter Goodwin (Dallas: Spring Publications, 1987), p. 27.

17. Ibid., p. 30.

18. Ibid., p. 41.

19. Ibid., p. 42.

20. David L. Miller, "Chiliasm: Apocalyptic with a Thousand Faces," in *Facing Apocalypse,* ed. Valerie Andrews, Robert Bosnak, and Karen Walter Goodwin (Dallas: Spring Publications, 1987), p. 18.

21. Ibid., p. 18.

22. Ibid.

23. Ibid., p. 19.

24. Ibid., p. 20.

25. Ibid., p. 21.

APPENDIX A

1. Ainslie T. Embree, ed., *Sources of Indian Tradition,* vol. 1, *From the Beginning to 1800,* 2d ed. (New York: Columbia University Press, 1988), pp. 60–61.

2. This description is an excerpt from the travel diary of Christopher Chapple (Loyola Marymount University in Los Angeles). On this particular day in December 1989, he was visiting the residence for Jain nuns in Ladnun in the Indian state of Rajasthan. Permission granted.

3. From *Japji* (the Sikh morning prayer), trans. Khushwant Singh and others, in *Universal Wisdom: A Journey through the Sacred Wisdom of the World,* comp. Bede Griffiths (London: Fount-HarperCollins, 1994), p. 292.

APPENDIX B

1. Ian Reader, *Religion in Contemporary Japan* (Honolulu: University of Hawaii Press, 1991), p. 9.

2. There are exceptions to this nonexclusivism; for example, Nichiren Buddhists and Christians often insist that their paths require undivided loyalty.

3. Ryusaku Tsunoda, William Theodore de Bary, and Donold Keene, eds., *Sources of Japanese Tradition,* vol. 2 (New York: Columbia University Press, 1964), p. 80.

4. Ichiro Hori et al., eds., *Japanese Religion: A Survey by the Agency for Cultural Affairs,* trans. Yoshiya Abe and David Reid (Tokyo: Kodansha, 1972), pp. 37–38.

5. Keiji Nishitani, *On Modernization and Tradition in Japan,* trans. Gene Sager (Nishinomiya, Japan: International Institute for Japan Studies, 1969); Yukitake Yamamoto, *Way of Kami* (Stockton, Calif.: Tsubaki American Publications, 1987), pp. 73–75.

6. Floyd Hiatt Ross, *Shinto: The Way of Japan* (Boston: Beacon Press, 1965), p. 155.

7. *Basic Terms of Shinto,* comp. Shinto Committee of the IXth International Congress for the History of Religions (Tokyo: Jinja Honcho [Association of Shinto Shrines], Kokugakuin University, and Institute for Japanese Culture and Classics, 1958), pp. 37–38.

8. Reader, *Religion in Contemporary Japan,* p. 7.

9. Ibid., p. 54.

10. The origins of Hachiman devotion are unclear. Shinto regards this powerful *kami* as the spirit of the third-century emperor Ojin of Japan, but the historicity of Ojin is in dispute. Some scholars (e.g., H. Byron Earhart) speculate that the origins of Hachiman may be Chinese, Buddhist, or both.

11. The term *kamikaze* was employed many centuries before its modern application to Japanese pilots in World War II.

12. Ryusaku Tsunoda, William Theodore de Bary, and Donold Keene, eds., *Sources of Japanese Religion,* vol. 1 (New York: Columbia University Press, 1958), p. 265.

13. Shigeru Matsumoto, *Motoori Norinaga, 1730–1801* (Cambridge, Mass.: Harvard University Press, 1970), p. 164.

14. H. Byron Earhart, *Japanese Religion: Unity and Diversity,* 3d ed. (Belmont, Calif.: Wadsworth, 1982), p. 158.

15. Tsunetsugu Muraoka, "Separation of State and Religion in Shinto: Its Historical Significance," in *Studies in Shinto,* trans. Delmer M. Brown and James T. Araki (Tokyo: Ministry of Education, 1964), p. 242.

16. A few Japanese writers have claimed that conservative elements in Japan have been attempting to revive state Shinto. These writers charge that public funds were used for a "state Shinto form of ritual" in Nagoya. They have also objected to official visits by the emperor and prime minister to the Ise and Yasukuni Shrines. However, most Japanese scholars feel these events do not constitute a revival of state Shinto. See Shigeyoshi Murakami, *Japanese Religion in the Modern Century* (Tokyo: University of Tokyo Press, 1980).

17. Sokyo Ono, *The Kami Way* (Tokyo: International Institute for the Study of Religions, 1959), p. 82.

18. Theodore Ludwig, *The Sacred Paths,* 2d ed. (Upper Saddle River, N.J.: Prentice-Hall, 1996), p. 331.

19. Reader, *Religion in Contemporary Japan,* p. 236.

INDEX

A

Abbasid caliphate, 608, 609–11
Abu Bakr, 588, 603–4
Abu Hanifa, 608
Accommodationist movements, 160
Acculturation, 159
Adept, 346
Adler, Morris, 460
Advaita, 226
Africa, tribal peoples of, 155
Agape, 527
Age of Kali, 211, 212, 639
Agnosticism, 81
Agriculture, prehistoric, 68
Ahad Ha-Am, 485
Ahimsa, 231, 653, 654
Akiva ben Josef, Rabbi, 458, 460, 473, 475
Al-Ashari, 610, 611
Alchemy, 368
Al-Ghazali, 611
Al-Hallaj, 611
Ali, 597, 604, 606, 607
Allah, 586, 588–89
Almsgiving, 593–94
Al-Shafii, 608–9
Ambedkar, B. R., 651
Ambrose, Saint, 542
Americas, tribal peoples of, 155–56
Amish, Old Order, 21
Amitabha Buddha, 18
Analects, 401, 404,
Anatman, 286
Ancestral spirits, 64
Ancestor worship, 408–10
Ancient spirituality, 51–99
Ancient urban religions
 beliefs and practices in, 75–93
 chronology of, 74–75
 cosmos in, 76–78
 death and human destiny and, 86–89
 divinities in, 78–82
 human nature in, 84–89
  morality in, 89–90
  sacred persons in, 82–84
  sacred texts of, 73
Ancient urban societies, 67–74
 characteristics of, 68–72
 chronology of, 74–75
Animism, 95
Anitya, 286
Anthrocentricity, 522–23
Anthropomorphism, 64
Anti-Semitism, 475
 Christian, 535
 Holocaust and, 455–56, 486–87, 489
 medieval Christian, 477–79
 modern, 483–87
 racial, 485–86
Antony of Egypt, 541, 542
Apocalypse, 640
Apostles, 533
Apostolic Age, 533–35
Apostolic See, 536
Applewhite, Marshall, 643, 644
Aquinas, Saint Thomas, 12, 14, 477, 521, 523, 545
Arabia before Muhammad, 602–3
Arab nationalism, 615
Arati, 217
Arhat, 300, 301
Arjun Dev, 655
Arian controversy, 537–38
Aristophanes, 82
Aristotle, 6, 87, 477, 521
Arius, 537, 538
Artha, 231
Asahara, Shoko, 24, 642
Asceticism, 541
Ascetics, 541–42
Ashkenazim, 477
Ashrama, 211
Asia, tribal peoples of, 155
Assimilation, 159
Athanasius of Alexandria, 537, 542
Atheism, 81, 82

Atman, 212, 283
Atonement, Christian doctrine of, 16
Attitudes, totalization of, 646
Augustine of Hippo, Saint, 475–76, 521, 523, 524, 525, 540, 542
Aum Shinrikyo, 24, 639, 642
Avatars, 17
Averroes, 610
Avicenna, 610
Axis mundi, 70, 140

B

Baal Shem Tov, 480
Bachofen, Johann J., 96
Baha Allah, 24
Bahadur, Tegh, 612
Baha'i, 20, 24, 30
Bar Kochba, 473
Barkun, Michael, 645
Bar mitzvah, 463
Barstow, Anne Llewellyn, 26
Basilian communities, 542
Basil of Caesarea, 542
Bat mitzvah, 463
Bedward, Alexander, 640
Belief system, 6, 15
Belief, 15
Benedict of Nursia, 542–43
Benedict's Rule, 543
Berdache, 142
Berg, David, 24
Berger, Peter, 592, 595
Bernard of Clairvaux, 544
Bhagavad Gita, 230–31
Bhakti, 212, 654, 655
Bhaktivedanta Swami Prabhupada, A. C., 24
Bharati, Baba Premananda, 238
Bible, 14
Biblical scholars, 530–33
Black Elk, 134, 136, 140, 144
Black Muslim movement, 618
Blasphemy, 520
Blood sacrifice, 11, 16
Bloom, Harold, 639
Bodhidharma, 306
Bodhisattva, 294, 295, 301
Body souls, 141
Bonhoeffer, Dietrich, 527
Bornkamm, Gunther, 531
Borromeo, Charles, 551
Brahman, 12, 212
   nirguna, 18
   saguna, 18
Brahmanism, 222–26

opposition movements to, 227
Branch Davidians, 24, 639, 642–43
Brethren, Church of, 552
Bright, William, 24
Brown, Raymond E., 531
Buber, Martin, 449
Buddha (Siddhartha Gautama), 6, 82, 84, 280
   Amitabha, 18
   Maitreya, 18
   Shakyamuni, 279, 281–83, 284, 285, 287, 288
Buddha-dharma, 280
Buddhism, 279–319
   absence of sacrifice in, 16
   beliefs of, 281–90
   in China, 302–5
   chronology of, 310–11
   Confucianism and, 420, 421
   contemporary, 311–19
   dependent co-origination in, 286–87
   in Digital Age, 317–18
   in East Asia, 305–9
   esoteric, 297–98
   Four Noble Truths of, 282, 284–86
   future of, 318–19
   gender issues in, 315–17
   history of, 299–311
   in India, 302
   in Japan, 307–8
   karma and rebirth in, 287
   in Korea, 307
   Mahayana, 288–90, 294–95, 300–302
   Nichiren, 13
   nirvana in, 288
   no-self in, 286
   Pure Land, 12, 281, 298–99, 306–7
   practice of, 290–99
   schools of, 303
   in Southeast Asia, 309–11, 312–13
   in Sri Lanka, 308–9
   Theravada, 303, 309–10
   in Tibet, 308
   in Vietnam, 310–11
   in the West, 315
   Zen, 12, 295–97, 306
Buddhist canon, 299–300
Buddhist cultures, traditional, 312–15
Buddhist scripture, 301
Bultmann, Rudolf, 531, 533
Burkert, Walter, 78
Bushido, 664
Byakko Shinkokai, 667

C

Caitanya, 237
Calendrical rites, 16, 78
    Jewish, 460–63
Caliph, 588
    four "Rightly Guided," 603–8
Calvin, John, 523, 549–50
Canaan, conquest of, 466
Cao Dai, 24
Cassian, John, 523, 542
Caste, 210–11, 246–47
Catholic Christians, 523, 524, 552, 555–57
Catholicism, 549
Cavanagh, Ronald, 584, 591
Celestial Masters, 348, 364–67
Cenobitism, 541
Chai, 346
Ch'an, 295
Chang Chi-hsien, 371
Chang Chueh, 367
Chang Lu, 352, 366
Chang Tao-ling, 365, 366, 368, 371
Chanting in Pure Land Buddhism, 298–99
Chao-chou, 296
Chapple, Christopher, 651
Ch'eng Hao, 422, 423
Ch'eng I, 422, 423
Chen Hsun, 420
Chen-I sect, 371, 372
Chernus, Ira, 640
Chiao, 341, 346–48, 375, 376
Chihangdaoren, 376
Childe, Gordon, 68
Chiliasm, 647
China
    Buddhism in, 302–5, 313
    Ch'ing dynasty, 372–73
    Chou dynasty, 355–58
    classical, 358–63
    dynasties of, 354
    Han dynasty, 364, 415–20
    Ming dynasty, 372
    People's Republic of, 374–75, 376, 377, 426–27, 428
    period of disunion in, 420–21
    prehistoric, 354–58
    Republic, 373
    Shang dynasty, 354–55
    Sung dynasty, 371
    T'ang dynasty, 370–71
    Yuan dynasty, 372
Ch'ing dynasty, Taoism in, 372–73
Ch'ing ming, 410
Chou dynasty, folk religion in, 355–58
Choueri, Youssef M., 619

Chou Tun-i, 422, 423
Christ, God in, 8
Christian Identity movement, 641, 645
Christianity, 4, 5, 7, 8, 515–59
    in Apostolic Age, 533–35
    beliefs of, 516–26
    competing worldviews in, 557–59
    contemporary, 554–59
    cosmos in, 521–22
    early modern, 552–54
    evil in, 524–26
    free will in, 525
    God in, 520–21
    good works in, 529–30
    grace in, 523–24
    history of, 530–54
    human nature and destiny in, 522–24
    immortality in, 524
    Islam's influence on, 544–45
    major divisions of, 556
    in Middle Ages, 540–46
    moral life in, 526–28
    original sin in, 523
    practice of, 526–30
    prayer in, 529
    premedieval, 535–40
    Protestant Reformation and, 547–52
    in Renaissance, 546–47
    worship in, 528
Christians
    Catholic, 523, 524, 525, 552
    Fundamentalist, 14, 521, 522, 533, 555
    Protestant, 523, 525, 552
Christian scripture, 532
Ch'uan-chen sect, 371–72
Chuang-tzu, 344, 358, 359, 362, 363
Chu Hsi, 6, 402, 403, 422, 423, 424
Chung-li Ch'uan, 344
Chung-tzu, 403
Cicero, 4
Circumcision
    female, 11, 596
    male, 16, 596
Cities, prehistoric, 70
Civilization, 68
Clement of Alexandria, 524
Clifford, James, 168
Cobb, John, 8
Codrington, Robert H., 95
Community, 17
Community well-being, 151–52
Compassion, wisdom and, 294–95
Complex ethnic religions, 19, 53
Comstock, W. Richard, 10

Concupiscence, 523
Confucianism, 8, 12, 397–428
    ancestor worship in, 408–10
    beliefs of, 398–405
    Buddhism and, 420, 421
    Ch'in suppression of, 415
    chronology of, 426–27
    contemporary, 427–28
    early, 413–15
    in Han dynasty, 415–20
    history of, 413–27
    human nature and destiny in, 403–5
    language and, 411
    literati and, 398–99, 411–12
    marriage in, 406–7
    in modern China, 424–26
    Neo-, 421–23
    parent-child relationship in, 407–8
    in period of disunion, 420–21
    practice of, 405–12
    in premodern China, 423–24
    public virtue in, 411
    Taoist, 402
    "triumph" of, 418–19
Confucian scripture, 417
Confucius, 32, 359, 399–401
    cult of, 410–11
    death of, 413
Conservative Judaism, 482, 483, 491
Contagious magic, 25
Convents of religious women, 542
Co-origination, dependent, 286–87
Coptic Christians, 539
Correspondence in Taoism, 340–41
Cosmic religion, 62
Cosmogenesis, 526
Cosmos
    in ancient China, 357
    in ancient urban religions, 76–78
    gestation of, 339–40
    in Hinduism, 211–12
    in Islam, 590
    in prehistoric religions, 62
    in Taoism, 338–41
    in tribal religions, 137–41
Covenant, Mosaic, 464–66, 467
Criticism, Christian scholarly, 530
Crow Dog, Mary, 151
Crusades, 544–45, 617
Cullmann, Oscar, 531
Cults, 23
Cultural diffusion, 132
Cyril of Alexandria, 538, 539

D
Da Costa, Uriel, 480
Dalai Lama, 308, 314
Dalits, 211, 651
Dancing Religion, 667
Darshan, 218
Death and human destiny
    in ancient urban societies, 86–89
    in tribal religions, 141–43
Death ritual
    in Confucianism, 410
    in Islam, 596–97
    in Judaism, 463
Deculturation, 158–59
Definitions of religion, 6–10
    denotative, 5
    functional definitions, 9–10
    intensional, 6
    monothetic definitions, 6–8
    open, 10
    polythetic definitions, 8–9
Deguchi, Nao, 667
Deities, Vedic, 224
Deloria, Vine, Jr., 167
Denny, Frederick M., 597, 620
Denominations, 21
Dependent co-origination, 286–87
De Poncins, Gontran, 152
De Sales, Francis, 551
Descartes, Rene, 151
Destiny
    in ancient urban societies, 86–89
    in Christianity, 522–24
    in Confucianism, 403–5
    in Islam, 590
    in Judaism, 452–54
    in Taoism, 344–45
    in tribal religions, 141–43
Desymbolization, 646
Deus otiosis, 133
Devi, 233, 235
Deviance amplification, 645
Dharma, 6, 208, 210–11
    buddha-, 280
    in everyday life, 213–14
    sanatana, 221, 247–48
Dharmic orthodoxy, 237
Dhayana, 285
Diaspora
    Hindu, 244
    Jewish, 471
Dickinson, Emily, 13, 27
Dietary rules, Jewish, 15, 16
Diffused monism, 136

Digambara, 654
Dissent, permissible, 558–59
Divination, 25, 85
    possession, 148
    Taoist, 357–58
    wisdom, 25, 148
Divine presence, in Hinduism, 212–13
Diviners, 85
Divinities
    in ancient urban religions, 78–82, 85–86
    in Taoism, 341–44
    interacting with, 85–86
    nature, 64–65, 134–35
Docetism, 539
Dodd, C. H., 531
Dogen, 308
Doi, Takeo, 408
Dominic de Guzman, 544
Do-ut des, 92
Durga, 235–36
Druze, 21
Dualism, cosmic, 525, 639
Duality, 288
Dumont, Louis, 27
Dupre, Louis, 26, 27
Durkheim, Emile, 9, 28, 95

E

Earhart, H. Byron, 666
Ebionites, 535
Ecological issues in Hinduism, 247
Eck, John, 548
Ecumenical councils, 535
Ehrenberg, Margaret, 56
Eightfold Path, 284
Eisler, Riane, 98
Eknath, 237
Eliade, Mircea, 7, 29, 62
Eliezar, Rabbi, 451
Ellison, James, 645
Ember, Melvin, 97
Embryonic breathing, 349–50
Emptiness, principle of, 289–90
End-time myths, 14
Epics, Hindu, 227–30
Epicurus, 525
Episcopacy, 536
Equilibrium, 402
Erasmus, Desiderius, 547
Esai, 308
Eschatologies, 14, 524, 591
Esoteric Buddhism, 297–98
Essenes, 472, 473
Ethics, Taoist, 351–53

Ethnic religions, 18–21
    complex, 19
Eucharist, 520, 528
Euhemerus, 82
Eurasia, tribal peoples of, 155
Euripides, 81
Europe, tribal peoples of, 153–55
Eusebius of Nicomedia, 537, 538
Eutyches, 539
Evans-Pritchard, E. E., 13, 136, 141
Evil
    in Christianity, 524–26
    in Judaism, 454–56
    in tribal religions, 143–44
Exorcism, 150, 348–49
Expedient means, 290
Ezra, 470

F

Fackenheim, Emil, 455, 456
Faith, 12, 592
Faith healing, 11
Falasafa, 609
Family *li*, 405–10
Farhah, Caesar E., 588
Farrakhan, Louis, 618
Feminist Judaism, 492
Festivals
    Hindu, 218–19
    Islamic, 597–99
    Jewish, 461–63
Fetishes, 133
Filial piety, 407
Five Classics, 416–18
Five Great Relationships, 405–6, 638
Five Pillars of Islam, 591–95, 638
Five Precepts, 291
Folk religions in China, 354–58
Form criticism, 530
Foundational events, 137
Foundational religious figures, 4
Four Noble Truths, 282, 284–86
Francis de Sales, 551
Francis of Assisi, 544
Frankel, Zacharias, 483
Free souls, 141
Free will, 525
Freud, Sigmund, 28–29, 95, 527
Functional definitions, 9–10
Fundamentalism, 555
    Islamic, 619–20
Fundamentalist Christians, 14, 521, 522, 533, 555, 619
Fung Yu-lan, 426

G

Galilei, Galileo, 552
Gandhi, Mohandas K., 5, 30, 230, 239–40, 654
Garvey, Marcus, 640
Gautama, 279, 281–82, 654
Geertz, Clifford, 9
Geiger, Abraham, 481
Gemara, 451, 474
Gender relations/roles/issues
    in Buddhism, 315–17
    in Christianity, 558
    in Hinduism, 214–16, 247
    in Islam, 601, 618–19
    in Judaism, 458–60
    prehistoric, 70
    in Shinto, 668
Genesis, 14–15
Gerhardsson, Birger, 533
Geronimo, 131
Ghost Dance movement, 160, 639
Gimbutas, Marija, 64, 95, 96, 97, 98
Ginsberg, Asher, 485
Girard, René, 16
Giver of Life, 13
Glossolalia, 148
Gnostics, 539
Gobind Singh, 656
Goddess(es), 95–96
    gods and, 65–66
    in Hinduism, 233, 235–36
God/ess, 10
God(s)
    in Christianity, 520–21
    goddesses and, 65–66
    high, 95
    in Islam, 588–89
    in Judaism, 446–49
    stratification of, 356
Good works, 12, 529–30
Gospels, 516–17
    synoptic, 531
Gould, Stephen Jay, 57
Government in Taoism, 345–46
Grace, 523–24
Graham, A. C., 413
Great Awakening, 554
Great Schism, 540
Great Ultimate, 402, 412, 422
Gregory of Nyssa, 524
Gross, Rita, 492
Gurus, 654, 655, 656
Gyatso, Tenzin, 314

H

Haddad, Yvonne Y., 592
Hadith, 608, 609
Hafiz, 588
Hajj, 594–95
Halakah, 456, 457, 459, 460
Halevy, Judah, 477
Hallowell, A. I., 136
Hanafite school, 608
Hanbalite school, 609
Handsome Lake, 163
    Han dynasty
        Confucianism in, 415–20
        religious milieu of, 364
Han Fei-tzu, 414
Hanif, 586, 603
Han Yu, 421–22, 423
Harris, Marvin, 98
Hart, Richard, 152
Hasidism, 480
Hauptman, Judith, 459
Heaven
    in Christianity, 524
    mandate of, 355–56, 415
Heavenly Journey, Prophet's, 599
Heaven's Gate, 639, 643–44
Hebrew scripture, 450
Hell, 524
Henotheism, 80
Henry VIII, 550
Heresy, 536, 545
Hermeneutics, 17, 645, 646–48
Hermits, groupings of, 541
Herzl, Theodor, 485
Heschel, Abraham, 460
Hesiod, 77
Hick, John, 30, 525
Hieros gamos, 66
High gods, 95
Hillel the Elder, 458, 459, 472, 474, 475
Hinayana, 300, 302
Hinduism, 207–48
    beliefs of, 210–13
    chronology of, 242–43
    contemporary, 241–48
    cosmos in, 211–12
    divine presence in, 212–13
    as emotional transformation, 219–21
    festivals in, 218–19
    gender roles in, 214–16
    history of, 221–41
    in Indian culture, 246
    life cycle rituals in, 214
    paths to release in, 212

Hinduism, continued
  philosophy and, 232–33
  pilgrimage in, 219
  practice of, 213–21
  sacrifice in, 16, 224–25
  sectarian, 233–34
  six schools of, 233
  social issues and, 246–47
  social structure in, 231–32
  tantras in, 236
  Westernization and, 238–40
  as "world" religion, 244–46
  yoga in, 216–17
Hindu scripture, 228–29
Hijra, 587
Hirsch, Samson R., 483
Historical-critical school, 531
Hoffman, Melchior, 550
Hogan, Linda, 130
Holding the Ones, 350
Holocaust, 455–56, 486–87, 489
Homo religiosus, 58
Hsiao, 407
Hsu Heng, 423
Hsun-tzu, 404, 413, 414–15, 421
Hua-yen philosophy, 307
Hubbard, L. Ron, 24
Hui-neng, 306
Hultkrantz, Ake, 141
Human-heartedness, 404–5
Humanism, 546
Humanistic Judaism, 482, 483
Humankind, 141, 356
Human nature, 84–85
  in Christianity, 522–24
  in Confucianism, 403–5
  in Islam, 590–91
  in Judaism, 452–54
  in Taoism, 344–45
Hume, David, 93, 525
Hung Hsin-ch'uan, 372–73
Hus, John, 547, 548
Husayn, 597, 606, 607

I

Ibn-Abd al-Wahhab, Muhammad, 613
Ibn-Arabi, 610–11
Ibn-Rushd, 610
Ibn-Sina, 609
I Ching, 357, 358, 416
Ideal state in Taoism, 345–46
Identity, sacralization of, 9–10
Idolatry, 589, 591
Idowu, E. Bolaji, 136

Ignatius of Loyola, 544, 551
Imam, 593, 606
Imitative magic, 25
Immortality, 86, 349, 524
Immortals in Taoism, 343–44
Index of Forbidden Books, 551
India
  Buddhism in, 302
  classical, 226–36
  medieval, 236–38
  modern, 238–40
  postcolonial, 240–41
  pre-Buddhist beliefs in, 283–84
Indian culture, Hinduism in, 246
Indigenous peoples, 153–66, 167–68
Indus Valley civilization, 221–22
Inerrancy, 533
Initiation cults, 72
Inquisition, 478, 551
International Society for Krishna Consciousness, 20, 24
Irenaeus, 525
Isaiah, 455, 469
Islam, 583–20
  in Abbasid caliphate, 609–11
  Allah in, 588–89
  beliefs of, 584–91
  chronology of, 616–17
  contemporary, 615–20
  cosmology of, 590
  definition of religion in, 4
  end of the world in, 591
  Five Pillars of, 591–95, 638
  gender roles in, 601, 618–19
  history of, 601–15
  human nature and destiny in, 590–91
  life cycle rituals in, 595–97
  in Mogul Empire, 611–12
  modern, 614–15
  moral life in, 599–601
  in Ottoman Empire, 612–14
  in postmodern world, 616–18
  practice of, 591–601
  Quran in, 587–88
  in Umayyad dynasty, 608–9
  in United States, 618
Islamic "fundamentalism," 619–20
Islamic scripture, 586
Ismaelis, 606–7
Israel, 8, 9, 10, 452
  kingdoms of, 466–69
  modern, 487–89
  Palestinians and, 487–88, 492
Israel ben Eleazer, 480

J

Jainism, 12, 20, 30, 282, 651–54
    beliefs of, 651–53
    history of, 653–54
    practice of, 653
Japan, Buddhism in, 307–8, 314–15
Jatis, 210
Jefferson, Thomas, 27
Jehovah's Witnesses, 24, 641
Jen, 404, 407, 409
Jeremias, Joachim, 531
Jesus of Nazareth, 472, 473, 475, 516–20, 530, 533
Jewish identity, 445–46, 489–92
Jews, 3, 7, 445–46
    Christians and, 475–76, 477–79
    Conservative, 482, 483, 491
    Hasidic, 457, 480
    Humanistic, 482, 483
    emancipation of, 481
    in Europe, 479–80
    in Middle East, 479
    Muslims and, 476–77
    Orthodox, 451, 457, 482–83, 491
    Reconstructionist, 457, 482, 483, 491
    Reform, 457, 463, 481, 482, 491
    worldwide dispersion of, 447
Jihad, 590–91, 600–601
Jinn, 586, 602
Jivas, 651, 652, 653
Jnana, 217
Jnaneshvar, 237
Joachim of Fiore, 11
Johanan ben Zakkai, 474, 475
John XXIII, Pope, 555, 557
John Chrysostom, Saint, 475
John the Baptist, 472, 473
Jones, Charles B., 316
Jones, James, 24, 640
Josephus, Flavius, 472, 473, 530, 531
Jouret, Luc, 643
Ju, 397, 398
Judah the Patriarch, 474
Judaism, 5, 8, 445–92
    beliefs of, 446–56
    in biblical period, 464–73
    chronology of, 490–91
    contemporary, 489–92
    dietary rules in, 15, 16
    feminist, 492
    gender roles in, 458–60
    God in, 446–49
    history of, 464–89
    Holocaust and, 455–56, 486–87, 489
    human nature and destiny in, 452–54
    Israel and, 452, 487–89
    modern, 480–88
    modern forms of, 481–83
    practice of, 456–63
    in rabbinic period, 473–80
    ritual in, 15, 16
    Roman rule and, 471–73
    Talmud and, 450–51, 474–75
    Torah and, 449–52, 456–58
    worship and ritual in, 460–63
    Zionism and, 485, 488
Kabbalism, 448, 454, 479
Kabir, 237
Kagura, 661, 668
Kahler, Martin, 530
Kalam, 609
Kali, 212, 236, 639
Kali *yuga*, 212, 639
Kama, 231
Kami, 659, 660, 661, 662
Kamidana, 661–62
Kamikaze, 664
Kannagara, 659
Kaplan, Mordecai, 449, 483
Karma, 211, 281, 287
    in Jainism, 652
    in Taoism, 345
Kashrut, 457
Kemal, Mustafa, 615
Keyes, Charles, 312, 317
Khalsa fellowship, 656
Kharijites, 604, 608
Khomeini, Ayatollah, 618
Kings, sacred, 82–84
Kinsley, David R., 210
Kirkland, J. Russell, 353
Kitabatake, Chikafusa, 660, 664
Kitamura, Sayo, 667
Knipe, David M., 210, 219
Knox, John, 551
Knowledge, 3, 645
Koan, 296
Ko Ch'ao-fu, 369
Ko Hung, 349, 367, 368, 369
Kojiki, 663
Korea, Buddhism in, 307, 314
Koresh, David, 24, 642, 643
Kosher laws, 457
Kotzk, Rabbi of, 448
K'ou Ch'ien-chih, 369–70
Kshatriya, 231
Kuei, 342
K'ung fu-tzu. See Confucius.
Kurozumikyo, 665, 666, 667

L

LaDuke, Winoma, 152
Lama, 308
Lame Deer, John, 11, 130, 163
Laming, Annette, 59
Language, religious uses of, 12–15
Lao-tzu, 338, 339, 343, 358, 363
    and *Tao Te Ching*, 359–61
Larson, Gerald, 213, 246
Latter-day Saints. See Mormons.
Le Bon, Gustave, 94
Legalism, 345, 359, 363, 364, 414–15
Leo X, Pope, 548
Leroi-Gourhan, Andre, 59
Levi-Strauss, Claude, 94
Levy-Buhl, Lucien, 94
Lewis, I. M., 149
Li, 398, 401, 404–10, 417
Li Ao, 422
Libationer, 365
Liberation, practice toward, 292
"Liberation theology," 558
Li Chi, 408, 409, 417–18
Lienhardt, Godfrey, 151
Life after death, 62–64. *See also* Immortality.
Life cycle rites/rituals, 16
    in Hinduism, 214
    in Islam, 595–97
    in Judaism, 463
    in tribal religions, 147–48
Lifton, Robert J., 645–46
Li Han-Kuang, 352
Lila, 217
Lin Chao-en, 423–24
Lindbeck, George, 9, 15
Lin Yutang, 408
Literalism, 647
Literati, 398–99, 411–12
Liu An, 363
Loftin, John D., 136, 140
Lombard, Peter, 545
Longevity, Taoist techniques of, 349–51
Lu Hsiu-ching, 369
Luria, Isaac, 479
Lutheranism, 549
Luther, Martin, 479, 523, 547–49, 552, 613
Lu Tung-pin, 351

M

Macrina, 542
Macrocosm, 340
Madhva, 232
Magic, 25
Mahavira, 20, 653, 654

Mahayana, 288, 300
Mahayanism, 288–90
    birth of, 300–302
    emptiness in, 289–90
    expedient means in, 290
    nonduality in, 288–89
    Six Perfections of, 294–95
    Two Truths of, 290
Mahdi, 606
Maimonides, Moses, 12, 446, 454, 459, 477, 483
Maitreya Buddha, 18
Makoto, 660
Malcolm X, 595, 596, 618
Malik ibn-Anas, 608
Malikite school, 608
Mana, 95, 132–33
Mandate of heaven, 355–56, 415
Mani, 4, 20
Manson, T. W., 533
Mantras, 223
Mao Tse Tung, 373, 374–75, 426
Marga, 216, 280
Marett, Robert B., 95
Marriage
    in Confucianism, 406–7
    in Islam, 596
    in Judaism, 463
Martin of Tours, 542
Marx, Karl, 28, 374, 481
Master of Animals, 65
Mbiti, John, 131, 135, 151
McCartney, Bill, 24
Mean, doctrine of, 414
Means, expedient, 290
Mecca, pilgrimage to, 16, 594–95
Medicine, traditional, 149–51
Meditation
    observational, 293–94
    stabilizing, 293, 294
    Zen, 295–97
Megaliths, 61
Meir, Rabbi, 460
Melanchthon, Philip, 549
Mellaart, James, 95, 97
Mencius, 359, 403, 407, 413–14, 421
Mendelssohm, Moses, 480–81
Meng-tzu. See Mencius.
Mennonites, 552
Mernissi, Fatima, 619
Merton, Thomas, 527
Messiah, 446, 473, 479, 516
Metaphors, 13
Methodism, 554
Mettles, Bonnie Lu, 641

Microcosm, 340, 341
Midrash, 449
Mihrab, 592
Miki, Nakayama, 21
Millennarian thought, 160
Millennialism, 639–40, 644–48
Millennial religions, 638–48
    twentieth-century, 640–44
Miller, Barbara Stoller, 219
Miller, David L., 647, 648
Ming dynasty, Taoism in, 372
Ming T'ang phenomenon, 418–19
Minyan, 460
Mishnah, 451, 458
    formation of, 474–75
Missionaries, Hindu, 244–46
Mitzvah, 457
Modernists, 94
Mogul Empire
    Hinduism under, 236–38
    Islam during, 611–12
Moism, 359
Moksha, 208, 211
Mol, Hans J., 9
Moltmann, Jurgen, 522
Monasticism, 540–44
    Basil's conception of, 542
Monism, diffused, 136
Monophysitism, 538, 539
Monotheism
    in ancient urban religions, 80, 81
    Monothetic definitions, 6–8
    supernatural beings, 6–7
Monuments, prehistoric, 70–72
Moon, Sun Myung, 24
Morality, 15
    in ancient urban societies, 89–90
    in tribal religions, 152–53
Moral life
    in Christianity, 526–28
    in Islam, 599–601
Moravians, 552
Mormons, 20, 24
    baptism of living on behalf of dead in, 12
Mortimer, John, 7
Morton, Samuel George, 93
Mosaic covenant, 464–66, 467
Mo-tzu, 358–59
Mughal Empire. See Mogul Empire.
Muezzin, 592
Muhammad, 4, 476, 584, 585–87, 590, 591
Muhammad, Elijah, 618
Muhammad, W. D., 618
Mujtahids, 606

Muller, F. Max, 30
Muslims, 583
    Shiite, 597, 606, 607, 608
    Sunni, 606, 607, 608
Mutazilites, 609, 610
Myoko, Naganuma, 24
Mystery religions, 72
Myths, 14–15
    as sacred "texts," 130

N

Nakamura, Miki, 666
Namdev, 237
Naming ritual in Islam, 595–96
Nanak, Guru, 20, 237, 612, 651, 655
Nathan of Gaza, Rabbi, 479
Naths, 654
National, 53
Native American Church, 24
Nature divinities, 64–65, 134–35
Nehru, Jawaharlal, 30, 240
Neo-Confucianism, 421–23
Neolithic Age, 59–61
    gender in, 60–61
    social stratification in, 60
Neolithic peoples, 54
Nestorius, 538, 539
Neusner, Jacob, 448, 456
Neville, A. O., 158
New Age thought, 643–44
New Religions of Japan, 667–68
New Testament, 16, 531
Nicene Creed, 538
Nichiren Buddhism, 13, 667
Nihonshoki, 663
Nikkyo, Niwano, 24
Nirvana, 288
Nishida, Kitaro, 11
Nonduality, 288–89
Nontheistic religions, 18, 19
Norinaga, Motoori, 659, 665
No-self, 286
Numinous, 11

O

Occultation, 606
Oceana, tribal peoples of, 155
O'Connell, Timothy, 527
Odorukyo, 667
Oedipus complex, 29
Old Europe, 98
Old Pierre, 132, 145, 149
Omoto religion, 639, 667
Oracles, 86

Origen, 524, 541
Original sin, 523
Origin myths, 14
Orphism, 88
Orthodox Judaism, 451, 457, 482–83, 491
Orthodox Unity movement, 371, 372
Otto, Rudolf, 7, 11, 29
Oyama Nezunomikoto Shinshikyokai, 667
Ozick, Cynthia, 492

P

Pachomius, 541, 542
"Pacifist churches," 552
Pagan, 52, 53
Pai-chang, 295
Paleolithic Age, 56–59
Paleolithic peoples, 54
Pantheism, 133
Papal schism, 546
Parables, 517
Parallel development, 132
Parsons, Talcott, 9
Passover, 16, 461, 462
Patriarchs, Age of, 464
Patrick, Saint, 542
Paul, Saint, 516, 523, 527, 533, 534, 535
Peace Religion, 667
Pelagianism, 523
Pelagius, 523
Pentateuch, 449, 450
Pentecost, 461, 533
Pentecostal Christian groups, 24
People's Temple, 24, 640
Perfect Liberty Fellowship, 667
Perfect Realization movement, 371, 372
Periodic rites, 16
Perrin, Norman, 531
Pesach, 461, 462
Pharisees, 472
Philo of Alexandria, 452, 460, 471
Philosophers
    in ancient urban societies, 81–82
    Hinduism and, 232–33
Pilgrimage
    in Hinduism, 219
    in Islam, 594–95
Pinsker, Leon, 485
Plaskow, Judith, 452, 492
Plato, 6, 81, 82, 87, 290, 471, 525
PL Kyodan, 667
Plotkin, Mark J., 150
Pluralism, religious, 27
Pliny the Younger, 531, 536
Poet-saints, Hindu, 237–38

Political systems, prehistoric, 68–70
Polytheism
    in ancient urban religions, 80–81
    Polythetic definitions, 8–9
Pontius Pilate, 520
Pope, 536
    infallibility of, 554
Possession divination, 148
Practice in Buddhism, 292
Prajna, 292
Prayer, 5
    in Christianity, 529
    in Islam, 592–93
Predestination, 550
Prehistoric religion, 61–67
    chronology of, 62–63
    cosmos in, 62
    in Japan, 662–63
    life after death in, 62–64
    sacred persons in, 66
    sacrifice in, 66–67
    spirit beings in, 64–66
Prehistory, 54–61
Priests, 17
Primal religions, 128, 129
Primitive, 52–53
"Primitive" minds, 93–94
Principle, 402
Prophets, 17
    Israelite, 469
Projectivists, 28
Protagoras, 81
Protestant Christians, 523, 525, 552
Protestantism, non-Lutheran, 550
Protestant Reformation, 547–52
    Catholic reaction to, 551–52
    spread of, 549–51
Psychic numbing, 646
Puja, 216, 217–18
Purdah, 618
Pure Land Buddhism, 12, 281, 306–7
    chanting in, 298–99
Purgatory, 524
Purim, 461
Pythagoras, 88

Q

Quakers, 529, 552
Quran, 4, 14, 585, 587–88
Quraysh, 602, 604, 608

R

Rabbi(s), 446
    at Yavneh, 474

Rabbinic period, 473–80
Raj, 238
Ramadan, 593, 598
Ramakrishna, Swami, 30, 239
Ram Das, 656
Rapture, 641
Rasa, 219–21
Rashi, 477
Rastafarianism, 24, 640–41
Ray, Benjamin, 144, 149
Rebirth, *karma* and, 287
Reconstructionist Judaism, 457, 482, 483, 491
Redaction criticism, 530
Reformation, 547–52
Reform Judaism, 457, 463, 481, 482, 491
Reincarnation, 142
Religio, 4, 5
Religion(s)
    as belief system, 6
    classifying, 17–25
    dead and living, 52
    defining, 4–6, 10
    definitions of, 6–10
    established, 21
    ethnic, 18–21
    functions of, 9
    magic and, 25–26
    national, 19
    new, 21–25
    nontheistic, 18, 19
    origin of, 94–95
    psychology and, 645–46
    in secular societies, 26–27
    sociology of, 645
    study of, 27–29
    theistic, 18, 19
    in traditional societies, 26
    tribal, 127–68
    truth and, 29–30
    universal, 18, 20–21
    world, 72–74
Religious experiences, 11
Religious expression, forms of, 15–17
Religious pluralism, 27
Ren, 404
Renaissance, 546–46
Renfrew, Colin, 98
Responsivists, 28
Restoration movements, 160
Restoration Shinto, 664, 665, 666
Revitalization movements, 160, 161
Riesser, Gabriel, 481
Rissho Koseikai, 24
Rites of passage, 16

Rituals, 9, 15–16
    Buddhist, 291–92
    Confucian, 404–5
    communal, 16
    Jewish, 460–63
    performative, 16
    repetitive, 16
Rosenzweig, Franz, 449
Rosh Hashanah, 461–62
Roy, Ram Mohan, 239
Rozman, Gilbert, 424
Ru, 397
Rubenstein, Richard, 456, 486
Ruether, Rosemary, 10
Russell, Charles Taze, 24, 641

S

Saadia of Sura, 476
Sabbath, 456, 460–61
Sacralization, 9
Sacramental system, 545
Sacraments, 13, 529
Sacred persons, 66
Sacred stories, 13–14
Sacred, the, 7
    defined, 10–11
    perceptions of, 10–15
    violence and, 16
Sacred kings, 82–84
Sacred persons, 82–84, 148–49
Sacred rites, 144–48
Sacred space, 139–41
Sacred texts, ancient, 73
Sacred time, 137–39
Sacrifice, 146
    in ancient urban religions, 90–93
    animal, 11
    blood, 11, 16, 90
    in Vedism, 224–25
    in prehistoric religions, 66–67
    sanctification through, 15
    in tribal religions, 146–47
Sadducees, 472
Sages, 17
Said, Edward, 209
"Saints," Islamic, 597
Sakorn, Phra Khru, 313
Samadhi, 285, 292
Samsara, 211, 283
Samskaras, 214
Samuel, 469
Sanatana dharma, 221, 247–48
Sanctification, 15
Sangha, 282

Sanhedrin, 472, 474, 520
Sannyasin, 211
Santería, 16, 25
Sants, 654
Sarasvati, Swami Dayananda, 239
Satya *yuga*, 639
Savonarola, Girolamo, 547
Sawm, 593
Sayyid Ahmad al-Badawi, 597
Schism
    Great, 540
    papal, 546
Schleiermacher, Friedrich, 7, 524
Schmidt, Wilhelm, 95
Schweitzer, Albert, 531
Scientology, 24
Scripture, 16–17
    Hindu, 228–29
    inerrancy of, 533
Sectarian Hinduism, 233–34
Sects, 23
Sect Shinto, 665
Secularism, 240–41
Secular societies, religion in, 26–27
Seder, 462–63
Sen, Keshub Chunder, 239
Sephardim, 477
Severus, Sulpicius, 542
Sexual minorities in Christianity, 558
Shabbat, 456, 460–61
Shafiite school, 608–9
Shahada, 592
Shaiva, 235, 652
Shakti, 236
Shakyamuni Buddha, 279, 281–83, 284, 285, 287, 288, 421
Shamanism, 66
Shamans, 17, 66, 148–49, 663
Shamatha, 293
Shang Ch'ing, 368
Shang dynasty, folk religion in, 354–55
Shang-ti, 355
Shan-tao, 306
Sharia, 600, 606
Shavuot, 461
Shekhinah, 448
Shema, 446, 463
Shen, 341
Shibayama, Zenkai, 7
Shiite Muslims, 597, 606
Shila, 285, 292
Shinto, 658–68
    beliefs of, 658–60
    celebrations in, 660–61
    contemporary, 666–68

ethics in, 660
formation of, 663–64
future of, 668
gender issues in, 668
history of, 662–66
in modern Japan, 665–66
practice of, 660–662
Restoration, 664, 665, 666
Sect, 665
Shrine (state), 665, 666, 667
Shirk, 589, 591, 616
Shiva, 235
Shotoku, 663
Shrine (state) Shinto, 665, 666, 667
Shruti, 223, 227, 228
Shudra, 231
Shunyata, 289
Shvetambara, 654
Siddhartha Gautama. See Gautama.
Sikhism, 20–21, 654–57
    beliefs of, 655
    contemporary, 656–57
    history of, 656
    practice of, 655–56
Silko, Leslie Marmon, 131
Simchat Torah, 461
Simeon ben Gamaliel, 474
Six Perfections, 294–95
Singer, Isaac Bashevis, 15
Smart, Ninian, 584
Smith, Wilfred Cantwell, 4, 5, 26
Smith, Jonathan Z., 6, 7–8, 145, 147
Smith, Joseph, Jr., 24, 30
Smriti, 227, 228
Social issues, Hinduism and, 246–47
Social relations, prehistoric, 70
Social structure, Hindu, 231–32
Sociology of knowledge, 645
Socrates, 6, 87
Soka Gakkai, 667
Solar Temple, Order of, 643
Solomon ben Isaac, Rabbi, 477
Songch'ol, 314
Sophocles, 84
Sorcery, 25
Soteriology, 280
Souls, 141
Source criticism, 530
Space, sacred, 139–41
Spinoza, Benedict (Baruch), 16, 449, 480
Spirit beings, 8, 10, 64–66, 132–36
Spirit possession, 66, 148
Spirituality, ancient, 51–99
Spiro, Melford E., 6, 7

Sri Lanka, Buddhism in, 308–9
Ssu-ma Cheng-chen, 352
Stoics, 525
Stone, Merlin, 96
Stone Age, 54
Suetonius, Gaius, 531
Sufis, 613
Sufism, 610–11, 613, 615
Sullivan, Lawrence E., 95
Sung dynasty, Taoism in, 371
Sunni Muslims, 606
Superhuman beings, 6
Supernatural beings, 6–7
Supreme Being, 133–34
Suras, 588
Sutras, 229
Suzuki, D. T., 315
Swearer, Donald, 297
Sword (Long Knife), George, 145, 148
Symbols, 12–13
Synagogues, 472
Synoptic Gospels, 531

T

Taboos, 28
Tacitus, Cornelius, 154, 472, 531
Tagore, Debendranath, 239
Taiwan, Buddhist culture in, 313–14
Tai Chen, 424
T'ai Chi, 402
Taiping movement, 372–73
Talmud, 450–51
    formation of, 474–75
Talmudic teaching, 475
Tanakh, 449, 450, 451
T'ang dynasty, golden age of, 370–71
T'an-luan, 306
Tantras, Hindu, 236
Tao, 338–41
Taocracy, 365, 370
T'ao Hung-ching, 369
Taoism, 5, 337–77
    beliefs of, 338–46
    Celestial Masters movement in, 348, 364–67
    in Ch'ing dynasty, 372–73
    contemporary, 375–77
    divination in, 357–58
    divinities in, 341–44
    early teachings of, 362–63
    ethics in, 351–53
    government and ideal state in, 345–46
    history of, 353–75
    human nature and destiny in, 344–45
    institutionalized, 364–67
    in Ming dynasty, 372
    movements and sects in, 368
    in North China, 369–70
    Orthodox Unity movement in, 371
    People's Republic of China and, 374–75
    Perfect Realization movement in, 371
    practice of, 346–53
    religious, 364–67
    republic and, 373
    ritual in, 346–48
    in South China, 367–69
    state, 370
    in Sung and Yuan dynasties, 371–72
    in T'ang dynasty, 370–71
    yoga in, 350–51
Taoist Confucianism, 402
Taoist scripture, 370
Tao Te Ching, 338, 339, 343, 345, 346
    Lao-tzu and, 359–61
Te, 352
Teilhard de Chardin, Pierre, 526
Tenrikyo, 21, 665, 666, 667, 668
Tetzel, John, 548
Thailand, Buddhist culture in, 313
Theistic religions, 18, 19
Theocentricity, 522
Theodicy, 525
Theology, 27–28
Theravada, 303, 309–10
Theriomorphic divinities, 64
Theudas, 473
Three Disciplines, 292–93
Three Pure Ones, 343, 344
    holding, 350
Three Worms, 344
Tibet, Buddhism in, 308, 314
T'ien, 356
Tikkun, 454
Tillich, Paul, 7, 29, 521
Time, 14, 137–39
Tirthankaras, 652
Tollefson, Kenneth, 153
Torah, 449–52
    as *halakah* and *mitzvot*, 456–58
    Simchat, 461
Totalization of attitudes, 644
Totemic spirits, 64, 65
Totemism, 29, 95
Townsend, Joan B., 96
Traditional medicine, 149–51
Tribal, 53
Tribal peoples
    adaptation and revitalization of, 160–63
    assimilation and acculturation of, 159

Tribal peoples, continued
    destruction and deculturation of, 158–59
    and modern states, 156–58
    and pre-modern states, 153–56
    self-determination of, 163–66
Tribal religions, 128
    beliefs in, 132–44
    chronology of, 164–65
    cosmos in, 137–41
    death and human destiny in, 141–43
    evil in, 143–44
    in historical times, 127–68
    humankind in, 141
    morality in, 152–53
    oral traditions in, 130–31
    practices in, 144–53
    sacred persons in, 148–49
    sacred rites in, 144–48
    spirit beings in, 132–36
    traditional medicine in, 149–51
    and tribal societies, 129–32
    values in, 151–53
Tribal societies, 129, 132
Tribal spirituality, 131–32
Tribulation, 641
Tricksters, 135, 143
Trinity, 520
Tripitaka, 300
Truth, 5, 7, 11
    inerrancy of scripture, 533
    religion and, 29–30
Tsong-kha-pa, 308
Tukaram, 219
Tulsidas, 237
Tumuli, 61
Tung Chung-shu, 357, 402, 415–16, 419, 421
Tu Wei Ming, 427
Two Truths, 290
Tylor, Edward Burnett, 6, 7, 28, 93, 95

U

Uisang, 307
Uji, 667
Ultimate (the), 7–8
    Great, 402, 412, 422
    manifestations of, 401–3
Umar, 604
Umayyad, 604, 609
Umayyad dynasty, 608–9
Unification Church, 24
Universal religions, 18, 20–21
Upanishads, 225–26
Urban societies, ancient, 67–74
Uthman, 604

V

Vaishnava, 218–19, 654
Vaishya, 231
Value Creation Society, 667
Van der Leeuw, Gerardus, 8, 29
Vardhamana, 653
Varna, 210
Vatican Council II, 555–57
Vedanta, 225
Vedas, 210, 223
Vedic deities, 224
Vedism, 222–26
    sacrifice in, 224–25
Venus figurines, 65
Vietnam, Buddhism in, 310–11, 313
Vinaya, 283
Violence, sacrifice and, 16
Vipassana, 297
Vishnu, 234
Vivekananda, Swami, 239, 244

W

Wach, Joachim, 11
Wahhabi movement, 613–14, 615
Wali, 597
Wang Che, 371
Wang Ch'u-i, 371
Wang Chung, 420
Wang Yang-ming, 412, 424
Weber, Max, 9
Weizmann, Chaim, 485
Wellhausen, Julius, 531
Wesley, Charles, 554
Wesley, John, 554
Westernization, Hinduism and, 238–40
Wiesel, Elie, 455, 456
Wine, Sherwin, 483
Wisdom, compassion and, 294–95
Wisdom divination, 25, 148
Wise, Isaac Mayer, 481
Witchcraft, 25–26
Wittgenstein, Ludwig, 8, 584
Wodziwob, 160
Wonhyo, 307
World religion(s)
    emergence of, 72–74
    Hinduism as, 244–46
Worldview, 10, 32
    competing, 557–59
World Wide Web resources, 669–71
Worship in Christianity, 528–29
Wovoka, 160
Writing, prehistoric, 72
Wu, 305

Wu Ching, 416–18
Wudu, 592
Wuquf, 595
Wu-wei, 351–52
Wycliffe, John, 547

X

Xenophanes, 80, 81

Y

Yang, 339–40, 357
Yang, C. K., 410, 427
Yang Hsi, 368
Yang Hsiung, 402, 420, 421
Yavneh, rabbis at, 474
Yazid, 606
Yeh Fa-Shan, 349
Yellow Turbans, 367, 420

Yen Yuan, 424
Yin, 339–40, 357
Yoga, 212, 216–17
    Taoist, 350–51
Yom Kippur, 461, 462
Yoshida, Kanetomo, 664
Yuan dynasty, Taoism in, 371, 372
Yun-ch'i Chu-hung, 424

Z

Zakat, 593
Zealots, 472, 473
Zen Buddhism, 7, 12, 295–97, 306
Zevi, Shabbatai, 479
Zionism, 485, 488, 615
Zohar, 448
Zoroaster, 20
Zuesse, Evan, 137, 138
Zwingli, Ulrich, 549